lonely planet

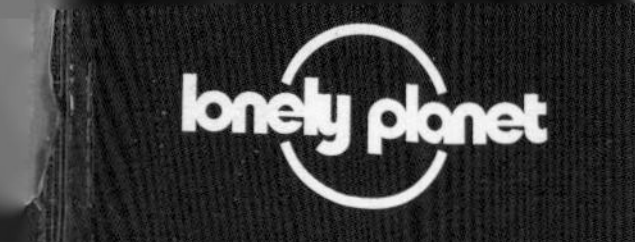

Estonia Latvia & Lithuania

Nicola Williams
Becca Blond, Regis St Louis

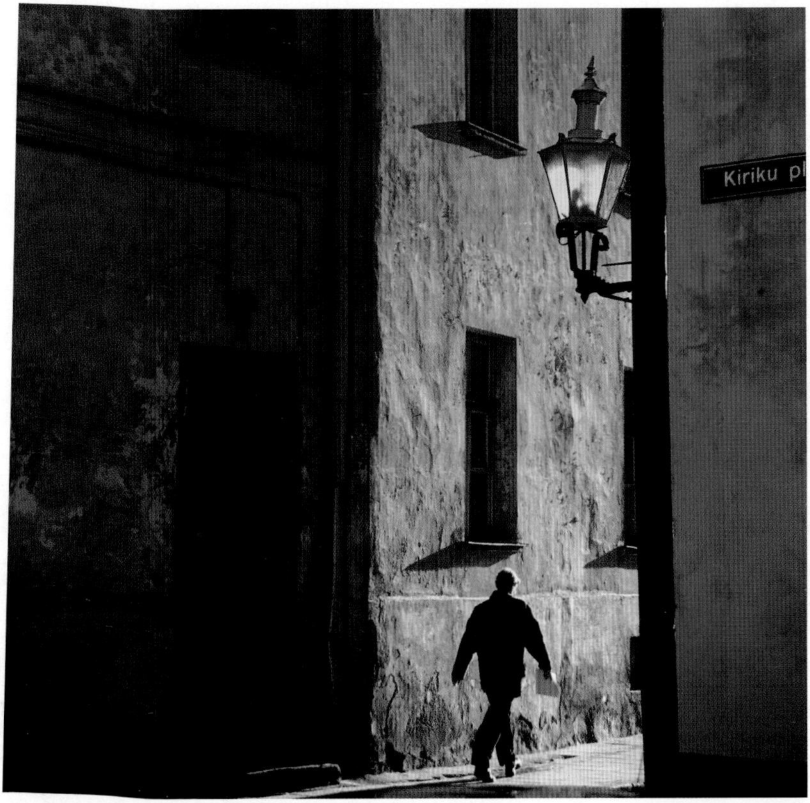

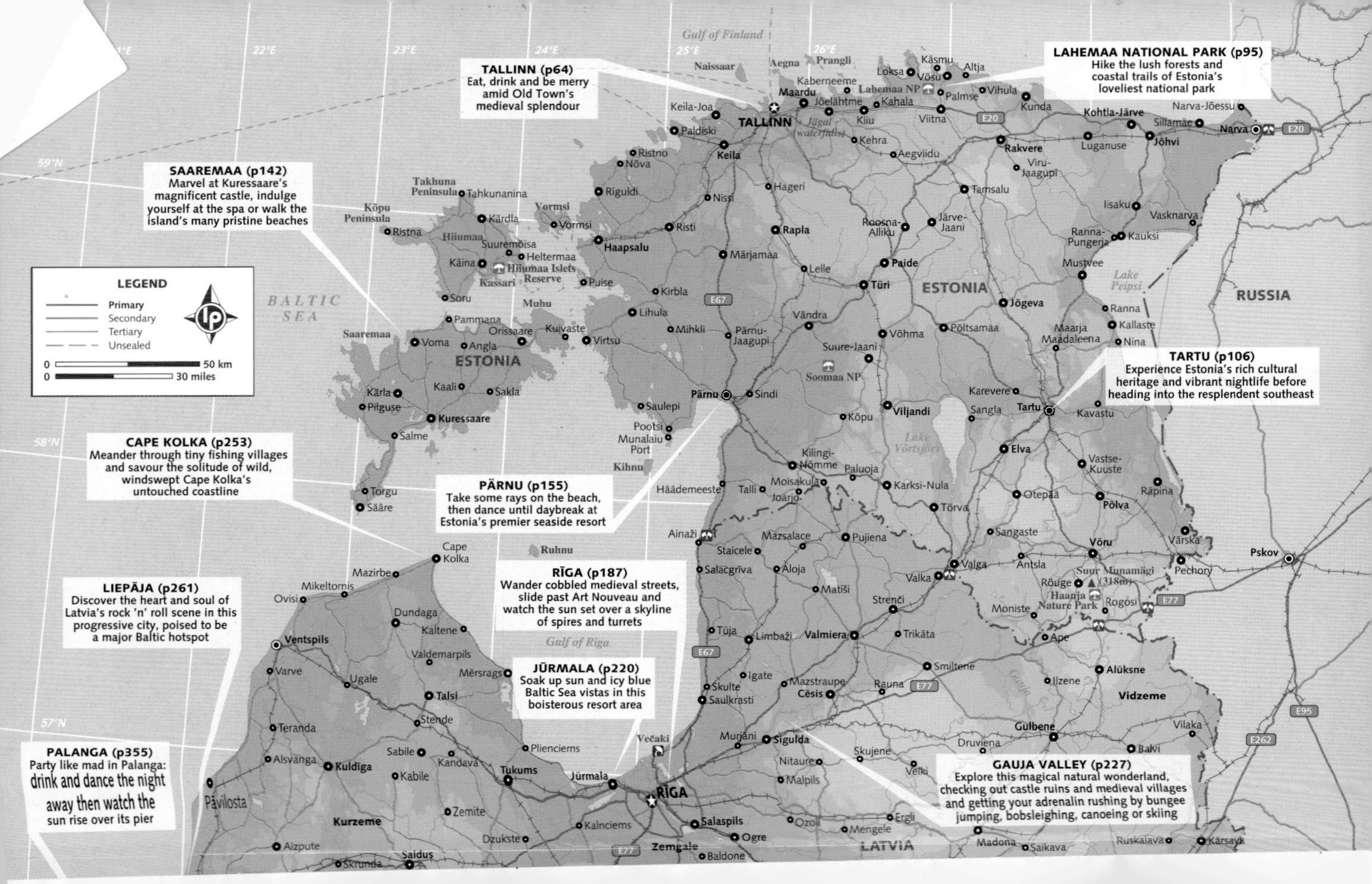
LAHEMAA NATIONAL PARK (p95)
Hike the lush forests and coastal trails of Estonia's loveliest national park
TALLINN (p64)
Eat, drink and be merry amid Old Town's medieval splendour
SAAREMAA (p142)
Marvel at Kuressaare's magnificent castle, indulge yourself at the spa or walk the island's many pristine beaches
TARTU (p106)
Experience Estonia's rich cultural heritage and vibrant nightlife before heading into the resplendent southeast
CAPE KOLKA (p253)
Meander through tiny fishing villages and savour the solitude of wild, windswept Cape Kolka's untouched coastline
PÄRNU (p155)
Take some rays on the beach, then dance until daybreak at Estonia's premier seaside resort
RĪGA (p187)
Wander cobbled medieval streets, slide past Art Nouveau and watch the sun set over a skyline of spires and turrets
LIEPĀJA (p261)
Discover the heart and soul of Latvia's rock 'n' roll scene in this progressive city, poised to be a major Baltic hotspot
JŪRMALA (p220)
Soak up sun and icy blue Baltic Sea vistas in this boisterous resort area
PALANGA (p355)
Party like mad in Palanga: drink and dance the night away then watch the sun rise over its pier
GAUJA VALLEY (p227)
Explore this magical natural wonderland, checking out castle ruins and medieval villages and getting your adrenalin rushing by bungee jumping, bobsleighing, canoeing or skiing
LEGEND
Primary
Secondary
Tertiary
Unsealed
0 50 km
0 30 miles
Gulf of Finland
BALTIC SEA
Gulf of Riga
ESTONIA
LATVIA
RUSSIA
Lake Peipsi
Lake Võrtsjärv
TALLINN
RĪGA
Tartu
Pärnu
Narva
Pskov
Ventspils
Kuressaare
Haapsalu
Viljandi
Valmiera
Sigulda
Cēsis
Jūrmala
Vidzeme
Kurzeme
Zemgale
Hiiumaa
Saaremaa
Muhu
Vormsi
Kihnu
Ruhnu
Naissaar
Aegna
Prangli
Lahemaa NP
Soomaa NP
Haanja Nature Park
Hiiumaa Islets Reserve
Suur Munamägi (318m)
Jägala (waterfalls)
Takhuna Peninsula
Kõpu Peninsula
Cape Kolka
E20
E67
E77
E95
E262
59°N
58°N
57°N
22°E
23°E
24°E
25°E
26°E

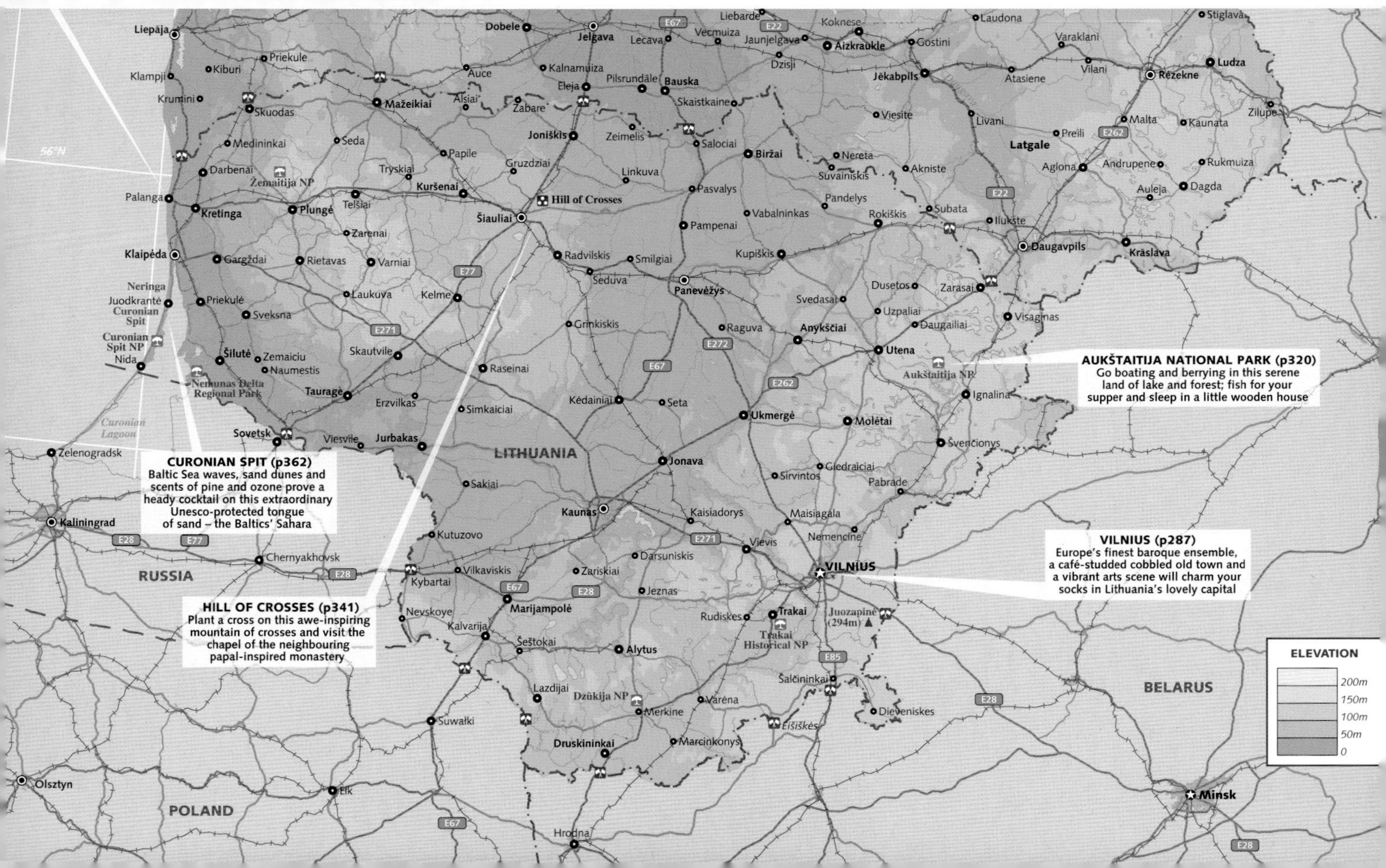

AUKŠTAITIJA NATIONAL PARK (p320)
Go boating and berrying in this serene land of lake and forest; fish for your supper and sleep in a little wooden house
CURONIAN SPIT (p362)
Baltic Sea waves, sand dunes and scents of pine and ozone prove a heady cocktail on this extraordinary Unesco-protected tongue of sand – the Baltics' Sahara
VILNIUS (p287)
Europe's finest baroque ensemble, a café-studded cobbled old town and a vibrant arts scene will charm your socks in Lithuania's lovely capital
HILL OF CROSSES (p341)
Plant a cross on this awe-inspiring mountain of crosses and visit the chapel of the neighbouring papal-inspired monastery
ELEVATION
200m
150m
100m
50m
0
LITHUANIA
RUSSIA
BELARUS
POLAND
Latgale
56°N
Curonian Lagoon
Liepāja
Dobele
Jelgava
Bauska
Jēkabpils
Aizkraukle
Daugavpils
Rēzekne
Ludza
Krāslava
Klaipėda
Palanga
Kretinga
Plungė
Telšiai
Mažeikiai
Šiauliai
Hill of Crosses
Joniškis
Biržai
Panevėžys
Rokiškis
Utena
Anykščiai
Ukmergė
Molėtai
Ignalina
Visaginas
Zarasai
Kaunas
Jonava
Kėdainiai
Marijampolė
Alytus
Druskininkai
Trakai
VILNIUS
Juozapinė (294m)
Šilutė
Tauragė
Jurbakas
Sovetsk
Nida
Neringa
Juodkrantė
Curonian Spit
Curonian Spit NP
Žemaitija NP
Nemunas Delta Regional Park
Aukštaitija NP
Trakai Historical NP
Dzūkija NP
Kaliningrad
Zelenogradsk
Chernyakhovsk
Suwałki
Ełk
Olsztyn
Hrodna
Minsk
E67
E22
E262
E77
E271
E272
E28
E85

Destination Estonia, Latvia & Lithuania

They're touted as Europe's best-kept secret or the new Prague – neither of which they'll remain for long. But one thing is sure: Estonia, Latvia and Lithuania are three small but priceless countries sporting sparkling idiosyncratic identities and jam-packed with brilliant surprises. From the picture-postcard cobbled streets and exquisite chocolate-box collections of brightly painted houses in the capitals' medieval old towns to rare and precious wildlife long gone elsewhere in Western Europe, this modest trio quite simply stuns. 'Why didn't I pack lighter clothes?' and 'Ooh, this is the furthest east I've been!' are classic observations made by first-time visitors who naively believe these old Soviet republics to be grey, drab and buried in snow. They're not.

Savouring Tallinn's bright white nights, scouring white Baltic shores for amber, scaling sand dunes in Lithuania's 'Sahara' and sampling local cuisine and drinks, including Lithuania's infamous *cepelinai* or zeppelins (special dumplings) and Latvia's disgusting black Balzāms (liqueurs), are Baltic joys to be revelled in. Vilnius boasts Eastern Europe's largest old town, a bohemian republic and a recommended overdose of baroque, while Rīga has the world's finest collection of Art-Nouveau architecture, a market housed in six WWI zeppelin hangars and one of the cheapest drinkable champagnes on the planet. Elegant Estonia, with its subtle hints of Scandinavia, boasts a coastline studded with 1521 beautiful islands, and a wave of outdoor pursuits.

Soviet recycling gives the region its quirk and its kick. A terror of the past the USSR might well be, but these young EU players – scarcely recognisable from the old days – are riding high on the back of their Soviet heritage: retro nightclubs, a Soviet sculpture park, terrifying warheads aimed at Europe and an antenna that poked its nose into Western satellite communications during the Cold War are all part of the unbelievable act. Don't miss it.

BRUCE YUAN-YUE B

Highlights

DONALD C & PRISCILLA ALEXANDER EASTMAN

Drink in the atmosphere while wandering around Tallinn's hub – Town Hall Square (p69), Estonia

BRUCE YUAN-YUE BI

Vilnius' Old Town (p296), Lithuania, has architecture that crosses the ages

Pay your respects at one of Lithuania's most iconic places, the haunting Hill of Crosses (p341)

JONATHAN SMITH

JONATHAN SMITH

Indulge your Gothic fantasies in the corner tower of the Baltics' finest fortress, Kuressaare Castle (p147), Estonia

Intoxicate your senses in vivid, vibrant (p155), Estonia's favourite beachside resort

CRAIG PERSHOUSE

Immerse yourself in stark and rugged beauty at Lahemaa National Park (p95), Estonia

DEBRA HERRMAN

JONATHAN SMITH

Art gallery, museum, concert and theatre venue – Trakai's Island Castle (p316), Lithuania, stands apart

BRUCE YUAN-YUE BI

Take in Rīga views, including the House of Blackheads (p178), from St Peter's Church (p191), Latvia

Weather the wind and breathe in bracing Baltic Sea air at Cape Kolka (p253), Latvia

AGEFOTOSTOCK/WOJTEK BUSS

DANITA DELIMONT/ALAMY

A crumbling castle tower highlights history in Latvia's most Latvian town, Cēsis (p232)

Come face-to-face with Europe's finest Art-Nouveau architecture (p199) in Rīga, Latvia

BRUCE YUAN-YUE

PHOTOLIBRARY

Gaze at Russia from the top of Parnidis Dune on the Curonian Spit (p362), Lithuania

Contents

The Authors 12

Getting Started 14

Itineraries 18

Snapshots 22

Activities 38

Estonia 43

Highlights 45
Itineraries 45
Current Events 45
History 46
The Culture 51
Sport 53
Religion 54
Arts 54
Environment 59
Food & Drink 62
TALLINN 64
History 65
Orientation 66
Information 67
Sights 69
Activities 78
Tallinn for Children 79
Tours 79
Festivals & Events 79
Sleeping 80
Eating 82
Drinking 86
Entertainment 87
Shopping 88
GETTING THERE & AWAY 89
GETTING AROUND 91
Around Tallinn 91
NORTHEASTERN ESTONIA 94
Lahemaa National Park 95
East Of Lahemaa 101
SOUTHEASTERN ESTONIA 106
Tartu 106
Around Tartu 115
Võru 120
Haanja Nature Park 122
Suur Munamägi 122
Rõuge 122
Luhasoo Trail & Karula National Park 123
Valga 124
Vastseliina Castle 124
Setumaa 124
Lake Peipsi (South) 127
WESTERN ESTONIA & THE ISLANDS 128
Haapsalu 130
Around Haapsalu 133
Vormsi 134
Matsalu Nature Reserve 135
Hiiumaa 135
Saaremaa 142
Muhu 152
SOUTHWESTERN ESTONIA 153
Pärnu 155
Kihnu 161
Ruhnu 162
Viljandi 162
Põltsamaa 165
ESTONIA DIRECTORY 167
Activities 167
Customs 167
Embassies & Consulates 167
Festivals & Events 168
Holidays 169
Internet Access 169
internet resources 169
Maps 170
Money 170
Post 170
Telephone 170
Tourist Information 170

Latvia 171

Highlights 173
Itineraries 173
History 175
The Culture 178
Sport 180
Religion 180
Arts 181
Environment 183
Food & Drink 184
RĪGA 187
History 187

Orientation 189
Information 190
Sights 190
Walking Tour 200
Rīga For Children 200
Tours 209
Festivals & Events 209
Sleeping 209
Eating 211
Drinking 214
Entertainment 216
Shopping 217
Getting There & Away 217
Getting Around 220
Around Rīga 220
VIDZEME 224
The Coast 224
Mazsalaca & Rūjiena 226
Gauja National Park 226
Sigulda 227
Līgatne 232
Cēsis 232
Āraiši 234
Valmiera 234
Valka 236
Alūksne, Gulbene & Around 237
Vidzeme Upland 237
LATGALE 238
Daugava Valley 238
Rēzekne & Around 241
Latgale Upland 241
Daugavpils 242
ZEMGALE 244
Bauska 244
Rundāle Palace 246
Mežotne Palace 247
Jelgava 248
KURZEME 248
Tukums 250
Talsi & Around 251
Northern Kurzeme 252
Abava Valley 255
Ventspils 256
Kuldīga 259
Liepāja 261
LATVIA DIRECTORY 265
Activities 265
Customs 265
Embassies & Consulates 266
Festivals & Events 266
Holidays 267
Internet Access 267
Internet Resources 267
Maps 267
Money 268
Post 268
Telephone 268
Tourist Information 268

Lithuania 269

Highlights 271
Itineraries 271
Current Events 271
History 273
The Culture 276
Sport 278
Religion 278
Arts 279
Environment 282
Food & Drink 284
VILNIUS 287
History 287
Orientation 287
Information 290
Dangers & Annoyances 291
Sights 294
Walking Tour 304
Vilnius For Children 305
Tours 305
Festivals & Events 306
Sleeping 306
Eating 308
Drinking 311
Entertainment 312
Shopping 312
Getting There & Away 313
Getting Around 314
Around Vilnius 315
EASTERN & SOUTHERN LITHUANIA 319
Aukštaitija National Park 320
Visaginas & Ignalina Nuclear Power Station 322
Labanoros Regional Park 323
Druskininkai 324
Dzūkija National Park 328
The Southwest 329
CENTRAL LITHUANIA 329
Kaunas 331
Šiauliai 339
Radviliškis & Around 343
Panevėžys 343
Anykščiai 345
WESTERN LITHUANIA 345
Klaipėda 347
Palanga 355
Žemaitija National Park 360
Curonian Spit National Park 362
Nemunas Delta 370
LITHUANIA DIRECTORY 372
Activities 372
Customs 372
Embassies & Consulates 372
Festivals & Events 373
Holidays 374
Internet Access 374
Internet Resources 374
Maps 374
Money 375
Post 375
Telephone 375
Tourist Information 375

Kaliningrad Excursion 376

KALININGRAD 377
Orientation & Information 377
Sights 377
Sleeping 379
Eating & Drinking 379
Getting There & Away 380
Getting Around 380

Regional Directory 381

Accommodation 381
Activities 383
Business Hours 383
Children 383
Climate Charts 384
Courses 384
Customs 385
Dangers & Annoyances 385
Disabled Travellers 385
Discount Cards 385
Embassies & Consulates 386
Festivals & Events 386
Food 387
Gay & Lesbian Travellers 387
Holidays 387
Insurance 387
Internet Access 387
Legal Matters 388
Maps 388
Money 388
Post 389
Shopping 390

Solo Travellers 390
Telephone 390
Time 390
Toilets 391
Tourist Information 391
Visas 391
Women Travellers 392
Work 392

Transport 393

GETTING THERE & AWAY 393
Entering Estonia, Latvia & Lithuania 393
Air 393
Land 396
Sea 400
GETTING AROUND 403
Air 403
Bicycle 403
Boat 404
Bus 404
Car & Motorcycle 405
Hitching 407
Local Transport 408
Train 408
Tours 409

Health 410

BEFORE YOU GO 410
Insurance 410
Recommended Vaccinations 410
Online Resources 410
IN ESTONIA, LATVIA & LITHUANIA 411
Availability & Cost of Health Care 411
Infectious Diseases 411
Traveller's Diarrhoea 411
Environmental Hazards 411
Travelling With Children 411
Women's Health 412
Sexual Health 412

Language 413

Glossary 424

Behind the Scenes 426

Index 436

World Time Zones 446

Map Legend 448

Regional Map Contents

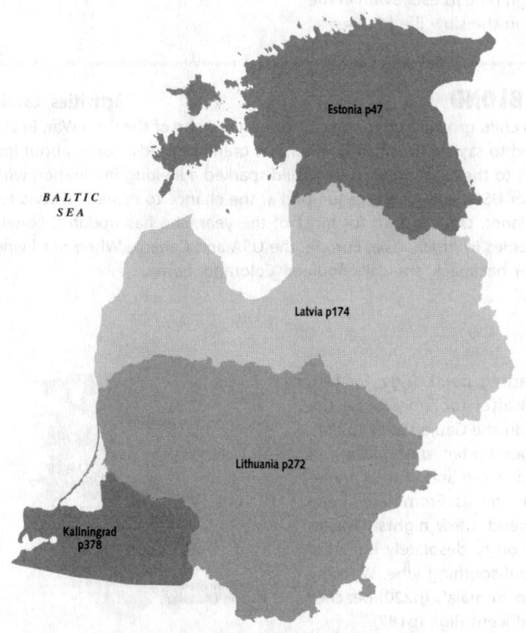

The Authors

NICOLA WILLIAMS

Coordinating Author, Lithuania

A year in Latvia before returning to London as an up 'n' coming young journalist never did work out: Nicola ended up staying a couple of years in Rīga, quitting her job as features editor for the *Baltic Times* only to move to Lithuania as editor-in-chief of the Vilnius-based *In Your Pocket* city guide series. Eventually, she did leave – to wed her German sweetheart in France where she now lives. Nicola wrote the 1st edition of *Estonia, Latvia & Lithuania* and has worked on many other Lonely Planet titles.

My Favourite Trip

I revel in the contrasts the three capitals proffer: quaint old Vilnius (p287), with its hidden courtyards and cobble maze, Tallinn (p64), with Scandinavian serenade, and Rīga (p187), the only capital sufficiently gritty and cosmopolitan to really feel like a capital. City-hopping aside, my favourite trip entails some serious eating and drinking in Vilnius, with an overnight flit to Trakai (p315) to Zen-out in the lakeside Jacuzzi and enjoy refined dining on the jetty restaurant at Akmeninė Užeiga (p317). Then it's a speed-drive west to the coast where party-mad Palanga (p355) contrasts with the indescribable beauty of the Curonian Spit (p362). Here, I could cycle through pine forests, swim in the sea, splash in wild sand and wallow in the slow life for ever.

BECCA BLOND

Activities, Latvia

Even as a child growing up in the USA during the end of the Cold War, Becca was proud to say she was half Russian. Her grandmother's stories about immigrating to the United States as a child sparked a lifelong fascination with the former USSR, and so Becca jumped at the chance to research Latvia for Lonely Planet. On the road for most of the year, she has updated Lonely Planet guides in Africa, Asia, Europe, the USA and Canada. When not living out of her backpack, she calls Boulder, Colorado, home.

My Favourite Trip

I enjoy leaving Latvia's obvious starting point, Rīga, for last. The city seems even more magical after tooling around the countryside. My favourite trip starts in the Gauja Valley (p224). Using Sigulda (p227) as a base, I spend a few days playing in this pine-scented wonderland. A canoe trip and visit to my favourite Latvian town, Cēsis (p232), are musts. From here I head to happening Liepāja (p261) and spend a few nights dancing to live Latvian rock music. Then it's on to desolately beautiful Cape Kolka (p253). I just love it's soul-soothing vibe. With my country cravings appeased, I head to Jūrmala's (p220) beaches before finishing up my trip in magnificent Rīga (p187).

REGIS ST LOUIS

Estonia, Kaliningrad Excursion, Regional Directory, Transport

Regis first became interested in Estonia during his student days at Moscow State University, when the Baltics were still referred to as wayward states rather than independent nations. Since then, he's avidly followed developments in this tiny country as it's gone from ex-Soviet to EU, becoming one of Europe's hottest destinations that almost no-one can point to on a map. The natural beauty of the landscape, the friendly people and the splendid cities and villages are just a few reasons why he can't stop raving about Estonia. Regis lives in New York City.

My Favourite Trip

My Estonian journey begins in Tallinn's alluring Old Town (p69). After a few days soaking up medieval splendour and café culture, I head south to charming Tartu (p106). Lovely parks, a meandering river and fascinating galleries preface an inspiring trip into the southeast (p106). There, I am immersed in Estonia's natural beauty: picturesque villages, lush forests and enchanting lakes. After rustic living beneath the gaze of Setu god Peko, I strike west for Saaremaa (p142), not overlooking its majestic castle nor its indulgent spa resorts. Assuming there's time (and money) to spare, I head to Haapsalu (p130) for lovely strolls along 19th-century lanes, and continue to Lahemaa (p95), a gem of a national park, fronting an idyllic stretch of deep-blue Baltic Sea.

LONELY PLANET AUTHORS

Why is our travel information the best in the world? It's simple: our authors are independent, dedicated travellers. They don't research using just the Internet or phone, and they don't take freebies in exchange for positive coverage. They travel widely, to all the popular spots and off the beaten track. They personally visit thousands of hotels, restaurants, cafés, bars, galleries, palaces, museums and more – and they take pride in getting all the details right, and telling it how it is. For more, see the authors section on www.lonelyplanet.com.

Getting Started

Astonishingly few people can pinpoint these three countries on a map, giving Baltic-bound travellers an instant head start. Accommodation is relatively easy to find (bar the capitals in July and August, which do get tourist-busy) and is still a steal compared with many other European countries. Dining is another unexpectedly tasty experience, in the capitals at least, with many meals at laughable prices. To top it all off, the arts scene is hot, young and vibrant.

WHEN TO GO

In spring, the weather is warm, the days are long, flowery cottage gardens blossom and the cultural calendar oozes fun. April and May, when the lucky stork returns to its nest, and the land and its people open up after winter, convey a real magic. June is midsummer-madness month (p17) and equally evokes the Baltic peoples' close ties to nature and their pagan past (p31).

See Climate Charts (p384) for more information

Summers are short but sweet. July and August (high season), the warmest and busiest months, and a time when many Balts go on holiday too, can also be the wettest and subject to the odd thunderstorm. Coastal waters at this time average between 16°C and 21°C, and daytime highs from May to September hover between 14°C and 22°C.

Winter (November to March – essentially low season), with just a few hours of semidaylight every 24 hours, is a long dark affair with temperatures rarely above 4°C and frequently dipping below zero. December to March sees snow-clogged streets, icy pavements and roofs laced with killer icicles. Ice skating, tobogganing, cross-country skiing, ice fishing and getting whipped in a sauna (p40) are this season's invigorating activities.

Avoid soggy March when the snow thaws, bringing with it far too much slush for enjoyment. Autumn, when snow falls then melts, is equally miserable.

COSTS & MONEY

Latvia and Estonia are the most expensive of the trio, with Rīga and Tallinn touting prices comparable to Scandinavia. Accommodation in the Baltics, especially in Rīga, is expensive and the biggest cost for travellers. Dining in

DON'T LEAVE HOME WITHOUT...

- Valid travel insurance (p387), ID card or passport, and visa (p391) if required
- Driving licence, car documents and car insurance (p397)
- Sunglasses, hat, mosquito repellent, a few clothes pegs and binoculars (summer)
- Thermals, ice skates and the thickest, warmest hat and coat you can find (winter)
- A universal sink plug (if you like baths)
- A good wad of tissues or toilet paper – to be carried at all times
- Your sea legs
- An indestructible pair of shoes or boots to combat cobblestones
- A taste for 'black magic' (p185)
- A travel pillow; some pillows in Latvia feel as though they're made of concrete.

rural Latvia and Lithuania, and across the board in Lithuania, is relatively cheap (p387); ditto for museum admission fees (free to €2) and overland travel (€2.55 to €4.50 per 100km) in the region. Discount cards (p385) in Rīga and Tallinn yield a bounty of money-savers for city-based visitors.

At the bottom of the accommodation barrel in the capitals, you can scrape a night's sleep in a dorm for as little as €12.80/8.50/5 in a Tallinn/Rīga/Vilnius hostel and €19.50/12.80/30 in a budget hotel; double rooms are cheaper per person than singles and most midrange and top-end hotels will put in an extra bed for kids for free or a small fee. Comfortable B&B accommodation in Tallinn/Rīga/Vilnius starts at €18/35/23 per person, while a night's stay in a midrange hotel costs €60 to €70 a head. Top-end rates can rocket as high as €200 per person, per night in all three capitals. Step away from the capitals into rurality and prices plummet: €10 gets you a blissfully quiet and peaceful night's sleep in budget/midrange/top-end accommodation in the Baltic countryside.

READING UP

Books

Among the Russians (Colin Thubron) Gloomy and resigned, yes, but that was precisely the mood when this Englishman motored everywhere he could in the pre-glasnost USSR.

Journey into Russia (Laurens van der Post) The three Baltic capitals are vividly painted in this travelogue through Soviet Russia in the 1960s.

The Last Girl & Amber (Stephan Collishaw) Collishaw (p276) won the heart of the literary world with these dark, haunting and highly emotive novels evoking two very different faces of modern-day Lithuania.

The Merry Baker of Riga (Boris Zemtzov) Hilarious and dry, this intuitive tale of an American entrepreneur setting up shop as a baker in Riga in 1992 is a true story.

To the Baltic with Bob (Griff Rhys Jones) A beach read easy enough to read with your eyes closed: sail with Griff 'n' Bob from London to Germany via Ventspils, Rīga, Saaremaa, Vormsi, Paldiski ('a wreck') and Tallinn.

Venusburg (Anthony Powell) For a taste of 1930s Latvia and Estonia, try this amusing tale of a journalist hobnobbing with exiled Russian aristocrats, Baltic-German intellectuals and local patriots.

Websites

In Your Pocket (www.inyourpocket.com) Insider city guides to a clutch of Baltic cities, with free PDF downloads to pop in your pocket.

Latvia: The Land That Sings (www.latviatourism.lv) Latvian tourist board website.

Latvians Online (www.latviansonline.com) Excellent Latvian-related features and loads of Latvian news, current affairs and hot topics.

Lonely Planet (www.lonelyplanet.com) Notes and posts on Baltic travel, plus the Thorn Tree bulletin board.

Official Lithuanian Travel Guide (www.travel.lt) Sexy name? No. Great site packed with useful information? Yes.

Welcome to Estonia (www.visitestonia.com) Estonian tourist board website.

FESTIVALS & EVENTS

The region enjoys a sumptuous festival calendar, embracing everything from religion and music to art, folklore, handicrafts, film and drama with gusto. Summer festival madness peaks with midsummer celebrations on 24 June (p17); the annual Baltika Folklore Festival in mid-July, which the three capitals take in turn to host; and the legendary Baltic song and dance festivals (p33).

All three countries celebrate magical festivals at other times of the year too; for a fat-cat calendar of country-specific festivals and events see the Festival & Events section in each country chapter.

TOP TEN BALTIC FESTIVALS

- **Midsummer** (regionwide) 24 June (opposite)
- **Black Nights Film Festival** (Tallinn) late November–early December (p80)
- **Kaziukas Crafts Fair** (Vilnius) 4 March (p306)
- **Jazzkaar** (Tallinn, Pärnu, Narva, Tartu & Viljandi) mid-April (p79)
- **Old Town Days** (Tallinn) early June (p79)
- **Song & Dance Festivals** Vilnius 2007, Rīga 2008, Tallinn 2009 (p33)
- **Baltika Folklore Festival** Rīga 2006, Tallinn 2007, Vilnius 2008 (p386)
- **Baltic Beach Party** (Liepāja) late July (p267).
- **Days of the White Lady** (Haapsalu) August (p132)
- **Visagino Country** (Visaginas) mid-August (p322)

RESPONSIBLE TRAVEL

Swelling tourist numbers coupled with local property development and an ever-increasing drive towards commercialism have accelerated the need to protect the region's fragile ecosystems, biological diversity and natural (relatively unspoiled) treasures. Ways to avoid placing pressure on the environment include conserving water and electricity, not littering or burying your rubbish, and taking care not to disturb wildlife. If you intend to camp or hike, seek permission to camp from the landowner or, in the case of national parks and protected nature reserves, only pitch your tent in designated areas. Forests – which carpet 44% each of Estonia and Latvia and 30% of Lithuania – are especially vulnerable. Do not light fires, discard cigarette butts or leave litter in these areas, and stick to assigned paths. Always observe the rules and recommendations set by park, nature reserve and forest authorities.

Erosion, fire and tourism pose an enormous threat to the unique sand spit and dunes on western Lithuania's Curonian Spit – a Unesco World Heritage natural treasure; a tableau at the foot of steps leading up to the Parnidis Dune shows just how much the mountain of sand has shrunk in the past 20 years. When walking on the spit don't blaze new trails across virgin sand or pick plant life that keeps the top sand in place; stick to marked wooden walkways.

Cities pose a whole different set of responsible travel rules. The cobbled old towns of Rīga, Tallinn and Vilnius all star on Unesco's list of World Heritage cultural and natural treasures. Pay them the respect they deserve. In Tallinn, after years of Finnish 'vodka' and 'Gin Long Drink' tourism, people are fed up with rowdy drunken behaviour and blokes peeing on the streets. You'll get better treatment if you indulge in moderation. The same applies to the increasing number of British stag parties hitting the Baltic capitals for cheap weekends of binge-drinking and sex. Drink by all means – but quietly and without offence to others.

Prostitution is rife in the capitals, particularly in Rīga where it is legal (prostitution is illegal in Estonia and Lithuania). While prostitution is legal in Latvia, pimping is punishable by up to four years in prison. Incidents do occur where Western clients are drugged, robbed and left lying in the gutter – literally. For your personal safety and for the sake of the young girls at hand, often forced by their parents to work the streets, it is better not to engage in this activity.

MIDSUMMER MADNESS

In pagan times it was a night of magic and sorcery when witches ran naked and wild, bewitching flowers and ferns, people and animals. In the agricultural calendar, it marked the end of the spring sowing and the start of the summer harvest. In Soviet times it became a political celebration; a torch of independence was lit in each capital and its flame used to light bonfires throughout the country.

Today Midsummer Day, summer solstice or St John's Day, falling on 24 June, is the Balts' biggest party of the year. On this night darkness barely falls – reason alone to celebrate in a part of the world with such short summers and such long, dark winters. In Estonia it is known as Jaanipäev, in Latvia Jāni, Jānu Diena or Ligo and in Lithuania Joninės or Rasos (the old pagan name).

Celebrations start on 23 June, particularly in Latvia, where the festival is generally met with the most gusto. Traditionally, people flock to the countryside to celebrate this special night amid lakes and pine forests. Special beers, cheeses and pies are prepared and wreaths strung together from grasses, while flowers and herbs are hung around the home to bring good luck and keep families safe from evil spirits. Men adorn themselves with crowns made from oak leaves, and women with crowns of flowers.

Come Midsummer's Eve, bonfires are lit and the music and drinking begins. No-one is allowed to sleep until the sun has sunk and risen again – anyone who does will be cursed with bad luck for the coming year. Traditional folk songs are sung, dances danced and those special beers, cheeses and pies eaten! To ensure good luck, you have to leap back and forth over the bonfire. In Lithuania, clearing a burning wheel of fire as it is rolled down the nearest hill brings you even better fortune. In Estonia, revellers swing on special double-sided Jaanipäev swings, strung from trees in forest clearings or in village squares.

Midsummer's night is a night for lovers. In Estonia the mythical Koit (dawn) and Hämarik (dusk) meet but once a year for an embrace lasting as long as the shortest night of the year. Throughout the Baltic region, lovers seek the mythical fern flower, which only blooms on this night. The dew coating flowers and ferns on midsummer's night is held to be a purifying force, a magical healer and a much sought-after cure for wrinkles! Bathe your face in it and you will instantly become more beautiful, more youthful. However, beware the witches of Jaanipäev/Jāni/Joninės, who are known to use it for less enchanting means.

Itineraries
CLASSIC ROUTES

BEST OF THE BALTICS
Two Weeks / Vilnius to Tallinn

Embark on the grandest of Baltic tours in the Lithuanian capital, **Vilnius** (p287). Take a day trip to castle-clad **Trakai** (p315) and/or the Soviet sculpture park at **Druskininkai** (p324), then push west to **Klaipėda** (p347) and the Unesco-protected **Curonian Spit** (p362). Next, hit **Rīga:** take the 3½-hour speed route via **Šiauliai** (p339) and the **Hill of Crosses** (p341); or the slow route of a few days along the tranquil Latvian coast via hip 'n' happening **Liepāja** (p261), **Cape Kolka** (p253) and **Jūrmala** (p220). In **Rīga** (p187), revel in Europe's best Art-Nouveau architecture, then delve into **Sigulda** (p227) and the Gauja Valley en route to university-driven **Tartu** (p106) and **Soomaa National Park** (p165). Those with bags of time could detour to the lazy old spa town of **Pärnu** (p155) or the fabulous islands of **Saaremaa** (p142) and **Hiiumaa** (p135).

The final leg is north to the Estonian capital, **Tallinn** (p64), where old-town medieval splendour jockeys for pride of place with hip wine bars, stylish lounges and a dizzying choice of cuisine.

Vilnius to Tallinn direct is only 588km, but throw in the slow route and detour cooked up by this itinerary to cover the very best of the Baltics and you'll easily clock up 1400km. The trip – minus deviations – can be done in a whirlwind fortnight, but definitely merits as much time as you can give it.

PAINT THE TOWN RED

One Month / Paldiski to Daugavpils

Tracking the Baltics' Soviet past is an eclectic trip. Start with the crumbling cliff-top Soviet barracks in Estonia's **Paldiski** (p93), then hit **Tallinn** (p64) for stained-glass Soviet-socialist realism in the TV tower and Soviet memorabilia shopping. Speed east next, through the USSR's first national park, **Lahemaa National Park** (p95), to **Sillamäe** (p103), a seaside museum of Stalinist architecture, and Russian-speaking **Narva** (p103), with its moody castle where Lenin lives. Villages settled by Soviet-persecuted Old Believers and Soviet-era resorts hug **Lake Peipsi** (p105; p127).

Cross the border into Latvia at twin-town **Valga/Valka** (p124; p236) and rip down the artificial bobsled track built for the Soviet team at **Sigulda** (p227). In **Rīga** (p187) meet die-hard reds in Victory Park, gawp at Stalin's birthday cake, dine retro-Soviet style, party in a Soviet train and learn about Soviet occupation in the Museum of Occupation, and Latvian resistance in the Latvian People's Front Museum. Then play I-spy at the world's eighth-largest parabolic antenna, 24km north of **Ventspils** (p256), and stroll around **Liepāja** (p261), taking in Karosta and its Soviet prison, where die-hards kip the night. Otherwise, try funky Hotel Fontaine.

In Lithuania, a tour of the **underground Soviet missile base** (p361) at **Žemaitija National Park** is terrifying. Sleep in the old Soviet barracks, then push east past the **Hill of Crosses** (p341) to **Vilnius** (p287) with its disturbing Museum of Genocide Victims and poignant reminders of bloody 1991. Afterwards, bear north to **Visaginas** (p322) and the dangers of a Soviet-designed nuclear power plant and overnight in the only Soviet city in the EU where nothing is more than 30 years old. Then it's north again to drab **Daugavpils** (p242) with its remarkable fortress where Soviet troops were stationed.

This trip takes you pretty much the length and breadth of the region, traversing north to south along its coastal western realm then heading back again via the more industrial, Russian-influenced east. Count 1720km, three border crossings and plenty of greenery to distract you when the concrete gets too much.

ROADS LESS TRAVELLED

GO GREEN

Two Weeks / Lithuania's Spit to Estonia's Islands

National-park hopping ensures mountains of discoveries off the beaten track. Witness the vulnerability of nature around the Sahara of Lithuania, **Curonian Spit** (p362), an unforgettable spit of sand where elks mingle with wild boar and Lithuania's largest colony of cormorants and grey herons. From **Nida** (p365), Lithuania, sail into the desolate **Nemunas Delta** (p370) where birdlife at the Ventės Ragas Ornithological Station enthrals. Complete the coastal ride with a look at innovative recycling in **Nida** (p357), Latvia; a blow-through at the end of the world at **Cape Kolka** (p253); and a walk through Latvia's oldest forest in the **Šlītere National Park** (p254). Next dive into the **Gauja National Park** (p226), where walking, biking, hiking and canoeing – and the rare black stork – thrill outdoor-lovers.

In week two go green in Estonia: stop at **Otepää** (p116) for skiing or summer swimming, and midsummer celebrations around Estonia's most sacred lake, **Pühajärv** (p118). Continue via pretty **Viljandi** (p162) to the wet, and wildlife-packed **Soomaa National Park** (p165), and explore myriad forested waterways by traditional *haabja* (canoe). Wallow in mud in **Pärnu** (p155), followed by a slice of island life: wooded islands lie off the lovely shores of Saaremaa in the **Vilsandi National Park** (p152), while **Matsalu Nature Reserve** (p135) is the Baltics' best bird-watching terrain. Alternatively, from Pärnu steer north to **Lahemaa** (p95), an alluring paradise with beautiful nature trails and coastline, and old-fashioned seafaring villages.

A fortnight gives you just enough time for a glimpse of the extraordinary Baltic flora, fauna and landscapes. A breath of fresh air after the tourist madness of the three capitals' medieval old towns, this green itinerary covering 1200km guarantees a foolproof getaway from the crowds.

TAILORED TRIPS

THE AMBER ROAD

Amber has been transported along amber roads since before the birth of Christ, and there's nowhere finer to feel its subtle magic than in the Russian-controlled **Kaliningrad Region** (p376), source of almost all Baltic amber. Stunning amber-studded jewellery and the world's second-largest hunk of amber add a sparkle to the Kaliningrad Amber Museum, while Kaliningrad's amber cabin aboard the *Vitiaz* is an interesting port of call. A tour of the industrial Yantarny Amber Mine from the capital is a must.

The region's finest amber gallery in **Nida** (p365), Lithuania, is a hop, skip and jump across sand dunes on **Curonian Spit** (p362) from the Russian province. Amber treasure was found in **Juodkrantė** (p364) in the 1850s but today you'll find only specks, washed up on the shore after fierce storms; professional amber fishers frequent **Karklė** (p351) and **Šventoji** (p355) beaches. **Palanga** (p355) sports a palatial amber museum and an innovative amber processing gallery, while wacky **Nida** (p357) across the border in Latvia presents amber-fishing from a home-spun perspective.

Lovely **Liepāja** (p261) boasts a 123m-long rope of amber beads and an amber clock. There are fine amber displays at Pāvilosta Ethnographic Museum, which also arranges amber-fishing trips, and inside the Livonian Order Castle in **Ventspils** (p256). **Vilnius** (p287), **Rīga** (p187) and **Tallinn** (p64) all have quality amber galleries.

WORLD HERITAGE SIGHTS

Estonia, Latvia and Lithuania safeguard nine Unesco-protected world treasures (http://whc.unesco.org), kicking off with each capital's extraordinary old town, inscribed on the World Heritage list since 1997: **Rīga** (p190) is a mind-blowing plethora of medieval, neoclassical and Art-Nouveau buildings dating from the 13th to 19th centuries, and its Art-Nouveau collection is Europe's best. Church-studded **Vilnius** (p294) is medieval, Gothic, Renaissance and classical, and has Europe's biggest baroque old town to boot. Nowhere better reflects the fabric of a medieval northern European trading city than **Tallinn** (p69). The archaeological site of **Kernavė** (p318) near the Lithuanian capital is another world gem, as is the extraordinary slither of sand linking Lithuania with Kaliningrad, **Curonian Spit** (p362), sculpted over millennia by Baltic Sea winds and waves.

Days of discovery surround the region's intangible treasures safeguarded by Unesco with a 'Masterpiece of the Oral and Intangible Heritage of Humanity' stamp: cross crafting and its symbolism in Lithuania; the Kihnu Cultural Space on **Kihnu Island** (p161); and the magnificent Baltic song and dance festivals.

Snapshots

CURRENT EVENTS

EU harmonisation is driving current affairs in the Baltics. Fully fledged EU members since 2004, Estonia, Latvia and Lithuania have realised their pipe dream: they've rejoined the West. Now they face the gargantuan task of bringing their laws, policies, economies and infrastructures in line with those of Europe while also realising their individual growth potentials: these are three of Europe's fastest-growing economies, after all.

The euro should replace Estonia and Lithuania's national currencies on 1 January 2007, and Latvia's in 2008.

Brussels' money is easing the transition: Estonia was allocated €695 million in structural and cohesion funds for 2004–06, Latvia just over €1 billion and Lithuania €1.5 billion. Building new roads, hotels and spas, rehabilitating railway tunnels, constructing waste-water treatment plants, decommissioning nuclear power plants and sorting out stinky sewage (not to mention drinking water) are among the kaleidoscope of projects flagged with a circle of stars on what feels like every second street corner.

But this is no easy ride. Every euro spent by Brussels is roughly matched with a euro from national coffers. The Baltic countries are the poorest of the 25 EU countries: one-third of households live below the poverty line. In 2005 the Latvian GDP per capita was 43.6% of the EU average, the Lithuanian 47.8% and the Estonian 50% (comparatively, France and Germany hover around the 110% mark, and Austria and Denmark are at 120%). Average net earnings better reflect the reality: €231 a month in Latvia, €264 in Lithuania and €379 in wealthier Estonia.

All three countries are parliamentary democracies run by a parliament (Estonia: *Riigikogu;* Latvia: *Saeima;* Lithuania: *Seimas*) and a president, both elected by universal suffrage for a four- or five-year term.

Incredibly the region remains on target to meet the economic requirements needed to trade in their national currencies for the common European currency, the euro. In Estonia and Lithuania, budget deficits are less than 3% of GDP, inflation has reached a constant low, and the Lithuanian litų and Estonian kroon have been pegged to the euro since mid-2004. Once Latvia has brought its 6% inflation down to 2.1%, it too can peg; curiously enough, Latvians – sticklers for language – are running a campaign to call the euro by its Latvian name, 'eiro'.

NATO hosted its spring parliamentary assembly in Vilnius in 2002 and returned to the Lithuanian capital in April 2005 for an informal meeting of foreign ministers – much to the consternation of Russia, which makes no bones about its fierce opposition to NATO's eastward expansion and its increasing influence on old USSR territory. Since Estonia, Latvia and Lithuania joined NATO in April 2004, Baltic air space has been policed by NATO aircraft based in Šiauliai – a bitter pill for Russia given that the Soviet-built base, large enough to land a space shuttle on, once defended the USSR's western border. Wrangles over shared borders, language laws, WWII celebrations and the citizenship rights of the region's sizable Russian-speaking community further exacerbate relations between the ex-Soviet republics and Russia, which are cool at best.

PRESIDENTIAL LINE-UP

Estonia: Arnold Rüütel (www.president.ee); elected in 2001 for five years.

Latvia: Vaira Vīķe-Freiberga (www.president.lv); re-elected in 2003 for four years.

Lithuania: Valdas Adamakus (www.president.lt); elected in 2004 for five years.

Players with the big boys they might be, but at heart these three Baltic countries remain extraordinarily young societies, as the extreme public opposition – including from the Latvian prime minister – to the region's first gay-pride march, held in Rīga in July 2005, clearly demonstrated. This emotive vent of anger was followed in September 2005 by all but one Latvian MP voting for a constitutional ban of same-sex marriages, which are already illegal under civil law. At time of research, the parliament had passed the amendment to the constitution, but it must be signed by

BALTIC LEXICON

Balkans Absolutely nothing whatsoever to do with the Baltics, beyond the fact that a shocking number of people confuse the two.
Baltic countries Estonia, Latvia and Lithuania.
Baltic states A generic term used to refer to the Soviet Baltic-Sea republics of Estonia, Latvia and Lithuania. Since independence, this has become a misnomer of convenience, but it is considered to be horribly outdated and politically incorrect by many. Avoid.
Baltic region The entire Baltic Sea catchment area, of which Estonia, Latvia and Lithuania make up approximately 11%. Finland, Sweden, Denmark, Germany, Poland and the Kaliningrad Region (Russia) are all in the Baltic region – but are not Baltic countries.
Balts A derivative of Mare Baliticum, the Latin for 'Baltic Sea' (coined by the German chronicler Adamus Bremen in the 11th century). It is used to describe people of Indo-European ethnolinguistic groups (Latvians and Lithuanians) who settled in the southeastern Baltic Sea area from 2000 BC.
Nordic countries Traditionally understood to be Scandinavia and Finland, but seen by many as including also Estonia, as the former Estonian foreign minister pointed out in the newspaper *Eesti Ekspress* in 1998. Toomas Hendrik argued that Estonia had closer historical and cultural ties to Finland than to Latvia and Lithuania, and concluded by saying that Estonia was Europe's 'only postcommunist Nordic country'.
Post-Soviet countries Assumed to be an indisputable tag, yet one that the Lithuanian parliament clearly rejected in early 1999 when it urged NATO not to describe Lithuania as 'former Soviet' or 'post-Soviet'. This, the parliament argued, implied that the Baltics legally belonged to Moscow in the Soviet era, as opposed to being 'illegally occupied'.

the president, Vaire Vīķe-Freiberga, before it becomes law. She is not in favour of the amendment, but is under immense pressure to sign it.

HISTORY

Until the early 20th century the ethnic identities of Estonia, Latvia and Lithuania were denied or suppressed. They emerged from the turmoil of WWI and the Russian Revolution as independent countries and enjoyed two decades of statehood until WWII, when all three fell under Soviet influence. Occupation by Nazi Germany in 1941 was followed by Soviet reconquest and the region was forcibly merged with the USSR. In 1991 Estonia, Latvia and Lithuania again won independence.

Ethnically speaking, Latvians and Lithuanians are closely related. The Estonians have different origins, with closer linguistic links to Finland than to their immediate Baltic neighbours.

However, in terms of the history of the past 800 years, Latvia and Estonia have more in common with each other than with Lithuania. The latter was once a powerful state in its own right – at its peak in the 14th to 16th centuries – but Latvia and Estonia were entirely subject to foreign rule from the 13th to the early 20th century. By the late 18th century the entire region had fallen under Russian rule. Until emancipation in the 19th century, most of its native people had been serfs for centuries.

UNEMPLOYMENT

In 2004, unemployment was at the following levels.

Estonia: 10.2%

Latvia: 9.8%

Lithuania: 10.8%

EU: 9%

From Settlers to Serfs

Human habitation in the region goes back to at least 9000 BC in the south and 7500 BC in the north, with the forebears of the present inhabitants –

TIMELINE

3000–2000 BC
Finno-Ugric hunters from the east and Balts from the southeast settle the region

13th century
By 1290 Germanic crusading knights have conquered almost all of Estonia and Latvia

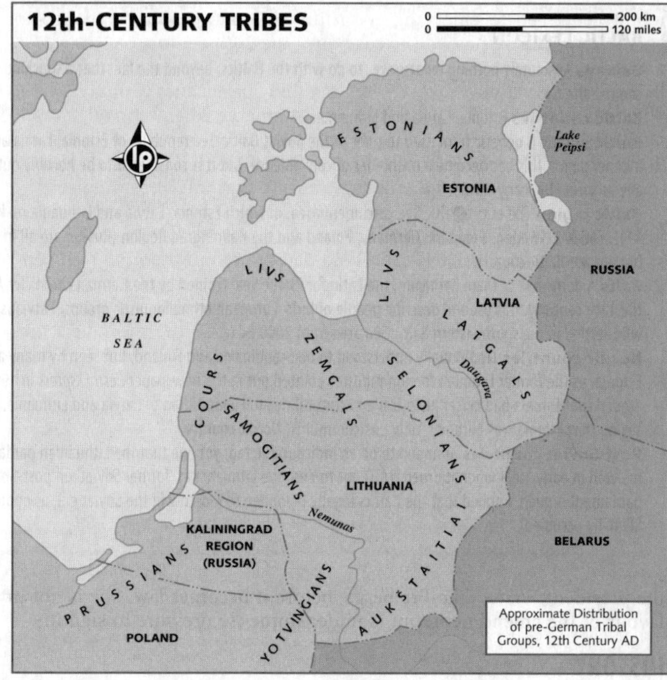

'In 1201 the Bishop of Rīga built the region's first Germanic fort'

Finno-Ugric hunters from the east and the Balts from the southeast – settling between 3000 and 2000 BC. The region rapidly became known as a rich source of amber, and local tribes traded the substance with German tribes, the Roman Empire and, later, Vikings and Russians.

The region was dragged into written history by the expansionist *Urge to the East* of Germanic princes, colonists, traders, missionaries and crusading knights. In 1201 the Bishop of Rīga, Albert von Buxhoevden, built the region's first Germanic fort and established the Knights of the Sword, an order of crusading knights whose white cloaks were emblazoned with blood-red swords and crosses. Their mission? To convert the region by conquest. And indeed, within a quarter of century these knights had subjugated and converted all of Estonia and most of Latvia, bar some regions in the west, which they would snatch in 1290. Cēsis became their castle-clad base. In 1237 they became a branch of the Prussian-based crusaders, the Teutonic Order, and renamed themselves the Livonian Order.

By 1346 Germanic rulers controlled the Baltic seaboard from west of Danzig (modern Gdansk in Poland) to Narva in northeastern Estonia. They divided the region into fiefdoms headed by Teutonics, Livonians or their vassals. In trade-rich towns like Rīga, Dorpat (Tartu), Pernau (Pärnu), Windau (Ventspils) and Wenden (Cēsis), a wealthy German

14th–16th century

Lithuania staves off Germanic attacks to emerge as a powerful state; its alliance with Poland sees it play second fiddle in the partnership

18th century

Peter the Great destroys Sweden as a regional power and establishes Russian rule in Estonia and much of Latvia nobility emerged to enjoy the good life while natives were reduced to feudal serfs. This remained the case until the 20th century.

The Germanic invaders made repeated attacks on Lithuania during the 14th century but were restricted to a thin coastal strip around Memel (Klaipėda), allowing the Baltic country to emerge as a powerful state in the 14th to 16th centuries. But its subsequent union with Poland saw Lithuanians play second fiddle to the Polish, with Lithuania's gentry adopting Polish culture and language and its peasants becoming serfs.

The Great Northern War was so devastating for Estonia and Latvia that neither bark of dog nor crow of cock could be heard anywhere from Narva to Rīga by the end of it, according to one Russian general.

Swedish, Polish & Russian Rule

As German control in Latvia and Estonia wavered in the mid-16th century, other powers cast interested eyes over the region. Ivan the Terrible of Muscovy seemed to ravage every town in mainland Estonia and eastern Latvia during the 25-year Livonian War and, after the war's end, the Baltic lands were fought over by Protestant Sweden and Catholic Poland-Lithuania, with Sweden the eventual victor. Seventeenth-century Swedish rule is regarded as an enlightened episode in Estonia and Latvia's long histories of foreign oppression: Swedish kings Gustaf II Adolf and Carl (Charles) XI raised Estonian and Latvian peasants from serfdom and introduced universal elementary education.

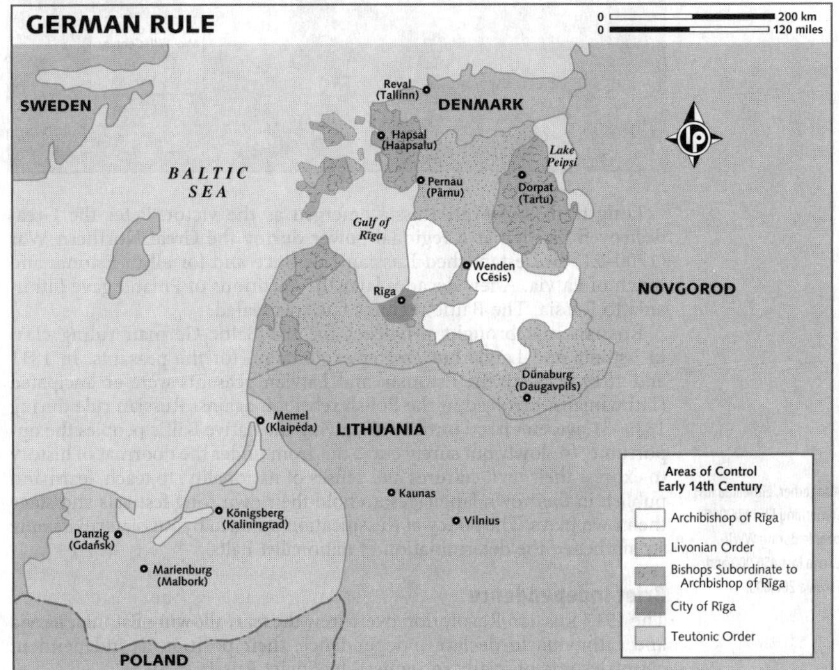

19th century

Emancipation marks the end of centuries of serfdom for most native Balts – and the birth of nationalism

1917

Estonia, Latvia and Lithuania emerge from WWI and the Russian Revolution as independent countries

Using original German and Soviet wartime newsreels, International Historic Films has produced an enthralling DVD depicting the true horror of WWII for the occupied Baltic nations. Buy *The Baltic Tragedy* online at www.ihffilm.com/22023.html.

Long term, however, Russia emerged as the victor. Peter the Great destroyed Sweden as a regional power during the Great Northern War (1700–21) and established Russian rule once and for all in Estonia and much of Latvia. A few decades later the Partitions of Poland gave Lithuania to Russia. The Baltic region's fate was sealed.

Russian rule brought privileges for the Baltic-German ruling class in Estonia and Latvia but greater exploitation for the peasants. In 1811 and 1819 respectively, Estonian and Latvian peasants were emancipated (Lithuanians, involved in the Polish rebellion against Russian rule during 1830–31, weren't freed until 1860), giving the native Baltic peoples the opportunity to slowly but surely crawl out from under the doormat of history to express their own cultures and senses of nationality; to teach, learn and publish in their own languages; to hold their own song festivals and stage their own plays. The policy of Russification pursued by Russian rulers only strengthened the determination of nationalist Balts.

Altogether, Lithuania lost something like 475,000 people during WWII. Latvia lost 450,000 and Estonia 200,000.

Brief Independence

The 1917 Russian Revolution overthrew the tsar, allowing Estonia, Latvia and Lithuania to declare independence; their position as independent countries was officially recognised by Soviet Russia in 1920.

1939–41

The Molotov-Ribbentrop Pact between Nazi Germany and the USSR puts Estonia, Latvia and Lithuania under Soviet control

1941–44

Hitler invades the USSR and the Baltic region; some Balts collaborate with the Nazi slaughter of Jews and other local people

But all three countries – caught between the ascendant Soviet Union and the openly expansionist Nazi Germany, which glorified the historic *Urge to the East* – lapsed from democracy into authoritarianism in 1930s, ruled by regimes that feared the Soviet Union more than the Third Reich.

The Singing Revolution (1992) by Clare Thomson tracks Estonia, Latvia and Lithuania's path towards independence through an account of the author's travels in the region in 1989 and 1990.

WWII & Soviet Rule

On 23 August 1939 Nazi Germany and the USSR signed the Molotov-Ribbentrop Pact, putting Estonia, Latvia and, soon after, Lithuania under Soviet control. Baltic Germans who hadn't already left for Germany departed, and by August 1940 the three countries were USSR republics. On 14 June 1941 mass deportations to Siberia began.

Hitler's invasion of the USSR and the subsequent Nazi occupation of the Baltic region between 1941 and 1944 created one of the most sensitive periods in Baltic history, as far too many Balts collaborated with the Nazis in their slaughter of Jews and other local people.

Between 65,000 and 120,000 Latvians, about 70,000 Estonians and 80,000 Lithuanians succeeded in escaping to the West in 1944–5 to avoid the Red Army's reconquest of the Baltics. Thousands more – known as 'forest brothers' – took to the woods rather than live under Soviet rule.

The postwar Soviet era saw the collectivisation of agriculture, the repression of religion and the death or deportation of thousands of Estonians, Latvians and Lithuanians. There was also a huge influx of migrant workers from Russia, Belarus and Ukraine, causing many Balts to fear that they'd become minorities in their own countries.

The Baltic Revolution (1994) by Anatol Lieven is a classic. Half Irish, half Baltic-German, Lieven was the Baltic correspondent for the London *Times* in the early 1990s and is a mine of information .

The Singing Revolution

Soviet leader Mikhail Gorbachev's encouragement of glasnost and *perestroika* in the late 1980s prompted the Baltic countries' pent-up dreams of independence to spill into the open. Popular fronts, formed in each republic to press for democratic reform, won huge followings, while rallies in 1988 saw thousands of Balts gather in the capitals to voice their longing for freedom by singing previously banned national songs. Several big rallies on environmental and national issues were held in Latvia, with 45,000 people joining hands along the coast in one antipollution protest; and an estimated 300,000 Estonians – about 30% of the population – attended one song gathering in Tallinn. On 23 August 1989 – the 50th anniversary of the Molotov-Ribbentrop Pact – two million people formed a human chain stretching from Tallinn to Vilnius, demanding secession.

Moscow granted the Baltic republics economic autonomy in November 1989 and a month later the Lithuanian Communist Party left the Communist Party of the Soviet Union – a landmark act in the break-up of the USSR. Lithuania became the first Soviet republic to legalise noncommunist parties and to declare its independence. Events turned bloody in Rīga and Vilnius in January 1991, but this didn't deter all three states voting overwhelmingly in favour of secession from the USSR in referenda a month later. Although there was little enthusiasm in the West for the Baltic independence movements, the 19 August 1991 coup attempt against Gorbachev in Moscow changed everything; on 6 September 1991 the West and the USSR recognised Estonian, Latvian and Lithuanian independence.

Keep abreast with the Baltic markets.

Tallinn Stock Exchange: www.tse.lt.

Rīga Stock Exchange: www.rfb.lv.

Vilnius Stock Exchange: www.nse.lt.

1944–52

Soviet reconquest sees the region become part of the USSR; Stalin kills or deports thousands of Estonians, Latvians and Lithuanians

1991

Estonia, Latvia and Lithuania win back their independence after five decades of Soviet rule; months later they join the UN

A couple of weeks later, Estonia, Latvia and Lithuania joined the UN, the first step to consolidate their new-found nationhood. In 1992 they competed independently in the Olympic Games for the first time since before WWII, and Estonia held its first elections under its own system (followed later that year by Lithuania, and by Latvia in June 1993). The pope visited all three countries in September 1993 but, such landmarks apart, the Baltic countries dropped out of the world's headlines.

The average monthly old-age pension in Estonia/Latvia/Lithuania is €103/99/93.

Postindependence

Zealous one-upmanship between Estonia, Latvia and Lithuania marked the immediate postindependence years as the three countries suddenly found themselves vying for the same foreign investment and aid. Each established its own currency, army and police force, and started the painful process of switching from a centralised economy to the free market. Runaway inflation topping 1000%, soaring unemployment, plummeting purchasing power, the collapse of several banks (wiping out life savings) and the end to the rudimentary-but-universal Soviet social-welfare system provided a harsh introduction to the 'joys' of consumer capitalism.

In politics a succession of coalition governments came and went, with no single party managing to form a mandate strong enough to gain an overall parliamentary majority.

PURGING THE PAST

Local collaboration with Nazi and Soviet occupiers during WWII has been confronted head-on by the Baltic countries, which have prosecuted several war criminals. They are the only post-Soviet countries to do so.

Among the first to be tried was Aleksandras Lileikis, head of the Vilnius security police during the 1941–44 German occupation of Lithuania. TV images of the feeble 91-year-old defendant in court in 1998, wheelchair-bound and scarcely able to speak, shocked the international community. Lileikis, who had fled to the US where he remained until 1996, when the US Department of Justice stripped him of his American citizenship and expelled him, was accused of sending hundreds of Jews to Nazi death squads. His case was dropped after the courts ruled him medically unfit to stand trial, and he died in 2000. His deputy commander, Kazys Gimzauskas, was found guilty of genocide in 2001 but escaped imprisonment after the courts ruled the 93-year-old pensioner medically unfit.

Neighbouring Estonia has succeeded in doling out one prison sentence. In 1999 79-year-old Mikhail Neverovski, Estonian citizen and former KGB agent, landed four years in prison for his role in deporting 300 Estonians to Siberia in 1949. Every other decrepit collaborator tried by Estonian courts has got a suspended sentence.

Ironically, the biggest trial in Baltic history, which saw some 4000 witnesses give evidence over the course of three years, was of Soviet hardliners who stormed the Vilnius TV tower in 1991. In August 1999 59-year-old Juozas Jarmalavičius and 71-year-old Mykolas Burokevičius, leaders of the Lithuanian Communist Party, were sentenced to eight and 12 years in prison respectively.

Purging the past remains a painful, controversial process. This was dramatically demonstrated in the Kalējs case in 2000, which saw the Latvian government refuse to prosecute 86-year-old Konrads Kalējs, accused of killing thousands of Jews, but – in the same breath – condemn 77-year-old WWII Soviet partisan Vasily Kononov to six years in prison. This was slammed as blatantly hypocritical by Russia and international critics.

2002

Latvia wins the Eurovision Song Contest with a sexy little number by Marie N

2004

Estonia, Latvia and Lithuania join the EU and NATO

Free-trade agreements with the EU were established in 1995, a watershed for the region; nervous of Russian sabre-rattling and hungry for economic stability, the Baltic countries also changed tack around this time, joining forces to present a united front to the world. In 1998 the USA signed the US-Baltic Charter of Partnership, pledging its support for Baltic integration into Western institutions, including NATO (which all three joined in 2002). The same year the three Baltic presidents publicly condemned Russia's political and economic pressure on Latvia, warning it was posing a danger to the region's future unity and integration with Europe.

The Balts are way more Internet and mobile-phone savvy than many of their EU counterparts. Paying for street parking by SMS is red-hot in all three capitals, with mobile phones the only way to fill the meter.

In October 1999, with the dismantling of the Skrunda radar site in Latvia, the last Russian military personnel left Baltic soil.

Citizenship, abolishing the death penalty, prosecuting Nazi and Soviet criminals and resolving border disputes with Russia were among the thorny issues the three countries were forced to tackle before starting accession talks with the EU in 1998 (Estonia) and 1999 (Latvia and Lithuania). For Latvia, the question of how to treat its substantial Russian-speaking minority was particularly contentious (see p179). All three countries were invited to join the EU in 2002 and became fully fledged members in 2004.

On a no-less serious note, the Balts' singing talents have made Europe sit up and take note. Mocked in music circles it might be, but the Eurovision Song Contest – hosted by Tallinn in 2002 and Rīga in 2003 – has served as a billion-dollar publicity campaign for the relatively unknown countries. The €8.2 million it cost Tallinn to host the show was a small price to pay for bringing Estonia to the attention of 166 million TV viewers worldwide – as well as the €5 million of business generated in the capital by the event.

The population is ageing and shrinking. The birth rate per 1000 inhabitants in Estonia/Latvia/Lithuania is 9.9/9/8.6.

PEOPLE

Lifestyle

Postindependent Estonia, Latvia and Lithuania are young societies in every sense of the word. Large chunks of all three economies are in the hands of energetic young dynamos with mobile phones and fast cars. For them, the world – certainly Europe – is their oyster. They speak a couple of languages at least, are comfortable mixing with most nationalities and are as at home on holiday in Spain or Greece as they are in their own country. Flitting off to the seashore to kitesurf at the first sign of good wind, regularly jetting abroad for work and indulging in the odd weekend shopping spree in London or Barcelona is what life is all about for this sizable group of city dwellers in their mid-30s.

But a fair few of the older generation look back with nostalgia to the Soviet era, when a certain equality of poverty prevailed. And indeed, stalling the ever-widening gap between rich and poor by 2015 is one of the Millennium Development Goals set for all three countries by the UN. Unless social policies are changed, life will only become harder for many people, including those living in rural areas (where the GDP per capita is generally half that in the capitals), families with several children or a handicapped child, and single-parent families.

The long, cold, hard Baltic winter casts a definite dampener over some Balts, who appear unnervingly glum, pessimistic and brusque during this dark time of year.

In all three countries, the birth rate is steadily declining (in Lithuania, it has decreased by 43.5% since 1990) and the mortality rate is rising. Male life expectancy in particular is notably lower than in the rest of Europe; on average, Baltic men only live until the age of 66, compared to 75 in the EU. Traffic accidents, violence and suicide remain higher-than-average forms of death.

Marriage and divorce trends reflect those in the rest of Europe: less people are marrying, more couples are having children out of wedlock and more are divorcing (around 60% of marriages end in divorce). Balts still

TIPS ON MEETING LOCALS

Don't lump Estonians, Latvians and Lithuanians into the one melting pot. They share common traits, but first and foremost they are three separate nationalities.

The stereotypical Estonian is reserved, efficient, polite and short on praise. Lithuanians are typically more gregarious, welcoming and emotional. Dubbed the 'Italians' of the region, they have a greater confidence in their national identity, being the only Baltic country to show its toppled Lenin to the world rather than keeping it under wraps. Latvians in general fall somewhere in between these two extremes, being least at ease with foreigners (partly because of ethnic tensions between Latvians and Russians) and probably the most entrepreneurial.

Baltic people do not greet each other with a hug or kiss. Most people are quite formal, and it takes a while to get onto first-name terms. Men always shake each other's hands and some women shake hands too. Don't mistake lack of smiles or a reserved attitude for indifference or hostility (Estonians are especially poker-faced – one national saying is 'May your face be as ice').

Flowers are a universal gift, but only give odd-numbered bouquets as even-numbered offerings (including a dozen red roses!) are for mournful occasions. If you are invited to a private home, take flowers or a bottle – but never money – as a gift for your host. Take your shoes off when you enter and do not shake hands across the threshold. Do not whistle inside either. Both actions bring bad luck and will be severely frowned upon.

Muttering just a few words in the local language will raise instant smiles. In Latvia and Lithuania, speaking Russian as a foreigner is generally (but not always) acceptable. In Estonia, you should try every other language you know first – be it English, German or Finnish – as speaking Russian can be met with a hostile response, or no response at all.

marry quite young – when they are around 24 (women) or 26 (men) – but more women are now waiting until their early 30s to have children.

Bureaucracy certainly seems its most Byzantine in Latvia, where armed Guards of Honour still stand, as rigid as stone, in front of Rīga's Freedom Monument from sunrise to sunset, come rain, hail or 3m of snow.

Multiculturalism

Ethnic identity is a sticky subject in the Baltic countries. Large-scale immigration of workers from Russia and other Soviet republics during the Soviet period dramatically changed the population make-up of Latvia and Estonia; ethnic Estonians and Latvians are barely in the majority (65.5% and 57.6% respectively), Latvians are a minority in Latvia's seven largest cities, and Russians easily swamp Estonians in industrial Narva (northeastern Estonia), where they account for 96% of the population.

The inability of some native Russian-speakers to speak Latvian has only added fuel to the fire. Interestingly, 42.2% of these are Latvian citizens. Education programmes aimed at teaching Latvian to non-Latvian speakers has dissolved some, but not all, linguistic barriers in Latvia. Twelve per cent of residents – mainly elderly people – still don't speak any Latvian; some Russian speakers, moreover, simply don't want to learn or speak Latvian, as the February 2004 street demonstrations in Rīga following education reform proved. Citizenship requirements are equally controversial (see p179).

The *Guide to Jewish Genealogy in Latvia and Estonia* (2001) by Rosemary E Wenzerul is a fascinating if unsettling read.

Odd incidents serve as an unnerving reminder of the ethnic tension that simmers beneath the surface. The violent attack by Russian nationalists on a 24-year-old Lithuanian border guard in May 2004 was a clear signal that the Balts' accession into the EU is not liked by Russian nationalists, who see it as a huge step in the wrong direction – ie away from Moscow.

Other ethnic groups present in smaller numbers include Poles, Jews, Roma, Tatars and Germans (in Lithuania), as well as nationals of the former Soviet Union.

ARTS

Folk Culture

The Balts' treasure-trove of oral folklore – inspired by the seasonal cycle, farming and the land, family life, love and myths – is considered the largest collection in the world. Latvia alone boasts more than 1.5 million *dainas* (short poetic songs somewhat like the Japanese haiku), vast collections of which were written down in the 19th century by people like Krisjānis Barons in Latvia and Jakob Hurt in Estonia. The first folkloric musical score was published in Lithuania, now guardian of some 600,000 folk songs and stories, as early as 1634.

During the Soviet era, Santa Claus didn't exist for Baltic children. Christmas Eve and Christmas Day were school days, and Santa Claus was replaced by the soulless Father Frost, who dropped gifts down chimneys on New Year's Eve.

Folk rhymes and music are very much living traditions, with numerous societies and groups devoted to them. Particularly unusual are chants of northeastern Lithuania, known as *sutartinės*, and of the Setumaa region in southeast Estonia. More immediately impressive are the national song and dance festivals (see boxed text, p33), evidence of the age-old power of song in Baltic culture.

With the mass production of identical crosses, the art of cross crafting (see p341), traditionally handed down from master to pupil in Latvia and Lithuania, is fast becoming a dying art – so much so that it is also Unesco-protected today.

Walking Since Daybreak: A Story of Eastern Europe, World War II and the Heart of our Century (1998) is a family history of acclaimed historian, Latvian-born Modris Eksteins, who spent most of his childhood in displaced-persons camps.

Literature

Baltic literature draws heavily on folklore. Modern Estonian and Latvian literature got going in the mid-19th century with the writing of national epic poems based on legends and folk tales that had been part of the oral tradition over preceding centuries. The giants of 20th-century literature are Estonian novelist Anton Hansen Tammsaare (1878–1940) and Latvian poet and playwright Jānis Rainis (1865–1929), who has been compared to Shakespeare and Goethe. More recently Estonian novelist Jan Kross and poet Jaan Kaplinski (both past Nobel Prize nominees) and

PAGANISM

Czech bishop Albert Waitiekus, the first Christian missionary to venture into the region, came here in the 10th century. Unfortunately for him, he wandered into a forest dedicated to pagan gods and was killed – leaving paganism to run rife in the region for another two centuries.

To pagan Latvians and Lithuanians the sky was a mountain and many of the leading gods lived on it, among humans: Dievs the sky god, Saule the sun goddess, Perkūnas (Pērkons in Latvia) the thunder god, who was particularly revered, and Mēness the moon god. There was also an earth-mother figure called Žemyna in Lithuania and Zemes māte in Latvia. In Latvia the Christian Virgin Mary has many of the attributes of Žemyna, and the two figures seem to be combined in the mythological figure of Māra. Also important were Laima the goddess of fate, Medeinė (Meža māte in Latvia) the forest goddess, and Velnias (Velns in Latvia) the guardian of wizards and sages, who was transformed into the devil in the Christian scheme of things. Many lesser deities presided over natural phenomena and objects, or human activities.

Today the pagan gods are enjoying a marked revival among those known as the Dievturība (literally 'Holding the Gods') in Latvia, and among the Romuva in Lithuania. The Romuva is particularly strong, perhaps because Lithuania was the last European stronghold of paganism until 1385, and it has congregations in Vilnius, Kaunas and in Lithuanian communities in Canada and the USA. It is named after an ancient temple site near Chernahovsk (in today's Kaliningrad Region) that attracted Lithuanian, Latvian and Prussian worshippers alike prior to Christianity's arrival in the Baltics. Founded as an organised pagan revival movement in 1967, it was banned under the Soviet regime in 1971 but revived under the jurisdiction of the 'Society for Ethnic Lithuanian Culture' in 1988.

Robert G Darst's *Smokestack Diplomacy* (2001) tackles the whole dirty issue of environmental protection in five former Soviet states, including Estonia, Latvia and Lithuania.

Lithuanian novelist Stephan Collishaw have received international acclaim. Lithuania also shares the credit for some major Polish writers who grew up in Lithuania, including Nobel laureate Czesław Miłosz.

In the Soviet years many leading writers and artists went into voluntary or forced exile and most other talent was stifled. Since 1991 the literary scene has changed so fast and there has been such a flood of outside influences that writers, artists and musicians in the Baltics seem to have been stunned, with many still struggling to assimilate their new freedom.

Music & Dance

Opera is big in Rīga thanks to Jāzeps Vītols, who founded the Latvian National Opera, and Andrejs Žagars, who revived that same opera in the mid-1990s. Before WWII the Latvian capital was likewise a pre-eminent performing-arts centre; its ballet company, which dates from the 1920s, was one of the best in the Soviet Union and produced Mikhail Baryshnikov and other notable dancers.

Rock and pop thrive, arguably at the expense of classical music, which was state-funded but is pretty strapped for cash these days. Both Estonia and Latvia host big annual rock festivals (see p169), and Lithuania is the Baltic jazz giant. The region's best-known composer is Estonian Arvo Pärt, who writes mainly choral works, including the haunting *Magnificat*.

Much-raved-about coffee-table book *Lithuania. 24 Hours* (Lietuva. 24 Vilandos) is the creation of 30-odd international photographers, who completed a 24-hour photography mission in Lithuania with awesome results.

Latvia's surprise victory in the 2002 Eurovision Song Contest – all the more remarkable given that Latvia didn't qualify originally (it replaced Portugal) – proved once and for all that the Balts' singing revolution and the previous Estonian victory in the 2001 Eurovision Song Contest were not one-off events: Balts really can sing. Eurovision-type pop and dance music remain the dominant forces in the Baltics' young music scene.

Architecture

The three capitals are architectural wonders. Their impressive collections of historical buildings prompted Unesco to protect the Old Towns in all three cities as World Heritage sites in 1997; Tallinn is particularly rich in medieval architecture, Vilnius in baroque and Rīga in Art Nouveau (p199). Both Rīga and Tallinn have excellent architecture museums hosting some great temporary exhibitions; Tallinn's is inside the city's beautifully restored salt cellars (see boxed text, p77).

City rejuvenation has created some noteworthy examples of contemporary architecture: Vilnius has a new skyline of skyscrapers (see p302); in Estonia, Pärnu central library is striking; and Urban Loop is the exciting glass concert hall crafted for Liepāja (in Latvia) by Austrian architects Giencke & Company.

Visual Arts

The contemporary scene is active, although few Baltic artists cause a stir internationally.

Peeling Potatoes, Painting Pictures (2001) by Renee Baigell and Matthew Baigell is an enlightened look at how female artists in Estonia and Latvia perceive themselves in the post-Soviet era. (The conclusion: art remains male-dominated.)

Only Lithuanians would be bold enough to create the tongue-in-cheek Republic of Užupis (see boxed text, p298) or turn Vilnius-based sessions of NATO's 2002 spring parliamentary assembly into a visual arts object – encasing the proceedings in glass walls so that the public could view what was happening. Outside the capital, contemporary art installations by Baltic artists are displayed at the Centre of Europe (p318), a highlight being a maze of 3000 second-hand TV sets that leads to a statue of Lenin. As with many works conceived by the region's artists today, the Soviet past inspired the work: the TV maze portrays the absurdity of Soviet propaganda and communism's ultimate burial by the Balts.

THE POWER OF SONG

Song is the Baltic soul. And nowhere is this expressed more eloquently than in the national festivals that unite Estonians, Latvians and Lithuanians worldwide in a spellbinding performance of song. The crescendo is a choir of up to 30,000 voices, singing its heart out to an audience of 100,000 or more, while 10,000-odd folk dancers in traditional dress cast a bewitching kaleidoscope of patterns across the vast, open-air stage.

Festivals are held every four years in Lithuania and every five years in Latvia and Estonia – the next taking place in Vilnius, Rīga and Tallinn in 2007, 2008 and 2009 respectively. To help ensure their survival, these Baltic song and dance celebrations were recognised by Unesco as one of 47 precious 'Masterpieces of the Oral and Intangible Heritage of Humanity' in 2003. As rural communities (and thus choirs) dwindle and city dwellers get increasingly wrapped up in modern life's frenetic pace, there are fears that these precious celebrations, which evoke the Balts' age-old relationship with nature, could die.

Although the first song festival did not take place in the Baltic region until the late 19th century, the Balts' natural lyricism and love of singing can be traced to pre-Christian times. Ancient Baltic beliefs in the pagan powers of sky god Dievs, god of thunder Perkūnas, and the mythological family of the sun, moon and stars found their way into Baltic folk rhymes, the lyrics of which were passed down orally between generations. Lines like 'once we sang so that the fields resounded with our songs' and choral titles like 'Song of Pain and Sun Disc', 'Lilac, Do You Bring Me Luck' and 'Blow Wind, Blow' remain an essential part of festivals. Dance, equally inspired by the agrarian cycle, relies on simple choreography, with dancing couples creating circles, lines, chains and other symmetrical formations. In the 'fisherman dance', giant ocean waves of dancers wash across the stage.

With songs, legends and proverbs being committed to paper in the 19th century, a political tool emerged. The revival of national spirit in Estonia and Latvia saw the first festivals in Tartu in 1869 and Rīga in 1873. In Lithuania, song filled interwar capital Kaunas for the first time, in 1924. Lyrics praising Stalin and later the USSR replaced many of the original Baltic songs during the early Soviet era. Following WWII's mass deportations, displaced Balts turned to song for solace in the refugee camps: the first song festival outside the region was held in 1946 for the estimated 120,000 Latvians in UN camps in Germany. Until 1991 loss and love of homeland dominated the symphony of festivals celebrated among Baltic immigrants in the USA, Canada and elsewhere. In Estonia and Latvia the power of song reached fever pitch during the 1990 national song festivals – two highly charged affairs climaxing with choirs of 30,000 singing in unison. The return of many Baltic exiles to the subsequent festivals in 1993–94 – the first since independence – was also incredibly emotive.

In Latvia today, the week-long festival peaks with a candlelit performance to an audience of 100,000 in Rīga's Mežaparks. Estonia's three-day festival kicks off with the centenary flame being brought by horse-drawn carriage from Tartu to Tallinn's song bowl. Lithuanians, meanwhile, sing for three to five days, parading along the streets from Vilnius Cathedral to the open-air festival stage in Vingis Park. For tickets (€15 to €80) and information contact festival organisers:

Estonian Song & Dance Foundation (☎ 6427 3120; www.laulupidu.ee; Suur-Karja 23, Tallinn)
Lithuanian Folk Culture Centre (☎ 22-611 190, 22-612 540; www.lfcc.lt; Barboros Radvilaitės gatvė 8, Vilnius)
Song Festival Foundation (☎ 722 8985; pasts@tmc.gov.lv; Pils laukums 4, Rīga, Latvia)

Zooming in on photography, it is another Lithuanian whose name is known internationally: Antanas Sutkas' works have been exhibited in galleries in Paris, New York et al.

ENVIRONMENT

The Land

…is small and flat: it's just 650km from Estonia's northernmost point to Lithuania's southern tip, and the highest point, Suur Munamägi in Estonia, peaks at a paltry 318m. Lakes are rife – there are 9000 in all, of which Lake Peipsi is the largest.

CLEAN BEACHES

Twenty-seven criteria must be met to get a **European Blue Flag** (www.blueflag.org), awarded annually to Europe's clean, safe beaches and marinas. In 2005 the region scored 16 flags, up from 12 in 2002. In Estonia, beaches in Pärnu, Võsu and Pühajärv (near Otepää) got the thumbs up, as did marinas in Lohusala, Pärnu, Roomassaare and Kuressaare. In Latvia, Jūrmala's Majori and Bulduri beaches, Ventspils beach and marina, and the beach in Liepāja were flagged – as were Lithuania's beaches in Nida, Juodkrantė and Smiltynė on the Curonian Spit, and the botanical-garden beach in Palanga.

The coastline clocks up 5000km, much of it either fronting the Gulfs of Finland and Rīga, or protected from the open Baltic Sea by islands. Estonia has over 1000 islands, but Latvia and Lithuania have none. The coast's most remarkable feature is the Curonian Spit, a Unesco-protected 98km sand bar divided between Lithuania and Kaliningrad (Russia).

LONGEST RIVERS

Daugava: 1005km from southeastern Latvia to the Baltic Sea.

Nemunas: 937km across southwestern Lithuania to the Curonian Lagoon.

Gauja: 452km within eastern Latvia.

Venta: 346km from Lithuania to western Latvia.

Narva: 77km north from Lake Peipsi to form the Estonia–Russia border.

Wildlife

There are more large mammals here than anywhere else in Europe, although spotting them invariably requires the help of a local guide. Forty-eight types of mammal alone live in Latvia's Gauja National Park. Elks, deer, wild boars, wolves, lynxes and otters inhabit all three countries, but brown bears, seals and beavers are only found Estonia and Latvia.

Some of Estonia's islands and coastal wetlands, as well as Lake Žuvintas in southern Lithuania and Ventės Ragas at the edge of the world in western Lithuania, are key breeding grounds and migration stops for water birds. Latvia and Lithuania harbour more white storks (see p282) than all of Western Europe, while the rare black stork nests in western Lithuania's Nemunas Delta and Latvia's Gauja National Park. The eagle owl and white-backed woodpecker – rare in the rest of Europe – also nest in abundance in the latter.

National Parks

Lithuania has five national parks, Estonia four and Latvia three – and they all have dozens more nature reserves that are protected to various degrees. See p60 (Estonia), p183 (Latvia) and p283 (Lithuania) for further details.

Environmental Issues

The Baltic Sea – particularly brackish and thus extra vulnerable – is the region's largest shared environmental burden. It is getting cleaner, but virtually all Estonian, Latvian and Lithuanian coastal waters remain polluted – partly by chemical pollution washing out from rivers and untreated sewage being pumped into rivers or the sea. Improving sewage systems, establishing more efficient waste-management systems and raising the quality of drinking water to EU norms are key concerns. The increase in shipping routes is not helping matters.

Forest covers 44% of Estonia, 44% of Latvia and 30% of Lithuania.

Oil transportation is equally dirty. The region occupies a key position in the Russian crude-oil pipeline system, with 16% of all Russia's crude oil exports in 2004 passing through Lithuania's Būtingė Oil Terminal and its own Baltic Sea port at Pirmorsk. Smaller quantities of crude oil, other petroleum products and coal – arriving by rail – pass through Tallinn. Russia is striving to reduce its dependency on these Baltic ports though; it reduced crude-oil shipments at Ventspils port in Latvia by 30% between 2000 and 2002, and halted shipments in 2003.

Energy production is hazardous. The EU has forced Lithuania into closing its Chornobyl-styled Ignalina Nuclear Power Plant (p322) in 2009, but Lithuania has already expressed interest in opening a new nuclear facility to meet energy needs. Estonia, meanwhile, relies heavily on its shale oil–fired power plant in Narva for electricity, but has been likewise compelled by EU environmental policies to switch to cleaner means by 2015. Its shale oil industry spews out 90% of the country's hazardous waste. Stringent renewable energy quotas – to be achieved by 2010 – have been set for all three countries by the EU.

Lithuania's Nemunas River is one of Europe's most polluted rivers.

For pointers on green travel, see p16.

FOOD & DRINK

Food

Baltic gastronomy has its roots planted firmly in the land, with livestock and game forming the basis of a very hearty diet. Potatoes add a generous dose of winter-warming stodge to national cuisines that are all too often dismissed as bland, heavy and lacking in spice.

Food preparation is plain and simple, and sauces are rarely used to brighten up meat and fish. In autumn, fruits of the land – mushrooms,

THE BALTIC AMBER ROAD

Amber – fossilised tree resin – was formed in the Baltic region 40 to 60 million years ago. Yet it was not until the mid-19th century that the trail for the so-called Baltic gold began in earnest.

Early humans burnt amber for heat, and in the Middle Ages it served as cash. For the tribal Prussians inhabiting the Baltic Sea's southeast shores around 12,000 BC, rubbing it was the best way to generate static electricity. During the 12th century, it was said to contain mystical qualities – amber worn next to the skin helped a person become closer to the spirits. In true crusader fashion, the Teutonic knights claimed Baltic amber as their own in the 13th century, yet they too failed to understand where amber was to be found and just how much there really was.

In 1854–55 and 1860 substantial amounts of amber were excavated near Juodkrantė on the Curonian Spit in Lithuania. Three separate clusters weighing 2250 tons in total were uncovered during the 'amber rush' to the sleepy seashore village, yet by 1861 the amber had dried up. Since 1869amber has been excavated at the Yantarny mine in Kaliningrad (Russia), the place where most amber sold in the Baltics today actually comes from!

Treasure seekers trailed Juodkrantė's shores once more in 1998, this time in search of the legendary Amber Room – a room comprising 10,000 panels (55 sq metres) of carved, polished amber given to Peter the Great by the Prussian king in 1716. For decades opportunists have been trying to track down the missing panels, which graced the Catherine Palace near St Petersburg until 1942 when invading Germans plundered the palace and shipped the jewels either to Königsberg (Kaliningrad) or, as the mayor of Neringa told the world in 1998, to the shores of the Curonian Lagoon, where wartime residents allegedly saw the SS burying large crates. Predictably, the search yielded few results.

Amber comes in 250 colours, ranging from green, pale yellow and black to brown or golden. White amber, contains one million gas bubbles per cubic millimetre. Some pieces sold are heated or compressed, combining pieces; others are polished (to test if a polished piece of amber is real put it in salt water – if it sinks, it's a dud). Rubbing unpolished amber should yield a faint pine smell. Old-fashioned ways of treating it include boiling in honey to make it darker, or in vegetable oil to make it lighter. Original, pieces with 'inclusions' – grains of dirt, shell, vegetation or *Jurassic Park*–style insects – are the most valuable.

The **Baltic Amber Road** (www.balticamberroad.net), an EU-funded tourism project, steers amber-curious tourists along a 418km route tracing the region's unique amber sights and experiences. See p21 for an itinerary, and p175 (Latvia), p282 (Lithuania) and p379 (Kaliningrad) for information on country-specific sights.

TRAVEL YOUR TASTEBUDS

We dare you to try these gastronomic highlights:

Cepelinai Lithuanian 'zeppelins' (potato dumplings covered with bacon, cream and butter sauce). A gastronomic legend.

Rīgas Melnais Balzāms Rīga Black Balsam – a thick, dark, bitter and potent liqueur.

Rūkytas ungurys Smoked eel, a lovely Lithuanian speciality to wrap your tongue around.

Saltibarsčiai Lithuanian cold beetroot soup; it's the pinkest soup you'll ever see.

Verikäkk Estonian balls of blood rolled in egg and flour and spiced with pig's fat.

Verileib Tasty Estonian blood bread.

cabbage, herrings and sausages – are salted, smoked or pickled and stored in cellars for the long hard Baltic winter.

STAPLES & SPECIALITIES

The national cuisines are meat-based and not for the faint-hearted. Be it an animal's tail, its blood or balls, the Balts eat every last bloody morsel – literally. *Šiupinys* (hodgepodge, alias pork snout stew) and *kraujinė sriuba* (blood soup) are Lithuanian delicacies, while Estonians deem *verivorst* (blood sausages wrapped in piggy intestines) to be a real treat.

Four common ways of cooking meat are as a *shashlik* (shish kebab), *carbonade* (a chop but in practice any piece of grilled meat), beefsteak (fried meat) and stroganoff (cubes of meat in stew).

Little salt is used, a reflection of the rarity it once was: if a dish is too salty, the cook is in love; if salt is spilled on the table, a quarrel will break out; and a loaf of bread and pot of salt is a traditional house-warming gift.

The Balts are big drinkers: annual beer consumption per capita is 81L in Estonia, 80L in Lithuania and 58L in vodka-fuelled Latvia.

Bread tends to be black, rye and dry. Other staples include pancakes filled with sweet fruit, jam, curd, sour cream or meat; sausage, usually cold and sliced; and a variety of dairy products – milk is turned to curd, sour cream and cottage cheese as well as plain old butter, cream and cheese.

Breakfast is generally bread with ham and cheese, a boiled egg or an omelette. Slices of tomato or cucumber are often served too, and coffee or milk is the usual drink. A typical lunchtime main course consists of a piece of grilled or fried meat or fish, along with potatoes and boiled vegetables.

Drinks

Tap water can be dodgy, so buy bottled mineral water, of which there are numerous local and imported brands. The fine art of brewing tea from the land's rich bounty of herbs, berries, leaves and fruits is a tradition very much honoured in the countryside and one that is suddenly hip in the capitals.

Excellent beer is brewed, and is widely available in restaurants, cafés and supermarkets alongside pricier imported German and Scandinavian beers (and even Guinness in some bars). Most Baltic beers are light, fairly flat and of medium strength. Four of the biggest brands – Saku in Estonia, Aldaris in Latvia, and Utenos alus and Švyturys in Lithuania – are the pride and joy of Baltic Beverages Holding (BBH), a Sweden-based joint venture between Carlsberg and Scottish & Newcastle. All four brands produce a dozen or so different labels, ranging from nonalcoholic beer to dark American-style iced beer. Highlights include Saku's seasonal Saku Porter, brewed strictly for Christmas; the ultradark Utenos Porteris (stout), which is reckoned to taste like wine; and the unfiltered Švyturys Baltas, served with a slice of lemon.

Other market leaders include Lithuanian brewers Kalnapilis (of which BBH owns 50%), Horn and Gubernija, and the heavier Saare beer from the Estonian island of Saaremaa. Across the region, small microbreweries brew great beer – many preservative-free and lasting no more than a week. Some breweries in Lithuania can be visited, and Estonia's five-day beer festival in July, Ollesummer (Beer Summer; p168), is a good tasting opportunity.

Estonians warm the cockles with *hõõgvein* (mulled wine) and Latvians rely on a shot of Rīga Black Balsam (see boxed text, p185) for a short, sharp pick-me-up. Vodka is less fashionable than it was but remains popular. Chart-topping brands like White Diamond Latvian vodka (which scooped the gold in the San Francisco World Spirit Competition in 2004) and Lithuanian Vodka are best drunk chilled and neat, or mixed as part of a martini. Lithuanians also merrymake in the company of *midus* (mead), *trauktinė* (bitters) and fruit liqueurs known as *likeriai*.

Wine is a niche drink rather than trend or tradition, but champagne – the thing to chink when celebrating – is enthusiastically consumed.

Where to Eat & Drink

The capitals burst with sophisticated restaurants, funky eateries, American-style diners and cosy bistros. International cuisines abound and there's ample choice, be it Armenian, Mexican, Italian or French. Places dishing up the Balts' meaty national cuisines are equally prevalent, with prices to suit budgets big and small. Many food products are imported though, and this, coupled with the Baltic indifference for spices, can mean you end up eating a tasteless, tamed-down version of a given ethnic dish.

Baltics Worldwide really is a fun tool for keeping tabs on political, economic and cultural action in the region. Check it out at www.balticsworldwide.com.

Restaurants in Rīga, Tallinn and, to a lesser extent, Vilnius command Western European city prices, but eating in the provinces is cheap. Many restaurants accept major credit cards and a few have English-language menus. Service ranges from superefficient to snail-pace slow. You can pay anything from €10 to €150 for a three-course meal in these places. Standard restaurant opening hours are 11am to midnight daily.

Canteen-style places – often with attractive rustic interiors and buzzing with local city dwellers – rarely have menus, but they display what's cooking, allowing you to point and order. While the food is generally no gourmet's delight, it's perfectly palatable. National dishes prevail and a fill-up typically costs between €3 and €6.

The café scene is vibrant and dynamic. Stylish design-led spaces, traditional places and everything in between serve up quality coffee, fresh breads and pastries, as well as alcoholic drinks and light hot meals. Many double as bars, opening from 8am to midnight daily. In Estonia and Lithuania, international fast-food chains are found in most larger towns and cities, but Latvia – with its own clutch of *pelmeņi* (meat dumpling) and *pīrāgi* (pasty) places – has yet to really embrace Western chains.

In provincial towns, dining is limited and is often accompanied by a blaring TV set. Cuisine is local, menus are limited and in the local language, and service can be bad: it is not unknown for a main course to arrive before the starter. In rural parts, simply finding somewhere to eat is tricky.

Practically every town has a daily market with a good choice of fruit and vegetables. Supermarkets are generally open from 8am to 10pm seven days a week.

Activities

Open space abounds in the Baltic region, and with major populations concentrated in relatively few urban areas, there's plenty to go around. Factor in low tourist numbers, especially in comparison with much of the rest of Europe, and you'll quickly realise the region offers some of the continent's best opportunities to ditch the crowds and just frolic in the wilderness.

A smorgasbord of active endeavours awaits the outdoor enthusiast. You can whet your appetite with berry picking before grabbing an alfresco meal-on-the-run of brisk, salty air, untouched white-sand beaches and icy-blue Baltic Sea vistas. Want seconds? Try cycling through dense forests scented with pine, canoeing down a fat, lazy river or checking out the flora and fauna in a quiet nature reserve. If you still have room for dessert, try baby-gentle downhill or cross-country skiing or birding, or maybe just sweat it all out in a sumptuously steamy sauna. In fact, whatever you're craving this hour, the Baltic countries can deliver it almost right to your door.

Visit www.bicycle.lt for the scoop on cycling in the Baltics. It has info about all three countries.

CYCLING

Cycling is taking off in a big way in the Baltics these days, with new tours and routes popping up all over the place. The region's flatness makes tooling around the countryside on a bicycle an option for anyone: casual cyclists can get the hang of things on gentle paved paths, while hard-core fanatics can rack up the kilometres on more challenging multiday treks. Although there's not much along the lines of steep single-track trails, dirt tracks through forests and hills abound, and the varied, but always peaceful, scenery ensures you'll never tire of the view. There are plenty of places to rent bicycles in Estonia and Latvia, and even the smaller towns usually have at least one hotel offering cycles for hire – although the quality of the gear varies greatly. Pickings are slimmer in Lithuania, with bike-hire outlets centred in major towns and cycling hubs.

For cycling info on all three countries, visit **BaltiCCycle** (www.bicycle.lt). The group, which incorporates the major cycling clubs in Latvia, Lithuania and Estonia, can hook up you with cycling maps (1:500,000), route descriptions and contacts for arranging biking tours.

BaltiCCycle also arranges an annual cycling tour through Eastern Europe. The trip lasts for two months and covers lots of terrain in the Baltic countries. Cyclists ride between 40km and 70km per day, and spend the nights in camp sites along the way. If you're serious about cycling and have some time to spare, this tour is a great way to experience the culture and natural beauty of the region. Check the website for more on dates, prices and routes.

CANOEING & RAFTING

Watching the landscape slide slowly by while paddling down a lazy river is a fabulous way to experience the natural world from a different angle. As the region's rivers are not known for their wild rapids, it is a great place for beginners to hone their skills or for families to entertain the kids. Even if you're usually more into wild than mild, the region's scenic beauty and tranquillity create such a Zen experience you'll quickly forget you haven't hit a single rapid.

Canoeing and rafting are particularly popular in Latvia. The Gauja, Salaca and Abava Rivers all offer uninterrupted routes stretching for several days, and you can join an organised tour or rent gear and run the routes on your own. In the capital, **Campo** (☎ 922 2339; www.laivas.lv; Blaumaņa iela 22/24, Rīga) is a good starting point for information. The club organises canoeing trips in Latgale, Zemgale, Kurzeme and Vidzeme and rents gear. For more info on paddling in this region, see p230.

BIKING THE BALTICS: A FEW EPIC RIDES

Whether you're yearning to pedal along the coast, through the forest or around the lake-flecked countryside, there are plenty of cycling routes to accommodate you. Here are a few of our favourites.

Riding the 'Sahara of Lithuania'

Western Lithuania boasts one of the most magical one-day cycling trips in the Baltics. The stupendous Curonian Spit, dubbed the 'Sahara of Lithuania', is a fragile stretch of spit coastline loaded with towering dunes, wild white beaches and pine forests. The biking trail starts in the sleepy little village of Nida and heads 30km north, mostly through pine forests, to bewitching, sculpture-studded Juodkrantė. Along the way you pedal through the Nagliai Strict Nature Reserve, past an authentic fish-smoking house in the tiny fishing village of Preila, and have the chance to marvel at the wondrous 67.2m-high Vecekrugas Dune – the highest on the spit. Lovely Nida or Juodkrantė are perfect spots to spend the night. For precise route details, see p367.

Estonian Island Jaunt

Loosely following part of Estonia's National Cycle Route No 1, this three-night trip is well signposted in English. To start your journey, catch a ferry to the island of Hiiumaa. Quiet and sparsely populated, the island is perfect for biking – think delightful coastal stretches, pine forests and plenty of fresh salty-sweet air. From the ferry pier, head north for 28km to the island's 'capital', Kärdla, a sleepy town filled with gardens and trees. From here pedal south through bog and forest for 33km until you reach Käina, the island's second-largest settlement and your stopping point for the night. The town is nothing special, but it does boast several decent hotels. Rise early, as day two is long. From Käina the route heads southwest for 25km to the small harbour of Sõru. It's a pretty ride, passing coastal marshlands, picturesque hamlets and isolated farmsteads. Catch your breath on the ferry to Saaremaa, which departs from Sõru. Despite being the country's biggest island and a favourite summer holiday spot, Saaremaa still retains an old-fashioned feel. Unspoiled rural landscapes, farmsteads, windmills and trees abound. From the pier it's a beautiful 30km ride to Orissaare, where you can bed down at the friendly hostel. The following morning, cross the 2.5km-long causeway to Muhu and spend the day cycling around the island, checking out fortress ruins and quaint villages. Spend the night on Muhu before catching the ferry back to the mainland from the Kuivastu pier.

City to Surf in Latvia

The 25km trail from Rīga to Jūrmala is a great day trip, perfect for novice riders or anyone just looking for a relaxing spin. Take the Vanšu bridge (on Valdemāra iela) out of Rīga and look for the red-painted trail behind the bus shelter at the edge of the road. Head past the Olympia shopping centre and over a canal, then follow the well-marked path to the right. Head straight for 600m before making a left onto Klinģeru iela and another left again onto Kuldīgas iela. At the end of the road, turn right onto the main road, Slokas iela, and follow this until you see a pedestrian crossing. Cross the road here and look for Kandavas iela, where you'll turn left. Take the first right onto Zārdu iela and you'll finally find yourself off the main roads and on the bike trail proper. From here it's a straight shot to Jūrmala on a paved path. You'll feel miles away from the city once you hit this tranquil, tree-lined trail. And since it's closed to motor vehicles, there's no need to worry about riding in traffic.

In northeast Lithuania, Aukštaitija National Park (p320) also offers excellent canoeing terrain, with a big network of interconnected lakes. Both the Aukštaitija National Park Office and the boatmen on the lakeshore in Palūse organise trips and rent equipment. In Dzūkija National Park (p328), canoeing trips along the Ūla River can likewise be arranged through the visitors centres in Marcinkonys and Merkinė.

Canoes or traditional *haabjas* (Finno-Ugric single-tree boats carved from aspen) serve as the primary vehicles for exploring Soomaa National Park (p165) in southwest Estonia. **Karuskoe** (☎ 0506 1896; www.soomaa.com), in Tohera, just outside the park's northwestern boundary, arranges canoeing and boating trips on Soomaa's rivers and bogs between April and September. The overnight trips are unique, and include a sweat in a floating sauna!

SKIING & SNOWBOARDING

They might not have anything even closely resembling a mountain, but Estonia and Latvia haven't let this little geographic hurdle hinder their ski-resort construction efforts. Instead these countries have become mas-

SWEAT IT OUT

Given that it's cold, dark and snowy for many months of the year, it's little surprise that the sauna is an integral part of Baltic culture. Most hotels have one, and some cities have public bathhouses with saunas. But it's the ones that silently smoulder next to a lake or river, by the sea or deep in the forest that provide the most authentic experience.

Balts split their saunas into two categories: Russian, and Finnish or Swedish. A 'Russian' or 'smoke' sauna is more traditional and is modelled after the great Russian *bahnia*. The sauna is housed in a one-room wooden hut; bathing begins when the open wood stove has roared for some three to four hours, turning the interior of the hut black with soot and the heated rocks a smouldering red. When taking a sauna, the often-boisterous bathers throw water onto the sizzling rocks to ensure the wood-perfumed air remains thick with steam (and sweat).

The 'Finnish' or 'Swedish' sauna, by comparison, can be a clinical, second-rate affair. This Nordic terminology refers to the clean and smokeless modern sauna that sprang up in the 1990s (despite the fact that until the 1950s Finns favoured the smoke sauna). Electric heaters are generally used to warm the modest mound of stones, contained in a small rack at one end of the neat, bench-clad sauna.

Balts use a bunch of birch twigs to lightly switch the body, irrespective of which sauna type they're sweating in. This gentle beating is said to increase perspiration, tingle the nerve endings and add to the overall sense of relaxation and revitalisation. Cooling down is an equally integral part of the sauna experience: most Finnish-style saunas have showers or pools, while the more authentic smoke saunas are usually next to a lake or river. In the depths of winter, cutting out a square metre of ice from a frozen lake in order to take a quick dip is not unheard of.

An invitation to share a sauna – said to come close to a religious experience on occasion – is a hospitable gesture that should be treated with great respect. Public or hotel saunas demand an hourly fee of around €5 and there are plenty of small, private saunas that can be rented for €15 to €23 per hour. Normally, you rent the entire sauna, which can usually fit at least eight people. In Estonia, the Reval Hotel Olümpia (p82) has a glass-windowed Finnish-style sauna noteworthy for its stunning views over Tallinn. For a sootier experience, try the smoke sauna at Kalma Suan, also in Tallinn (p78), and the traditional Russian-style sauna, dating from 1915, at the Mihkli Farm Museum (p151) on Saaremaa.

At the Zevynos Hostel (p329), in southern Lithuania, you'll find a serene sauna nestled into the forests of Dzūkija National Park.

In Latvia, soak up some sky-high city views – 180 degrees worth – while working up a sweat in the top-floor sauna at Riga's Reval Hotel Ridzene (p211). The traditional lakeside sauna at Cakuli (p242), a guesthouse in the Latgale Upland, is also fabulous.

ters at working with what they've got – and that means constructing lifts and runs on the tiniest of hills, and using rooftops and dirt mounds to create vertical drops. At least they've got the climate working for them, with cold temperatures ensuring snow cover for at least four months of the year. The Alps this ain't – don't expect much in the way of technical terrain or long powder runs – but you've got to admit that saying you've skied or snowboarded the Baltics is pretty damn cool!

Otepää (p116), in southeast Estonia, is probably the best of the Baltic winter resorts. It offers a variety of downhill-skiing and snowboarding areas, myriad cross-country trails, a ski jump and plenty of outlets from which to hire gear. Lively nightlife and a ski-town vibe heighten the appeal for skiers and boarders.

The Gauja Valley is the centre of Latvia's winter-sports scene. Sigulda (p227), Cēsis (p232) and Valmiera (p234) all offer short-but-semisweet downhill runs as well as loads of cross-country trails. Adrenaline junkies disappointed by Sigulda's gentle slopes can get their fix swishing down the town's 1200m-long artificial bobsled run – the five-person contraptions reach speeds of 80km/h!

'Bobsleds on Sigulda's artificial bobsled run can reach a speed of 80km/hr'

Lithuania hasn't really joined the downhill game, but you can cross-country ski amid deep, whispering forests and frozen blue lakes in supremely beautiful Aukštaitija National Park (p320).

BIRD-WATCHING

Thanks to a key position on north–south migration routes, the Baltic countries are a bird-watcher's paradise. Each year, hundreds of bird species descend upon the region, attracted by fish-packed wetlands and wide-open spaces relatively devoid of people. White storks arrive by the thousands each spring, nesting on rooftops and telegraph poles throughout the region. Other annual visitors include corncrakes, bitterns, cranes, mute swans, black storks and all types of geese.

In Estonia, some of the best bird-watching in the Baltics is found in the Matsalu Nature Reserve (p135), where 275 different species (many migratory) can be spotted. Vilsandi National Park (p152), off Saaremaa, arranges bird-watching tours. The Hiiumaa Islets Landscape Reserve (p142) is another other great birding spot. Visit the **Estonian Ornithological Society** (Eesti Ornitoloogiauhing; ☎ 0742 2195; www.eoy.ee; Veski tanav 4, Tartu) for all the latest regional birding info.

Home to some 270 of Lithuania's 325 bird species, the Nemunas Delta Regional Park (p370) is a must for serious birders. Park authorities can help organise bird-watching expeditions during the mid-September, late October and March–mid-May migratory seasons. The nearby Curonian Spit National Park (p362) offers opportunities for spotting up to 200 different species of birds amid dramatic coastal scenery.

In Latvia, keep an eye out for some of Europe's rarest birds in splendid Gauja National Park (p226). With thick forests and numerous wetlands, Ķemeri National Park (p252), in northern Kurzeme, is another great bird-watching spot. The boggy Teiči Nature Reserve (p238), in the Vidzeme Upland, is an important feeding and nesting ground for many bird species. Lake Engure (p253), in northern Kurzeme, is a major bird reservation with 186 species (44 endangered) nesting around the lake and its seven islets. The **Engure Ornithological Research Centre** (☎ 947 4420; Bērzciems; 🕒 by appt only) arranges bird-watching expeditions to an observation tower in the middle of the lake. For the scoop on everything bird-related in Latvia, check out **Latvian Birding** (www.putni.lv). This highly informative site is in English, has exhaustive lists of common

Latvian birds, notes on recent rare species sightings and tips on hot bird-watching spots.

BERRYING & MUSHROOMING

For info on berrying and mushrooming tours, check out www.countryside.lt (Lithuania), www.maaturism.ee (Estonia) and www.traveller.lv (Latvia).

The Balts' deep-rooted attachment to the land is reflected in their obsession with berrying and mushrooming – national pastimes for all three countries. Accompanying a local friend into the forest on a berrying or mushrooming expedition is an enchanting way to appreciate this traditional rural occupation.

If you're keen on picking, but lack a local invitation, join an organised tour. **Countryside Tourism of Lithuania** (☎ 37-400 354; www.countryside.lt; Donelaičio gatvė 2-201, Kaunas), **Estonian Rural Tourism** (☎ 600 9999; www.maaturism.ee in Estonian; Vilmsi tänav 53B, Tallinn) and Latvia's **Baltic Country Holidays** (☎ 761 7600; www.traveller.lv; Kuģu iela 11, Rīga) all offer ecotourism-oriented trips that include rural homestays and mushroom- and berry-picking excursions with your host.

FISHING

Abundant lakes and miles upon miles of rivers and streams provide ample fishing opportunities in all three countries. Visit a regional tourist office for the scoop on the best angling spots and information pertaining to permits.

In the dark depths of the Baltic winter there is no finer experience than dabbling in a touch of ice-fishing with vodka-warmed local fishermen on the frozen Curonian Lagoon (p362), off the west coast of Lithuania. The Nemunas Delta Regional Park (p370) is another good western Lithuanian fishing spot. The park information office sells the required permits and offers assistance on where to pick up gear.

An angling permit is compulsory in Latvia, Estonia and Lithuania; visit a regional tourism office to arrange one. Staff can also give you the low-down on the best fishing spots.

The Estonian coastline has some fine angling spots. You'll need a permit to fish anywhere along this coast; stop by the nearest tourist office to find out where to get one. In northeast Estonia, the **Lahemmaa National Park Visitors' Centre** (☎ 0329 5555; www.lahemaa.ee) has all the information on the regional fishing scene.

Latvia's numerous lakes and rivers are packed with all sorts of fish. You'll need a permit to fish anywhere in the country; these can be bought at local post offices or angling stores. The Latgale Upland (p241) is packed with hundreds of deep-blue lakes offering ample fishing opportunities. In northern Kurzeme, Lake Engure (p253) is another favourite angling spot.

Estonia

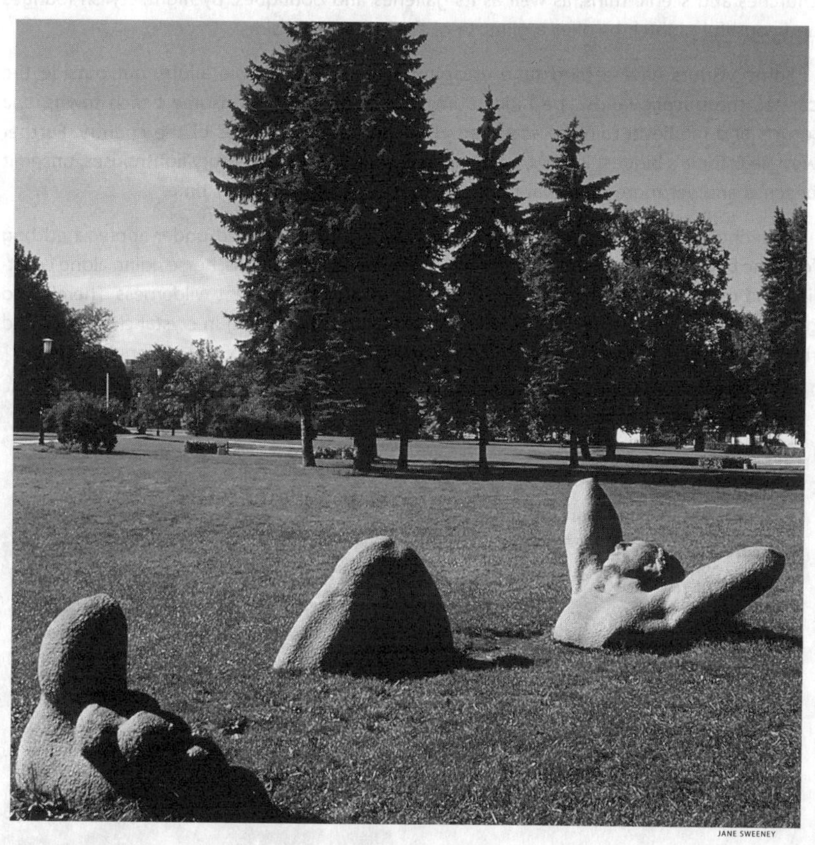

JANE SWEENEY

Estonia

Although the smallest of the Baltic countries, Estonia (Eesti) makes its presence felt in the region.

Lovely seaside towns, quaint country villages and verdant forests and marshlands set the scene for discovering many cultural and natural gems. Yet Estonia is also known for magnificent castles, pristine islands and a cosmopolitan capital amid medieval splendour. It's no wonder Estonia is no longer Europe's best-kept secret.

Tallinn, Estonia's crown jewel, boasts cobbled streets and rejuvenated 14th-century dwellings. Dozens of cafés and restaurants make for an atmospheric retreat after exploring historic churches and scenic ruins, as well as its galleries and boutiques. By night, stylish lounges and youthful nightclubs offer a glimpse of the city's sexier side.

Some visitors have a hard time escaping Tallinn's undeniable allure, but outside the capital, the bucolic landscape hides numerous attractions. Handsome beach towns, spa resorts and medieval ruins lie scattered about the western shores of the country. Further west lie Estonia's biggest islands, where iconic windmills, 19th-century lighthouses, unspoilt beaches and yet more medieval ruins transport visitors to another time.

Covering vast swaths of Estonia, forests, wooded meadows and under-appreciated bog form the backdrop to numerous activities. Hiking over wooded trails, horse riding along coastline and canoeing over flooded forests can link you to the ancient wilderness. There's also great bird-watching, cross-country skiing in winter and swimming in crystal-clear lakes and rivers in summer. This all makes a nice prelude to a sauna, one of the national pastimes.

FAST FACTS

- **Area** 45,227 sq km
- **Birthplace of** Carmen Kass, supermodel; Kalevipoeg, mythological hero
- **Capital** Tallinn
- **Country code** ☎ 372
- **Departure tax** none
- **Famous for** song festivals, lush woodlands and resplendent coastlines
- **Money** Estonian Kroon; €1 = 15.64Kr; US$1 = 13.07Kr; UK£1 = 15.64Kr
- **Population** 1.3 million
- **Visas** not needed for most nationalities. See p391 for details.

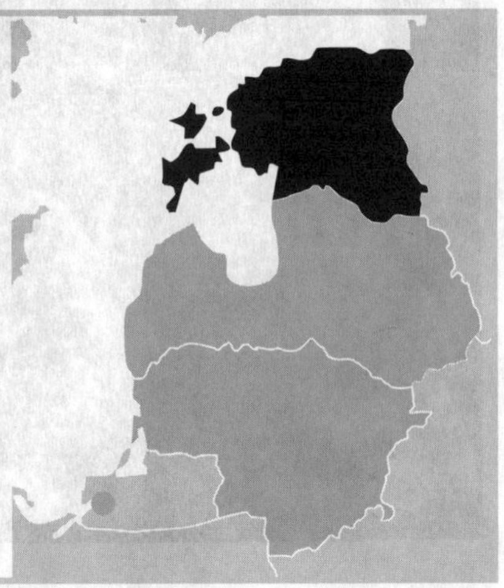

HIGHLIGHTS

- **Tallinn** (p64) Wander the medieval streets, and drink in lovely cafés, eclectic restaurants and steamy nightclubs.
- **Pärnu** (p155) Join this party town, home to sandy beaches, spa resorts and plenty of night-time distractions.
- **Saaremaa** (p142) Escape to Estonia's largest island, with lovely, long stretches of empty coastline and medieval ruins, and abundant opportunities for outdoor adventure.
- **Tartu** (p106) Discover the magic of this splendid town, gateway to the beautiful land of the mystical Setu community, with myriad lakes and forests.
- **Lahemaa National Park** (p95) Relish the natural beauty of this area's lush landscape and immaculate coastline.

ITINERARIES

- **Three Days** Spend your first 48 hours drinking in the splendour of Tallinn's Old Town. On the third day, head to leafy Kadriorg, the Botanical Gardens and TV Tower, or take a daytrip west to nearby beaches.
- **One Week** After Tallinn, go to the island of Saaremaa, where spa resorts, windswept beaches and a castle await. Alternatively, aim eastward for magnificent Lahemaa National Park.
- **Two Weeks** To the above, add Tartu, a vibrant university town and gateway to the lushly landscaped southeast, and/or Pärnu, a youthful seaside town near vast Soomaa National Park and charming Viljandi.

CURRENT EVENTS

To some degree Estonia has found it hard to escape its past, notably when Arnold Rüütel, the former head of Estonia's Soviet parliament, won the 2001 presidential election. Viewed by many as a politically inept communist dinosaur, 73-year-old Rüütel won on his dedication to social problems (such as unemployment) – an issue given short shrift as EU hysteria swept the country. His communist credentials and agricultural background were particularly deficient compared with the skills of his predecessor, the brilliant and charismatic Lennart Meri.

Still Rüütel had no intention of leading Estonia astray – and had little opportunity to do so, since the president has little involvement in the day-to-day running of the country (the domain of the prime minister).

Rüütel's administration, which ended in 2005, was marked by a few scandals. Some classified documents went missing on two occasions, leading to the resignation or firing of two high-ranking ministers. There were also the usual parliamentary shake-ups, which have become fairly commonplace in Estonian politics. Yet more important than the setbacks were the enormous twin achievements. Following a referendum in September 2003, approximately 60% of Estonians voted in favour of joining the EU. The following spring, the country officially joined NATO and the EU.

At last count in 2005, 65% of Estonians still believed EU membership had positive results. Assuming Estonia keeps its inflation down, it has a good chance of adopting the euro as its currency in 2007.

In many ways, Estonia is the outstanding economic success story of the Baltic region, having made a remarkable transition to capitalism. Its large-scale privatisation, free-trade agreements and low corporate taxes have brought in enormous foreign investment, mainly in the finance, manufacturing and transport sectors. The effect on economic growth has been pronounced: from 2000 to 2005, real GDP growth averaged 6.1% per year, a remarkable achievement for such a tiny newcomer.

HOW MUCH?

- **Coffee** 30Kr
- **Taxi fare (10 minutes)** 50Kr
- **Bus ticket (Tallinn to Tartu)** 80Kr
- **Bicycle hire (daily)** 150Kr
- **Sauna** 65Kr

LONELY PLANET INDEX

- **Litre of petrol** 14Kr
- **Litre of bottled water** 15Kr
- **Half-litre of Saku beer in a store/bar** 15/28Kr
- **Souvenir T-shirt** 150Kr
- **packet of roasted nuts** 25Kr

Meanwhile, Estonia's ongoing disputes with Russia have continued apace. These stem largely from the unresolved border treaty, first put forth in 1996. Estonia had to give up its claim to two frontier areas: a slice of land east of the Narva River and a larger area in Setumaa, around Pechory, across Estonia's existing southeastern border. These pieces of land, totalling 2300 sq km, had been in Estonia's possession only between the wars, after the signing of the 1920 Tartu Peace Treaty. The Estonian parliament finally ratified the border treaty in June 2005, but added a few oblique references to the 1920 Tartu treaty. Russia resented the comments and withdrew from negotiations in September 2005.

The tensions extend to other areas as well: in 2005, during the 60th anniversary of the Allied victory in WWII, Rüütel declined an invitation to attend the celebrations in Moscow, which the Russians found insulting.

HISTORY

Beginnings

Estonia's oldest human settlements date back 10,000 years, with Stone Age tools found around Pulli near present-day Pärnu. Finno-Ugric tribes from the east (probably around the Urals) came centuries later – probably around 3500 BC – mingling with Neolithic peoples and settling in present-day Estonia, Finland and Hungary. They took a liking to their homeland and stayed put, spurning nomadic ways that characterised most other European peoples over the next six millennia.

The Christian Invasion

By the 9th and 10th centuries AD, Estonians were well aware of the Vikings, who seemed more interested in trade routes to Kiev and Istanbul than in conquering the land. The first real threat came from Christian invaders from the west.

Following papal calls for a crusade against the northern heathens, Danish troops and German knights invaded Estonia, conquering the Southern Estonian castle of Otepää in 1208. The locals put up fierce resistance, and it took well over 30 years before the entire territory was conquered. By the mid-13th century Estonia was carved up between the Danish in the north and the German Teutonic Order in the south. The Order, hungry to move eastward, was powerfully repelled by Alexander Nevsky of Novgorod on frozen Lake Peipsi (marvellously imagined in Eisenstein's film *Alexander Nevsky*).

The conquerors settled in at various newly established towns, handing over much power to the bishops. By the end of the 13th century cathedrals rose over Tallinn and Dorpat (Tartu), around the time that Cistercian and Dominican religious orders set up monasteries to preach to the locals and (try to) baptise them. Meanwhile, the Estonians continued to rebel.

The most significant uprising began on St George's night (23 April) in 1343. It started in Danish-controlled Northern Estonia when Estonians pillaged the Padise Cistercian monastery and killed all of the monks. They subsequently laid siege to Tallinn and the Bishop's Castle in Haapsalu, and called for Swedish assistance to help them finish the job. The Swedes did indeed send naval reinforcements across the gulf, but they came too late and were forced to turn back. Despite Estonian resolve, by 1345 the rebellion was crushed. The Danes, however, decided they'd had enough and sold Estonia to the Livonian Order.

The first guilds and merchant associations emerged in the 14th century, and many towns – Tallinn, Tartu, Viljandi and Pärnu – prospered as trade members of the Hanseatic League (a medieval merchant guild). Tartu's St John's Church (Jaani Kirik) with its terracotta sculpture is testament to its wealth and western trade links.

Estonians continued practising pagan rites for weddings, funerals and nature worship, though by the 15th century these rites became interlinked with Catholicism, and

THE SOURCE OF EESTI

In the 1st century AD the Roman historian Tacitus described a people known as the 'Aestii'. In rather crude fashion he depicted them as worshipping goddess statues and chasing wild boars with wooden clubs and iron weaponry. These peoples collected and traded amber. Although Tacitus was describing the forerunners to the Lithuanians and Latvians, the name 'Aestii' was eventually applied specifically to Estonians.

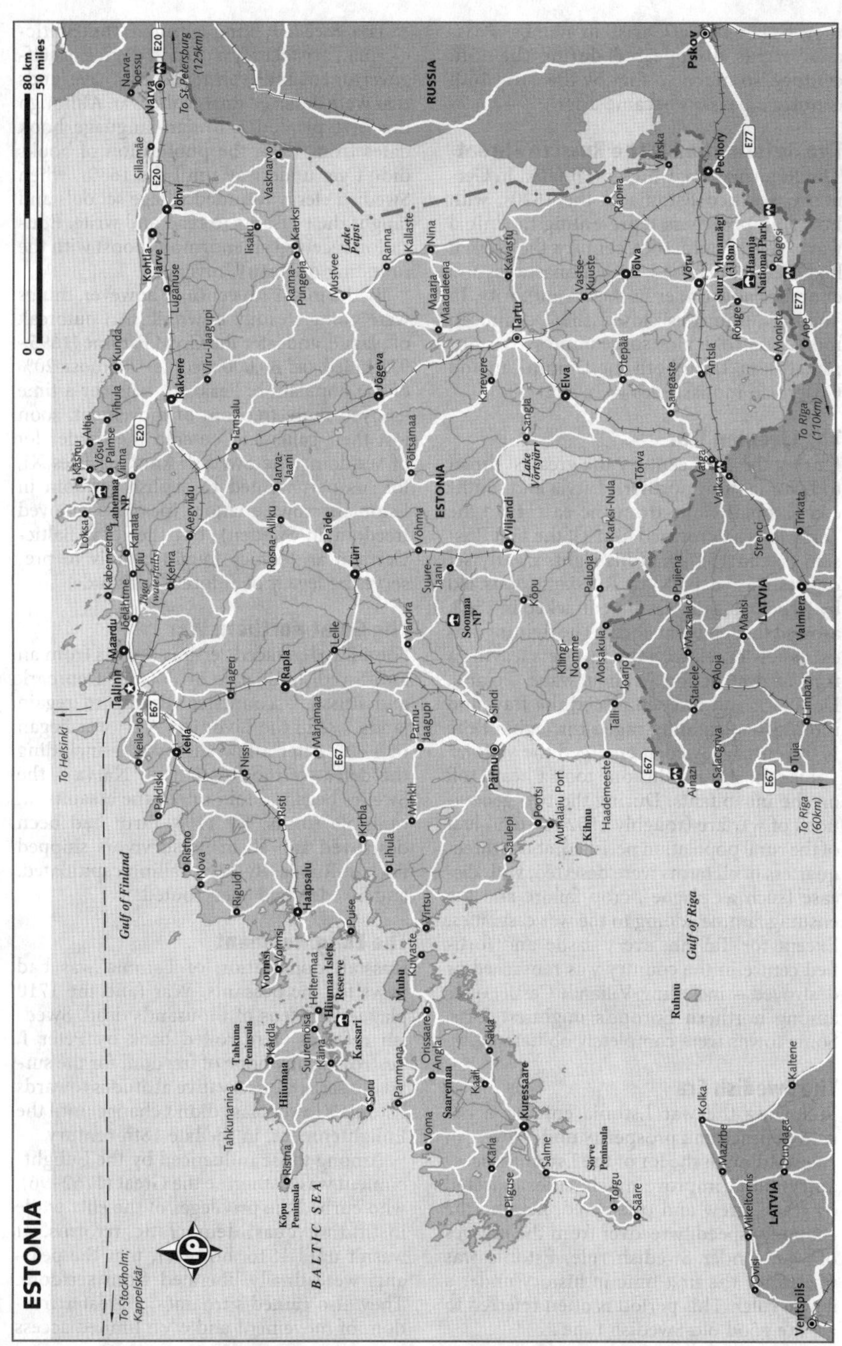
ESTONIA
0 80 km
0 50 miles
To Stockholm; Kappelskär
To Helsinki
To St Petersburg (125km)
To Riga (60km)
To Riga (110km)
Gulf of Finland
BALTIC SEA
Gulf of Riga
RUSSIA
LATVIA
Lake Peipsi
Lake Võrtsjärv
Tallinn
Maardu
Keila
Paldiski
Rapla
Paide
Türi
Rakvere
Kunda
Kohtla-Järve
Jõhvi
Sillamäe
Narva
Narva-Jõesuu
Pskov
Pechory
Tartu
Jõgeva
Põltsamaa
Viljandi
Elva
Põlva
Võru
Otepää
Valga
Valka
Valmiera
Pärnu
Sindi
Haapsalu
Hiiumaa
Kärdla
Saaremaa
Kuressaare
Muhu
Vormsi
Kihnu
Ruhnu
Lahemaa NP
Soomaa NP
Haanja National Park
Suur Munamägi (318m)
Ventspils
E20
E67
E77

they began using Christian names. Peasants' rights disappeared during the 15th century, so much so that by the early 16th century a peasant became a serf.

The Reformation & the Russian Threat

The Reformation, which originated in Germany, reached Estonia in the 1520s, with Lutheran preachers representing the initial wave. By the mid-16th century the church had been reorganised, with monasteries and churches now under Lutheran authority. In Tallinn authorities closed the Dominican monastery (of which some impressive ruins remain); in Tartu both the Dominican and Cistercian monasteries were shut.

The Livonian War

During the 16th century the greatest threat to Livonia (now northern Latvia and southern Estonia) came from the east. Ivan the Terrible, who crowned himself the first Russian tsar in 1547, had his sights clearly set on westward expansion. Russian troops, led by ferocious Tatar cavalry, attacked in 1558, around the region of Tartu. The fighting was extremely cruel, with the invaders leaving a trail of destruction in their wake. Poland, Denmark and Sweden joined the fray, and intermittent fighting raged throughout the 17th century. Sweden emerged the victor.

Like most wars, this one took a heavy toll on the inhabitants. During the two generations of warfare (roughly 1552 to 1629) half of the rural population perished, about three-quarters of all farms were deserted, with disease (such as plague), crop failure and the ensuing famine adding to the war casualties. Except for Tallinn, every castle and fortified centre in the country was ransacked or destroyed – including Viljandi Castle, once among northern Europe's mightiest forts. Some towns were completely obliterated.

The Swedish Era

Following the war Estonia entered a period of peace and prosperity under Swedish rule. Although the lot of the Estonian peasantry didn't improve much, cities, boosted by trade, grew and prospered, helping the economy speedily recover from the ravages of war. Under Swedish rule, Estonia was united for the first time in history under a single ruler. This period is often referred to as 'the good old Swedish time'.

The Swedish king granted the Baltic-German aristocracy a certain degree of self-government and even generously gave lands that were deserted during the war. Although the first printed Estonian-language book dates from 1535, the publication of books didn't get underway until the 1630s, when Swedish clergy founded village schools and taught the peasants to read and write. Education received an enormous boost with the founding of Tartu University.

By the mid-17th century, however, things were going steadily downhill. An outbreak of plague, and later the Great Famine (1695–97) killed off 80,000 people – almost 20% of the population. Peasants, who for a time enjoyed more freedom of movement, soon lost their gains and entered the harder lot of serfdom. The Swedish king, Charles XI, for his part wanted to abolish serfdom in Estonian crown manors (peasants enjoyed freedom in Sweden), but the local Baltic-German aristocracy fought bitterly to preserve the legacy of enforced servitude.

The Great Northern War

Soon Sweden faced serious threats from an anti-Swedish alliance of Poland, Denmark and Russia – countries seeking to regain lands lost in the Livonian War: war began in 1700. After a few successes – including the defeat of the Russians at Narva – the Swedes began to fold under the assaults on multiple fronts. By 1708 Tartu had been destroyed and all of its survivors shipped back to Russia. By 1710 Tallinn capitulated, and Sweden had been routed.

The Enlightenment

Russian domination of Estonia was bad news for the peasants. War (and the 1710 plague) left tens of thousands dead. Swedish reforms were rolled back by Peter I, destroying any hope of freedom for the surviving serfs. Conservative attitudes towards Estonia's lower class didn't change until the Enlightenment, in the late 18th century.

Among those influenced by the Enlightenment was Catherine the Great (1762–96), who curbed the privileges of the elite while instituting quasi-democratic reforms. It wasn't until 1816, however, that the peasants were finally liberated from serfdom. They also gained surnames, a greater freedom of movement and even limited access to self-government. By the second half of the 19th century, the peasants started buying farmsteads from the estates, and earning an income from crops such as potatoes and flax (the latter commanding particularly high prices during the US Civil War and the subsequent drop in American cotton export to Europe).

National Awakening

The late 19th century was the dawn of the national awakening. Led by a new Estonian elite, the country marched towards nationhood. The first Estonian-language newspaper, *Perno Postimees,* appeared in 1857. It was published by Johann Voldemar Jannsen, one of the first to use the term 'Estonians' rather than *maarahvas* (country people). Other influential thinkers included Carl Robert Jakobson, who fought for equal political rights for Estonians; he also founded *Sakala*, Estonia's first political newspaper. (Jakobson's house and farm, p161, provide insight into this unique man).

Numerous Estonian societies emerged, and in 1869 the first song festival was held, a major event foregrounding Estonia's unique choral traditions. Estonia's rich folklore also emerged from obscurity, particularly with the publication of *Kalevipoeg*, Friedrich Kreutzwald's poetic epic that melded together hundreds of Estonian legends and folk tales. Other poems, particularly works by Lydia Koidula, also helped shape the national consciousness – one imprinted with the memory of 700 years of slavery.

Rebellion & WWI

The late 19th century was also a period of rampant industrialisation, marked by the rise of large factories and an extensive railway network that linked Estonia with Russia. Socialism and discontent accompanied those grim workplaces, with demonstrations and strikes led by newly formed worker parties. Events in Estonia mimicked those in Russia, and in January 1905 as armed insurrection flared across the border, Estonia's workers joined the fray. Tension mounted until autumn that year, when 20,000 workers went on strike. Tsarist troops brutally responded by killing and wounding 200.

Tsar Nicholas II's response incited the Estonian rebels, who continued to destroy the property of the old guard. Subsequently, thousands of soldiers arrived from Russia, quelling the rebellions and then executed 600 Estonians and sent hundreds off to Siberia. Trade unions and progressive newspapers and organisations were closed down, and political leaders fled the country.

More radical plans to bring Estonia to heel – such as sending thousands of Russian peasants to colonise the country – were never realised. Instead, Russia's bumbling tsar had another priority: WWI. Estonia paid a high price for Russia's involvement – 100,000 men were drafted, 10,000 of whom were killed in action. Many Estonians went off to fight under the notion that if they helped defeat Germany, Russia would grant them nationhood. Russia, of course, had no intention of doing so. But by 1917 the matter was no longer the tsar's to decide. In St Petersburg Nicholas II was forced to abdicate, and the Bolsheviks seized power. As chaos swept across Russia, Estonia seized the initiative and on 24 February 1918, effectively declared its independence.

The War of Independence

Estonia faced threats from both Russia and Baltic-German reactionaries. War erupted as the Red Army quickly advanced, overrunning half the country by January 1919. Estonia fought back tenaciously, and with the help of British warships and Finnish, Danish and Swedish troops, it defeated its longtime enemy. In December Russia agreed to a truce and on 2 February 1920 it signed the Tartu Peace Treaty, which renounced forever Russia's rights of sovereignty over Estonian territory. For the first time in its history, Estonia was completely independent.

THE EARLIEST HERALD OF NATIONHOOD

One particularly insightful thinker of the Enlightenment was the German Garlieb Merkel, who in 1796 postulated the idea that serfdom was bad economics. He also referred to the Estonians (and Latvians) not as suppressed peasants, but as distinct nations forced into servitude. Revolutionary for the time, Merkel's thinking became highly influential in the national awakening a century later.

Days of Wine, Roses & Dictatorship

In many ways, the independence period was a golden era. The economy developed rapidly, with Estonia utilising its natural resources and attracting investments from abroad. Tartu University became a university for Estonians, and the Estonian language became the lingua franca for all aspects of public life, creating new opportunities in professional and academic spheres. Secondary education also improved (per capita the number of students surpassed most European nations), and an enormous book industry arose, with 25,000 titles published between 1918 and 1940 (again surpassing most European nations in books per capita).

On other fronts – notably the political one – independence was not so rosy. Fear of communist subversion (such as the failed 1924 coup d'état supported by the Bolsheviks) drove the government to the right. In 1934 Konstantin Päts, leader of the transitional government, along with Johan Laidoner, commander-in-chief of the Estonian army, violated the constitution and seized power, under the pretext of protecting democracy from extremist factions. Thus began the 'era of silence', a period of gross authoritarian rule that dogged the fledgling republic until WWII.

The Soviet Invasion & WWII

Estonia's fate was sealed when Nazi Germany and the USSR negotiated a secret pact in 1939, essentially handing Estonia over to Stalin. Thousands of Russian soldiers arrived, along with military, naval and air bases, between 1939 and 1941. Apparatchiks (Communist Party members) orchestrated a sham rebellion whereby 'the people' demanded to be part of the USSR. President Päts, General Laidoner and other leaders were sacked and sent off to Russian prison camps, a puppet government was installed, and on 6 August 1940 the Supreme Soviet accepted Estonia's 'request' to join the USSR.

Deportations and WWII devastated the country. Tens of thousands were conscripted and sent not to fight but to work (and usually die) in labour camps in northern Russia. Thousands of women and children were also sent to gulags.

When Russia fled the German advance, Estonia welcomed the Nazis as liberators. Fifty-five thousand Estonians joined home-defence units and Wehrmacht Ost battalions. The Nazis, however, would not grant statehood to Estonia and viewed it merely as occupied territory of the Soviet Union. Hope was crushed when the Germans began executing communist collaborators. Seventy-five thousand people were shot (5000 of whom were ethnic Estonians). Thousands fled to Finland, while those who remained faced conscription into the German army (nearly 40,000 were conscripted).

In early 1944 the Soviet army bombed Tallinn, Narva, Tartu and other cities. Narva's baroque Old Town was almost completely destroyed as Russia exacted revenge upon 'Estonian traitors'.

The Nazis retreated in September 1944. Fearing the advance of the Red Army, many Estonians also fled and around 70,000 reached the West. By the end of the war one in 10 Estonians lived abroad. All in all, Estonia lost over 280,000 people: in addition to those who emigrated, 30,000 were killed in action; others were executed, sent to gulags or exterminated in concentration camps.

The Soviet Era

After the war Estonia was immediately annexed by the Soviet Union. This began the grim epoch of repression, with many thousands tortured or sent to prison camps and 19,000 Estonians executed. Farmers were brutally forced into collectivisation, and thousands of immigrants flooded the country from different regions of the Soviet Union. Between 1939 and 1989 the percentage of native Estonians fell from 97% to 62%.

As a result of the repression, beginning in 1944, Estonians formed a large guerrilla movement. Calling themselves the 'Forest Brothers', 14,000 Estonians armed themselves and went into hiding, operating in small groups throughout the country. Unfortunately, the guerrillas had little success against the Soviet army, and by 1956 the movement had been effectively destroyed.

Although there were a few optimistic periods during the tyranny (notably the 'thaw' under Khrushchev), Estonia didn't see much hope until the mid '80s. With the ravaging war in Afghanistan and years of disastrous state planning under its belt, the Soviet Union teetered on the brink of economic catastrophe.

The dissident movement in Estonia gained momentum, and on the 50th anniversary of the Stalin-Hitler pact, a major rally took place in Tallinn. Over the next few months, more and more protests were held, with Estonians demanding the restoration of statehood. The song festival was one of Estonia's most powerful vehicles for protest. The biggest took place in 1988 when 250,000 Estonians gathered on Tallinn's Song Festival grounds. This brought much international attention to the Baltic plight.

In November 1989 the Estonian Supreme Soviet declared the events of 1940 an act of military aggression and therefore illegal. Disobeying Moscow's orders, Estonia held free elections in 1990. Despite Russia's attempts to stop it, Estonia regained its independence in 1991.

Postindependence

In 1992 the first general election under the new constitution took place, with a proliferation of newly formed parties. The Pro Patria (Fatherland) Union won a narrow majority after campaigning under the slogan 'Cleaning House', which meant removing from power those associated with communist rule. Pro Patria's leader, 32-year-old historian Mart Laar, became prime minister.

Laar set to work transforming Estonia into a free-market economy, introducing the very solid Estonian kroon and negotiating the complete Russian troop withdrawal. (The latter was a source of particular anxiety for Estonians, and the whole country breathed a collective sigh of relief when the last garrisons departed in 1994. Unfortunately, the Russians left a few things behind: ecologically devastated lands in the northeast, polluted ground water around air bases and nuclear waste in naval bases.)

Despite Laar's successes, he was considered a hothead, and in 1994, he was dismissed when his government received a vote of no confidence by the Riigikogu (National Council). Laar returned to the political arena in 1999, when he was elected prime minister a second time. During this time in office, he helped correct the Estonian financial crisis brought on by Russia's financial collapse in 1998. Laar cut business taxes and reduced social benefits, and continued the march to privatisation. His remedies worked, pulling Estonia out of its negative growth in 1999, which allowed it to begin accession talks with the EU. There was much political wrangling, however, among the coalition government, and in 2002 Laar resigned.

> **TALLINN'S CHECHEN HERO**
>
> In January 1991 Soviet troops seized strategic buildings in Vilnius and Rīga, and soldiers were ordered to do the same in Tallinn. The commander of the troops at the time, however, disobeyed Moscow's orders, and refused to open fire upon the crowd. He even threatened to turn the artillery under his command against any attempted invasion from Russia. That leader was Dzhokhar Dudayev, who would go on to become the president of Chechnya and lead its independence movement. He was brutally assassinated by the Russian military in 1995. In Estonia he is fondly remembered for his role in bringing about Estonian independence.

THE CULTURE

The National Psyche

Despite centuries of occupation by Danes, Swedes, Germans and Russians, Estonians have tenaciously held onto their national identity. Estonians are deeply connected to their history, folklore and national song tradition. The Estonian Literary Museum (p111) in Tartu holds over 1.3 million pages of folk songs, the world's second-largest collection (Ireland has the largest), and Estonia produces films for one of the world's smallest audiences (only Iceland produces for a smaller audience). Despite this inward-focus, Estonians are equally interested in what's happening in the outside world, particularly now that they're part of the EU and feel like they have a stake in things.

In person, Estonians tend to be reserved and standoffish. Some believe it has much to do with the weather – those long dark nights breeding endless introspection, as the stereotype goes. This reserve also extends to gross displays of public affection, brash behaviour and intoxication – all frowned upon. This is assuming that there isn't a festival underway, such as Jaanipäev, when friends, family and acquaintances gather in the countryside for drinking, dancing and revelry.

Despite the self-composure, Estonians try not to take themselves too seriously, and are known for their wit and good humour. Being rooted for so long in one place, it's no surprise that Estonians have a deep, some might say spiritual, connection to the land.

Lifestyle

The long, grey days of Soviet rule are well behind Estonia. Today first-time visitors are astonished to find a thriving society, with urban streetscapes awash in colourful design, and a savvy populace setting its own fashions and trends.

The new economy has created previously unimagined possibilities. Entrepreneurship is widespread (the developers of Kazaa, the peer-to-peer, file-sharing software, and Skype, which allows free telephone calling over the Internet, are both Estonian), and the economy has diversified considerably since 1991.

Estonians are known for their strong work ethic, but when they're not toiling in the fields, or putting long hours in at the office, they head to the countryside. Ideal weekends are spent at the family cottage, picking berries or mushrooms, walking through the woods, or sitting with friends soaking up the quiet beauty. Having a countryside sauna is one of the national pastimes.

In the realm of education, Estonia is making enormous steps in ensuring students are prepared for the future, and today its schools and towns are among the most wired-up in the world. Internet and mobile-phone usage per capita is higher here than it is in France. Estonians pay for parking using their mobile phones, and in 2005 even began voting online.

Yet despite the ongoing IT revolution, the country has some nagging social problems. Although the number of people living below the poverty line has fallen in recent years, wage disparities continue to grow, and the cost of goods continues to rise faster than salaries. Pensioners have been the hardest hit, as Estonia's social-welfare infrastructure doesn't quite meet the demands. Many Russians also feel alienated from the new Estonia, facing what they feel are enormous obstacles – one of the most daunting being the requirement to learn Estonian – in order to succeed in the new economy.

On a positive note, Estonia continues to experience huge economic growth (over 7% in 2005 compared with under 2% elsewhere in Europe), with unemployment around 9%; less than France and Germany. Earnings per capita in 2005 stood at €13,700, placing it below the EU average of €23,480, but well up from its Soviet days. Perhaps most discouraging for blue-collar Estonians is that the average worker earns only 20% of what their Finnish counterpart earns.

Population

Estonia ranks near the bottom of the world scale in terms of population (with slightly fewer residents than the Gaza Strip, but a fraction more than Mauritius). The country also has a low population density, with only 32 people per sq km, compared with 380 people per sq km in the Netherlands – good news for those sick of wading through crowds.

Only 68% of the people living in Estonia are ethnic Estonians. Russians make up 26% of the population, with 2% Ukrainian, 1% Belarusian, 1% Finnish and 2% other. Ethnic Russians are concentrated in the industrial cities of the northeast, where in some places (such as Narva) they make up 96% of the population. Russians also have a sizable presence in Tallinn (40%).

Seventy percent of Estonians reside in cities; 40% of the national population lives in the capital. Literacy is almost universal in Estonia (99.8%).

Multiculturalism

The ethnic make-up of present-day Estonia differs markedly from that of 70 years ago. In 1934 native Estonians comprised over 90% of the population. This changed a few years later with the Soviet takeover. Migration from other parts of the USSR occurred on a mass scale from 1945 to 1955, with many of the immigrants arriving with military troops. Over the course of the next three decades, Estonia had the highest rate of migration of any of the Soviet republics.

While much was made of the strife between ethnic Russians and Estonians in the '90s, today the two communities live together in relative harmony. While older Russians and Estonians in general have little to do with one another, the younger generation mix quite freely. This isn't to say

CITIZENSHIP

When Estonia regained independence, not every resident received citizenship. People who were citizens of the pre-1940 Estonian Republic and their descendants automatically became citizens. Other people had to be naturalised, an ongoing process that includes a language test (with questions about the constitution); so far, 133,000 people made up of Russians and other nationalities have become citizens in this way. Anyone living in Estonia before 1 July 1990 can apply for citizenship automatically; anyone who arrived after that date must hold a residency permit for five years before applying. However, anyone born in the country after 26 February 1992 is automatically a citizen. Only citizens may vote in parliamentary elections. Noncitizens can vote in local government elections providing they have legal residency.

In 2005 there were still 245,000 people classified as 'foreigners' living in Estonia: 103,000 held foreign passports (most of them Russian), and the remainder held a so-called 'alien's passport' (dubbed 'grey passport'). The latter gives legal residency in Estonia and freedom to travel to most countries but essentially renders the holders stateless – unless they choose to become naturalised or take up Russian or other citizenship.

One reason Russians do not apply for citizenship is their easier, visa-free travel to Russia to visit relatives (Estonian passport holders need visas). Another deterrent for young Russian men is that they avoid Estonian army service if they are not citizens until after the age of 27.

One deterrent to Russian speakers learning enough Estonian to pass a language test has been a perceived lack of goodwill on the part of the government to encourage them to learn. The Estonian government has spent relatively little on language immersion and integration programmes, the funding for which has come largely from foreign sources. Instead, efforts have concentrated on discouraging the 'illegal' use of Russian. The Language Department enforces laws forbidding the display of foreign-language words (excluding trademarks) in public places such as on billboards and in store windows (inside a store is allowed in certain cases). Another law regulates the minimum Estonian language requirements in all public and private enterprises (even including a Russian cultural centre in Narva, which is 92% Russian). As the majority of Russians are far from proficient in Estonian, this has prompted concern from the UN over limitations on freedom of speech and reduced opportunities for advancement and representation for many of Estonia's Russian speakers. Perhaps in response to international criticism, in recent years the Estonian government has begun addressing the problems – albeit slowly. In 2004 the government passed an amendment shortening the time required for obtaining citizenship, and the costs of language courses will be reimbursed to those who pass the exams. It has also committed to an extension of the time frame for phasing out Russian language tuition, and has requested assistance both politically and financially from organisations such as the EU to implement larger-scale language and integration programmes.

that life is smooth. Russians have a higher unemployment rate (20%) and make up a disproportionate share of prisoners (58%). A drive through some of the crumbling towns of the northeast, where work and hope are both in short supply, gives some clue to the Russian plight. To make matters worse, the higher social problems in the Russian community in turn feeds the negative stereotypes that some Estonians have of them.

One of the most overlooked ethnic groups in Estonia is the Setu people, a native group of mixed Russian-Estonian ancestry who live in southeastern Estonia and in neighbouring Russia. They are a Finno-Ugric people with rich cultural traditions, and they speak their own language (Võru Seto). There are about 4000 in Estonia (and 3000 in Russia), though their numbers continue to dwindle. Worst of all is the border that separates the two countries, cutting whole communities in half. For now, the Setus are destined to remain a divided people.

SPORT

For years, basketball was considered Estonia's national sport, but recently football mania has been sweeping the nation. Estonia's victory over Russia in 2002 certainly added more football fans to the pile. Abroad, meanwhile, Estonians are following the successes of Mart Poom, nicknamed the Estonian Giant, who is a goalkeeper for Arsenal, in the English Premier League.

Estonia has 10 football teams in its masters league, four of which are based in Tallinn. FC Flora is the long-standing favourite of many local fans. Those who want to catch a live match can do so in Tallinn at the A Le Coq Arena (p88).

Basketball aficionados will find courts large and small scattered around the country. Tallinn's Kalev Stadium (p88) is your best bet for seeing a game.

Once the summer arrives, locals take advantage of Estonia's 3700km of coastline, where avid windsurfers, kayakers, swimmers and mere beach spectators all fill the shoreline. There are some fantastic places to sail, and even a remote spot on the islands where you can surf some waves (see p139).

Estonia's flat landscape attracts loads of cyclists. Major bike marathons take place in Tartu (p112) and Otepää, which is also the country's cross-country ski capital. Skiing through snowy forests followed by a refreshing sauna is a much-vaunted combo in Estonia. Another well-known name in the sports world is Erki Nool, the decathlon gold-medal winner at the 2000 Olympics in Sydney.

A sport that you're unlikely to encounter elsewhere in the world is kiiking, where the gentle pleasure of riding a swing becomes an extreme sport. Devised in Pärnu in 1997, contestants attempt to complete a 360-degree loop around the top bar. For more information on kiiking, and info on upcoming events check out www.kiiking.ee.

RELIGION

Historically, Estonia was Lutheran from the early 17th century, though today only a minority of Estonians profess religious beliefs. From 1987 to 1990 there was a surge of interest in religion as the state Lutheran Church allied itself to the independence cause. Since then, enthusiasm has tapered off. More visible are the numerous sects and religious organisations that have recently set up shop in Estonia, including the Church of Latter Day Saints (the well-dressed and clean-cut representatives of which can be seen daily on the streets of Tallinn), Seventh Day Adventists, Jehovah's Witnesses, Hare Krishnas and even the Children of God. These groups have made inroads primarily in the Russian-speaking population. There are several thousand Muslims in Estonia and 260 Jews.

The Russian community is largely Orthodox, with beautiful brightly domed churches sprinkled around eastern Estonia.

One of Estonia's most intriguing religious groups arrived in Estonia over 300 years ago. In 1652 in Russia, Patriarch Nikon introduced reforms to consolidat his power and bring Russian Orthodox doctrine into line with the Greek Orthodox church. Those who rejected his reforms suffered torture or were executed, and many homes and churches were destroyed. Over the next few centuries, thousands fled to the western shores of Lake Peipsi, where they erected new villages and worship houses. Although they escaped persecution, they were still governed by tsarist Russia and weren't allowed to openly practise their religion until Estonia gained its independence in 1918. Sadly, the Soviet occupation led to the destruction of more churches, and religious persecution. Since 1991 they've been left alone to live a peaceful existence along the bucolic shoreline.

Today there are 15,000 Russian Old Believers living in 11 congregations along the shore of Lake Peipsi. Tiny villages such as Raja, Kasepää and Kolkja have some fascinating architecture and comprise one of the least visited corners of the country. Raja is also known for its icons, as this is where the famed icon painter Gavrila Frolov founded his painting school.

ARTS

Music

Estonia is widely known for its serious classical music tradition, and most notably its choirs. The Estonian Boys Choir has been acclaimed worldwide. Hortus Musicus, formed in 1972, is probably Estonia's best known ensemble, performing mainly medieval and Renaissance music.

The main Estonian composers of the 20th century all wrote music dear to the heart of the people, and remain popular today. Rudolf Tobias (1873–1918) wrote influential symphonic, choral and concerto works as well as fantasies on folk song melodies. Mart Saar (1882–1963) studied under Rimsky-Korsakov in St Petersburg but his music shows none of this influence. His songs and piano suites were among the most performed pieces of music in between-war concerts in Estonia. Eduard Tubin (1905–82) is another great Estonian composer whose body of work includes 10 symphonies. Contemporary composer Erkki-Sven Tür (1959–) takes inspiration from nature and the elements as experienced on his native Hiiumaa.

Estonia's most celebrated composer is Arvo Pärt (1935–), the intense and reclusive master of hauntingly austere music many have misleadingly termed minimalist. Pärt emigrated to Germany during Soviet rule, and his *Misererie Litany*, *Te Deum* and *Tabula Rasa* are among an internationally acclaimed body of work characterised by dramatic bleakness, piercing majesty and nuanced silence. His music draws inspiration from prayers or Bible passages and corresponds with a time in the Middle Ages when performers and composers were not celebrated as individuals for their creations but driven to find expression for collective aspirations. Pärt himself refers to his music as the tintinnabular style, a sparse method of creating tension and beauty with outwardly simple but actually complex, even mathematical, structures. Many believe his musical structures are like none other before.

Internationally renowned Tõnu Kaljuste, director of the Estonian Philharmonic Chamber Orchestra, has frequently recorded the music of Arvo Pärt. Neeme Järvi, Estonia's most lauded conductor, recently stepped down as director of the Detroit Symphony Orchestra after a heralded 15-year run. His son Paavo Järvi, also a conductor, is already making a name for himself in the world of music. In 2003 he, along with the Estonian Male Choir, the Ellerhein Girls' Choir and the Estonian National Symphony Orchestra, won the Grammy Award for best choral performance for *Sibelius: Cantatas*. Today he is the conductor and music director of the Cincinnati Symphony Orchestra.

Bridging the gap between old and new is one of Estonia's more clever groups. Rondellus, an ensemble that has played in a number of early music festivals, performs on medieval period instruments and isn't afraid of experimentation. Its well-received album *Sabbatum* is a tribute album of sorts to Black Sabbath – the only difference being the music is played on medieval instruments, and the songs are sung in Latin.

In jazz, the duo of saxophonist Villu Veski and piano-accordionist Tiit Kalluste incorporate Nordic elements into their work. Violinist Camille fuses classical with pop. In the world of New Age, Kirile Loo, who mixes sparse folk music with incantations and harp music, might be described as Estonia's Enya. Peeter Vähi's music has been influenced by Tibetan, Siberian, Turkish and Asian themes. Veljo Tormis, a leading Estonian choral composer, writes striking music based on old runic chants. His best-known works include the difficult-to-perform *Curse Upon Iron* and *The Ingrian Evenings*.

Hard rock thrives in Estonia with groups such as Venaskond, Tuberkuloised and the U2-style Mr Lawrence. The more approachable Ultima Thule and Compromise Bule are two of the country's most beloved bands. Jäääär is also at the top, with the album *Tartu – Small Wooden Town* (Tartu – Väike Puust Linn) ranking among the best Estonian albums. Excellent folk bands include Untsakond and Väikeste Lõõtspillide Ühing. Linnu Tee and Echosilence are highlights of the progressive rock scene.

The pop and dance-music scene is strong in Estonia, with slinky girl bands being the latest rage in the country: Vanilla Ninja, a group which formed in 2002, has been topping charts not only in Estonia but abroad for their catchy dance tunes (sung in English and Estonian). Their popularity seems to have no bounds: they've even had an ice cream named after them. Another all-girl band favourite is Nexus, whose 'hingetuna' was on every dance club's playlist in 2005.

Other singers with a following include Maarja, Liisi Koikson and Hedvig Hanson, primarily a jazz singer who moves seamlessly between genres with her captivating voice.

Literature

Although records indicate that there was an Estonian text from the 16th century, the history of written Estonian is little more than 150 years old. A New Testament had been published in Southern Estonian in 1686, and a complete Bible in Northern Estonian (the 'dialect' that became the standard Estonian of today) by 1739, but texts until the mid-19th century were mainly pious tracts read only by the clergy. Baltic-Germans published an Estonian grammar book and a dictionary, but it wasn't until the national awakening movement that the publication of books, poetry and newspapers began. This elevated Estonian from a mere 'peasants' language' to one with full literary potential.

Estonian literature grew from the poems and diaries of a young graduate of Tartu University, Kristjan Jaak Peterson. Also a gifted linguist, he died when he was only 21 years old in 1822.

Until the mid-19th century Estonian culture was preserved only by way of an oral folk tradition among peasants. The national epic poem *Kalevipoeg* (Son of Kalev), written between 1857 and 1861 by Friedrich Reinhold Kreutzwald (1803–82), made brilliant use of Estonia's rich oral traditions; it was also inspired by Finland's *Kalevala*, a similar epic created several decades earlier. Fusing hundreds of Estonian legends and folk tales, *Son of Kalev* relates the adventures of the mythical hero, which ends with his death and his land's conquest by foreigners, but also a promise to restore freedom:

> But one day an age will dawn when
> A bright flame bursts forth to free
> His hand from the vise of stone
> Then Kalev's son will return home
> To bring happiness to his children
> And build Estonia's life anew.

Lydia Koidula (1843–86), the face of the 100Kr note, was the poet of Estonia's national awakening and first lady of literature.

Anton Hansen Tammsaare is considered the greatest Estonian novelist for *Truth and Justice* (Tõde ja Õigus), written between 1926 and 1933. A five-volume saga of village and town life, it explores Estonian social, political and philosophical issues.

Eduard Vilde (1865–1933) was an influential early-20th-century novelist and playwright who wrote *Unattainable Wonder* (Tabamata Ime). *Unattainable Wonder* was to be the first play performed at the opening of the Estonia Theatre in 1913 but was substituted with *Hamlet,* as his scathing critique of the then intelligentsia was deemed too controversial. In most of his novels and plays, Vilde looked with great irony at what he saw as Estonia's mad, blind rush to become part of Europe. For Vilde, self-reliance was the truest form of independence.

Oskar Luts is often revered as Estonia's Mark Twain for his childhood tales including *Spring* (Kevade), written between 1912 and 1913. Paul-Eerik Rummo (1942–) is one of Estonia's leading poets and playwrights, dubbed the 'Estonian Dylan Thomas' for his patriotic pieces, which deal with contemporary problems of cultural identity.

More recently, Mati Unt has played an important role in cementing the place of Estonian intellectuals in the modern world, and has written, from the 1960s onwards, quite cynical novels (notably *Autumn Ball* or Sügisball), plays and articles about contemporary life in Estonia. The novelist Jaan Kross has won great acclaim for his historical novels in which he manages to tackle Soviet-era subjects. His work has been translated into 23 languages, making him Estonia's most internationally acclaimed author. His most renowned book, *The Czar's Madman* relates the story of a 19th-century Estonian baron who falls in love with a peasant girl and later ends up in prison. It's loosely based on a true story, though the critique of past- and present-day authoritarianism is the crux of his work.

Another leading novelist is Arvo Valton, who, like Kross, spent some time as an exile in Siberia. His work *Depression and Hope* (Masendus ja Lootus) deals with that experience.

Estonia also has a number of outstanding contemporary poets. Jaan Kaplinski has had two collections, *The Same Sea in Us All* and *The Wandering Border*, published in English. His work expresses the feel of Estonian life superbly. Kross and Kaplinski have both been nominated for the Nobel prize for Literature.

Tõnu Õnnepalu's *Borderland* (Piiri Riik, published under the pseudonym Emil Tode), is about a young homosexual Estonian who travels to Europe and becomes a kept boy for an older, rich gentleman. This leads him down a tortuous road of self-discovery. Not a mere confessional, *Borderland* is a clever and absorbing critique of modern Estonian values. In popular fiction, Kaur Kender's *Independence Day* tells the misadventures of young and ambitious entrepreneurs in postindependence Estonia.

Theatre

Many of the country's theatres were built solely from donations by private citizens, which gives an indication of the role theatre has played in Estonian cultural life. The Estonian Drama Theatre (p88) in Tallinn, the Vanemuine Theatre (p114) in Tartu and the Drama Theatre in Rakvere, the last civic building erected in Estonia before WWII, were all built on proceeds from door-to-door collections.

The popularity of theatre is also evidenced in the high attendance of theatre-goers. Estonians visit the theatre almost as often as they go to the cinema, with 800,000 tickets sold annually. Per capita, Estonians attend theatrical performances more often than any other country in Europe.

Modern Estonian theatre is considered to have begun in Tartu, where Lydia Koidula's *The Cousin from Saaremaa* became the first Estonian play to be performed in public. The Vanemuine Theatre (an outgrowth of the Vanemuine Society, an amateur troupe) launched professional theatre in 1906. Quickly thereafter the Estonia Theatre (p87) opened its doors in Tallinn, and the Endla Theatre (p159) in Pärnu followed suit in 1911. Within the first decade, theatre took off with talented directors and actors performing the works of August Kitzberg and Eduard Wilde.

During the country's independence days (1918–40), Estonian theatre thrived, displaying a number of styles: experimentation, which flourished in the other arts of the '20s, slowly made its way into drama, with symbolist and later expressionist works fed into the repertoire. However, by the 1930s there was a noticeable retreat from experimentation. (Some attribute this to a wealthier, more conservative populace now filling the theatre seats.) The number of native Estonian plays being produced also grew during this time. Playwrights such as Hugo Raudsepp and the novelist Tammsaare wrote widely acclaimed pieces for the stage.

Theatre, like the other arts, suffered heavily during Soviet rule, with heavy-handed censorship and a dumping of lifeless Soviet drama onto the stage. Things began to change after Stalin's death in 1953, as theatres gained more poetic freedom in stage productions. Although the '60s were still a time of repression in other spheres of life, on the stage the avant-garde emerged once again, with the staging of plays wild in subject matter and rich in symbolism. Anger, aggression and downright hysteria – fuelled perhaps by political frustration – were the characteristics of late '60s drama. At that time, some of the leading playwrights were better known as poets.

Paul-Eerik Rummo, perhaps Estonia's most famous poet of the time, wrote The Cinderella Game (*Tuhkatriinumäng*), a brilliant satire of Soviet-era repression that was performed in 1969. It was later performed at New York's La Mama theatre and in playhouses throughout Europe.

With the return to independence in 1991 and the disappearance of censorship, the stage once again held wide-open possibilities. Yet some critics contend that along with Estonia's new-found freedom, radicalism died in the theatre – for the very reason that the object of satire (Big Brother) had also died. Whatever the case, stage life continues to flourish, and today the halls are rarely empty. The most original people currently on the theatre scene are Jaanus Rohumaa, Katri Kaasik-Aaslav and Elmo Nüganen, all particularly sensitive directors who often work out of Tallinn's City Theatre (Linnateater; p88).

Cinema

The first 'moving pictures' were screened in Tallinn in 1896, and the first theatre opened in 1908. Johannes Päsuke (1892–1918), although primarily a photographer, is considered the first Estonian film maker. Estonia's cinematographic output has not been prolific, but there are a few standouts. The most beloved film of Estonians is Arvo Kruusement's *Spring* (Kevade, 1969), an adaptation of Oskar Luts' country saga. Its sequel, *Summer* (Suvi, 1976), was also popular though regarded as inferior. Kaljo Kiisk's *Happy-Go-Lucky* (Nipernaadi, 1983) is a much adored film, about an itinerant bohemian (an Estonian Peer Gynt) who wanders around Estonia, and the relationships he establishes with people he meets along the way.

Grigori Kromanov's *Last Relic* (Viimne Reliikvia, 1969) was a brave and unabashedly anti-Soviet film that has been screened in 60 countries. Some excellent Estonian documentaries include Andres Söt's *Midsummer's Day* (Jaanipäev, 1978), Mark Soosaar's *Miss Saaremaa* (1988) and Peeter Tooming's *Moments* (Hetked, 1976).

THE ANIMATED ART

Although Estonian feature film making has seen better days, the country continues to dazzle audiences around the globe with its brilliantly inventive animated films. For over half a century, Estonian film makers have been garnering awards at international film festivals and attracting critical acclaim with a brand of animation often described as witty, absurd, political, surreal and provocative.

Estonian animation essentially began in 1957 when Elbert Tuganov, an Azerbaijan transplant, created *Little Peter's Dream*. This marked the launch of Nukufilm, which would later become the largest animation studios in northern Europe, producing well over 200 animations and cartoons over the years. At press time Nukufilm was nearing its 50th year – an astonishing achievement given the tumultuous times it has lived through.

Following his initial success, Tuganov went on to make dozens of films, taking aim at Soviet bureaucracy while making artfully produced films. *Inspiration* (1975) is widely hailed as his greatest work. Although it's a simply told story – showing the preparation on the day of the song festival – the film ends with young singers filling the theatre with song, a powerful Estonian overture with enormous political implications.

Humorous, self-reflective, complex, even philosophical – these are just some of the adjectives appended to the films of Priit Pärn over the years. Estonia's most famous animator, he was the successor to early efforts, and led a new wave of film makers into the international spotlight. Some of his most important works are *Luncheon on the Grass* (1987), *Hotel E* (1991) and *Night of the Carrots* (1998). He continues to produce films (*Frank and Wendy*, 2005, is one of his most recent), though he also teaches at film schools around Europe and hosts solo exhibitions worldwide.

Other great Estonian animations worth watching include the *Cabbagehead Trilogy* (1993–2000), Riho Unt's thinly veiled critique of Estonia's transition to independence. Mati Kütt's incisive *Smoked Sprat Baked in the Sun* (1992) addresses environmental destruction, while the films of Ülo Pikkov, Priit Tender and Kaper Jancis have all won critical acclaim.

Sulev Keedus' unforgettably lyrical *Georgiça* (1998), about childhood, war and life on the western islands, and *Crossing the Highway* (Ristumine Peataga, 1999), a comedy by Arko Okk, have done the rounds of the international film festivals.

Estonia's most popular locally made film is *Names in Marble* (2002), which tells the story of a group of young friends in the late 1930s and their decision to fight against the Soviet army in WWII. It was directed by acclaimed Estonian stage director Elmo Nüganen and it's based on the book of the same name that was banned during Soviet times.

More recent productions include *Revolution of Pigs* (Sigade Revolutsioon, 2004), about an anti-Soviet uprising at a teenage summer camp.

Visual Arts

The undisputed national treasure here is eclectic graphic artist Eduard Wiiralt, an Estonian born near St Petersburg in 1898 who later studied art in Tallinn and Tartu. He is considered not only a superb local artist, but a truly international talent based on the diverse themes embodied in his progressive style, inspired by extensive travels and studies abroad. His subjects range from cabaret dancers and North African villagers to boxers and the majestic landscapes of Sami Land. He emigrated to Paris in 1925, where he lived until his death in 1954.

Kristjan Raud (1865–1943), who illustrated *Son of Kalev*, was the leading national idealist figure of the 19th century in Estonia. Ants Laikmaa (1866–1942), known for his sensitive landscape paintings, was so dedicated to his craft that he walked from Estonia to Düsseldorf in Germany to study art, and later opened an art school in Tallinn. Contemporary Estonian art from the 1970s has leaned towards geometrical abstraction, and leading exponents include Raul Meel and Siim-Tanel Annus.

The artist with the most recognisable style is Navitrolla. His bright, fanciful landscapes populated by wildly imagined clouds, trees and giraffes represent a world in which humans play no part. Although he is the most popular contemporary artist in Estonia, his style owes much to another great artist, Jüri

Arrak. Navitrolla's work is also rooted in hyper-reality, with portraits of fantastically imagined creatures, though Arrak's work seems weightier and more introspective.

Mark Kalev Kostabi is one of the most famous foreign-born Estonian artists. A diversely talented New York transplant, Kostabi in 1988 created Kostabi World, a studio, gallery and office complex that churns out 1500 paintings a year. His work has been shown in the Guggenheim and in other museums worldwide; he also composes music, designs album covers (including Guns N' Roses and the Ramones), produces a weekly cable TV show, and has written seven books.

Jaan Toomik is a modern, young Estonian artist emerging on the international scene. A long-time Tallinn resident, Toomik experiments with new artistic forms in his paintings and video installations, often bringing the viewer deep into his work.

ENVIRONMENT

The Land

Slightly larger than Switzerland, Estonia is the smallest Baltic country at 45,227 sq km. It is part of the East-European plain, extremely flat though marked by extensive bogs and marshes. At 318m, Suur Munamägi (Great Egg Hill; p122) is the highest point in the country – and in the Baltics. It lies in the southeast near Võru. Along with swamps and wetlands, forests make up about half of Estonia's territory.

Although it is smaller than the other Baltic countries, Estonia gets the lion's share of coastland. Along with Hiiumaa and Saaremaa – Estonia's biggest islands – the country boasts over 1500 islands (to Latvia and Lithuania's none), making up 10% of the landmass and 2500km out of its 3800km of coastline.

The coast is also where one of Estonia's most outstanding geographical features, the Baltic Glint, lies; a long stretch of raised limestone banks, the glint extends 1200km, from Sweden to Lake Ladoga in Russia. Although 500km of this lies underwater, there are some stretches of impressive cliffs along Estonia's north coast – at Ontika the cliffs rise over 50m above the coast.

Estonia has the biggest lakes in the Baltic region; Lake Peipsi, which straddles the Estonian-Russian border, is the fifth largest in Europe, at 3555 sq km (though its maximum depth is only 15m). Võrtsjärv, in southern Estonia, is the biggest lake lying entirely within Estonia, covering 266 sq km (but just six metres deep). The deepest lake, believed by some to emit magical energy, is the 38m-deep Suurjärv in Rõuge.

Some of the country's landforms owe their existence to the ice age. Immediately following the last glacial period, 9000 to 12,000 years ago, much of Estonia was flooded by ice-dammed lakes and the Baltic Sea. Later the western mainland and islands emerged as the earth's crust gradually rose – a process that is still underway (northwestern Estonia rises at a rate of 2.5mm annually). One of the more fascinating effects of the last ice age can be seen in various places; the march of glaciers and continental ice across the country deposited some truly gigantic rocks (called 'erratic' boulders), some of which were large enough to warrant a name – Kabelikivi (Chapel Boulder) east of Tallinn, for instance, stretches 19m long and 7m tall and hails originally from Scandinavia.

Perhaps proof of its powers of attraction, Estonia has one of the world's highest concentrations of documented meteor craters. At Kaali, in Saaremaa, lies the country's most famous meteor crater. It is now filled with water forming a lake 16m deep and 100m wide.

Wildlife

ANIMALS

Estonia has abundant bird life, with 335 recorded species. It holds the European record for the most species seen in one day, at 191. Owing to the harsh winters, most birds here are migratory. They typically arrive at the end of April (some arrive as early as March) and begin the return migration as early as August (though some birds stay until December). Long-tailed ducks are among the most numerous migrants (more than 1 million a year pass through). You're also likely to see whooper swans, Bewick's swans and other duck species that thrive in shallow coastal waters and seaside wetlands.

About half of Estonia's bird population inhabits the forest. Chaffinches and willow warblers are the most numerous, though you're also likely to see robins, thrushes and pippits. Bogs are also a rich source of avian life, with the swamplands in particular supporting some of the large raptors, such as the osprey, spotted eagle, golden eagle, eagle owl and white-tailed eagle.

Although it's found throughout much of the world, the barn swallow in Estonia receives an almost regal status, and became the national bird over 50 years ago. The swallow appears in April or late May following its winter retreat. Another bird with pride of place in Estonia is the stork. While their numbers are declining elsewhere in Europe, here in Estonia they are on the increase. You can see stork nests on telephone poles and chimneys; and storks can also be seen when they're out hunting through freshly mown fields all over the country. If you see the rare black stork, consider yourself lucky indeed.

Estonia also has its share of mammals, with 64 recorded species. Some animals, which have been declining elsewhere, are doing well in Estonia. The brown bear, Estonia's largest mammal, faced extinction at the turn of the 20th century (when the killing of large carnivores was all the rage). Today Estonia has around 500 bears, making it one of Europe's highest populations. The European beaver, which was hunted to near extinction, was successfully reintroduced in the 1950s, and today the population is well over 10,000. Other introduced species include the racoon dog, the North American muskrat and the American mink. These exotic species, introduced for their fur, have all posed potential threats to the native wildlife. The American mink, for example, has completely wiped out the previous population of European mink.

Other animals have also fared poorly. Roe deer and wild boar are dwindling, which some chalk up to predators – though these animals, along with elks, are commonly hunted and may appear on the menu in more expensive restaurants. Estonia still has wolves (around 100 to 150), though our favourite animal is the lynx (around 600 to 800), a handsome furry creature with an almost formal appearance and large, impressive feet that act as snowshoes.

Sadly, lynxes, bears, wolves and beavers are just a few of the animals that are hunted each year. Wolves, which numbered 700 in 1994, are in particular danger of disappearing from Estonia.

Protected species include grey seals and ringed seals, which you can see along the western coast of Saaremaa and in several islets in the Väinameri. Although there are several thousand in Estonian waters, worldwide their numbers are declining.

The **Estonian Green Movement** (Eesti Roheline Liikumine; ☎ 742 2084; www.roheline.ee), founded in 1988, was one of the country's first environmental organisations and continues to play an active role in addressing the ecological problems facing Estonia.

Another admirable environmental non-profit organisation is the **Estonian Fund for Nature** (☎ 742 8443; www.elfond.ee; Magasini tänav 2, Tartu), the mission of which is to help preserve Estonia's rich natural diversity.

PLANTS

Estonia's rich flora includes 1470 varieties of indigenous plants. Pine trees represent the dominant species in forests, making up 41% of the woodlands. Silver and downy birch are also common (28%), followed by Norway spruce (23%), adlers and aspen. Oak, willow, linden and maple are also found. Juniper groves are most common on the western islands. Many species of rare northern orchids can be found in western Estonia's wooded meadows. Arctic lichen can be found in the Hiiumaa Islets Reserve.

Fungi are found throughout Estonia's forests, meadows and bogs. The quest for some of the 400 edible species, particularly prominent in the north and southeast, is a widely enjoyed pursuit. For more information on Estonian plant life, visit the **Estonian Institute** (www.inst.ee)

National Parks & Reserves

Some of Europe's few remaining original landscapes have been preserved within Estonia, much of this inadvertently through isolation under the Soviet regime. Almost 20% of Estonia's lands are protected to some degree, which is more than double the European average. Estonia has four national parks, three of them established since independence, and a number of nature reserves. National parks are administered by **RMK** (☎ 372-628 1500; www.rmk.ee; Viljandi maantee 18B, Tallinn), the Estonian State Forest Management Centre. The most popular national parks to visit are Lahemaa and Haanja.

The following provide some information on Estonia's national parks.

RMK (www.rmk.ee) Manages all the forests and protected areas of Estonia, including its hiking trails, camp sites, forest huts and nature centres.

Union of Protected Areas of Estonia (www.ekal.org.ee) Information on Estonia's national parks and reserves.

Environmental Issues

While relatively few environment-friendly programmes are in place yet in Estonia, the Soviet regime's disregard for ecology was staggering; it left a populace traditionally bound to nature with a heightened sensitivity to the dangers of pollution. Large-scale clean-up programmes, often foreign-funded, greatly reduced pollution as well as the concentration of dangerous emissions in industrial areas throughout the 1990s.

Estonia is a signatory to the UN's 1997 Kyoto Protocol targeting reductions in greenhouse gas. Legislation enacted between 2000 and 2001 brought tougher restrictions on industrial pollution with offenders liable to penalties for improper handling and cleanup of waste; unfortunately this doesn't extend to the burning of oil shale, the country's biggest environmental problem. Although Estonia produces its own energy, it does so by burning a fuel that pollutes the air, soil and water. Ida Virumaa county (near the power plants of Narva) reveals the ecological damage: rivers are polluted (no swimming or fishing), with artificial hills made of ash from the oil-shale power plants, and barren trees silhouetted against the sky. The European Commission (the executive body of the EU) has given Estonia until 2009 to modernise its power plants, and

NATIONAL PARKS & RESERVES

National parks or reserves	Area	Features	Activities	Best time to visit
Elva Vitipalu (p115)	9 sq km	pine forest, lakes & river	hiking, biking	May-Sep
Endla Nature Reserve (p105)	101 sq km	wetlands, nature trails	hiking	May-Sep
Käina Bay Bird Reserve (p140)	35 sq km	protected coastal reserve	bird-watching (70 species)	May-Sep
Hiiumaa Islets Landscape Reserve (p142)	27 sq km	small, protected islands, rare grey & ringed seals, boar, lynxes	bird-watching (110 species)	May-Sep
Lahemaa National Park (p95)	725 sq km	striking Estonian coast & hinterland with beaches, rivers, lakes & waterfalls	hiking, wildlife-watching, swimming	May-Sep
Matsalu Nature Reserve (p135)	486 sq km	wetlands & major bird habitat	bird-watching	Apr-Oct
Nigula Nature Reserve (p161)	28 sq km	treeless peat bog with bog islands	hiking, bird-watching (144 species)	May-Sep
Soomaa National Park (p165)	367 sq km	swampland & flat meadow	hiking, canoeing,wildlife-watching (46 mammal species,172 bird species)	Jun-Sep
Viidumäe Nature Reserve (p150)	19 sq km	forest with rare plant species	walking along nature trails, bird-watching	May-Sep
Vilsandi National Park (p152) near Saaremaa	182 sq km	small islands & bird sanctuary (ringed seals, rare orchids 247 bird species)	wildlife-watching	May-Sep

although it's clear that Estonia must invest in a cleaner technology to save the ecology of the northeastern region, the government claims it hasn't the financial resources to do so.

In 2004 the UN's International Maritime Organisation designated the heavily polluted Baltic Sea one of the planet's five particularly sensitive areas (despite Russia's protests), which opens the way for greater protection and stricter standards. Toxic emissions in the industrialised northeast of Estonia have been reduced sharply and new environmental-impact legislation aims to minimise the effects of future development.

The purest air in the country is found on the western islands, and in the southeast, areas barely touched by industry.

FOOD & DRINK

Although Tallinn has a fantastically diverse dining scene, many parts of Estonia offer visitors little variety beyond what type of meat they'd like with their potatoes. This owes much to Estonia's roots. For centuries Estonia was largely a farming country. In fact, until the 20th century, 65% of the population was involved in agriculture. Country folk who worked the fields (serfs prior to emancipation in the 1800s) sought heavy nourishment to fuel their long days. Food preparation was simple and practical, using whatever could be raised, grown or gathered from the land. Daily fare was barley porridge, cheese curd and boiled potatoes. On feast days and special occasions, meat made its appearance. Coastal dwellers also garnered sustenance from the sea, mainly cod and herring. To make foods last through the winter, people dried, smoked and salted their fish. They also ate canned and preserved foods.

Traditionally the seasons played a large role in the Estonian diet. When spring arrived, wild leek, rhubarb, fresh sorrel and goat's cheese appeared, and the spring lambs were slaughtered. During the summer, there were fresh vegetables and herbs along with berries, nuts and mushrooms gathered from the forests – still a popular pastime for some Estonians. Autumn was the season of the traditional goose; it was also the prime hunting season – elk, pheasant, boar and even wild goat. To sustain themselves through the long harsh winters, Estonians would eat hearty roasts and stews, soups and plenty of sauerkraut.

Despite its simple culinary roots, or perhaps because of them, Estonia has a growing world dining scene. In Tallinn, and to a lesser extent Pärnu, Tartu and Kuressaare, you'll find French, Italian, Japanese, Thai, Indian and even Russian cuisine. (After 1991, Russian restaurants quickly disappeared from the capital and re-emerged only recently – long after the first Mexican restaurant opened.)

The hunger for innovation has led to an ever-changing scene in the capital. At last count, Middle Eastern cuisine was the latest rage, but this probably had more to do with the after-dinner practice of smoking from hookahs than the craving for *baba ganoush* (pureed eggplant) or *kibbe* (ground lamb).

Staples & Specialities

Although it was a rarity in the diet of 19th-century peasants, meat is an integral part of most meals. Beefing out most menus are red meat (particularly pork), chicken and sausage, alongside which you'll see cabbage and the beloved potato, a staple of Estonian cooking.

Although Estonia has an extensive coastline, fish doesn't take pride of place, as one might expect. Smoked-fish-lovers, however, have much to celebrate. Lake Peipsi is a particularly good place for tracking down *suitsukala* (smoked fish, usually trout or salmon); look for roadside stands along the shore road. You'll also find it on the islands; Kuressaare has one of the best fish shops, (p150), in the country.

In summer fresh fruits and vegetables are particularly plentiful. Be sure to take

FOR THE LOVE OF SPRATS

For such a tiny fish, sprats have been a large part of the Estonian diet. They've been a local favourite since at least the Middle Ages; many Russians who've never crossed the border picture 'sprats' when they think of Estonia. This is because of the ubiquity of Tallinn Sprats, a can of spicy sprats with the silhouette of Tallinn's skyline. Owing to this sprat tin, the capital is sometimes joshingly called 'Spratsville'.

EAT YOUR WORDS

Don't know your *kana* from your *kala*? Your *maasikas* from your *räim*? Get a head start on the cuisine scene by learning the words that make the dish. For pronunciation guidelines, see the Language chapter.

Useful Phrases

May I have a menu?	*kas* mah *saahk*·sin menüü	*Kas ma saaksin menüü?*
I'd like ...	ma *saw*·vik·sin ...	*Ma sooviksin ...*
The bill, please.	*pah*·lun *ahrr*·ve	*Palun arve.*
I'm a vegetarian.	mah *o*·len *tai*·me·toyt·lah·ne	*Ma olen taimetoitlane.*
Bon appetit!	head *i*·su	*Head isu!*
To your health! (when toasting)	*ter*·vi·seks	*Terviseks!*
breakfast	*hom*·mi·ku·serrk	*hommikusöök*
lunch	*lyu*·na	*lõuna*
dinner	*er*·tu·serrk	*õhtusöök*

Food Glossary

biifsteek	steak	*biifstrogonoff/ böfstrooganov*	beef stroganof
eelroad	starters	*kala*	fish
juust	cheese	*kana*	chicken
kalamari	caviar	*karbonaad*	grilled 'chop'
kapsas	cabbage	*kilud*	sprats
kartul	potato	*leib*	rye bread
köögivili	vegetables	*liharoad*	meat/main dishes
liha	meat (red)	*maarjad*	berries
lõhe	salmon	*pannkook*	pancake
maasikas	strawberry	*räim*	herring
puuvili	fruit	*salat*	salad
sai	white bread	*seen*	mushroom
šašlõkk	kebab	*suitsukala*	smoked fish
sealiha	pork	*vorst*	sausage
supp	soup		

advantage of the local *turg* (market) and load up on strawberries.

Given Estonia's rustic origins, it's not surprising that bread is a major staple in the diet, and that Estonians make a pretty good loaf. Rye is by far the top choice. Unlike other ryes you may have eaten, here it's moist, dense and, yes, delicious (assuming it's fresh).

Kama, a powdery meal made from different grains, is similar to bread in nutritional value, but quite different in consistency. This high-fibre food mixes well with *kefir* (a drink made from fermented cow's milk), yogurt and fruit juices; it may be served for breakfast or dessert.

Kalev chocolate is yet another iconic Estonian product. The candies and chocolates first appeared in Tallinn when its first factory opened in 1806; look for them in supermarkets.

Drinks

Beer is the favourite alcohol in Estonia, and the local product is very much in evidence. The best brands are Saku and A Le Coq, which come in a range of brews. On Saaremaa and Hiiumaa, you'll also find homemade beer, which is flatter than traditional beer, but still the perfect refreshment on a hot day. In winter Estonians drink mulled wine, the antidote to cold wintry nights.

Estonia's ties to Russia have led to vodka's long-time popularity. Viru Valge is the best brand, and it comes in a range of flavours, which some Estonians mix with fruit juices (try the vanilla-flavoured vodka mixed with apple juice).

Vana Tallinn is in a class of its own. No-one quite knows what the syrupy liqueur is made from, but it's sweet and strong and has a pleasant aftertaste. It's best served in coffee, over ice with milk, over ice cream, or in champagne or dry white wine. If you need a quick fix, go ahead and chug it straight from the bottle. There are several other locally made liqueurs, including the unbearably sweet, strawberry-flavoured Metsa Maasika and an egg-based liqueur, Kiiu Torn, named after the smallest fortress in Estonia.

Eesti Kali, a sweet dark beverage, is Estonia's answer to Coca-Cola. It's made of fermented bread but contains no alcohol.

Even without vineyards, Estonia is beginning to develop a wine culture. Wine bars are quite fashionable in Tallinn. The capital also boasts the largest wine cellars in the Baltics and plenty of medieval settings in which to imbibe (see p86).

Celebrations

At Christmas, sausages are made from fresh blood and wrapped in pig's intestine – joy to the world indeed! These *verivorst* (blood sausages), which locals insist are delicious and healthy, are served in most traditional Estonian restaurants, and sold in shops all year round. For the bloodthirsty, *verileib* (blood bread) and *verikäkk* (balls of blood rolled in flour and eggs with bits of pig fat thrown in for taste) will surely satisfy.

Where to Eat & Drink

For a meal, you can eat in a *restoran* (restaurant) or *kohvik* (café); pubs also serve meals. Nearly every town has a *turg*, where you can buy fresh fruits and vegetables, as well as meats and fish. For standard opening times, see the Regional Directory.

Habits & Customs

Estonian eating habits are similar to other parts of northern Europe. Lunch or dinner may be the biggest meal of the day. Tipping is fairly commonplace, with 10% the norm.

If invited over to an Estonian's house, you can expect abundant hospitality and generous portions. It's fairly common to bring flowers to the host. Just be sure to give an odd number (even-numbered flowers are reserved for the dead).

TALLINN

pop 412,000

One of Europe's most enchanting cities, Tallinn is a heady blend of medieval and modern, with narrow, cobbled streets set beneath the spires of 14th-century churches, and a wild mix of restaurants, cafés, boutiques and nightclubs hidden in the carved stone walls.

The World Heritage–listed Old Town has plenty of distractions for even the most ambitious itinerary. Although large art museums are nonexistent, you'll find some historic gems that illuminate both Tallinn's medieval past and its long grey days under the Soviet yoke. Meanwhile, its growing gallery scene showcases Estonia's most creative 21st-century artists.

Colour isn't limited to the art world. The flare of the streets is decidedly fashion-forward, with Tallinn's boutiques bearing the imprint of rising Estonian designers. This contrasts with the centuries-old artisan traditions of glassblowing, weaving and pottery, all of which make Tallinn such a shoppers' paradise.

Tallinn's café culture is hard to match. Art-Deco patisseries, cosy, candlelit anterooms and breezy, sunlit patios are the settings for strong coffee and people-watching – a fine prelude to the city's alluring restaurants and bars. Decadent old-world dining rooms, charming wine cellars and super-stylish bistros provide the backdrop to exquisite dishes from every savoury corner of the globe.

Tallinn's nightlife rages until the morning, with steamy nightclubs, slinky lounges, expat bars and colourful gay clubs, all hidden inside the Old Town walls. Culture seekers can sate themselves with choral concerts, classical recitals, theatre (human or puppet) and plenty of pop, rock and jazz.

Outside the medieval quarters, there's lots to see. Delve into the past at Peter the Great's Kadriorg Palace, a baroque masterpiece surrounded by idyllic woodlands. Or when the summer sun arrives, make like a local and head to Pirita or Väna-Jõesuu for a slice of beach action. There are also coastal islands and a bizarre old cliff-top military base. But don't stop there; you'll find plenty more to discover in this vibrant city.

HISTORY

The site of Tallinn is thought to have been settled by Finno-Ugric people around 2500 BC. There was probably an Estonian trading settlement here from around the 9th century AD, and a wooden stronghold was built on Toompea (*tom*-pe-ah; the hill dominating Tallinn) in the 11th century. The Danes under King Waldemar II (who conquered Northern Estonia in 1219) met tough resistance at Tallinn and were on the verge of retreat when a red flag with a white cross fell from the sky into their bishop's hands. Taking this as a sign of God's support, they went on to win the battle; the flag became their national flag. The Danes set their own castle on Toompea. The origin of the name Tallinn is thought to be from *Taani linn,* Estonian for 'Danish town'.

The Knights of the Sword took Tallinn from the Danes in 1227 and built the first stone fort on Toompea. German traders arrived from Visby on the Baltic island of Gotland and founded a colony of about 200 beneath the fortress. In 1238 Tallinn returned to Danish control, but in 1285 it joined the German-dominated Hanseatic League as a channel for trade between Novgorod, Pihkva (Russian: Pskov) and the west. Furs, honey, leather and seal fat moved west; salt, cloth, herring and wine went east.

By the mid-14th century, when the Danes sold Northern Estonia to the Teutonic Order, Tallinn was a major Hanseatic town with about 4000 people. A conflict of interest with the knights and bishop on Toompea led the mainly German artisans and merchants in the Lower Town to build a fortified wall to separate themselves from Toompea. However, Tallinn still prospered and became one of northern Europe's biggest towns. Tallinn's German name, Reval, coexisted with the local name until 1918.

Prosperity faded in the 16th century. The Hanseatic League had weakened, and Russians, Swedes, Danes, Poles and Lithuanians fought over the Baltic region. Tallinn survived a 29-week siege by Russia's Ivan the Terrible between 1570 and 1571. It was held by Sweden from 1561 to 1710, when, decimated by plague, Tallinn surrendered to Russia's Peter the Great.

In 1870 a railway was completed from St Petersburg, and Tallinn became a chief port of the Russian Empire. Freed peasants converged on the city from the countryside, increasing the percentage of Estonians in its population from 52% in 1867 to 89% in 1897. By WWI Tallinn had big shipyards and a large working class of over 100,000.

Tallinn suffered badly in WWII, with thousands of buildings destroyed during Soviet bombing in 1944. After the war, under Soviet control, large-scale industry was developed in Tallinn – including the USSR's biggest grain-handling port – and the city expanded, its population growing to nearly 500,000 from a 1937 level of 175,000. Much of the new population came from Russia, and new high-rise suburbs were built on the outskirts to house the workers.

Not surprisingly, the days of Soviet occupation (1940–91) were hard on the capital. The explosion of Soviet-style settlements in the suburbs meant a loss of cultural life in the centre. Old Town by the 1980s was run-down, with most people preferring to live in the suburbs rather than the centre. Old Town began to be renovated in the late '80s, with independence largely playing out on the streets of Tallinn.

The 1990s saw the city transformed into a contemporary midsized city, with a beautifully restored Old Town and a modern business district. Today a look around the centre indicates that the city is booming. Cranes all around town show that building is underway. Some of the more recent projects include the shiny glass Viru Centre mall, which opened in 2004. Tallinn shows a taste for all things new, extending to IT-driven business at the fore of the new economy, and an Internet-savvy populace that makes other parts of the world seem outmoded. Internet banking and paying parking tickets online are just a few of the conveniences Tallinnese wouldn't do without.

In addition to increasing arrivals by ferry –and close ties to Finland – there's a newly renovated airport, wiping out gloomy vestiges of the Soviet past. Discount airlines carry passengers from Western Europe, which has contributed to Tallinn's reputation as a weekend party getaway.

Meanwhile, the outskirts of the city have yet to get the face-lift that the centre has received. In these parts of the city that few tourists see, you'll find poverty, unemployment and less infrastructure.

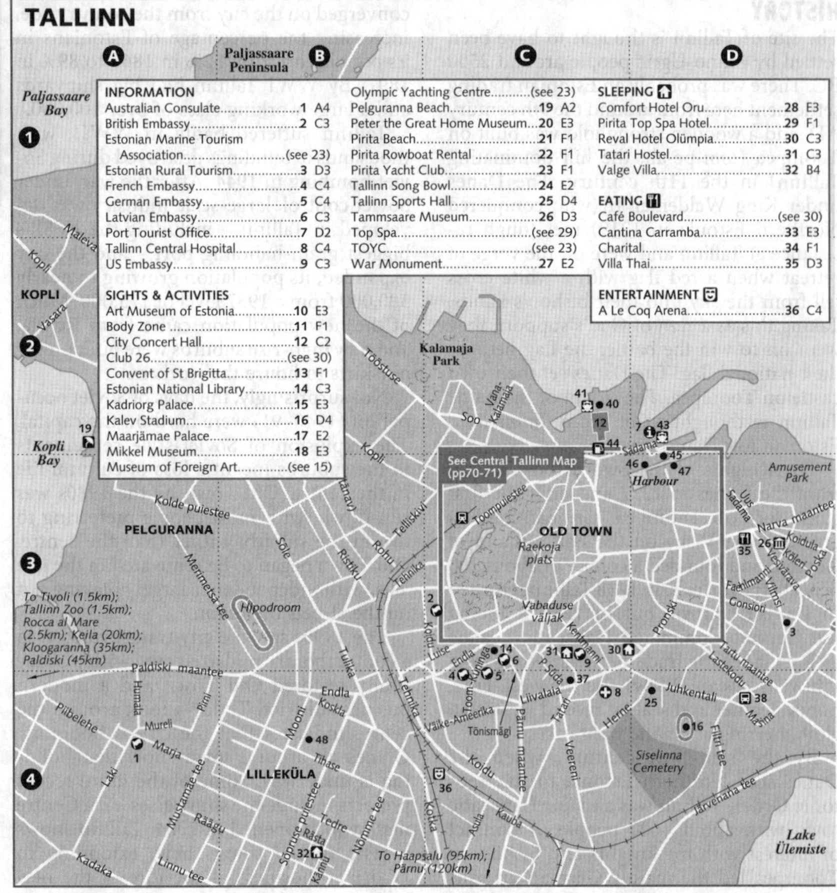

ORIENTATION

Tallinn spreads south from the edge of Tallinn Bay (Tallinna Laht) on the Gulf of Finland. Just south of the bay is Old Town (Vanalinn), the city's heart. It divides neatly into Upper Town and Lower Town. Upper Town on Toompea was the medieval seat of power, and it still features the parliament buildings. Lower Town spreads around the eastern foot of Toompea, and a 2.5km defensive wall still encircles much of it. The centre of Lower Town is Raekoja plats.

Around Old Town a belt of green parks follows the line of the city's original moat defences. Radiating from this old core is New Town, dating from the 19th and early 20th centuries. Vabaduse väljak (Freedom Sq) is today's city centre on the southern edge of Old Town.

The airport lies 3km southeast of the centre on the Tartu road. It's best reached by bus 2. The passenger-ferry terminal lies just 350m from the edge of Old Town, reachable on foot or by tram or bus. For more details on getting into town, see p91.

Maps

EO Map (www.eomap.ee) produces a good map of Tallinn (50Kr), with detailed coverage of Old Town and the modern centre. Many sights are marked, as are public transport routes, and it includes a useful street index. Walking tour and basic orientation maps are available

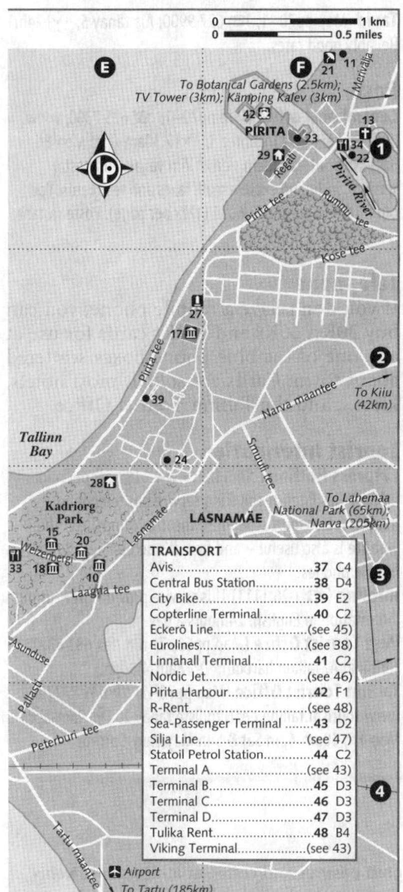

from the tourist office and throughout Old Town, some free of charge.

INFORMATION

Bookshops

Central bookshops stock city and regional maps covering most destinations in Estonia.

Allecto (Map pp70–1; ☎ 681 8731; Väike-Karja tänav 5) Excellent selection of English-language books.

Apollo (Map pp70–1; ☎ 654 8485; Viru tänav 23) Loads of Lonely Planet and other travel titles as well as foreign-language novels and periodicals, plus a comfy café on the 2nd floor.

Euro Publications (Map ppp70–1; ☎ 661 2210; Tartu maantee 1) Art and design books are the speciality. It's opposite the Kaubamaja and connected to the Tallinna Academy of Art.

Felix & Fabian (Map pp70–1; ☎ 683 0758; Harju tänav 1) Small collection of books on Tallinn and Estonia.

Lõmatult Raamat (Map pp70–1; ☎ 683 7710; Viru väljak 21) Stocks used books in English and other languages. Don't miss the selection of vinyl records on the 2nd floor.

Rahva Raamat Pärnu maantee (Map pp70–1; ☎ 644 3682; Pärnu maantee 10); Viru väljak (Map pp70–1; ☎ 644 6655; Viru väljak 4) Guidebooks, maps, Lonely Planet titles and Estonian-language books. The Viru väljak branch stocks English-language titles.

Cultural Centres

British Council (Map pp70–1; ☎ 631 4010; www.britishcouncil.ee; Vana-Posti tänav 7)

French Cultural Centre (Map pp70–1; ☎ 644 9505; www.france.ee; Kuninga tänav 4) Sponsors cultural events.

Goethe Institute (Map pp70–1; ☎ 627 2960; www.goethe.de/tallinn; Suurtüki tänav 4b)

Emergency

Central police station (Map pp70–1; ☎ 612 4200; Pärnu maantee 11)

First-Aid Hotline (☎ 110) English-language advice on treatment, hospitals, pharmacies.

Internet Access

There are over 500 wireless Internet (wi-fi) areas throughout Estonia, with 225 in Tallinn alone. Visit www.wifi.ee for a complete list of locations. If you're not packing a laptop, try the following places:

Central post office (Map pp70–1; ☎ 661 6616; 2nd fl, Narva maantee 1; per hr 60Kr; 🕑 9am-8pm Mon-Fri, to 6pm Sat)

Estonian National Library (Map pp66–7; ☎ 630 7381; room C-2118, Tõnismägi 2; per hr 40Kr; 🕑 10am-8pm Mon-Fri, noon-7pm Sat Sep-Jun, noon-7pm Mon-Fri Jul-Aug)

Internet café (Map pp70–1; ☎ 667 3100; Tallinna Kaubamaja, Gonsiori 2; per hr 40Kr; 🕑 9am-9pm)

Matrix Club (Map pp70–1; ☎ 641 9442; Tartu maantee 31; per hr 20Kr; 🕑 24hr)

Reval Café (Map pp70–1; Aia tänav 3; per hr 40Kr; 🕑 9am-9pm)

Libraries

Central Library (Map pp70–1; ☎ 661 4202; www.keskraamatukogu.ee; Estonia puiestee 8; 🕑 10am-7pm Mon-Fri, to 5pm Sat)

Estonian National Library (Map pp66–7; ☎ 630 7381; Tõnismägi 2; 🕑 10am-8pm Mon-Fri, noon-7pm Sat Sep-Jun, noon-7pm Mon-Fri Jul-Aug)

Media

In Your Pocket (www.inyourpocket.com) Tallinn's best listings guide, this quarterly publication contains up-to-date info on hotels, restaurants, clubs and what's on in the city. Buy it at bookshops or the tourist information office (35Kr).

Medical Services

You'll find English-speaking staff at all of the following places.

Aia Apteek (Map pp70–1; ☎ 627 3607; Aia tänav 10; ⌚ 8.30am-midnight) One of many well-stocked pharmacies in town.

Tallinn Central Hospital (Map pp66–7; ☎ 620 7015; Ravi tänav 18) Just south of Liivalaia, some 300m west of the Reval Hotel Olümpia, this hospital has a full range of services, a polyclinic and a 24-hour emergency room, and is used to foreigners dropping in.

Tallinna Linnaapteek (Map pp70–1; ☎ 644 0244; Pärnu maantee 10) A good 24-hour pharmacy.

Money

Currency exchange is available at all transport terminals, exchange bureaus, the post office and inside all banks and major hotels. ATMs are widespread. You can also receive wire transfers through the central post office, a Western Union agent.

Estravel (Map pp70–1; ☎ 626 6266; www.estravel.ee; Suur-Karja tänav 15; ⌚ 9am-6pm Mon-Fri, 10am-4pm Sat) Travel agency and official Amex agent.

Hansapank (☎ 631 0310; Liivalaia tänav 8) This bank will cash travellers cheques and give cash advances on credit cards.

Tavid (Map pp70–1; ☎ 627 9900; Aia tänav 5; ⌚ 24hr) Reliably good rates.

Post

Central post office (Map pp70–1; ☎ 625 7300; www.tallpost.ee; Narva maantee 1; ⌚ 7.30am-8pm Mon-Fri, 8am-6pm Sat) Northern side of Viru väljak. Full postal services, including express mail, faxes and telegrams. You can receive a fax at 661 6054 (12Kr per page). Poste restante is kept for one month.

Telephone

If you don't have a mobile phone, you can buy 30Kr, 50Kr and 100Kr cards for use at any one of the blue phone boxes scattered about town. Cards are sold at most hotels, kiosks, and the Tallinn Tourist Office.

Tourist Information

Ekspress Hotline (☎ 1182; www.1182.ee; per min 2.60Kr) This English-speaking service has telephone numbers, transport schedules, theatre listings, etc. The website is also useful – and free. It's accessible only from mobile phones.

Infoline (☎ 626 1111) This service provides free, useful information in English, 24 hours a day.

Port Tourist Office (Map pp66–7; ☎ /fax 631 8321; Terminal A, Tallinn harbour; ⌚ 8am-4.30pm)

Tallinn Tourist Office (Map pp70–1; ☎ 645 7777; www.tourism.tallinn.ee; Niguliste tänav 2; ⌚ 9am-8pm Mon-Fri, 10am-6pm Sat & Sun May-Aug, 9am-6pm

TALLINN IN...

Two Days

Start your day with breakfast at **Pegasus** (p83) or grab pastries and coffee at atmospheric **Kehrwieder** (p85). Get your bearings over the city by climbing up the Town Hall tower on splendid **Raekoja plats** (opposite). Follow this by an in-depth exploration of the streets down below. After getting your fill of **handicrafts shops** (p88), pay a visit to the **City Museum** (p73), a fine introduction to 700 years of city history. Grab a light lunch at **Café Anglais** (p85) before heading to Upper Town, where you can pay a visit to the jewel box of a church, **Alexander Nevsky Cathedral** (p75). You won't want to miss the view nearby at the **Danish King's Courtyard** (p75). That night treat yourself to dinner at the candlelit **Olde Hansa** (p82), a medieval restaurant, or the aptly named **Grandma's Place** (Vanaema Juures; p83).

On your second day, head to **Kadriorg Park** (p75), where Peter the Great's baroque **palace** (p76) stands. Afterwards, stroll through the surrounding streets – once home to Tallinn's elite.

Four Days

Follow the two-day itinerary, then on your third day add a trip to **Pirita beach** (p77), rent a **rowboat** (p78) on the Pirita River or have a picnic in the **Botanical Gardens** (p77). On your fourth day, get out of town: visit the surreal old Soviet base of **Paldiski** (p93) or if the weather's lovely, take in more beach action at **Väna-Jõesuu** (p92). Back in the city, be sure to get your fill of café culture, wine bars and the city's heady nightlife scene.

Mon-Fri, 10am-6pm Sat & Sun Sep, 9am-5pm Mon-Fri, 10am-3pm Sat & Sun Oct-Apr) Near Raekoja plats, this office has a full range of services and loads of brochures covering every corner of Estonia. This office also sells the Tallinn Card (see p386).

Travel Agencies

City tours, guided trips to provincial Estonia and accommodation in other towns are most travel agencies' stock in trade. Most have branches throughout Estonia.

Estonian Holidays (Map pp70–1; ☎ 627 0500; www.holidays.ee; Rüütli tänav 28)

Estravel (Map pp66–7; ☎ 626 6266; www.estravel.ee; Suur-Karja tänav 15)

Leon Travel (Map pp70–1; ☎ 641 1106; www.leontravel.ee; Lai 7) Good agency for help with Russian visas.

SIGHTS

Tallinn's major sights are found in and around Old Town. Only a fraction of visitors make it outside the medieval walls to see other attractions east of there, including Kadriorg Park, Pirita beach, the Botanical Gardens and the looming TV Tower. West of Old Town, the biggest draw is the Open Air Museum, where you can see some of Estonia's old wooden architecture.

Old Town

The medieval jewel of Estonia, Old Town (Vanalinn) is a wanderer's paradise. Picking your way along the narrow, cobbled streets is like strolling back to the dawn of the 14th century. You'll pass old merchant houses, hidden medieval courtyards, looming spires and winding staircases leading to sweeping views over the city. No matter which direction you head, you'll see plenty of cafés, restaurants and bars along the way.

If it's your first day in town, here's a tip: read the following section, then put your book away and head into town. One of the best ways to approach this fantastic old city is simply to lose yourself among its enchanting old lanes. If you happen to get lost (which is also recommended), a useful landmark is the 64m-high Town Hall tower.

RAEKOJA PLATS & AROUND

Raekoja plats (Town Hall Sq) has been the centre of Tallinn life since markets began here in the 11th century (the last was in 1896). Today it's a vibrant place ringed with cafés and restaurants, and during the summer hosts Tallinn's liveliest street scene. Rising over the square is the **Town Hall** (Raekoda; Map pp70-1; ☎ 645 7900; tower admission adult/concession 25/15Kr; 11am-6pm Tue-Sun Jun-Aug), the only surviving Gothic town hall in northern Europe. Built between 1371 and 1404, it was the seat of power in the medieval Lower Town. According to legend, its minaretlike tower was modelled on a sketch made by an explorer following his visit to the Orient. Tallinn's symbol, the pike-bearing guardsman named **Old Thomas** (Vana Toomas), stands atop the tower (and serves double duty as a weather vane), a post he's held since 1530. The teeming market from the Middle Ages was held beneath the ground-level arches on the north side.

Inside the Town Hall, the **Citizens' Hall** (☎ 645 7900; adult/concession 35/20Kr; 10am-4pm Tue-Sun Jul-Aug, by appt Sep-Jun) has an impressive vaulted roof, while the fine bench-ends (built in 1374) in the **Council Hall** are Estonia's oldest woodcarvings. There is a **tower** you can climb, and occasional exhibitions are held in the Citizens' Hall.

The former **Town Jail** (Linnavangla), in a lane behind the Town Hall, is now home to the **Museum of Estonian Photography** (Raevangla Fotomuuseum; Map pp70-1; ☎ 644 8767; Raekoja tänav 4/6; adult/concession 15/7Kr; 10.30am-6pm Thu-Tue Mar-Oct, 10.30am-5pm Thu-Mon Nov-Feb), which has a small exhibition spanning photography's earliest days in Estonia up to the present (don't miss the changing contemporary exhibits). Those travelling with finicky children can point out the irons still hanging outside the Town Hall. This is where lesser offenders where shackled in olden times.

On the northern side of the square, the **Town Council Pharmacy** (Raeapteek; Map pp70-1; ☎ 631 4860; Raekoja plats 11; 9am-7pm Mon-Fri, to 5pm Sat) is one of the world's oldest continuously running pharmacies. The building has served as a pharmacy or apothecary shop since at least 1422, once passing through 10 generations of the same family. Its present façade dates from the 17th century. An arch beside the pharmacy on Raekoja plats leads into the charming, narrow **White Bread Passage** (Saiakang), once filled with the aromas of a popular bakery. At its end is the striking 13th-century Gothic **Holy Spirit Church** (Pühavaimu Kirik; Map pp70-1; ☎ 644 1487; Pühavaimu 2; admission 10Kr; 9am-5pm Mon-Sat May-Aug, 10am-4pm Mon-Sat Sep, 10am-3pm Mon-Fri Oct-Apr), used by

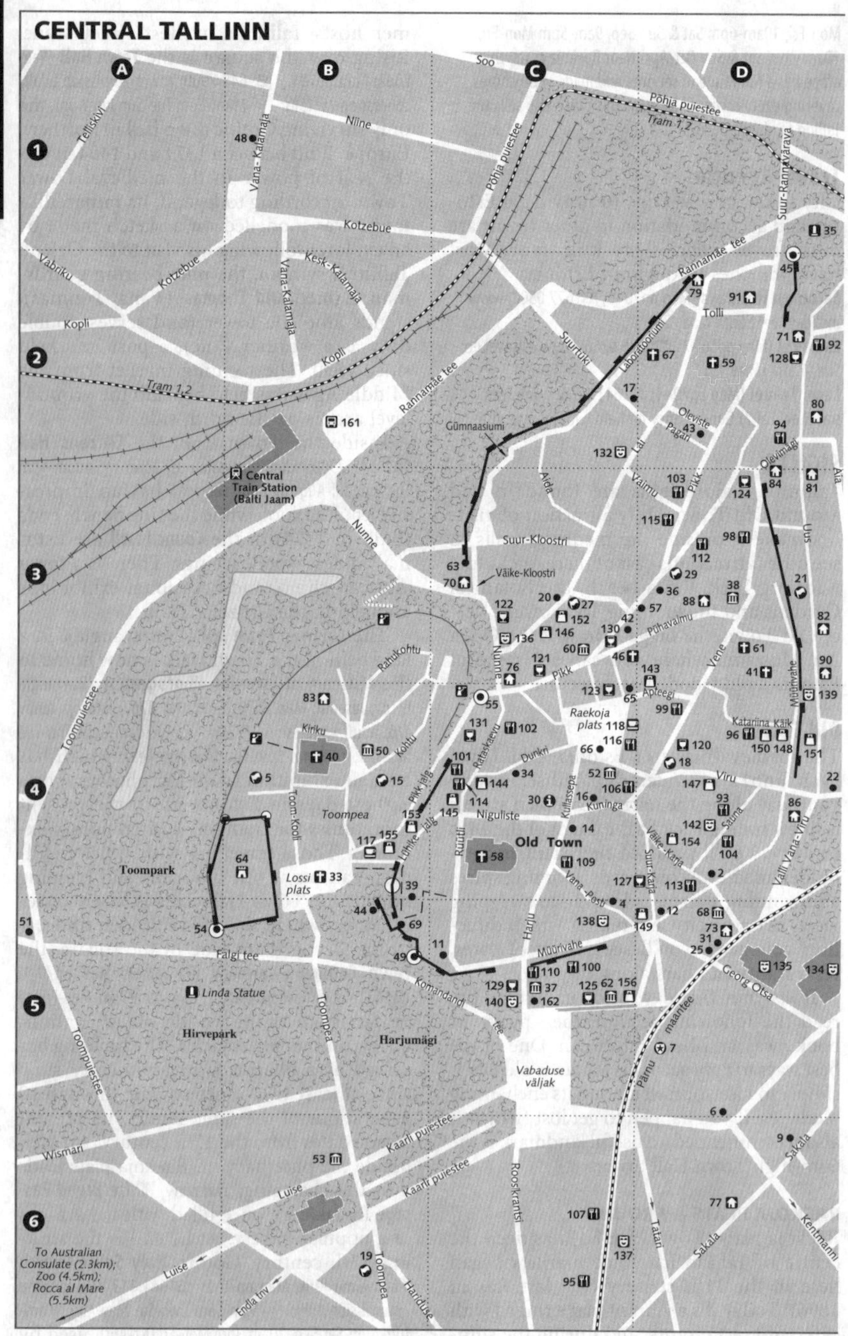
CENTRAL TALLINN
Soo
Põhja puiestee
Tram 1,2
Telliskivi
Vana-Kalamaja
Niine
Kotzebue
Vabriku
Kesk-Kalamaja
Kopli
Rannamäe tee
Suur-Rannavärava
Tolli
Suurtüki
Laboratooriumi
Oleviste
Pagari
Gümnaasiumi
Central Train Station (Balti Jaam)
Lai
Vaimu
Pikk
Aida
Olevimägi
Uus
Aia
Nunne
Suur-Kloostri
Väike-Kloostri
Pühavaimu
Vene
Rahukohtu
Apteegi
Raekoja plats
Kiriku
Kohtu
Rataskaevu
Dunkri
Kullassepa
Kuninga
Viru
Katariina Käik
Müürivahe
Sauna
Toompuiestee
Toom-Kooli
Toompea
Pikk jalg
Lühike jalg
Rüütli
Niguliste
Old Town
Väike-Karja
Suur-Karja
Valli
Vana-Viru
Toompark
Lossi plats
Vana-Posti
Falgi tee
Harju
Müürivahe
Georg Otsa
Komandandi tee
Linda Statue
Hirvepark
Harjumägi
Pärnu maantee
Vabaduse väljak
Wismari
Kaarli puiestee
Roosikrantsi
Tatari
Sakala
Luise
Kentmanni
Endla tnv
Hariduse
To Australian Consulate (2.3km); Zoo (4.5km); Rocca al Mare (5.5km)

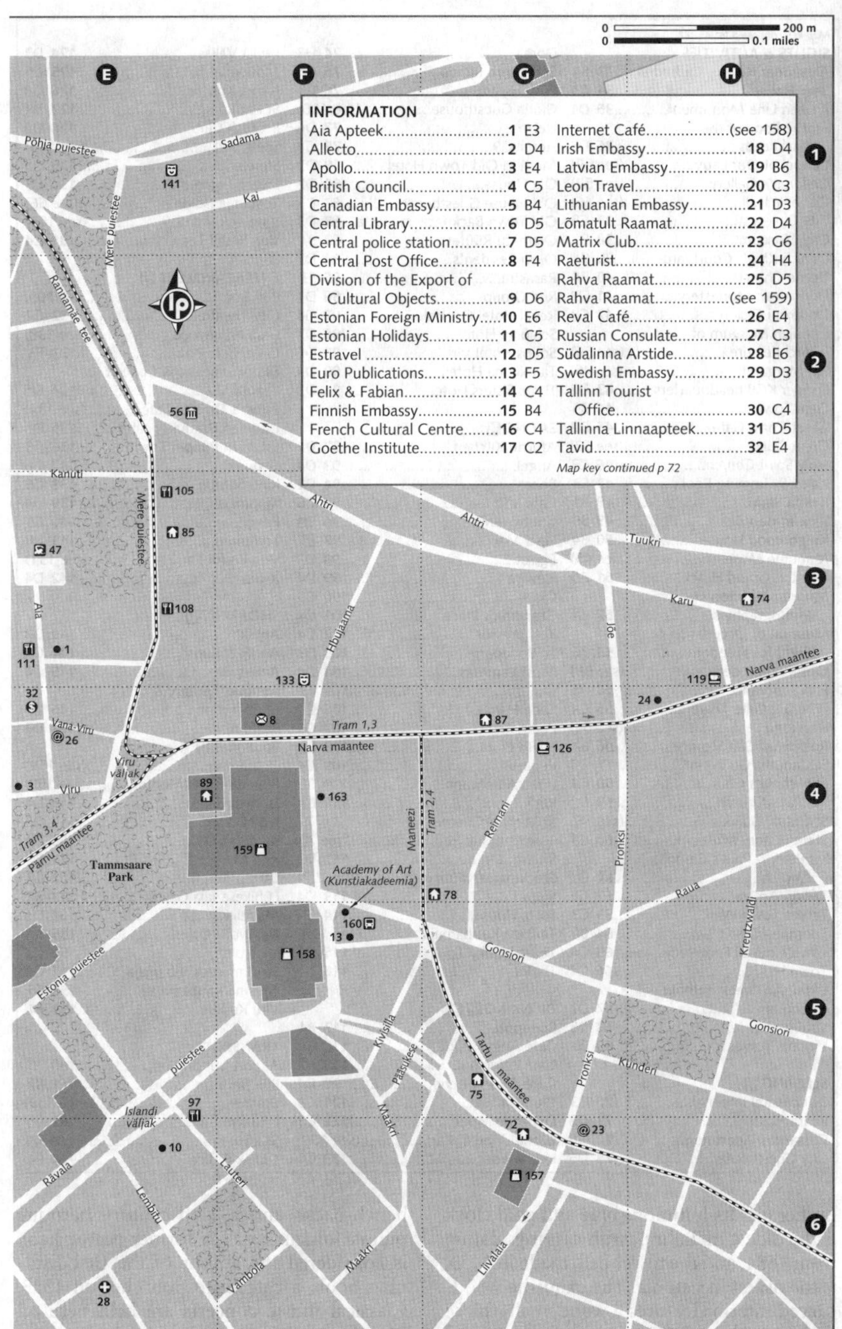
0 200 m
0 0.1 miles
E
F
G
H
1
2
3
4
5
6
INFORMATION
Aia Apteek....1 E3
Allecto....2 D4
Apollo....3 E4
British Council....4 C5
Canadian Embassy....5 B4
Central Library....6 D5
Central police station....7 D5
Central Post Office....8 F4
Division of the Export of Cultural Objects....9 D6
Estonian Foreign Ministry....10 E6
Estonian Holidays....11 C5
Estravel....12 D5
Euro Publications....13 F5
Felix & Fabian....14 C4
Finnish Embassy....15 B4
French Cultural Centre....16 C4
Goethe Institute....17 C2
Internet Café....(see 158)
Irish Embassy....18 D4
Latvian Embassy....19 B6
Leon Travel....20 C3
Lithuanian Embassy....21 D3
Lõmatult Raamat....22 D4
Matrix Club....23 G6
Raeturist....24 H4
Rahva Raamat....25 D5
Rahva Raamat....(see 159)
Reval Café....26 E4
Russian Consulate....27 C3
Südalinna Arstide....28 E6
Swedish Embassy....29 D3
Tallinn Tourist Office....30 C4
Tallinna Linnaapteek....31 D5
Tavid....32 E4
Map key continued p 72
Põhja puiestee
Sadama
Kai
Mere puiestee
Rannamäe tee
Kanuti
Ahtri
Tuukri
Karu
Ala
Hobujaama
Jõe
Narva maantee
Tram 1,3
Vana-Viru
Viru väljak
Viru
Tram 3,4
Pärnu maantee
Tammsaare Park
Maneezi
Tram 2,4
Reimani
Pronksi
Raua
Kreutzwaldi
Academy of Art (Kunstiakadeemia)
Gonsiori
Estonia puiestee
puiestee
Kivisilla
Pääsukese
Tartu maantee
Kunderi
Islandi väljak
Maakri
Rävala
Lauteri
Lembitu
Vambola
Liivalaia
141
56
105
85
47
108
1
111
32
26
3
133
8
87
119
24
126
74
89
163
159
78
160
13
158
97
10
75
72
23
157
28

Map key continued from p 71

SIGHTS & ACTIVITIES
Alexander Nevsky Cathedral.....33 B4
Beer House.....34 C4
Broken Line Monument.....35 D1
Brotherhood of the Blackheads.....36 D3
Chapel of Our Lady.....(see 59)
Children's Gallery.....(see 52)
Citizens' Hall.....(see 66)
City Gallery.....37 C5
City Museum.....38 D3
Danish King's Courtyard.....39 B4
Dome Church.....40 B4
Dominican Monastery.....41 D3
Draakoni Gallery.....42 C3
Estonian Museum of Architecture.....(see 56)
Fat Margaret.....(see 45)
Former KGB headquarters.....43 D2
Gate Tower.....44 B5
Great Coast Gate.....45 D2
Great Guild.....(see 60)
Holy Spirit Church.....46 C3
Kalev Swimming Pool.....47 E3
Kalma Saun.....48 B1
Kiek-in-de-Kök.....49 B5
Knighthood House.....50 B4
Maritime Museum.....(see 45)
Meriton Grand Hotel.....51 A5
Museum of Estonian Photography.....52 C4
Museum of Occupation & Fight for Freedom.....53 B6
Observation deck.....(see 59)
Pikk Herman.....54 A5
Pikk Jalg Gate Tower.....55 C4
Riigikogu.....(see 64)
Rotterman Salt Storage.....56 E2
St Canutus Guild Hall.....57 D3
St Nichola's Church.....58 C4
St Olaf's Church.....59 D2
St Olaus' Guild.....(see 36)
State History Museum.....60 C3
Sts Peter & Paul's Catholic Church.....61 D3
Tallinn Art Hall.....62 C5
Tallinn Town Wall.....63 C3
Toompea Castle.....64 B4
Town Council Pharmacy.....65 C4
Town Hall.....66 C4
Ukrainian Greek Catholic Church.....67 D2
Vaal.....68 D5
Virgin's Tower.....69 B5

SLEEPING
Baltic Hotel Imperial.....70 C3
Beata Hostel.....71 D2
Cassandra Apartments.....72 G6
City Guesthouse.....73 D5
Dorell.....74 H3
Erel International.....75 G5
Euro Hostel.....76 C3
Gloria Guesthouse.....(see 100)
Helke.....77 D6
Hotell G9.....78 G4
Meriton Old Town Hotel.....79 D2
Old House.....80 D2
Old House Guesthouse.....81 D3
Old Town Backpackers Hostel.....82 D3
Olematu Rüütel.....83 B4
Olevi Residents.....84 D3
Rasastra.....85 E3
Red Group.....86 D4
Reval Hotel Central.....87 G4
Schlösse Hotel.....88 D3
Sokos Hotel Viru.....89 E4
Taanilinna Hotell.....90 D3
Three Sisters Hotel.....91 D2

EATING
African Kitchen.....92 D2
Angel.....93 D4
Bocca.....94 D2
Café VS.....95 C6
Controvento.....96 D4
Eesti Maja.....97 E5
Egoist.....98 D3
Elevant.....99 D4
Gloria.....100 C5
Grandma's Place.....101 C4
Kompressor.....102 C4
Le Bonaparte.....103 D3
Must Lammas.....104 D4
Ö.....105 E3
Olde Hansa.....106 C4
Peetri Pizza.....107 C6
Peetri Pizza.....108 E3
Pegasus.....109 C4
Pizza Americana.....110 C5
Rimi.....111 E3
St Michael Cheese Restaurant.....(see 70)
Sisalik.....112 D3
Stockmann Kaubamaja.....(see 157)
Sultan.....113 D4
Sushi House.....114 C4
Tallinna Kaubamaja.....(see 158)
Texas Honky Tonk.....115 D3
Troika.....116 C4

DRINKING
Bogapott.....117 B4
Café Anglais.....118 C4
Café Peterson.....119 H3
Café-Chocolaterie.....120 D4
Club Havana.....121 C3
Depeche Mode.....122 C3
Gloria Wine Cellar.....(see 100)
Kehrwieder.....123 C4
Levist Väljas.....124 D3
Moskva.....125 C5
Narva Kohvik.....126 G4
St Patrick's.....127 D4
Scottish Club.....128 D2
Spirit.....(see 105)
Stereo.....129 C5
Sweet Tooth.....130 C3
Tristan ja Isolde.....(see 66)
Vinoteek V & S.....(see 105)
Von Krahli Teater Baar.....131 C4

ENTERTAINMENT
Bon Bon.....(see 105)
City Theatre.....132 C2
Club Hollywood.....(see 138)
Coca-Cola Plaza.....133 F3
Estonia Theatre & Concert Hall.....134 D5
Estonia Theatre Café.....(see 134)
Estonian Drama Theatre.....135 D5
Estonian Puppet Theatre.....136 C3
G-punkt.....137 C6
Kino Sõprus.....138 C5
Kinomaja.....139 D4
Privé.....140 C5
Terrarium.....141 E1
Von Krahli Theatre.....(see 131)
X-Baar.....142 D4

SHOPPING
Antiik.....143 D3
Antiik & Kunst.....144 C4
Antikvaar.....145 C4
Antique, Military & Collections.....146 C3
Bastion.....147 D4
Boutiques BT (Hoochi Mama).....(see 159)
Boutiques BT (Monton).....(see 159)
Domini Canes.....148 D4
Ivo Nikkolo.....149 D5
Katariina Gild.....150 D4
Knit Market.....151 D4
Lai.....152 C3
Lühikese Jala Galerii.....153 B4
Madeli Käsitöö.....154 D4
Navitrolla Galerii.....155 B4
Nu Nordik.....156 C5
Stockmann Kaubamaja.....157 G6
Tallinna Kaubamaja.....158 F5
Viru Keskus.....159 F4

TRANSPORT
Airport-bus Station.....160 F5
Bus Platform.....161 B2
Ecolines.....(see 159)
Estonian Air.....162 C5
Silja Lines.....(see 157)
Tallink Office.....163 F4

Lutherans. Its luminous blue and gold clock is the oldest in Tallinn, with carvings dating from 1684, and the tower bell, made in 1433, is the oldest in Estonia. The exquisite wood-carved interior features a wooden altarpiece dating back to 1483, 16th-century carved bench-backs and a 17th-century baroque pulpit. Johann Koell, a former pastor here, is considered the author of the first Estonian book, a catechism published in 1535. Classical music concerts are held here on Mondays at 6pm.

AROUND VENE

Several 15th-century warehouses and merchant residences surround Raekoja plats, notably when heading towards Vene (the Estonian word for Russian, named for the Russian merchants who traded here centuries ago). Vene is now one of Old Town's favourite restaurant precincts. Set in a medieval merchant's house, the **City Museum** (Linnamuuseum; Map pp70-1; ☎ 644 6553; Vene tänav 17; adult/concession 35/10Kr; 🕑 10.30am-6pm Wed-Mon Mar-Oct, to 5pm Wed-Mon Nov-Feb) traces the city's development from its earliest days, and its displays of clothing, furnishings and curios help take you back in time. The 3rd floor presents a politicised (but quite accurate we imagine) portrait of life under the Soviet yoke, and there's a fascinating video of the events surrounding the collapse of the regime. In addition to permanent displays, curators host temporary shows, and you never know what's in store – on a recent visit, we caught a baffling exhibition on women's undergarments from the 1930s.

Further down on Vene stands one of Tallinn's oldest buildings: the **Dominican Monastery** (Dominiiklaste klooster; Map pp70-1; ☎ 644 4606; www.kloostri.ee; Vene tänav 16; adult/concession 45/25Kr; 🕑 9.30am-6pm mid-May–mid-Sep, visits other times by appt), founded in 1246, once housed Scandinavian monks who aimed to convert Estonians to Christianity and educate the local population. In its glory days the coffers were full, and the monastery had its own brewery and hospital. Once the reformation began, however, its days were numbered. A mob of angry Lutherans torched the place in 1524, and the monks fled town. The monastery languished for the next 400 years until its restoration in 1954. Today it houses Estonia's largest collection of stone carvings (dating from the 15th to the 17th centuries), and the inner garden is a peaceful refuge from the summertime crowds.

Next door to the monastery is **Sts Peter & Paul's Church** (Peeter-Paul Kirik; Map pp70-1; ☎ 644 6367; Vene tänav 16; 🕑 10am-6pm mid-May–mid-Sep, visits outside season by appt), which dates back to 1844. A handsome whitewashed church, it was designed by the famed architect Carlo Rossi, who left his mark on the neoclassical shape of St Petersburg. It still functions as one of Tallinn's only Catholic churches, largely for the Polish and Lithuanian community.

PIKK

Pikk (Long St) runs north from Raekoja plats towards Tallinn port and is lined with the houses of medieval German merchants and gentry. Many of these were built in the 15th century, and contained three or four storeys, with the lower two used as living and reception quarters and the upper ones for storage.

Also on Pikk are the buildings of several old Tallinn guilds (associations of traders or artisans, nearly all German dominated). The **Great Guild** (Map pp70-1; Pikk tänav 17), to which the most eminent merchants belonged, is set in a striking building dating from 1410. Its vaulted halls now contain the **State History Museum** (Ajaloomuuseum; Map pp70-1; ☎ 641 1630; www.eam.ee; Pikk tänav 17; adult/concession 15/10Kr; 🕑 11am-6pm Thu-Tue), with a rather dry permanent exhibition of Estonian historical artefacts dating from the 14th to the 19th centuries. (Coin-collectors, don't miss this place.) Changing temporary shows, however, are often quite interesting: check the website to see what's on.

Another old artisans guild on this street is the 1860 **St Canutus Guild Hall** (Kanuti Gildi Saal; Map pp70-1; Pikk tänav 20), with its black statues of Martin Luther and St Canute looking down from their second-storey perch. The adjoining buildings of the **Brotherhood of the Blackheads** (Mustpeade Maja; Map pp70-1; ☎ 631 3199; www.mustpeademaja.ee; Pikk tänav 24) and **St Olaus' Guild** (Olevi Gildi Hoone; Map pp70-1; Pikk tänav 26) are closed to the public except for regular concerts. The Blackheads were unmarried merchants who took their name not from poor hygiene, but from their patron saint, Mauritius, a legendary African warrior whose likeness is found between two lions on the building façade (dating from 1597). Concerts are held here most nights during the summer and less frequently the rest of the year. St Olaus' Guild – probably the first guild in Tallinn – began in the 13th century, and developed a membership of more humble non-German artisans and traders.

At the northern end of Pikk stands **St Olaf's Church** (Oleviste Kirik; Map pp70-1; Pikk 48), its 124m spire being yet another of Tallinn's icons (formerly used as a surveillance centre by the KGB). The entrance is on Lai. Tallinn's best view awaits at the top of the **observation deck** (Map pp70-1; ☎ 621 4421; www.oleviste.ee; adult/concession 20/10Kr; 🕑 10am-6pm Jun-Aug). Although dedicated to the 11th-century King Olaf II of Norway, the church is linked in local lore with another Olaf –its architect who ignored the prophesies of doom to befall the one who completed the church's construction. Accordingly, Olaf fell to his death from the tower, and it's said that a toad and snake then crawled out of his mouth. The incident is shown in one of the carvings on the eastern wall of the 16th-century **Chapel of Our Lady**, adjoining the church.

Just south of the church is the former **KGB headquarters** (Map pp70-1; Pikk tänav 46/48), the basement windows of which were bricked up to prevent the sounds of violent 'interrogations' from being heard by those passing by on the street.

The **Great Coast Gate** (Map pp70–1), the medieval exit to Tallinn port, lies just north of the church. It's joined to **Fat Margaret** (Paks Margareeta), a rotund 16th-century bastion that protected this entrance to the town. Fat Margaret's walls are more than 4m thick at the base. Inside is the **Maritime Museum** (Meremuuseum; ☎ 641 1408; Pikk tänav 70; adult/concession 25/10Kr; ⏲ 10am-6pm Wed-Sun), with displays of old charts, model ships, antiquated diving equipment and other artefacts from Estonia's seafaring history. There are good views from the platform on the roof. Just outside the bastion stretch two strands of a long sculpture entitled *Broken Line*, which is dedicated to the victims of the *Estonia* ferry-sinking, Europe's worst peacetime maritime tragedy. Nearby, a 3m-long granite tablet lists the 852 people who died the night of 28 September 1994, travelling from Stockholm to Tallinn.

LOWER-TOWN WALLS & ST NICHOLAS' CHURCH

The longest-standing stretch of the Old Town wall, with nine towers, spans from Väike-Kloostri tänav, along Laboratooriumi to the northern end of Lai.

At the northern end of Aida tänav is a tiny passageway through the town wall; on the other side there's a picturesque spot to photograph a line-up of four **towers** (another can be found along Kooli). To access the walkway atop the walls, visit the **Tallinn Town Wall** (Map pp70-1; adult/concession 10/7Kr; ⏲ 11am-7pm Mon-Fri, to 4pm Sat & Sun). Three empty towers are connected here and visitors can explore their nooks and crannies for themselves. There are good views from the tower windows.

Nearby, the **Ukrainian-Greek Catholic Church** (Map pp70-1; ☎ 5668 2369; Laboratooriumi 22; ⏲ 1-2.30pm Sun & by appt) is a fascinating monastery with a 14th-century wooden church full of old relics. Visits include a free guided tour, where you'll learn all about the history and legends of the place. Donations accepted (and go towards the recently opened school and cultural centre).

The Gothic **St Nicholas' Church** (Niguliste Kirik; Map pp70-1; ☎ 644 9903; Niguliste tänav 3; adult/concession 35/20Kr; ⏲ 10am-5pm Wed-Sun) is another of the city's medieval treasures. Dating from the 13th century, St Nicholas' now houses artworks from medieval Estonian churches. Its most famous work is the eerie *Dance Macabre,* Berndt Notke's 15th-century masterpiece. Other artefacts here include baroque chandeliers, a 15th-century altar and a silver chamber. The church was badly damaged by Soviet bombers in 1944 and a fire in the 1980s, but today stands fully restored. The acoustics are first-rate, with organ recitals held most weekends (beginning at 4pm on Saturday and Sunday).

At the foot of the slope below St Nicholas' Church, along Harju tänav, you can see more ruins wrought by Soviet bombers on the night of 9 March 1944. A sign in English facing Harju details the damage inflicted on the city that night.

Also near the church in front of Rataskaevu No 16 is a well where many stray cats perished. In medieval times animals were sacrificed to appeal for prosperity in the year ahead. Some believe the house that stands near the well is haunted. The devil apparently hosted a wild party there some time ago, and if you happen to pass late one night, some say you can still hear sounds of the party.

TOOMPEA

A winding stairway connects Lühike jalg, off Rataskaevu, to Toompea. According to Estonian legend, Toompea is the burial mound of Kalev, the heroic first leader of the Estonians, built by his widow Linda. In German times this was the preserve of the feudal nobility and bishop, looking down on the traders and lesser beings of the Lower Town.

Although the most impressive – and until the 17th century the only – approach to

Toompea is through the red-roofed **Long Leg Gate Tower** (Pikk jalg; Map pp70–1), which dates from 1380, **Short Leg** (Lühike jalg), at the western end of Pikk, is not without character. A number of ghostly apparitions have been reported inside the **Gate Tower** (Lühike jalg 9), including a crucified monk and a black dog with burning eyes. It's thought to be the most haunted house in Tallinn.

At the top of Lühike jalg is Estonia's parliament building, the **Riigikogu**, which meets in the photogenic **Toompea Castle** (Map pp70-1; ☎ 631 6537; Lossi plats 1; by appt only ⏰ 10am-4pm Mon-Fri). Nothing remains of the Danish castle built here in 1219, but three of the four corner towers of its successor, founded between 1227 and 1229, still stand. The pink baroque façade dates from the 18th century when, under Catherine the Great, it was rebuilt and the moat was filled.

The finest of the castle towers is the 1371 **Pikk Hermann** at the southwest corner, topped by the national flag. The two other surviving towers, plus most of the northern wall of the old castle, can be seen from the yard of Toom-Kooli 13.

Toompea is named after the magnificent Lutheran **Dome Church** (Toomkirik; Map pp70-1; ☎ 644 4140; Toomkooli tänav 6; admission free; ⏰ 9am-4pm Tue-Sun) founded in 1233. The edifice dates from the 15th and 17th centuries, with the tower added in 1779. The church was a burial ground for the rich and noble. The finest of the **carved tombs** inside are those on the right as you approach the altar, including the 16th-century Swedish commander Pontus de la Gardie and his wife. The Swedish siege of Narva, where de la Gardie died, is depicted on the side of their sarcophagus. The Greek temple-style sarcophagus belongs to Admiral Samuel Greigh, an 18th-century Scot who joined the Russian navy and became a hero of Russo-Turkish sea battles. Admiral Adam Johann von Krusenstern, a German-Estonian who was the first Russian citizen to sail around the world, has another elaborate tomb. From the Dome Church, follow Kohtu tänav to the city's favourite lookout over the lower town.

The location of the Russian Orthodox **Alexander Nevsky Cathedral** (Map pp70-1; Lossi plats), opposite the parliament buildings, was no accident: the church was one of many Orthodox cathedrals built between 1894 and 1900 as part of a general wave of Russification in the Russian Baltic provinces in the last quarter of the 19th century. Orthodox believers still come here in droves.

A path leads down from Lossi plats to the **Danish King's Courtyard** (Map pp70–1), which offers sweeping views over the lower town. In the summer artists set up their easels. One of the towers here, the **Virgin's Tower** (Neitsitorn; Lühike jalg 9a), is said to have been a prison for medieval prostitutes.

One of Tallinn's most formidable cannon towers is the tall, stout **Kiek-in-de-Kök** (Map pp70-1; ☎ 644 6686; Komandandi 2; adult/concession 25/8Kr; ⏰ 10.30am-6pm Tue-Sun Mar-Oct, 10.30am-5pm Nov-Feb). Its name is Low German for 'Peep into the Kitchen'; from the upper floors lonely soldiers could peer into the houses of Lower Town. Built around 1475, it was badly damaged during the Livonian war, but it never collapsed (nine of Ivan the Terrible's cannon balls remain embedded in the walls). Today it houses a museum tracing the birth and development of Tallinn.

From Kiek-in-de-Kök, a pleasant downhill stroll southwest leads to the grassy **Hirvepark** (Map pp70–1) with a **statue** of Linda grieving. This has come to symbolise the tragic fate of those deported from Estonia during and after WWII.

Nearby, you can get a more in-depth look at the Estonian struggle at the fairly new **Museum of Occupation & Fight for Freedom** (Map ppp70-1; ☎ 668 0250; Toompea 8; adult/concession 10/5Kr; ⏰ 11am-6pm Tue-Sun). Photos and multimedia displays illustrate five decades of oppressive rule.

East of the Centre

Getting There & Away

Trams 1 and 3 go to the Kadriorg stop right by Kadriorg Park. Buses 1, 8, 34 and 38 all run between the city centre and Pirita, stopping on Narva maantee near Kadriorg Park, and at Maarjamäe. Buses 34 and 38 go to the Botanical Gardens (Kloostrimetsa stop) and the TV Tower (Motoklubi stop).

KADRIORG

The pleasant, wooded **Kadriorg Park** (Map pp66-7; Narva maantee) lies about 2km east of Old Town, and remains a long-time favourite of city dwellers seeking a bit of green space. Oak, lilac and horse chestnut trees are the setting for strollers, cyclists and picnickers, and the park's ample acreage never makes the paths feel crowded. Together with the baroque Kadriorg Palace, it was designed for the Russian tsar Peter the Great by the Italian Niccolo Michetti, soon after Peter's conquest of Estonia in the Great Northern War.

The centrepiece of the forest is **Kadriorg Palace**, which houses the **Museum of Foreign Art** (Väliskunsti Muuseum; Map pp66-7; Kadrioru loss; ☎ 606 6400; Weizenbergitänav 37; adult/concession 45/20Kr; 🕑 10am-5pm Tue-Sun May-Sep, 10am-5pm Wed-Sun Oct-Apr), built between 1718 and 1736 – with the help of Peter himself who laid no less than three sturdy bricks. The museum holds Dutch, German and Italian paintings from the 16th to the 18th centuries, along with Russian works from the 18th to 19th centuries. It's a nostalgic place to stroll for an hour or two among the mostly Romantic works, and there's a handsome flower garden at the back. In the 1930s the palace was the private domain of the president of independent Estonia. Since Estonia's re-independence, part of the palace complex has again become the presidential home.

Behind the palace, in the former kitchen building, the small **Mikkel Museum** (Map pp66-7; ☎ 601 5844; Weizenbergi 28; admission 15Kr; 🕑 11am-6pm Wed-Sun) has a small but interesting assortment of art. Russian and Chinese paintings, 15th-century icons and works in porcelain are all part of the eclectic collection.

Nearby is the cottage Peter the Great occupied on visits to Tallinn while the palace was under construction. Today it houses the **Peter the Great Home Museum** (Map pp66-7; ☎ 601 3136; Mäekalda tänav 2; admission 15Kr; 🕑 11am-4pm Wed-Sat May-Sep) where you may examine his clothes and the boots he made. There's also a small collection of 18th-century furnishings.

Also in Kadriorg is the futuristic **Art Museum of Estonia** (Map pp66-7; ☎ 602 6001; www.ekm.ee; Weizenbergi tänav 34), a massive seven-storey building that houses some 60,000 works by Estonian and foreign artists. Opened in early 2006, the Art Museum contains the largest art collection in the Baltics.

Just west of the park, the last home of the great Estonian novelist Anton Hansen Tammsaare now contains the small **Tammsaare Museum** (Map pp66-7; ☎ 601 3232; Koidula tänav 12A; admission 5Kr; 🕑 11am-6pm Wed-Mon) with period furnishings from the 1930s. The house lies on a tree-lined street among other charming 19th-century homes, and the whole neighbourhood makes a great setting for a stroll. Between the wars, this was Tallinn's most affluent area.

TALLINN SONG BOWL

The **Tallinn Song Bowl** (Lauluväljak; Narva maantee), site of the main gatherings of Estonia's national song festivals, is an open-air amphitheatre said to have a capacity of 150,000 people. In September 1988 300,000 squeezed in for one songfest and publicly demanded independence during the 'Singing Revolution'. Approximately half a million people, including a large number of Estonian émigrés, were believed to have been present at the 21st Song Festival in 1990, the last major festival before the restoration of independence. An Estonian repertoire was reinstated and around 29,000 performers sang under the national flag for the first time in 50 years.

PIRITA TEE

This coastal road curving northwards alongside Tallinn Bay is an ideal walk, affording a sea view that's particularly striking during late-night summer sunsets. It's a popular stretch for joggers, cyclists and Rollerbladers.

A kilometre north of Kadriorg Park, the seldom-visited **Maarjamäe Palace** (Maarjamäe loss; Map pp66-7; ☎ 601 4535; Pirita tee 56; adult/concession 10/8Kr; 🕑 11am-6pm Wed-Sun) covers Estonian history from the mid-19th century onwards. The neo-Gothic limestone palace was built in the 1870s as a summer cottage for the Russian general A Orlov-Davydov.

Further north along Pirita tee is an unmistakably Soviet **war monument** rising in its concrete glory to a sharp point on the eastern side of the street. It was erected in 1975 over the graves of German soldiers who died fighting the Soviets on the Leningrad front. Most of the graves were bulldozed for the purpose, but some remain in a small cemetery behind the statue. Postindependence, a memorial was added to the Nazi war dead (Estonians, after all, fought on both sides; see p50 if this has you baffled). Today the monument has an air of desolation about it, and it's a fascinating relic from 1960s USSR.

PIRITA

Approximately 1.5km beyond Maarjamäe, just before Pirita tee crosses the Pirita River, a short side road leads down to **Pirita Yacht Club** (Map pp66–7) and the **Tallinn Olympic Yachting Centre** (Map pp66-7; ☎ 639 8980; www.piritatop.ee), near the mouth of the river. This was the base for the sailing events of the 1980 Moscow Olympics, and international regattas are still held here. If you're just passing through, the Yacht Club is a relaxing spot for a drink alfresco. You can also hire rowboats nearby (see p78).

From there it's 50m to the ruined **Convent of St Birgitta** (Map pp66-7; ☎ 605 5000; adult/concession 20/10Kr; 🕑 10am-6pm). Only the Gothic gable still stands, which is the last remnant of this early-15th-century convent. The rest was destroyed courtesy of Ivan the Terrible during the Livonian War in 1577. In 1996 Birgittine nuns in Estonia were granted the right to return to and reactivate the convent. The convent's completed new headquarters are adjacent to the ruins.

North of the bridge is **Pirita beach** (Pirita rand; Map pp66–7), the city's largest and most popular beach (and it's only 6km from the city centre). Although it's no Bondi beach (or Pärnu, p155, for that matter), Pirita is a quick getaway for urbanites; there are plenty of young, bronzed sun-lovers filling the sands, with a handful of laid-back cafés nearby.

BOTANICAL GARDENS & TV TOWER

Set on 1.2 sq km and surrounded by lush woodlands, the **Botanical Gardens** (☎ 606 2666; Kloostrimetsa tee 52; adult/concession 40/20Kr, family ticket 60Kr; 🕑 11am-4pm Tue-Sun) boast 8000 species of plant scattered in a series of greenhouses and along a 4km nature trail. The gardens lie 2.5km east of Pirita.

The 314m **TV Tower** (☎ 623 8258; www.teletorn.ee; Kloostrimetsa tee 58a; adult/child 50/15Kr; 🕑 10am-midnight) is 400m further east. There's a Russian-style restaurant and panoramic viewing platform at the 170m point. At the base there are still a few bullet holes from events during the August 1991 attempted Estonian breakaway (it was as violent as things became in Estonia's bid for independence).

THE STATE OF THE ART

If you've had your fill of old stone churches and Baltic antiquities, take a detour from the medieval street and check out the state of contemporary Estonian art, c early 21st century. Although Tallinn's Warhols and Pollocks have yet to emerge, in the last few years the capital has become an increasingly fertile place for cerebral and often daring young artists on the make. A growing number of galleries have opened their doors, ensuring a wide array of talent is always on view, from the old and nostalgic to the neofuturistic. Keep an eye out for art openings, which are good opportunities to connect to the local scene. Otherwise, drop in at one of the following, and get a taste of Tallinn's *other* side.

Rotterman Salt Storage (Map pp70-1; ☎ 625 7000; www.arhitektuurimuuseum.ee; Ahtri tänav 2; adult/concession 30/10Kr; 🕑 11am-6pm Wed-Sun) East of Old Town, this beautifully restored limestone warehouse once served the unpoetic but utilitarian function as the city's saltcellar. Today the massive space houses the **Estonian Museum of Architecture**, with its permanent architecture exhibitions. Less of a yawn is the incredible array of temporary exhibitions – often the city's best – held here throughout the year. Check the website for details.

City Gallery (Map pp70-1; ☎ 644 2818; www.kunstihoone.ee; Harju tänav 13; admission free; 🕑 noon-6pm Wed-Mon) Hosts rapidly changing exhibits – often the most experimental pieces in Tallinn.

Vaal (Map pp70-1; ☎ 627 0161; www.vaal.ee; Väike-Karja tänav 12; admission free; 🕑 noon-6pm Wed-Sun) This versatile exhibition space in Old Town displays the works of some of Estonia's best artists. For getting a grip on the contemporary scene, this is the place to be.

Tallinn Art Hall (Map pp70-1; ☎ 644 2818; www.kunstihoone.ee; Vabaduse Väljak 8; admission 25Kr; 🕑 noon-6pm Wed-Sun) Daring, avant-garde Estonian art is on the menu at this imposing pre-Soviet-era building overlooking Vabaduse väljak (Freedom Sq). After getting your fill of art, pop next door to stylish Moskva (p85) for a different brand of intoxicant.

Draakoni Gallery (Map ppp70-1; ☎ 646 4110; Pikk tänav 18; admission free; 🕑 10am-6pm Mon-Fri, to 5pm Sat) This cosy Old Town space hosts small, sometimes stimulating, exhibitions. More than anything, though, we like this place for its fabulous sculpted façade.

Southwest of the Centre

The impressive, fortresslike façade of the **Estonian National Library** (Map pp66-7; ☎ 630 7611; Tõnismägi 2; ⏰ 10am-8pm Mon-Fri, noon-7pm Sat) is one example of the mini renaissance Estonia's national stone, dolomite limestone, has undergone in recent years. Built in 1982 by Raine Karp (who also designed the similar Sakala conference and cultural centre on Rävala puiestee and the enormous Linnahall concert hall by the port), the library is worth seeing for its cavernous interior. Frequent exhibitions take place on the upper floors (though you may need a day pass from reception).

About 4km due west of the centre (or a 15-minute ride on bus 40 or 48 from Viruväljak) is **Pelguranna beach** (Map pp66–7), which is purported to be the cleanest beach in the Tallinn area. It has a distinctly local feel but is a pleasant alternative to Pirita.

Tallinn Zoo (Loomaaed; ☎ 694 3300; Paldiski maantee 145; www.tallinnzoo.ee; adult/concession 50/20Kr; ⏰ 9am-7pm May-Aug, to 5pm Sep, Oct & Apr, to 3pm Nov-Mar) boasts the world's largest collection of wild goats, and 334 species of animals, birds, reptiles and fish. It's a good place for your kids to meet other kids – the entire child population of northern Estonia is there on summer weekends. Opposite the zoo is **Tivoli** (☎ 656 0110; day pass adult/child 175/120Kr; ⏰ noon-8pm Mon-Fri, 11am-8pm Sat & Sun, closed Oct-Apr) a small amusement park for the kids.

One kilometre beyond the zoo, Rannamõisa tee branches right towards Rocca al Mare and its **Open Air Museum** (☎ 654 9100; Vabaõhumuuseumi tee 12; adult/child May-Sep 30/15Kr, Oct-Apr 15/10Kr; ⏰ buildings 10am-6pm, grounds 10am-8pm). Most of Estonia's oldest wooden structures, mainly farmhouses but also a chapel (1699) and windmill, are preserved here. If you're not heading to villages in the south, this is a good place to see traditional wooden architecture and get an overview of 150 years of rural life. Along those lines, the audio tour (80Kr) is worthwhile. There are also views back to the city and you can walk through the woods or down to the sea. On Sunday mornings there are folk song-and-dance shows. There's also the **Kolu Kõrts tavern** (meals from 80Kr; ⏰ 10am-6pm), where you can sample traditional Estonian cuisine. Every June, Rocca al Mare celebrates its *Memme-taadi* days, with folk dancing, songs and craft fairs. Most kids love this place, particularly for the pony rides.

Buses 21 and 21B go from the train station straight to Rocca al Mare. The zoo is best reached by bus 22 or trolleybus 6 from Vabaduse Väljak, just south of Old Town.

ACTIVITIES

Boating

In summer **Pirita Rowboat Rental** (Map pp66-7; ☎ 621 2105; Kloostri tee 6a; rowboats/paddle boats per hr from 75/50Kr), beside the road-bridge over the Pirita River, rents rowboats and paddle boats. It's an idyllic place for a leisurely float, with thick forest edging towards the water. There's also a pleasant café and restaurant (p84) nearby.

Saunas

Locals attribute all kinds of health benefits to a good old-fashioned sweat out, and truth be told a trip to Estonia just won't be complete until you've paid a visit to the sauna. You won't have to look far: nearly every place listed in the Sleeping section has one. For something a little different, try one of the following:

Beer House (Map pp70-1; ☎ 627 6520; www.beerhouse.ee; Dunkri 5; per hr 300-600Kr; ⏰ 10am-midnight Sun-Thu, to 2am Fri & Sat) Two private saunas for rent (the larger has a Jacuzzi) in this large beer hall in Old Town.

Club 26 (Map pp66-7; ☎ 631 5585; www.revalhotels.com; 26th fl, Liivalaia tänav 33; before/after 3pm 300/600Kr; ⏰ 6:30am-11pm Mon-Fri, 7:30am-11pm Sat & Sun) On the top floor of the Reval Hotel Olümpia (p82), this is one of the most luxurious saunas in town.

Kalma Saun (Map pp70-1; ☎ 627 1811; Vana-Kalamaja 9A; per person 60-90Kr; ⏰ 10am-11pm) In a grand building behind the train station, Tallinn's oldest public bath still has the aura of an old-fashioned Russian-style *banya* (bathhouse).

Meriton Grand Hotel (Map pp70-1; ☎ 667 7000; www.meriton.ee; Toompuiestee 27; per 2hr before/after 5pm 500/800Kr) Cosy and stylish private sauna that can accommodate up to 10 people.

Spas, Health Clubs & Swimming Pools

Body Zone (Map pp66-7; ☎ 630 0940; www.bodyzone.ee; Merivälja tee 5; day pass 300-400Kr; ⏰ 7am-10pm Mon-Fri, 9am-6pm Sat, 11am-8pm Sun) If you need a day at the gym, Body Zone is a good choice. Guests have access to the pool, squash courts, several rooms full of machines and weights, and a wide variety of classes (aerobics, yoga, cardio dance, spinning etc). There's also a full-service spa, and once you're feeling toned and ready, Pirita beach lies just outside.

Club 26 (Map pp66-7; ☎ 631 5585; www.revalhotels.com; 26th fl, Liivalaia tänav 33; per visit 60-130Kr; 🕑 6.30am-11pm Mon-Fri, 7.30am-11pm Sat & Sun) Atop the Reval Hotel Olümpia (p82), this small health club has a gym and 16m swimming pool with superb views over the city. Good choice for a workout without breaking the bank.

Kalev Swimming Pool (Map pp70-1; ☎ 644 2286; Aia tänav 18; per visit 50-70Kr; 🕑 7am-9:30pm Mon-Fri, 9am-8:45pm Sat & Sun) For serious swimming in an indoor pool of Olympic proportions. Sauna is also available.

Tallinn Sports Hall (Map pp66-7; ☎ 646 6346; Herne tänav 30; per visit 25-75Kr; 🕑 7am-9.30pm Mon-Fri, 9am-8.45pm Sat & Sun) State-of-the art facilities draw Tallinn's most serious athletes (including Erki Nool, Olympic gold medallist). Huge indoor running track, top-notch gym and the all-essential sauna are on hand.

Top Spa (Map pp66-7; ☎ 639 8718; www.topspa.ee; Regati puiestee 1; per person 60-90Kr; 🕑 spa 8am-6pm Mon-Fri, 8am-3pm Sat, swimming pool 6.30am-10pm Mon-Fri, 8am-10pm Sat & Sun) Inside the Pirita Top Spa Hotel (p81), this spa offers a number of pampering options (massages, salt chamber, solarium, pedicures etc). The adjoining health club has a gym where you can work out, catch a yoga or aerobics class or swim the 25m, six-lane pool. Swimming ticket includes sauna use.

TALLINN FOR CHILDREN

If you're travelling with kids, Tallinn's Old Town with its medieval setting, colourful restaurants and lively street scene is pure eye candy for the under-12 crowd. One place particularly worth visiting is the **Children's Gallery** (Kullo Lastegalerii; Map pp70-1; ☎ 644 6873; Kuninga 6; adult/child 6/3Kr; 🕑 11am-6pm Wed-Mon), which hosts workshops for children, and showcases the work of Estonia's youngest artists. Other youthful attractions in Old Town include the highly recommended **Estonian Puppet Theatre** (Eesti Nukuteater; Map pp70-1; ☎ 667 9555; www.nukuteater.ee; Lai tänav 1; admission 45-60Kr; 🕑 box office 10am-6pm), where the animator's art has been going strong since 1952. Performances are held on one of three stages, including the outdoor summer stage. Outside Old Town, the Open Air Museum (opposite) is always a hit with the younger crowd. In the same area, you'll also find Tallinn Zoo (opposite) and the summer-only amusement park Tivoli (opposite), with plenty of rides and games.

TOURS

The Tallinn Tourist Office (p68) and any travel agent (p69) can arrange tours in English or other languages with a private guide for around €15 to €20 per hour. The city also offers the following organised tours.

Audioguide Old Town Walking Tour (www.audioguide.ee; 280Kr) On this self-guided tour, you follow a prescribed route through the medieval quarters, listening to historical details and anecdotes along the way. You can find the audio player at the Tallinn Tourist Office and at some hotels.

City Bike (☎ 511 1819; www.citybike.ee; Pirita tee 28; 220Kr; 🕑 tours 11am & 5pm Apr-Oct, 11am Nov-Mar) This 14km bicycle tour covers Kadriorg Park, the Song Festival grounds, Pirita and Old Town, and includes commentary in English by the bicycle guide. The tour begins on Pirita tee, but staff can pick you up from Old Town. Book the day before. Price includes bike, helmet and a very stylish emergency green safety vest.

City Bus Tour (☎ 627 9080; www.citytour.ee; adult/child under 7 320Kr/free; 🕑 10am-4pm May-Oct) This red double-decker bus won't exactly help you blend in with the locals. It will, however, give you quick and easy access to a number of the city's top sights. The 48-hour bus pass allows you to hop on and off at the following stops: Virju Väljak, Toompea, Kadriorg, TV Tower, Botanical Gardens and Pirita, among others. A recorded audio tour accompanies the ride (English, German, French, Spanish, etc).

Old Town Walking Tour (☎ 610 8616; with 24hr, 48hr or 72hr Tallinn Card free, without 100Kr; 🕑 tours 11.30am, 2pm, 4pm) Offered in English or Finnish, this one- to 1½-hour tour covers Alexander Nevsky Cathedral, Toomkirik, the viewing platform on Kohtu tänav, Lühike Jalg and ends at Raekoja plats. Tours depart daily from the corner of Toompea and Komandandi.

FESTIVALS & EVENTS

For a complete list of Tallinn's festivals, visit www.kultuur.info.

Jazzkaar (☎ 611 4405; www.jazzkaar.ee) Jazz greats from around the world converge on Tallinn in mid-April during this excellent two-week festival. Don't miss it if you're in town.

Old Town Days One of Tallinn's biggest annual events, this four-day fest in early June features dancing, concerts, costumed performers and plenty of medieval merrymaking on nearly every corner of Old Town.

Beer Summer (www.ollesummer.ee; 1-/5-day ticket 100/300Kr) This extremely popular ale-guzzling, rock-music extravaganza takes place under and around big tents near the Song Festival grounds (Laulaväljak) in early July.

Birgitta Festival (www.filharmoonia.ee; per show 150-250Kr) An excellent place to see some of Estonia's vibrant singing tradition, with choral, opera and classical concerts held at the Convent of St Birgitta (p77) over a five-day period in mid-August. Book early; tickets sell out.

Dance Festival (☎ 646 4704; www.saal.ee; per show around 75Kr) Held in the last two weeks in August, this highly recommended contemporary dance festival features troupes from all over Europe and the Baltics. Most performances are held at St Canutus Guild Hall (p88).

Black Nights Film Festival (☎ 631 4640; www.poff.ee) Featuring films and animations from all over the world, this festival brings much life to cold winter nights from late November to early December.

SLEEPING

Tallinn has wide-ranging accommodation, from charming and inviting guesthouses to lavish four-star hotels. Old Town undoubtedly has the top picks, with plenty of atmospheric rooms set in beautifully refurbished medieval houses – though you'll have to pay a premium for them. Midrange and budget hotels are scarcer in Old Town, though apartment rental agencies probably have the best deals. In summer book far in advance: Tallinn's medieval charm is no longer a state secret.

Apartment Rental

Cassandra Apartments (Map pp70-1; ☎ 630 9820; www.cassandra-apartments.com; 7th fl, Tartu maantee 18; per night 1500-6000Kr; ☒) This agency rents bright, modern apartments (with one to three bedrooms), some with saunas and fantastic views. It's located in a high-rise near Old Town.

Erel International (Map pp70-1; ☎ 610 8780; www.erel.ee; Tartu maantee 14; per night from 1450Kr; ☒) Offers dozens of handsomely furnished apartments in Old Town. Airport pick-up included.

Old House Guesthouse (Map pp70-1; ☎ 641 1464; www.oldhouse.ee; Uus tänav 22; apt 850-1900Kr; ☒) Sixteen beautifully furnished apartments are scattered through Old Town.

Rasastra (Map pp70-1; ☎ 661 6291; www.bedbreakfast.ee; Mere puiestee 4; per night from 800Kr; ☒) Rasastra can set you up in a private home in central Tallinn. In addition, it arranges rooms in private homes throughout Estonia and the Baltics starting at 275/500Kr per single/double.

Red Group (Map pp70-1; ☎ 620 7877; www.redgroup.ee; Valli 4; per night from 1200Kr; ☒) Specialising in Old Town accommodation, this friendly outfit has a number of modern apartments in excellent locations (some overlook Raekoja plats). Airport pick-up included.

THE AUTHOR'S CHOICE

Schlössle Hotel (Map pp70-1; ☎ 699 7700; www.schlossle-hotels.com; Pühavaimu 13/15; s/d from €307/351; ☒) Individually designed rooms are nothing less than breathtaking in this medieval complex in the heart of Old Town. This lovingly restored hotel features details from the original 17th-century building (such as original wooden beams and old stone walls) and its sumptuously decorated rooms are among the country's finest. If you manage to make it out of your room, you can enjoy the fireplace in the antique-laden great hall, the courtyard garden and the historically set restaurant in the cellar.

Budget

Old Town Backpackers Hostel (Map pp70-1; ☎ 517 1337; www.balticbackpackers.com; Uus tänav 14; dm with/without HI card 200/225Kr; ☒) Young travellers flock to this recently opened hostel in Old Town. The space is small (just one big room of bunk beds), and if you're not up for the party atmosphere, look elsewhere. Bonuses: kitchen and sauna. In the summer the staff arrange excursions out of town.

Euro Hostel (Map pp70-1; ☎ 644 7788; www.eurohostel.ee; 2nd fl, Nunne 2; dm/d 280/650Kr; ☒) Opened in 2005, this hostel has clean but nondescript quarters, shared kitchen use and a fantastic location around the corner from Raekoja plats. It was still undiscovered when we passed through, but will surely emerge as a backpackers' favourite in Old Town.

Tatari Hostel (Map pp66-7; ☎ 646 6287; www.tatarihostel.ee; Tatari tänav 21B; dm/d 250/500Kr; ☒) Just outside Old Town, this fairly new hostel (2002) has clean rooms with tall ceilings on two renovated floors of an old building. It's a friendly place popular with a mix of travellers. Kitchen use and sauna available.

City Guesthouse (Map pp70-1; ☎ 628 2236; www.cityguesthouse.ee; Pärnu maantee 10; dm/s/d/ste 350/500/700/1200Kr; ☒) This recently opened hostel on the edge of Old Town has bland but clean rooms with blue carpeting and fluorescent lights (its office-building days aren't far behind it), and handsome suites with wooden floors and private bathroom (all other rooms have shared bathrooms in the corridor). Kitchen for guest use.

Beata Hostel (Map pp70-1; ☎ 641 1171; Uus tänav 35; dm/s/d 270/555/750Kr; ☒) There's little to recommend this spartan hostel aside from its excellent location. Dorms feel cluttered, and the smell of cigarettes lingers. Private rooms are a better bet – though all use shared bathrooms. A guest kitchen is available.

Helke (Map pp70-1; ☎ 644 5802; fax 644 5792; Sakala 14; s/d with shared bathroom incl breakfast 450/500Kr; ⊠) In an old wooden house 10 minutes' walk from Old Town, this worn favourite has small battered rooms with linoleum floors. It's a friendly place, but be prepared to rough it.

Kämping Kalev (☎ 623 8686; motoklubikalev@hot.ee; Kloostrimetsa tee 56a; camp site/caravan 240/300Kr, 2-/4-bed cabins 350/530Kr; 🕑 mid-May–mid-Sep; ⊠) Near the TV Tower, this small grassy area has secure camp sites, rustic wooden cabins (four-bed cabins are the least claustrophobic) and caravan sites. Meals are available in the pub nearby and there's a shop for self-caterers. Take bus 34A or 38 from Viru väljak in the centre to the Motoklubi stop.

Midrange

Meriton Old Town Hotel (Map pp70-1; ☎ 614 1300; www.meritonhotels.com; Lai 49; s/d €60/75, Bella Vita r €80; ⊠) This nicely located hotel has small but comfortable modern rooms, and it's hard to beat this price for en-suite quarters inside Old Town. Worth the extra are the six Bella Vita rooms, which are smarter and roomier (two have balconies).

Reval Hotel Central (Map pp70-1; ☎ 633 9800; www.revalhotels.com; Narva maantee 7; s/d from €70/80; ⊠ 💻) This large hotel remains the cheapest of the city-centre hotels. Bright, decent-sized rooms and friendly service come without a lick of pretence, and it's a short walk to Old Town.

Dorell (Map pp70-1; ☎ 626 1200; www.dorell.ee; Karu tänav 39; s/d with private bathroom 700/800Kr, with shared bathroom 550/600Kr; ⊠) In an ageing building near Old Town, this simple guesthouse has clean and simple carpeted rooms. While it lacks in aesthetics, it's convenient (12 minutes' walk to Old Town), and the prices are reasonable. Sauna available.

Hotell G9 (Map pp70-1; ☎ 626 7100; www.hotelg9.ee; 3rd fl, Gonsiori 9; s/d/tr from €47/45/57; ⊠) A few blocks from Old Town, Hotell G9 is a good choice for budget travellers who don't feel like bunking in a hostel. Rooms are simple and clean, with Spartan furnishings. Shared bathrooms; sauna.

Olematu Rüütel (Map pp70-1; ☎ 631 3827; www.hot.ee/olematuryytel.ee; Kiriku põik 4a; d with private/shared bathroom from 800/650Kr; ⊠) This small, three-room guesthouse is one of only a few accommodation options on Toompea. The quarters are pretty basic, but for the price and location, you can't beat it. Reservations essential.

Valge Villa (Map pp66-7; ☎ 654 2302; www.white-villa.com; Kännu tänav 26/2; s/d/ste €50/63/83; ⊠) This charming, family-run bed and breakfast has pleasant rooms with wooden floors and wood-panelled walls. Rooms get good light, and the owners will make you feel right at home. It's 3km from the centre on trolleybus 2, 3 or 4 to the Tedre stop.

Pirita Top Spa Hotel (Map pp66-7; ☎ 639 8600; www.topspa.ee; Regati puiestee 1; s/d from €66/86; ⊠ 🏊) On the seafront, next door to the Olympic Yachting Centre, this large five-storey hotel is Tallinn's premier spa hotel. Rooms are airy and bright with parquet floors and a minimalist design, and some rooms have fine balconies facing the sea (be sure to book the sea-facing 'marine class' rooms). All guests enjoy free access to the pool and sauna, with a full-service spa on site (see p79).

Comfort Hotel Oru (Map pp66-7; ☎ 603 3302; www.oruhotel.ee; Narva maantee 120B; s/d from €65/80; ⊠) Set close to Kardriorg Park and Pirita tee, this modern hotel is a decent option for those who don't mind being outside the town centre. Rooms are spacious but uninspiring, with comfortable furnishings and big windows, giving a light, airy feel (some rooms have balconies or saunas). Numerous buses travel Narva maantee to Old Town (19, 29, 35, 44 etc). Sauna available.

Old House Guesthouse (Map pp70-1; ☎ 641 1464; www.oldhouse.ee; Uus tänav 22; dm/s/d incl breakfast 290/450/650Kr, apt 850-1900Kr; ⊠) This cosy guesthouse with wooden floors and tasteful furnishings offers warm and friendly hospitality in a superb neighbourhood.

A second branch, the **Old House** (Map pp70-1; Uus tänav 26) up the street functions more as a hostel, and has similarly charming features.

Top End

Three Sisters Hotel (Map pp70-1; ☎ 630 6300; www.threesistershotel.com; Pikk tänav 71; s/d from €310/340; ⊠) Offering sumptuous luxury in a lovingly refurbished medieval building, Three Sisters has spacious rooms, each unique but with uniformly gorgeous details, including old-fashioned bathtubs in the rooms, original wooden beams, tiny balconies and canopy beds. Outside of the rooms, there are plenty of romantic nooks to secret yourself on chilly nights: the wine cellar, the fireside seats in the lounge, the inviting library, the warmly lit lounge and the lavish restaurant.

Gloria Guesthouse (Map pp70-1; ☎ 644 6950; www.gloria.ee; Müürivahe 2; s/d from 800/1500Kr; ☒) This small guesthouse has colourful rooms featuring lovely Art-Deco details, and some beautiful antique furnishings (the owner is one of Estonia's biggest antique dealers). Artwork and old-fashioned wallpaper gives a nostalgic feel to these charming rooms. Don't miss the exquisite restaurant and wine cellar downstairs.

Olevi Residents (Map pp70-1; ☎ 627 7650; www.olevi.ee; Olevimägi tänav 4; s/d/ste from €77/103/224; ☒) The unique rooms in this medieval dwelling make for a delightful stay. Among the differing features are antique furnishings, arched ceilings, old oil paintings and those beautiful sea views in top-floor rooms.

Baltic Hotel Imperial (Map pp70-1; ☎ 627 4800; www.baltichotelgroup.ee; Nunne 14; s/d from €122/154; ☒) This small luxury hotel has comfortable, modern rooms in an old stone building with loads of character. Other pluses are the atmospheric lounge, the elegant cheese restaurant (with brown-robed waiters), and the adjoining indoor-outdoor pub.

Sokos Hotel Viru (Map pp70-1; ☎ 680 9300; www.viru.ee; Viru väljak 4; s/d from €115/135; ☒) This high-rise hotel outside Old Town isn't much to look at, but inside the rooms are inviting with hardwood floors, colourful furnishings and excellent views over Old Town.

Taanilinna Hotell (Map pp70-1; ☎ 640 6700; www.taanilinna.ee; Uus 6; economy tw €95, deluxe d €179, standard s/d €124/137; ☒) Set in a converted 19th-century home, this four-star hotel has a range of wood-floored rooms: from cramped economy rooms to modest but cosy standards, to more spacious, tastefully furnished deluxe rooms with tubs in the bathrooms. The restaurant and wine cellar are equally atmospheric.

Reval Hotel Olümpia (Map pp66-7; ☎ 631 5333; www.revalhotels.com; Liivalaia tänav 33; s/d from 2000/2400Kr; ☒) Built for the 1980 Moscow Olympics, this massive 26-storey hotel has modern, comfortable rooms with meticulous service, loads of amenities and enviable views from the top floors. It lies about 700m south of Old Town.

EATING

Tallinn has an enormous variety of cuisine, from Estonian to Thai with French, Italian, Indian and even Japanese options. Headquartered in Old Town, the restaurant scene has unbeatable atmosphere: whether you want to dazzle a date or just soak up the medieval digs alfresco, you'll find plenty of choices. A word to the wise: it's easy to blow a hole in the eating budget; lunchtime specials offer the best deals.

Restaurants

AFRICAN

African Kitchen (Map pp70-1; ☎ 644 2555; Uus tänav 32; meals 70-150Kr; ☒) Featuring authentic African cuisine and a cosy welcoming ambience, African Kitchen has earned many fans since opening in 2005. In summer the upstairs patio is an unbeatable place to linger over a meal, while at night, a festive atmosphere prevails in the loungelike rooms downstairs. Dishes feature flavourings of coconut cream, peanuts and red pepper, and there's a good selection of meat, seafood and vegetarian options.

ESTONIAN

Olde Hansa (Map pp70-1; ☎ 627 9020; Vana Turg 1; meals 75-225Kr) Amid candlelit rooms, with peasant-garbed servers labouring beneath large plates of wild game, Olde Hansa is the place to indulge in a sinfully gluttonous feast. Juniper cheese, forest mushroom soup and exotic meats (such as wild boar and elk) are among the numerous selections available (as well as honey beer). And

THE AUTHOR'S CHOICE

Le Bonaparte (Map pp70-1; ☎ 631 1755; Pikk 43; meals €15-23) The general himself would've been hard-pressed to find fault with this venerable French restaurant in a 17th-century merchant house. The delectable dishes are French with Estonian notes (grilled monkfish wrapped in Parma ham, grilled veal, Hiiumaa eel fillet with eggplant caviar), the service is impeccable and the dining room is restrained but elegant – not unsuitable for captious aristocrats, in other words. There's also a more intimate wine cellar down below and a handsome café (p85) in the foyer.

if the medieval music, communal wooden tables, and thick fragrance of red wine and roast meats sound a bit much, you can take heart – the chefs have done their research in producing historically authentic fare. Besides, where else are you going to see wandering chamber musicians playing 14th-century ballads?

Eesti Maja (Map pp70-1; ☎ 645 5252; Lauteri tänav 1; meals 120-185Kr; 11am-11pm) This fun folksy restaurant is a good place to sample authentic Estonian fare. Traditional favourites such as blood sausage, jellied pork and marinated eel aren't for the timid, but there are plenty of tasty dishes for the unadventurous (salmon, steak etc). There's a small weekday lunch buffet, which is a good place to sample the goods.

Grandma's Place (Map pp70-1; Vanaema Juures; ☎ 626 9080; Rataskaevu tänav 12; meals 140Kr; noon-10pm Mon-Sat, to 6pm Sun) One of Tallinn's most stylish restaurants in the 1930s, this restaurant still rates as a top choice for Estonian fare. The antique dining room is slightly formal, and the menu has plenty of options aside from pigs' feet.

FRENCH

Egoist (Map pp70-1; ☎ 646 4052; Vene tänav 33; meals 160-360Kr) Another of Tallinn's decadents, Egoist has a small menu showcasing the classics of French *haute cuisine*: duck, lamb, wild trout etc, served with panache in a 1600s-era building.

GEORGIAN

Must Lammas (Map pp70-1; ☎ 644 2031; Sauna tänav 2; meals 110-300Kr; noon-11pm Mon-Sat, to 6pm Sun) Preceded by a complimentary shot of house schnapps, meals at Must Lammas are a rewarding experience. Hearty, tasty plates of traditional fare go down nicely with the Georgian wine. Try an entrée of *hatšapuri* (cheese bread) or dolmas (stuffed vine leaves) before diving into a sizzling kebab.

INDIAN

Elevant (Map pp70-1; ☎ 631 3132; Vene tänav 5; meals 120-180Kr) Boasting a wide selection of vegetarian dishes and expertly prepared Indian cuisine, Elevant is an attractive spot for lingering over a meal. The winding wrought-iron staircase, airy furnishings and eclectic rhythms (bossa nova, progressive sitar etc) add to the charm.

Café VS (Map pp70-1; ☎ 627 2627; Pärnu maantee 28; meals 180Kr) The velvet walls, coloured lights and profusion of polished metal may not be a setting you associate with chicken tikka masala, but in fact, this popular bar and late-night spot serves a tasty assortment of Indian cuisine. It's trashy and fun late at night – and you can watch the chefs through the glass wall in the back room.

INTERNATIONAL & FUSION

Angel (Map pp70-1; ☎ 641 6880; Sauna 1; meals 65-90Kr; noon-1am Sun-Tue, to 4am Wed-Sat) One of Tallinn's most ebullient and diverse crowds gathers at this stylish 2nd-floor restaurant just off the beaten path. Exposed brickwork, rich woodwork and a trim loungelike feel provide a warm setting to the small but eclectic menu (salads, pastas and an unbeatable cheeseburger). Best of all, the kitchen stays open late – perfect for those craving chicken curry at 3am some Wednesday night. Adjoining the space downstairs is Tallinn's best gay nightclub, Angel (p87).

Gloria (Map pp70-1; ☎ 644 6950; Müürivahe 2; meals 260-380Kr) Mick Jagger, Pope John Paul II and Jacques Chirac have all eaten here (though presumably not together). What they enjoyed, you can, too: a sumptuous pre-WWII dining room, professional service and savoury dishes such as Estonian lamb with vegetables in puff pastry, blanched Norwegian salmon and duck with mango and raisins. The largest wine cellar in the Baltics is just downstairs (see p86).

Pegasus (Map pp70-1; ☎ 631 4040; Harju 1; meals 123-325Kr; 8am-1am Mon-Fri, 11am-2am Sat) Amid one of the most beautifully designed spaces in town, Pegasus serves eclectic, award-winning dishes such as pan-fried sea bass with truffle sausage and tiger prawn curry, with risottos, salads and grilled meats rounding out the menu. The breakfasts are among Tallinn's best (eggs Benedict, muesli, smoothies), and by night the party people converge. Upstairs rooms (reached via the curving staircase) offer a vibe that's pure lounge, with an attractive crowd checking each other out over brightly coloured cocktails.

Sisalik (Map pp70-1; ☎ 646 6542; Pikk 30; meals 85-240Kr; noon-11pm Mon-Sat) Featuring a diverse Mediterranean menu and a handsome interior, Sisalik is a welcome newcomer to the dining scene. Spanish tapas, grilled tuna, and gnocchi with pesto and cherry tomatoes are among the selections.

Ö (Map pp70-1; ☎ 661 6150; Mere puiestee 6e; meals 135-340Kr; noon-midnight Mon-Sat, 1-10pm Sun) Named after a vowel that exists in few other languages, Ö has certainly carved a unique space in Tallinn's culinary world. The dining room, with its wild chandelier-sculptures and grey and white overtones, is an understated work of art – no less so than the plates of fresh seafood dishes, featuring inventive touches and Asian accents.

St Michael Cheese Restaurant (Map pp70-1; ☎ 627 4845; Nunne 14; meals 260-380Kr; 5pm-midnight) A cheese-lover's paradise, this warmly lit, cosy restaurant features cassock-wearing waiters serving plates of Chateaubriand with feta, basil-and-cheese stuffed rockfish and seafood wok (for the non-cheese-lovers) amid medieval decor.

Charital (Map pp70-1; ☎ 623 7379; Kloostri tee 6; meals 150-350Kr) This lavish dining room boasts a superb setting along the Pirita River (and a fairly crusty clientele). Traditional Euro fare is the norm here, but the lobsters are tops. Upstairs is a more laid-back café, a good stop-off after boating along the river (see p78).

ITALIAN

Bocca (Map pp70-1; ☎ 641 2610; Olevimägi 9; meals 140-340Kr) Sophistication and style don't detract from the fresh, delectable cuisine served at this much-lauded restaurant. Creative dishes such as artichoke soup with grilled scallops, and baked monkfish in creamy fennel sauce with black truffles are matched to a strong wine list. Bocca also has a cosy lounge and bar, where Tallinn's A-list gathers over evening cocktails.

Controvento (Map pp70-1; ☎ 644 0470; Katariina käik; meals 130Kr; noon-11.30pm) Hidden away on Tallinn's most atmospheric alleyway, this longtime favourite serves nicely prepared Italian dishes in a pleasant old-fashioned setting.

JAPANESE

Sushi House (Map pp70-1; ☎ 641 1900; Rataskaevu 16; meals 120-185Kr; 11am-11pm) Boasting a surprising combination of 21st-century chic and 14th-century aesthetics, Sushi House has style in spades. It also serves tender fresh sushi and sashimi as well as *yakitori* (grilled meats), stir-fries, *ramen* (noodles) and some artfully arranged salads. Old wooden rafters, exposed brickwork and other medieval details add to the allure – as does its supposedly haunted past.

RUSSIAN

Troika (Map pp70-1; ☎ 627 6245; Raekoja plats 15; meals from 115Kr) Tallinn's best Russian restaurant is an experience in itself, with wild hunting-themed murals, live accordion music, and an old-style country tavern upstairs. Even if you don't opt for a plate of delicious *pelmeni* (dumplings) or a bowl of heavenly sweet borscht, make sure you stop in for an ice-cold glass of vodka. It's a charming place.

TEX-MEX

Cantina Carramba (Map pp66-7; ☎ 601 3431; Weizenbergi tänav 20a; meals from 100-175Kr) Boasting a delightful pueblo-esque colour scheme and a tasty selection of dishes, Cantina Carramba is ideally placed for a bit of indulgence after a walk in leafy Kadriorg Park. Burritos, fajitas and salads go down oh-so-nicely with the margaritas and Coronas.

Texas Honky Tonk (Map pp70-1; ☎ 631 1755; Pikk 43; meals 80-150Kr; closed Sun) Decked out like an old Texas saloon – complete with creaky wooden floors and the smell of sawdust in the air – this lively restaurant is the best place in Old Town to load up on tacos, burritos, pork ribs and other dishes you wouldn't expect to find this side of the Mason-Dixon Line. Kitschy ambience and a fun crowd.

THAI

Villa Thai (Map pp66-7; ☎ 641 9347; Vilmsi 6; meals 95-250Kr) Villa Thai has a sublimely decorated interior: the use of bamboos, dark woods and richly coloured fabrics is in perfect harmony with the nicely prepared Thai and tandoori specialities.

TURKISH

Sultan (Map pp70-1; ☎ 644 4666; Väikke-Karja 8; meals 70-155Kr) Tasty little platters of Turkish dishes (with Iberian accents) are the specialities at this airy restaurant. Lamb is the focus, though vegetarian options are available. Following the meal, retreat to the downstairs den for a bit of hookah action.

TOP 10 CAFÉS

Forget Paris and Rome – Tallinn's Old Town is so packed with cafés that you can spend your whole trip wandering wide-eyed and jittery from one charming, espresso-scented coffee house to the next. These warm and cosy settings are fine spots to retreat to with a new friend on a chilly afternoon; or if the setting inspires you, have a go at that murder mystery you've been aiming to write.

- **Kehrwieder** (Map pp70-1; ☎ 644 0818; Saiakäiak 1) This little cellar of a café is a perfect spot to stretch out on a couch, read by lamplight and bump your head on those old arched ceilings.
- **Tristan ja Isolde** (Map pp70-1; ☎ 644 8759; Raekoja plats; 🕑 8am-11pm) A java-lovers' dream, this café built into the Town Hall features heavenly scents and a splendid medieval setting.
- **Le Bonaparte** (Map pp70-1; ☎ 646 4444; Pikk tänav 45; 🕑 8am-10pm) Flaky croissants, moist strawberry truffle cake, warm *pain au chocolat* – these are just a few of the reasons why Le Bonaparte ranks as Tallinn's best patisserie. The coffee and tea selections are also splendid, as is the medieval setting in which to enjoy it all. For more indulgence, try dining at the restaurant (p82).
- **Café-Chocolaterie** (Map pp70-1; ☎ 641 8061; Vene tänav 6; 🕑 10am-11pm) Nestled inside a tiny courtyard in Old Town, this inviting café seems like a hideaway at Grandmother's place. Filled with antiques, it also has delectable handmade chocolates – impossible to resist.
- **Café Anglais** (Map pp70-1; ☎ 644 2160; Raekoja plats 14; 🕑 11am-11pm) A favourite with Tallinn's eccentrics and expats, this elegant café has a vaguely Parisian vibe and a delicious assortment of homemade cakes, coffees and light meals (try the warm salads). Despite the location, it somehow eludes the tour-bussing masses.
- **Spirit** (Map pp70-1; ☎ 661 5151; Mere puiestee 6e) This very inviting café and lounge is awash with rich textures: white stonework on the back wall, plush carpets, marble tabletops, a fire in the fireplace, and some poor creature's antlers on the wall. Like a page torn from a fashion mag, Spirit draws the young and fashionable who hold court here regularly. The entrance is at the back.
- **Moskva** (Map pp70-1; ☎ 640 4694; www.moskva.ee; Vabaduse väljak 10; 🕑 9am-midnight Mon-Thu, 9am-4am Fri, 11am-4am Sat, 11am-midnight Sun) An attractive mix of Estonians, Russians and a few straggling out-of-towners gather at this *tres chic* café and nightspot on the edge of Old Town. In addition to cocktails and cappuccinos, Moskva serves *bliny* (small pancakes served with various fillings), salads and other light fare. The upstairs lounge is a slightly swankier place to imbibe, with DJs spinning to young crowds most weekends (cover around 75Kr).
- **Café Peterson** (Map pp70-1; ☎ 662 2195; Narva maantee 15; 🕑 9am-11pm Mon-Sat, 10am-11pm Sun) If you want a dash of culture with your style, head to this charming café outside Old Town. A mix of local residents and students from neighbouring Tallinn Pedagogical University gather here. The café has an art gallery with colourful openings throughout the year, and there's live piano music some nights.
- **Sweet Tooth** (Map pp70-1; Maiasmokk; ☎ 646 4066; Pikk tänav 16; 🕑 8am-7pm Mon-Sat, 10am-6pm Sun) Open since 1864, the city's oldest café still draws a crowd of greying admirers who appreciate the classic décor and pre-WWII feel. The pastries may taste like they were made on opening day, but who cares – the ambience is fantastic!
- **Narva Kohvik** (Map pp70-1; ☎ 660 1786; Narva maantee 10; 🕑 10am-8pm Mon-Sat, to 6pm Sun) Travel back in time to the days of Brezhnev at this unintentionally kitsch coffee house and restaurant outside Old Town. Serving up *stolovaya* (cafeteria) favourites such as sausages, borscht and *plov* (meat and vegetable pilaf), Kohvik Narva offers brusque service, faded brown décor and a heavy dollop of unmitigated Soviet nostalgia. In short, it's the perfect place for brooding when life (or your entrée) has you down. Meals start at 40Kr.

Cafés

See boxed text, p85, for a list of our favourite 10 places to get jazzed. If you'd rather visit 11 or 12, try these instead.

Bogapott (Map pp70-1; ☎ 631 3181; Pikk jalg 9; 🕑 10am-6pm) One of few cafés in Upper Town, Bogapott serves coffee, pastries and fresh sandwiches amid medieval gloom. There's a pleasant courtyard out front, and an art shop and ceramics studio next door.

Café Boulevard (Map pp66-7; ☎ 631 5891; Reval Hotel Olümpia, Liivalaia 33; 🕑 24hr) Situated in Reval Hotel Olümpia and open all hours, this bright and cheery café/patisserie is the place of choice for insomniacs and late-night partygoers. The ambience here is late-Soviet, the crowd is hyped, and the pies and cakes are pure decadence.

Quick Eats

Kompressor (Map pp70-1; ☎ 646 4210; Rataskaevu tänav 3; meals from 45Kr; 🕑 11am-1am Mon-Thu, to 2am Fri-Sun) This popular student hang-out is known for its inexpensive pancakes. By night, the casual but colourful ambience makes a nice detour for a drink.

Pizza Americana (Map pp70-1; ☎ 644 8837; Müürivahe 2; pizzas from 90Kr) Thick, tasty pizzas of every possible permutation are on offer here, including several vegetarian and seafood options. Red booths, blue walls and creamy white milkshakes will take you to the land of Uncle Sam.

Peetri Pizza (pizzas from 80Kr; Mere puiestee Map pp70-1; ☎ 661 6181; Mere puiestee 6; 🕑 11am-10pm; Pärnu maantee Map pp70-1; ☎ 641 8203; Pärnu maantee 22) This chain opened when Estonia broke free from the USSR and so was practically synonymous with freedom. Pizzas are thin-crust and a bit flimsy, but the outfit remains very popular with locals. They also deliver.

Self-Catering

Load up on provisions at the city's best grocery stores.

Tallinna Kaubamaja (Map pp70-1; Gonsiori tänav 2; 🕑 9am-10pm) Inside Viru Keskus.

Stockmann Kaubamaja (Map pp70-1; Liivalaia 53; 🕑 9am-10pm Mon-Fri, to 9pm Sat & Sun)

Rimi (Map pp70-1; Aia tänav 7; 🕑 8am-10pm)

DRINKING

You've probably heard by now that Tallinn has pretty vibrant nightlife. It's also diverse: whether you seek a romantic wine cellar, an uber-chic locals-only lounge or a raucous pub full of pint-wielding punters, you'll find plenty to choose from.

Von Krahli Teater Baar (Map pp70-1; ☎ 626 9096; Rataskaevu tänav 12; live music cover charge 50-75Kr; 🕑 noon-1am Sun-Thu, to 3am Fri & Sat) One of the city's best bars, Von Krahli hosts live bands and the occasional fringe play, and it's a great place to meet some of Tallinn's more interesting locals.

Levist Väljas (Map pp70-1; ☎ 507 7372; Olevimägi 12; 🕑 3pm-3am Sun-Thu, 3pm-6am Fri & Sat) Inside this cellar bar you'll find broken furniture, cheap booze and a refreshingly motley crew of punks, has-beens and anyone else who strays from the well-trodden tourist path.

Stereo (Map pp70-1; ☎ 631 0549; Harju 6) White vinyl is the texture of choice at this painfully stylish club on the edge of Old Town. By night this sleek cubelike interior becomes the backdrop to DJs spinning a mix of global tunes to crowds of style mavens and their poseur friends. Love it or hate it, Stereo is worth checking out – just don't forget your iPod and sunglasses.

A few other stylish places where the beautiful people tend to flock include Spirit (p85), Moskva (p85), Bocca (p84) and Pegasus (p83).

Depeche Mode (Map pp70-1; ☎ 644 2350; Nunne 4; 🕑 noon-4am) For fans of the '80s New Wave band, this is liable to be the holy grail of drinking establishments. The bar itself is small and fairly nondescript – aside from the DM played in heavy (some would say 'endless') rotation. Ask the owner about the time the Essex lads stopped in for a drink back in 2001.

Gloria Wine Cellar (Map pp70-1; ☎ 644 8846; Müürivahe 2) This mazelike wine cellar and tapas restaurant has a number of nooks and crannies where you can secret yourself with a date and/or a good bottle of Shiraz. The dark wood, antique furnishings and flickering candles add to the allure.

Vinoteek V & S (Map pp70-1; ☎ 660 1818; Mere puiestee 6e; 🕑 2pm-midnight Sun-Thu, to 1am Fri & Sat) Boasting fabulous views over Tallinn, this unpretentious wine bar is another enticing setting for a glass (or a bottle).

Scottish Club (Map pp70-1; ☎ 641 1666; Uus 31; 🕑 noon-11pm Mon-Sat) Featuring an extensive whisky menu and plenty of pub fare, this cosy bar and restaurant is a fine place to sit by the fire with single malt or even haggis (sheep offal) in hand. A laid-back crowd meets on the manicured garden terrace in warmer weather.

St Patrick's (Map pp70-1; ☎ 641 8173; Suur Karja 8) One of the dozen or so of its ilk, this lively wooden bar has plenty of beer to go round and the comfy lounge in the adjoining room attracts a surprising number of Estonians. Expect plenty of tourists in the warmer months.

Club Havana (Map ppp70-1; ☎ 640 6630; Pikk 11; ⏲ closed Sun) A few locals and many tourists gather at this Latin-themed bar near Raekoja plats. On weekends you'll find dancing in the back room, deafening music and a raucous, inebriated crowd. For a more local, but no less sedate experience, check out Cafe VS (p83).

ENTERTAINMENT

It's a small capital as capitals go, but there's never a dull moment in Tallinn, whether in a wild club, laid-back bar or concert hall. Buy tickets for concerts and main events at **Piletilevi** (www.piletilevi.ee) and its central locations, including inside Viru Keskus (p89). Events are posted on city centre walls, advertised on flyers found in shops and cafés, and listed in newspapers as well as in *Tallinn in Your Pocket*.

Nightclubs

Club Hollywood (Map pp70-1; ☎ 627 4770; www.club-hollywood.ee; Vana-Posti tänav 8; admission 50-100Kr; ⏲ 10pm-5am Wed-Sat) A multilevel emporium, this one draws the biggest crowds. Plenty of tourists and Tallin's young party crowd mix it up.

Terrarium (Map pp70-1; ☎ 661 4721; www.terrarium.ee; Sadama 6; admission 50-100Kr; ⏲ 10pm-4am Wed-Sat) A more down-to-earth club experience is ensured here, with less attitude than in the posher Old Town clubs. Nevertheless, DJs still kick out the disco and the 20-something crowd laps it up. The outdoor terrace is a big draw – anything can happen in the little pool there.

Privé (Map pp70-1; ☎ 631 0545; Harju tänav 6; admission 100-200Kr; ⏲ 10pm-6am Wed-Sat) Tallinn's most elite club (note the deep-red curtains and oxygen bar) gets rowdiest on Saturdays. Despite the high prices, good DJs attract a beautiful and foreign crowd.

Bon Bon (Map pp70-1; ☎ 661 6080; Mere puiestee 6e; admission 130-150Kr; ⏲ 11pm-4am Fri & Sat) With enormous chandeliers and a portrait of Bacchus, the god of decadence, overlooking the dance floor, Bon Bon is a recent favourite on the club circuit. Friday-night Brazilian fests are the draw.

Be sure to check out dance parties at Moskva (p85) as well.

Gay & Lesbian Venues

Angel (Map pp70-1; ☎ 641 6880; www.clubangel.ee; Sauna 1; admission 75-125Kr; ⏲ 10pm-5am Wed-Sat) Tallinn's best gay club, Angel packs a festive, celebratory crowd. There's a balcony overlooking the dance floor, a men-only dark room and plenty of fine tunes pumping over the dance floor.

X-Baar (Map pp70-1; ☎ 692 9266; Sauna tänav 1; admission free; ⏲ 2pm-1am) The only place in Old Town flying the rainbow flag, X-Baar is Tallinn's oldest gay bar. The miniscule dance floor comes alive late on weekends.

G-Punkt (Map pp70-1; ☎ 688 0747; Pärnu maantee 23; admission free; ⏲ 6pm-1am Sun-Tue & Thu, to 4am Wed, Fri & Sat) Unsigned and hidden in an alley behind Pärnu maantee, this club recalls the secrecy of old Eastern European gay bars. Once inside, however, you'll join the cosy atmosphere, with a steady stream of regulars holding down the small dance floor until late most nights.

Cinemas

Check out what's on at www.superkinod.ee. Films are shown in their original language, subtitled in Estonian and Russian. Tickets cost around 100Kr.

Kino Sõprus (Map pp70-1; ☎ 644 1919; Vana-Posti 8) Set in a magnificent Stalin-era theatre, this art-house cinema has an excellent repertoire of European, local and independent productions.

Kinomaja (Map pp70-1; ☎ 646 4164; Uus tänav 3) Another great art-house cinema.

Coca-Cola Plaza (Map pp70-1; Hobujaama tänav 5) Supermodern 11-screen cinema playing the latest Hollywood releases.

Theatre & Dance

Tallinn has several companies staging productions (including translations of Western plays) from September until the end of May. Everything is in Estonian. A useful website for listings is www.concert.ee.

Estonia Theatre & Concert Hall (Map pp70-1; theatre ☎ 626 0215, concert hall 614 7760, opera 683 1201;

www.concert.ee & www.opera.ee; Estonia puiestee 4; box office noon-7pm Mon-Fri, to 5pm Sat) The premier venue for classical concerts, theatre and opera, this hall also hosts some big-name performers.

City Theatre (Linnateater; Map pp70-1; ☎ 665 0800; www.linnateater.ee; Lai tänav 23) The most beloved theatre in town always stages something memorable. Watch for its summer plays on an outdoor stage.

Estonian Drama Theatre (Map pp70-1; ☎ 680 5555; Pärnu maantee 5) The Estonian Drama Theatre stages mainly classical plays and tends to avoid contemporary fare.

Estonian Puppet Theatre (Eesti Nukuteater; Map ppp70-1; ☎ 667 9555; www.nukuteater.ee; Lai tänav 1) Stages lively and colourful performances – not just for kids!

Von Krahl Theatre (Map pp70-1; ☎ 626 9090; www.vonkrahl.ee; Rataskaevu tänav 10) Known for its experimental and fringe productions.

St Canutus Guild Hall (Map pp70-1; ☎ 646 4704; www.saal.ee; Pikk tänav 20) Tallinn's temple of modern dance also hosts the rare classical dance performance.

Live Music

For major concerts, see what's on at the **Estonia Concert Hall** (Map pp70-1; ☎ 614 7760; www.concert.ee; Estonia puiestee 4).

City Concert Hall (Linnahall; Map pp66-7; ☎ 641 1500; www.linnahall.ee; Mere puiestee 20) Housed in the rather ugly 4200-seat monolith by the harbour, Linnahall hosts pop concerts.

Chamber, organ, solo and a few other smaller-scale concerts are held at several halls around town, such as the Town Hall (p69) and the Brotherhood of the Blackheads (p73), which has concerts almost nightly.

St Nicholas' Church & Concert Hall (Map pp70-1; ☎ 631 4330; Niguliste tänav 3) This church has incredible acoustics, and holds organ and chamber-music concerts at 4pm on Saturdays and Sundays.

Sport

A Le Coq Arena (Map pp66-7; ☎ 627 9940; Asula tänav 4c) About 1.5km southwest of town, this sparkling, newly refurbished arena is home to Tallinn's football team FC Flora, Estonia's largest sporting club. If you have the chance, don't miss a lively match.

Kalev Stadium (☎ 644 5171; Juhkentali tänav 12) Basketball ranks as one of Estonia's most passionately watched games, and the best national tournaments are held in this stadium just south of town.

SHOPPING

Old Town is packed with shops and boutiques selling Estonian-made handicrafts. You'll see leather-bound books, ceramics, jewellery, silverware, hand-blown glassware, objects carved out of limestone, and traditional knitwear. You'll also find a plethora of antique stores selling Soviet memorabilia, old Russian icons and other fantastic curiosities. In addition to that battered airman's jumpsuit, don't forget to bring back a bottle of Vana Tallinn (local liqueur).

Antiques

Whether you're looking for that brass pocket watch with Stalin's profile, the Lenin-head belt buckle or perhaps an old marching uniform, you'll find plenty of Soviet nostalgia buried in Tallinn's antique shops. There are tons of other gems waiting to be unearthed (gramophones, furniture, silverware); you just have to dive in. These are some of our favourite spots:

Antique, Military & Collections (Map pp70-1; ☎ 641 2606; Lai 4; 10am-6pm)

Antiik & Kunst (Map pp70-1; 644 0923; Dunkri tänav 9; 11am-6pm)

Antiik (Map pp70-1; 631 4725; Raekoja plats 11; 10am-6pm Mon-Fri, to 4pm Sat)

Antikvaar (Map pp70-1; 641 8269; Rataskaevu 20; 10am-6pm Mon-Sat)

Handicrafts & Artwork

Madeli Käsitöö (Map pp70-1; ☎ 620 9272; Väike-Karja 1; 10am-6pm Mon-Fri, to 4pm Sat & Sun) This small but delightful shop features a unique selection of regional handicrafts, such as slippers from Muhu.

Domini Canes (Map pp70-1; ☎ 644 5286; Kateriina Käik; 11am-6pm) The ancient craft of glassmaking is kept alive at this lovely gallery workshop. Vases, stemware and stained-glass works are for sale.

Katariina Gild (Map pp70-1; ☎ 641 8054; Kateriina Käik; 11am-6pm) Next door to Domini, this row of workshops is a great place to browse. You'll find ceramics, leather-bound books, quilts and loads more.

Lühikese Jala Galerii (Map pp70-1; ☎ 631 3181; Lühike jalg 6; 10am-6pm Mon-Fri, to 5pm Sat & Sun) Fantastic jewellery, some of which

BOUTIQUES

Tallinn's designers have emerged from the postindependence lull and are slowly carving a niche for themselves in Europe's fashion scene. To see what's hot in the Estonian design world, visit the following stores:

Nu Nordik (Map pp70-1; ☎ 644 9392; Vabaduse Väljak 8; 10am-6pm Mon-Fri, 11am-6pm Sat) Unafraid of the avant-garde, this small boutique has youthful, edgier designs. It's a fun place to browse.

Ivo Nikkolo (Map pp70-1; ☎ 644 4828; Suur-Karja 14; 10am-7pm Mon-Fri, to 5pm Sat, to 4pm Sun) Stylish but staid, Ivo Nikkolo has neat, trim designs made with high-quality fabrics. Nikkolo is one of Estonia's most successful young designers.

Monton (☎ 660 1847; Viru Väljak 4; 9am-9pm) Features a diverse collection of elegant, versatile designs. Like Ivo Nikkolo, Monton keeps things pretty classic, for women as well as men (the suits here are nicely cut). Inside Viru Keskus shopping mall.

Bastion (Map pp70-1; ☎ 644 1555; Viru 12; 10-7pm Mon-Fri, 11am-6pm Sat, 11am-4pm Sun) One of Estonia's most successful fashion houses, Bastion has a small but splashy women's collection, aimed towards an older market.

Hoochi Mama (☎ 641 8866; Viru Väljak 4; 11am-8pm Mon-Thu, 11am-10pm Fri & Sat, noon-6pm Sun) Not just for halter-topped hotties from the Bronx, this youthful boutique has plenty of clubwear and other youthful fashions that run the gamut between the wild, the stylish and the indecent. Inside Viru Keskus shopping mall.

resemble art pieces. There are also ceramics, textiles and glassware.

Navitrolla Galerii (Map pp70-1; ☎ 631 3716; Pikk jalg 7; 10am-6pm Mon-Fri, to 4pm Sat & Sun) Find Navitrolla's fanciful paintings as original artworks or on T-shirts.

Bogapott (Map pp70-1; ☎ 631 3181; Pikk jalg 9; 10am-6pm) Sip coffee (p86) while watching the potters at work.

If that ceramic cup wasn't quite what you had in mind, take a browse around Tallinn's art galleries; see boxed text, p77, for recommendations.

Markets & Second-Hand Stores

Knit Market (Map pp70-1; Müürivahe & Viru; 9am-5pm) Along the Old Town wall, there are a dozen or so vendors selling their handmade linens, scarves, sweaters and socks.

Lai (Map pp70-1; 641 1743; Lai tänav 10; 10am-8pm Mon-Sat) The only second-hand store in Old Town, this funky place occasionally has some good finds – though you'll have to dig. If you collect records, don't miss the back room.

Shopping Malls

Estonia has them, too.

Viru Keskus (Map pp70-1; ☎ 610 1400; Viru Väljak 4; 9am-9pm) Tallinn's shiniest, newest mall lies just outside Old Town.

Tallinna Kaubamaja (Map pp70-1; ☎ 667 3100; Gonsiori 2; 9am-9pm Mon-Sat, 10am-7pm Sun)

Stockmann Kaubamaja (Map pp70-1; ☎ 633 9539; Liivalaia 53; 9am-9pm Mon-Sat, to 8pm Sun)

GETTING THERE & AWAY

This section concentrates on transport between Tallinn and other places in the Baltics. For listings of some useful travel agencies, see p69.

Air

For information on international flights (including helicopters to Helsinki), see p393. **Tallinn Airport** (☎ 605 8888; www.tallinn-airport.ee) is 3km southeast of Old Town on Tartu maantee.

Estonia has limited domestic routes. **Avies Air** (☎ 605 8022; www.avies.ee) flies from Tallinn to Kuressaare on Saaremaa (45 minutes) once or twice daily from Sunday to Friday. It also flies once or twice daily to Kärdla on Hiiumaa (30 minutes).

Boat

See p400 for information about the many services available between Tallinn and Helsinki or Stockholm. Tallinn's sea-passenger terminal (Map pp66–7) is at the end of Sadama, about 1km northeast of Old Town. Trams 1 and 2 and buses 3, 4 and 8 go to the Linnahall stop, by the Statoil Petrol Station (Map pp66–7), five minutes' walk from terminals A, B and C. Terminal D is at the end of Lootsi tänav,

ISLAND ESCAPE

Who says you can't relive your favourite scenes from *The Blue Lagoon* in Nordic Estonia? Sure, it's no Bora Bora, but the country offers its share of lovely shoreline and remote island landscapes. An excellent gateway from Tallinn is to the idyllic settings of Aegna and Naissaar islands.

Tiny **Aegna**, just 3 sq km, has been populated for centuries by local fishermen and, from 1689, postal workers who operated mail boats from there to Sweden via Finland. During Soviet times it was an off-limits military base, but since the 1990s Tallinners have been building summerhouses there or just using it for a quick escape into remote nature. There are some military remnants, an old church and cemetery, remains of a medieval village and long stretches of nearly always deserted beach.

Naissaar, much larger at 44 sq km, has an even livelier history, thick forests (covering 85% of the island), and even a boulder with a circumference of nearly 27m! There's a 19th-century cemetery for English sailors from the Crimean and Russo-Swedish wars, which attests to the island's military history. In fact, Naissaar has been a bulwark for defending the capital since the Great Northern War. A railway was even built before WWI for a speedier build-up of armaments. Curiously, from 1917 to 1918, tsarist troops took the island and tried to form their own government. Soviet military traces remain (the island was closed until 1995), with an old army village, gun batteries, empty mines and deep-sea mine anchors. There are dreamy stretches of unblemished beach and two nature trails: south takes you to historical sights, such as memorials, military ruins, a wooden church from 1856, a cemetery for English sailors from the Crimean (1854–55) and Russo-Swedish (1808–09) wars; north leads through forests, mires and past large 'erratic' boulders. Just up the hill from the dock is the Nature Park Centre where you can get lots of info, a warming coffee and a meal.

The Tallinn Tourist Office (p68) can suggest accommodation on both islands, or contact the **Aegna Hostel** (☎ 510 3653; d from 250Kr). To stay at Naissaar's **Männiku Küla** (camp site 25Kr, s 100-200Kr, d 200-400Kr) or book tours (100Kr) of Naissaar, contact **Naissaare Reisid** (☎ 639 8000).

MS Monika (☎ 5657 7021; www.saartereisid.ee; round trip to Aegna adult/concession 50/35Kr, round trip to Naissaar adult/concession 180/120Kr) has two boats daily (three on Sunday) from Tallin's Linnahall terminal to Aegna (60 minutes). If you come just for the day you'll have eight hours on Aegna.

The boat to Naissaar (60 minutes) also leaves from the Linnahall terminal, and it sails twice daily on Saturdays and Sundays only. If you're day-tripping, you'll have five hours on the island.

Schedules change seasonally, so check the website for the latest.

although there is better access from Ahtri tänav. A taxi between the centre and any of the terminals will cost about 45Kr.

For yachting information, yacht hire and activities contact the Tallinn Olympic Yachting Centre (p77).

Bus

Buses to places within 40km or so of Tallinn depart from the platform next to the **Central Train Station** (Balti Jaam; Map pp70-1). You can get information and timetables from **Harjumaa Liinid** (☎ 641 8218).

For detailed bus information and advance tickets for all other destinations, go to the **Central Bus Station** (Autobussijaam; ☎ 680 0900; www.bussireisid.ee; Lastekodu tänav 46), about 2km southeast of Old Town. Tram 2 or 4 will take you there.

For information regarding bus travel to other countries, see p396. For travel within the Baltic countries see also p404.

Here's the low-down on daily services from Tallinn to other Estonian cities.

Haapsalu 65Kr to 80Kr, 1½ hours, more than 20 buses.
Kärdla 140Kr to 160Kr, 4½ hours, three to five buses.
Kuressaare 170Kr to 195Kr, 4½ hours, eight to 10 buses.
Narva 85Kr to 110Kr, four hours, 15 buses.
Pärnu 80Kr to 115Kr, two hours, more than 20 buses.
Tartu 80Kr to 110Kr, 2½ to 3½ hours, about 30 buses.
Võru 85Kr to 110Kr, 3½ to 4½ hours, eight to 10 buses.

Car & Motorcycle

There are 24-hour fuel stations in the city and on major roads leading to and from Tallinn. The Pärnu maantee Neste (petrol station) has a car-repair service.

Car hire in Tallinn is pricey, around 1000Kr a day. You can hire cars in Tartu or Pärnu instead and save a bundle. The tourist offices in both of those cities have extensive lists of rental agencies.

If you prefer to rent in Tallinn, try one of the following:

Avis (www.avis.ee) Liivalaia tänav (Map pp66-7; ☎ 667 1515; Liivalaia tänav 13/15); Tallinn Airport (☎ 605 8222; Tallinn Airport)
Budget Tallinn Airport (☎ 605 8600; www.budget.ee; Tallinn Airport)
Hertz Tallinn Airport (☎ 605 8923; www.hertz.ee; Tallinn Airport)
R-Rent Tihase (Map pp66-7; ☎ 605 8929; www.rrent.ee; Tihase 34) From 500Kr daily.
Sixt Tallinn Airport (☎ 605 8148; www.sixt.ee; Tallinn Airport)
Tulika Rent Tihase (Map pp66-7 ☎ 612 0012; www.tulika.ee; Tihase 34) From 600Kr daily.

Train

The **Central Train Station** (Balti Jaam; Map pp70-1; ☎ 615 6851; www.edel.ee; Toompuiestee 35) is on the northwestern edge of Old Town, a short walk from Raekoja plats, or three stops on tram 1 or 2, north from the tram stop at the southern end of Mere puiestee.

The Central Train Station has three ticket areas: the main hall, for travel around Estonia; upstairs, for international tickets; and the separate *elektriraudtee* ticket office, next to the train platforms (and just to the right of the R-kiosk) for *elektrirong* (electric trains) within the Tallinn area.

Most Estonians think train travel is antiquated and old-fashioned, hence domestic routes are pretty limited. Here are some places you can still reach by train:
Narva 75Kr, 3½ hours, one daily.
Paldiski 16Kr, 1¼ hours, 10 daily.
Pärnu 50Kr, three hours, two daily.
Tartu 80Kr, 2½ hours, four daily.
Valga 115Kr, 5½ hours, one daily.
Viljandi 65Kr, three hours, two daily.

GETTING AROUND

To/From the Airport

Bus 2 runs every 20 to 30 minutes from terminals A and D at the **Airport-bus Station** (Map pp70–1) via Gonsiori tänav in the centre. From the airport it's just five bus stops to the centre. A taxi to or from the airport should cost about 60Kr.

Public Transport

Tallinn has an excellent network of buses, trams and trolleybuses that usually run from 6am to midnight. Buy *piletid* (tickets) from street kiosks (adult/concession 10/7Kr) or from the driver (15Kr). Validate your ticket using the hole puncher inside the vehicle (or face a 600Kr fine). All public transport timetables are posted on www.tallinn.ee.

Taxi

Taxis are plentiful in Tallinn. Rides are metered and should cost from 5.50Kr to 7Kr per kilometre. However, if you merely hail one on the street, there's a fair chance you'll be overcharged. To save yourself the trouble, order a taxi by phone. Operators speak English; they'll tell you the car number (license plate) and estimated arrival time (usually five to 10 minutes).

Here are some good choices:
Kiisu Takso (☎ 655 0777; per km 5.50Kr)
Krooni Takso (☎ 638 1111; per km 5.50Kr)
Linnatakso (☎ 644 2442; per km 7Kr) It also has vehicles for the disabled.

PEDI-CAB

Throughout central Tallinn, the ecologically sound **Velotakso** (☎ 508 8810) offers rides in egg-shaped vehicles run by pedal power and enthusiasm. Rates are 35Kr for anywhere within Old Town.

Train

Few of the suburban rail services from the central station in Tallinn go to places of much interest in the city. The one line that may be useful heads south to Nõmme, Pääskula and Laagri. There are approximately 40 trains along this line from about 5.30am to midnight. Most continue beyond the city bounds to Keila, Paldiski or Kloogaranna, but some only go as far as Pääskula.

AROUND TALLINN

Countryside and unspoiled coast are not far from Tallinn and there are several places worth making time to visit. All are local telephone calls from the city.

West of Tallinn

Getting There & Away

Buses travelling west along the coast, including 108 and 126 to Rannamõisa, Väna-Viti and Väna-Jõesuu, go from the terminal beside Tallinn's Central Train Station (Balti Jaam). Buses 108, 110 and 136 go from there to Keila-Joa (40 minutes). Call **Harjumaa Liinid** (☎ 641 8218) for timetables and the best buses for your destination. From the Central Train Station 10 trains go to Paldiski

AROUND TALLINN

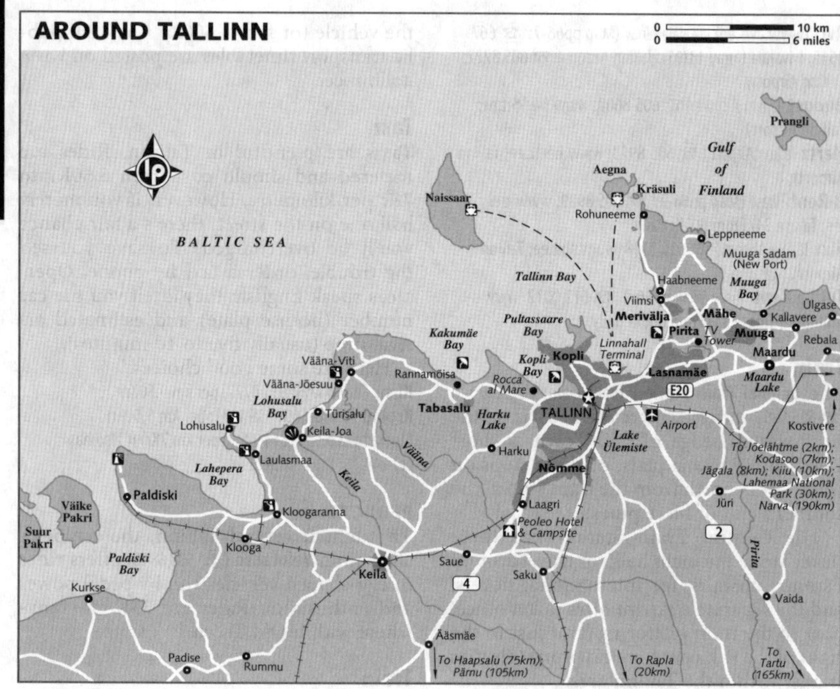

(1¼ hours) via Keila; three trains travel to Kloogaranna.

BEACHES & CLIFFS

The coast west of Tallinn is a favourite summer escape for city folk and the first long, sandy beach is at **Väna-Jõesuu**, 24km from the city centre. From the main coast road it's about 600m down a sidetrack to the beach. The beach continues south across the mouth of the Väna River, where there's a stretch of 30m cliffs, one of the highest on the Estonian coast. The road runs right along the cliff top to a very popular lookout called Türisalu (45m), about 2km after the Naage bus stop (the Russian film version of *Hamlet* was filmed here). There are more beaches further west at **Lohusalu**, and at **Laulasmaa** and **Kloogaranna** on Lahepera Bay, all 35km to 40km from Tallinn.

KEILA-JOA & LAULASMAA

About 30km west of Tallinn, the small village of Keila-Joa near the coast boasts a lovely little **waterfall** (at 6.1m the second highest in the country), with an unrestored manor house (built in 1883) on the edge of the falls. The large park and forest surrounding it make a fine setting for picnicking or hiking (1.7km to the sea). There's a basic restaurant beside the falls, but a more delightful option is **Vana Suvemaja** (☎ 672 3380; Kungla talu; meals 95-150Kr; 🕑 noon-10pm Wed-Sun), about 1km west (on the main road to Laulasmaa) of the falls. This pleasant old cottage serves a range of tasty dishes.

Five kilometres west of Keila-Joa is the area's loveliest hotel, **Laulasmaa Resort** (☎ 687 0815; www.laulasmaa.ee; Puhkekodu 4; s/d from 1240/1490), in the town of Laulasmaa. It has an attractive natural setting overlooking a sandy beach. It boasts nicely designed rooms, a full range of spa services, an indoor pool and stylish 2nd-floor restaurant (meals 75Kr to 225Kr; open 11am to 11pm), complete with outdoor terrace, that makes it a worthwhile stop. Fish soup, spinach gnocchi and flambéed shrimp are among the options.

Another lodging option is the rustic **Laulasmaa Side Holiday Camp** (☎ 672 1989; www.puhkekeskus.ee; tw from 400Kr), with small, pleasant wooden rooms, most with private bathrooms. Kitchen and sauna are available, and you can also join an excursion here. It's located off the Laulasmaa Klooga-ranna road (follow the signs).

If you're camping, you'll find a handful of good RMK camp sites, set right along the beach, about 3km from Laulasmaa, just off the main road heading to Keila-Joa.

PALDISKI

pop 4200

'Welcome to Hell.' Hands down the most surreal place within a day's travel of Tallinn, Paldiski was once the most heavily militarised Soviet base along the Estonian coast. Today you'll find crumbling old barracks, an eerie nuclear submarine station and a decaying town with a feeling of utter desolation. Not sold yet? Paldiski also has an appealing natural setting near some striking limestone cliffs, as well as a bright-red old lighthouse – Estonia's tallest.

But cliffs and lighthouses aside, it's that weird Soviet past that draws most people here. You'll witness one of the grimmest legacies of the former occupiers – as well as postindependence commentary such as the graffiti that's scrawled on one of the abandoned buildings, alerting us that we're not in Kansas anymore.

This area was the first Estonian area to be occupied by Soviet troops in 1939 and was the last to see them leave in 1994. It became the main Soviet naval base in Estonia, and Paldiski was a completely closed nuclear submarine station until 1994; only in 1995 were the decommissioned reactors removed. The reactors functioned continuously from the early 1970s until 1989. In 1994 a civilian died after stumbling upon radioactive materials (allegedly stolen from the disused base) on wasteground near Tallinn.

The most prominent landmark in Paldiski is the submarine training base – the darkly imposing concrete structure visible from anywhere in town. Locals dubbed this the 'Soviet Pentagon' owing to its monumental stature. In its day the building served as the main training facility for submariners throughout the Soviet Union. It is not open to visitors and entering the grounds is not recommended as the facility is guarded and potentially unsafe.

A trip to the **lighthouse** on the northwestern tip (follow the main road straight out of town), leads through destroyed army barracks and missile sheds, where 16,000 soldiers were stationed. The former training sites are deteriorating but the odd bunker and a staircase built into the limestone, with markers showing strata of rock formation on the exposed sides of the cliff, are still visible.

Paldiski's only hotel – and its only restaurant (meals from 90Kr) – is the **White Boat** (Valge Laev; ☎ 674 2095; www.valgelaev.ee; Räe tänav 32; s/d from 450/860Kr). Set on the main street, this nautically themed place has clean, nicely maintained rooms with big windows. Oil paintings of ships at sea add to the décor.

PADISE

At Padise, about 15km south of Paldiski on a back road between Tallinn and Haapsalu, is an atmospheric Cistercian monastery and cemetery dating back to the 13th century. It was damaged in the Livonian War in the 16th century and again in a 1766 fire. Padise is 4km west of Rummu (the site of Estonia's best-known prison), on the Haapsalu–Rummu–Keila–Tallinn bus route.

East of Tallinn

Getting There & Away

The Maardu area is served by city buses 183, 184 and 186, which leave from the Kivisilla stop, a block east of the Gonsiori tänav bus stop. Buses also occasionally leave from the train station. To reach Ülgase, take any of these buses to Kallavere, then change to bus 185. Call **Harjumaa Liinid** (☎ 641 8218) to find the best route for your destination and for information on buses headed further east.

From the bus stop next to the train station, take bus 134 to Jägala (one hour), or bus 151, 152 or 155 to Kiiu (one hour). Bus 143, departing from near the train station, will go through Jõelähtme (45–55 minutes); a small visitor centre with a large information symbol by the highway marks the site of the burial cysts.

MAARDU & REBALA RESERVE

On Tallinn's eastern border, the Tallinn–Narva highway crosses the Maardu area, which is partly an industrial wilderness thanks to phosphate mining and other industries that raged unchecked here in the Soviet era. Phosphate mining in Estonia was stopped in 1991.

As early as 1987, a 25 sq km area to the east and south of Maardu Lake (which lies beside the highway) was declared the **Rebala Reserve** (☎ 603 3097). There are 300 archaeological sites here, with traces of historic and prehistoric settlements and cultures (the oldest are about 5000 years old).

Within the reserve is the Maardu Manor, an 18th-century building that stands on the site where the original manor was built in 1379. There are also sites of pre-Christian cults and 'sliding rocks' said to cure infertility in women who slide down them bare-bottomed. If you want to give the rocks a try, they are just south of **Kostivere** village, a few kilometres from the main highway.

At Jõelähtme a number of late-Bronze-Age stone burial cysts lie beside Peterburgi maantee around 30 minutes by bus from Tallinn, on the main route to Narva. Inside the visitor centre adjoining the site (and posted outside for after-hours visitors) you can find details of the graves, their origins and objects found during excavations.

The **Wolf Piles** near Muuksi, east of Jõelähtme towards Lahemaa, is also a couple of kilometres off the Tallinn–Narva highway. It's the site of approximately 80 more burial chambers, the largest concentration in Estonia.

JÄGALA, ÜLGASE & KIIU TORN

There's a northbound turn-off from the Tallinn–Narva highway leading towards **Jägala**, the site of 'Estonia's Niagara Falls', the country's largest waterfall (7.2m), with the waters of the Jägala River tumbling over pretty limestone banks. On your way, you'll pass under a triple-arched stone bridge from the 19th century.

Several abandoned phosphate mines have been preserved in **Ülgase**, near the coast, north of Rebala village. The area between Ülgase and the highway is vast industrial wasteland, with eerie mountains of soil.

Kiiu Torn (☎ 607 3434; Kiiu; adult/concession 5Kr/free; ⏲ 10am-8pm), housed in the smallest fortress in Estonia, 6km east of Maardu on the Narva road, was built in the 16th century. The four-storey tower was restored in 1975 and is now a cute little restaurant. A popular sweet egg liqueur is named after this fortress.

NORTHEASTERN ESTONIA

The crown jewel of Estonia's national parks, Lahemaa occupies an enormous place – literally and figuratively – when talk of the northeast arises. Lahemaa, the 'land of bays', comprises a pristine coastline of rugged beauty, lush inland forests teeming with wildlife, and sleepy villages scattered along its lakes, rivers and inlets. Visitors are well looked after here: there are cosy B&Bs, remote camp sites along the sea and an extensive network of pine-scented forest trails.

The park lies about one-third of the way between Tallinn and the Russian border. Travelling beyond the park's eastern borders, the bucolic landscape slowly transforms into an area of ragged, industrial blight. The scars left by Soviet industry are still visible in towns such as Kunda, home to a mammoth cement plant; Kohtla-Järve, the region's centre for ecologically destructive oil-shale extraction; and Sillamäe, once privy to Estonia's very own uranium processing plant. Before reaching for that biohazard suit, however, visitors should know that despite lingering pollution in some areas, the region has vastly improved in the last decade. Those willing to take the time will find some rewarding sites here, including the youthful up-and-coming city of Rakvere, the picturesque limestone cliffs around Ontika, some enchanting castle ruins and the curious spectacle of the seaside city of Sillamäe, a living monument to Stalinist-era architecture. The most striking city of this region is Narva, with its majestic castle dating back to the 13th century.

For those seeking a taste of Russia without the hassle of visas and border crossings, northeastern Estonia makes an excellent alternative. The vast majority of residents here are native Russians, and you'll hear Russian spoken on the streets, in shops and in restaurants; and you'll have plenty of opportunities to snap photos of lovely Orthodox churches, frightening communist-bloc high-rises and other legacies left behind by Estonia's mystifying eastern neighbours.

National Parks

In addition to the very worthwhile Lahemaa National Park, Northeastern Estonia

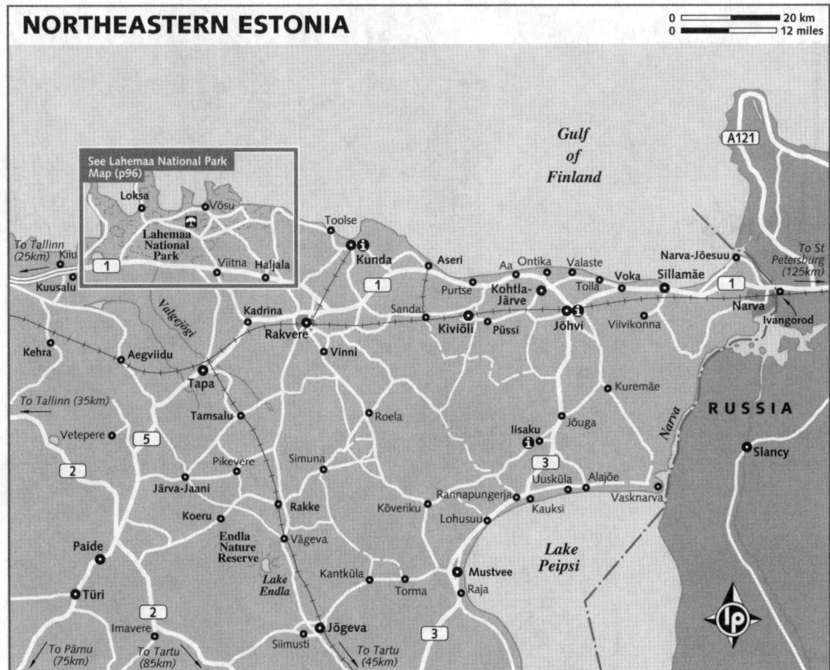

also contains the more modest Endla Nature Reserve, a fine place for a bog walk.

Getting There & Away

Unfortunately, bus travel is infrequent between Tallinn and towns inside Lahemaa. Hiring a car is the best way to reach and explore the many different areas inside the park. From Tallinn to Narva or Rakvere, there are numerous daily buses, as well as trains (see p89).

Getting Around

Lahemaa National Park is spread out and not well served by public transport. You can try hitching inside the park or getting around by bicycle, but bus isn't recommended. Elsewhere in the region, buses will be your best means of getting around.

LAHEMAA NATIONAL PARK

Estonia's largest *rahvuspark* (national park), Lahemaa is an alluring, unspoiled section of rural Estonia with varied coastal and inland scenery. It takes in a stretch of deeply indented coast with several peninsulas and bays. There are 475 sq km of forested hinterland, including 14 lakes, eight rivers and four waterfalls, plus 250 sq km of marine area.

The natural attractions of the coast, forests, lakes, rivers and bogs encompass many areas of historical, archaeological and cultural interest. About 24% of the park is human-influenced, 68% is forest or heath and 8% is bog. Roads traverse the park from the Tallinn–Narva highway to the coast, with a few parts accessible by bus. Walking, hiking and cycling trails encourage exploration of a more active kind.

Around 300,000 people now visit the Lahemaa National Park every year, but only a small number go out of season, when the park is transformed into a magical winterland of snowy shores, frozen seas and sparkling black trees.

Geography & Geology

The landscape is mostly flat or gently rolling, with the highest point just 115m above sea level. Geologically, much of the park is on the North Estonian limestone plateau, the

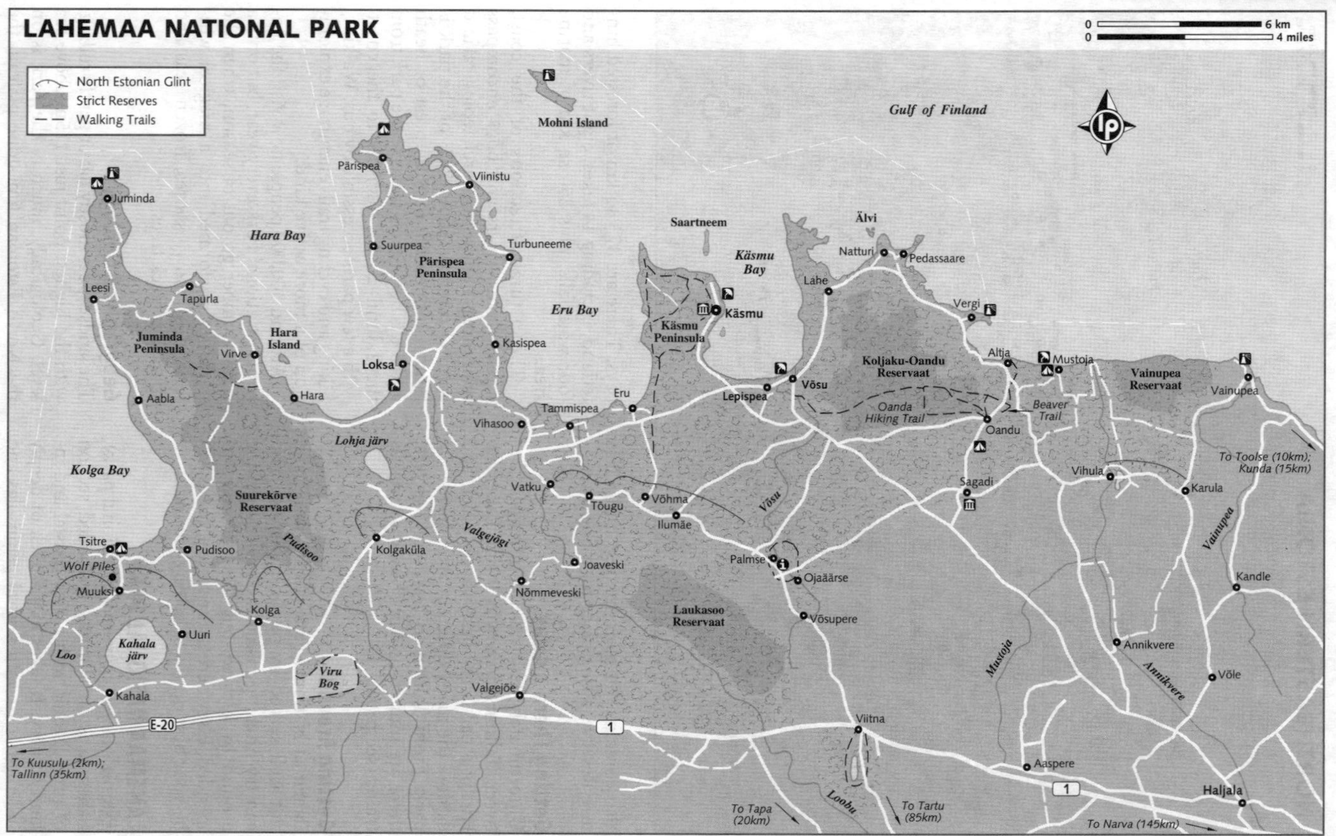
LAHEMAA NATIONAL PARK
0 6 km
0 4 miles
North Estonian Glint
Strict Reserves
Walking Trails
Gulf of Finland
Mohni Island
Saartneem
Älvi
Käsmu Bay
Eru Bay
Hara Bay
Kolga Bay
Hara Island
Juminda Peninsula
Pärispea Peninsula
Käsmu Peninsula
Koljaku-Oandu Reservaat
Vainupea Reservaat
Laukasoo Reservaat
Suurekõrve Reservaat
Oanda Hiking Trail
Beaver Trail
Viru Bog
Wolf Piles
Kahala järv
Lohja järv
Pudisoo
Valgejõgi
Võsu
Mustoja
Annikvere
Vainupea
Loobu
Loo
Juminda
Leesi
Tapurla
Aabla
Virve
Hara
Loksa
Pärispea
Suurpea
Viinistu
Turbuneeme
Kasispea
Vihasoo
Tammispea
Eru
Käsmu
Lepispea
Võsu
Lahe
Natturi
Pedassaare
Vergi
Altja
Mustoja
Vainupea
Oandu
Sagadi
Vihula
Karula
Annikvere
Võle
Kandle
Haljala
Aaspere
Viitna
Võsupere
Ojaäärse
Palmse
Ilumäe
Võhma
Tõugu
Vatku
Joaveski
Nõmmeveski
Valgejõe
Kolgaküla
Kolga
Pudisoo
Uuri
Tsitre
Muuksi
Kahala
E-20
1
To Kuusulu (2km); Tallinn (35km)
To Tapa (20km)
To Tartu (85km)
To Narva (145km)
To Toolse (10km); Kunda (15km)

northern edge of which, stretching east–west across the park, forms a bank up to 65m high, known as the North Estonian Glint, which forms part of the Baltic Glint (see p59). The highest parts are inland and therefore barely visible. In Lahemaa, the glint is most visible at Muuksi, where it is 47m high, but only 23m above ground level. At Nõmmeveski and Joaveski, rivers flowing over the bank become waterfalls.

Stone fields, areas of very thin topsoil called 'alvars', and large rocks called 'erratic' boulders, brought from Scandinavia by glacial action, are typically Estonian. There are as many as 50 large boulders in the country – eight in Lahemaa. The biggest one (580 cubic metres) is the House Boulder (Majakivi), while the Tammispea boulder is the highest at 7.8m. The best known stone field is on the Käsmu Peninsula.

Wildlife

Almost 850 plant species have been found in the park, including 34 rare ones. There are 50 mammal species, among them brown bear, lynx and American mink – none of which you're likely to see without specialist help. Some 222 types of birds, including mute swan, black stork, black-throated diver and crane, nest here, and 24 species of fish have been sighted. Salmon and trout spawn in the rivers. Check out www.estonica.org for more wildlife info.

History

When it was founded in 1971, Lahemaa was the first national park in the Soviet Union. Though protected areas existed before that, the authorities believed that the idea of a national park would promote incendiary feelings of nationalism. Sly lobbying (including a reference to an obscure decree signed by Lenin which mentioned national parks as an acceptable form of nature protection) and years of preparation led to eventual permission. Latvia and Lithuania founded national parks in 1973 and 1974 respectively, but it wasn't until 1983 that the first one was founded in Russia.

Information

Lahemaa National Park Visitor Centre (Lahemaa Rahvuspark Külatuskeskus; ☎ 329 5555; www.lahemaa.ee; 🕒 9am-7pm May-Aug, 9am-5pm Sep, 9am-5pm Mon-Fri Oct-Apr) is located in Palmse, 8km north of Viitna in the southeastern part of the park. Here you'll find helpful staff members, the essential map of Lahemaa, as well as information on hiking trails, island exploration and guide services. Staff can also book accommodation for you. It's worth contacting them before heading out.

Sights

PALMSE

The restored **manor house** (☎ 329 5555; adult/concession 40/25Kr; 🕒 10am-7pm May-Sep, to 3pm Oct-Apr) and park at Palmse, 8km north of Viitna, is the showpiece of Lahemaa. In the 13th century a Cistercian monastery occupied the land, and it was later developed as a private estate by a Baltic-German family (the von der Pahlens) who ran the property from 1677 until 1923 (when it was expropriated by the state).

Fully restored to its former glory, the manor house, dating from the 1780s, contains period furniture and fittings. Other estate buildings have also been restored and put to new use: the *ait* (storage room) is a summer exhibition hall; the *viinavabrik* (distillery) houses a hotel and restaurant (see p99); the *kavaleride maja* (house of Cavaliers), once a summer guesthouse, is now a souvenir and book shop; and the *supelmaja* (bathhouse), which overlooks a pretty lake, is now a charming café (see p100).

BEACHES, PENINSULAS & COASTAL VILLAGES

With their long sandy beaches, the small coastal towns of **Võsu** and, to a lesser extent, **Loksa**, are popular seaside spots in summer. During peak season Võsu fills up with young revellers, which can detract from the park's natural beauty. There are also good beaches at **Käsmu** (Captains' Village), an old sailing village across the bay from Võsu; and between **Altja** and **Mustoja**. A scenic hiking and biking route runs east along the old road from Altja to **Vainupea**.

Several peninsulas that make for lovely exploration include **Juminda** and **Pärispea**. Juminda has an old 1930s **lighthouse** at its northern tip; nearby is a WWII monument to the several thousand civilians who were killed (by mines and German ships) trying to flee Estonia in 1941.

The former Soviet coastguard barracks at Käsmu now shelters the **Sea Museum** (Käsmu

Meremuuseum; ☎ 323 8136; Merekooli tee 4; adult/concession 10/5Kr; 9am-7pm). In the 1920s a third of all registered boats in Estonia belonged to this village; at one time there were 62 long-distance captains living here. From 1945 to 1991 the entire national park's coastline was a military-controlled frontier, with a 2m-high barbed wire fence ensuring villagers couldn't access the beach or sea. The museum has photographs and memorabilia tracing the history of the village and exhibits on marine life from the area. It also hosts the **Viking Days** festival in August, when Vikings of all nations congregate for a bloodless battle.

The fishing village of Altja was first mentioned in 1465, though today no building older than 100 years is left. The park has reconstructed traditional net sheds here and set up an open-air museum of stones along the protected coastline. Altja's Swing Hill (Kiitemägi), complete with traditional Estonian swings, has long been the centre of Midsummer's Eve festivities in Lahemaa. Other coastal villages with an old-fashioned flavour are **Natturi** and **Virve**.

ISLANDS

Until 1992 **Hara Island** was a Soviet submarine base and hence a closed area. Soviet-era maps of the park did not mark the island. During the 1860s, Hara enjoyed a successful sprat industry and about 100 people worked there. If you're interested in a trip over, the visitor centre can help find someone to take you. When the water's low enough, you can walk (check with the visitor centre for best times).

When waters are low it's also possible to walk to **Saartneem** and **Älvi**, two other small islands. Again, check with the centre before rolling up your trousers. Älvi is a strictly protected nature reserve and Saartneem is only open to visitors from mid-July, after the bird nesting season is finished.

From **Viinistu** it's possible to cross over to **Mohni Island**, and guided tours (see opposite) are available.

LAKES, TOMBS & MANORS

Although technically outside the park, there are three lakes near **Viitna** that make lovely settings for a swim or hike along the pine-covered shoreline.

Old farm buildings still stand in villages such as **Muuksi**, **Uuri**, **Vatku**, **Tõugu** and **Võhma**. On the small hill of Tandemägi, near Võhma, four stone tombs from the 1st century AD and earlier have been reconstructed after excavation.

There are more old German manors at **Kolga**, **Vihula,** and **Sagadi**, the most impressive of the bunch. Now fully restored, Sagadi Manor houses a **Forest Museum** (☎ 325 8888; adult/concession incl entry to manor 30/10Kr; 11am-6pm Tue-Sun 15 May-30 Sep, by appt 1 Oct-14 May), with exhibits on the park's flora and fauna. The collection of chainsaws and hunting rifles is impressive indeed. On the grounds is a decent hotel.

The classical-style manor house at **Kolga** dates from the end of the 17th century but was largely rebuilt in 1768 and 1820, and is long overdue for restoration. It currently houses a restaurant and hotel.

Activities

BIKING

Lahemaa is a splendid place to ride. You can work up a sweat along forest-lined roads, then take a dip in a lake or in the sea. The Sagadi Manor rents mountain bikes (150Kr per day). The Kolga Manor rents for similar prices but only to guests.

HIKING

Some excellent hikes course through the park's diverse landscapes. Pick up maps and trail info from the visitors centre.

Altja 3.5km circular trail beginning at 'Swing Hill' on the coast at Altja, taking in traditional net sheds and fishing cottages, and the open-air museum of stones.

Beaver Trail 1.7km trail, 900m north of Oandu; a beautiful trek past beaver dams, although you're unlikely to see the shy creatures.

Käsmu 8.5km circuit from Käsmu village, taking in coast, pine forest, 'erratic' boulders and the Lake Käsmu (Käsmujärv); a longer route takes you to Eru.

Majakivi 3.5km trail on the Juminda Peninsula taking in the 7m-high Majakivi boulder.

Oandu 4.7km circular trail, 3km north of Sagadi, that is perhaps the park's most interesting. Note the trees that wild boars and bears have scratched, bark eaten by irascible moose, and pines scarred from resin-tapping.

Viitna Three paths (2km, 4km and 7km) that take in the lakes and forest shaped by glacier. Just south of busy Viitna bus stop.

Viru Rapa 3.5km trail across the Viru Bog, starting at the first kilometre off the road to Loksa off the Tallinn–Narva highway; look for the insectivorous sundew (Venus flytrap, Charles Darwin's favourite plant).

HORSE RIDING

Kuusekännu Riding Farm (Kuusekännu Ratsatalu; ☎ 325 2942; www.kuusekannu.maaturism.ee) arranges horse riding for all levels, and trail rides through Lahemaa. Sample trips: a six-hour ride to Lahemaa Streams passing two waterfalls (€55), a two-day trek to Altja coastal village (€157). Prices include the ride, meals and accommodation in a guesthouse. To reach the farm, head 68km east of Tallinn along the Tallinn–Narva highway. Take the turn-off to Tapa city, drive 300m and turn right at the first intersection, then follow the signs to the farm. Be sure to call before showing up.

Tours

The Lahemaa National Park Visitor Centre keeps lists of guides operating in the park. Contact the centre far in advance, as many guides get completely booked out during the summer. **Anne Kurepalu** (☎ 323 4100; anne@phpalmse.ee) arranges tours through the fragile ecosystem of Mohni Island.

Sleeping

Käsmu, set near a tiny beach, has plenty of low-key B&Bs. If you want rowdier beach action, head to Võsu, a popular summertime hang-out for Estonian students. Other guesthouses are sprinkled throughout the region. The Lahemaa National Park Visitor Centre in Palmse can arrange accommodation. Also, many small guesthouses have dogs (big ones). Keep that in mind before vaulting over fences.

Merekalda B&B (☎ 323 8451; www.merekalda.ee; Neeme tee 2, Käsmu; d with private bathroom 550-750Kr, 2-person cabin with shared bathroom 220Kr, apt 1100Kr) You'll have to book early if you want a spot in this peaceful B&B by the sea. Rooms are elegant, some with balconies and sea views. Cabins are more rustic (summer only) with shared bathrooms. There are also four attractive two-room apartments with kitchens. Sauna and boat hire are available.

Uustula B&B (☎ 325 2965; Neeme tee 78, Käsmu; camp site per person 25Kr, d 600Kr) Also in Käsmu, at the end of the road/start of the hiking trail, this quaint B&B has four simple, pleasant wooden rooms (three have bathrooms inside, one is outside the room). B&B guests can use the kitchen. Campers can pitch a tent on the grassy lawn. It offers bike rental and a sauna.

Postimaja Hostel (☎ 529 2722; rakvere@post.ee; Mere 63, Võsu; s/d 400/500Kr) Set back from the main street in Võsu, this bright-yellow house has trim and tidy rooms, some with balconies. Kitchen use, sauna (150Kr per hour).

Toomarahva Tourist Farm (☎ 325 2511; Altja; d 500Kr, camp site per person 25Kr) This friendly place has several handsome wooden ensuite cabins and a yard for camping. It's on the main road in Altja, just beyond the Altja Kõrts restaurant.

Hara Guesthouse (☎ 607 7323; www.aivel.ee; Hara; camp site 50Kr, r per person 260Kr) Along the main road in Hara (not the island but the town facing it), this countrified house has small wood-panelled rooms with shared bathrooms. There's a kitchen, a sauna and a billiards table. It's 150m to a sandy beach.

Viitna Holiday Centre (☎ 329 3651; camp site per person 25Kr, d from 240Kr) Overlooking a pretty lake, this place has rustic wooden cabins surrounded by forest. Several rooms have private bathrooms, but most share facilities. You can also pitch a tent. It's located in Viitna, about 600m east of the bus stop on the Tallinn–Narva highway (look for the 'Viitna Landscape Reserve' sign). It also has a beautiful lakeside sauna, which costs 270Kr for three hours.

Ojaärse Holiday Home (☎ 628 1532; www.rmk.ee; dm 225Kr) Run by RMK, this handsome converted 1850s farmhouse has tidy rooms with two to 10 beds each. There's a small lake (sometimes algae-covered) on the property. There's a guide service, a kitchen, and a sauna (250Kr per hour). Travelling from Palmse to Sagadi, it's signposted on the right. It's essential to book in advance (sometimes closed).

Park Hotel Palmse (☎ 322 3626; www.phpalmse.ee; s/d 690/890Kr) This hotel offers pristine and pine-fresh rooms inside the Palmse Manor distillery; book well ahead as it's favoured by groups.

Sagadi Manor (☎ 325 8888; sagadihotell@rmk.ee; dm from 200Kr, hotel s/d from 700/900Kr) In Sagadi, this restored governor's house offers charming quarters amid grand surroundings. The adjoining hostel with spotless rooms is a good, affordable option. Bike rental; sauna.

Kolga Mansion (☎ 607 7477; www.kolgahotell.ee; s/d with private bathroom 600/900Kr, with shared bathroom from 400/600Kr) Set on the grounds of a rundown manor, this guesthouse, formerly occupied by lucky horses, has pleasant wood-floored rooms amid lots of greenery. It has a restaurant, and also rents out bikes (guests only).

The camping is simply fantastic in Lahemaa, with lots of free RMK-administered camp sites. You will find them near Tsitre at Kolga Bay, at the northern tip of Juminda and Pärispea peninsulas, on the Mustoja–Vijula road near the bridge in a river bend, and by the Sadi–Altja road, 300m south of the Oandu trail. When looking for these sites, keep your eyes peeled for the small wooden signs with the letters 'RMK'. All camp sites (free RMK ones and private ones) are marked on the excellent *Lahemaa Rahvuspark* map available in the visitor centre.

Eesti Karavan (☎ 324 4665; caravan site 100Kr; ⌚ May-Aug) In Lepispea, 1km from Võsu; 100 caravan places.

Eating

Café Isabella (☎ 322 3626; meals 40-85Kr) In the grounds of Palmse Manor, this elegant café overlooks a swan-filled lake. Skip the mains (sausages etc) and concentrate on coffee, rhubarb cake and those idly floating birds.

Sagadi Manor (☎ 325 8888; meals 80-160Kr) This pleasant restaurant on the 2nd floor of the manor serves a decent selection of international fare (salmon soup, duck fillet, risotto with vegetables).

Võsu Kõrts (☎ 516 5115; Jõe 3, Võsu; meals 70-200Kr; ⌚ 11am-midnight) Võsu's best restaurant is a fine wooden tavern with indoor/outdoor seating. Smoked-fish salad, roasted codfish and grilled lamb are among the choices. Live music some nights.

> **THE AUTHOR'S CHOICE**
>
> **Altja Kõrts** (Altja; meals 50-130Kr; ⌚ 11am-11pm) Set in an old wooden farmhouse with a thatched roof and traditionally attired waiters, this charming place serves delicious plates of home cooking. Cauliflower soup, salmon pie (the best!) and omelettes can't be beaten. Follow it up with fresh blueberry pie (in season). The menu is posted in Estonian, but the staff will gladly translate. It's on the main road leading into Altja, overlooking a yard full of swings.

Viitna Kõrts (☎ 325 8681; tavern ⌚ 7.30am-8pm, restaurant ⌚ noon-11pm; meals from 60Kr) Almost opposite the eastbound bus stop at Viitna is this reconstruction of an 18th-century tavern serving a bare-bones buffet, with a more peaceful restaurant next door.

Võsu Grill Baar (☎ 325 8681; Mere 49, Võsu; meals 70-200Kr; ⌚ noon-11pm) Remains popular despite the basic fare: chicken, Wiener schnitzel, salmon.

If you're camping, you can load up on your provisions at the small, crowded **food shop** (⌚ 9am-9pm) in Võsu or in Loksa at the much bigger **Loksa Kauplus** (⌚ 9am-10pm) store on the main road. There's a simple café next door.

If you're staying at a tourist farm, don't bypass the traditional home cooking. Just ask your host in advance.

Getting There & Away

Visit www.bussireisid.ee for bus timetables.

PALMSE

From Tallinn there are one or two buses daily to Palmse (80Kr, 1½ to 2½ hours).

VIITNA

There are 19 buses daily from Tallinn to Rakvere, which stop at Viitna (50Kr, one hour). To go from Narva to Viitna take a bus to Rakvere (80Kr to 95Kr, about seven daily) and then a bus to Viitna (20Kr, 18 daily). From Tartu there's a bus to Võsu, stopping at both Viitna and Palmse (80Kr, 2½ hours).

VÕSU & KÄSMU

There are six buses daily from Tallinn to Võsu (55Kr to 85Kr, 1½ to 2½ hours), one of which goes on to Käsmu (40Kr, 1¼ to 1½ hours). A bus also connects Viitna and Käsmu, but runs only once daily, four days per week.

Getting Around

A car is extremely handy for getting around; this is also a great cycling region, though distances between points can be great. Hiking and cycling routes are marked in blue and red respectively; maps and trail information are available from the visitor centre. Some tourist farms and hotels rent out bikes. See p98 for information on renting bicycles.

You can also rent a bike in Tallinn and take it on the bus to Viitna as cargo.

You can also use the buses running to the coastal villages to get around the park, though these are infrequent. Ask at the visitor centre for the latest schedule.

EAST OF LAHEMAA

The territory from Lahemaa to the Russian border at Narva has for decades been Estonia's main industrial corridor. Oil shale, used in power generation, comes from the region, and for years its by-product of sulphur dioxide has been the largest pollutant in Estonia.

Aside from marvelling at the destruction wreaked upon the landscape, there are other things you can do here: explore the headland castle (p102) at Toolse, photograph the handsomely wrought Stalinist architecture of Sillamäe (p103), make an offering at the Russian Orthodox convent of Pühtitsa (p104), and get a taste of Russian history in Narva (p103). The biggest surprise in this region is Rakvere, a city with some stylish cafés and restaurants, and a fantastic castle perched on a hill.

If you're travelling in this rarely visited corner, you'll be among a handful of Western pioneers. Most visitors are Russians who come for a soak in one of the institutional sanatoriums in Narva-Jõesuu or a holiday along the northern shores of Lake Peipsi. Many Estonians are wary of this predominantly Russian-speaking area, but don't let them scare you off – see it with your own eyes first.

Rakvere

pop 17,000

Set with a magnificent castle – and very large bull sculpture – Rakvere is a small city, the tiny centre of which contains pleasant streets, nicely manicured parks and a lively, youthful population. In addition to the castle there are a few museums and historic churches, but the real charm of this town lies in simply strolling the streets.

Your first stop should be the **tourist information office** (☎ 324 2734; www.rakvere.ee; Laada 14; 🕑 9am-6pm Mon-Fri, 10am-3pm Sat & Sun May 15-Sep 14, 10am-5pm Mon-Fri Sep 15-May 14), where you can pick up a town map and walking-tour guide from the affable staff. It's located a block south of the main square.

SIGHTS & ACTIVITIES

Rakvere's star attraction, **Rakvere Castle** (☎ 322 5500; www.svm.ee; Tallinna 3a; adult/concession 40/25Kr; 🕑 11am-7pm Jun-Aug, 11am-5pm Wed-Sun Sep-May) was built by the Danish in the 14th century, though the hillside has served many masters over its 700 years: Danes, Russians, Swedes and Poles. The fortress was badly damaged in the battles of the 16th and 17th centuries and later turned into an elaborate manor in the late 1600s. Extensive reconstruction was completed in 2004, and today the castle contains exhibits related to its medieval history with medieval-style amusement that's aimed mostly towards small children (make a candle, make a nail at the blacksmiths, pony rides), though the adults can try their hand at archery. Don't miss the medieval torture chamber. Concerts and plays are held at the castle in summer; ask at the tourist information office to see what's on.

In front of the castle is Rakvere's other icon – a massive seven-ton **bull statue**, which was completed by local artist Tauno Kangro to commemorate the city's 700th-year anniversary.

In town, the **Rakvere Museum** (☎ 322 5503; Tallinna 3; adult/concession 15/10Kr; 🕑 10am-5pm Thu-Sat), housed in a late-18th-century building, contains modest expositions related to the town's history. A few blocks south, on one of Rakvere's most historical streets, is the interesting **Citizen's House Museum** (☎ 322 5503; Pikk 50; adult/concession 10/5Kr; 🕑 10am-5pm Thu-Sat). Displays here show what an early-20th-century apartment looked like; several workshops tap into Rakvere's rich artisan tradition.

SLEEPING

Hotell Wesenbergh (☎ 322 3480; www.wesenbergh.ee; Tallinna tänav 25; s/d 600/890; ⊠) Rakvere's best hotel has comfortable, modern rooms with wooden floors.

Katariina Kelder (☎ 322 3943; www.katariina.ee; Pikk tänav 3; d with private/shared bathroom 550/400Kr; ⊠) This small well-located guesthouse has decent rooms and friendly staff. There's a restaurant on the ground floor.

EATING

Art Café (☎ 325 1710; Lai tänav 13; meals 45-65Kr; 🕑 9am-11pm Mon-Fri, 11am-10pm Sat & Sun) This stylish space features a loungelike interior with an outdoor patio in back. Serving eclectic fare, this café is a good spot for a drink in the evening.

Berlini Trahter (☎ 322 3787; Lai tänav 15; meals 60-90Kr; 🕑 11am-midnight) Facing the main square, this old wooden pub is a Rakvere favourite for its cosy ambience and tasty international fare. Live music Saturdays.

Virma (☎ 322 3907; Tallinna tänav 8; meals around 70Kr; 🕑 11am-midnight Mon-Sat) This handsome pub serves up a mix of Thai and Chinese fare. Live music on Friday and Saturday nights.

Old Victoria (☎ 322 5345; Tallinna tänav 27; meals 90-150Kr; 🕑 11am-midnight Mon-Sat) Amid antique wallpaper and leather sofas, this English-style pub is the place to go for cottage pie, salmon-filo pastry and English breakfasts. There's also a peaceful backyard garden.

Turu Kaubamaja (Tallinna tänav 27; meals 90-150Kr; 🕑 11am-midnight Mon-Sat) Overlooking the main square (Turu plats), this is the best grocery shop in town (hint: grab some picnic food and head to the park).

ENTERTAINMENT

Rakvere Theatre (Rakvere Teater; ☎ 329 5420; Kreutzwaldi tänav 2) This historic theatre hosts an assortment of both classic and avant-garde performances in Estonian throughout the year.

GETTING THERE & AWAY

Rakvere is well connected by bus to Tallinn (20 daily, 55Kr to 65Kr, 1½ hours), Narva (10 daily, 70Kr to 75Kr, two to 2½ hours). There are also decent links to Lahemaa towns like Viitna (14 daily, 20Kr to 30Kr, 30 minutes), Võsu (six daily, 17Kr to 20Kr, one hour), Käsmu (five daily, 18Kr to 24Kr, 1½ hours) and Palmse (four weekly, 15Kr, 40 minutes). The bus station is on the corner of Laada and E Vilde, one block south of the information centre.

Rakvere has one or two trains daily to Tallinn (46Kr, 1¾ to two hours) and Narva (46Kr, 1¾ hours). The train station is on Jaama puiestee, 1200m northeast of the main square.

Lahemaa to Sillamäe

On a headland at **Toolse**, 8km west of Kunda, are the evocative ruins of a **castle** (adult/concession 30/15Kr; 🕑 11am-7pm mid-May–Sep) built in 1471 by the Livonian Order as defence against pirates. Summer visits include a 20-minute tour (English available) led by young guides who can point out the old medieval toilet, where the kitchen and livestock were, and relate some of the legends of the castle. Children can scramble around on the tiny pirate ship nearby.

At **Purtse**, 10km north of Kiviõli, there's more medieval action in the picturesque, restored, 16th-century **castle** (☎ 335 9388; 🕑 10am-6pm Apr-Sep, visits by appt). The coast between Aa and Toila is lined by cliffs where it coincides with the edge of the Baltic Glint. At **Ontika**, north of Kohtla-Järve, these cliffs reach their greatest height of 56m. The views out to sea are spectacular, though getting a good look at the cliffs is near impossible as they're obscured by trees, and climbing down can be a deadly affair. To save lives, a 2-million-Kroon metal staircase was built in 1999, 5km east at **Valaste**, facing Estonia's highest waterfalls (25.6m), which, depending on the month, may be a mere trickle.

Along a former Viking trade route, **Toila**, a lovely village on the coast 12km northeast of Jõhvi, is famous for its parklands. Here stood the majestic Oru Castle, built by famous St Petersburg businessman Yeliseev in the 19th century, which was later used as President Konstantin Päts' summer residence between the wars and subsequently destroyed. Parts of the park have been reconstructed, including the old terrace, making it a pleasant place for a stroll or picnic. The views from the Baltic Glint in the Toila region are spectacular, and here the glint forms part of the Saka-Ontika-Toila landscape reserve. There are seven buses daily to Toila from Jõhvi, and two to Ontika (none on Sundays).

SLEEPING & EATING

Sanatoorium Toila (☎ 332 5233; www.toilasanatoorium.ee; Ranna tänav 12; camp site per person 50Kr, caravan 110Kr, d/tr cabin 250/350Kr, s/d from 600/800Kr) In Toila, this large institutional sanatorium offers affordable spa treatments (massages, salt baths, salt chamber) on a fine spot overlooking a rocky beach. Rooms are clean but dated with old yellow wallpaper but fine sea views. Simple wooden cabins with shared bathrooms lie behind the hotel, with space for camping and caravans. There are tennis courts, bike rental and a 25m swimming pool, with a new water centre (pool, slide, steam rooms) planned, which might be ready by the time you read this.

Fregatt (☎ 336 9647; Pikk tänav 18; meals 60-120Kr; ⏲ noon-10pm) A local favourite, this friendly Toila restaurant serves eclectic dishes (pepper steak, pad Thai), amid a polished chrome setting. It's along the main road in town.

Sillamäe

pop 16,700

Located on the coast between Kohtla-Järve and Narva, Sillamäe is a pleasant, rarely visited town with a tree-lined main street that functions as a living museum of Stalinist-era architecture. Planned by Leningrad architects, Sillamäe features grand, solid buildings with gargoyles and a cascading staircase ornamented by large urns. Around the central square, there's a **town hall** specially designed to resemble a Lutheran church, a **cultural centre** (constructed in 1949) that still has reliefs of Marx and Lenin on the walls inside, and a very Soviet-style monument erected in 1987 to commemorate the 70th anniversary of the October Revolution. This is one of few places in Estonia where the aura of the USSR still lives on, and it feels caught between two worlds.

The region's fate was sealed in the post-WWII years upon the discovery that oil shale contains small amounts of extractable uranium. The infamous uranium processing and nuclear chemicals factory was quickly built by 5000 Russian political prisoners, and the town centre by 3800 Baltic prisoners of war who had previously served in the German army. By 1946 the city was strictly off limits; it was known by various spooky code names (Leningrad 1; Moscow 400) and was often omitted from Soviet-era maps.

Only unfinished uranium was processed at the plant, though the eerily abandoned buildings on the city's western border are testament to Soviet plans to process pure, nuclear reactor–ready uranium; only the disbanding of the USSR saved Estonian ecology from this. The plant was closed in 1991 and today the radioactive waste is buried under concrete by the sea; fears of leakage have alarmed environmentalists. The **Sillamäe Museum** (☎ 397 2425; Mayakovsky tänav 18a) details the history of the area. But the real attraction of this town is wandering its classical alleys and leafy boulevards.

Krunk (☎ 392 9030; www.krunk.ee; Kesk tänav 23; d 690Kr) In an attractive yellow building on the main street, this hotel has simple rooms and a beautifully set restaurant (open noon to 9pm Monday to Saturday). Sauna available.

At least 20 buses travel daily between Tallinn and Sillamäe (100-110Kr, three hours); and more than 30 buses go between Narva and Sillamäe (15Kr to 30Kr, 30 minutes).

Narva & Around

pop 67,000

Estonia's easternmost town is separated only by the thin Narva River from Ivangorod in Russia. Narva, which has the look and feel of a Russian city, has a magnificent castle and an intriguing history that spans many centuries. Although the most outstanding architecture was destroyed in WWII, Estonia's third-largest city is an intriguing place to wander – as you'll find no other place in Estonia (or in Russia for that matter) quite like it.

People have lived here since the Stone Age, and it was a fortified trading point in 1172. It was embroiled in border disputes between the German knights and Russia; Ivan III of Muscovy built a fort at Ivangorod in 1492. In the 16th and 17th centuries Narva changed hands often from Russian to Swede, until falling to Russia in 1704.

Narva was almost completely destroyed in 1944 during its recapture by the Red Army. Afterwards it became part of the northeastern Estonian industrial zone and one of Europe's most polluted towns. Today emissions have been greatly reduced, with investment in cleaner technology well underway.

ORIENTATION & INFORMATION

The castle, Narva's biggest landmark, is by the river, just south of the Russian-Estonian bridge. The train and bus stations are next to each other on Vaksali tänav 2; from there it's a 500m walk north along Pushkini tänav to the castle. You'll pass the friendly **tourist information office** (☎ 356 0184; www.narva.ee; Pushkini tänav 13; ⏲ 10am-6pm Mon-Fri, 10am-3pm Sat & Sun mid-May–mid-Sep, 10am-5pm Mon-Fri mid-Sep–mid-May), where you can get maps and city information. They can recommend guides in town.

A block east is the **public library** (2nd fl, Maimi tänav 8; ⏲ 11am-7pm Mon-Fri, 10am-5pm Sat; 💻), with free Internet access.

SIGHTS

The imposing **Narva Castle** is an absolute must-visit. Built by the Danes at the end of the 13th century, it faces Russia's matching Ivangorod Fortress across the river, creating an architectural ensemble unique to Europe. Restored after damage during WWII, Narva Castle houses the **Town Museum** (☎ 359 9230; www.narvamuuseum.ee; adult/concession 30/10Kr; 🕒 10am-6pm Wed-Sun) and the castle grounds are the refuge of Narva's statue of Lenin – the only fully intact one left in the Baltics. North of the castle, the baroque **Old Town Hall** (Raekoja väljak), built between 1668 and 1671, is impressive, as is the 19th-century **home of Baron von Velio** (cnr Sepa & Hariduse tänav), two blocks north. The Russian Orthodox **Voskresensky Cathedral** (Bastrakovy tänav), built in 1898, is situated north of the train station. On the square in front of the train station is a monument to the Estonians who were loaded into cattle wagons here and deported to Siberia in 1941.

SLEEPING & EATING

Hotel Vanalinn (☎ 352 2486; Koidula tänav 6; s/d 490/640Kr; ☒) The rooms are well worn, but you can't beat the setting: inside a 17th-century house with tall wooden ceilings and views overlooking the river.

King Hotel (☎ 357 2404; Lavretsovi tänav 9; s/d 590/790Kr; ☒) Featuring cosy modern rooms, King Hotel is an excellent option. There's a decent restaurant next door.

Rondel (☎ 359 9257; Peterburi maantee 2; meals 15-100Kr; 🕒 noon-8pm) On the castle grounds, this casual restaurant serves fresh-grilled meats, sandwiches and salads.

German Pub (☎ 357 3060; Tiimani tänav 5; meals 50-120Kr) Trout *shashlik* and other grilled favourites are on offer at this cosy pub. It has several outdoor tables.

Gulliver Pub (☎ 359 1551; Lavretsovi tänav 7; meals from 50Kr) This animated two-storey pub is a good place to stop in for a pint or a simple, hearty meal.

Alexander Kohvik (☎ 357 1350; Pushkini tänav 13; meals from 30Kr) Serving a good selection of salads, soups, and fish and meat dishes, this no-nonsense coffee shop and restaurant is a blast from the USSR past.

GETTING THERE & AWAY

Over 15 daily buses travel between Tallinn and Narva (85Kr to 110Kr, 3½ hours) and one train (75Kr, three to four hours) runs daily, stopping in Rakvere. There are also 10 daily Narva–Tartu buses (85Kr to 105Kr, three to 3½ hours).

Narva-Jõesuu

Lying about 12km north of Narva, the holiday resort of Narva-Jõesuu is a pretty but dilapidated town, which has been popular since the 19th century for its long golden-sand beach backed by pine forests. There are a number of unique, impressive early-20th-century wooden houses and villas throughout the town. This town makes a good base for exploring Narva. Here you'll find a dozen hotels and spas to choose from, all overlooking a fine sandy beach.

SLEEPING & EATING

Guesthouse Valentina (☎ 357 7468; keeping@hot.ee; Aia 49; s/d from 300/400Kr; ☒) Boasting pleasant, simply furnished rooms, this charming new guesthouse is also the best place for a meal. It has a small outdoor patio where you can have grilled trout, stuffed peppers and delectable desserts.

Narva-Jõesuu Sanatoorium (☎ 359 9529; sanator@hot.ee; Aia 3; s/d/ste from 450/800/990Kr; ☒) Resembling a large white cruise ship (that's going nowhere), this aging hotel has decent rooms and a range of spa services. Bike rental is available.

Mereranna Hostel (☎ 357 2826; www.narvahotel.ee; Aia 17; s/d 300/350Kr; ☒) Rooms here have old wooden floors, faded wallpaper and tiny bathrooms; but the beach is right outside the door.

GETTING THERE & AWAY

Nine daily buses and numerous daily *marshrutkas* (minibuses) connect Narva with Narva-Jõesuu (20Kr, 20 minutes).

Kuremäe

Originally the site of ancient pagan worship, the village of Kuremäe, 20km southeast of Jõhvi, is home to the stunning Russian Orthodox **Pühtitsa Convent** (☎ 339 2124; admission free; 🕒 noon-6pm Mon-Fri). Built between 1885 and 1895, the magnificent nunnery has five towers topped with green onion domes and is a place of annual pilgrimage for Russian Orthodox believers, operating a fully self-sufficient entity. Murals by the convent gate depict the Virgin Mary, who, it is said, appeared to a 16th-century shepherd by an oak tree. An icon was later found in the area and it is still in the main church of the convent. There is also a revered holy spring that never freezes.

Downhill from the monastery is a coffeeshop, where you can enjoy cakes and caffeine on the outdoor patio.

Two weekly buses connect Kuremäe with Tallinn (100 Kr, 3½ hours). A daily bus connects Kuremäe with Narva, with a stop in Jõhvi en route.

Lake Peipsi (North)

Estonia's finest (and least crowded) beaches are found on the northern coast of Lake Peipsi; 42km of clean, sandy dunes hug the shoreline of what appears to be a sea rather than a lake. The area had popular resorts during Soviet times but many of them have been left to crumble. Development has been slowly arriving to this beautiful area with enormous tourism potential.

On the northeastern shore of the lake, is **Vasknarva**, an isolated fishing village with about 100 residents. There is an evocative Orthodox church here that, according to some, held a KGB radio surveillance centre in Soviet times. Scant ruins of a 1349 Teutonic Order castle stand by the shore of Lake Peipsi. At **Alajõe**, is the area's main Orthodox church and a few shops. **Kauksi**, where the Narva–Jõhvi–Tartu road reaches the lake, is the area's most popular beach.

From **Lohusuu** extending southwards is Old Believers' territory (for more details, see p127). Further south, towards Jõgeva, are the lakeside towns of **Mustvee** and **Raja**. Mustvee, a town of just 2000, has four **churches** (there used to be seven): Orthodox, Baptist, Lutheran and Old Believer. There is also a forlorn WWII memorial by the sea, the **Mourning Lady**, a young woman with her head hung low. Some 8km south is the charming, one-street village of Raja, where a wooden church contains some rare **icons** dating from the 19th century when a prestigious school of icon painting was founded there.

Locally caught and smoked fish (trout or salmon) is a speciality of the area. Some would say the delicious catch alone warrants the journey. Look for *suitsukala* (smoked fish) stands scattered all along the main road curving around the lake.

SLEEPING & EATING

There are a number of resorts around Alajõe, but many are in dire need of repair. The following are off the main road that follows the shoreline.

Uusküla Holiday Centre (☎ 339 3249; tasandik@hot.ee; s/d from 300/400Kr) This sprawling complex of cottages and lodges has old, worn rooms and a restaurant on site.

Kauksi Beach (☎ 339 3835; telklager@hot.ee; camp site/wooden cabin per person 20/70Kr) Several kilometres further south, this popular camp site gets packed with young partygoers on weekends. It has tiny two-person cabins and a café on the grounds.

Peipsi Lained Hostel (☎ 339 3723; www.peipsi-lained.ee; d from 500Kr) Another two kilometres leads to this friendly place with clean cosy rooms and shared bathrooms. The beach is 50m from the door. There are numerous free RMK camp sites, just outside the gate (closer to the beach), and also about one kilometre south of Uusküla Holiday Centre.

GETTING THERE & AWAY

Getting to this area is tricky without your own wheels. To Kauksi and Alajõe, two buses a day leave from Kohtla-Järve and Jõhvi (two to 2½ hours). There are also about 10 Tartu-bound buses a day from Narva, many of which will stop in Kauksi.

There are 10 buses connecting Mustvee with both Jõhvi (one to 1½ hours) and Tartu (one hour).

Endla Nature Reserve

Endla Nature Reserve (Endla Looduskaitseala), covering a boggy area inhabited by beavers, begins south of Koeru, approximately 10km north of Jõgeva. The nature reserve includes Lake Endla and a number of springs in the western part of the reserve, including the 4.8m-deep Sopa spring (Estonia's deepest) and the Võlingi and Oostriku springs. Endla Nature Reserve was established in 1981.

The **reserve headquarters** (☎ 774 5339) is in Torma. You can visit the reserve and follow a 1.5km nature trail on boards across the bog, taking in two watchtowers along the way. Guided tours are also available, by advance arrangement through the headquarters.

SOUTHEASTERN ESTONIA

Set with rolling hills, picturesque lakes and vast woodlands, the southeast boasts some of Estonia's most attractive countryside. It also contains one of Estonia's most important cities: the heart of this region, the vibrant university centre of Tartu, the cobbled streets of which mark a rich history that spans centuries. This is where the national awakening began over 100 years ago, making it in some ways the spiritual birthplace of modern Estonia. Its lush parks, stimulating galleries and eclectic cafés and restaurants make for some fine exploring.

Beyond the city – no matter which direction you head – you'll find resplendent natural settings. In the south lie the towns of Otepää and Võru, the gateway to outdoor adventuring: hiking and lakeside swimming in summer and cross-country skiing in winter. Quaint towns set on wandering rivers or in picturesque valleys add to the allure. For a serious dose of woodland, head to Haanja National Park or Karula National Park.

To the east stretches Lake Peipsi, one of Europe's largest lakes. Along its shores are beautiful sandy beaches and a surprisingly undeveloped coastline. Aside from swimming, boating, fishing and soaking up the scenery, you can travel up its western rim stopping at roadside food stands and in tiny villages dotting the lakeside. Further north, the lake is also traditionally the land of Old Believers, Russians who came in the 18th and 19th centuries fleeing persecution in the east.

One of Estonia's most intriguing regions is also among its least visited. In the far southeast, clustered in villages near Lake Pihkva, live the Setus, ancestors of Balto-Finnic tribes who settled here in the first millennium. Today this proud group continues to preserve their culture and language, with colourful festivals staged throughout the year. Sadly, the Russian border now divides this previously united community.

National Parks

Highly recommended is the 200-sq-km Haanja Nature Park with its crisp lakes, lush woodlands and gently rolling hills. There are ample opportunities for hiking, camping and just absorbing the subtle beauty of Estonia's scenery.

Further west, the smaller Karula National Park is another decent choice for hikes. Its highlight is the sparkling Lake Ähijärv. The Luhasoo Nature Study Trail acquaints visitors with one of Estonia's most underappreciated geographic features, the swamp.

Getting There & Away

Frequent buses connect Tallinn with Tartu; though more nostalgic travellers will enjoy the train, which stops in Tartu before continuing on to Valga on the Latvian border. From Tallinn you can also catch direct buses to other southeastern cities (Põlva, Võru and Otepää), though all buses will go through Tartu. Tartu is also a sensible gateway to Lake Peipsi.

Getting Around

If you plan only to dip into the region, then you'll be fine getting around by bus. For more in-depth exploring – particularly around Haanja National Park, Setumaa and Lake Peipsi – bus services are infrequent and you'll save loads of time by renting a car. You'll also want a car – or a bicycle for the very fit – to explore the scenic countryside around Otepää. Tartu has plenty of affordable car-hire agencies.

TARTU

pop 101,000

Tartu lays claim to being Estonia's spiritual capital. Locals talk about a special Tartu *vaim* (spirit) inhabiting its 19th-century streets, old wooden houses, green parks and peaceful riverfront. Small and quaint, with the quietly flowing Emajõgi River running through it, Tartu is also Estonia's premier university town, with students making up nearly one-fifth of the population. This injects a boisterous vitality into the leafy, historic setting and grants it a surprising sophistication for a city of its size.

Tartu was the cradle of Estonia's 19th-century national revival and it escaped Sovietisation to a greater degree than Tallinn. Its handsome centre is lined with classically designed 18th-century buildings, many of which have been put to innovative uses by the city's idealists. Today visitors can get a more authentic depiction of Estonian life

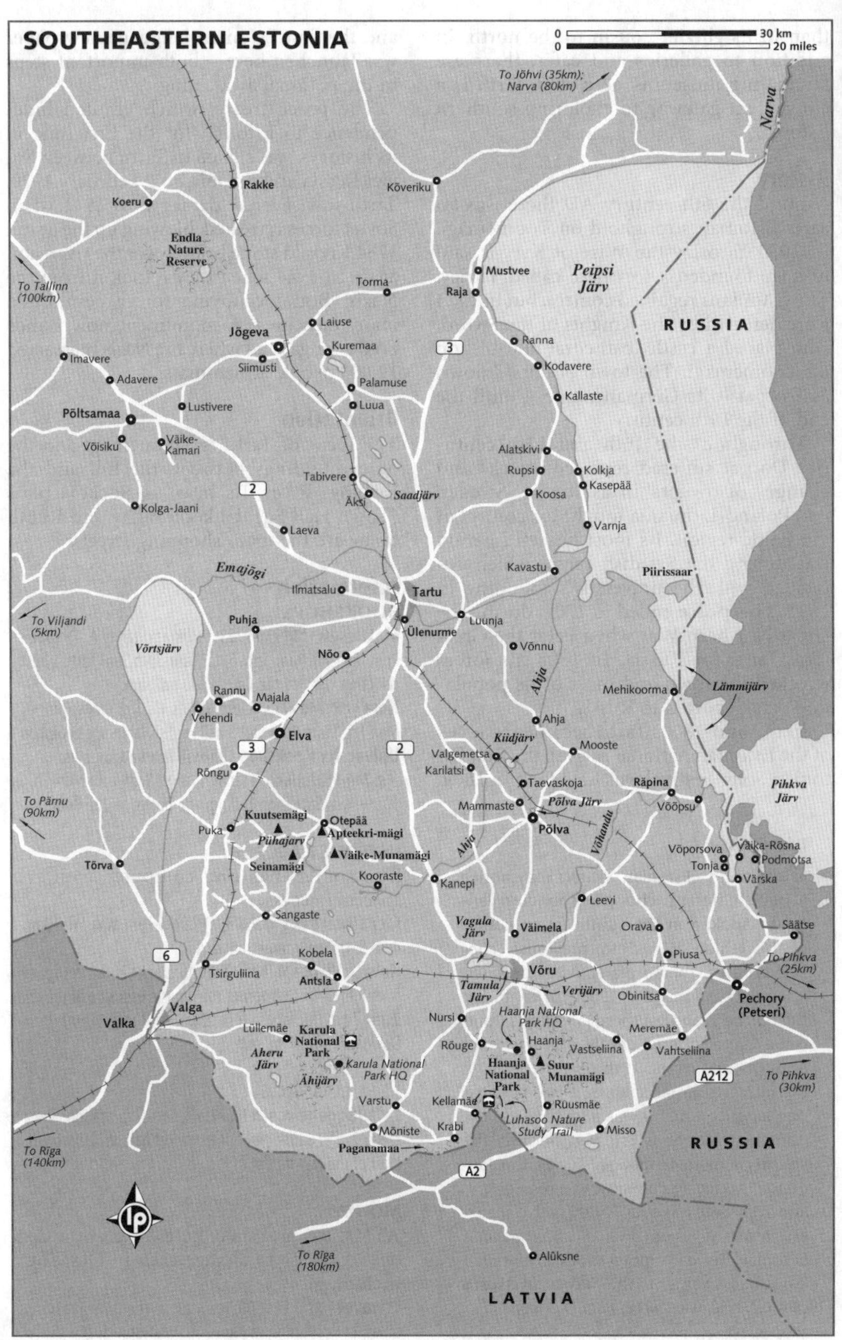
SOUTHEASTERN ESTONIA
0 30 km
0 20 miles
To Jõhvi (35km); Narva (80km)
Narva
Rakke
Kõveriku
Koeru
Endla Nature Reserve
To Tallinn (100km)
Mustvee
Peipsi Järv
Torma
Raja
RUSSIA
Laiuse
Jõgeva
Kuremaa
3
Ranna
Imavere
Siimusti
Kodavere
Adavere
Palamuse
Kallaste
Lustivere
Luua
Põltsamaa
Võisiku
Väike-Kamari
Alatskivi
Rupsi
Kolkja
Kasepää
Tabivere
2
Äksi
Saadjärv
Koosa
Kolga-Jaani
Varnja
Laeva
Emajõgi
Kavastu
Piirissaar
Ilmatsalu
Tartu
To Viljandi (5km)
Puhja
Luunja
Ülenurme
Võrtsjärv
Nõo
Võnnu
Ahja
Mehikoorma
Lämmijärv
Rannu
Majala
Vehendi
Ahja
Elva
3
2
Kiidjärv
Mooste
Valgemetsa
Karilatsi
Räpina
Pihkva Järv
Taevaskoja
Rõngu
Mammaste
Põlva Järv
Võõpsu
To Pärnu (90km)
Kuutsemägi
Otepää
Apteekri-mägi
Puka
Pühajärv
Põlva
Võhandu
Ahja
Võporsova
Väika-Rõsna
Podmotsa
Tõrva
Seinamägi
Väike-Munamägi
Tonja
Kooraste
Kanepi
Värska
Leevi
Sangaste
Vagula Järv
Väimela
Orava
Säätse
6
Kobela
Piusa
To Pihkva (25km)
Tsirguliina
Antsla
Võru
Tamula Järv
Verijärv
Obinitsa
Pechory (Petseri)
Valga
Valka
Haanja National Park HQ
Lüllemäe
Karula National Park
Nursi
Meremäe
Haanja
Aheru Järv
Rõuge
Vastseliina
Vahtseliina
Karula National Park HQ
Suur Munamägi
Ähijärv
Haanja National Park
A212
To Pihkva (30km)
Varstu
Kellamäe
Ruusmäe
Luhasoo Nature Study Trail
Mõniste
Krabi
Misso
To Rīga (140km)
Paganamaa
RUSSIA
A2
To Rīga (180km)
Alūksne
LATVIA

than in its glitzier cousin to the north. In addition to galleries and cafés, there are fascinating museums here, and Tartu is a convenient gateway to exploring southern Estonia.

History

Around the 6th century AD there was an early Estonian stronghold on Toomemägi. In 1030 Yaroslav the Wise of Kyiv is said to have founded a fort here called Yuriev. The Estonians regained control, but in 1224 were defeated by the Knights of the Sword, who placed a castle, cathedral and bishop on Toomemägi. The town became known as Dorpat – its German name – until the end of the 19th century.

Throughout the 16th and 17th centuries Dorpat suffered repeated attacks and changes of ownership as Russia, Sweden and Poland-Lithuania fought for control of the Baltic region. Its most peaceful period was during the Swedish reign, which coincided with the university's founding in 1632. This peace ended in 1704, during the Great Northern War when Peter the Great took Tartu for Russia. In 1708 his forces wrecked the town and most of its population was deported to Russia.

In the mid-1800s Tartu became the focus of the Estonian national revival: the first Estonian Song Festival was held here in 1869, and the first Estonian-language newspaper was launched here – both important steps in the national awakening.

The peace treaty, which granted independence to Estonia (for the first time in its history), was signed in Tartu between Soviet Russia and Estonia on 2 February 1920. Tartu was severely damaged in 1941 when Soviet forces retreated, blowing up the grand 1784 Kivisild stone bridge over the river, and again in 1944 when they retook it from the Nazis. Both occupying forces committed many atrocities. A monument now stands on the Valga road where the Nazis massacred 12,000 people at Lemmatsi.

LANGUAGE

In addition to Estonian, visitors may notice a quite different, choppier-sounding language spoken in the southeastern corner of this region. Võro-Seto, previously considered an Estonian dialect, was declared a separate language in 1998. For centuries, the northern and southern languages flourished quite independently of each other until the end of the 19th century. Then, in the interests of nationalism, a one-country, one-language policy was adopted, and the dominant Northern Estonian became the country's main language. Today the language is once again enjoying a resurgence, and Võro-Seto has over 70,000 native speakers, most of whom live in Võrumaa and Setumaa. To learn more about this unique language, contact the **Võro Institute** (☎ 782 1960; www.wi.ee; Tartu 48, Võru).

Orientation

The focus of Tartu is Toomemägi and the older buildings between the hill and the Emajõgi River. Its heart is Raekoja plats (Town Hall Sq). Ülikooli tänav and Rüütli tänav are the main shopping streets.

Information

BOOKSHOPS

Mattiesen (☎ 730 9723; Vallikraavi tänav 4; 🕒 9am-7pm Mon-Fri, 9am-5pm Sat, 10am-3pm Sun) Tartu's best selection is inside the Café Wilde building.

Nora (☎ 740 7715; Raekoja plats 11; 🕒 11am-7pm Mon-Fri, 11am-3pm Sat) Small English-language bookshop.

University Bookshop (Ülikooli Raamatukauplus; ☎ 744 1102; Ülikooli tänav 11; 🕒 9am-7pm Mon-Fri, 10am-4pm Sat) English-language books on 2nd floor.

INTERNET ACCESS

The tourist has one computer with free Internet access.

City Library (Kompanii 3; 🕒 9am-7pm Mon-Fri, 10am-4pm Sat) Free Internet upstairs.

Kohvik Virtuaal (Pikk tänav 40; per hr 20Kr; 🕒 11am-midnight) A sleek Internet café on the east side of the river.

Zum Zum (Küüni 2; per hr 25Kr; 🕒 11am-11pm) Downstairs from the pub.

LEFT LUGGAGE

Left-luggage room (pakihoid; Tartu bus station, Soola tänav 2; 🕒 6am-9pm) Off the ticket hall on the ground floor of the bus station.

MONEY

ATMs are prevalent here. There are dozens of places to change cash in Old Town including:

Estravel (☎ 744 0300; www.estravel.ee; Vallikraavi tänav 2; 🕒 9am-6pm Mon-Fri, 10am-3pm Sat)

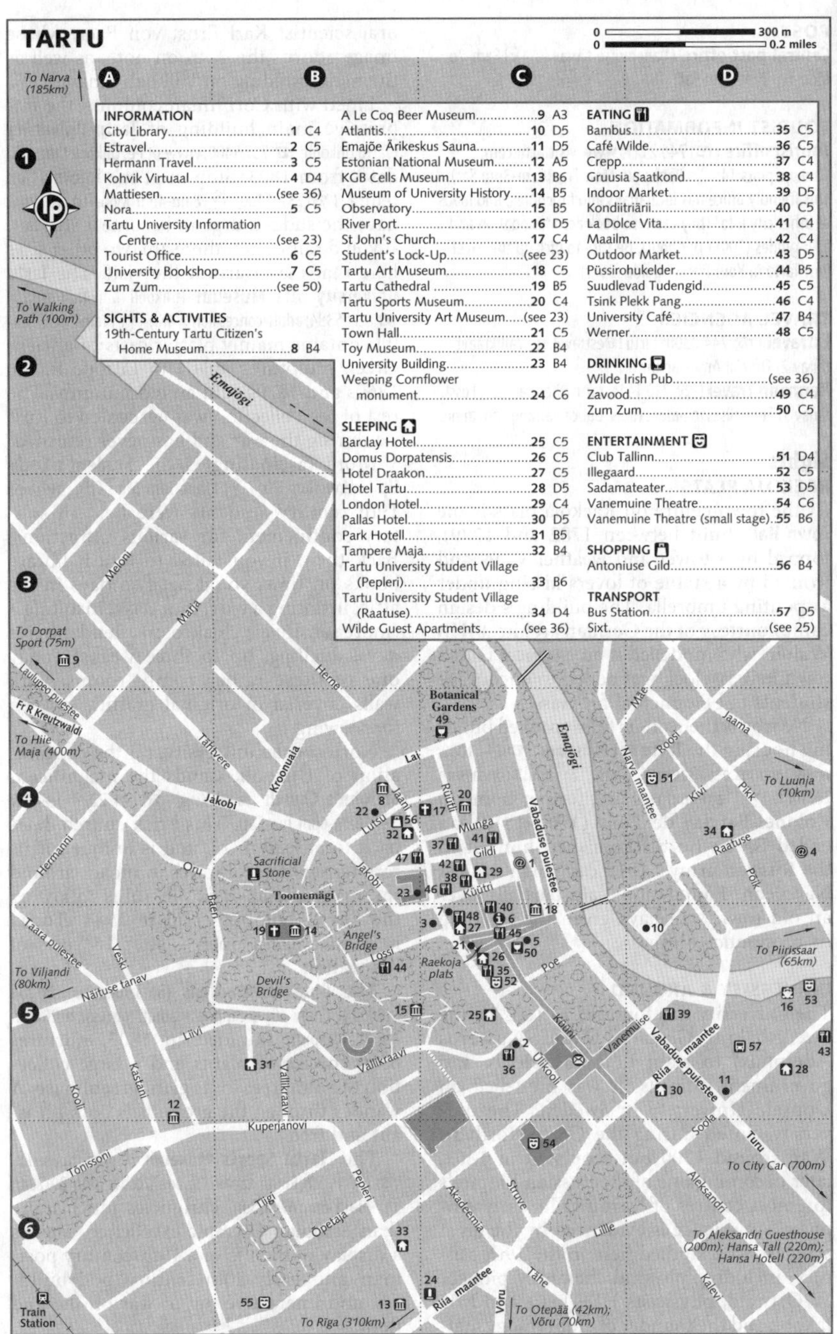
TARTU
0 300 m
0 0.2 miles
A
B
C
D
1
2
3
4
5
6
INFORMATION
City Library 1 C4
Estravel 2 C5
Hermann Travel 3 C5
Kohvik Virtuaal 4 D4
Mattiesen (see 36)
Nora 5 C5
Tartu University Information Centre (see 23)
Tourist Office 6 C5
University Bookshop 7 C5
Zum Zum (see 50)
SIGHTS & ACTIVITIES
19th-Century Tartu Citizen's Home Museum 8 B4
A Le Coq Beer Museum 9 A3
Atlantis 10 D5
Emajõe Ärikeskus Sauna 11 D5
Estonian National Museum 12 A5
KGB Cells Museum 13 B6
Museum of University History 14 B5
Observatory 15 B5
River Port 16 D5
St John's Church 17 C4
Student's Lock-Up (see 23)
Tartu Art Museum 18 C5
Tartu Cathedral 19 B5
Tartu Sports Museum 20 C4
Tartu University Art Museum (see 23)
Town Hall 21 C5
Toy Museum 22 B4
University Building 23 B4
Weeping Cornflower monument 24 C6
SLEEPING
Barclay Hotel 25 C5
Domus Dorpatensis 26 C5
Hotel Draakon 27 C5
Hotel Tartu 28 D5
London Hotel 29 C4
Pallas Hotel 30 D5
Park Hotell 31 B5
Tampere Maja 32 B4
Tartu University Student Village (Pepleri) 33 B6
Tartu University Student Village (Raatuse) 34 D4
Wilde Guest Apartments (see 36)
EATING
Bambus 35 C5
Café Wilde 36 C5
Crepp 37 C4
Gruusia Saatkond 38 C4
Indoor Market 39 D5
Kondiitriärii 40 C5
La Dolce Vita 41 C4
Maailm 42 C4
Outdoor Market 43 D5
Püssirohukelder 44 B5
Suudlevad Tudengid 45 C5
Tsink Plekk Pang 46 C4
University Café 47 B4
Werner 48 C5
DRINKING
Wilde Irish Pub (see 36)
Zavood 49 C4
Zum Zum 50 C5
ENTERTAINMENT
Club Tallinn 51 D4
Illegaard 52 C5
Sadamateater 53 D5
Vanemuine Theatre 54 C6
Vanemuine Theatre (small stage) 55 B6
SHOPPING
Antoniuse Gild 56 B4
TRANSPORT
Bus Station 57 D5
Sixt (see 25)
To Narva (185km)
To Walking Path (100m)
Emajõgi
Meloni
Marja
Herne
To Dorpat Sport (75m)
Laulupeo puiestee
Fr R Kreutzwaldi
To Hiie Maja (400m)
Tähtvere
Kroonuaia
Jakobi
Botanical Gardens
Lai
Jaani
Rüütli
Lutsu
Munga
Gildi
Küütri
Sacrificial Stone
Toomemägi
Oru
Hermanni
Baeri
Taara puiestee
Veski
Angel's Bridge
Lossi
Raekoja plats
Devil's Bridge
To Viljandi (80km)
Näituse tanav
Liivi
Vallikraavi
Kastani
Kooli
Kuperjanovi
Tõnissoni
Pepleri
Tiigi
Õpetaja
Akadeemia
Struve
Lille
Tähe
Riia maantee
Võru
To Otepää (42km); Võru (70km)
To Riga (310km)
Train Station
Ülikooli
Küüni
Poe
Vanemuise
Vabaduse puiestee
Riia
Soola
Turu
Aleksandri
Kalevi
To City Car (700m)
To Aleksandri Guesthouse (200m); Hansa Tall (220m); Hansa Hotell (220m)
To Piirissaar (65km)
To Luunja (10km)
Narva maantee
Mäe
Roosi
Jaama
Kivi
Pikk
Raatuse
Põik

POST

Central post office (Vanemuise tänav 7; 8am-7pm Mon-Fri, 9am-4pm Sat)

TOURIST INFORMATION

Tourist office (744 2111; www.visittartu.com; Raekoja plats 14; 9am-5pm Mon-Fri, 10am-3pm Sat) This friendly office has local maps and brochures, and loads of other city info. They can also book accommodation and tour guides (200Kr per hour). Be sure to pick up the excellent Tartu in Your Pocket guide (25Kr).

TRAVEL AGENCIES

Estravel (744 0300; tartu1@estravel.ee; Vallikraavi tänav 2) Official Amex agent.

Hermann Travel (730 1444; tartu@hermann.ee; Lossi tänav 3) Specialises in nature tours, but can arrange anything.

Sights

RAEKOJA PLATS

At the town centre on Raekoja plats is the **Town Hall** (built between 1782 and 1789), topped by a tower and weather vane, and fronted by a statue of lovers kissing under a spouting umbrella. The building's design came courtesy of the German architect JHB Walter, who modelled it on a typical Dutch town hall. A clock was added to encourage students to be punctual for classes.

Nearby is the wonderfully crooked building housing the **Tartu Art Museum** (744 1080; www.tartmus.ee; Raekoja plats 18; adult/concession 20/10Kr; 11am-6pm Wed-Sun), former home of Colonel Barclay de Tolly (1761–1818), an exiled Scot who distinguished himself in the Russian army's 1812 campaign against Napoleon. Foundations laid partially over an old town wall have given the building its pronounced lean.

UNIVERSITY & AROUND

The university was founded in 1632 by the Swedish king Gustaf II Adolf (Gustavus Adolphus) to train Lutheran clergy and government officials. It was modelled on Uppsala University in Sweden. The university closed during the Great Northern War around 1700 but reopened in 1802, later becoming one of the Russian Empire's foremost centres of learning. Its early emphasis on science is evidenced by the great scholars who studied here in the 19th century, including physical chemistry pioneer W Ostwald, physicists HFE Lenz and MH Jakobi, and the founder of embryology, natural scientist Karl Ernst von Baer, whose image adorns the 2 kroon note, as well as the main building on Ülikooli tänav.

Lined with Corinthian columns, the impressive main building of **Tartu University** (Tartu Ülikooli; 737 5400; www.ut.ee; Ülikooli tänav 18) dates from 1803. Stop in at the **information centre** (737 5100; 8am-4pm Mon-Fri) if you have the sudden urge to become a student. If you'd rather not, there are two other sites here that may warrant the visit. The **Tartu University Art Museum** (Ülikooli Kunstimuuseum; 737 5384; adult/concession 7/4Kr; 11am-5pm Mon-Fri) contains mainly plaster casts of ancient Greek sculptures, made in Europe in the 1860s and 1870s, and an old mummy. The rest of the collection was evacuated to Russia during the war and has never returned.

More fascinating is the **Student's Lock-Up** (admission 5Kr; 11am-5pm Mon-Fri), where 19th-century students were held in solitary confinement for various infractions. Back then, if you failed to return library books on time, you'd net two days in the attic; insulting a lady, four days; insulting a (more sensitive?) cloakroom attendant, five days; duelling, up to three weeks. Today one of these rather comfy rooms, with walls covered in original graffiti, is open for viewing.

North of the university, on the continuation of Ülikooli, stands the magnificent **St John's Church** (Jaani Kirik; 744 2229; Jaani 5; 10am-6pm Tue-Sat). This brick church dates back to at least 1323, and is unique for its rare terracotta sculptures in niches around the main portal. It lay in ruins following the Soviet bombing raid in 1944. Today it is once again open – after 16 years of renovation.

The **Botanical Gardens** (Botaanikaaed; 737 6180; Lai tänav 40; greenhouse adult/concession 20/7Kr; 10am-5pm), founded in 1803, nurtures 6500 species of plants and a large collection of palm trees in its giant greenhouse. A wander through the grounds is both pleasant and free.

The **Tartu Sports Museum** (Spordimuuseum; 730 0750; Rüütli tänav 15; adult/concession 30/20Kr; 11am-6pm Wed-Sun) chronicles much more than Estonian Olympic excellence. There's a display of the life of a 19th-century postman and early-20th-century bodybuilders, and interactive tug-of-war on the 2nd floor.

Amid period furnishings, the **19th-century Tartu Citizen's Home Museum** (☎ 736 1545; Jaani 16; adult/concession 10/5Kr; ⏲ 11am-6pm Wed-Sun) shows how a burgher from the 1830s lived.

Set in one of Tartu's oldest buildings (dating back to the 1770s), the **Toy Museum** (☎ 736 1551; Lutsu 8; adult/concession 15/10Kr; ⏲ 11am-6pm Wed-Sun) is a big hit with the under-eight crowd. Dolls, model trains, rocking horses, toy soldiers and tons of other toys on display date back 100 years. If all those unobtainable toys have unearthed your inner child, there's a playroom upstairs for more hands-on activity.

TOOMEMÄGI

Toomemägi (Cathedral Hill), rising behind the Town Hall, is a splendidly landscaped park, with walking paths meandering through the trees. This hill is the original reason for Tartu's existence, functioning on and off as a stronghold from around the 5th or 6th century. The approach from Raekoja plats is along Lossi tänav, which passes beneath the **Angel's Bridge** (Inglisild), which was built between 1836 and 1838. A bit further up the hill is **Devil's Bridge** (Kuradisild).

Atop the hill is the imposing Gothic **Tartu Cathedral** (Toomkirik). It was built by German knights in the 13th century, rebuilt in the 15th century, despoiled during the Reformation in 1525, used as a barn, and partly rebuilt between 1804 and 1807 to house the university library, which is now the **Museum of University History** (☎ 737 5677; adult/concession 20/5Kr; ⏲ 11am-5pm Wed-Sun). Inside you'll find a reconstructed autopsy chamber and other exhibits chronicling student life.

Also on the hill is the old **observatory** (☎ 737 5798; www.ahhaa.ee), set in a grand 1810 building. It's open by appointment, so phone ahead.

SOUTH OF TOOMEMÄGI

Tartu, as the major repository of Estonia's cultural heritage, has an abundance of first-rate museums. Among them is perhaps the country's best: the **Estonian National Museum** (☎ 742 1311; www.erm.ee; Kuperjanovi tänav 9; adult/concession 20/14Kr; ⏲ 11am-6pm Wed-Sun) traces the history, life and traditions of the Estonian people. Don't miss the regional displays of folk costumes and exhibits of uniquely handcrafted tankards. Temporary exhibits here are also noteworthy.

The former KGB headquarters, known infamously as the 'Grey House', is now the sombre **KGB Cells Museum** (KGB Kongide; ☎ 746 1717; Riia maantee 15b, entrance on Pepleri; adult/concession 5/3Kr; ⏲ 11am-4pm Tue-Sat), chronicling the deportations and life in the gulags. In 1990 the **weeping cornflower monument** was erected in front of the KGB buildings in memory of the victims of Soviet repression. The blue cornflower is Estonia's national flower.

One of the country's most important archives, the **Estonian Literary Museum** (Kirjandusmuuseum; ☎ 737 7700; www.kirmus.ee; Vanemuise tänav 42; admission free; ⏲ 9am-4.30pm Mon-Fri) is a national research museum housing an immense collection of Estonian folklore, ethnomusicology and cultural history. The museum hosts periodic exhibitions of historical artefacts and photographs from the collection.

BEER & BEACHES

North of Toomemägi, the **A Le Coq Beer Museum** (☎ 744 9711; Tähtvere 56; 25Kr; ⏲ tours 2pm Thu, 10am, noon & 2pm Sat), at the brewery, briefly covers the history of beer-making, but focuses mainly on the machinery and techniques A Le Coq has used to churn out their trademark beverage since 1879. Free samples at the end.

If you can't make it to Pärnu, there's a pleasant **beach** (with sand volleyball court) along the north side of the Emajõgi, a 1km walk west of Kroonuaia tänav. Another **beach** is on the south side of the Emajõgi, at the start of the walking path (see p123).

Activities

HIKING

Lovely walks into the countryside begin just at the edge of Tartu. A 5km **walking path** begins just west of Emajõe tänav at the signpost that reads 'Jänese rada' (rabbit path). From here you'll hike along the river through birch groves and past the ruins of the Jänese tavern (an 18th-century pub destroyed in WWII) as well as an old archaeological site. Bring mosquito repellent.

RIVER CRUISES

Throughout the summer months **Atlantis** (☎ 738 5485; Narva maantee 2; 50Kr; ⏲ cruise 2pm daily) runs a motor ship, *Pegasus*, which leaves from the dock in front of the restaurant for an hour-long cruise along the Emajõgi.

A hydrofoil, *Polaris*, also sails three times a week to Piirissaare, leaving from the city harbour.

SAUNAS

Many hotels have saunas, but if you're looking for something a little different, head to **Emajõe Ärikeskus Sauna** (☎ 737 1001; Soola 8; per hr from 500Kr; 🕒 8am-11pm Mon-Fri, 10am-10pm Sat & Sun). In a shiny building that resembles a hip flask, this sauna provides unbeatable views. You can reserve by phone or at the information desk on the ground floor.

TENNIS

If you're hungering for a match, head to **Dorpat Sport** (☎ 509 0705; Laulupeo puiestee 19; court per hr 60-100Kr; 🕒 8am-8pm Mon-Sat, 9am-8pm Sun), where you can play on one of three new clay courts. Racket and ball hire available.

Festivals & Events

Ski Marathon (www.tartumaraton.ee) In mid-February the city hosts this 60km race, which goes along the cross-country tracks near Otepää.

University Spring Days festival You can catch a glimpse of modern-day student misdeeds at the end of April. Students take to the streets to celebrate winter's end in every way imaginable. Raucous fun, parades and boat rallies are the order of the five sleepless days.

Tartu Bicycle Marathon (www.tartumaraton.ee) One of Tartu's big sporting events is this 136km race held at the end of May, with a second race held in mid-September.

Sleeping

Some hotels give discounts just for asking.

APARTMENT RENTAL

Domus Dorpatensis (☎ 733 1345; www.dorpatensis.ee; Raekoja plats 1; apt €28-50; ☒) This foundation rents out three apartments ranging from small to large in an unbeatable location next to the Town Hall. Apartments are simple, comfortably furnished affairs that offer great value for money.

Wilde Guest Apartments (☎ 730 9765; www.wilde.ee/kylaliskorterid.php; Vallikraavi 4; apt 1100-1500Kr; ☒) Rents beautiful modern apartments (one has a sauna and balcony) with old-world details. All are within a short distance of the pub.

BUDGET

Tartu University Student Village (☎ 740 9955; www.kyla.ee; s/d 250/400Kr; ☒; Pepleri dorm Pepleri tänav 14; Raatuse dorm Raatuse tänav 22) These student dorms offer cheap, clean accommodation. The Raatuse dorm is brand-new but somewhat institutional and every three rooms share a kitchen and bathroom. It's set up for disabled access. The Pepleri dorm is older but a bit cosier, with a kitchenette and bathroom in each room.

Tähtvere Hostel (☎ 742 1708; Laulupeo puiestee 19; s/d from 250/350Kr; ☒) A 1km walk west of the centre, this no-frills hostel has fairly worn rooms. It's next to tennis courts and a leafy park. Bike hire next door.

Hiie Maja (☎ 742 1236; www.bed.ee; Hiie 10; r per person €15; ☒) In a peaceful residential neighbourhood 15-minutes' walk west of the centre, this friendly bed and breakfast offers small clean rooms in a private house.

MIDRANGE

Tampere Maja (☎ 738 6300; www.tamperemaja.ee; Jaani 4; s/d/apt incl breakfast from €40/60/80; ☒ 💻) Boasting an excellent location in the old quarters, this small guesthouse has trim, cosy rooms in a historic building. The apartment has a kitchen; room guests have access to a shared kitchen. Sauna available.

Aleksandri Guesthouse (☎ 736 6659; www.aleksandri.ee; Aleksandri 42; s/d with shared bathroom 400/500Kr, with private bathroom 450/550Kr; ☒) A 15-minute walk southeast of the main square, this pleasant guesthouse has clean, simple rooms on a quiet street.

Park Hotell (☎ 742 7000; www.parkhotell.ee; Vallikraavi tänav 23; s/d 800/1080Kr; ☒) Nestled to the side of Toomemägi, the Park Hotell has pleasant wood-floored rooms painted in pale shades of green (others in cream). The lush greenery through the windows and parkland outside the door is the big draw.

Hotel Tartu (☎ 731 4300; www.tartuhotell.ee; Soola tänav 3; dm/s/d 300/715/1045Kr; ☒) Across from the bus station, this hotel isn't in the most charming locale, but its nicely renovated rooms are trim and comfortable with big windows. 'Youth rooms' are triples with shared bathrooms. Sauna available.

TOP END

Pallas Hotel (☎ 730 1200; www.pallas.ee; Riia maantee 4; s/d from 975/1250Kr; ☒) On the top two floors of a renovated building that used to house a famous art school, the Pallas has some of the most uniquely decorated rooms in Estonia, with vibrantly colourful walls and decent furnishings. Some rooms boast floor-to-ceiling windows, giving sweeping views over the city.

London Hotel (☎ 730 5555; www.londonhotel.ee; Rüütli tänav 9; s/d from 1125/1600Kr; ⊠) This handsome modern hotel has comfortable, nicely set rooms – some with enviable views over the old streets. The pond and fountain in the lobby and the inviting restaurant are nice features.

Barclay Hotel (☎ 744 7100; www.barclay.ee; Ülikooli tänav 8; s/d/ste/ste with sauna 990/1520/1800/2300Kr; ⊠) This charming hotel has elegant rooms with high ceilings and abundant greenery surrounding the 1912 building. The Barclay has a surprising past: the Red Army was headquartered here until 1992; you can also stay in the room where Chechen president Dudayev kept his office.

Hansa Hotell (☎ 737 1800; www.hansahotell.ee; Aleksandri 46; s/d/apt €60/80/105; ⊠) A 15-minute walk southwest of Raekoja plats, this charming hotel has decent, comfortably furnished rooms and more spacious apartments with wood-beamed ceilings, exposed brick and full kitchens. There's a lively bar and restaurant in the courtyard.

Hotel Draakon (☎ 744 2045; www.draakon.ee; Raekoja plats 2; s/d/ste from 975/1550/2600Kr; ⊠) Overlooking Raekoja plats, this elegant hotel has tastefully furnished rooms with deep wood tones, large windows and classic colour schemes. The double room with private sauna is worth the upgrade.

Eating

University Café (☎ 737 5405; Ülikooli tänav 20; meals 60-120Kr, 1st fl buffet per kilo 10Kr; 🕑 7.30am-1am Mon-Sat, 10am-10pm Sun) This old-world café with beautiful wooden floors and an outdoor patio is one of the gems of Tartu. Palm trees, high ceilings and black-and-white photographs give a colonial charm to the upstairs airy space. Downstairs there's a simpler buffet (decent breakfasts), also with outdoor patio, that makes a good spot for coffee or a quick meal.

Café Wilde (☎ 730 9764; Vallikraavi tänav 4; 🕑 9am-8pm Mon-Wed, 9am-10pm Thu-Sat, 10am-6pm Sun) This richly decorated place serves good coffees, decadent homemade cakes and light sandwiches. Its namesake is Peter Ernst Wilde, who opened a publishing house on the premises in the 18th century, though the pub also pays tribute to two literary Wildes: Oscar Wilde and Eduard Wilde. For heartier dining (and drinking) head to the upstairs pub (p114).

La Dolce Vita (☎ 740 7545; Kompanii 10; meals 45-80Kr) Thin-crust pizzas come straight from the wood-burning oven at this charming pizzeria. You'll also find pastas, salads and classic but casual décor (red-and-white checked tablecloths, Fellini posters). There's a patio at the back.

Crepp (☎ 742 2133; Rüütli 16; meals from 55Kr) This Parisian-style café serves delicious crepes, fresh salads and sandwiches in a cosy, candlelit setting. Outdoor tables are used in summer.

Gruusia Saatkond (☎ 744 1386; Rüütli 8; meals 45-90Kr) A rustic but colourfully decorated dining room sets the scene for feasting on hearty plates of Georgian cuisine. Eggplant with walnuts, *hatšapuri*, trout with walnuts and *shashlik* are among the favourites.

Suudlevad Tudengid (☎ 730 1893; Raekoja plats 10; meals 50-150Kr) One of several outdoor cafés on the main square, this one serves nicely prepared international fare (pasta, gazpacho, burgers, mushroom risotto). Downstairs there's a cosy brick-lined café. The restaurant incidentally means 'Kissing Students' – presumably named after the fountain rather than the sometimes frisky customers.

Maailm (☎ 742 9099; Rüütli 12; meals from 50Kr) The old wooden floors, beamed ceilings and wildly decorated walls may make you feel like you've stumbled across Greg Brady's secret Tartu hideaway. The food is just as eclectic: curry chicken, fish soup, vegetarian enchiladas and milkshakes.

Bambus (☎ 742 2448; Ülikooli tänav 5; meals 75-125Kr) Serving Indian, Thai and other dishes from the East, this loungelike space is beautifully set with bamboo furniture, exposed brick walls and other warm touches. The food is excellent.

Tsink Plekk Pang (☎ 744 1789; Küütri tänav 6; meals 50-200Kr) Named after the zinc buckets that are suspended from the ceiling as lampshades, this warmly lit Chinese pub serves decent meals with plenty of vegetarian fare. The outdoor patio up top is particularly inviting.

Püssirohukelder (☎ 730 3555; Lossi tänav 28; meals 50-100Kr) Set majestically in a cavernous old gunpowder cellar, this place doubles as a boisterous pub and it's a good choice for tasty meat and fish dishes. A more secluded wine cellar joins the space.

Werner (☎ 744 1274; Ülikooli tänav 15; 🕒 9am-8pm) This old-world classic serves fresh pastries, teas and coffees. It's a Tartu favourite.

Kondiitriärii (☎ 740 0366; Rüütli tänav 5; 🕒 8am-7pm Mon-Fri, 9am-5pm Sat, 10am-4pm Sun) Another lovely spot for cakes, pastries and coffee.

Outdoor Market (🕒 8am-5pm Mon-Fri, to 3pm Sat & Sun) The outdoor market, just east of the bus station, is a fun place to browse for fresh produce, flowers and other goodies.

There's a more extensive **indoor market** (🕒 8am-4pm Tue-Fri) across Riia maantee from the bus station.

Drinking

Wilde Irish Pub (☎ 730 9765; Vallikraavi tänav 4; meals from 60Kr) Upstairs from Café Wilde (p113), this pub has good food (both Estonian and Irish), live music and a popular terrace.

Zavood (☎ 744 1321; Lai 30) This battered cellar bar attracts an alternative, down-to-earth crowd with its inexpensive drinks and lack of attitude. Student bands sometimes play here.

Hansa Tall (☎ 737 1802; Aleksandri 46) Set like an old-fashioned tavern, this lively pub also has an extensive outdoor courtyard that draws a fair mix of locals and tourists on warm summer days. If it's not your scene you can always try Õlle Tare, a popular pub next door.

Zum Zum (☎ 744 1438; Küüni 2) Just off Raekoja plats, this indoor-outdoor pub and restaurant is a fun, welcoming place for a drink.

Entertainment

NIGHTCLUBS

Illegaard (☎ 742 3743; Ülikooli tänav 5; 🕒 5pm-2am) This New Wave–inspired jazz vault attracts an artsy crowd who cluster around tables for lively conversations. Live jams happen during the school year (September to May), and infrequently in the summer.

Atlantis (☎ 738 5485; www.atlantis.ee; Narva maantee 2; 🕒 10pm-3am Tue-Sat) Overlooking the Emajõgi River, Atlantis is a popular place that's pretty short on style; the riverside setting, however, is nice, and if you're in the mood, the retro hits make for a cheesy good time.

Club Tallinn (☎ 740 3157; www.clubtallinn.ee; Narva maantee 27; 🕒 10pm-3am Wed, Fri & Sat) Tartu's best nightclub is a multifloored dance fest with many nooks and crannies. Top-notch DJs spin here, drawing an eager, young crowd. Unfortunately, it's open only during the school year. During the summer, Club Tallinn (p160) packs up and moves to Pärnu.

THEATRE

Vanemuine Theatre (☎ 744 0165; www.vanemuine.ee; Vanemuise tänav 6) Named after the ancient Estonian song god, this theatre hosted the first Estonian-language theatre troupe, which performed here in 1870. The venue still hosts an array of classical and alternative theatrical and musical performances. It also stages performances at its **small stage** (☎ 744 0160; Vanemuise tänav 45) and **Sadamateater** (☎ 734 4248; Soola 5b).

Shopping

You'll find handicrafts stores scattered about the old streets.

Antoniuse Gild (Lutsu 5; 🕒 11am-5pm Tue-Fri) One of the best places to shop. Here you'll find ceramics, stained glass, leather-bound books, quilts, woodcarvings, as well as clothing made by some of Tartu's talented young fashion designers.

Getting There & Away

BUS

Daily buses run between Tartu and Tallinn (80Kr to 110Kr, 2½ to 3½ hours) every 15 to 30 minutes from 6am to midnight. International bus tickets are sold from the Eurolines office inside the **Tartu bus station** (☎ 733 1277; Soola tänav 2).

Daily bus services to and from Tartu include the following:

Haapsalu 110Kr to 170Kr, 4½ hours, one bus.
Kuressaare 200Kr to 220Kr, six to seven hours, two buses.
Narva 85Kr to 105Kr, three to 3½ hours, 10 buses.
Pärnu 85Kr to 115Kr, two to 3 hours, 16 buses.
Rīga 120Kr, four hours, one morning bus.
St Petersburg 240Kr, eight hours, one bus.
Valga 55Kr to 65Kr, 1½ to 2½ hours, eight buses.
Viljandi 50Kr to 60Kr, 1½ to 2 hours, 16 buses.
Võru 45Kr to 55Kr, one hour, 26 buses.

TRAIN

The seemingly abandoned **train station** (☎ 737 3200; Vaksali tänav 6) is 750m west of Toomemägi. Timetables are posted outside; tickets are sold on the train.

Four trains make the daily journey to Tallinn (80Kr, 2½ hours). One daily train also travels from Tartu to Elva (12Kr, 50 minutes), continuing on to Valga (36Kr, two hours).

Getting Around

The central stop for city buses is on Riia maantee, opposite the old Kaubamaja department store.

Bikes can be rented from **Jalgratas** (☎ 742 1731; Laulupeo 19; per day 120Kr), adjoining the Tähtvere Hostel.

The tourist office keeps up-to-date lists of car-hire agencies with prices. Among the many options are **City Car** (☎ 523 9699; www.citycar.ee; Jõe 9a) and **Sixt** (☎ 744 7260; www.sixt.ee; Ülikooli 8), which is handily located in the Barclay Hotel but isn't the cheapest. Call first before stepping out, as most agencies can pick you up, and many of these places are quite a hike.

By far, the cheapest place to rent a car is at **Olev's** (☎ 503 0151; per day from €10) in Elva, where you can hire a refurbished Audi; Olev, the friendly owner, can help arrange transport down.

AROUND TARTU

Piirisaar

This island in Lake Peipsi lies on the border with Russia, 50km due east of Tartu. It used to be a refuge for young men fleeing from conscription into tsarist armies. In its heyday at the end of the 1920s, the island had 700 inhabitants. Now less than 100 Russian Old Believers live on Piirisaar, scattered among three villages. There's a working church with services every Sunday morning, a border guard station (climb the observation tower for a great view), a general store, the villages, marshland and not much else. A visit on the two biggest feast days in the Orthodox Old Believers' calendar could prove interesting: 12 July is Peter and Paul Day, and 28 August is Uspeniya (Lady Day). For more information on the Old Believers, see p127

The *Polaris* **hydrofoil** (☎ 734 0066; 200Kr) departs from Tartu on Thursdays at 10am, returning at 5.30pm; and on Sundays at 10am, returning at 4pm. There's also a Friday 5.30pm boat, but it returns at 8.30pm, leaving little time to explore. Check with the Tartu tourist office for the latest schedule. Accommodation on the island can be arranged by the **general store** (☎ 743 4160).

Half the fun is the 90-minute boat trip along the Emajõgi. The *Polaris* leaves from the river port, 100m northeast of the bus station.

Elva & Around

pop 6300

A small town 27km from Tartu in a hilly, forested landscape on the Tartu–Valga road, Elva is set between two pretty lakes, Verevi and Arbi. Just outside town is Elva Vitipalu, a small, beautiful nature reserve with hiking trails, pristine rivers and lakes.

For more lake action, you can head 15km further west of Elva to **Võrtsjärv** (www.hot.ee/vjarv), Estonia's second-biggest lake. The best beaches lie on the northern and western shores.

The friendly **tourist information office** (☎ 735 6057; www.elva.ee; Pikk 2; 🕒 10am-5pm Mon-Fri, to 3pm Sat) near the train and bus stations is a good place to pick up maps and hiking guides, and get info on boating and horse riding in the area. The same building also contains the small **Tartumaa Muuseum** (☎ 745 6141; www.tartumaamuuseum.ee, in Estonian; Pikk 2; 🕒 10am-5pm Mon-Fri, to 3pm Sat), featuring exhibits on local history, folklore and artists.

From there, you can stroll west along Kesk street, the town's main street, which has banks, restaurants and a supermarket. Abutting Kesk street to the north is the pine-shrouded Arbi järv, the pleasant lake with a 1.5km walking path circling it. In the winter Arbi järv transforms into a skating rink.

About 1km northwest of Arbi järv off Tartu maantee is Verevi järv. With its sandy beach, refreshing water and views of the forest on the far shores, this lake makes a good setting for a swim on summer days.

Elva Vitipalu lies about 2km southeast of town. If you're on foot, you can take the walking path from the information office. Inside the reserve, hiking and biking trails pass near idyllic lakes, through pine forests and along the wandering Elva River. You can overnight in the reserve inside wooden cabins or camp sites. Pick up trail maps from the Elva information office.

SLEEPING & EATING

Waide Motel (☎ 730 6606; www.waide.ee; camp site/caravan/s/d 50/150/500/700Kr; ⊠) Some 2.5km southwest of Elva towards Rannu is this small complex. Here you'll find comfortable,

THE BLUE, BLACK AND WHITE: THE BIRTH OF A NATIONAL SYMBOL

Estonia's tricolour dates back to 1881, when a theology student named Jaan Bergmaan wrote a poem about a beautiful flag flying over Estonia. The only problem, for both Jaan and his countrymen, was that no flag in fact existed. Very clearly, something had to be done about this. This was, after all, the time of the national awakening, when the idea of independent nationhood was on the lips of every young dreamer across the country.

In September of that year, at the Union of Estonian Students in Tartu, 20 students and one alumnus gathered to hash out ideas for a flag. All present agreed that the colours must express the character of the nation, reflect the Estonian landscape, and connect to the colours of folk costumes. After long discussions, the students came up with blue, black and white. According to one interpretation, blue symbolised hope for Estonia's future; it also represented faithfulness. Black was a reminder of the dark past to which Estonia would not return; it also depicted the country's dark soil. White represented the attainment of enlightenment and education – an aspiration for all Estonians; it also symbolised snow in winter, light nights in summer and the Estonian birch tree.

After the colours were chosen, it took several years before the first flag was made. Three young activist women – Emilie, Paula and Miina Beermann – carried this out by sewing together a large one made out of silk. In 1884 the students held a procession, which went from Tartu to Otepää, a location far from the eyes of the Russian government. All members of the students' union were there as the flag was raised over the vicarage. Afterwards it was dipped in Puhajärv (a lake considered sacred to Estonians, see p118), and locked safely away in the student archive.

Although the inauguration of the flag was a tiny event, word of the flag's existence spread, and soon the combination of colours appeared in unions and choirs, and hung from farmhouses all across Estonia. By the end of the 19th century the blue-black-and-white was used in parties, and at wedding ceremonies. Its first political appearance, however, didn't arrive until 1917, when thousands of Estonians marched in St Petersburg demanding independence. In 1918 Estonia was declared independent, and the flag was raised on Pikk Hermann in Tallinn's Old Town. There it remained until the Soviet Union seized power in 1940.

During the occupation the Soviets banned the flag, and once again the blue-black-and-white went underground. For Estonians, keeping the flag on the sly was a small but hopeful symbol of one day regaining nationhood. People hid flags under floorboards or unstitched the stripes and secreted them in bookcases; those caught with the flag faced severe punishment – including a possible sentence in the Siberian gulags. Needless to say, as the Soviet Union teetered on the brink of collapse, blue, black and white returned to the stage. On February 1989, 45 years after its first time up, the flag was raised again on Pikk Hermann. Independence had been regained.

all-wooden en-suite rooms (some with balconies) and a pleasant café, and the property is backed by woods. Staff can help arrange activities – cycling, canoeing, sailing – if you arrange in advance.

Tartumaa Health & Sport Centre (Tervisespordikeskus; ☎ 745 6333; cabin from 300Kr; ⊠) Inside the nature reserve, these tidy wooden cabins are rich with the scent of pine, and sleep from two to four. Bathrooms, shower and sauna are inside the main building.

Free RMK camp sites are scattered throughout the park.

Kolmas Eesti (☎ 730 3616; Kesk 10; meals 50-80Kr; ⏲ 9am-midnight; ⊠) A few blocks from the information office, this handsome wooden pub serves good soups, *shashlik*, perch fillet, and many other selections.

GETTING THERE & AWAY

Between 6.30am and 9.30pm, more than 25 buses travel daily between Elva and Tartu (20Kr to 30Kr, 30 minutes to one hour). There's also a daily train to Elva (12Kr, 45 minutes).

Otepää

pop 2200

The small hilltop town of Otepää, 44km south of Tartu, is the centre of a picturesque area of forests and lakes, scenic hillsides and crisp rivers. The district is beloved by

Estonians for both its natural beauty and its many possibilities for hiking, biking and swimming in summer, and cross-country skiing in winter. Some have even dubbed this the 'Estonian Alps' – a teasing reference not to its 'peaks' but to its lovely ski trails.

ORIENTATION & INFORMATION

The centre of town is the triangular main 'square', Lipuväljak, with the bus station just off its east corner. There you'll find the **Otepää Tourist Office** (☎ 766 1200; www.otepaa.ee; Lipuväljak 13; 🕑 9am-5pm Mon-Fri, 10am-3pm Sat) with well-informed staff who can distribute maps and brochures, and make recommendations for activities, guide services and lodging in the area. Near the bus station, you'll find the **post office** (Lipuväljak 24) and a Hansapank **bank** (Lipuväljak 11) with ATM.

For information about hiking in the area, stop in at the **Otepää Nature Park headquarters** (☎ 765 5876; otepaa.looduspark@mail.ee; Kolga tee 28; 🕑 9am-4pm Mon-Fri) near Pühajärv.

SIGHTS

Church

Otepää's pretty little 17th-century church is on a hill top about 100m northeast of the bus station. It was in this church in 1884 that the Estonian Students' Society consecrated its new blue, black and white flag (see boxed text, opposite) which later became the flag of independent Estonia. Facing the church's west door is a small mound with a monument

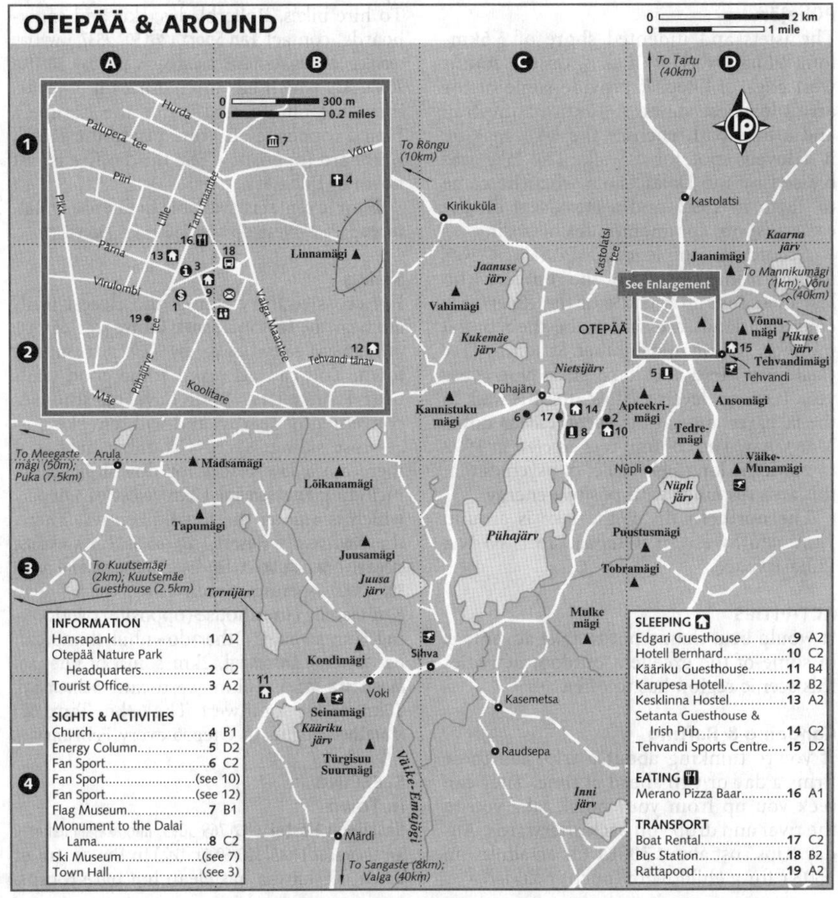

to those who died in the 1918–20 independence war. The former vicar's residence now houses two museums: **Flag Museum** (Eesti Lipu Muuseum; ☎ 765 5075; admission free) and **Ski Museum** (Suusamuuseum; ☎ 766 3670; adult/child 10/7Kr; 9am-2pm Tue-Fri, 10am-1pm Sat); both museums can be viewed by appointment.

Linnamägi

The tree-covered hill south of the church is Linnamägi (Castle Hill), a major stronghold from the 10th to 12th centuries. There are traces of old fortifications on top, and good views of the surrounding country. Archaeological finds indicate that the area around the hill was inhabited as early as the 1st century AD.

Pühajärv

The islets and indented shore of 3.5km-long Pühajärv (Holy Lake), on the southwest edge of Otepää, provide some of the area's loveliest views. A 12km nature trail and a bike path encircle the lake, making it a lovely spot for a walk. The lake was blessed by the Dalai Lama when he came to Tartu in 1992, and a **monument** on the eastern shore commemorates his visit.

According to legend, Pühajärv was formed from the tears of the mothers who lost their sons in a battle of the *Kalevipoeg* epic. Its islands are said to be their burial mounds. Major midsummer St John's Day (Jaanipäev) festivities take place here every year. If energy levels are low after the walk to the lake, recharge at the **energy column** down Mäe tänav. The column was erected in 1992 to mark the long-held belief of psychics that this area resounds with positive energy.

The northern tip of the lake is around 2km southwest of Otepää, reached via Pühajärve tee.

ACTIVITIES

It would be a shame not to take advantage of some of the excellent outdoor activities this scenic region has to offer.

Canoeing & Rafting

If you're thinking about a trip, call these firms a day or two ahead of time. They can pick you up from your hotel, take you to the river and drop you back afterwards. All-day trips cost about 300Kr for an adult and 150Kr for a child, with lunch included.

Veetee (☎ 767 9963; www.veetee.ee) offers a range of canoeing and rafting trips along the Ahja River, the Võhandu River and in Lake Kooraste.

Toonus Pluss (☎ 505 5702; www.toonuspluss.ee), near Arula and about 10km south of Otepää, specialises in canoeing trips, which can include combined hiking and mountain-biking tours.

In addition to rentals, Fan Sport (see Hotell Bernhard, opposite) also offers five-hour canoeing excursions on the Võhandu River.

If you want to just get in a boat and go, you can rent **rowboats** (☎ 5343 6359; 10am-7pm) and water-bikes on the north shore of Puhajärv.

Cycling & Rollerblading

To hire bikes, Rollerblades, skis and snowboards, contact **Fan Sport** (☎ 507 7537; www.fansport.ee; blades/skis/bikes/snowboards per day 80/150/200/275Kr), which has three offices in Otepää, including one located inside the Karupesa Hotell (opposite and one inside the Hotell Bernhard (opposite). The third office is just north of Pühajärv.

Bicycle rental is available in Otepää at **Rattapood** (Pühajärve tee; per day 150Kr; 10am-6pm).

Skiing

For cross-country skiing, the closest trails are near the **Tehvandi Sports Centre** (☎ 766 9500; www.tehvandi.ee; trail use per day 50Kr), just outside town. You can also find some good trails near **Kääriku järv**. Both have guesthouses conveniently nearby, and will rent skis.

Most skiing is cross-country here, but there are a few places for downhill skiing, including **Kuutsemägi** 12km west of Otepää, which is among the top ski centres. There, the **Kuutsemäe Resort** (☎ 766 9007; www.kuutsemae.ee; 1-day lift ticket 120-190Kr, ski/snowboard rental 300/400Kr) operates seven runs; there's also Kuutsemäe Guesthouse (opposite) overlooking Kuutsemägi. Other downhill skiing can be done at **Ansomägi**, 2km south of Otepää; **Meegaste mägi**, 10km west; and **Seinamägi**, 10km to the southwest. The 63km Tartu **Ski Marathon** begins in Otepää every February.

SLEEPING

In Town

Kesklinna Hostel (☎ 765 5095; info@kesklinnahotell.ee; Lipuväljak 11; s/d 300/600Kr; ☒) In the centre of town, Kesklinna has clean but bare rooms.

The place is short on charm, but at least there's a guest kitchen.

Edgari Guesthouse (☎ 765 4275; Lipuväljak 3; d from 400Kr; ⊠) Undergoing extensive renovations at the time of research, Edgari has small, clean rooms with decent light and wooden furnishings. There's also a communal kitchen, a pleasant 1st-floor pub, and bigger, better rooms are on the way.

Karupesa Hotell (☎ 766 1500; www.karupesa.ee; Tehvandi tänav 1a; s/d incl breakfast 650/800Kr; ⊠) Karupesa has a range of comfortable rooms, with nicely sized windows but an uninspiring colour scheme. The cosy lounge with fireplace makes a nice hideaway during chilly weather. It also has a good restaurant, tennis courts, a sauna, and you can hire bikes, Rollerblades and other gear here.

OUT OF TOWN

Setanta Guesthouse & Irish Pub (☎ 766 8200; www.setanta.ee, in Estonian; Núpli Village; d 500-1200Kr; ⊠) Better known for its Irish pub, Setanta has nine pleasantly furnished rooms, the best of which have terraces and splendid views over the lake.

Tehvandi Sports Centre (☎ 766 9500; www.tehvandi.ee; off Tehvandi tänav; s/d/tr 400/550/750Kr; ⊠) Just outside Otepää, Tehvandi has neat and functional rooms with balconies, housed in the rather Soviet octagonal building. Ski gear and other equipment can be hired on the trails just outside.

Hotell Bernhard (☎ 766 9600; www.bernhard.ee; Kolga tee 22a; d/ste from 890/1600Kr; ⊠) On the eastern edge of Pühajärv, this long, three-storey hotel has excellent rooms set with hardwood floors, big windows, and balconies overlooking the lake and forest. There's a good restaurant and tennis courts, and you can hire sports gear.

Kuutsemäe Guesthouse (☎ 766 9007; www.kuutsemae.ee; d 300-700Kr, cottage 1000-2000Kr; ⊠) Right at the slalom course and downhill slopes, this pleasant guesthouse has nice, simple rooms set among abundant greenery. You can also rent handsome three-bedroom wooden cottages (sleeping six to eight), complete with kitchens and electric saunas.

Kääriku Guesthouse (☎ 766 5600; www.kaariku.com; s/d 450/680; ⊠) Overlooking Lake Kääriku, this modern place has clean, comfortable rooms, but they're a bit nondescript. What most people come here for though are the lovely swimming lakes nearby as well as the many kilometres of trails through the surrounding forest. You can hire skis and other gear here. You can also hire one of two wooden saunas right on the lake.

Sangaste Castle (Sangaste Loss; ☎ 767 9300; www.sangasteloss.ee; dm/s/d from 125/250/390Kr; ⊠) About 22km south of Otepää, this fairy-tale brick castle is one of the most unusual places to stay in the Baltics. Erected between 1874 and 1881, it's said to be modelled on Britain's Windsor Castle. Rooms here are pretty basic with thin mattresses and bare walls. The castle is also open to visitors (museum adult/concession 20/15Kr, open 9am to 6pm). Five buses run daily, connecting Sangaste with Otepää (25Kr, 30 minutes) and Tartu (50Kr, one hour).

EATING & DRINKING

In general, the dining scene here is pretty disappointing.

Setanta Irish Pub (☎ 766 8200; Núpli Village; meals 70-140Kr) Hands down Otepää's best restaurant, this pleasant wooden pub has a lovely outdoor terrace overlooking the lake, and eclectic dishes: pesto pasta, paella and salmon steak among the options.

Merano Pizza Baar (☎ 767 9444; Tartu maantee 1a; pizzas 35-65Kr; 🕑 10am-midnight Mon-Sat, to 10pm Sun) Opposite the Town Hall, this place remains popular despite its flimsy pizzas.

GETTING THERE & AWAY

Buses connect Otepää with Tartu (45 minutes to one hour, 10 daily); Elva (45 minutes, four daily Monday–Saturday); Valga (one hour, one daily); Võru (1½ hours, one daily) and Tallinn (three hours, three daily). If you're heading to Põlva or towns further east, you'll have to go through Tartu first.

Põlva & Taevaskoja

pop 6500

Põlva lies in an attractive valley 48km southeast of Tartu, and makes for a pleasant stop on the way to Võru, 25km to its south. Aside from its tiny sand **beach** on the shoreline of the **lake**, Põlva has little to entice tourists. It does, however, have some enticing countryside nearby.

If you stop in town for a swim, you'll pass by Põlva's oldest building, St Mary's Church, which sits just back from the shore. This handsome country church dates from

1452, although its original foundations were laid in 1240. You can also check out the two war monuments in town, visit a lively food and clothing market, and perhaps stop in a wooded cemetery on your way out of town.

The amiable **tourist office** (☎ 799 4089; www.polvamaale.ee; Kesk tänav 42; 🕒 10am-6pm Mon-Fri, to 3pm Sat & Sun) can provide you with a map and hints on how to make the most of your time. Another excellent outfit is the **Kagureis travel agency** (☎ 799 8530; www.kagureis.ee; Uus tänav 5), located inside the Hotell Pesa. Staff here can organise hiking, biking, canoeing, riding and skiing trips. This agency also handles excursions with Timmo Tallid (right), which is located 1km north of Põlva on the road to Tartu. In addition to horse-riding excursions (two/four hours 400/600Kr), this riding centre offers sleigh rides in the winter (300Kr per hour) and they maintain a hostel year-round.

Taevaskoja, 7km north of Põlva, is in the valley of the Ahja River and is an idyllic base for expeditions of all kinds, or even just for a picnic. The area is noted for two large caves, Väike and Suur Taevaskoja, which are about 2km past the train tracks coming from the Tartu–Põlva road. There are strikingly beautiful red sandstone embankments above the caves, up to 24m high and 190m long, pockmarked by swallows and kingfishers, which nest in them. Signposted multilingual commentaries detail the myths that surround these formations. There are walking and biking paths in the surrounding woods, and you can also follow the river to **Kiidjärv**, 6km north, where you can hire a canoe.

For more in-depth exploration of the Ahja River, you can take a one-hour boat trip on the good ship *Lonny*, which in good weather departs on the hour between 10am and 6pm (50Kr). The ship docks at the entrance to the trails, just up from the car park. You can also book a canoe trip with the **Taevaskoja Holiday Centre** (☎ 799 2067; ttpk@estpak.ee).

SLEEPING & EATING

Pesa Hotel (☎ 799 8530; www.kagureis.ee; Uus tänav 5; s/d €38/57; 🅿) In Põlva, this modern hotel has trim, nicely designed rooms with wooden floors and warm colours. A decent restaurant (with outdoor patio in the summer) adjoins the space. You can also book outdoor activities here.

Ääl Klubi (☎ 799 8542; Tuglase tänav 2; meals 30-70Kr) Overlooking the lake, this simple restaurant offers basic Estonian fare. The tables out front are a nice setting for coffee.

Timmo Tallid (☎ 799 8530; beds 150-200Kr) In addition to horse-related activities, Timmo Tallid has a hostel with plain two- to four-bed rooms with shared bathrooms in the hall. There's also a pub where you can mingle with other admirers of those dashing four-legged animals. Bookings can be made through Kagureis at the Pesa Hotel.

Taevaskoja Tourism & Holiday Centre (☎ 799 2067; ttpk@estpak.ee; camp site/dm 40/170Kr) In Taevaskoja, this centre offers a wide range of activities from canoeing the sparkling Ahja River to rock climbing, bike tours, birdwatching, skiing and winter sled picnics. Guests can stay in basic wooden cabins, and have access to cooking facilities.

GETTING THERE & AWAY

From Tartu you can reach Põlva either by bus (28Kr to 45Kr, one hour, 15 daily) or by train (22Kr, one hour, one daily except Saturday).

Taevaskoja is 2km east of the Tartu–Põlva road, which is the nearest a bus will take you. There are six to 10 buses daily between Põlva and Võru (14Kr to 30Kr, 30 minutes to one hour), and four between Põlva and Tallinn (80Kr to 110Kr, 3½ hours).

An evening train from Tartu stops at Taevaskoja (daily except Saturday), which is a 1km walk from the Tourism & Holiday Centre and 2km from the caves.

VÕRU

pop 15,000

A small pleasant town on the eastern shore of Lake Tamula, Võru has a bucolic feel with its leafy parks and picturesque churches, and 19th-century houses lining its old lanes. Võru's sandy shoreline is perhaps its most attractive feature, and its refreshing lake attracts plenty of beachgoers in summer.

The town was founded in 1784 by special decree from Catherine the Great, though archaeological finds here date back several thousand years. Its most famous resident, however, was neither a tribesman nor a tsarina, but the writer Friedrich Reinhold Kreutzwald (1803–1882), who is known as the father of Estonian literature for his folk epic *Kalevipoeg*.

Information

The **tourist office** (☎ 782 1881; www.vorulinn.ee; Tartu maantee 31; 🕑 9am-6pm Mon-Fri, 9am-3pm Sat & Sun May-Sep, 9am-5pm Mon-Fri Oct-Apr) is a good place to pick up a map and get info about festivals, attractions and tourist farms throughout Võru and Setu counties.

Banks, including **Ühispank** (Tartu maantee 25), are scattered about town. Free Internet access is available at the **public library** (Jüri; 🕑 10am-6pm Mon-Fri, to 4pm Sat).

Sights & Activities

Võru's most interesting museum is the **Kreutzwald Memorial Museum** (Kreutzwaldi tänav 31; adult/concession 10/5Kr; 🕑 11am-4pm Wed-Sun), set in the former house where the great man lived and worked as a city doctor from 1833 to 1877. In addition to personal relics, there's a lovely garden at the back.

In front of the 18th-century **Lutheran Church** (Jüri tänav 9) overlooking the central square is a granite **monument** to 17 local town council officials who lost their lives in the 1994 *Estonia* ferry disaster. Up the road is the classical yellow and white Russian Orthodox **Jekateriina kirik** (Tartu tänav 26), built in 1793 and named in honour of Catherine II.

Located in one of the town's ugliest buildings, the **Võrumaa Regional Museum** (☎ 782 1939; www.hot.ee/muuseumvoru; Katariina tänav 11; adult/concession 10/6Kr; 🕑 11am-6pm Wed-Sun) has mildly interesting exhibits on regional history and culture.

Undergoing renovation at research time, the **Cultural Centre** (Liiva tänav 11) should be open again by the time you read this. The garden behind the building hosts concerts and folk festivals. Check the tourist office to see if anything is on when you're in town.

Silja Sport (☎ 782 1916; Vabaduse 1; bikes per day 200Kr; 🕑 9am-7pm) hires out bikes, snowboards and ski equipment. It's on the ground floor of the Semu department store. Ask at the tourist office about December snow-safari tours.

Sleeping & Eating

Tamula Hotel (☎ 783 0430; www.tamula.ee; Vee tänav 4; s/d 500/800Kr; 💻) Võru's loveliest hotel has

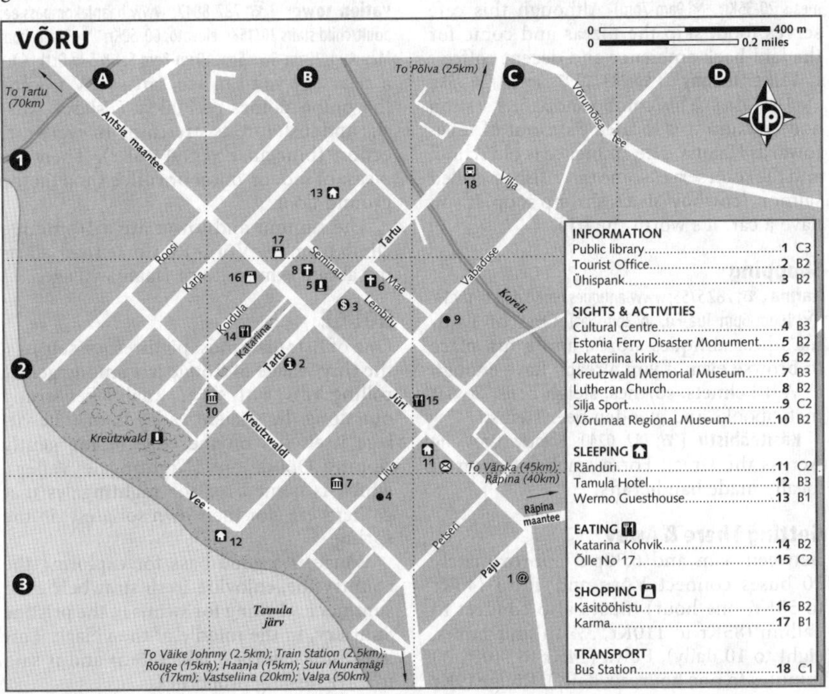

a minimalist, Scandinavian design with bright airy rooms, big windows and lake-front balconies. Best of all, the beach is right outside your door.

Ränduri (☎ 786 8050; www.randur.ee; Jüri tänav 36; s/d with private bathroom from €28/45, with shared bathroom €24/35) Ränduri has handsomely set 2nd-floor rooms, each decorated around a different motif and colour scheme (Japanese, Egyptian, Russian etc). Third-floor rooms are pleasant but more basic, with shared bathrooms. Downstairs, the wood-lined pub serves fairly good food: schnitzel, salmon, soups and salads (meals cost from 30Kr to 80Kr).

Wermo Guesthouse (☎ 782 3418; Koidula tänav 6; s/d from 250/400Kr) This basic hotel has a range of rooms. The best are newly renovated with clean lines and nice views; the worst have linoleum floors and sagging mattresses.

Õlle no 17 (☎ 782 8461; Jüri tänav 17; meals 40-70Kr) This Irish-style pub is a friendly place for a pint or some hearty food. The pleasant outdoor terrace is a popular meeting spot during the summer.

Katarina Kohvik (☎ 782 4490; Koidula tänav 4; meals 20-35Kr; 🕑 9am-7pm) Although this café serves food, skip the pizzas and come for the laid-back ambience and decent coffee.

Väike Johnny (☎ 783 0192; meals 50-75Kr; 🕑 11am-11pm) This combo shop, fuel station and restaurant is located 3km out of town towards Haanja. The ambience is old school and the cook serves some tasty dishes: grilled salmon, 'cowboy' steak, shrimp soup. If you have a car, it's worth the trip.

Shopping

Karma (☎ 782 5755; www.antiques.ee; Koidula tänav 14; 🕑 10am-6pm Tue-Fri, to 2pm Sat) One of Estonia's best antiques stores, and a fun place to browse even if you already have enough WWII helmets, scythes, sleigh bells, Soviet matchbooks and wooden beer steins.

Käsitööhistu (☎ 782 0240; Koidula tänav 16) Across the street. For a small selection of locally made handicrafts.

Getting There & Away

Between 6am and 6.30pm approximately 20 buses connect Võru and Tartu (45Kr to 55Kr, one hour). Buses also connect to Tallinn (85Kr to 110Kr, 3½ to four hours, eight to 10 daily), Põlva (14Kr to 30Kr, 30 minutes to one hour, six daily), Rõuge (9Kr to 14Kr, 30 minutes, nine daily), Haanja (9Kr to 18Kr, 30 minutes to one hour, seven daily) and Krabi (18Kr to 23Kr, 45 minutes to two hours, four daily). There's a daily bus to Võru (60Kr, two hours). The **bus station** (☎ 782 1018) can provide the latest schedules. Entrance is on Vilja.

HAANJA NATURE PARK

Thick forests, rolling hills and dozens of sparkling lakes and rivers make up this lovely national park south of Võru. This 200-sq-km protected area also includes charming rural villages and some excellent tourist farms. The **Haanja Nature Park headquarters** (☎ 782 9090; www.haanjapark.ee, in Estonian) in the village of Haanja can provide detailed information about the area.

SUUR MUNAMÄGI

Great Egg Hill (Suur Munamägi), about 17km south of Võru, is the highest hill in the Baltics at just over 318m. Still, the tree-covered 'summit' is easy to miss if you're not looking out for it. The best way to enjoy the Great Egg is to ascend its 29m **observation tower** (☎ 787 8847; www.haanjakompass.ee; adult/child stairs 30/15Kr, elevator 60/60Kr; 🕑 10am-8pm May-Aug, 10am-5pm Sep, 10am-8pm Sat & Sun Oct). On a clear day you can see Tartu's TV towers, the onion domes of Pihkva (Pskov), Russia, and lush forests stretching in every direction (binocular rental 15Kr). There's a pleasant indoor-outdoor coffee shop on the ground floor.

The summit and tower are a 10-minute climb from the Võru–Ruusmäe road, starting about 1km south of Haanja village.

RÕUGE

One of Estonia's most picturesque settings, the tiny village of Rõuge lies among gently rolling hills, with seven small lakes strung out along the ancient valley floor. The village itself sits on the edge of the gently sloping Ööbikuorg (Nightingale Valley), which is named for the nightingales that gather here (for their own songfest) in the spring.

Rõuge is a good base for exploring the countryside, enjoying fresh strawberries in summer and going for swims in the pristine Suurjärv, in the middle of the village. This is Estonia's deepest lake (38m) and is said to have healing properties.

You can pick up maps and obtain regional information at Rõuge's well-signed **tourist office** (☎ 785 9245; raugeinfo@hot.ee; Haanja maantee 1; 🕑 10am-4pm Mon-Fri, to 2pm Sat & Sun), 30m from the bus stop.

Opposite **Santa Maria**, Rõuge's attractive 18th-century village church, stands a **monument** to the local dead of the 1918–20 independence war. The memorial was buried in one local's backyard through the Soviet period to save it from destruction.

Rõuge's **Linnamägi** (Castle Hill), by Lake Linnjärv, was an ancient Estonian stronghold during the 8th to 11th centuries. In the 13th century Rougetaja, a man who healed people with his hands, and to whom the ailing travelled from afar to see, lived here. There's a good view here, across the valley.

For a unique tour of the area and historical explanations of local sites and lore, call **Padimees** (☎ 785 9271), who works out of the Saarsilla Café. Padimees can guide you (in Estonian) through nearby places to assess whether you are sensitive to the area's energy fields. His granddaughter sometimes translates the tour into English for him.

Rõuge lies 10km west of Suur Munamägi by dirt road, or by paved road from Võru.

Sleeping & Eating

Ööbikuoru Kämping (☎ 509 0372; www.hot.ee/oobikuorg; camp site 30Kr, cabin per person 75-90Kr, r per person 175-190Kr, cottage 1450Kr; ☒) Set on a lovely spot overlooking Nightingale Valley, this outfit offers lodging in simple wooden cabins with bathrooms in another building. You can also bunk in a winterised cottage with a private bathroom (or rent the whole cottage yourself). Rowboat rental is available. Located 600m from the main road; heading south, take the first left after Saarsilla Café.

Rõuge Suurjärve Guesthouse (☎ 524 3028; Metsa 4; r per person 250-350Kr; ☒) This pleasant guesthouse has a range of comfortable rooms, the best of which have a private balcony overlooking the lake. Sauna available. The turn-off to the guesthouse is opposite Rõuge's church.

Rohtlätte Talu (☎ 787 9315; www.rohtlatte.ee; camp site/r per person €4/16; ☒) Near the village of Nursi, 12km from Võru on the Valga road, this comfortable country place lies in a lush setting overlooking a creek. There are hiking trails (guided excursions available), a sauna and trout fishing.

Vaskna Talu (☎ 782 9173; info@vaskna.ee; s/d from 350/600Kr; ☒) Just south of Haanja by Lake Vaskna is this farmhouse in a particularly pretty spot. Try swimming, boating and water-biking here.

Saarsilla Café (☎ 785 9271; Haanja maantee 2; 🕑 10am-11pm; ☒) Situated just outside Rõuge, Saarsilla boasts a lovely terrace by Lake Suurjärv.

Several shops, a few cafés, a restaurant and a post office lie 1km out of town on the road to Nursi.

LUHASOO TRAIL & KARULA NATIONAL PARK

Located in wild swampland on the border with Latvia, some 15km south of Rõuge, the **Luhasoo Nature Study Trail** provides a fascinating glimpse into Estonia's primordial past. The 4.5km well-marked trail passes over varied bogs and along a velvety black lake, with Venus flytraps, water lilies and herbivorous shrubs among the scenery.

To get there, take the Krabi road from Rõuge and, after the Pärlijõe bus stop, turn right towards Kellamäe, then continue another 5km.

Further along the main road that borders Paganamaa, and about 12km along dirt roads north of the village of Mõniste, is an area of round, wooded hills dotted with many small lakes and ancient stone burial mounds, which forms Karula National Park. The **National Park Visitors Centre** (☎ 782 8350; kiri@karularahvuspark.ee) in Ähijärve, past Lüllemäe, 25km east of Valga, distributes maps and hiking trail information. The highlight is Ähijärv, a 3km long lake with several bays, inlets and promontories. There are four marked trails in the park, the longest beginning in Lüllemäe. This area can also be reached via Antsla to the north.

Set in the Forest Fairy Park (Metsamoori Perepark), **Veetka Farm** (☎ 786 7633; www.metsamoor.ee; camp site 50Kr) is one of several tourist farms in the area offering some unusual attractions. In addition to hiking trails, you can camp here, spend a sleepless night out on a raft floating in the lake and learn about healing herbs and forest spirits.

In Vastse-Roosa near Mõniste, 8km west of Paganamaa, there is **Metsavenna Talu** (☎ 789 1280; info@metsavennatalu.ee; camp site/chalet bed 25/200Kr), an authentic reconstruction of typical living quarters used by the Forest

Brothers resistance (Metsavendlus). Being the initiative of one of the original brothers, authenticity is assured. It is also possible to camp overnight or sleep in a dorm bed in the chalet. Sauna and guided nature tour are also available.

VALGA

pop 16,000

The once-battered border town of Valga is enjoying a slow process of gentrification, and its old wooden houses and curious history make it an interesting place to wander through before moving on. The town, contiguous with Valka in Latvia, is set in the only region that was seriously contended between Estonia and Latvia after WWI. A British mediator had to be called in to settle the dispute and suggested the current border line, effectively splitting the town in two.

The **information centre** (☎ 766 1699; www.valgalv.ee; Kesk 11; 🕒 9am-6pm Mon-Fri, 10am-3pm Sat & Sun), located near the border crossing in town, can provide you with a town map and recommend inexpensive homestays in the area.

Sites of interest include the 19th-century **St John's Church** (Jaani Kirik) and a local history **museum** (Valga Koduloomuuseum; ☎ 766 8867; Vabaduse 8; 🕒 11-6pm Tue-Fri; 10am-3pm Sat & Sun).

An estimated 30,000 people were murdered at the Nazi death camp Stalag-351, located in converted stables at Priimetsa on Valga's outskirts.

You can also stay in the lovely new **Metsis Hotell** (☎ 766 6050; www.hotellmetsis.com; Kuperjanovi 63; s/d from 500/700Kr), which also has a good restaurant (meals 75Kr to 150Kr). On the same road is **Voorimehe Pubi** (☎ 767 9627; Kuperjanovi 57; meals 40-65Kr), an atmospheric darkwood pub that serves filling salmon, pork and the like.

Around eight daily buses connect Valga with Tartu (55Kr to 65Kr, 1½ to 2½ hours), and one bus daily goes to Võru (two hours). One daily train runs between Tallinn and Valga (115Kr, 5½ hours). Twice daily trains travel from Valga to Tartu (36Kr, two hours) via Sangaste Castle (6Kr, 20 minutes).

VASTSELIINA CASTLE

Vastseliina Castle (Vastseliina linnus) was founded by the Germans on their border with Russia in the 14th century. The evocative ruins stand on a high bluff above the Piusa River on the eastern edge of the village of **Vahtseliina**, 4km east of the small town of **Vastseliina**, itself 12km southeast of Võru along the road to Pihkva (Pskov). The area prospered from its position on the Pihkva–Rīga trade route until the mid-19th century and was also the scene of many battles.

The castle stands on the Meremäe road out of Vahtseliina. In the valley, down to the left as you walk from the former inn to the castle, is the park of the old Vastseliina manor, where a pretty 15km hiking trail (piusa matkarada) along the river begins a circuit north to Suuremetsa. A map near the ruins details the region's hiking and mountain-biking routes.

To reach Vahtseliina turn east off the Võru–Pihkva road 1km south of the southernmost turning to Vastseliina (which is just west of the road) and go 2km. Several buses from Võru go to Vastseliina daily and some, including most of those to Misso, continue along the Pihkva road to the Vahtseliina turning and beyond.

SETUMAA

In the far southeast of Estonia lies the (politically unrecognised) area of Setumaa, stretching over into Russia. It's one of the most interesting and tragic areas of the country, politically and culturally. Its native people, the Setus, have a mixed Estonian-Russian culture. They are originally Finno-Ugric but the people became Orthodox, not Lutheran, because this part of the country fell under Novgorod and later Pihkva's (Russian: Pskov) subjugation and was not controlled by Teutonic and German tribes and barons, as was the rest of Estonia. They never fully assimilated into Russian culture and throughout the centuries retained their language (today known as Võro-Seto), many features of which are actually closer in structure to Old Estonian than the modern Estonian language. The same goes for certain cultural traditions, for instance leaving food on a relative's grave; this was practised by Estonian tribes before Lutheranism.

All of Setumaa was in independent Estonia between 1920 and 1940, but the greater part of it is now in Russia. The town of Pechory (Petseri in Estonian), 2km across the border in Russia and regarded as the 'capital' of Setumaa, is famed for its fabulous 15th-century monastery, considered the

DEVIL'S RUN

Along the Latvian border just south of the village of Krabi lies **Paganamaa** (Devil's Land), another scenic area with four lakes strung out along the Estonian side of the border in the Piiriorg Valley. Legend has it that this was the home of Vanapagan (Old Heathen), a devil who set about building a bridge across Lake Kikkajärv to his friends in Latvia. As he was collecting boulders, a thunderstorm frightened him (thunder was the god of heaven to ancient Estonians) and he ran, creating the craters and sharp valleys that are characteristic of the area (glacier-formed, to us modern sceptics). The small island in Kikkajärv is supposed to be one of the boulders he dropped on the run. There's an observation tower and bathing spot at Liivajärv, a lake which lies half in Estonia, half in Latvia. Three buses per day go to Krabi from Võru (one hour), passing through Rõuge en route.

most breathtaking in Russia (it looks more like an Italian villa than a monastery).

Today the Setu culture is in the sad, slow process of disappearing. There are approximately 4000 Setus in Estonia (and another 3000 in Russia), which is half the early-20th-century population. While efforts are made to teach and preserve the language, and promote customs through organised feasts, the younger generation are being quickly assimilated into the Estonian mainstream. The impenetrable border with Russia that has split their community since 1991 has further crippled it.

A rough look at the Setu landscape illustrates how unique it is in the Estonian context. Notably, their villages are structured like castles, with houses facing each other in clusters, often surrounded by a fence. This is in stark contrast to the typical Estonian village where open farmhouses are separated from each other as far as possible. Here, the Orthodox tradition has fostered a tighter sense of community and sociability.

Setumaa is particularly known for its women folk singers who improvise new words each time they chant their verses. Setu songs, known as the *leelo*, are polyphonic and characterised by solo, spoken verses followed by a refrain chanted by a group.

Obinitsa & Piusa

The village of Obinitsa, near a pristine lake, makes for a pleasant stopoff on the road. The chief attraction is the one-room **Setu House Museum** (Setu Tare Muuseum; adult/concession 15/10Kr; 11am-5pm Tue-Sun May-Oct, other times by appt), which has a few folk costumes, tapestries, cookware and some old photos. It also functions as the **tourist office** (☎ 785 4190; setotour@hot.ee). A few blocks away, you can have a traditional Setu meal – if you arrange it in advance. The town also has a church (built in 1897), a cemetery and a sculpture to the Setu 'Song Mother', which stares solemnly over Lake Obinitsa. There's a swimming platform by the lake.

Obinitsa has several big Setu celebrations, the most important being the 19 August **Feast of the Transfiguration**. Thousands of Setus come for a procession from the church to the cemetery, which ends with a communal picnic and the leaving of food for the departed souls.

The road north from Obinitsa passes under a railway bridge after some 5km. The first dirt road east, following the sign for the Piusa Pood (shop), will take you to one of Estonia's more intriguing sights, the **Piusa sand caves** (Piusa Koopad), the result of a sand mining industry, which began in the area in 1922. (Sand is still mined for glass production 1km north of this spot.) You can visit the smaller of the two unused caves; the larger one remains plunged in darkness and home to some 2000 bats (one of Europe's largest colonies), just behind the friendly **shop/café** (10am-4pm). There's a small **RMK office** (10am-6pm) here where you can pick up maps of the nearby regions.

You can wander through a maze of cathedral-like caves (bring a flashlight) and look for the sand altar, made by some well-known modern-day Estonian witches in the early 1990s. If you place your palms on the altar top and they feel warm, your spiritual energy is derived from the land, if they feel cold, your energy comes from the sky.

Seltsimaja (☎ 786 1412; meals 100Kr) is a private Setu home doubling as Obinitsa's community centre, and if you call the day before, you can order a very filling home-cooked

DAY OF THE SETUS

Peko, the pagan god of fertility, is as important to the Setus as the Orthodox religion they follow. The 8000-line Setu epic *Pekolanõ* tells the tale of this macho god, the rites of whom are known only to men. The epic dates back to 1927 when the Setus' most celebrated folk singer, Anne Vabarna, was told the plot and spontaneously burst into song, barely pausing to draw breath until she had sung the last (8000th) line.

According to folklore, Peko sleeps night and day in his cave of sand. So on the Day of the Setu Kingdom – proclaimed around 20 August each year – an *ülemtsootska* (representative) for the king has to be found. The Setus then gather around the statue of their 'Song Mother' in search of someone worthy of bearing the crown of the sleeping king's royal singer. Competitions are also held to find a strongman for the king.

The Setu king's dress, and the bread, cheese, wine and beer he consumes are also important. On the same day that his kingdom is declared for another year, people from the Setu stronghold are selected to serve the king as his mitten and belt knitters, and bread, beer, wine and cheese makers.

And so completes the royal throne. Amid the day's celebrations, traditional Setu songs and dances are performed and customary good wishes exchanged. The women are adorned with traditional Setu lace and large silver breastplates and necklaces, said to weigh as much as 3kg each. Later in the day respects are paid to the dead.

meal. You can also buy a few handicrafts. It's on the main road into town, and is well-signed.

Set on a small lake, **Setomaa Turismitalo** (☎ 508 7399; http://setotalu.maaturism.ee; d/tr 440/660Kr, 7-room cabin 2800Kr) has a few simple wooden rooms with shared bathrooms, and several sizable, very comfortably furnished cottages for rent. There's a sauna and a place for bonfires.

You're welcome to camp for free on the small grounds next to the Piusa sand caves. No fires.

Värska & Around

The pretty town of Värska is known for its rich mineral water, sold throughout Estonia, and its healing mud. There's plenty of rural charm here, including a picturesque stone church and a leafy cemetery surrounding it. The best reason for coming here is the **Setu Farm Museum** (Setu Talu Muuseum; ☎ 505 4673; adult/concession 20/10Kr; 🕑 10am-5pm May-Sep, 10am-4pm Tue-Sun Oct-Apr) on the south edge of town. Presided over by a wooden carving of Peko, the museum comprises a re-created 19th-century farmhouse complex, with stables, granary and the former workshops for metalworking and ceramics. Don't bypass the charming restaurant here or the excellent gift shop – the region's best – selling handmade mittens, socks, hats, dolls, tapestries, books and recordings of traditional Setu music.

Võporzova and **Tonja**, a few kilometres north of Värska on the west side of Värska Bay, are classic Setu villages. In Võporzova there's a monument to folk singer Anne Vabarna, who knew 100,000 verses by heart. Võporzova homesteads typically consist of a ring of outer buildings around an inner yard, while Tonja's houses face the lake from which its people get their livelihood.

Traditional Setu holidays are still celebrated. The biggest feast of the year, **Lady Day**, falls on 28 August (though it is celebrated only in Pechory), close to which the **Day of the Setu Kingdom** is held. The **Day of Setu Lace** is 1 March and **midsummer** celebrations are held on 6 July in accordance with the Julian calendar. Värska also celebrates **St George's Day** (Jüripäev) in spring (6 May) and winter (9 December).

Other exotic features of this area are the borders. There are only a few official border crossing points with Russia, the rest are abandoned control points, or seemingly unguarded wooden fences, creepy dead ends or lonely plastic signs. One road, from Värska to Saatse even crosses the zigzagging border line into Russian territory for 2km. You're not allowed to stop on this stretch.

Near the tiny, ancient village of **Podmotsa**, northeast of Värska, a beautiful Orthodox church in the Russian village of Kulje is visible across the inlet – as is the border guard watchtower. Be aware that crossing the border at any nonofficial point (even if you have a Russian visa) is illegal and can lead to your arrest.

SLEEPING

The Obinitsa tourist office is the best source of information on farmstays in the area.

Hirvemäe Puhkekeskus (☎ 797 6105; www.hirvemae.ee; Silla tänav 2a; s/d with breakfast 350/560Kr; ⊠) Set on a pretty lake, this guesthouse has wood-floored rooms and a café. There's a tiny beach, tennis courts and a playground. It's located 500m south of the church.

Setu Farm Restaurant (☎ 505 4673; meals around 60Kr; 🕑 11am-7pm Tue-Sun) Across from the museum, this handsome wooden farmhouse makes an unbeatable setting for a delicious home-cooked meal. The fare is nothing fancy – roast vegetables, pork, mashed potatoes, pancakes, omelettes and the like – but it's a real gem nonetheless.

GETTING THERE & AWAY

There are five buses daily between Tartu and Värska (50Kr to 65Kr, 1½ to two hours) via Räpina, three of which continue to Koidula, 2km across the border from Pechory. There's one bus daily between Põlva and Värska (1¼ hours).

From Võru, three to five buses go daily to Meremäe (22Kr, 45 minutes to one hour) and Obinitsa (18Kr to 29Kr, 45 minutes). There are no buses running between Võru and Värska.

LAKE PEIPSI (SOUTH)

In the 18th and 19th centuries Russian Old Believers, a sect of the Orthodox Church persecuted for refusing to accept liturgical reforms carried out in 1666, took refuge on the western shores of Lake Peipsi (Chudkoye Ozero in Russian), particularly in Kallaste. They founded several coastal villages, namely Kolkja, Kasepää and Varnja, and settled the island of Piirissaar.

About 37km north of Tartu lies the spectacular **Alatskivi Castle** (Alatskivi loss; ☎ 528 6598; info@muusa.ee; adult/concession 15/5Kr; 🕑 9am-7pm Wed-Sun), which was built in the late 1500s, though its neo-Gothic centrepiece dates from the 19th century. It's on the main road, easily spotted once you reach Alatskivi.

Four kilometres south of **Alatskivi**, in the hamlet of Rupsi, is the **Liiv Museum** (☎ 745 3846; info@muusa.ee; adult/concession 15/5Kr; 🕑 9am-7pm Wed-Sun), another worthwhile stop. It houses exhibitions on both Juhan Liiv, a celebrated writer and poet who died in 1913, and Eduard Tubin, a composer of some of Estonia's best-known songs and symphonies (No 5 is highly regarded). Both were born in the area. Occasional concerts and poetry competitions are held at the museum, which also doubles as the region's tourist office.

From Alatskivi, it's 6km southeast to **Kolkja**, a village of Russian Old Believers with a dainty, green wooden Orthodox church, an **Old Believers' Museum** (☎ 745 3431; 25Kr; 🕑 by appt) in the new schoolhouse, and some of the most charming village architecture in the country. Unlike most of Estonia's Russian population, the people and their descendants have been living here for centuries, and most also speak Estonian. Few tourists make it out here, and even the dogs stop and stare at strangers.

Kallaste (pop 1285), 8km north of Alatskivi, is where a settlement of Old Believers has existed since 1720, when the area was known as Red Mountains (Krasniye Gori) because of the red sandstone cliffs, up to 11m high, that surround this town. Nearly all the villagers are Russian-speaking. There's a large Old Believers' cemetery at the southern end of town, a sandy beach with small caves, and a lakeside café.

The northern half of Lake Peipsi (p105) is covered in the Northeastern Estonia section.

Sleeping & Eating

The best places to stay in the area are just north of Kallaste.

Piirioja Holiday Centre (☎ 501 8990; www.peipsi.com; camp site per person/4-person cabin 50/400Kr) A few kilometres south of Mustvee, this open grassy space contains new small wooden cabins and room for camping. In addition to beach activities, you can hire a rowboat, fishing tackle or use the sauna.

Hansu Farm (☎ 745 2518; hans.turism@mail.ee; bed per person/camp site from 240/40Kr) About 3km north of Kallaste at the village of Kodavere, and 50m west of the main road, this pleasant farmhouse near the shore has simple, comfortable rooms, a sauna, home cooking, and boat and bicycle hire.

Getting There & Away

A car is the handiest way of getting around this area. Ten buses go daily between Tartu and Kallaste (35Kr, 1¼ hours), with fewer runs on Saturdays and Sundays. Around 15 buses go from Tartu to Alatskivi (27Kr to 35Kr, one hour), again with limited service on weekends. About five daily buses go from Tartu to Kolkja (33Kr, 1½ hours), most via Alatskivi, others via Varnja.

WESTERN ESTONIA & THE ISLANDS

One of the Baltics' most alluring regions, the west coast of Estonia is the gateway to forest-covered islands, idyllic countryside, and seaside villages slumbering beneath the shadows of picturesque medieval castles.

Pine forests and juniper groves cover Saaremaa and Hiiumaa, Estonia's largest islands. Dusty roads loop around them, passing desolate stretches of coastline, with few signs of development aside from 19th-century lighthouses and old wooden windmills – both iconic symbols of the islands. Here you'll find peaceful settings for hiking, horse riding or simply rambling through the countryside in search of hidden stone churches and crumbling fortresses – ruins left behind by both 14th-century German Knights and 20th-century Soviet military planners.

Saaremaa, the largest and most visited of the islands, boasts spa resorts, a magnificent castle and a pretty town that comes to life during the summer months. It's also the departure point for the wildlife-rich islands in Vilsandi National Park and the pastoral setting of Abruka, an island with less than two dozen permanent residents.

Vormsi is another peaceful island of tiny villages and pristine coastline, as is Muhu, which offers unusual attractions, including an ostrich farm and a preserved traditional 19th-century village now functioning as a living museum.

On the mainland, Haapsalu is an enchanting but ragged town that was once a resort for 19th-century Russian aristocrats. The jewel of its Old Town is a 14th-century bishop's castle, today the setting for open-air festivals and summer concerts. The town's bayside promenade, its small but attractive beach and the narrow tree-lined lanes make for an idyllic wander into the past.

The bird life in this region is the best in the country. Bird-watchers, and those interested in experiencing Estonia's verdant forest and marshlands, should head to the Matsalu Nature Reserve, where some 275 bird species can be found.

National Parks & Reserves

Rich in natural beauty, Western Estonia boasts a range of attractive national parks and reserves. On the mainland, the Matsalu Nature Reserve is one of the country's most important bird habitats. Other important bird sanctuaries are the Käina Bay Bird Reserve in Hiiumaa, and the Hiiumaa Islets Landscape Reserve, just off Hiiumaa, where you can spend the night on one of several tiny islands. Off Saaremaa's west coast, the Vilsandi National Park is the largest and most outstanding choice for nature seekers. Comprising numerous uninhabited islands, this reserve also contains rare orchids, seals and more than 200 species of bird.

Getting There & Away

If you don't want to waste time, you can fly directly from Tallinn to either Kärdla in Hiiumaa or Kuressaare in Saaremaa (see p89). Haapsalu is situated just a short bus ride from Tallinn. To reach Hiiumaa, you can also take a bus there directly from Tallinn (see p90). The same bus that drives onto the ferry will drive to its end destination on the island. This also holds true for Saaremaa. If you're not going direct, you can catch ferries from Rohuküla, south of Haapsalu, to both Vormsi and Hiiumaa. To reach Saaremaa by ferry, you'll go via the port of Virtsu to Muhu Island, which is connected to Saaremaa by a causeway. A summer ferry links Saaremaa with the remote island of Ruhnu (p162).

Getting Around

Both Saaremaa and Hiiumaa are quite large and bus service around the islands is highly inadequate. Plenty of people thumb rides, but you'll need time on your hands. Hiring a car is a better alternative. You can rent in both Kuressaare (Saaremaa) and Kärdla (Hiiumaa). Travelling between the two islands, there is a year-round car-ferry service between Sõru in Hiiumaa and Triigi in Saaremaa.

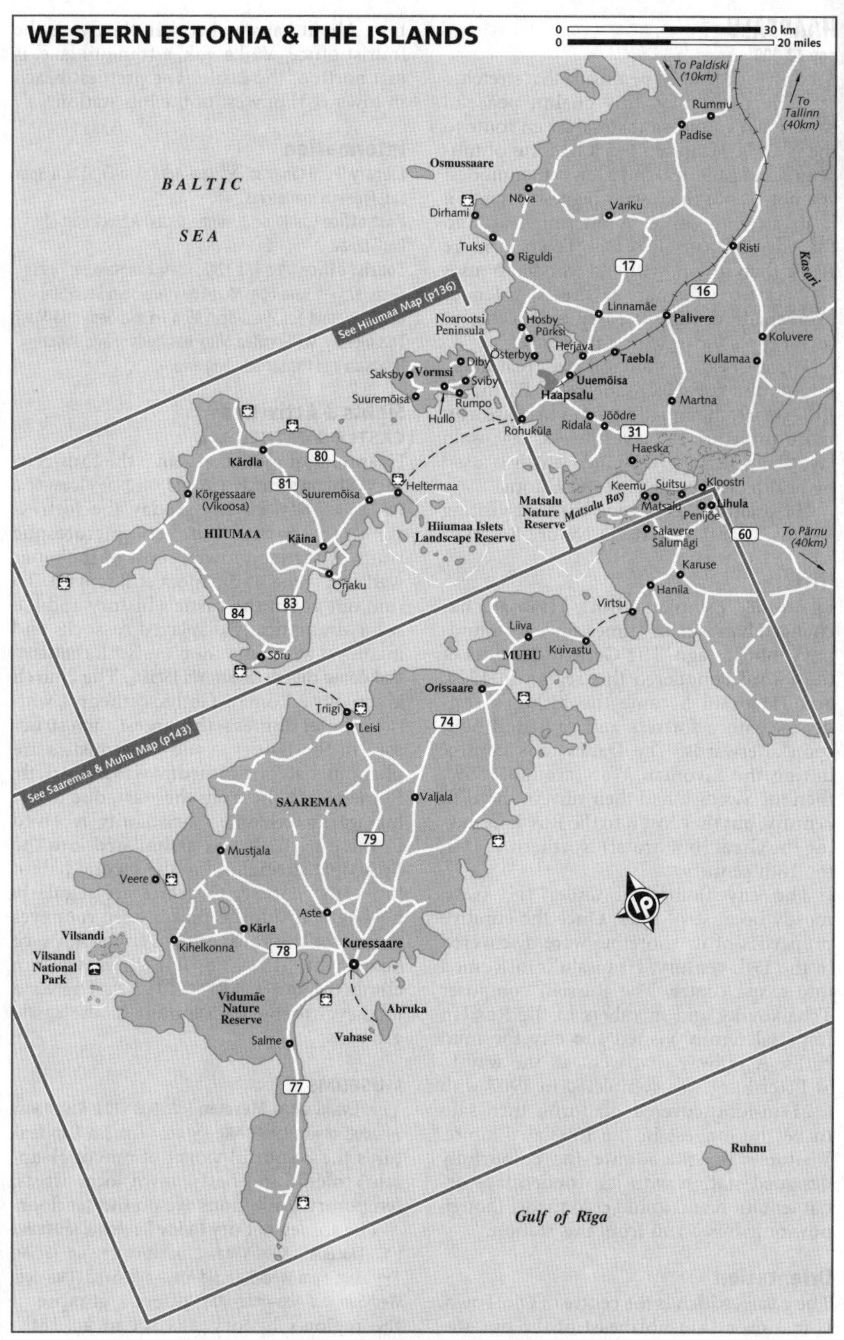
WESTERN ESTONIA & THE ISLANDS
0 30 km
0 20 miles
BALTIC
SEA
To Paldiski (10km)
To Tallinn (40km)
Rummu
Padise
Osmussaare
Nõva
Variku
Dirhami
Tuksi
Riguldi
Risti
Kasari
17
16
See Hiiumaa Map (p136)
Noarootsi Peninsula
Hosby
Pürksi
Linnamäe
Palivere
Koluvere
Herjava
Taebla
Kullamaa
Österby
Diby
Saksby
Vormsi
Sviby
Uuemõisa
Haapsalu
Suuremõisa
Rumpo
Martna
Hullo
Rohuküla
Ridala
Jõõdre
31
Haeska
Kärdla
80
81
Heltermaa
Körgessaare (Vikoosa)
Suuremõisa
Keemu
Suitsu
Kloostri
Matsalu Nature Reserve
Matsalu Bay
Matsalu
Lihula
Penijõe
HIIUMAA
Käina
Hiiumaa Islets Landscape Reserve
Salavere
Salumägi
60
To Pärnu (40km)
Orjaku
Karuse
Hanila
84
83
Virtsu
Liiva
MUHU
Kuivastu
Sõru
Orissaare
Triigi
Leisi
74
See Saaremaa & Muhu Map (p143)
SAAREMAA
Valjala
79
Mustjala
Veere
Vilsandi
Vilsandi National Park
Aste
Kärla
Kihelkonna
78
Kuressaare
Vidumäe Nature Reserve
Abruka
Vahase
Salme
77
Ruhnu
Gulf of Rīga

HAAPSALU

pop 12,000

Set on a fork-shaped peninsula that stretches into Haapsalu Bay, this quaint, peaceful town makes a pleasant stopover en route to the islands. Haapsalu has a handful of museums and galleries, and a few rather modest spa hotels, but the town's biggest attraction is its striking castle. A bit rough around the edges, Haapsalu's Old Town is more rustic than urban, with old wooden houses set back from the narrow streets, a slender promenade skirting the bay, and plenty of secret spots for watching the sunset.

Those seeking mud or spa treatments might opt for Haapsalu over Pärnu or Kuressaare, though the centres here are a bit more proletarian. Nevertheless, Haapsalu lays claim to superior mud, which is used by health centres throughout Estonia.

Haapsalu makes a good base for visiting Vormsi Island or Matsalu Nature Reserve.

History

Like other Estonian towns, Haapsalu has changed hands many times since its founding centuries ago. The German Knights of the Sword conquered this region in 1224, and Haapsalu became the bishop's residence, with a fortress and cathedral built soon afterwards. The Danes took control during the Livonian War (around 1559), then the Swedish had their turn in the 17th century, but they lost it to the Russians during the Great (but brutal) Northern War in the 18th century.

The city flourished under the tsars, mostly because of mud. Once the curative properties of its shoreline were discovered in the 19th century, Haapsalu transformed into a spa centre. The Russian composer Tchaikovsky and members of the Russian imperial family visited the city for mud baths. A railway that went all the way to St Petersburg was completed in 1907 with a 214m-long covered platform, then said to be the longest in the Russian Empire. Visitors can still admire the colourfully designed station with its wooden lace ornamentation and grand colonnade, though now only buses run from this station.

Orientation

The castle, which is the centre of Old Town, is just over 1km northeast of the bus station. About halfway between the two is the tourist office. Väike viik, a tranquil lake, is just north of the castle. The prettiest beach in town is 1km west of the bus station.

Information

Library (Posti tänav 3; ⌚ 9am-4pm Mon-Fri, 10am-3pm Sat) Free Internet access.

Post office (cnr Niine & Nurme tänav) A block east of Posti tänav.

Tourist office (☎ 473 3248; www.haapsalu.ee; Posti tänav 37; ⌚ 9am-6pm Mon-Fri, 10am-3pm Sat & Sun mid-May–mid-Sep, 9am-5pm Mon-Fri mid-Sep–mid-May) This friendly, well-staffed office has loads of info about Haapsalu and the surrounding area.

Sights & Activities

CASTLE & CATHEDRAL

Haapsalu's unpolished gem is the 13th-century **Bishop's Castle** (☎ 472 4470; ⌚ 10am-6pm Tue-Sun mid-May–mid-Sep). Today the fortress stands in partial but very picturesque ruins. A turreted tower, most of the outer wall and some of the moat still remain. To find out about the castle's history and see some dramatically displayed cassocks and medieval weaponry, don't miss the **museum and dome church** (adult/child 15/5Kr). The church is actually a Roman-Gothic cathedral, with three inner domes – the largest such structure in the Baltics – and its acoustics are phenomenal. The cathedral was not strictly Roman Catholic from the start, due to the lukewarm welcome Christianity received in these parts. It was assimilated into the Episcopal stronghold in the second half of the 13th century. Concerts are regularly held here. Inside the church keep your eyes peeled for the ghost of the White Lady (see boxed text, p132). For fine views, you can climb the **tower** (adult/child 15/5Kr). There's a medieval-themed restaurant in the castle grounds.

MUSEUMS

The **Evald Okas Museum** (☎ 508 9105; Karja tänav 24; adult/concession 10/5Kr; ⌚ noon-6pm Jun-Aug) features the colourful works of one of Haapsalu's oldest and best-known local artists; temporary exhibitions are on the 1st floor.

The somewhat dry **Lääne Regional Museum** (☎ 473 6065; Kooli tänav 2; adult/concession 15/5Kr; ⌚ 10am-6pm Wed-Sun mid-May–mid-Sep, 11am-4pm Wed-Sun mid-Sep–mid-May) offers a glimpse of the region's history. It's set in an 18th-

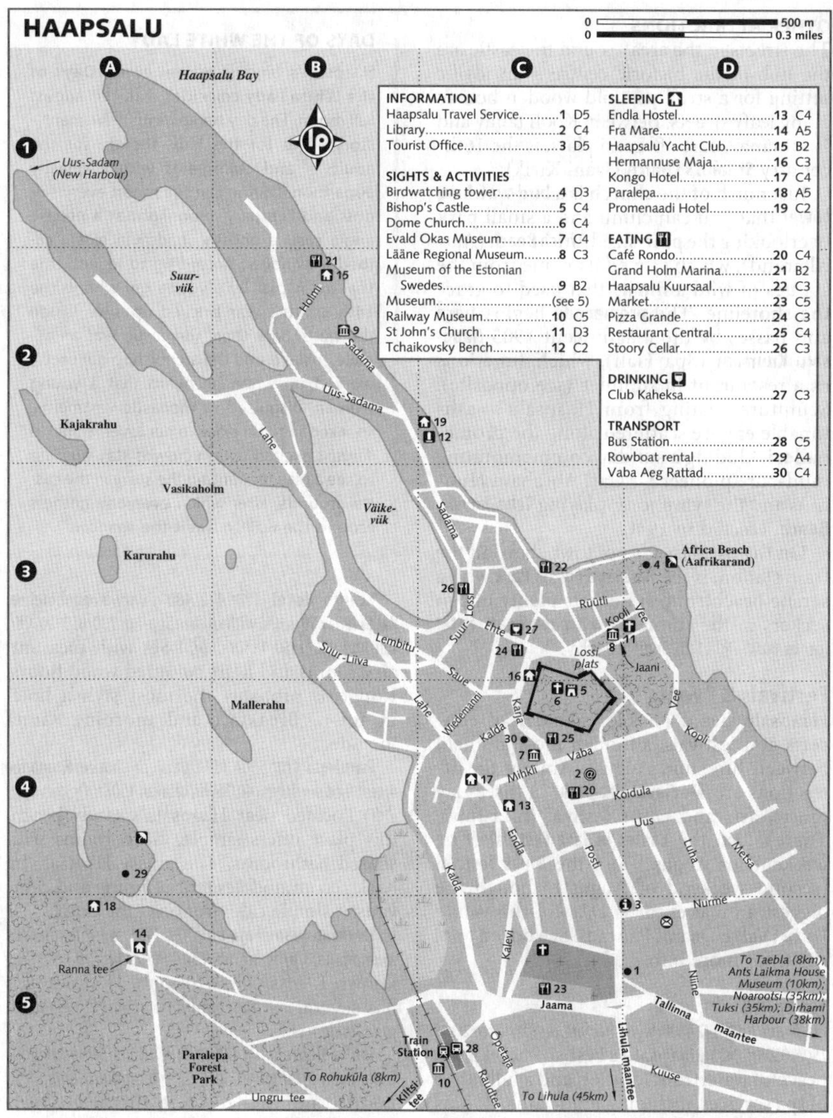

century building that was at one time the town hall.

The quaint **Museum of the Estonian Swedes** (Rannarootsi Muuseum; ☎ 473 7165; Sadama tänav 32; adult/concession 20/10Kr; ⌚ 10am-6pm Wed-Sun 15 May-Aug, 11am-4pm Sep-Apr) has relics, photos, old fishing nets and a marvellous tapestry tracing the history of Swedes in Estonia from the 1200s to their flight back to Sweden on the *Triina* in 1944.

The boxcar-sized **Railway Museum** (Raudteemuuseum; ☎ 473 4574; Raudtee 2; admission 5Kr; ⌚ 10am-6pm Wed-Sun) on the station's west side records the golden years of train travel. You're free to check out the old locomotives nearby.

OTHER ATTRACTIONS

The streets in the area around the castle are the hub of the historic centre – an idyllic setting for a stroll past old wooden houses along leafy streets. Between Kooli tänav and Jaani tänav, east off Lossi plats, is the 16th-century **St John's Church** (Jaani Kirik).

Just north of the church is a **bird-watching tower** that you can climb and a small park overlooking the pint-sized **Africa Beach** (Aafrikarand), which earned its name from the statues of wild animals that used to grace the shoreline. The **promenade** begins here and passes by the magnificent 1905 **Haapsalu Kuursaal** (Spa Hall), which functions as a restaurant in summer (see opposite). Sculptures dating from Haapsalu's fashionable era are scattered along the promenade, including a sundial commemorating mud-cure pioneer Dr Carl Abraham Hunnius and the symphony-playing **Tchaikovsky Bench**, erected in 1940.

On the western edge of town, beyond the train station, is the **Paralepa Forest Park** with a serene beachfront. It attracts plenty of sun seekers in the summer, with **rowboat rental** (per hr 60Kr; 11am-5pm) nearby.

Festivals & Events

Haapsalu has a packed calendar of concerts and festivals, although most are held between June and August. Among the attractions are **'Medieval Haapsalu'**, a three-day music, arts and crafts festival (mid-July). There's also the **Ladies in Jazz Festival** (first weekend of August) and the **Blues Festival** (second weekend of August), though the biggest annual event is Days of the White Lady (Valge Daami Päevad). See boxed text, right, for more info.

Sleeping

Fra Mare (☎ 472 4600; www.framare.ee; Ranna tee 2; s/d 750/1050Kr; ⊠) Haapsalu's best spa hotel has a peaceful waterfront location and a full range of spa services, including mud baths. Rooms are comfortable but a bit heavy-handed with the floral theme. It has a seawater pool, an outdoor café and a restaurant.

Promenaadi Hotel (☎ 473 7250; www.promenaadi.ee; Sadama tänav 22; s/d €45/55Kr; ⊠) Set on the water's edge, Promenaadi has attractive rooms, all with balconies and sea views. The all-glass bar and restaurant also offers great views (but hit-and-miss food).

DAYS OF THE WHITE LADY

Haapsalu's biggest annual event, **Days of the White Lady** coincides with the August full moon. The day begins with merriment – storytelling for the kids, theatre for the adults – and culminates with a ghastly apparition. During the full moon every August and February, moonlight at a precise angle casts a ghostly shadow across a cathedral window. According to legend, the shadow is cast by a young girl who in the 14th century was bricked up alive inside the walls. Back then, the castle was an all-male enclave, and the archbishop got pretty worked up when he heard that a young woman, disguised in monastic vestments, sneaked in to be close to her lover-monk. In August excited young crowds stay out late to see a play recounting the story in the castle grounds, after which everyone gathers around the wall to await the shadow.

Kongo Hotel (☎ 472 4800; www.kongohotel.ee; Kalda tänav 19; s/d/d with kitchen Sep-Apr 700/850/1000Kr, Jun-Aug 950/1150/1350Kr; ⊠) Set with pleasant, airy rooms and light-coloured wood floors, Kongo is probably the most stylish hotel in town. Breakfast and morning sauna included.

Paralepa (☎ 5564 1674; paralepa@hot.ee; Ranna tee 4; tent/bed per person 40/150Kr, caravan 150Kr; Jun-Aug; ⊠) Located near Haapsalu's sandy beach, this place offers simple, clean rooms with shared bathrooms. The grassy lawn at the back accommodates tent camping and caravans; a simple café overlooks the beach.

Hermannuse Maja (☎ 473 7131; www.hermannus.ee; Karja 1a; s/d/tw/ste 500/650/750/950Kr; ⊠) Better known for its colourful pub, Hermannuse has several comfortably furnished en-suite guestrooms.

Endla Hostel (☎ 473 7999; www.hot.ee/hostelendla; Endla tänav 5; tw/tr 360/500Kr; reception 1-6pm; ⊠) Located on a quiet street, this white two-storey building has small basic quarters with shared bathrooms and a guest kitchen. It's popular with budget travellers.

Eating & Drinking

Grand Holm Marina (☎ 565 2887; Westmeri 3; meals 50-175Kr) Haapsalu's best restaurant has an outdoor terrace overlooking the marina and a beautifully set dining room. The food is delicious. For something different try the juniper-smoked duck breast with polenta, followed by warm rhubarb tart.

Hermannuse Maja (☎ 473 7131; Karja 1a; meals 40-150Kr) With eclectic South Pacific furnishings, and a warm and inviting atmosphere, this pub serves hearty meals, though it's a cosy spot just for a drink.

Restaurant Central (☎ 473 5595; Karja tänav 21; meals 180Kr) This elegant dining room offers tasty varied selections such as *farfalle* with smoked cheese, and oven-baked trout. The music is bad, but the service is friendly, and the *crème brûlée* is not to be missed. There's also an outdoor terrace and an atmospheric bar downstairs.

Stoory Cellar (☎ 473 5568; Suur-Lossi 15; meals 75-135Kr) During the summer this café's grassy backyard, perched on the edge of the lake, makes a lovely setting for a drink. It serves food, but the only thing commendable is the freshly grilled *shashlik*.

Club Kaheksa (☎ 5665 7963; Ehte 8; meals from 45Kr) This stylish lounge, café and restaurant features a large outdoor terrace and often has live music on weekends.

Haapsalu Kuursaal (☎ 509 7795; www.kuursaal.ee; Promenaadi 1; meals around 175Kr; 🕒 May-Aug) Inside a beautiful 1898 spa hall, you'll find international, somewhat overpriced fare, but the seaside setting and surrounding rose garden are a big draw. Come for coffee, cocktails or the concerts and performances held here. Check website for listings.

Pizza Grande (☎ 473 7200; Karja tänav 6; meals 40-110Kr) This casual, popular spot serves decent pizzas and Italian dishes. Outdoor terrace at the back.

Café Rondo (☎ 474 4592; Posti tänav 7; 🕒 8.30am-5.30pm Mon-Fri, 9am-4pm Sat & Sun) A charming old café with freshly baked apple cakes and cinnamon buns.

For fresh fruits and vegetables visit the **Market** (Turg; Jaama tänav; 🕒 7am-2pm Tue-Sun) a few blocks east of the bus station. Don't miss fresh strawberries in summer.

Getting There & Away

The **bus station** (☎ 473 4791; Jaama tänav 1) is inside the pretty but defunct train station. At least 17 daily buses connect Haapsalu and Tallinn (65Kr to 80Kr, 1½ hours, 100km). There's also one daily bus to/from Tartu (110Kr to 170Kr, 4½ hours), and two daily buses to Kärdla, Hiiumaa (three hours). Unfortunately, the fastest way to reach Pärnu, Virtsu or Kuressaare, Saaremaa, is to go to Tallinn first.

Ferries to Hiiumaa and Vormsi leave from Rohuküla, 9km west of Haapsalu. See p137 and p135 for ferry details.

Getting Around

You can rent bicycles at **Vaba Aeg Rattad** (☎ 521 2796; Karja 22; bikes per hr/day 25/100Kr; 🕒 10am-6pm Mon-Fri, to 3pm Sat). Car and bicycle rental is available from **Grand Holm Marina** (☎ 565 2887; Westmeri 3). Bus 1 runs almost hourly between Lossi plats, the train station and Rohuküla; timetables are posted at Lossi plats and the bus station. Bus 2 goes about hourly between the bus station and the Yacht Club. For taxi service, call **ESRA Taxi** (☎ 473 4555).

AROUND HAAPSALU

Taebla

pop 3000

About 10km east of Haapsalu, and 2km beyond Taebla, is **Ants Laikmaa House Museum** (Ants Laikmaa majamuuseum; ☎ 472 9756; adult/concession 15/5Kr; 🕒 10am-6pm Wed-Sun mid-May–mid-Sep, 10am-4pm Wed-Sun mid-Sep–mid-Apr), in the eclectic house of inexhaustible artist Ants Laikmaa (1866–1942), who walked more than 2600km from Rīga to Düsseldorf in Germany (in six weeks apparently) to study art. His efforts extended to designing and building the house itself. Buses along the Tallinn–Haapsalu road will drop you at Taebla.

Haapsalu's tourist office can arrange accommodation in the region, with rooms from 200Kr per person.

Kiige Farm (☎ 479 5492; www.hot.ee/kiigefarm; Linnamäe, Oru district; r per person 140-240Kr), 10km north of Taebla at Linnamäe, is a small family homestead with beds in a pretty wooden summerhouse or in the main house. It's well liked by young Estonian travellers, and there are ample opportunities for leisure – volleyball, walks in the forest, or a go round on the giant swing (aka kiiking).

Tuksi & Around

Some of Estonia's loveliest – and least discovered – beaches lie along the northern coastline between Nõva and Dirhami. You can camp along this stretch, take some sun or just enjoy the fabulous expanse of isolated light-sand beach.

Roosta Holiday Village (☎ 479 7230; www.roosta.ee; Tuksi; 1-/2-/3-bedroom cottage incl breakfast from €75/110/144) is an attractive holiday cottage complex in a pine forest beside a lovely, relatively deserted beach. These neat all-wood cottages are equipped with kitchenette, living room, shower and veranda. Two cottages have disabled facilities; there's also caravan space. On site are a restaurant, bar, sauna and tennis courts. Bicycle, sailboard and rowboat rentals are available.

Roosi Talu (☎ 525 3408; www.hot.ee/roosituris mitalu; d per person 220Kr), not to be confused with Roosta, is a little further north at Nõva. Accommodation is provided in this friendly private home within a stone's throw of the sea and forest. The kitchen is available for guest use, and excursions to Osmussaare Island can be arranged. From Roosi, it's 1.5km to a sandy beach.

To get to Tuksi from Haapsalu, turn north off the main Tallinn–Haapsalu road 2km east of Herjava and continue about 30km through Linnamäe and Riguldi. It's well off the beaten track and the only buses that go there are Haapsalu–Variku–Nõva–Dirhami buses, which go once each way daily except Monday and Thursday.

There's a **harbour** at Dirhami, a few kilometres north of Tuksi, where a knowledgeable captain can take you to **Osmussaare** (round trip in a 10-person boat 1300Kr), a small island 7.5km from the mainland that was once inhabited by Estonian Swedes. It's known to them as Odensholm, the legendary burial place of the Viking god Oden. The island's **cemetery** and **chapel ruins** are reminders of the Swedish presence prior to their forced exodus by the USSR. After they were driven out a Soviet army base was built here in the early 1940s. The island is uninhabited, so if you plan to camp, bring food and water with you.

Noarootsi Peninsula

pop 750

The Noarootsi Peninsula is 2km across the bay from Haapsalu but about 35km by road. Estonian Swedes lived here for several centuries before their exodus in 1944. There's an old church from the Swedish era at **Hosby**, a fine manor park at **Pürksi** and views to Haapsalu from the old village of **Österby**.

One daily bus goes between Haapsalu and Österby via Pürksi, taking 1¼ hours.

VORMSI

pop 340

Vormsi, Estonia's fourth biggest island (93 sq km), lies covered in pine and spruce forests, mixed with coastal pastures and wooded meadows, with tiny lakes dotting the landscape. Vormsi's topography is fascinating: this is the only place in the world where Arctic lichen grows south of the Arctic Circle. There's even coral reef hidden in one forest – brought by retreating glaciers 10,000 years ago. (Some believe that trolls now lie buried under the rocklike coral). Vormsi has remained largely undisturbed owing to sparse human settlements, largely Swedes until 1944. Today cars are rarer than peregrine falcons – along with 200 other bird species.

Orientation & Information

More information about the wildlife and landscape, including the 30 protected islets in Hullo Bay, is available through **Vormsi Landscape Reserve** (☎ 472 9430; http://vormsi.silma.ee; Rumpo Village).

Vormsi lies 3km off the Noarootsi Peninsula. Ferries make the 10km-crossing to Sviby on Vormsi's south coast from Rohuküla, 9km west of Haapsalu.

Sights

Vormsi – 16km from east to west and averaging 6km from north to south – is a good place to tour by bicycle, but you could also take a car or walk. There are about 10km of paved road. **Hullo**, Vormsi's largest village, lies about 3km west of Sviby. A further 7km by paved and dirt road will bring you to Saksby, the westernmost village, where it's a short walk to a **lighthouse**. Rumpo is due south of the stretch between Sviby and Hullo.

Other highlights include the **14th-century church** at Hullo, which has a fine baroque pulpit and a collection of old Swedish-style, wheel-shaped crosses in the graveyard; the southern **Rumpo Peninsula**, dotted with juniper stands (and the famous Arctic lichen); and the 5.8m-high boulder, **Church Rock** (Kirikukivi), near Diby in the northeast.

Sleeping

You can find more options online (www.vormsi.ee) or at the tourist office in Haapsalu. Both places listed here rent out bicycles and boats, have saunas, and include breakfast in the price.

Rumpo Mäe Talu (☎ 472 9932; www.hot.ee/streng; per person camp site/bed 35/240Kr; Apr-Nov;) Near Rumpo, and just a few steps from the coast, this handsome farmhouse offers Vormsi's best accommodation. Rooms have an authentic, old-style feel, and guests have access to kitchen and grill.

Elle-Malle Boarding House (☎ 473 2072; www.vormsi.ee/ellemall; r per person from 240Kr;) Another good option is this cosy spot in Hullo. There's a romantic double room inside a windmill (summer only) or rooms inside a separate wooden cottage (year-round).

Getting There & Away

A vehicle and passenger ferry (adult/concession/car 30/14/110Kr, 45 minutes) leaves Rohuküla for Sviby two to three times daily. If you're taking a vehicle in the summer, reserve a place in advance by calling ☎ 443 1069. For the latest timetable and fares visit www.kihnu.ee/veeteed (in Estonian) or check with the Haapsalu tourist information office.

Haapsalu town bus 1 runs regularly (10 times daily) to Rohuküla from Lossi plats and the bus station, where timetables are posted. All the Vormsi ferries wait for this bus except on Sunday morning. There are also daily buses to/from Tallinn.

MATSALU NATURE RESERVE

A bird-watcher's paradise, Matsalu Nature Reserve is a prime bird-migration and breeding ground, both in the Baltics and in Europe. Some 275 different bird species have been counted here, and the reserve has been around since 1957. The reserve encompasses Matsalu Bay, which is over 20km long and is also the deepest inlet in the west Estonian Coast.

Spring migration peaks in April/May, but some species arrive as early as March. Autumn migration begins in July and can last until November.

Bird-watching towers, with extensive views of resting sites over various terrain, have been built at Penijõe, Kloostri, Haeska, Suitsu and Keemu. There are two marked **nature trails**, one at Penijõe (5km), another at Salevere Salumägi (1.5km). Bring reliable footwear, as the ground is wet and muddy. The reserve's headquarters is 3km north of the Tallinn–Virtsu road at Penijõe, near Lihula. There you'll find a small **visitor centre** (☎ 472 4236; www.matsalu.ee; 8am-5pm Sat-Thu, 8am-3.45pm Fri mid-Apr–Sep, 8am-5pm Mon-Fri Oct–mid-Apr) and a permanent exhibition with slide show. The centre can hook you up with guides offering tours of the reserve, from two-hour canoe trips around the reed banks to several days of bird-watching. It can also recommend lodging in the area. It's best to contact the centre in advance. If you're planning an extensive bird-watching trip, consider contacting **Kumari** (☎ 477 8214; www.kumari.ee) before you head out. This outfit employs naturalist guides who have a wealth of knowledge on Matsalu's avian riches.

HIIUMAA

pop 11,000

Hiiumaa, Estonia's second-biggest island, is a peaceful and sparsely populated place with some delightful stretches of coastline and a forest-covered interior. Though there's plenty to do on the island, most visitors come here to breathe in the fresh sea air and simply relax amid pastoral splendour.

Scattered about Hiiumaa you'll find picturesque lighthouses, eerie old Soviet bunkers, empty beaches and a nature reserve with over 100 different bird species. Those seeking a bit more activity can hike, horse ride or, on rare days, even surf – the only place in the Baltics with a bit of swell.

Given their relative isolation from mainland Estonia, it's not surprising that the islanders have a unique take on things, and a rich folklore full of legendary heroes, such as Leiger, who had nothing to do with Kalevipoeg (the hero over on the mainland). People who move onto the island must carry the name *isehakanud hiidlane* (would-be islanders) for 10 years before being considered true residents. Hiiumaa is also said to be a haven for fairies and elves, ancestors of those born on the island. Modern-day Hiiumites rarely discuss this unique aspect of their family tree, however, as this can anger their elusive relatives.

Hiiumaa (1000 sq km) is not quite visible from the mainland, 22km away.

GETTING THERE & AWAY

A passenger and vehicle ferry runs between Rohuküla on the mainland and Heltermaa at Hiiumaa's eastern end. Buses from Tallinn

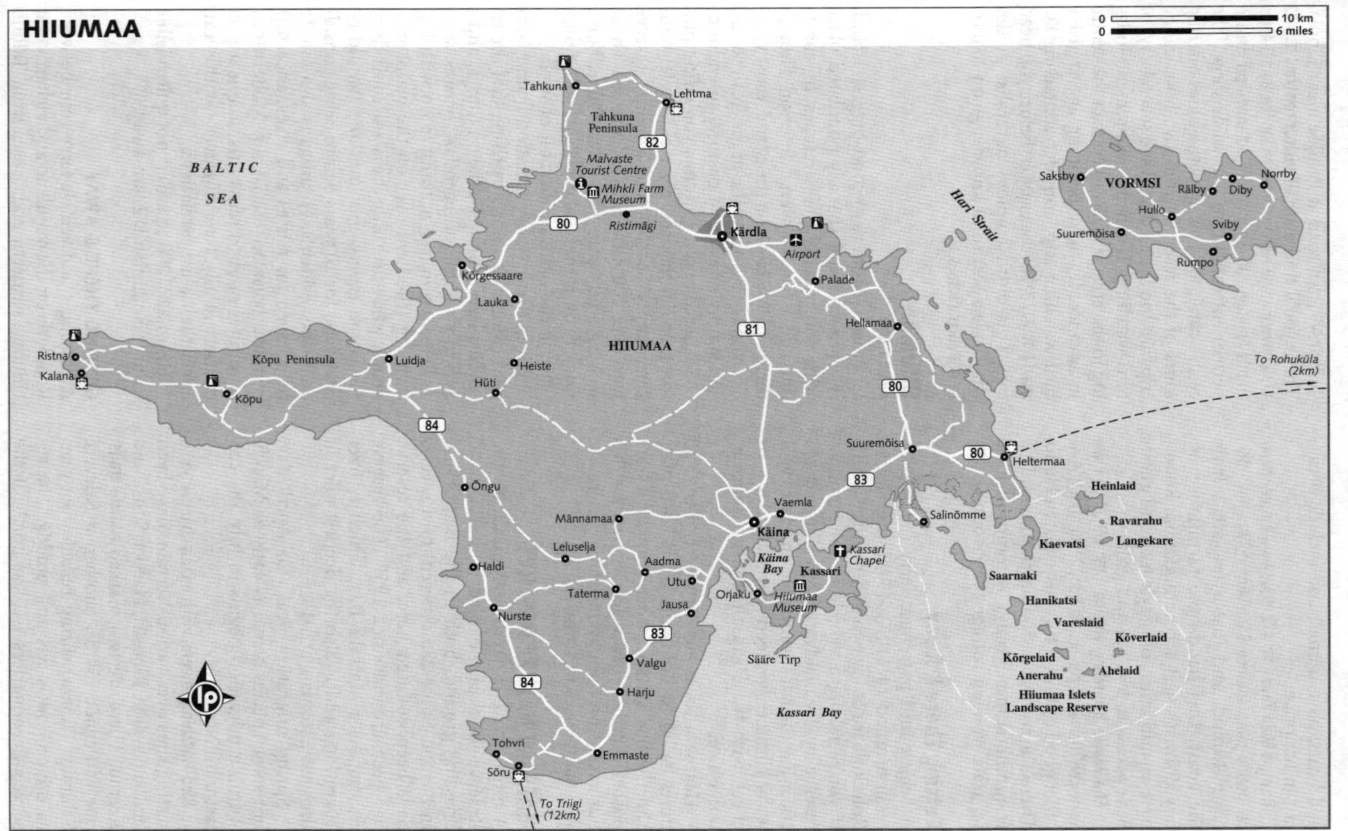
HIIUMAA
0 10 km
0 6 miles
BALTIC SEA
Tahkuna
Lehtma
Tahkuna Peninsula
82
Malvaste Tourist Centre
Mihkli Farm Museum
Ristimägi
80
Kärdla
Airport
Palade
Kõrgessaare
Lauka
Ristna
Kalana
Kõpu Peninsula
Kõpu
Luidja
Heiste
Hüti
HIIUMAA
81
Hellamaa
Hari Strait
Saksby
VORMSI
Rälby
Diby
Norrby
Hullo
Sviby
Suuremõisa
Rumpo
To Rohuküla (2km)
84
Suuremõisa
Heltermaa
83
Õngu
Vaemla
Käina
Männamaa
Salinõmme
Heinlaid
Ravarahu
Kaevatsi
Langekare
Leluselja
Aadma
Haldi
Utu
Käina Bay
Kassari
Kassari Chapel
Taterma
Orjaku
Hiiumaa Museum
Saarnaki
Hanikatsi
Vareslaid
Kõverlaid
Nurste
Jausa
Valgu
Harju
Sääre Tirp
Kõrgelaid
Anerahu
Ahelaid
Hiiumaa Islets Landscape Reserve
Kassari Bay
Tohvri
Emmaste
Sõru
To Triigi (12km)

via Haapsalu run all the way to Hiiumaa; the ferry crossing is included in the trip. Other buses will drop you off or pick you up at either ferry terminal. It's also common to hitch or ask for lifts off the ferries at either end.

A ferry also connects Hiiumaa and Saaremaa, just 5.5km away.

Air

Avies Air (☎ 605 8002; www.avies.ee) flies twice per day Monday to Friday, and once on Saturdays and Sundays between Tallinn and Kärdla (adult/concession one way 245/215Kr, 30 minutes).

Boat

SLK Ferries (Saaremaa Laevakompanii; ☎ 452 4444; www.laevakompanii.ee) runs ferries between Rohuküla and Heltermaa four to six times daily (adult/child/vehicle 45/20/95Kr one way, 1½ hours). Check website for departure times.

Most people don't bother calling ahead, but if you're taking a car and you want to be on the safe side, book ahead, and show up at least 20 minutes before the ferry departs. Have your vehicle registration handy. You can also purchase tickets at either port: **Rohuküla ticket office** (☎ 473 3666) or **Heltermaa ticket office** (☎ 463 1630), a small building on the right as you leave the pier.

SLK Ferries also operates a year-round ferry (adult/vehicle 20/75Kr one way, one hour) two to three times daily from Sõru ferry terminal, on the southwesternmost tip of Hiiumaa, to Triigi on Saaremaa.

Bus

There are two to three buses daily from Tallinn to Kärdla (140Kr to 160Kr, 4½ hours), which can also be caught in Haapsalu and Rohuküla.

GETTING AROUND

Paved roads circle Hiiumaa and cover several side routes; the rest are dirt roads. In Kärdla, **Jaanus Jesmin** (☎ 511 2225; www.carrent.hiiumaa.ee; Põllu 2a) rents out cars from 300Kr per day. Padu Hotell (p138) also rents cars as well as bicycles. There are fuel stations at Kärdla and Käina.

Jalgrattarent (☎ 5660 6377; www.hot.ee/jalgrattalaenutus; per day €7) rents bicycles in Heltermaa, near the ferry landing.

Buses, nearly all radiating from Kärdla but some from Käina, get to most places on the island, though not very often. Schedules are posted inside the bus station in Kärdla or are available through **Tiit Reisid** (☎ 463 2077; www.tiitreisid.ee; Sadama tänav 13, Kärdla). Hitching is fairly common on Hiiumaa's roads.

Heltermaa to Kärdla

At Suuremõisa, 6km inland from Heltermaa, you can visit the chateaulike, late-baroque **Suuremõisa manor and park** (adult/concession 10/5Kr; ⌚ 10am-4pm Jun-Sep), created in the mid-18th century. The property once belonged to the rich baronial Ungern-Sternberg family. The nearby **Pühalepa Church** dates from the 13th century. Legends surrounding a mound of rocks known as the **Stones of the Ancient Agreement** (Põhilise leppe kivid), about 1km northeast of the manor, suggest that they mark the grave of a ruler of Sweden.

Kärdla

pop 3950

Hiiumaa's 'capital' grew up around a cloth factory founded in 1829 and destroyed during WWII. It's a green town full of gardens and tree-lined streets, with a sleepy atmosphere and few diversions except that it's Hiiumaa's centre for services of all kinds.

ORIENTATION

The centre of town is Keskväljak (Central Square), a long plaza 500m north of the main Heltermaa–Kõrgessaare road. The bus station lies 200m north of its northern end. To the west is Rannapark, which runs down to the sea.

INFORMATION

Cultural Centre (☎ 463 2192; Rookopli tänav 18) Hosts occasional exhibitions and performances.

Hiiumaa Protected Areas Administration (☎ 462 2101; Vabrikuväljak 1; www.bka.hiiuloodus.ee) Oversees Hiiumaa's landscape reserves and protected areas. Maps and brochures available.

Library (☎ 463 2142; Rookopli tänav 18) Next door to the cultural centre, the library provides Internet access.

Post office (Keskväljak 3)

Tiit Reisid (☎ 463 2077; www.tiitreisid.ee; Sadama tänav 13) Run by Hiiumaa experts, this travel agency inside the bus station arranges accommodation and tours.

Tourist office (☎ 462 2232; www.hiiumaa.ee; Hiiu tänav 1; ⌚ 9am-6pm Mon-Fri & 10am-3pm Sat & Sun mid-May–mid-Sep, 10am-5pm Mon-Fri mid-Sep–mid-May)

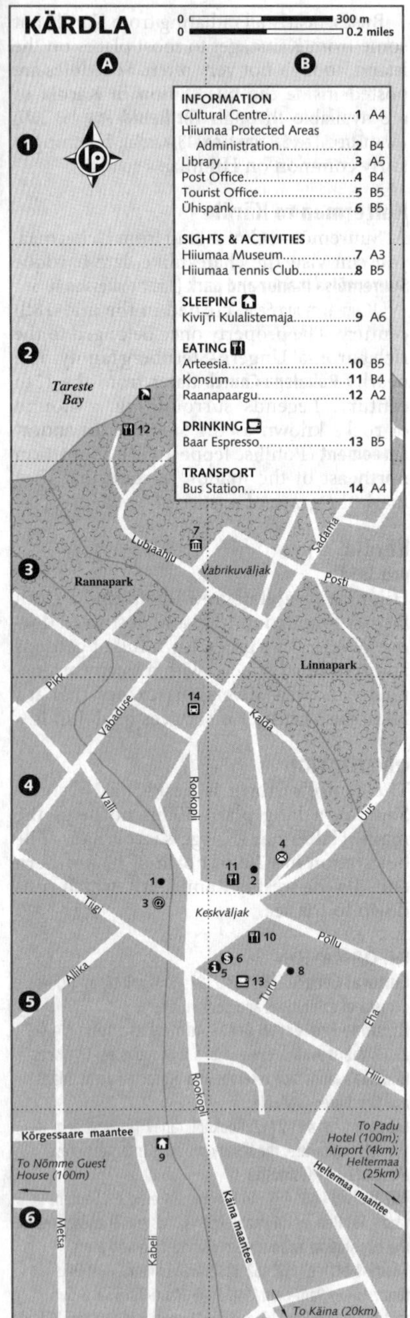

This friendly centre distributes maps and can help arrange accommodation and guide service. It also sells the *Lighthouse Tour*, a 40-page driving tour of the island in English. The office is housed in an old fire tower. Climb up the steps for a great view over the area.

Ühispank (Keskväljak 7) Money exchange and ATM.

SIGHTS & ACTIVITIES

On a rainy day, visit the small **Hiiumaa Museum** (☎ 463 2091; Vabrikuväljak tänav 8; adult/concession 10/5Kr; ⌚ 10am-5pm May-Jun, 10am-5pm Mon-Fri Jul-Apr), which has displays related to the cloth factory, and work from local artists.

Call the Hiiumaa **tennis club** (Tenniseklubi; ☎ 463 3010; Turu tänav 2) about court hire. At the **beach** (follow Lubjaahiu tänav) there's a clean, sandy shore, a café and minigolf.

You can hire bicycles and cars from Padu Hotell.

SLEEPING

Padu Hotell (☎ 463 3037; www.paduhotell.ee; Heltermaa maantee 22; s/d/apt incl breakfast 450/650/800Kr; ⊠) One of Kärdla's better options, this pleasant two-storey hotel has cosy wooden rooms, all with balconies. There's a sauna with a small pool, and a relaxing café.

Kivijüri Kulalistemaja (☎ 469 1002; www.hot.ee/kivijuri; Kõrgessaare maantee 1; s/d incl breakfast 300/500Kr; ⊠) This bright-red, warm country house has simple rooms. There's a backyard patio and lots of greenery nearby.

EATING & DRINKING

Raanapaargu (☎ 463 2053; Lubjaahju tänav 3; meals 35-65Kr) Overlooking the beach, this pyramid-shaped restaurant with outdoor patio offers a pleasant setting for a meal. Dance parties are held here on weekends (entrance 25Kr).

Baar Espresso (☎ 463 1213; Hiiu tänav 1a; ⌚ 10am-6pm Mon-Sat noon-6pm Sun) This tiny café serves the best coffee in town. It's a pleasant pit stop before sightseeing.

Arteesia (☎ 463 2173; Keskväljak 5; ⌚ 9am-11pm Mon-Sat, 11am-10pm Sun) This cheery place serves basic fare (meat and potatoes, anyone?), but there are few other options.

Konsum (Keskväljak; ⌚ 9am-9pm) Load up on provisions at the island's largest grocery store.

GETTING THERE & AWAY

Several buses a day travel along the main road from Kärdla past the Malvaste turn-off, a 15-minute ride.

Tahkuna Peninsula

The sparsely populated Tahkuna Peninsula stretches 8km north into the Baltic Sea, west of Kärdla. Northern Hiiumaa had a population of free Swedish farmers until the late 18th century, when they were forced to leave, with many ending up in Ukraine on the false promise of a better life. At Ristimägi, 7km west of Kärdla, there's a **Hill of Crosses**, a small dune decked with handmade crosses just off the main road. These mark the spot where the last 1200 Swedish people living on Hiiumaa performed their final act of worship before leaving the island in 1781. It has become a tradition for first-time visitors to Hiiumaa to lay a cross there.

At Tahkuna, on the peninsula's northwest tip, there's a **lighthouse** dating from 1875. This area was the scene of a battle between German and Russian troops during WWII; the official Soviet story was that the Soviets bravely fought to the bitter end, and the last man climbed to the top of the lighthouse and flung himself off while still firing at the Germans. Behind it stands an eerie **memorial** to the victims of the *Estonia* ferry disaster. Facing out to sea, the 12m-tall metal frame encases a huge cross, from the bottom of which a bell with carved, sculpted faces is suspended; it only rings when the wind blows with the same speed and in the same direction as that fatal night in September 1994, when the *Estonia* went down.

On the road south of Tahkuna, and especially on the winding dirt road eastwards towards Lehtma, you'll see deserted **Soviet army bases**, including a complete underground bunker to wander through; bring a torch.

At Malvaste, 2km north of the Kärdla–Kõrgessaare road from a turning 10km west of Kärdla, there's the open-air **Mihkli Farm Museum** (☎ 523 2225; adult/concession 10/5Kr; ⏲ 10am-6pm mid-May–mid-Sep). It has a working smoke sauna (built in 1915) for hire, which can hold up to 10 people. It's a unique, old-fashioned experience – but not recommended for sensitive eyes.

SLEEPING

If you're looking for a dose of nature, there are several good options on Tahkuna Peninsula.

Kalda Puhketalu (☎ 462 2122; www.kaldapuhketalu.ee; cabin per person 180Kr, holiday house 2000-2500Kr; ⊠) Less than 1km north of Malvaste, this friendly tourist farm rents out simple wooden cabins (with separate shared bathrooms) and much larger holiday houses, each with kitchen, fireplace and bathroom. It's an excellent location 200m from a sandy beach. Sauna, bike and boat hire are available.

Randmäe (☎ 5691 3883; www.hot.ee/puhketalu/etutvustus.htm; camp site 50Kr, cabin per person 150Kr; ⊠) Just south of Kalda, this place offers more rustic accommodation in small wooden cabins. It's close to the beach. Sauna available.

Western Hiiumaa

The harbour village of **Kõrgessaare**, 20km west of Kärdla, offers little by way of distractions except a quaint restaurant and guesthouse (see below) on your way westward.

The best-known landmark in Hiiumaa is the inland **Kõpu lighthouse** (☎ 469 3474; adult/concession 20/10Kr; ⏲ 9am-10pm May–mid-Sep), the third-oldest, continuously operational lighthouse in the world. A lighthouse has stood on this raised bit of land since 1531, though the present white limestone tower was built in 1845. At 37m high, it can be seen 55km away. East of here, near the 61km highway mark, is the 1.5km Rebastemäe **nature trail**, which takes in forest paths along the highest (therefore oldest) parts of the island.

You can get more information at the small information booth next door to the restaurant near the lighthouse base.

A second lighthouse stands at the western end of the peninsula near **Ristna** (Stockholm is just over 200km west of here). It was brought to Hiiumaa by freighter from Paris, where it was made, together with the lighthouse at Tahkuna.

Near Ristna is **Surf Paradiis** (☎ 5625 1015; www.paap.ee), set on a stretch of lovely sandy beach. You can hire sea kayaks, surfboards and wetsuits or have a sauna. Check surf conditions (Paradiis' website has a webcam) before you come. Remember, this is the Baltic Sea we're talking about.

SLEEPING & EATING

At Kõpu lighthouse, you can arrange **camping** (☎ 469 3476; camp site 20Kr) at the information booth. You can also camp for free along Tõnupsi beach north of there.

Viinakök (☎ 469 3337; Kõrgessaare; d 500Kr) Set in a picturesque 1880s building (formerly a vodka factory), this place offers fairly shabby rooms painted in undersea colours, and shared bathrooms. The more attractive restaurant downstairs serves an OK buffet lunch (110Kr), and there's a well-stocked bar to help it all go down.

GETTING THERE & AWAY

Kärdla buses run several times most days to/from Kõrgessaare and Luidja at the start of the Kõpu Peninsula, and two or three times daily to/from Kalana near the end of the peninsula.

Käina & Käina Bay Bird Reserve

pop 2390

Hiiumaa's second-largest settlement is a fairly nondescript place, apart from the ruins of a fine **15th-century stone church**, which was wrecked by a WWII bomb, near the main road. On the western edge of Käina is the **Tobias Museum** (☎ 463 2091; adult/concession 10/5Kr; ⏰ 10am-5pm mid-May–mid-Sep), former home of Rudolf Tobias (1873–1918), composer of some of Estonia's first orchestral works.

The main appeal of the town is its proximity to the shore of **Käina Bay**, an important bird reserve that is virtually cut off from the open sea by the twin causeways to **Kassari Island**. You can get a good view over the action from the bird-watching tower north of Orjaku on Kassari, where you'll also find a short walking trail. During the hot summer months a large part of the bay dries up and becomes nothing more than a mud field. About 70 different species breed at Käina Bay. The headquarters of the Hiiumaa Protected Areas Administration (p137) publishes a variety of leaflets to take you through nature trails within the reserve.

Four kilometres from Käina, at Vaemla on the road to Kassari, is a small **wool factory** (Hiiu Vill; ☎ 463 6121; admission free; ⏰ 10am-6pm), which still uses original 19th-century weaving and spinning machines to produce some fine traditional knitwear. In addition to sweaters and mittens, the factory sells wool in bulk if you want to do your own knitting. There's a decent café on site.

SLEEPING & EATING

Hotell Liilia (☎ 463 6146; www.liiliahotell.ee; Hiiu maantee 22; s/d/tr incl breakfast 700/800/1000Kr; ⊠) Set in a Spanish colonial two-storey building, Liilia has bright, airy rooms with hardwood floors and private bathrooms. There's also a popular restaurant and bar serving Estonian and international dishes.

Tondilossi (☎ 463 6337; Hiiu maantee 11; s/d 250/500Kr; ⊠) This is a comfortable, wooden lodge that also has a café (open 11am to 6pm Monday to Saturday). Boat and car rental are available.

Lõokese Hotel (☎ 463 6107; www.lookese.com; Lõokese tänav 14; s/d from 600/670Kr; ⊠) This uninspiring brick building hides clean rooms with wild carpeting and bright drapes. There's a small pool and a children's playground.

GETTING THERE & AWAY

A good paved road runs 20km across the island from Käina to Kärdla. Five or six buses daily go between Kärdla and Käina, with fewer runs on weekends.

Kassari

pop 90

This pleasant 8km-long island is thickly covered with mixed woodland and boasts some striking coastal scenery. It's linked to Hiiumaa by two causeways.

Southern Kassari narrows to a promontory with some unusual vegetation and ends in a thin 3km spit of land the tip of which, **Sääre Tirp**, juts out into the sea. It's a beautiful place for a walk. On the way towards Sääre Tirp you'll pass by a small **swimming beach** (about 500m past the fork to Orjaku).

You'll also notice a **statue** of the local hero, Leiger, carrying a boulder on his shoulder. He was a relative of Suur Tõll, Saaremaa's hero. Legend has it that the Sääre Tirp is the result of an aborted bridge he started to build to Saaremaa, to make it easier for Suur Tõll to visit and join in various heroic acts.

Just inland of the main road, a short distance west of the Sääre Tirp fork, is the single-storey **Hiiumaa Museum** (☎ 463 2091; adult/concession 10/5Kr; ⏰ 10am-5pm Mon-Fri, 11am-2pm Sat), which was formerly servants' quarters on the Kassari estate. It has a small collection of artefacts and exhibits on Hiiumaa's history and biodiversity. Among the curiosities: the jewel-like prism of the 1874 Tahkuna lighthouse and the stuffed body of the wolf that allegedly terrorised the island in the 1960s.

M/S *ESTONIA:* CONSIGNED TO MYSTERY

About 30 nautical miles northwest of Hiiumaa's Tahkuna Peninsula lies the wreck of the ferry *Estonia*, which sank during a storm just after midnight on 28 September 1994. Only 137 people survived the tragedy, which claimed 852 lives in one of Europe's worst maritime disasters.

In 1993 the Swedish-Estonian joint venture Estline launched the *Estonia* to service the increasingly popular route between Tallinn and Stockholm. The 15,000-tonne roll-on/roll-off ferry was already a veteran of Scandinavian seas, having sailed between Sweden and Finland for 14 years. The ferry was a source of pride and a symbol of freedom to the newly independent Estonians, even for those whose only experience of it would be seeing the huge white vessel dock at Tallinn's port.

The cause of the tragedy remains the subject of contention and burgeoning conspiracy theory. In 1997 the final report of the Joint Accident Investigation Commission (JAIC), an official inquiry by the Estonian, Swedish and Finnish governments, concluded that the ferry's design was at fault and the crew were probably underskilled in safety and emergency procedures. The report claimed the bow gate, or visor, was engineered inadequately for rough sailing conditions and that during the storm the visor was torn from the bow and in the process breached the watertight seal of the loading ramp. This exposed the car deck to tonnes of seawater that sank the *Estonia* completely within one hour. Escape time for the 989 people on board was estimated at only 15 minutes and they were denied access to lifeboats due to the sudden list and sinking of the ferry. For those who did escape, the freezing conditions of the water that night reduced survival time to only minutes.

The integrity of the report was questioned after dissent within the JAIC became public. Allegations followed that vital information had been withheld and that the Commission did not act impartially. The report also met with criticism from relatives of the victims, the majority of whom were Swedes. In 2000 a Swedish newspaper survey claimed over 70% of victims' families were still calling for a new investigation. Subsequent reports from Sweden and an inquiry commissioned by the ferry's German manufacturers argued that, contrary to the JAIC findings, the *Estonia* was not seaworthy, it had been poorly serviced and the visor-securing mechanisms were in need of repair.

In 2000 a joint US-German diving expedition and new analyses of the *Estonia's* recovered visor prompted theories of an explosion on board, which explosive experts believe would be the most feasible explanation for the damage sustained and the ferry's rapid sinking. Estline suspected an underwater mine, while it has also been suggested that the ferry collided with another vessel. Conspiracy theorists claim that the *Estonia* was transporting unregistered munitions cargo, as an illicit trade in weapons was to be curtailed with new export laws about to come into effect. Claims of a cover-up have been bolstered by the alleged disappearance of eight crew members, initially listed as survivors.

Unexplained interference with the wreck, along with the Swedish government's dumping of sand to stabilise it in 2000, further fuelled conspiracy claims and calls for a new inquiry. The governments of Estonia, Finland and Sweden are resolute that the ferry will remain where it sank as a memorial to the dead; an estimated 700 people are thought to be inside. To date no-one has been found liable and no compensation has been paid to the victims or their families.

Another enjoyable walk, ride or drive is to a pretty, whitewashed, 18th-century **chapel** at the east end of Kassari. A sign 'Kassari Kabel 2' directs you down a dirt road from the easternmost point of the island's paved road. A path continues nearly 2km to a small bay in Kassari's northeastern corner.

Along the way to the chapel, you'll also pass Hiiumaa's largest horse farm, the **Kassari Ratsamatkad** (☎ 469 7102; www.kassari.ee; 1hr/day tour €10/40), which offers a range of horse-riding excursions through forests and along untouched coastline.

SLEEPING & EATING

Vetsi Tall (☎ 462 2550; www.vetsitall.ee; camp site/r per person/apt 40/200/1200Kr; ⊠) On the main road between Orjaku and the fork to Säära Tirp, Vetsi Tall offers accommodation in simple, wooden, barrel-shaped cabins. It also rents a comfortable three-room apartment with kitchen. You can camp, use the sauna or have a meal at the pleasant tavern (meals 50Kr to 80Kr; restaurant open 10am to 10pm). The food is basic but among Hiiumaa's better options.

Seeba (☎ 5661 8036; www.hot.ee/seebatalu; d incl breakfast 790Kr; ☒) Near the horse farm (Kassari Ratsamatkad), Seeba rents small but charming wooden cabins, with tiny kitchenettes and bathrooms. There's also one large room with a balcony. Sauna available.

Camping (☎ 5625 3535; camp site 50Kr) is available near the swimming beach on the way to Sääre Tirp. Stop in at the snack stand by the side of the road.

GETTING THERE & AWAY

There are only two buses a day between Kärdla and Kassari. Check with the tourist office in Kärdla for the latest times. It's also possible to hitch.

Southern Hiiumaa

The main paved road from Käina runs southwest through Valgu and Harju, villages separated from the coast by a 3km-wide marshy strip. **Harju** has two restored windmills. At Emmaste the main road turns northwest to end at Haldi, just past Nurste. Hamlets and isolated farmsteads dot the west-facing stretch of coast and its hinterland. The southern tip of Hiiumaa around the harbour of Sõru (where ferries to Saaremaa depart) is bleaker with few trees. North of Haldi, dirt roads continue through Õngu to the western Kõpu Peninsula and to Luidja, the end of the paved road west from Kärdla.

There are buses from Kärdla and Käina to Valgu, Harju, Emmaste, Tohvri (in the south near Sõru), Nurste and Õngu every day.

Hiiumaa Islets Landscape Reserve

Saarnaki, Hanikatsi, Vareslaid, Kõrgelaid and other islets off southeastern Hiiumaa form the Hiiumaa Islets Landscape Reserve, now incorporated into the Hiiumaa Protected Areas Administration which has its headquarters (p137) in Kärdla. This is a breeding place for some 110 bird species, including avocets, eider ducks and goosanders, as well as a migration halt for swans, barnacle geese and other species. Over 600 plant species – almost half Estonia's total – grow here, including the rare red helleborine.

Saarnaki and **Hanikatsi**, the two largest islands at almost 1.5 and 1 sq km respectively, were inhabited until the 1960s or 1970s. They were depopulated, like many other Estonian coastal villages, because of Soviet bans on seagoing boats, which meant people could no longer earn a living from fishing.

Birds on the islands have been carefully monitored since 1974. A number of observation towers have been built within the reserve, including one near the **Hiiumaa Islets Reserve Centre** (☎ 469 4299; www.laiud.hiiuloodus.ee) at Salinõmme on Hiiumaa. It is possible to spend a night on deserted and peaceful Saarnaki or Hanikatsi Islands but you have to get permission from the reserve centre first. It can arrange for a guide to take you by boat to the islands. Note some of the smaller islands are off limits until the beginning of July, after the nesting season has ended.

SAAREMAA

pop 35,600

Estonia's largest island still lies covered in thick pine and spruce forests, while old windmills, slender lighthouses and tiny villages still appear as if unchanged by the passage of time. Saaremaa, more than any other place in Estonia, offers a glimpse of 'old Estonia'. There are long empty stretches of sparkling coastline, juniper bushes slumbering beneath the ruins of a 15th-century church, and the stray sheep staring out from an old stone wall.

This unique old-time setting goes hand-in-hand with inextinguishable Saaremaan pride. Saaremaa has always had an independent streak and was usually the last part of Estonia to fall to invaders. Its people have their own customs, songs and costumes. They don't revere mainland Estonia's Kalevipoeg legend, for Saaremaa has its own hero, Suur Tõll, who fought many battles around the island against devils and fiends.

Yet this vision of the idyllic clashes somewhat with the modernity that Kuressaare has thrust upon it. With its magnificent castle, charming Old Town and picturesque bayside setting, Saaremaa's capital has clearly established itself as a premier summer destination. When the long days arrive so do the crowds of Finns and Swedes, jostling for beach space

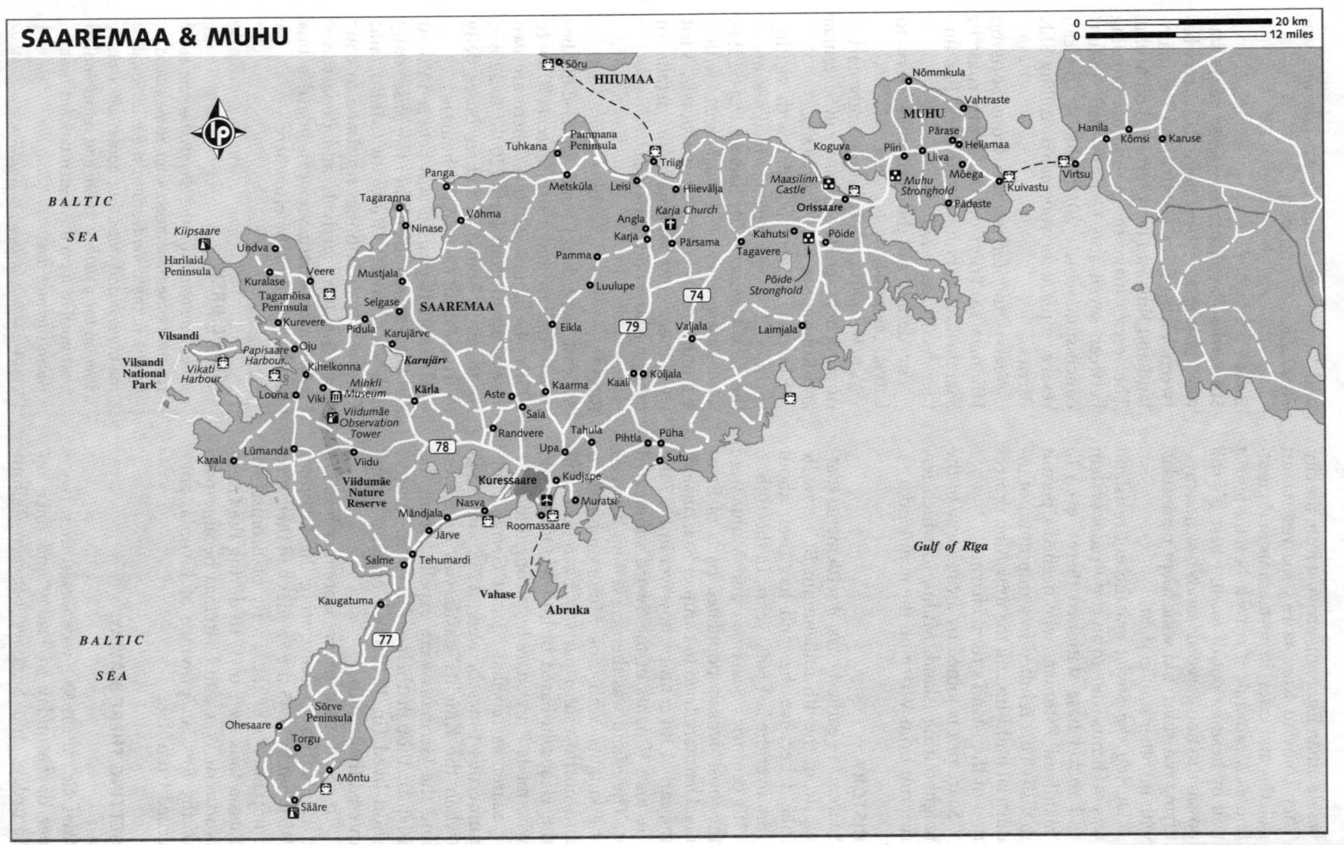
SAAREMAA & MUHU
0 20 km
0 12 miles
Sõru
HIIUMAA
Nõmmkula
Vahtraste
MUHU
Pärase
Hellamaa
Hanila
Kõmsi
Karuse
Koguva
Piiri
Liiva
Mõega
Muhu Stronghold
Pädaste
Kuivastu
Virtsu
Tuhkana
Pammana Peninsula
Triigi
Panga
Metsküla
Leisi
Hiievälja
Maasilinn Castle
Orissaare
BALTIC
SEA
Tagaranna
Võhma
Ninase
Karja Church
Angla
Karja
Pärsama
Kahutsi
Tagavere
Põide
Kiipsaare
Harilaid Peninsula
Undva
Kuralase
Veere
Tagamõisa Peninsula
Kurevere
Mustjala
Selgase
Pidula
SAAREMAA
Pamma
Luulupe
74
Põide Stronghold
Eikla
79
Valjala
Laimjala
Vilsandi
Vilsandi National Park
Papisaare Harbour
Oju
Vikati Harbour
Kihelkonna
Karujärve
Karujärv
Kõljala
Kaali
Loona
Viki
Mihkli Museum
Kärla
Aste
Kaarma
Saia
Viidumäe Observation Tower
Randvere
Tahula
Pihtla
Püha
Sutu
Upa
78
Lümanda
Karala
Viidu
Viidumäe Nature Reserve
Kuressaare
Kudjape
Muratsi
Mändjala
Nasva
Roomassaare
Järve
Salme
Tehumardi
Gulf of Rīga
Vahase
Abruka
Kaugatuma
77
BALTIC
SEA
Sõrve Peninsula
Ohesaare
Torgu
Mõntu
Sääre

beside urban Estonians arriving from the city. They come to Kuressaare's spa resorts, art galleries and cafés, its restaurants and guesthouses. Meanwhile, it's easy to beat the tourist trail by heading out of town, where it's still possible to find gorgeous sandy beaches, mystifying old ruins and windswept peninsulas, with no other soul in sight.

During the Soviet era the entire island was off limits (due to an early-radar system and rocket base stationed there), even to 'mainland' Estonians who needed a permit to visit. This resulted in a minimum of industrial build-up and the unwitting protection of the island's rural charm.

Saaremaa is joined by a causeway to the neighbouring island, Muhu, to which ferries run from Virtsu on the mainland.

HISTORY

Saaremaa's earliest coastal settlements (dating from the 4th millennium BC) now lie inland because the land has risen about 15m over the last 5000 years. In the 10th to 13th centuries Saaremaa and Muhu were the most densely populated parts of Estonia. Denmark tried to conquer Saaremaa in the early 13th century; however in 1227 the German Knights of the Sword subjugated it. The island was then carved up between the knights, who took Muhu and eastern and northwestern parts of Saaremaa, and the Haapsalu-based bishop of Ösel-Wiek, who made Kuressaare his stronghold.

Saaremaa rebelled against German rule numerous times between 1236 and 1343 (when the Knights' castle was destroyed and the Germans were expelled from the island), though their efforts were always short-lived (in 1345 the Germans reconquered the island).

In the 16th century Saaremaa became a Danish possession during the Livonian War, but by 1645 the Swedes had their turn compliments of the Treaty of Brömsebro. Russia took over in 1710 during the Great Northern War and Saaremaa became part of the Russian province of Livonia, governed from Rīga.

GETTING THERE & AWAY

Air

Avies Air (☎ 605 8002; www.avies.ee) flies twice per day Monday to Friday and once on Saturdays and Sundays between Tallinn and Kuressaare (adult/concession one way 385/255Kr, 45 minutes).

Boat

SLK Ferries (Saaremaa Laevakompanii; ☎ 452 4444; www.laevakompanii.ee) operates a daily ferry between Virtsu ferry terminal on the mainland and Kuivastu ferry terminal on Muhu. The ferries make the 30-minute crossing between seven and 12 times daily (adult/concession/vehicle 20/10/55Kr). You can reserve a place for your car by calling SLK Ferries.

Year-round ferries run from Sõru on Hiiumaa to Triigi on the north coast of Saaremaa at varying frequencies. For further details, see p137.

For details on the Saaremaa ferry to Latvia, see p404.

A new summer-only line recently started running between Roomassaare in Saaremaa and Ruhnu. See p162 for details.

Saaremaa is very popular with visiting yachties. The best harbour facilities are at the new **Kuressaare City Harbour** (☎ 453 3540, 503 1953; www.kuressaare.ee/yachtharbour), within a stone's throw of three spa hotels. Visit www.tt.ee/renza/sadamad for details of other harbours on Saaremaa.

Bus

At least eight direct buses travel daily between Tallinn and Kuressaare (170Kr to 195Kr, 4½ hours, 220km). There are two buses daily to/from Tartu (200Kr to 220Kr, six to seven hours) and three buses daily to/from Pärnu (140Kr, 3¼ hours).

There are five buses daily between Virtsu and Saaremaa, and another five buses daily each way between Kuivastu (Muhu) and Kuressaare; a 1½-hour trip timed to connect with ferry arrivals and departures. Likewise, at Virtsu you can board a bus bound for Tallinn or elsewhere.

ISLAND BREW

When you're out on the islands, be sure to try the homemade beer. A longtime island tradition, the brew features the traditional malt, yeast and hops, but comes off a bit sour on the palate. It's light and refreshing, best quaffed from a wooden tankard on a warm summer day.

GETTING AROUND

There are over 400km of paved road on Saaremaa and many more dirt roads. Hitching is not uncommon on the main routes (but there's not much traffic on minor roads). Buses do get around the island, but not very frequently. It's possible to put a bike or two in the baggage compartments, though you have to ask the driver for permission. Before you head out, call the friendly folks at **Kuressaare bus station** (☎ 453 1661) for help in route planning.

Eastern Saaremaa

The first place you reach on Saaremaa is **Orissaare**, the island's second-largest town. The small **tourist office** (☎ 454 5051; Sadama 1; 9am-5pm Mon-Fri, to 3pm Sat & Sun) can provide maps and general info. The German knights built **Maasilinn Castle** just north of Orissaare during the 14th to 16th centuries. It was badly damaged in 1576 but you can still see the ruins, and wander through a restored underground chamber. The town itself is a quaint, sleepy settlement, with a tiny handicrafts shop, **Uku** (Rana puiestee 9; 9am-4pm Mon-Fri, 10am-1pm Sat), where you can watch Orissaare's old weavers in action.

Pöide, 3km south of the main road, was the German knights' headquarters on Saaremaa. Their fortress was destroyed in 1343 in the St George's Night Uprising, but Pöide Church, built by the Germans in the 13th and 14th centuries a short distance east of the road, remains an imposing symbol of their influence.

Kaali

At Kaali, 18km north of Kuressaare, stands a 100m-wide, water-filled **meteorite crater** blasted into existence about 2700 years ago. In Scandinavian mythology, the site was known as 'the sun's grave'. It's Europe's largest and most accessible meteorite crater, though it looks small up close. There's a new museum and hotel here as well as an old-style tavern with Estonian fare (and home-made beer). To get there, take Rd 10 north from Kuressaare, and keep your eyes peeled for the well-marked turn-off on the left.

Angla, Karja, Triigi & Tuhkana

If you are arriving on the ferry from Hiiumaa, this region provides a bucolic introduction to the island.

Angla, 40km from Kuressaare on the main road to the north coast, is the site of the biggest and most photogenic grouping of Saaremaa's old **windmills** – five of them of various sizes lined up together on the roadside. Opposite the windmills is the turn-off to the 14th-century **Karja Church**, 2km east, which has a fortresslike façade and an elaborate crucifixion carving on one of its inner walls.

North of Angla, the road continues 5.5km to Leisi, the venue for **Õlletoober** (www.olletoober.ee), a beer festival each July showcasing both sophisticated and feral brews. From Leisi it's 3.5km to the harbour of Triigi, a picturesque bay on Saaremaa's north coast with views across to Hiiumaa. If arriving from Hiiumaa, the **Leisi tourist office** (☎ 457 3073; noon-7pm Jun-Aug) on the main road is a good place to pick up maps and get general Saaremaa information.

There's a sandy beach at Tuhkana, 3km north of Metsküla, which is 10km west of Leisi, mostly by unpaved roads.

SLEEPING

Kuressaare tourist office (p147) can arrange accommodation in the region.

Püharisti Hostel (☎ 454 5149; www.eelk.ee/orissaare; Ranna puiestee 11, Orissaare; camp site/bed per person from 200/50Kr; ⊠) Overlooking the sea, Püharisti offers hostel-like accommodation in a warm, superfriendly environment. Kayaks are available (100Kr per hour). You can also pitch a tent nearby.

GETTING THERE & AWAY

Buses between Kuressaare and the mainland take the main road passing within 1km of Valjala, while the local Kuressaare–Kuivastu service takes the more southerly road through Laimjala and within 1km of Pöide. There are 10 buses daily between Kuressaare and Orissaare (30Kr, 1¼ hours) and 10 between Orissaare and Kuivastu (30Kr), mostly in the morning and afternoon.

Up to 14 buses daily run between Kuressaare and Leisi, a trip of about an hour, passing right by the Angla windmills and close to Karja Church. Those via Pärsama go right by Karja Church. Kaali is halfway between the Kuressaare–Valjala and Kuressaare–Leisi roads, about 3km from each, so you could use a bus along either road to get within walking distance.

Kuressaare

pop 16,000

Saaremaa's star attraction, Kuressaare is a picturesque town with peaceful leafy streets, charming guesthouses and cafés, and a magnificent castle rising up in its midst. The town is also famous for its spas, which range from Eastern-bloc sanatoriums to sleek and stylish resorts. Its reputation as a health centre began as early as the 19th century, when the ameliorative properties of its coastal mud were discovered and the first health spas opened.

Kuressaare's reason for being is its castle, which was founded in the 13th century as the Haapsalu-based Bishop of Ösel-Wiek's stronghold in the island part of his diocese. Kuressaare became Saaremaa's main trading centre, developing quickly after passing into Swedish hands in 1645. In the Soviet era Kuressaare was named Kingisseppa, after Viktor Kingissepp, an Estonian communist of the 1920s.

ORIENTATION

The road from Kuivastu and the mainland enters Kuressaare as Tallinna tänav, passing southwest through modern suburbs to the central square, Keskväljak. Kuressaare Castle and its surrounding park, which reaches down to the coast, are 750m beyond Keskväljak, along Lossi tänav. The **bus station** (Pihtla tee 25) is located northwest of Keskväljak.

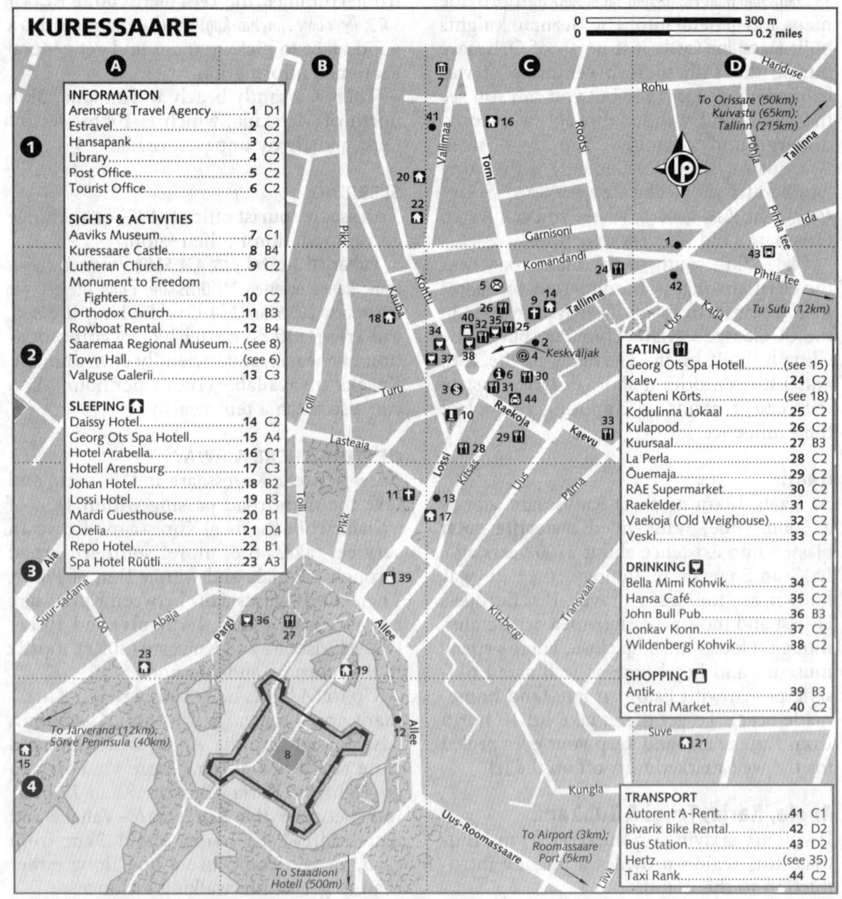

INFORMATION

There are several banks, ATMs and exchange bureaus on Keskväljak.

Arensburg travel agency (☎ 453 3360; abr@tt.ee; Tallinna maantee 25; 9am-5pm Mon-Fri) Extremely knowledgeable about the island and offers arranged boat trips to Vilsandi.

Estravel (☎ 454 5345; www.estravel.ee; Tallinna maantee 8) Good all-purpose travel agent.

Hansapank (Kohtu tänav 2)

Library (Tallinna maantee 6; 10am-7pm Mon-Fri, to 4pm Sat) Free Internet access.

Post office (Torni tänav 1) Public phones (telephone-card only).

Tourist office (☎ 453 3120; www.kuressaare.ee; Tallinna tänav 2; 9am-7pm Mon-Fri, 9am-5pm Sat, 9am-3pm Sun May-Sep, 9am-5pm Mon-Fri Oct-Apr) Inside the old town hall. It sells maps and guides, arranges accommodation, and books boat trips and island tours.

SIGHTS & ACTIVITIES

Kuressaare Castle

The majestic Kuressaare Castle stands at the southern end of the town, on an artificial island ringed by a partly filled moat. It's the best-preserved castle in the Baltics and the region's only medieval stone castle that has remained intact.

A castle was founded in the 1260s, but the mighty dolomite fortress that stands today was not built until the 14th century, with some protective walls added between the 15th and 18th centuries. It was designed as an administrative centre as well as a stronghold. The more slender of its two tall corner towers, Pikk Hermann to the east, is separated from the rest of the castle by a shaft crossed only by a drawbridge, so it could function as a last refuge in time of attack.

Inside the castle is a warren of chambers, halls, passages and stairways to fuel anyone's fantasies about Gothic fortresses. It houses the **Saaremaa Regional Museum** (Saaremaa Koduloomuuseum; ☎ 455 6307; adult/concession/audiotour 30/15/60Kr; 10am-7pm Wed-Sun). On the ground floor look for the *hüpokaust* (hypocaust) on the southwestern side, a furnace that fuelled a medieval central-heating system. According to legend, condemned prisoners were dispatched through a small floorless room near the bishop's chamber, to be received by hungry lions. Legends also tell of a knight's body found when a sealed room was opened in the 18th century. It's said that, upon discovery, the knight's body dissolved into dust, which has given rise to varying accounts of how he met his tragic fate.

SAAREMAA'S SEDUCTIVE SPAS

Saaremaa's reputation as a major spa destination may be a bit premature, but there are still some excellent opportunities for pampering, detoxing and/or sliding into a bathtub full of slippery coastal mud – a Saaremaa remedy for over 150 years. You'll also encounter some downright bizarre (some would say innovative) treatments – anyone up for a NeoQui Energy Cocoon? But whatever your yin, if you've come to Saaremaa, give a treatment a try.

Although the island has a number of spas, if you don't want to feel like you're checking into a hospital, you have only two options: the elegant **Georg Ots Spa Hotell** (p148) or the **Spa Hotel Rüütli** (p148) up the road. While both spas offer the standard classical massage, Thai massage (where they roll you all over the floor until you're nice and supple), aromatherapy and herbal baths, the Georg Ots Spa tends to lean more in the pampering direction. For instance, you can soak in a juniper bath, get a body wrap or have a chocolate massage. Meanwhile, the Rüütli, which may not be as stylish as the Georg Ots, has a much wider range of offerings – some of them clearly leaning towards the category of 'punishment' – like the full body massage with hot lava stones, the caviar facial, and our favourite, Charcot's shower, where someone sprays you with streams of water from a hose (improves circulation while lowering self-esteem). There's also music therapy, a salt chamber (good for asthmatics), and you can even go 'grossing' (they strap you into a harness suspended from the ceiling and you bounce across a gym floor). Both of these places offer package deals, though you can also reserve a treatment or two (best to book ahead).

Incidentally, a NeoQui Energy Cocoon (with or without cream) isn't for sissies. It involves lying in an enclosed capsule and undergoing the effects of infrared sauna, steam sauna, vibration massage, aromatherapy, Vichy douche and hydrobath massage. In the sandwich world, this would be called 'the works'. Both spas have 'em. What are you waiting for?

On the top floor, the castle has a café boasting fine views over the bay and surrounding countryside. Down below, outdoor concerts are held throughout the summer just inside the fortress walls. There's also a few targets where you try your hand at **archery** (four arrows 15Kr; ⌚ 10am-5pm).

The shady park around the castle moat that extends to Kuressaare Bay was laid out in 1861 and there are some fine wooden resort buildings in and around it, notably the 1889 **Spa Hall** (Kuursaal).

Other Attractions

The best of Kuressaare's other old buildings are grouped around the central square Keskväljak, notably the **town hall** (built in 1670), on the eastern side, with a pair of fine stone lions at the door, and the **weighhouse** (now Vaekoja pub) across from it, both 17th-century baroque. There's a handsome **Lutheran Church** at the northeast end of Keskväljak and an **Orthodox Church** (Lossi tänav 8).

Aaviks Museum (☎ 455 7553; Vallimaa tänav 7; adult/child 10/5Kr; ⌚ 11am-6pm Wed-Sun) is dedicated to the life and works of linguist Johannes Aavik (1880–1973), who introduced major reforms to the Estonian language, and his musically talented cousin, Joosep Aavik (1899–1989). One of several galleries on Lossi, **Valguse Galerii** (☎ 513 0921; Lossi tänav 13; ⌚ 10am-6pm) contains a small variety of works by Estonian artists. You'll find ceramics, woodblock prints, sculptures and paintings.

Boating

If the weather's nice, you can hire rowboats and float idly around the castle. **Boat hire** (Allee tänav 8; per hr 80Kr; ⌚ noon-6pm) is available at Lossi Konn café.

Beaches

The best beach in the Kuressaare area is Järverand at Järve, about 14km west, some 2km past Mändjala. There's also a beach at Sutu, 12km east. Salme, Torgu or Sääre buses from Kuressaare go to Järverand.

FESTIVALS & EVENTS

The biggest event in Kuressaare is the **Castle Days** fest held in early July. Vespers, an old-time feast, Renaissance tournaments, a handicrafts market and lots of medieval fanfare take place. If you're in town, don't miss it. Other events include the **Waltz Festival** (June), the **Saaremaa Summer Days** classical music festival (July), **Opera Days** (August), the **chamber-music festival** (August) and **Maritime Days** (August), which features lots of sea-related activities. There are also fortnightly concerts held in the castle grounds. Find out what's underway at the tourist office.

SLEEPING

Town Centre

The tourist office can arrange accommodation in private flats around town (starting at 200Kr) or advise on out-of-town options.

Lossi Hotel (☎ 453 3633; lossihotel@tt.ee; Lossi tänav 27; s/d/ste 850/990/1290Kr; ⊠) Set on the castle grounds, this beautifully restored mansion has elegant Art-Nouveau rooms, many of which boast stunning views of the castle.

Georg Ots Spa Hotell (☎ 455 0000; www.gospa.ee; Tori tänav 2; s/d from €101/112; ⊠ 🖳) Kuressaare's most stylish hotel, the Georg Ots has attractive modern rooms with wildly striped carpeting (most people like it, but be warned), enormous beds and a warm but minimalist design. Most rooms have balconies, and there's a lovely pool, fitness centre and spa services just down the hall.

Spa Hotel Rüütli (☎ 454 8100; www.sanatoorium.ee; Pargi tänav 12; s/d €81/102; ⊠ 🖳) This large spa hotel has airy and comfortable wood-floored rooms, all of which have balconies. There are many spa services available, as well as a large swimming pool with waterslide, a sauna and a small gym. Even if you don't stay here, you can use the sauna, pool and gym (a bargain for 70Kr).

Hotell Arensburg (☎ 452 4700; www.sivainvest.ee; Lossi tänav 15; s/d/ste 1050/1290/2100Kr; ⊠) In a historic building near the main square, this hotel has great service and a lovely terrace out back. Rooms are decent, if a bit formal and heavy-handed with the colour green.

Daissy Hotell (☎ 453 3669; www.hot.ee/daissyhotell; Tallinna maantee 15; s/d/ste 950/1190/1600; ⊠) Daissy has simple elegant rooms, though the suites – with either a fireplace or a balcony – are less cramped than the attic rooms. Good restaurant housed in the old brick cellar. Can arrange scooter rental.

Johan Hotel (☎ 453 3036; www.saaremaa.ee/johan; Kauba tänav 13; s/d/ste 750/900/1700Kr; ⊠) This peaceful guesthouse has small, simple rooms painted in warm colours, but the place could use new carpeting. There's a handsome wood-toned pub next door.

Repo Hotel (☎ 453 3510; Vallimaa tänav 1a; www.saaremaa.ee/repo; s/d incl breakfast 560/790Kr; ⊠) A short walk from Raekoja plats, Repo has small, charming rooms painted in different colours. Good buffet breakfasts.

Staadioni Hotell (☎ 453 3556; www.staadionihotell.ee; Staadioni tänav 4; s/d 590/750Kr; ⊠ 💻) Good views are on offer at this pleasant, secluded spot, 1km south of the centre. Clean, modern rooms have big windows facing either towards the castle or the sea. There's an athletics stadium next door.

Hotell Arabella (☎ 455 5885; www.arabella.ee; Torni tänav 12; s/d 575/800Kr; ⊠) Although not terribly popular, this guesthouse offers clean, comfortable if slightly dated rooms. Try to snag the double room with balcony.

Mardi Guesthouse (☎ 452 4633; mardi@ametikool.ee; Vallimaa tänav 5a; s/d/tr incl breakfast 370/470/600Kr; ⊠) This centrally located budget place has clean, basic rooms, every two of which share a bathroom.

Ovelia (☎ 455 5732; Suve tänav 8; d with private/shared bathroom 400/200Kr; ⊠ 💻) One of the cheapest places in town, friendly Ovelia has small, poorly furnished rooms, and rustic cabins in the garden. Ovelia has a following among student travellers. You can cook on the outdoor grill or have a sauna (50Kr per person). It's a 12-minute walk southwest of the town square.

Out of Town

Owing to infrequent bus service, these places are mainly geared towards people with cars.

Puhkemaja Nasva (☎ 453 3603; jurigo@hot.ee; r/ste/house 220/700/1300Kr) Seven kilometres west of Kuressaare, this small homey property contains several basic cabin rooms with shared bathrooms, and more spacious, cosier suites. Some rooms have kitchenettes and look out over a pretty garden. You can also rent the whole house – a good option for four. The beach is nearby.

Kämping Mändjala (☎ 454 4193; www.mandjala.ee; camp site/cabin per person 60/200Kr, cabin with private bathroom 700Kr; 🕑 May-Sep; ⊠) Ten kilometres west of Kuressaare, Mändjala offers rustic wooden cabins and camping amid lots of greenery. You can also book a cabin with kitchen and private bathroom. It's a short walk to the beach. Three buses per day from Kuressaare to Torgu or Sääre go to the Mändjala bus stop, about 500m beyond the site.

Hotel Saaremaa (☎ 454 4100; www.saarehotell.ee; d/ste 1140/1410Kr; ⊠) About 600m past Kämping Mändajala, this pleasant whitewashed hotel has trim, modern rooms and a pleasant outdoor terrace. Best of all, it's right on the beach.

EATING & DRINKING

Georg Ots Spa Hotell (☎ 453 3020; Tallinna maantee 3; meals from 70Kr; 🕑 9am-10pm) Saaremaa's best restaurant is found inside this attractive spa hotel. Amid a lovely dining room with big windows facing onto the sea, you can feast on seafood favourites such as trout with vegetable ratatouille, fish and shellfish stew, and salmon steak with sweet chilli sauce.

La Perla (☎ 453 6910; Lossi tänav 3; meals 50-140Kr) A handsome new addition to the dining scene, this Italian restaurant serves tasty brick-oven baked pizzas and plenty of other Italian options.

Vaekoja (☎ 453 3020; Tallinna maantee 3; meals from 70Kr; 🕑 9am-10pm) One of several inviting restaurants on the main square, Vaekoja serves eclectic fare (rainbow trout with blue cheese, grilled ostrich, salads) amid historic elegance. The front terrace is a popular meeting/drinking spot in the summer.

Õuemaja (☎ 453 3423; Uus tänav 20a; meals 20-65Kr; 🕑 10am-9pm Mon-Sat, 11am-8pm Sun) This popular no-frills restaurant serves decent, not terribly healthy food in a hurry. Noted writer and linguist Johannes Aavik and his musician cousin Joosep Aavik once lived here.

Veski (☎ 453 3776; Pärna tänav 19; meals 55-125Kr) This cosy multilevel restaurant is set inside a windmill; unfortunately, the chef is wildly inconsistent. The menu features grilled fish, roasted meats and other dishes.

Kodulinna Lokaal (☎ 453 1178; Tallinna maantee 11; meals 80-165Kr) This is an atmospheric cellar restaurant and bar that makes a pleasant retreat during chilly weather. Grilled fish, meats and salads are on offer.

Hansa Café (☎ 455 4321; Tallinna Maantee 9; 🕑 9.30am-5.30pm Mon-Sat) One of Kuressaare's finest cafés, Hansa exudes old-world bohemian ambience. Fresh homemade pastries and a vibrant art gallery next door add to the charm.

Bella Mimi Kohvik (☎ 454 5123; Kauba tänav 6; 🕑 8am-6pm) This superfriendly café provides a cosy setting for lattes, waffles and fresh-baked cakes. Entrance on Kohtu.

Kalev (☎ 453 3088; Tallinna Maantee 19a; 🕑 8.30am-7pm Mon-Fri, 9am-4pm Sat) Sample Estonia's famous chocolates here.

Kuursaal (☎ 453 9749; Pärgi tänav 1; meals 50-120Kr) Inside a former early-20th-century spa hall, Kuursaal is a fine stop-off for a coffee or light meal, but time your visit well to avoid tour-bus troops.

Kulapood (Torni tänav & Kiriku; 🕑 9am-7pm Mon-Fri, to 4pm Sat) If you're self-catering, this is the place for fish-lovers. Don't miss the delicious smoked salmon. An iron fish marks the downstairs entrance.

RAE Supermarket (☎ 453 3776; Raekoja tänav 10; 🕑 9am-10pm) This is the best grocery store in Saaremaa.

Wildenbergi Kohvik (☎ 454 5325; Tallinna maantee 1; 🕑 9am-midnight) Also on the main square, this charming café is a lovely place for a drink – it has a fantastic tea selection.

Kapteni Kõrts (☎ 453 3406; Kauba tänav 13; meals from 65Kr) With its old saloon-like feel and summer terrace, the Kapteni Kõrts pub draws a lively crowd.

Raekelder (☎ 453 1170; Raekoja plats; meals 90-175Kr) Another winner for the ambience, the stone floors, old beamed ceiling and antique sitting room of the town hall basement is a fine place for coffee. The food and service is less enticing.

John Bull Pub (☎ 453 9988; Pärgi tänav 4) This friendly bar has a pleasant outdoor deck facing the castle; an unbeatable spot in summer.

Lonkav Konn (☎ 455 3240; Kauba tänav 6) This battered, easy-going pub attracts a mix of locals and tourists. It sometimes gets lively on the weekends.

SHOPPING

Central market (Raekoja plats) You'll find dolomite vases, wool sweaters, honey, strawberries and other Saaremaa treats at this small market near the square.

Antik (Lossi tänav 19) Antik sells all sorts of antiques, from 19th-century farm tools to Soviet memorabilia. It's a fun place to browse.

GETTING THERE & AWAY

For direct bus/ferry connections between Kuressaare, the mainland and Hiiumaa, see p144. Kuressaare's **bus station** (☎ 453 1661; Pihtla tee 25) is the terminus for most buses on the island; schedules are posted inside.

GETTING AROUND

Kuressaare airport is at Roomassaare, 3km southeast of the town centre. Buses 2 and 3 run throughout the day to/from Keskväljak. There's a **taxi rank** (Raekoja tänav) just off Keskväljak.

For car hire, try **Autorent A-rent** (☎ 453 6620; Vallimaa tänav 5) or **Hertz** (☎ 453 3660; Tallinna maantee 9). It's wise to book ahead in the summer. You can rent bicycles at **Bivarix** (☎/fax 455 7118; Tallinna maantee 22; bike per day 150Kr; 🕑 10am-6pm Mon-Fri, to 4pm Sat) and scooters at Daissy Hotel (p148).

Western Saaremaa

SÕRVE PENINSULA

Small cliffs, such as the Kaugatuma pank (bank) and Ohessaare pank, rear up along the west coast of the 32km southwestern Sõrve Peninsula. Legend has it that the cliffs were formed when the Devil tried in vain to wrench this spit of land from the mainland to separate Suur Tõll, who was vacationing on Sõrve, from Saaremaa. This is where the island's magic can really be felt. A bike or car trip along the coastline will reveal fabulous views.

This sparsely populated strip of land saw heavy fighting during WWII, and the battle scars remain; by the lighthouse at Sääre on the southern tip, you can walk around the ruins of an old Soviet army base. Other bases and the remnants of the Lõme-Kaimri antitank defence lines still stand. There's a large monument at Tehumardi, south of the beach at Järve, which was the site of a gruesome night battle in October 1944 between retreating German troops and an Estonian-Russian Rifle Division. The horror defies belief: both armies fought blindly, firing on intuition or finding the enemy by touch. Russian-Estonian dead lie buried in double graves in the cemetery nearby.

Near the village of Torgu on the Sõrve Peninsula in rugged windswept surrounds, **Sõrve Holiday House** (☎ 452 3061; www.saaremaa.ee/sorve; bed per person €8, d/cottage from €33/87) is a 20-minute walk to the coast. Here you'll find rustic cabins, comfy cottages with kitchens and a range of excursions on offer (boating, hiking, bird-watching).

VIIDUMÄE NATURE RESERVE

Founded in 1957, Viidumäe Nature Reserve covers an area of 19 sq km, with a 22m observation tower on Saaremaa's highest point (54m) at Viidumäe, about 25km west of Kuressaare. The tower, about 2km along a dirt road off the Kuressaare–Lümanda road at Viidu, offers a panoramic view of the reserve and the wonders of the island itself. The view is particularly memorable at sunset. There are two nature trails (2.2km and 1.5km), marked to highlight the different habitats of the area. Viidumäe is a botanical reserve, its favourable climate and conditions making it home to rare plant species such as the blunt-flowered rush, the Saaremaa yellow rattle and the whitebeam. Some plants are indigenous to the island.

At the reserve's **headquarters** (☎ 457 6321; ⏰ 10am-6pm Wed-Sun Jun-Aug) in Viidu, you can see a small exhibition and book guided tours.

THE NORTH COAST

At Viki on the road to Kihelkonna, about 30km from Kuressaare, a 19th-century farm has been preserved as the **Mihkli Farm Museum** (Talumuuseum; adult/concession 15/10Kr; ⏰ 10am-6pm). Here you can tour the old wooden farmhouses, rent out the sauna (200Kr per hour) or pitch a tent (camp site 25Kr). Kihelkonna, 3km beyond, has a tall, austere, early German church.

On the western side of the Tagamõisa Peninsula north of Kihelkonna there's an old **watchtower** and the ruins of a port where Saaremaans were shipped to Siberia. Further up the peninsula stretches a beautiful and rarely visited coastline. At its northwestern tip is the striking **Kiipsaare lighthouse**, which leans at a steep angle towards the sea.

East of the peninsula and 1km west of Pidula is the **Pidula Fish Farm** (☎ 454 6513; trout per kg 110Kr; ⏰ 10am-2pm), where you can 'fish' for trout in stocked ponds. They'll even clean it and cook it for you if you wish. Camping and simple wooden cabins (350Kr) are available.

Heading east from here, you'll pass the town of Mustjala, where you'll find **Musta Jala Galerii** (☎ 5342 1215; ⏰ 11am-7pm), an art gallery where you can see colourful works by Navitrolla and other Estonian artists. There's a handicrafts shop and a homy café with a garden patio.

North of Mustjala along the Ninase Peninsula is one of Saaremaa's kitschier icons. You can't miss the clunky wooden **folk windmill**, built to resemble a giant man in traditional costume. Sadly, his counterpart, a giant clothed female windmill, burned down in 2004.

Panga pank, Saaremaa's highest cliffs, run along the northern coast near Panga and offer some lovely panoramic views from the top.

Sleeping & Eating

Loona Manor (☎ 454 6510; www.loona.ee; camp site/s/d/ste/50/450/700/1200Kr; ⊠) This handsome 16th-century manor house offers simple, clean-swept guestrooms in a historic setting. There's a pleasant restaurant on the 1st floor, a sauna, and the manor arranges guided trips to Vilsandi National Park. Reserve far in advance – or plan on pitching a tent on the extensive grounds.

Pilguse Manor (☎ 454 5445; www.pilguse.ee; s/d 550/860Kr; ⊠) Housed in the stables of an old country estate west of Lümanda, Pilguse has nicely refurbished rooms with stone floors, simple furnishings, bathrooms and kitchenettes, and large windows facing onto grazing sheep next door. Incidentally, this manor was once home to Fabian von Gellingshausen, the early-19th-century Russian explorer who achieved fame for his Antarctic voyages.

Värava Tourist Farm (☎ 518 4814; www.varava.fie.ee; cabin/camp site per person 150/25Kr; ⊠) In a forested area along the idyllic northern coast, this well-kept place offers rustic accommodation in wooden cabins. Camping is possible, and the owners rent bicycles and offer hiking tours. It's located near Selgase, just off the Kihelkonna–Mustjala road.

Kämping Karujärve (☎/fax 454 2034; cabin per person 270Kr; ⏰ mid-May–mid-Sep) Among the trees on the east side of Lake Karujärv, some 9km east of Kihelkonna, this campground offers basic facilities. Boat hire possible.

If you're camping and you have a car, you'll find some of Estonia's loveliest camp sites (for free no less) along the shoreline on the eastern and western sides of the Pammana Peninsula.

Lümanda Söögimaja (☎ 457 6493; meals 85-175Kr) In a red house on the main road in Lümanda, this cosy country place serves tasty freshly prepared meals (fish soup, pork with turnips, white fish and potatoes) made with only organic ingredients. Beer-lovers should try the somewhat sour home-brew.

Getting There & Away

At least three buses daily go from Kuressaare down the Sõrve Peninsula to Sääre or Torgu, and six daily to Kihelkonna along different routes. A good combination bus/bike trip is bussing from Kuressaare to Viidu (bikes in the baggage compartment), then cycling north through Viidumäe Nature Reserve towards Kihelkonna or further on to the Tagamõisa Peninsula. Be sure to arrive early for your return trip as buses in these remote parts can deviate from their schedules.

VILSANDI & VILSANDI NATIONAL PARK

Vilsandi, west of Kihelkonna, is the largest of 161 islands and islets off Saaremaa's western coast protected under the Vilsandi National Park (containing about 10% of Estonia's islands). The park covers an area of 181.6 sq km and is an area of extensive ecological study. The breeding patterns of the common eider and the migration of the barnacle goose have been monitored very closely here. Ringed seals can also be seen here in their breeding season and 32 species of orchid thrive in the park.

Vilsandi, 6km long and in places up to 3km wide, is a low, wooded island. The small islets surrounding it are abundant with currant and juniper bushes. Up to 247 bird species are observed here, and in spring and autumn there is a remarkable migration of waterfowl: up to 10,000 barnacle geese stop over on Vilsandi in mid-May, and the white-tailed eagle and osprey have even been known to drop by.

The **Vilsandi National Park headquarters** (☎/fax 454 6554), at Loona, can arrange accommodation and wildlife-watching tours given advance notice, as can the Arensburg travel agency (p147) in Kuressaare.

Aside from camping, the only place to stay on the island is at **Kusti Talu** (☎ 5623 0606; bed per person 250Kr; ⏲ May–mid-Sep), a tourist farm offering an idyllic setting amid the island's beauty.

Süla Talu (☎ 454 6927, 5649 0503; sylla.talu@mail.ee) offers boating excursions to Vilsandi or around the Tagamõisa Peninsula. It's located in Oju, a tiny village 4km northwest of Kihelkonna. It also offers horse-riding excursions (on Saaremaa).

The best time to visit the island is from the beginning of May to mid-June. In summer a **private boat** (☎ 520 2656; adult/concession one way 35/20Kr) makes between one and three trips per day on Tuesday, Friday and Sunday. It travels between Papisaare Harbour and Vikati Harbour. You can also book the boat at nonscheduled times for 300Kr. In July, if the waters are shallow enough, an old bus ploughs its way across from Papisaare to Vikati instead, a one-way journey taking about 20 minutes.

ABRUKA & VAHASE

Known as a 'Mecca for naturalists' by Estonians, the 10-sq-km island of Abruka and neighbouring Vahase stretch 6km from Roomassaare, off Saaremaa's south coast. The wooded meadows are lined with lush ferns and rare plant species, with a small deer population (now endangered) scattered about the island. There are two 1920s lighthouses but very few people: less than 20 permanent residents live year-round on Abruka, though the population increases during the summer.

In summer a **private boat** (☎ 513 6961; one way 30Kr) departs three times weekly for the island from Saaremaa. Stop by the tourist office in Kuressaare (p147) for the latest times. During particularly cold winters it's possible to walk across the ice to Saaremaa, but not recommended without local advice.

There are several tourist farms on the island open in the summer only. Inquire at the Kuressaare tourist office.

Innu Farm (☎ 452 6633; bed per person 200Kr; ⏲ mid-May–mid-Sep), on the island, provides accommodation with kitchen facilities; tents can also be pitched. The family running the centre rents out bicycles and can pick you up by boat from Roomassaare Port for an extra charge. Horse-riding tours of the island can be arranged.

MUHU

pop 1900

Muhu, unfortunately, has a reputation for being the Kansas of the archipelago – lots of people passing through, but no-one stopping. In fact, Estonia's third-biggest island has a traditional old village, now functioning as a living museum, where you can get a grasp on the culture and history of this region. There's also a quirky ostrich farm, more Teutonic ruins and some downhome country hospitality that may make you want to stick around a while.

Near the main road about halfway across the island is the 13th to 14th century **Liiva Church**, with some unusual ship murals. Southwest of there is the **Muhu stronghold**, which is where the islanders surrendered to the Knights of the Sword in 1227, marking the end of Estonian resistance. The nearby **Eemu Tuulik** (windmill; ☎ 452 8130; adult/concession 5/3Kr; 🕑 10am-6pm Wed-Sun) has a small exhibit and sells bread baked with its milled flour.

The turn-off to the **Ostrich Farm** (☎ 452 8148; adult/concession 15/10Kr; 🕑 10am-6pm) is 200m east of the windmill. The quirky owners will give you an earful about these strange creatures and even let you feed them (mind your fingers). A small shop sells feathers, eggs, purses and shoes made from a certain leather.

Koguva, on the western tip of Muhu, 6km off the road, is an exceptionally well-preserved, old-fashioned island village, now protected as an **open-air museum** (☎ 454 8885; adult/concession 25/15Kr; 🕑 10am-5pm). One ticket allows you to wander through a number of interesting houses: an old schoolhouse, a museum containing beautiful traditional textiles from the area, including the painstakingly detailed folk costumes once worn by the locals in the area. You can also peer into author Juhan Smuul's ancestral home.

Also on the grounds of the village is the handsome modern art gallery and café **Koguva Kunstitallis** (🕑 11am-5pm).

Sleeping & Eating

Pädaste Manor (☎ 454 8800; www.padaste.com; s/d/ste from 1560/1820/3050Kr; ☒) Housing one of Estonia's grandest hotels, this lovely bayside manor dates from the 19th century. Elegant rooms, a cosy lobby with fireplace and beautifully manicured grounds make for a decadent stay. There's also an excellent restaurant (meals 160Kr to 350Kr).

Vanatoa Farm (☎ 454 8884; www.vanatoa.ee; camp site/s/d/from 40/400/550Kr; 🕑 May-Sep; ☒) In an idyllic setting near the open-air museum, Vanatoa has homy, down-to-earth rooms and friendly service, as well as boat trips and bicycle hire. The country-style restaurant serves decent meals, though it's sometimes booked with tour groups.

Muhu Restoran (☎ 5333 4005; meals 40-125Kr) Located in Liiva, this pleasant, airy restaurant serves wholesome food, which you can enjoy on the front terrace in the summer.

Getting There & Away

Use the Kuivastu–Kuressaare bus; it's also possible to hitch to reach the points along the main road.

SOUTHWESTERN ESTONIA

Southwestern Estonia contains the country's most popular resort town, as well as charming country villages, a vast national park and two remote islands that see few foreign visitors every year.

Perched along a lovely, sandy coastline, Pärnu attracts legions of holidaymakers during the summer. Young partygoers appear from Tallinn and Tartu en route to the city's nightclubs, cafés and restaurants, just as busloads of elderly out-of-towners arrive seeking spa treatments and mud cures. Perhaps owing to the odd mix, Pärnu has a little something for everyone – colourful museums and galleries, boutiques and handicraft markets, good theatre, and amusements for the kids – and plenty of mud baths and drinking spots.

East of Pärnu stretches Soomaa National Park, a biodiverse region of meandering rivers, wooded meadows and swamp forest. Full of wildlife, Soomaa is an excellent place to experience Estonia's natural beauty – whether floating along streams in a dugout canoe or hiking through ancient bogs.

Among the most charming country towns, Viljandi lies just beyond Soomaa. It has a tiny but historic centre, old castle ruins and breathtaking views over a forested valley and the pristine Lake Viljandi. Põltsamaa, another pleasant town in the region, is noted for its pleasant river, old stone church and fragrant rose gardens.

Visitors yearning to get off the beaten path can find peaceful settlements and deserted coastline on the island of Kihnu, one of Estonia's most traditional places. Ruhnu, even tinier and more remote, has a few sandy beaches, an old wooden church and plenty of spots for connecting to the land in that almost spiritual Estonian fashion.

National Parks & Reserves

The star attraction is Soomaa National Park, a 367 sq km region comprising some of the

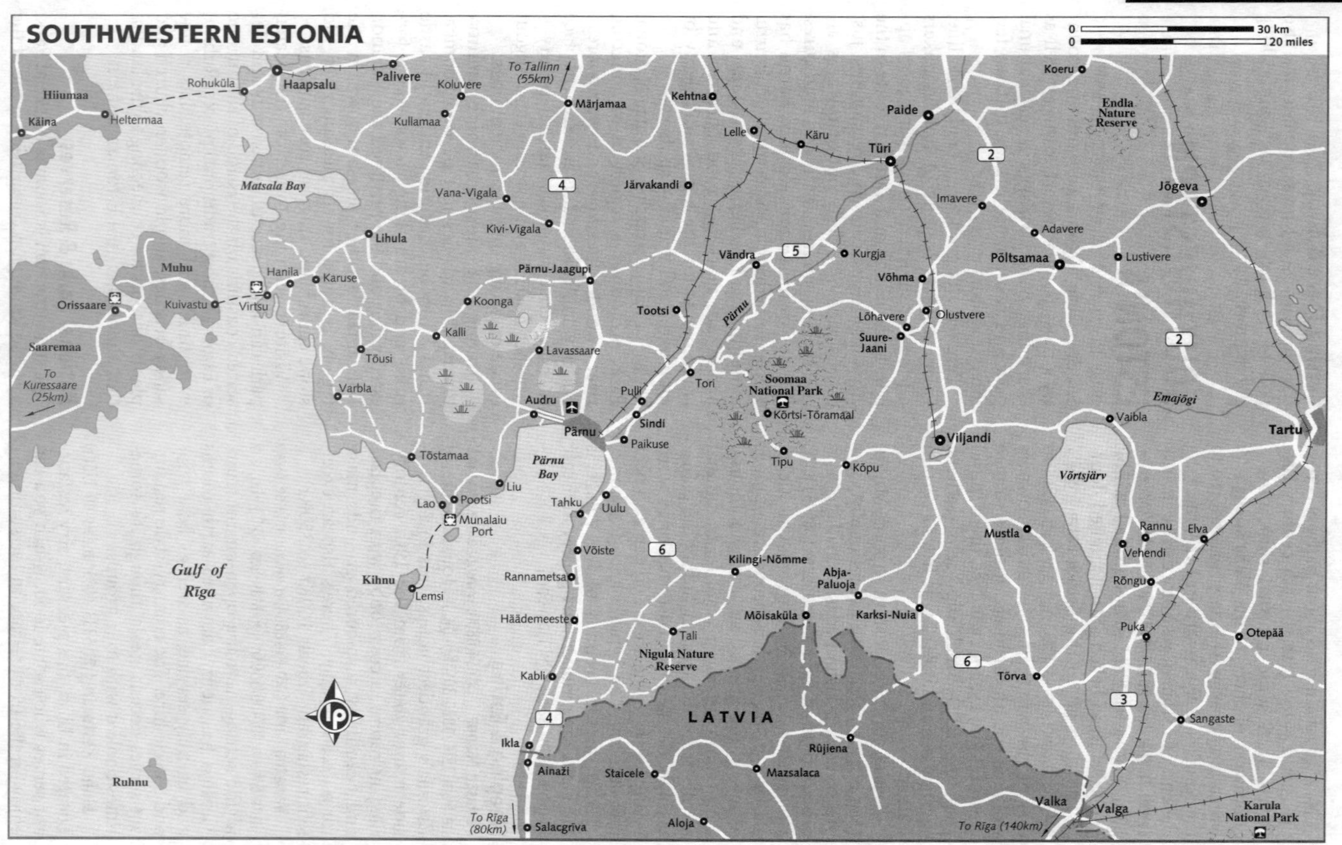
SOUTHWESTERN ESTONIA
0 30 km
0 20 miles
Hiiumaa
Käina
Heltermaa
Rohuküla
Haapsalu
Palivere
Koluvere
Kullamaa
To Tallinn (55km)
Märjamaa
Kehtna
Lelle
Käru
Türi
Paide
Koeru
Endla Nature Reserve
Jõgeva
Matsalu Bay
Vana-Vigala
Kivi-Vigala
Järvakandi
Imavere
Adavere
Lustivere
Põltsamaa
Lihula
Muhu
Hanila
Karuse
Virtsu
Kuivastu
Orissaare
Saaremaa
To Kuressaare (25km)
Pärnu-Jaagupi
Vändra
Kurgja
Võhma
Koonga
Kalli
Tõusi
Varbla
Lavassaare
Tootsi
Pärnu
Lõhavere
Olustvere
Suure-Jaani
Tori
Soomaa National Park
Kõrtsi-Tõramaal
Tipu
Kõpu
Viljandi
Emajõgi
Vaibla
Tartu
Audru
Pulli
Sindi
Paikuse
Pärnu Bay
Tõstamaa
Liu
Lao
Pootsi
Munalaiu Port
Tahku
Uulu
Võiste
Võrtsjärv
Mustla
Rannu
Vehendi
Elva
Rõngu
Gulf of Rīga
Kihnu
Lemsi
Rannametsa
Kilingi-Nõmme
Abja-Paluoja
Mõisaküla
Karksi-Nuia
Häädemeeste
Tali
Nigula Nature Reserve
Puka
Otepää
Kabli
Tõrva
Sangaste
LATVIA
Ikla
Ainaži
Staicele
Mazsalaca
Rūjiena
Ruhnu
To Rīga (80km)
Salacgrīva
Aloja
Valka
Valga
To Rīga (140km)
Karula National Park
2
3
4
5
6

biggest mires, floodplain grasslands and forests in Estonia. In addition to the rich flora, 46 mammal species and 172 species of bird have been spotted in the area. The Nigula Nature Reserve, known for its path through the Nigula bog, lies further south.

Getting There & Away

Numerous buses and two daily trains run between Tallinn and Pärnu (p90). There are also numerous buses between Pärnu and Tartu (p160), and several daily buses to Kuressaare, Saaremaa (p144). The island of Ruhnu can be reached by boat from Saaremaa, but only in summer.

Getting Around

Ten daily buses connect Viljandi and Pärnu. To reach the islands, there are a few options. To Kihnu, summertime boats depart from both Munalaiu port and from Pärnu city port. Air Livonia flies between Pärnu and Kihnu, but only from October to April. Air Livonia flies year-round to Ruhnu Island (twice weekly), with one plane continuing on to Kuressaare, Saaremaa. Soomaa National Park is not reachable by public transport. Cars can be hired in Pärnu or Viljandi.

PÄRNU

pop 45,000

Boasting golden-sand beaches, lush sprawling parks and a historic, picturesque centre, Pärnu (*pair*-nu) is Estonia's premier resort town. On warm summer nights, young revellers pack the city's beachside bars and nightclubs, its cosy wine bars and outdoor cafés. By day, people head to the pleasant seaside, though Pärnu has first-rate museums and galleries, with colourful boutiques and shops sprinkled about Old Town.

Yet youth and bacchanalia aren't the only spirits moving through town. Pärnu is a popular health resort for older visitors from the Baltics, Finland and Eastern Europe who come seeking rest, amelioration and Pärnu's vaunted mud treatments, available in both old-school Soviet-style sanatoriums and more modern, glitzier spa resorts.

Pärnu lies 130km south of Tallinn on the main road to Rīga.

History

Stone-Age objects from around 7500 BC found at Pulli, near Sindi on the Pärnu River about 12km inland, are among the oldest human artefacts found in Estonia. At that time the mouth of the river was at Pulli and the site of Pärnu was still sea bed.

There was a trading settlement at Pärnu before the German crusaders arrived, but the place entered recorded history when the Pärnu River was fixed as the border between the territories of the Ösel-Wiek bishop (west and north) and the Livonian knights (east and south) in 1234. The town, joined by rivers to Viljandi, Tartu and Lake Peipsi, became the Hanseatic port of Pernau in the 14th century. (Sinking water levels have since cut this link.) Pernau/Pärnu had a population of German merchants from Lübeck origin till at least the 18th century. It withstood wars, fires, plagues, and switches between German, Polish, Swedish and Russian rule, and prospered in the 17th century under Swedish rule until it had its trade devastated by the Europe-wide blockades during the Napoleonic wars.

From 1838 it gradually became a popular resort, with mud baths proving a draw as well as the beach. Only the resort area was spared severe damage in 1944 as the Soviets drove out the Nazis, but many parts of Old Town have since been restored.

Orientation

Pärnu lies on either side of the Pärnu River estuary, which empties into Pärnu Bay. The southern half of the town contains the major attractions, including Old Town, which begins a few blocks south of the river, and the beach, which lies half a kilometre further on the far southern end. Between Old Town and the shoreline are a series of parks extending westward towards the bay.

The bus station is at the western end of Old Town, walking distance to many hotels.

Information

BOOKSHOPS

Apollo (☎ 654 8485; Rüütli 41; ⌚ 9am-7pm Mon-Fri, 10am-5pm Sat) Sells books, maps and English-language books.

INTERNET ACCESS

Central Library (Keskraamatukogu; Akadeemia tänav 3; ⌚ 10am-6pm Mon-Fri, to 5pm Sat) Free Internet.

Pärnu New Art Museum (Esplanaadi tänav 10; per hr 30Kr; ⌚ 24hr)

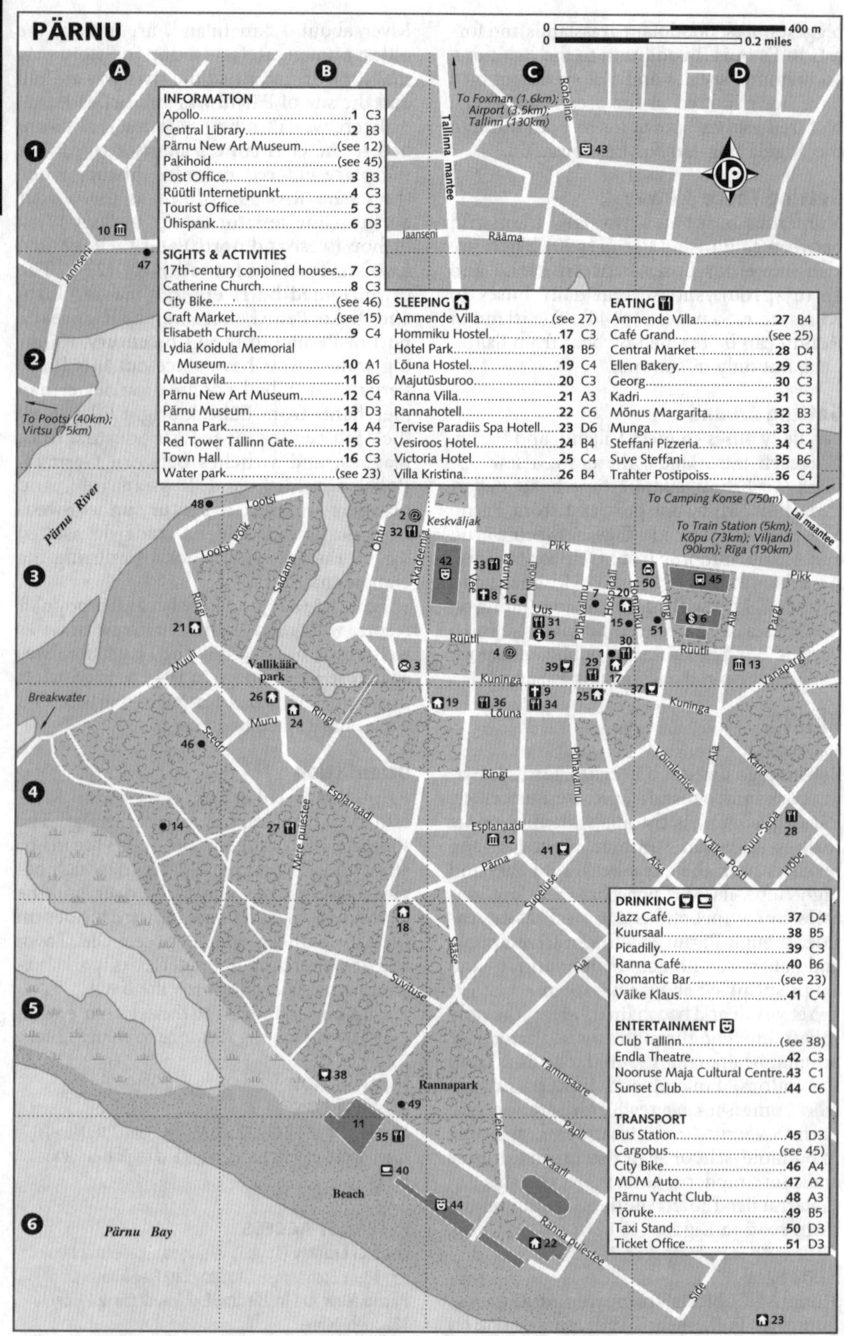
PÄRNU
0 400 m
0 0.2 miles
INFORMATION
Apollo....1 C3
Central Library....2 B3
Pärnu New Art Museum....(see 12)
Pakihoid....(see 45)
Post Office....3 B3
Rüütli Internetipunkt....4 C3
Tourist Office....5 C3
Ühispank....6 D3
SIGHTS & ACTIVITIES
17th-century conjoined houses....7 C3
Catherine Church....8 C3
City Bike....(see 46)
Craft Market....(see 15)
Elisabeth Church....9 C4
Lydia Koidula Memorial Museum....10 A1
Mudaravila....11 B6
Pärnu New Art Museum....12 C4
Pärnu Museum....13 D3
Ranna Park....14 A4
Red Tower Tallinn Gate....15 C3
Town Hall....16 C3
Water park....(see 23)
SLEEPING
Ammende Villa....(see 27)
Hommiku Hostel....17 C3
Hotel Park....18 B5
Lõuna Hostel....19 C4
Majutüsburoo....20 C3
Ranna Villa....21 A3
Rannahotell....22 C6
Tervise Paradiis Spa Hotell....23 D6
Vesiroos Hotel....24 B4
Victoria Hotel....25 C4
Villa Kristina....26 B4
EATING
Ammende Villa....27 B4
Café Grand....(see 25)
Central Market....28 D4
Ellen Bakery....29 C3
Georg....30 C3
Kadri....31 C3
Mõnus Margarita....32 B3
Munga....33 C3
Steffani Pizzeria....34 C4
Suve Steffani....35 B6
Trahter Postipoiss....36 C4
DRINKING
Jazz Café....37 D4
Kuursaal....38 B5
Picadilly....39 C3
Ranna Café....40 B6
Romantic Bar....(see 23)
Väike Klaus....41 C4
ENTERTAINMENT
Club Tallinn....(see 38)
Endla Theatre....42 C3
Nooruse Maja Cultural Centre....43 C1
Sunset Club....44 C6
TRANSPORT
Bus Station....45 D3
Cargobus....(see 45)
City Bike....46 A4
MDM Auto....47 A2
Pärnu Yacht Club....48 A3
Tõruke....49 B5
Taxi Stand....50 D3
Ticket Office....51 D3
To Foxman (1.6km); Airport (3.5km); Tallinn (130km)
To Pootsi (40km); Virtsu (75km)
To Camping Konse (750m)
To Train Station (5km); Kõpu (73km); Viljandi (90km); Rīga (190km)
Tallinna mantee
Roheline
Jannseni
Rääma
Pärnu River
Lootsi
Lootsi Põik
Sadama
Ringi
Muuli
Breakwater
Vallikäär park
Muru
Seedri
Keskväljak
Ohtu
Akadeemia
Vee
Munga
Nikolai
Pikk
Uus
Rüütli
Kuninga
Lõuna
Pühavaimu
Hospidali
Hommiku
Aia
Pargi
Vanapargi
Lai maantee
Võimlemise
Karja
Suur-Sepa
Väike Posti
Hõbe
Aisa
Esplanaadi
Mere puiestee
Pärna
Supeluse
Sääse
Suvituse
Tammsaare
Papli
Kaarli
Lehe
Ranna puiestee
Side
Rannapark
Beach
Pärnu Bay

Rüütli Internetipunkt (Rüütli tänav 25; per hr 25Kr; 10am-9pm Mon-Fri, to 6pm Sat & Sun) A basement-level café.

LEFT LUGGAGE

Pakihoid (per day 15Kr; 8am-7.30pm Mon-Fri, 9am-5pm Sat & Sun) At the southern end of the bus terminal, near platform 8.

MONEY

Ühispank (Rüütli tänav 40a) Behind the bus station, this bank provides many services.

POST

Central post office (Akadeemia 7; 8am-6pm Mon-Fri, 9am-3pm Sat & Sun)

TOURIST INFORMATION

Tourist office (447 3000; www.parnu.ee; Rüütli tänav 16; 9am-6pm Mon-Fri, 10am-4pm Sat, 10am-3pm Sun Jun-Aug, 9am-5pm Mon-Fri Sep-May) Pick up maps, brochures and the helpful *Pärnu in Your Pocket*, published annually (25Kr).

Sights & Activities

The wide, sandy beach, and Ranna puiestee, the buildings along which date from the early 20th century, are among Pärnu's finest attractions. A new beach promenade should be completed by the time you read this.

You can experience Pärnu's famous mud baths inside the neoclassical **Mudaravila** (445 9020; Ranna puiestee 1; mud therapy 160Kr; 10am-6pm Mon-Sat), which offers a large selection of mud to wallow in. A more upscale mud/spa experience can be had at Tervise Paradiis (p159), which also boasts a sparkling new **water park** (Veepark; 445 1606; Side tänav 14; adult 90-135Kr, concession 65-90Kr; 10am-10pm), with pools, slides, tubes and other slippery fun.

The main thoroughfare of the historic centre is **Rüütli tänav**, lined with splendid buildings dating back to the 17th century. Just off the main street is the **Red Tower** (Punane Torn; Hommiku tänav 11; 10am-6pm), the city's oldest building, which dates from the 15th century. Originally bigger, this was the southeast corner of the medieval town wall, of which nothing more remains. At one stage the tower was used as a prison. Today a small gallery is housed on the top floor, and a **craft market** fills the courtyard.

Two blocks west, on Pühavaimu tänav, is a pair of large **17th-century conjoined houses**, a fascinating example of ambitious early home-renovation efforts. Originally separate residences, the buildings received a neoclassicist face-lift in the 1840s. One block further west is the former **Town Hall** (Raekoja Hoon; cnr Nikolai tänav & Uus tänav), a yellow and white classical edifice originally built in 1797 as the home of a rich merchant. The grey and white Jugendstil north wing with its little spire was added in 1911.

Across Nikolai from the main Town Hall building there's a half-timbered house dating from 1740, and a block down the street on the corner of Nikolai and Kuninga is the baroque Lutheran **Elisabeth Church**, also from the 1740s, named after the Russian empress of the time. The Russian Orthodox **Catherine Church** (Ekatarina Kirik; cnr Uus & Vee tänav), from the 1760s, is named after another Russian empress, Catherine the Great.

At the western end of Rüütli tänav a stretch of Pärnu's **Swedish ramparts** overlooks the **moat**, from where the west side of Old Town was defended. Where the rampart meets the western end of Kuninga tänav it's pierced by the tunnel-like **Tallinn Gate** (Tallinna Värav), which once marked the main road to Tallinn. It was one of three gates in the ramparts built as part of the strengthening of Pärnu's defences.

The **Pärnu New Art Museum** (443 0772; www.chaplin.ee; Esplanaadi tänav 10; adult/concession 25/15Kr; 9am-9pm), in the former Communist Party headquarters, is among the cultural highlights in Estonia, and often features some of the country's most forward-thinking exhibitions. Founded by film maker Mark Soosaar, it also hosts an annual film festival. There's a café and art shop near the entrance, and a decapitated Lenin statue out back.

The **Lydia Koidula Memorial Museum** (443 3313; Jannseni tänav 37; adult/concession 15/10; 10am-6pm Wed-Sun) stands north of the river. Here you can learn about one of Estonia's great poets in the former school she attended.

Despite its modest size, the **Pärnu Museum** (443 3231; www.pernau.ee; Rüütli tänav 53; adult/concession 30/15Kr; 10am-6pm Wed-Sun) covers 11,000 years of regional history. Archaeological findings along with relics from the country's German, Livonian, Russian and even Soviet periods are on display.

Open in summer, **Ranna Park**, west of Seedri tänav, is a small amusement park with a Ferris wheel, bumper cars and bouncy rides.

Tours

Offering summer cycling, walking, canoeing and horse riding excursions, **City Bike** (☎ 5660 8990; www.citybike.ee; Seedri 4; ⏲ Jun-Aug) is based in the Maritime Hotel.

Festivals & Events

The biggest annual event is the **Pärnu Film Festival** (first week of July), featuring documentary and anthropology films. It's held at the Pärnu New Art Museum and other venues in town. See www.chaplin.ee for details.

The tourist office distributes the annual *Pärnu This Week*, which lists events happening around town.

Sleeping

For inexpensive accommodation in private flats, contact the **Majutüsburoo** (☎ 443 1070, 518 5319; Hommiku 7; r from 200Kr; ⊠).

BUDGET

Lõuna Hostel (☎ 443 0943; www.hot.ee/hostellouna; Lõuna tänav 2; dm €13-17; ⊠) This spotless, well-located hostel has quality budget accommodation in two- to seven-bed rooms. The shared kitchen doubles as social room; it's a good place to meet other travellers.

Camping Konse (☎ 5343 5092; www.konse.ee; Suur-Jõe 44a; camp site/caravan/d/tr from €4/9/36/50) One of several camping options near the city, this one is barely 1km from the centre on a perfect spot on the river, and offers tent, rowboat and bike rentals. Most rooms share bathroom. Open year-round.

MIDRANGE

Vesiroos Hotel (☎ 443 0940; www.pina.ee; Esplanaadi tänav 42A; d/tr 900/1250Kr; ⊠ 🅿) The only hotel in town with an outdoor swimming pool, Vesiroos was fully renovated in 2001 and features bright, airy rooms painted in cheery pastels, with wooden floors.

Villa Kristina (☎ 442 9803; www.zone.ee/villakristina; Suvituse tänav 1; d/ste 680/1200Kr; ⊠) This small family-run guesthouse has spotless rooms with wooden floors. The owner, a doctor, has made the place hypoallergenic and can arrange mud baths and other therapies.

Hommiku Hostel (☎ 445 1122; www.hot.ee/pav; Hommiku tänav 17; d/tr 700/1000Kr; ⊠) Nicer than your average hostel, this stylish modern place has handsome rooms with private bathrooms and kitchenettes, and old beamed ceilings throughout.

> **THE AUTHOR'S CHOICE**
>
> **Ammende Villa** (☎ 447 3888; www.ammende.ee; Mere puiestee 7; meals 190-310Kr) This lovely villa boasts beautiful rooms (below), but the food is the real reason we love coming here. If the weather is warm, bypass the splendid Art-Nouveau dining room and go instead to the lovely garden at the back. There you can dine on roast beef with morel sauce, seared tuna steak and a range of French and Mediterranean dishes. In the morning don't miss the superb buffet breakfasts (fresh fruit, French toast, smoked salmon and champagne). Weekly classical concerts are held on the lawn in summer.

Ranna Villa (☎ 444 1120; www.rannavilla.ee; Ringi 52; d/ste €66/80; ⊠) This pleasant guesthouse has good-sized rooms with big windows, wood floors and a splash of colour (usually orange); some rooms have balconies.

Hotel Park (☎ 447 6915; www.spaestonia.ee; Pärna tänav 12; s/d 500/700Kr; ⊠) Packed full of convalescing elders, this unattractive seven-storey hotel screams 'sanatorium'. Once you're past the uninspiring corridors, however, you'll find tidy rooms with faux-wood floors and a balcony with sea views. The top floor bar has panoramic views (and a telescope).

TOP END

Ammende Villa (☎ 447 3888; www.ammende.ee; Mere puiestee 7; s/d cottages 1200/1550Kr, d 3100Kr, ste 4300-6500Kr; ⊠) Class and luxury abound in this fabulously refurbished 1905 Russian Art-Nouveau building, set amid handsomely manicured grounds. Suites contain period furnishings while the other rooms are quite comfortable. Top-notch service includes surprises for the guests, such as a winter picnic outside with bonfire and vodka or schnapps. See boxed text, above for a review of the hotel's restaurant.

Rannahotell (☎ 443 2950; www.scandic-hotels.ee; Ranna puiestee 5; s/d from €71/95; ⊠) Inside this stunning 1930s building you'll find beautifully renovated rooms with wood floors and big windows (overlooking the beach or the park); some rooms have balconies. For beach action, it's the best location in town.

Victoria Hotel (☎ 444 3412; www.victoria.ee; Kuninga tänav 25; s/d from 945/1265Kr; ⊠) In the town centre, this 1920s gem has lavish rooms with curved walls, soft colours and lots of old-fashioned touches; on the ground floor is one of Pärnu's most elegant restaurants, the Café Grand.

Tervise Paradiis Spa Hotell (☎ 445 1600; www.terviseparadiis.ee; Side tänav 14; s/d/ste €82/102/159; ☒) This enormous spa hotel near the water has nicely designed rooms with wooden floors and balconies; guests have access to spa services, fitness club, pool and waterpark. There's a good restaurant on the ground floor, and a handsome bar on the top floor.

Eating

Trahter Postipoiss (☎ 446 4864; Vee tänav 12; meals 80-230Kr) One of Pärnu's new additions, this converted 17th-century postal building houses a delightful Russian tavern, with excellent Russian cuisine, a garrulous crowd (especially after a few vodka shots) and imperial portraits watching over the proceedings. The spacious patio opens during the summer.

Mõnus Margarita (☎ 443 0929; Akadeemia tänav 5; meals 65-145Kr) This colourful Tex-Mex restaurant serves freshly prepared Mexican fare, with vegetarian options, and seductive strawberry margaritas.

Café Grand (☎ 444 3412; Kuninga tänav 25; meals 130-220Kr) Pärnu's most stately dining room serves up delicately prepared Chateaubriand, rack of lamb and other favourites amid 1920s grandeur. The plush chairs in the bar and café make a cosy spot for coffee and *crème brûlée*.

Munga (☎ 443 1099; Munga tänav 9; meals around 70Kr) In a tucked-away 19th-century cottage, this charming café has lots of homy touches. Meals are fairly standard, but the eclectic appetizers and ambience warrant the visit.

Steffani Pizzeria (☎ 443 1170; Nikolai tänav 24; meals 65-80Kr) A good choice for thin-crust and pan pizzas, particularly in summer when you can dine alfresco in the courtyard.

Suve Steffani (☎ 449 5505; Ranna puiestee 1) A second branch of Steffani Pizzeria, this recently opened near the beach.

Kadri (☎ 442 9782; Nikolai tänav 12; meals 22-45Kr; ⏰ 7.30am-9pm Mon-Sat, 9am-5pm Sun) This longtime local favourite serves tasty, inexpensive, home-cooked meals.

Georg (☎ 443 1110; Rüütli tänav 43; meals 30-50Kr; ⏰ 7.30am-7.30pm Mon-Fri, 9am-7.30pm Sat & Sun) This streamlined diner has inexpensive soups, salads and basics such as beef stroganoff, served buffet style.

Ellen Bakery (☎ 447 0044; Kuninga tänav 32; tarts 6-8Kr; ⏰ 7.30am-4pm) A tiny bakery serving rhubarb tart, strudel and other fresh delights.

Provisions abound at the **central market** (Turg; Suur-Sepa 18; ⏰ 8am-3pm Tue-Sun), southeast of the centre.

Drinking

Ranna Café (☎ 446 4890; Ranna puiestee 3) Overlooking the beach, this handsome new three-storey café boasts several outdoor terraces and a laid-back ambience perfect for sipping cocktails at sunset.

Picadilly (☎ 442 0085; Pühavaimu 15) This cosy wine bar has plush chairs you can sink into while you sample some of the vintages. Colourfully painted walls decked with local artwork and a small front patio add to the allure.

Jazz Café (☎ 442 7546; Ringi 11; ⏰ 10am-midnight) A bit disappointing for jazz-lovers, this indoor-outdoor café still makes a lively spot for a drink. Live performances most Fridays.

Kuursaal (☎ 442 0368; www.kuur.ee; Mere puiestee 22) This early-20th-century spa hall has been transformed into a spacious countrified beer hall with a large terrace at the back. An older mix of tourists and locals come for draft beer and occasional rock shows.

Romantic Bar (☎ 445 1600; Tervise Paradiis Spa Hotell, 8th fl, Side tänav 14) Although the name is uninspiring, this glass-sided hotel bar has extraordinary views over the water, and we can't deny the appeal of the stylish lounge-like interior or the patio outside.

Väike Klaus (☎ 447 7208; Supeluse 3) A casual, welcoming ambience prevails at this German-inspired pub; it's a popular meeting spot over drinks or billiards games.

Entertainment

Pärnu Town Orchestra holds classical concerts every weekend in summer. Check with the tourist office.

THEATRE

Endla Theatre (☎ 442 0667; www.endla.ee; Keskväljak 1) This is Pärnu's best theatre and it stages a wide range of performances. It also houses an art gallery and an open-air café on the rooftop.

Nooruse Maja Cultural Centre (☎ 444 1768; www.noorusemaja.ee; Roheline tänav 1b) This cultural centre stages periodic folk shows and concerts.

NIGHTCLUBS

Club Tallinn (www.clubtallinn.ee; Mere puiestee 22; entrance 40-100Kr; Tue-Sat Jun-Aug) This summertime-only club is held in one section of Kuursaal (p159). It's the city's hottest spot, with excellent DJs and an eager young crowd.

Sunset Club (443 0670; www.sunsetclub.ee; Ranna puiestee 3; entrance 60-100Kr; closed Sun & Mon) In a grandiose building dating from 1939, this club has an outdoor beach terrace and a sleek multifloor interior with plenty of cosy nooks when the dance floor gets crowded.

Getting There & Away

AIR

Pärnu's **airport** (447 5001; www.eepu.ee) lies on the northern edge of town, west off the Tallinn road. Bus 23 runs from the bus station to the airport (20 minutes).

Air Livonia (447 5007; www.airlivonia.ee) flies twice weekly from Pärnu to Ruhnu (adult/concession 300/200Kr one way, 25 minutes); one of these flights continues on to Kuressaare (adult/concession 300/200Kr one way, one hour), Saaremaa. Air Livonia also has daily flights from Pärnu to Kihnu, but only from October to April (120Kr, one way). Book well in advance.

BOAT

It's possible to take a ferry or private boat trip from Pärnu to Kihnu (see p162). **Pärnu Yacht Club** (Pärnu Jahtklubi; 447 1740; Lootsi tänav 6) has a harbour with a customs point and passport control.

BUS

The **bus station** (447 1002; 5am-8.30pm) is at the north end of Ringi tänav, just off Pikk. **Cargobus** (442 7845) near platform 8 sells Eurolines tickets to Rīga, Vilnius and beyond, though you can purchase tickets from the driver. For destinations throughout Estonia, the **ticket office** (6am-7.30pm), a red-brick building, is 100m south on the opposite side of Ringi tänav. More than 20 daily buses connect Pärnu with Tallinn (80-115Kr, two hours). Buses depart three times daily (one hour) for Munalaiu Port, the departure point for ferries to Kihnu. See p397 for information on getting from Pärnu to Russia. Other buses to/from Pärnu include:

Kuressaare 140Kr, 3¼ hours, three daily.
Rīga 110Kr, three hours, two daily.
Tartu 85Kr to 115Kr, two to three hours, 16 daily.
Viljandi 65Kr, 1½ to two hours, 10 daily.
Vilnius 280Kr, eight hours, two weekly.
Virtsu 55Kr, 1¼ hours, three daily.

TRAIN

Two daily trains run between Tallinn and Pärnu (50Kr, three hours). The **Pärnu station** (Riia maantee 116) is 5km east of the town centre along the Rīga road. There's no station office there; buy tickets on the train.

Getting Around

A main local bus stop in the town centre is the Sidesõlm stop on Akadeemia tee in front of the main post office. **Taxis** (cnr Pikk & Ringi tänav) line up near the bus station. You'll get better rates by calling **E-Takso** (443 1111) or **Pärnu Takso** (443 1200).

BICYCLE

During the summer you can rent bicycles from **Tõruke** (502 8269; Supeluse; bike per hr/day 40/150Kr), a bike stand near the beach, and **City Bike** (5660 8990; www.citybike.ee; Seedri 4; bike per hr/day 35/150Kr).

CAR & MOTORCYCLE

Neste, Shell and Statoil stations along Riia maantee are all open 24 hours. There's a fuel station next to the Port Artur Shopping Centre. There are numerous car-hire agencies in town. Get a list from the tourist office for the best rates. A couple of budget rentals are **MDM Auto** (443 2113; Jannseni 36b) – look out for the sign that says 'SEAT' – and **Foxman** (443 4800; Roheline tänav 64).

Around Pärnu

LAVASSAARE

Railways are used in the peat-extraction industry at Lavassaare, in an area of bogs 25km northwest of Pärnu, and there's a **railway museum** (527 2584; www.museumrailway.ee; 11am-6pm Mon-Sat, 11am-5pm Sun Jun-Aug, 11am-5pm Sat & Sun Sep) close to the peat fields with locomotives from all over the Baltics. It's best to come on Saturday, when the museum offers rides on its little old steam engine along the narrow-gauge tracks. To reach Lavassaare turn north off the Lihula road 13km west of central Pärnu, then go about 12km north.

TORI

A tiny town along the Pärnu river, Tori has a **stud & horse-riding farm** (446 6080;

www.hot.ee/torihobune; Pärnu maantee 13; rides per person per hr 150-250Kr; 8am-5pm Mon-Fri) that's been in operation since 1856, when attempts began to breed bigger, stronger Estonian farm and cart horses. Learn more about Estonia's finest breeds at the **horse-breeding museum**. You can also go riding, by horse or carriage – or sleigh in winter. Just be sure to call at least one day in advance.

Across the road from the farm is **Tori Matkakeskus** (☎ 511 4253; www.tori.ee, in Estonian), a friendly adventure outfit that offers one- and two-day kayaking trips (from 300Kr) along the nearby rivers and in Soomaa National Park. You can also pitch a tent here (per person 25Kr) or hire a kayak (per hour 100Kr) to paddle around the Pärnu river, which stretches downhill from the house.

Tori lies 20km northeast of Pärnu.

KURGJA

At Kurgja, on the Pärnu River 15km east of Vändra and 65km northeast of Pärnu, stands the **Carl Robert Jakobson farm & museum** (☎ 445 8171; adult/concession 15/8), where you can learn about the much revered leader of the Estonian nationalist movement. Jakobson was a professional educator and edited the radical newspaper *Sakala* in Viljandi. (His face adorns the 500Kr banknote.) Jakobson's farm, which he founded in 1874, still operates using 19th-century methods. In addition to touring the old country estate, you can take a swim in the river or camp on the grounds (50Kr per person), a popular activity with school groups.

PÄRNU TO THE LATVIAN BORDER

Highway 4 from Pärnu to the Latvian border, a 65km stretch, runs through forest much of the way, usually 2km to 3km inland. The border on the older, more pleasant coastal road from Hädemeeste is no longer operational.

Sights & Activities

Konstantin Päts, the semidictatorial president of independent Estonia before WWII, was born at **Tahku**, 20km down the coast from Pärnu. His statue here was the first **political monument** to be restored in post-Soviet Estonia. Estonia's biggest dunes are off the highway at **Rannametsa**, about 3km north of Häädemeeste, but they are forested and inland, so there's little to see. Ten kilometres south of Rannametsa is **Kabli**, a seaside town fronted by sandy **beaches**.

The **Nigula Nature Reserve** protects the **Nigula bog** (Nigula raba), just north of the Latvian border, about 10km east of Highway 4. This treeless peat bog is filled with pools and hollows, in the western part of which there are five 'bog islands'. It's also an important bird-breeding area: golden eagles and black-throated divers are occasionally sited, as are 144 other bird species. You can follow a 6.8km trail along wooden planks that pass through the wild scenery here.

For more information about the bog, stop in the **Nigula Nature Reserve office** (☎ 445 6668; www.loodus.ee/nigula; Pärnu tänav 2) in Kilingi-Nõmme.

Sleeping

Lepanina Hotell (☎ 446 5024; www.lepanina.ee; camp site/caravan €3/8, s/d/cottage incl breakfast €46/66/33; ⊠) This sprawling, modern complex lies near the coast, just south of Kabli, following the old border road. Rooms inside the hotel are comfortably set with sea-facing balconies. There are also some simple wooden cottages on the grounds. It's a stone's throw to the beach.

KIHNU

pop 500

Kihnu Island, 40km southwest of Pärnu in the Gulf of Rīga, is one of the most traditional places in Estonia. Most women still wear the colourful striped skirts nearly every day. There are three main villages on the 7km-long island, plus a school, church, and combined village hall and bar in the centre of the island. Long, quiet beaches line the western coast. Kihnuans are among the few non-Setu Estonians who follow the Russian Orthodox religion.

In December 2003 Unesco declared the Kihnu Cultural Space a masterpiece of the Oral and Intangible Heritage of Humanity. This honour is a tribute to the rich cultural traditions that are still practised, in song, dance, the celebration of traditional spiritual festivals and the making of handicrafts. In part, the customs of Kihnu have remained intact for so many centuries owing to the island's isolation.

Many of the island's first inhabitants, centuries ago, were criminals and exiles from the mainland. Kihnu men made a living from fishing and seal hunting, while women effectively governed the island in their absence. The most famous Kihnuan was the sea captain Enn Uuetoa (better known as Kihnu Jõnn), who became a symbol of lost freedom for Estonians during the Soviet period when they were virtually banned from the sea. Kihnu Jõnn, said to have sailed on all the world's oceans, drowned in 1913 when his ship sank off Denmark on what was to have been his last voyage before retirement. He was buried in the Danish town of Oksby but in 1992 his remains were brought home to Kihnu and reburied in the island's church.

You can learn more about him and life on Kihnu at the **Kihnu Muuseum** (☎ 446 9983; adult/child 15/6Kr; 🕑 10.30am-4pm), across the street from the picturesque Orthodox church. Town information and Internet access is available 50m up the road at the **tourist office** (🕑 10am-4pm Tue-Sat, 11am-3pm Sun).

In the south stands a picturesque lighthouse, shipped over from Britain.

After WWII a fishery collective was established. Fishing and cattle herding continue to be the mainstay of employment for Kihnu's inhabitants.

Sleeping & Eating

Tolli Tourist Farm (☎ 446 9908; r/camp site per person 250/60Kr; ☒) Offers accommodation in the main house or in a more rustic log cabin. You can also pitch a tent. Sauna available. Tolli offers bike rental, boating excursions, and guests can order meals. The farm is located about 2km north of the port.

Rock City (☎ 446 9956; d 350Kr; ☒) Near Tolli, this place offers simple wood-floored rooms with shared bathroom. The restaurant (meals 18Kr to 45Kr) serves hearty country fare.

Kurase Pood Kohvik (☎ 446 9938; meals from 20Kr) Near the church and museum in the island centre, this food shop has a pleasant restaurant with a patio out the back. It's Kihnu's best place to pop in for a meal.

Getting There & Away

From mid-May through September, the ferry **Amalie** (☎ 448 9924; one way 30Kr) departs from Munalaiu Port for Kihnu twice daily Sunday to Friday, once daily on Saturday, taking about 50 minutes. Munalaiu Port is in the village of Pootsi, 40km southwest of Pärnu; buses from Pärnu are theoretically timed to meet the ferries.

From the Pärnu city port (Kalda tänav 2), the ferry **Liisi** (☎ 5344 1294; one way 70Kr) sails between Pärnu and Kihnu daily from Thursday to Monday, taking about 2½ hours.

The Pärnu tourist office keeps updated ferry departure times.

Air Livonia (☎ 447 5007; www.airlivonia.ee; one way 120Kr) has one or two daily flights from Pärnu to Kihnu but only from October to April.

Getting Around

Once you reach Kihnu, bicycle is the best way to get around. You can rent bikes and pick up a map (10Kr) of the island at **Jalgrattaläe nutus** (bikes per hr/day from 25/125Kr), in a brick building 150m from the port.

RUHNU

pop 65

Ruhnu, smaller than Kihnu at just 11 sq km, is 100km southwest of Pärnu and nearer to Latvia than the Estonian mainland. For several centuries Ruhnu had a mainly Swedish population of about 300, but they all fled in August 1944, abandoning homes and livestock, to avoid the advancing Red Army. Ruhnu has some sandy beaches, but the highlight is a very impressive **wooden church** (dating back to 1644), making it the oldest surviving wooden structure in Estonia. It has a wooden altar and pulpit dating from 1755 in its atmospheric interior. The island is flat but there's a forest of 200- to 300-year-old pines on its eastern dunes.

If you're arriving in summer (19 May to 31 August), you can reach Ruhnu by boat from Saaremaa. **SLK Ferries** (Saaremaa Laevakompanii; ☎ 452 4444; www.laevakompanii.ee) sails five times weekly between Roomassaare and Ruhnu (200Kr one way, two hours).

Air Livonia (☎ 477 5007; www.airlivonia.ee; adult/concession one way 300/200Kr) operates twice weekly flights between Pärnu and Ruhnu; it flies once weekly between Kuressaare and Ruhnu.

VILJANDI

pop 20,500

One of Estonia's most charming towns, Viljandi overlooks a picturesque valley with the lovely Lake Viljandi at its centre. The town is relaxed and peaceful, with some evocative castle ruins, historic buildings and abundant surrounding greenery. It makes a good base for exploring the natural wonders of Soomaa National Park, or for just unwinding in a pretty country town.

The Knights of the Sword founded a castle at Viljandi in the 13th century. The town around it later joined the Hanseatic League, then was subject to the usual comings and goings of Swedes, Poles and Russians. Today its tiny centre, with an eclectic mix of 19th-century architecture, makes for lovely strolls, and it's easy to feel like you've stepped back in time.

Viljandi is 160km south of Tallinn en route to Valga on the Latvian border.

Orientation

The centre of town is about 500m back from Lake Viljandi, with steps leading down to the shoreline. The central square is Keskväljak, where Tartu tänav meets Lossi tänav. Lossi tänav leads south to the castle park. The **bus station** (Tallinna maantee) is 500m north of the centre, past the **main post office** (Tallinna maantee 22); the **train station** (Metalli tänav 1) is 2km west of the centre along Vaksali.

Information

The **Viljandi tourist office** (☎ 433 0442; www.viljandi.ee; Vabaduse plats 6; 🕑 10am-5pm Mon-Fri, to 2pm Sat) can help with accommodation; it has many brochures on the area. For free Internet access, try the public **Library** (Tallinna maantee 7; 🕑 10am-6pm Tue-Fri, 9am-4pm Sat). You can change money and use the ATM at **SEB Ühispank** (Vaksali tänav 2).

Sights & Activities

One of the highlights is visiting **Castle Park** (Lossimäed), a lush area containing the ruins of the 13th-century **Viljandi Order Castle**, founded by the Knights of the Sword. The castle park has sweeping views over the primeval valley and the lake directly below. Also in the castle park are the medieval **St John's Church** (Jaani Kirik; Tasuja puiestee) and a **suspension footbridge** built in 1931. The ravines surrounding the castle ruins are what remain of the castle moat; trenches from WWII came later. A small cemetery to the rear of the castle area is the final resting place of the Germans killed in the fighting.

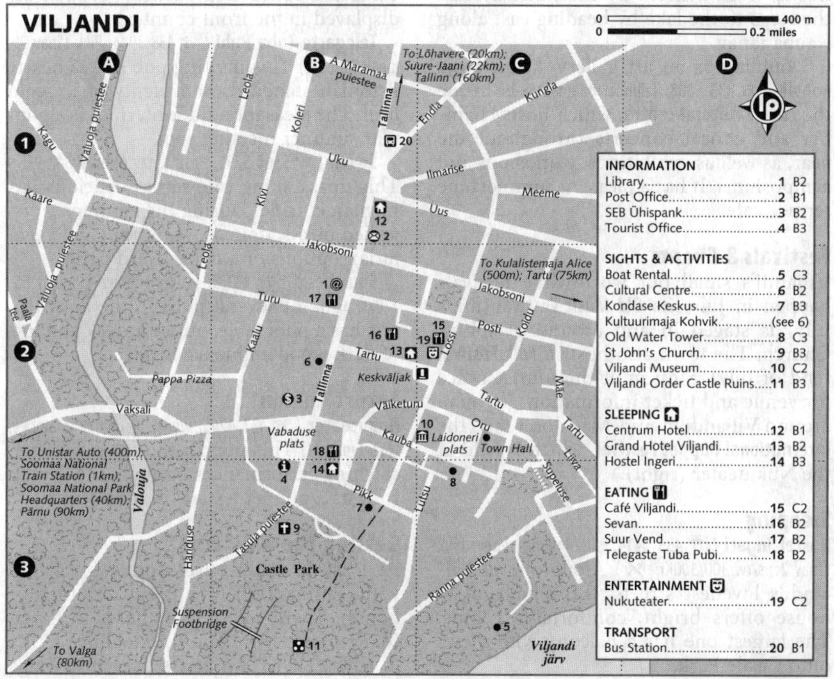

The old part of town is lined with brick streets and handsome wooden buildings with finely wrought details. Facing the old market square stands the modest two-storey **Viljandi Museum** (☎ 433 3316; Laidoneri plats 10; adult/concession 10/5Kr; ⏲ 10am-5pm Wed-Sun), which has displays tracing Viljandi's history from the Stone Age to the mid-20th century. There are folk costumes, black-and-white photos of the city, and a mock-up of what the original castle probably looked like. Nearby, the **old water tower** (Vana Veetorn; Kauba tänav; adult/concession 10/5Kr; ⏲ 11am-6pm May-Sep) offers fine views over the countryside.

A few blocks south is the excellent **Kondase Keskus** (☎ 433 3968; Pikk tänav 8; adult/concession 15/5Kr; ⏲ 10am-7pm Wed-Sun), with some vibrantly colourful works by the painter Paul Kondas and other self-taught artists working outside the mainstream. It's the country's only gallery dedicated to naive art.

The **lake** (Viljandi järv) is a lovely place for a swim on warm summer days. There's a pleasant café near the water and a swim platform just offshore. You can rent **boats** (paddleboats/rowboats per hr 30/40Kr; ⏲ 10am-8pm Jun-Aug) from a shack by the water. Access the steps to the lake by heading east along Kauba tänav.

Doubling as an art gallery, **Kultuurimaja kohvik** (☎ 433 5888; Tallinna maantee 5) is inside the main **cultural centre**, which hosts chamber and choral concerts throughout the year, as well as exhibitions, workshops and symposiums. It has a pleasant summertime terrace café.

Festivals & Events

Viljandi's small but worthwhile festivals happen in July; its **Old Music Festival** (mid-July) is staged in and around St John's Church. The town also hosts a **Folk Festival** (end of July). Stop in at the tourist office for venue and ticket information. If you're around Viljandi in mid-May don't miss the **International Puppet Festival**, which is held at the Nukuteater (right).

Sleeping

Hostel Ingeri (☎ 433 4414; valeriinkeri@hot.ee; Pikk tänav 2c; s/tw 300/500Kr; ⊠) Along one of Viljandi's loveliest streets, this small guesthouse offers bright, comfortable rooms. The largest one has a balcony with views onto Castle Park.

Grand Hotel Viljandi (☎ 435 5800; www.ghv.ee; Tartu tänav 11; s/d 1100/1400Kr; ⊠) The town's most elegant hotel has sumptuous rooms with dark wood trim, satiny chairs, large windows and wildly patterned carpets. There's a pleasant indoor-outdoor café in front.

Kulalistemaja Alice (☎ 434 7616; alice@matti.ee; Jakobsoni tänav 55; s 400Kr, d 500-700Kr; ⊠) In a peaceful neighbourhood 10 minutes' walk east of the centre, this small, friendly guesthouse has neat, airy rooms with wooden floors. Most rooms have private bathrooms, and guests can use the kitchen. Prices include breakfast.

Centrum Hotel (☎ 435 1100; www.centrum.ee; Tallinna maantee 24; s/d 700/900Kr; ⊠) Near the bus station, Centrum has large but uninspiring rooms with modern furnishings. There's a sauna and a restaurant on site.

Eating & Drinking

Café Viljandi (☎ 433 3021; Lossi tänav 31; meals 28-55; ⏲ 8am-10pm Mon-Fri, 9am-10pm Sat & Sun) This cosy café has lots of old-world charm; the full menu offers basic meals, or you can come for coffee and pastries (seductively displayed in the front counter).

Telegaste Tuba Pubi (☎ 433 3944; Pikk tänav 2b; meals 35-65Kr) This inviting pub serves hearty Estonian standards and plenty of ice-cold beer. The pleasant outdoor terrace is a popular summer meeting spot.

Sevan (☎ 5566 5295; Posti tänav 6; meals 40-95Kr) This unassuming café serves delicious Armenian cuisine. During the summer enjoy grilled meats, dolmas, *shawerma* and vegetarian options on the backyard patio.

Suur Vend (☎ 433 3644; Turu tänav 4; meals 65-120Kr) One of several pubs in the area, this one has a pool table, outdoor deck and lots of dark wood ambience inside.

Entertainment

Nukuteater (☎ 433 4295; www.viljandinukuteater.ee; Lossi tänav 31) This puppet theatre stages eye-catching performances throughout the year. It hosts a puppet festival in mid-May.

Getting There & Away

At least 13 daily buses connect Viljandi with Tallinn (70Kr to 85Kr, 2½ to four hours). There are 10 daily buses to Pärnu (65Kr, 1½ to two hours), 16 to Tartu (50Kr to 60Kr, 1½ to two hours), seven to Valga

(1¾ hours) and three to Kuressaare, Saaremaa (4¾ hours).

Two trains run daily to/from Tallinn (65Kr, three hours). For bus schedules, call ☎ 433 3680; for train schedules, call ☎ 434 9425.

Car hire is available at **Unistar Auto** (☎ 345 5921; Tenika tänav 2; cars from 600Kr). This is a good option for reaching and exploring Soomaa National Park.

Around Viljandi

At **Lõhavere**, just northeast of the lovely town of **Suure-Jaani** on the Viljandi–Vändra–Pärnu road, is the site of the fortress of Lembitu, the 13th-century Estonian leader who put up the most resistance to the invading Knights of the Sword. There's a large granite monument near a hill but little more. A few kilometres east is **Olustvere Manor**, a 1730s manor house with a watermill, distillery and English-style gardens housing the **Olustvere tourist office** (☎ 437 4280; www.olustvere.edu.ee/loss; 10am-5pm Mon-Fri, 11am-4pm Sat & Sun May-Aug, 10am-4pm Mon-Sat Sep-Apr). You're free to tour the manor, and if you call the day before, you can also order a meal, which will be served in the elegant dining room. From Viljandi at least eight daily buses (25–45 minutes) stop in Olustvere on the Viljandi–Tallinn route. Tallinn-bound trains from Viljandi (two or three daily) also stop at Olustvere, taking a little over two hours.

Vaibla is a sandy beach with **camping facilities** (☎ 504 9102; www.vaibla.ee, in Estonian; camp sites/caravans/cabins 50/150/280Kr) at the northern end of Võrtsjärv, just off the Viljandi–Tartu road. Nearby hamlets of Paissu, Kaalgu-Jaani, Leie and Paistu lay claim to scenes from the *Kalevipoeg* epic and sacrificial stones from pre-Christian times. A detailed map is available from the Viljandi tourist office. You'll find loads of information on Lake Võrtsjärv at www.hot.ee/vjarv.

SOOMAA NATIONAL PARK

Embracing Estonia's largest area of swamps, flat meadows and waterside forests, Soomaa National Park (Soomaa: literally 'land of wetlands') is primarily made up of four bogs – Valgeraba, Öördi, Kikepera and Kuresoo – the peat layer of which measures 7m in places. The bogs are split by tributaries of the Pärnu River, the spring flooding creating a 'fifth season' for the inhabitants of this boggy land, where the waters can rise to 5m in March and April.

Up to 46 different mammal species inhabit the surrounding forests, among them the wolf, lynx, brown bear, elk, wild boar and otter. Thousands of birds migrate to Soomaa every year, with 172 observed species.

The best way to explore the national park and it numerous meandering waterways, is by canoe or by *haabja*, a traditional Finno-Ugric single-tree boat carved from aspen and used for centuries for fishing, hunting, hauling hay and transportation.

Bogs, as forest, have historically provided isolation and protection to Estonians. Witches were said to live there. According to Estonian folklore, it is the evil will-o'-the-wisp who leads people to the bog, where they are forced to stay until the bog gas catches fire, driving the grotesque bog inhabitants out for all to see. Closer to reality, bogs were also hiding places for partisans escaping from outside invaders who couldn't penetrate the bogs as easily as forests (probably because they were scared of the witches).

Park information is available from the **Soomaa National Park visitor centre** (☎ 435 7164; www.soomaa.ee), which is a welcoming, highly professional outfit in Kõrtsi-Tõramaal. It distributes hiking maps and arrange accommodations and guide service (best to contact the centre in advance).

Soomaa.com (☎ 506 1896; www.soomaa.com; excursions from €30) offers a number of excursions, from five-hour canoeing trips to multiday bird-watching, mushroom-picking and wolf-tracking excursions. They also offer four-day *haabja*-building workshops each June. Call in advance, and they'll arrange a meeting time at the visitor centre. Pick up in Pärnu or Tori available at extra charge.

PÕLTSAMAA

pop 5100

Known for its rose gardens, Põltsamaa is a quaint town set along an idyllic river, with quiet leafy streets, a restored 17th-century church and the cinematic ruins of a medieval castle. It makes a pleasant stop when heading into the region.

During the 13th century the Knights of the Sword set up a fortification along the Põltsamaa River. The ruins of the **castle** date from the 1770s, although it – along with the 17th-century church adjoining it –

THE FOREST BROTHERS' RESISTANCE AND THE UNDERGROUND WAR

Today the sleepy marshes and quiet woodlands of Estonia are a haven only for wildlife, but between 1944 and 1956 much of what is now national park and nature reserve was a stronghold of the Metsavendlus pro-independence movement. The Metsavennad (Forest Brothers) fiercely resisted the Soviet occupation. Many resorted to an underground existence in the woods and some remained there for years. They knew their terrain well and used this knowledge to their advantage both for their own survival and in the fight to restore the republic.

The Soviets claimed Estonia in the Molotov-Ribbentrop pact of 1939 and, after the Germans retreated from a difficult three-year occupation, secured this claim by advancing on Tallinn in 1944. The early resistance, believing this latest occupation would not be recognised in accordance with the British–US Atlantic treaty of 1941 (which states that sovereignty and self-governance should be restored when forcibly removed), rallied support for what some thought would be a new war. As international assistance did not eventuate, the independence cause remained Estonia's own.

Resistance action began with isolated attacks on Red Army units that claimed the lives of around 3000 soldiers. Tactical expertise and secure intelligence networks resulted in damaging offensives on Soviet targets. At the height of the resistance there were over 30,000 Metsavennad and their supporters, which included women, the elderly, young people and a network of 'Urban Brothers'. The impact of resistance activity is found in Soviet records from the time, which detail incidents of sabotage on infrastructure such as railways and roads that hindered early attempts at moulding Estonia into a new Soviet state.

In the years that followed the Metsavendlus suffered high casualties, with varied and increasing opposition. The NKVD (Soviet secret police) provided incentives to some of the local population who were able to infiltrate the resistance. The Soviets coordinated mass deportations of those suspected to be sympathetic to the resistance cause and some Metsavennad supporters were coerced into acting against the resistance. By 1947 15,000 resistance fighters had been arrested or killed. The greatest blow to the Metsavendlus came in 1949 with the deportation of 20,000 people – mainly women, children and the elderly – many of whom had provided the support base and cover for resistance activities.

The movement continued for some years but was greatly impeded by the strength of the Soviets and loss of local support due to ongoing deportations and the clearing of farmhouses for collectivisation. Some of the Metsavennad who were not killed or imprisoned escaped to Scandinavia and Canada.

There are many heroes of the Metsavendlus; most came to a tragic end. Kalev Arro and Ants Kaljurand (*hirmus,* or horrible Ants to the Soviets) were famous for their deft disguises and the humour and tact with which they persistently eluded the Soviets. It was only in 1980 that the final active Forest Brother, Oskar Lillenurm, was found – shot dead in Lääne county.

Much work has been done to compile a history of the movement by recording accounts of local witnesses. Enemies of Metsavennad are still finding themselves in court, while surviving members are regarded as national heroes and are awarded some of the country's highest honours.

was badly damaged in WWII. The church boasted one of Estonia's most magnificent organs, which was out of commission until its restoration in 2004. Concerts are held here throughout the year.

Also inside the castle walls is the town **museum** (☎ 775 1390; Loss tänav 1; adult/concession 8/5Kr; ⏲ 10am-6pm May-Sep, 10am-4pm Mon-Sat Oct-Apr), which has photos of the original castle, as well as history about Põltsamaa's development and its notable residents. The museum has an **information centre** (☎ 775 1390; Loss tänav 1; ⏲ 10am-6pm May-Sep, 10am-4pm Mon-Sat Oct-Apr), and is probably one of Estonia's friendliest bureaus. Pick up a town map and get excellent local and regional info here. If the church is closed when you arrive, the centre can open it for you.

Several **islands** in the river are a short stroll southeast of the castle. This is a good area for seeing the summer rose gardens. Upstream from the islands is a swimming spot – and a good area for a picnic.

A more extensive collection of roses is found at the **Roosiaed** (☎ 776 9877; Karja tänav; admission 10Kr), which contains over 3000 types. The Roosiaed is 1½km north of the bridge over the river (off the main road, Pajusi maantee).

Rivaal (☎ 776 2620; www.rivaal.ee; s/d 400/600Kr; 🕑 8am-10pm Mon-Sat; ⊠) On Flower Island, along the east side of the river, this pleasant spot rents out small but comfortable rooms in the attic of the house. Downstairs is a popular café and restaurant (meals 20Kr to 65Kr), serving tasty dishes, with outdoor seating in the summer.

One or two buses daily connect Põltsamaa with Viljandi (one to two hours); Põltsamaa has more frequent connections with Tartu (two hours, 10 buses daily) and Tallinn (two hours, 10 buses daily).

ESTONIA DIRECTORY

The following contains practical information related to travelling in Estonia. For regional information pertaining to all three countries, see the Regional Directory.

ACTIVITIES

Estonia offers plenty of adventure and relaxation amid pastoral splendour. One of the most enjoyable summer activities is simply heading to the country's beautiful lakes and rivers for swimming in pristine, refreshing waters. Southeastern Estonia is particularly well served by lakes ideal for swimming.

Whatever you do, don't leave Estonia without a trip to the sauna. You'll find them on lakesides, tucked away in forests and in most hotels. It's the true Estonian experience.

For a complete list of activities in the Baltics, see the Activities chapter.

CUSTOMS

If arriving from another EU country, the limits for alcohol and tobacco are generous; see www.customs.ee for the latest restrictions. Antique objects made outside Estonia before 1850 or in Estonia before 1945 need special permits to be taken out of the country. These can be obtained from the **Division of the Export of Cultural Objects** (☎ 644 6578; Sakala tänav 14, Tallinn).

EMBASSIES & CONSULATES

For up-to-date contact details of Estonian diplomatic organisations as well as foreign embassies and consulates in Estonia, contact the **Estonian Foreign Ministry** (631 7600; www.vm.ee; Islandi Väljak1, Tallinn).

Estonian Embassies & Consulates

Estonia has diplomatic representation in a number of overseas countries, including the following:

Australia Sydney (☎ 02-9810 7468; eestikon@ozemail.com.au; 86 Louisa Rd, Birchgrove, NSW 2041)
Canada Toronto (☎ 416-461 0764; estconsu@ca.inter.net; 202-958 Broadview Ave, Toronto, Ontario M4K 2R6)
Finland Helsinki (☎ 9-622 0260; www.estemb.fi; Itäinen Puistotie 10, 00140 Helsinki, Suomi)
France Paris (☎ 01 56 62 22 00; 46 rue Pierre Charron, 75008 Paris)
Germany Berlin (☎ 30-25 460 600; www.estemb.de; Hildebrandstrasse 5, D-10785 Berlin); Hamburg (☎ 40-450 4026; fax 40-450 40 515; Badestrasse 38, 20143 Hamburg)
Ireland Dublin (☎ 1-219 6730; embassy.dublin@mfa.ee; Riversdale House, St Ann's, Ailesbury Rd, Dublin 4)
Latvia Rīga (☎ 781 2020; www.estemb.lv; Skolas iela 13, Rīga LV 1010)
Lithuania Vilnius (☎ 5-278 0200; www.estemb.lt; Mickevičiaus gatvė 4a, Vilnius)
Netherlands Amsterdam (☎ 3120-316 54 40; embassy.hague@mfa.ee; Snipweg 101, 1118 DP Amsterdam Schiphol Airport)
Russia Moscow (☎ 095-290 5013; www.estemb.ru; Malo Kislovski 5, 103009 Moscow); St Petersburg (☎ 812-109 0920; fax 812-109 0927; Bolsaja Monetnaja 14, 197101 St Petersburg)
Sweden Stockholm (☎ 08 5451 2280; www.estemb.se; Tyrgatan 3, 10041 Stockholm)
UK London (☎ 020-7589 3428; www.estonia.gov.uk; 16 Hyde Park Gate, London SW7 5DG)
USA New York (☎ 212-883 0636; www.nyc.estemb.org; 26th fl, 660 3rd Ave, New York 10016); Washington DC (☎ 202-588 0101; www.estemb.org; 2131 Massachusetts Ave, NW, Washington DC 20008)

Embassies & Consulates in Estonia

Most of the following embassies or consulates are in or near Tallinn's Old Town unless otherwise indicated.

Australia (Map pp66–7; ☎ 650 9308; mati@standard.ee; Marja tänav 9) Southwest of the centre.
Canada (Map pp70–1; ☎ 627 3311; tallinn@canada.ee; Toom-Kooli tänav 13)
Finland (Map pp70–1; ☎ 610 3200; www.finland.ee; Kohtu tänav 4)
France (Map pp66–7; ☎ 631 1492; www.ambafrance-ee.org; Toom-Kuninga 20)
Germany (Map pp66–7; ☎ 627 5300, www.germany.ee; Toom-Kuninga tänav 11)

PRACTICALITIES

- For news, the best English-language weekly is the *Baltic Times* (www.baltictimes.com).
- The bimonthly *City Paper* is a glossy magazine with in-depth articles and sometimes quirky features.
- For events listings pick up the excellent *In Your Pocket* series (www.inyourpocket.com), published quarterly for Tallinn and twice yearly for Tartu and Pärnu (also available as pdf downloads).
- Tallinn visitors can pick up three Finnish channels in addition to Estonia's three channels (Eesti TV, www.etv.ee, is the state-run network).
- Radio 2 (101.6 in Tallinn) and Sky Plus (95.4) are the two most popular radio stations among Estonia's pop and Euro-disco lovers. You can also listen to the BBC World Service (100.5 FM) 24 hours a day.
- PAL is the main video system used in Estonia.
- Electrical current is 220V, 50Hz AC. Sockets require a European plug with two round pins.
- Estonia uses the metric system for weights and measures. Food and drink often appears on menus listed by the gram (200g of wine, 500g of schnitzel, etc).

Ireland (Map pp70–1 ☎ 681 1888; embassytallinn@eircom.net; Vene tänav 2)
Latvia (Map pp66-7; ☎ 646 1313, consular 646 13 10; embassy.estonia@mfa.gov.lv; Tõnismägi 10, EE10119 Tallinn)
Lithuania (Map pp70–1; ☎ 631 4030; www.hot.ee/lietambasada; Uus tänav 15)
Russia Narva (☎ 356 0652; fax 356 0654; Rüütli tänav 8); Tallinn (Map pp70–1; ☎ 646 4175; www.estonia.mid.ru; Lai tänav 18)
Sweden (Map pp70–1; ☎ 640 5600; www.sweden.ee; Pikk tänav 28)
UK (Map pp66–7 ☎ 667 4700; www.britishembassy.ee; Wismari tänav 6)
USA (Map pp66–7 ☎ 668 8100; www.usemb.ee; Kentmanni tänav 20) Southeast of the centre.

FESTIVALS & EVENTS

Estonia has a long list of festivals and cultural events, especially during the summer months. The tourist office in Tallinn (p68) has information on events around the capital and further afield. For a complete listing of Estonia's festivals, visit www.culture.ee.

February

Student Jazz Festivalu (www.tudengijazz.ee) This international festival held in mid-February in Tallinn attracts musicians from around the Baltic region.
Tartu Ski Marathon Held outside Tartu in mid-February, this 63km cross-country race brings a bit of cheer to an otherwise dreary season.

March

World Music Days (www.maajailm.ee, in Estonian) Taking place in mid-March, Tartu's small world-music festival attracts some colourful performers.

April

Jazzkaar (www.jazzkaar.ee) This international jazz festival is headquartered in Tallinn, though events happen in towns throughout the country. Held in late April.
Estonian Music Days (www.ehl.kul.ee) In Tallinn, this event features both classical Estonian performances and new, emerging works during mid-April.
Tartu Student Days (www.studentdays.ee) Tartu's students let their hair down in late April in this wild, pagan celebration marking the end of term and the dawn of spring.

May

International Puppet Festival (www.hot.ee/viljandinukuteater) Viljandi's puppet theatre gathers a specialist crowd at this four-day fest in mid-May.

June

St John's Day (Jaanipäev) Held on June 23, Estonia's biggest annual night out is a celebration of the pagan Midsummer's Night, best experienced out in the country where huge bonfires flare for all-night revellers.
Tallinn Old Town Days (www.vlp.ee) Held in Tallinn's cinematic 14th-century quarters in early June, this fest features lots of medieval amusement.

July

Beer Summer A hugely popular festival in Tallinn (at the Song-Festival Grounds on the road to Pirita) in early July.

Tallinn Rock Summer The Baltics' biggest three-day international rock-music festival takes place in the Tallinn Song Bowl.
Pärnu International Documentary & Anthropology Film Festival (www.chaplin.ee) Pärnu's big-name film fest features dozens of films from all over the world in early July.
Saaremaa Summer Festival This week-long largely classical event takes place mostly in Kuressaare, but is also held in venues throughout the island in mid-July.
Kuressaare Castle Days Against the backdrop of one of the Baltics' most magnificent castles, this two-day fest in early July features lots of medieval chicanery.
Muhu Future Music Festival (www.nordicsounds.ee) Jazz, experimental music, progressive rock and much more are on offer at this colourful event held on the island of Muhu in early July.
Viljandi Folk Festival (www.folk.ee) This four-day festival in late July features bands from Estonia and abroad.

August

Ladies in Jazz Festival (early August) One of Haapsalu's many music fests. Held in early August.
International Organ Music Festival Features concerts held in Tallinn and throughout Estonia during early August.
Blues Festival (www.haapsalu.ee/kk) Another of Haapsalu's popular musical events, held in mid-August.
White Lady Festival (www.haapsalu.ee/kk) On Haapsalu's castle grounds, this festival culminates in the appearance of a mysterious visitor during late August.

September

Matsalu Nature Film Festival One of the more unusual film festivals in the Baltics, this one features nature films submitted by a wide variety of film makers. It's held in Lihula near the lush Matsalu Nature Reserve in late September.

November & December

Black Nights Film Festival (www.poff.ee) Estonia's biggest film festival showcases world cinema in its myriad forms: feature-length films, animated films and student films. Held in late November–early December.

> **ON THE HORIZON**
>
> - **All-Estonian Song Festival** (www.laulupidu.ee) Convenes every five years and culminates in a 30,000-strong traditional choir, due in Tallinn in 2009.
> - **Baltika Folklore Festival** A week of music, dance and displays focusing on Baltic and other folk traditions, this festival is shared between Rīga, Vilnius and Tallinn; Tallinn will host it in 2007.

HOLIDAYS

New Year's Day 1 January
Independence Day Anniversary of 1918 declaration, 24 February.
Good Friday March/April
Easter Monday March/April
Spring Day 1 May
Võidupüha Victory Day Commemorating the anniversary of the Battle of Võnnu (1919), 23 June.
St John's Day (Jaanipäev; Midsummer's Night) 24 June. Taken together, Victory Day and St John's Day are the excuse for a week-long midsummer break for many people.
Day of Restoration of Independence (1991) 20 August
Christmas Day (Jõulud) 25 December
Boxing Day 26 December

INTERNET ACCESS

Wireless Internet access (wi-fi) is widespread in Estonia. You'll find over 200 hot spots in Tallinn and in many places connection is free (see www.wifi.ee for a complete list). If you can't find a free connection, prices are around 35 senti per minute. The only adjustment you may have to make is to set your outgoing mail server (SMTP) to a local host such as mail.hot.ee. If you're not packing a laptop, there are numerous Internet cafés (charging around €2 to €4 per hour) with speedy connections in virtually every corner of the country. Most public libraries (Tallinn, Tartu, Narva, Pärnu, Haapsalu, Kuressaare etc) have Web-connected computers that anyone can use free of charge. During peak times, however, you may have to wait in line.

INTERNET RESOURCES

For more information about Estonia, check out the following websites:
Estonia Directory (www.ee) This Estonia-wide directory has links to national parks, car-hire agencies, guesthouses and hundreds of other businesses in Estonia. Start your search on 'tourism'.
Estonica (www.estonica.org) Nicely designed website with information on Estonian history, culture, the economy and nature.
Estonian Institute (www.einst.ee) This site has 'publications' that you can click on, which provide colourful info on Estonian cuisine, art, song traditions and more.
Tallinn Tourism (www.tourism.tallinn.ee) This is the portal to Tallinn's events and attractions.

MAPS

EO Map (www.eomap.ee) has fold-out maps for every Estonian county, and city- and town-centre maps. If you're driving, pick up EO's excellent road atlas or its *Estonia in Your Pocket*, featuring detailed street maps for several dozen cities. **Regio** (www.regio.ee) produces road atlases and maps for professional reference, and digital maps on CD-ROM. Maps are available at most bookstores.

MONEY

See the inside front cover for exchange rates.

Estonia's currency is the kroon (pronounced krohn), which is pegged to the euro at 15.64Kr. The kroon comes in two, five, 10, 25, 50, 100 and 500Kr notes. One kroon is divided into 100 senti (cents), and there are coins of five, 10, 20 and 50 sents, as well as one- and five-kroon coins. Estonia has a fair chance of adopting the euro by 2007.

POST

Mail service in and out of Estonia is highly efficient. Most letters or postcards take about one or two days within Estonia, three or four days to Western Europe and about a week to North America and other destinations outside Europe. There is a poste-restante bureau, where mail is kept for up to one month, in the basement of Tallinn's **central post office** (Narva maantee 1, Tallinn 10101).

To post a letter up to 20g to Scandinavia/Europe/rest of the world costs 6/6.50/8Kr.

TELEPHONE

Estonia phased out all city codes in 2004. If you're calling anywhere within the country, just dial the number as it's listed here. All land-line phones have seven digits. All mobile phone numbers have seven or eight digits, and all begin with ☎5. Estonia's country code is ☎372. To make a collect call dial ☎16116. To make an international call dial 00-country code-area code-subscriber number.

About 95% of Estonia is covered with digital mobile-phone networks. Mobile phones that work on the GSM mobile network in Europe and the UK will work here. To avoid the high roaming charges, you can get a starter kit (around 150Kr), which will give you an Estonian number, a SIM card that you pop into your phone and around 100Kr of talk time (incoming calls are usually free with most providers). You can buy scratch-off cards for more minutes as you need them. SIM cards and starter kits are available from mobile-phone stores, post offices and kiosks.

Public telephones accept chip cards (30Kr, 50Kr or 100Kr), available at post offices, hotels and most kiosks. For placing calls outside Estonia, an international telephone card with PIN, such as *Voicenet* (available at many kiosks), is better value.

EMERGENCY NUMBERS

- 24-hour roadside assistance ☎1188
- Fire, ambulance and urgent medical advice ☎112
- Police ☎110
- Tallinn's First Aid hotline (☎697 1145) can advise you in English about the nearest treatment centres.

TOURIST INFORMATION

There are tourist offices in many of the larger centres, national parks and reserves throughout Estonia, and at nearly every one you'll find English-speaking staff. See the Information sections in each section for individual addresses. The main administrative office of the **Estonian Tourist Board** (www.visitestonia.com; Liivalaia tänav 13/15) is in Tallinn.

Latvia

JONATHAN SMITH

Latvia

If you're yearning to hit Europe's untrodden jackpot, cash in your chips in Latvia (Latvija). Still undiscovered by the tourism masses, this sizzling Baltic sexpot is poised to become the continent's next A-list star. A country in transition, hellbent on shedding its stalwart old-Soviet image, the Latvia of today is vibrant, enigmatic and altogether mesmerising. Refreshingly unpretentious, Latvia manages to tantalise even the most jaded traveller. Many arrive expecting little and leave overwhelmed, certain they've uncovered long-buried treasure.

Bustling Rīga, with its pumping nightlife, cobbled streets and marvellous Art-Nouveau architecture is one of Eastern Europe's most fun cities. Away from the capital, the pace slows. Historic villages, miles from anywhere, sit frozen in time. Despite growing popularity, Latvia is still one of those places where you can embrace the unbeaten path and become an intrepid adventurer exploring virgin terrain. From crumbling castles in pine-scented forests to alluring resorts on the edge of the ice-blue Baltic Sea, it's very easy to just get away. Summer is an especially magical time – twilight comes near midnight and by 4am it's light again. After long, dark winters, Latvians seem determined to soak up as much light as possible and the whole country exudes a frenetic, turbocharged energy. Beer gardens pop up in even the smallest villages and revellers slug pints well into the night.

It's hard to believe this tiny, vivacious nation shed its Russian stranglehold less than two decades ago because, despite years of intense suffering under Soviet and Nazi occupations, Latvia has a serenity and charm rarely found elsewhere in Europe.

This is Latvia's moment. Visit before everyone else does.

FAST FACTS

- **Area** 64,600 sq km (twice the size of Belgium)
- **Birthplace of** the world's first miniature camera, the VEF Minox
- **Capital** Rīga
- **Country code** ☎ 371
- **Departure tax** none
- **Famous for** winning the 2002 Eurovision Song Contest
- **Money** Latvian lats €1 = 0.70Ls; UK£1 = 1.02Ls; US$1 = 0.58Ls
- **Population** 2.4 million
- **Visa** not required for visits of up to 90 days for citizens of the EU, the US, Canada, Australia, New Zealand and Japan. See p391 for details.

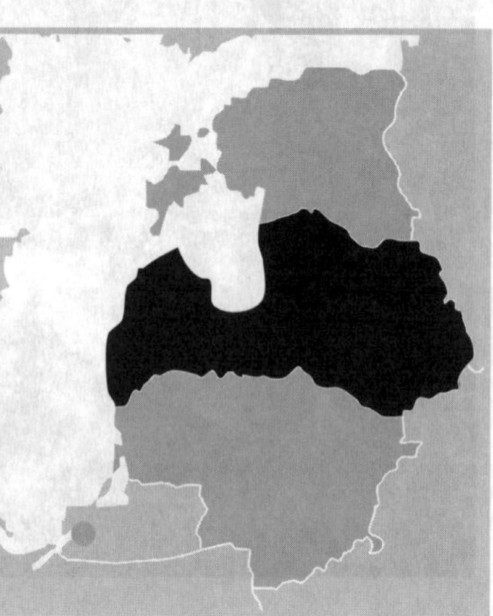

HIGHLIGHTS

- **Rīga** (p187) Wander cobbled medieval streets, slide past Art-Nouveau flourishes and watch the sun rise over a skyline of spires and turrets.
- **Gauja Valley** (p227) Get your adrenaline rushing by bungee jumping, bobsleighing or skiing amid this exquisite landscape.
- **Jūrmala** (p220) Soak up sun and Baltic Sea vistas in this boisterous resort area.
- **Liepāja** (p261) Discover the heart and soul of Latvia's rock 'n' roll scene in this progressive city poised to become a major Baltic hot spot.
- **Cape Kolka** (p253) Feast on fresh fish, gulp mouthfuls of crisp air and savour the solitude of wild and windswept Cape Kolka.

ITINERARIES

- **Three days** Visit Rīga, with a choice of day trips to Sigulda and the Gauja Valley, Jūrmala, the Ķemeri National Park, Rūndale Palace, the Pedvāle Open-Air Art Museum and nearby Kuldīga or Tukums.
- **One week** Do Rīga and some day-trip destinations, then take the Rīga–Kolka coastal road stopping in Jūrmala, Ķemeri and some of the fishing villages around Roja. See where the Gulf of Rīga and the Baltic Sea meet at Cape Kolka, then nose-dive into the Slītere National Park and its Livonian villages. Dip south to happening Liepāja, stopping in wealthy Ventspils along the way.
- **Two weeks** Explore western Latvia at a more leisurely pace, allowing time to scale Slītere Lighthouse, follow a few nature trails in the national parks and enjoy some boating, bird-watching or other activity. Or split the fortnight in two and spend a week exploring eastern Latvia – include the Gauja Valley and Alūksne's narrow-gauge railway.

CURRENT EVENTS

From political shake-ups to 'get tough now' economic policies, there's a lot going on in Latvia today. Although one-third of Latvians voted against joining the EU in 2004, today the general mood in the country towards membership is optimistic and Latvia has moved quickly to embrace the free market.

HOW MUCH?

- **Cup of coffee** from 0.50Ls
- **Taxi fare per kilometre** 45Ls to 65Ls
- **Public transport ticket** 0.2Ls
- **Bicycle hire (daily)** 4.50Ls
- **Sauna per hour** 10Ls

LONELY PLANET INDEX

- **Litre of petrol** 0.54Ls
- **Litre of bottled water** 0.50Ls
- **50cl bottle of beer** 0.40Ls
- **Souvenir T-shirt** 5Ls
- **Street snack** 1.50Ls

High inflation has hindered efforts to peg the lats to the euro (the first step towards making the euro the country's currency), but the government has imposed tough measures to curb inflation while still boosting growth, and the country is now establishing formal links with the common currency and hopes to adopt the euro within a few years. The EU invested more than €1 billion in the country between 2004 and 2006, and the funds are benefiting key economic development projects.

Since independence in 1991 Latvia has held four elections and had a string of governments, all leaning centre-right. The country's latest political shake-up came in 2004, when Prime Minister Indulis Emsis resigned following a parliamentary vote to reject the 2005 draft budget. Emsis, of the Greens and Farmers union, was Europe's first Green premier. His minority coalition government lasted only eight months. Aigars Kalvitis, of the centre-right People's Party, was given the task of picking up the pieces. Kalvitis' four-party coalition was approved in December 2004 and the new prime minister promised to work towards political stability.

Latvia made lots of world headlines in 2005. In May of that year US President George W Bush visited the country as part of a tour commemorating the end of WWII. Before Bush's arrival, the local media encouraged anyone living in Rīga to stay inside during the visit, or better yet, sojourn

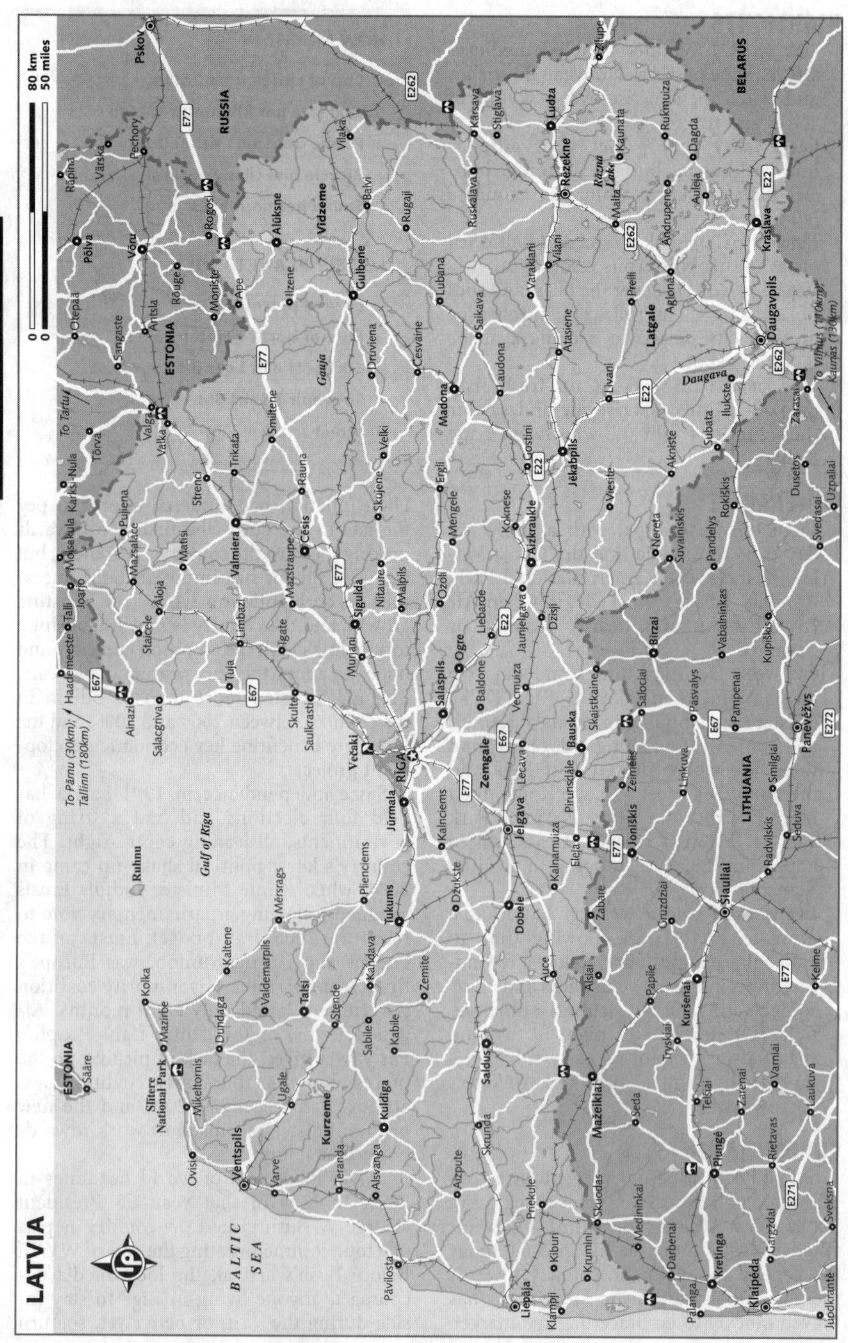
LATVIA
0 80 km
0 50 miles
BALTIC SEA
Gulf of Riga
Ruhnu
ESTONIA
RUSSIA
BELARUS
LITHUANIA
Kurzeme
Zemgale
Vidzeme
Latgale
Gauja
Daugava
Rāzna Lake
Slītere National Park
To Pärnu (30km); Tallinn (180km)
To Tartu
To Vilnius (110km); Kaunas (130km)
Rīga
Jūrmala
Vecāķi
Ventspils
Liepāja
Kuldīga
Talsi
Tukums
Saldus
Dobele
Jelgava
Bauska
Sigulda
Cēsis
Valmiera
Valka
Valga
Alūksne
Gulbene
Madona
Jēkabpils
Aizkraukle
Ogre
Salaspils
Daugavpils
Rēzekne
Ludza
Krāslava
Limbaži
Salacgrīva
Ainaži
Kolka
Mazirbe
Pāvilosta
Šiauliai
Klaipėda
Palanga
Panevėžys
Pskov
Võru
Põlva
E67
E77
E22
E262
E272
E271

THE LATVIAN AMBER ROAD

Although the precious fossilised resin is not found as prolifically in Latvia as it is in Lithuania, *dzintars* (amber) is a ubiquitous shop staple throughout the country. Amber animal figurines dating back to the 4th millennium BC have been uncovered in Latvia, and traditional folk costumes include amber beads, brooches and *kniepkeni* (fastening for women's blouses).

The region's 'Amber Road' starts in the northwestern Latvian port town of Ventspils, where many fine pieces have washed ashore. Check out the Livonian Order Castle (p256) to see some fine samples. South of Ventspils, the next stop on the country's 80km amber discovery route is tranquil Pāvilosta. Large quantities of amber often wash ashore here, especially during strong spring and autumn storms. Amber fishers scour the coast for the substance and make a portion of their living from selling it. Following the professionals on an amber hunt is not only a great way to learn more, it is also a fabulous day-in-the-life experience. To get the scoop, visit the **Pāvilosta Ethnography Museum** (☎ 379 8276; Dzintara iela 1; 🕙 9am-5pm Mon-Fri) and ask the staff how to set up a trip. The museum also houses an extensive amber collection.

The large, vibrant city of Liepāja has two not-to-be-missed amber attractions. During Liepāja's 750th birthday celebration in 2003, residents and visitors donated more than 50 litres of amber to the city. The pieces came in all shapes and sizes – the biggest were threaded into 123m beaded ropes, the rest used to construct a stunning 4m-high **sundial**. You can check out the 'amber clock' on the promenade along the town's Tirdzeniecibas canal – on a bright day it makes a wonderful photo. The beads are displayed at the **Liepāja craftsmen's association** (☎ 342 3286; Barinu iela 33; 🕙 9am-5pm Mon-Fri). The Liepāja History & Art Museum (p263) also boasts a fine amber exhibit.

If you haven't had your fill of Latvian amber, take a side trip to the Lithuanian-border town of Nida (p357).

to the countryside. Residents were asked not to make any sudden movements near their windows when Bush was in the vicinity – they were told this was a precaution against possible sniper bullets! To make matters more complicated, Bush's entourage was so big there were not enough hotel beds to accommodate them. The Latvian government solved the conundrum by hiring a large ship on which to sleep them. Prior to the visit, anti-Bush posters popped up in cafés and bars around town. The bright posters featured slogans such as 'Welcome Peace Duke' (you'll have to ask a Russian speaker what 'peace duke' sounds like in their language to get the negative gist…).

President Vaira Vīķe-Freiberga was the only Baltic leader to accept Moscow's invitation to attend end of WWII celebrations, and her decision created quite a controversy – with demonstrations by veterans of Latvia's SS brigade and clashes with anti-fascist protestors in Rīga.

The Baltics' first gay pride event – a march in Rīga in July 2005 – was a milestone for gay rights activists. Even though the Latvian prime minister publicly condemned the march, the event went ahead and drew large crowds. The event had little impact on the government's stance on gay rights, however. In September 2005 parliament took the first step towards making a ban on same-sex marriage part of the constitution. Same-sex marriage is illegal under civil law.

Other still-to-be-resolved issues in Latvia include a controversial language law passed in September 2004 stipulating that 60% of all lessons in state schools must be conducted in Latvian, and tensions between Latvia and Russia regarding issues over their mutual border, as Russia has yet to sign a treaty formally delineating the border.

In June 2005 Latvia's parliament ratified the proposed EU constitution.

Rīga is hosting the November 2006 NATO Summit, just further proof that Latvia has taken its place on the world players' map.

HISTORY

The history of Latvia is best described as a troubled whirlwind of fierce struggle and downright rebellion.

Early History

The Latvians and Lithuanians are the two surviving peoples of the Balt branch of the

Indo-European ethnolinguistic group. The Balts are thought to have spread into the southeastern Baltic area around 2000 BC from the region that is now Belarus and neighbouring parts of Russia. (The term Balt, which was derived from the Baltic Sea, was first used in the 19th century.) Those people who stayed behind were assimilated, much later, by Belarusian or Russian Slavs (who are ethnically the Balts' nearest relatives). By the 13th century the Balts were divided into a number of tribal kingdoms.

The Latvians are descended from those tribes who settled in the territory of modern Latvia, such as the Letts (or Latgals), the Selonians, the Semigallians and the Cours. The Latgals, Semigallians and Cours gave their names to Latvian regions: Latgale, Zemgale and Kurzeme.

The Selonians settled between the Daugava River and northern Lithuania. During succeeding centuries of foreign rule, these tribes (and to a large extent the Finno-Ugric Livs who inhabited the northern coastal regions of Latvia) lost their separate identities and became merged in one Lettish, or Latvian, identity.

The first Christian missionaries arrived in Latvia in 1190 and tried to persuade the pagan population to convert. It was an uphill battle: as soon as the missionaries left, the new converts jumped into the river to wash off their baptism. In subsequent years more missionaries would arrive, and more Latvians would submit and then renounce Christianity.

In 1201, at the behest of the pope, German crusaders, led by Bishop von Buxhoevden of Bremen, conquered Latvia and founded Rīga. Von Buxhoevden also founded the Knights of the Sword, who made Rīga their base for subjugating Livonia. Colonists from northern Germany followed, and during the first period of German rule, Rīga became the major city in the German Baltic, thriving from trade between Russia and the West and joining the Hanseatic League (a medieval merchant guild) in 1282. Furs, hides, honey and wax were among the products sold westward from Russia through Rīga.

Power struggles between the church, knights and city authorities dominated the country's history between 1253 and 1420. Rīga's bishop, elevated to archbishop in 1252, became the leader of the church in the German conquered lands, ruling a good slice of Livonia directly and further areas of Livonia and Estonia indirectly through his bishops. The church clashed constantly with knights, who controlled most of the remainder of Livonia and Estonia, and with German merchant-dominated city authorities that managed to maintain a degree of independence from 1253 to 1420.

Latvia was conquered by Poland in 1561 and Catholicism was firmly rooted. Sweden colonised Latvia in 1629 and occupied the country until the Great Northern War (1700–21), after which it became part of Russia.

Soviet occupation began in 1939 with the Molotov-Ribbentrop Pact, nationalisation, mass killings and about 35,000 deportations, 5000 of whom were Jews, to Siberia.

Latvia was then occupied by Nazi Germany from 1941 to 1945, when an estimated 75,000 Latvians were killed or deported. The Jewish population suffered greatly during this period. The Germans captured Rīga on 1 July 1941.

At the end of WWII the Soviets reclaimed Latvia and occupied the country for another 40 years.

Road to Independence

The first public protest against Soviet occupation was on 14 June 1987, when 5000 people rallied at Rīga's Freedom Monument to commemorate the 1941 Siberia deportations. New political organisations emerged in the summer of 1988. The Popular Front of Latvia (PLF) quickly rose to the forefront of the Latvian political scene. The PLF, representing the interests of many Latvian social and political groups, garnered much grass-roots support and on 31 May 1989 the group called for the full independence of Latvia. Less than two months later, on 23 August 1989, two million Latvians, Lithuanians and Estonians formed a 650km human chain from Vilnius, through Rīga, to Tallinn, to mark the 50th anniversary of the Molotov-Ribbentrop Pact.

The PLF won a big majority in the March 1990 elections, but Russia barged back in on 20 January 1991. Soviet troops stormed the Interior Ministry building in Rīga, killing five people and injuring hundreds. However, the parliament in Rīga was barricaded, the people stayed calm, the violence drew

Western condemnation of Moscow and the immediate threat subsided. In referendums in February and March 1991, big majorities in Latvia voted in favour of secession from the USSR. However, the West, not wanting to weaken Gorbachev further, gave only lukewarm support to the Baltic independence movements.

A 19 August 1991 coup attempt against Gorbachev in Moscow loosened the political stranglehold against full-fledged autonomy and Latvia declared full independence on 21 August 1991.

On 17 September 1991 Latvia, along with Estonia and Lithuania, joined the UN and began taking steps to consolidate their newfound nationhood, such as issuing their own postage stamps and currencies. In 1992 Latvia competed independently in the Olympic Games for the first time since before WWII. The pope visited all three Baltic countries in September 1993, but with the exception of these milestones, Latvia silently disappeared from the world's headlines.

Towards Europe

June 1993 saw Latvia's first democratic elections. Valdis Birkavs, of the centre-right moderate nationalist party, Latvijas Ceļš (LC; Latvian Way) became the country's first postindependence prime minister. Guntis Ulmanis of Latvijas Zemnieku Savieniba was elected president – an office he held for two terms.

The country's postindependence government lurched from crisis to crisis, and a game of prime-minister roulette followed the Baltija Bank crash in 1995, when Latvia's biggest commercial bank went bust. With a staggering 204 million lati in liabilities – and thousands of Latvians deprived of their life savings – the crisis spread, and by the time the blood-letting was over, 40% of Latvia's banking system had disappeared. Elections that year saw Andris Šķēle emerging as prime minister.

Formal Russian recognition of Latvian independence was achieved in 1996 in exchange for Latvia reluctantly ceding the Abrene (Russian: Pytalovo) region – a 15km-wide, 85km-long sliver of territory down its northeastern border.

Nervous of Russian sabre-rattling and hungry for economic stability, Latvia became desperate to join NATO and the EU. By 1998 the West seemed less concerned about annoying Russia, which was fiercely opposed to eastward expansion by NATO, than previously, and the USA publicly pledged its support for Latvia, as well the other two Baltic nations, by signing the US-Baltic Charter of Partnership, in which it gave its support to Baltic integration into Western institutions, including NATO.

Latvia made world headlines again in May 1998, when the presidents of Estonia and Lithuania joined forces with the president of Latvia to publicly condemn Russia's political and economic pressure on Latvia, warning it was posing a danger to the region's future unity and integration with Europe. A medal awarded by Latvia to the former Russian president Boris Yeltsin for his role in helping Latvia secure its independence was spurned by Yeltsin following Latvia's imprisonment of a former WWII Soviet partisan in January 2000.

Presidential elections in 1999 saw Guntis Ulmanis defeated by Vaira Vīķe-Freiberga, Latvia's current president and the first woman president of an ex-USSR country. The fact that Vīķe-Freiberga was not among the five presidential candidates – all voted out in the first round of voting – made her final election all the more unusual. A long-time Canadian resident, Vīķe Freiberga brought experience in a multiethnic democracy to Latvia and assumed office unburdened by petty political connections. On the other hand, she only took Latvian citizenship the year before her election, prompting critics to claim she was less 'in tune' with the real Latvia than a lifelong resident.

Vīķe-Freiberga faced a tough challenge during her first days in office. On 5 July 1999 Prime Minister Vilis Kristopans resigned, prompting Andris Šķēle's appointment as PM at the head of a conservative government formed by Šķēle's People's Party, the LC and For Fatherland and Freedom. Three days later the Latvian parliament approved a controversial language law that invited criticism from the EU and made international headlines. Among the law's requirements, employees of private enterprises and self-employed people had to use Latvian at public functions. Latvian was also made obligatory at major public events, and was the language for all publicly displayed signs and notices. Heeding massive international pressure, Vīķe-Freiberga vetoed the bill and sent it back to parliament. The law was amended in December 1999, the same year Latvia was invited to start accession talks with the EU.

But the language issue remained hot. Another amendment to the language law in late 2000 stipulated that lawyers, taxi drivers, telephone operators and a host of other professions in the private sector had to speak a certain level of Latvian. Throughout 2001 debate raged as to whether those standing for political office should speak the official state language, climaxing in mid-2002 with parliament, heeding the advice of NATO, decreeing that they don't. A couple of months previously all hell had broken loose after an Organization for Security and Co-operation in Europe (OSCE) official in Rīga had suggested to Vīķe-Freiberga that Russian be made an official state language alongside Latvian. The response was an immediate amendment to the constitution by parliament declaring Latvian to be its only working language, and a statement of support from the EU saying that it was up to Latvia alone to decide its state language. By 2004 the primary language that school pupils were being taught in was Latvian.

Merriment spilled across Rīga's streets in 2001 as the capital celebrated its 800th birthday. To herald the event, the city council raised old Rīga's 14th-century House of Blackheads from the ashes and built itself a new town hall too – allegedly based on the city's original town hall but in fact a complete fabrication on the part of architects. This, coupled with the heady rash of commercial development enveloping the old city, prompted a subtle warning from Unesco that it was not unheard of for cities to be struck off the World Heritage List (a status Latvia's capital was awarded in 1997).

On 1 May 2004, the EU opened its doors to 10 new members, including Latvia, amid huge expectations of a secure border with Russia and better times to come.

THE CULTURE

The National Psyche

Latvia's inhabitants are very different in temperament from their neighbours, the flamboyant Lithuanians and calm Estonians. At first glance folks appear a bit standoffish. You won't hear many hellos from strangers on the streets, and even shop owners may not greet you with as much enthusiasm as you'd expect. Latvians are a withdrawn people who have to be coaxed into friendship, but if you succeed you'll discover a steely strength hidden beneath their stoic façade. A prime example of this stoicism can be gleaned by watching the armed Guards of Honour standing rigid as stone in front of Rīga's freedom monument from sunrise to sunset each day, come rain, hail or 3m of snow. This guarded nature is hardly surprising, however, considering the country's history of oppression – and the fact that Latvians are still a minority group in each of their main cities.

Lifestyle

Latvians generally adore nature – their traditions and customs reach back to their pagan past. In many rural households it's counted as lucky to have a green snake (nonvenomous grass snake) living in the home. Latvians like flowers; if you go to a birthday party or some other special event, it's nice to bring a bouquet – but make sure it's an odd number of flowers! Even numbers are reserved for funerals and other sad occasions. Latvian women are a tad less emancipated than in the West, so female drivers, for instance, might provoke some mildly sexist but harmless commentary. In addition Latvians have perhaps the best-developed entrepreneurial sense of all three Baltic countries, perhaps following the example set by the enterprising, predominately Russian population found in Rīga.

Population

Of Latvia's population of 2.33 million, just 58.3% are ethnically Latvian. Russians account for 29.1% of the total population (compared to 32.8% in 1995) and Belarusians (4%), Ukrainians (2.6%), Poles (2.5%) and a small Jewish community (0.4%) round out the rest of the demographics. Latvians make up less than 50% of the population in Daugavpils, Jūrmala, Liepāja, Rēzekne, Ventspils and the capital, Rīga, where 43.7% are Russian and 41.2% Latvian.

Of particular concern is the country's declining population, which dropped 13.8% between 1999 and 2000 and made Latvia the fourth-slowest-growing country in the world. Some of this is due to the migration of ethnic Russians back to Russia, but the main factor is an extremely low birth-rate – at 20.3 births per 1000 people (compared to 32.2 deaths), Latvia is reckoned to have the world's lowest crude birth rate: nine births per 1000 inhabitants.

The divorce rate in Latvia remains among the highest in Europe: more than 60% of marriages end in divorce and almost 40% of children are born into one-parent families.

Up to 200,000 Latvians live in Western countries as a result of emigration around the turn of the 20th century, and during and after WWII. Most live in the USA, followed by Australia, Canada, Germany and Britain.

Multiculturalism

Citizenship has been one of Latvia's most contentious – and complicated – issues. Upon gaining independence, the new state proclaimed that residents of the pre-1940 Latvian Republic and their descendants – including about 300,000 nonethnic Latvians (mainly Russians) – automatically became citizens of modern Latvia. Former Soviet soldiers, settled in Latvia after demobilisation, were understandably barred from citizenship, as were former Soviet secret-service employees.

But other residents – roughly 35% of the population and the vast majority of native-Russian speakers – were not allowed to vote in the 1993 elections because they were not citizens. This was widely seen as unjust.

Citizenship rules passed in 1994 stated that would-be citizens must have lived in Latvia for at least five years, must pass a test on Latvia's language, history and constitution, and take a loyalty oath. Additionally, only those of certain ages could apply at certain times (only Latvian-born residents aged from 16 to 20 could apply in 1996, those aged up to 25 in 1997, and so on), provoking an outcry from the large Russian community in Latvia.

Finally, in 1998 the Latvian parliament repealed the harsh 'windows' restriction on who could apply, meaning all noncitizens, irrespective of age, could apply for citizenship through naturalisation – a process

LATVIAN FOLKLORE

From the myth of *Lāčplēsis* (the Bear Slayer) to the custom of only giving odd numbers of flowers as welcome gifts, Latvian culture is rich in folklore. Customs and rituals, many dating back to pagan times, play integral roles in traditional Latvian life to this day. Step into a Latvian cemetery and you'll notice the sandy paths around the gravestones are meticulously raked, void of any footprints. This practice stems from the ancient belief that the spirit of the dead could follow the mourner home unless all living footprints were erased.

Another ancient tradition, still embraced wholeheartedly today, is the celebration of Midsummer's Day, or Jāņi. In pagan times, this was a night of magic and sorcery when witches ran naked and wild, bewitching flowers and ferns, people and animals. Today Jāņi is Latvia's biggest celebration, with festivities beginning on 23 June. People flock to the countryside to party amid lakes and pine forests. Special beers, cheese and pies are prepared, and flowers and herbs, meant to bring good luck and keep families safe from evil spirits, are hung around homes. Men adorn themselves with oak-leaf crowns, while women wear wreathes of flowers on their heads. Legend has it that if you sleep before the sun has sunk and risen again you'll be riddled with a year of bad luck. To help people stay awake giant bonfires are lit, traditional folk songs sung, dances danced and those special cheeses, beers and pies consumed. Lovers seek out the mythical fern flower, which supposedly only blooms on this night – finding the flower ensures a lifetime of happiness!

Latvian folklore has strong ties to the natural world. Many locals believe that when a child is born a new star appears and stays bound to the child throughout their life. When the person dies, the star falls to earth, a symbol of the disappearance of their soul. It is also believed that children born under sunny skies have better luck than those who enter the world on a grey or rainy day. Storks are another symbol of luck, especially if the bird decides to nest near a Latvian home. Trees, flowers and animals are also featured prominently in Latvian folklore, and stories about animals with human attributes are common.

requiring a test in Latvian and an exam about Latvian history. The law also granted automatic citizenship to children born in Latvia after 1991 whose parents were non-citizens.

Fierce opposition to the changes raised sufficient public support for a referendum to be twinned with parliamentary elections. Latvian voters narrowly approved the repeal, and European human-rights groups breathed a sigh of relief. So too did those waiting for citizenship. After the referendum was passed, applications tripled to around 1000 a month. The law was finally ratified by parliament in January 1999.

The problem is far from resolved, however, and today more than 450,000 Russians and native-Russian speakers (about 25% of the population) are still classified as 'non-citizens', because they have either refused, or failed, the required naturalisation test in Latvian language and history.

SPORT

Though it has exported its top talent to the USA-based National Hockey League, Latvia's sporting forte remains ice hockey. Although league games throughout the country draw only a few hundred hard-core fans, Latvians are fiercely devoted to their national team, and televised games, especially during the IIHF World Ice Hockey Championships, are closely followed. On big game nights devoted fans pack Rīga's sports pubs, their eyes locked on the giant-screen TVs broadcasting the match. If you're interested in the sport, stop by a pub on a night when the Latvian national team is playing and join the chaotic party: Latvians may be a reserved bunch, but after a few pints they'll cut loose and cheer their home team on with some seriously raw enthusiasm!

Latvia hosted the IIHF World Ice Hockey Championships in 2006. To prepare for the event, the country constructed a state-of-the-art arena. One of the largest construction projects launched in Latvia since independence, the 12,500-seat Arena Rīga is being used for both concerts and sporting events. To get an idea just how devoted Latvians are to the sport on a national level check out this figure: 17,000 ticket packages for the 2006 championships went on sale in September 2005 and sold out within the first hour and a half!

Bobsledding is another popular winter sport and Sigulda's bobsled track, one of Europe's longest, plays host to international competitions.

Basketball also draws crowds, though its following is not quite as large as in Lithuania. Latvian basketball player Uljana Semonova ranks among the best female players of all time. Of Russian origin, Semonova was born in Daugavpils in 1952 and won over 45 medals (including two Olympic golds for the USSR in 1976 and 1980) in an 18-year career that saw her team never lose an international game. At 2.1m tall, she was the tallest female player in Olympic history.

RELIGION

Christianity long ago superseded Latvia's ancient religion, which was based on a belief in natural deities and the divinity of all living things, though a movement in the 1920s tried to revive and preserve these ancient traditions.

Christianity first came to Latvia in the 12th century, and the crusades of the following century firmly entrenched it as the dominant religion. The type of Christianity practised today largely follows a historical pattern: eastern Latvia, which was under the Polish empire, tends to be Roman Catholic, while other areas are Lutheran.

The first Latvian Bible was published in 1689. Its translator was the Reverend Ernest Glück, and a memorial museum to him stands in the town of Alūksne. During the Soviet occupation, the power of the church was seen as a threat, and religious practice of any kind was condemned. The regime attempted to suppress the faithful by killing or deporting many priests and clergy and converting places of worship into secular buildings such as museums, concert halls and cinemas. When the Soviet stranglehold began to loosen in the 1980s, faith-based practices experienced a revival. The PLF included the right to religious freedom as a core of its political platform, and churches began to reassert their power. In Latvia today, the Roman Catholic Church has the largest following with roughly 500,000 adherents, followed by Lutheran (300,000), Russian Orthodox (100,000) and Old Believers (70,000).

ARTS

Latvian folklore plays an integral role in the country's art and music scene.

Cinema

Since Latvia's first full-length sound film, *Zvejnieka dēls* (The Fisherman's Son), came out in 1940, Latvian filmmaking has taken off, with occasional international recognition. The state-owned **Rīga Film Studio** (www.rigafilmstudios.com), prominent for its feature films during Soviet times, is less successful today, in part due to the dozen or so other film studios that have stepped up since independence.

Production studio Dauka is Latvia's leader in animation; its film *The Cat's Mill* won second prize at the Chicago International Film Festival in 1994. Other film makers of note include Laila Pakalnina, whose 1998 feature film *The Shoe,* about occupied Latvia, was an official selection at the Cannes 1998 film festival. Pakalnina's film *The Mail* shows the isolation of Latvia, as symbolised by the lonely delivery of the morning mail.

Latvian director Jānis Streičs (1936–) has produced a number of films pertinent to Latvia's turbulent past. *Limousine in the Colour of Summer Solstice Night* (1981) and *The Child of Man* (1991) remain popular for their blend of irony and comedy. The latter, about a boy growing up and falling in love in Soviet-occupied Latvia, won the Grand Prix at San Remo in 1992 and was nominated for an Academy Award for best foreign film in 1994. Streičs' more recent film, *The Mystery of the Old Parish Church* (2000), addresses the prickly issue of local collaboration with Nazi and Soviet occupiers during WWII, as the victims of a former KGB agent set out to haunt their killer. The film, partly set during summer solstice, stars the lead singer of Latvian band Brainstorm, Renars Kaupers.

The website www.latfilma.lv has a wealth of information on Latvian films, directors, festivals and more.

JURIS PODNIEKS

Latvian film director Juris Podnieks, arguably the most influential filmmaker in the former USSR, had that rare gift of being at the right place at exactly the right time. During the 1970s, '80s and early '90s, Podnieks and his film crew worked tirelessly to produce riveting documentaries that in many ways predicted the collapse of the Soviet monolith.

Born in Rīga in 1950, Podnieks worked in a Rīga studio after graduating from film school in 1975. He began first as a cameraman and rose quickly, becoming a director in 1979.

Podnieks' breakthrough film was 1986's *Is It Easy to Be Young?,* which broke Soviet box-office records – and wooed an international crowd of 28 million – by depicting the Soviet Union's troubled youth. His cinematic triumph was managing to get footage of some youthful Latvians vandalising a train after a rock concert.

Another Podnieks landmark was the five-part 1989 series *Hello Do You Hear Us?* The series, broadcast in the USA, painted a gloomy portrait of the Soviet Union, from the Baltic police to the workers' strike in a Yaroslavl factory.

Even more important were *Homeland* and *Homeland Postscript*, which captured the events of the early 1990s. The film *Homeland* was completed and due to be released in February 1991. The turbulent events of January 1991, however, clearly required an addendum. When Podnieks was in Vilnius on 11 January 1991 to present *Homeland*, he was on the scene to film the storming of the Vilnius TV tower. He and his assistant, though caught in the crossfire, escaped unharmed and slipped back to Rīga with their footage.

Nine days later a shoot-out took place in Rīga as Soviet troops stormed the Ministry of the Interior. Two of Podnieks' crew heard the confrontation and ran out to film it. Both were killed in the crossfire. Endowed with new and sombre meaning, *Homeland* and *Homeland Postscript* opened on 7 February.

Podnieks died just a little more than a year later, on 23 June 1992, in a midsummer scuba-diving accident. The **Juris Podnieks studio** (☎ 721 69 67; jps@parks.lv; Citadeles iela 2, LV-1010 Rīga) carries on under his name, however, and continues to produce documentaries. The studio can make copies of the films, some of which have English subtitles, for €17 to €20 (plus €30 postage within Europe).

Literature

Latvia's national epic – *Bear Slayer*, written by Andrējs Pumpurs in the mid-19th century – is based on traditional Latvian folk stories. The hero struggles against his enemy, a German Black Knight, only to drown in the Daugava River at the moment of triumph. The anticipated rebirth of *Bear Slayer*, however, leaves hope for new freedom. The first Latvian novel, *The Time of the Land Surveyors*, written in the 1860s and 1870s by the brothers Reinis and Matiss Kaudzīte, has become a classic for its humorous portrayal of Latvian characters.

Rūdolfs Blaumanis (1863–1908) wrote psychologically penetrating novelettes and comic and tragic plays; among them, *Tailor's Days in Silmači* (Skroderdienas Silmačos) is still one of Latvia's most popular plays. Anna Brigadere (1861–1933) wrote many fairy-tale dramas and well-loved tales of rural life. Kārlis Skalbe (1879–1945) was another major writer of fairy tales.

Music & Dance

Traditional folk songs have always played an integral role in Latvian culture, although the recognition of music as an established art form did not come about until the mid-19th century. In 1869 Jānis Cimze started cataloguing folk tunes, some dating back 1000 years, and his collection of about 20,000 melodies quickly gained popularity. His collected works were sung in school choirs and became the basis for Latvia's first song festival, where thousands of singers joined together in huge choirs to celebrate traditional folk music. During the Soviet occupation the song festivals were pivotal in forging a strong sense of national identity and pride, and became part of the battle cry that rallied Latvians to fight for independence.

Today music is very popular and there are many big annual festivals (p266). Latvia's third-largest city, Liepāja, is considered the heart and soul of Latvia's rock 'n' roll scene. Artists come from across the country to perform in its lively bars and clubs, and even the smallest pubs often host live acts (although the quality of music is varied).

Perkons (Thunder) and award-winning mainstream rockers Rebel (formed out of Dr Blues, a band that had been on the scene since the late 1980s) were among the first bands to make it big in rock. Rebel notably sings in English and Russian on its album *Sarovaja Molnija* (1999). Acoustic blues is represented by Hot Acoustic, formed in 1994, while the eccentric Karl and Cuckoo-Bite contribute a new wave sound to the Rīga club scene. A more recent female vocalist to listen out for is Linda Leen with her mix of rhythm and blues.

Patra Vetra, otherwise called Brainstorm, is the best-known band outside Latvia, breaking into the European market with its first album in English *(Among the Suns)* in 1999, finishing third in the Eurovision Song Contest in 2000, and going on tour with the Cranberries in 2002. Lead singer Renars Kaupers, who wrote one of the band's best-known hit songs, 'My Star', has also indulged in a brief but successful film career. The surprise win of sexy Russian-Rīgan Marija Naumova (Marie N) in the 2002 Eurovision Song Contest served to tell the world that Brainstorm's third place was not a fluke and that Latvia really could sing.

The godfather of Latvian rock is the eclectic composer Imants Kalņins, founder of the country's first rock band, Menuets, in the mid-'70s. A graduate of the Latvian State Conservatory, Kalņins has written everything from film scores to symphonies and operas. His son, Mart Kristiāns Kalņins, lead singer of the 'art rock' band Autobuss

LIFE AFTER EUROVISION 2002

Marija Naumova's life changed forever on 25 May 2002, the day she won the Eurovision Song Contest in Tallinn. Relatively unknown outside Latvia prior to her win, Naumova (who goes by the name Marie N) hit the world music scene in a big way following the contest when her winning single *I Wanna…* was released in countries as far away as Saudi Arabia, South Africa and Brazil. The last few years have brought their share of momentous moments for the young singer. She starred in a Rīga production of *The Sound of Music*, played clubs in Europe, the USA and Canada and even managed to record a few albums. Her latest endeavour, released in 2004 and titled *On My Own*, features original songs, along with a few well-known covers, and has Marie N belting out lyrics in English, Latvian, French and even Portuguese!

debesīs, which released its debut album in 2001, is another name to look out for.

The National Opera House, reopened in 1996 after renovation, is the home of the Rīga Ballet, which produced Mikhail Baryshnikov and Aleksander Godunov during the Soviet years. The Latvia National Symphonic Orchestra is highly regarded. Song composers Joseph Wihtol (Jāzeps Vītols) and Alfrēds Kalniņs are important early-20th-century figures in classical music. Inga Kalna is among Latvia's leading female soloists.

Contemporary classicists include internationally renowned conductor Mariss Jansons, winner of the Latvian 1995 Grand Prix in music. Another major figure in the Latvian music scene is Raimonds Pauls, light music orchestra conductor for the Latvian State Philharmonic in the late 1960s. He later rose to become minister of culture (1988–93).

Visual Arts

Jānis Rozentāls was really the first major Latvian painter. At the turn of the 20th century he painted scenes of peasant life and portraits, with some influence from impressionism and Art Nouveau. Vilhelms Purvītis and Jānis Valters were the outstanding landscape artists of the time. Both – especially Purvītis – were influenced by impressionism. Olegs Tillbergs is one of the most interesting modern Latvian artists. He collects and assembles garbage and other unwanted materials. Ivars Poikans is another contemporary artist to watch for. Karlis Rudēvics is known for his translations of Roma poetry and for his striking paintings inspired by Gypsy legends.

ENVIRONMENT

The Land

Latvia is 64,589 sq km in area – a little smaller than Ireland. Unlike its relatively compact Baltic neighbours, Latvia is a lot wider from east to west than from north to south. A good half of its sweeping 494km coast faces the Gulf of Rīga, a deep inlet of the Baltic Sea shielded from the open sea by the Estonian island of Saaremaa.

Latvia's borders include Estonia to the north, Russia and Belarus to the east and Lithuania to the south. Rīga lies on the Daugava River, just inland from the Gulf of Rīga. The country has four regions: Vidzeme, the northeast; Latgale, the southeast; Zemgale, the centre; and Kurzeme, the west.

The Vidzeme Upland in eastern Latvia is the largest expanse of land with elevation over 200m in the Baltics; it is topped by Latvia's highest point, Gaiziņkalns (312m).

Wildlife

Forests dominate 44% of Latvia's landscape, with northern Vidzeme and northern Kurzeme the most forested parts of the country. The country's oldest forest, in Kurzeme's Slītere National Park and protected since 1921, is a broad-leaf forest with a calcium-rich bog and several rare orchids. This national park alone protects 23 forest types and three types of swamp. The Gauja National Park also has a vibrant ecosystem, and is the breeding ground for 900 plant types.

Latvia, along with the other Baltic countries, has more large wild mammals than anywhere else in Europe, although seeing them in the wild requires patience, determination and, often, the services of a local guide. Elks, deer, wild boar, wolves and even a few bears inhabit the country's forests in varying numbers, although you're not likely to bump into any without some guidance. There are also beavers on inland waters, seals along the coasts and large otter populations (between 2000 and 4000 live in Latvia). Gauja National Park is home to 48 types of mammal. South of Liepāja, Latvia's branch of the Worldwide Fund for Nature (WWF) has reintroduced konick horses – descendants of wild horses that once roamed free in Europe – on abandoned farmland around Lake Pape. The country also has a large white stork population. In fact, in conjunction with Lithuania, the two countries have more storks than all of Western Europe. The rarer black stork is also found in Latvia and builds nests in the Gauja National Park.

National Parks & Reserves

An increasingly large area of the country is becoming protected as new nature parks and reserves are established. **WWF Latvia** (☎ 750 5640; www.wwf.lv; Elizabetes iela 8-4, Rīga LV-1010) is involved in several nature-protection projects around the country, aimed at restoring natural ecosystems. The most noteworthy national parks and reserves are the following.

NATIONAL PARKS & RESERVES

National park or reserve	Area	Features	Activities	Best time to visit
Abava Valley Nature Park (p255)	149 sq km	the small towns of Kandava & Sabile	hiking	summer
Gauja National Park (p226)	917 sq km	castles & lovely valley scenery	hiking	summer
Ķemeri National Park (p252)	428 sq km	Latvia's oldest forest, wetlands, many bird species, nature trails & boardwalks across bogs	birding, hiking	summer
Krustkalni Nature Reserve (p138)	30 sq km	nine lakes & 48 protected species of flora	hiking	summer
Moricsala Nature Reserve (p251)	8 sq km	part of Lake Usma & its shores	fishing	summer
Slītere National Park (p254)	164 sq km	coastal & hinterland nature reserve	hiking	summer
Teiči Nature Reserve (p238)	190 sq km	an important feeding & nesting ground for many bird species	bog-walking, birding	summer

Environmental Issues

Rapid industrialisation during the Soviet occupation and the failure to address the environmental impact of endeavours such as the construction of manufacturing centres, hydroelectric plants and dams led to high levels of water and air pollution. Since independence the Latvian government and various national organisations have made cleaning up the environment a priority and Latvia's pollution problems are now being addressed. Ironically, some areas are threatened more today than during Soviet times: the Livonian coastline in northern Kurzeme – a former Soviet border-control post once off limits but now threatened by forestry and property development – is a classic example.

Financial assistance from Scandinavia and Germany has helped reduce the pollution generated by industrial centres such as Daugavpils and Liepāja. Ventspils, smothered in potash dust in the late 1980s, has witnessed a huge cleanup: a new water-supply system aimed at reducing the amount of sewage dumped in the Baltic Sea, air monitoring and the construction of a new heating system to decrease sulphur dioxide and nitrogen dioxide omissions are all part of the city's long-term environmental plan, drawn up to last until 2010 and estimated to cost €23 million. Despite these efforts, Latvia's Municipal Air Control Management admits Rīga's air is still unhealthy and that pollution-induced damage to some of Old Rīga's historic buildings remains a problem (although it's starting to be tackled).

Rīga's upgraded sewage treatment facilities are reducing the flow of sewage into the Daugava River and making swimming in the Gulf of Rīga safer. The European Blue Flag (a water safety rating; see p34) has been awarded to beaches in Jūrmala, Ventspils and Liepāja, but the safety of swimming in other areas is still questionable.

Latvia is making a concerted effort to use renewable sources to generate energy. Currently 40% of the country's energy is obtained in this manner, with hydroelectric energy accounting for most of this figure. Latvia's 2004 entrance into the EU brought with it a new set of environmental obligations, and the government is committed to fully complying with EU environmental directives by 2010.

FOOD & DRINK

Farming and fishing have long been economic mainstays in Latvia, and as a result Latvian cuisine is of the hearty, sustenance-providing variety. Fish and meat, especially bacon, along with dairy products, grains, berries and vegetables are all staples.

Staples & Specialities

Step into a Latvian eatery and your nose will be assaulted with a melange of smells: roasting meats, salted fish, boiled peas dripping in bacon grease and smelling of onion are only some of the varied offerings. Latvians consume a lot of dairy products, and *biezpiens* (cottage cheese), *siers* (cheese) and *rūgušpiens* (curdled milk) are main ingredients in many dishes. *Sprotes* (sprats) are popular starters in many places. If they're *ar sīpoliem*, they'll be with onions. Fish is another staple, and you will find *siļķe* (herring), *līdaka* (pike), *zutis* (eel), *forele* (trout) or *lasis* (salmon) on many menus. If fish is *cepts*, it's fried; if *sālīts* or *mazsālīts*, it's salted; and *kūpīnats* means it'll be smoked. *Žāvēta desa* (smoked sausage) is another popular dish. Dill seems to be Latvia's favourite herb and is sprinkled liberally on almost all savoury dishes. (Where else can you buy dill-flavoured crisps?) *Zupas* (soups) and *salāti* (salads) are listed on almost every menu, and often vary. *Pankūki* (pancakes) stuffed with cheese, meats or potatoes are popular snacks, although you could easily make a meal out of two or three. *Pīrāgi* (small pies or pasties) are another favourite, and usually come stuffed with cabbage and boiled egg.

During the summer months berry picking is almost a national obsession, and you'll find fresh strawberry stalls everywhere, from the side of the highway to outside the town pub. During autumn fresh-picked mushrooms, cranberries and nuts replace strawberries and raspberries at the little stalls. Honey is another popular delicacy. Latvians are intrepid beekeepers and many farms have beehives and honey production facilities.

The sweet toothed won't be left disappointed. In summer and autumn good use is made of those fresh-picked berries – fruit pies and tarts *(kūka)* are abundant. Throughout the year you will find a mouth-watering choice of freshly baked cakes, breads and pastries for under 0.10Ls.

Drinks

Latvians like their booze; when it comes to alcoholic beverages, Latvians are among the heaviest drinkers in Europe. *Alus* (beer) has long been a traditional favourite, and for such a small country Latvia has more than its share of breweries. The leading beer is Aldaris. It comes in varying degrees of darkness and costs around 0.50Ls in kiosks (every kiosk stocks beer) and from 0.70Ls a litre in bars. Cēsu is another popular beer, and has been produced at Latvia's oldest brewery since 1590. Small breweries are scattered around the country, and different regions are known for their beers. Keep an eye out for Bauskas, Piebalgas, Tērvetes and Užavas, each with a distinct taste.

Rīga *sampanietis* (champagne) comes in two varieties: *sausais* (sweet), which is very sweet, and *pussaldais* (semisweet). It's dirt-cheap at 2Ls a bottle. It's not up to French standards, but it tastes OK. Many restaurants feature extensive wine lists, incorporating the world's famous wine-producing regions as well as offerings from countries you never knew produced wine – like Georgia.

Not to be missed is Latvia's famous Balzāms (see boxed text, below), a thick,

BLACK MAGIC

It's as black as ink, as thick as custard, as sharp as lemon, and has been produced in Latvia – and nowhere else – since 1752. Its recipe remains a closely guarded secret: orange peel, oak bark, wormwood and linden blossoms are among some 14 fairy-tale ingredients known to stew in the wicked witch's cooking pot.

It steels the nerves, settles the stomach and stops Jack Frost from biting. A shot a day keeps the doctor away, so say most of Latvia's pensioners. In the 18th century it was administered to Catherine the Great when she was struck down by a mystery illness in Rīga. Two sips later she made an instant recovery – and left town.

Rīga druggist Abraham Kunze created the insidious concoction. Its name originates from *balsamon*, the ancient Greek word for a sweet-smelling medicinal balm or ointment. Its opaque ceramic bottle, labelled with a black and gold Rīga skyline, is reminiscent of the clay jars the potent liquid used to be stored in during the 18th and 19th centuries to keep it safe from sunlight.

It is 45% proof and guaranteed to knock the hind legs off a donkey. Drink it with coffee or Coca-Cola; down it with a shot of vodka if you dare.

That's what you call Rīga Black Balsams *(Rīgas Melnais Balzāms)*.

EAT YOUR WORDS

Menus in smaller towns are often in Latvian; so if you're craving pasta and not wanting to end up with salted fish, check out the Language chapter. We've listed a few of the more useful eating phrases here.

Useful Phrases

I have a reservation.	muhn ir *puh*·soo·teets	*Man ir pasūtīts.*
A table for ... people, please.	*loo*·dzu *guhl*·du ... *per*·so·nahm	*Lūdzu galdu ... personām.*
Do you have a menu?	vai yums ir *eh*·dean·kuhrt·e	*Vai jums ir ēdienkarte?*
I'm a vegetarian.	es as·mu ve·jye·tah·rea·tis/·te	*Es esmu veģetārietis/te* (m/f)
What do you recommend?	kaw yoos *ea*·suh·kuht	*Ko jūs iesakat?*
I'd like ...	es *vaa*·laws ...	*Es vēlos ...*
The bill, please.	*loo*·dzu *reh*·kyi·nu	*Lūdzu rēķinu.*
breakfast	bro·kas·tis	*brokastis*

Food Glossary

biešu zupa	beetroot soup (similar to borscht)
cepts lasis ar piedevām	fried salmon with potatoes, pickled and fresh vegetables
dārzeņu salāti	diced vegetable salad in sour cream and mayonnaise
desa	sausage (usually smoked)
dīpolu diyrnid	beefsteak with fried onions
kāpostu salāti	fresh grated cabbage
karbonāde ar piedevām	fried pork chop with potatoes, pickled and fresh vegetables
kokteiju salāti	sausages, peas and cucumber in sour cream and mayonnaise
kotletes	meatballs
lasis poju mērcē	salmon in cream sauce
lasis sēņu un dijju mērcē	salmon in mushroom and dill sauce
mednieku desiņas	Hunter's sausages (pork)
pelēkie zirņi ar speķi	grey peas with pork fat and onions
šašliks	shish kebab (usually lamb)
siļķe kažokā	pickled herring with sour cream, egg and beetroot
svaigo gurķu salāti	fresh cucumbers with sour cream
zivju zupa	fish soup

jet-black, 45% proof concoction that tastes strange, if not downright revolting. Apparently, it's best served with coffee or mixed with equal parts of vodka.

Those not interested in alcoholic beverages will find the usual assortment of soft drinks as well as coffee, tea and fruit juices.

Celebrations

Food plays an integral role in Latvian festivals and holiday celebrations. Fishermen's or Sea Festivals are staples in the small towns and villages in Kurzeme and Vidzeme, with eating freshly caught fish and drinking locally brewed beer the main activities. During Jāņi (St John's Night), Latvia's most important celebration, a special beer is brewed. Latvians also create a cheese, known as *Jāņi siers* (John's cheese), made with caraway seeds, for the day. For more on the festival, see boxed text, p179.

A special type of *pīrāgi* filled with cubes of fatty bacon and tender onion is a staple at pretty much every Latvian celebration. Another celebration favourite is sweetbreads topped with berries or apples in summer and dried apples or sweetened cottage cheese in autumn.

Where to Eat & Drink

Restorāns (restaurants) in Latvia are generally more formal affairs, while *kafejnīca* (cafés) are usually simpler self-service joints, although some have full menus. Bars, especially in Rīga and other major cities, often serve a full range of food. In the last 10 years Latvian restaurants have gone international – especially in Rīga. Here you'll discover everything from classic French to rowdy British and Irish pubs to Greek, Thai, Italian, Chinese and even more than a few fusion restaurants. In smaller towns most restaurants serve traditional Latvian fare, although even the smallest villages now often boast a Western-oriented restaurant. Pizza and pasta dishes are your most likely non-Latvian choices outside the bigger cities.

A Latvian *brokastis* (breakfast) usually consists of bread and cheese, cold meat and smoked fish. Eggs and bacon can also be found, although the British fry-up is a rarity outside Rīga or the big international hotels. Yogurt, cereal and milk are also common, and breakfast drinks include coffee, tea and fruit juices. Most hotels in Latvia include some sort of breakfast in their rates.

Pusidienas (lunch) and *vakariņas* (dinner) are more substantial affairs, often consisting of a starter, such as a soup or salad, followed by a main course and finished off with a dessert. Restaurants serve lunch from 11am onwards. Dinner usually starts around 5pm. Many places serve food until 11pm or even later, and some Latvian cafés stay open 24 hours.

RĪGA

pop 760,000

Rīga has always been the big boy of the Baltics – a metropolis with a big-city atmosphere hard to find elsewhere in the region. Funky and vibrant, it pulsates with a magnetism that traps travellers long after their planned departure date. Set on a flat plain divided only by the 500m-wide Daugava River, the city answers the quaintness of Tallinn and Vilnius with impressive Art-Nouveau architecture of its own, a historic old quarter and large parks. You won't want to leave once you're settled into a candle-lit bar or lost on winding, sun-dappled or snow-covered cobbled streets. Rīga manages to couple its toy-town cuteness of steeples and turrets with a glitzy nightlife and thriving restaurant scene. Business is booming, with eager backers pouring much-needed money into its infrastructure. Old Town may be a Unesco World Heritage site, but this fairy-tale city, once dubbed the 'Paris of the East,' is building so fast that Unesco has warned Rīga it may withdraw its protected status due to the number of glittering glass hotels and business centres springing up faster than mushrooms after the rain.

With lavish beauty, timeless elegance and a restless fusion of old and new, Rīga has a charm as potent as the Rīga Black Balsams liquor it's known for.

Fewer than half of Rīgans are ethnic Latvians (41.2% at last count), with Russians accounting for 43.7% of the population. Despite Latvians being a minority in their own capital, ethnic harmony prevails in the city, with street- and shop-talk a natural blend of Russian and Latvian.

HISTORY

Scandinavian and Russian traders and raiders used the Latgal, or Liv, fishing village on the site of modern Rīga for centuries before German traders first discovered it in the mid-12th century. In 1201 Bishop Albert von Buxhoevden from Bremen founded the first German fort in the Baltics here, as a bridgehead for the crusade against the northern heathens. He also founded the Knights of the Sword, who made Rīga their base for subjugating Livonia. Colonists from northern Germany followed, and Rīga became the major city in the German Baltic, thriving from trade between Russia and the West.

Sweden captured Latvia in 1621, and during this period Rīga was, effectively, the second city of Sweden. It was during this time that the city first expanded beyond its fortified walls. In 1710 Russia snatched Latvia from Sweden's grip and Rīga grew into an important trading and industrial city. Its population jumped to 28,000 in 1794 and 60,000 by the 1840s. While the old part of the city remained a preserve of Rīga's approximately 30,000 Germans, around it grew suburbs of wider, straighter streets with wooden houses, inhabited by the largest Russian community in the Baltic provinces as well as a growing number of Latvians.

Between 1857 and 1863 city walls were torn down to assist in the free flow of commerce. Rīga soon developed into the world's busiest timber port and Russia's third-greatest industrial city (after Moscow and St Petersburg). Russia's first cars were

LATVIA

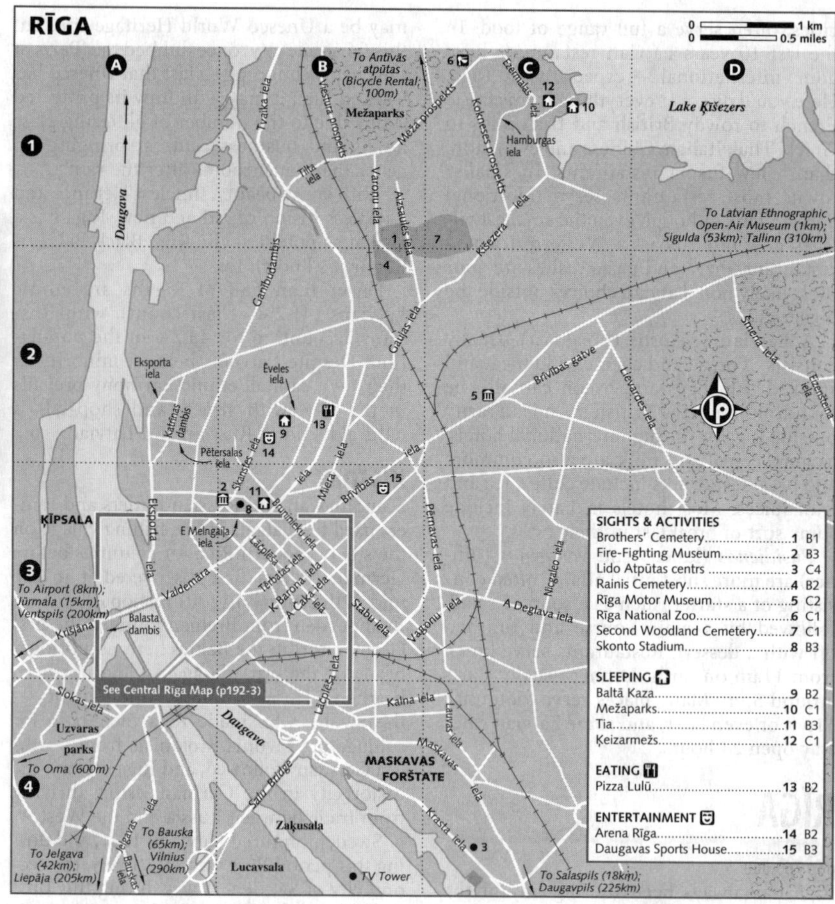

built here. And Rīga was renowned for the quality of the Lithuanian and Belarusian hemp and flax it exported to the outside world.

The city population skyrocketed in the 19th century, as Latvians recently freed from countryside serfdom migrated to Rīga and pushed their way into its trades, business, civil service and intellectual circles. By the 1860s about a quarter of the population was made up of former serfs. The Rīga Latvian Association, formed in 1868, became the core of the Latvian national awakening, inspiring a Latvian national theatre, opera, encyclopaedia and, in 1873, the first Latvian song festival. The number of Latvians in Rīga grew until they formed about half the city's population of 500,000 on the eve of WWI. There were significant communities of Jews and Western merchants – the city's last mayor before the war, George Armitstead, came from an English merchant family.

Rīga was badly damaged in both world wars. Following evacuations and other ravages, it was left with only 181,000 people at the end of WWI. The Germans departed after the Latvian land reform of the 1920s and Hitler's 'come home' call in 1939. In the Latvian independence era between the wars, Rīga was the centre chosen by Western diplomats, journalists and spies to eavesdrop on Stalin's Soviet Union. Flourishing nightclubs, restaurants and intellectual life earned it the nickname 'Little Paris'.

RĪGA IN...

Two Days

Start your day meandering around the fairyland wonder of **Old Town** (p196), wander down narrow cobbled streets and gape at 17th-century and Art-Nouveau architecture before taking in the views from atop the spire at **St Peter's Church** (p196). After lunch, stroll through the **parks and boulevards** (p195) east of old Rīga and watch the changing of the guard at the **Freedom Monument** (p196). Head back to Old Town in the afternoon and stop at a beer garden for a cold drink and some serious people-watching. Bar hop around Old Town in the evening; end your night with a drink at **Skyline** (p215).

Visit the famous **Central Market** (p218) on day two, then wander the less touristy streets of **new Rīga** (p198), checking out funky boutiques, slick bars and hip restaurants. In the afternoon take a boat **tour** (p209) on the Daugava River. Spend the evening delving deeper into Rīga's lively nightlife scene.

Four Days

Follow the two-day itinerary, but devote more time to exploring Old Town. Head to the suburbs and visit the **Latvian Ethnographic Open-Air Museum** (p199). Take a day-trip to **Jūrmala** (p220) on day four and spend some time sunbathing and soaking up the pleasant beach-resort atmosphere.

During WWII Rīga was occupied by the Germans from 1941 to 1944, and virtually all its Jewish community (estimated variously at 45,000 to 100,000) was exterminated. Thousands of Latvians left for the West towards the end of the war to avoid Soviet rule.

After the war the city became the industrial and commercial powerhouse of the USSR's Baltic region, and many migrated here to work. Rīga became the USSR's main source of railway engines and carriages, producing half its mopeds and a third of its washing machines, as well as trams, radios, telephone exchanges, robots and computers. The city sprawled as large numbers of migrants arrived, and Rīga became known as the most Western city in the USSR, with a liberal arts and music scene that attracted people from all over the union.

Today Rīga remains a bustling arts centre and, as the largest city in the Baltics, has acquired a reputation for its vibrant nightlife. The success of the city's 800th birthday party in 2001 – marked by a rash of historical buildings miraculously rising from the ashes – was sealed in 2002 by a budding young Russian-Rīgan singer striking gold in the Eurovision Song Contest. The city went on to host the great event in May 2003. In 2006 Rīga welcomed the World Ice Hockey Championships to its brand new state-of-the-art arena.

ORIENTATION

Rīga straddles the Daugava River, about 15km inland from its mouth in the southeastern corner of the Gulf of Rīga. Old Rīga (Vecrīga), the historic heart of the city, stretches 1km along the eastern side of the river and 600m back from its banks.

Three steeples dominate Old Rīga's skyline. From south to north these are: St Peter's (the tallest), the square bulk of the Dome Cathedral tower, and the simpler St Jacob's. Around most of Old Town is a wide band of 19th-century parks and boulevards; beyond lies new Rīga, beginning with the areas built up in the 19th and early 20th century. Further out are the newer, mainly residential suburbs and Soviet industrial enclaves.

The boundaries between these zones are clear if you trace the street running northeast from Akmens Bridge (Akmens tilts) over the Daugava. First it cuts across the middle of Old Town as a narrow, mainly pedestrian artery called Kaļķu iela. Then, becoming Brīvības bulvāris (Freedom Boulevard), it widens to cross the ring of boulevards and parks and passes the Freedom Monument, a key landmark. At the Reval Hotel Latvija, 1.25km from the river, it enters the new town and becomes Brīvības iela.

The train and bus stations border the central market and are a five-minute walk apart on the southeastern edge of old Rīga. The ferry terminal is 600m north of old Rīga.

Maps

Latvian, Lithuanian and Estonian maps are sold at **Jāņa sēta** (Map p188; ☎ 709 2277; www.kartes.lv; Elizabetes iela 83-85). The *Rīga Pilsētas plāns* (Rīga City Plan, 1:20,000, 1.50Ls), with a 1:7000 city centre inset, is one of several city maps it produces. Stock up on road and city maps for Latvia while you're here.

INFORMATION

Bookshops

Globuss (Map p196; ☎ 722 6957; Valņu iela 26) Small selection of classic English-language books and lots of newspapers, and an added bonus of an upstairs reading café.

Jāņa Rozes (Map pp192-3; ☎ 728 4388; Elizabetes iela 85a) Sells English-language novels, classical literature and Latvian-language learning cassettes. Its branch at K Barona iela 5 stocks reference books in English on Rīga and Latvia.

Jāņa Sēta (Map pp192-3; ☎ 709 2277; Elizabetes iela 83-85) Plenty of Lonely Planet guides and other travel titles.

Emergency

For an ambulance dial ☎ 03; see also Quick Reference on the inside front cover of this book.

Internet Access

Rīga has reams of Internet cafés.

Arēna (Map pp192-3; ☎ 731 4514; Ģertrūdes iela 46; per hr 0.50Ls; 24hr)

Dual Net Café (Map p196; ☎ 781 4440; Peldu iela 17; per hr 0.50Ls; 24hr)

Internet Kafe (Map p196; ☎ 724 0030; Valņu iela 41; per hr 0.50Ls; 24hr)

Laundry

City Clean (Map pp192-3; ☎ 727 2471; K Barona iela 52) Also does dry-cleaning.

Left Luggage

Baggage store (Map pp192-3; luggage 1Ls) In the bus station.

Left-luggage room (Map pp192-3; bagāžas glabātava; luggage 1Ls) In the basement of the train station.

Medical Services

ARS Clinic (Map pp192-3; ☎ 720 1001/3; Skolas iela 5; 24hr) English-speaking service and an emergency home service.

Rīgas vecpilsētas aptieka (Map p196; ☎ 721 3340; Audēju iela 20; 24hr) Pharmacy on the edge of Old Town.

Money

There are plenty of ATMs all over Rīga, although some will only accept local cash cards; if one machine doesn't work keep trying your luck at others – it can be very frustrating, but eventually you're likely to find a machine that works with your card.

Chequepoint Exchange (Map p196; ☎ 722 1219; Kaļķu iela 28)

Parex Banka (☎ 701 0873; Smilšu iela 3) Offers currency exchange, ATM and money transfer.

Post

Central post office (Map pp192-3; ☎ 701 8804; Stacijas laukums 1) Next to the train station.

Tourist Information

City of Rīga Information Centre (www.rigatourism.com) airport (☎ 720 7005); bus station (Map pp192-3; Rīgas starptautiskā autoosta; Prāgas iela 1); House of Blackheads (Map p196; ☎ 704 4377; Rātslaukums 6; ☎ 10am-7pm) English-speaking staff provide city book, brochures, free maps and regional tourism info.

Travel Agencies

Latvia Tours (www.latviatours.lv) Kaļķu iela (Map p196; ☎ 708 5001; Kaļķu iela 8); Marijas iela (Map pp192-3; ☎ 724 3391; Berga bazārs, Marijas iela 13) One of Latvia's largest agencies and offers a bounty of services. Has branches in Ventspils and Liepāja.

Student & Youth Travel Bureau (SJCB; Map pp192-3; ☎ 728 4818; www.sjcb.lv; Lāčplēsa iela 29) Handles International Student Identity Cards (ISIC).

Via Rīga (Map pp192-3; ☎ 728 5901; www.viaRīga.lv; K Barona iela 7-9) Ferry and plane tickets.

World Travel Service (Map pp192-3; ☎ 733 2233; K Valdemāra iela 33) Ferry and plane tickets.

SIGHTS

Old Rīga

A joyous cacophony of 17th-century architecture, crumbling streets and church spires, the fairyland wonder of the World Heritage–listed Old Town is ideal for Rīga's main activity – strolling. Pick any of the narrow, now mainly pedestrian, streets and take a wander. You'll discover a gem of a boutique tucked behind a crumbling stone wall, a delicious aroma bursting from a brightly painted little restaurant, or a café made for people-watching. Simply walking around here – not forgetting to gaze up at the playful statuettes and carvings that adorn many building façades – is one of the chief pleasures of visiting Latvia's capital. The crumbling yet stunning golden façade known as **Pie Kristapa** (Map p196; Jaun iela 25-29) is a classic example of but one of Rīga's many different faces.

Kaļķu iela neatly divides old Rīga in half, each half focusing on a towering church – Dome Cathedral in the north, St Peter's in the south.

ST PETER'S CHURCH

Rīga's skyline centrepiece is **St Peter's** (Sv Pētera baznīca; Map p196; ☎ 722 9426; Skārņu iela; admission 1.5Ls; 🕑 10am-5pm, closed Mon). Don't miss the view from the spire, which has been built three times in the same baroque form: originally in wood in the 1660s; again in wood in the 18th century, after it burnt down from a lightning strike; and then in steel (1967–73) after it was burnt in 1941, by attacking Germans or the retreating Red Army, depending on whom you ask. The spire is 123.25m, but the lift only whisks you up to 72m.

DOME CATHEDRAL

The largest church in the Baltics, this humungous **cathedral** (Doma baznīca; Map p196; ☎ 721 3498; admission 0.50Ls; 🕑 1-5pm Tue-Fri, 10am-2pm Sat) boasts the fourth-largest organ (1880) in the world. Alternatively known as Rīgas Doms (from the German *Dom*, meaning cathedral), it towers beside Doma laukums, the main square within Old Town, surrounded by an unusual brew of architecture.

Founded in 1211 as the seat of the Rīga diocese, Mass is held at 8am Monday to Saturday, and at noon on Sunday. In the Soviet era services were banned; the first service for over 30 years, in 1988, was a major event of the *perestroika* era.

Rīga's oldest museum, the **Museum of the History of Rīga & Navigation** (Rīgas vēstures un kuģniecības muzejs; Map p196; ☎ 721 2051; Palasta iela 4; adult/child 1/0.50Ls; 🕑 11am-5pm Wed-Sun), founded in 1773, is housed in the cloister of the monastery next to the cathedral.

RĪGA'S VITAL ORGAN

Architecturally, the Dome Cathedral is an amalgam of styles from the 13th to the 18th centuries: the eastern end, the oldest, has Romanesque features; the tower is 18th-century baroque; and much of the rest dates from a 15th-century Gothic rebuilding. The floor and walls of the huge interior are dotted with old stone tombs – note the carved symbols on some of those on the north side, denoting the rank or post of the occupant. Eminent citizens would pay to be buried as close to the altar as possible. In 1709 a cholera and typhoid outbreak, which killed a third of Rīga's population, was blamed on a flood that inundated the tombs.

The cathedral's pulpit dates from 1641 and the huge organ (which has 6768 pipes) was built in the 1880s; today it's the world's fourth-largest organ, but it was the largest in the world when it was originally built.

RĪGA CARD

Rīga Card yields a juicy range of discounts in selected restaurants, cafés, theatres and museums, and includes a free walking tour of the city, free admission to many museums, a free copy of *Rīga in Your Pocket* and other goodies. Prices for one-/two-/three-day cards are 8/12/16Ls (4/6/12Ls for under 16 years) and are sold at **Tūrinfo** (Map pp192-3); ☎ 721 7217; Lāčplēsa iela 29) and at select hotels (such as Reval Hotel Latvija and Hotel de Rome) and travel agencies.

RĪGA CASTLE

Originally built as the headquarters for the Livonian Order, **Rīga Castle** (Map p196; Pils laukums) dates to 1330 and served as the residence of the order's grand master. Today Latvia's president lives here. Painted canary yellow, the castle appears younger than it really is following modifications through the centuries, and not very castlelike from its inland side. You get a more turreted aspect from the river or Akmens Bridge.

Part of the castle houses a **Museum of Foreign Art** (Ārzemju mākslas muzejs; ☎ 722 6467; Pils laukums 3; adult/child 1.20/0.70Ls; 🕑 11am-5pm Tue-Sun), exhibiting Latvia's largest treasury of artwork dating back to the 15th century. Also here is the **History Museum of Latvia** (Latvijas vēstures muzejs; ☎ 722 1357; www.history-museum.lv; adult/child 0.70/0.40Ls, free Wed; 🕑 11am-5pm Wed-Sun), which traces the national history.

ARSENĀLS MUSEUM OF ART

East of the square is the **Arsenāls Museum of Art** (Mākslas muzejs Ars-enāls; ☎ 721 3695; Torņa iela 1; adult/child 0.70/0.40Ls; 🕑 11am-5pm Tue, Wed & Fri-Sun,

CENTRAL RĪGA

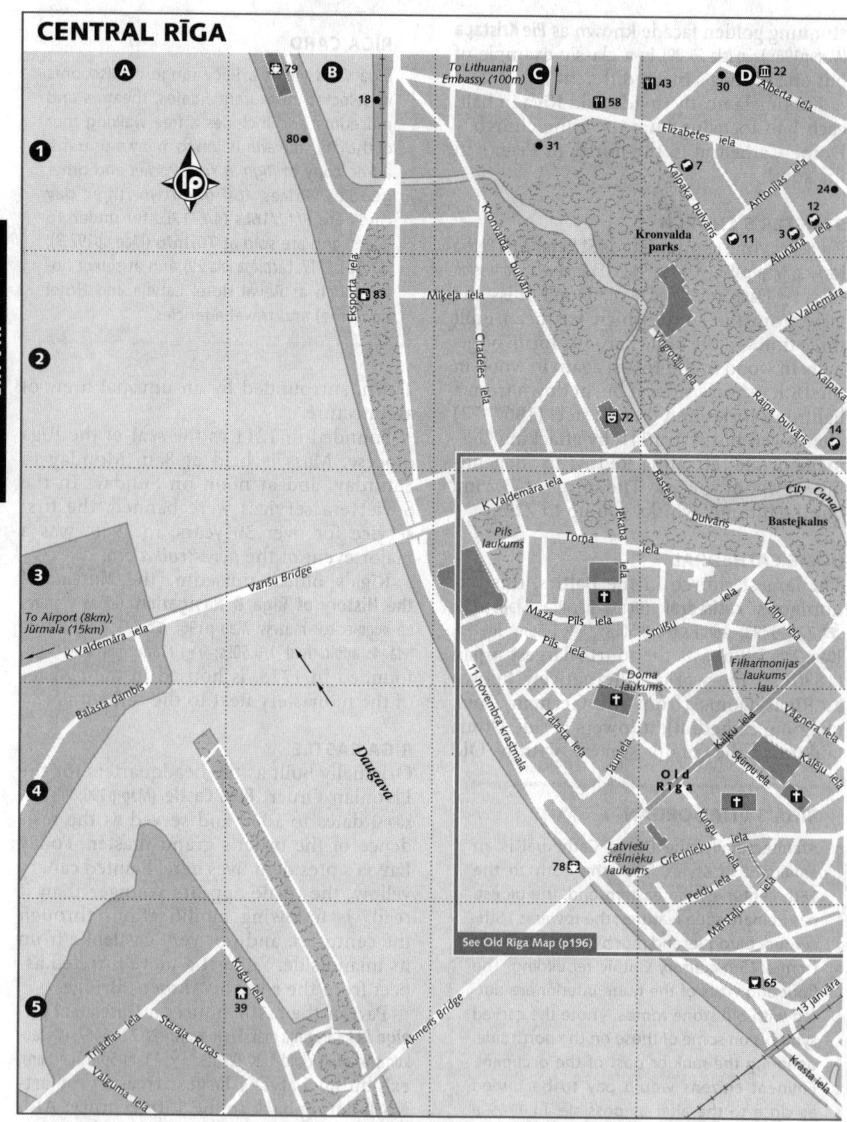

to 7pm Thu), the exhibition hall of the State Museum of Art (p197). Its interior magnificently frames a large modern-art collection.

LATVIESU STRĒLNIEKU LAUKUMS & RĀTSLAUKUMS

The square immediately east of Akmens Bridge is known as **Latviesu strēlnieku laukums** (Latvian Riflemen Sq; Map p196), once home to Rīga's central market but today dominated by the big, dark-red **Latvian Riflemen statue**. The said marksmen were eight regiments formed in WWI to fight in the Russian imperial army. When the Russian Revolution rolled around, most of them supported the Bolsheviks. They provided a palace guard for Lenin

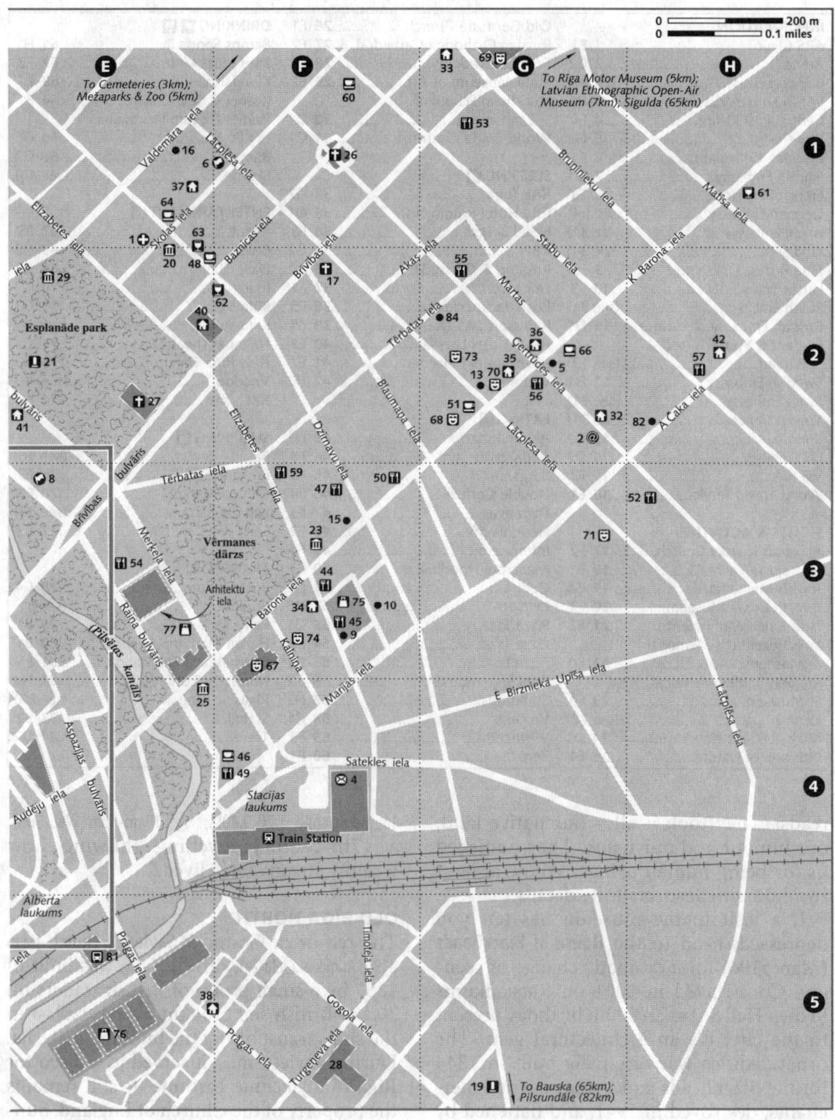

and formed key units of the Red Army during the Russian civil war – although some sided against the Bolsheviks in the concurrent Latvian independence war. During the Soviet era the riflemen were known as the Latvian Red Riflemen.

Behind the statue, in a controversial bunker – at one point almost razed for its ugliness – is the chilling yet spirited **Museum of Occupation in Latvia** (Latvijas okupācijas muzejs; Map p196; ☎ 721 2715; www.occupationmuseum.lv; Latviesu Strēlnieku laukums 1; admission free; 🕑 11am-5pm, closed Mon). The worthy museum gives an impressive account of the Soviet and Nazi occupations of Latvia between 1940 and 1991. An anonymous inscription inside

INFORMATION
- ARS Clinic 1 E1
- Arēna 2 G2
- Baggage Store (see 81)
- British Embassy 3 D1
- Central Post Office 4 F4
- City Clean 5 G2
- Estonian Consulate 6 F1
- Finnish Embassy 7 D1
- French Embassy 8 E3
- German Embassy (see 54)
- Israeli Embassy (see 31)
- Jāņa Sēta (see 34)
- Jāņa Rozes 9 F3
- Latvia Tours 10 F3
- Polish Embassy (see 31)
- Russian Embassy 11 D1
- Student & Youth Travel Bureau (see 13)
- Swedish Embassy 12 D1
- Swiss Embassy (see 31)
- Tourist Office (see 81)
- Tūrinfo 13 G2
- US Embassy 14 D2
- Via Rīga 15 F3
- World Travel Service 16 E1

SIGHTS & ACTIVITIES
- Alexandr Nevsky Church 17 F2
- Andrejosta Yacht Club 18 B1
- Jewish Memorial 19 G5
- Jews in Latvia Museum 20 E2
- Jānis Rainis Monument 21 E2
- Jānis Rozentaāls Memorial Museum 22 D1
- Krisjānis Barons Memorial Museum 23 F3
- Liepāja (see 78)
- Mikhail Eisenstein's House 24 D1
- Museum of Nature 25 E4
- Old Gertrude Church 26 F1
- Russian Orthodox Cathedral 27 E2
- Science Academy 28 F5
- State Museum of Art 29 E2
- Stockholm School of Economics 30 D1
- World Trade Centre 31 C1

SLEEPING
- B&B Rīga 32 G2
- City Hotel Bruņinieks 33 G1
- Hotel Bergs 34 F3
- KB 35 G2
- Krišjānis & Gertrude 36 G2
- Laine 37 E1
- Posh Backpackers 38 E5
- Radisson-SAS Daugava 39 B5
- Reval Hotel Latvija 40 E2
- Revel Hotel Rīdzene 41 E2
- Viktorija 42 H2

EATING
- Ai Karamba! 43 D1
- Andalūzijas Suns 44 F3
- Bergs 45 F3
- Double Coffee 46 F4
- Dzirnavas 47 F3
- Hedonia 55 48 E2
- Interpegro 49 F4
- Macaroni Noodle Bar 50 F3
- Osiris 51 G2
- Pelmeņi 52 H3
- Pizza Jazz 53 G1
- Pizza Jazz 54 E3
- Pizza Lulū 55 G2
- Rimi Supermarket 56 G2
- Staburags 57 H2
- Vincents 58 C1
- Vērmanītis 59 F3
- Zen 60 F1

DRINKING
- Barons Sports Bar 61 H1
- Bites Blūzs Klubs 62 F2
- Klondaika 63 E1
- Kosher Cafe L'Chaim 64 E1
- Paldies Dievam Piektdiena ir Klāt 65 D5
- Rāma 66 G2
- Skyline (see 40)

ENTERTAINMENT
- Circus 67 F3
- Daile 68 G2
- Daile Theatre 69 G1
- Indigo 70 G2
- Kino 52 71 G3
- Kino Suns (see 44)
- National Theatre 72 C2
- New Rīga Theatre 73 G2
- Voodoo (see 40)
- XXL 74 F3

SHOPPING
- Barona Centrs (see 56)
- Berga bazārs 75 F3
- Central Market 76 E5
- Latvijas Balzams (see 49)
- Senā Klēts 77 E3

TRANSPORT
- Boat Station 78 C4
- Ecolines (see 81)
- Ferry Terminal 79 B1
- Hanza Maritime Agency 80 B1
- International Bus Station 81 E5
- Norma-A (Ecolines) 82 H2
- Rīgas SeaLine (see 80)
- Statoil 83 B2
- Trase 84 G2

reads: 'They took it all – our native land, our honour and our name. They punished us for being human beings.' Allow at least two hours to absorb all the details.

If a visit to the museum has left you depressed, head to the **House of Blackheads** (Map p196) for a dramatic change of scenery. Constructed in 2001 on Rātslaukums (Town Hall Sq) as an 800th birthday present to the city, it's an architectural gem. The ornate edifice was originally built in 1344 for the Blackheads guild of unmarried merchants, destroyed in 1941, and flattened by the Soviets seven years later. In front is a recent sword-wielding **statue of Roland**, Roland being the medieval defender of the accused. The **town hall**, on the opposite side of the square, was built from scratch in 2002 – after chopping Rīga's former technical university in half to accommodate it, that is.

East of here is **Mentzendorff's House** (Mencendorfa nams; Map p196; ☎ 721 2951; Grēcinieku iela 18; adult/child 1.20/0.40Ls; 🕑 10am-5pm Wed-Sun), a 17th-century dwelling showing how wealthy Rīgans once lived.

OLD RĪGA NORTH

The red-brick Gothic **St Saviour's Church** (Map p196; Anglikāņu iela 2a), off Pils iela, was built in 1857 by a small group of British traders on 30ft of British soil brought over as ballast in the ships transporting the building material. During Soviet times, it served as a disco for Rīga's Polytechnic Institute. It still remains the property of the Church of England. Sunday services in English are held at 10am.

Nearby are the **Three Brothers** (Map p196; Mazā Pils iela 17, 19 & 21), a quaint row of houses. No 17 dates from the 15th century, making it Latvia's oldest house; No 19 houses the **Latvian Museum of Architecture** (Latvijas arhitektūras muzejs; Map p196; ☎ 722 0779; Mazā Pils iela 19; admission free; 🕑 9am-6pm Mon-Fri). Nearby, **St Jacob's Cathedral** (Sv Jēkaba katedrāle; Map p196; Klostera iela) has an interior dating back to 1225 and is the seat of Rīga's Roman Catholic archbishopric. Latvia's **Parliament** (Saeima; Map p196; Jēkaba iela 11), in a Florentine Renaissance building, is next door.

Between Torņa iela and Aldaru iela, the picturesque **Swedish Gate** (Map p196) was built onto the city walls in 1698 during the Swedish period and is the only remaining old city gate. The round, peaked **Powder Tower** (Map p196) is a 14th-century original and the only survivor of the 18 towers in the old city wall. Nine Russian cannonballs from 17th- and 18th-century assaults are embedded in the tower's walls. In the past it has served as a gunpowder store, prison, torture chamber, museum and students' party venue. Today it is the **Museum of War** (Kara muzejs; Map p196; ☎ 722 8147; www.karamuzejs.lv; Smilšu iela 20; adult/child 0.50/0.25Ls; 🕑 10am-6pm Wed-Sun May-Sep, to 5pm Wed-Sun Oct-Apr). Exhibitions on permanent display include 'Proclamation of the Latvian State and Liberation War' and 'Latvian Soldiers during WWII'.

The 19th-century Gothic exterior of the **Great Guild** (Lielā gilde; Map p196; Amatu iela 6) encloses a fine 1330 merchants' meeting hall, now a concert hall for the Latvian State Philharmonic Orchestra. The yellow-painted **Cat House** (Map p196; Meistaru iela 19) is the one you see pictured on many a postcard.

SKĀRŅU IELA & MĀRSTAĻU IELA

A row of particularly pretty restored buildings faces St Peter's on Skārņu iela. The former St George's Church – an original chapel of the Knights of the Sword dating to 1208 – is now the absorbing **Museum of Decorative & Applied Arts** (Dekoratīvi lietišķās mākslas muzejs; Map p196; ☎ 722 7833; Skārņu iela 10/20; admission 0.70Ls; 🕑 11am-5pm, closed Mon). It is full of fine Latvian work; the pottery and wall hangings are particularly outstanding.

Yet more ceramics and porcelain can be viewed in the **Porcelain Museum** (Map p196; ☎ 750 3769; Kalēju iela 9-11; adult/child 0.50/0.40Ls; 🕑 11am-6pm, closed Mon), tucked away in Konventa sēta, the restored Convent Courtyard of the **former convent** (Map p196; Skārņu iela 22) that stood here in the 15th century. Next door, **St John's Church** (Jāņa baznīca; Map p196; Skārņu iela 24) is a 13th- to 19th-century amalgam of Gothic, Renaissance and baroque styles.

Further south, near the corner of Audēju iela, is the 17th-century **House of Johannes Reitern** (Map p196; Mārstaļu iela 2-4), with its elaborate stone carvings. Reitern was a rich German merchant. Next door is the interesting **Latvian Photography Museum** (Latvijas fotogrāfijas muzejs; Map p196; ☎ 722 7231; Mārstaļu iela 8; adult/child 1/0.50Ls; 🕑 10am-5pm Tue, Fri & Sat, noon-7pm Wed & Thu), an 18th- to 19th-century former merchant's house with unique photographs of 1920s Rīga. The baroque **House of Dannenstern** (Map p196; Mārstaļu iela 21) was also home to a wealthy 17th-century merchant.

Nearby, the one-room **Latvian People's Front Museum** (Latvijas tautas frontes muzejs; Map p196; ☎ 722 4502; Vecpilsētas iela 13-15; admission free; 🕑 2-7pm Tue, noon-5pm Wed-Fri, noon-4pm Sat) remains furnished exactly as it was when it served as the office of the Latvian People's Front prior to 1990. There are several tall **medieval warehouses** both on this narrow street and the parallel Alksnāja iela – at Vecpilsētas iela 10 and 11, and Alksnāja iela 5, 7, 9 and 11. Both streets lead south to **Alberta laukums**, a small square that was the site of Bishop Albert's original German settlement.

Parks & Boulevards

East of old Rīga's confined streets, the city opens out into a perfectly contrasting band of parks and wide boulevards laid out in the 19th century. Along the boulevards are many fine 19th- and early-20th-century buildings. Some of these belong to the eclectic school of design, which drew on a multitude of past styles, while others are flamboyant examples of Jugendstil which crops up all over Rīga. The old defensive moat, known as the **City Canal** (Pilsētas

CAT HOUSE

At the beginning of the 20th century, the Latvian owner of the Cat House had statuettes made of the back ends of his two black cats – backs arched and tails up. He placed them on the building's topmost pinnacles facing the Big Guild Hall across the road as a gesture of defiance against the guild that refused him entry – it was strictly reserved for rich German traders. Following a lengthy court case, he was admitted to the guild on the condition that he his cats be turned around to a more elegant position.

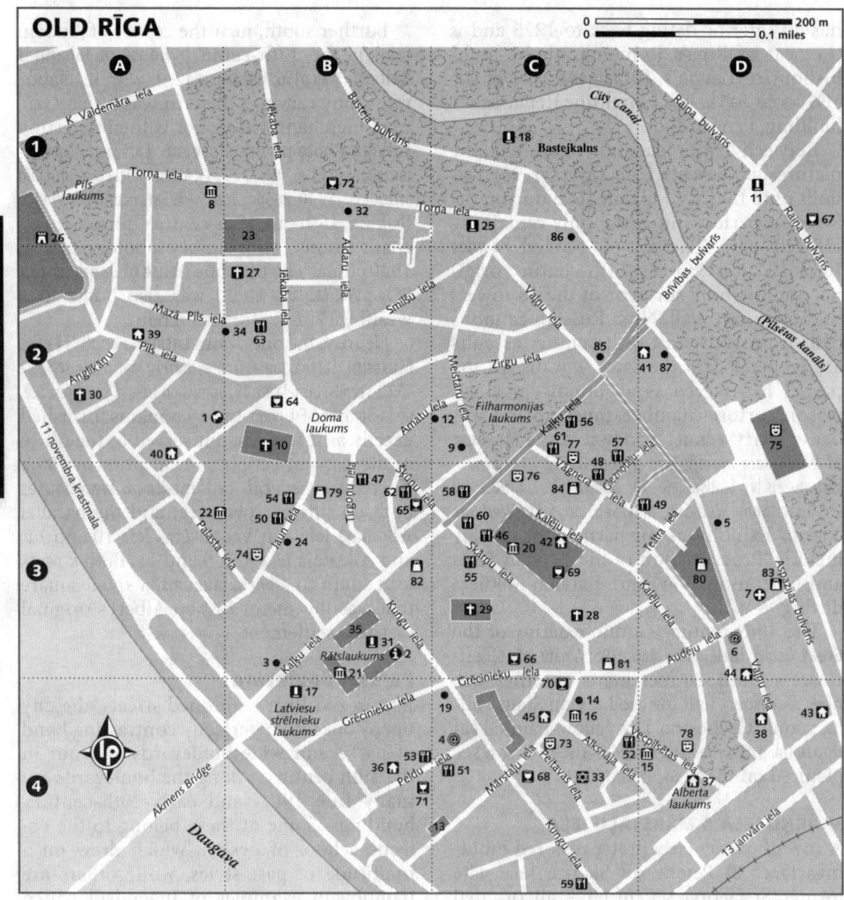

kanāls; Map p196), snakes through the parks and marks the line of the old city walls that were knocked down in the mid-19th century.

FREEDOM MONUMENT

The central landmark of the park ring is the **Freedom Monument** (Map p196; Brīvības bulvāris), near the corner of Raiņa bulvāris. Paid for by public donations, the monument was erected in 1935, in a style best described as '30s nationalism, on a spot where a statue of Peter the Great had stood. Topped by a bronze female Liberty holding up three stars facing west, representing three regions of Latvia – Kurzeme, Vidzeme and Latgale – it bears the inscription 'Tēvzemei un Brīvībai' (For Fatherland and Freedom). During the Soviet years the Freedom Monument was off limits, and a statue of Lenin, facing the other way down Brīvības iela, was placed two blocks east. Lenin was removed on the night of 20 August 1991, after the collapse of the Moscow coup attempt.

In the late 1980s and early '90s the Freedom Monument became a focus of the Latvian independence movement, which started on 14 June 1987, when 5000 people rallied here illegally to commemorate the victims of Stalin's deportations. Several later rallies and marches focused on the monument, which still functions as an unofficial centre for animated political debate. Come here to watch the changing of the guards,

INFORMATION
Canadian Embassy....1 A2
Chequepoint Exchange....(see 41)
City of Rīga Information Centre..2 B3
Country Holidays....3 B3
Dual Net Café....4 C4
Dutch Embassy....(see 72)
Globuss....5 D3
Internet Kafe....6 D3
Latvia Tours....(see 60)
Rīgas vecpilsētas aptieka....7 D3

SIGHTS & ACTIVITIES
Arsenāls Museum of Art....8 A1
Cat House....9 C2
Dome Cathedral....10 B2
Freedom Monument....11 D1
Great Guild....12 C2
History Museum of Latvia....(see 26)
House of Blackheads....(see 2)
House of Dannenstern....13 C4
House of Johannes Reitern....14 C4
Latvian Museum of Architecture....(see 34)
Latvian People's Front Museum....15 D4
Latvian Photography Museum..16 C4
Latvian Riflemen Statue....17 B4
Memorials to Victims of 20 January 1991....18 C1
Mentzendorff's House....19 C4
Museum of Decorative & Applied Arts....20 C3
Museum of Foreign Art....(see 26)
Museum of Occupation in Latvia....21 B3
Museum of the History of Rīga & Navigation....22 A3
Museum of War....(see 25)
Parliament....23 B1
Pie Kristapa....24 B3
Porcelain Museum....(see 42)
Powder Tower....25 C1
Rīga Castle....26 A1
St Jacob's Cathedral....27 B2
St John's Church....28 C3
St Peter's Church....29 C3
St Saviour's Church....30 A2
Statue of Roland....31 B3
Swedish Gate....32 B1
Synagogue....33 C4
Three Brothers....34 B2
Town Hall....35 B3

SLEEPING
Ainavas Boutique Hotel....36 B4
Argonaut Backpackers Hostel...37 D4
Forums....38 D4
Grand Palace Hotel....39 A2
Gutenbergs....40 A2
Hotel de Rome....41 D2
Konventa Sēta....42 C3
Metropole....43 D4
Old Town Hostel....44 D3
Radi un Draugi....45 C4

EATING
1739....46 C3
Alus sēta....47 B3
Austrumu robeža....48 C3
Bella Italia Restaurant....49 D3
Cuba Cafe....50 B3
Habibi....51 C4
Indian Raja....52 C4
John Lemon....53 B4
Kamāla....54 B3
Lotoss....55 C3
Nostalģija....56 C2
Palete....57 C2
Pelmeņi XL....58 C3
Salt & Pepper....59 C4
Sievasmātes pīrādziņi....60 C3
Zivju....61 C2
Šetpavārs Vilhelms....62 B3
Ķiploka krogs....63 B2

DRINKING
B-bārs....64 B2
de Lacy's....65 B3
Dickens Pub....66 C3
Melnai Kaķis....67 D1
Nautilus....68 C4
Orange Bar....69 C3
Paddy Whelan's....70 C4
Pulkvedim neviens neraksta....71 B4
Rīgas Balzams....72 B1

ENTERTAINMENT
Far & Gate....73 C4
Groks....(see 56)
Kinogalerija....74 B3
National Opera House....75 D2
Russian Drama Theatre....76 C3
Wagner Hall....77 C2
Četri balti krekli....78 D4

SHOPPING
A&E Gallery....79 B3
Centrs Universālveikals....80 D3
Musikas salons....81 C3
Nordwear....82 B3
Sakta....83 D3
Upe....84 C3

TRANSPORT
AirBaltic....85 C2
Estonian Air....(see 85)
Europcar....86 C1
Sixt....87 D2

who stand still as stone in front of her, every hour on the hour from 9am to 6pm daily.

NORTH OF FREEDOM MONUMENT

Bastion Hill (Bastejkalns; Map p196), the mound beside Basteja bulvāris, is what remains of one of the bastions of Rīga's fortifications. Beside the paths either side of the canal, below Bastion Hill, stand five polished stone slabs – **memorials to the victims of 20 January 1991**. Edijs Riekstins, Sergey Kononenko, Vladimir Gomanovich, Andris Slapins and Gvido Zvaigžne were all killed or fatally wounded here when Soviet special forces stormed the Interior Ministry nearby at Raiņa bulvāris 6. Slapins and Zvaigžne were members of the film crew of the Latvian documentary maker Juris Podnieks. No-one who has seen the films *Baltic Requiem* or *Homeland Postscript*, or the documentary *Homeland*, will forget the last footage shot by Slapins that night or his gasped words 'keep filming…' as he lay dying.

Raiņa bulvāris was 'Embassy Row' during Latvian independence between the world wars and has assumed that status again, with the Stars and Stripes fluttering in front of No 7, France installed at No 9 and Germany at No 13. To the west, opposite the corner of Basteja bulvāris, the **National Theatre** (Nacionālais teātris; Map pp192-3; K Valdemāra iela) is an interesting baroque building (1899–1902); Latvia's independence was declared here on 18 November 1918. To the north, Rīga's **World Trade Centre** (Map pp192-3; Elizabetes iela 2) is also home to some foreign embassies: Israel, Poland and Switzerland. The building used to be the Latvian Communist Party headquarters.

The **State Museum of Art** (Valsts mākslas muzejs; Map pp192-3; ☎ 732 4461; K Valdemāra iela 10a; adult/child 1.20/0.40Ls; 11am-5pm Wed-Mon) has collections of Russian work downstairs and Latvian work upstairs, plus interesting

JEWS OF RĪGA

The history of Rīga's Jews has been tumultuous. Pre-18th century Rīga had less than 1000 Jewish residents, a consequence of social policy that granted residency only to successful Jews. Even then, laws barred them from being buried in Rīga; the Jews had to shuttle their own dead to Polish cemeteries. A more flexible policy was instituted in 1725, when clearance came through for the first Jewish cemetery to be built.

Prior to the 19th century, most Jews were concentrated in the ghetto in the Maskavas suburb, about 1km southeast of the train station. It was a 750-sq-metre area bounded by Lāčplēsa iela, Maskavas iela, Ebreju iela, Lauvas iela and Kalna iela. There's little trace of the area's old character now due to Nazi destruction. In the late 1800s restrictions were lifted and the Jews were able to move to other parts of Rīga.

The first **synagogue** (Map p196; ☎ 721 0827; Peitavas iela 6-8), built in 1905, was the only synagogue to survive the Nazi terror. It's proximity to Old Town, and the danger of destroying the entire city, made them afraid to burn it. Call in advance to sample kosher food at the synagogue.

When WWII began about 5000 Jews were among the thousands of Latvians deported to Siberia by the Soviet authorities from 1940 to 1941. The city fell to the Germans on 1 July and new atrocities began that day with hundreds of Jews executed as 'retribution' for the Germans killed in the taking of Old Town. Others were forced to scrub the bloodstains from the site of the battle with toothbrushes. A few days later, on 4 July 1941, 300 or more Jews were taken from the streets and locked in the Big Choral synagogue. Grenades were thrown through the windows and the building was set on fire. No-one survived. The Jewish cemetery buildings were also burned that day; later the Soviets razed the old cemetery and converted it into the 'Park of the Communist Brīgades'.

Several thousand more Rīga Jews were murdered before the remaining thousands were herded into the ghetto in October 1941. Half-starved, they endured forced labour until most were taken and killed in Rumbula Forest, east of Maskavas, between 30 November and 8 December. Latvian collaborators as well as Germans were responsible for the holocaust – indeed the collaborators had a reputation for greater cruelty. Other Jews transported from Germany took some of the dead victims' places in the ghetto.

After the 1943 Warsaw-ghetto uprising, the Rīga ghetto, along with others, was liquidated on Himmler's orders, but those inmates capable of work were moved to the Kaiserwald prison camp in Mežaparks. Later they were brought back to other camps with the retreating German forces.

A **memorial** (Map pp192-3; Gogola iela 25) marks the former site of the Jewish community's Big Choral synagogue. The Jewish community headquarters shares the same building as **Jews in Latvia** (Ebreji Latvijas; Map pp192-3; ☎ 728 3484; ebreji.latvija@apollo.lv; Skolas iela 6; admission free; 🕑 noon-5pm Sun-Thu), Rīga's small Jewish museum that recounts Latvian Jewish history from the 16th century to 1945.

temporary exhibitions. On the Kalpaka bulvāris side of the Esplanāde is the **Jānis Rainis Monument** to Latvia's national poet.

The domed 19th-century **Russian Orthodox Cathedral** (Pareizticīgo katedrāle; Map pp192-3; Brīvības bulvāris) fronting the boulevard was a planetarium under Soviet rule but is once more used as a church.

New Rīga

The heart of everyday Rīga life lies outside the once fortified confines of Old Town and the park-boulevard ring in the areas built up in the 19th and early 20th centuries. Here you'll find funky boutiques selling discount designer wares and other non-tourist-oriented shops, as well as slick bars and hip restaurants. For a less touristy side of Rīga and a glimpse into the core of Latvian urban life, take a stroll through streets north of Old Town (coming from Old Town look for the Reval Hotel Latvija – it's the tallest building around – and head northeast from it).

The **central market** (Centrāl tirgus), south of the train station, always presents a lively scene and is a barometer of the city's standard of living. For more on the market, see p218.

Other landmarks to look for include the Russian Orthodox **Alexandr Nevsky Church** (Map pp192-3; Brīvības iela 56), built in the 1820s; the Gothic **Old Gertrude Church** (Map pp192-3; Ģertrūdes iela 8), built in 1865; and the towering Stalin-era wedding-cake-like **Science Academy** (Map pp192-3; Turgeņeva iela).

Krišjāņis Barons, the father of Latvian folk songs, lived the last years of his life in the building which now houses the **Krišjāņis Barons Memorial Museum** (Krišjāņis Barons memorialais muzejs; Map pp192-3; ☎ 728 4265; K Barona iela 3; adult/child 0.40/0.20Ls; ⌚ 1-7pm Tue & Wed, 11am-5pm Thu-Sun).

Suburbs

MOTOR MUSEUM

The stars of the collection at the fantastic **Rīga Motor Museum** (Rīgas motormuzejs; Map p188; ☎ 709 7170; Eizenšteina iela 6; adult/child 1/0.50Ls; ⌚ 10am-3pm Mon, to 6pm Tue-Sun) are cars once belonging to Soviet luminaries Gorky, Stalin, Khrushchev and Brezhnev – complete with irreverent life-sized figures of the men themselves. Stalin, pockmarked cheeks and all, sits regally in the back of his seven-tonne, 6005cc armoured limousine. The car has 1.5cm-thick iron plating everywhere except on the 8cm-thick windows. It drank a litre of petrol every 2.5km. Brezhnev sits, with appropriate surprise registered on his features, at the wheel of his crumpled Rolls-Royce Silver Shadow, written off in 1980 when he strayed from the safety of an official convoy into the path of a truck.

The museum was opened in 1989, but its seeds were sown in 1975 when a Latvian car enthusiast, Viktors Kulbergs, saved a rare 16-cylinder 1938 German Auto Union racer from being scrapped in Moscow. The racer is today shown with 100 or so other Eastern and Western cars, motorcycles and bicycles – including an 1886 Daimler Motorkutsche (a genuine horseless carriage, maximum speed 16km/h), a 1984 Cadillac Fleetwood limo and a 1942 Harley Davidson – packed into this modern, purpose-built museum.

The museum is 8km east along Brīvības iela, then 2km south to the Mežciems suburb. Take bus 21 from the Russian Orthodox Cathedral to the Pansionāts stop on Šmerļa iela.

LATVIAN ETHNOGRAPHIC OPEN-AIR MUSEUM

The not-to-be-missed **Latvian Ethnographic Open-Air Museum** (Latvījas etnogrāfiskais brīvdabas muzejs; ☎ 799 4515; Brīvības gatve 440; adult/child 1/0.50Ls; ⌚ 11am-5pm mid-May–mid-Oct) sits on the shores

LATVIA

ART-NOUVEAU ARCHITECTURE

Rīga's architectural distinction is its Art-Nouveau style, also called Jugendstil and credited by Unesco as being the finest in Europe. Crafted in the late 19th and early 20th century, it has survived in Rīga more than in many German cities, which were damaged during WWII.

The Jugendstil architectural features emphasise the ornate: monsters, flowers, masks and grotesques peer out from the upper storeys of the buildings. Different coloured tiles may be used to make the designs stand out. Often the buildings' plain interiors offer an almost comical contrast to the elaborate style of the façade.

One place that showcases the ornate Jugendstil style is along the combined residential, office and commercial streets east of Elizabetes iela, where a number of low, wooden buildings survive from the 19th century. One of the best examples, designed by Mikhail Eisenstein, father of the renowned film-maker, is the beautifully renovated blue-and-white house at Elizabetes iela 10b, just north of the State Museum of Art.

Around the corner on **Alberta iela** – famous as a confluence of architectural schools: national romanticism, historicism, neoclassicism and rationalism – the buildings become even more fantastical. All were designed by Mikhael Eisenstein except for No 12, an Art-Nouveau apartment, formerly home to the Latvian painter Jānis Rozentāls (1866–1916) and now the **Jānis Rozentāls Memorial Museum** (Map pp192-3; ☎ 733 1641; Alberta iela 12-9; adult/child 0.60/0.30Ls; ⌚ 11am-5pm Thu-Mon). The houses at Nos 2, 4, 6 and 8 have grandiose Art-Nouveau façades; the façade at 2a towers above the building itself.

Equally fabulous is the beautifully renovated 1905 façade of the **Stockholm School of Economics** (Map p192-3 Central Riga; Strēlnieku iela 4a), considered by many to be the city's most stunning example of Art-Nouveau architecture.

of Lake Jugla on the city's eastern edge. Dozens of predominantly wooden buildings from rural Latvia – churches, windmills and farmhouses from Latvia's different regions – can be discovered here. Thousands of artefacts inside the buildings provide a record of bygone country life. On summer weekends folk-dance performances are held and there's a crafts fair in early June.

Take bus 1 from the corner of Merķeļa iela and Tērbatas iela to the Brīvdabas muzejs stop.

MEŽAPARKS & CEMETERIES

Rīga's biggest park is **Mežaparks** (Woodland Park; Map p188; ☎ 754 0288), about 7km north of the centre, beside Lake Ķīšezers. Here you'll find pine woods, playgrounds, lots of boats and jet skis to rent in summer, the Rīga National Zoo (p209) and the stage for the main concerts of Latvian song festivals.

South of Mežaparks are three cemeteries: **Rainis Cemetery** (Raiņa kapi), where Jānis Rainis, his wife (feminist poet Aspazija) and other Latvian cultural figures are buried; **Second Woodland Cemetery** (Meža kapi II), with a monument to the five dead of 20 January 1991; and the **Brothers' Cemetery** (Brāļu kapi), the resting place of Latvian soldiers who died in WWI and the independence war, and notable for its monuments and sculptures.

WALKING TOUR

Start at the northern half of old Rīga, which centres on **Doma laukums (1)**, then head towards the riverside and walk halfway over **Akmens Bridge (2)** for a classical view of old Rīga. Return to the southern half of old Rīga and ride the lift up the spire of **St Peter's Church (3**; p191) for another rewarding view. From there head down Skārnū iela and gaze at the varied architecture. Further along the street you'll find the whitewashed bricks of Rīga's oldest building, the former **St George's Church (4)**, today home to the **Museum of Decorative & Applied Arts** (p195). Just a few buildings up the street you'll find **St John's Church** (**5**; p195), with a baroque-style altar and enticing stained-glass windows. Wander east out of old Rīga to the **Central Market** (**6**; p198), a focus of the city's modern and historical life. Head north, first along Valņu iela then Brīvības bulvāris till you reach the **Freedom Monument** (**7**; p196), set in the band of boulevards and parks

WALK FACTS

Distance 5km
Duration three hours (leisurely pace)

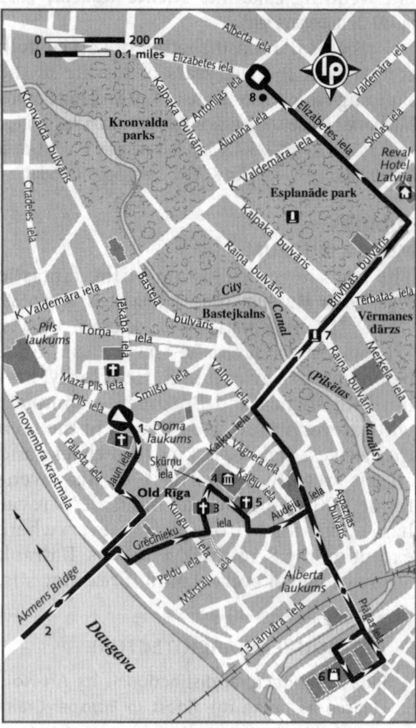

that border Old Town. From here you can stroll around the city parks, ride the lift to the 26th floor of Reval Hotel Latvija for yet another stunning city view, and – if you still have the energy – head northwest to view Rīga's sumptuous **Jugendstil** (**8**; p199), German Art Nouveau–style architecture.

RĪGA FOR CHILDREN

Rīga is not a particularly child-friendly destination. It's not that travelling with the kiddies is discouraged; it is just there's simply not that much to keep them interested. Rīga's greatest delights are discovered by foot, and while strolling the streets and checking out the architecture of Old Town is a fascinating experience for adults, younger children will probably bore quickly.

(Continued on page 209)

TIIT VEERMAE/ALAMY

Sun-dappled Estonian forest (p60)

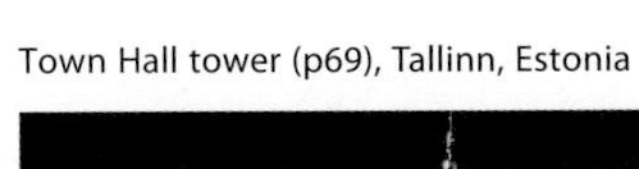

Town Hall tower (p69), Tallinn, Estonia

JONATHAN SMITH

Wares for sale at the knit market (p89),Tallinn, Estonia

JONATHAN SMITH

Turaida Castle tower (p228), Sigulda, Latvia (opposite)

PHILIP GAME

JONATHAN SMITH

St Olaf's Church (p73), Tallin, Estonia

Kissing Students, by Mati Karmin, Tartu (p106), Estonia

TIIT VEERMAE/ALAMY

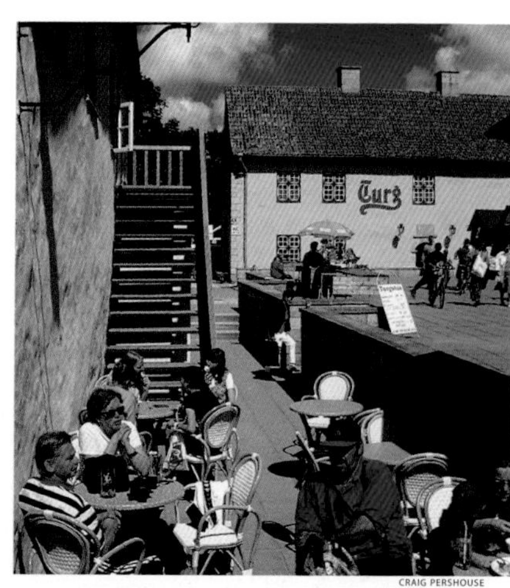

CRAIG PERSHOUSE

Café culture in Kuressaare (p146), Estonia

JONATHAN SM

Estonia Theatre & Concert Hall (p87), Tallinn

Stork mural on the side of a house, Rīga (p187), Latvia

MARTIN LLADÓ

BRUCE YUAN-YUE BI

Girl jumping into Lake Galve, Trakai (p315), Lithuania

JONATHAN SMITH

Bridge across the Daugava River (p189), Rīga, Latvia

BRUCE YUAN-YUE BI

The 17th-century Swedish Gate (p195), Rīga, Latvia

Nightlife (p216), Rīga, Latvia

PHOTOLIBRARY

JONATHAN SMITH

Snow-covered trees in a forest, near Kaunas (p331), Lithuania

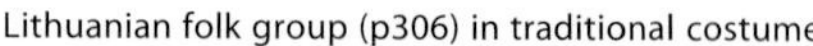

Lithuanian folk group (p306) in traditional costume

JONATHAN SMITH

19th century façades on Lukiškių Square in New Town (p300), Vilnius, Lithuania

JONATHAN SM

JONATHAN SMITH

Clock tower seen through the columns of Vilnius Cathedral (p296), Lithuania

JONATHAN SMITH

19th-century wooden fishing cottage, Klaipėda (p347), Lithuania

Light and shadow highlighting the belfry of St John's Church (p296), Vilnius, Lithuania

TOM COCHREM

PHOTOLIBRARY

Woman mushrooming (p328) in Lithuania

Rowing boats on the Danė River (p347), Lithuania

JONATHAN SMITH

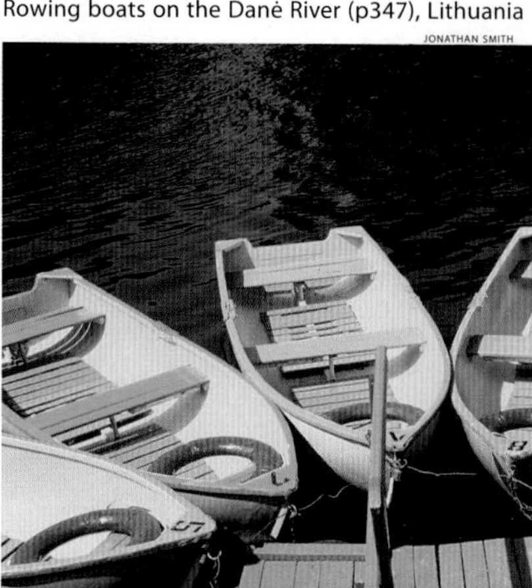

Man (p335), by Petras Mazūras, opposite St Michael the Archangel Church (p335) in Kaunas, Lithuania

BRUCE YUAN-Y

(Continued from page 200)

That said, there are a few options sure to bring a smile to a child's face. Rīga's biggest park, Mežaparks (p200) is packed with playgrounds and you can rent boats and jet skis in summer. You'll also find the **Rīga National Zoo** (Zoologiskais dārz; Map p188; ☎ 751 8669; Meža prospekts 1; admission 2Ls; 🕙 10am-6pm) here. Set in a hilly pine forest, the zoo has a motley collection of animals, including a few bears, zebras and even the odd camel or two.

Museum of Nature (Dabas Muzejas; Map pp192-3; ☎ 722 6078; K Barona iela 4; adult/child 0.60/0.30Ls; 🕙 10am-5pm Tue, Wed & Sat, to 6pm Thu, to 4pm Sun) is another kid-friendly attraction. The top floor features pickled body parts and child-oriented interactive computer programmes in English. There is also a zoology exhibit featuring stuffed lions, tigers and bears and a collection of ancient creepy critters and fossilised fish.

Young wannabe firefighters will dig the collection of fire engines, uniforms and old photos at the **Fire-Fighting Museum** (Latvijas ugunsdzēsības muzejas; Map p188; ☎ 733 1334; Hanzas iela 5; admission 0.20Ls; 🕙 10am-5pm Wed-Sun).

If your kids just want to play in the water, you'll have to head to Jūrmala (p220), just a short ways out of town. Here you'll find Latvia's largest indoor water park, **Līvu Akvaparks** (☎ 775 5636; www.akvaparks.lv; Vienībaws gatve 36; admission 8Ls, child under 6 free; 🕙 noon-11pm Mon-Fri, 10am-10pm Sat & Sun), in the village of Lielupe. A wave pool, children's pool and waterslides are among the attractions.

TOURS

Most travel agencies, including the ones listed earlier in this chapter, arrange city tours and day trips to other places in Latvia, including Sigulda, Cēsis, Kurzeme, Latgale and Rundāle.

Liepāja (Map pp192-3; ☎ 953 9184; Novembra krastmala 11; admission 2Ls) This company offers Daugava River boat tours. Trips depart from the boat station by Akmens Bridge (opposite the tram 4 stop) two to five times daily – stop by to check the schedule. River tours last one to two hours.

Rīga Sightseeing (☎ 702 7801; amberway@inbox.lv; adult/child 6/3Ls) Organises two-hour bus tours of the city, departing from in front of the House of Blackheads on Rātslaukums at noon daily. The tourist office sells tickets or you can buy them direct from the bus driver.

FESTIVALS & EVENTS

Rīga hosts dozens of annual and one-off festivals. The following are among the most famous:

International Baltic Ballet Festival (www.ballet-festival.lv) Takes place over five days in late April; performances by Latvian and international companies.

National Ethnic Arts and Crafts Fair (www.muzeji.lv/index_e.html) Big arts and crafts fair held at the Open-Air Ethnography Museum on the first weekend in June.

Rīga Opera Festival (www.music.lv/opera) The Latvian National Opera's showcase event, it takes place over 10 days in June and includes performances by world-renowned talent.

Arēna New Music Festival (www.arenafest.lv) Contemporary music festival showcasing various genres and held at venues throughout Rīga during the first two weeks of October.

SLEEPING

Although it seems a new hotel is opening in Rīga every day, there still aren't enough rooms to go around. Unless you've booked in advance (highly recommended), there ain't no rooms to be found between May and August. If you arrive without a reservation, you'll probably have to shop around. Don't despair, with enough sleuthing you'll probably find a place to lay your head, but be prepared to have to check out and start the search all over again the next day – frustratingly hotels seem to have one room left for only one night. Although budget and midrange places are becoming more prevalent, the majority of accommodation in Rīga still falls in the top-end price bracket.

Budget

New hostels are opening every day, and Rīga's definitely becoming more budget-friendly. If the hostels are full, or just not your thing, some of the nicer hotels have cheaper rooms with shared bathrooms.

Old Town Hostel (Map p196; ☎ 722 3406; www.rigaoldtownhostel.lv; Valņu iela 43; dm/r 10/30Ls; 💻) Marble floors, chandeliers on all four floors, a spiral staircase and sauna make this smart place a star find. Dorms are large and clean, and the on-site bar is a great place to meet people and party. There's a self-catering kitchen.

Argonaut Backpackers Hostel (Map p196; ☎ 614 7214; www.argonautbackpackers.com; Kalēju iela 50; dm from 6Ls, r 25-60Ls; ⊠ 💻) The new kid on the block. Smack in the middle of Old Town, it was packed when we stopped by. Highlights at this Aussie-owned place include a chill lounge, bold colour scheme, friendly reception and free Internet. Dorms are a little cramped.

Viktorija (Map pp192-3; ☎ 701 4111; www.hotel-viktorija.lv; A Čaka iela 55; s/d from 12/17Ls; Ⓟ) If you don't want to stay in a hostel, Viktorija wins the prize hands down for Rīga's best-value budget accommodation. The cheapest rooms share bathrooms (for around 40Ls, you can get a more modern room with en suite and breakfast), but are very clean and spacious with high ceilings and sinks.

Posh Backpackers (Map pp192-3; ☎ 721 0917; www.poshbackpackers.lv; Pūpolu iela 5; dm/d 8/16Ls; Ⓟ 💻) Dorms feel spartan, but the place is clean and friendly. In an old warehouse, it sits within the central market precincts and can feel bustling. Those with heavy packs will be happy to know it's just a minute's walk from the bus and train stations. A lounge, laundry and free Internet are pluses.

Krišjānis & Gertrūde (Map pp192-3; ☎ 750 6604; www.musbalt.com/hotel.htm; Ģertrūdes iela 39; r from 17Ls; ⊠) This five-room setup is named after the Latvian couple who run it. The cheapest rooms share bathrooms, but all are clean and uniquely decorated. It's a cosy place.

Baltā Kaza (Map p188; ☎ 737 8135; Ēveles 2; dm/d 4/25Ls) With the cheapest dorm beds in the city, the 'White Goat' is an option for the financially strapped. It's a 15-minute tram ride from the centre of town, so it's not the most convenient place, but the four-bed dorms are clean and safe.

Mežaparks (Map p188; ☎ 755 7988; mezaparks@tvnet.lv; Sakses iela 19; d from 9Ls; Ⓟ) One of Rīga's top cheap hotels comes complete with outstanding lake views, although it's a ways out of town. The cheapest rooms are clean, no-frills affairs with shared bathrooms. Pay a bit more for a renovated room with private facilities and TV. Take trolleybus 2 for 30 minutes to the last stop.

Midrange

Prices include breakfast unless mentioned otherwise. The bathroom-clad rooms at the Viktorija (above) offer excellent-value midrange accommodation too.

Radi un Draugi (Map p196; ☎ 722 0372; www.draugi.lv; Mārstaļu iela 1; s/d from 37/46Ls; 💻) Owned by British-Latvians, Radi un Draugi is very popular and often fully booked. An Old Town gem, it consistently gets rave reviews for its value, cleanliness and Scandinavian feel. There's disabled access and a lift.

B&B Rīga (Map pp192-3; ☎ 652 6400; www.bb-Rīga.lv; Ģertrūdes iela 43; r from 25Ls; Ⓟ) A small, family-run B&B, this features eight spacious, modern rooms with fridges and microwave ovens. It's tucked back from the street in a quaint, flower-filled courtyard and offers travellers good-value accommodation.

Laine (Map pp192-3; ☎ 728 8816; www.laine.lv; Skolas iela 11; s/d from 40/50Ls; Ⓟ 💻) In a courtyard off the main street, Laine is a great central find. A colourful, spacious place, most rooms here come with satellite TV and minibars. There are a few cheaper rooms with shared bathrooms. For the best views, ask for digs on the top floors.

KB (Map pp192-3; ☎ 731 6953; www.kbhotel.lv; Barona iela 37; d from 27Ls; 💻) This great new B&B has restored frescos in the foyer and a marble staircase leading to bright and modern rooms. There's a communal kitchen.

Forums (Map p196; ☎ 781 4680; www.hotelforums.lv; Valņu iela 45; d from 46Ls) The elegant rooms at this modern hotel are done up in dark reds with gold upholstered furnishings. If you're looking to splurge, try a top-floor suite, complete with private sauna (85Ls).

City Hotel Bruņinieks (Map pp192-3; ☎ 731 5140; www.cityhotel.lv; Bruņinieku 6; r from 50Ls) Rooms are clean and newly refurbished with nice touches like heated bathroom floors and minibars. The big, airy and very modern lobby has a 24-hour bar. Service is professional, and the place is good midrange value.

Tia (Map p188; ☎ 733 3918; www.tia.lv; K Valdemāra iela 63; s/d/tr 50/62/78Ls; 💻) Tia has simple, soulful rooms, done up in blues and greys, with unusually nice bathrooms. All are renovated and come with satellite TV and fridges.

Metropole (Map p196; ☎ 722 5411; www.metropole.lv; Aspazijas bulvāris 36-38; s/d from 55/65Ls; ❄ 💻) Down towards the bus station, Metropole was renowned as a centre of diplomatic intrigue and espionage in the 1930s. Rīga's oldest continuously running hotel has a Scandinavian influence and modern rooms done up in tasteful pastels.

Ķeizarmežs (Map p188; ☎ 751 7510; www.keizarmezs.lv; Ezermalas iela 30; s/d 40/48Ls; ❄) A modern hotel overlooking Lake Ķišezers, 7km north of the centre in Rīga's green and flowery Mežaparks. Rooms are sparkling clean, and the swimming pool, air-con and fabulous fitness centre make it great value if you're willing to be a bit outside town.

Top End

Rīga boasts scores of top-end hotels ready to cater to your every whim. Rates include breakfast.

Grand Palace Hotel (Map p196; ☎ 704 4000; www.schlossle-hotels.com; Pils iela 12; r from 140Ls; P ✕ 💻) With some of Rīga's most attractive rooms, this lavish place caters to visiting celebrities. Rooms are truly luxurious, done up in white, blue and gold colour schemes. The service is attentive and professional.

Reval Hotel Rīdzene (Map pp192-3; ☎ 732 4433; www.revalhotels.com; Reimersa 1; s/d €180/200; P ✕ 💻) There's a rubber duck in every bathroom at this renovated hotel, which once catered to the Soviet elite. Rooms are comfortable with cherry-wood furnishings and include all the modern conveniences. One of the city's most deluxe hotels, this comes with sauna and fitness centre, which are on the top floor. They come with 180-degree city views.

Ainavas Boutique Hotel (Map p196; ☎ 781 4316; www.ainavas.lv; Peldu iela 23; s/d €135/175; P 💻) Ainavas markets itself as a boutique hotel and, indeed, it is stylish. Each room flaunts a different landscape depicted in a painting above the bed. Heated bathroom floors and web TV are among the perks at this original spot inside a 15th-century town house.

Konventa Sēta (Map p196; ☎ 708 7501; www.konventa.lv; Skārņu iela 22; s/d €80/86; P 💻) Within the restored courtyards of a 15th-century convent, this unique hotel is excellent value. The 10 medieval buildings are named after their original uses and the rooms are exquisitely furnished, many making use of the building's existing oak beams. Wheelchair-accessible rooms are available.

Gutenbergs (Map p196; ☎ 781 4090; www.gutenbergs.lv; Doma laukums 1; d 70Ls; P 💻) A gorgeous place in the heart of Old Town, Gutenbergs is worth a stay, if only to dine in its stunning rooftop restaurant overlooking the spire of St Peter's Church. Try for a room in the newer wing – these feature rustic furnishings and wooden ceilings.

Reval Hotel Latvija (Map pp192-3; ☎ 777 2222; latvija@revalhotels.com; Elizabetes iela 55; d from 100Ls; P ✕ 💻) Once an Intourist hotel that sent shivers down the spine of many a Latvian, today it's a sparkling 27-storey tower of wealth and luxury. Views from the 26th-floor bar are the best in Rīga (even better than St Peter's). Rooms are rather simple, but come with fabulously comfortable linens. The staff attends to every whim.

> **THE AUTHOR'S CHOICE**
>
> **Hotel Bergs** (Map pp192-3; ☎ 777 0900; www.hotelbergs.com; Elizabetes iela 83/85; r from 90Ls; P ✕ 💻) In the trendy Berga bazārs shopping plaza, this luxurious hotel was made for pampering. One of Rīga's best hotels, it has rooms that are spacious and tastefully decorated with quality linens and a mix of 19th century and contemporary furnishings. The exotic-looking bar is filled with African artefacts.

Hotel de Rome (Map p196; ☎ 708 7600; www.derome.lv; Kaļķu iela 28; s/d from €142/156; P 💻) With a fabulous central location and jam-packed with amenities, this prestigious hotel is often fully booked. Rooms are lux and the views fantastic.

Radisson-SAS Daugava (Map pp192-3; ☎ 706 1111; www.radisson.com/Rīgalv; Kuģu iela 24; s/d €122/142; P ✕ 💻 🏊) Considered to be on the 'wrong' side of the river by many, the Radisson has great views of the Old Town skyline, and every imaginable facility: fitness centre, indoor swimming pool, sauna and a restaurant renowned for its Sunday brunch. It caters to business travellers, and rooms are well appointed and comfortable.

EATING

Dining out in Rīga is dizzying. The choice of cuisine – be it Korean, Caribbean or Caucasian – can be overwhelming. For those seeking good old-fashioned Latvian fare, there are loads of self-service, cafeteria-style eateries run by the hugely successful Lido chain.

In summer, tables and chairs spill out onto Doma laukums and the open-air plaza along Kaļķu iela, transforming Old Town into a fun-packed plaza of cheap cafés, beer tents and late-night bars.

Cafés

The city's café scene is fun, fun, fun and never more so than during Latvia's short but sweet summer when outdoor terraces fill most of the many Old Town squares and side streets.

LATVIA

THE AUTHOR'S CHOICE

John Lemon (Map p196; ☎ 722 6647; Peldu iela 21; meals 4Ls) With orange walls and a pink bar, this is a popular spot for late-night noshing (it serves food until 5am on Friday and Saturday nights). John Lemon dishes up lots of Western favourites (you won't find any pork or sour cream here): eggy breakfasts, soul-soothing soups, sumptuous wraps and loads of salads. It's a very chill joint with a decidedly bohemian edge, the kind of place where you can curl into slinky green '60s space-station sofas and read the night away in relative peace and quiet. Solo women travellers will feel comfortable here.

Cuba Cafe (Map p196; ☎ 722 4362; Jaun iela 15; light meals 3-6Ls) A new, very hip spot with dark walls and ultramod, classically smoky environs and cramped, but oh-so-trendy tables outside. The light tapas menu is hearty and delicious. The cocktail menu is extensive, and includes Cuban favourites like *mojitos*.

Osiris (Map pp192-3; ☎ 724 3002; K Barona iela 31; meals 6-12Ls) A Rīga institution, Osiris remains one of the city's best spots for a leisurely breakfast or romantic evening glass of wine. It's very slick with green marble counters and framed photos on the walls.

Hedonia 55 (Map pp192-3; ☎ 724 2855; Dzīrnavu iela 55; meals 2-7Ls) Minimalist Asian meets pseudo-industrial at this popular café/bar featuring a spinning disco ball and red plastic chairs. Bar food is served until 3am and the extensive menu features dishes from around the globe. If you just want to drink, the crowd is young, hip and well dressed. The cocktail menu includes more than 70 concoctions.

Zen (Map pp192-3; ☎ 731 6521; Stabu iela 6) It's as zen as zen can be at this oriental teahouse. Loll on floor cushions, watch the candles flicker, and chill out while your tea is prepared tableside – the full ritual takes a very thirsty 20 minutes. If you want to smoke while you're waiting, tobacco water pipes are available for 5Ls.

Double Coffee (Map pp192-3; ☎ 722 6548; Raiņa iela 25; meals 2-4Ls; ⊠) This is one of the best coffee shops in Latvia. It features a large menu of espresso and tea drinks as well as the richest hot chocolate you'll ever taste. There are also sandwiches, breakfast options, more substantial mains and cocktails on the glossy menu. The nonsmoking section is a real plus.

Habibi (Map p196; ☎ 722 8551; Peldu iela 24) Run by an English- and Russian-speaking Egyptian, Habibi has a rich and exotic interior clad with cushions and carpets. Local belly dancers shake their stuff in front of a water-pipe smoking clientele in the back room. Fruit-flavoured tobacco costs 5Ls per pipe.

Rāma (Map pp192-3; ☎ 727 2490; K Barona iela 56; meals 2Ls) The café of the Society for Krishna Consciousness lolls in a lovely pink-and-violet wooden house and is the cheapest place to stuff yourself with veggie fodder in Rīga. Choose from rice, cabbage and tofu dishes flavoured with chilli and curry. The food is often hit or miss, but all proceeds go to the poor, so you never feel you're wasting money.

Kosher Café L'Chaim (Map pp192-3; ☎ 728 0235; Skolas iela 6; meals 3-5Ls) Popular with Rīga's Jewish community, this small café guarantees all food to be 100% kosher. The menu includes *tsimmes*, *latkes*, *gefillte fish* and *challa*, along with loads of freshly baked pastries.

Restaurants

OLD RĪGA

Palete (Map p196; ☎ 721 6037; Gleznotāju iela 8; meals 15-25Ls) A *très* elegant restaurant, delectably designed Palete is the place to go for fine dining; the Latvian cook spent five years cooking for Latvia's former president, and makes a tender champagne-poached sea bass and a sumptuous salmon teriyaki. There's piano or guitar music most nights.

Salt & Pepper (Map p196; ☎ 722 6836; Kungu iela 33; meals 6Ls) Looking out on the river, this is a stylish joint in super spacious environs and definitely one of the hot places to see and be seen in Rīga. Lavish and lux, with a sort of pseudo-Soviet industrial vibe, it also offer lots of hidden nooks and crannies for getting intimate. The 2Ls breakfast buffet gets rave reviews. The menu is arty Parisian café meets greasy American diner.

Indian Raja (Map p196; ☎ 721 2614; Vecpilsētas 3; meals 13Ls) An expat place offering some of the best Indian food in the Baltics, this is where to go if you're craving a sumptuous, spicy curry or a perfectly cooked tandoori.

Lotoss (Map p196; ☎ 721 2665; Skārņu iela 7; meals 9Ls) Serving a refreshing range of tantalising light lunches – everything from samosas to fillet mignon to lots of meatless entrées – Lotoss also attracts the people-watching set who flock in for one of Old Riga's best views.

Bella Italia Restaurant (Map p196; ☎ 722 3587; Vāgnera iela 16; meals 6-12Ls) Tucked into a corner of Old Town, this popular Italian place has a congenial vibe – think warm hues, stone tables, rattan chairs and heaping plates of Italy's favourite comfort food, pasta. There's also a decent selection of seafood and pizza.

Alus sēta (Map p196; ☎ 722 2431; Tirgoņu iela 6; meals 7Ls; 🕒 10am-1am) Lido's only Old Town outlet has fabulous outside seating overlooking Doma laukums and serves hearty Latvian cuisine at unbeatable prices. Favourites include chicken or pork shashlik and Latvian grey peas. Wash your meal down with home-brewed Lido ale.

Ķiploka krogs (Garlic Bar; Map p196; ☎ 721 1451; Jēkaba iela 3; meals 7Ls) Probably not the place for a first date – although the intimate ambience just might lure you inside for a romantic evening – Ķiploka krogs dishes up garlic in all shapes, sizes and guises. This also doubles as a bar (albeit a smelly-breathed one).

Austrumu robeža (Eastern Border; Map p196; ☎ 781 4203; Vāgnera iela 8; meals 6Ls, admission for shows 2Ls) Decked out like some demented person's dream of a WWII bunker, this independent theatre and restaurant is at least worth a peep for its Soviet memorabilia. Eastern Border is 1011km from Moscow, and the menu is old school red Baltic and Caucasian cuisine. It even boasts a hammer and a sickle on its front.

Kamāla (Map p196; ☎ 721 1332; Jaun iela 14; meals 6Ls) This vegetarian restaurant exudes spiritualism. Incense smoke, Indian music, ornately carved furniture and bright embroidered tablecloths set the dreamy vibe.

1739 (Map p196; ☎ 721 1398; Skārnu iela 6; meals 12Ls) Inside a historic home, this classy Italian restaurant serves authentic pastas, meat dishes and soups in calm, refined environs. If you can't afford dinner, the menu at lunch is very similar but with much lower prices.

Zivju (Map p196; ☎ 721 6713; Vāgnera iela 4; meals 18-36Ls) One of Rīga's only true seafood restaurants, Zivju serves some fabulous fish and seafood. Its cooked tiger shrimps in fennel sauce (a mere 9.40Ls) are sublime. The ambience is soothing, yet elegant, with a blue and beige colour scheme.

THE AUTHOR'S CHOICE

Nostalģija (Map p196; ☎ 722 2338; Kaļķu iela 22; meals 10Ls; 🕒 10am-2am) This gaudy, gilded monument to all things communist is where to head for a solid meal of *pelmeņi* (meat dumplings fried, boiled or swimming in soup) and caviar. At this retro Soviet restaurant, which also serves Western classics, you'll be able to feast your eyes on glossy murals glorifying the old revolution. Late on Thursday through Saturday nights, the place turns into a chaotic disco.

CENTRAL RĪGA

Bergs (Map pp192-3; ☎ 777 0949; Elizabetes iela 83/85; meals 10-20Ls) Serving international fusion cuisine, Bergs, in the Berga bazārs shopping mall, is one of Rīga's top restaurants. The menu changes constantly, but the elegantly presented mains are consistently delicious. The restaurant's easy-on-the-eyes interior only serves to enhance the experience.

Andalūzijas Suns (Map pp192-3; ☎ 728 8418; Elizabetes iela 83/85 3; meals 8-12Ls) Thanks to some seriously devoted patrons, this restaurant in the Berga bazārs is a perennial expat favourite. You'll dig the industrial flavour and the American brewpub grub – think juicy burgers, plump burritos and endless glasses of ale.

Macaroni Noodle Bar (Map pp192-3; ☎ 721 7981; K Barona iela 17; meals 6-12Ls) A very modern and ultrahip joint where ambient House plays softly in the background. The menu includes every type of pasta, sauce, meat and seafood combo imaginable along with loads of sushi platters. In the evenings it turns into a trendy, and popular, cocktail lounge.

Vincents (Map pp192-3; ☎ 733 2634; Elizabetes iela 19; meals 12-20Ls) Inspired by Van Gogh, Vincents is a bit of a local institution and has served more than one head of state and international movie star. Every summer the restaurant adopts a European theme – Catalonian and French have already rolled around, but future choices promise to be equally delicious. Other perks are a separate sushi menu and a three-course business lunch (from 6Ls).

Ai Karamba! (Map pp192-3; ☎ 733 4672; Pulkveža Brieža 2; meals 6Ls) It's about as kitschy Americana as Rīga gets, and the food at this Canadian-owned restaurant is about as close to American country kitchen-cum-greasy-spoon diner as you'll find in Latvia. A good bet if you're craving one of those hangover-curing breakfast fry-ups.

Vērmanītis (Map pp192-3; ☎ 728 6289; Elizabetes iela 65; meals 6Ls; 8am-1am) With fabulous park views and the whole gamut of Baltic fare – meat, potatoes, rice, salads, desserts – it's no wonder Vērmanītis is another local favourite. Those not in the mood for pork and potatoes can choose from pizza on the ground floor and fast food in the basement.

Dzirnavas (The Mill; Map pp192-3; ☎ 728 6204; Dzirnavu iela 76; meals 6Ls) This authentic Latvian kitchen, also run by Lido, packs in hordes of hungry Latvians, tourists and expats alike. The giant buffet fills several rooms and offers all sorts of greasy, yet tempting, local favourites.

Staburags (Map pp192-3; ☎ 729 9787; A Čaka iela 57; meals 6Ls) A rustic Latvian joint serving great ribs, peas and beer in an inviting farmhouse setting. It's a favourite with locals.

Lido atpūtas centrs (Map p188; ☎ 781 2187; Krasta iela 76; meals 5Ls) This vast eating and drinking complex has food galore, lots to entertain the kids (animals, electric cars, playground) and folk musicians playing every evening from 7pm. Take bus 107 from in front of the train station to the Lido stop.

Quick Eats

For Rīga's most popular fast-food options, see boxed text, below.

Pizza Jazz (Map pp192-3; ☎ 800 0005; Raiņa bulvāris 15; pizza from 3Ls; 10am-midnight Mon-Sat, 11am-midnight Sun) This Lithuanian-run chain is said to serve the biggest and best pizza in town. They'll deliver directly to your hotel room. You can find another branch of Pizza Jazz at Brīvības iela 76 (Map pp192–3).

Pizza Lulū (Map pp192-3; Ģertrūdes iela 27; meals 4Ls) Run by a Canadian-Latvian team, it serves yummy American-style pizzas by the slice or pie. A slice, soda and a salad will only set you back about 2Ls. There are seven locations around town, one of which is at K Valdemāra iela 143/145 (Map p188).

Self-Catering

Central market (Map pp192-3; Prāgas iela; 7.30am-6pm Tue-Sat, to 4pm Sun & Mon) Rīga's colourful market is housed in five great zeppelin hangars behind the bus station. You can buy everything from slabs of meat to fresh fruits and veggies; see p218 for more info.

Interpegro (Map pp192-3; Marijas iela 1) You'll find this well-stocked supermarket opposite the train station.

Rimi (Map pp192-3; K Barona iela 46) A large supermarket inside the Barona Centrs, a small shopping centre on three floors.

DRINKING

Nightlife in Rīga is pumping and there is no shortage of great places to grab a pint and while away the evening.

PASTIES, PANCAKES & DUMPLINGS

Latvia's answer to fast food can be found stuffed inside *pelmeņi* (meat dumplings fried, boiled or swimming in soup), *pīrāgi* (meat pasties baked in the oven) and *pankuki* (pancakes). Which is maybe why the big international fast-food chains are refreshingly few and far between in the Latvian capital.

Dozens of places dish up pasties, pancakes and dumplings. Temples devoted exclusively to the latter include **Pelmeņi** (Map pp192-3; A Čaka iela 38a; 8am-9pm Mon-Fri, 9am-8pm Sat) and **Pelmeņi XL** (Map p196; Kalķu iela 7; 9am-4am), two calorie-heavy spots where you can indulge to your heart's content – eat in or take away – for 0.55Ls a dumpling. Pelmeņi, a cheerful polka-dotted place with its entrance on Ģertrūdes iela, cooks up soup (from 0.45Ls) too.

The mother-in-law bakes the best pīrāgi at **Sievasmātes pīrādziņi** (Map p196; Kaļķu iela 10), quite literally called Mother-in-Law's Pīrāgi. The cute little pasties come stuffed with meat, mushrooms, fruit or cheese.

Pancakes with sweet and savoury toppings and fillings are the reason behind that long lunchtime queue that spills into the street outside **Šetpavārs Vilhelms** (Chef William; Map p196; Šķūņu iela 6), another cafeteria-style place in old Rīga.

Rīgas Balzams (Map p196; ☎ 721 4494; Torņa iela 4) Not ordering at least one shot or cocktail made from black Balzāms is sacrilege at this intimate bar. The ambience is warm and tingling, just like you'll feel inside after partaking of the potent elixir. The bar attracts a mix of tourists, diplomats and well-dressed locals, all looking to have a good time.

Orange Bar (Map p196; ☎ 722 8423; Jāņu sēta 5) Attracting a mixed crowd, this tiny place is always packed and usually a little crazy; where the beautiful people swig champagne straight from the bottle then dance on tables to alternative grooves.

Klondaika (Map pp192-3; ☎ 724 0366; Dzīrnavu iela 59) This cellar joint serves lots of food and beer, much to the delight of the mainly foreign crowd. This well-loved pub is so extravagantly kitsch you can't help falling for it. With an American West theme (cow skulls and wagon wheels), it also boasts one of the best people-watching patios in town. Inside you'll find slots, billiards.

Pulkvedim neviens neraksta (No-one Writes to the Colonel; Map p196; ☎ 721 3886; Peldu iela 26/28) An old favourite that's still going strong, this is a bar and disco rolled into one. Dedicated party animals dance the night away to alternative grooves in the industrial digs up top or amid the trippy colours down below.

THE AUTHOR'S CHOICE

Skyline (Map pp192-3; ☎ 777 2222; Elizabetes iela 55) Sky high on the 26th floor of the Reval Hotel Latvija, Skyline is a must for every first-time visitor to the capital. The crowd is glam and the city view is nothing short of stunning. Window tables are hard to score, but with enough patience you're likely to snag one at some point.

B-bārs (Map p196; ☎ 722 8841; Doma laukums 2) An inviting place with well-spaced brown leather couches and chairs, Rīga's second Balsams bar is a hot spot these days. Filled with trendsetters, it serves some of the best cocktails in town, especially ones made with Latvia's national drink.

Paldies Dievam piektdiena ir klāt (Thank God It's Friday; Map pp192-3; ☎ 750 3964; 11 Novembra krastmala 9) A Caribbean bar-cum-restaurant in Old Town, it's favoured for its imaginative and exhaustive cocktail menu and the bikini-clad women dancing on the bar.

Dickens Pub (Map p196; ☎ 721 3087; Grēcinieku iela 9/1) This British pub is where most Anglophone expats kick off a night out. Guinness/Kilkenny costs 1.70/1.60Ls a pint. Loud and rowdy, it's popular with stag parties.

TOP FIVE RĪGA BEER GARDENS

When the snow begins to melt and the days grow longer, Old Town fills with merry revellers pounding pints well into the white summer nights under the tents and umbrellas of Rīga's numerous beer gardens. The cigarette smoke is thick, the gossip juicy, the heat lamps warm and the vibe frenetic. Most of these seasonal watering holes don't have proper names, so we've used the name of the sponsor embossed on the tents to identify our favourites. They are open most of the day and well into the night.

- Head to **Piebalga** (Līvu laukums) if you're looking for attention. This is Rīga's most popular beer garden, and a place where patrons dress to impress. It's often impossible to find a table amid the hubbub, and the service is less than quick, but the vibe is always rowdy and upbeat.
- A bit more sophisticated than its neighbouring establishments, **Capri** (Līvu laukums) is where to go for creamy Italian gelatos, glasses of champagne or shots of Sambuca. In a central, bustling location, it's a great place to just sit back and watch the night unfold.
- The food and brew at **Konventa Sēta** (Jāņu sēta), in St John's Courtyard, is quite good, but the beers are a little overpriced. It's popular with tourists and good for people watching.
- Although not as trendy as it once was, **Doma dārzs** (Doma laukums) has a long cocktail menu, making it the obvious choice for those not interested in another pint of ale.
- Sandwiched between two colourful churches, **Labais krasts** (The Right Bank; Anglikāņu 5) is an atmospheric spot with great river views. It appeals to those looking to have a quiet drink away from the deafening crowds.

LATVIA

LATVIA

Paddy Whelan's (Map p196; ☎ 721 0249; Grēcinieku iela 4) Rīga's first Irish pub pours pints of Aldaris to Latvian youngsters downstairs, while older foreigners down glasses of Guinness upstairs. Good pub grub, sports on the telly and bands are other drawcards.

Barons Sports Bar (Map pp192-3; ☎ 729 9707; K Barona iela 108) Rīga's biggest sports bar, this place takes up three floors and is filled with TVs, including a huge screen in the back where clients can bet on live matches. It's the place to go to sip pints and catch the game.

de Lacy's (Map p196; ☎ 722 9045; Skūņu iela 4) Rīga's latest expat watering hole, this Irish pub packs in crowds nightly. Sports jerseys hang from the ceilings and patrons can sip Guinness while watching sport on the telly behind the bar.

Melnais kaķis (Map p196; ☎ 781 4190; Raiņa bulvāris 15) A slick spot at any time of night, the Black Cat was recently renovated and now boasts classy, colourful environs and a potent cocktail menu. The kitchen stays open all night.

ENTERTAINMENT

Rīga has a giddying entertainment and cultural scene. Upcoming events are listed in the *Baltic Times*, *Rīga in Your Pocket* and *Rīga This Week*. If you'd rather have someone else arrange your big night out, **Rīga by Night** (☎ 927 6072) does a city bar and club tour four times nightly for €50 per person. There's no office, so call to book.

Nightclubs

Far & Gate (Map p196; ☎ 722 1221; Mārstaļu 6; cover 5Ls) The new kid on the clubbing block, Far & Gate is quickly becoming the town's hottest spot. Upstairs the place is an ultrahip, retro-meets-modern joint, with eccentric lighting, Art-Nouveau décor and crazy plastic chairs. In the basement you'll find a dance floor and dark corners for discreet cuddling.

Četri balti krekli (Map p196; ☎ 721 3885; Vecpilsētas iela 12; cover 5Ls) Literally 'Four White Shirts', this is the top place to listen to Latvian rock bands. It's popular with well-known local writers and artists.

Bites Blūzs Klubs (Map pp192-3; ☎ 733 3125; Dzirnavu iela 34a; Fri & Sat cover 3Ls) For a taste of the blues in the Baltics, head to this unpretentious club. Dark and smoky, you'd never call it trendy. The patrons here are more interested in listening to the fabulous live acts, some hailing from as far away as New Orleans, than worrying about the hip factor.

Groks (Map p196; ☎ 721 6381; Kaļķu iela 12; cover 2Ls) A flashback to life under communism. The modern club is decked out as a Soviet train, complete with the cloakroom in a re-created train compartment and the DJ in the driver's cabin. It's popular with young Russians who come to drink and dance to pounding techno.

Voodoo (Map pp192-3; ☎ 777 2355; Elizabetes 55; cover 3-5Ls) Inside the Reval Hotel Latvija, this African-themed small club is one of Rīga's poshest. Dress to impress. The patrons are mostly the stylish, well-heeled local and expat variety. The music varies, but there's never techno. No one under 21 allowed.

Indigo (Map pp192-3; ☎ 728 4263; K Barona iela 31; Fri & Sat cover 2Ls) Off the main clubbing circuit, this is a very local joint attracting a slightly older crowd. The music is a mix of Russian top 40 and smash pop hits.

Nautilus (Map p196; ☎ 781 4477; Kungu iela 8; cover 3-8Ls; 🕑 10pm-7am Wed-Sat) In the same building as a Japanese restaurant, Nautilus is throbbing hot spot inside a faux submarine. There's a chill-out room with plush red couches, a frantic dance floor and a little too much uniformed security.

XXL (Map pp192-3; ☎ 728 2276; Kalniņa iela 4) Rīga's sole gay club and video bar makes no bones about the 'face kontrole' that bouncers rigorously exercise at the door. If you make it inside, you'll find a thriving disco on Friday and Saturday nights, go-go dancers and plenty of dark rooms to get cosy.

Classical Music

Great Guild (Lielā ģilde; Map p196; ☎ 721 3643; Amatu iela 6; tickets 2-7Ls; box office 🕑 noon-6pm & 2hr before performances) The main concert hall of the renowned Latvia National Symphonic Orchestra hosts numerous other concerts too.

Wagner Hall (Vāgnera Zālē; Map p196; ☎ 721 0814; Vāgnera iela 4; box office 🕑 noon-3pm & 4-7pm) Chamber and solo concerts are often held at Wagner Hall.

The Dome Cathedral's acoustics, as well as its huge organ, are spectacular (see p191) and the twice-weekly evening organ concerts (Wednesday and Friday at 7pm) are well worth attending. Tickets (1Ls to 3Ls) and concert programmes are available from the cathedral **ticket office** (☎ 721 32 13; 🕑 noon-3pm & 4-7pm), opposite the western door of the

Wagner Hall box office and 30 minutes before performances start.

Cinemas

Films are generally shown in their original language – often English – with Latvian or Russian subtitles. Tickets cost about 2.50Ls; some cinemas give 10% discounts to ISIC cardholders. Call ☎ 722 2222 or 777 0777 (English spoken) to find out what's showing where. On the Internet, see www.filmas.lv and www.baltcinema.lv.

There are several cinemas:

Daile (Map pp192-3; ☎ 728 3854; K Barona iela 31) Mainstream fare.

Kino 52 (Map pp192-3; ☎ 728 8778; Lāčplēsa iela 52-54) Also mainstream.

Kino Suns (Map pp192-3; ☎ 728 5411; Elizabetes iela 83-85) Artsy cinema.

Kinogalerija (Map p196; ☎ 722 9030; Jaun iela 24) Hosts the British Film Club on Friday.

Opera, Ballet & Theatre

Ballet, opera and theatre break for summer holidays, around June to September.

National Opera House (Map p196; information ☎ 707 37777; www.opera.lv; Aspazijas bulvāris 3; tickets 1-10Ls; box office 10am-7pm) The home of the highly rated Rīga Ballet, where Mikhail Baryshnikov made his name. Performances start most nights at 7pm.

There are several theatres:

Daile Theatre (Dailes teātris; Map pp192-3; ☎ 727 0278; Brīvības iela 75) Stages plays in Latvian.

New Riga Theatre (Rīgas jaunais teātris; Map pp192-3; ☎ 728 0765; www.jrt.lv; Lāčplēsa iela 25) Plays in Latvian.

Russian Drama Theatre (Krievu drāmas teātris; Map p196; ☎ 722 5395; www.trd.lv; Kaļķu iela 16) Plays in Russian.

Circus

Circus (Cirks; Map pp192-3; ☎ 721 3279; circusRīga@apollo.lv; Merķela iela 4; tickets 1-3Ls; shows twice daily Fri-Sun Oct-Apr) Rīga's permanent circus is close to the train station.

Sport

Football is the most popular spectator sport (posters around town announce big games), followed closely by basketball. The city's leading football clubs, PFK Daugava and FC Skonto, play at Rīga's 5000-seater **Daugava Sports House** (Daugavas Sporta Nams; Map p188; ☎ 727 2030; K Barona iela 107); and the **Skonto Stadium** (Map p188; ☎ 702 0909; E Melngaila iela 1a), which holds 8300. Ice hockey is played at the **Arena Rīga** (Map p188; ☎ 738 8200; www.arenaRīga.com; Skanstes iela 21), a multipurpose arena built for the 2006 World Ice Hockey Championships.

SHOPPING

Street sellers peddle their wares – amber trinkets, knitwear, paintings and Russian dolls – outside St Peter's Church on Skarnu iela and along the southern end of Valņu iela. Rīga's large crafts fair, the Gadatirgus, is held on the first weekend in June.

Berga bazārs (Map pp192-3; Dzirnavu iela 84) Literally 'Bergs Bazaar', this upmarket mall was built in the late 19th century by Kristaps Bergs (1840–1907), and reconstructed in the late 1990s. The maze of courtyards, sandwiched between Elizabētes, Marijas and Dzirnavu, has fine boutiques and galleries.

Nordwear (Map p196; ☎ 750 3546; www.nordwear.com; Kaļķu iela 2) This is where Australian-born Aldis Tilēns sells Nordic wool sweaters patterned with tiny Latvian symbols and other 'amber-free' souvenirs.

Latvijas Balzams (Map pp192-3; ☎ 722 8715; Marijas iela 1) This place sells Latvian Balzāms and other alcohol.

Centrs Universālveikals (Map p196; cnr Valņu iela & Audēju iela) In Old Town, this is the only department store. A large branch of the newspaper and magazine shop, Narvesen, is on the ground floor.

Among the mind-boggling plethora of craft and souvenir shops in Rīga, consider shopping at the following:

A&E Gallery (Map p196; Jaun iela 17) Off Doma laukums, this is the place to shop for amber. It's a favourite with visiting dignitaries and celebs.

Musikas salons (Map p196; Audēju iela 6) Latvian rock, pop and classical music.

Sakta (Aspazijas iela 30) Latvian flags and wooden jewellery.

Senā Klēts (Merķeļa iela 13) Latvian national costumes.

Upe (Map p196; Vāgnera iela 5) Folk music, traditional instruments and unusual toys beautifully carved from wood.

GETTING THERE & AWAY

See p393 for links with countries outside the Baltics.

Air

Rīga Airport (Lidosta Rīga; ☎ 720 7009; www.riga-airport.com) is at Skulte, about 8km west of the city centre. Most major European airlines have an office here, including Latvia's national

CENTRAL MARKET

Whatever your heart desires – be it CDs, a pig's head, bloodied sheep carcasses or Ecuadorian bananas – Rīga's bustling, colourful central market will supply them in abundance. As well as being a fantastic place for cheap shopping, this colourful collage of people and products is a worthy attraction in itself. It is one of Europe's largest markets and also its most ancient, dating back at least to the city's founding in 1201.

Rīga's market was not always so large – nor was it always in its present location. Historians believe that a tiny market operated along the banks of the Daugava in the Dark Ages. When German crusaders, on a northward sweep, founded Rīga in 1201, this fledgling market logically relocated within the new city.

A 1330 manuscript provides the first written reference, alluding to the market near the Dome Cathedral being moved to what is now called Latviesu strēlnieku laukums (Latvian Riflemen Square), east of Akmens Bridge. The market remained in Riflemen Sq until 1570, when it was moved to the banks of the Daugava to facilitate trading along the river.

The market stayed on the Daugava banks for more than 350 years. Its growth corresponded to that of Rīga itself. By the mid-1600s when Rīga, then under Swedish rule, outgrew Stockholm, the market flourished with over 1000 merchants trading goods from all over the region. But in 1930 the market was moved once more, to its present location by the train and bus stations. This final move was prompted by the need to have the market closer to the railway, which had replaced the river as the principal route for trade. Confronted with the market's vast size, the city of Rīga decided to bring in five enormous zeppelin hangars from the town of Vainode in western Latvia. At a cost of 5 million lati, these hangars – each 35m high – were erected on the current site between 1924 and 1930. All told, the hangars provide 57,000 sq metres of space for up to 1250 sellers and – crucially – central heating for Rīga's long, cold winters.

When Latvia was absorbed into the Soviet Union, the market shrank briefly, but it rebounded with produce from the southern Soviet republics. These days it is larger than ever, seemingly bursting at the seams. If you get lost wandering through the forest of carcasses and cheese in the mammoth zeppelin hangars, don't despair – you're not the first.

carrier, **AirBaltic** (Map p196; ☎ 720 7777; www.airbaltic.com; airport & Kaļķu iela 15). Its Estonian counterpart, **Estonian Air** (Map p196; ☎ 721 4860; www.estonian-air.ee; Kaļķu iela 15) is in town.

AirBaltic flies twice daily Monday to Friday to/from Tallinn (code-sharing with Estonian Air) and twice a day Tuesday to Thursday to/from Vilnius. Return fares to Tallinn/Vilnius start at 76/75Ls (three-day advance purchase, maximum stay of five days).

Boat

Rīga's **ferry terminal** (Map pp192-3; ☎ 732 9882; www.rop.lv; Eksporta iela 1) is about 1.5km downstream (north) of Akmens Bridge. It is served by a twice-weekly ferry to/from Kiel, Germany. Tickets are sold at the **Hanza Maritime Agency** (Map pp192-3; ☎ 732 3569; www.hanza.lv; Eksporta iela 3a). There is also a twice-weekly ferry to/from Lübeck, Germany.

Between mid-April and mid-September the Max Mols ferry sails every second day between Nynashamn, 60km south of Stockholm, and Rīga. For fare details, see p403.

The service is operated by **Rīgas Jūras Līnija** (RJL; Rīga Sea Line; Map pp192-3; ☎ 720 5460; www.rigasealine.lv; Eksporta iela 3a). Ferry tickets are also sold at travel agencies (see p190).

In January 2006 Tallinn-based Tallink started ferry operations between Rīga and Stockholm; check with the tourist office for more details.

Andrejosta (Map pp192-3; ☎ 732 3225; support.rsc@apollo.lv; Eksporta iela 1a), Rīga's yacht centre, rents out yachts from 10Ls per day. It has a mooring depth of up to 4m.

Bus

Buses to/from other towns and cities use Rīga's **international bus station** (Rīgas starptautiskā autoosta; Map pp192-3; www.autoosta.lv; Prāgas iela 1), behind the railway embankment just beyond the southern edge of Old Town. Up-to-date timetables and fares are displayed in the station (with final destination and departure platforms) and on the bus station's well-organised website. Most staff in the **information office** (izziņas; ☎ 900 0009) speak English.

Ecolines (☎ 721 4512; www.ecolines.lv) has an office at the bus station and another called **Norma-A** (Map pp192-3; ☎ 727 4444; A Čaka iela 45) in town. It runs weekly services to/from Bremerhaven in Germany, Brussels, Kyiv, London, Moscow, Paris and Prague (for details, see p396).

Weekly buses to Berlin and other cities in Germany, St Petersburg (via Jēkabpils and Rēzekne) and Kaliningrad are operated by **Eurolines** (☎ 721 4080; www.eurolines.lv), based at the bus station. Eurolines also runs daily inter-regional services to/from Valga (4.50Ls, 3¼ hours, one daily), Tartu (8.50Ls, 4¾ hours, one daily), Tallinn (8.50Ls, 5¼ hours, five daily), Vilnius (6Ls, five hours, four daily), Kaunas (6Ls, 3½ hours, one daily) and Klaipėda (6Ls, six hours, twice daily).

The bus services within Latvia include, among others, the following:

Bauska 1.20Ls, 1½ hours, hourly btwn 5.30am and 5.10pm.
Cēsis 1.30Ls, two hours, hourly btwn 6.30am and 6.55pm.
Daugavpils 3Ls, four hours, up to seven daily.
Jelgava 0.80Ls, one hour, one or two daily.
Kolka 3Ls, 5¾ hours, three daily.
Kuldīga 2.50Ls, three to four hours, six to 10 daily.
Liepāja 3Ls, 3½ hours direct, four to 4½ hours via Kalnciems, five to seven hours via Jelgava or Tukums, hourly between 6.40am and 4.45pm.
Rēzekne 3Ls, 4½ hours, up to six daily.
Sigulda 1Ls, one hour, hourly between 8.15am and 8.10pm.
Talsi 2Ls, 2½ hours, hourly between 7.55am and 8.45pm.
Tukums 1Ls, 1¼ hours, eight daily.
Valka 2Ls, 3¾ hours, up to four daily.
Valmiera 1.50Ls, 2½ hours, hourly between 6.20am and 10.20pm.
Ventspils 3Ls, 2½ to four hours, hourly between 7.05am and 10.30pm.

Car & Motorcycle

Motorists have to pay 5Ls per hour to enter Old Town, payable with a *viedkarte* – a magnetic strip card, sold and recharged at the information desk inside the Centrs Universālveikals (p217) and out of town at the **Statoil** (Map pp192-3; Eksporta iela 1c; 🕒 24hr) petrol station.

Car-hire firms include the following:

Avis Airport (☎ 720 7535); Krasta iela (☎ 722 5876; www.avis.lv; Krasta iela 3)
Budget Airport (☎ 720 7327; www.budget.com)
Europcar Airport (☎ 720 78 25); Basteja bulvāris (☎ 722 2637; www.europ car.lv; Basteja bulvāris 10)
Hertz Airport (☎ 720 7980; www.hertz.com)
Sixt Airport (☎ 720 71 31); Aspazijas bulvāris (☎ 722 4036; www.sixt.lv; Aspazijas bulvāris 8)

Train

Rīga **train station** (centrālā stacija; Map pp192-3; ☎ 583 3095, advance reservations ☎ 721 6664; Stacijas laukums), at the southern end of the park-and-boulevard ring, underwent a €5.8 million face-lift in 2003.

Tickets are sold in the main departures hall: window Nos 1–6 sell tickets for *starptavtiskie vilcieni* (international trains); window Nos 7–9 sell tickets for long-distance *dizeļvilcienci* (diesel trains); and window Nos 10–13 sell tickets for slower *elektrovilcienci* (electric suburban trains).

Staff at the **information desk** (izziņas; ☎ 583 2134) don't appear to be very cooperative – a less frustrating bet for schedules is to consult the train timetable on Latvian Railways' website at www.ldz.lv.

SUBURBAN

There are six suburban lines out of Rīga, served in the main by *elektrovilcienci*. Speedier diesel trains serve some larger suburban stations, like Valmiera.

Ergļi–Suntaži Three trains daily take this line.
Jelgava One or two trains an hour go to Jelgava between 5.40am and 11.05pm. Some long-distance trains to Ventspils, Šiauliai, Kaunas and Vilnius stop at Jelgava too.
Ogre–Krustpils This line follows the Daugava River inland to Krustpils, opposite Jēkabpils. Trains run between 5.10am and 11.12pm. Destinations include Ogre, Lielvārde, Aizkraukle or Krustpils. Long-distance trains heading to Daugavpils, Rēzekne, Zilupe and Moscow also take this line.
Priedaine–Dubulti–Sloka–Ķemeri–Tukums This is the line to take for Jūrmala. Two to five trains an hour leave for each of Ķemeri, Sloka and Tukums II between 5.45am and 11.10pm. All call at Dubulti and most at Majori.
Saulkrasti–Skulte Two to three trains an hour leave for varying destinations, including Skulte and Vecāķi, between 5.52am and 11.08pm.
Sigulda–Cēsis–Valmiera There are four trains daily to Sigulda, two to Cēsis and four to Valmiera. All call at Sigulda; Valmiera trains also call at Cēsis. The long-distance train to St Petersburg also takes this line. This line runs from 5.42am to 10.36pm.

LONG-DISTANCE

The timetable for *atiesanas laiks* (departures) listing the final destination, platform number, name of train and departure time is bang opposite you when you enter the station. To check *pienaksanas laiks* (arrivals), consult the printed timetables on the wall.

It is quicker to get to Tallinn by bus (see p218). There is a slow overnight train to/from Vilnius (6/8/11Ls for a seat/couchette/bunk in four-bed compartment, 7½ hours) via Kaunas (but again, the bus is easier to both places), and an overnight train to St Petersburg (10/20/31Ls for a seat/couchette/bunk in four-bed compartment, 50Ls in 1st class, 12¾ hours) that stops in Krustpils, Rēzekne and a handful of other towns. Other mainline services include the following.

Daugavpils 3Ls, 3½-4¼ hours, four daily.
Liepāja 2.50Ls, five to 5¾ hours, two daily.
Valga via Sigulda, Cēsis & Valmiera 2Ls, three to 3½ hours, one daily.
Ventspils 2.50Ls, 4¾ hours, two daily.

GETTING AROUND

To/From the Airport

Bus 22 runs about every 20 minutes between Rīga airport and the stop on opposite the bus station in central Rīga. Tickets (0.20Ls) are sold by the bus driver. A taxi to the centre should cost no more than 10Ls.

Bicycle

You can hire two wheels from **Trase** (Map pp192-3; ☎ 728 8617; Terbatas iela 34) for 2/1.50Ls for the first/each consecutive hour.

Bus, Tram & Trolleybus

Rīga has 123km of tram lines serving eight different routes and 23 trolleybus lines covering 217km, all operated by TTP. The usual ticket-punching system is used on trams, trolleybuses and buses too, but different tickets are used on each. Tickets cost 0.20Ls, and are sold at most news kiosks and by the driver. City transport runs daily from 5.30am to 12.30am. Some routes have an hourly night service. Updated timetables are posted on TTP's website (www.ttp.lv).

Taxi

Officially, taxis charge 0.30Ls per kilometre (0.40Ls between 10pm and 6am), but as a foreigner you could get ripped off. Insist on the meter running before you set off. There are taxi ranks outside the bus and train stations, at the airport and in front of the major hotels.

AROUND RĪGA

A bounty of white-sand beaches and a WWII concentration camp where the earth still groans (or, rather, beats) lie within easy reach of Rīga.

Jūrmala

pop 56,000

Latvia's version of the French Riviera, Jūrmala (Seashore) is the name of a string of small towns and resorts stretching 20km along the coast west of Rīga. Vehicles clog the roads on summer days when it seems everyone from day-tripping Rīgans to families on holiday from far-flung country villages descends on Jūrmala for serious fun in the sun. In fact, beautiful fresh air and a relaxed atmosphere have drawn vacationers in droves since the 19th century. In Soviet times 300,000 visitors a year from all over the USSR flooded in to boarding houses, holiday homes and sanatoriums owned by trade unions and other institutions. Today Jūrmala's long, sandy beaches backed by dunes and woods of pine and its shady streets lined with low-rise wooden houses are only

...THE EARTH GROANS

Between 1941 and 1944 about 45,000 Jews from Rīga and about 55,000 other people, including Jews from other Nazi-occupied countries and prisoners of war, were murdered in the Nazi concentration camp at Salaspils, 15km southeast of Rīga. Giant, gaunt sculptures stand as a memorial on the site, which stretches over 0.4 sq km. The inscription on the huge concrete bunker, which forms the memorial's centrepiece, reads 'Behind this gate the earth groans' – a line from a poem written by the Latvian writer Eizens Veveris, who was imprisoned in the camp. Inside the bunker a small exhibition recounts the horrors of the camp. In its shadow lies a 6m-long block of polished stone with a metronome inside, ticking a haunting heartbeat, which never stops.

To get there from Rīga, take a suburban train on the Ogre–Krustpils line to Dārziņi (not Salaspils) station. A path leads from the station to the *piemineklis* (memorial), about a 15-minute walk.

slightly less packed. Although once polluted, the beaches at Majori and Bulduri have been cleaned up in recent years; the water, while quite cold, is safe for swimming.

During Soviet times the Rīga–Jūrmala highway, Latvia's only six-laner, was dubbed '10 minutes in America' because local films set in the USA were always filmed on it.

ORIENTATION

Jūrmala lies between the coast, which faces north, and the Lielupe River, which flows parallel to the coast, 1km or 2km inland. The Lielupe finally empties into the Gulf of Rīga 9km west of the mouth of the Daugava. The main townships that make up Jūrmala are, from the eastern (Rīga) end: Priedaine (inland), Lielupe, Bulduri, Dzintari, Majori, Dubulti, Jaundubulti, Pumpuri, Melluži, Asari, Vaivari, Kauguri (on the coast) and Sloka (2km inland). The busiest part is the 4km to 5km between Bulduri and Dubulti, centred on Majori and Dzintari.

Majori's main thoroughfare is the 1km-long, pedestrianised Jomas iela, where you'll be able to find most lodging, restaurants and bars. A number of streets and paths lead through the woods on the left, heading northwards, to the beach.

INFORMATION

Datorklubs (☎ 781 1411; Jomas iela 62; per hr 0.60Ls; ⌚ 24hr) In Majori; Internet access.

Latvijas Unibanka (Jomas iela 46) One of several Majori ATMs.

Post office (Jomas iela 2) In front of the town hall.

Tourist office (☎ 776 4676; www.jurmala.lv; Jomas iela 42; ⌚ 9am-5pm Mon-Fri Oct-May, 9am-5pm Mon-Fri, 9.30am-5pm Sat & Sun Jun-Sep) Sells maps, provides info, and arranges accommodation and guided tours. Distributes the free *Jūrmala This Week*, a quarterly listings guide.

SIGHTS & ACTIVITIES

Walking along the beach, over dunes and through the woods before popping into a couple of cafés are reason enough to come to Jūrmala. Dubulti is its oldest township, while the highest **sand dunes** are at Lielupe. Further west, Vaivari is home to the wet and wonderful **Nemo Water Park** (Nemo ūdens atrakciju parks; ☎ 773 6392; www.nemo.lv; Atbalss iela 1; admission before/after 8pm & all day Mon 5/2.50Ls; ⌚ 11am-11pm Mon-Thu & Sun, to 4am Fri & Sat May-Sep), with five waterslides, a sauna and two heated pools right on the beach. The centre also rents bicycles for 5Ls per hour. For more on another Jūrmala water park, Līvu Akvaparks, see p209.

In Majori, north off Jomas iela, is poet Jānis Rainis' country cottage, where he died in 1929; now the **Rainis & Aspazija Memorial Summer Cottage** (Raiņa un Asparijas vasarnīca; ☎ 766 4295; Pliekšāna iela 5-7; adult/child 0.50/0.30Ls ⌚ 10am-6pm Wed-Sun), it showcases various exhibitions and houses Rainis' personal library. Across Jomas iela, in the **Jūrmala City Museum** (Jūrmalas pilsētas muzejs; ☎ 776 4746; Tirgoņu iela 29; adult/child 0.50/0.20Ls; ⌚ 11am-5pm Wed-Sun), you can view works by local artists and learn how the resort has developed since the 19th century.

Anyone who makes it as far as Buļļuciems, the tiny town beyond Lielupe, will be rewarded by the intriguing open-air **Fishery Museum** (Jūraslīcis; ☎ 775 1121; Tiklu iela 1a; admission free; ⌚ 10am-6pm Mon-Sat). It has exhibits (with Latvian captions) about the region's fishing history, displayed in small cottages and linked by a planked wooden walking path.

SLEEPING

Jūrmala is a spread-out place, so you may have to put in a bit of legwork to find a room. The tourist office can usually guide you to accommodation in your price bracket. It also keeps a list of families that rent private rooms and can help with apartment rentals for longer stays.

Budget

Dzintaru (☎ 775 4539; iestātnes 6-14; s/d/ste 11/14/30Ls; P) In Dzintari, this former Soviet monster doesn't sport a sign, but it's a great deal for those travelling on a shoestring. The reception and hallways are drab, but rooms, while sparsely furnished, are clean and have private bathrooms. Splurge on a renovated suite – these are spacious and include refrigerators and TVs.

Kempings Nemo (☎ 773 6392; www.nemo.lv; Atbalss iela 1; cottages 5-24Ls, camp sites 1Ls plus per person 1Ls; P) Adjoining the Nemo Water Park in Vaivari and right on the beach, this place sports little wooden cottages as well as green grass on which to pitch tents.

Midrange & Top End

Jūrmala has many lovely small hotels and even a swanky high-end spa resort to choose

LATVIA

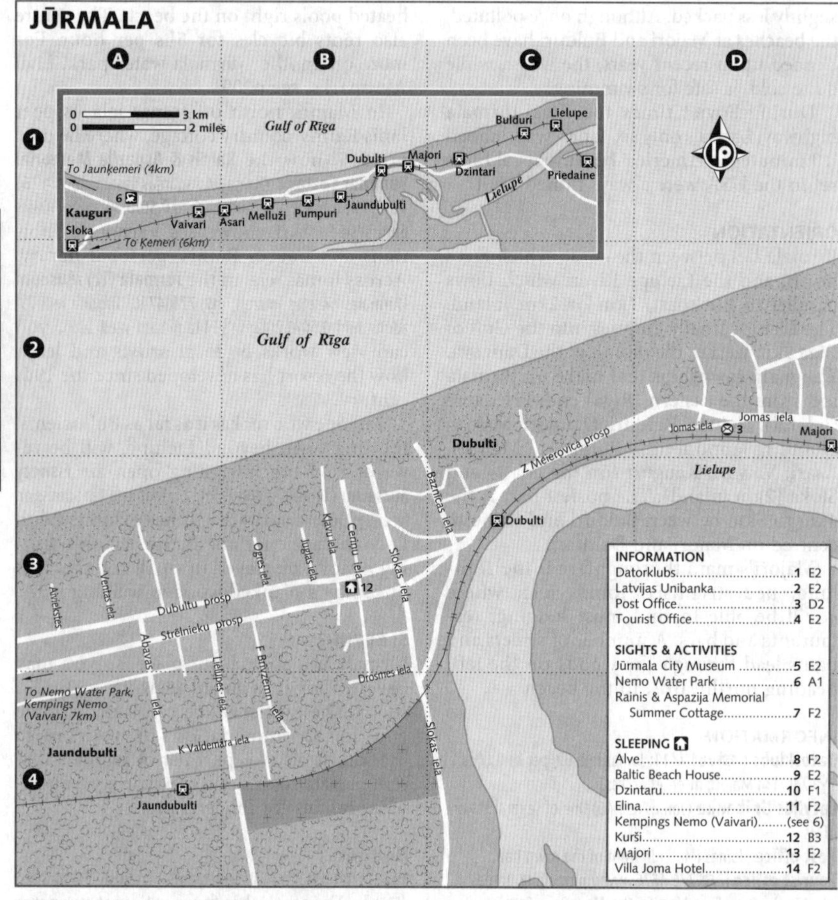

from. Unless otherwise noted, breakfast is included at the following places.

Villa Joma Hotel (☎ 777 1999; www.villajoma.lv; Jomas iela 90; r from 40Ls; P) This boutique hotel is great value. The airy, immaculate rooms are all different, but a minimalist theme presides throughout. Try for a room with a skylight. The breakfasts are fabulous: you get to choose from the restaurant menu.

Baltic Beach House (☎ 777 1400; www.balticbeach.lv; Jūras iela 23-25; s 50-100Ls, d 55-120Ls; P) Right on the beach, Jūrmala's showcase swanky establishment somehow manages to cater to all budgets. The most expensive rooms have luxury furnishings, satellite TV, bathrobes and sea-view balconies. The cheapest have Soviet-era trappings and no air-con, but are comfortable, and a good deal to boot. Amenities include a top-notch spa, tennis courts and a good restaurant.

Alve (☎ 775 5971; www.alve.times.lv; Jomas iela 88A; s/d 45/55Ls; P) The handrails are made from braided rope at this chichi place with an eclectic interior design. Rooms come with nice linens and Scandinavian-style light-wood furnishings. Spa treatments and steam baths are available.

Elina (☎ 776 1665; www.elinahotel.lv; Lienes iela 43; d from 25Ls; P) Often fully booked, Elina has 24 rooms of varying size. All are simple, but cheery, and come with TVs. The attached café and friendly English- and German-speaking staff are pluses at this family run hotel. Breakfast is not included.

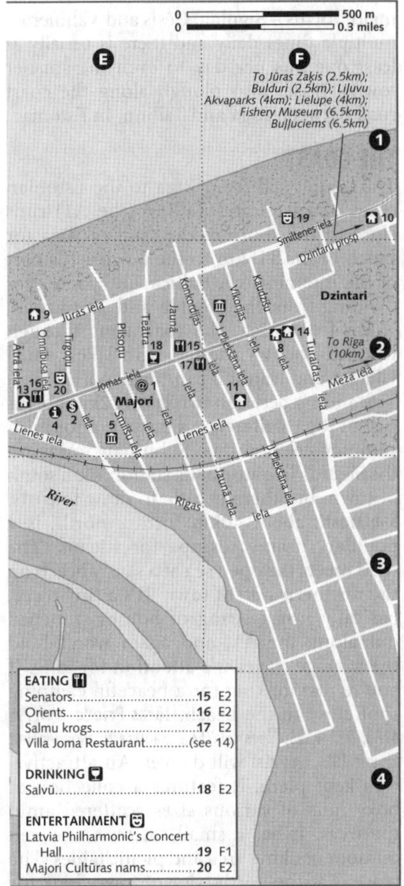

Kursi (☎ 777 1606; www.augstceltne.lv; Dubultu prospekts 30; apt 40-75Ls; P 💻) In Dubulti, this pleasant place has modern two-storey apartments. They come with kitchens, microwaves and satellite TV. Rates depend on size. Prices drop in low season.

Majori (☎ 776 1380; www.majori.lv; Jomas iela 29; s/d 35/50Ls; P) It's got a bold paint job, but rooms aren't quite as glam as you'd expect from a place with such a swanky lobby. Done up in a sort of retro '70s style, the digs are smallish but feature big bathrooms with old tubs. It's not bad if other places are full.

EATING & DRINKING

Every second building on Jomas iela offers an eating or drinking option. In summer the street is lined with beer tents and pavement-terrace bars and cafés. Jūrmala is a year-round resort, and most places are open.

Villa Joma Restaurant (☎ 777 1999; Jomas iela 90; meals 6-12Ls) The food is fabulous at this restaurant attached to the hotel of the same name. The gourmet menu is Western and seafood oriented, quite eclectic and very reasonably priced. Try the crab soup; it's mouth-watering.

Orients (☎ 776 2082; Jomas iela 33; meals 4-10Ls) A Middle Eastern restaurant with a great pavement terrace in Majori, Orients is well worth a nibble. It's definitely got the most eclectic décor in town – sort of French bistro meets Asian-style bar with an electronic buffalo head thrown in for good measure.

Salmu krogs (☎ 776 1393; Jomas iela 70/72; meals 4-10Ls) This charming, rustic bar is topped with a thatched roof and plenty of wooden benches around shared tables. Meats are grilled outside on the terrace and the place emits delicious smells. There's a long cocktail menu and a decent wine list.

Jūras Zaķis (Sea Rabbit; ☎ 775 3005; Vienības prospekts 1; meals 6Ls) In Bulduri, the Sea Rabbit is a good place to try local fish. Fishing nets suspended from the ceiling and weathered wooden furniture support the seafaring theme. The restaurant is about 30m from the beach.

Senators (☎ 781 1163; Jomas iela 55; meals 5-10Ls) A charming little place with a glass-enclosed patio and lots of greenery along with outdoor seating in a prime people-watching locale, Senators features a large menu with pizza, pastas, sandwiches, meats and seafood.

Salvū (☎ 776 1401; Jomas iela 57; meals 4-9Ls) Jūrmala's late-night hot spot, this place offers a big and airy covered patio for drinking or dining on Russian favourites and a second-storey nightclub that rocks late into the night. There is live music on weekends.

ENTERTAINMENT

In summer there are discos several nights a week in and around Majori. Look out for flyers on billboards down Jomas iela. Nemo Water Park (p221) organises pop concerts, disco nights and raves on summer weekends.

Majori Culture House (Majori Cultūras nams; ☎ 776 2403; Jomas iela 35) The Majori Culture House hosts films, music concerts and various art and craft exhibitions.

Latvia Philharmonic's Concert Hall (Dzintari Koncertzāle; Turaidas iela) At the northern beach end of Turaidas iela, this hall hosts a season of summer concerts from June to August.

GETTING THERE & AWAY

Between 5.45am and 11.10pm, two to five trains per hour run from Rīga to Jūrmala along the Ķemeri–Tukums line (see p219). All stop at Dubulti (0.50Ls, 35 minutes), but not all stop at Majori (0.50Ls, 40 minutes) and other stations.

Motorists driving into Jūrmala have to pay a toll of 1Ls per day, at self-service machines at control posts either end of the resort. Bicycle tracks wind through pine forests from Rīga to Jūrmala; ask at the tourist office or bike-hire places in Rīga for details.

GETTING AROUND

You can use trains to go from one part of Jūrmala to another. There are also buses along the main roads. The Nemo Water Park (p221) hires bicycles.

VIDZEME

With a heady mix of long sandy stretches of unspoilt, wild coastline, ancient forested valleys sprinkled with historic castles and deep ravines, tranquil and alluring small towns and the wondrous Gauja Valley, Vidzeme is Latvia's most scenically enticing region.

After Rīga, Vidzeme, embracing the northeast, is the country's biggest tourism draw. If you only have time to explore one region in Latvia, we'd suggest heading here. Be warned though: the intoxicating scent of pine forest in the exquisite Gauja National Park, could make you dizzy. The sight of castle turrets peeping through dense woodland in Sigulda may seduce you into extending your stay. An outdoor enthusiast's paradise, there is always something to see and do. Ride the country's only operating narrow-gauge railway through bucolic countryside, frolic in the watery playground known as the Vidzeme Upland, canoe down a fat, lazy river or check out one of the fabulous medieval town's – Cēsis is our favourite.

Getting There & Away

Vidzeme is accessible by private vehicle, bus or train. Buses and trains serve the region's major towns – Sigulda, Cēsis and Valmiera – multiple times daily and there is usually at least one bus per day to even the smaller towns. Buses also plough along the coast road between Rīga and Tallinn, in Estonia.

THE COAST

The main road from Rīga to the Estonian cities of Pärnu and Tallinn (the A1) runs close to the shore of the Gulf of Rīga for much of the 115km to the border. It's part of the infamous via Baltica, and soon after dividing from the Sigulda and Tartu road, 15km from Rīga, the road runs through wooded country, dotted with lakes, small villages and tranquil camping spots.

Standing between two lakes 12km northeast of Rīga, **Baltezers** is a busy spot for midsummer celebrations. Suburban trains on the Sigulda line stop at its station, 3km south of town, but there is little to draw tourists. **Saulkrasti**, about 40km further north, is a popular summer escape for Rīgans. The road meets the open sea at a sandy beach on the northern side of town. It's a tiny place, basically just a string of houses stretched out along the A1, and again won't hold the average traveller's attention for long. If you're just looking for a peaceful camping spot close to the beach, **Jūras Priede** (☎ 795 4780, 922 7523; Ūpes iela 56a, Saulkrasti; wooden hut around 10Ls, tent 2Ls) will deliver. An attractive, well-kept place, it features a collection of boxy huts of various sizes scattered amid the trees. It has a small cafeteria, covered outdoor cooking area and picnic tables. The place is at the north edge of town; look for the sign north of the bridge after crossing the Aga River.

The area's most substantial town, **Salacgrīva** sits on a harbour at the mouth of the Salaca River. It's still a blink-or-you'll-miss-it type of place, not really worth going out of your way to visit, but if you're hungry on the way to Estonia it makes a good lunch stop. The **tourist office** (☎ 404 1254; Rīgas iela 10a; 🕑 10am-4.30pm Mon-Fri) runs tours to Livonian sacrificial caves on the coast. **Zvejnieku Sēta** (Rīgas iela 1, Salacgrīva; meals 2-6Ls) is a friendly restaurant, with a pleasing, rustic old-time seafaring vibe – creaky wood floors, a fishing boat moored outside and nets draped across the terrace. The menu is mostly seafood oriented, although it does sandwiches, soups and salads. The food is hearty and surprisingly tasty.

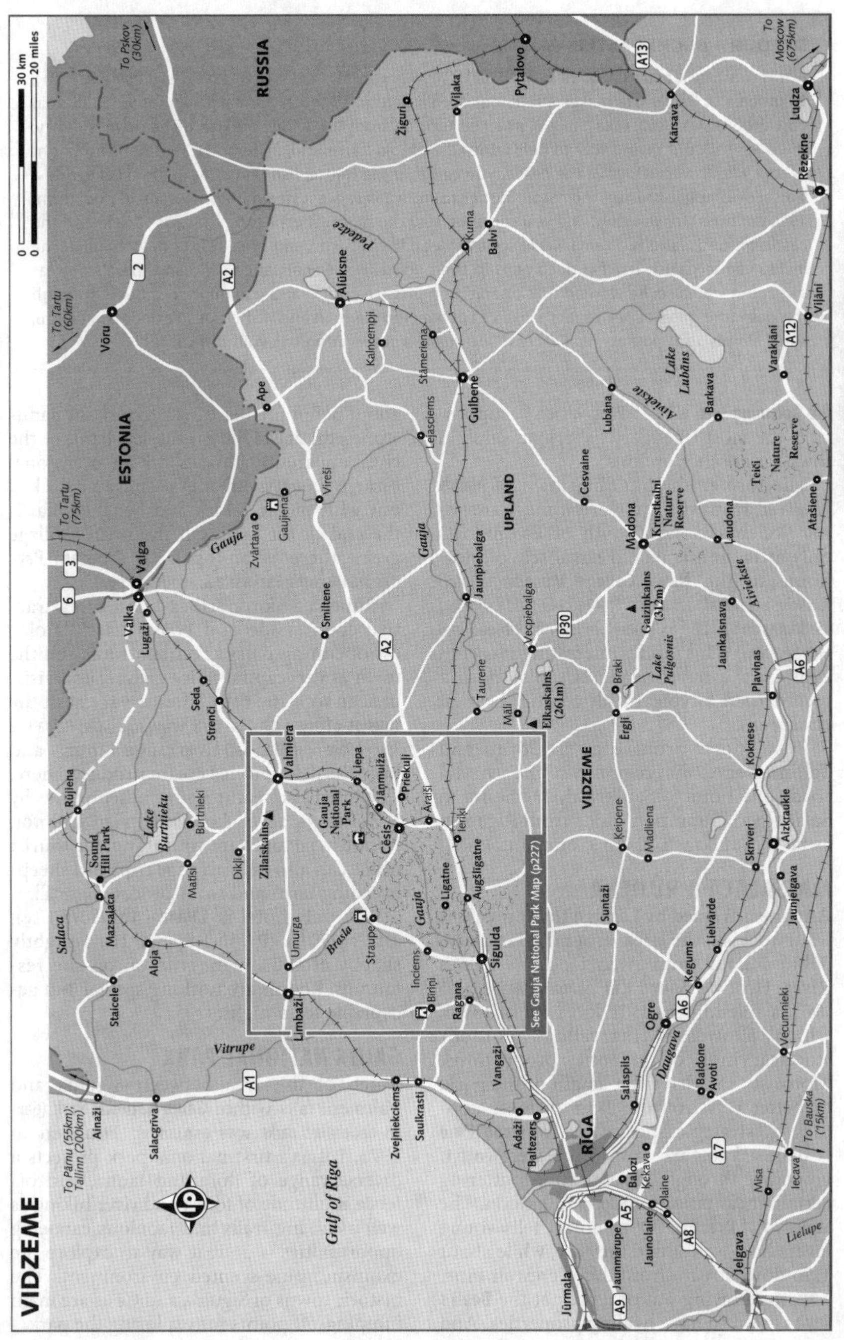
VIDZEME
0 30 km
0 20 miles
ESTONIA
RUSSIA
To Pskov (30km)
To Tartu (60km)
To Tartu (75km)
To Pärnu (55km); Tallinn (200km)
To Moscow (675km)
To Bauska (15km)
Võru
Valga
Valka
Lugaži
Ape
Alūksne
Pededze
Kalncempji
Stāmeriena
Gulbene
Lejasciems
Vireši
Gaujiena
Zvārtava
Gauja
Smiltene
Seda
Strenči
Rūjiena
Sound Hill Park
Lake Burtnieku
Burtnieki
Mazsalaca
Salaca
Matīši
Dikļi
Zilaiskalns
Valmiera
Liepa
Jānmuiža
Priekuļi
Gauja National Park
Cēsis
Āraiši
Ieriķi
Straupe
Brasla
Ligatne
Augšlīgatne
Umurga
Limbaži
Aloja
Staicele
Ainaži
Salacgrīva
Vitrupe
Inciems
Biriņi
Ragana
Sigulda
See Gauja National Park Map (p227)
Zvejniekciems
Saulkrasti
Vangaži
Adaži
Baltezers
Gulf of Rīga
RĪGA
Jūrmala
Jaunmārupe
Jaunolaine
Olaine
Ķekava
Baloži
Salaspils
Daugava
Ogre
Ķegums
Lielvārde
Baldone
Avoti
Vecumnieki
Iecava
Misa
Jelgava
Lielupe
Skrīveri
Aizkraukle
Jaunjelgava
Koknese
Pļaviņas
Suntaži
Madliena
Ķeipene
VIDZEME
Ērgļi
Braki
Lake Pulgosnis
Mālī
Elkaskalns (261m)
Taurene
Vecpiebalga
Jaunpiebalga
Gaiziņkalns (312m)
Jaunkalsnava
Aiviekste
Madona
Krustkalni Nature Reserve
Laudona
Cesvaine
UPLAND
Lubāna
Lake Lubāns
Barkava
Teiči Nature Reserve
Atašiene
Varakļāni
Viļāni
Rēzekne
Ludza
Kārsava
Pytalovo
Viļaka
Žīguri
Balvi
Kurna
A1
A2
A5
A6
A7
A8
A9
A12
A13
P30
2
3
6

DETOUR – BĪRIŅI CASTLE

A trip to **Bīriņi Castle** (Bīriņu pils; ☎ 406 6316; www.birinupils.lv; admission & tour 0.80Ls, r from 34Ls; P), 17km east of Saulkrasti, makes a fabulous scenic detour. To reach the baronial manor, built amid vast grounds in 1860, take the well-marked turn-off from the A1 in Saulkrasti. The drive is pretty: the trees thin out giving way to fields dotted with old barns and, in summer, mesmerising bright yellow wildflowers. Once at the castle, you can tour the house; fish and boat in Bīriņi Lake; ride a horse; or simply picnic on the magnificent grounds. There are a steam bath, sauna and pool (from 19Ls per hour) for relaxing, and you can even stay the night. The 11-room hotel is situated on the castle grounds, and is a remarkable spot to sleep like a baron and breakfast beneath vaults. The inside of the palace itself is decorated in the original neo-Renaissance style and there's a great sweeping staircase. Be warned that operating hours are erratic, and you might not be let through the gate (the gatekeeper speaks a mix of Latvian and German and if she doesn't understand you, she'll simply turn you away). Call first and make a reservation to avoid difficulties.

Pie Bocmaņa (☎ 407 1455; Pērmavas iela 6), supposedly 'the most legendary fisherman's pub in town', is another option.

The former shipbuilding town of **Ainaži** (derived from the Liv word *annagi*, meaning 'lonely') is 1km south of Estonia. Its only attraction is its old naval school, now home to the **Naval College Museum** (Ainaži Jūrskolas memorialais muzejs; ☎ 404 3349; Valdemāra iela 45; admission 0.30Ls; 🕑 10am-4pm Jun-Aug, closed Sun & Mon Sep-May). This mildly interesting museum exhibits the naval academy's history and reconstructs a typical 19th-century Latvian classroom.

Buses north from Rīga to Pärnu and Tallinn serve the region via the coastal road (one hour to Saulkrasti, 1¾ hours to Salacgrīva). Suburban trains from Rīga run as far as Saulkrasti (0.70Ls, one hour).

MAZSALACA & RŪJIENA

Anyone intrigued by Latvian folklore might want to visit the area around Mazsalaca, 55km inland from Ainaži on the Salaca River. Head to **Sound Hill** (Skaņāis kalns; ☎ 425 1945), a splendid park 1.7km west of town, which showcases marvellous outdoor woodcarvings of gigantic proportions. Motorists can drive the length of the park, or better yet stroll the 2km on foot, stopping at strategic spots. The **Werewolf Pine** is believed to turn you into a werewolf if you crawl through its roots after muttering certain incantations under a full moon. The **Stairway of Dreams**, 300m north, tells young lovers how well suited they are, while about 1km downstream from the Werewolf Pine, a spring flowing out of a rock at the **Devil's Cave** is said to have healing properties. And about 800m further downstream, the sandstone cliff **Sound Hill** on the left bank of the river apparently throws off an occasional bizarre acoustic effect. A picnic area decked out with picnic tables and benches marks the end of the trail. On the town's village green there is an open-air **Dinosaur Park** (Dinozauru parks; Parka iela 8; admission free).

Rūjiena, 15km northeast, is set in attractive countryside and boasts Latvia's oldest operating dairy. Tourism touts sell the town as the 'capital of ice cream', and visitors can tour the **dairy** – hours vary, visit the **tourist office** (☎ 426 3278; www.rujiena.lv; Raiņa iela 3; 🕑 9am-5pm Mon-Sat) to arrange a tour – and taste the delicious ice cream produced here. The town also features several sculptures by K Zemdegs, a well-known Latvian sculptor. If industrial tours are your thing, the tourist office can also help arrange trips to a sheep-breeding farm and wool-processing mill.

The only hotel is **Tālava** (☎ 426 3767; Rīgas iela 12; r 15-25Ls; P) in Rūjiena. It's a slightly shabby establishment with an on-site restaurant. Rooms are nothing special, but acceptable for a night.

GAUJA NATIONAL PARK

Much of the area between Sigulda and Valmiera falls within **Gauja National Park** (Gaujas nacionālais parks; www.gnp.gov.lv). Founded in 1973, Latvia's first national park protects a diverse range of flora and fauna, and offers a multitude of forest and river hiking as well as biking trails and fabulous canoeing opportunities – a great way to explore the exquisite, pine-scented environment. The historic towns of Sigulda and Cēsis are main jumping-off points for exploring the park.

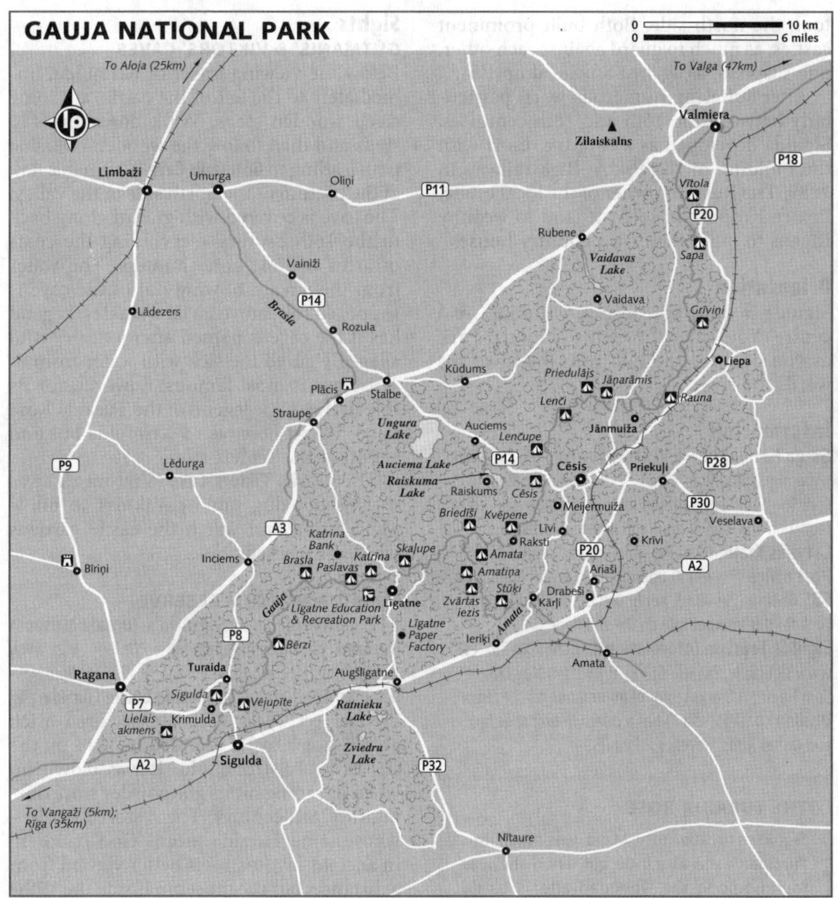

SIGULDA

pop 10,855

This enchanted town stands on the southern edge of a picturesque, steep-sided, wooded section of the Gauja Valley and is spanned by a string of medieval castles and legendary caves. Just 53km east of Rīga, it is known locally as the 'Switzerland of Latvia', although that title is a bit deceptive – the surrounding area is very pretty, but don't expect towering snowcapped peaks. That said, the bogs, green rolling hills, old wooden farmhouses and fields of yellow flowers create some pretty dreamy-looking countryside.

Sigulda is a minor health resort and winter sports centre, with an Olympic bobsled run snaking down into the valley. It also is the primary gateway to the beautiful Gauja National Park, located northeast of town. Sigulda itself offers some excellent sleeping options – get away from hotels and check out the charming country guesthouses.

History

Finno-Ugric Liv tribes inhabited the area as far back as 2000 BC; by the 12th century they had built several wooden hill-top strongholds. In 1207, when the German crusaders were dividing up their spoils, the Gauja was chosen as the boundary in this area between the territories of the Knights of the Sword, who took the land south of the river, and of the archbishop of Rīga, who took the north side. Both built prominent castles, as much to guard against each other, one suspects, as against any local uprising.

After suffering numerous wars, particularly between the 16th and 18th centuries, Sigulda developed as a country resort with the building of the Pskov–Rīga railway in 1889. The Russian owner of the local estate, Prince Kropotkin, sold off land to wealthy Rīgans to build their own country houses.

Orientation

Sigulda is quite spread out, without a real centre. You enter the Gauja National Park as you descend the hill from the town towards the river.

Information

Gauja National Park Visitors Centre (☎ 797 1345; www.gnp.lv; Baznīcas iela 3; 🕑 9.30am-5pm Mon, to 6pm Tue-Sun) Sells park and town maps, arranges accommodation and guided tours and organises activities.
Latvijas Krājbanka (Pils iela 1) One of several ATMs.
Post office (Pils iela 2) Opposite the Latvijas Krājbanka.
SBS Online (Pils iela 3; per hr 0.70Ls; 🕑 9am-11pm) Look for this Internet café on the 2nd floor.
Sigulda Tourism Information Centre (☎ 797 1335; www.sigulda.lv; Pils iela 6; 🕑 10am-7pm May-Oct, to 5pm Nov-Apr) Stocks reams of information on the region.
Unibanka (Rīgas iela 1) Has a currency-exchange facility and cashes AmEx traveller's cheques.

THE TURAIDA ROSE

Sigulda's local beauty, Maija, was taken into Turaida Castle as a little girl when she was found among the wounded after a battle in 1601. She grew into a famous beauty courted by men from far and wide, but she loved Viktors, a gardener at Sigulda Castle. They would meet in a cave halfway between the two castles.

One day a particularly desperate Polish officer among Maija's suitors lured her to the cave by means of a letter forged in Viktors' handwriting. Maija offered to give the Pole the scarf from around her neck, which she said had magical protective powers, if he let her go. To prove the scarf's powers, she suggested he swing at her with his sword. Whether this was a bluff or she really believed in the scarf isn't clear. Either way, the Pole duly took his swing, killed her and then fled.

Sights

GŪTMAŅIS' & VIKTORS' CAVES

Below the viewing tower of Krimulda, immediately to the left of the castle, are some steep wooden steps. Walk down the 410 steps and then follow the wooden riverside path leading to **Gūtmaņis Cave** (Gūtmaņa ala), at the bottom of the north side of the valley. The cave is covered with graffiti going back to the 16th century – including the coats of arms of long-gone hunters. The water from the stream flowing out of the cave is supposed to remove facial wrinkles. Legend has it the cave is named after a healer who allegedly cured the sick with water from it. This cave is most famous, however, for its role in the tragic legend of the Turaida Rose (left). To get here take a Krimulda bus and get off at the Senleja stop.

The nearby **Viktors' Cave** (Viktora ala) was supposedly dug out by Viktors to allow Maija to sit and watch the castle gardens where he worked.

TURAIDA MUSEUM RESERVE

The centrepiece of Sigulda's **Turaida Museum Reserve** (Turaidas muzejrezervats; ☎ 797 1402; www.turaida-muzejs.lv; admission 1.50Ls; 🕑 9.30am-8pm May-Oct, 10am-5pm Nov-Apr) is **Turaida Castle** (Turaidas pils; 🕑 10am-6pm May-Oct, to 5pm Nov-Apr), a red-brick archbishop's castle founded in 1214 on the site of a Liv stronghold. It was blown up when lightning hit its gunpowder store during the 18th century. The restored castle – whose name, Turaida, means 'God's Garden' in ancient Livonian – is better viewed from a distance, but the museum inside the 15th-century **granary** offers a rather interesting account of the Livonian state from 1319 to 1561. Further exhibitions can be viewed in the 42m-high **Donjon Tower**, and the castle's western and southern towers.

On the path between the castle and the road is the small wooden-spired **Turaida Church** (Turaidas Baznīcas; 🕑 10am-6pm Wed-Sun May-Oct), built in 1750 and housing a small history exhibition. In the churchyard two lime trees shade the grave of the legendary Turaida Rose. The headstone bears the inscription 'Turaidas Roze 1601–1620'. Viktors himself is said to have buried Maija and planted one of the trees, then disappeared without trace. The hillside behind the church is known as Daina Hill (Dainu kalns) and shelters the **Daina Hill Song Garden**. The *daina* (poetic folk

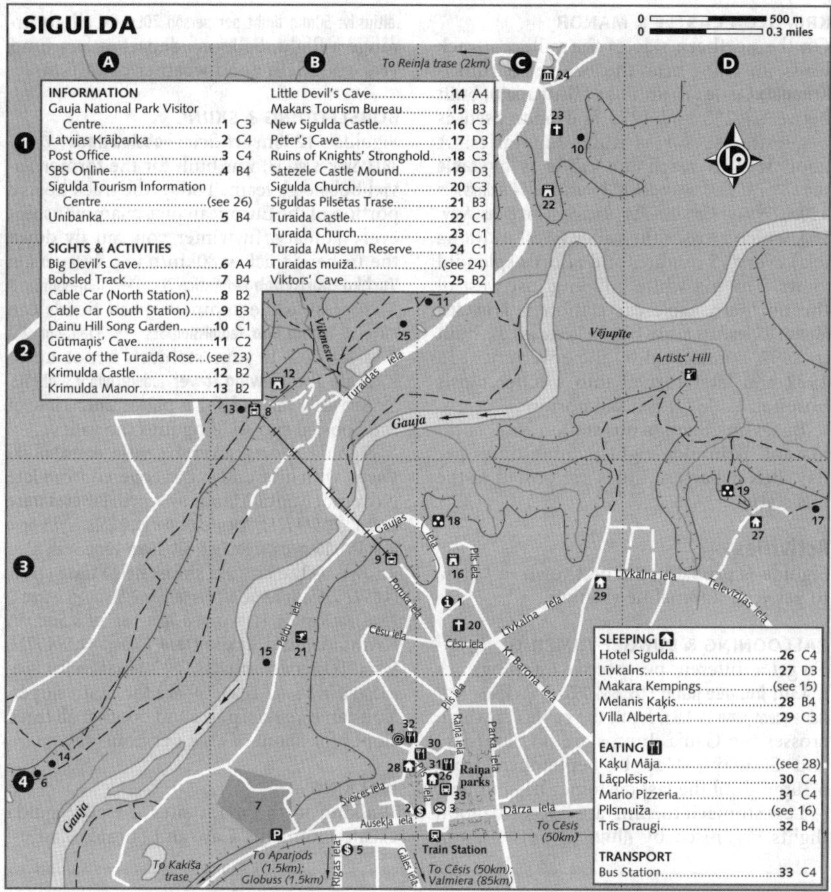

song) is a major Latvian tradition, and the hillside is dotted with sculptures dedicated to epic Latvian heroes immortalised in the *dainas*.

More paths twist around the estate past the **estate manager's house**, home to an exhibition on collective farming in the 1950s; the **dog keeper's house**, where wood craft tools are displayed; the **smithy**, still operational; the **cart house**, which hosts various farming exhibitions; and the old 19th-century **sauna**. All these exhibitions are open 10am-6pm from Wednesday to Sunday, May to October.

Kārļa Hill (Kārļa kalns), facing Turaida Castle across the ravine which the road ascends, was another old Liv stronghold.

SIGULDA CASTLES & CHURCH

Little remains of the **knights' stronghold** (Siguldas pilsdrupas), built between 1207 and 1226among woods on the northeastern edge of Sigulda. The castle hasn't been repaired since the Great Northern War, but its ruins are perhaps more evocative because of that. There's a great view through the trees to the archbishop's reconstructed Turaida Castle, on the far side of the valley.

On the way to the ruins from town, you pass **Sigulda Church** (Siguldas baznīca), built in 1225 and rebuilt in the 17th and 18th centuries, and also the 19th-century **New Sigulda Castle** (Siguldas jaunā pils), the former residence of Prince Kropotkin and now a sanatorium.

KRIMULDA CASTLE & MANOR

On the northern side of the valley, a track leads up from near the bridge to ruined **Krimulda Castle** (Krimuldas pilsdrupas), built between 1255 and 1273 and once used as a guesthouse for visiting dignitaries. A good way to reach the castle is by **cable car** (☎ 797 2531; www.lgk.lv; Poruka iela 14; admission 0.50Ls; 🕑 9am-5pm Jun-Aug, 9am-5pm Sat & Sun May-Sep), which crosses the valley (west of Raiņa iela) every 15 minutes and affords splendid views. The big white building just west of the northern cable-car station is **Krimulda Manor** (Krimuldas muižas pils; Mednieku iela 3), built in 1897, confiscated by the government in 1922 and later turned into a tuberculosis hospital. Today it is a sanatorium.

Buses link Sigulda bus station with Turaida and Krimulda eight or nine times per day. Bus departure times are posted at the bus station.

Activities

Sigulda is probably the best town in Latvia to get your adrenaline rushing.

BALLOONING & BUNGEE JUMPING

To get a different perspective on things, try a 43m **bungee jump** (☎ 664 0660; www.lgk.lv; first/subsequent jump 15/13Ls) from the cable car which crosses the Gauja. Jumps are on Saturdays and Sundays, May to September, from 6.30pm until the last customer has jumped.

Less stomach turning are hot-air balloon flights organised by **Altius** (☎ 761 1614; www.altius.lv; 50min flight per person 70Ls). Call to arrange a flight; balloons depart at any time, year-round, in good weather conditions.

BOBSLEDDING & SKIING

Sigulda's 1200m artificial **bobsled track** (☎ 797 3813; Sveices iela 13) was built for the former Soviet bobsleigh team. Today, the track hosts a portion of the European luge championships every January. In winter you can fly down the 16-bend track at 80km/h in a five-person **Vuchko tourist bob** (admission 2Ls; 🕑 11am-6pm Sat & Sun Nov-Feb), while summer speed fiends can ride a **wheel bob** (admission 3Ls; 🕑 11am-6pm Sat & Sun May-Sep). If your stomach is not up to it, scale the **viewing tower** (adult/child 0.30/0.15Ls; 🕑 8am-dusk) instead for a panoramic view of the bobsled run snaking into the valley.

Sigulda sports several gentle **downhill ski slopes**, with lifts, and snow-covered from late November until March or April. **Pilsētas trase** (350m; ☎ 944 7713; Peldu iela 4; per lift 0.25Ls; 🕑 3-6pm Mon-Thu, 10am-midnight Fri & Sat, 10am-10pm Sun), also known as the city ski slope; **Reiņa trase** (150m; ☎ 927 2255; Kalnzaķi; lift per hr/day 2/5Ls; 🕑 3-6pm & 7pm-1am Mon-Fri, 11am-6pm & 7pm-1am Sat & Sun), in Krimulda; and **Kakīša trase** (300m; ☎ 944 7713; Senču iela 1; per lift from 0.20Ls; 🕑 2-10pm Mon-Thu, 2pm-midnight Fri & Sat, 2-11pm Sun) are the main slopes. You can hire skis, poles and boots at all three slopes for about 3/12Ls per hour/day.

WALKING

Walking to the main sites – New Sigulda Castle, Gūtmaņis' Cave and Turaida Castle –

CANOE TRIPS

Vidzeme's Gauja and Salaca Rivers are both fine canoeing terrain. The 220km stretch of the Gauja between Vireši and Sigulda is particularly good, flowing through some of Latvia's best scenery with nothing more hazardous than some fairly gentle rapids. Riverside camp sites dot this whole stretch; above Valmiera the river flows through almost entirely unspoilt country.

You can set up a Gauja canoe trip through many organizations. On the banks of the river in Sigulda, inside the Gauja National Park, **Makars Tourism Agency** (☎ 924 4948; www.makars.lv; Peldu iela 1) arranges one- to three-day water tours in two- to four-person boats from Sigulda, Līgatne, Cēsis and Valmiera, ranging in length from 3km to 85km. Tours cost between 10Ls and 40Ls per boat including equipment, transportation between Sigulda and the tour's starting point, and camp-site fees for up to four people. Tents, sleeping bags and life jackets can also be rented for a nominal fee. For the less intrepid paddler, Makars rents out canoes and rubber boats seating between two and six people for about 10Ls per day.

Valmiera's **Sporta Bāze Baiļi** (☎ 422 1861; www.baili.lv) arranges various one-day canoe trips that cost 22Ls (24km, Valmiera–Strenči), 40Ls (83km Valmiera–Sigulda) or 30Ls (45km, Valmiera–Cēsis). Trips spread across two days or more cost more. The company also offers one-day rafting trips for 115Ls. The price includes a boat, paddles, life jackets and transport.

is a fabulous way to stretch your legs. Within the Turaida Museum Reserve a series of gentle nature trails is marked, ranging from 200m to 800m in length.

A good circular walk on the castle's eastern side – about 6km to and from Sigulda Church – heads first to **Satezele Castle Mound** (Satezeles pilskalns), another Liv stronghold, then on to **Peter's Cave** (Pētera ala), found on a steep bank of the Vējupīte River, before reaching **Artists' Hill** (Gleznotāju kalns), which offers an excellent 12km panorama.

On the northern bank you could walk downstream from the bridge to the **Little Devil's Cave** (Mazā velnala) and **Big Devil's Cave** (Lielā velnala), then return along the top of the escarpment to Krimulda Castle – about 7km. The Little Devil's Cave has a **Spring of Wisdom** (Gudrības avotiņs). The Big Devil's Cave has black walls from the fiery breath of a travelling demon that once sheltered for a day here to avoid sunlight.

The Gauja National Park Visitors Centre (p228) has details of plenty more walks in the national park. Particularly interesting are its day- and night-time bird-watching and birdsong-discovery walks.

CYCLING, ROLLERBLADING & HORSE RIDING

In summer you can rent bicycles and Rollerblades from **Eži** (☎ 942 8846; Pils iela 4a; per day 5Ls; ⏰ 10am-8pm May-Oct).

Turaidas muiža (☎ 912 4360; Turaidas iela 10; ⏰ 11am-8pm) organises various horse-riding activities, including treks (from 16Ls per person per hour) and horse-drawn carriage rides (5Ls for four people for 20 minutes) around the national park.

Sleeping

Wild camping is permitted in certain designated areas in the national park. Apart from camping, budget options don't really exist. Unless otherwise mentioned, all places listed here include breakfast.

Villa Alberta (☎ 797 1060; www.zl.lv/villaalberta; Līvkalna iela 10A; r 35-55Ls; P) A classy option in town, a lot of time went into decorating the uniquely furnished and spacious rooms. The deluxe rooms, with rich tapestries, Jacuzzis and satellite TV, are huge and a steal at just 55Ls. The attached bar and restaurant serves a variety of food (meals 4Ls to 8Ls), including pastas, Mexican dishes and Latvian fare.

Līvkalns (☎ 797 0916; www.livkalns.lv; Pēteralas iela; s/d from 24/30Ls; P) A peaceful and romantic choice, Līvkalns overlooks a lake and has well-maintained grounds. The large wooden thatched-roof house has eight spacious rooms with pale wooden furnishings and muted colours. All are spotless and comfortable. The restaurant gets good reviews.

Aparjods (☎ 770 5225; www.aparjods.lv; Ventas iela 1b; s/d/tr 28/30/40Ls; P) A rustic reed- and shingle-roofed place 1.5km south of town, Aparjods merges old and new styles with solid results. Soft duvets and sturdy oak doors are highlights of the cosy rooms.

Hotel Sigulda (☎ 797 2263; www.hotelsigulda.lv; Pils iela 6; s/d 30/42Ls; P) A comfortable and modern hotel, it has spacious rooms with sloping ceilings and bright bedcovers. The pool with steam room (2Ls per hour) and sauna (up to four people 30Ls per hour) are oddly open only on Thursday, Saturday and Sunday.

Melanis Kaķis (☎ 797 0272; Pils iela 8; r 25Ls; P) This new place has immaculate rooms with bright walls and sturdy furniture. The rooms are a bit cramped, and were rather hot when we stopped by, but the central location and on-site bar and restaurant (Kaķu Māja) make it a decent find. If you can't locate reception, ask about rooms at the restaurant.

Makara Kempings (☎ 924 4948; www.makars.lv; Peldu iela 1; person/tent/car/caravan 3/1.50/1.50/4.50Ls; ⏰ 15 May-15 Sep) Pitch your tent at this riverside camping place inside the national park. Enjoy a traditional Latvian sauna for 15Ls per hour. Two-person tents can be rented for 4Ls a day.

SLEEPING BENEATH THE STARS

Twenty-two 'wild' camp sites, which are intended for hikers and canoeists, are strung along the banks of the Gauja between Sigulda and Cēsis – the most scenic stretch of valley. They're mostly on the northern bank, but there's one opposite Katrīna Bank at Līgatne (accessible by car or on foot from Līgatne Education and Recreation Park; p232) and a couple more on the Amata River between Zvārtas iezis and the Gauja. Both the information centre at the Līgatne Education and Recreation Park, and the national park visitor centre (p228) in Sigulda can tell you where they are.

Eating & Drinking

Aparjods (☎ 770 5225; www.aparjods.lv; Ventas iela 1b) This place dishes up delicious food (meals 12Ls) in an elegant dark-wood setting with fireplace and interesting B&W photos of old Sigulda on the walls. Sample traditional herrings with curd or for a splash out with friends order an entire roasted piglet (110Ls). Retire to the on-site dance club after dinner.

Kaķu Māja (☎ 797 0272; Pils iela 8; meals 4-10Ls) Artsy and modern, the restaurant and nightclub part of this slick complex features steel and wood décor and very funky orange-striped chairs – a rather unexpected find. The food is meat and fish oriented. The adjacent canteen-style café has a sumptuous pastry selection.

Mario Pizzeria (☎ 797 3322; Pils iela 4b; meals 4-12Ls) If you're tiring of Latvian fare, head to this quaint little pizzeria with lots of choices and fabulous English translations – 'fowl ham' pizza was our favourite. The thin-crust pizza is quite tasty, and cooked just right.

Trīs Draugi (☎ 797 3721; Pils iela 9; meals from 2Ls) Trīs Draugi is a bright and sparkling place where you can be served – canteen-style – with large, tasty helpings of cheap food. Sit at the outside picnic tables under the trees.

Lāčplēsis (☎ 797 4640; Pils iela 8; meals 4Ls; 🕒 8am-2am) Directly opposite Trīs Draugi, this place is mainly a bar with lots of pool tables, darts and one-armed bandits (slot machines). It's very clean with funky red curtains and serves light meals in a pub-style setting.

Pilsmuiža (☎ 797 1425; Pils iela 16; meals 7Ls) Inside New Sigulda Castle, this eatery overlooks the ruins of the castle and has panoramic views of the Gauja Valley. The food is typical Latvian fare.

Globuss (Ventas iela 1; meals from 1Ls; 🕒 24hr) This supermarket has a small bistro for those needing to eat on the cheap.

Getting There & Away

Buses trundle the 50-odd kilometres between Sigulda bus station and Rīga (1Ls, two hours, six daily).

Ten trains a day on the Rīga–Sigulda–Cēsis–Valmiera line stop at Sigulda. Fares from Sigulda include Rīga (2Ls, 1¼ hours), Valmiera (1.5Ls, 1¼ hours), Līgatne (0.50Ls, 10 minutes) and Cēsis (1Ls, 50 minutes).

LĪGATNE

pop 1365

Although the village of Līgatne, in the heart of the Gauja National Park, is in itself unremarkable, some of Latvia's loveliest countryside is a mere hop, skip and jump from the village, making it a good base from which to explore the area.

On the southern side of the river, about 4km west of Līgatne village and 15km northeast of Sigulda, is **Līgatne Education and Recreation Park** (Līgatnes mācību un atpūtas parks; ☎ 415 3313; adult/child 1/0.50Ls; 🕒 9.30am-5pm Mon, to 6.30pm Tue-Sun May-Oct), a nature park where elks, beaver, deer, bison, lynxes and wild boar roam in sizable open-air enclosures in the forest. A 5.1km motor circuit and a network of footpaths link a series of observation points, and there's a 22m observation tower with a fine panorama. Marked footpaths include a 5.5km nature trail with wild animals, a botanical trail (1.1km), a wild nature trail (1.3km) and a fun fairy-tale trail (900m), which winds its way through a fantastical path of 90-odd wooden sculptures.

One of the national park's camp sites (see boxed text, p231) is opposite Katrīna Bank in Līgatne. It is accessible by car or foot from Līgatne Education and Recreation Park. In a log-style building, **Lāču Miga** (☎ 750 6604; www.lacumiga.lv; Gaujas iela 22; s/d 22/35Ls; P 🅧) has rooms with TVs and coffee makers. There are nearby trails for walking and cross-country skiing, along with a restaurant, terrace bar and grocery store selling takeaway.

Public transport is poor. The bus stop nearest to the nature park is Gaujasmala, 2km from the entrance. Five buses daily are scheduled from Cēsis to Zvārtas iezis, but the service is erratic. You can always get a bus or suburban train to Līgatne village's main road or to Ieriķi, then walk or hitch.

Coming from the north (Straupe direction), you can catch a **car ferry** across the Gauja to Līgatne. A single fare is 0.40Ls per person, plus 1Ls per car. Boats run from May to September between 6am and 11pm. From Līgatne village, follow the signs for 'Līgatnes Pārceltuve'.

CĒSIS

pop 19,471

We just loved historic Cēsis, Latvia's most Latvian town. Decidedly romantic, Cēsis is made for wandering. The main drag, Rīgas iela, has loads of character and is lined with old tan and brown stone buildings. Check out the crumbling castle, the country's oldest brewery (although the famous beer is now produced in a slick facility outside town) or meander down to the small murky lake and nap on grassy grounds shaded by ancient trees. About 30km northeast of Sigulda, Cēsis was once the headquarters of the Livonian Order. Open-air concerts are often held in summer on the castle grounds.

Orientation

The bus and train stations are on the eastern fringe. From here Raunas iela leads to the main square, Vienības laukums.

Information

Capital Datorsalons (☎ 410 7111; Rīgas iela 7; per hr 0.50Ls; 9am-6pm Mon-Fri, 10am-2pm Sat) Internet access.

Cēsis tourist office (☎ 412 1815; www.cesis.lv; Pils laukums 2; 9am-6pm Mon-Sat, 10am-5pm Sun mid-May–mid-Sep, 9am-5pm Mon-Fri rest of year)

Latvijas Krābanka (Vienības laukums) There's an ATM outside.

Vidzeme Tourism Association (☎ 412 2011; info@vta.apollo.lv) This is based at the Cēsis tourist office. It arranges accommodation in private homes in rural Vidzeme.

Sights

CASTLE, MUSEUM & PARK

Cēsis Castle (Cēsu pils) was founded in 1209 by the Knights of the Sword. Its dominant feature is two stout towers at the western end. To enter, visit **Cēsis History & Art Museum** (Cēsu Vēstures un mākslas muzejs; Pils laukums 9; adult/child 0.30/0.20Ls; 10am-5pm Tue-Sun), in the adjoining 18th-century 'new castle', painted salmon pink. Temporary art exhibitions and chamber-music concerts are held in **Cēsis Exhibition House** (Cēsu Izstāžu nams; ☎ 412 3557; 10am-5pm Tue-Sun) next to the tourist office on the same square. The yellow-and-white building housed stables and a coach house (1781) in the 18th and 19th centuries.

Pretty **Castle Park** (Pils park) has a song bowl, lake and a Russian Orthodox church. On the far side from the church is the 19th-century building of **Cēsu Alus** (Cēsis Brewery; ☎ 412 2245; Lenču iela 9/11). It has brewed beer since 1590. Opening hours vary; just stop by.

LATVIA

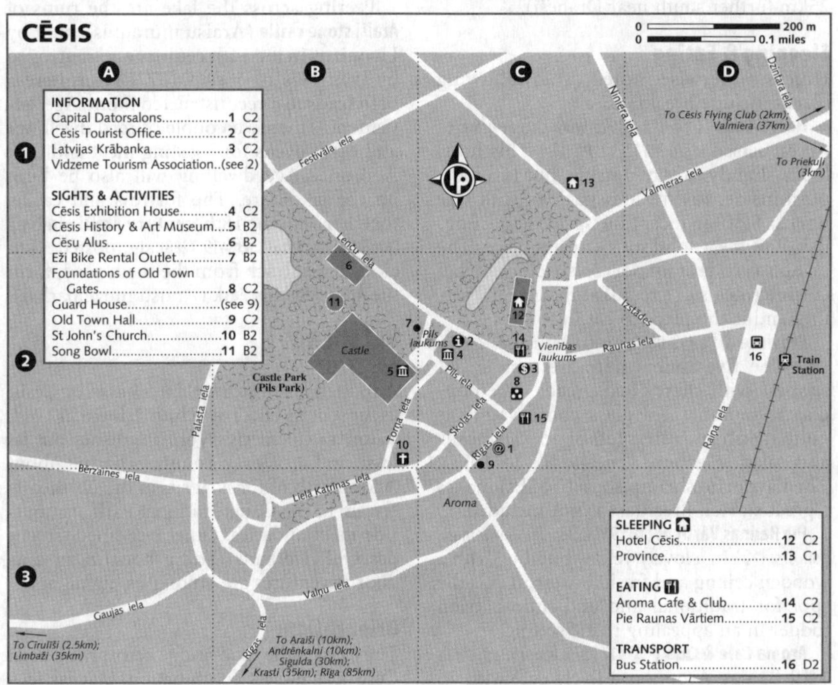

LATVIA

OLD TOWN
Old Town runs south from the bottom end of Vienības laukums. Just off this square, at the top of Rīgas iela, the foundations of the Old Town gates have been excavated and left exposed. Nearby, the **Old Town hall** and **guard house** (Rīgas iela 7) dates to 1767.

The main landmark is **St John's Church** (Svēta Jāņa baznīca; Skolas iela), which dates back to 1287 and makes for an impressive photo. Its original Gothic form has been altered, with the towers dating back to 1853. Inside, the church has some fine stained glass and a baby-blue ceiling.

Activities

Cyclists can hire wheels from the **Eži bike rental outlet** (☎ 428 1764; Pils laukums 1; per hr/day 1/5Ls; 9am-6pm Mon-Sun Apr-Sep).

In winter skiers and snowboarders poodle down the gentle slopes and cross-country trails at **Cirulīši** (☎ 412 5225; cirulkalns@e-apollo.lv; Cirulīšu iela 70), on Cēsis' southwesternmost fringe. The tourist office has details of other places to ski in the region, such as **Andrēnkalni** (10km south near Skujenes) and **Krasti** (some 25km further south near Drabeši).

Sleeping & Eating

Unless otherwise noted, the following places include breakfast.

Hotel Cēsis (☎ 412 2392; www.danlat-group.lv; Vienības laukums 1; s/d 30/42Ls; P) This hotel looks slightly dreary outside, but is almost posh inside. Rooms are spacious with fine linens. Staff at reception speak good English, and it's a solid tourist-class place. The in-house restaurant serves strictly Latvian cuisine (meals 4Ls to 10Ls) in a formal setting and is the place to eat in town.

Province (☎ 412 0849; Niniera iela 6; s/d 17/28Ls; P) The five rooms here are simple but spotless with cherry bedspreads. The popular restaurant in a glass conservatory is quite stylish and offers lots of pork, pancake and salad selections (meals 4Ls to 10Ls). The flavourful shrimp soup (0.85Ls) makes a great starter. Breakfast is not included.

Pie Raunas Vārtiem (☎ 919 2938; Rīgas iela 8; meals from 6Ls; ⊠) In a lovely yellow building with a wooden ceiling and fresh flowers, this is the spot for traditional and authentic Latvian fodder in an appealing rustic setting.

Aroma Café & Club (☎ 412 7575; Lencū iela 4; meals 4-8Ls) By day Aroma is a lively café with 70 types of coffee and tea on, along with light Latvian snacks and pastries. At night the back opens into a slick club with an industrial vibe, with red walls and silver piping.

Getting There & Away

Cēsis bus station is served by at least hourly buses daily to/from Rīga (1.30Ls, two hours) and about 10 daily to/from Valmiera (0.50Ls, 45 minutes). There are six daily trains between Cēsis and Rīga (1.30Ls, 1¼ to two hours).

ĀRAIŠI

Plopped on an islet in the middle of Āraiši Lake, about 10km south of Cēsis, **Āraiši Lake Fortress** (Āraišu ezerpils; ☎ 419 7288; adult/child 0.60/0.20Ls; 10am-6pm May–mid-Oct) is a reconstruction of a settlement inhabited by ancient Latgalans in the 9th and 10th centuries. A wooden walkway leads across the water to the unusual village, which was built on a low flooded islet, fortified like a hill fort and discovered by archaeologists in 1965. About 40 log houses originally stood on the site – 15 have been rebuilt in recent times.

Peering across the lake are the ruins of **Āraiši stone castle** (Āraišu mūra pils), built by Livonians in the 14th century and destroyed by Ivan IV's troops in 1577. From here a path leads to a reconstructed Stone Age settlement – there's a couple of reed dwellings and earth ovens for roasting meat and fish. A Bronze Age dwelling will also be built on the lakeshore. The fortress and castle, together with the 18th-century **Āraiši windmill** (Āraišu vējdzirnavas; ☎ 419 7288) signposted 1km along a dirt track from the main road, form the **Āraiši Museum Park** (Āraišu muzejparks).

VALMIERA

pop 28,732

Although less historic than Sigulda or Cēsis, as most of its Old Town burnt down in 1944, Valmiera (formerly Wolmar) dishes out its own brand of easy country charm. About 30km north of Cēsis, it sits at the northeastern tip of the Gauja National Park, just outside its boundaries. Quiet tree-lined streets, peaceful riverbanks and a bonanza of outdoor adventures are among its highlights.

Orientation

The focus is the road bridge across the Gauja. Cēsu iela and its continuation, Stacijas iela, leads south from the bridge to the bus station (100m or so), opposite the corner of Cēsu iela, and on to the train station (800m). The centre is on the northern side of the bridge.

Information

Datocentras (☎ 428 1818; info@devia.lv; Tērbatas iela 1; per hr 0.50Ls; 9am-11pm) Internet access.

Tourist office (☎ 420 7177; www.valmiera.gov.lv; Bruņinieku iela 2; 7am-9pm Mon-Fri, 9am-5pm Sat May-Sep) Sells maps and arranges private accommodation.

Sights

Valmiera's pinprick historic area stands on a point of land between the Gauja River and a tributary called the Ažkalna. **St Simon's Church** (Svētā Simaņa Baznīca; Bruņinieku iela 2) dates to 1283 and shelters a fine 19th-century organ. You can climb its church tower for a nominal fee. Along the same street are the ruins of **Valmiera Castle**, founded by the Livonian Order.

Continue to **Valmiera Regional Museum** (Valmieras Novadpētniecības muzejs; ☎ 423 2733; Bruņinieku iela 3; adult/child 0.50/0.30Ls; 10am-5pm Mon-Fri, to 3pm Sat). Its collection is of limited interest, but it's a good source of information on the district – if you read Latvian.

The curtains rose for the first time at **Valmiera Drama Theatre** (☎ 422 3300; Lāčplēsa iela 4) in 1885. The current building dates to 1987.

There's an **observation tower** on the hillock Valterkalniņs, just above the meeting of the Ažkalna and the Gauja. Across a small bridge over the Ažkalna, a loop of land surrounded by the Gauja has been preserved as a woodland **park**.

Activities

In town, **Eži** (☎ 420 7263; www.ezi.lv; Valdemāra iela; 9am-7pm Mon-Sat, to 1pm Sun), once a popular hostel, now concentrates solely on outdoor adventures. It organises all sorts of active pursuits – from themed one- or two-day hiking and biking excursions to river rafting to zip-wires through the trees (trips start at 20Ls per day). It also rents out mountain bikes (2/6Ls per hour/day), helmets (2Ls per day), saddlebags and seats for kids (each 2Ls per day) along with canoes (10Ls per day). In winter the company does cross-country skiing tours across lakes and through snow-covered forests complete with picnic lunch cooked over a bonfire in the woods.

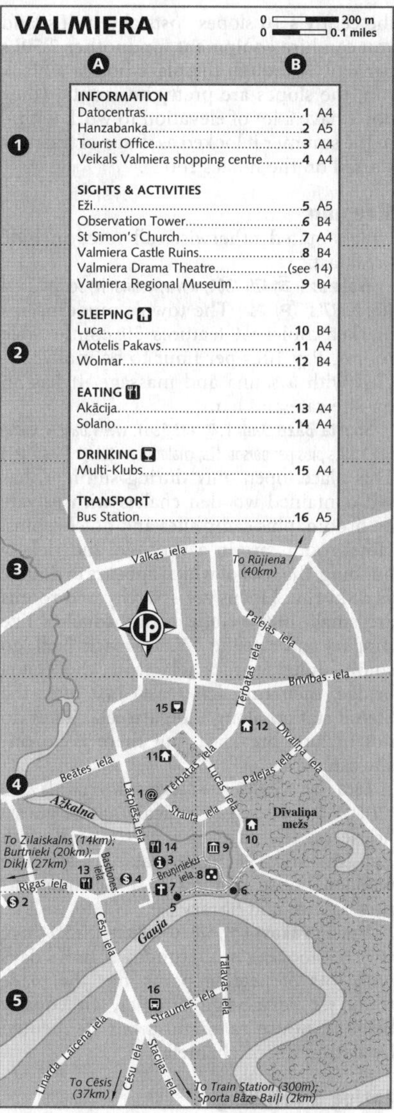

Sporta Bāze Baiļi (p236) is another option for water sports, organising raft and canoe trips on the Gauja and Salaca Rivers; for more on these trips see the boxed text, p230. The place also has a short mountain-bike trail through forest and there's winter skiing. A half-day ski pass (valid from 11am to 4pm or from 4pm to 11pm) for the centre's 10 slopes costs about 6Ls, and you can hire equipment for another 2.50Ls per day. Although the place boasts a black run, the slopes are pretty horizontal (they don't have a lot of elevation to work with – in the summer it looked as if one of the runs started on the hotel's roof!).

Sleeping

Unless stated otherwise, all rates include breakfast.

Wolmar (☎ 420 7301; www.wolmar.lv; Tērbatas iela 16a; 20/27Ls; P) The town's modern, upmarket choice, it features 30 comfortable rooms. Pay 10Ls per hour to be mollycoddled with a sauna and massage. It has an on-site café and bar.

Sporta Bāze Baiļi (☎ 422 1861; www.baili.lv; camp site 1.50Ls plus per person 1Ls, chalet from 30Ls, r 15Ls; P) This place, open only during summer, has self-contained wooden chalets with private bathroom, plus camp sites and hotel rooms. Hotel rooms are in a very old and rickety building, the roof of which appears to double as a ski run. Linens are scratchy and rooms are small, but include comfy touches like slippers and satellite TV. To reach Baiļi, go south along Stacijas iela from the Gauja bridge, then turn left (east) just after the Statoil station along Kauguru iela. Rates do not include breakfast, but there is an on-site café.

Luca (☎ 422 3988; luca-haus@one.lv; Lucas iela 2; s/d 12/18Ls; P) Luca is a squeaky-clean guesthouse on the edge of a pretty park, with English- and German-speaking staff. The wooden house doubles as a German cultural centre and library.

Motelis Pakavs (☎ 428 1050; Beātes iela 5; 14/19Ls; P) It's looking a bit rundown these days with lots of peeling paint, but the place touts six very beige doubles, an equally beige in-house café, and a bar frequented by a stony-faced clientele.

Eating & Drinking

Dining options are frustratingly limited. In a nutshell, the choice is the café at the Wolmar (above) or the following.

Akācija (☎ 423 3812; Rīgas iela 10; meals 4Ls) This busy bar with a token handful of tables dishes up a vast array of satisfying creations. Its veal cooked in wine with mushrooms and potato pancakes is recommended. There's an attached nightclub.

Solano (Lāčplēša iela 4; meals 2Ls) Known for cheap but tasty traditional Latvian cuisine, Solano is inside the drama theatre.

Multi-Klubs (☎ 423 2114; Tirgu iela 5) In a big red building, it's the place to sink bar snacks and beer. Air hockey and a machine to test alcohol levels are other features of this surprisingly with-it nightclub.

Getting There & Away

From Valmiera **bus station** (☎ 422 4728; www.autobusunoma.lv; Stacijas iela 1) buses run hourly between 4.55am and 7.55pm to/from Rīga (1.50Ls, 2½ hours). Other services include 10 to 15 buses a day to/from Cēsis (0.50Ls, 45 minutes).

The **train station** (☎ 582 7232; Stacijas laukums) is served by five trains daily to/from Rīga (1.55Ls, 1¾to three hours) via Cēsis (0.60Ls, 40 minutes) and Sigulda (1Ls, 20 minutes).

Around Valmiera

Heading 18km northeast on the Valmiera–Valka road, you hit Strenči, known for the Strenči Rapids, 4km below the town on the Gauja. With its steep, high banks, this is reckoned to be the most scenic stretch of the entire river. To get paddling, contact a canoeing centre; see boxed text, p230. The village hosts a raft festival on the third Sunday in May.

Blue Hill (Zilaiskalns), topped by a lookout tower 14km west of Valmiera, and **Lake Burtnieku**, about 23km north, off the Mazsalaca road, are other local beauty spots. **Burtnieki** village, on the southern edge of the lake, is known for its **horse-breeding centre** (Burtnieku zirgaudzētava; ☎ 425 6444). When the Latvian show-jumping team isn't in training, you can ride (5Ls per hour) or be driven around the exceptionally pretty village in a horse-drawn carriage (15Ls). The centre is signposted 'stallis' (stables) from the village.

VALKA

pop 6927

Unless you're heading to Estonia, there's little reason to visit the border town of Valka about 45km northeast of Valmiera. On the road and train line to Tartu in Estonia, Valka is the Latvian (and smaller) part of the unique twin town of Valga/Valka – divided between Latvia and Estonia when the republics were declared in 1920. The border, ironically nonexistent in Soviet times, is marked by a fence and can now be crossed in town.

The history of the 'great divide' and the 142 buildings Valka was allocated is explained in the **Valka Regional Museum** (Valkas novadpētniecības muzejs; ☎ 472 2198; Rīgas iela 64; adult/child 0.50/0.30Ls; 10am-5pm Mon-Fri, to 4pm Sat), which doubles as an unofficial tourist office.

Valka's sole hotel, **Oltrā Elpa** (☎ 472 2280; Zvaigžņu iela 12; s/d 17/20Ls; P) is modern, with tastefully furnished rooms and a decent restaurant. Saunas (8Ls per hour) and meals (4Ls) are also available.

From Valka bus station, at the northern end of Rīgas iela, daily buses run to/from Rīga (2Ls, 3¾ hours, up to four daily). There are no buses to/from Estonia; a **taxi** (☎ 987 1999) to Valka from the rank in front of the bus station should cost no more than 4Ls.

The main train station is on the Estonian side, but one or two trains daily to/from Rīga (2Ls; via Cēsis and Sigulda) stop on the Latvian side in Lugaži (1km off the main road, down a dirt road).

ALŪKSNE, GULBENE & AROUND

The primary reason to visit this area is to take a ride on the **Gulbene–Alūksne Narrow-Gauge Railway** (☎ 953 1097; www.banitis.lv; one-way ticket 0.70Ls), the only narrow-gauge railway still operating in Latvia today. Trains depart from Gulbene at 6am, 1.25pm and 6pm and meander through 33km of lovely, hilly countryside to Alūksne. The journey, by diesel locomotives and modern carriages, takes 1½ hours. Trains depart Alūksne at 7.50am, 3.20pm and 7.50pm.

Gulbene is a run-down town that holds little interest for tourists. By contrast, sleepy Alūksne is rather delightful and one of Latvia's prettier small villages. Still, there's not a lot to see or do, and you'll really only need a few hours to wander around. Alūksne, located 202km east of Rīga, is best known as being home to Ernest Glueck (1654–1705), a Lutheran clergyman who was the first person to translate the Bible into Latvian. You can study sermons and check out hymns at the **Ernest Glueck Bible Museum** (Ernsta Glika Bībeles muzejs; ☎ 432 3164; Pils iela 25a; adult/child 0.40/0.20Ls; 10am-5pm Tue-Thu, 8am-5pm Fri, 10am-2pm Sat), located in his old home. The nearby **Museum of Local Studies & Art** (Mākslas muzejs; ☎ 432 1363; Pils iela 74; adult/child 0.30/0.10Ls; 10am-5pm Tue-Thu, 8am-5pm Fri, 10am-2pm Sat) features exhibits pertaining to the region, and a small collection of oil paintings by Leo Kokles.

Or, take a day trip to the **Museum of Local Studies** (kalncempju novadpētniecības muzejs ates dzirnavas; ☎ 434 5452; admission 1Ls; 9am-5pm Wed-Mon) midway between Alūksne and Gulbene (as the crow flies) in Kalncempji. Granaries, a smithy, barns, a watermill, and 4000 exhibitions and photos are among this open-air farm museum's exhibits. During the lively harvest festival, on the second Saturday in September, test your threshing and rope-making skills, then relax with a slab of home-made bread and mug of home-brewed beer.

Nearby, in the small town of Stāmeriena, you can spend the night at the tranquil **Vonadziņi Guesthouse** (☎ 924 2551; www.vonadzini.lv; Skolas iela 1; r from 18Ls; P). On the shores of Lake Ludza, the thatched-roofed guesthouse offers 16 tidy rooms, a restaurant and a children's playground.

Anyone driving west from Alūksne to Valmiera might consider a side trip to **Zvārtava Manor**, built in a neo-Gothic style in 1882. The park-clad estate in Zvārtava is about 2km northwest of Gaujiena, signposted off the P23. Gaujiena itself is home to **Anniņas** (☎ 435 7101; 9am-5pm Mon-Sat), the house where Latvian song composer Joseph Wihtol (Jāzeps Vītols) spent most of his summers between 1922 and 1944 and composed some of his most important works.

Alūksne tourist office (☎ 432 2804; www.aluksne.lv/tourism; Dārza iela 8a; 9am-6pm Mon-Fri mid-Oct–mid-Apr, 9am-6pm Tue-Fri, 9am-3pm Sat mid-Apr–mid-Oct) stocks plenty of information on accommodation options in and around Alūksne.

VIDZEME UPLAND

Latvia's highest hills give way to the low-lying plains of Lubāna in the unique outdoor paradise of the Vidzeme Upland (Vidzemes Augstiene). Sandwiched between Cēsis and Madona, 80km southeast, forests and farms converge and two nature reserves offer ample opportunity for ecotourism adventures. From castle mounds to strange rock forms, from sacred springs of medicinal and mythological importance to baronial estates, churches and windmills, the Upland is both scenically and culturally appealing. Hills flag the approach to **Madona**, climaxing in Latvia's highest point, **Gaiziņkalns** (312m), 10km west of the small country town.

LATVIA

Picturesque lakes are sprinkled throughout the Upland, and the Gauja River, rising on the southern side of **Elkaskalns** (261m), flows in a big lazy circle around the region: east through Jaunpiebalga and Lejasciems, north past Vireši and Gaujiena to form the Latvian–Estonian border for a stretch, then southwest through Strenči and Valmiera.

Ērgļi, 28km southwest of Vecpiebalga, is a small ski resort. Latvian writer Rūdolfs Blaumanis (1863–1908) was born in **Braki**, 3km east, and his former home can be visited. Traditional musical instruments are exhibited in **Meņģeļi** (☎ 487 1077; adult/child 0.40/0.30Ls; 🕑 11am-4pm Thu-Sun), a picturesque farmstead by Lake Pulgosnis. It has a sauna and bathhouse (advance reservations only) and tents can be pitched on the lakeshore for 2Ls.

South of Madona, **Krustkalni Nature Reserve** (Krustkalni rezervāts; 30 sq km) and **Teiči Nature Reserve** (Teiču reservāts; 190 sq km) serve up titillating treats for outdoor buffs. Fish or splash around in one of Krustkalni's nine lakes, or search for rare birds and plants in its forests and swamps. Teiči, 11km southeast, features even more lakes, 19 in total, along with Latvia's largest bog and a migrating crane population. Both reserves offer ample opportunities for mushroom and berry picking (the cranberries are particularly delicious). Ļaudona village, wedged between the two, is a handy base for forays into either reserve. Both parks are headquartered at **Madona tourist office** (☎ 486 0573; Saieta laukums 1; 🕑 8am-5pm Mon-Fri). You must visit the tourist office before entering either reserve; both are open by appointment only.

The Rīga–Rēzekne–Moscow trunk road crosses the Upland from west to east (through Madona), but the north–south route from Cēsis to Madona (the P30 through Taurene and Vecpiebalga) is more scenic. The Rīga–Pskov–St Petersburg road (the A2) crosses the northern part of Vidzeme Upland.

LATGALE

Anyone searching for the heart and soul of Latvia just might find their elixir in Latgale. Another scenic beauty queen, Latvia's poorest region is well off the mainstream tourist's radar screen. With placid, bright-blue lakes, timeworn, gracefully decaying castles and centuries-old churches still packing in the faithful for Sunday Mass, Latgale has a timeless quality about it. From faded villages to the Soviet relic of Daugavpils, Latvia's second-largest city, the evidence of hard times is omnipresent. Life passes slowly here, but folks are friendly and this region's real attraction lies in its lack of serious attractions. Unless you're the type that relishes exploring one-shop towns, you'll probably want to head straight for the Latgale Upland. The region's most scenically enticing area, the Upland is packed with thousands of lakes to play in. It's also home to the shimmering white Aglona Basilica, Latvia's leading Roman Catholic shrine.

The southeastern region gets its name from the Latgal (Lettish) tribes who lived here at the time of the German invasion in the 12th century. It's also the main bastion of Roman Catholicism in Latvia, having been under Polish control from 1561 to 1772.

Getting There & Away

Buses and trains run between Rīga and Daugavpils several times per day. Buses also travel between the capital and other Latgale towns. The Latgale Upland is best explored by private vehicle, as public transport in this area is unreliable.

DAUGAVA VALLEY

Latvia's Daugava River rises in western Russia then flows through Belarus and Latvia before emptying into the Gulf of Rīga. The most impressive and longest river in the country, it has served as inspiration for myriad folk songs and mythical tales pertinent to Latvian culture. The Daugava Valley has been Latvia's main northwest–southwest transport corridor for centuries. Prior to hydroelectric construction projects, goods were transported downriver by rafts and barges. Today goods travel via a road and railway following the northern bank of the river and linking Rīga to Daugavpils.

The area is neither spectacularly beautiful nor profoundly interesting, but has a few worthwhile sights. Those interested in poetry may find a stop particularly worthwhile, as the Daugava Valley was home to two of Latvia's best-known poets, who are remembered in local museums.

From Rīga, the first worthy stopping place is **Ķegums**, 50km east of the city. Visit the hydroelectric plant, dam and on-site

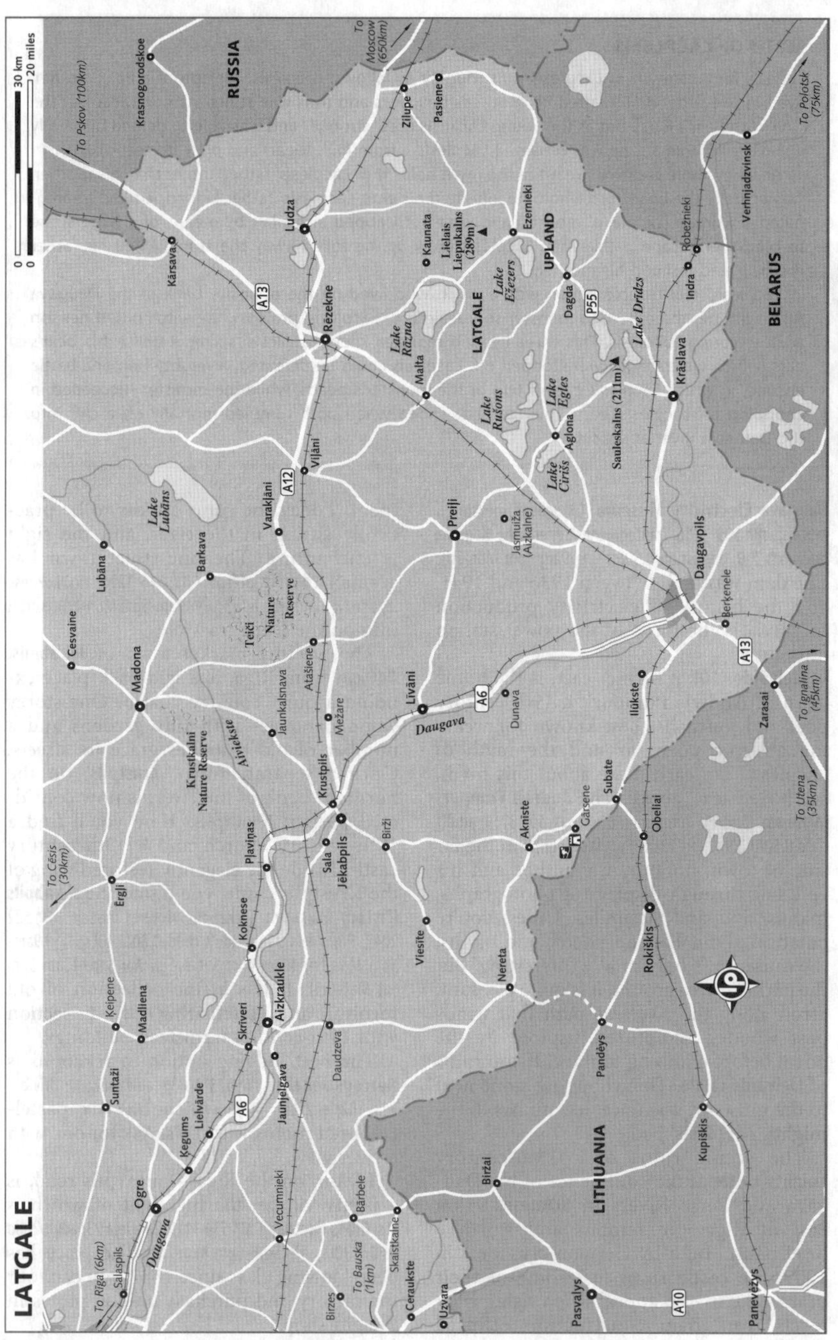
LATGALE
0 30 km
0 20 miles
RUSSIA
To Pskov (100km)
Krasnogorodskoe
To Moscow (650km)
Zilupe
Pasiene
Kārsava
Ludza
Kaunata
Lielais Liepukalns (289m)
Ezernieki
Rēzekne
A13
Lake Rāzna
Lake Ežezers
LATGALE
UPLAND
Dagda
P55
Lake Drīdzis
Indra
Robežnieki
Verhnjadzvinsk
To Polotsk (75km)
BELARUS
Malta
Lake Rušons
Lake Egles
Sauleskalns (211m)
Krāslava
Aglona
Lake Cirišs
Viļāni
A12
Lake Lubāns
Varakļāni
Preiļi
Jasmuiža (Aizkalne)
Lubāna
Barkava
Teiči Nature Reserve
Daugavpils
Berķenele
Cesvaine
Madona
Atašiene
Līvāni
A6
Dunava
Ilūkste
Zarasai
To Ignalina (45km)
Jaunkalsnava
Mežare
Daugava
Aiviekste
Krustkalni Nature Reserve
Krustpils
Jēkabpils
Sala
Birži
Akniste
Gārsene
Subate
Obeliai
To Utena (35km)
Pļaviņas
Ērgļi
To Cēsis (30km)
Koknese
Viesīte
Rokiškis
Nereta
Aizkraukle
Keipene
Madliena
Skrīveri
Pandėlys
Daudzeva
Suntaži
Jaunjelgava
Lielvārde
Ķegums
Kupiškis
LITHUANIA
Ogre
Vecumnieki
Bārbele
Biržai
Skaistkalne
Salaspils
To Rīga (6km)
Birzes
To Bauska (1km)
Ceraukste
Uzvara
Pasvalys
A10
Panevėžys

MYTH OF LĀČPLĒSIS

Latvia's famous myth of Lāčplēsis runs roughly as follows: Lāčplēsis, the son of a bear mother, lived in Lielvārde. He inherited his mother's bear ears and thus was at first named Lāčausis (The One With Bear's Ears). But as the young Lāčausis grew stronger and was able to defend his family against wild animals, he was renamed Lāčplēsis – from *lāčis* (bear) and *plēst* (to tear apart).

Another, more creative variant of the myth holds that Lāčplēsis' father, rather than his mother, was actually the bear from whom he inherited his ears. Lāčplēsis' father kidnapped and impregnated a woman (Lāčplēsis' mother) and kept her trapped in his lair by means of a large stone to block her escape path. When Lāčplēsis grew up, he rolled away the stone, killed his father the bear and rescued his mother.

Lāčplēsis' real trouble began with a witch who lived on the opposite bank of the Daugava River with her three-headed monster-son. Jealous of Lāčplēsis' prowess, the witch pitted her son against young Lāčplēsis. This three-headed monster knew Lāčplēsis' secret – that if his bear's ears (which were magic) were lopped off, Lāčplēsis could be defeated. A mighty Homeric battle ensued, in which Lāčplēsis cut off two of the monster's heads, while the monster succeeded in chopping off Lāčplēsis' ears. Their combat ended when both tumbled mortally off a cliff into the Daugava River at sunset.

Daugava Electricity Museum (Daugavas spēkstaciju muzejs; ☎ 505 3256; zaliteg@dhesk.energo.lv; Ķeguma prospekts 7-9; admission 0.50Ls; 🕑 9am-4pm Mon-Fri). The dam was built between 1936 and 1941, and the history of electricity production in Latvia is the focus of the power-station museum.

Lielvārde, 10km further east, is the home town of Andrejs Pumpurs, a 19th-century poet and journalist best known for weaving an epic poem around the myth of Lāčplēsis. To learn more about this myth, see boxed text, above. The **Andrejs Pumpurs Museum** (Andreja Pumpura muzejs; ☎ 505 3759; adult/child 0.50/0.20Ls; 🕑 10am-5pm Wed-Sun), on the far side of town, honours the author and his epic tale through displays of photographs, manuscripts and facsimiles. Unless you're fanatical about Latvian poetry and myths, the museum is only mildly interesting. But the parklike area around it is quite pleasant. Stroll along the riverside path that winds past wooden sculptures inspired by the poem before climbing to the cliff-top ruins of **Lielvārde castle**. The whopping stone next to the museum was once, legend has it, the mighty Lāčplēsis' bed.

The scenic ruins of a 13th-century **knights' castle** at the confluence of the Daugava and Perse Rivers in **Koknese**, 95km east of Rīga, are famous and worth a brief pause. Built by German crusaders in 1209, the castle ruins lost some of their dramatic cliff-top appeal when rising river levels from dam construction eclipsed them. Today the ruins appear to be practically sitting in the river, and the sight is enchanting. The one-street town has a small **tourist office** (☎ 516 1296; tic@koknese.apollo.lv; Blaumaņa iela 3; 🕑 9am-5pm Mon-Fri), with info on the Daugava Valley.

The wealthy market town of **Jēkabpils**, 140km from Rīga, is a laid-back place exuding a quiet country charm. One-storey wooden houses with tidy gardens and a number of old churches grace its streets. Once a separate town, **Krustpils**, on the northern bank of the river, is now considered part of Jēkabpils. Here you'll find a 17th-century church and a 13th-century castle. Inside the elegantly restored wing of the Krustpils castle, you'll find the **Jēkabpils History Museum** (Jēkabpils vēstures muzejs; ☎ 522 1042; Rīgas iela 216b; adult/child 0.80/0.40Ls; 🕑 9am-5pm Mon-Fri, 10am-4pm Sat & Sun Apr-Sep, 10am-3pm Sat May-Oct). It has a fine collection of old furniture and a fascinating open-air section with 19th-century farmstead buildings.

The best lodging option in Jēkabpils is **Hercogs Jēkabs** (☎ 523 3433; saule@niko.lv; Brīvības iela 182; r 25Ls; Ⓟ), which has six pastel-coloured rooms with TVs. Ask for one with a river view.

Līvāni, on the Rīga–Daugavpils road, is a pretty village, the highlight of which is its **Glass Factory** (☎ 534 1129; Zala iela 23; adult/child 0.50/0.30Ls; 🕑 9am-6pm Mon-Fri). The place has been blowing glass since 1887; you can tour the factory and purchase unique pieces in the gift shop.

Dunava, 27km further southeast, is the birthplace of Latvia's great poet Jānis Rainis. The village is said to be 'the cradle of the poet's soul'. The Rainis museum, **Tadenava** (☎ 525 2522; adult/child 0.40/0.20Ls; ⏰ 10am-5pm Tue-Sun), inside the house where he lived until the age of four, recounts Rainis' childhood. For details on other Rainis' museums in Latgale, see p242.

An alternative route to Daugavpils from Jēkabpils is via **Gārsene**, about 50km west of Daugavpils in the gentle Saara hills near the Lithuanian border. In winter you can ski here.

RĒZEKNE & AROUND

pop 44,000

Predominantly Russian Rēzekne, 235km east of Rīga, took a heavy beating during WWII when most of its historic buildings were pulverised by artillery fire. Tourist information says the town stands on seven hills like Rome, although this is hard to see. In reality, Rēzekne is a rather depressing place filled with drab grey buildings. We mention it, however, because it forms the northwestern gateway to the Latgale Upland, and you may find yourself spending a night here if you're heading in that direction.

The main street, Atbrīvoš anas alejā, runs from Rēzekne II train station (north) to the bus station (south), and crosses the central square en route. In the square's middle stands **Māra**, a statue twice destroyed by the Soviet authorities in the 1940s and only re-erected in 1992. Its inscription 'Vienoti Latvijai' means 'United Latvia'.

More enticing, and also the place for regional tourism information, is **Untumi** (☎ 463 1255; untumi@e-apollo.lv), a country ranch 7km northwest of town signposted off the Rīga road (the A12). It's a tranquil place where you can ride horses (2Ls to 5Ls per hour). Open fields surround the ranch and there's plenty of space to pitch your tent (1Ls per pitch) or have a picnic.

If you need to stay the night, the only real option is the **Hotel Latgale** (☎ 462 2180; latgale@hotel.apollo.lv; Atbrīvosvanas alejā 98; s/d from 13/22Ls; Ⓟ). Overlooking Māra, the hotel is not bad as far as Soviet-era hulks go. Prices reflect room size and extent of renovation. Try for an upper floor room, all of which have good city views.

Little Italy (☎ 462 5771; Atbrīvosvanas alejā 10; meals 4Ls), opposite the Hotel Latgale, is a relaxing spot for an evening meal. It dishes up pizza, pasta, meats and other Italian-inspired fodder in congenial environs.

The **bus station** (Latgales iela 17) has services to/from Daugavpils (2Ls, two hours, seven daily) and Rīga (2.70Ls, 4½ hours, up to six daily), among other destinations. The Eurolines bus from Rīga to St Petersburg stops here every second day.

Rēzekne II train station (Stacijas iela) has one train daily each way between Rīga and St Petersburg, and Moscow–Rīga. In all, there are four trains daily to/from Rīga (2.50Ls; four hours).

The St Petersburg–Vilnius train (every second day) is the only service to stop at the southern **Rēzekne I train station** (☎ 588 3801).

LATGALE UPLAND

A land of a thousand lakes (okay, really just a few hundred, but doesn't the other way sound better?), the Latgale Upland (Latgales Augstiene) is an angler's paradise and the region's star attraction. The shimmering blue lakes come in various shapes, sizes and hues and include **Lake Drīdzs**, Latvia's deepest at 65m, and **Lake Lubāns**, Latvia's largest, covering 82 sq km. Some of Latgale's prettiest scenery is found around **Lake Rāzna**, Latvia's second-biggest lake. Sheltered by rolling green hills, its easily accessible eastern and southern shores are perfect for strolling. With sweeping blue bays and dozens of islands, **Lake Ežerzers**, 45km from Rēzekne, is perhaps the region's most beautiful lake.

To say you've stood at the top of the Upland, visit its highest point, **Lielais Liepukalns** (289m), located 3km east of the Lake Rāzna–Ezernieki road. Other fine views are found at the Catholic church in **Pasiene**, 8km south of Zilupe and 4km from the Russian border. From here you can see across the plains of Russia, which stretch endlessly to the east.

The Latgale Upland is also home to Latvia's most important Roman Catholic shrine, **Aglona Basilica**. Even if you're not religious, the shimmering white, twin-towered church is a majestic sight worthy of a visit. Overlooking Lake Egles, south of Aglona village, the 18th-century church is engulfed by a vast grass courtyard, created when Pope John Paul II visited in 1993. The disproportionately large pulpit where he addressed the congregation still stands, as does the regal archway built at the entrance to the site. One of the basilica's 10 altars guards a miraculous icon of the Virgin Mary, said to have saved Aglona from the plague in 1708.

Every year on Ascension Day (15 August) pilgrims gather here. A candlelight procession the night before precedes the religious celebration. During the Soviet era Peteris Jakovels, then dean of Aglona, was sent into forced labour after rigging up loudspeakers outside the basilica on 15 August 1959.

Aglona village, wedged between Lake Egles (east) and Lake Cirišs (west), is 35km north of Krāslava and 8km off the main Daugavpils–Rēzekne road (the A13), which crosses the western part of the lake district.

Anyone keen on slightly obscure poetry might want to visit **Jasmuiža** (also called Aizkalne). The renowned Latvian poet Jānis Rainis (1865–1929) wrote some of his earliest works here, 9km west of Aglona. The **Rainis Memorial Museum** (☎ 535 4677; adult/child 0.60/0.40Ls; ⌚ 10am-6pm Fri-Sun) showcases traditional Latgalian pottery as well as changing literary exhibitions devoted to the Shakespeare of Latvia. True fans will find the **Rainis House Museum** (☎ 542 2515; adult/child 0.30/0.15Ls; ⌚ 10am-4pm Tue-Sat) in Berķenele, about 10km south of Daugavpils, equally interesting. The poet lived in the cottage for nine years.

One of the best places to stay in the area is **Cakuli** (☎ 537 5465; Ežera iela 4; dm 5Ls, r from 8Ls; P), a family-run guesthouse by Lake Cirišs. Choose from a dorm-style summer house, cosy attic digs with shared bathroom or a proper room with a balcony and lake view. A beating in its traditional lakeside Latvian sauna (10Ls) is an absolute must, and you can rent paddleboats (3Ls per hour).

DOWN & OUT DAUGAVPILS?

Daugavpils had 40,000 inhabitants before WWII, about two-thirds of them Latvians and one-third Russians or Poles. Today less than 15% of the population is Latvian (the lowest percentage of any town in Latvia), and Russian seems to be the only language used in shops, bars and on the street.

This massive population shift took place during the Soviet era when industries located here lured mainly Russian workers. Most industries were large, specialist, all-union plants performing a single service for the whole USSR, like the 4000 people who made bicycle and tractor chains or the 3500 repairing one type of railway locomotive. When the Soviet Union collapsed, so too did these industries – and Daugavpils.

More than a decade on, the city has yet to recover – it remains more economically depressed than other Latvian towns. Unemployment in the Daugavpils region clocks in at about 18%, close to the highest in the country.

Getting There & Away

Public transport is limited, making a car or bicycle the only way to get around the Latgale Upland. Despite the numerous lakes, there is nowhere to hire canoes in the region. A handful of daily buses run between Rēzekne and Ludza, and several daily between Daugavpils and Krāslava, Aglona and Ludza – although service is erratic and fares were not available.

DAUGAVPILS

pop 114,000

Daugavpils, Latvia's second-largest city, dates from 1275 and has a chequered past in which it has, at various times, been called Dünaburg by the Germans, Borisoglebsk by the Russians and Dvinsk by the Poles. Today it's a drab, post-WWII Soviet creation and so depressing to visit it's almost a national joke – a skyline of smoke stacks and the lumbering grey hulk of Daugavpils prison overlook the southern approach. But the city, perched on the northern bank of the Daugava River, 225km upstream from Rīga, does provide a gateway to the decidedly lovelier Latgale Upland. And intrepid travellers looking for a grittier, harder-edged slice of Latvian life just might find the place appealing.

Information

Datoruklubs (☎ 542 4457; Vienības iela 11; per hr 0.50Ls; ⌚ 10am-6am) Internet access.

Hansabanka (Rīgas iela 22) There's an ATM outside.

Tourist office (☎ 543 3818; Rīgas iela 22a; ⌚ 9am-5pm Mon-Sat) City and regional information.

Sights

Downtown Daugavpils is a typical Soviet city centre of straight streets arranged in a strict grid, a couple of large squares, a desolate park

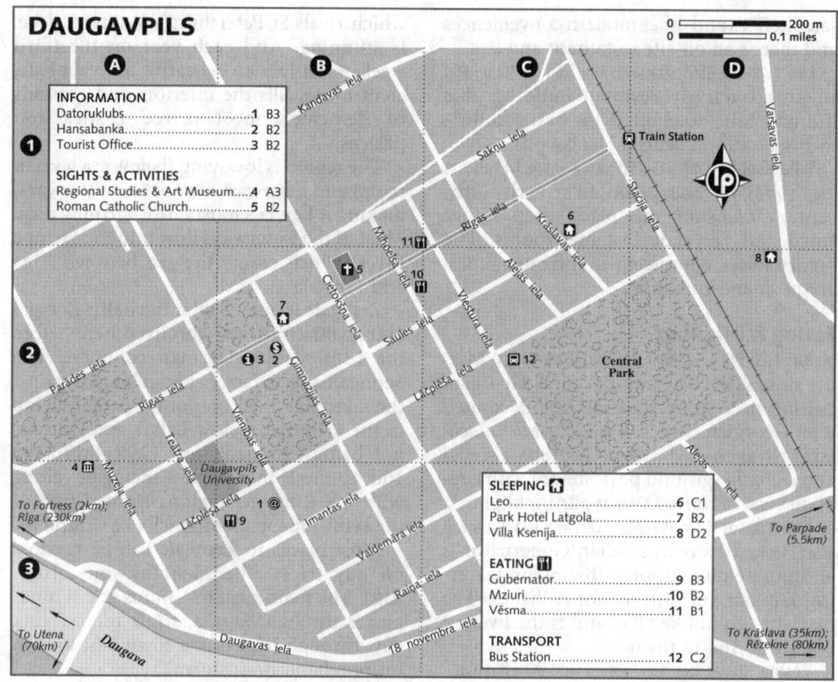

with a black-marble **monument** to those who died in WWII (and an eternal flame that no longer burns), and a mixture of pre-WWII and Soviet-era buildings. Ugly Hotel Latvija is the dominant landmark – a dramatic contrast to the white-domed **Roman Catholic church** next to it across Cietoksņa iela.

The **Regional Studies & Art Museum** (Novadpētniecības un mākslas muzejs; ☎ 542 4073; Rīgas iela 8; adult/child 0.40/0.20Ls; 🕑 11am-6pm Tue-Sat), inside an Art-Nouveau house guarded by stone lions, exhibits high-quality reproductions of abstract painter Mark Rothko's paintings. Rothko was born in Daugavpils in 1903 and lived there until 1913, when his family moved to the USA. Although long recognised in the West, Rothko's work remained relatively anonymous in Latvia until the collapse of the Soviet Union. Today the museum is striving to awaken national interest in the artist through its exhibition and educational programmes in local schools.

Daugavpils' most remarkable feature is the huge **fortress** (cietoksnis; ☎ 542 6398; adult/child 0.20/0.10Ls; 🕑 8am-6pm), built by the Russians in 1810 on the northwestern side of town and occupied by the Soviet army until 1993. A red-brick bunker monument by the entrance states (in Russian and Latvian) that the Tatar poet Musa Jalil languished here from September to October 1942, in what was then the Nazi concentration camp Stalag 340.

Tickets to the inner compound are sold at the former checkpoint. Once inside, you can follow the abandoned, run-down streets past boarded-up buildings and desolate parade areas. Part of the barracks – once home to 6000 army personnel including 2500 army cadets attending the engineering school – are occupied today by pensioners and those in need of state assistance. From town, a quiet riverside road leads 2km from the western end of Imantas iela to the fortress.

Sleeping

The following places include breakfast.

Park Hotel Latgola (☎ 542 0932; www.hoteldaugavpils.lv; Ģimnāzijas iela 46; r 40-60Ls; Ⓟ 💻) Once a dreary Soviet hotel, this place recently received a total face-lift and is now the classiest place to stay in town. The comfortable, although rather antiseptic, rooms feature

LATVIA

satellite TVs and other modern conveniences and there's an on-site restaurant and bar.

Leo (☎ 542 6565; Krāslavas iela 58; r 20-40Ls; P) In an attractively restored building, this intimate little hotel offers the best comfort-to-price ratio in central Daugavpils.

Villa Ksenija (☎ 543 4317; www.villaks.lv; Varšavas iela 17; s/d 35/45Ls, luxury ste 90Ls) In an early-20th-century mansion, this place offers rather small, but very comfortable, rooms. The luxury suites, complete with private saunas, are posh and romantic.

Eating & Drinking

Mziuri (☎ 542 1518; Mihoelsa iela 60; meals 5Ls) Mziuri shines. It dishes up delicious Georgian cuisine in a stone-clad interior decorated with Georgian castles. Eating its *kuchmachi* (spicy liver cooked with pomegranate seeds) and *chanahi* (ground pork stewed with eggplant) is a definite Daugavpils highlight.

Gubernator (☎ 542 2455; Lačpleša iela 10; meals 4Ls) Tucked away in a cellar, Gubernator is an unpretentious spot with a menu featuring Latvian and international dishes. The place has a publike vibe, and is the liveliest place to drink in town.

Vēsma (Rīgas iela 49; meals 2-4Ls) Multifunctional Vēsma features a self-service canteen with a decent salad bar on one side and a rather hip café and bar on the other. It's a popular place with the local crowd.

Getting There & Away

From the **bus station** (☎ 542 3000; www.buspark.lv; Viestura iela 10) buses run to/from Rīga (3Ls, 3½ hours, eight daily), Rēzekne (2Ls, two hours, seven daily) and Aglona (1Ls, 1½ hours, three daily).

Daugavpils is served by trains to/from Rīga (3Ls, four hours, four daily). For international rail service information to/from Gomel (Belarus) and St Petersburg (Russia), see p398. Trains also run to/from Vilnius (3Ls, three to four hours, three daily).

ZEMGALE

Architecture, art and history buffs will relish a visit to Zemgale, in central Latvia west of the Daugava River between Rīga and the Lithuanian border. Quaint country towns, and castles and palaces are the reason to come. Rastrelli's majestic Rundāle Palace, which rivals St Petersburg's Winter Palace, is stunning. And each year on the third weekend in July an evocative festival of ancient music fills the interiors and grounds of Zemgale's most prized castles and palaces.

The region is low lying (below sea level in parts) and has a vast network of waterways, making it Latvia's most fertile farming area. Most of the waterways flow into the Lielupe River, which enters the sea between Rīga and Jūrmala.

Zemgale is named after the Baltic Zemgal (Semigallian) tribes, who lived here before the 13th-century German conquest. The Semigallians, in fact, held out longer against the Germans than any other people living in the area that is now Latvia and Estonia, not being subdued until 1290. From the 16th to the 18th centuries, Zemgale (along with the Kurzeme region) formed part of the semi-independent Duchy of Courland.

Most places in Zemgale can be reached on day trips, albeit lengthy ones, from Rīga. The main road to Vilnius and Kaunas passes through Bauska, while the rail link cuts through Jelgava – a town best known for pop band Brainstorm.

Getting There & Away

Bauska, Rundāle and Jelgava can be visited on day trips from Rīga. Buses run between the capital and Bauska every half-hour or so. From Bauska, you can catch a bus to Rundāle, though Rundāle is best reached by private vehicle. Jelgava is best reached by train; these depart Rīga hourly.

BAUSKA

pop 10,620

Bauska is a country town with a small textile industry, 65km south of Rīga on the main Rīga–Vilnius road. A staging post on the way to Rundāle Palace, it's worth a brief stop in its own right to see its large castle.

As well as the music festival in July, Bauska Castle hosts a **medieval arts festival** in September.

Orientation & Information

The city centre is on the southern side of the main road bridge over the Mēmele River. Its **tourist office** (☎ 392 3797; www.bauska.lv; Rātslaukums 1; 🕑 9am-6pm Mon-Fri, to 3pm Sat) stocks lots of information on the Bauska region.

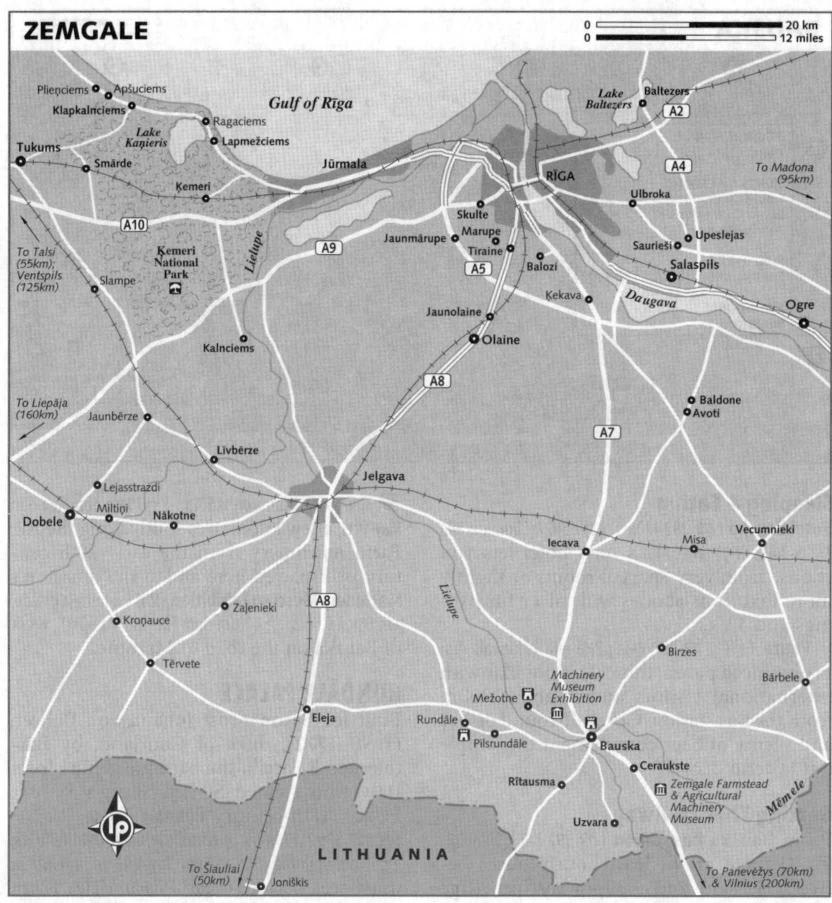

Sights

On a hillock between the Mēmele and Mūsa Rivers, 1km from the centre on the town's western edge, are the **Bauska Castle Ruins** (Bauskas pilsdrupas; ☎ 392 3793; 🕓 9am-7pm May-Sep, to 6pm Oct). From the bus station, walk towards the centre along Zaļā iela then branch left along Uzvaras iela beside the park at the top of Kalna iela. You can also approach the ruins along any street westward off Kalna iela. The castle was built between 1443 and 1456 as a stronghold for the Livonian knights. The imposing edifice was destroyed in warfare, rebuilt as a residence for the duke of Courland in the 16th century, and destroyed again during the Great Northern War (1706).

Despite the impressive reconstruction job carried out in the 1970s, it is still possible to see where parts of the old castle remain. Inside, **Bauska Castle Museum** (☎ 392 3793; adult/child 0.50/0.25Ls; 🕓 9am-7pm, to 6pm Oct) displays archaeological finds and a collection of 16th- and 17th-century art.

Around the centre are several 18th- and 19th-century houses and the local **History Museum** (Bauskas novadpētniecība un mākslas muzejs; ☎ 392 2197; bnmuzejs@apollo.lv; Kalna iela 6; admission 0.50Ls; 🕓 10am-6pm Tue-Sun May-Oct, 10am-5pm Tue-Fri, 10am-4pm Sat & Sun Nov-Apr). A 1930s hairdressing shop and exhibition on Bauska's pre-WWII Jewish community – 15% of Bauska's prewar population – are among the exhibits.

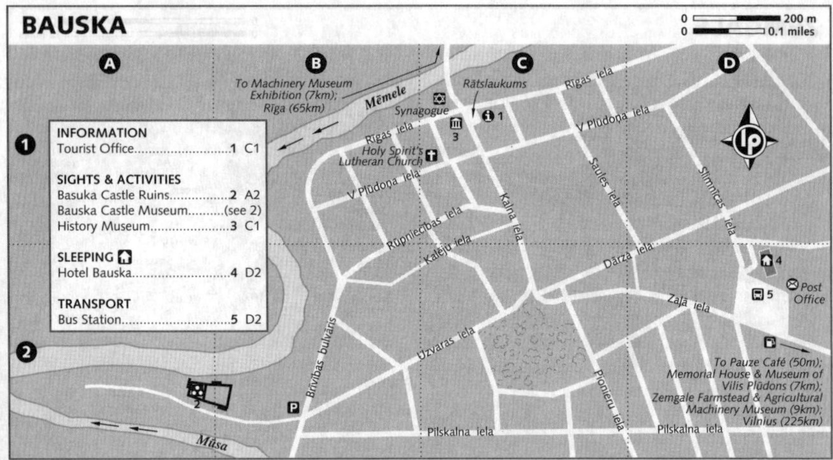

Sleeping & Eating

Hotel Bauska (☎ 392 4705; fax 392 3027; Slimnīcas iela 7; r 5-24Ls; P) Bauska's only hotel lets you choose from very Spartan rooms or slightly more luxurious abodes with nicer furnishings and TVs.

Pauze Café (☎ 392 7408; Zaļā iela 25; meals 4Ls) Pronounced pauza, this café is popular with international visitors and is about 300m from the bus station. Good all-round dishes and plenty of beer complement the simple but tasteful décor.

Getting There & Away

From Bauska **bus station** (☎ 392 2477; Slimnīcas iela 11) there are at least hourly buses between 5.30am and 5.30pm to/from Rīga (1.20Ls, 1¼ hours). All long-distance buses from Rīga to Panevėžys, Vilnius and Kaunas also stop here.

Around Bauska

Latvian poet Vilis Plūdons (1874–1940), best remembered for his children's poetry and romantic lyrics, was born just south of Bauska in **Ceraukste**. The farmstead where he grew up is now the **Memorial House & Museum of Vilis Plūdons** (māja muzejs; ☎ 919 4975; adult/child 1.50/1Ls; ⌚ 10am-6pm Wed-Sun May-Oct), which gives you all the details about his life. Wooden sculptures dot the garden and there is a traditional Latvian sauna.

19th-century rural life is captured at the **Zemgale Farmstead & Agricultural Machinery Museum** (Zemnieku sētas un lauksaimniecības maš imuzejs; ☎ 395 6316; admission 0.50Ls; ⌚ 10am-5pm Tue-Sun May-Oct), a few kilometres south along the A7. Farm machinery from the early 20th century is displayed here and at the museum's **Machinery Museum Exhibition** (Maš inu muzeja izstāde; admission 0.50Ls; ⌚ 10am-5pm Tue-Sun May-Oct), west of Bauska on the road to Mežotne.

RUNDĀLE PALACE

Built for Baron Ernst Johann von Bühren (1690–1772), duke of Courland, by Bartolomeo Rastrelli, the baroque genius from Italy who created St Petersburg's Winter Palace, 18th-century **Rundāle Palace** (Rundāles pils; ☎ 396 2197; www.rpm.apollo.lv; adult/child 1.50/1Ls; ⌚ 10am-6pm May-Oct, to 5pm Nov-Apr) is a Latvia must-see. Located near Pilsrundāle, 12km west of Bauska, this lavish creation is a monument to aristocratic ostentatiousness and is provincial Latvia's architectural highlight.

Restoration of the palace began in the 1970s, with most period furnishings being bought or donated. Its façade was restored in 2001. Of the palace's 138 rooms, about 40 are open to visitors. The Gold Room (Zelta zāle) was the throne room; its ceiling paintings display the baron's virtues as a ruler. The White Room (Baltā zāle) was the ballroom. The main staircase in this wing, with multiple mirrors in its walls, is perhaps the outstanding original Rastrelli creation here.

On the ground floor of the eastern wing you can visit the palace kitchens; the western wing was for the duchess' apartments. The

Rundāle Palace Museum (Rundāles pils muzejs) on the ground floor showcases paintings, silverware and other treasures from the Courland dukes' collections. In the old stables there is an interesting exhibition on Latvia's Lutheran churches in Soviet times.

A stroll through the gardens is a pleasant way to end a visit.

Sleeping & Eating

Straumeni (☎ 910 9388; Rundāle; d 10-12Ls; Ⓟ) Strau-meni is a countryside guesthouse with 10 beds 3km west of Rundāle Palace. Fish and boat here, or get beaten with birch twigs in the Latvian sauna. Breakfast is included.

Rundāle Palace Restaurant (☎ 396 2116; meals from 6Ls) Inside the palace kitchens, this place dishes up excellent steak, veal and fish entrees, although there's little for vegetarians.

Getting There & Away

Rundāle Palace is about 1km south off the Bauska–Eleja road. Unless you're on a tour or have your own transport, take a bus to Bauska, then a Rundāle-bound bus to Pilsrundāle; make sure you get off at Pilsrundāle, a different village to Rundāle, 2.5km west. From Bauska there are seven Pilsrundāle buses daily between 8am and 4.30pm; if you're coming from Rīga the tourist office there has updated schedules.

MEŽOTNE PALACE

On the northern bank of the Lielupe River, **Mežotne Palace** (Mežotnes pils; ☎ 392 8796; adult/child 0.50/0.20Ls; 🕑 8am-5pm), 11km west of Bauska in Mežotne, is worth a side trip. The palace was built in a classical style from 1797 to 1802 for Charlotte von Lieven, the governess of Russian empress Catherine II's

FROM RUSSIA WITH LOVE

How the Italian master Bartolomeo Rastrelli came to build the splendid Rundāle Palace in such a remote corner of Europe, which wasn't even part of the Russian Empire at the time, is a curious tale. It begins with the marriage in 1710 of Anna Ioannovna, a niece of Russia's Peter the Great, to Frederick, Duke of Courland – no doubt an affair of state as Russia clawed its way into Poland's sphere of influence. In 1730, following Peter the Great's death, Anna of Courland found herself crowned empress of Russia.

Baltic German baron Ernst Johann von Bühren (Latvian: Bīron) had been something of a failed adventurer in Courland and Russia before becoming Anna's chief adviser (and lover) a few years before she succeeded to the Russian throne. With more interest in the trappings than the exercise of power, Anna handed over much of the management of the empire to von Bühren and a small clique of German advisers. Von Bühren's heavy-handed and corrupt style soon made him unpopular with the Russian nobility, but as long as Anna ruled Russia, the baron's star waxed. When he decided he needed a new home to go with his new status, Anna dispatched Rastrelli to Courland, and in 1736 work began on the summer palace for von Bühren, at Rundāle. It proceeded quickly with as many as 1000 people working on it at one time.

In 1737 the duke of Courland died heirless and, thanks to Russian influence, von Bühren was handed the dukedom. He then began work on an even grander Rastrelli-designed palace at Jelgava, intended as his main residence. Rundāle was put on the back burner – and came to a halt altogether in 1740 when Empress Anna died and von Bühren's enemies took their revenge, forcing him into exile for the duration of Empress Elizabeth's reign in Russia.

Only in 1763 – with a German, Catherine the Great, now on the Russian throne – was von Bühren allowed to return and finish Rundāle, also restoring the parts that had decayed in his absence. This time Rastrelli brought the Italians Francesco Martini and Carlo Zucchi, who had worked on the St Petersburg Winter Palace, to do the ceiling paintings. JM Graf, who had worked on Prussian royal palaces in Berlin, came to do the elaborate wall decorations.

In contrast to Rastrelli's initial baroque work, Rundāle, completed in 1768, was in the newer rococo style. Von Bühren was able to enjoy the palace until 1795 when, in the third Partition of Poland, Courland became Russian territory, and Catherine gave Rundāle to one of her favourites, Subov. Von Bühren managed to shift most of the fixtures and fittings to some of his other estates in Germany.

grandchildren. Catherine II bequeathed the estate to von Lieven (ancestor of contemporary writer Anatol Lieven) in 1795. Agrarian reforms in 1920 transformed the family palace into an agricultural school (1921–41).

Mežotne Palace was restored in 2001 and a handful of rooms, including the dining room and grandiose Cupola Hall, can be visited. Part of the palace is a lovely live-like-royalty **hotel** (☎ 392 8796; mezotnepils@apollo.lv; r 30-40Ls; Ⓟ), one of rural Latvia's most charming. The surrounding 0.14-sq-km park is landscaped in English style. The rooms feature old-world décor – think cast-iron bed frames and lots of antiques.

Mežotne, an ancient Zemgalian hill fort settlement, is signposted west off the northbound Bauska–Rīga road (A7). The best way to reach it is by car.

JELGAVA

pop 63,000

Jelgava, 42km southwest of Rīga, is Zemgale's biggest town and home to Latvia's best known boy band, Brainstorm (Patra Vetra). From the 16th to 18th centuries, it was the capital of the duchy of Courland. Afterwards, it was the capital of the Russian province of Courland and a place of renowned society and hospitality where gentry would gather in winter.

Unfortunately, much of Jelgava was ruined in the two world wars. But lovers of Rastrelli architecture should stop here to see the 300-room, baroque **Jelgava Palace** (Jelgavas pils; ☎ 300 5617; Leilā iela 2; adult/child 0.50/0.30Ls; 🕙 10am-4pm Mon-Fri), built in 1783. The palace, now Latvia's Agricultural University, houses the family vault of the dukes of Courland. The palace is beside the main river bridge on the Rīga road, a 750m walk from the central square on the eastern side of town.

Jelgava **tourist office** (☎ 302 3874; Čakstes bulvāris 7; 🕙 10am-4pm Mon-Fri) has accommodation details.

Hotel Jelgava (☎ 302 6193; jelgava@apollo.lv; Leilā iela 6; s/d from 8/12Ls; Ⓟ) is the best sleeping option in the city. It has English-speaking staff and pleasant rooms in a lovely 1938 building near the palace.

Buses run every half-hour between Rīga and Jelgava (0.80Ls, 1¼ hours). One or two suburban trains an hour run from Rīga to Jelgava (0.75Ls, 50 minutes).

KURZEME

Latvia's sparsely populated western region, Kurzeme (Courland in English), with coasts on both the Baltic Sea and the Gulf of Rīga, is perfect for off-the-beaten-path exploring. The region's allure lies in its subtleties, and you'll need to prod beneath the surface to unearth its quiet charm. With the exception of its largest town, Liepāja, you won't find much rollicking nightlife or many big-city restaurants, but Kurzeme will enchant those searching for a taste of rural Latvian life. The wild coastline, crowned by glorious Cape Kolka, has long, untouched stretches of beautiful white-sand beaches and is home to Latvia's tiny ethnic minority, known as the Livs. The wealthy port town of Ventspils boasts brisk, clean air and a vibrant vibe. Slightly eccentric Liepāja is quickly turning hip and has become the epicentre of Latvia's burgeoning rock 'n' roll scene. It proudly boasts that it's home to Latvia's only 'rock café', a multilevel venue where bands play late into the night. The sleepy country town of Kuldīga is a real gem, perfect for wandering and immersing yourself in local life.

Getting There & Away

Multiple buses run between Rīga and Kuldīga, Ventspils and Liepāja each day, while Tukums can be reached by train from the capital. It is possible to journey to Cape Kolka by bus, but it is easier to explore this region by private vehicle.

History

Kurzeme is very much a region apart from the rest of Latvia. When Germany signed its unconditional surrender in Berlin in 1945, the Red Army had succeeded in reconquering the whole of the Baltic countries – except Courland. The region became sadly famous as the 'Courland Fortress' for the fight Latvian troops put up against the Red Army. The troops suffered heavy losses in the struggle.

Kurzeme is named after the Cours, a Baltic tribe who lived here before the 13th-century German invasion. They were an adventurous lot who would raid Scandinavia from time to time – and even occasionally join forces with the Vikings to attack Britain. Their leader, Lamekins, accepted Christian

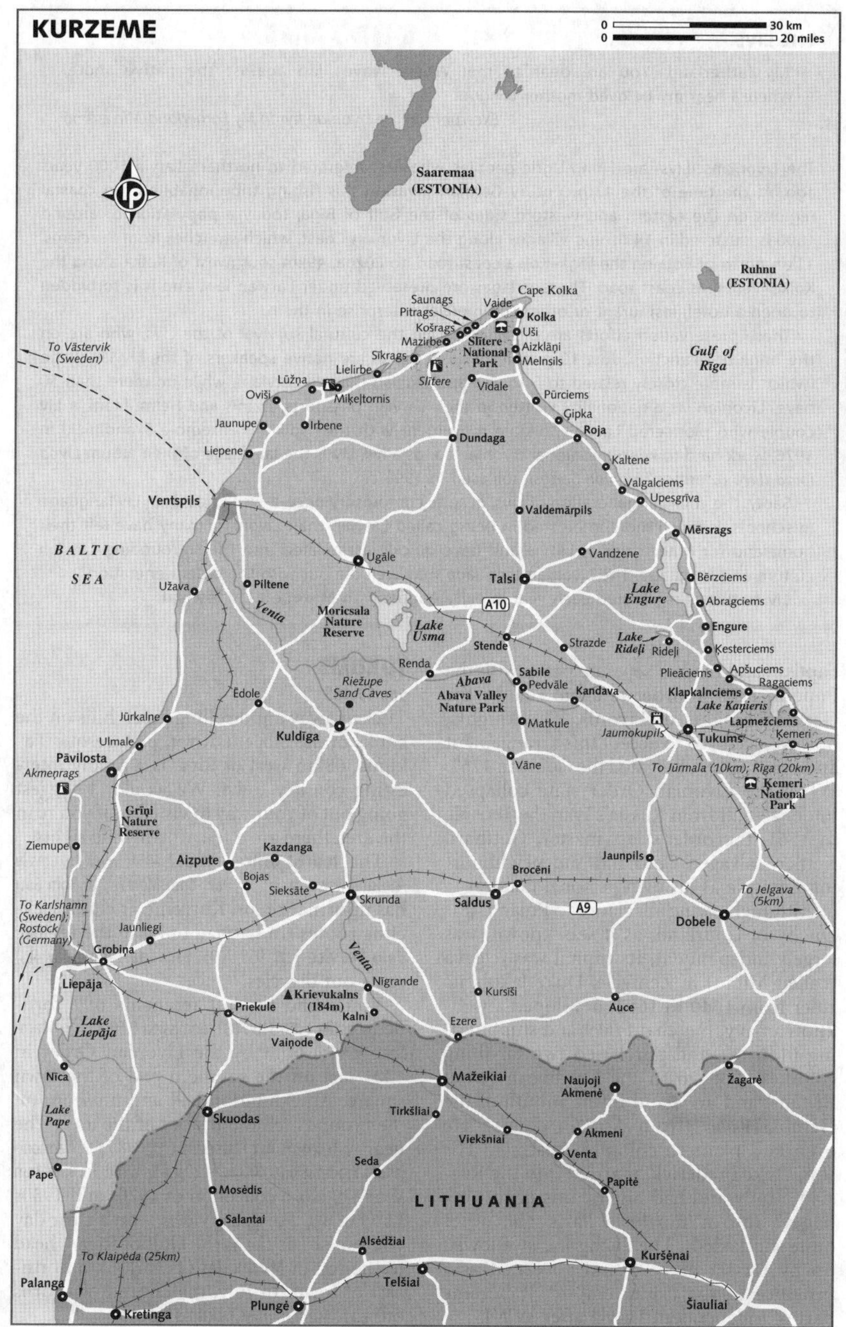
KURZEME
0 30 km
0 20 miles
Saaremaa (ESTONIA)
Ruhnu (ESTONIA)
Cape Kolka
Saunags
Pitrags
Vaide
Kolka
Košrags
Uši
Mazirbe
Slītere National Park
Aizklāņi
Melnsils
Sīkrags
Lielirbe
Slītere
Vīdale
Lūžņa
Miķeļtornis
Oviši
Pūrciems
Ģipka
Roja
Jaunupe
Irbene
Dundaga
Liepene
Kaltene
Valgalciems
Upesgrīva
To Västervik (Sweden)
Gulf of Rīga
Ventspils
Valdemārpils
Mērsrags
Vandzene
BALTIC SEA
Ugāle
Talsi
Bērzciems
Užava
Piltene
Venta
Lake Engure
Abragciems
Moricsala Nature Reserve
Lake Usma
A10
Engure
Stende
Strazde
Lake Rideļi
Rideļi
Ķesterciems
Renda
Sabile
Pedvāle
Plieņciems
Apšuciems
Abava
Ragaciems
Riežupe Sand Caves
Abava Valley Nature Park
Kandava
Klapkalnciems
Ēdole
Lake Kaņieris
Jūrkalne
Kuldīga
Matkule
Jaumokupils
Tukums
Lapmežciems
Ķemeri
Ulmale
Vāne
Pāvilosta
Akmeņrags
To Jūrmala (10km); Rīga (20km)
Ķemeri National Park
Grīņi Nature Reserve
Ziemupe
Kazdanga
Jaunpils
Aizpute
Bojas
Brocēni
Sieksāte
Skrunda
Saldus
To Jelgava (5km)
To Karlshamn (Sweden); Rostock (Germany)
A9
Dobele
Jaunliegi
Grobiņa
Venta
Liepāja
Nīgrande
Krievukalns (184m)
Kursīši
Priekule
Kalni
Auce
Lake Liepāja
Ezere
Vaiņode
Nīca
Mažeikiai
Naujoji Akmenė
Žagarė
Lake Pape
Skuodas
Tirkšliai
Akmeni
Viekšniai
Venta
Pape
Seda
Papitė
Mosėdis
LITHUANIA
Salantai
To Klaipėda (25km)
Alsėdžiai
Kuršėnai
Palanga
Telšiai
Kretinga
Plungė
Šiauliai

LATVIA

THE LIVS

'My fatherland, You are dear to me! Where waves lap against the native shore, Where I hear my beloved mother tongue!'

Excerpt from the Livonian hymn My Fatherland/Min izāmō

The Livonians (Livs) are Finno-Ugric peoples who first migrated to northern Latvia 5000 years ago. At the time of the 13th-century German invasion this fishing tribe inhabited the coastal regions on the eastern and western sides of the Gulf of Rīga; today a population of around 1600 is clustered in 14 fishing villages along the Livonian Coast, which stretches from Pūrciems, 11km north of Roja on the Rīga–Kolka coast road, to Lūžņa, 49km southwest of Kolka along the Kolka–Ventspils coast road. These villages are preserved under Latvian law, and it is forbidden to open a hotel, restaurant or other commercial enterprise in them.

These preservation efforts are intended to aid the cultural survival of the Livs, who are on the brink of extinction. Just 10 people or so in Latvia are native speakers of the Liv language (which is more closely related to Estonian and Finnish than to Latvian), while no more than 50 have 'Livonian' as a nationality written in their Latvian passports. Dainis and Helmi Stalti, a Liv couple who pioneered Latvia's folklore movement with their folklore ensemble Skandinieki in 1976, work hard to keep traditional Livonian songs alive. Liv is the language of their album *Livod lolod (Livu dziesmas/Livonian Songs)*, released in 1998.

Sadly, the younger generation of Livs, despite compulsory once-a-week classes in Liv language in schools, is much more interested in being called Latvian than Livonian; many have left their homeland for other cities in Latvia and have quickly assimilated into the surrounding Latvian culture and language. The Livonian language may well die out with the older generation.

Liv culture is celebrated each year in early August with Mazirbe's **Liv festival**.

baptism and made a separate peace with the Pope in 1230 in order to avoid rule by the German knights of Livonia. The knights, however, refused to accept this arrangement and eventually subjugated the Cours in 1267. When the Livonian Order state collapsed under assault from Russia's Ivan the Terrible in 1561, the order's last master, Gotthard Kettler, salvaged Courland and neighbouring Zemgale as his own personal fiefdom.

Although owing allegiance to Poland, this Duchy of Courland, as it was known, was largely independent. Its capital was Jelgava (called Mitau) in Zemgale. Duke Jakob, its ruler from 1640 to 1682, developed a well-known navy, merchant fleet and shipbuilding industry, and purchased two far-flung colonies: Tobago in the Caribbean (from Britain) and an island in the mouth of the Gambia River (from African chiefs). He even laid plans to colonise Australia! His son, Duke Frederick, married into the Russian family and had big dreams of turning Jelgava into a 'northern Paris' (he never quite succeeded). The duchy was swallowed up by Russia in 1795 and governed as a province of the tsarist empire. It became part of independent Latvia after WWI.

TUKUMS

pop 19,465

Tucked away amid rolling green hills on the banks of the Slocene River, picturesque Tukums, 68km west of Rīga, is a mildly interesting country town. We wouldn't suggest going out of your way to visit, but if you're in the area there are a few worthwhile sights.

The **tourist office** (☎ 312 4451; www.tukums.lv/turisms; Pils iela 3; 🕑 9am-6pm Mon-Fri, to 3pm Sat) has information on Kurzeme, including cycling routes (in Latvian only) in the region. **Velo Service** (☎ 950 7095; Raiļa iela 14; per day 4Ls) rents out bicycles.

You'll find the last remnants of a fortified **castle** (☎ 310 7081; admission 0.50Ls; 🕑 10am-5pm Mon-Fri) built by the Livonian Order in 1301 just off the southern end of the town square. An exhibition hall and museum on the grounds tell the history of the area. The nearby **Tukums Art Museum** (☎ 318 2392; Harmonijas iela 7; admission 0.40Ls; 🕑 10am-5pm Tue-Fri, 9am-1pm Mon & Sat) has a collection of 1920s and 1930s Latvian art. For great views – on a clear day you can see as far as the Gulf of Rīga – head to the top of **Milzukalns** (113m), 5km north-east of town. In July, the entire town turns out for the annual **Tukums festival**.

Pastel-themed **Hotel Arka** (☎ 312 5747; ervins@arka.apollo.lv; Pils iela 9; d/tr from 24/36Ls; P) is both spacious and comfortable and boasts a great spiral staircase. On weekends its cellar restaurant turns into a popular disco. Alternatively, opt for a night in a castle. Signposted some 12km northwest of Tukums off the Ventspils road (A10), **Jaumokupils** (☎ 310 7125; dm 7Ls, s 7-15Ls, d 10-25Ls; noon-6pm Mon, 9am-6pm Tues-Fri, 10am-6pm Sat, 11am-6pm Sun May-Oct, until 5pm daily Nov-Apr) was built in 1901 as a hunting residence for George Armitsted, mayor of Rīga between 1901 and 1912. During WWII the former aristocratic palace, turned over to the state by land reforms in 1919, served first as a Russian military school, then a German transmitting station and later a German hospital. The Latvian State Forestry Commission now owns the **castle** (adult/child 0.50/0.25Ls), hotel and restaurant. The original ceramic-tiled stove featuring 50 different drawings of early-20th-century Rīga and Jūrmala is in the entrance hall and is stunning. Spending a night here lets you get a feel for the way Latvia's royalty lived in the old days.

There are buses to Rīga (1Ls, 1¼ hours, eight daily). You could combine a visit to Tukums with one to Jūrmala, since they're both on the same suburban railway line from Rīga. Tukums I station (1Ls, 1½ hours), the first station you reach coming from the east, is nearer the town centre than Tukums II (1.50Ls), where the trains terminate four minutes later. At least 10 trains run in each direction daily.

TALSI & AROUND

pop 12,391

Once a medieval war zone, today peaceful Talsi, 115km from Rīga, is the cultural and economic centre of northern Kurzeme. Nine hills, which locals are fiercely proud of, ring the village. Cobbled streets twist around the slopes above the town's two small lakes, making it a pleasant place to wander. Quiet as it might be, Talsi does serve as good base for exploring. About 30km west lies **Lake Usma**, a 39-sq-km puddle of water polka-dotted with seven islands and backed by leafy forests. The **Moricsala Nature Reserve**, established in 1912, is one of Europe's oldest nature reserves. It protects the lake's western waters, shores and several islands. The heavily wooded reserve makes a great camping place, with several serene spots around the sandy shores; see below. The reserve's **tourist office** (☎ 324 2542; Dakterlejas iela 3, LV 3270 Dundaga) is in Dundaga village.

Orientation

A shallow valley runs north–south through Talsi making it surprisingly hilly for such a flat region. There are two lakes, one on the southern edge of town (Lake Talsu), and a bigger one (Lake Vilku) towards the north. The town centre is at the top of the valley's western slope, with the central square at the meeting of Valdemāra iela and Lielā iela. The **market** (Ezera iela 7) is north off Lielā iela in the lower part of town.

Information

Latvijas Krājbanka (Lielā iela 3) Has an ATM.
Tourist office (☎ 322 4165; www.talsi.lv; Lielā iela 19/21; 10am-1pm & 1.30-5pm Mon-Fri) Inside Talsi Culture House.

Sights

There's really not a great deal to do in Talsi except wander around and enjoy the surroundings. Rising above **Lake Talsu** on the eastern side of town is **Pilsētas dārzs**, an ancient Cour castle mound topped by **Freedom Sun**, a statue of a man sitting Buddha-style. It was erected in 1996 in remembrance of Latvia's freedom fighters.

Above the mound, local history is documented at the **Talsi District Museum** (Talsu novada muzejs; ☎ 322 2770; Milenbaha iela 19; adult/child 0.50/0.30Ls; 11am-5pm Tue-Sun summer, 10am-4pm Tue-Sun winter). The museum is in a baronial manor dating to 1880.

South of town, the **Museum of Agriculture Machinery** (Lauksaimniecības tehnikas muzejs; ☎ 328 1343; Celtnieku iela 11; adult/child 1/0.50Ls; 8am-6pm Mon-Fri) exhibits tractors from the 19th and 20th centuries.

Sleeping & Eating

Usma Camping (☎ 633 4500; www.usma.lv; Priežkalni; camp site 1Ls plus per adult/child 1/0.50Ls, cabin from 10Ls; May-Oct; P) Usma is the get-away-from-it option for those who seek peace. You can camp, fish, sail, row, swim and play volleyball at this lakeside site, 1km south of the A10 on the road to Usma village. Although a bit more rustic, it's a much better option than Talsi's sole hotel.

Talsi (☎ 322 2689; viesnica_talsi@e-apollo.lv; Kareivju iela 16; r 12-40Ls; P) A Soviet-era block of 95

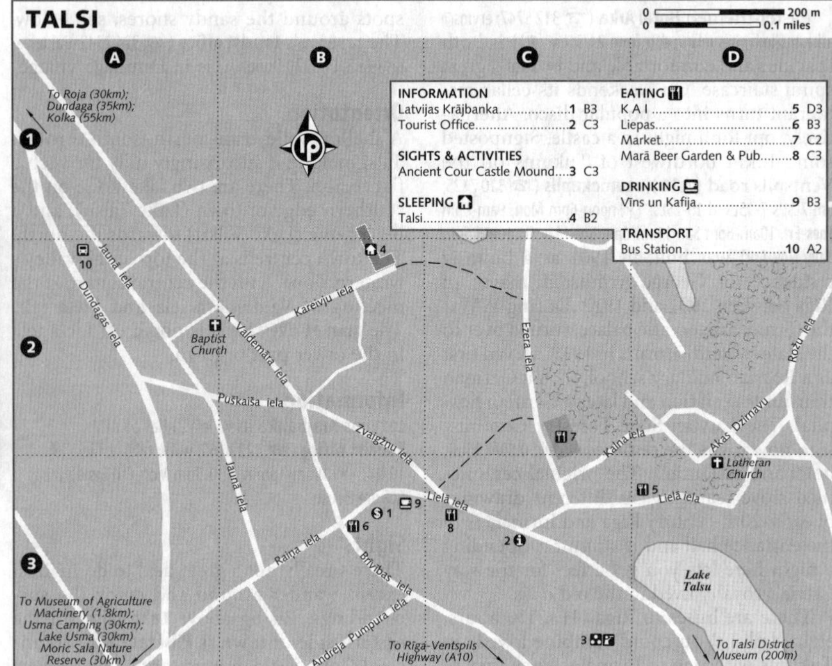

rooms situated atop a hill, Talsi's only hotel boasts a striped yellow-and-beige exterior and a renovated interior.

Marā Beer Garden & Pub (Lielā iela 16; meals 3Ls) A hip bar (at least by Talsi standards), this place has a cafeteria-style eatery on the ground level and a cellar beer bar serving big platefuls of grilled meats and lots of salads.

KAI (☎ 928 8407; Lielā iela 30; meals 2Ls; 🕑 11am-3am) KAI competes for the title of the most kitsch spot in the Baltics. Munch on unremarkable food and watch fish bob in plastic tubes of florescence. The place has a pool table and late-night disco.

Liepas (Lielā iela 1; meals 2Ls) Liepas is a food shop and café rolled into one. Be sure to try the *platmaize*, a sponge cake topped with curd, particular to this region.

Vīns un Kafija (☎ 328 1049; Lielā iela 7) The place to taste and buy wine (albeit wine produced everywhere but Latvia) and coffee. It runs a beer tent out front in summer.

Getting There & Away

From the **bus station** (Dundagas iela 15), on the road north to Dundaga, there are buses to/from Rīga (2Ls, 2½ hours, hourly), Ventspils (1.50Ls, 1½ hours, twice daily) and Liepāja (2.50Ls, 4½ hours, six daily).

NORTHERN KURZEME

You could visit the remote northern tip of Kurzeme in a day trip from Talsi, or make a long loop on the way to Rīga or Ventspils. The area remains fairly untravelled and is worth taking time to explore.

Getting There & Away

Northern Kurzeme is best seen by private transport, although there are sporadic buses; always check return schedules before setting out. Buses to Rīga (3Ls, four hours, twice daily) pass through Mērsrags and Roja.

Ķemeri National Park

Well off the beaten track, **Ķemeri National Park** (☎ 776 5387; www.kemeri.gov.lv; 🕑 May-Oct 15) is one of Latvia's most beautiful reserves and well worth visiting. Established in 1997, the park spans 427.9 sq km from just west of Jūrmala to Klapkalnciems, and inland to Kalnciems. It is easily accessible from the

Rīga–Kolka coastal road (P128). Ancient bogs, swamps, lakes and forests, dating back about 8000 years, are all found here, along with a wealth of flora and fauna. Check the website for updated information as the park was undergoing major restructuring and the information centre was in the process of moving when we stopped by.

Hiking is the main activity in the park, and a vast network of wooden boardwalks and nature trails traverse the beautiful landscape. The 1930s spa town of **Ķemeri**, in the middle of the park, is known for its sulphurous springs and is also the starting point for the **Dumbrāja laipa**. This 600m, raised plank trail (look for the signs in the centre of town) takes about 30 minutes to hike and winds past rivers and forests. The quiet hamlet is also the starting point for the 3km **Laipa Lielajā Ķemeru tīrelī**. Slightly more strenuous, this boardwalk jaunt crosses the large bog that fills the entire southern half of the park. To reach the trailhead turn right on the A10/E22 at the Ķemeri train station then take your first left by the cemetery. In the park opposite town, 12 cutely named bridges – Musical Bridge, Bridge of Sighs, Bridge of Caprices etc – cross the Vēršupite River and are scenic spots to snap a picture.

The information centre arranges **bat-watching** expeditions and runs half-day **nature workshops** in summer. For birding buffs, there's **Lake Kaņieris**, home to 237 bird species nestled around 14 islets.

Fish canning and smoking remain traditional occupations in the national park. Nowhere smells fishier than **Lapmežciems**, overlooking Lake Kaņieris, 3km west of Jūrmala. Sprats are canned in the factory on the right at the village's eastern entrance. The village market sells freshly smoked eel, sprat, salmon and tuna, as does the market in **Ragaciems**, 2km north.

There are plenty of places to stay along this coastal stretch. The Soviet-era **camp site** (☎ 314 3146; dm 2Ls; ⏰ summer only), 2km north of Apšuciems, is rather uninspiring and offers beds in very rustic wooden huts with shared bathrooms. The roadside car park across the street is much more appealing, and you can camp for free amid pretty wooded sand dunes. There are motels on either side of the road at the eastern entrance to Ragaciems. The very modern **Lindaga café-bistro** (☎ 316 3544; meals 2-6Ls) is a good place to fill up before or after a hike. It serves big plates of simple, but hearty, Latvian fare.

Lake Engure to Roja

Two kilometres north of the fishing village of Engure, **Lake Engure** is the country's third-largest lake and a major bird reservation; 186 species (44 endangered) nest around the lake and its seven islets. The **Engure Ornithological Research Centre** (☎ 947 4420; Bērzciems; ⏰ by appt only) arranges bird-watching expeditions to the observation tower in the middle of the lake. The centre, signposted 600m north of Bērzciems village, is at the end of a 2.5km dirt track.

You can rent a boat to row around the lake (1/5Ls per hour/day) from the *laivu bāze* (boat station) off the main road in Bērzciems. **Abragciems Kempings** (☎ 316 1668; camp site 8Ls), a site by the sea 4km north of Engure (open only during summer), also offers boat rentals and has a serene sauna.

At **Lake Rideļi**, a tiny lake 15km inland (west), you can visit **Rideļi Watermill**, still in operation, and munch on pancakes made with local flour at the adjoining **Cope Café & Guest House** (☎ 316 1373; s/d incl breakfast 9/16Ls, camp site 2Ls; P). The camp site is open only during summer. Boat hire costs 4.50Ls per day.

Roja, 50km further north, is another fishing town, the history of which is told at small **Maritime & Fishing Museum** (Jūras un zvejniecības muzejs; ☎ 326 9594; Selgas iela 33; admission 0.50Ls; ⏰ 10am-6pm Tue-Sat). The most interesting exhibits are those relating to the development of Roja's collective fishing farms and state fish cannery in the 1950s.

The **Roja Hotel** (☎ 326 0209; Jūras iela 6; d 20Ls; P), just past the harbour, is one of the few lodging options in the area. It's a decent, comfortable place with simple but brightly furnished rooms.

Kolka & Cape Kolka

Enchantingly desolate and hauntingly beautiful, a journey to Cape Kolka (Kolkasrags) feels like visiting the ends of the earth. Kurzeme's most northerly village, Kolka stands on the Gulf of Rīga just south of Cape Kolka – the dividing point between the gulf and the Baltic Sea. The village is not pretty, but its dramatic position on the tip of the cape is reason enough to spend time strolling along sandy beaches, over dunes and through forests. During the Soviet era

LATVIA

the area was a military reserve, out of bounds to civilians, and today the region's sparsely populated villages have an almost eerie, long-forgotten feel about them. But the rugged coastline here is some of the Latvia's most captivating, with long uninterrupted stretches of white-sand beaches set against forests of spruce and pine. The cape itself is the point where the line of beach and dunes changes direction – making it possible to stand with one foot in the Gulf of Rīga and the other in the Baltic Sea.

Simple, but quite friendly, **Ūši** (☎ 327 7350; www.kolka.lv; camp site/r 3/10Ls; P) has little wooden chalets with sea views, a communal kitchen and places to pitch tents in the garden. To find it, look for the brick house, opposite the onion-domed Orthodox church on the main road at the village's northern end. Featuring clean and modern rooms, **Zitari** (☎ 324 7145; d 15Ls; P) is Kolka's only hotel. Its ground-floor café (meals 4Ls) is popular for a drink and a plate of herrings (0.80Ls) or smoked eel (2.45Ls) after a trip to the windy cape. Look for it on Kolka's only real street.

Slītere National Park

Overlooking the Gulf of Rīga and the Baltic Sea, **Slītere National Park** (☎ 328 1066; www.slitere.gov.lv) is a magnificent pocket of spectacular sand dunes and forests covering 163.6 sq km on Latvia's most savage coastal tip. Beginning at Cape Kolka, and extending 5km to 10km inland, the park stretches 26km west along the Baltic Coast to Sikrags, and shelters deer, elks, buzzards and beaver. Rare species include the yew tree, pond turtle, golden eagle and osprey. In mid-April, during spring migration, the Kolka peninsula buzzes with 60,000-odd birds. The park's population (1300) doubles in summer when rich Rīgans flock to their summer cottages.

The information centre, inside Slītere lighthouse (right), runs a guide service (0.30Ls per hour) and is the starting point for a 1.3km **nature trail** through Latvia's oldest forest. Protected since 1921, the broad-leaf forest shelters a calcium-rich bog and is prime ground for rare orchid species (which flower in June or July).

THE KOLKA–VENTSPILS COAST ROAD

Far removed from the 21st century's hustle and bustle, the remote villages along Latvia's northernmost coastal road are nestled among a natural wilderness of sea, sand and breathtakingly beautiful beaches and pine forests. Feel the centuries slide backwards as you explore these sleepy fishing hamlets where time all but stands still.

Elk antlers hang from street signs in **Vaide**, 10km west of Kolka, where there is little to see or do except wonder at the simple wooden houses. If the antlers spark your curiosity, there are 518 more in the **Museum of Horns & Antlers** (Ragu kolekcija; ☎ 324 4217; admission 0.50Ls; 9am-8pm May-Oct). The collection, creatively arranged in an attic, is the result of one man's lifetime of work as a forest warden in the region (none are hunting trophies). In summer you can **camp** (camp site per person 0.50Ls) in the field behind the museum; there's a pond, toilets and picnic tables.

Eighteenth-century wooden buildings line the sand-paved streets in pleasant **Košrags**, 6km to the west. Spend the night at **Jaunitmači viesu nams** (☎ 941 2974; r 30Ls), a quaint B&B with charming rooms and onsite sauna.

Behind a gorgeous stretch of dune-backed beach, neighbouring **Mazirbe**, 18km southwest of Kolka, is home to the **Livonian People's House** (Lībiešu tautas nams; Livlist rovkuoda in Livonian). In a modernist white-cube 1930s building, it hosts exhibitions on Livonian culture. Livonian ethnographical treasures, including a small costume display, are found at the **Rundāli Museum** (Muzejs Rundāli; ☎ 324 8375; by appointment only), located inside a squat, barnlike building on your right when entering the village. To experience village life first-hand, spend the night at **Kalēji** (☎ 324 8374; d from 5Ls; P), a 12-bed guesthouse with sauna in a private home. It is well signposted.

From Mazirbe a gravel road leads inland to Dundaga and Talsi. About 5km south of Mazirbe you will see a sign for **Slītere Lighthouse** (Slīteres bāka; ☎ 324 9215), 1.4km down an even rougher track. Pay 0.30Ls and climb 101 steps for an aerial view of the national park and the Estonian island of Saaremaa. The lighthouse was built in 1849 and hosts the national park information centre.

Latvia's tallest lighthouse at 55.6m, **Miķeļ Lighthouse** (Miķeļ bāka; ☎ 368 1501), built in 1957, is further down the coast in **Miķeļtornis**. The caretaker lives opposite the lighthouse entrance on the 1st floor; ask nicely and he'll take you up the 277 steps for yet another stunning view.

DUNDAGA

Set amid three lakes, 20km from the Gulf of Rīga and 40km north of Talsi, Dundaga is known for its **crocodile statue** (cnr Talsu & Dinsberga iela). The 3m concrete crocodile, which lazes on a bed of stones, was given to the town by the Latvian consulate in Chicago in September 1995. The statue honours Arvids von Blumenfelds, a Latvian born in Dundaga but forced to flee his home town during WWII for Australia. Here he spent his days hunting crocodiles in the outback, and local lore has it that the film *Crocodile Dundee* was based on this Dundaga hero. As you enter Dundaga from the north, the crocodile is on your left.

If you're looking for ghosts, pay a visit to **Dundaga Castle** (Dundagas pils; ☎ 324 2093; Pils iela 14; adult/child 0.50/0.20Ls; 10am-noon & 1-4pm Mon-Fri, 11am-4pm Sat & Sun). Constructed in 1249, it is the largest castle in northern Courland. Legend has it that a fair maiden made the mistake of intruding upon a gnomes' wedding and as punishment she was walled up here alive. She haunts the castle to this day, appearing when the moon is full.

Pūpoli (☎ 324 0100; pupoli@dundpag.apollo.lv; Gipka iela; camps site/d 2/20Ls; P) is a wooden terraced guesthouse with four comfortable rooms and oodles of green space for campers. It arranges berry- and mushroom-picking trips, forest walks and sauna soaks. Pūpoli is 600m east of Dundaga centre along the Gipka road.

ABAVA VALLEY

Carved by glaciers a few millennia ago, the U-shaped Abava Valley is a picturesque place popular with outdoor enthusiasts. The Abava River from near Kandava to its confluence with the Venta River is a popular canoe route, and the area also offers lots for hikers and bikers.

Kandava

Split in two by the Abava River, Kandava is a charming town located 20km south of Strazde. A mound fortified by the ancient Cours and the ruins of a **Livonian Order castle** appear to the north. From the top of the mound, there is an excellent view of the fine **stone bridge** (1875) – one of Latvia's oldest – across the Abava River. Bikes can be rented at **Velotūre** (☎ 941 5842; Sabiles iela 6; per day 4Ls) or **Plosti** (☎ 313 1349; www.plosti.lv; Rēdnieki; per day 4Ls; dm 3Ls; P). The latter is a recreational centre that also offers canoe hire, guided paddles down the Abava, horse rides and fishing trips. The place doubles as a small hostel, offering accommodation in basic dorms. For a simple meal, visit **Pils** (meals 2-4Ls) a green-and-white cottage café below the castle ruins. It has a wonderful fireplace in winter and a sunny terrace in summer.

Sabile & Pedvāle

The sleepy, cobbled-street village of Sabile, 14km downstream from Kandava, is famed for its vineyard – listed in the *Guinness Book of Records* as the world's most northern. A Council of Europe flag marks the legendary patch of land, called **Vīna kalns** (Wine Hill), located on a hill just north of town. Founded in the 17th century by Duke Jakob of Courland, the vineyard was never very productive and fell into disuse. Although operations resumed in 1936, the vineyard's focus lay in researching hardy strains of vines rather than producing high-quality wines. The only chance to taste local wine (it's impossible to buy) is at Sabile's **wine festival** in July, but the **tourist office** (☎ 325 2269; Ventspils iela 14; 10am-3pm Mon-Fri) sells tickets (0.15Ls) that allow you to check out the wine terraces. The self-guided tours are worthwhile, providing great views over the town. Other Sabile highlights include a 17th-century **Lutheran Church**, at the western edge of town. The blazing white church features an arresting baroque pulpit held up by four gryphon-headed snakes. Follow the trail behind the church to the summit of **Castle Hill**, where there's an ancient fort and excellent valley views.

Across the river from Sabile the road climbs to the **Pedvāle Open-Air Art Museum** (Pedvāles brīvdabas mākslas muzejs; ☎ 762 2335; www.pedvale.lv; adult/child 1/0.50Ls, guide 5Ls; 9am-6pm May-Oct), located about 1.5km south of the tourist office. The museum spreads over 2km and features over a hundred works of art created by artists from around the world. Many of the sculptures, installations and paintings were created in memory of those deported to Siberia. The graves of Latvian soldiers who died during WWII are also on the estate. Also located here is **Firkspedvāle**

LATVIA

(☎ 325 2249; pedvale@pedvale.lv; camp site 1Ls, r per person 5Ls; Ⓟ), an atmospheric guesthouse with a handful of simply furnished rooms featuring wooden floors and rustic beams. The camp site is closed during winter. Opposite the guesthouse, **Krodziļš Dāre** (☎ 325 2273; meals 4Ls) dishes up satisfying food, from simple salads to hearty plates of freshly caught trout. Sit outside on the wooden terrace in summer.

In winter you can ski at **Zviedru cepure** (☎ 651 4001; www.zviedrucepure.lv; lift ticket per hr/day 1/6Ls; 🕑 10am-1am Mon-Thu, 9am-1am Fri-Sun winter, 10am-10pm Mon-Thu, 9am-midnight Fri-Sun summer), a recreational centre 3.5km south of Sabile on the road to Matkule. You can rent ski or snowboarding gear here (2Ls to 5Ls per hour) and whiz down its two short downhill runs. In summer get your thrills by flying down its dry toboggan run. The place also rents bikes and boats and you can pitch a tent for 2Ls.

Abavas rumba is a small waterfall 4km northwest of Sabile. The **Rendas rumba**, off the Abava River at Renda, 20km downstream on a tributary called the Ivanda, falls 2m and is Latvia's highest natural waterfall.

This area is best explored by car.

VENTSPILS

pop 44,000

Viewed by Latvians as the country's most dynamic city after Rīga, Ventspils is a tidy oil-transit port renowned for the riches it reaped from black-gold exports. The air is brisk and clean, and the well-kept buildings are done up in various pastel and yellow hues. Small shops and outdoor cafés abound, and the city is home to the country's best skate park and an Olympic training centre. However, Ventspils, 200km west of Rīga, is an industrial town at heart. Its port is Latvia's busiest, and much of its tourism is business-oriented.

There was a Cour settlement here before the Livonian Order founded a castle in 1244. Ventspils was in the Hanseatic League from the 14th to 16th centuries, and in the 17th century Duke Jakob of Courland based his navy here. After a spell in the doldrums the town revived with the arrival of a railway from Rīga in the early 20th century. During the Soviet era Ventspils was a key USSR port and attracted a workforce mainly from non-Latvian parts of the USSR – 32% of the population remains Russian today.

When in Ventspils, do as locals do – drink Užavas, a light beer brewed locally.

Orientation

The Venta River flows up the eastern side of the town then turns west for its final 2.5km to the sea. Old Town, south of the river, was the real town centre until the Soviet navy took over the riverside area, and a new centre was created around Ganību iela and Kuldīgas iela, 750m or so further south.

Information

Baltijas Tranzītu Banka (cnr Liela & Kuldīgas iela) Currency exchange and ATM.

Planet Internet Club (Andrejs iela 7; per hr 1Ls; 🕑 10am-10pm) On the top floor of the Andrejs Nams shopping centre.

Post office (Jūras iela)

Tourist office (☎ 362 2263; www.tourism.ventspils.lv; Tirgus iela 7; 🕑 8am-7pm Mon-Fri, 8am-5pm Sat, 10am-5pm Sun May-Oct, 9am-5pm Mon-Fri, 10am-3pm Sat Nov-Apr) Reams of tourist info; reserves accommodation.

Sights & Activities

Ventspils' prime attraction is its coastline, which is laced with a sandy, dune-backed beach stretching south from the river mouth, about 2km west of the town centre. You can reach it along Viļņu iela (or Medņu iela), which branches off Vasarnīcu iela, or take bus 10 along Lielais prospekts.

Breakwaters poke 1km or so out to sea from the mouth of the river to form Ventspils' Sea Gates, with a narrow entrance that makes it treacherous for shipping if there's any sea running. A popular pastime is to walk or cycle 1km from the northern end of the beach, along the **South Mole** (Dienvidu mols) walkway, to the lighthouse at the end of the southern breakwater.

Ventspils' beach is overlooked by a **water amusement park** (Ūdens atrakciju parks; ☎ 366 5853; Mednu iela 19; per hr adult/child 1/0.50Ls, per day adult/child 2/1Ls; 🕑 10am-8pm), a vast complex in **Seaside Park** (Piejūras parks). Towards the south is the **Seaside Open-Air Museum** (Ventspils jūras zvejniecibas brīvdabas muzejs; ☎ 322 4467, Riņķu iela 2; adult/child 0.60/0.30Ls, railway adult/child 0.50/0.25Ls; 🕑 11am-6pm May-Oct, 11am-5pm Wed-Sun Nov-Apr), with a collection of fishing craft, anchors and other seafaring items. On weekends between May and October you can ride around the museum's extensive grounds on a narrow-gauge railway dating to 1916. A little further south there's an **open-air concert hall** (Vasarnīcu

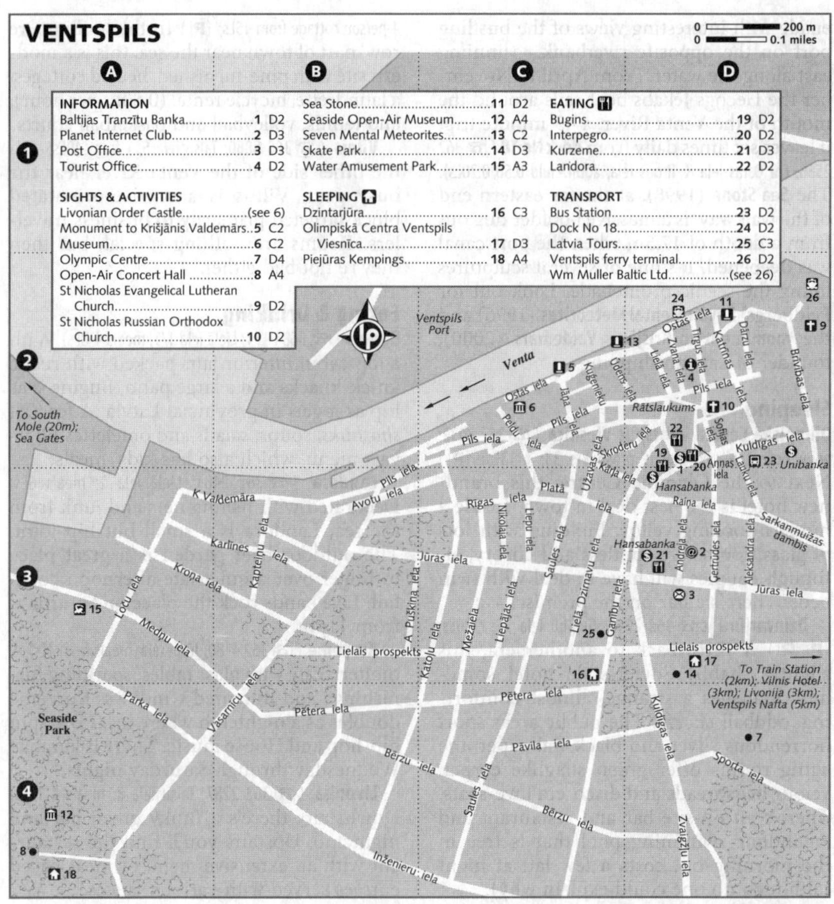

iela). Buses 6 and 11 run here regularly from Lielais prospekts.

Boarders, bladers and BMX bikers can leap around in the region's only **skate park** (Skeitparks; ☎ 362 2172; Sporta iela 7-9; admission free; 24hr), with 18 jumps. Ice skaters can twirl around the city's ice-skating rink inside the modern **Olympic Centre** (☎ 362 1996; Sporta iela 7-9; per hr 1Ls, skate rental adult/child 0.50/0.20Ls).

There is little to see or do in Old Town except wander its streets and absorb the 18th-century architecture. Pils iela is the main street, cutting east–west across Old Town. Peering across Brīvibas iela is the neo-Byzantine **St Nicholas Russian Orthodox Church** (Sv Nivolaja pareizticīgo baznīca; Plosu iela 10), built in 1901 and crowned with five onion domes. Walking west along Pils iela, you can detour south down Tirgus iela to Rātslaukums, a pretty cobbled square overlooked by **St Nicholas Evangelical Lutheran Church** (Sv Nivolaja luterāļu baznīca; Tirgus iela 2), built in 1835.

Ventspils' 13th-century **Livonian Order Castle** (☎ 362 2031; Jana iela 17; adult/child 1/0.50Ls; 9am-6pm May-Sep, 10am-5pm Oct-Apr) hosts a cutting-edge interactive museum on castle history, with digital displays and two panoramic telescopes for visitors to enjoy an eagle's-eye view of the port and city. The museum also showcases fine pieces of amber discovered on archaeological digs in the region.

From the castle, it's a two-minute walk to the Venta River. Ostas iela is a riverside promenade with interesting views of the bustling port on the opposite riverbank, runnimg east along the water. From April to November the Hecogs Jēkabs boat sails around the mouth of the Venta River, a 45-minute trip; it leaves six times daily from **dock No 18** (☎ 362 2586; cnr Ostas iela & Tirgus iela; adult/child 0.50/0.20Ls). The **Sea Stone** (1998), at the far eastern end of the walkway, is a massive boulder dug out from a depth of 17.5m when the port canal was deepened. It's one of several sculptures lining the scenic promenade. Look out for Feldbergs' **Seven Mental Meteorites** (1996) and the **monument to Krišjānis Valdemārs** (2000), founder of Latvian shipping.

Sleeping

Olimpiskā Centra Ventspils Viesnica (☎ 362 8032; www.ocventspils.lv; Lielais prospekts 33; r 13Ls; P) Next to the Olympic Centre, this brand-new hotel is the best deal in town. Inside a modern-looking yellow building with lots of glass, rooms are spotless and cheery, although couples will have to deal with twin beds. There's a bar on the premises.

Dzintarjūra (☎ 362 2719; Ganību iela 26; r 30Ls; P) A throwback to another era, this slightly shabby Soviet-style hotel somehow manages a strange, almost comforting, oddball charm. The public areas sport horrendous silver and black wallpaper; the aging rooms offer green shaglike carpet, velour bedspreads and disco-era love-seats. There's an on-site bar and restaurant and an indoor swimming pool that is free in the morning but costs a few lati at night (although no one could explain why).

Piejūras Kempings (☎ 362 7925; www.camping.ventspils.lv; Vasarnicu iela 56; camp site per person 1.50Ls, 4-person cottage from 15Ls; P) In the 'millionaire row' part of town near the sea, this is a modern site with pine-furnished, heated cottages, a laundrette, bicycle rental (0.80Ls per hour), and tennis, volleyball and basketball courts.

Vilnis (☎ 366 8880; Talsu iela 5; r from 40Ls) On the other side of the Venta River near the busy port, Vilnis is a service-orientated block targeted primarily to business travellers. Rooms are nothing special, but then they're not bad either.

Eating & Drinking

Bugins (☎ 368 0151; Lielā iela 1/3; meals 4-8Ls) With a log-cabin interior jam-packed with rustic knick-knacks and a large patio, Bugins is as hip as it gets in provincial Latvia. A feast of *shashliks*, soups, salads and omelettes fill its vast menu, which also has kids' meals.

Landora (☎ 362 2481; Lielā iela 2; meals 6Ls) Decorated with fishing nets and junk from the sea, Landora is a small but hip joint. The outdoor beer garden is a great place to linger over a quiet late-afternoon cocktail. Live bands rock the place on Saturdays from 11pm.

Kurzeme (☎ 362 4180; Jūras iela; meals from 4Ls) A modern café with glass tables, sparkling furnishings and mirrored windows, Kurzeme doubles as a nightclub where local DJs spin hip-hop and House music. There is karaoke Wednesday through Saturday nights.

Livonija (☎ 362 2287; Talsu iela 8; meals 4-12Ls) Downstairs there's a funky green bar and nightclub. Upstairs you'll find the restaurant with an extensive menu of meat-based entrées served with various sauces.

Interpegro (Annas iela 1) Interpregro is a central supermarket.

I-SPY

The Soviets used the 32m-diameter radio telescope in Irbene to eavesdrop on Western satellite communications. Today scientists gaze at the stars, moon and sun through it.

Hidden in the forest 24km north of Ventspils, Irbene's superpowerful antenna was one of three used to spy on the world by the Soviet army at the USSR Space Communication Centre. When the last Russian troops left in 1994, they took one antenna with them but left the remaining two – too large to move – to Latvia.

The R-32 – a 600-tonne dish mounted on a 25m-tall concrete base – was built by the USSR in the 1980s and is the world's eighth-largest parabolic antenna. Since 1994 the former military installation has belonged to the **Ventspils International Radio Astronomy Centre** (VIRAC; Ventspils starptautiskais radioastronomijas centrs), which is part of the **Latvian Academy of Sciences** (☎ 722 8321; www.lza.lv; Akademijas laukums 1, LV-1524 Rīga). Essentially a research centre, the antennae can be visited by guided tour, arranged in advance by calling ☎ 368 1541.

Getting There & Away

Ventspils' **bus station** (☎ 362 2789; Kuldīga iela 5) is served by buses to/from Rīga (3Ls, 2½ to four hours, hourly), Liepāja (3Ls, three hours, twice daily), Talsi (1.50Ls, 1½ hours, twice daily), Kuldīga (1.50Ls, 1½ hours, four daily) and Jelgava (3Ls, 4¾ to 5½ hours, four daily) via Kandava and Tukums.

Two trains run daily to/from Rīga (2.50Ls, 4¼ hours) from the **train station** (Dzeizceļnieku iela), on the Rīga road 2km east of the centre, across the river.

VV Line LV (☎ 360 7358; www.vvline.com; Plostu iela 7) runs seasonal ferries six times weekly from **Ventspils ferry terminal** (☎ 360 7357; Plostu iela 7) to Västervik in Sweden. **Latvia Tours** (☎ 362 5413; www.latviatours.lv; Ganību iela 8) also sells tickets.

KULDĪGA

pop 13,335

Untouristy Kuldīga, 54km southeast of Ventspils, is a sleepy country town on the Venta River. There's not a lot to see or do, but the place has an almost romantic air about it and offers a glimpse into rural life. If you're tired of big-city hustle, stop here for a night. The medieval-looking town – with crumbling buildings, cobbled streets and quiet riverside parks – is perfect for lazy wandering. Settle down at an outdoor café and watch life slowly pass by.

An important Cours settlement and most likely the Cour capital at the time of the 13th-century German invasion, Kuldīga (then called Goldingen) later became an important stronghold of the Livonian Order. In its heyday it served as the capital of the Duchy of Courland (1596–1616), but the town suffered greatly in the Great Northern War (1700–21) and never quite regained its former importance.

Kuldīga throws its annual **town festival** in mid-July.

Orientation

The Venta River flows east of town and is crossed by the bridge leading out to the Rīga road. The old part of the town centre is 500m or so west and southwest of the bridge. The newer part of the centre focuses on Pilsētas laukums, 500m west along Liepājas iela.

Information

Hansabanka (Liepājas iela 15) Has an ATM outside.
Post office (Liepājas iela 34)
Tourist office (☎ 332 2259; www.kuldiga.lv; Baznīcas iela 5; 🕑 9am-5pm Mon-Sat, 10am-2pm Sun mid-May–mid-Sep, 9am-5pm Mon-Fri rest of year)

Sights

OLD TOWN

Start your explorations in Rātslaukums, the old town hall square, which gets its name from the **17th-century town hall** (Rātslaukums 5). The new town hall, built in 1860 in Italian Renaissance style, is at the southern end of the square, and Kuldīga's oldest house – built in 1670, reconstructed in 1742 and renovated in 1982 – stands here on the northern corner of Pasta iela.

From Rātslaukums, Baznīcas iela leads north to the Lutheran **St Katrina's Church** (Sv Katrīnas baznīca), built in 1655 and largely rebuilt in the 1860s and 1960s. The wooden altar and pulpit date from 1660; the large organ, with 996 pipes, is c 1712. Another fine church, the 1640 Roman Catholic **Holy Trinity Church** (Sv Trisvienības baznīca; Raiļa iela), with an ornate baroque/rococo interior, is also a short way off Rātslaukums, along Liepājas iela – the main Old Town street.

From Baznīcas iela a bridge leads across the Aleksupīte, a tributary of the Venta, to a **water mill** (1807). Across the river is the site of the **Livonian Order Castle**, built from 1242 to 1245, but ruined during the Great Northern War. The **castle watchman's house** (Pils iela 4) was built in 1735 to protect the ruins. Legend has it that the house was the site of executions and beheadings and the stream behind the house ran red with the victims' blood. Today all that remains of the castle are a few mounds and ditches. On the grounds you'll find the mildly interesting **Kuldīga District Museum** (Kuldīgas novada muzejs; ☎ 332 2364; Pils iela; adult/child 0.40/0.20Ls; 🕑 11am-5pm Tue-Sun), located inside a home built in Paris in 1900 to house the Russian pavilion at the World Exhibition.

From Pils iela there's an excellent view of the Venta and the **Kuldīga waterfall**, which is only a metre or so high but stretches the width of the river – at 275m it's said to be Europe's widest waterfall. You can fish and swim here and, when the water's low, you can walk across the top of the falls.

OTHER ATTRACTIONS

The large **old castle hill** (pilskalns), 2.5km north of town on the western bank of the

Venta, was the fortress of Lamekins, the Cour who ruled much of Kurzeme before the 13th-century German invasion. Legend has it that the castle was so staggeringly beautiful – copper pendants hanging from the roof glistened in the sunlight and tinkled in the wind – that invaders were magnetically drawn to it. To get to the hill, follow Ventspils iela then Virkas iela north from the centre, then take the right fork off Virkas iela.

Immediately after the old bridge –the eastern extension of Baznīcas iela – turn left to get to **Riežupe Sand Caves** (Smilšu alas; ☎ 332 6236; adult/child 2/1Ls; 🕓 11am-5pm May-Oct), 5km further along unpaved Krasta iela in Riežupe. The labyrinthine caves can be visited by candlelight; they're a chilly 8°C, so bring a warm sweater. The forested area around the caves is equipped with picnic tables and outdoor games.

Sleeping & Eating

Jāņa nams (☎ 332 3456; fax 332 3785; Liepājas iela 36; r 22-40Ls; Ⓟ) The best sleeping option in town. Rooms are cosy, rustically inspired and very clean. The funky in-house café has bright-yellow walls, a varied Latvian menu (meals 2Ls to 5Ls) and possibly the coolest curtains in the country. Rates include breakfast.

Kursa (☎ 332 2430; fax 332 3671; Pilsētas laukums 6; s/d 12/16Ls; Ⓟ) Recently renovated, this Soviet-era hotel features lovely public areas, but rather shabby rooms with twin beds,

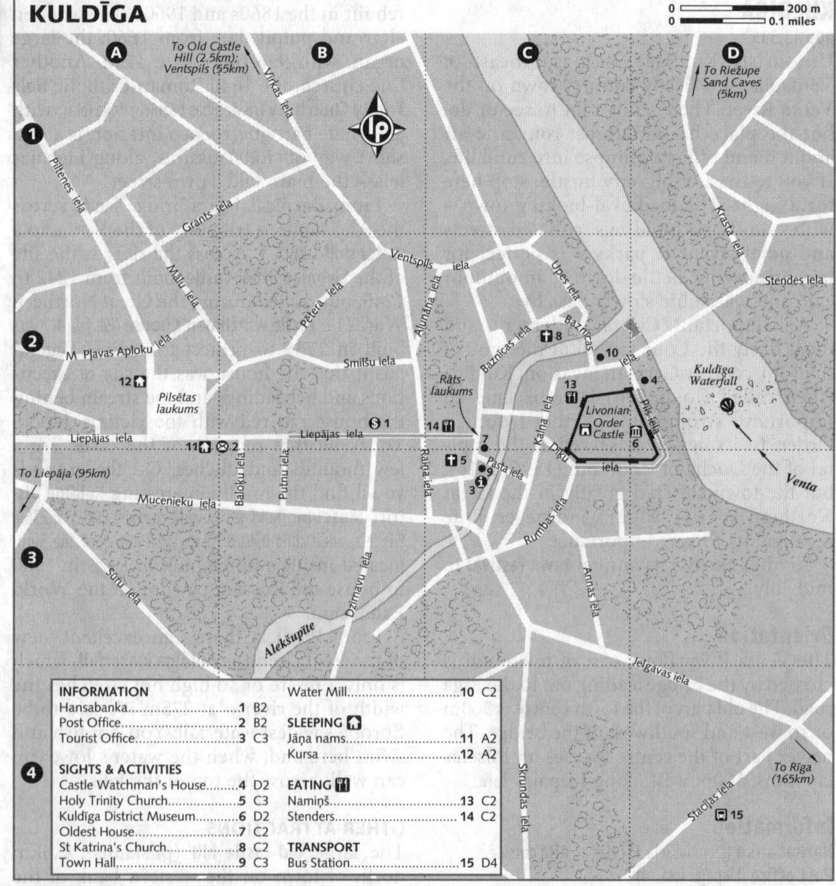

lumpy pillows and scratched wooden furniture. The English-speaking staff is friendly, however, and the place is clean and OK for a short stay.

Stenders (☎ 332 2703; Liepājas iela 3; meals 4Ls) A fabulous find, Stenders is the town's funkiest joint. Housed in an 18th-century granary, it features a great upper-level wooden porch that's perfect for people-watching. Live bands often play here.

Namiņš (☎ 332 2697; Kalna iela 25a; meals 3-6Ls) With bright-orange walls and mod white leather chairs, this is the place to curl up by the fireplace in winter. In summer the outdoor terrace offers tranquil dining. The long cocktail menu features everything from pina coladas to margaritas. If you're hungry, choose from pasta, salads, soups, traditional Latvian fare and even a few vegetarian options.

Getting There & Away

From the **bus station** (☎ 332 2061; Stacijas iela) buses run to/from Rīga (2.50Ls, three to four hours, six to 10 daily), Liepāja (1.50Ls, 2¼ hours, six daily) and Ventspils (1Ls, 1½ hours, four daily).

Motorists must buy a 0.50Ls ticket to cross the old road bridge (the Rīga road) across the Venta in the town centre. Looping around town to cross the river at the new bridge (the Ventspils road) instead is free. Namiņš (above) sells tickets.

LIEPĀJA

pop 89,400

Latvia's third-largest city has a gritty, urban vibe. A port city on the Baltic Coast, Liepāja, 205km west of Rīga and 111km south of Ventspils, is a city lost in transition, not sure which way it wants to go. Decaying and abandoned Soviet-era buildings sit next to slick Western-style bars, and the feel is at once edgy and eccentrically upbeat. Part of the Latvian Amber Road (see boxed text, p175), Liepāja is home to 123m ropes of amber beads and an impressive amber sundial. The city also hosts Latvia's largest rock festival, *Liepājas Dzintars* (Amber of Liepāja), in August each year, although the town is cashing in on Latvia's burgeoning rock 'n' roll scene year-round. Its multistorey 'rock café' is unique in the country, and hosts live bands nightly. Smaller venues are drawing up-and-coming bands from as far away as Rīga, and the nightlife here is often raging. Though lacking in sightseeing attractions, Liepāja has a pleasant beachfront, unique boutique hotels, some funky galleries – and a glass concert hall. Bizarrely, the local city council markets Liepāja today as the place where wind is born! The city still has rough edges to polish, but it's progressing quickly. In 10 years it just might be considered ultrahip. You'll have to visit to decide.

History

Founded by the Livonian Order in the 13th century, the city only really took off with the deepening of the harbour and arrival of a railway track in the 19th century. Tsar Alexander III built a naval port in Liepāja in 1890, becoming home to the first Baltic fleet of Russian submarines. Heavily bombed during WWII, Liepāja became a virtual ghost town in the postwar years. The Soviets used its port as a military base and kept everyone away. After the Iron Curtain fell, life returned, with residents working hard to turn it into the progressive hub it is today.

Orientation

Liepāja occupies the neck of land (about 2km to 3km wide) between Lake Liepāja and the sea. The city straddles Tirdzniecības Canal, the narrow canal flowing from the lake to the sea. The former naval port, and train and bus stations sit north of the canal, while the city centre lies south of the canal.

Information

Liva Hotel Hansabanka (Lielā iela 11) There's an ATM outside.

Post office (cnr Pasta iela & Radio iela) A block west of Lielā iela.

Sapņu sala (☎ 348 5333; Lielā iela 12; per hr 0.50Ls; 9am-9pm) Internet access.

Tourist office (☎ 348 0808; www.liepaja.lv; Lielā iela 11; 9am-6pm Mon-Fri, to 5pm Sat) Inside the Liva Hotel, the tourist office offers a limited amount of English-speaking help to visitors.

Sights

OCCUPATION MUSEUM

This sobering **museum** (Okupāciju režīmos; ☎ 342 0274; K Ukstiņa iela 79; admission free; 10am-5pm Wed-Sun) traces the bloody history of the Soviet and Nazi occupations in Latvia, with an emphasis on Liepāja. A visit here is a

LATVIA

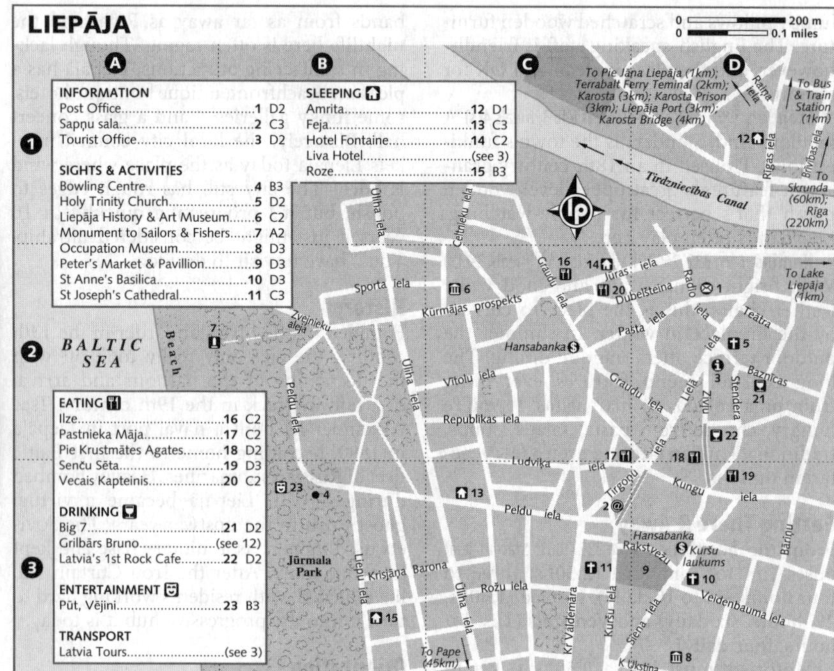

moving, albeit disturbing, experience and should be on any Liepāja agenda. Captions are in Latvian, but no words are needed to explain the powerful images of the 1939–40 deportations to Siberia (an estimated 2000 people from Liepāja were deported), the genocide committed against Latvian Jews and the 1991 fight for independence.

KAROSTA

Off limits to everyone – including Latvians – during the Soviet occupation, Karosta is a former Russian naval base encompassing about one-third of Liepāja's city limits. From aging army barracks to ugly Soviet-style, concrete apartment blocks (many abandoned), evidence of the occupation still remains, but the Karosta of today is a vibrant place with a bohemian air. Home to artists, musicians, writers and other free thinkers, this progressive area is worth exploring.

A detention facility until 1997, today ghostly **Karosta Prison** (Karostas cietums; ☎ 636 9470; www.karostascietums.lv; Invalīdu 4; admission from 0.50Ls; 🕑 10am-6pm May-Sep, by appointment only Oct-Apr) offers a variety of tours. Originally built as an infirmary in 1900, the Soviets, Nazis and most recently the Latvians used the place as a military prison. Graffiti left behind by former inmates reveals the horrors incurred doing hard time here. Supposedly haunted, your tour guide will be happy to try to explain the unexplainable – light bulbs that mysteriously screw out of their sockets, doors that open without assistance and sudden eerie chills that descend upon a heated room. If you're craving some serious punishment, or just want to brag that you've spent the night in Latvian jail, sign up to become a prisoner for the night. You'll be subjected to regular bed checks, verbal abuse by guards in period garb and forced to relieve yourself in the most disgusting of latrines. It's a very different experience, all right. For more details, check the website.

HOLY TRINITY CHURCH

Built between 1742 and 1758, the baroque-style **Holy Trinity Church** (Sv Trīsvienības baznīca; ☎ 943 8050; Lielā iela 9; admission by donation; 🕑 10am-6pm) has a dazzling gilded rococo interior. Its centrepiece is its fabulous organ, at one time the world's largest, boasting more than 7000 pipes, 131 registers and four manuals. For a small fee (usually 1Ls), the church caretaker will escort you up the myriad of creaky wooden steps to the clock tower, where fabulous city views await.

LIEPĀJA HISTORY & ART MUSEUM

A collection of carved amber ornaments dating back 1500 years is just one of the highlights of a visit to the **Liepāja History & Art Museum** (Liepājas vēstures un mākslas muzejs; ☎ 342 2327; Kūrmājas prospekts 16/18; adult/child 0.50/0.30Ls; 🕒 10am-5pm Wed-Sun Sep-May, 11am-6pm Wed-Sun Jun-Aug). Other exhibits include impressive Stone and Bronze Age artefacts unearthed on local archaeological digs, an interesting collection of old jewellery and weapons and vintage memorabilia from both world wars. At the seaside end of the same street is a **monument** to sailors and fishers who died at sea.

PETER'S MARKET

Vendors have touted their wares at the outdoor market on Kuršu laukums since the mid-17th century. The market expanded in 1910, when a **pavilion** (Pētertirgus; ☎ 343 4517; Kuršu laukums 5-9; 🕒 8am-6pm) was constructed adjacent to the square. Today you'll find stalls inside and out at this bustling complex, selling everything from second-hand tables, pirated CDs, DVDs and local crafts to fruits, vegetables and fresh slabs of meat.

ST JOSEPH'S CATHEDRAL & ST ANNE'S BASILICA

The Roman Catholic **St Joseph's Cathedral** (Sv Jāzepa katedrāla; ☎ 342 9775; K Valdemāra 28) is a towering yellow-brick church with a notable interior – it's ornately decorated with Bible scenes. Nearby, **St Anne's Basilica** (Sv Annas basilica; ☎ 342 3384; Veidenbauma 1) is a red-brick, neo-Gothic edifice constructed in 1587. Its highlights include a sky-high steeple and an impressive baroque altar painting that is 5.8m high and 9.7m wide.

Activities

If you're travelling with the kids, head to the **Bowling Centre** (Dzintara boulings; ☎ 348 0080; Peldu iela 66; 🕒 noon-midnight Mon-Thu, noon-2am Fri & Sat, 10am-midnight Sun). The giant recreation complex houses eight bowling lanes, air hockey and pool tables, a children's play area and a bar and restaurant. Adults will likely dig the complex too, especially if it's freezing outside.

The **beach**, west of the city centre, is long, clean and sandy. Once considered unsafe for swimming (rumour has it the Soviet navy dumped several hundred thousand tonnes of toxic waste and unexploded bombs here during the days of the military base), the water has subsequently been cleaned up, and the beach has been awarded the internationally recognised Blue Flag rating.

At the far west end of Peldu iela, right behind the beach, nearly 0.5 sq km of parkland have been designated as **Jūrmala Park**. With woodlands and dunes, this park is perfect for strolling. Grand wooden Art-Nouveau summer homes, constructed by Liepāja's wealthy citizens from the 1870s onward, grace the streets around the park. If your wanders have left you parched, stop by one of the many beer gardens or cafés scattered around the grounds. You can also partake in a game of miniature golf or tennis or check out the skate park.

Festivals & Events

Liepaja throws a giant beach bash every year at the end of July. The **Baltic Beach Party** (www.balticbeachparty.lv) takes place over two days and includes live music, discos, carnivals, fashion shows, sporting events and other hoopla all right on the beach.

Sleeping

Unless stated otherwise, room rates in the listings in this section include breakfast.

Roze (☎ 342 1155; www.parkhotel-roze.lv; Rožu iela 37; s/d from 32/40Ls; P ⊠) Stylish and comfortable, this Art-Nouveau wooden guesthouse near the sea was once a summer home for the elite. Rooms are spacious, and each is uniquely decorated. Amenities include satellite TVs and minibars.

Feja (☎ 342 2688; www.feja.lv; Kurzemes iela 9; s 18-30Ls, d 20-40Ls; P) This turreted red-brick guesthouse, with a rather strange grey and silver colour scheme, offers very large rooms with all the mod cons and a couple of luxury suites. The entrance is on Peldu iela.

Amrita (☎ 340 3434; www.amrita.lv; Rīgas iela 7; s/d from 40/60Ls, presidential ste 205Ls; P 💻) Liepāja's classiest hotel offers comfortable digs with all modern conveniences, done up in a pseudo-Scandinavian style, although they seem a bit bland for the price. The two-floor

LATVIA

LATVIA

THE AUTHOR'S CHOICE

Hotel Fontaine (☎ 342 0956; www.fontaine.lv; Jūras iela 24; r from 20Ls; P 💻) A real gem, this boutique joint is one of those places you'll either fiercely love or absolutely abhor. The rooms are ultrahip, but the beds are less than comfortable. Whatever, it's definitely Latvia's funkiest hotel. A shrine to everything rock 'n' roll, it's kitsch to the max. Each retro room is different (see a few before deciding), but all feature loads of rock memorabilia as well as satellite TV with DVD players. Old Soviet army–issue footlockers serve as tables in some; others boast private balconies, hardwood floors, oriental rugs or garish bedspreads. Walls sport a mix of '70s disco-style wallpaper and bright, bright paint. Downstairs there's a communal kitchen and a chill-out lounge with hookahs. The reception is in the on-site curiosity shop, crammed with dusty Soviet-era gas masks and uniforms, woollen coats and other assorted knick-knacks – dig hard enough and you might just find a cheap treasure (we discovered a vintage Gucci purse selling for pennies).

presidential suite is a luxurious affair complete with Jacuzzi, and is where the president stays when she's in town. The lobby bar and restaurant are swanky enough, and reception is very friendly and accommodating.

Pie Jāna Liepāja (☎ 342 5075; piejana@one.lv; Raiņa iela 43; dm/r 8/21Ls; P) Backpackers on a budget will appreciate the clean, cheap and renovated dorm rooms here. Those with a little extra cash will dig the cosy doubles, decked out with antique furnishings. To book a room, visit the travel agency on the 1st floor; the same friendly folks run the hotel.

Liva Hotel (☎ 342 0102; www.liva.lv; Lielā iela 11; s 10-25Ls, d 15-32Ls; P 💻) Liva makes up for its lack of character by offering clean, good-value rooms in a very central location. The cheapest share bathrooms, the more expensive have modern en-suite facilities. Couples will have to deal with twin beds in double rooms.

Eating

Pastnieka Māja (☎ 340 7521; Brīvzemnieka iela 53; meals 6-12Ls) This very modern, ultraslick two-level restaurant is housed in a vast mansion. The menu features traditional Latvian favourites, as well as a few very exotic offerings: the 'spicy nuts' are bulls' balls stuffed with a garlic nut sauce served on a bed of warm bean and potato salad. This is also one of the few places that serves Liepāja's local beer, Līvu alus.

Ilze (☎ 342 6724; Graudu iela 23; meals 4-8Ls) Candles and flowers set the mood at this inviting cellar restaurant with an international menu that includes dozens of salad choices. One of the city's oldest privately run cafés, Ilze has live jazz performances on weekends.

Senču Sēta (☎ 342 5453; Stendera iela 13a; meals 2-8Ls) Located on a quiet side street, this fisherman's cottage has a modern red and green theme inside and an outdoor flower-filled beer garden strewn with fishing nets. The big menu offers lots of salads, vegetarian options, hearty Latvian meals and light snacks. It's also a popular drinking spot.

Pie Krustmātes Agates (Zivju iela 4/6; meals 2Ls) Pie Krustmātes Agates is a real gem. This canteen-style spot dishes up mains for 0.35Ls in a lovely rustic setting, decorated with cartwheels, dried flowers, pumpkins and the like.

Drinking & Entertainment

Liepāja has a reputation throughout Latvia as the centre of the country's rock-music scene, and taking in a concert is a real treat. Even if you can't understand the lyrics, just being a part of the screaming, pulsating masses is a cultural experience you won't soon forget.

Upcoming concerts, cinema and theatre productions are listed in *Liepāja This Week*, a weekly eight-page entertainment magazine; pick up a free copy at the tourist office. In summer open-air concerts are held at **Pūt, Vējini** (☎ 342 5268), an outside theatre in Jūrmala Park.

Latvia's 1st Rock Café (☎ 348 1555; Zivju iela 4/6; www.pablo.lv; cover 2-3Ls) It goes by a variety of names, including Pablo's Place, but there's no way you'll miss this massive four-storey structure with loads of glassy windows and a pseudo-industrial look. Restaurants, bars, dance floors, billiards and a rooftop beer garden are all housed here. The walls are plastered with old concert posters and the club features live music every night, as well as frequent rave parties.

THE AUTHOR'S CHOICE

Vecais Kapteinis (Old Captain; ☎ 342 5522; Dubelsteina iela 14; meals 4-14Ls) Hands down, the best meal we had in Latvia. The innovative dishes, best described as upmarket Latvian fusion, are rich in flavour and nothing short of delicious. Meat, fish and seafood comprise much of the giant menu, but there are a few pasta and vegetarian offerings as well. The ambience is almost as delightful as the cuisine. In a stunning timber-framed building dating to 1773, whitewashed walls, candles and a seafaring theme cultivate a romantic vibe. Other highlights include a long, global wine list, quiet music and glasses of absinthe served in the traditional fashion and guaranteed to knock your socks off.

Grilbārs Bruno (☎ 340 0888; Rīgas iela 7/9) Exposed brick walls and sturdy wooden tables dominate at this cosy cellar bar inside the Amrita hotel. Enjoy a game of chess, darts or *novuss* – a Latvian creation that's part shuffleboard, part billiards – with a glass of the nation's favourite beer, Užavas, served on draught.

Big 7 (☎ 342 7318; Baznīcas 14/16) This giant complex offers a little bit of everything. Divided into multiple sections for dancing, drinking, eating and chilling, it also offers stripteases, pool and slot machines. Head upstairs to King 7 if you want to zone out on couches and pillows or fill your lungs with hookah smoke (5Ls per hookah).

Getting There & Away

Liepāja's **bus & train stations** (☎ 342 7552; Rīgas iela) are rolled into one, linked by tram 1 with Lielā iela in the town centre.

There are daily bus services to/from Rīga (3Ls, 3½ hours direct, four to 4½ hours via Kalnciems, five to 5½ hours via Jelgava, and seven hours via Tukums, hourly), Kuldīga (2Ls, 2¼ hours, six daily), Talsi (3Ls, 4½ hours, six daily) and Ventspils (3Ls, three to 3¾ hours, six daily). Updated timetables are online at www.liepaja-online.lv/lap.

There are six trains to/from Rīga (3.50Ls, 4¾ to six hours, four daily).

In town, **Latvia Tours** (☎ 342 7172; www.latviatours.lv; Lielā iela 11), inside the Liva Hotel, sells tickets for ferries and Eurolines buses.

Terrabalt (☎ 342 7214; www.terrabalt.lv; Pier No 46) runs ferries from Liepāja to Karlshamn (Sweden) and Rostock (Germany). Ferries depart for Karlshamn three times weekly (17½ hours); seats cost 40Ls, beds in two/four-bed cabins cost 60/70Ls. There's a 5Ls port tax per person and it costs 7/46Ls to transport a bicycle/car.

Terrabalt ferries to Rostock depart twice weekly (seven hours). A seat costs €80 and beds in two-/four-bed cabins cost €110/140; port tax is €10. It costs €10/115 to transport a bicycle/car.

On both routes children aged three to 15 pay approximately 50% less.

LATVIA DIRECTORY

The following contains practical information related to travelling in Latvia. For regional information pertaining to all three countries, see the Regional Directory.

ACTIVITIES

Mushrooming, berrying, canoeing and cycling in summer, and hitting the sauna, skiing, snowshoeing and snowboarding in winter are but some of the uplifting pursuits Latvia offers to active visitors. All three national parks plus Latvia's many nature reserves sport some well-marked nature trails that help visitors discover the country's rich flora and fauna collection. See the Activities chapter for more regional activity info.

CUSTOMS

The **Latvian Tourism Development Agency** (www.latviatourism.lv) posts the latest customs rules on its website.

People over 18 can bring in and take out 1L of alcohol and 200 cigarettes, 20 cigars or 200g of tobacco without paying duty. You can import and export duty-free any amount of hard currency.

Works of art or of cultural significance (including antique books) that date from before 1945, but are less than 100 years old, are subject to a 50% customs duty; those older than 100 years attract 100% duty. They may only be taken out of the country with a licence issued by the **State Inspection for Heritage Protection** (☎ 722 9272), inside the **Ministry of Culture** (☎ 704 7400; www.km.gov.lv; Valdemāra iela; LV-1050 Rīga).

PRACTICALITIES

- The English-language paper *Baltic Times* (www.baltictimes.com) is published every Thursday in Rīga and has an entertainment guide that includes cinema listings. For news, the Latvian daily newspaper *Diena* (www.diena.lv) provides the best politically independent coverage and comes out in a separate Russian-language edition.
- *Rīga in Your Pocket* (www.inyourpocket.com) and *Rīga This Week* (www.rigathisweek.lv) are bimonthly English-language guides with Rīga hotel, restaurant and nightlife reviews.
- On air, tune into Latvian State Radio (www.radio.org.lv), which transmits daily short-wave broadcasts at 5935 kHz in English; FM frequencies are listed on its website. Popular commercial channels are Mix FM on 102.7 FM, Radio SWH at 105.2 FM and Super FM on 104.3 FM. Listen to the BBC World Service 24 hours a day at 100.5 FM.
- Latvian State Television (Latvijas Televizija; www.ltv.lv) broadcasts two state-run TV channels, LTV1 and LTV2, while TV5 (www.tv5.lv) is Rīga's city channel, broadcasting programmes strictly about the capital and its inhabitants. The country's most popular private TV broadcast station is Latvian Independent Television (Latvijas NeatkaRīga Televizija; www.lnt.lv).
- PAL is the main video system used in Latvia.
- Electrical current is 220V, 50Hz AC. Sockets require a European plug with two round pins.
- Use the metric system for weights and measures.

EMBASSIES & CONSULATES

Latvian Embassies & Consulates

A complete list of Latvian diplomatic missions abroad is posted on the website of Latvia's **Ministry of Foreign Affairs** (www.am.gov.lv). They include the following:

Australia (☎ 02-9744 5981; 32 Parnell St, Strathfield, NSW 2135)

Belarus (☎ 0172-849 393, consular 84 74 75; daile@anitex.by; 6a Doroshevica Str, BY-220013 Minsk)

Canada (☎ 613-238 6014, consular 238 6868; www.magma.ca/~latemb; 208 Albert St, Suite 300, Ottawa, K1P 5G8 Ontario)

Estonia (☎ 627 7850; embassy.estonia@mfa.gov.lv; Tõnismägi 10, EE10119 Tallinn)

Finland (☎ 09-4764 7244, consular 4764 7233; consulate.finland@mfa.lv; Armfeltintie 10, SF-00150 Helsinki)

France (☎ 01 53 64 58 10, consular 01 53 64 5816; embassy.france@mfa.gov.lv; 6 Villa Said, F-75116 Paris)

Germany (☎ 030-8260 0222; www.botschaft-lettland.de; Reinerzstrasse 40-41, D-14193 Berlin)

Lithuania (☎ 5-213 1260; embassy.lithuania@mfa.gov.lv; Čiurlionio gatvė 76, LT-2600 Vilnius)

Russia (☎ 095-925 2703, consular 923 8772; embassy.russia@mfa.gov.lv ulitsa Chapligina 3, RUS-103062 Moscow)

Sweden (☎ 08-700 6300; lettlands.ambassad@swipnet.se; Odengatan 5, Box 19167, S-10432 Stockholm)

UK (☎ 020-7312 0040; embassy@embassyoflatvia.co.uk; 45 Nottingham Place, London W1U 5LR)

USA (☎ 202-726 8213; www.latvia-usa.org; 4325 17th Street NW, Washington, DC 20011)

Embassies & Consulates in Latvia

The following embassies are in Rīga:

Canada (Map p196; ☎ 722 6315; canembr@bkc.lv; Doma laukums 4)

Estonia (Map pp192-3; ☎ 781 2020; www.estemb.lv; Skolas iela 13, Rīga LV 1010)

Finland (Map pp192-3; ☎ 707 8800; www.finland.lv; Kalpaka bulvāris 1)

France (Map pp192-3; ☎ 703 6600; www.ambafrance-lv.org; Raiņa bulvāris 9)

Germany (Map pp192-3; ☎ 722 9096; www.deutschebotschaft-Rīga.lv; Raiņa bulvāris 13)

Lithuania (Map p188; ☎ 732 1519; lithemb@ltemb.vip.lv; Rūpniecības iela 24)

Netherlands (Map p196; ☎ 732 6147; www.netherlandsembassy.lv; Torņa iela 4)

Russia (Map pp192-3; ☎ 733 2151; rusembas@mail.junk.lv; Antonijas iela 2)

Sweden (Map pp192-3; ☎ 733 8770; www.swedenemb.lv; Andreja Pumpura iela 8)

UK (Map pp192-3; ☎ 777 4700; www.britain.lv; Alunāna iela 5)

USA (Map pp192-3; ☎ 703 6200; www.usembassy.lv; Raiņa bulvāris 7)

FESTIVALS & EVENTS

Latvia shares a number of regular cultural events with Estonia and Lithuania, the most important being the national song festival (which occurs every five years) and the Baltika Folklore Festival (see p386) and midsummer celebrations. Information on the dozens of one-off festivals is online at www.km.gov.lv.

Latvia's major annual festivals include the following:

International Baltic Ballet Festival (www.ballet-festival.lv) Takes place over five days in late April; performances by Latvian and international companies.

National Ethnic Arts and Crafts Fair (www.muzeji.lv/index_e.html) Big arts and crafts fair held at the Open-Air Ethnography Museum in Rīga on the first weekend in June.

Rīga Opera Festival (www.music.lv/opera) The Latvian National Opera's showcase event, it takes place over 10 days in June and includes performances by world-renowned talent.

Baltic Beach Party (www.balticbeachparty.lv) Giant festival featuring live music, discos, carnivals, fashion shows, sporting events and other hoopla on the beach in Liepāja; late July.

Festival of Ancient Music (www.bauska.lv) Music festival held at Bauska Castle and Rundāle Palace in late July.

Opera Music Festival (www.sigulda.lv) Open-air festival in Sigulda's castle ruins; late July.

Tukums Town Festival (www.tukums.lv) Small town festival, held in Tukums in late July.

Ascension Roman Catholic processions, celebratory masses in Aglona; 14-16 August.

Arēna New Music Festival (www.arenafest.lv) Contemporary music festival showcasing various genres and held at venues throughout Rīga during the first two weeks of October.

Lāčplēsis Day (Lāčplēsu Diena) Commemoration of dead heroes, named after Latvia's mythical warrior hero, whose name means 'Bear Slayer'; 11 November.

HOLIDAYS

Latvian national holidays:

New Year's Day 1 January

Good Friday (Easter Monday is also taken as a holiday by many.)

Labour Day 1 May

Mothers' Day Second Sunday in May

Ligo (Midsummer festival) 23 June

Jāni or Jānu Diena (St John's Day) 24 June

National Day 18 November; anniversary of proclamation of Latvian Republic, 1918

Christmas (Ziemsvētki) 25 December

Second Holiday 26 December

New Year's Eve 31 December

INTERNET ACCESS

Wi-fi access is becoming quite prevalent in Latvia. There are wi-fi hot spots in all the major cities, and many hotels, especially in Rīga, offer the service to their guests. Fees vary, sometimes it's free, other times there is a slight charge. Wi-fi is also available in many cafes around the country.

Internet cafés – many open 24 hours – are abundant in Rīga and most large towns and seaside resorts. Online access generally costs 0.50Ls per hour.

In provincial Latvia an Internet café tends to translate as a *datorsalons*, crammed with square-eyed kids playing killer computer games. Make it clear you want to access the Internet (rather than tangle with Lara Croft) and a kid will be kicked off to make way for you.

INTERNET RESOURCES

The official website of the **Latvian Tourism Development Agency** (www.latviatourism.lv) is packed with oodles of intelligently written cultural, historical and practical information about Latvia, as well as some excellent links to other Latvia-related sites.

The other indispensable site for serious background information and up-to-date cultural listings is **Latvians Online** (www.latviansonline.com). Its section on Latvian music reviews all the latest releases and is particularly useful, as are its links to other sites on Latvia. **Music in Latvia** (www.music.lv) is another inspiring site for those keen to tune in to Latvian jazz, opera, folk and other classical genres.

Sports fans can follow Latvia's football, basketball and ice hockey clubs with **Sports News** (www.sportsnews.lv). Those interested in what the president has to say can click on www.president.lv. For articles on everything Latvian, check out www.allaboutlatvia.com.

MAPS

Country, city and town maps of Latvia are available from Rīga-based **Jāņa sēta** (Map p188; ☎ 709 2277; www.kartes.lv; Elizabetes iela 83-85, LV-1009 Rīga), which runs an excellent map shop in the capital. Its town-plan series covers practically every town in Latvia; individual maps range in scale from 1:15,000 to 1:20,000 and cost 0.70Ls to 1.50Ls.

With the exception of Jāņa sēta's detailed *Gaujas Nacionālais parks* (Gauja National Park, 1;100,000, 1.35Ls), hiking maps don't exist. But Jāņa sēta does stock topographical map sheets (1:50,000, 1.98Ls) of Latvia published by **Kartogrāfijas Pārvalde** (☎ 703 8610; www.vzd.gov.lv; 11 Novembre krastmala 31, LV-1050 Rīga) covering western Latvia. The satellite-generated sheets (1,50:000, 0.98Ls) by the same cartographer and available on CD (13.90Ls) are less accurate.

MONEY

Latvia's currency, the lats (plural: lati), was introduced in March 1993 and has remained stable ever since. The lats (Ls) is divided into 100 santīmi (singular: santīms). Lati come in coin denominations of 1Ls and 2Ls and notes of 5Ls, 10Ls, 20Ls, 50Ls, 100Ls and 500Ls; and santīmi come in coins of 1, 2, 5, 10, 20 and 50. The 100Ls gold coin, minted in 1998, is a rarity.

The national bank **Latvijas Bankas** (Latvian Bank; www.bank.lv) posts the lats' daily exchange rate on its website. For exchange rates, see inside front cover.

POST

Latvia's postal system is almost completely reliable. It costs 0.15/0.30/0.30Ls to send a postcard/letter under 20g to Latvia/Europe/elsewhere; a letter weighing 20g to 100g costs 0.50Ls to send within Latvia or Europe and 0.80Ls to the US. Mail to North America takes about 10 days, and to Europe about a week.

TELEPHONE

Public cardphones are widespread throughout Latvia, but coin-operated phones are a rarity. Calls can be made from cardphones using a *telekarte*, worth 2Ls, 3Ls or 5Ls and sold at kiosks and post offices, or with a major credit card; instructions in English are included in every booth.

Latvian telephone numbers have seven digits and need no city or area code. To make a local or national call, simply dial the seven-digit number. To make an international call, dial the international access code (00), followed by the appropriate country code, city code if applicable and subscriber's number. To call a Latvian telephone number from abroad, dial the international access code, then the country code for Latvia (371) followed by the subscriber's number. Telephone rates are posted on the website of the partly state-owned **Lattelekom** (www.lattelekom.lv), which enjoys a monopoly on fixed-line telephone communications in Latvia.

Telephone numbers kicking off with 900 or 999 are pricier than normal calls; those starting with 800 are free. To contact directory inquiries, try www.118.lv, or dial ☎ 118 or ☎ 722 2222; English is spoken.

Mobile telephones likewise have seven digits and need no area code; they generally start with the digit nine. Mobile phones are difficult to rent, but providing your phone is GSM900/1800-compatible, you can buy a SIM-card package from one of Latvia's two mobile telephone operators, **Latvijas Mobilais Telfons** (LMT; www.lmt.lv) or **Tele2** (www.tele2.lv). Tele2's Zelta zivtiņa (literally 'gold fish') start-up kit costs 8.50Ls (SIM plus 7Ls credit) and local calls cost 0.168Ls to 0.234Ls per minute. LMT's OKarte package costs 9.70Ls (SIM plus 7Ls credit) and calls cost 0.036Ls to 0.216Ls per minute. The LMT network extends further than Tele2, but coverage in the countryside can be patchy with either network.

TOURIST INFORMATION

A small network of tourist offices overseas represents the **Latvian Tourism Development Agency** (☎ 722 9945; www.latviatourism.lv; Pils laukums 4, LV-1050 Rīga). In Latvia practically every town and city has a tourist office, listed both on the Latvian Tourism Development Agency's excellent website and under Information in the respective city/town sections of this chapter.

Some tourist offices are substantially more efficient than others, although practically all have an English-speaking staff and distribute printed information in English on its respective town and region.

Lithuania

BRUCE YUAN-YUE BI

Lithuania

Rebellious, quirky and vibrant, Lithuania (Lietuva) is Europe's best-kept secret. Shoved successively between Russian pillar and Nazi post, tenacious little Lithuania stunned the world when it played David and Goliath with the might of the Soviet Union – and won its independence just over a decade ago. Today the nation that vanished from the maps of Europe is back with a vengeance: it's part of the EU, was the first of the 25 EU players to give the European Constitution a stamp of approval and is a fully fledged 'n' fighting partner of NATO – home no less to four F-16 military alliance jet fighters used to police Baltic skies.

Politicians have come and gone, including the young, tenacious Rolandas Paksas, who wooed electors with big talk of a land of plenty and flamboyant aerial stunts in a small plane – until his fall from grace on corruption charges in 2004. Now the country is back in the hands of a couple of old stalwarts who, age aside (we're talking 74 for the prime minister, 80 for the president), lend little Lithuania a definite air of confidence.

This is a country with a colourful history, once boasting an empire stretching from the Baltic to the Black Sea. Its raw pagan roots fuse with Catholic fervour – the Polish inheritance that sets it apart from its Baltic brothers – to create a land where Catholics and Orthodox mingle happily in the forest to pick wild berries and mushrooms from nature's altar. Its capital, Vilnius, is an incredibly small place (can this really be a capital city?) with astonishing contrasts – eerie shadowy courtyards, eccentric artist community, awesome arts and beautiful baroque. Its natural treasures – forests, lakes, a magical spit of sand and a soggy delta – shimmer, while its oddities – the Hill of Crosses and a Soviet sculpture park – add a flavour found nowhere else.

FAST FACTS

- **Area** 65,303 sq km
- **Birthplace of** composer and painter Čiurlionis
- **Capital** Vilnius
- **Country code** ☎ 370
- **Departure tax** none
- **Famous for** causing the USSR to collapse; Europe's largest baroque old town
- **Money** Lithuanian litas; €1 = 3.45Lt; UK£1 = 5.04; US$1 = 2.84Lt
- **Population** 3.4 million
- **Visa** most nationalities don't need one; see p391 for more information.

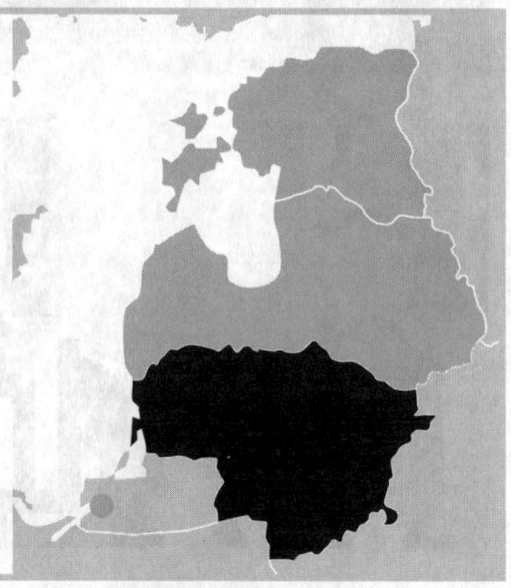

HIGHLIGHTS

- **Vilnius** (p287) Get lost by day in the cobbled heart of this beautiful baroque capital; dine come dusk on an atmospheric street terrace.
- **Curonian Spit** (p362) Gaze in awe at the drifting sands of Nida's golden Parnidis Dune (p368); cycle through pine to Juodkrantė (p364) and sail to Venice (p370).
- **Hill of Crosses** (p341) Plant a cross on this awe-inspiring mountain of crosses; visit the chapel of the neighbouring papal-inspired monastery.
- **Palanga** (p355) Party like mad in Palanga: drink and dance the night away then watch the sun rise over its pier.
- **Aukštaitija National Park** (p320) Go boating and berrying in this serene land of lake and forest; fish for your supper and sleep in a little wooden house.

HOW MUCH?

- **Cup of coffee** 1.70Lt to 5Lt
- **Taxi fare** 1Lt/km to 1.5Lt/km
- **Public transport ticket** 1.40Lt
- **Bicycle hire** 6/35Lt per hour/day
- **Sauna** 80Lt to 150Lt

LONELY PLANET INDEX

- **Litre of petrol** 2.6Lt
- **Litre of bottled water** 2.5Lt
- **50cl bottle of Švyturys beer** 2Lt
- **Souvenir T-shirt** 20Lt to 35Lt
- **pancake** 3.45Lt

ITINERARIES

- **Three Days** Devote two days to Vilnius (see p290) and spend the third day in Trakai (catch your own lunch and sleep in style on the lakeshore).
- **One Week** Combine a few days in Vilnius with day trips to Trakai and Druskininkai's Soviet sculpture park, plus a couple of days canoeing in the Aukštaitija National Park or dune dancing on the Curonian Spit.
- **Two Weeks** Vilnius to Klaipėda: explore Smiltynė, the gateway to the Curonian Spit. Explore the dunes of Nida, sweat it out in a seaside sauna in Smiltynė, then head down the mainland to Rusnė and explore the backwaters of the Nemunas Delta by boat. Double back, go to the eerie Hill of Crosses via the Orvydas Garden, the Soviet missile base and Lake Plateliai. Back to Vilnius via Kaunas.

CURRENT EVENTS

Valdas Adamkus (b 1926) made Lithuania's EU dream come true. Smashed at the polls in 2003 by a man 30 years younger, the 80-year-old Lithuanian émigré and former US citizen was re-elected president for a five-year term in June 2004. His return followed the impeachment of charismatic young dynamo Rolandas Paksas, whose alleged dealings with Russian mafia served as a harsh reminder of Lithuania's relative immaturity. In a country where public accountability is scarcely more than a decade old (not to mention where everyone led a different life pre-1991), the past is sensitive: in January 2005 a national newspaper exposed Lithuanian foreign minister Antanas Valionis as a former officer in the KGB reserves, prompting a parliament inquiry into his Soviet past.

True to form, bold Lithuania unabashedly ratified the EU constitution in November 2004, becoming the first of the 25 EU member countries to do so. Giving the green light with practically no political debate or public referendum, the move highlighted the nation's over-riding eagerness for all things European, including the euro, which many Lithuanians are gagging for.

Former president and current Prime Minister Algirdas Brazauskas (b 1932), picked by the president and backed by the 141-seat *seimas* (parliament) to form a government in late 2004, is one of its staunchest supporters. Leader of the Communist Party in Soviet Lithuania, the wily leftist politician subsequently reinvented himself as Social Democrats party leader and currently heads a power-sharing coalition with a clutch of other political parties, including the young Labour Party, formed in 2003.

Since joining NATO, Lithuania has been the first former Soviet republic to host the military alliance. It has also taken it upon itself to mediate between old East and West. This was made quite clear, to the disconcertion of some fellow EU members, during

LITHUANIA

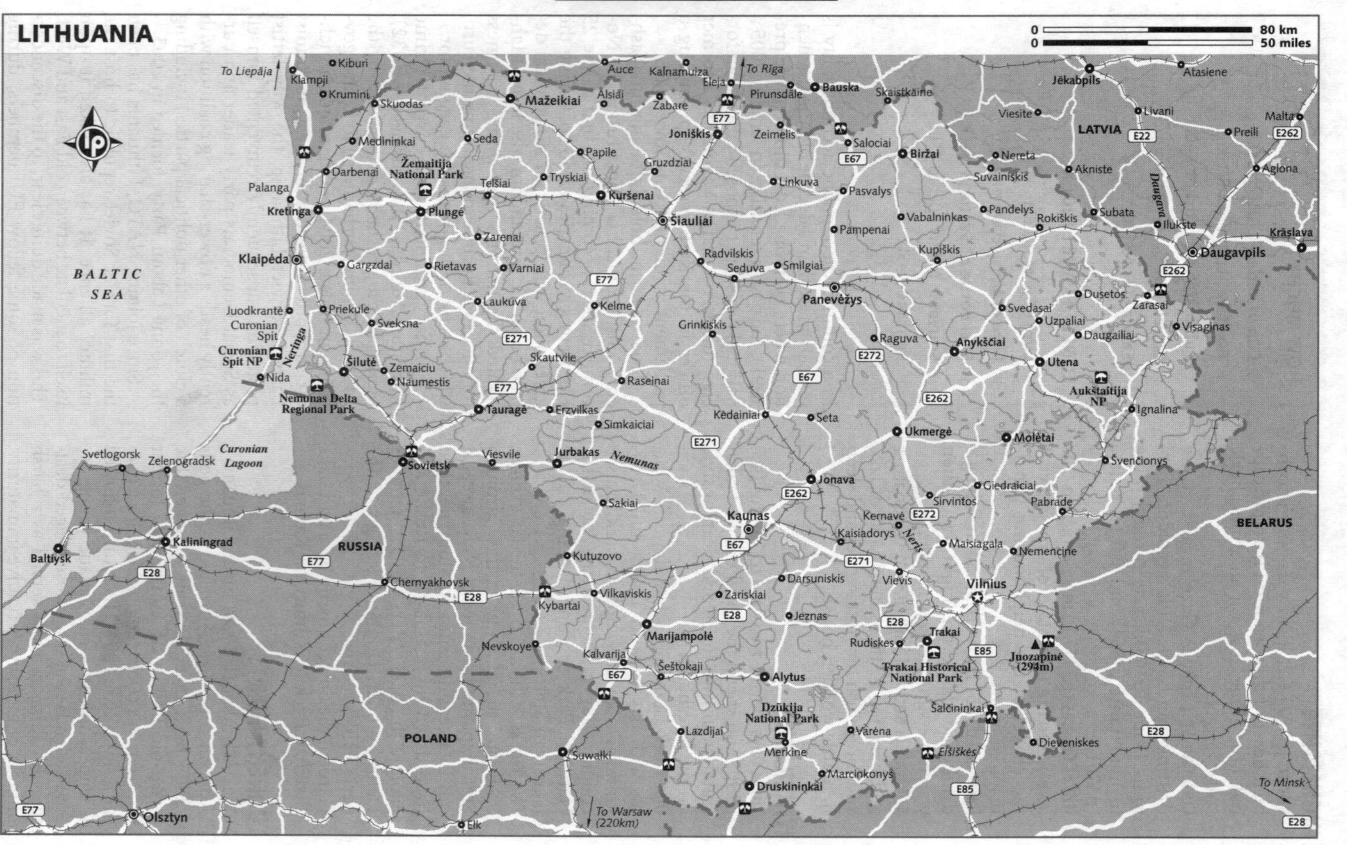
LITHUANIA
0 80 km
0 50 miles
BALTIC SEA
Curonian Lagoon
Curonian Spit
Curonian Spit NP
Neringa
Nemunas Delta Regional Park
To Liepāja
Kiburi
Klampji
Krumini
Skuodas
Medininkai
Darbenai
Palanga
Kretinga
Klaipėda
Juodkrantė
Nida
Žemaitija National Park
Seda
Plungė
Telšiai
Zarenai
Gargzdai
Rietavas
Varniai
Laukuva
Priekule
Sveksna
Šilutė
Zemaiciu Naumiestis
Auce
Alsiai
Mažeikiai
Kalnamuiža
Zabare
Papile
Tryskiai
Gruzdziai
Kuršenai
Šiauliai
Eleja
To Riga
Joniškis
Pirunsdāle
Bauska
Zeimelis
Saločiai
Skaistkaine
Linkuva
Pasvalys
Biržai
Radvilskis
Seduva
Smilgiai
Pampenai
Vabalninkas
Panevėžys
Kupiškis
Kelme
Grinkiskis
Raguva
Skautvile
Raseiniai
Tauragė
Erzvilkas
Simkaiciai
Kėdainiai
Seta
Sovietsk
Viesvile
Jurbakas
Nemunas
Svetlogorsk
Zelenogradsk
Baltiysk
Kaliningrad
RUSSIA
Chernyakhovsk
Kutuzovo
Sakiai
Kaunas
Jonava
Ukmergė
Anykščiai
Utena
Svedasai
Uzpaliai
Daugailiai
Dusetos
Zarasai
Visaginas
Aukštaitija NP
Ignalina
Molėtai
Švenčionys
Giedraiciai
Sirvintos
Pabrade
Kernavė
Neris
Kaisiadorys
Maisiagala
Nemencine
Vievis
Vilnius
Darsuniskis
Zariskiai
Jeznas
Kybartai
Vilkaviskis
Marijampolė
Nevskoye
Kalvarija
Šeštokaji
Alytus
Rudiskes
Trakai
Trakai Historical National Park
Juozapinė (294m)
Dzūkija National Park
Lazdijai
Varėna
Merkine
Šalčininkai
Eišiškės
Dieveniskes
Marcinkonys
Druskininkai
POLAND
Suwałki
To Warsaw (220km)
Olsztyn
Ełk
To Minsk
BELARUS
Jēkabpils
Atasiene
Viesite
Livani
LATVIA
Malta
Preili
Aglona
Nereta
Suvainiškis
Akniste
Daugava
Pandelys
Rokiškis
Subata
Ilukste
Krāslava
Daugavpils
E22
E28
E67
E77
E85
E262
E271
E272

Ukraine's Orange Revolution in January 2005, when Adamkus got heavily involved in negotiations with the country's disputing presidential contenders.

HISTORY

A powerful state in its own right at its peak in the 14th to 16th centuries, Lithuania subsequently fell under the Polish then Soviet yoke. Bar a brief interwar period of independence, Lithuania was not independent again until 1991. Kaunas' Military Museum of Vytautas the Great and Vilnius' National Museum cover the whole span of Lithuania's history.

Tribal Testosterone

Human habitation in the wedge of land that makes up present-day Lithuania goes back to at least 9000 BC. Trade in amber started during the Neolithic period (6000 to 4500 years ago), providing the Balts – the ancestors of modern Lithuanians – with a ready-made source of wealth when they arrived on the scene from the southeast some time around 2000 BC.

Two centuries on, it was this fossilised pine resin and the far-flung routes across the globe its trade forged – brilliantly explained in Palanga's Amber Museum – that prompted a mention of the amber-gathering *aesti* on the shores of the Baltic Sea in *Germania,* a beast of a book about Germanic tribes outside the Roman Empire written in 1009. The same year Lithuania was mentioned for the first time in written sources (the *Kvedlinburgh Chronicle*) as the place where an archbishop called Brunonus was struck on the head by pagans in Litae (Latin for Lithuania). Its 1000th anniversary will be celebrated in Vilnius, where an entire palace is being rebuilt brick by brick to mark the event; visit the site for the full story.

By the 12th century Lithuania's peoples had split into two tribal groups: the Samogitians (lowlanders) in the west and the Aukštaitiai (highlanders) in the east and southeast. Around this time a wooden castle was built atop Gediminas Hill in Vilnius.

Medieval Mayhem

In the mid-13th century Aukštaitiai leader Mindaugas unified Lithuanian tribes to create the Grand Duchy of Lithuania, of which he was coronated king in 1253 at Kernavė, the 'Pompeii of Lithuania'. Mindaugas accepted Catholicism in a bid to defuse the threat from the Teutonic Order – Germanic crusaders who conquered various Prussian territories, including Memel (present-day Klaipėda). Unfortunately neither conversion nor unity lasted very long: Mindaugas was assassinated in 1263 and Christianity rejected. Vilnius did reap its first cathedral, though, from this sacred decade of peace.

In 1290 Lithuania was reunified and under Grand Duke Gediminas (1316–41) its borders extended south and east into modern-day Belarus. After Gediminas' death two of his sons shared the realm: in Vilnius, Algirdas pushed the southern borders of Lithuania past Kyiv, while Kęstutis – who plumped for a pretty lake island in Trakai as a site for his castle – fought off the Teutonic Order. After Algirdas' death in 1377, Kęstutis drove Algirdas' son and successor, Jogaila, from Vilnius and made himself sole ruler of Lithuania. But in 1382 Jogaila captured Kęstutis and son Vytautas, and threw the pair into prison (where Kęstutis died).

With the Teutonic threat increasing, Jogaila found himself in a quandary. His Orthodox princes advised alliance with Moscow, the rising Russian power in the east, and conversion to Orthodoxy, while his pagan princes suggested conversion to Catholicism and alliance with neighbouring Poland.

Jogaila's decision was a watershed in Eastern European history. In 1386 he wed Jadwiga, crown princess of Poland, to become Władysław II Jagiełło of Poland and forge a Lithuanian-Polish alliance that would last 400 years. The Aukštaitiai were baptised in 1387 and the Samogitians in 1413, making Lithuania the last European country to accept Christianity.

Glory Days

Jogaila patched things up with Vytautas, who became Grand Duke of Lithuania on condition that he and Jogaila share a

> **TIP OFF**
>
> To keep abreast of the latest current events, surf the Ministry of Foreign Affairs' website (www1.urm.lt) – an invaluable, reliable and well-organised news source.

common policy. The decisive defeat of the Teutonics by their combined armies at Grünwald (in modern-day Poland) in 1410 ushered in a golden period of prosperity, particularly for its capital Vilnius, which saw its legendary Old Town born.

Vytautas ('the Great') extended Lithuanian control further south and east. By 1430 when he died, Lithuania stretched beyond Kursk in the east and almost to the Black Sea in the south, creating one of Europe's largest empires. Nowhere was its grandeur and clout better reflected than in 16th-century Vilnius, which, with a population of 25,000-odd, was one of eastern Europe's biggest cities. Fine late-Gothic and Renaissance buildings sprung up, and Lithuanians such as Žygimantas I and II occupied the Polish-Lithuanian throne inside the sumptuous Royal Palace. In 1579 Polish Jesuits founded Vilnius University and made the city a bastion of the Catholic Counter Reformation. Under Jesuit influence, baroque architecture also arrived.

Polonisation & Partitions

But Lithuania gradually sank into a junior role in its partnership with Poland, climaxing with the formal union of the two states (instead of just their crowns) at the Treaty of Lublin in 1569 during the Livonian War with Muscovy. Under the so-called Rzeczpospolita (Commonwealth), Lithuania played second fiddle to Poland. Its gentry adopted Polish culture and language, its peasants became serfs and Warsaw usurped Vilnius as political and social hub.

A century on it was Russia's turn to play tough. In 1654 Russia invaded the Rzeczpospolita and snatched significant territory from it. By 1772 the Rzeczpospolita was so weakened that the Prussia-Brandenburg state of Russia, Austria and Prussia simply carved it up in the Partitions of Poland (1772, 1793 and 1795–96). Most of Lithuania went to Russia, while a small chunk around Klaipėda in the west went to Prussia.

Power to the People

While neighbouring Estonia and Latvia were governed as separate provinces, Russian rule took a different stance with rebellious Lithuania.

Vilnius had quickly become a refuge for Polish and Lithuanian gentry dispossessed by the region's new Russian rulers and a focus of the Polish national revival, in which Vilnius-bred poet Adam Mickiewicz was a leading inspiration. When Lithuanians joined a failed Polish rebellion against Russian rule in 1830 and 1831, Tsarist authorities clamped down extra hard. It shut Vilnius University, closed Catholic churches and monasteries and imposed Russian Orthodoxy. Russian law was introduced in 1840 and the Russian language was used for teaching. From 1864 books could only be published in Lithuanian if they used the Cyrillic alphabet, while publications in Polish (spoken by the Lithuanian gentry) were banned altogether.

In 1861 Lithuanian (and Russian) peasants were emancipated: power to the people! National revival became a hot trend in the 19th and early 20th century, the rapid industrialisation of Vilnius and other towns simply lending nationalist drives more clout. Vilnius became an important Jewish centre during this period, Jews making up around 75,000 of its 160,000-strong population in the early 20th century to earn it the nickname 'Jerusalem of the North'.

Independence

Ideas of Baltic national autonomy and independence had been voiced during the 1905 Russian revolution, but it was not until 1918 that the restoration of the Independent State of Lithuania was declared. During WWI Lithuania was occupied by Germany and it was while still under German occupation on 16 February 1918 that a Lithuanian national council, the Taryba, declared independence in Vilnius in the House of Signatories, open to visitors today. In November Germany surrendered to the Western Allies, and the same day a Lithuanian republican government was set up.

With the re-emergence of an independent Poland eager to see Lithuania reunited with it or cede it the Vilnius area, which had a heavily Polish and/or Polonised population, things turned nasty. On 31 December 1918 the Lithuanian government fled to Kaunas, and days later the Red Army installed a communist government in Vilnius. Polish troops drove the Red Army out on 2 January 1919, only for the Red Army to recapture it three days later. The Poles hit back on 19 April, but were again thwarted. Following the Peace

Conference of Paris on 1 June 1919, Lithuanian independence was recognised, and on 15 May 1920 the first parliament met in Kaunas at the State Theatre Palace (today the Kaunas Musical Theatre). But on 9 October 1920 the Poles occupied Vilnius for a third time and on 10 October 1920 annexed the city once and for all.

Thus from 1920 until 1939, Vilnius and its surrounds was an isolated corner of Poland while the rest of Lithuania enjoyed independence, for the most part under the iron-fist rule (1926–40) of Lithuania's first president, Antanas Smetona (1874–1944). See the politician's statue and learn how he ruled along similar lines to Mussolini in Italy at Kaunas' Presidential Palace, now a museum. Kaunas was Lithuanian capital throughout this interwar period. In 1923 Lithuania annexed Memel (present-day Klaipėda).

WWII & Soviet Rule

With the fatal signing of the Molotov-Ribbentrop nonaggression pact, Lithuania fell to the Nazis and soon after (when it refused to join the Nazi attack on Poland in September 1939) into Soviet hands. The 'mutual-assistance pact' the USSR insisted on signing with Lithuania regained it Vilnius in October 1939 (the Red Army had taken the city in its invasion of eastern Poland at the same time as Germany had invaded western Poland). But this was little consolation for the terror Lithuania experienced as a USSR republic – a fate and history it shared with its immediate neighbours, Estonia and Latvia. Soviet purges saw thousands upon thousands of Balts killed or deported.

Following Hitler's invasion of the USSR and the Nazi occupation of the region in 1941, nearly all of Lithuania's Jewish population – between 135,000 and 300,000 people according to varying estimates – were killed; most Vilnius Jews were killed in its ghetto or in Paneriai Forest, a horribly unnerving place to visit today. An estimated 45,000 Lithuanians were enlisted in German military units; others were conscripted for forced labour; and 80,000 Lithuanians escaped to the West between 1944 and 1945 to avoid the Red Army's reconquest of the Baltic countries. In all some 475,000 Lithuanians perished during WWII.

Between 1944 and 1952 under Soviet rule, a further 250,000 Lithuanians were killed or deported, suppression of spirit and free thought being the order of the day. Nowhere is this dark, dark period in Lithuanian history explained more powerfully than at the Museum of Genocide Victims in the old KGB headquarters in Vilnius.

1989–91

A yearning for independence had simmered during the glasnost years, but it was with the storming success of Lithuania's popular front, Sajūdis, in the March 1989 elections for the USSR Congress of People's Deputies (Sajūdis won 30 of the 42 Lithuanian seats) that Lithuania surged ahead in the Baltic push for independence. The pan-Baltic human chain formed to mark the 50th anniversary of the Molotov-Ribbentrop Pact a few months later confirmed public opinion, and in December that year the Lithuanian Communist Party left the Communist Party of the Soviet Union – a landmark in the break-up of the USSR.

Vast proindependence crowds met Gorbachev when he visited Vilnius in January 1990. Sajūdis won a majority in the elections to Lithuania's supreme soviet in February, and on 11 March this assembly declared Lithuania an independent republic. In response, Moscow carried out weeks of troop manoeuvres around Vilnius and clamped an economic blockade on Lithuania, cutting off fuel supplies. The pressure was finally removed after 2½ months, when Sajūdis leader Vytautas Landsbergis agreed to a 100-day moratorium on the independence declaration in exchange for independence talks between the respective Lithuanian and USSR governments. No foreign country had yet recognised Lithuanian independence.

Soviet hardliners gained the ascendancy in Moscow in winter 1990–91, and in January 1991 Soviet troops and paramilitary police occupied and stormed Vilnius' TV tower and TV centre, killing 14 people; tourists bungee jump from this tower today. Some of the barricades put up around the parliament remain. On 6 September 1991 the USSR recognised the independence of Lithuania.

Towards Europe

Lithuanians have a sense of irony: they led the Baltic push for independence, then, at their first democratic parliamentary elections, in 1992, raised eyebrows by voting

LITHUANIA

in the ex-communist Lithuanian Democratic Labour Party (LDDP). Presidential elections followed in 1993, the year the last Soviet soldier left the country, with former Communist Party first secretary Algirdas Brazauskas landing 60% of the vote. Corruption scandals dogged his term in office – a painful time as inflation ran at 1000% and thousands of jobs were lost from inefficient heavy industry. The collapse of the country's banking system in 1995–96 did little to aid economic performance.

But change was underway: Lithuania's currency, the litas, replaced the talonas (coupon), the transitional currency used during the phasing out of the Soviet rouble in Lithuania; Lithuania opened a stock exchange, abolished the death penalty and joined the NATO Partnership for Peace programme; and Lithuanian became the official language and an association agreement was signed with the EU. Presidential elections in 1998 ushered in wild card Valdas Adamkus, a 71-year-old Lithuanian émigré and US citizen, resident in the US since his parents fled the Soviets in 1944. Hopes that Adamkus would inject some Western life into the failing economy ran higher still when he appointed a member of the ruling Conservative Party, 43-year-old Rolandas Paksas, prime minister in 1999. The popular Vilnius mayor and champion stunt pilot won instant approval as 'the people's choice' – so much so in fact that he ran against Adamkus in 2003 presidential elections and won.

By 2001 the Lithuanian economy was being praised by the International Monetary Fund as one of the world's fastest growing, thanks to large-scale privatisation in 1997–98 and a rigorous campaign to lure international cash by focusing on the country's low operating costs, cheap workforce and its status as a transport hub between East and West. When deep recession struck following the 1998 Russian economic crisis (GDP shrank by 4.1%), forward-thinking Lithuanians clawed their way back by diversifying into new EU electronic, chemical and manufacturing markets. Lithuania joined the World Trade Organization in 2000, and in 2002 – in a bid to make exports competitive and show determination to join Europe – pegged its currency to the euro instead of the US dollar.

In 2001 Lithuania took over as annual chair of the Council of Europe Committee of Ministers at its 109th session in Strasbourg, and the Dalai Lama paid a visit. In 2003 it became the first Baltic country to resolve border disputes with Russia (over its shared land and maritime borders with Russian-owned Kaliningrad).

THE CULTURE

National Psyche

With their warm and welcoming emotional natures, tendency towards mysticism and fierce pride in their national identity, gut-driven Lithuanians really are the Italians of the Baltics. Their pride in being part of the EU and home to the geographical centre

TOP FIVE HISTORICAL READS

- *The Last Girl* (Stephan Collishaw) Absolutely spellbinding, this superb historical novel set in Vilnius flits between WWII and the 1990s.
- *Lithuania Awakening* (Alfred Senn) From 'new winds' (the birth of the independence movement in the 1980s) to a 'new era' (independence), Senn's look at how the Lithuanians achieved independence remains the best in its field; read the entire thing free online at http://ark.cdlib.org/ark:/13030/ft3x0nb2m8/.
- *Lithuania – Independent Again: The Autobiography of Vytautas Landsbergis* The scene outside parliament on 13 January 1991 is among the dramatic moments Landsbergis brings vividly to life in his autobiography.
- *Forest of the Gods* (Balys Sruoga) The author's powerful account of his time spent in the Stutthof Nazi concentration camp in the early 1940s was censored, hence not published until 1957.
- *Showdown: The Lithuanian Rebellion and the Break Up of the Soviet Union* (Richard J Krickus) A look at the USSR and the huge part played in its break-up by Lithuania.

LITHUANIA

DO'S & DON'TS

- When visiting a Lithuanian bring an odd number of flowers: even-numbered bouquets are for dead-solemn occasions – and the dead!
- Don't shake hands across the threshold; it brings bad luck.
- Always maintain eye contact when toasting your host or they'll think you're shifty.

of Europe is reflected in their willingness to speak English, German, Russian or any other language they can twist their nimble tongues around.

Lithuania oozes confidence, boldly exuding a happy-go-lucky assurance that manifests itself in the toppled Lenins it happily shows off in a Soviet sculpture park (p326) and the 'republic' (p298) that artists have created in the capital.

Tradition and a deep-rooted attachment to the land play an integral part in the national psyche – a trait Lithuania shares with its Baltic neighbours.

Lifestyle

The contrast in lifestyle between Vilnius and elsewhere is stark.

Capital-city slickers are young, buoyant, cash-happy and party-mad. Many live in stylish loft apartments in Old Town, are professionals and car-owners, and end the day with friends in the latest trendy bar or café. Pumping iron in the gym, yoga and catching a movie are run-of-the-mill pursuits, while weekends mean shopping, kitesurfing and dancing till dawn in Palanga or snowboarding in Latvia. With supermarkets and many shops open sunrise to sunset, seven days a week, Sunday is no different to any other day; Mass has less allure for the upwardly mobile set in increasingly commercial, diverse and international Vilnius, where casinos and strip joints rapidly threaten to outnumber churches (quite an achievement in Vilnius where a church studs practically every Old Town street corner!).

Then there is the rest of Lithuania – a monochrome mix of provincial town and rural scape, where poverty is about the only prevalent excess. The government might well have bumped up the minimum monthly salary by 10% to 500Lt (€145) in 2004, and the average monthly wage might well have reached a record 1270Lt (€368) in 2005, but for many living and working in the countryside, such figures are meaningless. These people work the land and that is about it, unemployment being way higher in rural areas than wealthier urban circles.

Until 1998 Vilnius was the only place in Lithuania to offer a university degree. Since then, nine state universities, five academies and four colleges have sprung up. More than 80% of pupils go on to further education; most students work full time alongside studying and live in university dorms or with friends rather than remaining in the parental nest. Family ties remain fiercely strong, however, many married couples living with elderly parents no longer able to live alone. Despite increased career prospects, especially for women, Lithuanians marry young – as a day trip from Vilnius to Trakai, full of blushing brides scarcely out of their teens, on a Saturday afternoon in summer instantly reveals! Many marriages – 57 of every 100 – end in divorce.

Population

The population is predominantly urban: a quarter of the population lives in and around Vilnius and 40% of people live in the country's five major cities – Vilnius plus

LIFESTYLE IN A NUTSHELL

- Lithuania's wealthiest 10% spend 7.7 times more a month than its poorest 10%.
- The country's richest spend 25% of their income on food, the poorest 62%.
- Fifty-one percent of urban households own a car compared to 37% in the countryside.
- Excluding kids' bikes, 64% of rural homes own a bicycle. In urban areas 31% of homes are pedal-powered.
- In rural areas just one home in 10 is computer-equipped, unlike in the five major cities – Vilnius, Kaunas, Klaipėda, Šiauliai and Panevėžys – where 38% of households have a PC.

Kaunas, Šiauliai and Panevėžys in central Lithuania and Klaipėda on the Baltic Sea. Population density was 46.6 people per sq km before WWII, peaked at 56.6 people per sq km prior to independence in 1990 (when contraception was illegal) and shrunk to 52.5 people per sq km in 2005.

Easily the most ethnically homogeneous population of the three Baltic countries, Lithuanians count for 83% of the total population, making multiculturalism less of a hot potato than in Latvia. Russians form 6.3% of the Lithuanian population, the bizarrely Soviet town of Visaginas (p322), created in the 1970s, being the country's Russian stronghold. Poles and Jews make up 6.7% and 0.1% respectively.

Lithuania's smallest ethnic community, numbering just 280, are the Karaites. An early 19th-century prayer house and ethnographic museum (p316) in Trakai provide insight into the culture and beliefs of this tiny Turkic minority.

Lithuanian Roma officially number 2500, but Vilnius' **Human Rights Monitoring Institute** (www.hrmi.lt) reckons the real figure is 3000, centred in Vilnius, Panevėžys and Šiauliai. Some 46% are aged under 20 and many, unlike the Roma elders they live with, don't speak Lithuanian. Since 1993 a government-initiated programme for the integration of Roma into Lithuanian society has paid lip service to improving education and living conditions for Roma: nothing has changed for this impoverished and discriminated-against minority. Getting the government to put antidiscrimination legislation in place is one of the goals of the Roma Rights Defense Legal Programme launched by the Human Rights Monitoring Institute in April 2005.

More than three million Lithuanians live abroad, including an estimated 800,000 in the USA. Other communities exist in Canada, South America, Britain and Australia.

SPORT

Basketball is akin to religion. The worshipped national team are reigning European champions and scooped bronze in three successive Olympic Games (1992, 1996 and 2000), only to lose it to the American Dream Team in Athens at the 2004 Games – after both teams turned up in the same coloured strips!

Basketball players of legendary status include retired Sarūnas Marčiulionis, the first Lithuanian to play in the NBA in 1989, and Arvydas Sabonis, one of baksetball's greatest centres. Marčiulionis and Sabonis have since founded basketball schools – and luxury hotels – in Vilnius and Kaunas respectively.

Popular ice-skaters and a married couple to boot, **Margarita Drobiazko & Povilas Vanagas** (http://drobiazko.vanagas.w3.lt), rather controversially lost out on medals both at the Salt Lake City Winter Olympics (they were placed 5th) and the Ice Dancing World Championship (4th) in 2002, amid accusations of biased judges. But their woe has raised the profile of the sport in Lithuania. Of equal elegance and excellence off ice are Lithuanian dancesport duo Arūnas Bižokas and Edita Daniūtė, whose incredible manoeuvres landed them gold at the 2005 Dance-sport World Games in Germany and a world ranking of No 2.

World-champion cyclist Diana Žiliūtė won the Tour de France in 1999 and silver at the Sydney 2000 Olympics. Raimondas Rumšas surprised everyone by finishing 3rd in the 2002 Tour de France, only for his wife to be stopped with a campervan full of drugs driving home. Rumšas was banned from racing for a year after testing positive for performance-enhancing drugs during the 2003 Giro d'Italia and in November 2005 appeared in court on charges of smuggling illegal drugs into France during the 2002 Tour. The Bicycle Museum (p339) in Šiauliai is a fun spot to learn about lesser-known Lithuanian riders.

Discus thrower Alekna Virgilijus –guard to the Lithuanian president during his spare time (at 2.02m tall and 130kg it's best not to mess with him) – scooped Lithuania's only gold medals at the 2000 and 2004 Olympics.

RELIGION

Lithuania was the last pagan country in Europe, not baptised into Roman Catholicism until 1387. This explains why so much of its religious art, national culture and traditions have raw pagan roots. During the Soviet years, Catholicism was persecuted and hence became a symbol of nationalistic fervour. Churches were seized, closed and turned into 'museums of atheism' or used for other secular purposes (such as a radio station in the case of Christ's Resurrection

Basilica in Kaunas, open for business as usual today) by the state.

Other minorities include Orthodox believers, Lutherans, Jews, Evangelical Christians and the pagan Romuva movement.

GODLY AFFAIRS

Of Gods and Holidays: The Baltic Heritage (1999) is a revealing look at Lithuania's pagan roots.

ARTS

Lithuania is Baltic queen of contemporary jazz, theatre and the avant-garde, while its arts scene is one of Europe's youngest, freshest and most dynamic.

Literature

The Renaissance ushered in the first book to be published in Lithuanian – a catechism by Martynas Mažvydas, whose statue stands in Klaipėda – in 1547 and the creation of Vilnius University in 1579. But it wasn't until a couple of centuries later that a true Lithuanian literature emerged.

The land was the focus of the earliest fiction: The Seasons *(Metai)*, by Kristijonas Donelaitis, described serf life in the 18th century in poetic form, and a century on Antanas Baranauskas' poem, *Anykščiai Pine Forest* (*Anykščių šilelis;* 1860–1), used the deep, dark forest around Anykščiai as a symbol of Lithuania, bemoaning its destruction by foreign landlords.

Russia's insistence on the Cyrillic alphabet for publishing from 1864 (until 1904) hindered literature's development – and inspired poet Jonas Mačiulis (1862–1932) to push for its national revival. A statue of the Kaunas priest, nicknamed Maironis, stands in Kaunas' Old Town. The city's Maironis Lithuania Literary Museum (p333), in Maironis' former home, tells his life story. Maironis' romantic *Voices of Spring* (*Pavasario balsai;* 1895) is deemed the start of modern Lithuanian poetry.

Several major Polish writers grew up in Lithuania and regarded themselves as partly Lithuanian, notably Adam Mickiewicz (1798–1855), the inspiration of 19th-century nationalists, whose great poem *Pan Tadeusz* begins 'Lithuania, my fatherland...' The rooms in Vilnius' Old Town, where he stayed while studying at Vilnius University, form a museum (p297). Winner of the 1980 Nobel prize, Czesław Miłosz (1911–2004) translated Lithuanian folk songs into French and wrote about intellectuals and the Soviet occupation in *The Captive Mind.*

Novelists at the fore of contemporary Lithuanian literature include Antanas Skėma, whose semiautobiographical novel *White Linen Shroud* (*Balta drobulė;* 1954) recounts a childhood in Kaunas, then emigration to Germany and New York. It pioneered stream of consciousness in Lithuanian literature. Realist novelist and short-story writer Ričardas Gavelis shocked the literary world with *Poker in Vilnius* (1989) and *Vilnius Jazz* (1993), which openly criticised the defunct

TOP FIVE CONTEMPORARY READS

Online, visit **Books from Lithuania** (www.booksfromlithuania.lt), a comprehensive literary information centre reviewing the latest in Lithuanian poetry and prose, including English-language translations.

- *The Earth Remains* (edited by Laima Sruoginis) Anthology of contemporary Lithuanian prose with lengthy excerpts from key works, including Gavelis' *Poker in Vilnius*.
- *Lithuanian Literature* (edited by Vytautas Kubilius) Read this to get the big picture.
- *Gone with Dreams* (Jurga Ivanauskaitė) A young Lithuanian woman travels to the Himalayas and hangs out with Tibetan monks in her quest for spiritual enlightenment.
- *Bohin Manor* (Tadeusz Konwicki) Set in the aftermath of the 1863 uprising, this novel by a leading modern Polish writer born in Lithuania uses the past to comment on current events and evokes tensions between locals, their Russian rulers and a Jewish outsider, as well as the foreboding and mysterious nature of the Lithuanian backwoods.
- *Raw Amber* (edited by Laima Sruoginis) Anthology of contemporary Lithuanian poetry.

Soviet system and mentality. Equally controversial was the story of a priest's love affair with a woman, The Witch and the Rain *(Ragana ir lietus)* by Jurga Ivanauskaitė, banned on publication in 1992. Her subsequent novel *Gone with Dreams* (2000) highlighted new issues and subjects, such as religion, travel and perceptions of others' religion and cultures, that couldn't be addressed in Lithuanian literature until after 1991.

Cinema & TV

Vilnius' Theatre, Music & Cinema Museum (p298) is the perfect place to find out about cinema and TV.

The 11 documentaries and one short film made by Audrius Stonys are acclaimed Europe-wide: *510 Seconds of Silence* (2000) – an angel's flight over Vilnius' Old Town, the lake-studded Aukštaitija National Park and Neringa – is awesome; watch it at www.stonys.lt.

Stonys codirected *Baltic Way* (1990) – which landed best European documentary in 1992 – with hot-shot director-producer Arūnas Matelis (b 1961). A frequent guest at Cannes, Matelis raised eyebrows by becoming the Minister of Changes and Migration in the Republic of Užupis (p298). Find him and his film crew at www.nominum.lt.

The grim reality of the post-Soviet experience is the focus for talented film director Šarūnas Bartas, whose silent B&W movie *Koridorius* (The Corridor; 1995) – set in a dilapidated apartment block in a Vilnius suburb – received international recognition. Bartas opened Lithuania's first independent film studio in 1987. Algimantas Puipa became prominent with *Vilko dantu karoliai* (The Necklace of Wolf's Teeth; 1998) and *Elze is Gilijos* (Elsie from Gilija; 1999).

With the onslaught of commercial box-office hits from abroad, the Lithuanian film industry relies heavily on its reputation as a cheap film location. Founded in Soviet Kaunas in 1940 and transferred to Vilnius in 1956, the **Lithuanian Film Studio** (www.kftv.com) has helped make dozens of big-name foreign movies since the mid-1990s: British TV serials *The New Adventures of Robin Hood* (1995–96) and *Elizabeth I* (filmed 2005) starring Jeremy Irons; feature films *The Devil's Arithmetic* (1998) and *Silence Becomes You* (2004) with one-time Batgirl Alicia Silverstone; and Brett Leonard's *Highlander: The Source*, filmed in late 2005 in Vilnius, Kaunas and Trakai.

Music

Lithuania is the Baltic jazz giant. Two noteworthy musicians are sparkling pianist Gintautas Abarius and cerebral saxophonist Petras Vysniauskas. As famed is the Ganelin Trio, whose avant-garde jazz stunned the West when discovered in the 1980s. Kurpiai (p352) in Klaipėda and Birštonas Jazz (p339) are *the* spots to catch Lithuanian jazz.

Romantic folk-influenced Mikalojus Konstantinas Čiurlionis is Lithuania's leading composer from earlier periods. Two of his major works are the symphonic poems *Miske* (In the Forest) and *Jūra* (The Sea; 1900–07). Čiurlionis wrote many piano pieces, played and recorded notably by contemporary Lithuanian parliament chairman Vytautas Landbergis.

Rytis Mažulis (b 1961) represents a new generation of composers with his neo-avant-garde stance expressed in minimalist compositions for voice. Prominent late-20th-century musicians include Lithuanian Symphony Orchestra conductor Gintaras Rinkevičius; his counterpart at the Lithuanian Chamber Orchestra, Saulius Sondeckis; opera tenor Virgilijus Noreika; and booming baritone Vytautas Juozapaitis. Country-and-western icon Virgis Stakėnas is the larger-than-life force behind the country's cult country music festival.

Home-brand pop music is dominated by girl band Mango, boy band B'avarija and Amberlife, whose debut album *My Way* (2003) saw critics dub the young male soloist 'the next Coldplay'. Skamp plays mainstream hip-hop and G&G Sindikatas mixes purer street sounds. Lemon's Joy plays popular electronic pop-rock, Rebel Heart plays hard rock and Lithuania's leading soloists are female blues singer Arina and Andrius Mamontovas, whose signature song is *Laužo āviesa* (Fire Light).

DJs Mamania and Element are proof that dance music has arrived in Lithuania. Gravity (p312), Cozy (p311) and Pascha (p312) in Vilnius are the places to catch the latest on the Lithuanian DJ scene. On air, tune into **Užupio Radijas** (www.uzupioradijas.lt; 94.9 FM).

The most innovative sound to come out of Lithuania for years is **Inculto** (www.inculto.net), an eclectic band whose creative

FOLK ART

The carved wooden crosses placed at crossroads, cemeteries, village squares and at the sites of extraordinary events across Lithuania are a beautiful expression of religious fervour – and a striking nationalistic statement. Pagan symbols of suns, moons and plants are intertwined, making the totems a unique cultural contradiction. Vincas Svirskis (1835–1916) was the master; see his carvings in Vilnius' Museum of Applied Arts (p294). In the Soviet period, such work was banned, although it has survived to amazing effect at the Hill of Crosses (p341) near Šiauliai. **Old Lithuanian Sculpture, Crosses and Shrines** (www.tradicija.lt) is an excellent online resource.

Several folk artists' workshops in Vilnius can be visited (p305), while galleries and museums such as Vilnius' Contemporary Art Centre (p297), Aukso Avis (p313) and Museum of Applied Arts and Kaunas' Čiurlionis Art Museum (p335) showcase contemporary creations. Ona Grigaitė and Dalia Laučkaitė-Jakimavičienė are big names in the ceramics world.

output reflects diverse world influences. This positive side of cultural globalisation was the message of Inculto's outstandingly successful no-name debut album (2005), a mix of traditional punk, rock, jazz and folk fused with Latin American rhythms and electronic beats. The album was meant to be called *PostSovPop* until the band's record label and sponsors persuaded it otherwise (the title was ditched from the cover but appeared on the inside jacket).

Visual Arts

Lithuania's finest painter and musician is Varėna-born Mikalojus Konstantinas Čiurlionis (1875–1911), who spent his childhood in Druskininkai, where his home is now a museum (p325). He wrote Lithuania's first symphony, *In the Forest*, created piano pieces and conducted and composed string-quartet pieces. Oh yes, and he also put paint to canvas and produced romantic masterpieces in gentle, lyrical tones, theatre backdrops and some exquisite stained glass. The best collection of these works is in the National Čiurlionis Art Museum (p335) in Kaunas. Depression dogged Čiurlionis, although when he died aged 35 it was of pneumonia.

Lithuania has a thriving contemporary art scene. Vilnius artists created the tongue-in-cheek Republic of Užupis (p298), which hosts alternative art festivals, fashion shows and exhibitions in its breakaway state. Some 19km north, Lithuanian sculptor Gintaras Karosas heads up a sculpture park, Europos parkas (p318).

From Lenin to rock legend, Konstantinas Bogdanas was famed for his bronzes of communist heroes (see some in Druskininkai's Soviet Sculpture Park; p326) and his bust of musician and composer Frank Zappa (p299).

Lithuanian photography has achieved international recognition. Vytautas Stanionis (b 1949) was the leading postwar figure, while artist Antanas Sutkus stunned the photographic world with his legendary shots of French philosopher Sartre and novelist Simone de Beauvoir cavorting in the sand on the Curonian Spit. Vitalijus Butyrinas' (b 1947) famous series *Tales of the Sea* uses abstract expressionism to make powerful images. For more on these and other hot shots, visit the **Union of Lithuanian Art Photographers** (www.photography.lt).

Theatre

Lithuanian theatre is becoming an international force, with several young experimental directors turning European heads left, right and centre. Theatres yield 15% of their income from box-office sales; 13 of Lithuania's 25-odd theatres are state funded.

Vilnius-based Oskaras Koršunovas (b 1969) has done Europe's theatre-festival circuit with *Old Woman, Shopping and Fucking, PS Files OK* and his 2003 adaptation of *Romeo and Juliet*. In 1999 the controversial director established his own theatre company in Vilnius, the Oskaras Koršunovas Theatre (OKT; p312), albeit one with no fixed stage. OKT won one of the country's most prestigious art awards for the best presentation of Lithuanian culture abroad in 2004 and was subsequently honoured with the additional title of Vilnius City Theatre.

Other big names include Gintaras Varnas, artistic director at the Kaunas Academic Drama Theatre (p337), voted Lithuania's

THE LITHUANIAN AMBER ROAD

The capital has some striking amber galleries (p312) and a couple of tip-top fashion designers (p313) who work with 'Baltic gold'. But it is on the coast that the Lithuanian amber road – part of a compelling 418km pan-Baltic trail (p21 & p35) – gets serious.

The world's sixth-largest collection of Baltic amber comprising 14,478 pieces is the star of the show; find it in Palanga (p357) alongside an innovative amber-processing gallery inspired by master amber crafters' workshops of old. Elsewhere, there are beaches to hunt amber (p21), and amber jewellery galleries (p367) in Nida.

best director of the year several times, including in 2005; and Rimas Tuminas, who directed a fantastic play called *Madagaskaras* (set in independent 1920s Lithuania) by budding Lithuanian playwright Marius Ivaškevičius in Vilnius.

The international theatre festival, Sirens, an annual event in late September, was created in 2004 to mark the Lithuanian capital on the European cultural map. A key online information source on Lithuanian theatre is www.theatre.lt.

ENVIRONMENT

The Land

The largest of the Baltic countries, Lithuania is dotted with lush forests, 4000 lakes (covering 1.5% of the country) and a 100km-wide lowland centre. Latvia neighbours it to the north, Belarus to the southeast, and Poland and the Kaliningrad Region (Russia) to the southwest. Juozapinės (294m), straddling the Belarusian border, is the country's highest point.

Half of Lithuania's short (99km) Baltic Coast lies along the Curonian Spit – the region's most breathtaking natural feature. Split between Lithuania and Kaliningrad, the golden sand spit stretches for 98km and is just 4km wide, with sand dunes majestically rising up to 60m high. Behind it spans the Curonian Lagoon, into which the Nemunas River – Lithuania's longest river – flows.

Wildlife

Lithuania is home to 70 species of mammal, including elks, wild boars and lynx, while the Nemunas Delta wetlands are an important breeding area for birds, including the stork (p282). The beaver, European bison and red deer have been reintroduced. Wolves breed in inland national parks; the Austrian grass snake slithers around in Dzūkija and large bat populations bat about everywhere. Occasionally, in a quiet spot in one of Lithuania's lovely lake lands, a rare freshwater turtle lays its eggs on an empty sandy shore.

Forest covers 30% of the country, pine, spruce and birch predominating. Predictably, trees are a source of great pride for Lithuanians, who honour their oldest with names like Kapinių pušis (Cemetery Pine) and Ragaonos uosis (Witch's Ash). In pagan times trees were said to shelter souls of the dead, soldiers killed in battle turning into trees. A century ago man hollowed out beehives high up (so brown bears didn't steal the honey) in pine tree trunks; dozens still stud the Dzūkija National Park.

STORKS

Spring is marked by the arrival of the majestic stork, which jets in for the summer from Africa.

The height of sensibility, this bird of passage usually settles back into the same nest it has used for years. Large and flat, the nest is balanced in a tree or atop a disused chimney or telegraph pole. Some are splayed out across wooden cartwheels, fixed atop tall poles by kindly farmers keen to have their farmstead blessed by the good fortune the stork brings. Lithuanians celebrate this traditional protector of the home with Stork Day (25 March), the day farmers traditionally stir their seeds, yet to be planted, to ensure a bigger and better crop.

Measuring 90cm in height, this beautiful long-legged, wide-winged creature is breathtaking in flight. Equally marvellous is the catwalk stance it adopts when strutting through meadows in search of frogs to feast on. It sleeps standing on one leg.

Lithuania, with approximately 13,000 pairs, enjoys Europe's highest density of storks. By contrast, the rare black stork numbers just seven pairs.

Dzūkija and Žemaitija are particularly rich in fauna, each protecting over 1000 species. Rare flowers found in the Aukštaitija National Park include the white water lily, ghost orchid, single-leafed bog orchid and hairy milk vetch. Sea holly is increasingly rare on the dunes of the Curonian Spit thanks to walkers who pick it to take home.

National Parks & Reserves

Five national parks (one of which so spectacular and precious that Unesco declared it a World Heritage site in 2000), five nature

NATIONAL PARKS & RESERVES

National Park/ Reserve	Area	Features	Activities	Best time to visit
Aukštaitija National Park (p320)	300 sq km	69% forest, 15.5% river/ lake; wolves & bears	walking, canoeing, kayaking, mushrooming & berrying, skiing	spring & summer
Čepkeliai Strict Nature Reserve (p328)	85 sq km	Lithuania's largest raised bog (54% of reserve) marsh, forest, cranes & woodgrouse	bird-watching (Jul-Mar) walking (Jul-Mar); walking forbidden during nesting season (Apr-Jun)	summer & autumn
Curonian Spit National Park (p362)	265 sq km	high dunes, pine forests, beaches, lagoon & sea coast; rare species of mammals, birds & butterflies	cycling, swimming, walking, bird-watching	summer
Dzūkija National Park (p328)	550 sq km	forest, historic settlements	handicrafts, walking, canoeing, cycling, bird-watching	spring, summer & autumn
Labanoras Regional Park (p323)	528 sq km	Lithuania's largest regional park; rare flora & fauna, ancient burial mounds	canoeing, berrying & mushrooming	spring & summer
Nemunas Crook Regional Park (p339)	252 sq km	steep forested river banks, ravines & tallest pine trees (42m) in Lithuania	bird-watching, cycling, self-pampering	spring & autumn
Nemunas Delta Regional Park (p370)	289 sq km	unique delta of waterways, dikes, polders & islands with varied birdlife	bird-watching, fishing, boating	spring & autumn
Trakai Historical National Park (p316)	80 sq km	old town, castle museum, Kairates culture, 32 lakes including Lake Galvė with its 21 islands	swimming, sailing, fishing, canoeing, getting married	summer
Žemaitija National Park (p360)	200 sq km	forest; Lake Plateliai, Žemaičių Kalvarija Catholic shrine centre, Polkštinė Soviet Missile base	boating, cycling, fishing	spring, summer & autumn
Žuvintas Nature Reserve (p329)	54 sq km	important bird & plant habitat with 255 bird species & rich wetland wildlife	bird-watching & boating	spring & autumn

reserves and 394 areas under varying degrees of control protect 11.5% of Lithuanian land and plenty of rare and wonderful wildlife. Plenty more information on these parks and their wildlife habitats can be found in the regional chapters.

Environmental Issues

A huge amount of EU money is being sunk into the environment: €307.05 million was allocated in cohesion funds and €32.8 million in structural funds alone to Lithuania between 2004 and 2006.

For years the hot potato has been Ignalina Nuclear Power Plant (p322), 120km north of Vilnius. One of two reactors similar in design to the Chornobyl plant in Ukraine was closed in December 2004, and with the final shutdown of the plant scheduled for 2009, the big question now is how to decommission the grim Soviet monstrosity with the least cost to the environment. The financial cost will be at least €3.2 billion – paid, for the most part, by Brussels. Those who don't make it to eastern Lithuania to witness the plant first-hand can view a scale model in Vilnius' Lithuanian Energy Museum (p302).

How future energy will be generated remains a big question. Just 3.7% of electricity is produced by renewable energy (including hydroelectric and wind power) at the moment, but EU directives demand that Lithuania ups this percentage to 12% by 2010.

Oil extraction at the D-6 oil field in the Kaliningrad Region, 22km from the coast and 500m downstream from the Lithuania–Russia border, threatens the Curonian Spit and Baltic Sea (see p34). Public protests in the late 1980s prevented the USSR cashing in on the estimated 24 million tonnes of oil. But in June 2004 Russian oil giant Lukoil started drilling. Large-scale demonstrations prompted the Council of Europe to intervene in 2005: it recognised good operating practises at the rig but emphasised the huge risks its proximity to the spit posed and called for Lithuania and Russia to cooperate more fully in protecting its shared coastline.

The transportation of oil, an environmental threat affecting all three Baltic countries (see p34), is as controversial as its exploitation.

GREEN LINKS

- **Lithuanian Fund for Nature** (☎ 5-231 0700; www.glis.lt; Algirdo gatvė 22-3, Vilnius)
- **Lithuanian Green Movement** (☎ 37-324 241; www.zalieji.lt; Kanto gatvė 6, Kaunas).

FOOD & DRINK

Long, miserable winters are to blame for Lithuania's hearty, waist-widening diet based on potatoes, meat and dairy products. Cuisine between regions does not vary enormously, although certain traits become noticeable as you eat your way around: mushrooms, berries and game dishes dominate in heavily forested eastern and southern Lithuania; beer sneaks its way into northern cooking pots; while fish reigns on the coast and in lake districts like Trakai. Bread everywhere tends to black and rye.

For a lowdown on Baltic food and drink, see p35.

Staples & Specialities

Lithuanian food is epitomised in the formidable *cepelinai* (parcels of thick potato dough stuffed with cheese, *mesa* [meat] or *grybai* [mushrooms]; sometimes also known as a zeppelin). They come topped with a rich sauce made from onions, butter, sour cream and bacon bits. Another artery-furring favourite is sour cream–topped *kugelis* – a 'cannon ball' dish borrowed from German cuisine that bakes grated potatoes and carrots in the oven. *Koldūnai* are hearty ravioli stuffed with meat or mushrooms and *virtiniai* are stodgy dumplings.

Lithuanians like the less savoury bits of animals: *liežuvis* (cow's tongue) and *alionių skilandis* (minced meat smoked in pork bladders) are delicacies, and Lithuanians pork out on *vėdarai* (fried pork innards). Hodgepodge or *šiupinys* – often mistakenly assumed to be hedgehog – is pork snout stewed with pork tail, trotter, peas and beans (try it in Vilnius at Žemaičių Smuklė, p309). Smoked pigs' ears, trotters and tails are popular beer snacks alongside *kepta duona* – sticks of black rye bread heaped with garlic and deep-fried. Order them with or without a gooey cheese topping.

Wild boar, rabbit and venison are popular in the Aukštaitija National Park, where

TASTY READING

Anyone wanting to build their own *cepelinai* (zeppelin), bake a rabbit or butter-braise a hen should invest in the excellent cookery book *Lithuanian Traditional Foods,* compiled by Birutė Imbrasienė.

hunted birds and animals were traditionally fried in a clay coating or on a spit over an open fire in the 18th century. When perpetually drifting sands on the Curonian Spit in the 17th to 19th centuries made growing crops impossible, locals took to hunting and eating migrating crows in winter: one bite (followed by a generous slug of vodka) at the crow's neck killed the bird, after which its meat was eaten fresh, smoked or salted.

Blyneliai (pancakes) – a real favourite – are sweet or savoury and eaten any time of the day. *Varskõčiai* are stuffed with sweet curd, and *bulviniai blyneliai* are made with grated potato and stuffed with meat, *varske* (cheese curd) or fruit and chocolate.

Common starters include *silkė* (herring), *sprotai* (sprats), salads and soups. *Lietuviškos salotos* (Lithuanian salad) is a mayonnaise-coated mix of diced gherkins, boiled carrots, meat and anything else that happens to be in the fridge. *Šaltibarsčiai* – infamous for its fabulous shocking-pink colour – is a cold beetroot summer soup served with dill-sprinkled boiled potatoes and sour cream. Nettle, sorrel, cabbage and bread soup (not to mention blood soup, which does indeed have goose, duck or chicken blood in it) are other soups that have fed Lithuanians for centuries. Eel soup is specific to the Curonian Spit, where eel also comes as a main course. In Aukštaitija, fish soup served in a loaf of brown bread is the dish to try.

Mushrooms are popular, especially in August and September when forests are studded with dozens of different varieties – some edible, some deadly. Mushrooms are particularly abundant in Aukštaitija; see p328 for advice on picking mushrooms. In spring and early summer the same forests buzz with berry pickers; locals stand at roadsides in the region selling glass jam jars of wild strawberries, blueberries, blackberries and so on.

Drinks

Alus (beer) is the most widespread drink, local brands being Švyturys (p353), Utenos (p323) and Kalnapilis (p345). Brewing traditions are oldest in the northern part of Lithuania, where small family-run breweries treat lucky palates to natural beer free of preservatives.

Midus (mead) – Lithuania's oldest and most noble drink, traditionally served in families to celebrate a baby's birth – was popular in the Middle Ages. Honey is boiled with water, berries and spices, then fermented with hops to produce an alcoholic drink of 10% to 15% proof. With the decline of beekeeping in the 18th century, Lithuanian mead disappeared and did not make a comeback until 1959, when Lietuviskas midus in Stakliškės near Prienai in central Lithuania started making authentic mead; it produces seven varieties today.

Gira (kvass) is made from fermented grains or fruit and brown rye bread. Particularly popular as a street drink in the USSR, it is served as a 'Soviet flashback' at Druskininkai's Soviet sculpture park (p326).

The more sober-minded might enjoy the honey liqueur *stakliskes* or *starka,* made from apple-tree and pear-tree leaves. Herbal and fruit teas and brews made from linden, thyme, caraway, ginger, mint, rhubarb and a bounty of other sweet ingredients are age-old; Skonis ir Kvapas (p310) in Vilnius provides a unique opportunity to taste some.

Celebrations

Christmas is the major culinary feast of the year. On 24 December families sit down to dinner in the evening around a candle-lit hay-covered table topped with a white linen cloth; the hay anticipates Jesus' birth and serves as a place for the souls of dead family members to rest. (Indeed, one place around the table is always laid for someone who died that year.) The Christmas Eve feast that unfolds comprises 12 dishes – one for each month of the coming year to ensure year-long happiness and plenty. Dishes are fish- and vegetarian-based and include festive *kūčiukai* – small cubed poppy-seed biscuits served in a bowl of poppy-seed milk; others like herrings, pike, mushrooms and various soups are not necessarily seasonal.

EAT YOUR WORDS

Don't know a pig's ear from its trotter? Here are a few useful phrases. For other words and phrases when ordering a meal see the Language chapter.

Useful Phrases

A table for…, please.	*stah*·lah… prah·*show*	*Stalą…, prašau.*
May I see the menu, please?	ahr gah·*leh*·chow gow·ti man·*yew* prah·*show*	*Ar galėčiau gauti meniu prašau?*
Do you have the menu in English?	ahr yoos *tu*·ri·ta man·*yew ahn*·glish·kai	*Ar jūs turite meniu angliškai?*
I'd like to try that.	ahsh naw·*reh*·chow ish·bahn·*dee*·ti taw	*Aš norėčau išbandyti to.*
I don't eat…	ahsh na·*vahl*·gow	*Aš nevalgau…*
meat	*meh*·sish·kaw	*mėsiško*

Food Glossary

arbata	tea
braškės	strawberries
blyneliai	pancakes
cepelinai	boiled potato dumplings stuffed with meat and covered with bacon, cream and butter sauce
erškėtas	sturgeon
jautiena	beef
karbonadas	breaded pork chop
kiauliena	pork
kotlietai	rissoles
kopūstų sriuba	cabbage soup
mėlynės	bilberries
pienas	milk
pupos	beans
silkė	herring
šernas	wild boar
šilkmedžio uogos	mulberries
sterkas	perch
sviestas	butter
upėtakis	trout
vėžiukas	shrimp
vištiena	chicken
žuvies asorti	fish assortment
avietės	raspberries
bifšteksas	beefsteak
burokėliai	beetroot
duona	black rye bread
ėriena	lamb
gervuogės	blackberries
grybai	mushrooms
kaldūnai	Lithuanian dim sims
kava	coffee
kiaušiniai	eggs
kopūstai	cabbage
menkė	cod
morkos	carrots
plekšnė	plaice
rūkytas ungurys	smoked eel
šaltibarščiai	beetroot and sour-cream soup (cold)
skilandis	salami-style pork sausage
sūris	cheese
ungurys	eel
varškė	curd; like cottage cheese
veršiena	veal
žirneliai	peas

Šakotis – 'egg cake' – is a large tree-shaped cake covered with long spikes (made from a rather dry, sponge-cake mixture of flour, margarine, sugar, sour cream and dozens and dozens of eggs), which is served at weddings and other special occasions.

Where to Eat & Drink

Dining Lithuanian-style can mean spending anything from €5 for a three-course meal in a self-service café in a provincial town well off the tourist trail to €100 in a swish upmarket restaurant in the capital. Restaurants rarely pin a menu up outside, making it impossible to do a price and dish check before committing yourself. In Vilnius, choice of cuisine and price range covers the whole gamut, and an English-language menu is usually available; elsewhere the choice is limited and menus are rarely translated. Service is at its best in the capital – and generally appalling everywhere else.

For more information on types of eateries and opening hours, see p37.

Habits & Customs

A traditional dose of hospitality means loosening your belt several notches and skipping breakfast. Feasting is lengthy and plentiful, punctuated by many choruses of *Išgeriam!* (Let's drink!) and *Iki dugno!* (Bottoms up!). Starter dishes can be deceptively generous, leading unsuspecting guests to think they're the main meal. To decline further helpings may offend and be taken to mean that you don't like the food or the hospitality.

The family meal is a ceremonious affair and one that is taken very seriously, albeit one increasingly reserved for feast days, birthdays and other occasions in urban Lithuania's quicker-paced society. Each member of the family has a set place at the table – father at the head, mother opposite. If you arrive at someone's home while the family is seated, be sure to say *skanaus* (enjoy your meal); *prašom* (you're welcome) in response is an invitation to sit down and share the meal, while *ačiū* basically means 'thanks but go away!'

VILNIUS

☎ 5 / pop 542,250

Bizarre, beautiful and bewitching, Lithuania's capital seduces visitors with its astonishing Old Town charm. Its chocolate-box baroque skyline littered with the spires of Orthodox and Catholic churches are intoxicating, decadent and fragile – so much so that Unesco has declared this, Europe's largest baroque old town, a World Heritage site. But there's more to this devilishly attractive capital than meets the eye. There is an underlying oddness that creates its soul.

Where else could there be the world's only statue of psychedelic musician and composer Frank Zappa? Or a self-proclaimed, unofficial, independent republic inhabited by artists and dreaming bohemians? Where else is there the spirit of freedom and resistance that existed during Soviet occupation? There are reminders of loss and pain everywhere, from the horror of the KGB's torture cells to the ghetto in the centre of all this beauty where the Jewish community lived before their mass wartime slaughter.

Strange bars glow inside dark courtyards and medieval archways frame the life of the narrow, cobbled streets through which change has swept with panache. Using foreign cash and local vision, this stylish little city has big plans. But new business and infrastructure – even a skyscraper skyline – won't disguise the curious charm of eccentric, soulful Vilnius.

HISTORY

Legend says Vilnius was founded in the 1320s when Lithuanian grand duke Gediminas dreamt of an iron wolf that howled with the voices of 100 wolves – a sure sign to build a city as mighty as their cry. In fact, the site had already been settled for 1000 years.

Moat, wall and tower atop Gediminas Hill protected 14th- and 15th-century Vilnius from Teutonic attacks (p273). Tatar attacks prompted inhabitants to build a 2.4km defensive wall (1503–22), and by the end of the 16th century Vilnius was among Eastern Europe's biggest cities. Three centuries on, industrialisation arrived: railways were laid and Vilnius became a key Jewish city.

Occupied by Germany during WWI, it became an isolated pocket of Poland afterwards. WWII ushered in another German occupation and the death knoll for its Jewish population (p300). Postwar Vilnius ushered in new residential suburbs populated by Lithuanians from elsewhere alongside immigrant Russians and Belarusians. In the late 1980s the capital was the focus of Lithuania's push for independence from the USSR.

Vilnius has fast become a European city. In 1994 its old town became a Unesco World Heritage site and four years later the **Old Town Renewal Agency** (www.vsaa.lt) was established to spearhead its dramatic revitalisation. Since his election at the tender age of 32 in November 2000, dynamic city mayor Artūras Zuokas, from the Liberal Union Party, has worked wonders in raising the city's profile internationally and transforming it into the tourist hot spot it is today.

ORIENTATION

The centre sits on the south bank of the Neris River. Its heart is cathedral-studded Katedros aikštė with Gediminas Hill rising behind it. Southward lies the cobbled Old Town, which has Pilies gatvė as the main pedestrian thoroughfare. East along the river is the self-proclaimed Užupis Republic.

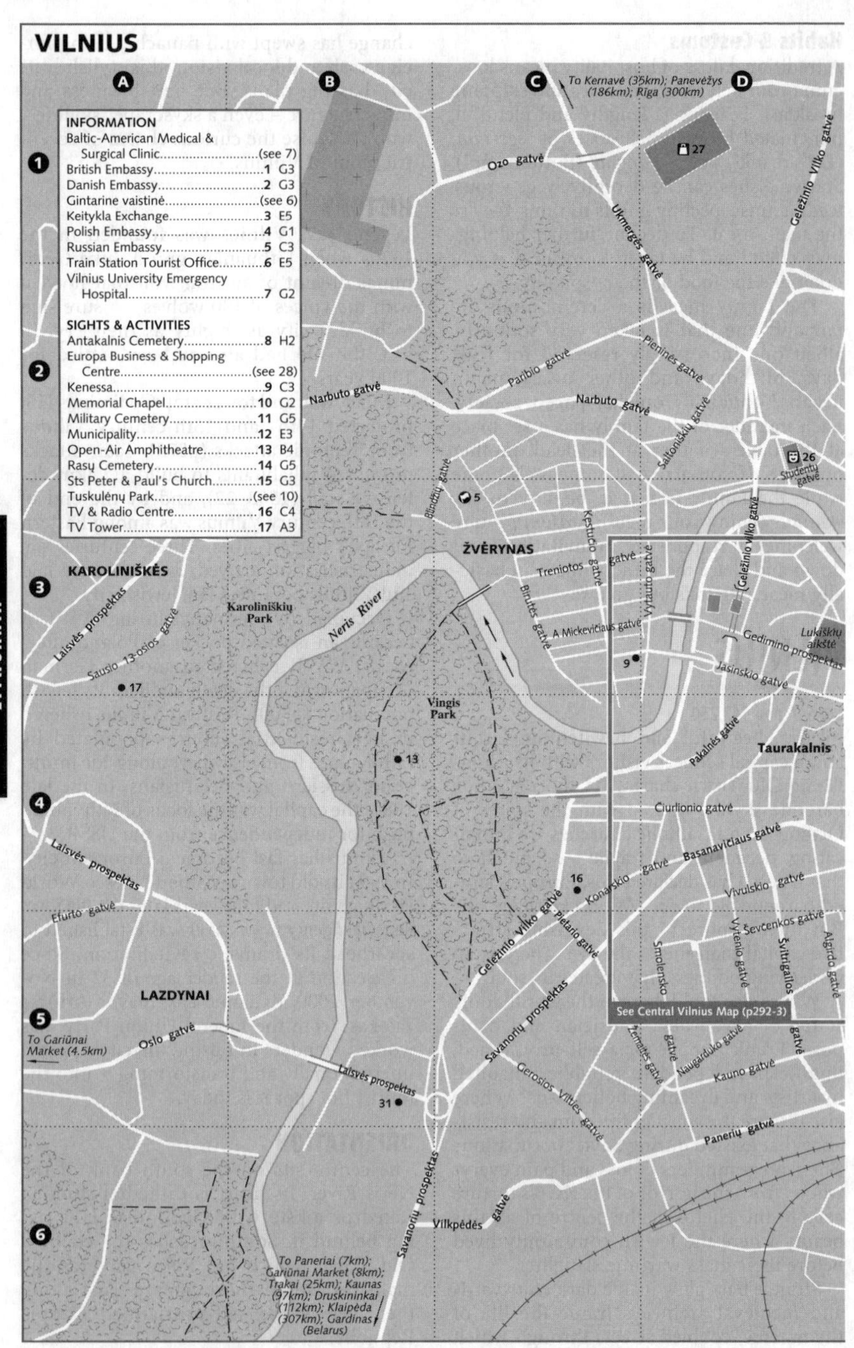

VILNIUS
INFORMATION
Baltic-American Medical & Surgical Clinic (see 7)
British Embassy 1 G3
Danish Embassy 2 G3
Gintarine vaistinė (see 6)
Keitykla Exchange 3 E5
Polish Embassy 4 G1
Russian Embassy 5 C3
Train Station Tourist Office 6 E5
Vilnius University Emergency Hospital 7 G2
SIGHTS & ACTIVITIES
Antakalnis Cemetery 8 H2
Europa Business & Shopping Centre (see 28)
Kenessa 9 C3
Memorial Chapel 10 G2
Military Cemetery 11 G5
Municipality 12 E3
Open-Air Amphitheatre 13 B4
Rasų Cemetery 14 G5
Sts Peter & Paul's Church 15 G3
Tuskulėnų Park (see 10)
TV & Radio Centre 16 C4
TV Tower 17 A3
To Kernavė (35km); Panevėžys (186km); Rīga (300km)
Ozo gatvė
Ukmergės gatvė
Geležinio Vilko gatvė
Pieninės gatvė
Paribio gatvė
Narbuto gatvė
Šaltoniškių gatvė
Studentų gatvė
Blindžių gatvė
ŽVĖRYNAS
Kęstučio gatvė
Treniotos gatvė
Vytauto gatvė
(Geležinio Vilko gatvė)
KAROLINIŠKĖS
Laisvės prospektas
Sausio 13-osios gatvė
Karoliniškių Park
Neris River
Birutės gatvė
A Mickevičiaus gatvė
Gedimino prospektas
Lukiškių aikštė
Jasinskio gatvė
Vingis Park
Pakalnės gatvė
Taurakalnis
Čiurlionio gatvė
Basanavičiaus gatvė
Konarskio gatvė
Vivulskio gatvė
Efurto gatvė
Pietario gatvė
Ševčenkos gatvė
Smolensko gatvė
Vytenio gatvė
Švitrigailos gatvė
Algirdo gatvė
LAZDYNAI
Savanorių prospektas
See Central Vilnius Map (p292-3)
To Gariūnai Market (4.5km)
Oslo gatvė
Žemaitės gatvė
Naugarduko gatvė
Kauno gatvė
Gerosios Vilties gatvė
Panerių gatvė
Vilkpėdės gatvė
To Paneriai (7km); Gariūnai Market (8km); Trakai (25km); Kaunas (97km); Druskininkai (112km); Klaipėda (307km); Gardinas (Belarus)
LITHUANIA

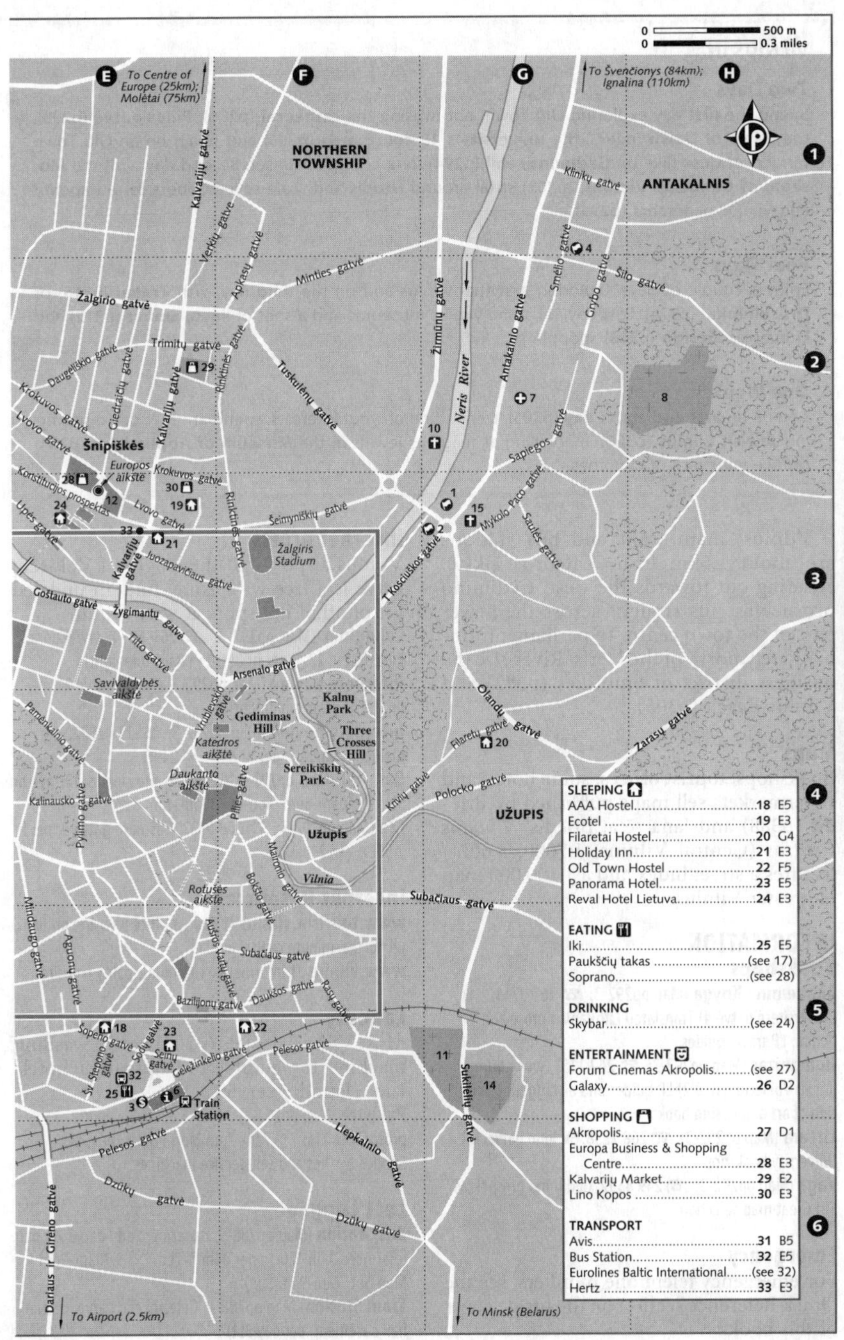

0 500 m
0 0.3 miles
To Centre of Europe (25km); Molėtai (75km)
To Švenčionys (84km); Ignalina (110km)
NORTHERN TOWNSHIP
ANTAKALNIS
Klinikų gatvė
Kalvarijų gatvė
Verkių gatvė
Apkasų gatvė
Minties gatvė
Žalgirio gatvė
Žirmūnų gatvė
Neris River
Antakalnio gatvė
Smėlio gatvė
Grybo gatvė
Šilo gatvė
Trimitų gatvė
Daugėliškio gatvė
Giedraičių gatvė
Rinktinės gatvė
Tuskulėnų gatvė
Krokuvos gatvė
Lvovo gatvė
Šnipiškės
Europos aikštė
Konstitucijos prospektas
Upės gatvė
Šeimyniškių gatvė
Sapiegos gatvė
Mykolo Paco gatvė
Saulės gatvė
T Kosciuškos gatvė
Žalgiris Stadium
Juozapavičiaus gatvė
Goštauto gatvė
Žygimantų gatvė
Tilto gatvė
Arsenalo gatvė
Savivaldybės aikštė
Vrublevskio gatvė
Gediminas Hill
Kalnų Park
Three Crosses Hill
Katedros aikštė
Daukanto aikštė
Sereikiškių Park
Pamėnkalnio gatvė
Kalinausko gatvė
Pylimo gatvė
Pilies gatvė
Užupis
Maironio gatvė
Vilnia
Bokšto gatvė
Rotušės aikštė
Aušros Vartų gatvė
Subačiaus gatvė
Mindaugo gatvė
Aguonų gatvė
Bazilijonų gatvė
Daukšos gatvė
Rasų gatvė
Olandų gatvė
Filaretų gatvė
Zarasų gatvė
Polocko gatvė
Krivių gatvė
UŽUPIS
Šopeno gatvė
Sodų gatvė
Seinų gatvė
Šv. Stepono gatvė
Geležinkelio gatvė
Pelesos gatvė
Train Station
Sukilėlių gatvė
Liepkalnio gatvė
Dzūkų gatvė
Darius ir Girėno gatvė
To Airport (2.5km)
To Minsk (Belarus)
SLEEPING
AAA Hostel 18 E5
Ecotel 19 E3
Filaretai Hostel 20 G4
Holiday Inn 21 E3
Old Town Hostel 22 F5
Panorama Hotel 23 E5
Reval Hotel Lietuva 24 E3
EATING
Iki 25 E5
Paukščių takas (see 17)
Soprano (see 28)
DRINKING
Skybar (see 24)
ENTERTAINMENT
Forum Cinemas Akropolis (see 27)
Galaxy 26 D2
SHOPPING
Akropolis 27 D1
Europa Business & Shopping Centre 28 E3
Kalvarijų Market 29 E2
Lino Kopos 30 E3
TRANSPORT
Avis 31 B5
Bus Station 32 E5
Eurolines Baltic International (see 32)
Hertz 33 E3

LITHUANIA

VILNIUS IN...

Two Days

Spend the first day exploring Old Town, not missing the **cathedral** (p296), **Pilies gatvė** (p296), the **Gates of Dawn** (p297), the **university's 13 courtyards** (p296) and lunch on an Old Town terrace. At dusk hike up **Gediminas Hill** (p294) for a city-spire sunset. Second day, visit the **Museum of Genocide Victims**, (p302) stroll around Užupis and scale several floors for an apéritif and Vilnius panorama (p295).

Four Days

Enjoy a couple of days exploring essential Vilnius and on the third day, visit **Trakai** (p315) or **Druskininkai** (p324). Last day, do some Vilnius museums and a spot of linen, **amber** (p312) and Lithuanian **design** (p313) shopping.

One Week

Add on an **arts and crafts day** (p305). Depending on your interests, spend another day discovering **Jewish Vilnius** (p300), marvelling at religious jewels in the **Museum of Applied Art** (p294) or take your pick of churches.

Vilnius' main train and bus stations are about 1.5km from Katedros aikštė. Heading out towards the west, Gedimino prospektas cuts straight across the newer part of the town centre to parliament. Immediately north of the Neris River rise the business district of Šnipiškės (p302) and Vilnius Beach (p305).

Maps

Bookshops, tourist offices, some hotels and supermarkets sell maps published by Briedis (p388) and Jāņa sēta. Briedis' *Vilniaus Centras* (Central Vilnius; 1:7000; 5.60Lt) features a street index and a 1:100,000 map of greater Vilnius.

INFORMATION

Bookshops

Akademinė Knyga (Map pp292-3; ☎ 261 9711; Universiteto gatvė 4) Translated Lithuanian prose and fiction, LP travel guides.

Humanitas (Map pp292-3; ☎ 262 1153; www.humanitas.lt; Vokiečių gatvė 2) LP guides and a staggering selection of art and design books.

Littera (Map pp292-3; ☎ 268 7258; Šv Jono gatvė 12) University bookshop.

Vaga (Map pp292-3; ☎ 249 8392; Gedimino prospektas 50) Great map selection.

Emergency

For emergency telephone numbers, see the Quick Reference section on the inside cover of this book.

Internet Access

Vilnius airport and the length of Vokiečių gatvė is a free wi-fi zone; find an updated list of other hot spots at www.wifi.lt.

Collegium (Map pp292-3; ☎ 261 8334; www.dora.lt; Pilies gatvė 22-1; per hr 8Lt; 🕑 8am-midnight)

Interneto Kavinė (Map pp292-3; Pylimo gatvė 21; per hr 3Lt; 🕑 9am-midnight)

Interneto Kavinė (Map pp292-3; ☎ 231 2622; Klaipėdos gatvė 3; per hr 4Lt; 🕑 24hr)

Omnitel (Map pp292-3; Gedimino prospektas 12; per hr 3Lt; 🕑 9am-6pm Mon-Fri, 10am-4pm Sat)

r2e (Map pp292-3; ☎ 268 5833; Goštauto gatvė 4; per hr 2.50Lt; 🕑 24hr)

Internet Resources

www.tourism.vilnius.lt Tourist office website; brilliant up-to-the-minute capital guide.

www.vilnius.lt Informative city municipality website.

Laundry

Most Vilnius hostels (p306) have a washing machine for guests, and upmarket hotels run a laundry service.

Palūstrė (Map pp292-3; ☎ 216 0000; Savanorių prospektas 11a; 🕑 7am-7pm Mon-Fri, to 2pm Sat) Service washes and self-service machines.

Left Luggage

Bus Station (Map pp288-9; Bagažinė; Sodų gatvė 22; bag less/more than 180cm per 24hr 3/7Lt; 🕑 5.30am-9pm Mon-Sat, 7am-9pm Sun)

Train Station (Map pp288-9; Geležinkelio gatvė; central hall basement; per day 3Lt)

Libraries

American Centre (Map pp292-3; ☎ 266 0330; webemailvilnius@state.gov; Pranciskonų gatvė 3/6; 🕑 10am-7pm Mon-Thu, to 5pm Fri) American media in a 14th-century monastery.

British Council (Map pp292-3; ☎ 264 4890; www.britishcouncil.lt; Jogailos gatvė 4; 🕑 11am-6pm Tue-Sat) Inside the Business Centre 2000; British papers, mags and free Internet access for members (25Lt a year).

Centre Culturel Français (Map pp292-3; ☎ 231 2985; www.centrefrancais.lt; Didžioji gatvė 1; 🕑 1.30-6.30pm Mon-Fri, 10am-3pm Sat)

Media

Exploring Vilnius (www.exploringcity.com) Detailed guide, free in hotels and bookshops.

Vilnius In Your Pocket (www.inyourpocket.com) Quality city guide published every two months, available as PDF download or in bookshops, tourist offices and newspaper kiosks (5Lt).

Medical Services

Baltic-American Medical & Surgical Clinic (Map pp288-9; ☎ 234 2020; www.bak.lt; Nemenčinės gatvė 54a; 🕑 24hr)

Euro vaistinė (Map pp292-3; ☎ 270 4704; Gedimino prospektas 8; 🕑 8am-8pm Mon-Fri, 9am-8pm Sat, 10am-5pm Sun)

Gedimino vaistinė (Map pp292-3; ☎ 261 0135; Gedimino prospektas 27; 🕑 24hr) Pharmacy.

Gintarine vaistinė (Map pp288-9; Geležinkelio gatvė 16; 🕑 7am-9pm Mon-Fri, 9am-6pm Sat & Sun) At the central hall of the train station.

Vilnius University Emergency Hospital (Map pp288-9; ☎ 216 9140; Šiltnamių gatvė 29; 🕑 24hr)

Money

The following all have ATMs accepting Visa and MasterCard.

American Express (Map pp292-3; ☎ 212 5809, 24hr service ☎ 8-616 81255; www.amextravel.lt; Vokiečių gatvė 13) Lithuania's only American Express agent issues emergency cheques and replaces lost AmEx traveller's cheques.

Keitykla Exchange (Map pp288-9; Parex Bankas; ☎ 213 5454; www.keitykla.lt; Geležinkelio gatvė 6; 🕑 24hr) Currency exchange with ATM; exit the train station and head left.

Hansa Bankas (www.hansabank.lt) Gedimino (Map pp292-3; Gedimino prospektas 56); Vilniaus (Map pp292-3; Vilniaus gatvė 16) Cashes Thomas Cook and AmEx traveller's cheques.

Vilniaus Bankas Gedimino (Map pp292-3; Gedimino prospektas 12); Jogailos (Map pp292-3; Jogailos gatvė 9a); Vokiečių (Map pp292-3; Vokiečių gatvė 9)

Post

Branch Post Office (Map pp292-3; Vokiečių gatvė 7)

Central Post Office (Map pp292-3; Gedimino prospektas 7)

Tourist Information

All three tourist offices sell maps and make accommodation bookings (6Lt).

Old Town tourist office (Map pp292-3; ☎ 262 9660; tic@vilnius.lt; Vilniaus gatvė 22; 🕑 9am-6pm Mon-Fri, 10am-4pm Sat & Sun Jun-Sep) Seasonal office with info on the city and surrounds; rents bicycles (p314).

Train station tourist office (Map pp288-9; ☎ 269 2091; Geležinkelio gatvė 16; 🕑 9am-6pm Mon-Fri, 10am-4pm Sat) In the central hall of the train station.

Town hall tourist office (Map pp292-3; ☎ 262 6470; turizm.info@vilnius.lt; Didžioji gatvė 31; 🕑 9am-6pm Mon-Fri, 10am-4pm Sat & Sun) Hidden in the former town hall, it organises city tours (p305) and English-speaking guides (140Lt/two hours).

Travel Agencies

Baltic Travel Service (Map pp292-3; ☎ 212 0220; www.bts.lt; Subačiaus gatvė 2) Reservations for country farmstays (p382).

Lithuanian Student & Youth Travel (Jaunimo kelionių centras; Map pp292-3; ☎ 239 7397; www.jaunimas.lt; Basanavičiaus gatvė 30) Cheap fares for International Student Identity Card holders.

West Express (Map pp292-3; ☎ 212 2500; www.westexpress.lt; Stulginskio gatvė 5) Ferry tickets for boats departing from Klaipėda for Rīga and Tallinn.

DANGERS & ANNOYANCES

Vilnius is provincial compared to most other world capitals. That said, it definitely pays to be streetwise here. Avoid walking alone on dark streets at night, stash your wallet in a front pocket, and watch for pickpockets in Old Town and on buses linking the airport with town. Don't hop in a taxi direct from the street; ask your hotel or the restaurant/bar you are leaving to call one for you.

Resident beggars are notorious for hassling tourists on Pilies gatvė. If someone asks for money, give them a yellow pocket-sized card (free at the tourist office) with information in Lithuanian on how they can find help.

Unsavoury tap water (you should drink bottled), crammed trolley buses, minibuses that don't stop when hailed and snail-slow service in some restaurants are minor irritations.

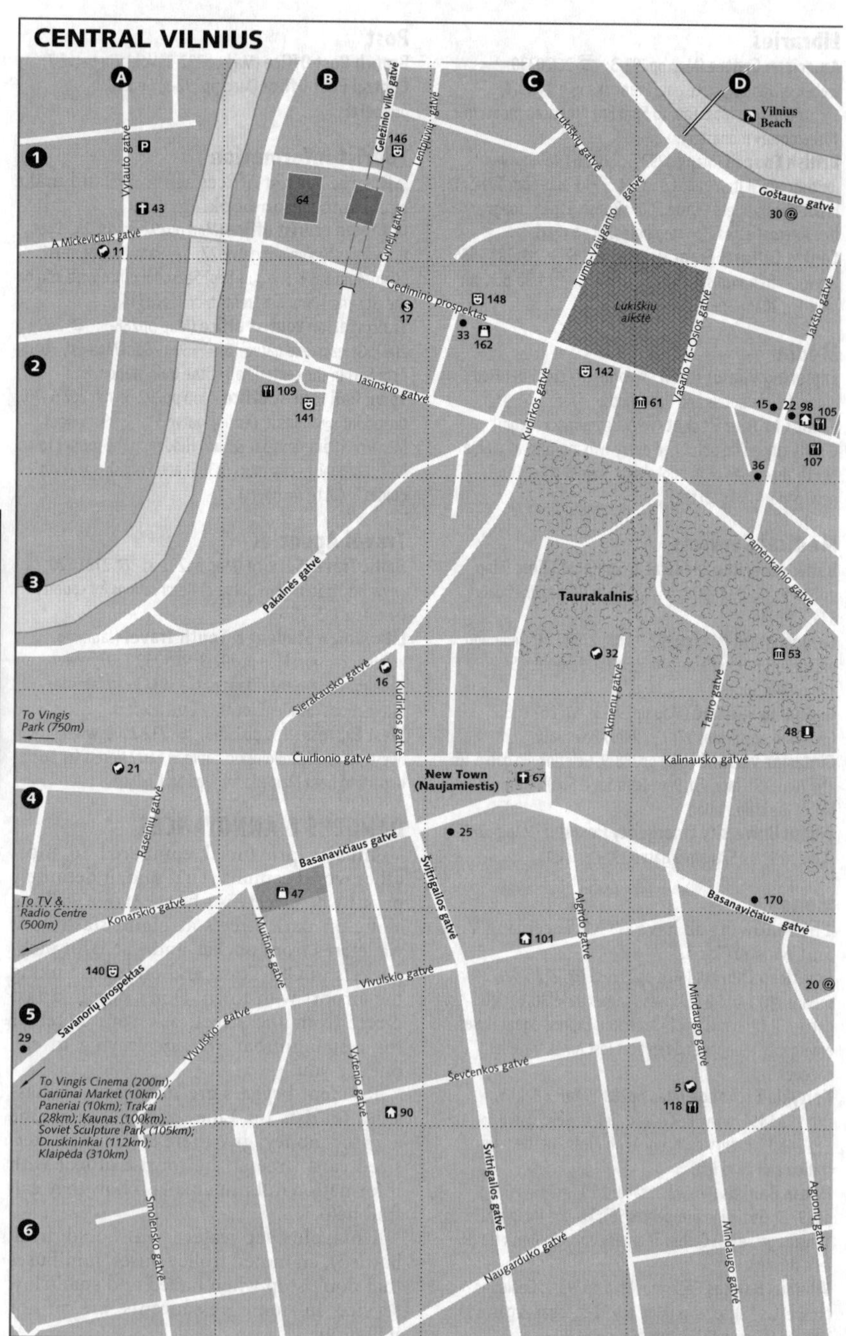
CENTRAL VILNIUS
Vilnius Beach
Vytauto gatvė
A Mickevičiaus gatvė
Geležinio vilko gatvė
Lentpjūvių gatvė
Gynėjų gatvė
Lukiškių gatvė
Tumo-Vaižganto gatvė
Goštauto gatvė
Gedimino prospektas
Lukiškių aikštė
Vasario 16-Osios gatvė
Jakšto gatvė
Jasinskio gatvė
Kudirkos gatvė
Pamėnkalnio gatvė
Pakalnės gatvė
Taurakalnis
Sierakausko gatvė
Akmenų gatvė
Tauro gatvė
To Vingis Park (750m)
Čiurlionio gatvė
Kalinausko gatvė
New Town (Naujamiestis)
Raseinių gatvė
Basanavičiaus gatvė
To TV & Radio Centre (500m)
Konarskio gatvė
Muitinės gatvė
Švitrigailos gatvė
Algirdo gatvė
Savanorių prospektas
Vivulskio gatvė
Mindaugo gatvė
To Vingis Cinema (200m); Gariūnai Market (10km); Paneriai (10km); Trakai (28km); Kaunas (100km); Soviet Sculpture Park (105km); Druskininkai (112km); Klaipėda (310km)
Ševčenkos gatvė
Vytenio gatvė
Smolensko gatvė
Naugarduko gatvė
Aguonų gatvė

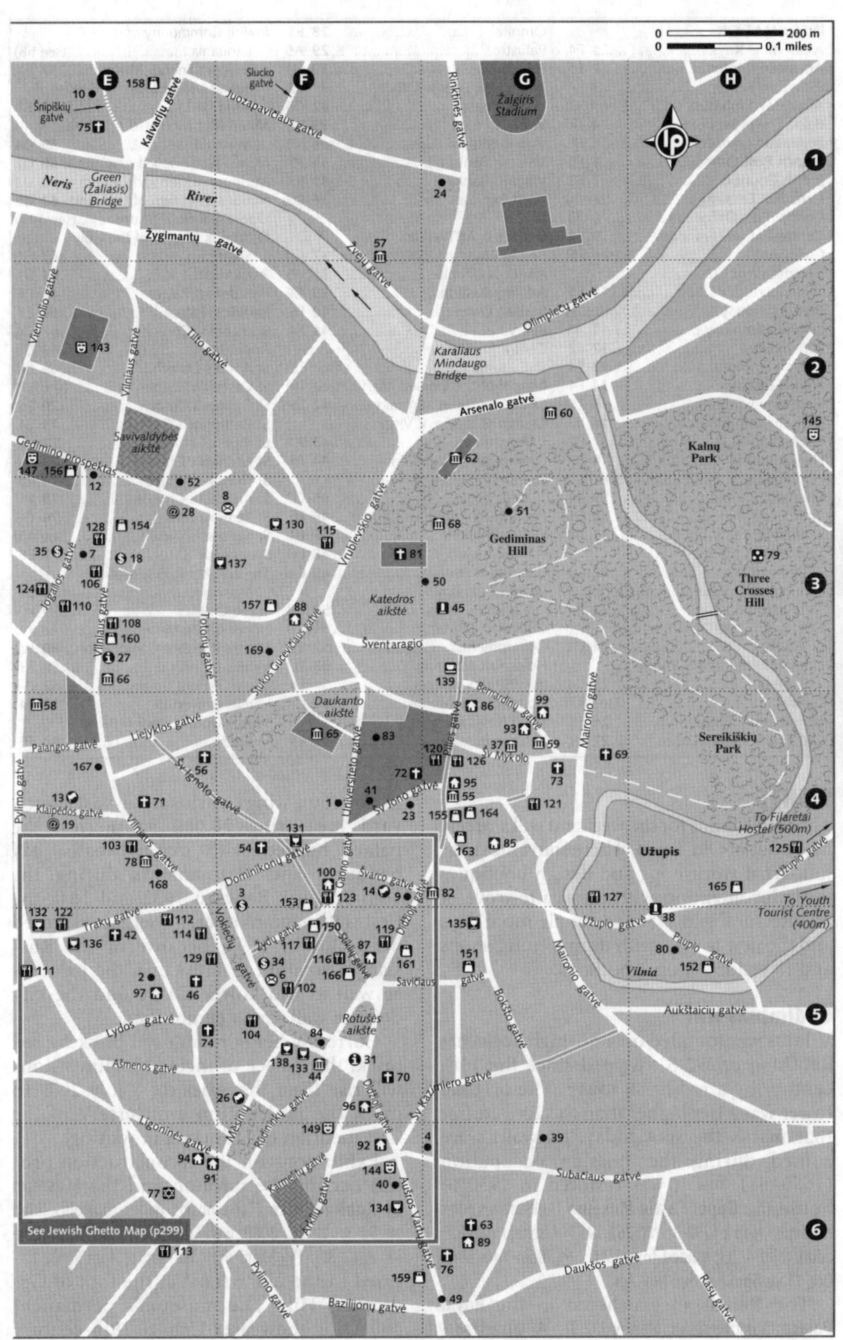
Neris River
Green (Žaliasis) Bridge
Karaliaus Mindaugo Bridge
Žalgiris Stadium
Gedimino prospektas
Savivaldybės aikštė
Katedros aikštė
Daukanto aikštė
Gediminas Hill
Kalnų Park
Three Crosses Hill
Sereikiškių Park
Užupis
Vilnia
Rotušės aikštė
To Filaretai Hostel (500m)
To Youth Tourist Centre (400m)
See Jewish Ghetto Map (p299)
LITHUANIA

INFORMATION

Akademinė Knyga....................**1** F4
American Centre....................**2** E5
American Express....................**3** F4
Australian Embassy..............(see 106)
Baltic Travel Service....................**4** G6
Belarusian Embassy....................**5** D5
Branch Post Office....................**6** F5
British Council....................**7** E3
Canadian Embassy....................(see 7)
Central Post Office....................**8** F3
Centre Culturel Français....................**9** F4
Collegium....................(see 95)
Committee of Cultural Heritage....................**10** E1
Dutch Embassy....................(see 7)
Estonian Embassy....................**11** A1
Euro vaistinė....................**12** E2
Finnish Embassy....................**13** E4
French Embassy....................**14** F4
Gedimino vaistinė....................**15** D2
German Embassy....................**16** B3
Hansa Bankas....................**17** B2
Hansa Bankas....................**18** E3
Humanitas....................(see 133)
Interneto Kavinė....................**19** E4
Interneto Kavinė....................**20** D5
Latvian Embassy....................**21** A4
Lithuanian Customs Department....................**22** D2
Lithuanian National Commission for Unesco....................**23** F4
Lithuanian State Department of Tourism....................**24** G1
Lithuanian Student & Youth Travel....................**25** C4
Littera....................(see 83)
Norwegian Embassy....................**26** F5
Old Town Tourist Office....................**27** E3
Omnitel....................**28** E3
Palūstrė....................**29** A5
r2e....................**30** D1
Town Hall Tourist Office....................**31** F5
USA Embassy....................**32** C3
Vaga....................**33** C2
Vilnias Bankas....................(see 28)
Vilniaus Bankas....................**34** F5
Vilniaus Bankas....................**35** E3
West Express....................**36** D2

SIGHTS & ACTIVITIES

Amber Museum-Gallery....................**37** G4
Angel of Užupis....................**38** H5
Artillery Bastion....................**39** G6
Basilian Gates....................**40** F6
Belfry....................**41** F4
Centre for Stateless Cultures....................(see 83)
Chapel of the Blessed Mary....(see 49)
Church of the Assumption....................**42** E5
Church of the Saint Virgin's Apparition....................**43** A1
Contemporary Art Centre....................**44** F5
Equestrian Statue of Gediminas....................**45** G3
Evangelical Lutheran Church....**46** E5
Flower Market....................**47** B4
Frank Zappa....................**48** D4
Gates of Dawn....................**49** G6
Gates of the Royal Palace Pavilion....................**50** G3
Gedimino Tower....................**51** G3
Government....................**52** E3
Holocaust Museum....................**53** D3
Holy Spirit Church....................**54** F4
House of Signatories....................**55** G4
Jesuit Noviciate with St Ignatius' Church....................**56** E4
Jewish Community of Lithuania....................(see 58)
Lithuanian Energy Museum....**57** F1
Lithuanian State Jewish Museum of Vilna Gaon....................**58** E4
Mickiewicz Memorial Apartment & Museum....................**59** G4
Museum of Applied Arts....................**60** G2
Museum of Genocide Victims...**61** D2
National Museum of Lithuania..**62** G2
Opera & Ballet Theatre.........(see 143)
Orthodox Church of the Holy Spirit....................**63** G6
Parliament....................**64** B1
Presidential Palace....................**65** F4
Radvilos' Palace....................**66** E3
Romanovs' Church....................**67** C4
Royal Palace....................**68** G3
St Anne's Church....................**69** G4
St Casimir's Chapel....................(see 81)
St Casimir's Church....................**70** F5
St Catherine's Church....................**71** E4
St John's Church....................**72** F4
St Michael's Church....................**73** G4
St Nicholas' Church....................**74** E5
St Raphael's Church....................**75** E1
St Teresa's Church....................**76** G6
Senamiesčio Gidas....................(see 40)
Synagogue....................**77** E6
Theatre, Music & Cinema Museum....................**78** E4
Three Crosses....................**79** H3
Upper Castle Museum............(see 51)
Užupis Republic Constitution... **80** H5
Vilnius Cathedral....................**81** F3
Vilnius Picture Gallery....................**82** G4
Vilnius University....................**83** F4
Yellow Double-Decker Bus Tours....................**84** F5

SIGHTS

Those in Vilnius for the weekend will scarcely move out of Old Town, where souvenir stalls, folk-artist workshops and design boutiques jostle for attention with a treasure-trove of architectural gems. Stay a couple more days and the new town – with its museums, shops and riverside action – beckons.

Gediminas Hill

Vilnius was founded on 48m-high **Gediminas Hill** (Map pp292-3), topped since the 13th century by a red-brick tower. The original tower was a tier higher than the 20m edifice that marks the spot today. Its walls were ruined during the Russian occupation (1655–61), but it was restored in 1930 to house the **Upper Castle Museum** (Aukštutinės pilies muziejus; Map pp292-3; ☎ 261 7453; Arsenalo gatvė 5; adult/child 4/2Lt, guided tour 15Lt; ⌚ 10am-7pm May-Oct, 11am-5pm Tue-Sun Nov-Apr).

The Renaissance ushered in the **Royal Palace** (Valdovų rumai; Map pp292-3). A quadrangle of four wings enclosing a vast courtyard measuring 10,000 sq metres, the palace buzzed with masked balls, gay banquets and tournaments during the 16th century. Between 1632 and 1648 the first Lithuanian operas were performed here. But in 1795, because of the Russian occupation of Lithuania, the palace – as well as the Lower Castle and the city defence wall – was demolished.

Currently being rebuilt red brick by red brick, this palace of incredible dimensions will rise from the ashes on 6 July 2009 to mark the millennium anniversary of the first mention of Lithuania in writing.

Exhibitions on the reconstruction project occupy the pavilion and the **Museum of Applied Arts** (Taikomosios dailės muziejus; Map pp292-3; ☎ 262 8080; www.muziejai.lt; Arsenalo gatvė 3a; adult 8Lt; ⌚ 11am-6pm Tue-Sat, to 4pm Sun), located in the old arsenal at the foot of Gediminas Hill. The museum's permanent collection showcases 15th- to 19th-century

SLEEPING

Arts Academy Hostel ... **85** G4
Atrium ... **86** G4
Centro Klubas ... **87** F5
CityPark Hotel ... **88** F3
Domus Maria ... **89** G6
E-Guest House ... **90** B5
Grotthaus ... **91** E6
Grybas House ... **92** F6
Litinterp ... **93** G4
Mano Liza ... **94** E6
Narutis ... **95** G4
Radisson SAS Astorija ... **96** F5
Šauni Vietelė ... **97** E5
Scandic Neringa ... **98** D2
Shakespeare ... **99** G4
Stikliai ... **100** F4
Telecom Guest House ... **101** C5

EATING

Aukštaičiai ... **102** F5
Balti Dramblai ... **103** E4
Čili Kaimas ... **104** F5
Čili Pica ... **105** D2
Da Antonio I ... **106** E3
Double Coffee ... **107** D2
Ephesus ... (see 112)
Guru ... **108** E3
Iki ... **109** B2
Ikiukas ... **110** E3
Ikiukas ... **111** E5
Keisti Ženklai ... **112** E5
Kineret ... **113** E6
La Pergola ... (see 91)
La Provence ... **114** E5
Literatų Svetainė ... **115** F3
Lokys ... **116** F5
Markus ir Ko ... **117** F5
Maxima ... **118** D5
Mini Maxima ... (see 12)
Pegasus ... **119** F5
Pilies kepyklėlė ... **120** G4
Saint Germain ... **121** G4
Skonis ir Kvapas ... **122** E5
Stikliai Aludė ... **123** F4
Sue's Indian Raja ... **124** E3
Tores ... **125** H4
Trattoria Da Antonio ... **126** G4
Užupio Kavinė ... **127** G4
Za Za ... **128** E3
Žemaičių Smuklė ... **129** E5

DRINKING

Avilys ... **130** F3
Cozy ... **131** F4
Fashionbar ... **132** E5
Gras'as ... **133** F5
Ibish Lounge ... **134** F6
Iki Aušros ... (see 134)
Mano Klubas ... **135** G5
Pablo Latino ... **136** E5
Paparazzi ... **137** F3
Šokoladas ... (see 112)
Savas Kampas ... **138** F5
Soprano ... **139** G3

ENTERTAINMENT

Club Connect ... (see 44)
Coca-Cola Plaza ... **140** A5
Gravity ... **141** B2
Lithuanian Music Academy ... **142** C2
Lithuanian National Drama Theatre ... **143** E2
Men's Factory ... (see 90)
National Philharmonic ... **144** F6
Open-air Amphitheatre ... **145** H2
Pacha Vilnius ... **146** B1
Small Theatre of Vilnius ... **147** E2
Trasa ... **148** C2
Youth Theatre ... **149** F6

SHOPPING

Aldona Mickuvienė's Workshop ... **150** F5
Aukso Avis ... **151** G5
Black Ceramics Centre ... **152** H5
Bronė Daškevičienė's Workshop ... (see 150)
Elementai ... **153** F4
Flagman ... **154** E3
Gedimino 9 ... (see 52)
Gintaras ... **155** G4
Gintaras ... (see 134)
Grand Duke Palace ... **156** E2
Jonas Bugailiškis' Workshop ... (see 159)
Juozas Statkrevičius ... **157** F3
Kalvarijų Market ... **158** E1
Kristijonas ir Karolina ... **159** F6
Lino Namai ... **160** E3
Ramunė Piekautaitė ... **161** F5
Šokoladas ... **162** C2
Šokoladas ... **163** G4
Sauluva ... **164** G4
Užupis Blacksmith Museum-Gallery ... **165** H4
Vitražo manufaktūra ... (see 116)
Zoraza ... **166** F5

TRANSPORT

Bikeworld ... **167** E4
Ecolines ... **168** E4
Eurolines Baltic International ... (see 7)
Europcar ... **169** F3
Krantas Travel ... (see 58)
Liturimex ... **170** D4
Rent a Car Litinterp ... (see 93)

Lithuanian sacred art. Much of it was only discovered in Vilnius cathedral in 1985 after being hidden in the walls by Russian soldiers in 1655. Because of the fear that they'd be seized by the Soviets, the gems, valued at €11 million, remained a secret until 1998, when they were finally displayed to the world.

Sitting stoically next door, the **National Museum of Lithuania** (Lietuvos nacionalinis muziejus; ☎ 262 9426; www.lnm.lt; Arsenalo gatvė 1; adult/child 4/2Lt, guided tour 15Lt; 10am-5pm Tue-Sat, 10am-3pm Sun May-Sep, 10am-6pm Wed-Sun Oct-Apr) has exhibits looking at everyday Lithuanian life before WWII.

Cathedral Square

Katedros aikštė – a square set to make your dreams come true (p296) – buzzes with local life. In the 19th century markets and fairs were held here and a moat ran around what is now the square's perimeter so ships could sail to the cathedral door. Within the moat were walls and towers, the only remaining part of which is the 57m-tall **belfry** (Map pp292–3) near the cathedral's western end.

At the square's eastern end is an **equestrian statue of Gediminas** (Map pp292–3), built on an ancient pagan site. Behind the grand old duke, **Sereikiškių Park** (Map pp292–3) leads to **Three Crosses Hill** (p299) and **Kalnų Park** (Map pp292–3).

TOP FIVE PANORAMAS

For a breathtaking cityscape scale:

- Upper Castle Museum (p294) while sightseeing.
- Europa (p313) during a shopping spree.
- Tores (p309) over lunch or dinner.
- Skybar (p311) apéritif in hand.
- TV Tower (p302) while bungee jumping.

WISH UPON A...

...star? No. Not in Vilnius. Rather a tile marked *stebuklas* (miracle). It marks the spot on Cathedral Sq where the human chain – formed between Tallinn and Vilnius by two million Lithuanians, Latvians and Estonians to protest Soviet occupation in 1989 – ended. To make a wish, do a clockwise 360-degree turn on the tile. Unfortunately superstition forbids the location of Vilnius' elusive-but-lucky spot to be revealed, meaning you have to search for it yourself.

CATHEDRAL

This national symbol was originally used for the worship of Perkūnas, the Lithuanian thunder god. Later the Soviets turned **Vilnius Cathedral** (Arkikatedra bazilika; Map pp292-3; ☎ 261 1127; Katedros aikštė 1; 🕑 7am-7.30pm, Sunday mass 9am, 10am & 11.15am, 7pm) into a picture gallery. It was reconsecrated in 1989 and Mass has been celebrated daily ever since.

The first wooden cathedral was built here in 1387–88. A grander edifice was constructed under Grand Duke Vytautas in the 15th century, which was in Gothic style, but has been rebuilt so often that its old form is unrecognisable. The most important restoration was completed from 1783 to 1801, when the outside was redone in today's classical style. The statues of Sts Helene, Stanislav and Casimir atop are replicas of wooden versions added in 1793 but destroyed under Stalin.

The statues on the cathedral's south side facing the square are Lithuanian dukes; those on the north side are apostles and saints. The interior retains more of its original aspect, though the entrances to the side chapels were harmonised in the late 18th century.

St Casimir's Chapel (Map pp292–3) is the showpiece. It has a baroque cupola, coloured marble and granite on the walls, white stucco sculptures, and fresco scenes from the life of St Casimir (who was canonised in 1602 and is Lithuania's patron saint). Find it at the eastern end of the south aisle.

Old Town

Eastern Europe's largest old town deserves its Unesco status. The area, stretching 1.5km south from Katedros aikštė, was built up in the 15th and 16th centuries, and its narrow, winding streets, hidden courtyards and lavish old churches retain the feel of bygone centuries. The main axis is along Pilies, Didžioji and Aušros Vartų gatvė. Its approximate boundary, starting from Katedros aikštė, runs along Stuokos-Gucevičiaus, Liejyklos, Vilniaus, Trakų, Pylimo, Bazilijonų, Šv Dvasios, Bokšto, Maironio, Radvilaitės and Sventaragio streets – an area of roughly 1 sq km.

PILIES GATVĖ

Cobbled Castle Street – the hub of tourist action and the main entrance to Old Town from Katedros aikštė – buzzes with buskers, souvenir stalls, pedal-powered taxis (p314) and the odd beggar (p291). Until the 19th century, the street was separated from the square by the lower castle wall, which ran across its northern end. Only a gate in the wall connected the two. Notice the 15th- to 17th-century brickwork of Nos 4, 12 and 16 towards the northern end of the street. The act granting Lithuania independence in 1918 was signed in No 26, the baroque **House of Signatories** (Lietuvos nepriklausomybės akto signatarų namai; ☎ 231 4442; Pilies gatvė 26; adult/child 2/1Lt; 🕑 8am-5pm Mon-Thu, noon-4pm Fri).

VILNIUS UNIVERSITY

Founded in 1579 during the Counter Reformation, **Vilnius University** (Map pp292-3; ☎ 268 7001; www.vu.lt; Universiteto gatvė 5), Eastern Europe's oldest, was run by Jesuits for two centuries and became one of the greatest centres of Polish learning. It produced many notable scholars, but was closed by the Russians in 1832 and didn't reopen until 1919. Today it has 22,500 students and Lithuania's oldest library, shelving five million books. The world's first **Centre for Stateless Cultures** (Map pp292-3; ☎ 268 7293; www.statelesscultures.lt; Universiteto gatvė 5) or those that don't have an army or navy, including Jewish, Roma and Karaimic cultures, is in the history faculty. The Tuesday evening seminars held at 6pm in room No 29 of the faculty are open to everyone; see the website.

The hidden but linked **13 university courtyards** (Map pp292-3; ☎ 268 7298; Universiteto gatvė 3; adult/child 5/2.50Lt; 🕑 9am-6pm Mon-Sat Mar-Oct, 9am-5pm Mon-Sat Nov-Feb) are accessed by passages and gates from surrounding streets. The south gate on Šv Jono gatvė brings you into the **Grand Courtyard.** Inside is **St John's Church** (Šv Jono bažnyčia; Map pp292-3; 🕑 10am-5pm Mon-Sat), founded in 1387 well before the university arrived. Its 17th-century bell tower, standing on the south side of the courtyard, is a distinctive feature in the Vilnius skyline. The arch through the 16th-century building opposite St John's leads to the **Astronomical Observatory Courtyard**, with an old two-domed **observatory**, the late 18th-century façade of which is adorned with reliefs of the zodiac.

DAUKANTO AIKŠTĖ

The exit from the university's **Sarbievijus Courtyard** to Universiteto gatvė brings you into the square opposite the former Bishops' Palace, now the **Presidential Palace** (Map pp292-3; ☎ 266 4011; www.president.lt; Daukanto gatvė 3; admission free; guided tours ⏲ 9am-2.30pm Sat), rebuilt in the classical Russian Empire style early in the 19th century. The palace was used by Napoleon during his advance on Moscow, and by his Russian adversary General Mikhail Kutuzov when he was chasing Napoleon back to Paris. Visits by guided tour (in Lithuanian) must be booked in advance; bring your passport to get in.

MICKIEWICZ MEMORIAL APARTMENT & MUSEUM

'Lithuania, my fatherland…' is Poland's national romantic masterpiece. It's not surprising when you realise it was Polish poet Adam Mickiewicz (1798–1855) – muse to Polish nationalists in the 19th century – who wrote the infamous line from his poem *Pan Tadeusz*. He grew up near Vilnius and studied at the university (1815–19) before being exiled for anti-Russian activities in 1824. The rooms where he wrote the well-known poem *Gražia* in 1822 are now the **Mickiewicz Memorial Apartment Museum** (Mickevičiaus memorialinis butas-muziejus; Map pp292-3; ☎ 260 0148; Bernardinų gatvė 11; ⏲ 10am-5pm Tue-Fri, to 2pm Sat & Sun).

ST MICHAEL'S & ST ANNE'S CHURCHES

Opposite the eastern end of Bernardinų gatvė, 17th-century **St Michael's Church** (Šv Mykolo bažnyčia; Map pp292-3; ☎ 261 6409; Šv Mykolo gatvė 9; ⏲ 11am-5pm Mon, to 6pm Wed-Sun) shelters a small museum focusing on 1918–90 architecture.

Vilnius' cobbled streets were lower than they are today. For a peek at street level in the 15th century, nip into the **Amber Museum-Gallery** (Gintaro Muziejus-Galerija; Map pp292-3; ☎ 262 3092; admission free; Šv Mykolo gatvė 8; ⏲ 10am-7pm). The usual array of amber trinkets and jewellery to buy are displayed on the ground floor, but the small exhibition on amber in the basement is interesting – not least for its archaeological excavations. Ceramics were fired in the two kilns in the 15th century.

Sixteenth-century **St Anne's Church** (Šv Onos bažnyčia; Map pp292-3; ☎ 261 1236; Maironio gatvė 8) is so fine that Napoleon wanted to take it back to Paris in the palm of his hand. A gem of Gothic architecture, its sweeping curves and delicate pinnacles frame 33 different types of red brick.

DIDŽIOJI GATVĖ

Old Town's main artery continues south from Pilies gatvė, past the **Vilnius Picture Gallery** (Vilniaus Galerija Paveikslų; Map pp292-3; ☎ 212 4258; Didžioji gatvė 4; adult/child 2/1Lt; ⏲ noon-6pm Tue-Sat, to 5pm Sun), filled with 16th- to 20th-century Lithuanian art, and the city's oldest baroque church, **St Casimir's** (Šv Kazimiero bažnyčia; Map pp292-3; ☎ 212 1715; Didžioji gatvė 34). Its dome and cross-shaped ground plan defined a new style for 17th-century churches when the Jesuits built it between 1604 and 1615. Under tsarist rule St Casimir's was taken by the Russian Orthodox church and given an onion dome, removed in 1942. Under Soviet rule it was an atheism museum.

Didžioji gatvė widens at its southern end into **Rotušės aikštė** (Town Hall Sq). The former town hall in the middle of the square has been here since the early 16th century, but its classical exterior dates from 1785 to 1799. Today it houses the tourist office.

Opposite, excellent installation art and photography by Lithuanian and foreign avant-garde artists fills the **Contemporary Art Centre** (Šiuolaikinio meno centras; SMC; Map pp292-3; ☎ 262 3476; www.cac.lt; Vokiečių gatvė 2; adult/child 6/3Lt; ⏲ 11am-6.30pm Tue-Sun).

AUŠROS VARTŲ GATVĖ

Vilnius' oldest street is laden with churches and souvenir shops. The famous 16th-century **Gates of Dawn** (Aušros Vartai; Map pp292-3) at the top of the street are the only gates of the original nine in the town wall still intact.

A door on the street's eastern side opens onto a staircase that leads to the 18th-century **Chapel of the Blessed Mary** (Map pp292-3; ⏲ 6am-7pm, mass 9am Mon-Sat, 9.30am Sun) above the gate arch. This houses a miracle-working icon of the Virgin, reputed to have been souvenired from the Crimea by Grand Duke Algirdas in 1363, though more likely dating from the 16th century. It is revered by the deeply Catholic Polish community and is one of Eastern Europe's leading pilgrimage destinations.

Heading north along Aušros Vartų gatvė, Catholic **St Teresa's Church** (Šv Teresės bažnyčia; Map pp292-3; Aušros Vartų gatvė 14) looms up large – early baroque outside and ornate late baroque inside. Underneath its entrance is a chamber for the dead.

The late baroque archway known as the **Basilian Gates** (Map pp292-3; Aušros Vartų gatvė 7) forms the entrance to the decrepit Holy Trinity Basilian monastery complex. Almost opposite is the pink-domed 17th-century **Orthodox Church of the Holy Spirit** (Šv Dvasios cerkvė; Map pp292-3; Aušros Vartų gatvė 10), Lithuania's chief Russian Orthodox church. In a chamber at the foot of a flight of steps in front of the altar (you can even see their feet peeping out) lie the preserved bodies of three 14th-century martyrs – Sts Anthony, Ivan and Eustachius.

LITHUANIA

ARTILLERY BASTION

Follow the old wall around from the Gates of Dawn on to Šv Dvasios gatvė, then continue north to reach the **Artillery Bastion** (Artilerijos bastėja; Map pp292-3; ☎ 261 2149; Bokšto gatvė 20/18; admission 2Lt; ⏲ 10am-5pm Wed-Sun). This 17th-century fortification houses a collection of old weaponry and armour. Lovers smooch here at sunset.

VILNIAUS GATVĖ & AROUND

Four sizable Catholic church and monastery complexes chiefly dating from the 17th- and 18th-century baroque era overlook the corner of Vilniaus gatvė and Dominikonų gatvė. Among them, **Holy Spirit Church** (Šv Dvasios bažnyčia; Map pp292-3; ☎ 262 9595; cnr Dominikonų & Šv Ignoto gatvė) is Vilnius' primary Polish church (1679). Once attached to a Dominican monastery, it has a splendid gold and white interior and a labyrinth of cellars concealing preserved corpses. The two towers of peach and creamy-white **St Catherine's Church** (Šv Kotrynos bažnyčia; Map pp292-3; Vilniaus gatvė 30) were once part of a Benedictine monastery.

Memorabilia from stage and screen stars at the **Theatre, Music & Cinema Museum** (Teatro, muzikos ir kino muziejus; Map pp292-3; ☎ 262 2406; www.ltmkm.lt; Vilniaus gatvė 41; adult/student 4/2Lt; ⏲ noon-6pm Tue-Fri, 11am-4pm Sat). Its show of traditional musical instruments – including a *pūslinė* (a primitive Baltic string instrument made from animal bladders) and several *kanklės* (plucked, fretted string instruments) – is enchanting.

Symbolic of the incredible renovation sweeping through Old Town is the recently reconsecrated **Church of the Assumption** (Map pp292-3; Trakų gatvė 9/1). Dubbed 'Sands Church' after the quarter in which it stands, this 15th-century Franciscan church was a hospital for the French army in 1812 and state archives from 1864 to 1934 and 1949 to 1989. The building was returned to the Archbishopric of Vilnius in 1995 and to Franciscan friars three years later.

REBELS WITH A CAUSE

The cheeky streak of rebellion pervading Lithuania flourishes in Vilnius' bohemian heart, where artists, dreamers, drunks and squatters in Užupis have declared a breakaway state.

The Užupis Republic (Užupio Republika) was officially, in an unofficial sense, born in 1998. The state has its own tongue-in-cheek president, anthem, flags and a 41-point **constitution**, which, among other things, gives inhabitants the right to hot water, heating in winter and a tiled roof; the right to be unique, to love, to be happy (or unhappy) and to be a dog. It ends 'Don't conquer. Don't defend. Don't surrender'. Read the entire thing in English, French or Lithuanian on a wall on Paupio gatvė (Map pp292–3).

On April Fool's Day, citizens of the Republic of Užupis celebrate their wholly unofficial state. Border guards wearing comical outfits stamp passports at the main bridge and the Užupis president makes speeches in the quarter's small square – the intersection of Užupio, Maluno and Paupio gatvės where the republic's symbol, the **Angel of Užupis** (Map pp292–3), stands. Increasingly hip and trendy, art galleries and folk artist workshops (p305) are mushrooming here like there's no tomorrow.

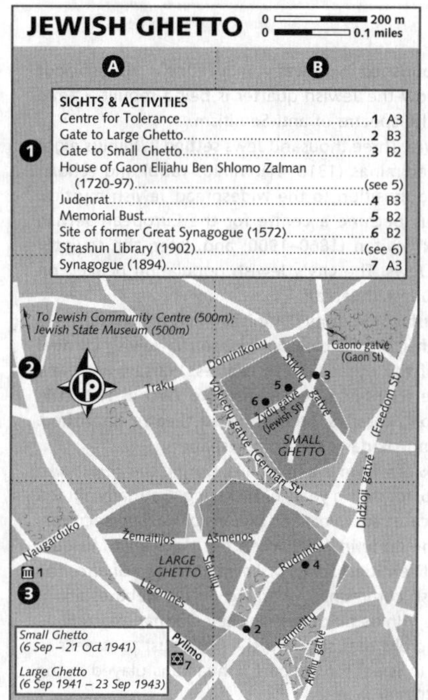

Other churches include the **Jesuit Noviciate with St Ignatius' Church** (Šv Ignoto bažnyčia; Map pp292-3; Šv Ignoto gatvė) and **St Nicholas' Church** (Šv Mikalojaus bažnyčia; Map pp292-3; Šv Mikalojaus gatvė), Lithuania's oldest Gothic church, founded by Germans around 1320. In a courtyard, the revamped **Evangelical Lutheran Church** (Evangelikų liuteronų bažnyčia; Map pp292-3; ☎ 262 6046; www.icvilnius.org; Vokiečių gatvė 20; English service 🕑 9.30am Sun), dating from 1553, is home to Vilnius' tiny Protestant community. Under the Soviets a concrete floor split the church into workshop and basketball court.

Radvilos' Palace (Radvilų rūmai; Map pp292-3; ☎ 212 1477; Vilniaus gatvė 41; adult/student 5/2.50Lt; 🕑 noon-6pm Tue-Sat, to 5pm Sun), a 17th-century residence, houses the foreign fine-arts section of the Lithuanian Art Museum.

West of Vilniaus gatvė, rock 'n' roll legend **Frank Zappa** (Map pp292-3; Kalinausko gatvė 1) is immortalised in a 4.2m-high bronze bust – flanked by a swirling psychedelic mural. It was the world's first memorial to the off-beat American who died from cancer in 1993.

East of Gediminas Hill

You could be in danger of crossing a border without realising it when you walk across the Vilnia River into Užupis. This Montmartre of Vilnius has declared itself an independent republic!

THREE CROSSES

East of Gediminas Hill, **Three Crosses** (Trys kryžiai; Map pp292–3) stand majestically atop Three Crosses Hill (Trijų kryžių kalnas). Crosses have stood here since the 17th century in memory of three monks who were crucified on this spot. The remains of three crosses lie in the shadow of the erect ones. These are the original hill monuments, which the Soviets bulldozed after WWII. In the spirit of Lithuania the people rebuilt them but left the twisted remains of the originals as a historical reminder of oppression. Walk to them from Kosciuskos gatvė.

STS PETER & PAUL'S CHURCH

Don't be fooled by the uninspiring exterior of **Sts Peter & Paul's Church** (Šv Petro ir Povilo bažnyčias; Map pp288-9; ☎ 234 0229; Antakalnio gatvė 1). Its baroque interior – an orgy of thousands of ornate white sculptures created by Italian sculptors between 1675 and 1704 – is breathtaking. The church was founded by Lithuanian noble Mykolas Kazimieras Paca, whose tomb is on the right of the porch.

ANTAKALNIS

One of Eastern Europe's most beautiful graveyards lies in this leafy suburb, a short stroll east of the centre. Those killed by Soviet Special Forces outside the parliament on 13 January 1991 are buried in **Antakalnis Cemetery** (Map pp288–9), off Karių kapų gatvė. A sculpture of the Madonna cradling her son memorialises them. Another memorial honours Napoleonic soldiers who died of starvation and injuries in Vilnius while retreating from the Russian army; the remains of 2000 of them were only found in 2002.

On All Saints' Day (1 November) thousands of people flock to the cemetery to light candles by the graves to respect the dead.

RASŲ & MILITARY CEMETERIES

Vilnius' **Rasų and Military Cemeteries** (Sukilėlių gatvė) face each other in the southeastern

JERUSALEM OF THE NORTH

One of Europe's prominent Jewish communities flourished in prewar Vilnius (Vīlne in Yiddish), but Nazi and Soviet brutality virtually wiped it out. Now the Jewish quarter is being rebuilt – amid raging controversy in a country still haunted by the spectre of anti-Semitism.

The history of Vilnius is indebted to Jewish culture. Three thousand Jews settled in Vilnius eight centuries ago at the invitation of Grand Duke Gediminas (1316–41). Vilnius rabbi and scholar Gaon Elijahu ben Shlomo Zalman (1720–97) led opposition to the widespread Jewish mystical movement Hassidism. In the 19th century Vilnius became a centre for the European Jewish language, Yiddish. Famous landscape artist Isaak Levitan (1860–1900) and, later, the sculptor Jacques Lipchitz (1891–1973; p325) were Vilnius Jews. The city's Jewish population peaked on the eve of WWI at almost 100,000 (out of 240,000 in Lithuania).

Plagued by discrimination and poverty, the Jewish community diminished in the interwar years when Vilnius was an outpost of Poland. Despite this, Vilnius blossomed into the Jewish cultural hub of Eastern Europe, and was chosen ahead of the other Yiddish centres, Warsaw and New York, as the headquarters of the Yiddish-language scientific research institute YIVO in 1925 (the institute stood on Vivulskio gatvė). Jewish schools, libraries, literature and theatre flourished. There were 100 synagogues and prayer houses and six daily Jewish newspapers.

Today there are just 5000 Jews in Lithuania, 80% of whom live in Vilnius. During the *perestroika* years an estimated 6000 Jews left for Israel. In 1996, following years of bickering, Germany agreed to pay €1 million to Lithuania to compensate holocaust survivors and victims of Nazi persecution. Further media attention was focused on the community in 1999 when the Holocaust Museum in Washington apologised for selling a satirical CD entitled *Songs of Kovno (Kaunas) Ghetto*. The lyrics blamed Lithuania for the death of the Jewish community, sparking off old debates about whether Lithuanian sidekicks were as cruel in the Vilnius holocaust as their German masters.

In 2002 Lithuania handed hundreds of Torah scrolls that survived the holocaust to Israelis in a ceremony in Vilnius. The move was an apology to Israel for the part Lithuanians played in the devastating massacre of most of the country's 240,000 Jews.

Jewish Quarter & Ghettos

The Jewish quarter lay in the streets west of Didžioji gatvė. Today the street names Žydų (Jews) and Gaono (Gaon) are among the few explicit reminders of this. The 1572 **Great Synagogue** (Map p299) and its famous 1902 **Strashun Library** (Map p299) stood at the western end of Žydų gatvė; the site is home to a nursery school today.

Virtually all Vilnius' Jewish organisations, except communist ones, were dissolved when the Soviet Union took over eastern Poland in September 1939. Many Jewish leaders were deported. Meanwhile Polish Jews fleeing the Nazis arrived here as refugees. Vilnius fell to the Nazis two days after their invasion of the USSR on 22 June 1941. In the next three months some 35,000 Jews – almost half those in the city – were murdered in Paneriai Forest (p315), before a ghetto was established in a small area north of Vokiečių gatvė, which was the heart of the Jewish quarter. This first ghetto – known as the **Small Ghetto** (Map p299) – was liquidated after 46 days and its inhabitants killed at Paneriai; a memorial plaque outside Gaono gatvė 3 remembers the 11,000 Jews marched to their death from this ghetto between 6 September and 20 October 1941. For 80 years preceding 1941, the building at Gaono gatvė 6 (today the Austrian embassy) was a Jewish

end of Old Town. Founded in 1801, Rasų Cemetery is the resting place for the Vilnius elite. More interesting, however, is the small military cemetery opposite, where the heart of the Polish Marshal Jósef Piłsudki, responsible for Poland's annexation of Vilnius in 1921, is buried. His mother shares his heart's grave and his body is buried in Kraków.

New Town

The 19th-century new town (Naujamiestis) stretches 2km west of the cathedral and Old Town.

Heading a little away from the action, **Romanovs' Church** (Map pp292-3; Basanavičiaus gatvė) is an eye-catching Russian Orthodox church with pea-green onion domes built in 1913. Further is Vilnius' fabulous house of prayer. At Žydų gatvė 3, outside the **former home of Gaon Elijahu** (Map p299), is a **memorial bust** (Map p299), erected in 1997 on the 200th anniversary of the death of the sage who recited the entire Talmud by heart at the age of six.

Vilnius' **Large Ghetto** (Map p299), created on 6 September 1941 south of Vokiečių gatvė, lasted until the general liquidation of ghettos on Himmler's orders in September 1943, when 26,000 people were killed at Paneriai and a further 10,000 herded off to concentration camps. About 6000 Vilnius Jews escaped. The single gate of the main ghetto stood at what's now Rūdninkų gatvė 18, marked with a plaque bearing a detailed map of the former ghetto. The former **Judenrat** (ghetto administration building; Map p299) was at Rūdninkų gatvė 8; its courtyard shelters a commemorative plaque to 1200 Jews selected to be sent to Paneriai.

Jewish Quarter Controversy

Restoration of the Jewish ghetto is underway at a cost of €32 million. The Great Synagogue, the area around Žydų gatvė, and plots in Rūdninkų gatvė and near the French embassy between Švarco gatvė and Šv Jono gatvė are being reconstructed. It is both a tribute to the perished community and a resurrection of the lost culture. Despite the plans being formally adopted by parliament in 2000, there was outspoken opposition. Most controversially, MP Vytautas Sustauskas claimed Lithuania would 'be turned into slaves of the Jews' in an outrageous outburst that inflamed simmering anti-Semitic sentiment. And as the project would develop much of the remaining lucrative property in the Old Town, there is little hope of it fizzling out. For more information, contact the **Centre for Tolerance** (Map p299; ☎ 663 818; Naugarduko gatvė 11), the rebuilding nerve centre.

Jewish Museums, Synagogues & Cemeteries

One of the few Vilnius ghetto survivors helped found the **Lithuanian State Jewish Museum of Vilna Gaon** (Lietuvos valstybinis Vilniaus Gaono žydų muziejus; Map pp292-3; ☎ 261 7907; www.jmuseum.lt; adult/child 4/2Lt; 10am-5pm Mon-Thu, to 4pm Fri & Sat) inside the **Jewish Community of Lithuania** (Map pp292-3; ☎ 261 3003; www.litjews.org; Pylimo gatvė 4; admission free; 9am-3pm Mon-Fri). Powerful B&W photographs portray the holocaust and those who helped save Jews, and guided tours of Jewish Vilnius in English can be arranged. A visit to the museum's other section, the **Holocaust Museum** (Map pp292-3; ☎ 262 0730; Pamėnkalnio gatvė 12; admission by donation; 9am-5pm Mon-Thu, 9am-4pm Fri, 10am-4pm Sun), in the so-called 'Green House', is equally moving. The exhibition is a stark reminder of the true horror suffered by Lithuanian Jews in an 'unedited' display of horrific images and words.

Modern Vilnius' only **synagogue** (Map pp292-3; ☎ 261 2523; Pylimo gatvė 39), currently being renovated, was built in 1894 for the wealthy and survived only because the Nazis used it as a medical store. Restored in 1995, it is used by a small Orthodox community.

The Soviets liquidated several Jewish cemeteries in the 1950s. The old Jewish cemetery where Rabbi Gaon Elijahu was originally buried was ripped up in 1957 and turned into a sports stadium (Žalgiris Stadium). The *maceivas* (tombstones) were recycled in the city as paving stones; the steps leading up Tauro Hill to the Trade Union Palace on Mykolaičio-Putino gatvė were originally built from Jewish gravestones. In 1991 the Jewish community retrieved many of these desecrated *maceivas*. Gaon Elijahu is now buried in the **new Jewish cemetery**, north of Vingas Park in the Virsuliskės district (entrance on Ažuolyno gatvė).

flower market (Map pp292-3; Basanavičiaus gatvė 42; 24hr).

West of Jasinskio gatvė is a **kenessa** (Map pp288-9; Liubarto gatvė 6), a traditional Karaites prayer house (p316).

GEDIMINO PROSPEKTAS

Sandwiched between the Roman Catholic cathedral's dramatic skyline and the silver domes of the Russian Orthodox **Church of the Saint Virgin's Apparition** (Map pp292–3), fashionable Gedimino is the main street of modern Vilnius. Its 1.75km length is dotted with shops, a theatre, banks, hotels, offices, a few park squares and the seat of various official bods, including that of the Lithuanian **government** (Map pp292-3; www.lrv.lt; Gedimino prospektas 11) and parliament. Laid out in

1852, the sparkling street has had 11 name changes since: the tsarists named it after St George, the Poles after Mickiewicz, and the Soviet rulers first after Stalin, then Lenin.

Gedimino 9 (Map pp292-3; Gedimino prospektas 9) – the Harrods or Bloomingdale of Vilnius – is scheduled to open for business in 2007 in a stunningly renovated historic building covering 18,000 sq metres. Investment in the upmarket mall is €50 million. Another classy shopping centre (Karen Millen has already bought up shop space in it) will open in the salmon-pink and cream **Grand Duke Palace** (Map pp292-3; Gedimino prospektas 20/1).

Outside **parliament** (Seimas; Map pp292-3; www.seimas.lt; Gedimino prospektas 53), concrete slabs with mangled barbed wire and daubed slogans are poignant reminders of Lithuania's violent past. Barricades were erected here on 13 January 1991 to protect parliament from Soviet troops. Thousands of people gathered at the building. The barricades to the north of the parliament building were left in place until December 1992, when the last Russian soldier left Vilnius.

Lenin stood on **Lukiskių aikštė**, a square that used to bear the name of the levelled statue, now displayed in Druskininkai's Soviet sculpture park (p326). The KGB – and during the Nazi occupation, the Gestapo – was headquartered in the late-19th-century building facing this square. Part of it today houses the horrific **Museum of Genocide Victims** (Genocido aukų muziejus; Map pp292-3; ☎ 249 6264; Aukų gatvė 2a; adult/audioguide 2/8Lt; 🕑 10am-5pm Tue-Sat, to 3pm Sun). Memorial plaques honouring those who perished in 1945 and 1946 tile the outside of the building. Inside, inmate cells and the execution cell where prisoners were shot or stabbed in the skull between 1944 and the 1960s can be visited. In 1994 the remains of 766 victims killed here between 1944 and 1947 were found in a mass grave in **Tuskulėnai Park** (Map pp288–9), north of the Neris. In 2005 they were reburied in the park in a state-of-the-art cone-shaped **memorial chapel** (Map pp288-9; Žirmūnų gatvė) built in memory of 20th-century terror victims. Disturbingly, the graveyard of those killed by the KGB in the 1950s, reckoned to be within a 30km radius of Vilnius, has not yet been found.

VINGIS PARK

Just over 1km southwest of parliament, at the western end of Čiurlionio gatvė, is the wooded **Vingis Park** (Map pp288–9), surrounded on three sides by the Neris and pierced with a large **open-air amphitheatre** (Map pp288–9) used for the Lithuanian Song and Dance Festival. Take trolleybus 7 from the train station or 3 from the Gedimino stop on Vrublevskio gatvė to the Kęstučio stop (the second after the bridge over the river), then walk over the footbridge from the end of Treniotos gatvė.

Like the more distant TV Tower (below), the **TV & Radio Centre** (Map pp288-9; cnr Konarskio gatvė & Pietario gatvė), near the southeastern edge of the park, was stormed by Soviet tanks and troops in the early hours of 13 January 1991. Wooden crosses remember Lithuania's independence martyrs.

ŠNIPIŠKĖS

On the north bank of the Neris, the quarter of Šnipiškės has been transformed: the tatty Soviet concrete blocks have gone and in their place is a new skyline of skyscrapers, including the **Europa Tower** atop the **Europa Business & Shopping Centre** (Map pp288-9; Europas aikštė), which – at 129m – is the Baltics' tallest skyscraper. The brainchild of Vilnius mayor Artūras Zuokas, this new business district dubbed 'Sunrise Valley' had reaped €142 million in investments by 2005 and promises to net €800 million in all by 2010. As part of the urban redevelopment project, two new bridges linking it with the centre have been built and the **municipality** (Map pp288-9; Konstitucijos prospektas 3) has moved here. A state-of-the-art conference centre is planned for Šnipiškės' rapidly growing skyline.

There are fine examples of Soviet architecture on this side of the river: **St Raphael's Church** (Map pp292-3; Šv Rapolo bažnyčia) near Žaliasis tiltas (Green Bridge) has a fine baroque interior. A nuclear power plant and other Soviet (and subsequent) energy-making means are the industrial focus of the **Lithuanian Energy Museum** (Map pp292-3; ☎ 278 2085; Žvejų gatvė 14a; 🕑 10am-4pm Mon-Fri), in the city's original power plant. The edifice went up in 1901, was destroyed during WWII, rebuilt, and powered the city until 1998.

TV Tower

The 326m **TV tower** (Televizijos Bokstas; Map pp288-9; ☎ 204 0333; www.lrtc.lt; Sausio 13-osios gatvė 10; adult/child 15/6Lt; observation deck 🕑 10am-10pm) symbolises Lithuania's strength of spirit. On

BEGINNING WITH A

'We want to show the world how a little nation fought for its independence; show how dear, how valuable, independence itself is.'

Juozas Aleksiejūnas, former inmate, KGB Prison

Juozas Aleksiejūnas, a tour guide at the Museum of Genocide Victims, was in his 80s when he died. Against all the odds, he survived Vilnius' KGB prison – an appalling house of horrors where blood still stains the walls of the cramped cells in which prisoners lived and died. His story, told before he died, is a proud but harrowing one.

Aleksiejūnas joined the partisan Resistance movement in 1944. As one of the country's estimated 40,000 'forest brothers', he roamed the forests around Molėtai, 75km north of Vilnius, with five other 'brothers'. His official task was to steal identity forms from the local passport office to pass on to fellow partisans.

On 26 March 1945 he was arrested by the KGB and tried for anti-Soviet activities. Within minutes he was found guilty and his ordeal in Vilnius' KGB prison, notorious for its high security and inhumane disciplinary measures, began.

Between 1944 and 1953, 200,000 Lithuanians passed through the Soviet prisons. The one in Vilnius was used for equally sinister purposes by the Gestapo during the Nazi occupation; its execution ward, various torture chambers and 9m-square cells where up to 20 prisoners were kept at any one time all remain today. Inmates were showered once a month and only allowed to go to the bathroom once a day; at other times, a bucket in the cell doubled as toilet pan.

Aleksiejūnas was interrogated and tortured for a week. 'How many of you are there?' and 'Who is your leader?' were the questions fired at him. Prisoners did not have names. They were called 'Beginning with A', 'Beginning with B' and so on to ensure prisoners knew as little about each other as possible. Inmates who attempted conversation were sent to an isolation cell, stripped to their underwear, rationed to 300g of bread and half a litre of water a day and deprived of sleep.

Inmates who refused 'to talk' to KGB officers were sent to the 'soft cell'. Its walls were padded in 1973 to muffle the hideous human cries and the sound of beatings. Prisoners were put in straitjackets and forced to sit in the pitch-black, silent cell until their spirit broke. Aleksiejūnas survived the soft-cell hell.

After three days in the 'wet room' he lost consciousness. This 8 x 10m punishment cell had a sunken floor covered with cold water, which turned to ice in winter. In the centre was a slippery metal pedestal, 30cm in diameter, which was the prisoners' only refuge from the wet floor.

Aleksiejūnas was later moved to another prison in Vilnius and on 29 June 1945 he was deported to Vorkuta, Siberia, where he spent five years in a hard labour camp followed by another five years in a high-security prison. In 1955 he was released on parole. But he was not allowed to leave Vorkuta and had to report twice a month (which he did for nine years) to the prison's special commander. His Lithuanian wife, whom he married in 1943 (but had barely seen since), joined him in Vorkuta where their first son was born. The Aleksiejūnas family returned home to Vilnius in 1963.

13 January 1991 Soviet special forces killed 12 people here. Lithuanian TV kept broadcasting until the troops came through the tower door. Wooden crosses remember the victims and on 13 January hundreds of people light candles here. At Christmas 6000-odd fairy lights are strung on the tower to create the world's largest Christmas tree!

From the observation deck (165m), accessible via an elevator, there is an extraordinary city panorama. Steel stomachs can eat while feasting on views at **Paukščių takas** (Map pp288-9; ☎ 252 5338; meals 15-40Lt; 🕑 10am-10pm; ☒), a revolving restaurant in the tower. The fearless/senseless can hurl themselves 168.8m off the tower at a petrifying 104km/h during Europe's highest **bungee jump** (☎ 8-635 17828; www.bungee.lt; rates per jump 200Lt, per person for groups of 5/7 170/150Lt; 🕑 May-Oct).

To get to the tower, take trolleybus 16 from the train station or 11 from Lukiskių aikštė to the Televizijos Bokstas stop on Laisvės prospektas. A trip here takes you to Vilnius' Soviet-era high-rise suburbs.

WALKING TOUR

Eastern Europe's largest old town is made for meandering. This itinerary is a taster for those with just a few hours to spare.

Kick off on Cathedral Sq, taking in its magical tile, **cathedral** (**1**; p296) and **Royal Palace** (**2**; p294) before climbing through the park to the **Upper Castle Museum** (**3**; p294) atop Gediminas Hill. From the tower survey the city then hike down into Old Town along Pilies gatvė. To shake off the crowd and get an authentic taste of quaint old Vilnius, cut left onto Bernardinų gatvė and zigzag along Volano gatvė, Literatu gatvė, Rusu gatvė and Latako gatvė to Bokšto gatvė. Midway along Bokšto, turn right onto Savučiaus gatvė for the best of Lithuanian textiles at **Aukso Avis** (**4**; p313). Continue along Savučiaus to Didžioji gatvė, turn left and follow the street past the **former town hall (5)** to its southern end. Continue along Aušros Vartų, past the **National Philharmonic** (**6**; p312), which is under renovation, the **Basilian Gates** (**7**; p298), the **Orthodox Church of the Holy Spirit** (**8**; p298), **St Teresa's Church** (**9**; p298) and **artist workshops (10)** before stopping at the sacred **Gates of Dawn** (**11**; p297).

WALK FACTS

Distance: 3.5km (plus two 700m add-ons)
Duration: one hour (brisk pace), half day (meandering)

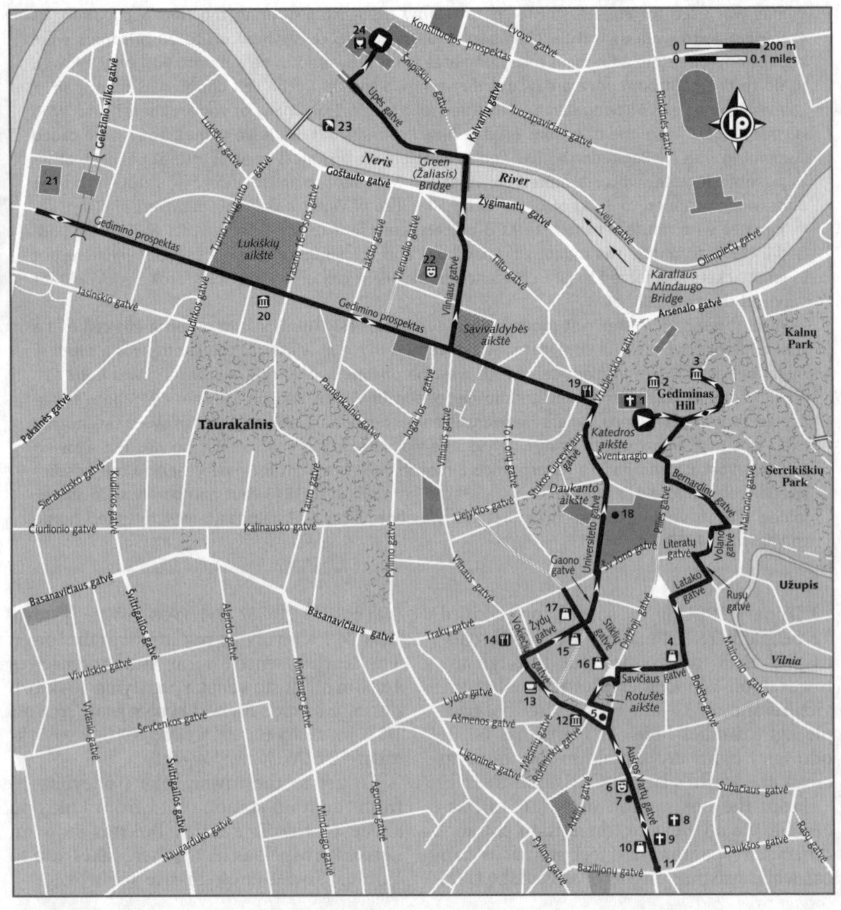

CRAFTY VILNIUS

Lithuanian folk art is alive and well, as the clutch of enchanting folk-artists' workshops tucked in Old Town proves.

Aldona Mickuvienė's workshop (Map pp292-3; ☎ 216 5063; Žydų gatvė 2-10) and **Bronė Daškevičienė's workshop** (Map pp292-3; ☎ 275 9116; vlado@delfi.lt; Žydų gatvė 2-9) Two elderly ladies have been weaving colourful wedding sashes in their neighbouring workshops for decades. Buy a ready-made sash (50Lt) or order one with your name on it (70Lt). Each sash takes a full day or more to weave.

Black Ceramics Centre (BCC; Map pp292-3; ☎ 8-699 42456; http://ceramics.w3.lt; Paupio gatvė 5) Ceramics as black as coal have been crafted since prehistoric times. See the end result at this innovative Užupis art centre.

Jonas Bugailiškis (Map pp292-3; ☎ 261 7667, 8-652 36613; Aušros Vartų gatvė 17-10) Angels, jumping horses, donkeys and a menagerie of other animals and toys carved from wood ensures this workshop buzzes with life. Making traditional folk-music instruments is the folk artist's other love.

Sauluva (Map pp292-3; ☎ 212 1227; Literatų gatvė 3; 🕑 10am-7pm) Learn how to make *verbos* (traditional woven dried flowers crafted to celebrate Palm Sunday) and paint traditional Lithuanian Easter eggs at this shop-cum-workshop.

Užupis Blacksmith Museum-Gallery (Užupio kalvystės muziejus galerija; Map pp292-3; Užupio gatvė 26) Forged-iron articles are sold at this traditional blacksmith's; demonstrations Tuesday, Friday and Saturday.

Vitražo manufaktūra (Map pp292-3; ☎ 212 1202; www.stainedglass.lt; Stiklių gatvė 6-8; 🕑 10am-6pm Tue-Fri, to 4pm Sat) Stained-glass sculptures, wall murals and mobiles fill this creative stained-glass workshop; daily demonstrations noon to 4pm.

Next, backtrack to Rotušės aikštė where the **Contemporary Art Centre** (**12**; p297) awaits. Quench your thirst on a **café terrace (13)** on Vokiečių gatvė or lunch at **Žemaičių Smuklė** (**14**; p309), then cross the street and cut through the alleyway onto Žydų gatvė for a glimpse of Jewish Vilnius. Wander north along Jewish St, pausing to watch wedding sashes being woven at more **folk-artist workshops (15)**. Take in the design boutiques, such as **Zoraza** (**16**; p313) and **Elementai** (**17**; p313), on Stiklių gatvė then continue south along Gaono gatvė to **Vilnius University** (**18**; p296) on Universiteto gatvė.

Exhausted? Cut back onto Cathedral Sq and flop on the terrace at **Literatų Svetainė** (**19**; p310). Still raring to go? Add on an amble west along Gedimino prospektas to the **Museum of Genocide Victims** (**20**; p302) and **parliament barricades** (**21**; p302) or cut north along Vilniaus gatvė, past the **Opera & Ballet Theatre** (**22**; p312), to the river. Cross the bridge and splash around on **Vilnius Beach (23)** or be dazzled in Šnipiškės' sky-high **Skybar** (**24**; p311).

VILNIUS FOR CHILDREN

Palm tree–studded **Vilnius Beach**, on the Neris' northern bank, keeps kids cool on steaming summer days. There's sand to play with, a pool to splash in, a snack bar, a couple of beach volleyball courts and a small skateboard park. In town, the **electric cars** in Sereikiškių Park (Map pp292–3) are popular, as are the horse-drawn carriages (p305) and pedal-powered taxis (p314) that loiter near the park entrance on Cathedral Square. Otherwise, there's nothing like a sky-high panorama (p295), spooky ghost walk or ride on an open-top bus (p306) to impress.

In winter the best place for kidding around is Akropolis (p313), which has an **ice-skating rink** (☎ 238 7852; 5/7Lt before/after 1.30pm Mon-Fri, 7/9Lt Sat & Sun; 🕑 8am-midnight), 20-lane **Apollo Bowling Alley** (☎ 238 7777; 30/40Lt per hr before/after 6pm Mon-Thu, 50Lt/hr Sat & Sun; 🕑 9am-4am) with eight automatic lanes for kids, and **soft play area** (☎ 238 7848; under/over 4yr 15/20Lt per week; 🕑 10am-10pm) for under 12s.

TOURS

Walking tours (in English) of Užupis (52Lt, 2½ hours), Old Town (35Lt, two hours) and Vilnius' ghostly haunts (69Lt, two hours) can be booked in advance at any tourist office (p291).

Horse-drawn carriages (☎ 260 8410; tourism .vilnius@mail.lt; Katedros aikštė; 🕑 May-Sep) In summer these carriages take tourists for romantic rides around Sereikiškių Park (60Lt/hr, daily) and Old Town (80Lt, Saturday and Sunday).

Senamiesčio Gidas (Old Town Guides; Map pp292-3; ☎ 8-699 54064; www.vilniuscitytour.com; Aušros Vartų gatvė 7) Organises half-day minibus tours of Vilnius (€23, 3½ hours) and Jewish Vilnius, as well as 'Trace your Family

Roots' tours and day trips to Trakai (p315) and Kernavė (p318), Lithuania's Soviet sculpture park (p326) and Europe's geographical centre (p318). Prices – see its website – depend on numbers.

Yellow double-decker bus (☎ 273 8625; www.vap.lt; 1hr tour adult/child 10/5Lt, departures 3pm, 5pm & 6.30pm Wed-Fri, 11am & 3pm Sat & Sun; 2hr tour adult/child 25/10Lt, departures 12.30pm Wed-Fri, 12.30pm & 5pm Sat & Sun) For a whirl in an open-top bus, pitch up at the bus stop on Rotušės aikštė and pay the driver.

FESTIVALS & EVENTS

Vilnius enjoys a rich pageant of festivals (www.vilniusfestivals.lt):

Užgavėnės Pagan carnival (Mardi Gras) on Shrove Tuesday, February.

Kaziukas crafts fair Held in Old Town to celebrate St Casimir's Day, 4 March.

Lygiadienis Pagan carnival marking spring equinox, March.

Vilnius Festival Classical music, jazz and folk music concerts in Old Town courtyards, June.

Christopher Summer Festival (www.kristupofestivaliai.lt) Music festival, July and August.

Vilnius Days International arts festival, mid-September.

Sirens International theatre festival, end September–mid-October.

SLEEPING

The hotel business is young, and while there is a plethora of magical top-end options the city does lack decent budget accommodation. That said, hoteliers are starting to pounce on this glaring gap in an otherwise well-filled market. Prices include breakfast unless stated otherwise.

Budget

GUESTHOUSES

Collegium (p290) has 12 Old Town rooms with shower and toilet for 90Lt per person.

Litinterp (Map pp292-3; ☎ 212 3850; www.litinterp.lt; Bernardinų gatvė 7-2; s/d/tr 100/160/210Lt, with shared bathroom 80/140/180Lt, apt from 200Lt; 🕑 8.30am-5.30pm Mon-Fri, 9am-3pm Sat; P ⊠) This efficient accommodation agency runs its own charming guesthouse above its office and arranges B&B accommodation in private homes. Rates are lower in winter and guests can check in after office hours providing they give advance notice.

Šauni Vietelė (Map pp292-3; ☎ 212 2189; sauni.vietele@takas.lt; Pranciškonai gatvė 3/6; s 120Lt, d 150Lt & 170Lt, 2-room apt 220Lt) This four-room guesthouse above a crumbling courtyard café in Old Town makes a refreshing change from the chic designer norm. Rooms – unbeatable value for money – are vast, boast dark furnishings and flouncy charm despite their age. The lovely old building was a Franciscan abbey in a previous life.

HOSTELS

Old Town Hostel (Map pp288-9; ☎ 262 5357; booking@lithuanianhostels.org; Aušros Vartų gatvė 20-15; dm 32Lt, d/tr with shared bathroom 100/120Lt, 2-/3-person apt 120/150Lt; 💻) These 25 beds – a two-minute signposted walk from the train and bus stations – fill up fast. A centuries-old courtyard location makes it Vilnius' most atmospheric hostel and *the* place to meet fellow backpackers. Non-HI members pay 2Lt more, sheets/laundry are 2/10Lt and Internet access is free on two computers in the noisy kitchen where guests slug free tea and coffee.

AAA Hostel (Map pp288-9; ☎ 8-680 18557; www.aaahostel.lt; Šv Stepano gatvė 15; dm in 4-bed r 41-51Lt, dm in 8-bed r 31Lt; 💻) Squeakier than squeaky-clean is the hallmark of this modern hostel where the interior decoration screams colour. Dorms are mixed and Internet access is free for 10 minutes then 7Lt an hour. Locker padlocks – to take home when you leave – cost 10Lt and breakfast (9Lt) is served in a café down the street.

Filaretai Hostel (Map pp288-9; ☎ 215 4627; www.filaretaihostel.lt; Filaretų gatvė 17; dm 28Lt, s/d/tr with shared bathroom 65/90/105Lt May-Sep, dm 23Lt, s/d/tr with shared bathroom 65/80/90Lt Oct-Apr; P 💻 ⊠) Affiliated with the Lithuanian Hostels Association,

GAY & LESBIAN VILNIUS

The scene is low-key and underground. For general information, chat rooms and guides, contact Vilnius-based **Lithuanian Gay League** (☎ 233 3031; www.gay.lt; PO Box 2862, Vilnius), which publishes a solid entertainment guide in English online. Gals can befriend the Lithuanian lesbian league **Sappho** (www.is.lt/sappho; PO Box 2204, Vilnius).

Men's Factory (Map pp292-3; ☎ 8-699 85009; www.gayclub.lt; Švencenkos gatvė 16/10; admission 5-40Lt; 🕑 7pm-6am Wed & Thu, 10pm-6am Fri & Sat) Buzz at the steely door of this ravishingly popular gay club to penetrate its hardcore underground scene. Door policy is strict but fair. Look for the line-up of flags outside.

Filaretai has five- to eight-bedded dorms; bed linen and towels are provided (pay a 3Lt surcharge the first night); and it has a washing machine (10Lt), kitchen and satellite TV. Breakfast costs 6Lt, a locker costs 3Lt and non-HI members pay 4Lt more per night. To get here take bus 34 from the bus and train stations to the seventh stop.

Arts Academy Hostel (VDA Hostel; Map pp292-3; ☎ 212 0102; Latako gatvė 2; dm 18Lt, bed in d 26-30Lt, bed in tr 22-26Lt mid-Jul–mid-Sep, s/d/tr 43/76/99Lt year-round) The budget-conscious won't get cheaper than this concrete block, stumbling distance from Pilies gatvė – home to Art Academy students in term time. Little English is spoken.

HOTELS

Ecotel (Map pp288-9; ☎ 210 2700; www.ecotel.lt; Slucko gatvė 8; s/d/tr 169/189/240Lt; P ⊠ ❄ 🖳) The first of a new breed of hotel, this economy-driven hotel is a steal. Simple but smart furnishings fill 168 squeaky-clean rooms, in which bathrooms have heated towel rails. There is a computer with free Internet access in the lobby, and some rooms are designed for both disabled travellers and tall people – beds are 2.10m long. Rates are 10Lt less per person on Saturday and Sunday.

Panorama Hotel (Map pp288-9; ☎ 273 8011; www.hotelpanorama.lt; Sodų gatvė 14; s/d/tr 149/179/249Lt; ⊠ 🖳) A Soviet-era hotel that surprises: dig beneath its kitsch, chocolate-brown tiled façade to find a bright and airy train-station hotel with great Old Town views from its northern side. A currency exchange, ATM and free Internet access in the lobby ease the ride for new arrivals.

Midrange

Mano Liza (Map pp292-3; ☎ 212 2225; www.hotelinvilnius.lt; Ligoninės gatvė 5; d 280Lt, 1-/2-bedroom ste 360/400Lt) Each room is different at Mano Liza, tucked in a late-19th-century building in the Old Town heart. Rooms on the top floor are smaller and have sloping ceilings and some have a fridge.

Grybas House (Map pp292-3; ☎ 212 1854; www.grybashouse.com; Aušros Vartų gatvė 3a; s/d 280/380-450; P) Stase and Vladas run Grybas House – the first independent family-run hotel to crop up after independence – with grace, charm and bags of smiles. Some rooms peep at a pretty courtyard off Aušros Vartų gatvė and breakfast happens in a cosy cellar bar.

THE AUTHOR'S CHOICE

Domus Maria (Map pp292-3; ☎ 264 4880; http://domusmaria.vilnensis.lt; Aušros Vartų gatvė 12; dm/s/d/tr/q/ste 75/179/249/279/299/250Lt; P 🖳) No guesthouse better reflects the Vilnius soul than Domus Maria. With rooms sheltered in the cells of a Carmelite monastery that was attached to St Theresa's Church and the Gates of Dawn in the 17th century, the place oozes atmosphere and charm. Architecturally faithful to its monastic origins, rooms off long corridors are arranged around an interior courtyard. Rooms 207 and 307 – the only hotel rooms in Vilnius with a Gates of Dawn view – are booked months in advance. Breakfast is served in the vaulted refectory, original 18th-century frescoes decorate the conference room and one floor is kitted out for disabled travellers. To top off its appeal, Domus Maria touts eight doubles and two six-bedded rooms with shared bathrooms – stunning value at 75Lt per person – for those with less worldly wealth.

Telecom Guest House (Map pp292-3; ☎ 264 4861; www.telecomguesthouse.lt; Vivulskio gatvė 13a; s/d/ste 240/328/320Lt, s/d/tr/q with shared bathroom 75/120/180/220Lt; P 🖳) One of Vilnius' best-kept accommodation secrets, this dynamic hotel within walking distance of the madding Old Town crowds touts cheaper rooms in an unrenovated building as well as regular rooms with three-star comforts. Hotel parking is free.

Scandic Neringa (Map pp292-3; ☎ 268 1910; neringa@scandic-hotels.com; Gedimino prospektas 23; d/ste from 297/456Lt; ⊠ 🖳) One of the few preindependence old girls still on the scene, 60-room Neringa has hit lucky again. The few fabulous 1970s Soviet touches it has retained (take its restaurant with mosaic floor, frescoed wall and tinkling fountain) are now retro, while recent renovations add a tasteful touch of comfort. Breakfast on the street terrace is a pleasure and every room is kettle-equipped.

Centro Klubas (Map pp292-3; ☎ 266 0860; www.centroklubas.lt; Stiklių gatvė 3; s/d 320/360Lt; P 🖳) The bizarre décor of this Old Town hotel – life-sized windmill in the lobby, horseshoe on each door and farm utensils on the walls – doesn't quite gel. That said, rooms are huge and some have a kitchenette and/or interior balcony (overlooking the windmill!). Parking/breakfast is 25/19Lt a night.

E-Guest House (Map pp288-9; ☎ 266 0730; www.e-guesthouse.lt; Ševčenkos gatvė 16; d/tr/apt 180/210/240Lt; P 💻) This hi-tech hotel with bold blue exterior and free Internet connection throughout runs a handy rent-a-laptop service. The quarter in which it stands is a building site as neighbours get spruced up, but it's definitely up-and-coming. The city's premier gay club (p306) shares the same courtyard.

Atrium (Map pp292-3; ☎ 210 7777; www.atrium.lt; Pilies gatvė 10; s/d/tr/ste 300/350/799Lt; P ❄ 💻) One floor inside this 15th-century town house is kitted out for disabled travellers. Its restaurant, in a courtyard off Pilies gatvė, cooks up meaty Argentinean cuisine. Rooms otherwise are standard midrange to top-end options in the tourist heart of Vilnius.

Reval Hotel Lietuva (Map pp288-9; ☎ 272 6272; www.revalhotels.com; Konstitucijos prospektas 20; s/d/ste from 380/449/794Lt; P ⊠ ❄ 💻) Once a seedy Soviet landmark, sky-rise Reval rose like a phoenix from the flames into the swankiest hotel in Vilnius' business sector. The 22nd-floor Skybar (p311) is a Vilnius highlight; the hotel is a free wi-fi zone and reception rents bicycles (25/50Lt per half/full day).

CityPark Hotel (Map pp292-3; ☎ 210 7461; www.citypark.lt; Stuokos-Gucevičiaus gatvė 3; s/d/ste from 360/480/660Lt; P ⊠ ❄ 💻) With a chef from Sicily and smart rooms overlooking the cathedral, this enviably located hotel hovers near the top-end fringe. Since its small 16-room beginnings, it has blossomed into a 77-room modern block. But be prepared to cough up extra for parking (€10 per night) and breakfast (28Lt).

Top End

Vilnius boasts a divine selection of hotels for the well-heeled; most lounge in Old Town.

Stikliai (Map pp292-3; ☎ 264 9595; www.stikliaihotel.lt; Gaono gatvė 7; s/d/ste 604/725/966Lt; P ⊠ ❄ 💻 🏊) The cream of the crop is tucked down a picture-postcard cobbled street in the old Jewish quarter and named after the glass-blowers who had their workshop in the 17th-century pad on Stikliai gatvė (Glass Blowers St).

Radisson SAS Astorija (Map pp292-3; ☎ 212 0110; reservations.vilnius@radissonSAS.com; Didžioji gatvė 35/2; s/d/ste €179/189/400Lt; P ⊠ ❄ 💻) This mint-green classical wonder – a hotel since 1901 – overlooks St Casimir's Church. Its wintertime Sunday brunches (65Lt) are renowned, and trouser press, safe and self-regulating heating/air-con are standard. Business-class rooms boast added luxuries, such as king-sized bed, bathrobe, slippers, iron, tea-/coffee-making facilities and free Internet access (everyone else pays €15 per 24 hours).

Narutis (Map pp292-3; ☎ 212 2894; www.narutis.com; Pilies gatvė 24; s/d/ste weekdays 450/680/900, weekends 383/578/850Lt; P ⊠ ❄ 💻 🏊) Housed in red-brick town house built in 1581, this classy pad has been a hotel since the 16th century. Breakfast and dinner is served in a vaulted Gothic cellar, wi-fi access is free in public areas, and free apples at reception add a tasty touch. Narutis earns five stars because of its cellar swimming pool.

Shakespeare (Map pp292-3; ☎ 266 5885; www.shakespeare.lt; Bernardinų gatvė 8/8; s/d/ste from €105/174; P ⊠ ❄ 💻) Striving to be the best of boutique hotels, Shakespeare is a refined Old Town gem that evokes a cultured, literary feel with its abundance of books, antiques and flowers. Each room pays homage to a different writer – in name and design.

Grotthaus (Map pp292-3; ☎ 266 0322; www.grotthusshotel.com; Ligoninės gatvė 7; d 420-560Lt, ste 700Lt; P ⊠ ❄ 💻) Step through the red-canopied entrance of this buttercup-yellow townhouse to find Villeroy & Boch bathtubs, 19th-century Titanic-style fittings, Italian-made furniture and curtains allegedly made with the same fabric as that used by the queen of England! The restaurant, La Pergola (meals 70Lt to 100Lt), with tables on an English lawn, is as regal.

Holiday Inn (Map p288-9; ☎ 210 3000; www.holidayinnvilnius.lt; Šeimyniškių gatvė 1; s/d/ste 483/587/656Lt; P ⊠ ❄ 💻) This chain hotel within a two-minute dash of the business district is sleek. Rooms have loudspeakers in bathrooms allowing guests to catch the morning news in the shower. Two floors are no smoking and the executive floor and small gym on the top floor proffers skyscraper views. Outside/garage parking costs 25/40Lt.

EATING

Whether it's curry, *cepelinai* or *kepta duona* you want, Vilnius has a mouth-watering selection of local and international cuisine. That said, traditional food has survived the Western dining take-over bid and it's still very easy to feast on delicious Lithuanian

THE AUTHOR'S CHOICE

Žemaičių Smuklė (Samogitian Tavern; Map pp292-3; ☎ 261 6573; Vokiečių gatvė 24; meals 50Lt) Sorrel soup with country sausage and quail eggs, duck soup, rabbit stew and wild boar roast with asparagus and green pepper sauce are delectables to gorge on at this rustic inn. A meat-eater's paradise, the culinary hardy can hog down boiled pigs ears and trotters or a half-metre long eel, while dining trios can share a Landlord's Skillet – a feast of piggie bits, duck thighs, pork shank, sausage and bacon with sauerkraut, mustard and horseradish sauce. An entire piglet, stuffed and roasted (order 24 hours in advance; 160Lt), is just the thing for a hungry party of five. Summertime seating is around wooden benches and cartwheels on cobbles or up top among Old Town church steeples and terracotta rooftops.

cuisine. Dining after midnight is more challenging. Listed prices include a starter or dessert, a main course and a soft drink.

Lithuanian

Aukštaičiai (Map pp292-3; ☎ 212 0169; Antokolskio gatvė 13; meals 40-100Lt) Boasting a fabulous terrace that fills half the length of a cutesy Old Town street, this traditional restaurant oozes charm. It cooks up breakfast until 11am, moves onto cabbage soup with mushrooms served in a loaf of bread for lunch, and proffers a wealth of tasty meats for dinner.

Markus ir Ko (Map pp292-3; ☎ 262 3185; Antokolskio gatvė 11; meals 50-100Lt) Next-door neighbour to Aukštaičiai, with an equally charming terrace on the other half of the same cutesy street, Markus is a long-time favourite that remains top-notch for sweet, succulent, melt-in-your-mouth steak – at half the price you'd pay in any other European capital.

Stikliai Aludė (Map pp292-3; ☎ 262 4501; Gaono gatvė 7; meals 50-100Lt) Waving distance from the latter two street terraces, this one is another gorgeous, shaded and busy place. Get here early to snag a table outside or descend to the cellar for an authentic Lithuanian dining experience at the hands of traditionally dressed maidens.

Tores (Map pp292-3; ☎ 262 9309; Užupio gatvė 40; meals 30-50Lt) Feast your tastebuds on a plentiful mix of Lithuanian and European dishes and your eyes on a stunning Old Town panorama at this well-placed eating and drinking hang-out, atop a hill in bohemian Užupis. Užupio Radijas airs tunes in the basement.

Čili Kaimas (Map pp292-3; ☎ 231 2536; Vokiečių gatvė 8; meals 15-30Lt; 10am-midnight Sun-Thu, to 2am Fri & Sat) Hens cluck around in a glass enclosure at this cheerful farmstead where waitresses wear traditional dress, and mushroom soup is served inside a brown-bread loaf (5.90Lt). This is very much a winter hide-out. There is a summer terrace opposite.

Lokys (The Bear; Map pp292-3; ☎ 262 9046; Stiklių gatvė 8; meals 50-100Lt) Hunt down the big wooden bear outside to find this Vilnius institution, a cellar maze going strong since 1972. Game is its mainstay, with delicacies like beaver-meat stew with plums and roast boar luring the culinary curious. Folk musicians play here in summer.

Za Za (Map pp292-3; Vilniaus gatvė 19; meals 25Lt) Pizza gets fused with dumplings and cocktails at this chic, far-from-strictly-Lithuanian hybrid eating and drinking spot where *koldūnai* (ravioli stuffed with meat or mushrooms) come boiled or roasted.

European

Saint Germain (Map pp292-3; ☎ 262 1210; Literatų gatvė; meals 30Lt) Paris is the inspiration behind this idyllic wine bar-cum-restaurant inside a convivial century-old brown-shuttered house on a quiet Old Town street. Advance reservations for its street terrace are essential.

Guru (Map pp292-3; ☎ 212 0126; Vilniaus gatvė 22/1; meals 25Lt; 7am-9pm Mon-Fri, 9am-8pm Sat & Sun) Guru is a Zen salad lounge, decked out in a soothing and minimalist fashion. Floor-to-ceiling windows and crisp white linen set off a bold choice of soups (eight) and salads (50) – a perfect and peaceful pad for lunch with the girls.

La Provence (Map pp292-3; ☎ 261 6573; Vokiečių gatvė 24; meals 100 Lt) Boiled veal tongue in port with king prawns, gorgonzola cheese and capers (46Lt) or pan-fried foie gras atop a bed of apple with caramelised apricot and pearl barley cooked in saffron-spiced orange juice are among the lavish dishes served with a typical French flourish at this elegant restaurant. Its motto is 100% gourmet.

LITHUANIA

Literatų Svetainė (Map pp292-3; ☎ 261 1889; www.literatai.lt; Gedimino prospektas 1; meals 50Lt) This is where the Polish-Lithuanian poet and Nobel Prize–winner Czesław Miłosz watched the Red Army march into Vilnius in June 1940. Today European food (the roast garlic soup is divine, as are its many vegetarian choices), impeccable service and a street terrace with a cathedral view ensures this 19th-century tavern remains top. Orange, amaretto or hazelnut cappuccino makes a sweet coffee stop.

Čili Pica (Map pp292-3; ☎ 261 9071; Gedimino prospektas 23; 7.30am-midnight Sun-Wed, to 3am Thu-Sat) The Lithuanian love affair with the humble pizza continues unabated at this pizza chain, which, unremarkable pizza aside, serves nosh well into the wee hours in Old Town and near the train and bus station.

Da Antonio I (Map pp292-3; ☎ 262 0109; Vilniaus gatvė 23; ☎ 261 8341; meals 30Lt) Italian-inspired joints come and go, but Da Antonio has staying power. Italian favourites conjured up in a classical interior woo a faithful crowd that rates Antonio's pizza and pasta – dished up here and at **Trattoria Da Antonio** (Map pp292-3; ☎ 261 8341; Pilies gatvė 20; meals 30Lt) – the best in town.

LITHUANIA

International

Pegasus (Map pp292-3; ☎ 260 9430; www.restaurantpegasus.lt; Didžioji gatvė 11; meals 50-100Lt) World cuisine takes centre stage at Pegasus, a crisp white lounge with a strong design-led interior and one solitary but fabulous table on a balcony overlooking Didžioji gatvė. Its discreet entrance and live jazz attracts a moneyed local crowd.

Sue's Indian Raja (Map pp292-3; ☎ 8-600 27788; Odminių gatvė 3; meals 30Lt) The food served here is by no means the hottest Indian nosh you'll find on the planet, but expats in Vilnius swear by Sue's – and where else in the world will you find an Indian serving curried *cepelinai*?

Kineret (Map pp292-3; ☎ 8-656 08927; Šv Stepano gatvė 5; meals 30Lt) The ambience might not be the most inspirational, but Kineret, just around the corner from the synagogue, is the city's only kosher restaurant.

Balti Drambliai (Map pp292-3; ☎ 262 0875; Vilniaus gatvė 41; meals 20Lt) An exhaustive choice of cheap vegan and veggie delights from all cuisines renders this heaven for non-meat-eaters.

Ephesus (Map pp292-3; ☎ 260 8866; Trakų gatvė 15; kebabs 5Lt; 11am-1am Mon, to 6am Tue-Sat) Ravenous night owls can munch on a kebab into the really wee hours at this small Turkish joint, complete with occasional belly dancers and water pipes.

Cafés

Užupio kavinė (Map pp292-3; ☎ 212 2138; Užupio gatvė 2;eals 30Lt) Well away from the trampled tourist trail, this legendary riverside café terrace with artsy clientele is unmatched. A plaque on the wall pays homage to its soul mate – Montmartre, Paris.

Pilies kepyklėlė (Map pp292-3; ☎ 260 8992; Pilies gatvė 19) A standout from the crowd on Vilnius' busiest tourist street, Pilies kepklėlė is an old-fashioned tearoom with a brick and beam interior. The apple strudel and sweet and savoury pancakes (7Lt to 10Lt) are delicious.

Double Coffee (Map pp292-3; ☎ 261 4175; Gedimino prospektas 5 & 26) Coffee in all sizes and guises is the speciality of this Starbucks-inspired chain where the menu is delivered to the table in the shape of the *Double Coffee Times* broadsheet.

Keisti Ženklai (Strange Signs; Map pp292-3; ☎ 261 0779; Trakų gatvė 13; meals 20Lt) 'Enjoy the spirit of modernity' is what you're meant to do at Strange Signs, a café with a strange sign outside and large tasty meals inside.

THE AUTHOR'S CHOICE

Skonis ir Kvapas (Map pp292-3; ☎ 212 2803; Trakų gatvė 8; 9.30am-11pm) Heaven for tea connoisseurs, this stylish courtyard café knows how to make a good cuppa. Pick from a myriad of designer teas (recommended: milky Masala loaded with cinnamon; sweet-and-sour ginger tea with orange juice and honey; or smoked tea with vodka), many of which take a good 15 minutes to brew – so come with your patience hat on. Tea comes by the cup (3Lt to 5Lt) or pot (7Lt), and a sublime array of creamy and homemade cakes, cucumber sandwiches and breakfasts (opposite) top off the tastebud-tempting picture. The terrace is Old Town's most peaceful and shaded; there are rugs to wrap up in on chillier days; and the red-brick fireplace inside is a great wintertime toe-toaster.

TOP FIVES PLACES TO BREAKFAST...

- if you're hot off the dance floor at 5am – **Cozy** (below)
- on an egg boiled in green tea with toast – **Skonis ir Kvapas** (opposite)
- on pancakes – **Pilies kepyklėlė** (opposite)
- in traditional Lithuanian style – **Aukštaičiai** (p309)
- on a Sunday brunch to last all day – **Radisson SAS Astorija** (p308)

Soprano (Central Vilnius Map pp292-3; ☎ 212 6042; Pilies gatvė 3; Vilnius Map pp288-9; Konstitucijos prospektas 3) Soprano sells fruit-topped *gelato Italiano.* Buy a cone (2Lt) to lick on the move or sit on its terrace for the ice cream of your dreams (2Lt to 10Lt).

Self-Catering

Shopping at the market (p313) for milk, honey and smoked eel aside, self-catering is a doddle with a supermarket on every second street corner. **Iki** (www.iki.lt; ☎ 249 8340; Jasinskio gatvė 16) and **Maxima** (Map pp292-3; www.maxima.lt; Mindaugo gatvė 11) are leading chains. Both run smaller corner shops: **Ikiukas** (Jogailos gatvė Map pp292-3; ☎ 231 3135; Jogailos gatvė 12; Pylimo gatvė Map pp292-3; ☎ 231 3403; Pylimo gatvė 21) and **Mini Maxima** (Map pp292-3; Gedimino prospektas 64).

DRINKING

Nightlife is a laid-back affair with many places offering something to eat too. Pubs and bars where punters stand around English-style drinking don't exist; drinking is very much done the Med Europe way, ie seated around tables. In summer Vokiečių gatvė, a street lined with wooden-decking terraces in summer, is an obvious starting point.

Cozy (Map pp292-3; ☎ 261 1137; www.cozy.lt; Dominikonų gatvė 10; 🕒 7.30am-6am) Run by hip Bernie and his beaming smile from Holland, Cozy is a hot address. Street level is lounge style with a chef who cooks until 6am, while local DJs spin tunes downstairs to a discerning crowd in the Friday and Saturday night DJ club.

Skybar (Map pp288-9; ☎ 272 6272; Konstitucijos prospektas 20; 🕒 4pm-1am Sun-Thu, to 2.30am Fri & Sat) Perched on the 22nd floor of the Reval Hotel Lietuva, this spacey blue bar with red swivel chairs proffers panorama after panorama. DJs play from 9pm Friday and Saturday.

Iki Aušros (Until Dawn; Map pp292-3; ☎ 8-610 04131; Aušros Vartų gatvė 15) Dress up to fit in at the city's premier cocktail bar, which shakes a mean Singapore Sling within a hair's breadth of the sacred Gates of Dawn.

Ibish Lounge (Map pp292-3; ☎ 8-680 75462; Aušros Vartų gatvė 11) Two suspended bubble chairs facing the street, sofa seating and a fireplace ensure chic times year-round at Ibish Lounge, a lounge bar owned by Turkish-German Ibish.

Mano Klubas (Map pp292-3; ☎ 8-698 27231; www.manoklubas.com; Bokšto gatvė 7) There's a definite industrial air to this student hang-out where the cocktail called Neprisikashkopustelaujancho punch might defeat the most nimble of linguists.

Fashionbar (Map pp292-3; ☎ 243 0777; www.ftv.lt; Trakų gatvė 2) Lithuanian beauties of both sexes converge at Fashionbar – part of the Fashion TV worldwide franchise – where the cream of Vilnius society hobnobs.

Contemporary Art Centre (Map pp292-3; ☎ 261 7097; Vokiečių gatvė 2) The art centre has a smoky hide-out bar filled with arty Lithuanian luvvies and one of the most simple but hip summer terraces in town. At weekends roll up your jeans and hold your nose to enter the aeroplane-style loo.

Paparazzi (Map pp292-3; ☎ 212 0135; www.paparazzi.lt; Totorių gatvė 3; 🕒 5pm-3am Mon-Thu, to 6am Fri & Sat, to 3am Sun) Plop yourself down on a green, red or black sofa and look cool –

THE AUTHOR'S CHOICE

Avilys (Map pp292-3; Gedimino prospektas 5; beer per litre 13-15Lt) Beehive – a brew pub with a cellar bar and summer street terrace – is *the* spot to sup authentic Lithuanian beer. The unstrained beer made from wholly natural products comes in three guises: Avilio, a light beer that notches 4.5% on the alcohol barometer; honey beer (hence the name of the place), a medium dark beer with honey aromas which, despite its sweet name, is not sweet; and Korio, which gets its kick from the ginseng thrown in with the hops. If that's not enough, there are beer soup (9Lt) and hot beer grog (9Lt) to warm the cockles in winter, and nonalcoholic beer ice cream (6Lt) to cool down on in summer.

LITHUANIA

INDUSTRY NEWS

Intimate, sexy, glamorous and funky is what the legendary **Pacha** (www.pacha.com) club franchise, started way back in 1967 in Ibiza, Spain, prides itself on. And that's precisely what Vilnius clubbers should get when **Pacha Vilnius** (Map pp292-3; www.pacha.com; Gyneju gatvė 14; admission €4-10; 🕑 10pm-6am Thu-Sat) opens its doors in Autumn 2006. Easily the most ambitious project of its kind to date in the Baltics, the venue – a new building being built from scratch behind parliament – will have two dance floors and a capacity of 2500. Europe's top DJs are expected to play here.

someone could be watching you. There are cameras in the loo allegedly.

Also recommended:

Gras'as (Map pp292-3; ☎ 212 2031; www.grasa.lt; Vokiečių gatvė 2) Merits one drink for its underground interior between rocks.

Pablo Latino (Map pp292-3; ☎ 262 1045; Trakų gatvė 3) Strictly Latin.

Savas Kampas (Map pp292-3; ☎ 212 3203; Vokiečių gatvė 4; 🕑 8.30-1am Mon-Wed, 8.30-2am Thu, 8.30-4am Fri, 10-4am Sat, 10-1am Sun) Breakfast, brunch, dinner and drink.

LITHUANIA

ENTERTAINMENT

The tourist office publishes events listings, as does the *Baltic Times*.

Nightclubs

The clubbing scene – young, fresh and dynamic – is at its best in winter when everyone's around. (In summer many go to the seashore to party.) Cozy (p311) is the top spot to pick up flyers for monthly dance parties held by non-club-based party organisers **Ore** (www.ore.lt) and **Boogaloo** (www.boogaloo.lt).

Gravity (Map pp292-3; ☎ 249 7966; www.clubgravity.lt; Jasinskio gatvė 16; admission 20-30Lt) Happening DJs, exotic cocktails and thumping House make this stylish club hot. Think London-style door policy: five bouncers and difficult to get into.

Galaxy (Map pp288-9; ☎ 263 6666; www.forumpalace.lt; Konstitucijos gatvė 26; admission variable) Very much an event-led club rather than a weekly haunt, Galaxy is a large amphitheatre-styled space that, DJ depending, draws a large crowd.

Club Connect (Map pp292-3; ☎ 212 2031; www.connectclub.lt; Vokiečių gatvė 2; admission 5-15Lt) A lairy Union Jack on the door sets the tone for this Old Town nightclub, which lures a bold, brash, mildly rough set – stags included.

Trasa (Map pp292-3; ☎ 249 8258; www.trasa.lt; Gedimino prospektas 39/1; admission 5-10Lt; 🕑 11am-3am Mon-Wed, 11am-4am Thu, 11am-6am Fri, 3pm-6am Sat, 3pm-3am Sun) The bold cellar bar of Trasa thumps with local DJ beats until well after sunrise. Watch your back.

Cinemas

Find movie listings at www.cinema.lt (Lithuanian only). Films are screened in English at **Coca-Cola Plaza** (Map pp292-3; ☎ 265 6565; www.forumcinemas.lt; Savanorių prospektas 7; admission before 1pm/1-4pm/after 4pm Mon-Fri 8/10/12.20Lt, before/after 1pm Sat & Sun 12.20/15Lt) and at the out-of-town **Forum Cinemas Akropolis** (☎ 248 4848; www.forumcinemas.lt; Ozo gatvė 25; admission before 1pm/1-4pm/after 4pm Mon-Fri 8/10/12.20Lt, before/after 1pm Sat & Sun 12.20/15Lt) in the Akropolis multiplex.

Theatre & Classical Music

Oskaras Koršunovas Theatre (OKT; Oskaro Koršuno teatro; ☎ 261 1877; www.okt.lt) Lithuania's most innovative, daring and controversial theatre company (p312).

Resident companies perform opera and ballet at the **Opera & Ballet Theatre** (Map pp292-3; Operos ir Baleto Teatras; ☎ 262 0636; www.opera.lt; Vienuolio gatvė 1).

The **Lithuanian National Drama Theatre** (Map pp292-3; Lietuvos nacionalinis dramos teatras; ☎ 262 9771; www.teatras.lt; Gedimino prospektas 4), **Small Theatre of Vilnius** (Map pp292-3; Vilniaus Mažasis Teatras; ☎ 261 3195; www.vmt.lt; Gedimino prospektas 22) and the **Youth Theatre** (Map pp292-3; Jaunimo teatras; ☎ 261 6126; www.jaunimoteatras.lt; Arklių gatvė 5) are the stages for Lithuanian and foreign plays in Lithuanian.

The country's most renowned orchestras perform at **National Philharmonic** (Map pp292-3; Nacionalinė filharmonija; ☎ 266 5233; www.filharmonija.lt; Aušros Vartų gatvė 5), which breaks for summer. The **Lithuanian Music Academy** (Map pp292-3; Lietuvos muzikos akademija; ☎ 261 2691; www.lma.lt; Gedimino prospektas 42) stages concerts all year.

SHOPPING

Pilies gatvė is something of a bustling craft market, with painters hanging out their masterpieces, and traders behind stalls laden with wooden chopping boards and spoons,

LITHUANIAN FASHION DESIGN

A stroll in Old Town reveals a band of Lithuanian designers, some well established on the international catwalk, others up and coming.

Crinkled linen designs with free-flowing feminine lines are the trademark of Rita Plioplienė, who named her small boutique for women near the Gates of Dawn after her two children, **Kristijonas ir Karolina** (Map pp292-3; ☎ 212 0398; Aušros Vartų gatvė 17). **Ramunė Piekautaitė** (Map pp292-3; ☎ 231 2270; Didžioji gatvė 20), a short strut away, is another well-known name to turn her hand to linen. Don't miss the imaginative collection of amber jewellery displayed beneath glass in her boutique.

The Lithuanian master of linen is 38-year-old Giedrius Šarkauskas, who stunned the world in Tokyo, Japan, with his 2005 autumn/winter collection entitled 'Century'. Inspired by life's natural cycle, the designer – who was born deaf – lives out his wholly naturalist philosophy with collections sewn solely from linen. Accessories are made from amber, wood, leather and linen. **Lino Kopos** (Linen Dunes; Map pp288-9; ☎ 275 1200; Krokuvos gatvė 6) is his design studio and shop.

Lithuania's other big name is the flamboyant **Juozas Statkrevičius** (Map pp292-3; ☎ 212 2029, 8-600 87491; Odminų gatvė 11), who is the country's best-known designer and has boutiques in Vilnius, Paris, Palm Beach and New York.

Daiva Urbonavičiūtė fronts the fun and funky fashion house **Zoraza** (Map pp292-3; ☎ 212 0084; Stiklių gatvė 6), where a riot of colours and textures – suede, glitter, beads, felt, crystal, leather and so on – creates an urban, vintage feel. Fashion fiends will adore this Pandora's box of glam funk. On the same street, local fashion designers still seeking fame and fortune pool their creations in **Elementai** (☎ 260 8588; elementai@takas.lt; Stiklių gatvė 14), a fantastic shop crammed with designs by non-names. It sells a few pieces of sculpture, pottery, ceramic and glassware too.

Final stop on the fashion design trail is **Aukso Avis** (Golden Sheep; Map pp292-3; ☎ 261 0421; Savičiaus gatvė 10), a textile gallery established by Vilnius fashion designer Julija Žilėniene, which sells bags, T-shirts, wall murals and jewellery (think necklaces in felt or wool) made from a rich range of material. The gallery runs courses in knitting, embroidery, wool felting and weaving for those seeking some know-how.

Online, shop for Lithuanian design with Vilnius-based **Ona** (www.ona.com).

cheap amber trinkets, clothing and so on. Amber and linen shops are a dime a dozen, both here and on Aušros Vartų gatvė:

Gintaras (Auðros Vartų Map pp292-3; Aušros Vartų gatvė 13; Pilies Map pp292-3; ☎ 8-612 40501; Pilies gatvė 32) Stands out with its beautiful collection of children's wooden toys and dolls as well as standard amber fare.

Lino Namai (Linen House; Map pp292-3; ☎ 212 2322; Vilniaus gatvė 22) For table and bed linen.

For clothes, visit a local designer (above). Gedimino prospektas – the main shopping street – is lined with mainstream fashion shops, the department store **Flagman** (Map pp292-3; Gedimino prospektas 16; 🕑 10am-8pm Mon-Sat, 11am-6pm Sun) and – in 2007– a couple of state-of-the-art shopping centres (p302). **Šokoladas** (Didžioji Map pp292-3; Didžioji gatvė 42; Gedimino Map pp292-3; Gedimino prospektas 46; Trakų Trakų gatvė 13) sells handmade chocolate.

Away from the centre, **Europa** (Map pp288-9; www.europa.lt; Konstitucijos prospektas 3; 🕑 8am-midnight) in Šnipiškės and **Akropolis** (Map pp292-3; www.akropolis.lt; Ozo gatvė 25; 🕑 10am-10pm) are shopping and entertainment complexes.

Vilnius has two main markets, the often disappointing **Gariūnai**, to the west, off the Kaunas road, and the food-driven **Kalvarijų** (Map pp292-3; Kalvarijų gatvė 6), where you can join the scrum of babushkas jostling for bargains. Both open sunrise to noon Tuesday to Sunday. Minibuses marked 'Gariūnai' or 'Gariūnų Turgus' ferry shoppers from the train station road every morning. By car it's 11km along Savanorių prospektas from Vilnius centre.

GETTING THERE & AWAY

See p393 for details on links with countries outside the region.

Air

For international flights to/from Vilnius, see p393. Domestic and inter-Baltic flights are limited. There are five flights weekly to/from Palanga (160Lt one way, 45 minutes) with Lithuanian Airlines, May to September only. There is at least one flight daily Monday to Friday to/from Rīga (from 265Lt one way) with Air Baltic, and to/from Tallinn (from 315Lt) with Air Baltic and Estonian Air. Up-to-date fares are online.

Major airline offices at Vilnius airport:

Estonian Air (☎ 273 9022; www.estonian-air.ee)
Lithuanian Airlines (☎ 252 5555; www.lal.lt)
Lufthansa (☎ 230 6300; www.lufthansa.com)
SAS/Air Baltic (☎ 235 6000; www.sas.lt, www.airbaltic.com)

Bus

Vilnius **bus station** (Autobusų stotis; Map pp288-9; ☎ 216 2977; Sodų gatvė 22) is opposite the train station. Inside its ticket hall, domestic tickets are sold at six ticket windows from 5.30am to 7.30pm, and information is doled out at the **information office** (informacija; ☎ 1661; www.autobusai.lt; 6am-9pm). Timetables are displayed on a board here and online. Passenger facilities include left luggage (p290), a pharmacy, ATM, Iki supermarket (p311), bistro and sandwich bar.

Tickets for international destinations, including Rīga and Tallinn, are sold at **Eurolines Baltic International** (Map pp288-9; ☎ 233 6666; www.eurolines.lt; Sodų gatvė 22; 8am-8pm Mon-Sat, 10am-1pm & 2-7pm Sun), with an office in the main hall and in **town** (Map pp292-3; ☎ 269 0000; Jogailos gatvė 4; 9am-6pm Mon-Fri, to 2pm Sat). Buses to destinations within the Baltics include the following:

Druskininkai 19Lt, two hours, 10 direct daily.
Kaunas 14.50Lt, two hours, about 20 daily.
Klaipėda 44Lt, five to seven hours, eight daily.
Lazdijai 18-19Lt, three hours, three to six daily.
Molėtai 10Lt, 1½ hours, two daily.
Palanga 47Lt, six hours, about nine daily.
Panevėžys 20Lt, 2¼ hours, about 12 daily.
Rīga 40Lt, five hours, four daily.
Šiauliai 29Lt, 4½ hours, seven daily.
Tallinn 90Lt, 12 hours, three daily.
Trakai 3Lt, 45 minutes, about 30 daily.
Visaginas 12Lt, three hours, nine daily.

Car & Motorcycle

Numerous 24-hour petrol stations selling Western-grade unleaded fuel are dotted around Vilnius.

If you hire a car and intend to cross the border in a Lithuanian-registered car, check the car is insured for inter-Baltic travel. Rental companies:

Avis Airport (☎ 232 9316); Town (Map pp288-9; ☎ 230 6820; www.avis.lt; Laisvės prospektas 3)
Budget Airport (☎ 230 6708; www.budget.lt)
Europcar Airport (☎ 216 3442); Town (Map pp292-3; ☎ 212 0207; www.europcar.lt; Stuokos Gucevičiaus 9-1)
Hertz Airport (☎ 232 9301); Town (Map pp288-9; ☎ 272 6940; www.hertz.lt; Kalvarijų gatvė14)
Rent a Car Litinterp Town (Map pp292-3; ☎ 212 3850; www.litinterp.lt; Bernardinų gatvė 7-2)
Rimas Rent a Car Town (☎ 277 6213, 8-698 21662; rimas.cars@is.lt) Charismatic Rimas rents cheap self-drive cars or you can hire a car with an English-speaking driver.
Sixt Airport (☎ 239 5636; www.sixt.lt)

Train

The **train station** (Geležinkelio stotis; Map pp288-9; ☎ 233 0087/6; Geležinkelio gatvė 16) is opposite the bus station. The domestic ticket hall is to the left as you face the central station building, and the international ticket hall to the right. Train information and timetables (in English) are available at the information office between the two halls and online at www.litrail.lt.

There is no rail link between Vilnius and Tallinn. For international trains, see p398. Direct daily services within the region to/from Vilnius:

Ignalina 10Lt, two hours, seven daily.
Kaunas 11Lt, 1¼ to two hours, 13 to 16 daily.
Klaipėda 40Lt, five to nine hours, three daily.
Rīga 46Lt, eight hours, two daily.
Šiauliai 26Lt, 2¾ to 3½ hours, five to eight daily.
Trakai 2.50Lt, 40 minutes, seven daily.

GETTING AROUND

To/from the Airport

Vilnius International Airport (☎ 232 9122, information desk ☎ 273 9305/6; www.vilnius-airport.lt; Rodūnė kelias 2) lies 5km south of the centre. Bus 1 runs between the airport and the train station; bus 2 runs between the airport and the northwestern suburb of Šeškinė via the Žaliasis bridge across the Neris and on to Lukiskių aikštė. Minibus 15 also links the airport with town.

A taxi from the airport to the city centre should cost no more than 20Lt.

Bicycle

The Old Town tourist office (p291) rents bicycles for 1Lt a day plus a copy of your passport. Otherwise, pick up a pedal-powered taxi (20Lt per 30 minutes) from Katedros aikštė or Pilies gatvė.

A key stop for serious cyclists is bike shop **Bikeworld** (Map pp292-3; ☎ 8-686 52924; www.bikeworld.lt; Vilniaus gatvė 37).

Car & Motorcycle

Vilnius is easy to navigate by car, its traffic burden being light compared to other capitals. Street parking is plentiful and costs 2Lt an hour payable by meter between 8am and 8pm. Cars are not allowed in part of the pedestrian Old Town.

Public Transport

The city is efficiently served by buses and trolleybuses from 5.30am or 6am to midnight; Sunday services are less frequent. Tickets cost 1.40Lt at news kiosks and 1.10Lt direct from the driver; punch tickets on board in a ticket machine or risk a 20Lt on-the-spot fine.

Nippier minibuses shadow most routes. Minibuses pick up/drop off passengers anywhere en route (not just at official bus stops) and can be flagged down on the street. Tickets costs 2Lt from the driver.

Bus 4 links the train station with Pylimo gatvė. Trolleybus 7 from the train station, or trolleybus 3 from the Gedimino stop on Vrublevskio gatvė near the cathedral, takes you along Jasinskio gatvė, a block south of Gedimino prospektas.

For route details see www.vilniustransport.lt (Lithuanian only).

Taxi

Taxis officially charge 1Lt to 1.50Lt per kilometre and must have a meter. To avoid getting ripped off or robbed, ask your hotel or the bar/restaurant you are leaving to call you a taxi by telephone (☎ 215 0505, 261 6161, 277 7777). Hopping into a taxi on the street, especially if you are drunk and don't speak Lithuanian, is asking for trouble.

Taxi ranks are numerous and include: outside the train station; in front of the old town hall on Didžioji gatvė; in front of the Contemporary Art Centre on Vokiečių gatvė; and outside the Radisson SAS Astorija hotel.

AROUND VILNIUS

The centre of Europe, a fairy-tale castle and ancient castle mounds lie within easy reach of the capital. Or there is the trip to Paneriai.

Paneriai

Here Lithuania's brutal history is starkly portrayed. Over 100,000 people were murdered here by the Nazis between July 1941 and July 1944 at this mass-murder site, 10km southwest of central Vilnius. About half the city's Jewish population – about 35,000 people – had already been massacred here by the end of the first three months of the German occupation (June to September 1941) at the hands of Einsatzkommando 9, an SS killing unit of elite Nazi troops. Lithuanian accomplices are accused of doing as much of the killing as their German overseers.

The forest entrance is marked by a **memorial**, the Panerių memorialas. The text in Russian, dating from the Soviet period, remembers the 100,000 'Soviet citizens' killed here. The memorial plaques in Lithuanian and Hebrew – erected later – honour the 70,000 Jewish victims.

A path leads to the shocking **Paneriai Museum** (Panerių muziejus; ☎ 264 1847, 260 2001; Agrastų gatvė 15; 🕑 11am-6pm Wed-Sat Jun-Sep, by appointment Oct-May). There are two monuments here, one Jewish (marked with the Star of David), the other one Soviet (an obelisk topped with a Soviet star). From here paths lead to a number of grassed-over pits where, from December 1943, the Nazis lined up 300 to 4000 victims at a time and shot them in the back of the head. The bodies were then covered with sand to await the next layer of bodies. The Nazis later burnt the exhumed corpses to hide the evidence of their crimes. One of the deeper pits, according to its sign, was where they kept those who were forced to dig up the corpses and pulverise the bones.

GETTING THERE & AWAY

There are about 20 trains daily (some terminating in Trakai or Kaunas) from Vilnius to Paneriai station (1.20Lt, 20 minutes). From **Paneriai station** (Agrastų gatvė) it's a 1km walk southwest along Agrastų gatvė straight to the site.

Trakai

☎ 528 / pop 6110

Lakeside Trakai, with its red-brick fairy-tale castle and blushing brides in meringue dresses who flock here on Saturdays to have their pic taken, is the quintessential day trip from Vilnius.

LITHUANIA

Gediminas probably made Trakai, 28km west of Vilnius, his capital in the 1320s and Kęstutis certainly based his 14th-century court here. Protected by the **Trakai Historical National Park** (www.seniejitrakai.lt), spanning 80 sq km since 1991, Trakai today is a quiet town blessed with pretty lakes and filled with song each July during the Trakai Festival.

Most of Trakai stands on a 2km-long, north-pointing tongue of land between Lake Luka (east) and Lake Totoriškių (west). Lake Galvė opens out from the northern end of the peninsula and boasts 21 islands.

INFORMATION

Snoras Bankas (Vytauto gatvė 56) ATM and currency exchange opposite the tourist office. Two more ATMs next door outside Iki.

Tourist Office (☎ 51 934; www.trakai.lt; Vytauto gatvė 69; 🕑 8.30am-noon & 12.45-4.15pm Mon, 8.30am-noon & 12.45-5.30pm Tue-Fri, 9am-3pm Sat Jun-Aug, 8am-noon & 12.45-5pm Mon-Thu, 8am-noon & 12.45-3pm Fri Sep-May) Sells maps and guides, books accommodation and proffers oodles of practical info.

SIGHTS

The ruins of Trakai's **Peninsula Castle**, built from 1362 to 1382 by Kęstutis and destroyed in the 17th century, are at the north end of town. The peninsula itself is dotted with old wooden cottages, many built by the Karaites, a Judaic sect and Turkic minority originating in Baghdad, which adheres to the Law of Moses. Their descendants were brought to Trakai from the Crimea around 1400 to serve as bodyguards. Only 12 families (60 Karaites) live in Trakai and their numbers – 280 in Lithuania – are dwindling, prompting fears that the country's smallest ethnic minority is dying out. The **Karaites Ethnographic Museum** (Karaimų etnografinė paroda; ☎ 55 286; Karaimų gatvė 22; adult/student & child 2/1Lt, camera 4Lt, guided tour 20Lt; 🕑 10am-6pm Wed-Sun) traces their ancestry. Their beautifully restored early-19th-century **Kenessa** (Karaite prayer house; Karaimų gatvė 30; admission by donation) can be visited.

The centrepiece of Trakai is its picture-postcard **Island Castle** on Lake Galvė. The painstakingly restored red-brick Gothic castle probably dates from around 1400, when Vytautas needed stronger defences than the peninsula castle afforded. A footbridge links it to the shore and a moat separates the triangular outer courtyard moat from the main tower with its cavernous central court and

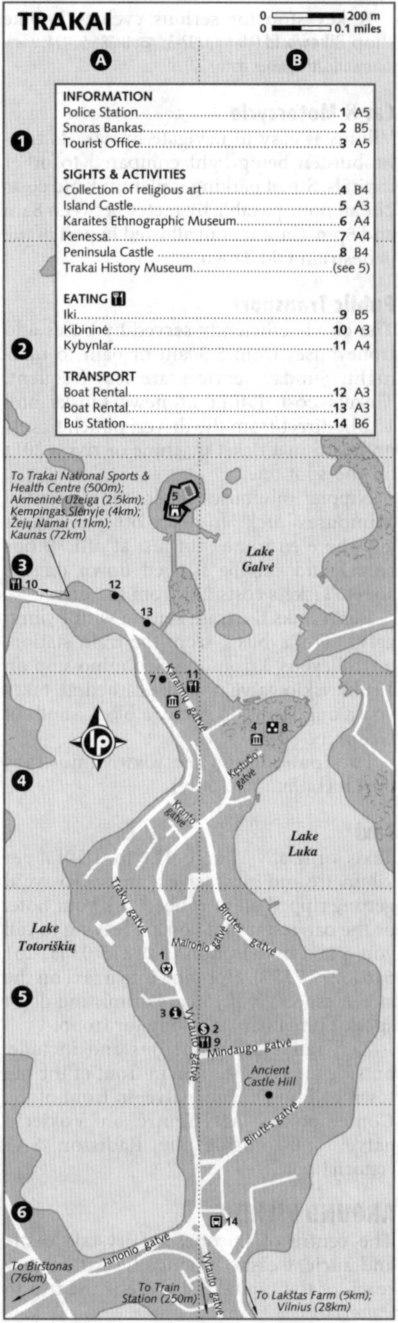

a range of galleries, halls and rooms. Some house the **Trakai History Museum** (Trakų istorijos muziejus; ☎ 53 946; www.trakaimuziejus.lt; adult/student & child 8/4Lt; ⏲ 10am-7pm May-Sep, 10am-5pm Tue-Sun Oct-Apr), which charts the history of the castle. The castle's prominence as a holy site is reflected in its **collection of religious art** (☎ 53 941; Kestučio gatvė 4; adult/student & child 4/2Lt; ⏲ 10am-6pm Wed-Sun). In summer the castle courtyard is a magical stage for concerts and plays.

ACTIVITIES

Pick up a **pedalo** or **rowing boat** (both 7Lt an hour) from boatmen near the footbridge leading to the Island Castle.

The tourist office has information on the 14km **bicycle route** around the main sights. Kempingas Slėnyje (below) and the **Trakai National Sports & Health Centre** (Trakų Poilsio ir pramogų centras; ☎ 55 501; www.sc.trakai.com; Karaimų gatvė 73) rent bikes for 35Lt/6Lt per day/hour. Fishing, sailing, scuba diving and horse riding are also available at this former training camp for Lithuanian sporting heroes. It rents rowing boats (8Lt per hour), water bicycles (8Lt per hour), canoes (50Lt/10Lt per hour/day) and kayaks (35Lt/10Lt per hour/day); has a fabulous sauna (50Lt per hour) by the lake; and arranges hot-air ballooning (350Lt per hour). Winter guests enjoy horse-drawn sled rides, skiing and ice-fishing.

SLEEPING

Accommodation options are limited.

Kempingas Slėnyje (☎ 53 380; www.camptrakai.lt; Slėnio gatvė 1; adult/car 16/6Lt plus 2-/4-person camp site 5/7Lt, lakeside hut for 2/4 people 80/100Lt, d/tr/q with shared bathroom 75/85/100Lt, cottage for 2-4 people 250Lt, d in guesthouse 120Lt; 🅿) Some 5km out of Trakai in Slėnje, on the northern side of Lake Galvė off the road to Vievis, this camp site has accommodation to suit all budgets and comfort requirements. Basic lakeside huts are fine providing you have mosquito repellent. A sauna and steam bath (both 160Lt per two hours), sandy beach, folklore evenings and various sporting activities (above) ensure guests don't get bored. Campers can buy firewood (5Lt) and rent a floating BBQ with skewers for 20Lt (now how cool is that?).

Lakštas Farm (☎ 59 043, 8-698 16533; Varnikų Forest; d 120Lt; 🅿) Ecotourists with their own wheels or hiking boots should head for this farm, some 5km east of Trakai in Varnikų Forest. Camp here, stay in a wooden cabin or in the main farmhouse. From Trakai, follow the Vilnius road to Lentvaris, then turn left (north) along Rubežiaus gatvė. The third road on the left leads to the farm.

THE AUTHOR'S CHOICE

Akmeninė Užeiga (Lake Stone Inn; ☎ 25 186, 8-698 30544; www.akmenineuzeiga.lt; standard/lux/superlux d 295/640/675Lt, cottage 795Lt; 🅿) Find this traditional wood and thatched-roof hotel complex hidden on a lakeshore 2.5km north of Trakai. Nothing short of gorgeous, it comprises several luxury thatched cottages with fireplace and kitchen, and a main building where terraced rooms peep onto the water. Stylish dining (meals 50Lt) is beneath thatch or on a wooden jetty above the water – very romantic. Ladders lead into the water to swim, you can fish from a rowing boat and self-pamperers can watch DVDs in bed, sweat in a sauna or wallow in an outdoor Jacuzzi above the lake shore. Ice-fishing with hot rum tea is the thing to do in winter. To find Trakai's most magical and unique hide-out (there are no signs), follow the road north (signposted Vievis) out of central Trakai and almost immediately after passing Lakes Akmenos (left) and Galvės (right), turn left towards the thatched rooftops.

EATING

Akmeninė Užeiga (above) offers the best dining.

Kibininė (☎ 55 865; Karaimų gatvė 65; meals 20Lt) This green wooden house with Karaite kitchen is *the* spot to munch on traditional Karaite pasties called *kibinai* (like a Cornish pasty, served with a bread-based drink similar to *gira*). But beware that first bite – scalding-hot juices pour out. The pretty garden with lake view is particularly peaceful and a hole in the wall doles out meat- or veg-stuffed *kibinai* (3Lt to 3.60Lt) to take away.

Kybynlar (☎ 55 179; Karaimų gatvė 29; meals 20-40Lt; ⊠) There is a definite Turkic feel to Trakai's other Karaite-driven restaurant, where piping-hot pastries are likewise cooked up alongside a predominantly meat-based fare. The writing on the wall in Arabic is native Karaim, a language belonging to the Kipchak branch of Turkish languages and spoken as mother tongue by 535 people worldwide.

Buy picnics at **Iki** (☎ 54 628; Vytauto gatvė 56).

LITHUANIA

THE AUTHOR'S CHOICE

Žejų Namai (☎ 26 008; trout per kg 30Lt) For trout, fresher than fresh, motor 11km north of Trakai through pretty lake land to this one-of-a-kind restaurant. Kitted out with a couple of trout pools, a playground for kids and shaded bench seating around lakeside tables, this is the spot to lunch and have fun at the same time. Pick up a rod, bait and bucket and catch your own lunch. Staff are on hand to bash friskier fish over the head, after which the fish is weighed, filleted, cooked in a choice of spices and brought to your table on a platter. Other fishy delights include salted or smoked trout, herrings and bouillabaisse (fish soup). Žejų Namai is signposted 11km north of Trakai, off the road to Vievis.

LITHUANIA

GETTING THERE & AWAY

For buses and trains to/from Vilnius see p314 . Seven daily trains leave **Trakai station** (☎ 51 055; Vilniaus gatvė 5).

Centre of Europe

Lithuania is proud of its supposed geographic **Europos centras** (centre of Europe), 25km north of Vilnius off the Molėtai highway. Despite contrary claims, the French National Geographical Institute pronounced this central position – at a latitude of 54° 54' and longitude of 25° 19' – in 1989, marking it with a boulder inscribed with the points of the compass and the words 'Geografinis Europos Centras'. When Lithuania joined the EU in 2004 it brightened up the bleak spot with 27 fluttering flags (the EU flag plus that of each member country), a wooden decking stage and a phallic white granite obelisk with a crown of gold stars. The surrounding rolling hills were landscaped and a wooden house marked 'tourist information' set up to issue 'I've been to the centre of Europe' certificates for 5Lt a throw! Plans include a café and an 18-hole **golf course** (☎ 8-616 26 366; www.golfclub.lt) around Europe's disputed centre; nine holes might be complete by 2007.

Some 17km from the centre of Europe, off the Utena road, is **Europos parkas** (☎ 237 7077; www.europosparkas.lt; adult/student/child 18/12/6Lt, camera 6Lt; 🕑 9am-sunset). Leading contemporary sculptors, including Sol LeWitt and Dennis Oppenheim, show works in wooded parkland (bring mosquito repellent in summer). The sculpture park was the brainchild of Lithuanian sculptor Gintaras Karosas in response to the centre of Europe tag. Every year international workshops are held here, attracting artists from all over the world. Its café serves light lunches. Say you're an artist and you might be able to kip here.

GETTING THERE & AWAY

To get to the centre of Europe, turn left off the Vilnius–Molėtai road at the sign saying 'Europos Centras'; park in the car park at the foot of the hill and walk. Follow the dirt road for another 600m to get to the golf club.

From Vilnius, minibuses marked 'Europos parkas' leave from the bus stop on Kalvarijų gatvė for the Centre of Europe Museum or take trolleybus 10 to the Žalgirio stop or bus 36 to the end of the line. By car, head north along Kalvarijų gatvė until you reach the Santasriskių roundabout, then bear right towards Žalieji ežerai, following the signs for 'Europos parkas'.

Kernavė

Deemed an 'exceptional testimony to 10 millennia of human settlements in this region' by Unesco who made it a world heritage site in 2004, Kernavė – the 'Pompeii of Lithuania' – is a must-see. Thought to have been the spot where Mindaugas (responsible for uniting Lithuania for the first time) celebrated his coronation in 1253, the rural cultural reserve comprises four old castle mounds and the remains of a medieval town.

The fascinating heritage of the **Kernavė Cultural Reserve** (Kernavės kultūrinio rezervato; www.kernave.org) can be explored in the **Archaeological & Historical Museum** (Archeologijos ir istorijos muziejus; ☎ 382-47 385; kernave.archeo@is.lt; Kerniaus gatvė 4a; adult/student & child 3/1Lt, guided tour 22Lt; 🕑 10am-5pm Wed-Sun Apr-Oct, to 3pm Wed-Sun Nov-Mar).

Medieval fun and frolics – axe throwing, catapulting, mead making, medieval fights, music making and so on – fill Kernavė with festivity on 23 June and during the three-day International Festival of Experimental Archaeology (lots of fun despite the deadly name) in mid-July.

To reach Kernavė, 35km northwest of Vilnius in the Neris Valley, follow the road through Dūkštos from Maisiagala on the main road north to Ukmergė.

EASTERN & SOUTHERN LITHUANIA

The deep, magical forests of Lithuania's eastern and southern corners are a tree-hugger's paradise. Some of the most spectacular scenery in the Baltic region is found in these wildernesses, with a lake district that extends into Belarus and Latvia.

Aukštaitija National Park is Lithuania's oldest park, framed by the 900-sq-km Laboranas-Pabradė Forest. Exquisitely sweet and tiny wild strawberries are the pick of the abundant berry crop in early summer, while mushrooms of all shapes and guises sprout by the bucketful from early spring until late autumn. Skiing, canoeing, hiking, windsurfing, watching golden eagles and spotting black storks (white ones are everywhere) are the tip of the iceberg as far as outdoor pursuits are concerned.

Dzūkija in the far south is the biggest national park, surrounded by the 1500-sq-km Druskininkai-Varėna Forest. Nearby, on the Nemunas River, is the increasingly hip spa resort of Druskininkai, where Čiurlionis compositions serenade fat-walleted self-pamperers who come here on weekend breaks for warm honey massages. Next door at Grutas sculpture park reside Lenin, Stalin and Co – the main reason most people travel here.

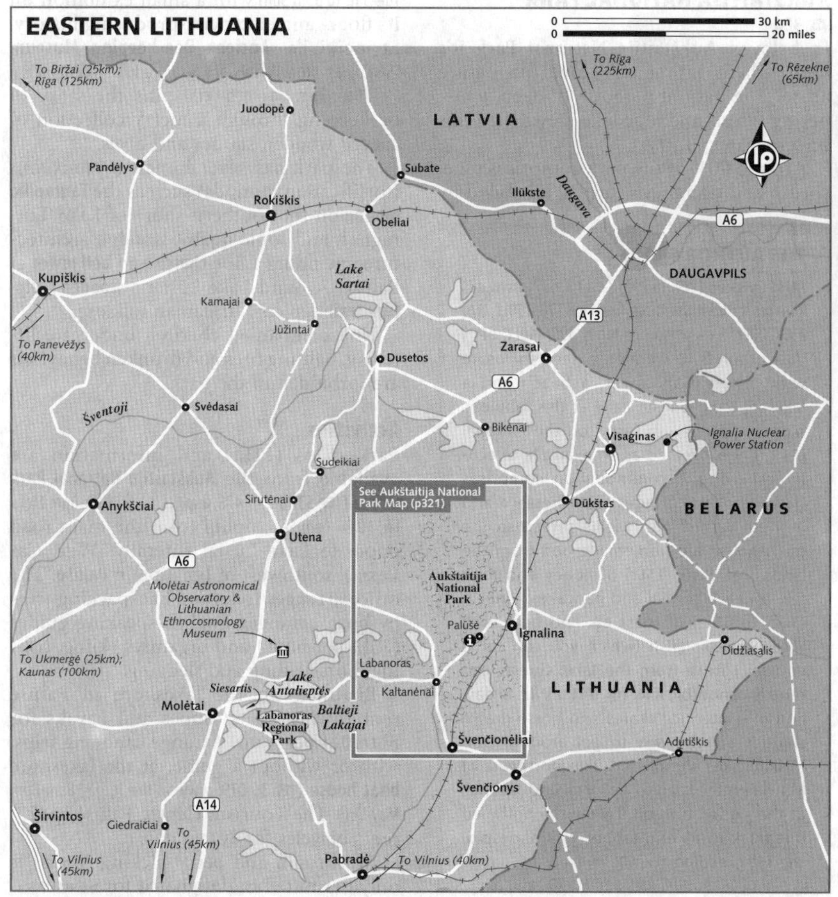

Dangers & Annoyances

Mosquitoes are a menace so bring insect repellent. Only pick mushrooms with a local guide and be aware that the stomach of the guide – reared on mushrooms since birth – is substantially more tolerant of certain species than your own.

Getting There & Around

The area is overwhelmingly rural and while travel to/from and around the region can be done by limited bus and train services to Druskininkai and other towns, nothing quite beats the freedom (buying mushrooms here) and flexibility (another extra night roughing it there) of your own wheels.

AUKŠTAITIJA NATIONAL PARK

☎ 386

In beloved Aukštaitija National Park it's clear where Lithuania's love for nature arose. The natural paradise of deep, whispering forests and blue lakes bewitched this once-pagan country.

Around 70% of the park comprises pine, spruce and deciduous forests, inhabited by elk, deer and wild boar. Its highlight is a labyrinth of 126 lakes, the deepest being **Lake Tauragnas** (60.5m deep). A footpath leads to the top of 155m **Ice Hill** (Ledakalnis), from where a panorama of some seven lakes unfolds. Particularly pretty is **Lake Baluošas**, ensnared by woods and speckled with islands. White-tailed and golden eagles prey here and storks are rife. The **Trainiškis Wildlife Sanctuary** and **Ažvinčiai Forest**, home to 150- to 200-year-old pine trees, can only be visited with park guides.

There are a hundred settlements within the park: **Šuminai**, **Salos II**, **Vaišnoriškės**, **Varniškės II** and **Strazdai** are protected ethnographic centres. **Ginučiai** has a 19th-century **watermill** (☎ 8-616 29366; adult/student 3/1Lt; ⏲ 10am-6pm Tue-Sat, to 5pm Sun) with a small exhibition on its flour- and electricity-producing history. Stripeikiai's **Ancient Bee-keeping Museum** (Senorinės bitininkystės muziejus; adult/student 3/1Lt; ⏲ 10am-7pm May–mid-Oct) spins the story of beekeeping through a merry collection of carved wooden statues and hives.

The park has several ancient *piliakalnis* (fortification mounds) such as the **Taurapilio mound** on the southern shore of Lake Tauragnas, and some quaint wooden architecture, including a fine **church** and **bell tower** at Palūsė. Around Lake Lūšiai a **wooden sculpture trail** depicts Lithuanian folklore.

Unaccompanied children under 16, littering, lighting fires and drunken behaviour are forbidden in the park.

THE AUTHOR'S CHOICE

Miškiniškės (☎ 36 296, 8-612 33577; www.miskiniskes.lt; d with/without fireplace 170/150Lt, tr/q 150/200Lt, 5-/6-person cottages 390/440Lt; Ⓟ) Vast grounds to wander, a deer enclosure with observation tower, a beach and a lake are icing on the cake at this fabulous hide-out, hidden in forest on the national park fringe. Created as an example of ecological living, accommodation comprises basic wooden cottages with fireplace and modern furnishings. Meals served in the main house are homemade and from the land: breakfasts (15Lt) of honey and mint tea, rhubarb cordial and pancakes; dinners (30Lt to 35Lt) of roast elk and boar with wild berries or fish (which you can catch yourself) fresh from the lake. Guests can rent a canoe/bicycle for 70Lt/35Lt a day, and in winter, ice skates and horse-drawn sledges are the way to get around. Find Miškininškės signposted 2km northeast of Minčia on the road to Apkartai and Jakenai; at the signed turn-off, follow the potholed dirt track to its end (about 2.5km, despite the sign reading '1km').

Activities

Park maps (11Lt) and information are available from the **Aukštaitija National Park Office** (☎ 53 135, 47 478; anp@is.lt; ⏲ 9am-6pm Mon-Fri, 10am-6pm Sat), uphill from the main road opposite Lake Lūsiai (literally 'Wild Cat Lake'), southwest of Ignalina in **Palūšė**. The office arranges treks and backpacking trips by boat, arranges English-speaking guides (30Lt per hour) and organises skiing, fishing, horse riding and sledging.

Boatmen on the lakeshore in Palūsė rent rowing boats/canoes and kayaks for 5Lt/10Lt per hour. Arrange canoeing trips, with or without a guide, at the lakeshore **boat house** (☎ 36 079; www.valtine.lt; ⏲ 8am-8pm May-Oct). The Tourism Centre Palūšė (p322) rents bicycles for 30Lt a day.

Mushroom and berry picking (p328) is only permitted in designated forest areas.

AUKŠTAITIJA NATIONAL PARK
0 5 km
0 3 miles
Minčia
Ažvintis
Miškininškės
Minčios Giria
Minčia
To Visaginas (25km); Zarasai (40km)
Rūgšteliškis
Ažvinčių Giria
Šeimatis
Utenas
Kazitiškis
Tauragnai
Tauragnas
Taurapilio Mound
Daunoriai
Ažvinčiai Forest Reserve
Lauksteniai
Būka
Miškas
Vaišnoriškės
Varniškės II
Pliaušė
Strazdai
Baluošas
Stripeikiai
Šuminai
Šiliniškės
Almajas
Trainiškis
Vaišniūnai
Ginučiai
Baltys
To Utena (20km)
Kirdeikiai
Trainiškis Wildlife Sanctuary
Ledakalnis
Drūkšis
Kemešys
Salos II
Asalnai
Gaveikėnai
Laimėstas
Ignalina
Saldutiškis
Antalksnė
Meironys
Lūšiai
Gavys
Pakalas
Palūšė
Linkmenys
Aisetas
Ūsiai
Kiauna
Gasiulių
Miškas
Vajuonis
Mekšrinis
Žeimenys
Labanoras
Baltas
Kaltanėnai
Pakretuonio Miškas
Kretuonas
Labanoras
Indrajai
Salaičiai
Liedis
Ilgis
Labanoras Regional Park
Peršokšna
Žeimena
Luknelė
Šventas
Dumblys
Girutiškis
Sirgėlis
Sibris
Žeimena
Kampuotis
Ešerinis
To Švenčionys (3km); Vilnius (85km)
Švenčionėliai

Sleeping

The national park office arranges homestay accommodation.

Tourism Centre Palūšė (☎ 52 891; www.paluse.lt; camp site for stays of less/more than 4 days 7/5Lt per day, wooden cabin 15Lt, d 60Lt, with shared bathroom 40Lt; P) The whole gamut of accommodation – camp sites to wooden cabins and comfy doubles with bathroom – is at this yellow wooden house opposite the national park office. Hire a tent/sleeping bag for 8Lt/6Lt per day.

Lithuanian Winter Sports Centre (Lietuvos žiemos sporto centras; ☎ 54 102, 54 193; www.lzsc.lt; Sporto gatvė 3, Ignalina; s/d/tr/apt 40/60/90/200Lt; P) Accommodation plays second fiddle at this Soviet-era sports centre where guests wake up, rent skis (5Lt/25Lt per hour/day) and leap on the ski lift (6Lt/30Lt per hour/day). Summer guests boat (5Lt per hour) on the lake or Rollerblade along a 7.5km track. From Ignalina centre, cross the train track and follow Budrių gatvė for 2km.

Getting There & Away

Hop in the car or jump on a train from Vilnius to Ignalina (10Lt, two hours, seven daily), from where you have to walk or hitch.

There is one bus daily from Vilnius (via Molėtai, Panevėžys and Marijampolė), two buses to/from Kaunas (29.50Lt, four hours) and three to/from Utena.

VISAGINAS & IGNALINA NUCLEAR POWER STATION

☎ 386 / pop 30,000

Doomed Visaginas is a town without a future: built in 1975 for workers of the Ignalina Nuclear Power Plant, the unlucky lakeside frontier was designed by the USSR for energy specialists seconded from the Soviet Union to oversee the plant's construction. With its EU-forced closure (scheduled for 2009), people are now leaving in droves – before they are left in a ghost town with no job and little prospect of getting one nearby.

The Soviet toy town, packed with identical-looking blocks of flats amid a forest, is circled by a ring road, along which buses shuttle 3500 shift workers between Visaginas and the plant, 2km east of the town centre. In its heyday 5000 people worked at Ignalina. A Geiger counter records the day's radiation level and Russian remains the language spoken on the streets.

There's **tourist office** (☎ 52 597; www.ignalina.lt; Taikos gatvė 11; 8am-6pm Mon-Fri, 9am-2pm Sat, 10am-3pm Sun) here and staying the night is a must if you're after the ultimate Soviet experience. This is, after all, the only Soviet city in the EU where nothing is more than 30 years old! **Hotel Aukštaitija** (☎ 50 686; www.mimina.surgardas.lt; Veteranų gatvė 9; d 250Lt; P) is the concrete block for the full Soviet throwback, and 10-room, spa-clad **Gabriella** (☎ 70 171; www.gabriella.lt; Jaunystės gatvė 21; s/d from 180/240Lt; P) is the place to avoid it.

In mid-August Visaginas bizarrely rocks with a bunch of cowboys – hats, boots and all – who groove on into town from across Europe for the two-day international country music festival, **Visagino Country** (www.visagino-country.lt). The tourist office knows all about it.

Getting There & Away

From Vilnius to Visaginas there are daily trains (12Lt, 1¾ to two hours, six daily) and the odd bus (12Lt, three hours).

IGNALINA

Ignalina (named after Ignalina region) looks uncannily like Springfield's nuclear power station in *The Simpsons* and it's just as safe say scientists. Unlike reactors in the West, its one remaining online RMBK reactor – the same design as Ukraine's Chornobyl reactor, which exploded in 1986 – is graphite-cooled and has no containment system. If an accident occurs, there is an increased chance of emissions escaping into the atmosphere. Until 2004 the plant met 80% of Lithuania's energy needs.

Enormous pressure from the EU forced a reluctant Lithuania to shut down the first reactor on 31 December 2004 and pledge to shut the second by the end of 2009. Millions of euros have been pumped into Ignalina to improve safety, and its eventual closure and the disposal of redundant radioactive material – the complete decommission process will take 30 years – will consume €3.2 billion at least.

To visit the site, see a video in English about Ignalina and play with a scaled-down model of the plant, ring Ignalina AE's **Information Centre** (☎ 29 911; www.iae.lt; 8am-4pm Mon-Fri).

LABANOROS REGIONAL PARK

West of Aukštaitija is 528 sq km of pretty parkland polka-dotted with 285 lakes. At its heart sits lovely **Labanoras**, home to the **Regional Park Information Centre** (☎ 838-731 357, 838-747 142; www.labanoroparkas.lt; 8am-noon & 1-5pm Mon-Fri, 8am-3pm Sat).

Canoeists can paddle until they drop with **Plaukių** (☎ 8-676 11086; www.plaukiu.com; Kalno gatvė 32) in Švenčionėliai. One-day canoe/kayak hire costs 40Lt/80Lt and those planning to stay overnight in the Labanoros or Aukštaitija parks can rent tent/sleeping bag/axe/kettle/skewers for 10Lt/10Lt/2Lt/5Lt/0.50Lt per day.

THE AUTHOR'S CHOICE

Hotel Restaurant Labanoras (☎ 8-655 70917; www.hotellabanoras.lt; meals 20-40Lt, d from 60Lt; P) This hotel-restaurant in Labanoras village, tucked in a pale peppermint-green house, is delightful. Its traditional wooden architecture and pretty terrace overlooking the village square make a bold contrast to the interior, crammed with collectables such as stuffed birds, padlocks and so on. The mushroom picker's stew, jam-packed with onions, lentils and locally picked and pickled green mushrooms, is delicious and the six rooms up top are divine. Guests can borrow a bike to explore the park.

Molėtai

☎ 383

A small town 30km west of the Aukštaitija National Park, Molėtai is unstartling bar its lake surrounds, on which its **tourist office** (☎ 51 187; www.infomoletai.lt; Inturkės gatvė 4; 8am-6pm Mon-Fri, 9am-1pm Sat) has information.

There are spectacular views of Molėtai's lake-studded landscape and the stars above from the **Molėtai Astronomical Observatory** (Molėtų astronomijos observatorija; ☎ 45 444; www.astro.lt/mao) on Kaldiniai Hill (193m). The observatory boasts northern Europe's largest telescope. Next door, hell, heaven and earth can be explored at the **Lithuanian Ethnocosmology Museum** (Lietuvos etnokosmologijos muziejus; ☎ 45 424/3). Ring in advance for opening hours and to book an English-speaking guide.

To get here, follow the Molėtai–Utena road for 10km, then turn right at the 'Lietuvos ethnokosmologijos muziejus' sign and follow the dirt track for 4km.

Utena

☎ 389 / pop 36,000

Utena, 34km north of Molėtai and a 101km drive from Vilnius, is famous for the Utenos beer it brews, and beer tourists should be able to visit the **Švyturys Utenos Alus brewery** (☎ 63 309; Pramonės gatvė 12). The **tourist office** (☎ 54 346; www.utenainfo.lt; Utenio aikstė 5; 9am-noon & 1-6pm Mon-Fri) can provide information.

Alaušynė (☎ 75 724; www.abuva.lt; wooden chalet 50Lt, d 250Lt; P), 12km northeast in the tiny village of Salos immediately north of Sudeikiai village, cooks up fish soup – swimming with six different of fish (including eel and carp) and served in a brown loaf of bread. This regional speciality must be ordered 48 hours in advance. The farmstead offers comfortable accommodation, meals for 30Lt, a sauna and also rents out boats.

LITHUANIA

THE AUTHOR'S CHOICE

Užeiga Prie Bravoro (☎ 385-56 653; cizoalus@takas.lt; Dusetų homestead; 10am-10pm Tue-Sun) It's not much to look at, but the story behind this brewery creates its soul. Four generations have brewed the light, thirst-quenching Čižo *alus* (beer) since 1863, teenage daughters Miglė and Rūta being let into the family secret on their 16th birthdays. The girls are now frequently found behind the bar at their family-run village inn, pulling a pint of the cloudy unfiltered beer, cooking up winter-warming beer soup or showing punters the old beer-making equipment their grandfather used to grind hops. Preservatives are a strict 'No No' and honey made by forest bees is the only sweetener.

Their father, Ramūnas, gave up his day job to run his brewery full time in 1995: brewing and selling beer was forbidden in the USSR, forcing the fourth-generation brewer to concoct in secret while working as an economist. Today he produces 12 tonnes annually and tours craft fairs and folk celebrations (he's always in Kernavė on 6 July). Find his brewery on the northern fringe of Dusetos village.

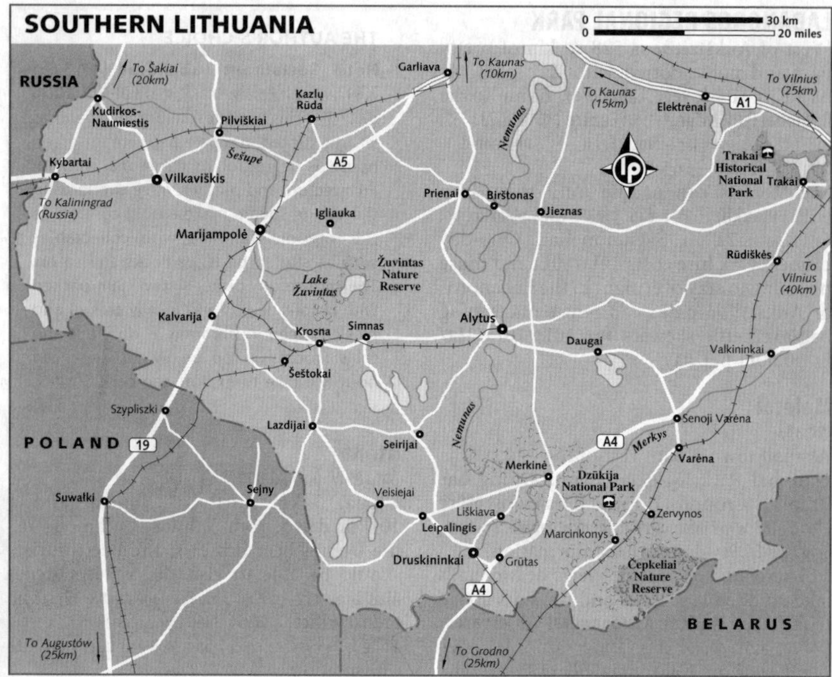

Geltonasis Submarine (☎ 50 223; www.submarinas.lt; Basanavičiaus gatvė 55; small/medium/large pizza 7/8/10Lt), a Beatles-inspired pizzeria that serves *pica su karka* (pizza with smoked pigs' trotters) is the cheeriest place to eat. **Iki** (Basanavičiaus gatvė 55; 8am-10pm) next door sells the makings of a lovely lakeside picnic.

From Utena **bus station** (☎ 61 740; Baranauskas gatvė 19) there are two daily buses to/from Ignalina (11Lt to 15Lt); up to eight daily to/from Vilnius (14.20Lt), a couple via Molėtai (10Lt to 12Lt) and eight daily to/from Kaunas (17.10Lt).

Around Utena

Some 34km northeast of Utena is **Dusetos**, known for its annual horse race held the first Saturday in February on frozen **Lake Sartai**. The race dates to 1865 and attracts horse enthusiasts, musicians and folk artists from all over the region, who pour into the small village to watch the race and slug local Čižo beer (p323).

A fun spot to play is **Bikėnų Uzeiga** (☎ 385-59 476; www.degesa.lt; 10am-10pm Apr-Sep), in Bikėnai on the eastern shore of **Lake Antalieptės**. The bar rents rowing boats, canoes and kayaks for 6Lt per hour, charters a 10-person speedboat (250Lt per hour), and has a water slide that snakes into the water at a terrifying pace. The centre also organises two-day canoeing expeditions (80Lt for a two-person canoe and tent hire) on the Šventoji River and has rooms to rent in lakeside houses – and in a floating wooden house (400Lt for eight people).

DRUSKININKAI

☎ 313 / pop 21,700

Nineteenth-century spa town Druskininkai on the Nemunas River is Lithuania's oldest and most chic. During the days of the USSR, the old and ailing flocked to this famous health resort in search of miracle cures for all sorts of ailments that its vast dinosaur sanatoriums treated. Today, as investments flood in, Druskininkai is shedding its fusty old grey-haired image. Chic weekend spa breaks for young, hip and wealthy Lithuanians seeking a quick detox from city life is what makes Druskininkai tick these days.

Salty mineral water aide, Druskininkai was the home of romantic painter and composer Mikalojus Konstantinas Čiurlionis (p281). Around the corner is the Baltics' only Soviet sculpture park.

Information

Internetas Visiems (www.vija.lt; Čiurlionio gatvė 4a; 9am-6pm Mon-Fri) Internet.
Post office (Kudirkos gatvė)
Tourist office former train station building (☎ 60 800; Gardino gatvė 3; 8.30am-12.15pm & 1-5.15pm Mon-Fri); Town Centre (☎ 51 777; www.druskininkai.lt; Čiurlionio gatvė 65; 10am-1pm & 1.45-6.45pm Mon-Sat, 10am-5pm Sun)
Vilniaus Bankas (Čiurlionio gatvė 40; Vilniaus alėja 16) Currency exchange inside, ATM outside.

Sights

Lithuania's most talented painter-musician spent his childhood in what is now the **MK Čiurlionis Memorial Museum** (☎ 52 755; Čiurlionio gatvė 41; adult/student 3/1.50Lt; 11am-5pm Tue-Sun). A **statue** of Čiurlionis stands at the northern end of Kudirkos gatvė. Both the museum and the open-air stage in front of the **Cultural Centre** (Vilniaus alėja 24) host beautiful classical concerts during the 'Druskininkai Summer with Čiurlionis' festival (June to September).

To see Druskininkai past and present, follow Čiurlionio gatvė to its northern end and turn right (east) along Liepu gatvė to Laisvės aikštė. On this vast tree-shaded square, one of the USSR's biggest and best, 10-storey **Nemunas Sanitorium** contrasts with the modern glass façade of Medūna (p327). The pretty, blue, multidomed **Russian Orthodox Church** in the square's middle dates to the 19th century.

Heading south, the **Jewish Museum** (☎ 53 100; Sv Jokūbo gatvė 17; 11am-5pm Tue-Thu May-Oct) commemorates Druskininkai-born sculptor Jacques Lipchitz.

The magical powers of local mineral water can be tested at the Dzūkija Fountain inside the **Mineralinio Vandems Biuvetė** (per cup 0.30Lt or per 10/20 days 5/9.50Lt; 11.30am-1.30pm & 4-7pm Mon-Fri, 10.30am-1.30pm Sat), a round green building with mosaic floor and stained-glass windows on the footpath running along the Nemunas. Continue north to the **Fountain of Beauty**

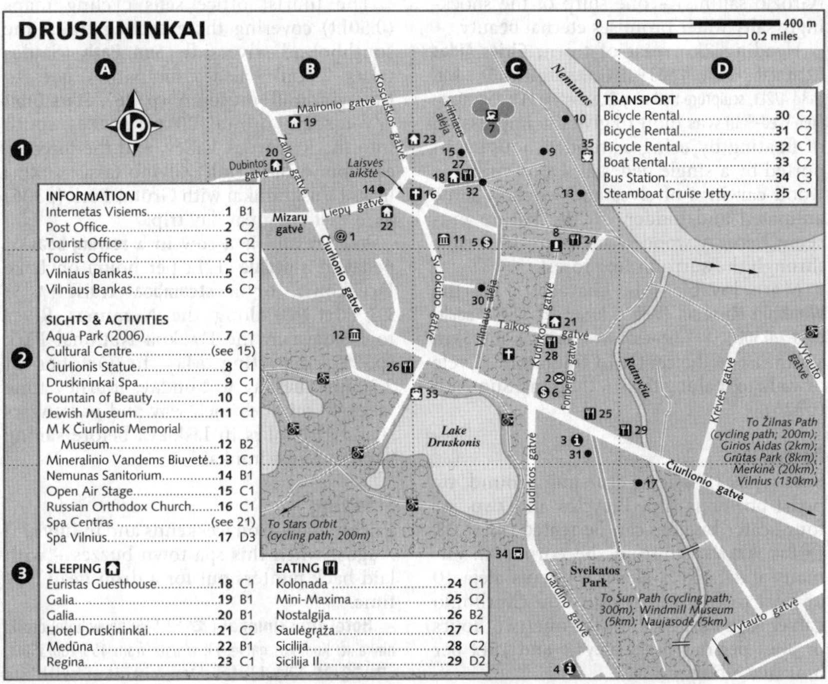

STALIN WORLD

Headline-grabbing Grūtas Park opened amid controversy in 2001. Dubbed Stalin World, this collection of bronze sculptures once stared down Big Brother–style at oppressed Lithuanians in parks and squares countrywide. The former head of a collective farm, Viliumas Malinauskas made his fortune canning mushrooms then won the loan of the hated objects from the Ministry of Culture in 1999 and transformed part of his 2-sq-km estate into a Soviet sculpture park.

Built to resemble a Siberian concentration camp, the park entrance is marked by a Soviet-Polish border crossing with barbed wire, red-and-white (Polish) and red-green (USSR) striped poles. Next to it is a single carriage in which Lithuanians were deported to Siberia. Once through the turnstile, Russian tunes blast from watchtowers, and in the restaurant, visitors eat vodka-doused sprats and onions with Soviet-made cutlery. Tacky souvenir stalls are rife; there is a playground with old Soviet swings and a mini children's zoo – all of which lends itself to critics branding the park a diabolical version of Disney.

Yet the park's attention to detail – reflected in the reconstructed rural Soviet polling station where visitors can sign the park's visitors' book – is impressive. In another building Soviet art is displayed and a stained-glass gallery is planned. Top of the bill are 13 Lenins, two Stalins, six Kapsukas and various other communist heroes.

Accused of trivialising Soviet horrors, Malinauskas, whose father spent 10 years in Siberian camps, said: 'This is a place reflecting the painful past of our nation which brought pain, torture and loss. One cannot forget or cross out history – whatever it is'.

Find **Grūtas Park** (Grūto parkas; ☎ 313-55 511; www.grutoparkas.lt; adult/5-16yr 10/3Lt, camera/video camera 5/10Lt; ⏲ 9am-8pm) 8km east of Druskininkai; entering Grūtas village from the south, turn left (west) off the main road and follow the road 1km to its end.

(Grožio šaltinis) – one slurp of the shockingly salty water promises eternal beauty.

Heading 2km east of town, **Girios Aidas** (Echo of the Forest; ☎ 53 901; Čiurlionio gatvė 102; adult/child 4/2Lt, sculpture trail only 2Lt, camera 2Lt; ⏲ 10am-6pm Wed-Sun) was built to give the impression of floating by using a wooden house supported by a single pedestal. Don't miss the wood carvings of elves and witches, some animated and hidden, in the nature museum here. A wooden sculpture trail runs through the surrounding forest.

More lovable folk characters fill the **Windmill Museum** (Vėjo malūnas; ☎ 52 448; adult/child 2/0.50Lt; ⏲ 10am-6pm Wed-Sun), about 5km southeast of the centre in Naujasodė. Cycle or walk to it along the southbound Sun Path (p326).

Activities

Spas (p327) aside, cruising around by pedal-power is hip. Bicycles and two- or four-seater buggies can be **rented** (☎ 52 318; ⏲ 8am-9pm May-Oct) from the corner of Vilniaus and Laisvės alėjas, Vilniaus alėja 10 or next to the tourist office on Čiurlionio gatvė. Rates are 5Lt/8Lt for one/two hours or 30Lt per day for a bicycle and 15Lt per hour for a buggy.

The tourist office sells cycling maps (0.50Lt) covering three cycling trails: the southbound riverside **Sun Path** (Saulės takas; 24km) – also a footpath – goes to the windmill museum (p326), **Stars Orbit** (Žvaigzdžių orbita; 20km) snakes south into the Raigardas Valley, and the forested eastbound **Žilnas Path** (Žilvino takas; 20km) links Druskininkai with Grūtas Park (p326) 8km east – a great day trip.

Very restful is a row in a **rowing boat** or pedal in a **pedalo** (12Lt per hour) on Lake Druskonis, or a **steamboat cruise** (☎ 53 393; ticket 24Lt) along the Nemunas River to Liškiava in the Dzūkija National Park (p328), departing May to October at 2.30pm Tuesday to Sunday. Journey time takes 45 minutes each way and passengers spend 1½ hours in Liškiava before sailing back to Druskininkai.

Sleeping

Prices increase on weekends and in July and August when this spa town buzzes – with laid-back punters out for a drop-dead lazy time.

Hotel Druskininkai (☎ 52 566; www.hotel-druskininkai.lt; Kudirkos gatvė 43; s/d/ste from 150/200/350Lt; P ⊠ ✲ 🖳) Hotel Druskininkai with its striking glass-and-wood façade is living proof that Soviet blocks can be transformed beyond recognition. Luxury suites have terrace and steam booth and everyone can use the Turkish bath, the Jacuzzi bubbling with Druskininkai mineral water, and the hotel gym.

Regina (☎ 59 060; www.regina.lt; Kosciuškos gatvė 3; s/d/ste from 129/179/400Lt, P) Regina strives to be an anywhere-in-the-world hotel, but trips up on the detail: no lift, amusing mistakes in the English menu and tiny, wafer-thin paper napkins in the restaurant (meals 40Lt to 80Lt).

Galia (☎ 60 510; www.galia.lt; Maironio gatvė 3, Dubintos gatvė 3 & 4; d from 250Lt; P) Galia surprises with a rainbow of colours. The hotel has several buildings, so confirm which is yours before checking in; the Maironio one is a candyfloss-pink affair with dark furnishings and Soviet stained glass.

Euristas Guesthouse (☎ 52 318, 8-618 00441; euris ta@one.lt; Laisvės alėja 1 22; d 80-100Lt; P) Scandinavian-style rooms lounge in a green-stained wooden house behind the souvenir stalls off the main pedestrian avenue. If no-one is at home, check in at the pizzeria next door.

Medūna (☎ 58 033; www.meduna.lt; Liepų gatvė 2; s/d/ste from 69/89/200; P) No English appears to be spoken at the Meduna, a bold example of contemporary architecture. Interior furnishings are less inspiring.

Eating

The dining scene is limited, rendering unremarkable hotel restaurants like Regina a serious option.

Kolonada (☎ 51 222, 8-612 11088; www.kolonada .lt; Kurdikos gatvė 22; meals 30-50Lt) This renovated late-1920s music hall propped up by classical columns oozes atmosphere. Have a terrace lunch with river view or sip apéritifs at dusk against a backdrop of local jazz (Friday), blues and rock 'n' roll (Saturday) or classical music (Sunday). A fireplace hangs inside.

Saulėgrąža (☎ 52 254; Vilniaus alėja 22; meals 20-30Lt) Saulėgrąža stands out as a happening bar with reliable Lithuanian- and American-style pizzas, a pool hall and a decking terrace with a view to slurp beer on.

Nostalgija (Čiurlionio gatvė 55; meals 30Lt) A shady terrace staring out across Lake Druskonis is the drawcard of Nostalgija, which has a beer hall like a boat and a minimalist café.

Sicilija (☎ 51 865; Taikos gatvė 9; meals 30Lt) Pizza – 60 varieties – is the speciality of this dining spot, which runs a second, industrial-styled outlet, **Sicilija II** (☎ 57 258; Čiurlionio gatvė 56).

Self-caterers can stock up at **Mini-Maxima** (Čiurlionio gatvė 50).

TOP DRUSKININKAI SPAS

Druskininkai is spa-riddled. But beware. Not all are swish. Step into the wrong place and you could be slapped around by a formidable babushka straight out of a horror movie.

Hot-choice **Spa Centras** (☎ 60 523; Kudirkos gatvė 43), inside Hotel Druskininkai, has separate bubbling pools, inviting serious wallowers to pick from Dead Sea water (36Lt per 20 minutes), local mineral water or good old tap water (25Lt per hr). On the massage front (65Lt per hr), the body pummel with warm honey – a stronger massage than with regular or aromatic oil – wins hands down, although the massage with silky-smooth hot Hawaii stones is heavenly.

Equally striking designwise is **Spa Vilnius** (☎ 53 811; www.spa-vilnius.com; Dineikos gatvė 1). This spa, with a retro 1950s-style café-bar inside an eight-storey hotel, sports the best indoor swimming pool (filled with local mineral water) and a clutch of baths, including one with seaweed (30Lt) and another with mud (10Lt). It also offers the full range of massages, including underwater body (25Lt per 30 minutes) and Shiatsu foot (40Lt per 30 minutes) ones. Scary-sounding things like intestine showers and gynaecologic irrigations are other mineral-water treatments on offer.

Then there's **Druskininkai Spa** (Druskininkų gydykla; ☎ 60 508; www.gydykla.lt; Vilniaus alėja 11), a peppermint-green, riverside building propped up by marble columns. Pearl, herbal, mineral, mud and even vertical baths are among its wonderful watery delights. It likewise treats a mind-boggling array of diseases – cardiovascular, cutaneous, vestibular, endocrinal etc.

Next door, a €12 million **aqua park** (Vendens parkas) promises to be Druskininkai's biggest attraction, opening in late 2006. It's set in a magnificent Soviet complex comprising three crab-shaped buildings joined together in a clover-leaf formation.

Getting There & Away

From the **bus station** (☎ 51 333; Gardino gatvė 1), there are up to 10 daily buses (19Lt, two hours) to/from Vilnius; seven buses daily to/from Kaunas (19Lt, two to three hours), one of which continues to/from Palanga (46.50Lt), one to/from Panevėžys (33Lt) and one to/from Šiauliai (39Lt).

DZŪKIJA NATIONAL PARK

☎ 310

This lush mushroom-picking and berrying spot (see p328) is the perfect place to evict a few gnomes from their mushroom homes. Covering 550 sq km, the park is Lithuania's largest with four-fifths covered by dense pine forest. Between Marcinkonys and the Belarusian border, the **Čepkeliai Strict Nature Reserve** safeguards the country's largest marsh. The Ūla and Grūda Rivers cross the park and 48 lakes polka-dot it.

Several villages, including **Zervynos**, between Varėna and Marcinkonys, are ethnographic reserves. **Liškiava**, 10km northeast of Druskininkai, has remnants of a 14th-century hill-top **castle**. The village **church** and former Dominican monastery is famous for its seven rococo-style altars and its crypt with glass coffins. **Merkinė**, 10km further down the Nemunas, is the starting point for a 12km **black potters' trail** around workshops where pots as black as soot are made from red clay. The extraordinary colour comes from pinewood resin fired with the pot in an outdoor kiln. Other traditions like woodcarving, weaving, basket-making and beekeeping come to life in Marcinkonys' **Ethnographic Museum** (Marcinkonių etnografijos muziejus; ☎ 8-616 52623; Miškininkų gatvė 7; adult/child 2/1Lt; 🕑 9am-4pm Tue-Sat May-Sep, 10am-4pm Tue-Sat Oct-Apr).

Visitor centres in **Marcinkonys** (☎ 44 466; info@dzukijosparkas.lt; Miškininkų gatvė 61; 🕑 8am-5.30pm Mon-Fri, 9am-6pm Sat) and **Merkinė** (☎ 57 245; merkine@dzukijosparkas.lt; Vilniaus gatvė 3; 🕑 8am-noon & 1-5pm Mon-Thu, 8am-3.45pm Fri) advise on walking, cycling and canoeing along the Ūla, and on arranging English-speaking guides (30/100Lt per hour/day) to take you mushrooming or berrying. The centres also have information on the 14km **Zackagiris Walking Trail**, with shorter 7km and 10.5km routes, which starts outside Marcinkonys visitor centre.

Falling just outside the boundaries of the park, 22km northeast of Marcinkonys and 58km northeast of Druskininkai, is **Varėna** (www.varena.lt). Founded in the 15th century when Grand Duke Vytautas built a hunting lodge here, it is the birthplace of Čiurlionis. The main road (A4) leading from Varėna to Druskininkai is lined with sculpted wooden 'totem' poles and sculptures, erected in 1975 in commemoration of the 100th anniversary of his birth.

Sleeping

The visitor centre arranges homestay accommodation (35Lt to 100Lt per person); camping is only allowed in designated areas.

MUSHROOMING & BERRYING

Mushrooming is a blooming business, particularly in the Aukštaitija and Dzūkija National Parks, which, come August and September, are carpeted with little white and yellow buttons. The forests lining the Varėna–Druskininkai highway (A4) and the Zervynos forests – best known for sand dunes, beehive hollows and substantial *grybas* (mushroom) populations – make rich *grybaula* (mushroom-hunting grounds) too. For mushroom addicts, there's Varėna's September mushroom festival.

The crinkle-topped, yellow chanterelle and stubby *boletus* are among the edible wild mushroom varieties hunted and exported to other parts of Europe. The less common *baravykas,* with its distinctive brown cap, is a stronger-tasting mushroom that ends up stuffed inside a *cepelinai* (zeppelin-shaped parcels of thick potato dough stuffed with cheese, meat or mushrooms) or dried and stored until Christmas Eve, when it is served as one of the 12 dishes (p285). Lithuania boasts 1200 mushroom species; 100 are poisonous and 380 edible.

Berrying is another trade and tradition. Red bilberries can only be picked in August and cranberries in September, but most other berries – wild strawberries, blueberries, buckthorn berries, sloe berries and raspberries – can be harvested whenever they are ripe.

The roadside rate for mushrooms is around 15Lt per kilogram. Look for locals selling at roadsides, glass jam jars overflowing with freshly picked forest goodies lined up on car bonnets. The mushroom season runs early spring to late autumn.

Zervynos Hostel (☎ 8-687 50826; dm 10Lt) Affiliated to the Lithuanian Hostels Association, this rural idyll has two wooden turn-of-the-20th-century cottages, one with wood-burning stove, the other with no heating. Both have basic bunks and no running water (bathe in the river and pee in the bushes). Meals cost 5Lt to 7Lt. There is a sauna (17Lt an evening) and it organises mushrooming, berrying and canoeing expeditions on the Ūla River. Call in advance (little English is spoken) and someone will meet you at Zervynos train station. By car, Zervynos Hostel is at the end of a 3km gravel road, signposted off the main Varėna–Marcinkonys road (take the right fork at the end).

Getting There & Away

In summer a **steamboat** (☎ 53 393; ticket 24Lt) makes half-day trips from Druskininkai to Liskiava.

The four buses to/from Druskininkai and Vilnius stop at the Merkinė intersection (Merkinės kryžkelė), 2km east of Merkinė town centre.

Six daily trains to/from Vilnius stop at Zervynos (10Lt, two hours).

THE SOUTHWEST

Southwestern Lithuania is a rural pocket few venture into bar Poland-bound travellers who drive through **Lazdijai**, 43km northwest of Druskininkai, or rattle by train through **Šeštokai**, 18km north of Lazdijai, en route to Suwałki (Poland).

The main approach to the Kalvarija–Suwałki road border crossing with Poland is through **Marijampolė** (population 69,900), the largest southwestern town, with an attractive 1920s train-station building, a neobaroque twin-towered basilica (1824) and a small Old Town. Six bridges cross the Šešupė River, dividing old town from new, and an **Ethnographic Museum** (☎ 343-93 042; Vytauto gatvė 31; adult/child 2/1Lt; 10am-6pm Tue-Sun) reflects daily southwestern life a couple of centuries ago. The **tourist office** (☎ 343-51 109; jotva@mari.omnitel.net; Kudirkos gatvė 41) and municipality website (www.marijampole.lt) are handy info sources.

Pretty **Alytus**, in a 16km loop of the Nemunas River 72km southeast, is the capital of the southern ethnographic Dzūkija region. Cycling paths are plentiful and the town is a springboard for forays into the **Žuvintas Nature Reserve**, an important breeding ground for birds. Alytus **tourist office** (☎ 315-52 010; www.alytus.lt; Rotušės aikšte 14a) has information on bird-watching, boats and bicycles.

Sleeping & Eating

Both towns have a handful of places to stay and eat. Standouts:

Hotel Sudavija (☎ 343-52 995; www.sudavija.com; Sodo gatvė 1a, Marijampolė; s/d/ste 150/180/200Lt; P) This atmospheric, cream-and-white mansion set amid parkland off Vytauto gatvė boasts three stars and a restaurant that makes tummies rumble.

Keta (☎ 315-52 264; Gedimino gatvė 1a, Alytus; meals 20Lt; 10am-midnight) There is no mistaking you're in provincial Lithuania at this rustic restaurant where traditional cuisine is served in a folkloric setting. Note the old weaving loom.

Getting There & Away

Buses run to Marijampolė from Kaunas, and to Lazdijai from Druskininkai, Kaunas and Vilnius. Four trains run to Šeštokai from Kaunas via Marijampolė, one from Vilnius (on even days). For details on getting to/from Poland, see p396.

CENTRAL LITHUANIA

Central Lithuania is a strange brew. More of an accidental stopover point en route to somewhere else rather than a destination in itself, this large flat area is invariably written off as dull and short on vision. Yet it proffers a couple of Lithuania's most bizarre and blackest sights.

Three cities form a neat triangle. Complacent Kaunas, primary kick-off point for central-country forays, still rides on its sterling reputation as alternative Lithuanian capital during the interwar period when Vilnius was part of Poland. And indeed, it's got a great palace to prove it presidential past. But, say critics, Kaunas must brush up and progress if it wants to stay in today's EU-driven game. The exciting arrival of no-frills budget airline Ryanair to Kaunas in September 2005, not to mention the hoards of Brits it brings on the cheap, could be the catalyst.

Then there's Šiauliai, a closed city in Soviet times that sheltered the USSR's largest military base outside Russia, and today the

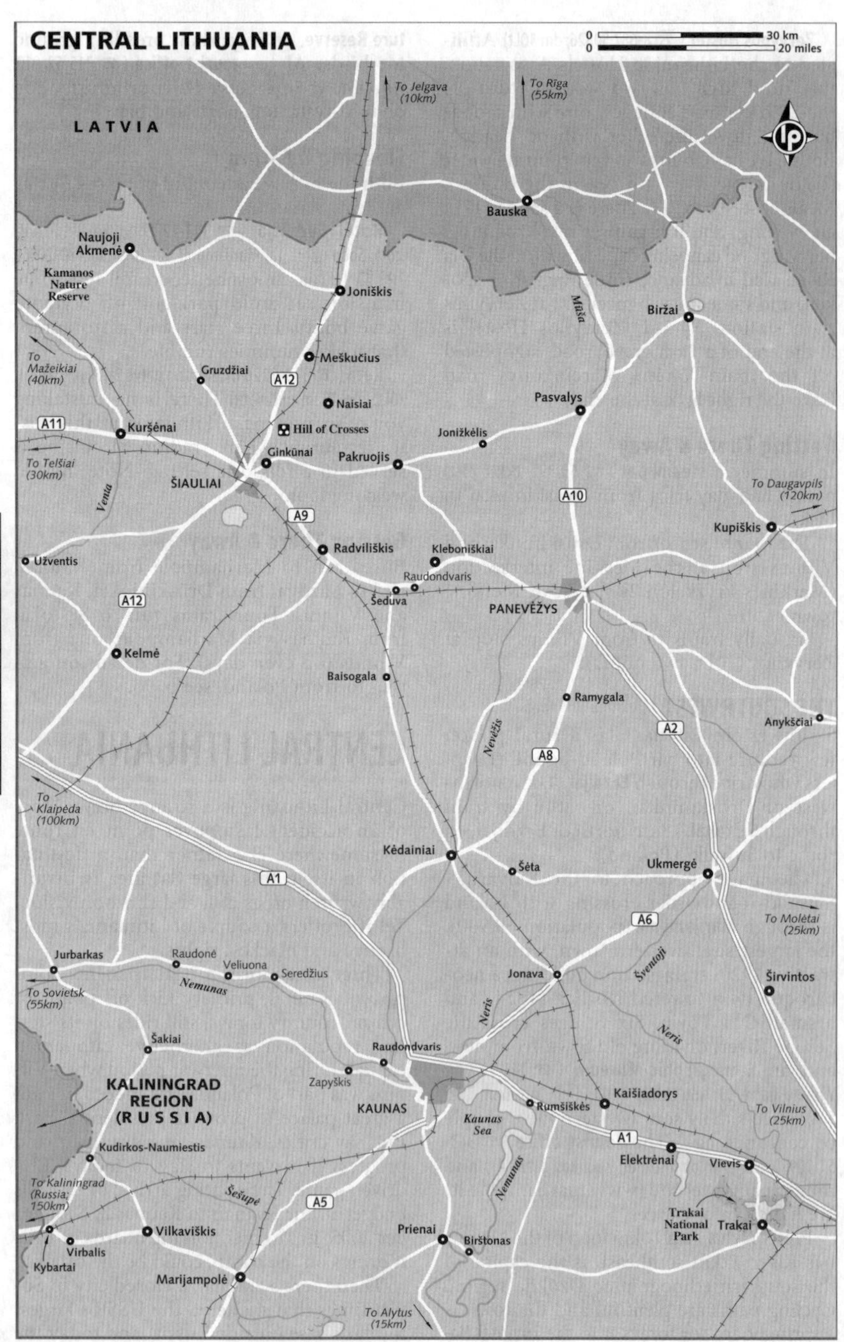
CENTRAL LITHUANIA
0 30 km
0 20 miles
LATVIA
To Jelgava (10km)
To Rīga (55km)
Bauska
Naujoji Akmenė
Kamanos Nature Reserve
Joniškis
Biržai
Mūša
To Mažeikiai (40km)
Meškučius
Gruzdžiai
A12
Naisiai
Pasvalys
A11
Kuršėnai
Hill of Crosses
Joniškėlis
To Telšiai (30km)
Ginkūnai
Pakruojis
ŠIAULIAI
Venta
A10
To Daugavpils (120km)
A9
Kupiškis
Radviliškis
Kleboniškiai
Užventis
Raudondvaris
Šeduva
PANEVĖŽYS
Kelmė
Baisogala
Ramygala
Anykščiai
A2
Nevėžis
A8
To Klaipėda (100km)
Kėdainiai
Šėta
Ukmergė
A1
A6
To Molėtai (25km)
Jurbarkas
Raudonė
Veliuona
Seredžius
Jonava
Šventoji
Širvintos
To Sovietsk (55km)
Nemunas
Neris
Šakiai
Raudondvaris
Zapyškis
KALININGRAD REGION (RUSSIA)
KAUNAS
Rumšiškės
Kaišiadorys
Kaunas Sea
To Vilnius (25km)
Kudirkos-Naumiestis
Elektrėnai
Vievis
To Kaliningrad (Russia; 150km)
Šešupė
A5
Nemunas
Trakai National Park
Trakai
Vilkaviškis
Prienai
Birštonas
Virbalis
Kybartai
Marijampolė
To Alytus (15km)

LITHUANIA

place from which Baltic skies are policed by NATO air forces. Learning how enterprising locals made a living from syphoned-off fuel intended for Soviet MiG-29 fighters is enlightening. The same incredible spirit of resilience pervades the obligatory pilgrimage tourists make 12km north to Lithuania's strangest monument, the papal-blessed Hill of Crosses.

Throw into the melting pot 'Chicago of Lithuania' Panevėžys, the black fort where Nazis murdered the region's Jewish population, a crook of a nature park, top-brand beers and the Baltic's biggest jazz festival – and that stop in the centre of the country might just become far from accidental.

Getting There & Away

The region is well linked by public transport to Vilnius, Klaipėda and other major towns (see p338), and Panevėžys is a major stop on the bus route to/from Rīga. By the time you read this, a hydrofoil will sail along the Nemunas River from Kaunas to/from Rusnė and Nida in Western Lithuania.

KAUNAS

☎ 37 / pop 415,800

Kaunas has a reputation as a sprawling urban city and a hotbed of post-Soviet mafia. Think again. This vibrant city, the second largest in Lithuania, is a thriving cultural and industrial centre with an interesting Old Town.

Legend has it that Kaunas, 100km west of Vilnius at the confluence of the Nemunas and Neris Rivers, was founded by the son of tragic young lovers. Beautiful maiden Milda let the Holy Eternal Flame go out while caring for her lover Daugerutis. They were sentenced to death by vengeful gods, thus they fled to a cave and gave birth to Kaunas.

Archaeologists insist the city dates from the 13th century and until the 15th century was in the front line against the Teutonic Order in Lithuania's west. Kaunas became a successful river-trading town in the 15th and 16th centuries. German merchants were influential here, and there was a Hanseatic League office. Its strategic position is the main reason it was destroyed 13 times before WWII – when it once again received a battering.

Today it is a town with a sizable student population, some fine architecture, plenty of museums and terrible food.

Orientation

Rotušės aikštė, the square wedged between the Nemunas and Neris Rivers, is the historic heart. From here pedestrian Vilniaus gatvė runs east to meet the city's main axis, Laisvės alėja – also pedestrian. The bus and train stations are 900m and 1.25km respectively south of the eastern end of Laisvės alėja.

MAPS

Jāņa sēta publishes the *Kaunas City Plan* (1:25,000), sold in bookshops and supermarkets.

Information

BOOKSHOPS

Centrinis Knygynas (☎ 229 572; Laisvės alėja 81) Maps, English-language newspapers and magazines.

Humanitas (☎ 209 581; Vilniaus gatvė 11) English-language books.

INTERNET ACCESS

Kavinė Internetas (☎ 407 427; www.café net.ot.lt; Vilniaus gatvė 26; per hr 4Lt; 🕒 8.15am-midnight) Old Town Internet café.

INTERNET RESOURCES

Kaunas (www.kaunas.lt) Official city website.

MEDICAL SERVICES

Gintarinė vaistinė (Vilniaus gatvė 35; 🕒 8am-8pm Mon-Fri, 9am-3pm Sat, 10am-5pm Sun) Pharmacy.

MEDIA

Kaunas In Your Pocket Annual city guide sold in hotels, art galleries and news kiosks for 5Lt; download it in PDF format at www.inyourpocket.com.

MONEY

For currency exchange inside; ATM accepting Visa and MasterCard outside:

Hansa Bankas (Vilniaus gatvė 13; Laisvės alėja 79)

Snoras Bankas (Laisvės alėja 60)

Vilniaus Bankas (Vilniaus gatvės 43)

POST

Post office (Laisvės alėja 102)

TOURIST INFORMATION

Tourist office (☎ 323 436; http://visit.kaunas.lt; Laisvės alėja 36; 🕒 9am-6pm Mon-Fri, 9am-1pm & 2-6pm Sat & Sun Jun-Sep, 9am-6pm Mon-Fri, 9am-1pm & 2-6pm Sat Oct-May) Books accommodation, sells maps and guides; arranges bicycle rental.

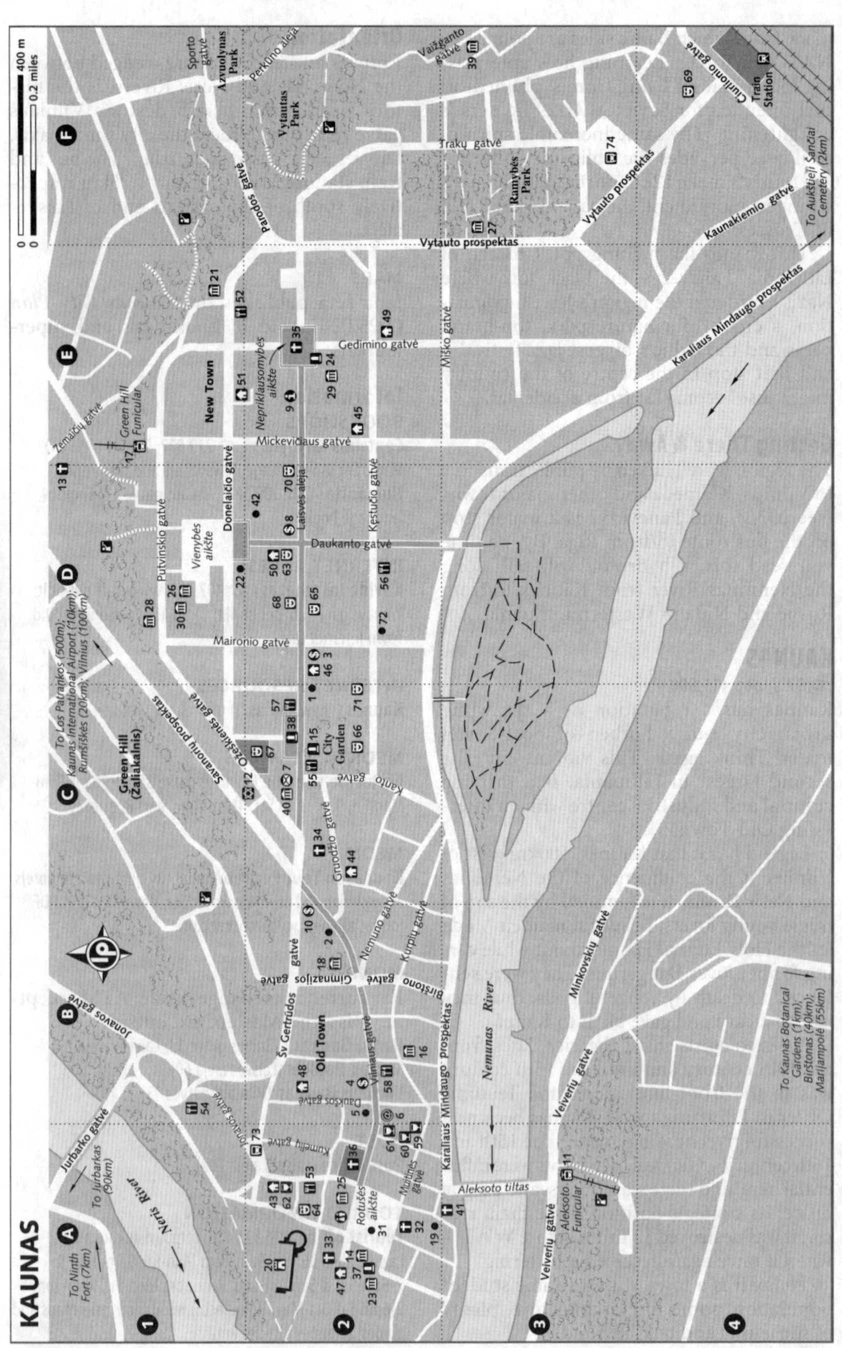
KAUNAS
LITHUANIA
Old Town
New Town
Green Hill (Žaliakalnis)
Vytautas Park
Azvuolynas Park
Ramybės Park
City Garden
Nemunas River
Neris River
Rotušės aikštė
Nepriklausomybės aikštė
Vienybės aikštė
Green Hill Funicular
Aleksoto Funicular
Aleksoto tiltas
Train Station
Laisvės alėja
Donelaičio gatvė
Kęstučio gatvė
Miško gatvė
Gedimino gatvė
Mickevičiaus gatvė
Daukanto gatvė
Maironio gatvė
Putvinskio gatvė
Savanorių prospektas
Ožeškienės gatvė
Vytauto prospektas
Karaliaus Mindaugo prospektas
Kaunakiemio gatvė
Čiurlionio gatvė
Trakų gatvė
Parodos gatvė
Perkūno alėja
Vaižganto gatvė
Sporto gatvė
Žemaičių gatvė
Šv Gertrūdos gatvė
Gimnazijos gatvė
Gruodžio gatvė
Kanto gatvė
Nemuno gatvė
Kurpių gatvė
Birštono gatvė
Vilniaus gatvė
Daukšos gatvė
Kumelių gatvė
Muitinės gatvė
Jonavos gatvė
Jurbarko gatvė
Veiverių gatvė
Minkovskių gatvė
To Los Patrankos (500m); Kaunas International Airport (10km); Rumšiškės (20km); Vilnius (100km)
To Ninth Fort (7km)
To Jurbarkas (90km)
To Kaunas Botanical Gardens (1km); Birštonas (40km); Marijampolė (55km)
To Aukštieji Šančiai Cemetery (2km)
0 400 m
0 0.2 miles

INFORMATION
Centrinis Knygynas......1 C2
Gintarinė vaistinė......2 B2
Hansa Bankas......3 D2
Hansa Bankas......4 B2
Humanitas......5 B2
Kavinė Internetas......6 B2
Post Office......7 C2
Snoras Bankas......8 D2
Tourist Office......9 E2
Vilniaus Bankas......10 B2

SIGHTS & ACTIVITIES
Aleksoto Funicular......11 A3
Ceramics Museum......(see 31)
Choral Synagogue......12 C2
Christ's Resurrection Basilica......13 D1
Communications Development Museum......14 A2
Field of Sacrifice......15 C2
Folk Music & Instruments Museum......16 B2
Green Hill Funicular......17 E1
Historical Presidential Palace of Lithuania......18 B2
Holy Trinity Church......(see 47)
House of Perkūnas......19 A2
Jesuit Monastery......(see 32)
Kaunas Castle......20 A2
Kaunas Picture Gallery......21 E1
Kaunas Technological University......22 D1
Maironis Lithuanian Literary Museum......23 A2
Maironis' Tomb......(see 36)
Man Statue......24 E2
Medicine & Pharmaceutical History Museum......25 A2
Military Museum of Vytautas the Great......26 D1
Museum of Deportation & Resistance......27 F3
Museum of Devils......28 D1
Mykolas Žilinskas Art Gallery......29 E2
National Čiurlionis Art Museum......30 D1
Palace of Weddings......31 A2
St Francis Church......32 A2
St George's Church......33 A2
St Gertrude's Church......34 C2
St Michael the Archangel's Church......35 E2
St Peter & St Paul's Cathedral......36 A2
Statue of Maironis......37 A2
Statue of Vytautas the Great......38 C2
Sugihara House......39 F3
Tadas Ivanauskas Zoological Museum......40 C2
Vytautas Church......41 A3
Vytautas Magnus University......42 D2

SLEEPING
Apple Hotel......43 A2
Best Western Santakos......44 C2
Daniela......45 E2
Kaunas Hotel......46 D2
Kauno Arkivyskupijos Svečių Namai......47 A2
Kunigaikščių menė......48 B2
Litinterp......49 E2
Metropolis......50 D2
Takioji Neris......51 E1

EATING
Avilys......(see 58)
Bernelių Užeiga......52 E1
Bernelių Užeiga......53 A2
Iki......54 B1
Miesto Sodas......55 C2
Minima......56 D2
Presto......57 C2
Senieji Rūsiai......58 B2

DRINKING
BO......59 A2
Bumerangas......60 A2
Crazy House Užeiga......61 A2
Kavos Klubas......62 A2

ENTERTAINMENT
City Metro......63 D2
Ex-It......64 A2
Kaunas Academic Drama Theatre......65 D2
Kaunas Musical Theatre......66 C2
Kaunas Philharmonic......67 C2
Kaunas Puppet Theatre......68 D2
Planeta......69 F4
Romuva......70 D2
Siena......(see 55)
Youth Chamber Theatre......71 C2

TRANSPORT
Air Lithuania......72 D2
Ecolines......(see 74)
Eurolines......(see 74)
Local Bus Station......73 A2
Long-Distance Bus Station......74 F3

Sights

OLD TOWN

Vilniaus gatvė is the main artery of charming Old Town. Its eastern end is dominated by the former **Presidential Palace of Lithuania** (Lietuvos Respublikos prezidentūra kaune; Vilniaus gatvė 33; adult/student 3/1.50Lt; 11am-5pm Wed-Sun, gardens 8am-9pm Tue-Sun), where the country was run between 1920 and 1939. Restored to its original grandeur, the palace hosts a great exhibition on independent Lithuania. Black and white photographs are interspersed with gifts given to past presidents, collections of family silver and presidential awards. Statues of the former presidents stud the palace garden.

Nearby, the **Folk Music & Instruments Museum** (Lietuvos tautinės muzikos muziejus; ☎ 422 295; Kurpių gatvė 12; adult/child 2/1Lt; 10am-6pm Wed-Sun Oct-May, 11am-6pm Wed-Sun Jun-Sep) strikes a musical note.

St Peter & St Paul's Cathedral (Vilniaus gatvė 1) with its single tower owes much to baroque reconstruction, especially inside, but the original 15th-century Gothic shape of its windows remains. It was probably founded by Vytautas around 1410 and now has nine altars. The **tomb** of Maironis stands outside the south wall.

Rotušės Aikštė

Soviet planners threatened to bulldoze a highway through this **central square** (they didn't) and its pretty 15th- and 16th-century German merchants' houses and 17th-century former town hall remain. The latter, now a **Palace of Weddings** where brides and grooms say *taip* ('I do') on Saturday, has a small **Ceramics Museum** (Keramikos muziejus; ☎ 203 572; Rotušės aikštė 15; adult/child 3/1.50Lt; 11am-5pm Tue-Sun) in its cellar. In the square's southwestern corner is a **statue of Maironis** (1862–1932), a Kaunas priest called Jonas Mačiulis who was the poet behind Lithuania's late-19th- and early-20th-century nationalist revival. Stalin banned his works. From 1910 to 1932 Maironis lived in the house behind, now the **Maironis Lithuanian Literary Museum** (Maironio Lietuvos literatūros muziejus; ☎ 200 410; Rotušės aikštė 13; adult/child 3/1Lt; 9am-5pm Tue-Sat). The square's southern side is dominated by the twin-towered **St Francis Church** (Rotušės aikštė 7-9), college and Jesuit monastery complex, built between 1666 and 1720; and the late-Renaissance (1624–34), terracotta-roofed **Holy Trinity Church** (Rotušės aikštė 22) fills the western side.

The **Medicine & Pharmaceutical History Museum** (Medicinios ir farmacijos istorijos muziejus; ☎ 201 569; Rotušės aikštė 28; adult/child 3/1Lt; ⏰ 11am-6pm Wed-Sun Apr-Oct, 11am-5pm Wed-Sun Nov-May) is gruesome and fascinating. The former post office contains the **Communications Development Museum** (Ryšių istorijos muziejus; ☎ 424 920; Rotušės aikštė 19; adult/child 2/1Lt; ⏰ 10am-6pm Wed, Thu, Sat & Sun) should old telephones be your thing.

Off the southeast of Rotušės aikštė, the curious **House of Perkūnas** (Perkūno namas; Aleksotas gatvė 6) was built in red brick in the 16th century as trade offices on the site of a former temple to the Lithuanian thunder god, Perkūnas. Beyond, on the bank of the Nemunas River, the Gothic-style **Vytautas Church** (Vytauto bažnyčia; Aleksoto gatvė 5) is the same red brick.

Kaunas Castle

A reconstructed tower, sections of wall, and part of a moat are all that remain of Kaunas Castle, around which the town originally grew. Founded in the 13th century, it was an important bastion of Lithuania's western borders.

Trolleybus 7 from the bus or train stations terminates at the castle site.

Lookout Points

Apparently there are nine lookout points of Kaunas. Don't bother finding all of them! The hill across the Nemunas from Vytautas Church offers a good view of old and new Kaunas. Cross the bridge and mount the hill via either the **Aleksoto funicular** (Aleksoto funikulierius; Skriaudžių gatvė 8 & Aušros gatvė 6; ticket 0.60Lt; ⏰ 7am-noon & 1-4pm Mon-Fri) – one of Europe's few surviving funiculars – or the steps beside it. A right turn from the top funicular station leads to the lookout point.

The **Green Hill funicular** (Žaliakalnio funikulierius; Putvinskio gatvė 22; ticket 0.50Lt; ⏰ 7am-7pm) glides up **Green Hill** (Žaliakalnis). Above the top station towers **Christ's Resurrection Basilica** (Kauno paminklinė Kristhaus Prisikėlimo bašničia; ☎ 200 883; Zemaicių gatvė 316; ⏰ 10am-7pm), a piece of history that took 70 years to build. A Nazi paper warehouse and a Soviet radio factory, the church was finally consecrated in 2004.

NEW TOWN

Kaunas expanded east from Old Town in the 19th century, giving birth to the modern centre and its striking 1.7km pedestrian street, **Laisvės alėja**. Also known as Freedom

KAUNAS HEROES

Beloved Lithuanian pilots Steponas Darius and Stanislovas Girėnas died on 15 July 1933, 650km short of completing the longest nonstop trans-Atlantic flight. Two days after the duo set off from New York, 25,000 people gathered at Kaunas airport for their triumphant return. They never arrived. Their orange plane *Lituanica* crashed in Germany; see the wreckage in the Military Museum of Vytautas the Great (p335). After being embalmed, then hidden during Soviet occupation, the bodies came to rest at **Aukštieji Šančiai Cemetery** (Asmenos gatvė 1) in 1964.

Kaunas-based Japanese diplomat Chiune Sugihara (1900–86) saved 12,000 Jewish lives between 1939 and 1940, issuing transit visas to stranded Polish Jews who faced being forced into Soviet citizenship. When the Soviets annexed Lithuania and ordered all consulates be shut he asked for a short extension. Dubbed 'Japan's Schindler', he disobeyed orders for 29 days by signing 300 visas per day, and handed the stamp to a Jewish refugee when he left. **Sugihara House** (Sugiharos namai; ☎ 423 277; www.sugihara-foundation.com; Vaižganto gatvė 30; admission free; ⏰ 10am-5pm Mon-Fri, 11am-4pm Sat & Sun) tells his life story.

The **Museum of Deportation & Resistance** (Rezistencijos ir tremties muziejus; ☎ 323 179; Vytauto prospktas 46; admission free; ⏰ 10am-4pm Thu-Sun) documents the Resistance spirit embodied by the Forest Brothers, who fought the Soviet occupation. Led by Jonas Žemaitis-Vytautas (1909–54), 100,000 men went into Lithuania's forests to battle the tyrannical regime. One-third were killed, the rest captured and deported. Fighting continued until 1954 when the last partisan was shot.

One of the most desperate anti-Soviet actions was the suicide of Kaunas student Romas Kalanta. On 14 May 1972 he doused himself in petrol and set fire to himself in protest at tyrannical communist rule. A suicide note was found in his diary explaining why.

Avenue, it was legendary for years as one of the few strips where smoking was banned – until 2000 when the city mayor butted in and permitted puffing again.

Independent Lithuania's first parliament convened in 1920 at the **Kaunas Musical Theatre**, the former State Theatre Palace overlooking **City Garden** (Miestos Sodas) at the western end of Laisvės alėja since 1892. **Field of Sacrifice** (2002) – a name engraved on paving slabs in front of the garden – is a tragic tribute to the young Kaunas hero (p335) who set himself alight in protest at Soviet rule. Across the street, a **statue of Vytautas the Great** and a stone turtle stand outside the **Tadas Ivanauskas Zoological Museum** (Tado Ivanausko zoologijos muziejus; ☎ 229 675; Laisvės alėja 106; adult/child 5/3Lt; 11am-7pm Tue-Sun). Inside, 13,000 stuffed animals jockey for attention.

A gothic gem of a church is tucked in a courtyard off Laisvės alėja: **St Gertrude Church** (Šv Gertrūdos bažnyčia; Laisvės alėja 101a) was built in the late 15th century. Its red-brick crypt overflows with burning candles, prompting a separate candle shrine to be set up in a shed opposite the crypt entrance.

The Soviets turned the blue neo-Byzantine **St Michael the Archangel Church** (Šv Mykolo Arkangelo igulos bažnyčioje; Nepriklausomybės aikštė 14), filling the skyline at the eastern end of Laisvės alėja, into a stained-glass museum. Built for the Russian Orthodox faith in 1895, the church was reopened to Catholic worshippers in 1991.

On the same square, **Man**, modelled on Nike the Greek god of victory, caused a storm of controversy when his glorious pose exposing his manhood was unveiled. The **Mykolas Žilinskas Art Gallery** (Mykolo Žilinsko dailės galerija; ☎ 222 853; Nepriklausomybės aikštė 12; adult/child 5/2.50Lt; 11am-5pm Tue-Sun) behind boasts Lithuania's only Rubens.

Close to Laisvės alėja, a memorial at Kaunas' only operational **Choral Synagogue** (Choralinė sinagoga; ☎ 206 880, 8-614 03100; Ožeškienės gatvė 17; admission free; 5.45-6.30pm Mon-Fri, 10am-noon Sat) remembers 1600 children killed at the Ninth Fort (p335). The WWII Jewish ghetto was on the western bank of the Neris, in the area bounded by Jurbarko, Panerių and Demokratų streets.

Vienybės Aikštė

Unity Sq houses **Kaunas Technological University** (Kauno technologijos universitetas), which has 14,000 students, and the smaller **Vytautas Magnus University** (Vytauto didžiojo universitetas), refounded in 1989 by an émigré Lithuanian.

The **Military Museum of Vytautas the Great** (Vytauto didžiojo karo muziejus; ☎ 320 939; Donelaičio gatvė 64; adult/child 2/1Lt; 11am-6pm Wed-Sun) covers Lithuanian history from prehistoric times to the present day. Of particular interest is the wreckage of the aircraft in which Steponas Darius and Stasys Girėnas died while attempting to fly nonstop from New York to Kaunas in 1933 (see boxed text, p335).

In the same building (entrance at the back) is the **National Čiurlionis Art Museum** (Nacionalinis Čiurlionio dailės muziejus; ☎ 221 417; Putvinskio gatvė 55; adult/child 5/2.50Lt; 11am-5pm Tue-Sun), Kaunas' leading museum. It has extensive collections of the romantic paintings of Mikalojus Konstantinas Čiurlionis (1875–1911), one of Lithuania's greatest artists and composers, as well as Lithuanian folk art and 16th- to 20th-century European applied art.

Diabolical is the collection of 2000-odd devil statuettes in the **Museum of Devils** (Velniukai; ☎ 221 587; Putvinskio gatvė 64; adult/child 5/2.50Lt; 11am-5pm Tue-Sun), collected by landscape artist Antanas Žmuidzinavičius (1876–1966). Note the satanic figures of Hitler and Stalin, performing a deadly dance over Lithuania.

Kaunas Picture Gallery (Kauno paveikslų galerija; ☎ 200 520; Donelaičio gatvė 16; adult/student 3/1.50Lt; 11am-5pm Tue-Sun) has a tribute to Jurgis Mačiūnas, the father of avant-garde movement, Fluxus.

NINTH FORT

Lithuania's brutal history is at some of its darkest at the **Ninth Fort** (IX Fortas; ☎ 377 715; Žemaičių plentas 73; adult/child 5/3Lt; 10am-6pm Wed-Mon Mar-Nov, 10am-4pm Wed-Sun Dec-Feb), built on Kaunas' northwestern outskirts in the late 19th century to fortify the western frontier of the tsarist empire. During WWII the Nazis made it a death camp where 80,000 people, including most of Kaunas' Jewish population, were butchered. Later it became a prison and execution site by Stalin's henchmen.

The museum has exhibits on the Nazi horrors against Jews, and also includes material on Soviet atrocities against Lithuanians. Take bus 35 or 23 from the bus station to the IX Fortas bus stop, 7km out of town, then walk for 1km.

PARKS & GARDENS

Vytautas Park occupies the slope up from the end of Laisvės alėja to the stadium, along which stretches the lovely **Ažuolynas Park**. South along Vytauto prospektas is **Ramybės Park**, home to the Old City Cemetery until the Soviets tore up all the graves in the 1960s.

Gardening buffs will enjoy the **Kaunas Botanical Gardens** (Kauno botanikos sodas; ☎ 390 033; www.vdu.lt; Žilibero gatvė 6; park adult/5-12yr 2/1Lt, park & greenhouses adult/5-12yr 4/1Lt; 🕒 8am-4.45pm Mon-Thu, 8am-6pm Fri, 10am-6pm Sat & Sun) where university gardeners tend rare and wonderful plants in a 1920s manor-house garden.

Festivals & Events

Kaunas' social diary highlights are April's four-day **International Jazz Festival** (www.kaunasjazz.lt) and the open-air **Operetta in Kaunas Castle**, held for two weeks in the castle ruins in late June–early July.

For classical fans, the **Pažaislis Music Festival** (p339) has concerts in the courtyards and churches of Pažaislis Monastery each year May to August.

Sleeping

The tourist office has a list of farms where you can stay for 20Lt to 200Lt a night.

BUDGET & MIDRANGE

Litinterp (☎ 228 718; www.lintinterp.lt; Gedimino gatvė 28/7; s/d/tr from 70/120/180Lt; 🕒 8.30am-5.30pm Mon-Fri, 9am-3pm Sat) comes to the rescue for budget travellers and those seeking homely touches, with a clutch of apartments and B&B rooms in private homes. It also rents bicycles. Take trolleybus 7 or 1 from the bus station and get off at the third stop.

Kauno Arkivyskupijos Svečių Namai (☎ 322 597; http://kaunas.lcn.lt; Rotušės aikštė 21; s/d/tr 50/80/100Lt) This charming guesthouse, run by the Lithuanian Catholic Church, sits smugly wedged between centuries-old churches in Old Town – making it the envy of every Kaunas hotelier. Accommodation at a price that won't break the bank makes it a dream come true for budget travellers.

Metropolis (☎ 205 992; metropolis@takiojineris.com; Daukanto gatvė 21; s/d/tr/ste 70/120/135/150Lt) This budget hotel with strong overtones of past grandeur is a rare breed. Sculpted-stone balconies overlook a leafy street; a hefty wooden turnstile door sweeps guests into a lobby with moulded ceiling; and age-old furnishings only add to the charm. As the name in Lithuanian and Russian outside says, it was called Hotel Lietuva in the USSR.

Kunigaikščių menė (☎ 320 872; mene@takas.lt; Daukšos gatvė 28; s/d 200/250Lt; P) This sweet choice down a cobbled street in Old Town consists of eight well-kept, comfortable rooms above a run-of-the-mill and unpretentious café.

Takioji Neris (☎ 306 100; www.takiojineris.com; Donelaičio gatvė 27; economy s/d/tr 120/200/300Lt, standard s/d/tr 180/300/260Lt, business s/d/apt with sauna 280/360/750; P) From outside, Kaunas' Soviet-era block holds zero appeal. But step inside and be surprised: Soviet stained glass fuses with contemporary renovations to make this 179-room hotel, popular for its size with tour groups, a nice place to stay. Economy rooms tout decades-old furnishings, but standard and business rooms are mod.

THE AUTHOR'S CHOICE

Apple Hotel (☎ 321 404; Valančiaus gatvė 19; www.applehotel.lt; s/d with shared bathroom 135/145Lt, standard s/d 140/150Lt, lux s/d 160/170; ⊠ 💻) Set on Old Town's edge in a courtyard, this budget hotel is fantastic. Inspired by a cheap, tasty green apple, its 14 rooms are stylishly furnished with white linens, modern white-tiled bathrooms with the odd dash of bold colour and minimalist white blinds. Six cheaper rooms share a bathroom between two, while lux doubles are bigger than their standard counterparts. Staff – recognisable by the apple-motif ties they sport – go out of their way to please and bring breakfast (6.50Lt) on a tray to your room. A computer sits in reception for guests to use.

TOP END

Kaunas Hotel (☎ 750 850; www.kaunashotel.lt; Laisvės alėja 79; d/tr/ste from 320/600/500Lt; P ⊠ ❄ 💻 ♿) This swanky five-floor, four-star pillow parlour, dates from 1892. Glass fronts the top floor where room 512 sports a peek-if-you-dare glass-walled bathroom overlooking Laisvės alėja and Žaliakalnis. The hotel is a free wi-fi zone and guests can use the business centre for 20Lt per hour. Hotel restaurant 55° in a red-brick cellar is a must-dine.

Daniela (☎ 321 505; www.danielahotel.lt; Mickevičiaus gatvė 28; s/d/ste from 320/370/500Lt; P ❄) A retro-

LITHUANIA

chic hotel owned by basketball hero Arvydas Sabonis, 30-room Daniela has plans to double in size – although rooms in the new block will be of a more midrange calibre. Furnishings are fun and bold; think soft pink chairs, steely mezzanines and extra-large bouncy sofas. Parking costs an extra 5Lt a night.

Best Western Santakos (☎ 302 702; www.santaka.lt; Gruodžio gatvė 21; s/d/ste 360/480/880Lt; P ⊠ ✣ 🖳) The industrial warehouse-style building in which this Best Western chain hotel resides is its most unique feature. Otherwise heavy furnishings add an oppressive air to the summer heat – as does the TV set that blares Soviet-style in reception. Sauna and pool are free to guests between 7am and 10am (100Lt an hour at other times).

Eating

Dining in Kaunas is cheaper than in Vilnius but lacks imagination and can be of poor quality.

Senieji Rūsiai (literally 'Old Cellars'; ☎ 202 806; Vilniaus gatvė 34; meals from 50Lt; 🕑 11am-midnight Mon-Thu & Sun, 11am-2am Fri & Sat) Hands down the tastiest street terrace at which to dine, drink and soak up Old Town, this candlelit 17th-century cellar grills great meats and serves a funky chicken filet with fruity curry sauce.

Avilys (☎ 203 476; Vilniaus gatvė 34; meals from 50Lt; 🕑 11am-midnight Mon-Thu & Sun, to 2am Fri & Sat) Sharing the same terrace as Senieji Rūsiai, Avilys is an award-winning brewery that serves unusual beers to a discerning crowd. Dining – reason itself to come here – overlooks the street or is underground.

Presto (☎ 221 087; Laisvės alėja 90; meals 30Lt) The food is nothing to write home about, but Presto punters don't seem to care. The terrace on the main drag proffers fine church-dome and people-watching views against a tasteful backdrop of jazz and blues.

Miesto Sodas (☎ 424 424; Laisvės alėja 93; meals 20-30Lt) Trendy Miesto Sodas has a cool club, Siena (p337) in its basement and a varied menu. Sip on fresh carrot or beetroot juice and pick from wok-fried BBQ spare ribs, a T-bone steak, cold berry soup or a typically Lithuanian herring filet in the company of marinated red onions, sour cream and baked potatoes. Service can be snail-slow.

Bernelių Užeiga (☎ 200 913; meals 30-50Lt); Valančiaus (Valančiaus gatvė 9); Donelaičio (Donelaičio gatvė 11) If it's rustic Lithuanian cuisine served by fair maidens in traditional dress that you're after, then this twinset of wooden country inns in the middle of town is for you.

Central supermarkets:

Iki (Jonavos gatvė 3)
Minima (Kęstučio gatvė 55)

Drinking

Kavos Klubas (Coffee Club ☎ 229 669; Valančiaus gatvė 19; 🕑 9am-11pm Mon-Sat, to 7pm Sun) There's a definite bookish air to Coffee Club, a cosy winter hide-out in Old Town where fresh, aromatic coffee beans rule. Thirty-odd coffee types straddle the central bar and seating is around small tables that almost shout 'sit up straight, shoulders back'.

B.O. (☎ 206 542; Muitinės gatvė 9; 🕑 6pm-2am Mon-Thu & Sun, to 3am Fri & Sat) This laid-back bar whose name is short for 'Blue Orange' is a student hang-out where a drunken bunch while away the wee hours of the weekend.

Bumerangas (Naugardo gatvė 6; 🕑 10am-midnight Mon-Fri, noon-midnight Sat) Around the corner and just as debauched.

Crazy House Užeiga (☎ 221 182; Vilniaus gatvė 16; 🕑 11am-midnight Mon-Thu & Sun, to 2am Fri & Sat) Love it or hate it (we hated it), this crazy house has pneumatic furniture that moves after 6pm.

Entertainment

Check daily newspaper **Kauno diena** (www.kaunodiena.lt) for listings.

NIGHTCLUBS

City Metro (☎ 8-683 73043; www.citymetro.lt; Daukanto gatvė 19; admission 5-10Lt) Mix Ibiza, Viva la Fiesta and City Mix with DJ Tomie are the varied sounds to blast out of this steely hip club inspired by a metro.

Other clubs:

Ex-It (☎ 202 813; Jakšto gatvė 4)
Siena (☎ 424 424; www.siena.lt; Laisvės alėja 93)
Los Patrankos (☎ 338 228; www.lospatrankos.lt; Savanorių prospektas 124)

CINEMAS

Watch an English-language film at **Planeta** (☎ 338 330; Vytauto prospektas 6) or **Romuva** (☎ 324 212; Laisvės alėja 54).

THEATRE & CLASSICAL MUSIC

Original dramas take to the stage at the innovative **Kaunas Academic Drama Theatre** (Akademinis dramos teatras; ☎ 224 064; www.dramosteatras.lt; Laisvės alėja 71) and the **Youth Chamber Theatre** (Jaunimo kamerinis teatras; ☎ 228 226; www.kamerinisteatras; Kęstučio gatvė 74a). Puppets enchant at the **Kaunas Puppet Theatre** (Kauno valstybinis lėlių teatras; ☎ 221 691; www.kaunoleles.lt; Laisvės alėja 87a).

The **Kaunas Philharmonic** (Kauno filharmonija; ☎ 200 478; www.kaunofilharmonija.lt; Sapiegos gatvė 5) is the main concert hall for classical music, and operas fill the **Kaunas Musical Theatre** (Muzikinis teatras; ☎ 200 933; www.muzikinisteatras.lt; Laisvės alėja 91).

Getting There & Away

AIR

From **Kaunas International Airport** (☎ 399 307; www.kaunasair.lt; Savanorių prospektas), 10km north of Kaunas, **Air Lithuania** (☎ 7007 0777, 399 401; kaunas@airlithuania.lt; Kęstučio gatvė 69) flies to/from Hamburg, Oslo, Billund, Munich and Cologne via Palanga.

No-frills airline **Ryanair** (www.ryanair.com) operates flights to/from London's Stansted Airport; see p394.

BOAT

By the time you read this **Nemuno Linija** (☎ 8-674 84898; www.nemunolinjia.lt) will operate regular boats between Kaunas and Rusnė (Nemunas Delta), and between Kaunas and Nida (Curonian Spit). Daily hydrofoils depart from Kaunas/Nida at 8am/3.30pm. Sailing time is four hours and a one-way fare for adult/children aged under six is 99Lt/48Lt.

BUS

At the **long-distance bus station** (☎ 409 060; Vytauto prospektas 24), buy tickets for domestic destinations in the main booking hall and tickets for international journeys at the **International Booking Office** (Tarptautinių autobusu bilietų kasa; ☎ 322 222; ⌚ 8am-7pm Mon, Tue & Fri, 8.30am-8pm Wed, 8.30am-6.45pm Sat, noon-8pm Sun). For bus info, consult the timetable on the wall or challenge the **information desk** (⌚ 7am-8pm).

Tickets for **Kautra** (www.kautra.lt) buses throughout Lithuania and most international destinations (p396) are also sold in town at **Eurolines** (☎ 209 836; Laisvės alėja 36; ⌚ 9am-1pm & 2-6pm Mon-Fri, 9am-1pm Sat), inside the tourist office.

Daily services within the Baltics include the following:

Druskininkai 19Lt, two to three hours, six buses via Alytus.
Klaipėda 334Lt, three hours, 10 buses.
Marijampolė 10Lt, 1½ hours, about nine buses.
Palanga 36Lt, 3½ hours, about 11 buses.
Panevėžys 17Lt, two hours, about 20 buses.
Rīga 40.50Lt, 3½ hours, one bus.
Šiauliai 22.50Lt to 26Lt, three hours, 20 buses.
Tallinn 100Lt, 12 hours, one bus.
Vilnius 14.50Lt, 1½ to two hours, about 20 buses.
Visaginas 29.50Lt, four hours, two buses.

CAR & MOTORCYCLE

Litinterp (☎ 228 718; www.lintinterp.lt; Gedimino gatvė 28-7) Car rental.

TRAIN

From the **train station** (☎ 221 093; Čiurlionio gatvė 16) there are up to 16 trains daily to/from Vilnius (11Lt, 1¼ to two hours) and an overnight bus to/from Klaipėda (25Lt, six hours).

Getting Around

Buses and trolleybuses run from 5am to 11pm and tickets cost 0.90Lt from newspaper kiosks or 1Lt from the driver. Minibuses shadow routes and run later than regular buses; drivers sell tickets for 1.20Lt. The tourist office sells a public transport map detailing all routes for 3Lt.

To get to/from the airport, take minibus 120 from the local bus station on Šv Gertrūdos gatvė. Buses depart every five minutes between 6am and 11pm.

Trolleybuses 1, 5 and 7 run north from the train station along Vytauto prospektas, west along Kęstučio gatvė and Nemuno gatvė, then north on Birštono gatvė. Returning, they head east along Šv Gertrūdos gatvė, Ožeškienės gatvė and Donelaičio gatvė, then south down Vytauto prospektas to the bus and train stations.

Ordering a taxi by telephone (☎ 366 666) is safer than hopping into a car on the street.

Around Kaunas

PAŽAISLIS MONASTERY

This fine example of 17th-century baroque architecture is 9km east of the centre, near the shores of **Kaunas Sea** (Kauno marios), a large artificial lake. The monastery church with its 50m-high cupola and sumptuous Venetian interior made from pink and black Polish marble is a sumptuous if shabby affair. Passing from Catholic to Orthodox to Catholic control, the monastery has a chequered history and was a psychiatric hospital for part of the Soviet era. Nuns inhabit it today. The best time to visit is between June and August during the **Pažaislis Music Festival** (www.pazaislis.lt). Take trolleybus 5, 9 or 12 to the terminus on Masiulio gatvė, a few hundred metres before **Pažaislis Monastery** (☎ 37-456 485; Masiulio gatvė 31; admission free; mass ⏲ 11am Sun).

Rumšiškės

Go back in time at the **Open-Air Museum of Lithuania** (Lietuvių liaudies buities muziejus; ☎ 346-47 392; Neries gatvė 6; adult/child with car 10/7Lt, on foot 6/3Lt; ⏲ 10am-6pm Wed-Sun May-Oct, upon request only Nov-Apr), where four villages of 18th- and 19th-century buildings represent Lithuania's four main regions. Potters, weavers and joiners demonstrate their crafts in the museum workshop. Rumšiškės is 20km east of Kaunas, about 2km off the Vilnius road.

BIRŠTONAS

☎ 319

Some 40km south of Kaunas is the small spa town of Birštonas, host to the springtime three-day jazz festival **Birštonas Jazz** (http://jazz.birstonas.lt), which in even-numbered years unites Lithuania's top jazz musicians with fans by the lorryload. At other times, its unique position in a loop of the Nemunas River makes it a sweet spot to relax.

The **tourist office** (☎ 65 740; www.birstonas.lt; Jaunimo gatvė 3) rents bicycles and boats and has information on accommodation options, including three old-style *sanatorijos*. For riverside activities, contact the visitor centre of the **Nemunas Crook Regional Park** (Nemuno kilpų regioninio parko; ☎ 65 610; nkrp@korbas.lt; Tylioji gatvė 1).

From Kaunas bus station there are buses every half hour to/from **Birštonas bus station** (☎ 52 333; Tumo Vaižganto gatvė 20).

ŠIAULIAI

☎ 41 / pop 147,000

Lithuania's fourth-largest city is overshadowed by the incredible Hill of Crosses 10km north. But despite this – and plague, fires and battles – Šiauliai has survived its troubled history to become an eccentric, thriving city 140km north of Kaunas. It is also the main centre of the northwestern Samogitia (Žemaitija) region.

TV sets, Black Panther bicycles, milk and Gubernija beer are in the mixed bag of products manufactured in town – a mildly shabby place yet to see better days. Its main pedestrian street, Vilniaus gatvė, is due a complete face-lift, while the transformation of its Soviet military airfield – the USSR's largest airbase outside Russia, not mapped until 1991 – into a tourist attraction promises an interesting new future for Šiauliai.

Information

Get cash with Visa/MasterCard from ATMs outside banks at Vilniaus gatvė 116, Tilžės gatvė 157 and Tilžės gatvė 149.

Post office (Aušros alėja 42)

Sela (Dvaro gatvė; per hr 2Lt; ⏲ 9am-8pm Mon-Fri, 10am-8pm Sat & Sun) Internet saloon.

Tourist office (☎ 523 110; www.siauliai.lt; Vilniaus gatvė 213; ⏲ 9am-6pm Mon-Fri, 10am-5pm Sat, 10am-4pm Sun) Sells maps and guides, including cycling itineraries to the Hill of Crosses; rents bicycles for 3Lt an hour; makes accommodation bookings and arranges guided tours of the Soviet airbase (p340).

Sights

TOWN CENTRE

St Peter & Paul's Cathedral (Šv Petro ir Povilo bažnyčia; Aušros takas 3), overlooking Priskėlimo aikštė, was constructed between 1595 and 1625 from the proceeds of the sale of four-year-old bulls donated by local farmers. It has a 75m spire – Lithuania's second highest – and legend says the hillock it stands on was created from sand and dust which blew over a dead ox that wandered into Šiauliai, sat down and died. **St George's Church** (Šv Jurgio bažnyčia; Kražių gatvė 17) was built for the local Russian garrison in 1909 but is Catholic today.

A distinctive city landmark is the mammoth **sundial** (cnr Salkauskjo gatvė & Ežero gatvė), topped by a bronze statue of an archer in what has become known as 'Sundial Square'. It was built in 1986 to commemorate the 750th anniversary of the Battle of Saulė (1236), the battle in which local Samogitians defeated the Knights of the Sword and founded the town.

Šiauliai has an eccentric museum collection: the **Radio & TV Museum** (Radio ir televijos muziejus; ☎ 524 399; Vilniaus gatvė 174; adult/child 2/1Lt; ⏲ 10am-6pm Tue-Fri, 11am-4pm Sat), **Museum of Cats** (Katinų muziejus; ☎ 523 883; igs@splius.lt; Žuvininkų gatvė 18; adult/child 2/1Lt; ⏲ 11am-5pm Wed-Sun), **Photography Museum** (Fotografijos muziejus; ☎ 524 396; Vilniaus gatvė 140; adult/child 2/1Lt; ⏲ 10am-6pm Tue-Fri, 11am-4pm Sat), and a **Bicycle Museum** (Dviračių muziejus; ☎ 524 395; Vilniaus gatvė

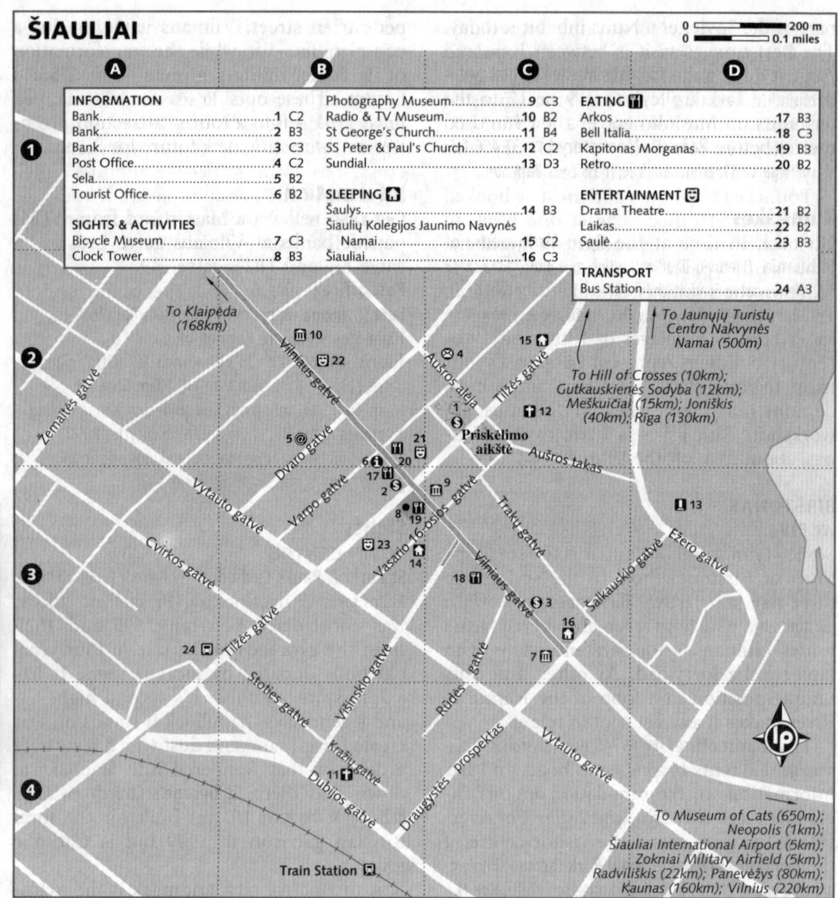

139; adult/child 2/1Lt; 10am-6pm Tue-Fri, 11am-4pm Sat) where bone-jolting wood and iron bicycles without tyres stand next to orange and pink communal bikes introduced by Vilnius City Municipality in the late 1990s (they were stolen within days) and mean speed machines made by Lithuania's biggest bicycle manufacturer, Šiauliai-based Balti Vairas (Black Panther).

ZOKNIAI MILITARY AIRFIELD

In Soviet times this airfield with two 3.5km-long and 45m-wide runways – large enough to land a space shuttle – was the USSR's biggest military base outside Russia, used to defend its western border. The last of its 55,000 troops based here left in 1993, and since 2004 the Lithuanian air base has been used by NATO forces to patrol Baltic skies.

Guided tours take you around the airfield, built in 1935 and much of it in a shocking state of crumbling disrepair after 10 years of abandonment. Many of the 50 or so Soviet aircraft hangars once housing MiG-29 fighters remain, as do the subterranean command post, sturdy enough to survive nuclear attack, and the fuel reserves, a lucrative source of income in Soviet times for enterprising locals who syphoned off fuel from the underground tanks!

About 120 NATO personnel and four F-16 jet fighters are currently stationed at Zokniai. NATO countries take three-month turns to defend Baltic air space: Belgium,

Denmark, the UK, Norway, the Netherlands and Germany and the US have already done QRA (Quick Reaction Alert) stints. By 2008 it is estimated that NATO will have invested €59 million into Zokniai; in 2004 €563,000 was allocated to rebuild its legendary runway, for which no aircraft is too big.

Tours last two hours and must be booked at the tourist office at least one week in advance. Price is dependent on numbers; groups of 30 pay 15Lt each and ride to the base, on the southeastern edge of town, in an old Soviet bus; groups of four can expect to pay 100Lt each.

HILL OF CROSSES

This 'Mecca of Lithuania' – thousands upon thousands of crosses on a hillock – has inspired countless pilgrimages. Large and tiny, expensive and cheap, wood and metal, the crosses are devotional, to accompany prayers, or finely carved folk-art masterpieces. Others are memorials, tagged with flowers, a photograph or other mementoes in memory of the deceased, and inscribed with a sweet or sacred message. Traditional Lithuanian *koplytstulpis* (wooden sculptures of a figure topped with a little roof) intersperse the crosses, as do magnificent sculptures of the Sorrowful Christ (Rūpintojėlis). If you wish to add your own, souvenir traders in the car park sell crosses big and small.

An alternative view of the cross-swamped hill is from inside the chapel of the modern brick **monastery**. Home to 10 Franciscan monks, it was built behind the hill between 1997 and 2000 – allegedly upon the wishes of John Paul II who said he wished to see a place of prayer following after his visit in 1993. Behind the altar in the church, the striking backdrop through the ceiling-to-floor window of the Hill of Crosses in place of a traditional crucifix is breathtaking; Italian architect Angelo Polesello designed it.

CROSS CRAFTING

Crosses were once symbols of sacred fervour and national identity, both Pagan and Catholic; cross crafting – a Unesco-protected tradition since 2001 – is the embodiment of Lithuanian contradiction.

Handed down from master to pupil, the crosses were carved from oak, the sacred pagan tree. They were made as offerings to gods, draped with food, coloured scarves (for a wedding) or aprons (for fertility). Once consecrated by priests, they became linked with Christian ceremonies in unmistakable sacred significance. The crosses, which measure up to 5m, then became symbols of defiance against occupation.

When it comes to explaining the origin of the Hill of Crosses, there are almost as many myths as crosses. Some claim it was built in three days and three nights by the bereaved families of warriors killed in a great battle. Others say it was the work of a father who, in a desperate bid to cure his sick daughter, planted a cross on the hill. Pagan traditions tell stories of sacred fires being lit here and tended by celestial virgins.

Crosses first appeared here in the 14th century. They multiplied after bloody antitsarist uprisings to become this potent symbol of suffering and hope.

During the Soviet era planting a cross was an arrestable offence – but pilgrims kept coming to commemorate the thousands killed and deported. The hill was bulldozed at least three times. In 1961 the Red Army destroyed the 2000-odd crosses that stood on the mound, sealed off the tracks leading to the hill and dug ditches at its base, yet overnight more crosses appeared. In 1972 they were destroyed after the immolation of a Kaunas student (p335) in protest at Soviet occupation. But by 1990 the Hill of Crosses comprised a staggering 40,000 crosses, spanning 4600 sq metres. Since independence, they have multiplied at least 10 times – and still are. In 1993 Pope John Paul II celebrated mass here (his pulpit still stands) and graced the hill a year later with a papal cross, adding his own message to the mountain of scribbled-on crosses: 'Thank you, Lithuanians, for this Hill of Crosses which testifies to the nations of Europe and to the whole world the faith of the people of this land'.

New crosses now stand to commemorate those who perished in the 2001 Twin Towers attack in New York and subsequent terrorist attacks elsewhere. The spirit continues, the hill grows and the sound of the crosses rattling in the wind becomes yet more sobering.

LITHUANIA

The Hill of Crosses (Kryžių kalnas) is 10km north of Šiauliai, 2km east off the road to Joniškis and Rīga, in the village of Jurgaičiai. To get here, take one of eight daily buses from Šiauliai bus station to Joniškis or one of eight to Rīga and get off at the Domantai stop, from where it is a 2km walk to the hill. Look for the sign 'Kryžių kalnas 2' on the A12. By taxi, the return taxi fare is 30Lt, with a 30-minute stop at the hill; ask Šiauliai tourist office or your hotel/hostel to order one for you by telephone to avoid being ripped off. By bicycle the Hill of Crosses is a 12km ride; allow at least three hours for the return trip. The tourist office rents bikes and has route maps.

Sleeping

The tourist office has information on homestay accommodation around Šiauliai.

Šiauliai College Youth Hostel (Šiaulių Kolegijos Jaunimo Navynės Namai; ☎ 523 764; administracija@siauliaikolegija.lt; Tilžės gatvė 159; s/d/tr/q 50/60/75/100Lt; reception 7am-11pm; P ⊠) Reception is unhelpful. That said, this former college has been renovated with EU funds to create a spanking clean and sparkling, state-of-the-art hostel with kitchen and TV room.

Šaulys (☎ 520 812; www.saulys.lt; Vasario 16-osios gatvė 40; s/d/tr/apt from 180/250/350/500Lt; P ⊠) With a pool and a sauna, this is Šiauliai's swankiest choice. Four stars twinkle from its deep-red façade, its bright and spacious lobby buzzes with activity and it organises paragliding and parachuting expeditions for the truly adventurous.

Šiauliai (☎ 437 333; Draugystės prospektas 25; s/d/tr from 70/100/180; P) The town's old Soviet hotel is spectacularly ugly but does have great views 14 storeys high!

THE AUTHOR'S CHOICE

Gutkauskienės sodyba (☎ 8-698 79544, 8-698 34256; www.horse-g.lt; Žačiai village; s/d 50/70Lt; P) This century-old, renovated stud farm is perfect for those keen to skip Šiauliai's drab hotel scene for a taste of rural life. The farmhouse has six charming rooms, an outdoor pool, sauna, plenty of surrounding forest to explore and berries to pick in season – and lots of horses to ride. To get here, head north out of town along the Rīga road and pick up the eastbound 150 to Pakruojis. After Ginkūnai turn left (north) towards Naisai and Pašvitinys; follow the road for 5km then turn right (east) towards Žačiai and continue for 1.3km to the farmstead. All up it's about 12km (20 minutes) from Šiauliai.

Eating

Arkos (☎ 520 205; Vilniaus gatvė 213; meals 20-30Lt) This eating-drinking joint in a brick cellar caters to all. Whether you want a simple beer with deep-fried garlic bread sticks, a teatime pancake or dinner, you'll be sure of a tasty time. Service can be slow but the detailed scenes of rural Lithuania painted on the walls provide distraction.

Bell Italia (☎ 520 866; Vilniaus gatvė 167; meals 20-30Lt) Bell Italia is a young, fun and sparkling yellow-blue pizza place that cooks up delicious Italian food, including a 'viagra pizza' – guaranteed to fire you up!

Retro (☎ 521 202; retro@splius.lt; Vilniaus gatvė 146; meals 40Lt) Discerning diners seeking fine art and sculptures to view while they eat should not miss this hybrid art gallery–restaurant.

Kapitonas Morganas (☎ 526 477; Vilniaus gatvė 183; meals 20-40Lt) Come to Captain Morgan's jolly pirate ship to meet happy punters busily eating European fodder, drinking local beer and merrymaking on a great street terrace.

Entertainment

Spend the evening at the **Drama Theatre** (☎ 432 940; Tilžės gatvė 155), watching an English-language flick at **Laikas** (☎ 525 208; Vilniaus gatvė 172) or **Saulė** (☎ 524 983; www.saule.lt; Tilžės gatvė 140), or bowling and boogieing at **Neopolis** (☎ 521 542; www.neopolis.lt; Vilniaus gatvė 47; bowling per hr 40-60Lt; noon-3am), an out-of-town entertainment centre with a nightclub.

Getting There & Away

AIR

Šiauliai International Airport (☎ 542 005; www.airport.siauliai.lt), adjoining Zokniai Military Airfield on the southeastern edge of town, has only been used by cargo planes since it opened in 1997, but there is talk of a no-frills budget German airline flying here soon.

BUS

Services from Šiauliai **bus station** (☎ 525 058; Tilžės gatvė 109):

Kaunas 22.50Lt to 26Lt, three hours, 20 buses.
Klaipėda 23Lt, 2½ hours, six buses.

LITHUANIA

Palanga 22Lt, 2½ hours, about 10 daily.
Panevėžys 11Lt, 1½ hours, 12 daily.
Rīga 16Lt, two to three hours, eight daily.
Vilnius 29Lt, 4½ hours, seven daily.

TRAIN

Services to/from Šiauliai **train station** (☎ 430 652; Dubijos gatvė 44):
Klaipėda 16.50Lt, two to three hours, six daily.
Rīga 16Lt, 2½ hours, one to three daily.
Vilnius 26Lt, 2¾ to 3½ hours, five to eight daily.

RADVILIŠKIS & AROUND

Grim, grimy **Radviliškis** (population 21,000), 22km southeast of Šiauliai, is notable only as the central hub of the rail network, but there are a couple of interesting stops on the 55km stretch of the A9 heading east towards Panevėžys.

Šeduva, a 16th-century architectural monument 10km east of Radviliškis, is a large village with a yellow-and-white baroque church framed by cobbled streets and a small **Ethnographic Exhibition** (Šeduvos kraštotyros ekspozicija; Veriskių gatvė 7; adult/child 1/0.50Lt; 🕑 9am-4pm Tue-Sun) in a tannery (1884). Its main draw is a naff restaurant inside a windmill (1905). Dining at **Šeduvos Malūnas** (☎ 422-56 300, 8-687 70690; meals 20-40Lt), also called Velnių Malūnas (Devil's Mill), is on four levels around the windmill's original central-core cog mechanism. Cuisine is Lithuanian and a hotel in a modern building next door provides accommodation (double 80Lt, parking available) without breakfast. The mill is signposted off the A9 immediately west of Šeduva.

In **Kleboniškiai**, signposted 5km further east along the A9 to Panevėžys, is another windmill (1884) and – 1km down a dusty road – the **Kleboniškiai Rural Life Exhibition** (Kleboniškių kaimo buites ekspozicija; ☎ 422-63674; adult/student 6/3Lt, camera 0.50Lt; 🕑 9am-6pm Tue-Sun). The beautiful farmstead, with 19th- and early-20th-century farm buildings, offers a picture-postcard peek at rural Lithuania. The exhibition is part of the **Daugyvenė Cultural History Museum Reserve** (Daugyvenės kultūros istorijos muziejus-draustinis; ☎ 422-51 747), which groups burial grounds, mounds and other local sights.

Getting There & Away

About 12 buses a day run between Šiauliai and Panevėžys, via Radviliškis. There are buses every half an hour to/from Radviliškis and Šeduva and one a day to/from Vilnius.

There are six to eight daily trains to/from Vilnius (20Lt, 2½ hours), three daily to/from Kaunas (14Lt, three hours) and six daily to/from Klaipėda (17.90Lt, 2½ hours).

PANEVĖŽYS

☎ 45 / pop 119,000

Known as the 'Chicago of Lithuania' for crime and mafia dealings, Panevėžys has done serious work on its image. Emerging from post-Soviet industrial collapse, it boasts a prestigious theatrical tradition, a charming riverbed lake and a thriving art scene.

Lithuania's fifth-largest city, it lies 140km north of Vilnius on the Nevėžis River and on the Rīga highway. It was founded in 1503 and it claims to be the most Lithuanian of Lithuanian towns: Lithuanians comprise 96% of its population.

Economic turnaround aide, Panevėžys is still largely a manufacturing base – and a far cry from a tourist hot spot. Few people really stop here bar to change bus or to stop for something to eat en route to Rīga from Vilnius.

Orientation

At the centre is Laisvės aikštė, bordered at its northern end by east–west Elektros gatvė and at its southern end by Vilniaus gatvė. Basanavičiaus gatvė runs north to the Rīga

THE AUTHOR'S CHOICE

Smuklė Žarija (☎ 422-43 340, 8-615 11527; www.smuklezarija.lt; meals 20Lt; Ⓟ) It might be next to the Panevežys–Šiauliai motorway (A9), 5km west of Šeduva and 10km east of Radviliškis, but this inn on the shore of Lake Arimaičių could not make a more original pit stop. Toothy-grinned gnomes and dozens of other intricately carved wooden sculptures greet punters who flock here for superb shashlik, grilled meats, fish and authentic Lithuanian cuisine. Stuffed birds and a snake add a unique touch to the décor, and a wooden playground outside – complete with old sledge as swing – keeps pint-sized punters amused. There is a lakeside sauna, floating bathhouse to relax and swim from, boats to rent and friendly staff at the inn arrange hot-air ballooning. If you eat too much and cannot move, it has a bunch of basic rooms up top (double from 60Lt).

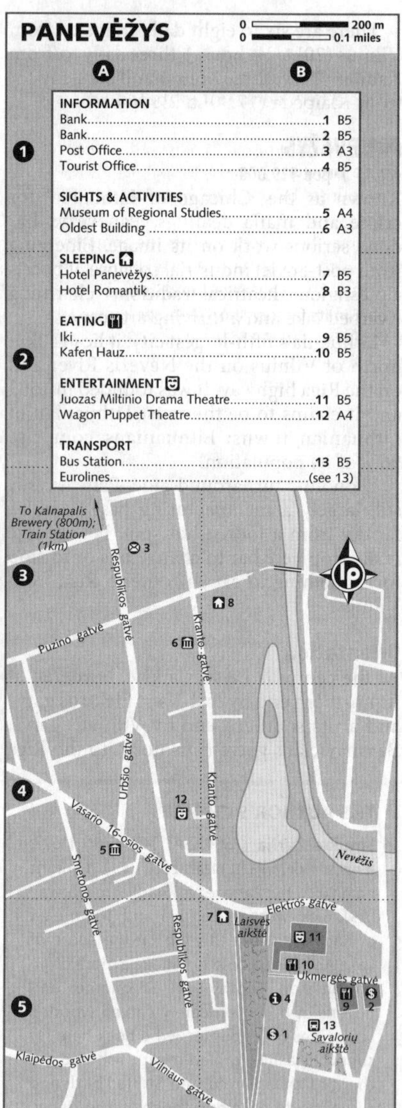

road and south to Kaunas and Vilnius. The train station is 2km northwest of the centre, the bus station is on Savanorių aikštė.

Information

For ATMs and currency exchange, try the banks at Laisvė aikštė 15 and Ukmerges gatvė 18a.

Left Luggage (bus station; per 24hr weight depending 2.50-20Lt; 6am-12.20pm & 1.50-7pm Mon-Fri, 7am-6pm Sat & Sun)

Post office (Respublikos gatvė 60)

Tourist office (508 080; www.panevezystic.lt; Laisvės aikštė; 10am-6pm Mon-Fri, 9am-2pm Sat) Ultrahelpful staff who, among other things, run beer tours (p345).

Sights

Triangular-shaped **Laisvės aikštė** is a central tree-lined pedestrianised spot, pleasant for two months in summer and deadly grey the rest of the year. It is surrounded by a few uninspiring cafés and shops and the **Juozas Miltinio Drama Theatre** (584 614; www.miltinio-teatras.lt; Laisvės aikštė 5), in action since 1940. By the riverbed, a **small bridge** and **statues** – including an irresistible one of a standing man playing chess – make for a pleasant stroll.

The tiny **Museum of Regional Studies** (Kraštotyros muziejus; 461 973; Vasario 16-osios gatvė 23; adult/child 2/0.50Lt; 10am-6pm Tue-Sat) focuses on ethnography and hosts temporary exhibitions in the city's **oldest building**, dating to 1614, at Kranto gatvė 21.

A great escape are the magical dolls and puppets in the **Fairytale Train** (Pasakų traukinukas; 511 236; Respublikos gatvė 30; admission 3-5Lt; 8am-noon & 1-5pm Mon-Fri)) of the **Wagon Puppet Theatre**. Lithuania's only travelling cart theatre is rarely at home (it travels all summer), but the characters displayed inside this old narrow-gauge train carriage will enchant.

Sleeping & Eating

Hotel Romantik (584 860; www.hotel-romantic.lt; Kranto gatvė 24; s/d/ste 190/320/600;) Romantic is the tone set by Hotel Romantik, housed in a converted old mill. A couple of original architectural features add an authentic rustic touch and the restaurant terrace – definitely the best place in town to dine – overlooking the park is a delight (meals 40Lt to 70Lt). Guests pay extra to use the adjoining fitness centre and spa.

Hotel Panevėžys (501 601; www.hotelpanevezys.lt; Laisvės aikštė 26; s/d 120/160Lt, standard s/d 140/180Lt, lux s/d 200/220Lt) The landmark Soviet ugliness of what used to be the town's only central hotel is infamous. Beige and brown colour schemes remain king in this 12-storey concrete wonder where the cheapest rooms – yet to be renovated – ensure an authentic Soviet experience.

BEER TALK

Northern Lithuania is the land of barley-malt beer, ale-makers keeping to ancient recipes and rituals practised by their ancestors 1000 years ago. People here drink 160L of beer a year, say proud locals.

Big-name brews to glug include **Horn** (www.ragutis.lt), brewed in Kaunas since 1853; Šiauliai-made **Gubernija**; and **Kalnapilis** from Panevėžys, whose **brewery** (www.kalnapilis.lt; Taikos alėja 1), currently closed for a refit, should be welcoming beer tourists by the time you read this. Book tours at Panevėžys tourist office.

Lakeside Biržai, 65km north and the true heart of Lithuanian beer country, hosts the annual two-day **Biržai Beer Festival**, a madcap fiesta of beer-keg throwing and general drunken behaviour. Its **Rinkuškiai Brewery** (☎ 450-35 293; www.rinkuskiai.lt; Alyvų gatvė 8) can be visited, and its beer – everything from light lager to lead-heavy stout – bought in bulk in its factory shop. A lesser-known label to look out for is the sweet **Butautų alaus bravoras**, an ale bottled in brown glass with a ceramic, metal-snap cap like Grolsch. It has been brewed in the village of Butautų since 1750.

Kafen Hauz (☎ 461 595; Ukmergės gatvė 3) German-named Coffee House is new, bright and adds a cheery sparkle to Panevėžys' glazed eye. Look for the elevated street terrace below retro stained glass.

Iki (Ukmerges gatvė 18a) This supermarket is in the three-storey *prekybos centras* (shopping centre) adjoining the bus station.

Getting There & Away

Bus tickets for international destinations are sold at **Eurolines** (☎ 582 888; panevezys@eurolines.lt; 9am-6pm Mon-Fri, to 3pm Sat), at the **bus station** (☎ 463 333; Savanorių aikštė 5). Domestic and regional services include buses to/from Vilnius (20Lt, 2¼ hours, about 12 daily), Kaunas (17Lt, two hours, 20 daily), Šiauliai (11Lt, 1½ hours, 12 daily), Rīga via Bauska (20Lt, four hours, six daily) and Tallinn via Rīga (74Lt, eight hours, three daily).

ANYKŠČIAI

☎ 381 / pop 13,000

Lovely Anykščiai, 60km southeast of Panevėžys, sits on the confluence of the Sventoji and Anyksta Rivers. Fanning eastwards are 76 lakes, the largest of which – **Lake Rubikiai** (9.68 sq km and 16m deep) – is freckled with 16 islands.

A pine forest 10km south of Anykščiai contains **Puntukas Stone** (Puntuko akmuo), a 5.7m-tall by 6.7m-wide by 6.9m-long boulder that legend says was put there by the devil. In trying to destroy Anykščiai's twin-steeple church, **St Mathew's** (1899–1909), a rooster crowed and the devil thundered to hell – prompting the boulder to thunder down from the sky. The **tourist office** (☎ 59 177, 8-655 27943; www.anyksciai.lt; Gegužės gatvė 1; 10am-6pm Mon-Fri, to 3pm Sat) can tell you precisely how to find it.

A steam locomotive is displayed at the **Narrow-Gauge Railway Museum** (Siaurojo geležinkelis istorijos ekspozicija; www.baranauskas.lt; Viltis gatvė 2; adult/child 1.50/0.50Lt; 10am-5pm May-Oct, by appt Nov-Apr), a fun museum for kids housed in Anykščiai's old station that used to be served by cargo trains to Panevėžys (60km west), Šenčionėliai (a major stop on the St Petersburg–Warsaw line, 84km east) and Pastavy in present-day Belarus. The narrow 75cm-wide track here was part of a narrow-gauge rail network operational until the 1970s as a cargo link to the wide-gauge railways. An old rail cycle is the most visitors can ride today.

From the **bus station** (☎ 51 333; Vienuolio gatvė 1) there are buses to/from Panevėžys (three to eight daily), Vilnius (six daily) and Kaunas (13 daily).

WESTERN LITHUANIA

Lithuania's coastline is magical. Vast empty tracts of wild white sand snuggle up against dunes and scented pine for much of its 99km Baltic stretch, climaxing with a world-unique gem – the Curonian Spit (Kursių Nerija), a skinny leg of sand that stalks into Russia. From the late 19th century East Prussian artists, as well Thomas Mann in the 1930s, artists sought inspiration in one of its fishing villages; French philosopher Sartre was photographed in this wind-sculpted Sahara in 1965; and in 2000 Unesco stepped in to safeguard this anorexic, fragile and extraordinary natural

LITHUANIA

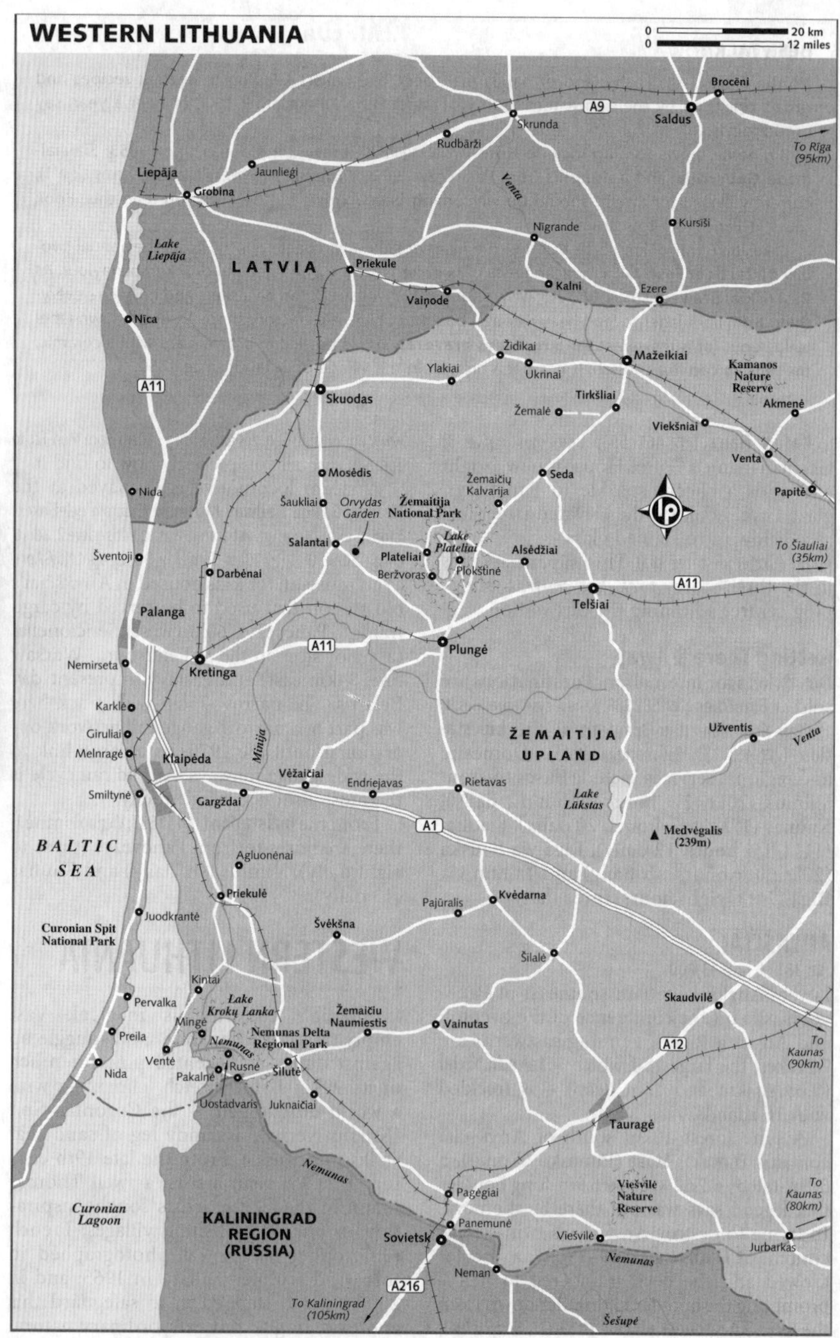
WESTERN LITHUANIA
0 20 km
0 12 miles
Brocēni
Saldus
Skrunda
Rudbārži
To Rīga (95km)
Liepāja
Jaunlieģi
Grobiņa
Venta
Nīgrande
Kursīši
Lake Liepāja
LATVIA
Priekule
Kalni
Vaiņode
Ezere
Nīca
Židikai
Ukrinai
Mažeikiai
Kamanos Nature Reserve
Ylakiai
Skuodas
Tirkšliai
Žemalė
Akmenė
Viekšniai
Venta
Mosėdis
Seda
Žemaičių Kalvarija
Papilė
Nida
Šaukliai
Orvydas Garden
Žemaitija National Park
Lake Plateliai
Salantai
Plateliai
Alsėdžiai
To Šiauliai (35km)
Šventoji
Darbėnai
Beržvoras
Plokštinė
Telšiai
Palanga
Plungė
Kretinga
Nemirseta
Karklė
Giruliai
Melnragė
Klaipėda
Minija
ŽEMAITIJA UPLAND
Užventis
Venta
Smiltynė
Vėžaičiai
Endriejavas
Rietavas
Gargždai
Lake Lūkstas
Medvėgalis (239m)
BALTIC SEA
Agluonėnai
Priekulė
Juodkrantė
Pajūralis
Kvėdarna
Švėkšna
Curonian Spit National Park
Šilalė
Kintai
Pervalka
Lake Krokų Lanka
Žemaičių Naumiestis
Skaudvilė
Mingė
Preila
Nemunas Delta Regional Park
Vainutas
Nemunas
Ventė
Nida
Pakalnė
Rusnė
Šilutė
Uostadvaris
Juknaičiai
To Kaunas (90km)
Tauragė
Nemunas
Pagėgiai
Viešvilė Nature Reserve
To Kaunas (80km)
Curonian Lagoon
KALININGRAD REGION (RUSSIA)
Panemunė
Sovietsk
Viešvilė
Jurbarkas
Nemunas
Neman
To Kaliningrad (105km)
Šešupė
LITHUANIA

DID YOU KNOW

Three widths of train track once snaked across Lithuania: narrow-gauge tracks were 75cm wide; Soviet trains ran on tracks 152cm wide; while European trains ran on tracks 143cm wide.

phenomenon, one of the world's most precious sights.

Klaipėda, the country's third-largest city and major port, is the curious gateway to all this overwhelming natural splendour. Called Memel by Germans (it wasn't part of Lithuania until 1923), this busy city with its tiny Old Town and constant flow of ferries forging across the Curonian Lagoon and into the Baltic Sea exudes a definite grit.

Heading north, romantic souls follow in the footsteps of 19th-century amber fishers in the remote seaside hamlet of Karklė and watch new days dawn from the pier in party-mad Palanga – the hottest spot on Lithuania's coast. And if you nip across the border into Latvia from here (best to ignore the vast storage terminals of Būtingė Oil Terminal you pass en route), there's a wacky surprise waiting.

Peace-lovers should head south to wallow in bird song in the Nemunas Delta Regional Park, a boggy wetland where Lithuania's largest river spills into the lagoon, and villagers boat around beneath bird-filled skies. During spring floods an amphibious tractor is the way to get around.

Then there's what many rate as Lithuania's most extraordinary experience – standing on the edge of an abandoned 30m-deep missile silo, built by the Soviets in the secret heart of a national park to fire deadly warheads at Europe.

Getting There & Around

Klaipėda – the region's transport hub – is easily reached by train from Vilnius (p354) and by bus (p354) from Vilnius, Kaunas and most other towns in Lithuania, as well as from Rīga and Tallinn.

Pedestrian and car ferries (p354) link Klaipėda with Smiltynė on the Curonian Spit, and river boats sail to/from Nida, Rusnė and Kaunas. The Nemunas Delta is impossible to get around without your own vehicle and/or boat.

KLAIPĖDA

☎ 46 / pop 202,500

Sea port Klaipėda, 315km west of Vilnius, is the springboard to the natural beauty of the Curonian Spit. But as Lithuania's third-largest city, it is worth a stop in its own right, notably for its Germanic flavour and architecture that reflects its fascinating past as Prussian capital Memel. The city was destroyed in WWII, during which it served as a Nazi submarine base, but a teeny weeny patch of its Old Town survived unscathed – as did one tower of its once magnificent red-brick castle.

Straddling the narrow strait where the Curonian Lagoon opens into the Baltic Sea, the city is Lithuania's only port of call for *Titanic*-sized cruise ships, and a vital sea link for cargo and passenger ferries between Lithuania, Scandinavia and beyond. Klaipėda celebrates its rich nautical heritage each July with a flamboyant five-day **Sea Festival** (www.juros.svente.lt).

History

Klaipėda was Memel until 1925. Founded in 1252 by the Teutonic Order who built the city's first castle, it was a key trading port from the 15th century until 1629 when Swedish forces destroyed it. After the Napoleonic wars it became part of Prussia (1807) and stayed in Prussian hands until WWI. The population at this time was an even split of Germans and Lithuanians.

Under the Treaty of Versailles, Memel town, the northern half of the Curonian Spit and a strip of land (about 150km long and 20km wide) along the eastern side of the Curonian Lagoon and the northern side of the Nemunas River were separated from Germany as an 'international territory'. It remained stateless until 1923, when Lithuanian troops marched in, annexed it and changed its name two years later to Klaipėda.

Klaipėda was rebuilt and repopulated after WWII, developing into an important city on the back of shipbuilding and fishing. In 1991 its university opened, followed in 2003 by a new cruise terminal. Few Germans remain today.

Orientation

The Danė River flows westward across the city centre and enters the Curonian Lagoon

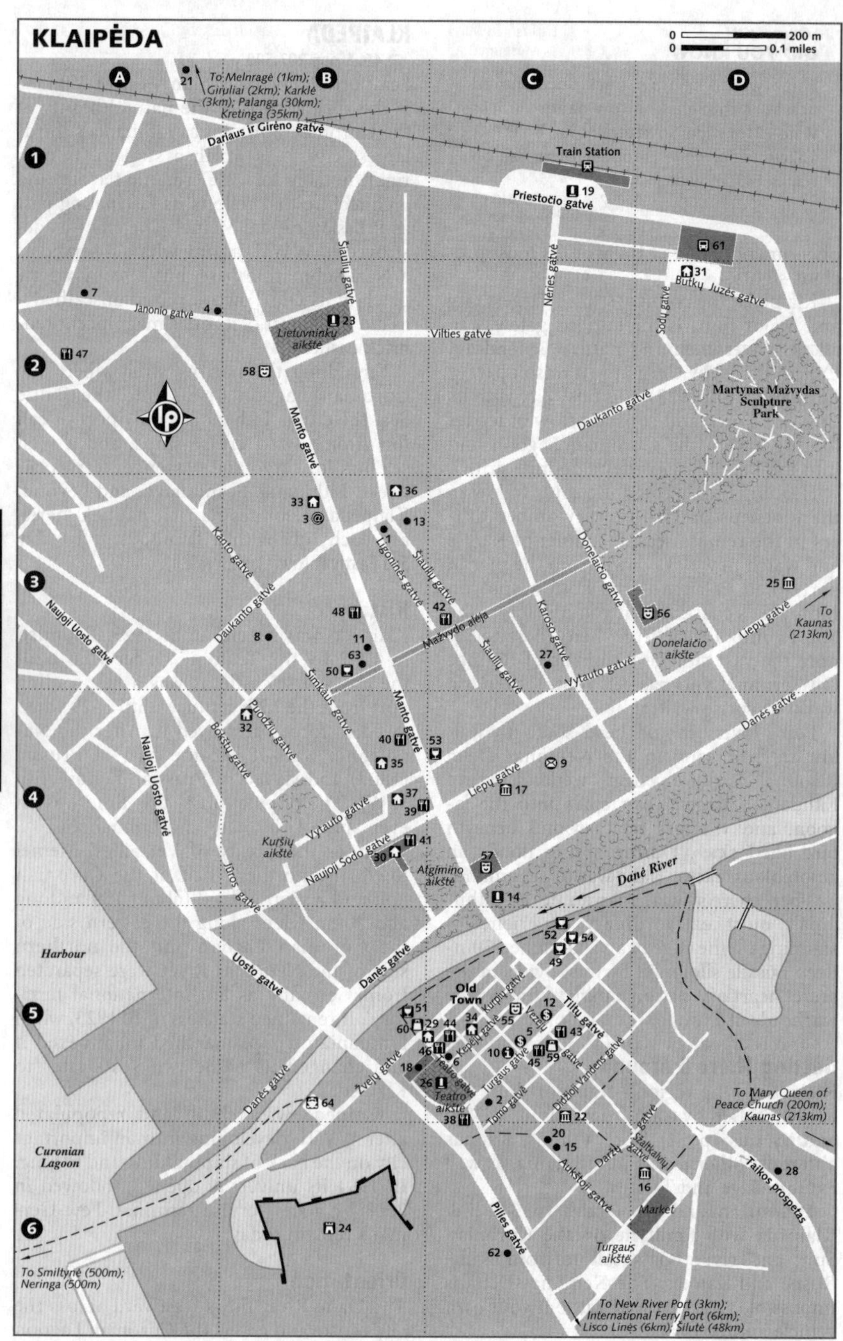
KLAIPĖDA
0 200 m
0 0.1 miles
To Melnragė (1km); Giruliai (2km); Karklė (3km); Palanga (30km); Kretinga (35km)
Dariaus ir Girėno gatvė
Train Station
Priestočio gatvė
Šiaulių gatvė
Nėries gatvė
Butkų Juzės gatvė
Sodų gatvė
Janonio gatvė
Lietuvninkų aikštė
Vilties gatvė
Martynas Mažvydas Sculpture Park
Daukanto gatvė
Manto gatvė
Kanto gatvė
Ligoninės gatvė
Donelaičio gatvė
Naujoji Uosto gatvė
Mažvydo alėja
Karoso gatvė
Donelaičio aikštė
Liepų gatvė
To Kaunas (213km)
Vytauto gatvė
Šimkaus gatvė
Puodžių gatvė
Bokštų gatvė
Danės gatvė
Kuršių aikštė
Naujoji Sodo gatvė
Atgimimo aikštė
Jūros gatvė
Danė River
Harbour
Uosto gatvė
Old Town
Kurpių gatvė
Tiltų gatvė
Vežėjų gatvė
Kepėjų gatvė
Žvejų gatvė
Teatro gatvė
Turgaus gatvė
Teatro aikštė
Tomo gatvė
Didžioji Vandens gatvė
Daržų gatvė
Šaltkalvių gatvė
To Mary Queen of Peace Church (200m); Kaunas (213km)
Taikos prospektas
Curonian Lagoon
Aukštoji gatvė
Market
Pilies gatvė
Turgaus aikštė
To Smiltynė (500m); Neringa (500m)
To New River Port (3km); International Ferry Port (6km); Lisco Lines (6km); Šilutė (48km)

INFORMATION
Akademija....1 B3
Baltic Clipper....2 C5
Baltų Lankų....3 B3
Bankas Snoras....(see 11)
Eurokalbos....4 A2
Hansa Bankas....5 C5
Krantas Travel....6 C5
Lithuanian Student & Youth Travel....7 A2
Mėja Travel....8 B3
Post Office....9 C4
Tourist Office....10 C5
Vaga....11 B3
Vilniaus Bankas....12 C5
West Express....13 B3

SIGHTS & ACTIVITIES
Äennchen von Tharau Statue...(see 26)
Arka....14 C4
Baroti Gallery....15 C6
Blacksmith's Museum....16 D6
Clock Museum....17 C4
Drama Theatre....18 B5
Farewell....19 C1
Klaipėda Art Exhibition Palace...20 C6
Klaipėda Castle Museum Entrance....(see 62)
Klaipėda Castle Museum....(see 24)
Klaipėda University....21 A1
Lithuanian Minor History Museum....22 C5
Martynas Mažvydas Statue....23 B2
Old Castle....24 B6
Picture Gallery....25 D3
Simon Dach Fountain....26 C5
Sothys Spa Centras....27 C3
Švyturys Beer Brewery....28 D6

SLEEPING
Europa Royale....29 C5
Hotel Klaipėda....30 B4
Klaipėda Travellers Hostel....31 D2
Litinterp Guesthouse....32 B4
Navalis....33 B3
Preliudija Guesthouse....34 C5
Prūsija....35 B4
Radisson SAS Klaipėda....36 B3
Viktorija....37 B4

EATING
Anikės Teatras....38 C5
Bambola Pizza....39 B4
Boogie Woogie....40 B4
Forto Dvaras....41 B4
Iki....42 C3
Ikiukas....43 C5
Kurpiai....44 C5
Pėda....45 C5
Senoji Hansa....46 C5
Skandalas....47 A2
XII....(see 30)
Čili Kaimas....48 B3

DRINKING
Glaja....49 C5
Juodojo Katino Smuklė....50 B3
Memelis....51 B5
Meridianas....52 C5
Onyx....53 C4
Žvejų Baras....54 C5

ENTERTAINMENT
Elcalor....55 C5
Honolulu....(see 30)
Klaipėda University Concert Hall....56 D3
Musical Theatre....57 C4
Žemaitija Cinema....58 B2

SHOPPING
Art Gallery Pėda....59 C5
Parko Gallery....(see 10)
Smelio Krantas....60 B5

TRANSPORT
Bus Station....61 D1
Cruise Ship Terminal Entrance...62 C6
Ecolines....63 B3
Old Castle Port....64 B5
Scandlines....(see 30)

4km from the Baltic Sea. The key street axis is the north–south Manto gatvė (north of the river), Tiltų gatvė (for its first 600m south of the river) and Taikos prospektas.

Old Town lies within the 400m south of the river, mostly west of Tiltų gatvė. Most hotels, the train and bus stations and Klaipėda University are north of the river.

Smiltynė, the northern tip of the Curonian Spit, sits 500m off the mouth of the Danė, across the narrow channel which forms the northern end of the Curonian Lagoon.

MAPS

Jāņa sēta's *Klaipėda Neringa* map covers Klaipėda's northern beach suburbs, Smiltynė and the Curonian Spit as well as central Klaipėda (1:10,000). Bookshops sell it for 6.25Lt.

Information

BOOKSHOPS

Akademija (Daukanto gatvė 16) Maps, guidebooks and English-language fiction.

Baltų Lankų (☎ 310 717; www.baltos.lankos.lt; Manto gatvė 21) Best bookshop in town with excellent website and Internet access, on top floor of the red-brick and glass-fronted Mega Plaza shopping centre.

Eurokalbos (☎ 311 076; Janonio gatvė 4) English-language novels.

Vaga (Manto gatvė 9) Maps, travel guides and the *Baltic Times*.

INTERNET ACCESS

The tourist office and Baltų Lankų bookshop have a couple of computers for surfing (2Lt per hour).

LEFT LUGGAGE

Bus station (Bagažinė; Priestočio gatvė; 7.30-11.30am & 12.30-8.30pm)

MEDIA

Klaipėda In Your Pocket (www.inyourpocket.com) Annual city guide published locally and sold in hotels and news kiosks for 5Lt.

MONEY

Change cash or withdraw it with Visa/MasterCard at an ATM at these locations:

Bankas Snoras (Manto gatvė 9)

Hansa Bankas (Turgaus gatvė 9)

Vilniaus Bankas (Turgaus gatvė 15) Cashes American Express traveller's cheques.

POST

Post office (Liepų gatvė 16)

TOURIST INFORMATION

Tourist office (☎ 412 186; tic@one.lt; Turgaus gatvė 5-7; 9am-7pm Mon-Fri, 10am-4pm Sat, 10am-2pm Sun Jun-

Aug, 9am-6pm Mon-Fri, 10am-4pm Sat May-Sep, 9am-5pm Mon-Fri Oct-Apr) Exceptionally efficient tourist office selling maps and locally published guidebooks. It arranges accommodation and English-speaking guides (50Lt per hour).

TRAVEL AGENCIES

Krantas Travel (☎ 395 111; www.krantas.lt; Teatro gatvė 5) Kiel and Karlshamn ferry tickets (p354).

Lithuanian Student & Youth Travel (☎ 314 672; klaipeda@jaunimas.lt; Janonio gatvė 16) Discounted air, plane and bus tickets.

Mėja Travel (☎ 310 295; www.klaipedamejatravel.com; Simkaus gatvė 21-8) Excursions for cruise-ship passengers and amber fishing.

West Express (☎ 310 311; www.westexpress.lt; Daukanto gatvė 20)

Sights

OLD TOWN

Little of German Klaipėda remains but there are some restored streets in the oldest part of town wedged between the river and Turgaus aikštė. Pretty **Teatro aikštė** (Theatre Sq) is the Old Town focus, dominated by the fine classical-style **Drama Theatre** (1857). Hitler proclaimed the *Anschluss* (incorporation) of Memel into Germany to the crowd on the square from the theatre's balcony.

In front tinkles a fountain dedicated to **Simon Dach**, a Klaipėda-born German poet (1605–59), who was the focus of a circle of Königsberg writers and musicians. On a pedestal in the middle of the water stands **Äennchen von Tharau** (1912), a statue of Ann from Tharau sculpted by Berlin artist Alfred Kune and inspired by a famous German wedding and love song originally written in the East Prussian dialect. The words of the song were originally ascribed to Dach, but it's now thought another Königsberg circle member, the composer Johann Albert, wrote them. The statue and fountain is a replica of the original destroyed during the war.

West of Pilies gatvė are the remains of Klaipėda's old moat-protected **castle**. The **Klaipėda Castle Museum** (Klaipėdos pilies muziejus; ☎ 410 524; www.mlimuziejus.lt; Pilies gatvė 4; adult/child 4/2Lt; 🕑 10am-6pm Wed-Sun Jun-Aug, 10am-6pm Tue-Sat Sep-May) inside the one remaining tower tells the castle's story from the 13th to 17th centuries. To get to the museum, walk through the Klaipėda State Sea Port Authority building and a ship-repair yard. Incredibly, this rundown ramshackle yard is the first thing the 20,000 passengers a year who step off luxury cruise ships in Klaipėda see! The **cruise ship terminal** (☎ 490 990; www.ports.lt; Pilies gatvė 4) shares the castle site.

Some excellent modern art hangs in the **Klaipėda Art Exhibition Palace** (Klaipėdos Dailės parodų rūmai; ☎ 410 412; Aukštoji gatvė 3; adult/child 3/1.50Lt; 🕑 noon-6pm Tue-Sun). Next door, **Baroti Gallery** (Baroti galerija; ☎ 313 580; Aukštoji gatvė 3/3) is partly housed in a converted fish warehouse (1819). Its exposed-timber style, called *Fachwerk*, is typical of German Memel.

Around the corner, the **Lithuanian Minor History Museum** (Mažosios lietuvos istorijos muziejus; ☎ 410 524; Didžioji Vandens gatvė 6; adult/child 2/1Lt; 🕑 10am-6pm Tue-Sat) traces the early history of Lithuania Minor. The cute **Blacksmith's Museum** (Kalvystės muziejus; ☎ 410 526; Šžaltkalvių gatvė 2 & 2a; adult/child 2/1Lt; 🕑 10am-6pm Tue-Sat) displays ornate forged-iron works.

NORTH OF THE RIVER

A **riverside park** skirts the northern bank of the Danė. Liepų gatvė – home to the **Picture Gallery** (Paveikslų galerija; ☎ 213 319; Liepų gatvė 33; adult/child 4/2Lt; 🕑 noon-6pm Tue-Sat, to 5pm Sun) with works by Lithuanian expressionist painter Pranas Domšaitis (1880–1965) – was called Adolf-Hitler-Strasse for a brief spell. **Martynas Mažvydas Sculpture Park** (Liepų gatvė), opposite, was a German cemetery in the 1820s.

All manner of clocks – from Gothic to nuclear – tick inside the **Clock Museum** (Laikrodžių muziejus; ☎ 410 413; Liepų gatvė 12; adult/child 4/2Lt; 🕑 noon-6pm Tue-Sat, to 5pm Sun). Carillon concerts are held in its back yard on summer weekends at noon; the 48-bell carillon is in the 44m bell tower of the neighbouring neo-Gothic **post office**.

Klaipėda University (☎ 398 900; www.ku.lt; Manto gatvė 84) is magnificent. Founded in 1991, it's located in red-brick 19th-century Prussian military barracks, home to the 3rd Coastal Division when Estonia was part of the USSR.

SMILTYNĖ

Smiltynė (Map p348) is a hop, skip and five-minute ferry ride away (p354) across the thin strait that divides Klaipėda from its achingly beautiful coastal sister – the Curonian Spit (p362). This strait-side patch of paradise – packed on summer weekends with Klaipėda residents – has beautiful beaches, sandy dunes and sweet-smelling pine forests.

CITY SCAPE

There is no higher spot from which to survey the city than atop the 46.5m tower of Klaipėda's **Mary Queen of Peace Church** (Švč Mergelės Marijos Taikos Karalienės bažnyčia; ☎ 410 120; Rumpiškės gatvė 6a; adult/child 2/1Lt). The enormous concrete church was built in 1957, shut by the Soviet authorities the moment it was complete in 1960 and used as a concert hall until 1988, when the church was reconsecrated and Mass celebrated for the first time. Book a visit through the tourist office.

Equally crowd-pleasing are the sea lion and dolphin shows at the **Lithuanian Sea Museum** (Lietuvos jūrų muzieujus; ☎ 490 740; www.juru.muziejus.lt; adult/student 9/5Lt, dolphin/sea lion show 13/3Lt, camera 5Lt; 🕐 10.30am-6.30pm Tue-Sun Jun-Aug, 10.30am-5.30pm Wed-Sun May & Sep; 10.30am-5pm Sat & Sun Oct-Apr), 1.5km from the passenger ferry landing (for Old Castle Port ferries) at the tip of the peninsula. Seals dance on the rocks and sea lions splash around in the moat around the 19th-century fort in which the aquarium is housed.

In July and August horse-drawn carriages (15Lt to 25Lt) ferry tourists from the ferry landing to the museum. Otherwise, it is a lovely waterside stroll past several local sights. The granite boulder at the start of the path honours past winners of the three- and six-nautical-mile races run around Smiltynė on the second Saturday in October. Next port of call is the National Park Visitors Centre (p363) of the Curonian Spit National Park and the **Curonian Spit National Nature Museum** (Kursių nerijos nacionalinis parkas gamtos muziejus ekspozicija; ☎ 391 179; Smiltynė plentas 12, 10 & 9; adult/child 2/1Lt; 🕐 11am-6pm Tue-Sun Jun-Aug, 11am-6pm Wed-Sun May & Sep), in three wooden houses, incorporating the birds and mammals, plants and insects, and landscape sections of the museum painted yellow, green and brown.

About 700m further north are **old fishing vessels**, including three Baltic Sea fishing trawlers built in the late 1940s and a 1935 **kurėnas** (a traditional 10.8m flat-bottomed Curonian sailing boat used for fishing). Next door, the **Ethnographic Sea Fishermen's Farmstead**, with its collection of traditional 19th-century buildings (the granary, dwelling house, cellar, cattle shed and so on) proffers a glimpse of traditional fishing life.

Activities

Grab your Speedos and hit Smiltynė, where footpaths cut through pine forests across the spit's 1km-wide tip to a bleached-white sandy **beach**. From the ferry landing, walk straight ahead across the car park, then bear left towards Nida; on your right a large sign marks a smooth footpath that leads through pine forest to a women's beach (*Moterų pliažas;* 1km), mixed beach (*bendras pliažas;* 700m) and men's beach (*Vyrų pliažas;* 900m). Nude or topless bathing is the norm on single-sex beaches.

Melnragė, 1km north of Klaipėda, has a pier-clad beach to which city dwellers flock at sunset; **Giruliai Beach** is 1km further north. Buses 6 and 4 respectively link Manto gatvė with both. **Karklė**, another kilometre north, is known for having amber specks washed up on its unusually stony beach after

SCULPTURE SCAPE

In true Lithuanian style, Klaipėda is studded with great sculptures, including 120-odd from the late 1970s in the Martynas Mažvydas Sculpture Park (p350) and a monumental 3.5m one in granite of the geezer the park is named after – **Martynas Mažvydas**, author of the first book published in Lithuanian in 1547 – on Lietuvninkų aikštė.

The red granite pillar propping up a broken grey arch of almighty proportions at the southern end of Manto gatvė is Lithuania's biggest granite sculpture. Engraved with the quote 'We are one nation, one land, one Lithuania' by local poet Ieva Simonaitytė (1897–1978), **Arka** (Arch) celebrates Klaipėda joining Lithuania in 1923.

No sculpture grabs you by the throat more than **Farewell** (2002), a heart-tearing statue of a mother with a headscarf, a suitcase in one hand, and the hand of a small boy clutching a teddy bear in the other. It was given by Germany to Klaipėda to remember Germans who said goodbye to their homeland after the city became part of Lithuania in 1923.

LITHUANIA

autumn storms and for the protected **Dutch Cap**, a 24m sea cliff. The tourist office rents bicycles (6/30Lt per hour/day plus €100 deposit) to cycle to the sand.

Winter visitors will like the luxurious spa **Sothys Spa Centras** (☎ 315 063; Mažoji Smilties gatvė 2; 🕑 8am-9pm Mon-Fri, 9am-8pm Sat), where Turkish sauna, pool and masseurs are at hand. The tourist office arranges **ice-fishing**.

Sleeping

BUDGET

Klaipėda Travellers Hostel (☎ 211 879, 8-685 33104; guestplace@yahoo.com; Butkų Juzės gatvė 7/4; dm/d 34/84Lt; reception 🕑 9am-noon; 💻) This bus-station hostel is small, friendly and eager to please. Two small dorms sleep 12 people and there's one double, a kitchen and free tea, coffee and Internet access. Please take your shoes off when you come in.

Litinterp Guesthouse (☎ 410 644; klaipeda@litinterp.lt; Puodžių gatvė 17; s/d/tr 100/160/210Lt, with shared bathroom 80/140/180Lt; 🕑 8am-7pm Mon-Fri, 10am-3pm Sat; P ♿) This accommodation agency arranges B&B in/around Klaipėda. The 16 rooms in its own guesthouse are clean and nonsmoking. Light pine furnishings create a fresh contemporary look and breakfast is delivered to your room in a basket.

Viktorija (☎ 412 190/88; Šimkaus gatvė 2; s/d/tr/q 45/68/90/96/Lt, d with bathroom 135Lt) Shabby old Viktorija is so horrendously awful it's hard to believe it's really open. But it has to be included for adventurous souls who select accommodation based on 'unforgettable experience' rather than 'comfort' factor. A shower costs 3.50Lt and left luggage at reception costs 1Lt/2Lt per small/big item.

MIDRANGE

Preliudija Guesthouse (☎ 310 077; www.preliudija.com; Kepėjų gatvė 7; s/d from 160/180Lt; 💻) Snug in an Old Town house dating to 1856, this guesthouse – a rare breed in Klaipėda – is charming. Despite its history, rooms are minimalist and modern; each has a single fresh flower in a vase and BBC World on the TV. Breakfast costs an extra 17Lt.

Hotel Klaipėda (☎ 404 372; www.klaipedahotel.lt; Naujoji Sodo gatvė 1; s/d/ste/apt from 280/300/450/1000Lt; P ❄ 💻 ♿) 'Big, friendly and perfectly equipped' boasts the city's landmark 12-storey former Intourist hotel – a magnificent 210-room red-brick monstrosity squatting north of the Danė River. Renovations lend the four-star hotel a contemporary boost; the top-floor XII restaurant (open noon to 3am) is a panoramic treat; and its stylish swimming pool with vast flat-screen TV is almost worth the 40Lt it costs per dip.

Prūsija (☎ 412 081; Šimkaus gatvė 6; d/tw/apt 160/200/240Lt) This bizarre place with an eclectic bunch of gilded mirrors on the walls, 11 rooms and a restaurant serving Caucasian food is – despite its age and odd manner – an inoffensive budget choice. Staff don't speak English but do smile ferociously.

TOP END

Navalis (☎ 404 200; www.navalis.lt; Manto gatvė 23; s/d/ste/apt 380/414/650/800Lt; P ❄ 💻 ♿) The architectural appeal of this fashionably industrial four-star pad is outstanding. In an old red-brick town house dating to 1863, Navalis – Latin for 'naval' – has a lobby large enough to moor a ship, vast rooms dressed in beech or mahogany furniture and a restaurant of sublime standing.

Europa Royale (☎ 404 444; www.europaroyale.com; Teatro gatvė 1; d/ste from €115/220; P ⊠ ❄ 💻 ♿) Slick sliding doors set the tone for this oasis of elegance overlooking Klaipėda's prettiest square. Rooms are refined.

Radisson SAS Klaipėda (☎ 490 800; www.radissonsas.com; Šaulių gatvė 28; s/d/ste from €100/110/235; P ⊠ ❄ 💻 ♿) Being geared towards business travellers, this international-standard hotel is cheaper at weekends when the suits go home. Other plus points include a three-hour express laundry service and superduper breakfast buffet.

THE AUTHOR'S CHOICE

Kurpiai (☎ 410 555; Kurpių gatvė 1a; meals 35-60Lt; 🕑 noon-3am) It's quite incredible really: this Old Town jazz club with cobbled terrace and dark old-world interior has been around for years, opening way before the postindependence bars and restaurants mushroomed. Yet it is not just the best place to eat in Klaipėda, but one of Lithuania's best bars too. (Hell no – it's *the* best.) A Klaipėda legend, not least because of 'Lithuanian Louis Armstrong' Kango and his amazing sax life, Kurpiai is the spot to come for funky live jazz nightly while sampling tender, juicy steaks and fish dishes. It heaves at weekends so get in well before 9.30pm.

Eating

Anikės Teatras (☎ 314 471; Sukilėlių gatvė 8-10; meals 20-40Lt) Just about the only restaurant with a terrace truly plump on Teatro aikštė, this theatrical dining spot with lavish interior is a Klaipėda must-dine. European is served in the *teatras;* Lithuanian in the adjoining *kuršiai.*

Čili Kaimas (☎ 310 953; Manto gatvė 11; meals 15Lt) A chain it might be, but Čili Kaimas deserves recognition on two counts: (a) for its smoked ears, potato pudding and other hearty Lithuanian fodder (b) for its atmospheric setting in a great Soviet-era cinema.

Forto Dvaras (☎ 300 211; Naujoji sodo gatvė 1; meals 20Lt) Another rustic choice: think thatched roof, painted wood and a chef who cooks like Grandma did years ago.

Scandal (Skandalas; ☎ 411 585; Kanto gatvė 44; meals 40Lt) Scandal is a brash American dream, part Wild West, part Mae West, where charcoal-grilled steaks are as big as states. The spare ribs and brownies are legendary.

Bambola Pizza (☎ 312 213; Manto gatvė 1; meals 20Lt) An eatery Klaipėda is famed for in Lithuania, Bambola is a fantastic pizzeria touting over 40 different *picos,* a retro brick interior and busy street terrace.

Boogie Woogie (☎ 411 844; Manto gatvė 5; meals 30Lt) This hugely popular but by no means spectacular food factory serves American and European fodder amid pop memorabilia set to get guests tapping their toes.

Senoji Hansa (☎ 400 056; Kurpių gatvė 1; meals 12-20Lt) This café sits wedged on a wooden decking terrace in the middle of a cobbled street with enviable Theatre Sq view. At 9.50Lt, the chef's lunchtime dish of the day is a gastronomic steal.

Pėda (☎ 310 234; Turgaus gatvė 10) A stylish cellar adjoining an art gallery (entrance around the corner), this old-timer is ideal for light evening snacks, sweet-centred *blyneliai* and live jazz at weekends.

Self-caterers should be able to find what they're looking for at **Iki** (Mažvydo alėja 7/11) and **Ikiukas** (Turgaus gatvė) supermarkets.

Drinking

Old Town boasts several traditional beer bars, including **Žvejų Baras** (Kurpių gatvė 8) and **Glaja** (Kepėjų gatvė 6), which have riverside terraces overlooking **Meridianas** (☎ 310 601; ⏲ noon-3am), an old sailing ship turned bar with sails sponsored by Švyturys (p353).

> **BEER TALK**
>
> Švyturys is the big-brand beer to drink. Brewed in Klaipėda by Lithuania's oldest operating brewery (since 1784), the market leader comes in eight types ranging from the light fresh golden Gintarinis to the old-style unfiltered Baltas (shake before opening) and the strong, dark, amber-coloured Baltijos.
>
> Danish beer giant Carlsberg Breweries bought a controlling stake in Švyturys in 1999 and four years later scooped Utenos (p323) into its corporate fold, managing the two breweries under controlling company Baltic Beverages Holding (p36).
>
> Tours of Klaipėda's **Švyturys brewery** (www.svyturys.lt), rebuilt after WWII, are organised by the tourist office; 1½-hour tours cost 40Lt per person and depart at noon Wednesday and Friday. Reservations are essential.

Memelis (☎ 403 040; www.memelis.lt; Žvejų gatvė 4) This red-brick brewery-restaurant by the river has been in operation since 1871. Interior is old-style beer hall; outside is industrial-feel riverside terrace.

Black Cat Pub (Juodojo Katino Smuklė; ☎ 411 167; Mažvydo alėja 1) Cushioned wicker chairs beneath trees make the Black Cat Pub a nice bar to drink at away from traffic fumes. Look for the Guinness sign and feline outside.

Onyx (☎ 411 995; Manto gatvė 4) A spiral staircase whirls trendy young punters up to mezzanine seating at this chic café with flat-screen TV and an overdose of steel. With no terrace to speak of, it's very much a winter hang-out.

Entertainment

The **Organ Summer Festival** in July and August brings organ concerts to the **Klaipėda University Concert Hall** (Donelaičio gatvė 4; tickets 10Lt). Kurpiai (p352) tops the live-jazz bill.

CINEMA

Watch a movie in English at the **Žemaitija Cinema** (☎ 400 514, 314 090; www.zemaitijoskinas.lt; Manto gatvė 31).

NIGHTCLUBS

Elcalor (☎ 256 186; www.eclalor.lt; Kepėjų gatvė 10; admission before/after 11pm 15/25Lt) With purpled-out windows, Elcalor in Old Town (entrance on

LITHUANIA

Jono gatvė) is Klaipėda's Latin soul. Bands play on Friday and DJs mix Latin, Latin pop and Latin House on Saturday. Entrance (over 21s) includes a free drink.

Honolulu (☎ 404 372; www.honolulu.lt; Naujoji Sodo gatvė 1) A kitsch neon-flashing palm tree sets the tone of this Hawaiian-inspired nightclub, in the basement of Hotel Klaipėda.

THEATRE

The curtain closes on mainstream plays at the **Drama Theatre** (Dramos teatros; ☎ 314 453; Teatro aikštė 2), and the Klaipėda Philharmonic plays at the **Musical Theatre** (Muzikinis teatras; ☎ 397 402; www.muzikinis-teatras.lt; Danės gatvė 19).

Shopping

Stalls selling amber souvenirs dot Teatro aikštė.

Smelio Krantas (☎ 315 110; Žvejų gatvė 4) For quality linen, amber, books and art.

Parko Gallery (☎ 310 501; park.gallery@takas.lt; Turgaus gatvė 9) One of the gallery highlights on Turgaus gatvė. It has contemporary paintings, sculptures and etchings.

Art Gallery Pėda (☎ 310 234; Vežejų gatvė) Has designs by contemporary jeweller Jurga Karčiauskaitė-Lago.

LITHUANIA

Getting There & Away

BOAT

From Klaipėda's **International Ferry Port** (Klaipėdos Nafta; ☎ 395 050; www.spk.lt; Perkėlos gatvė 10), **Scandlines** (☎ 310 561; www.scandlines.lt; Naujoji Sodo gatvė 1) sails to/from Kiel (Germany), Aarhus and Aabenraa (Denmark); and **Lisco Lines** (☎ 395 050; www.lisco.lt; Perkėlos gatvė 10) at the port runs passenger ferries to/from Kiel and Sassnitz (Germany), Karlshamn (Sweden) and Gdansk (Poland). For details on schedules and fares, see p400.

BUS

Ecolines (☎ 310 103; www.ecolines.lt; Mažvydo alėja 1; 🕑 9am-7pm Mon-Fri, 10am-5pm Sat) sells tickets for international destinations (p396).

At the **bus station** (☎ 411 547; Priestočio gatvė) the **information window** (🕑 4.30am-noon & 1-10.30pm) has timetable information. Most buses and minibuses to/from Juodkrantė and Nida depart from the ferry landing at Smiltynė on the Curonian Spit.

Services to/from Klaipėda bus station include the following:

Kaunas 34Lt, three hours, 10 buses daily.
Kretinga 3.20Lt, 1¼ hours, half-hourly between 6.25am and 9.30pm.
Liepāja 13Lt, 2¾ hours, four buses daily.
Nida 8Lt, 1½ hours, two buses daily from the bus station, plus minibuses every half-hour from Smiltynė.
Palanga 2.50Lt to 3.50Lt, 45 minutes, at least half-hourly between 4.15am and 11.35pm.
Pärnu 65Lt, eight hours, three overnight buses weekly.
Rīga 41Lt, six to seven hours, two buses daily (one via Liepāja and Palanga).
Šiauliai 23Lt, 2½ hours, six buses daily.
Tallinn 82Lt, 10 hours, three overnight buses weekly.
Vilnius 44Lt, six hours, around 14 buses daily.

TRAIN

The **train station** (☎ 313 677; Priestočio gatvė 1), 150m from the bus station, has an unusual helmeted clock tower and a moving sculpture (p351) in front.

Daily services include three trains to/from Vilnius (40Lt, five to nine hours), one via Kaunas (25Lt, six hours); six trains to/from Šiauliai (16.50Lt, two to three hours) and Kretinga (3Lt, 20 to 30 minutes).

Getting Around

BOAT

Everything about **Smiltynė ferries** (Smiltynės perkela; 24hr information line ☎ 311 117; www.keltas.lt) – timetables, fares, news flashes – is online. Smoking on ferries is forbidden.

The passenger ferry for Smiltynė leaves from **Old Castle Port** (Senoji perkėla; ☎ 314 257; Žvejų gatvė 8). It docks on the eastern side of Smiltynė, at the start of the Nida road. Ferries sail at least every half-hour between 6.30am and 2.15am June to August (at least hourly until 2am the rest of the year). The crossing takes 10 minutes and a return passenger fare is 1.50Lt/0.75Lt per adult/child, and 2Lt for a bicycle; children under seven sail for free. Except between 9.30am and 7.30pm daily in July and August when it is reserved for foot passengers and cyclists only, motorists can also use Old Castle Port ferries. The return fare for car and passengers is 32Lt.

Year-round, vehicles can use the **New River Port** (Naujoji perkėla; ☎ 310 974; Nemuno gatvė 8), 3km south of the mouth of the Danė River. Ferries sail half-hourly from 6.50am to 8.30pm Monday to Friday, and 7.30am to 9.30pm Saturday and Sunday (hourly in winter). On the Curonian Spit this ferry docks 2.5km south of the Smiltynė ferry landing.

Bus 1 links Klaipėda city centre with the New River Port; in summer an **electric tourist train** (adult/7-10yr 1/0.50Lt) ferries passengers from the New River Port (the train boards the ferry) to the Lithuanian Sea Museum in Smiltynė.

BUS

Buy tickets for local buses from news kiosks for 0.80Lt or from the driver for 1Lt. Bus 8 (known for pickpockets) links the train station with Manto gatvė, the city centre and the Turgaus stop, on Taikos prospektas. Bus 11 links the bus station with Manto gatvė. Minibuses follow the same route, can be flagged down on the street and cost 1.50Lt/2Lt before/after 11pm; pay the driver.

PALANGA

☎ 460 / pop 19,550

Palanga is a seaside resort with a split personality – peaceful pensioner paradise in winter, pounding party spot in summer. Tourists from all over Lithuania and abroad flock to its idyllic 10km sandy beach backed by sand dunes and scented pines.

You'll find Palanga, if you don't hear it first, 25km north of Klaipėda and 18km south of the Latvian border. Blink and you'll miss another hotel or bar opening. Yet despite the crowds and encroaching neon Palanga retains its traditional charm with wooden houses and the ting-a-ling of bicycle bells and pedal-powered taxis adding a quaint air to red-brick Basanavičiaus gatvė – the pedestrian heart of the action.

Brash **Šventoji**, 12km north, lacks the panache of Palanga but – with its inflatable fish that spit out kids, dodgem cars and merry-go-round of restaurant entertainers and fun-fair rides – it entertains. **Nemirseta**, a couple of kilometres south of Palanga, is known for its incredible sand dunes and for being the furthest east the Prussians ever got.

History

Lying on what was for centuries a stretch of Lithuanian Coast, between German territory to the south and German- or Polish-dominated territory to the north, Palanga has often been Lithuania's only port – or potential port, for it was destroyed by the Swedish in 1710. It was a resort in the 19th century, and a Soviet hot spot. After 1991, villas and holiday homes nationalised under the Soviets were slowly returned to their original owners, and family-run hotels and restaurants opened. In 2005 the city's main pedestrian street had a face-lift befitting the sparkling reputation Palanga now enjoys.

Orientation

Vytauto gatvė runs parallel to the coast about 1km inland; the tourist office and bus station are a few steps east at Kretingos gatvė. Busy Basanavičiaus gatvė – pedestrian-only between 11am and midnight in summer and lined with bars and restaurants – heads west from amber stalls at its eastern end to Palanga's famous pier on the sea. Klaipėdos plentas, the main road between Klaipėda and the Latvian border, skirts the town to the east.

MAPS

Jāņa sēta's *Palanga* town plan (1:15,000), featuring Palanga and Šventoji, costs 6.25Lt.

Information

INTERNET ACCESS

Laukinių Vakarų Salūnas (☎ 52 831; Basanavičiaus gatvė 16; per hr 3Lt; 🕓 8am-6am) Saloon bar with Internet room.

EMERGENCY

Police station (☎ 53 837; Vytauto gatvė 4)

MEDICAL SERVICES

Gintarinė vaistinė (www.gintarine.lt; Vytauto gatvė 49; 🕓 9am-9pm)

Palangos vaistinė (Vytauto gatvė 33; 🕓 9am-8pm) Pharmacy in the former KGB headquarters (1944–51).

MONEY

Bankas Snoras Basanavičiaus (Basanavičiaus gatvė; 🕓 8am-noon & 1-8pm Mon-Sat, 9am-6pm Sun); Jūratės (cnr Vytauto & Jūratės gatvė; 🕓 11am-8pm Mon-Sat, to 5pm Sun) Blue booths with currency exchange and ATM.

Hansa Bankas (Jūratės gatvė 15)

Vilniaus Bankas (Vytauto gatvė 61)

POST

Post office (Vytauto gatvė 53)

TOURISM INFORMATION

Tourist office (☎ 48 811, 8-606 05083; www.palangatic.lt; Kretingos gatvė 1; 🕓 9am-6pm Mon-Fri, 9am-5pm Sat & Sun, until 3.30pm Sat & Sun Sep-May) Books accommodation and sells maps and guides; at Palanga bus station.

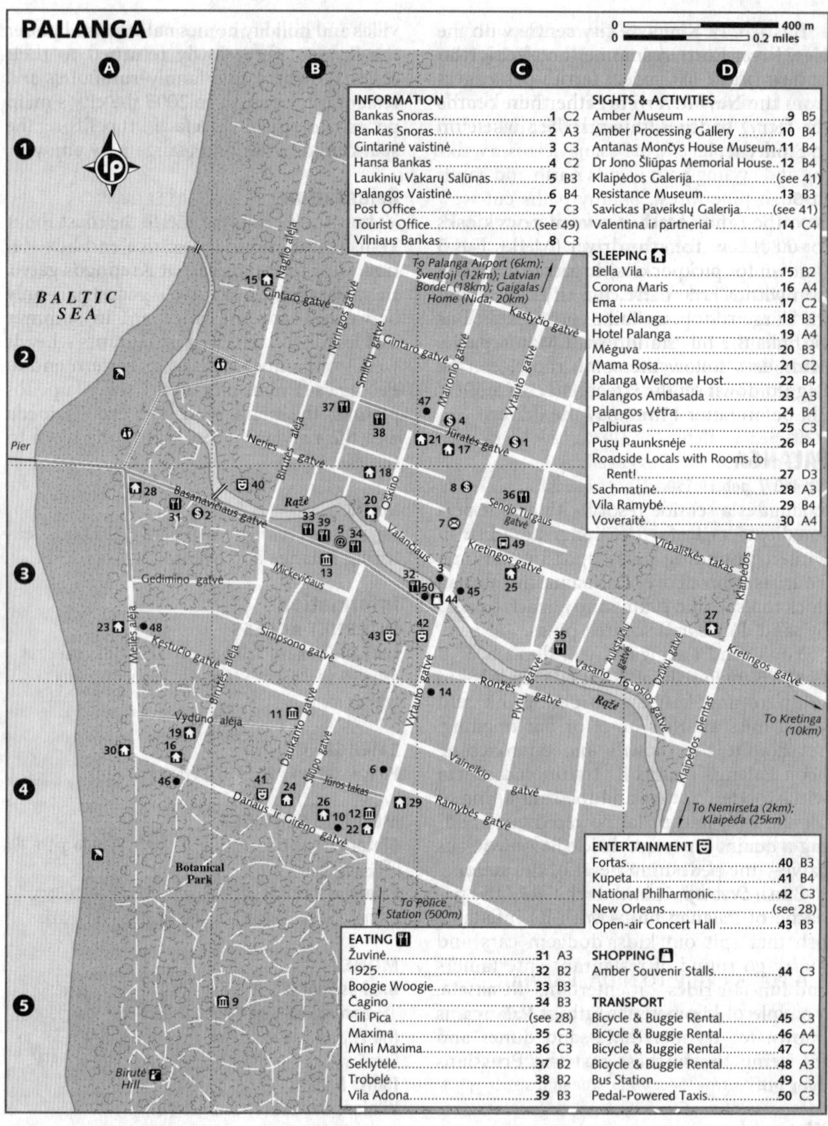

Sights & Activities

A **stroll along Basanavičiaus gatvė** is a sight in itself – and the way most holidaymakers pass dusky evenings. Stalls selling amber straddle the eastern end and amusements dot its entire length – inflatable slides, bungee-jump simulators, merry-go-rounds, electric cars, portrait artists, buskers, and street performers with monkeys. A discordant note amid all this party madness is struck by the small photographic display inside the **Resistance Museum** (Basanavičiaus gatvė 19; 3-5pm Wed, Sat & Sun).

From the end of Basanavičiaus gatvė, a boardwalk leads across the dunes to the **pier**. The original wooden pier dated to

1888. By day, street vendors sell popcorn, *ledai* (ice cream), *dešrainiai* (hot dogs), *alus* and *gira* here. At sunset (around 10pm in July) families and lovers gather here on the sea-facing benches to watch the sunset.

From the pier end of Basanavičiaus, a walking and cycling path wends north and south through pine forest. Skinny paths cut west onto the sandy **beach** at several points and, if you follow the main path (Meilės alėja) south onto Darius ir Girėno gatvė, you reach the **Botanical Park** where cycling and walking tracks are rife. Fascinating B&W photos of old Palanga fill the **Dr Jono Šliūpas Memorial House** (Jono Šliūpo memorialinė sodyba; ☎ 54 559; Vytauto gatvė 23a; adult/child 2/1Lt; 🕒 11am-5pm Tue-Sun).

Contemporary artworks are showcased at **Klaipėdos Galerija** (☎ 410 401; Daukanto gatvė 24; 🕒 2-7pm) and **Savickas Paveikslų Galerija** (☎ 8-685 62637; Daukanto gatvė 24), a twinset of galleries in an interior courtyard. The **Antanas Mončys House Museum** (Antonio Mančio namai muzeijus; ☎ 49 366; Daukanto gatvė 16; adult/child 2/1Lt; 🕒 noon-5pm Tue, to 7pm Wed-Sun) displays sculptures, collages and masks by Lithuanian émigré artist Antanas Mončys (1921–93).

BOTANICAL PARK & AMBER MUSEUM

Lush greenery and swans gliding on still lakes make Palanga's Botanical Park a haven of peace after the frenetic-paced beach and town centre. The 1-sq-km park includes a rose garden, 18km of footpaths and **Birutė Hill** (Birutės kalnas), once a pagan shrine. According to legend, it was tended by vestal virgins, one of whom, Birutė, was kidnapped and married by Grand Duke Kęstutis. A 19th-century chapel tops the hill.

The highlight is the **Amber Museum** (Gintaro muziejus; ☎ 51 319, 53 501; Vytauto gatvė 17; adult/child 5/2.50Lt; 🕒 10am-8pm Tue-Sat, to 7pm Sun), inside a sweeping classical palace (1897). The museum showcases 20,000-odd examples of Baltic gold (p35).

AMBER PROCESSING GALLERY

A key stop on Lithuania's Baltic Amber Road (p282) is an old barn that has been renovated and painted yellow to become an amber workshop. In the 17th century there were a dozen or so such workshops, which today's **Amber Processing Gallery** (Gintaro dirbtuvės galerija; ☎ 8-652 36719; Vytauto gatvė 21; admission free; 🕒 10am-8pm May-Sep), run by the Palanga guild of amber masters, emulates. In the late 1880s Palanga was one of the largest amber-processing centres in the Baltics, its amber products being transported to Russia then mailed on to the Caucasus, Germany and France. A gallery sells finished amber pieces (jewellery, sculptures, chessboards etc), as does upmarket amber jeweller **Valentina ir partneriai** (☎ 51 386; Vytauto gatvė 66; 🕒 10am-6pm).

KRETINGA

This winter garden has seen better days but the green-fingered might still enjoy the tropical mirage of 850 species of exotic plants blooming forth in a tatty classical glasshouse at the **Kretinga Museum** (Kretingos muziejus; ☎ 445-53 505; Vilniaus gatvė 20; adult/student 3/1Lt; museum 🕒 10am-6pm Mon, 9am-8.30pm Tue-Sun, café 🕒 noon-11pm), 10km east in Kretinga. The hot house opened in 1875 in one of the many homes of the Tyszkiewicz family of Polish nobles, but

A WACKY TRIP TO NIDA, LATVIA

Wackier than wacky is the Gaigalas family home, a crumbling homestead – a stone's throw from the sea – with a garden decorated solely from trash washed up on the 3.5km stretch of beach in front. Life rings, 'women only' signs from the beach, toothbrushes, hard hats, fishing nets, driftwood, buoys by the barrow load: you name it, it's strung on the branch of a tree, studded on a bush or retooled as a sculpture. Carefully wrapped in plastic are 25 letters washed up in bottles since 1995.

Totally ridiculous it might seem, but a visit here is a unique opportunity to peek into a local home and see how far too many people in these tough postindependent climes live: water is from a well, the only sink is beneath the stars and Birutė's only real income in the past 10 years has been from the odd camper she lets camp in her field and the 15kg of amber specks she's found on the beach after autumn storms.

Find the Gaigalas home in pinprick Nida, 20km north of Palanga and 2km north of the Lithuanian border in Latvia. After crossing, turn left after 200m down a mud track signposted Nida and follow it for 4km. All donations welcome: look for the orange buoy with the money-box slit.

THE AUTHOR'S CHOICE

Hotel Palanga (☎ 41 414; www.palangahotel.lt; Birutės alėja 60; d 500-800Lt, 1-/2-room apt 1200/1600Lt; P ⊠ ⊠ ⊒ ⊠) A breathtaking vision of glass and wood wrapped inside 80-year-old pine trees, this chic hotel was built from new – lopping down just three trees in the process. The result is stunning: rooms peer out on blue sky and tree trunk, treetop or sea (in the case of the top floor), while furnishings are subtle, luxurious, with natural hues of amber, cream and sand predominating. The outdoor pool is a sparkling expanse of blue between trees while the sauna complex (free to hotel guests between 8am and noon; 200Lt per hour at other times) is, as the hotel bumf phrases it, 'an oasis for body and soul'. Best of all, the imaginative souls behind Palanga's swishest project to date are all set to open a three-star counterpart on the same street very soon. Call Hotel Palanga for an update.

a fire devastated it in 1915 and in 1940 the Soviet Army destroyed it.

LITHUANIA

Festivals & Events

The summer season opens on the first Saturday of June and closes with a massive street carnival, song festival and pop concert on the last Saturday in August. Summer is one long merry-go-round of music concerts of all genres.

The three-day **Palanga Seals** (Palangos ruoniai) festival in mid-February sees thousands of hardy swimmers frolic and squeal in the freezing waters of the Baltic Sea.

Sleeping

Prices listed are for the high season (June to September) when everything gets booked up fast; winter sees rates slashed by up to 50%.

Palanga Welcome Host (☎ 48 723; www.palangawelcomehost.lt; Vytauto gatvė 21) is an association of 150 private homes with self-catering rooms, apartments and villas to rent.

BUDGET

Try haggling with one of the many locals who stand at the eastern end of Kretingos gatvė touting *'Nuomojami kambariai'* (rooms for rent) signs. Most houses on Nėries gatvė and Birutės alėja tout the same sign. Count on paying 25Lt to 100Lt a night, room quality and facilities depending. Alternatively, contact room-rental agency **Palbiuras** (☎ 51 500, 8-675 37222; www.palbiuras.lt; Kretingos gatvė 12) or Litinterp Guesthouse (p352) in Klaipėda.

Voveraitė (☎ 52 532; 8-699 88808; voveraite24@one.lt; Meilės alėja 24; d 120-350Lt) Find these 'excellent luxury rooms' wedged between a café and the beach. Jacuzzi-clad rooms on the top floor can apparently view the sea.

Ema (☎ 48 608; www.ema.lt; Jūratės gatvė 32; s/d 60/100Lt) Blue, pink, green, yellow – there is a wall for every colour at this basic but bold guesthouse. A cactus marks the spot.

Mėguva (☎ 48 839; Valančiaus gatvė 1; s/d/tr 60/120/75Lt) Tucked behind Palanga's red-brick church, this old Soviet block touts three sets of seasonally adjusted prices and a clutch of rooms sporting varying degrees of renovation. Triples with shared bathroom remain rock bottom.

MIDRANGE

Vila Ramybė (☎ 54 124; www.vilaramybe.lt; Vytauto gatvė 54; d 80-200Lt) It is tricky to snag a room at this stylish, unpretentious standout. This 1920s wooden villa is the pick of the crop as far as Vilnius trendies are concerned. Pine-clad rooms come in soothing pastel hues of blues and greens, seven of the 12 have a terrace and most have a little lounge. Its terrace restaurant is equally hip.

Hotel Alanga (☎ 49 215; www.alanga.lt; Nėries gatvė 14; d/ste 160/390Lt, apt with/without kitchen 270/250Lt; P ⊠) This family-friendly hotel might not be the most fashionable, but its rooms are attractive, spotlessly clean and comfortable, and unbeatable value for money. They also have balconies and heated towel rails. Breakfast/parking costs an extra 20Lt/15Lt and a hotel nanny cares for kids for 5Lt per hour.

Bella Vila (☎ 26 815; www.bellevila.lt; Gintaro gatvė 1a; d/apt €50-150; P) Beautiful Villa is superbly placed in pine forest. Favoured by sports enthusiasts, it rents canoes (15Lt per hour), arranges wind- and kitesurfing, and has a sauna. The 12 basic but comfortable rooms are kitchenette-equipped.

Palangos Ambasada (☎ 8-698 08333; www.palangosambasada.lt; Meilės alėja 16; d 160Lt; P) This quiet villa backing onto dunes is the closest you'll get to the beach. Half of its dozen spacious rooms face the water but room 21 is the only one to boast a Real McCoy sea view. Breakfast is DIY with the aid of a fridge, kettle and crockery in each room.

Corona Maris (☎ 51 329; www.coronamaris.lt; Darius ir Girėno gatvė 5; d/apt 220/350Lt; P) With cottages and apartments rather than hotel rooms, this smart modern guesthouse is worth noting. Built from red brick, glass and wood, it is a striking complex framed by well-tended lawns. Doubles have microwave and fridge; apartments have proper kitchens. Guests can rent bikes for 5Lt per hour.

Palangos Vėtra (☎ 53 032; www.vetra.lt; Daukanto gatvė 35; s/d 270/320Lt; P) An oasis of Scandinavian glass and wood, Palangos Vėtra accommodates every need. Standouts include an ATM in the lobby, the quick-service coffee bar and the inflatable slide set up on the green lawn opposite in summer. The hotel pool, sauna, Jacuzzi and steam bath are free to guests between 8am and 10am; otherwise pay 100Lt per hour.

TOP END

Sachmatinė (☎ 51 655; www.sachmatine.lt; Basanavičiaus gatvė 45; d 190-600Lt, tr 330-450Lt; P) Pride of place party- and location-wise, this trendy design hotel is near the pier. But don't expect peace; its 11 stylish rooms are above a busy pizza joint and nightclub.

Mama Rosa (☎ 48 581; www.mamarosa.lt; Jūratės gatvė 28a; s/d from 220/395Lt; P) The height of romance, Mama Rosa has eight sweet rooms, each cosily clad English-style with fireplace, trouser press and heated bathroom floor. There is a stylish lounge, sauna complex (150Lt per hour) and Jacuzzi (75Lt per hour) for guests.

Pusų Paunksnėje (☎ 49 080; www.pusupaunksneje.lt; Dariaus ir Girėno gatvė 25; d P) Lithuanian basketball fans, watch out! This beautiful wooden tavern, arranged around a courtyard big enough to host a full-sized tennis court on ground level and a subterranean car park below, feels as giant as its owner – basketball hero Arvydas Sabonis.

Eating

The focus is on Basanavičiaus gatvė, where the good, bad and ugly line up for a parade of kitsch dining, flaunting everything from fake Hawaiian sunshades to Wild West taverns. From 7pm until midnight, bands blast out cheesy Lithuanian and Russian pop tunes on practically every restaurant terrace.

Those seeking peace – not to mention style – should head for the outside terrace restaurant of achingly cool Vila Ramybė (p358) or Pusų Paunksnėje (p359); pay from 35Lt per head.

Opening hours listed below are for high season; many places don't open in winter.

1925 (☎ 52 526; Basanavičiaus gatvė 4; meals 25Lt) Sunk down from Basanavičiaus, this old wooden house provides relief from the main-street madness. Cuisine is simple and its back garden with church view is the least Disneylike you'll find.

Vila Adona (☎ 40 313; Basanavičiaus gatvė 24; meals 20-50Lt; 9-3am) Vast manicured terrace gardens front this majestic villa, draped in flower boxes. Service is slick (earpieces ensure waiters stay in touch with the kitchen) and a menu in full colour suits every gastronomic mood. Breakfast is served until 11am.

Boogie Woogie (☎ 30 413; Basanavičiaus gatvė 28; meals 20-50Lt; 10am-2am Sun-Thu, to 3am Fri & Sat) Interior designers adopted a definite Disney approach at this enormous tavern with elaborate water garden out back. Cuisine is Lithuanian with a generous pinch of European.

Čili Pica (☎ 8-686 23355; Basanavičiaus gatvė 45; 20/50cm pizza from 9/45Lt; 8am-2am Mon-Thu, to 6am Fri & Sat) This pizzeria is the face of Palanga, with its mixed crowd of kid-clad couples, noisy families and young beauties out to party. Find it propped up on candyfloss-pink pillars. Pizzas come in 53 varieties.

On the main street, **Žuvinė** (☎ 53 555; Basanavičiaus gatvė 37a; meals 20-50Lt) cooks up fish and **Čagino** (☎ 53 555; Basanavičiaus gatvė 14; meals 20-50Lt; 10am-midnight), Russian cuisine, both behind striking glass façades.

Away from the main street:

Seklytėlė (☎ 57 415, Jūratės gatvė 18; meals 20Lt) This delightful wooden house is painted a cheery canary yellow and cooks up home-made Lithuanian food in a quaint flowery garden. Granny-knitted rugs are provided for nippier evenings.

Trobelė (Jūratės gatvė; meals 20Lt) Drinkers and diners soak up a beer-garden atmosphere at this informal restaurant where kids run riot on swings, slides and cars while grown-ups munch smoked pigs' ears, boiled pig's leg and the Lithuanian like.

Self caterers should check out **Maxima** (Plytų gatvė 9) and **Mini Maxima** (Senojo Turgaus gatvė 1) supermarkets.

LITHUANIA

Entertainment

The tourist office knows what's on where. Watch out for posters outside the **National Philharmonic** (Nacionalinė filharmonija; Vytauto gatvė 45) and nearby **Open-air Concert Hall** (Vasaros koncertų salė; ☎ 52 210; Vytauto gatvė 43).

Kupeta (Daukanto gatvė 24) For live jazz, folk and blues, try this hip jazz club.

Vila Aldona (p359), **Fortas** (☎ 51 555; Neries gatvė 39; admission 15Lt) and **New Orleans** (☎ 48 296; Basanavičiaus gatvė 45) are nightclubs.

Getting There & Away

Reach Palanga by road or air; services are substantially more frequent in summer.

AIR

Palanga Airport (☎ 52 020; www.palanga-airport.lt; Liepojos plentas 1), 6km north of the centre, is served by a once-weekly Lithuanian Airlines flight to/from Vilnius.

Air Lithuania handles international flights to Hamburg, Oslo, Billund (Denmark), Munich, Cologne and Moscow. SAS, Air Baltic, Avitrans and Palanga-based Amber Air all fly to/from Copenhagen. For more details, see p393.

Amber Air (☎ 56 338; www.amberair.lt) and **Air Lithuania** (☎ 53 431) have an airport office.

BUS

Services at the tiny **bus station** (☎ 53 333; Kretingos gatvė 1):

Kaunas 36Lt, 3½ hours, about 11 buses daily.
Klaipėda 2.50Lt to 3.50Lt, 45 minutes, at least half-hourly between 4.15am and 11.35pm.
Rīga (via Liepāja) 40Lt, five hours, three buses weekly.
Šiauliai 22Lt, 2½ hours, about 10 daily via Panevėžys and Plungė.
Vilnius 47Lt, six hours, about nine daily.

Getting Around

Bus 2 runs to/from the airport, roughly every hour from 6am to 10pm. Timetables are posted at its town centre stop on Požėlos gatvė behind the bus station.

The main taxi stand is on Kretingos gatvė in front of the bus station; a taxi from the airport into town costs 20Lt.

Pedal-powered taxis (☎ 8-606 55928) are at the eastern end of Basanavičius gatvė. May to September, bicycle-hire stalls pepper the town. Hourly rates are 6Lt for a bicycle, 15Lt/20Lt for a three-/four-wheel buggie for two and 35Lt for a two-kid buggie.

ŽEMAITIJA NATIONAL PARK

☎ 460 / pop 3500

Head 50km inland from Palanga and you hit this 200-sq-km national park, enshrined in fables of devils, ghosts and buried treasure amid its carpet of fir trees. It's named after the historical region of Samogitia (Žemaitija), and people in this neck of the woods flaunt a fierce sense of ethnic identity. The presence of an underground Soviet

GET STONED

A stony silence reigns over 'Lithuania's Stonehenge', as the **Orvydas Farmstead** (adult/child 4/2Lt; 🕑 10am-7pm Tue-Sun) is known. Some say divine intervention was behind the prolific, obsessional carvings and fantastical creations of stonemason Kazys Orvydas (1905–89) and oldest son turned Franciscan monk Vilius (1952–92), which struggle for space today between the weeds that threaten to smother the once well-kept garden.

Originally carved from stone and wood for the village cemetery in Salantai, the collection was hoarded at the Orvydas homestead after Khrushchev's wrath turned on religious objects in the 1960s. But most of the bizarre collection dates to the 1980s, the site being blockaded by the Soviets to prevent visitors getting to the persecuted Orvydas family. A traditional Samogitian roadside cross marks the farmstead entrance, 5km south of Salantai on the road to Plungė.

Stone-lovers heading in the opposite direction can get stoned at the **Museum of Unique Stones** (☎ 76 291; Salantų gatvė 2; adult/child 2/1Lt, museum guide 5.50Lt; 🕑 8am-6pm summer, 8am-noon & 1-5pm Mon-Fri winter) in Mosėdis, 12km north of Salantai. Ranging from boulders to pebbles labelled with their origin from Scandinavia and the bottom of the Baltic Sea, the eclectic collection of stones spills out around the entire village.

Four daily buses between Klaipėda and Skuodas stop in Salantai and Mosėdis. Buses also run to Salantai and Mosėdis from Plungė. For the Orvydas Garden get off at the last stop before Salantai and walk about 1km.

FROM RUSSIA WITH LOVE

Deep in the forests of Žemaitija National Park a secret Soviet underground missile base has been discovered. It once housed mighty nuclear missiles – with enough power to destroy most of Europe. The 22m R12 rockets with 3m warheads were smuggled into the heart of Lithuania so that they were in range of their targets.

This terrifying arsenal lay hidden from the Lithuanian people for at least two decades. The base, a circular underground centre, was flanked by four missile silos, only visible from the ground by their domed tops. The James Bond–style pad, which lies in Plokštinė, just a few kilometres east of the idyllic rural village Plateliai, was equipped with electrical and radio stations, and control rooms. Ten thousand soldiers were secretly drafted in from USSR satellite states to construct the base in 1960, taking eight months to dig out the enormous 25m-deep silos. It was home to the 79th Rocket Regiment until 1978 – when the missiles mysteriously disappeared and the base was left to rot. During its history the base deployed rockets to Cuba during the crisis in September 1962 and was put on red alert during the 1968 Czechoslovakia aggression. The military town, once home to 320 soldiers, stands nearby: travellers can sleep in its barracks (p361).

In summer the base can be visited by **guided tour** (adult/child 4/2Lt; tours 10am, noon, 2pm, 4pm & 6pm May-Aug); at other times you need to ring Žemaitija National Park HQ (p361) in Plateliai to arrange a tour and/or book an English-speaking guide (30Lt per hour). Tours take you into the heart of the base: you see the control room, heating room, enormous diesel engine used to power the place and, most terrifyingly of all, one of the 27m-deep silos (6m across) where a warhead once stood ready. It is cold underground so bring a warm jumper. Sturdy shoes are also recommended; 30 years of abandonment renders the bat-infested site hazardous. A **3.2km nature trail** leads from the site into the surrounding forest and past the remains of security lines.

By car take the road to Plateliai off the A11 (Kretinga–Šiauliai road), follow signs to Plateliai, then turn right (east) to Plokštinė following the 'Militarizmo Ekspozicija' (Military Exhibition) signs; find the base at the end of the gravel road, 5km from the Plateliai road turn-off. It's impossible to get to without your own wheels.

missile base only adds to the mysterious charm.

Lake Plateliai (Platelių ežeras), renowned for its seven islets and seven ancient shore terraces, is the park's most stunning natural feature – the site of midsummer celebrations (p15). Legend says the lake was swept into the sky by a storm before dropping where it lies now after the magic words 'Ale plate lej' (the rain goes wide) were uttered.

Many traditional Samogitian festivals are celebrated in small-town **Plateliai** on its western shore, including the amazingly colourful **Shrove Tuesday Carnival**. See elaborate masks worn during the Shrovetide festivities in the old granary of **Plateliai Manor** (Didžioji gatvė 22).

About 20km northeast is **Samogitian Calvary** (Žemaičių Kalvarija), built on the site of 9th- to 13th-century burial grounds. Pilgrims flock here during the first week of July to climb the seven hills where 20 chapels form a 7km 'Stations of the Cross' route in commemoration of Christ's life, death and resurrection.

Plungė, 5km south of the park and the main gateway into it, is of no interest bar the modern Samogitian art (carvings, metal works, sun crosses) displayed in the **Žemaitija Art Museum** (Žemaičių dailės muziejus; ☎ 54 731; 10am-5pm Wed-Sun), inside a run-down 19th-century manor house.

Information

In Plateliai the **national park headquarters** (☎ 49 231; www.zemaitijosnp.lt; Didžioji gatvė 8; 8am-noon & 12.45-5pm Mon, 8am-7pm Tue-Fri, 8am-5pm Sat) issues fishing permits (1Lt/3Lt per day/month), arranges guides (15Lt to 30Lt an hour), has information on yacht, windsurf and boat hire, and can direct you to the workshops of local folk artists. It also hosts a small exhibition on park flora and fauna.

Sleeping & Eating

In July and August die-hards can kip the night in the former military barracks: 15Lt gets you a bed (no hot water, no shower, one loo between everyone); the park headquarters can book you in.

Otherwise the park headquarters arranges B&B (around 50Lt per person) in

LITHUANIA

some fabulous farms and private homes in the park, including the flowery lakeside home of **Marija Striaukienė** (☎ 49 152, 8-698 03485) in the village of Beržoras. In Plateliai, **Morta Mikašauskienė** (☎ 49 117, 8-682 05059; Ežero gatvė 33; 4-bed cottages 160Lt; P) rents little wooden houses for four people (160Lt) and has a traditional sauna (80Lt for three hours).

Getting There & Away

See Klaipėda (p354), Palanga (p342) and Šiauliai (p360) for limited public transport to/from Žemaitija.

CURONIAN SPIT NATIONAL PARK

☎ 469 / pop 2600

The western Lithuanian scent of ozone and pine is at its headiest on this thin tongue of sand. Waves from the Baltic Sea pound one side, the Curonian Lagoon laps the other. The winds and tree-felling have sculpted the Curonian Spit (Kursių Nerija) over time. But this precious natural treasure is by nature a fragile one – being made up of millions of grains of constantly shifting sand. As the dunes creep closer to the Baltic Sea there are fears it may one day disappear.

In 1991 the Curonian Spit National Park was created to protect the dunes, lagoon and surrounding sea. Lush pine forests filled with deer, elk and wild boar cover 70% of the park; the dunes make up 25% of it; and just 1.5% is urban, namely the four traditional villages where fishermen smoke their catch according to an old Curonian recipe. The main industry is tourism, the double-edged sword that yields both its main source of income and biggest environmental threat.

SPIT RULES

- National park entrance fee: car, driver and passengers 20Lt, bus passenger or foot 3Lt.
- Speed limit: 40km/h in villages, 60km/h or 70km/h on open roads.
- Don't bathe in the lagoon: it's polluted.
- Don't romp in the dunes, pick flowers or stray off designated footpaths.
- Don't damage flora or fauna, mess with bird nests, pitch a tent or light campfires.
- Beware of elks crossing the road.
- Break a rule and risk an on-the-spot fine of up to 300Lt.
- In case of forest fire: Juodkrantė ☎ 8-259 53273, Preila and Pervalka. ☎ 8-259 55125; Nida ☎ 8-259 52224.
- To alert a lifeguard: ☎ 8-469 52239.

SHIFTING SANDS & DELICATE DUNES

Legend has it that motherly sea giantess Neringa created the spit, lovingly carrying armfuls of sand in her apron to form a protected harbour for the local fishing folk. The truth is as enchanting. The waves and winds of the Baltic Sea let sand accumulate in its shallow waters near the coast 5000 or 6000 years ago to create an original beauty found nowhere else.

Massive deforestation in the 16th century started the sands shifting. Trees were felled for timber, leaving the sands free to roam unhindered at the wish of the strong coastal winds. At a pace of 20m a year, the sands swallowed 14 villages in the space of three centuries.

Dubbed the 'Sahara of Lithuania' due to its desert state, drastic action was needed. In 1768 an international commission set about replanting. Today this remains a priority of the national park authorities. Deciduous forest (mainly birch groves) covers 20% of the national park; coniferous forest, primarily pine and mountain pine trees, constitutes a further 53%. Alder trees can be found on 2.6 sq km (3% of the park's area). Lattices of branches and wooden stakes have pinned down the sand.

But the sands are still moving – 5.5m north in 2002 and at least 1m a year since. Slowly the spit is drifting into the Baltic Sea. Each tourist who scrambles and romps on Parnidis Dune – the only remaining free-drifting dune – meanwhile pushes down several tonnes of sand. With 1.5 million people visiting the dunes each year, the threat of people wandering off designated paths – not to mention forest fire – is high.

The dunes are also shrinking. Winds, waves and humans have reduced them by 20m in 40 years. Its precious beauty may yet be lost forever.

The entire Curonian Spit was Prussian territory until WWI. It used to have a hugely magnetic attraction for German exiles who returned to the spot where they once lived to holiday instead, but today dozens of world languages are heard among tourists.

The southern half of the spit belongs to Russia; a road runs the whole length to Kaliningrad (see the Kaliningrad Excursion chapter), in the neighbouring Russian-owned Kaliningrad Region. The main settlement on the Lithuanian side is Nida, a quaint summer resort north of the border, which forms the Neringa administrative district with Juodkrantė, Pervalka and Preila.

Information

There is a tourist office (www.neringainfo.lt) in Nida (p366) and Juodkrantė (p364), and the national park website (www.nerija.lt) is invaluable. For spit accommodation, surf www.kopos.lt.

National Park Visitors Centre Nida (Lankytojų centras; ☎ 51 256; Naglių gatvė 8; 🕒 9am-noon & 1-5pm Mon-Sat, 9am-2pm Sun May-Sep); Smiltynė (☎ 46-402 257; kinfo@takas.lt; Smiltynės plentas 11; 🕒 8am-noon & 1-5pm Mon-Fri, 9am-4pm Sat, 9am-2pm Sun Jun-Aug, 9am-noon & 1-5pm Mon-Fri Sep-May). Arranges guides (40Lt per hour) and stocks an abundance of information on walking, cycling, boating and lazing activities in the park.

Festivals & Events

The summer season – early June to the end of August – ushers in the **Summer Extravaganza Neringa** (Vasaros pramogų kolekcijos; ☎ 1588; www.vasaraneringoje.lt), a fiesta of concerts, craft days and cultural events.

Getting There & Away

The Klaipėda–Smiltynė ferry (see p354) is the main access route. From Smiltynė, microbuses – timed to coincide with ferry arrivals/departures – ply the route to/from Nida via Juodkrantė. Some stop in Pervalka and Preila too; see p370 for details. In low season, team up with fellow Nida-bound travellers in Smiltynė and share a taxi; a fare per person to Nida is around 10Lt, excluding park entrance fee. A daily river boat links the Curonian Spit with Kaunas (p338).

You can also reach Kaliningrad (south) in Russia. The Russian border post is 3km south of Nida on the main road. Don't contemplate this without the necessary Russian visa and paperwork (see p392).

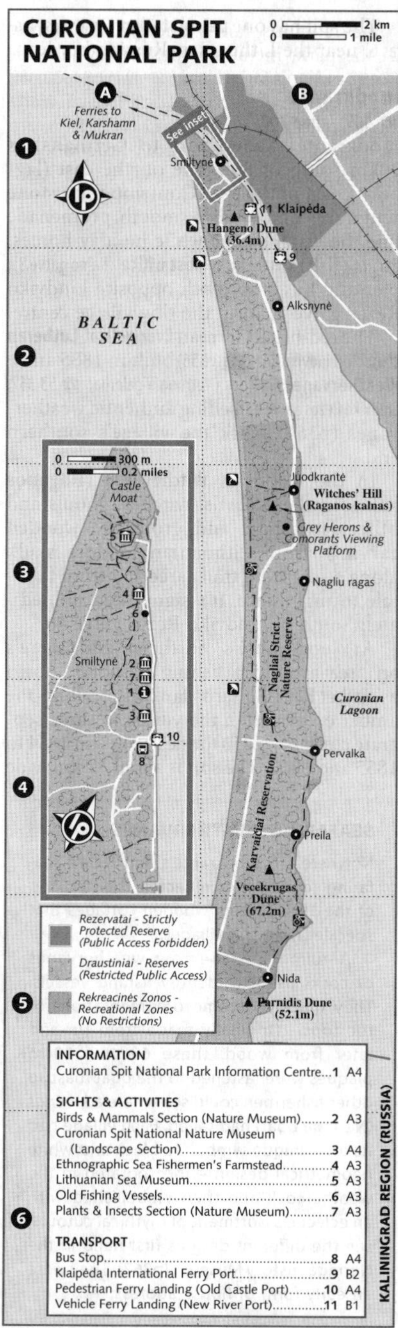

The spit has one **petrol station** (Smiltynės plentas 6) near the Lithuanian-Russian border.

Juodkrantė

☎ 469 / pop 700

Juodkrantė (Schwarzort to Germans) is 20km south of Smiltynė on the east (lagoon) coast of the spit. Contemporary stone sculptures and a silky-smooth promenade line the water's edge while holiday homes, *žuvis* (fish) outlets, a **post office** (Kalno gatvė 3), pier and bus stop (both opposite Liudviko Rėzos gatvė 8) form the tiny village centre.

The red-brick German **Evangelical-Lutheran church** (Liudviko Rėzos gatvė 56) built in 1885 and a **Weathervanes Gallery** (Vetrungių galerija; ☎ 53 357; Liudviko Rėzos gatvė 13) selling authentic weathervanes (p364) mark the village's southern end.

In the woods is **Witches' Hill** (Raganos kalnas), where devils, witches, ghouls and other fantastical and grotesque wooden carvings from Lithuanian folklore skulk along a sculpture trail careering from fairytale to nightmare. It's signposted immediately south of Liudviko Rėzos gatvė 46.

At Juodkrantė's northern end there's an area around a fishing harbour known as **Amber Bay** (Gintaro įlanka), recalling the amber excavated in the village in three separate clusters – 2250 tonnes in all – in 1854 to 1855 and 1860. The spit is about 1.5km wide at this point and the fine stretch of forest – good for spotting elk in the early morning and evening – is among the loveliest you will find on the peninsula. Fauna and flora abounds along the gorgeous cycling path (p367) linking Juodkrantė with Nida.

SEAFARING WEATHERVANES

Nowhere are Juodkrantė's and Nida's seafaring roots better reflected than on top of the 19th-century wooden cottages that speckle these spit villages.

A ruling in 1844 saw weathervanes or cocks used to identify fishing vessels. They quickly became ornamentation for rooftops. Originally made from tin and later from wood, these 60cm x 30cm plaques were fastened to the boat mast so other fishermen could see where a *kurėnas* (Neringa boat) had sailed. Each village had its own unique symbol – a black-and-white geometrical design – incorporated in the weathercock and then embellished with an eclectic assortment of mythical cutouts; see the different designs first-hand in the Neringa History Museum (p367). They were an early form of house address.

THE AUTHOR'S CHOICE

Vila Flora (☎ 53 024; www.vilaflora.lt; Kalno gatvė 7a; s/d/tr 180/220/250Lt; Ⓟ) Tucked across a green lawn in an attractive rust- and wine-red building, Vila Flora cooks up the most imaginative cuisine on the spit (meals 30Lt). It bans fries from its menu and stuffs bog-standard Lithuanian *blyniai* (pancakes) with seafood to come up with a dish that is traditional, tasty and – amazingly – found nowhere else. Its chicken filet filled with mozzarella cheese and topped with a curry sauce is equally delicious while its cool covered terrace, equipped with a play bench for kids, keeps the whole family happy. Seventeen stylish rooms upstairs ensure a perfect night's sleep.

INFORMATION

Pharmacy (Liudviko Rėzos gatvė 54; 9am-1pm & 5-7pm Mon-Fri) Located in Hotel Ažuolynas, which also contains an ATM.

Tourist office (☎ 53 490; juodkrante@neringa.lt; 9am-5pm Tue-Sat May-Sep) Mildly useful and also located in Hotel Ažuolynas.

SLEEPING

The tourist office has a list of private rooms and flats to rent. A new hotel should be open by the time you read this, in a new wooden house behind Sorrento (p367) near the water's edge.

Hotel Ažuolynas (☎ 53 310; www.hotelazuolynas.lt; Liudviko Rėzos gatvė 54; s/d/tr/q Jun-Aug 179/228/399/529, May & Sep 132/170/345/524Lt, Oct-Apr 111/141/294/440Lt;) A stuffed brown bear stands in the lobby of this rambling hotel, laden with facilities: Italian restaurant, billiard hall, minigolf opposite, gift shop, Turkish bath and sauna (150Lt per hour), swimming pool with superduper curly-wurly water slide and tennis courts. Breakfast (22Lt) is not included in high-season (June to August) rates.

Kurėnas (☎ 53 101, 8-698 20549; Liudviko Rėzos gatvė 10; d/tr/q 250/270/340Lt; Apr-Sep) Named after a flat-bottomed Curonian boat, this busy and bright café-bar with street-side terrace sports seven rooms up top. Some peep onto the lagoon.

EATING

Eating options are limited and self-caterers should buy everything bar smoked fish (sold at Liudviko Rėzos gatvė 16, 20, 22, 36 and 44) in Klaipėda before arriving.

Sorrento (☎ 53 100; www.sorrento.lt; Liudviko Rėzos gatvė 1a) The contemporary kid on the block, this hot sunset-watching spot is a kiss away from the water's edge in a painted wooden villa. Cuisine is upmarket and Italian.

Family-run choices in flower-filled gardens of quaint wooden cottages;

Pamario takas (Liudviko Rėzos gatvė 42; meals 20Lt)
Švejonė (Liudviko Rėzos gatvė 30; meals 20Lt)

GETTING THERE & AWAY

Buses to/from Nida (5Lt, 25 minutes) and Smiltynė (3Lt, 30 minutes) stop in Juodkrantė; see p367.

Juodkrantė To Nida

South of Juodkrantė is Lithuania's largest colony of **grey herons and cormorants**, observed here since the 19th century. Wooden steps lead from the road to a **viewing platform** where the panorama of thousands of nests amid pine trees – not to menton the noise of the 6500-strong colony – is astonishing. Cormorants arrive in early February (herons a little later) to pick and rebuild their nests. By May chicks are screaming for food. Starlings, thrushes, warblers, and grey, spotted and black woodpeckers can also be seen here.

Almost immediately afterwards, the road switches from the eastern side of the peninsula to the western. The 16.8-sq-km **Naglių Strict Nature Reserve** (Naglių rezervatas) here protects the **Dead** or **Grey Dunes** (named after the greyish flora that covers them) that stretch 8km south and are 2km wide; a marked footpath leads into the reserve from the main road.

Shifting sands in the mid-19th century forced villagers here to flee to **Pervalka** (population 40) and **Preila** (population 200) on the east coast, accessible by side roads from the main road. Pine-forested **Vecekrugas Dune** (67.2m), the peninsula's highest dune, near Preila, stands on a ridge called Old Inn Hill – named after an inn that stood at the foot of the dune before being buried by sand; view it from the Juodkrantė–Nida cycling path (p367).

THE AUTHOR'S CHOICE

Kuršmarių vila (☎ 55 117; 8-685 56317, 8-620 58630; kursmariuvila@walla.conm; Preilos gatvė 93; d 170-350Lt; Ⓟ) Not only does this thatched wooden seaside abode make a great pit stop for cyclists; it is also a fine place to be welcomed by a soothing lagoon view. At the southern end of Preila village, Kuršmarių vila is run by a fishing family. Smoke pours from its old smokehouse in the garden, smoked fish are strung up to buy out front and there's always the fresh catch of the day waiting to be eaten in the lagoon-facing café, which has a wooden jetty jutting out over the water. Roach and bream are the most frequent catch in the Curonian lagoon – pike, perch, ling and eel are less common. Smelts – migratory fish – are the terrain of winter's ice-fishers, who bore a hole through the ice, pop their line in and wait for a bite.

Nida

☎ 469 / pop 1500

Lovely Nida is an old-fashioned fishing village bathed in natural beauty. The allure of sparkling lagoon waters, yellow sands, hazy pine forests and wooden cottages with fishing nets strung outside have made it the hub of the spit. Each year 50,000 tourists swamp this tiny village.

Nida (Nidden in German) is the largest settlement on the Lithuanian half of the Curonian Spit, 48km from Klaipėda and 3km from the Russian border. White-sand beaches are a 2km walk away through pine forest, or there's a shuttle bus in summer from pier to beachfront. To the south is the most impressive dune on the peninsula, Parnidis Dune (Parnidžio kopa), which has steps up to its 52m summit from where there are stunning views of rippling, untouched dunes stretching into Russia.

From the late 19th century a colony of mainly East Prussian artists drew inspiration from the area. Nida developed as a tourist resort and there were five hotels by the 1930s, when the German writer Thomas Mann (1875–1955) had a summer home built here. In 1965 French philosopher Jean Paul Sartre and companion Simone de Beauvoir were

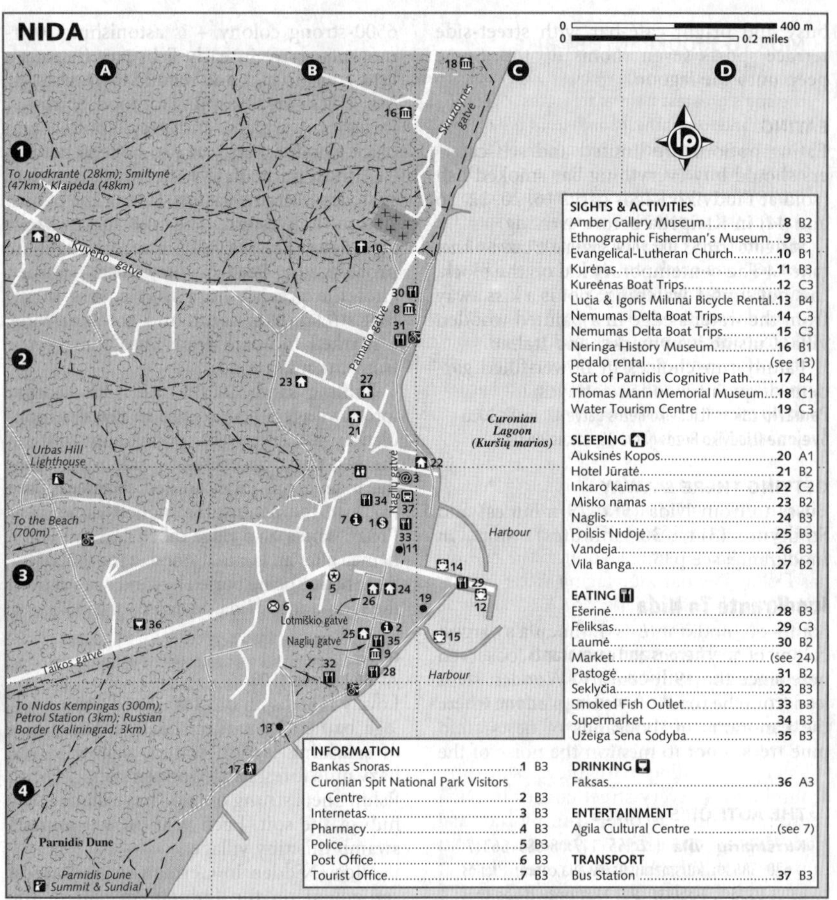

granted special permission by Khrushchev to spend five days on the dunes, Lithuanian photographer Antanas Sutkus being allowed to shoot the pair in the sand.

Nida stretches for 2km, but its centre is at the southern end, behind the harbour.

INFORMATION

Bankas Snoras (Naglių gatvė 27) Currency exchange and ATM opposite the bus station.

Internetas (Naglių gatvė 22; per 10/60min 1/5Lt; ⌚ 10am-1pm & 3-10pm)

Pharmacy (☎ 52 138; Taikos gatvė 11; ⌚ 8.30am-8pm Mon-Sat, 9am-3pm Sun May-Sep)

Police (☎ 52 202; Taikos gatvė 5)

Post office (Taikos gatvė 15)

Tourist office (☎ 52 345; agilainfo@is.lt; Taikos gatvė 4; ⌚ 9am-8pm Mon-Sat, to 3pm Sun Jun-Aug, 10am-6pm Mon-Fri Sep-May) Sells maps, books accommodation (5Lt) and stocks loads of information (including photographs) of private rooms and flats to rent.

National Park Visitors Centre (Lankytojų centras; ☎ 51 256; Naglių gatvė 8; ⌚ 9am-noon & 1-5pm Mon-Sat, 9am-2pm Sun May-Sep)

SIGHTS & ACTIVITIES

Chill out. Go for walks. Relax. During the spring and autumn storms, speckles of amber are washed up on the shores. In the depths of winter the frozen lagoon is dotted with people ice-fishing for smelt and burbot. In summer hire a pedalo (8/15Lt per 30/60 minutes) from the coastal path leading to Parnidis Dune

NIDA TO JUODKRANTĖ BY BIKE

An ab fab cycling path wends its way 30km from Nida to Juodkrantė, passing en route some of the spit's greatest natural treasures – Vecekrugas Dune (p365), an authentic fish smoker in Preila (p365) and footpaths leading from the cycling path in Karvaičiai Reservation where entire villages were buried by sand. At Pervalka you can cycle through or around the village (the quicker route), arriving 4km later at the entrance to the Naglių Strict Nature Reserve (p365). Shortly afterwards, the cycling path crosses the main road to take cyclists along the opposite western side of the spit for the remaining 9km to Juodkrantė; the first 5km snake beneath pine trees alongside the main road and the final 4km skirt seaside sand dune. Once you're out of the reserve, leap into the sea for a quick cool down before the last leg – an uphill slog through forested dune to arrive in Juodkrantė behind the village.

To pick up the cycling path in Nida, follow the red-paved cycling track north along the lagoon promenade and after passing Thomas Mann's house up top (left), follow the track left around the corner onto Puvynės gatvė. On the road, turn immediately right and follow it for 3.5km until you see a dirt track forking off left into pine forest: this is the start of the cycling path, complete with 0.0km marker.

At the harbour, opt for a boat trip aboard a handsome replica of a **kurėnas** (☎ 8-689 93335; ⏲ Jul & Aug), a traditional 19th-century fishing boat, or sail across the lagoon to the Nemunas Delta. The harbour-facing **Water Tourism Centre** (Vandens turizmo centras; ☎ 8-682 70504; Naglių gatvė 14; ⏲ 10am-10pm Jun-Sep) has information on boats to hire, organises trips, arranges bass-fishing expeditions in the lagoon (15Lt) and rents tackle (4Lt per hour). It also transports bicycles across the lagoon for cyclists wanting to pedal only one way.

There are outlets with bicycles to hire around almost every street corner in Nida centre, including a couple run by **Lucia and Igoris Milunai** (☎ 8-682 14798; 9am-sunset May-Oct) midway along the lagoon promenade that runs parallel to Pamario gatvė and on the path leading to Parnidis Dune. Count on paying 6Lt/10Lt per hour for a bicycle/children's buggy; cheaper day rates can be negotiated (up to 30Lt/50Lt per bike/buggy).

North of the Harbour

Breathtaking views of Parnidis Dune can be had at the harbour, from where a pleasant waterfront lagoon promenade stretches for over 1km to a flight of steps that leads up to the **Thomas Mann Memorial Museum** (Tomo Mano memorialinis muziejus; ☎ 52 260; www.mann.lt; adult/child 2/0.50Lt; ⏲ 10am-6pm Tue-Sun Jun-Aug, 11am-5pm Tue-Sat Sep-May). The German writer spent just two summers with his wife and six children in the peacock-blue cottage between 1930 and 1932, before returning to Germany.

Back towards the town centre, a path leads to an 1888 red-brick **Evangelical-Lutheran Church** (Mass ⏲ 11am Sun May-Sep). The church's peaceful woodland cemetery is pinpricked with *krikstai* – crosses carved from wood to help the deceased ascend to heaven more easily. Opposite is an **Amber Gallery Museum** (Gintaro galerija muzeijus; ☎ 52 712; www.ambergallery.lt; Pamario gatvė 20; ⏲ 9am-9pm mid-Apr–Sep) with a small amber garden and fantastic pieces of amber jewellery. It runs a second gallery, **Kurėnas** (Naglių gatvė 18c; ⏲ 9am-9pm mid-Apr–Sep), in a striking glass box encased in an old wooden boat near the harbour.

B&W photographs of Nida in its more brutal spear-fishing, crow-biting days fill the thoughtfully laid-out **Neringa History Museum** (Neringos istorijos muzeijus; ☎ 52 372; Pamario gatvė 53; adult/child 2/1Lt; ⏲ 10am-6pm Jun–mid-Sep, 10am-5pm Mon-Sat mid-Sep–May) where Nida's tale from the Stone Age to 1939 is told. Particularly brilliant are the shots of local hunters biting a crow's neck to kill the bird followed by a shot of vodka to kill the taste. Eating crows and seagulls' eggs was common on the spit in the 17th to 19th centuries, when continually drifting sands rendered previously arable land useless.

West of the Harbour

All westward routes lead to the beach. One way is to turn north off Taikos gatvė, opposite the post office. The street bends sharply left after 150m and climbs. A path leads up the hill to the 29.3m **Urbas Hill Lighthouse** (closed to visitors), atop the highest point in

LITHUANIA

the area. Continue 700m along the path behind the lighthouse to come out on a straight path that leads back down to the main road and, 400m beyond that, to the beach.

A less adventurous option is to follow Taikos gatvė westwards until it meets the main Smiltynė–Nida road, then continue in the same direction along a paved footpath (signposted) through pine forest until you hit sand.

South of the Harbour

Heading south are two or three streets of fishing cottages with pretty flower-filled gardens. The **Ethnographic Fisherman's Museum** (Žejo etnografinė sodyba; ☎ 52 372; Naglių gatvė 4; adult/child 1Lt; 10am-6pm May-Sep, 11am-5pm Tue-Sat Sep-May) is a peek at Nida in the 19th century, with original weathervanes decorating the garden, and rooms inside arranged as they were a couple of centuries ago.

Beyond Lotmiškio gatvė a path leads along the coastline and through a wooded area to a meadow at the foot of the **Parnidis Dune** (Parnidžio kopos), an unforested, 7km thread of golden sand that snakes south into Russia. In the meadow, dubbed 'Silence Valley', walkers can pick up the **Parnidis Cognitive Path** (Parnidžio pažintinis takas), a 1.8km nature trail with information panels highlighting dune flora and fauna. At the bottom of the flight of 180 steps, two dune photographs are displayed – one taken in 1960, the other in 2002. The difference in dune height – 20m in 40 years – is a warning to those keen to romp in the sand.

At the top of the spectacularly high bare dune, a panorama of sand, both coastlines, the forests to the north, and a mixture of sand and forests to the south is heart-stopping and unforgettable. Park authorities have left the smashed remains of the **granite sundial** that stood 12m tall atop the 52m dune peak until 1999 when a hurricane sent it crashing to the ground as a symbol of 'nature's uncontrollable forces' – another warning to wannabe sand rompers.

From here, the Kaliningrad border is 3km south – see the signs. If you stick to the designated wooden footpaths, you have no chance of wandering into Russia by mistake. From the dune, the Parnidis Cognitive Path continues past the lighthouse and pine forest to Taikos gatvė.

LITHUANIA

SLEEPING

Prices in Nida fluctuate wildly between winter and summer; high-season prices (June, July and August) are listed here.

Guesthouses

Naglis (☎ 51 124, 8-699 33682; www.naglis.lt; Naglių gatvė 12; d 200-250Lt) This charming guesthouse in a wooden house between the market, main street and harbour is full of smiles. Doubles comprise two rooms, and most have a door opening out to the table-clad, tree-shaded garden. There's a dining room and kitchen for guests to share, one room has a fireplace and sauna (80Lt per hour), and the guesthouse rents bikes (6Lt/2Lt per hour/day).

Poilsis Nidojė (☎ 31 698; www.neringahotels.lt; Naglių gatvė 11; d 200-250Lt; ⊠) Another wooden-house favourite, Poilsis Nidojė sports five spacious doubles and three two-room apartments with kitchen and fireplace. Interior design is rustic, an optional breakfast (20Lt) is served in the kitchen around a shared table and guests can cook up dinner on a barbecue in the pretty garden.

Inkaro kaimas (☎ 52 123; Naglių gatvė 26-1; d from 200Lt; P) Blue pillars prop up this beautifully maintained red wooden house on the water's edge. The place dates from 1901 and a couple of pine-furnished rooms boast a balcony overlooking the lagoon. Look for the giant anchor in its small but sweet garden.

THE AUTHOR'S CHOICE

Misko namas (☎ 52 290; www.miskonamas.com; Pamario gatvė 11-2; d/ste from €33/74; P) This unpretentious guesthouse was a *poliklinic* (outpatient facility) until 1991, when it was privatised to the workers. Among them was lovely Jovita, an enterprising woman who'd worked at the clinic for 18 years and who set about buying out her fellow workers from the business and transforming the traditional wooden house into the guesthouse of her dreams. Several years of jolly-hard work later, the result is an appealing sky-blue cottage laden with flower boxes and oozing charm. Every room has a fridge, sink and kettle and a couple have fully fledged kitchens and balconies. Guests can cook meals in a communal kitchen and Jovita is always on hand to help. Upon entering, note the original twisting wooden staircase.

Vila Banga (☎ 51 139, 8-686 08703; www.nidosbanga.lt; Pamario gatvė 2; d 230-280Lt, apt 340-400Lt) This pristine wooden house with bright-blue shutters and perfect thatched roof makes most visitors say 'Wow, look at that one!' It has seven comfortable rooms in its pine-wood interior. Prices include breakfast.

Vandeja (☎ 8-614 67196, 8-655 21127; vandeja@forelle.lt; Naglių gatvė 17; d 120-200Lt, apt 350-600Lt; P) A dune view and a less snooty attitude are about the only things that could improve the enviable location of this luxurious wooden house, which has a couple of doubles and several small kitchen-equipped apartments in a separate building. Water is filtered, quality furnishings are modern and there is a sauna (100Lt per hour).

Hotels

Hotel Jūratė (☎ 52 618; jurate-nida@takas.lt; Pamario gatvė 3; s/d 105/225Lt; P) Hotel Jūratė's history is a colourful one, given its pride-of-place position on the spot where a Prussian post house stood from 1745. Burnt down in 1829, it was rebuilt as an inn, which survived until the mid-20th century. Soviet die-hards will be thrilled to know that the hotel's most recent face-lift didn't get rid of the kitsch glitter cement on the corridor walls. Austere rooms on the 3rd floor are not yet renovated.

Auksinės Kopos (☎ 52 387, 52 212; relita@klaipeda.omnitel.net; Kuverto gatvė 17; s/d 140/225Lt;) A Soviet-era rest home still going strong thanks to the tour groups who flock to Nida, Golden Dunes surprises with its cathedral-hall lobby, stylishly pebbled outdoor-pool area and cool, crisp rooms. Find it an uphill stroll from the centre amid pines.

Camping

Wild camping can land you a 300Lt fine.

Nidos Kempingas (☎ 52 045, 8-682 41150; www.kempingas.lt; Taikos gatvė 45a; small/big tent 10/15Lt, adult/child/car 15/5/10Lt, d 180-200Lt, 2-/6-room studios with garden 250/450Lt; May-Sep; P) Set in pine forest at the foot of a path that leads to Parnidis Dune, this spruced-up camp site has accommodation to suit all budgets. Double rooms have satellite TV and fridge, and apartments are fully equipped for self-caterers.

EATING

Opening hours follow the Nida standard: 10am to 10pm daily May or June to September. Out of season, little is open.

Seklyčia (☎ 50 000; Lotmiškio gatvė 1; meals 50-70Lt) There is nothing quite like sitting on the small terrace up top at this rust-coloured house to watch the sun sink behind the dune while wolfing down Curonian pike-perch in orange sauce or smoked eel.

Feliksas (Taikos gatvė 38; small/medium/large pizza from 6/9/18Lt) A hub of Nida nightlife, the former harbour building shelters an atmospheric pizzeria with a pavement terrace overlooking bobbing boats and a nightclub up top. In summer a sax and piano duo accompanies the 13 types of pizza served on the terrace.

Užeiga Sena Sodyba (☎ 52 782; Naglių gatvė 6; meals 30Lt) Note the swans on the gables at this delightful wooden cottage restaurant where traditional Lithuanian fare can be enjoyed in a small flowery summer garden. Its June-time pancakes stuffed to the gills with fingernail-sized wild strawberries are gastronomic heaven.

Laumė (☎ 52 335; Pamario gatvė 24-3a; meals 20-40Lt) Herrings with walnuts, smoked eel and pigs' ears are traditional Lithuanian delights to nibble on while taking in awesome views and fresh air on this delightful flower-bedecked terrace.

Pastogė (☎ 51 149; Kuverto gatvė 2) If Laumė is full, try Pastogė, its pretty sister. This place boasts an identical menu. Find both on the promenade skirting the lagoon.

Ešerinė (☎ 52 757; eserine@takas.lt; Naglių gatvė 2; meals 25-40Lt) This odd but attractive Hawaiian-style wooden building with thatched roof pulls in the crowds with its vast waterfront terrace. Munch *fermentinis sūris* (cheese sticks) and watch the sun set behind Parnidis Dune.

Self-caterers are likely to give up gracefully after trying to shop at Nida's only **supermarket**

> **SMELLS FISHY TO ME**
>
> And believe you me, it is. There is nothing fishier than the tasty choice of smoked fish waiting to be munched on in fine Curonian fashion at Nida's **smoked fish-outlet** (Rūkyta žuvis; Naglių gatvė 18; 10am-10pm May-Sep), next to the bus station. So you know what you're eating – *ungurys* is long slippery eel, *starkis* is pikeperch, *stinta* is smelt, *ešerys* is perch and flat round *karšis* is bream. Prices displayed, calculated by weight, are per fish.

LITHUANIA

(Taikos gatvė), a Soviet hand-me-down inside the Prekybos Centras Gilija, next to the Agila Cultural Centre. The one-stall market (opposite Naglių gatvė 17) sells plastic cups of wild strawberries, cranberries and other berries picked fresh from the forest.

ENTERTAINMENT

Agila Cultural Centre (Taikos gatvė 4) Discos, films, art exhibitions and other cultural events fill this centre adjoining the tourist office.

People don't come to Nida to party. Should you have the uncontrollable urge, try Feliksas (p369) or **Faksas** (☎ 8-698 33261; Taikos gatvė 32a), the only place to catch a live band.

GETTING THERE & AWAY

Buses use the **bus station** (☎ 54 859; Naglių gatvė 20). From Nida there are microbuses every half-hour to/from Smiltynė (7Lt, 1¼ hours) between 6am and 10pm (until 8pm from September to May), stopping en route in Juodkrantė (5Lt, 25 minutes); a couple daily to/from Kaliningrad (16.30Lt, three hours) and Klaipėda bus station (8Lt, 1½ hours); and one daily to/from Kaunas (44Lt, 3½ hours) and Vilnius (55Lt, six hours).

NEMUNAS DELTA

☎ 441

The low-lying, marsh-dotted eastern side of the Curonian Lagoon (Kursių marios) could be the end of the world. Remote and rural, tourism has scarcely touched this isolated landscape where summer skies offer magnificent views of the spit's white dunes across the lagoon. In winter ice-fishermen sit on the frozen lagoon – up to 12km wide in places – waiting for a smelt to bite.

The gateway into the extraordinary Nemunas Delta (Nemuno Delta), where the Nemunas River ends its 937km journey from its source in neighbouring Belarus, is **Šilutė** (population 25,000), a sleepy town 48km south of Klaipėda. The cluster of islands forms a savage but beautiful landscape protected since 1992 by the **Nemunas Delta Regional Park** (Nemuno Deltos Regioninis Parkas). One-fifth of the park is water – which freezes most winters, exposing hardy residents to extreme weather conditions. **Rusnė Island**, the largest island, covers 48 sq km and increases in size by 15cm to 20cm a year.

Boat is the main form of transport, villagers being transported in and out of the park by an amphibious tractor from March to mid-May, when merciless spring floods plunge about 5% of the park under water. In 1994 flood waters rose to 1.5m in places, although 40cm to 70cm is the norm. From Nida there are seasonal boats across the lagoon to the delta settlement of **Mingė** (also called Minija after the river that forms the main 'street' through the village). No more than 100 people live in Mingė – dubbed the Venice of Lithuania – and only two families still speak Lietuvinkai, an ethnic dialect of Lithuanian distinct to the delta. The 19th-century riverside houses are made of wood with reed roofs and are protected architectural monuments. A good way to explore this area is by bicycle; from Mingė a **cycling track** runs around **Lake Krokų Lanka**, the largest lake in the park at 4km long and 3.3km wide.

Information

Getting up-to-date information on this underfunded park is tantamount to squeezing

NEMUNAS BIRDLIFE

This wetland is a twitcher's heaven. Some 270 of the 325 bird species found in Lithuania frequent the Nemunas Delta Regional Park, many rare birds breeding in the lush marshes around Rusnė, including rare black storks, white-tailed eagles, black-tailed godwits, pintails, dunlin, ruff and great snipe. The common white stork breeds like there's no tomorrow in Ventė.

The Arctic–European–East African bird migration flight path cuts through the park, making it a key spot for migratory waterfowl. But it's not just a stopover or feeding site – the park is a breeding ground for 169 species of birds, and some, such as the pintail, don't breed anywhere else in Lithuania.

Rare aquatic warblers, corncrakes, black-headed gulls, white-winged black terns and great crested grebes have their biggest colonies in the delta. In autumn up to 200,000 birds – 80% of which are tits and finches – fly overhead at any one time in the Ventės Ragas Ornithological Station sky, and up to 5000 are ringed each day for research into world migration.

blood out of a stone. The **regional park headquarters** (☎ 75 050; p.deltosrp@takas.lt; Lietuvininkų gatvė 10) in Šilutė is not officially open to visitors, but you might be able to persuade them otherwise. **Šilutė tourist office** (☎ 77 795; www.silute.lt; Lietuvininkų gatvė 10; 8am-noon & 1-5pm Mon-Fri), on the ground floor of the same building, is totally unhelpful but does sell the indispensable *Rusnės sala* (Rusnė Island) map.

Sights & Activities

In the heart of the Nemunas Delta is **Rusnė**, 8km southwest of Šilutė, where the main stream divides into three: the Atmata, the Pakalnė and the Skirvytė. In this fishing village there's nothing to do except gawp at its two badly stocked food shops, regret not bringing a picnic to enjoy on its pretty riverbanks, and visit the tiny **Ethnographic Farmstead Museum** (Etnografine Sodyba Muziejus; admission by donation; variable), signposted 1.8km from the village. Exhibitions of tools, furnishings and farm buildings reflect the harsh face of delta life centuries ago – and today.

Dike-protected polders (land reclaimed from the sea) cover the park, the first polder being built in 1840 to protect Rusnė. The red-brick **water-pumping station** (1907) near the **lighthouse** *(švyturys)* in Uostadvaris, 8km from the bridge in Rusnė, can be visited upon request; you can swim in the river from the small beach here. Many lower polders are still flooded seasonally and serve as valuable spawning grounds for various fish species (there are some 60 in the park).

Ventės Ragas ('world's edge') is a sparsely inhabited area on the south-pointing promontory of the delta, which, with its dramatic nature and uplifting isolation, is beautifully wild. A Teutonic Order castle was built here in the 1360s to protect shipping, only for it to collapse within a couple of hundred years due to severe storms on this isolated point. The church was rebuilt, only to be storm-wrecked again in 1702. Its stones were used to build a new church at **Kintai**, 10km north on the regional park's northeastern boundary. Bar a few fishers' houses and the lighthouse (1862), the main attraction here is the **Ventės Ragas Ornithological Station** (☎ 54 480; adult/child 2/1Lt; 10am-5pm Jun-Sep, 10am-5pm Mon-Fri Oct-May), 66km south of Klaipėda at the end of the Kintai–Ventė road. The first bird-ringing station was established here in 1929, but it was not until 1959 to 1960 that large bird traps were installed. Today, one million birds pass through the station each migratory period, zigzag, snipe, cobweb and duck traps ensnaring birds to be ringed. Two exhibition rooms inside the station explain the birdlife (p371) and an observation deck encourages visitors to spot species first-hand. **Vytas** (☎ 68 541, 8-617 78410; vros@takas.lt) is a local English-speaking ornithological guide.

Sleeping & Eating

Campers can pitch tents at designated spots in the park – the regional park office can tell you where – but bring food provisions with you. Farm accommodation organised by the regional park is an exhilarating way to experience delta life; beds cost around 30Lt a night and a delicious dinner can be cooked for a little extra. Šilutė's only hotel is too grim to mention.

Kintai (☎ 47 339, 8-686 70490; www.kintai.lt; d/tr 140/180Lt, 5-bedded room 300Lt; P) The top spot to stay in the delta, this hotel-restaurant and boating complex entertains guests with awesome views and total peace bar the sweet sound of fish biting and oars dipping in lake water. Carp is the main catch. You can rent a boat to motor around the Curonian Lagoon and seven doubles (140Lt) float on a boat. Find Kintai 6km east of Kintai village on the Minija River.

Ventainė (☎ 47 422, 8-686 70490; www.ventaine.lt; Ventės Ragas; adult/car/tent 10/8/8Lt, d 160Lt, with shared bathroom 100Lt, lux d 310Lt; P) This complex, a two-minute walk from the ringing station, sits on the lagoon shore. Comfy villa rooms have fridge and heated bathroom floors, and campers are well catered for with wooden huts, camp sites and a clean, modern shower/toilet block. A traditional sauna (80Lt per two hours) sits on the water's edge and eel soup (13Lt) is served on the café terrace.

Laimutės (☎ 59 690; www.silec.lt/laimute; d/apt Oct-Mar 80/120Lt, Jun-Aug 100/150Lt; P) About 15km east of Šilutė in Žemaičių Naumiestis, this 16-room guesthouse slumbers between forest and lake. Facilities include a sauna, bicycle and riverboat rental (free to guests, 10Lt an hour to everyone else) and it arranges boat trips, summer and winter lake fishing, horse riding, berrying and mushrooming.

Getting There & Around

Getting to the area without your own wheels is tough. In summer Šilutė is served by 10

LITHUANIA

buses a day to/from Klaipėda (6.50Lt), five to/from Kaunas (20.50Lt, 180km) and four to/from Vilnius (32Lt, 280km).

Boats are the best means of exploring the delta (it's 8km from Pakalnė to Kintai by boat but 45km by road). The main routes follow the three main delta tributaries – the Atmata (13km), Skirvytė (9km) and Pakalnė (9km) Rivers – which fan out westwards from Rusnė.

Kintai, Ventainė and Laimutės rent boats with a boatman-guide. The park office in Šilutė might be able to help.

LITHUANIA DIRECTORY

For regional information pertaining to all three countries, see the Regional Directory.

ACTIVITIES

Lithuanians love nature. People were still worshipping ancient oak trees a mere six centuries ago, and these days in their free time they make regular pilgrimages to their country's many luscious lakes and forests.

Boating, berrying, mushrooming, birdwatching and ballooning are uplifting pursuits. Travellers can cycle into the wilderness, sweat in traditional lakeside saunas and enjoy ice-fishing or skiing.

For more details see the Activities chapter and individual destinations.

CUSTOMS

For pointers on customs regulations, see p385. The **Lithuanian Customs Department** (Map pp292-3; ☎ 5-266 6166; www.cust.lt; Jakšto gatvė 1/25) in Vilnius has online updates.

From outside the EU you can import duty-free into Lithuania: 1L of spirits, 2L of wine or champagne, 3L of beer and 200 cigarettes or 250g of tobacco. Meat and dairy products cannot be brought in as hand luggage from outside the EU. Upon entering, you must declare foreign currency in cash above 10,000Lt, and above 5000Lt when exiting.

When travelling within the EU, there are no restrictions on what you can take in and out of Lithuania providing it's for personal use – with the exception of cigarettes, which are limited to 200 when leaving Lithuania for Austria, Denmark, Finland, Germany, Ireland, Sweden and the UK.

Lithuania limits amber exports, but a few souvenirs should be okay providing the value doesn't exceed 3500Lt. You need a Culture Ministry permit, and pay 10% to 20% duty, to export artworks over 50 years old. Contact the **Committee of Cultural Heritage** (Map pp292-3; ☎ 5-272 4005; Snipiškių gatvė 3, Vilnius) for info.

EMBASSIES & CONSULATES

Lithuanian Embassies & Consulates

Find a complete list of Lithuanian diplomatic representations at the **Lithuanian Ministry of Foreign Affairs** (www.urm.lt). They include the following:

Belarus Minsk (☎ 017-285 24 48; ulitsa Zacharova 68, 220088 Minsk)

Canada Ottawa (☎ 613-567 5458; www.lithuanianembassy.ca; 130 Albert St, Suite 204, Ottawa, Ontario K1P 5G4)

Czech Republic Prague (☎ 02-57 21 01 22; amb.cz@urm.lt; Pod Klikovkou 1916/2, 1500 Prague 5)

Denmark Copenhagen (☎ 39-63 62 07; Bernstorffsvej 214, DK-2920 Charlottelund, Copenhagen)

Estonia Tallinn (☎ 631 4030/4053; www.hot.ee/lietambasada; Uus tänav 15, 0100 Tallinn)

Finland Helsinki (☎ 09-608 210; embassy@liettua.pp.fi; Rauhankatu 13a, 00170 Helsinki)

France Paris (☎ 01 40 54 50 50; www.amb-lituanie-paris.fr; 22 Blvd de Courcelles, 75017 Paris)

Germany Berlin (☎ 030-890 68 10; www.botschaft-litauen.de; Charitestr 9, 10711 Berlin)

Ireland Dublin (☎ 01-668 8292; 90 Merrion Rd, Ballsbridge, Dublin 4)

Israel Tel Aviv (☎ 3-695 8685; Top Shaul Hameleh Blvd 8, Amot Mishpat Bldg, Tel Aviv 64733)

Latvia Rīga (☎ 732 1519; lithemb@ltemb.vip.lv; Rūpniecības iela 24, 1010 Rīga)

Netherlands The Hague (☎ 070-385 54 18; http://amb.urm.lt; Koninginnegracht 78, 2514 AH The Hague)

Norway Oslo (☎ 221-292 00; Drammensveien 40, Oslo 0244)

Poland Warsaw (☎ 02-625 33 68; www.lietuva.pl; aleje Szucha 5, 00-580 Warsaw)

Russia Kaliningrad (☎ 0112-957 688; kons.kaliningradas@urm.lt; Proletarskaja 133, Kaliningrad); Moscow (☎ 095-785 8605; Borisoglebsky per 10, 121069 Moscow); St Petersburg (☎ 812-327 02 30; st.peterburgas@peterstar.ru; Ryleyeva ulitsa 37, 191123 St Petersburg)

UK London (☎ 020-7486 6401/2; http://lithuania.embassyhomepage.com; 84 Gloucester Place, London W1U 6AU)

USA Chicago (☎ 312-397 0382; kons.cikaga@urm.lt; 211 E Ontario St, Suite 1500, Chicago, IL 60611); New York (☎ 212-354 7840; info@ltconsny.org; 420 Fifth Ave, New York, NY 10018); Washington DC (☎ 202-234 5860; www.ltembassyus.org; 2622 16th St NW, Washington, DC 20009)

PRACTICALITIES

- The *Baltic Times* (www.baltictimes.com) is published every Thursday, and has an entertainment guide that includes cinema listings.
- Listen to the BBC World Service 24 hours a day at 100.5 FM.
- For national news, pick up the most popular independent daily *Lietuvos Rytas* (www.lrytas.lt), its tabloid counterpart *Respublika* or quality business daily *Verzlio Žinios* (www.vz.lt).
- Lithuanian Airlines in-flight magazine *Lithuania in the World*, sold in Vilnius bookshops (p290), is a brilliant source for insightful features on cultural and current affairs.
- Tune into state-run Lithuanian Radio (102.6 FM); M1 (106.8 FM; www.m-1.fm) for news and views; commercial channel Radiocentras (101.5 FM); or M1 Plus (106.2FM) for non-stop music.
- Public broadcaster Lithuanian TV (www.lrt.lt) puts up a good fight with LTV and its culture-driven Channel 2 against the stiff competition posed by the commercial channels, among them TV3 (www.tv3.lt), popular for American films, soaps and concerts; and TV4 (www.tv4.lt).
- Buy or watch videos on the PAL system.
- Plugs have two round pins; the electric current is 220V, 50Hz.
- Use the metric system for weights and measures.

Embassies & Consulates in Lithuania

Foreign embassies in Vilnius include the following:

Australia (Map pp292-3; ☎ 5-212 3369, emergency 8-687 11117; australia@consulate.lt; Vilniaus gatvė 23)
Belarus (Map pp292-3; ☎ 5-266 2200; www.belarus.lt; Mindaugo gatvė 13)
Canada (Map pp292-3; ☎ 5-249 0950; www.canada.lt; Jogailos gatvė 4)
Denmark (Map pp288-9; ☎ 5-264 8760; www.denmark.lt; Kosciuškos gatvė 36)
Estonia (Map pp292-3; ☎ 5-278 0200; www.estemb.lt; Mickevičiaus gatvė 4a)
Finland (Map pp292-3; ☎ 5-212 1621; www.finland.lt; Klaipėdos gatvė 6)
France (Map pp292-3; ☎ 5-212 2979; www.ambafrance-lt.org; Švarco gatvė 1)
Germany (Map pp292-3; ☎ 5-210 6400; www.vilnius.dilpo.de; Sierakausko gatvė 24)
Latvia (Map pp292-3; ☎ 5-213 1260; embassy.lithuania@mfa.gov.lv; Čiurlionio gatvė 76)
Netherlands (Map pp292-3; ☎ 5-269 0072; www.netherlandsembassy.lt; Jogailos gatvė 4)
Norway (Map pp292-3; ☎ 5-261 0000; www.norvegija.lt; Mėsinių gatvė 5/2)
Poland (Map pp288-9; ☎ 5-270 9001; ambpol@tdd.lt; Smėlio gatvė 20a)
Russia (Map pp288-9; ☎ 5-272 1763; www.lithuania.mid.ru; Latvių gatvė 53/54)
UK (Map pp288-9; ☎ 5-246 2900; www.britain.lt; Antakalnio gatvė 2)
USA (Map pp292-3; ☎ 5-266 5500; www.usembassy.lt; Akmenų gatvė 6)

FESTIVALS & EVENTS

Lithuania's most important cultural events include its national song festival (the next will be in 2007; p32), midsummer celebrations and the Baltika Folklore Festival (p386). The State Department of Tourism (p391) posts a complete list online. Key dates:

February

Horse Race First Saturday of the month; on Lake Sartai in Dusetos, near Utena, if the lake is frozen, or in the town.
Užgavėnės Animal, bird and beast masquerades in towns and villages of Žemaitija to celebrate Mardi Gras.

March

St Casimir's Day Held on 4 March. Lithuania's patron saint's day, with the Kaziukas crafts fair in Vilnius around this date.
Birštonas Jazz Festival Held late March in even-numbered years. Three-day jazz event, with top Lithuanian and foreign musicians.

April

Kaunas International Jazz Festival Four-day festival, with acts in Kaunas and Vilnius, attracting top jazz musicians from all over the world.

July

Vilnius Summer Music Festival A week-long summer festival of street theatre, dancing, masked parades and craft fairs in the streets of Vilnius' Old Town.
Žemaičių Kalvarija Church Festival First week of the month. Thousands of pilgrims from all over Lithuania

LITHUANIA

flock to the Žemaičių Kalvarija to celebrate this week-long church festival.
Klaipėda Sea Festival Late July. Celebrations in the port city.

August

Visagino Country (www.visagino-country.lt) Two-day international country-and-western music festival in Visaginas, mid-August.

September

Vilnius City Days Mid-month. Three days of musical and cultural events in theatres, concert halls and the streets of Vilnius.

October

Vilnius Jazz Festival One of Eastern Europe's leading contemporary jazz gatherings, held in the capital city.

November

Vėlinės (All Souls' Day) Held on 2 November. Commemoration of the dead, with visits to cemeteries.

LITHUANIA

HOLIDAYS

Lithuania also celebrates such days as the Day of the Lithuanian Flag (1 January), St Casimir's Day (4 March), Earth Day (20 March), Partisans' Day (fourth Sunday in May), Black Ribbon Day (23 August) and the Genocide Day of Lithuanian Jews (23 September). People still work on these days, but the national flag flutters outside most public buildings and private homes.

Public holidays

New Year's Day 1 January
Independence Day (Nepriklausomybės diena) 16 February; anniversary of 1918 independence declaration
Lithuanian Independence Restoration Day 1 March
Good Friday
Easter Monday
International Labour Day 1 May
Mothers' Day First Sunday in May
Feast of St John (Midsummer) 24 June
Statehood Day 6 July; commemoration of coronation of Grand Duke Mindaugas, 13th century
Assumption of Blessed Virgin 15 August
All Saints' Day 1 November
Christmas (Kalėdos) 25, 26 December

INTERNET ACCESS

Internet cafés grow like mushrooms (as they say in Lithuania!) in Vilnius (2.50Lt to 8Lt per hour). Outside the capital, prices are higher and speeds are slower. In remote areas such as the Nemunas Delta in western Lithuania the whole concept is nonexistent.

Most top-end hotels and a good few midrange places advertise free or paying hook-up in hotel rooms. What is actually meant by hook-up varies enormously, though. Many simply have a telephone plug in the room, which, if you have a laptop, you can use to dial up using your modem, access number etc. Others will provide the cable if you have the laptop. Many hotels (as well as Vilnius airport and Vokiečių gatvė in Vilnius) are wi-fi zones, allowing you to hook-up wirelessly for free or a small fee. A complete listing of wi-fi hot spots can be found on www.wifi.lt.

A couple of top-end hotels in Vilnius and Kaunas have computer-equipped business centres for guests to use at a fairly substantial fee. Many budget and midrange places, meanwhile, have a computer terminal in the lobby, on which guests can surf for free.

INTERNET RESOURCES

Useful general Baltic websites are on p15. Recommended sites pertaining solely to Lithuania include the following:
Countryside Vacation in Lithuania (www.countryside.lt) Key site for booking farm and homestay accommodation in rural Lithuania or contacting local folk artists.
Entertainment Bank (Pramagos Lietuvoje; www.eb.lt) Entertainment and culture website, jammed with invaluable info on what's happening when across the entire country; eating, drinking and Lithuania with kids too.
European Information Centre (www.eic.lrs.lt) Lithuania in Europe! Read all about it.
Lithuania (www.lietuva.lt) Information portal packed with useful links.
Lithuania Statistics (www.std.lt) Crunch figures with the national statistics office.
Lithuania Travel Information (www.travel.lt) Precisely what its name says; set up by the Lithuanian Tourism Fund.
Litrail (www.litrail.lt) Train timetable and information by Lithuanian Railways.
Parliament of Lithuania (www.lrs.lt) Read all about the latest laws.
President of Lithuania (www.lrp.lt) Brush up on who's ruling the country.
Toks (www.toks.lt) Comprehensive national and international bus information.

MAPS

For regional maps, see p388. For Lithuania nothing can beat the interactive and searchable maps covering the entire country at **Maps.lt** (www.maps.lt).

In print, Lithuania is best covered by the *Lietuva* (1:400,000) road map, published by Vilnius-based map publisher **Briedis** (www.briedis.lt; Parodu gatvė 4, LT-04133 Vilnius) and sold by the publisher online. Bookshops, tourist offices and supermarkets in Lithuania sell it for 8Lt.

For stress-free navigation buy Jāņa sēta's *miesto planas* (city maps) covering Vilnius, Kaunas and Klaipėda at a scale of 1:25,000, with a 1:10,000 inset of the centre, and Palanga (1:15,000), Šiauliai and Panevėžys (1:20,000). They cost 6Lt to 8Lt apiece in bookshops and some tourist offices.

MONEY

The Lithuanian litas (Lt) will remain firmly in place until at least 2007 when Lithuania could possibly trade in its litas for the euro (p22). Some hotels and restaurants already list prices in euros as well as litų, but payment is still in litų only.

The litas (plural: litų or litai) is divided into 100 centai (singular: centas). It comes in note denominations of 10Lt, 20Lt, 50Lt, 100Lt, 200Lt and 500Lt and coins of 1Lt, 2Lt and 5Lt alongside the virtually worthless centai coins. Since 2002 the litas has been pegged to the euro at a fixed rate of 3.45Lt; see the inside front cover for exchange rates. For seven years previously, the US dollar served as the peg.

POST

Lithuania's postal system (www.post.lt) is quick and cheap. Letters/postcards cost 1.70Lt/1.20Lt internationally and 1Lt/0.80Lt domestically. Mail to the USA takes about 10 days, to Europe about a week. State-run EMS is the cheapest express mail service; find it in Vilnius at the central post office (p291).

TELEPHONE

Lithuania's digitised telephone network, run by **Lietuvos Telekomas** (Lithuanian Telecom; www.telecom.lt), is quick and efficient, although knowing what code to dial can be confusing.

To call other cities within Lithuania, dial ☎ 8, wait for the tone, then dial the area code and telephone number.

To make an international call from Lithuania, dial ☎ 00 followed by the country code.

To call Lithuania from abroad, dial Lithuania's country code (☎ 370), the area code and telephone number.

Then of course there are mobile telephones. No self-respecting Lithuanian would be seen without a mobile surgically attached to their ear, and indeed, many a hotel and restaurant – especially in more rural parts – lists a mobile telephone as its main number. Mobile numbers comprise a three-digit code and a five-digit number.

To call a mobile within Lithuania, dial ☎ 8 followed by the three-digit code and mobile number. To call a mobile from abroad, dial ☎ 370 followed by the three-digit code and mobile number. This guide lists full mobile numbers, ie ☎ 8-xxx xxxxx.

Mobile companies **Bitė** (www.bite.lt), **Omnitel** (www.omnitel.lt) and **Tele 2** (www.tele2.lt) sell prepaid SIM cards; Tele2 is only one to offer free roaming with its prepaid cards, making it the best choice for those travelling in Estonia, Latvia and Poland too.

Public telephones – increasingly rare given the widespread use of mobiles – are blue and only accept phonecards, sold in denominations of 50/75/100/200 units for 9/13/16/30Lt at newspaper kiosks.

TOURIST INFORMATION

Most towns have a tourist office with staff who usually speak at least a little English. Tourist offices range from the superbly helpful, useful and obliging to the downright useless and are coordinated by the Vilnius-based **State Department of Tourism** (Map pp292-3; ☎ 5-210 8796; www.tourism.lt; Juozapavičiaus gatvė 13). For a list of its representatives overseas, see p391. Details of tourist offices in cities and towns are given in the Information sections throughout the chapter.

For more info on Lithuania's three Unesco World Heritage sights – Neringa, Vilnius' Old Town and the fine tradition of cross crafting – visit the Vilnius-based **Lithuanian National Commission for Unesco** (Map pp292-3; ☎ 5-210 7340; www.unesco.lt; Šv Jono gatvė 11, Vilnius).

LITHUANIA

Kaliningrad Excursion

Overlooking the Baltic Sea, the Kaliningrad Region boasts some striking scenery. Among the region's attractions, is a vibrant city with 700 years of Prussian history and the region's main amber producer.

Yet more than its natural wonders, Kaliningrad is known for its history. From the 13th century until 1945, the entire region was German, part of the core territory of the Teutonic knights and their successors, the dukes and kings of Prussia. Its capital, now named Kaliningrad, was the famous German city of Königsberg, capital of East Prussia, where Prussian kings were crowned. After WWI, East Prussia was separated from the rest of Germany when Poland regained statehood. The three-month campaign in which the Red Army took Kaliningrad in 1945 was one of the fiercest of WWII, with hundreds of thousands of casualties on both sides.

FAST FACTS

- **Area** 15,100 sq km
- **Birthplace of** Emanuel Kant
- **Country** Russia
- **Country code** ☎ 22 within the region, ☎ 0112 from elsewhere
- **Departure tax** none
- **Money** rouble; €1 = R33.84; UK£1 = R49.33; US$1 = R28.26
- **Population** 955,000
- **Official language** Russian
- **Visa** unless you're flying, to reach the Kaliningrad Region from any of the Baltic countries, you must be in possession of a visa for one of the neighbouring countries. This must be arranged in advance. It can be done at the main **PVU office** (☎ 228 274, 228 282; room 9, Sovetsky pr 13) in Kaliningrad.

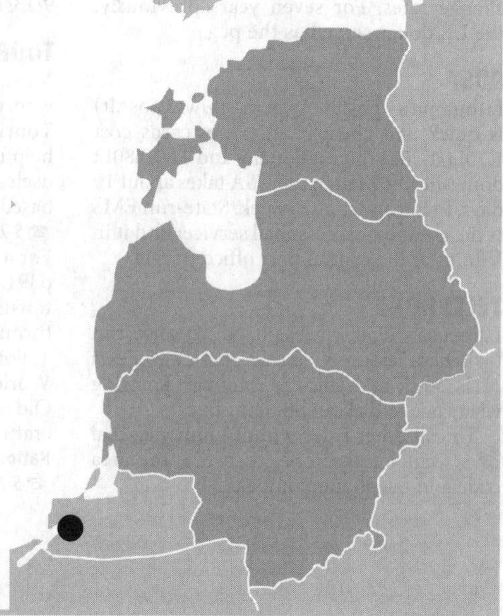

KALININGRAD

Old photos attest that until 1945 Königsberg was one of Europe's finest-looking cities: regal, vibrant, cultured and an architectural gem. But WWII, later Soviet destruction of German-era constructions and misguided building projects saw to it that today's Kaliningrad is not exactly eye-candy.

However, there are lovely residential corners of the city that predate the war, a forestlike park and a few large ponds that work as effective antidotes to all the concrete. A number of central areas have been given a recent and friendly face-lift. It's also a vibrant, fun-loving city that feels larger than its population would suggest.

ORIENTATION & INFORMATION

Leninsky prospekt, a broad north–south avenue, is Kaliningrad's main artery, running over 3km from the bus and main train station, Yuzhny Vokzal (South Station), to the suburban Severny Vokzal (North Station). About halfway along it crosses the Pregolya River and passes the cathedral, the city's major landmark. The city's real heart is further north, around the sprawling pl Pobedy.

A free Russian/English guide to the region and city called *Welcome to Kaliningrad* is available in hotel lobbies. **In Your Pocket** (www.inyourpocket.com/russia/kaliningrad/en; available only online) has the latest city listings. **Baltma Tours** (☎ 211 880; www.baltmatours.com; pr Mira 49; 🕑 9.30am-6.30pm Mon-Fri, 11am-3pm Sat) is the best travel agency in town and by far the best source of regional information.

Change money at **Sberbank** (ul Chernyakhovskogo 38; Leninsky pr 2). To keep in touch, head to **Internet Café** (pr Mira; per hr about R80; 🕑 11am-11pm) or to the **telephone & fax centre** (Teatralnaya ul 13/19; 🕑 24hr) for good value calls.

SIGHTS

Cathedral & Around

A Unesco World Heritage site, the red-brick Gothic **cathedral** (☎ 446 868; adult/student R70/35; 🕑 9am-5pm) is an outstanding remnant from the German past. Founded in 1333, it was severely damaged during WWII and since 1992 has been undergoing total reconstruction. On the top floor is an austere room with the death mask of Emanuel Kant, whose rose-marble **tomb** lies outside on the outer north side. The 18th-century philosopher was born in Königsberg and studied and taught here too.

The fine blue Renaissance-style building, just across the river to the south of the cathedral, is the **Former Stock Exchange** (Leninsky pr 83), built in the 1870s and now a 'Sailors' Culture Palace'.

North of the cathedral is Tsentralnaya ploshchad (Central Square), on which sits one of the dourest, ugliest of Soviet creations, the upright H-shaped **Dom Sovietov** (House of Soviets). On this site stood a magnificent 1255 castle, damaged during WWII but dynamited out of existence by narrow-minded Soviet planners in 1967–8 to rid the city of a flagrant reminder of its Germanic past. Over 10 long years this eyesore was built in its place, but it has never even been used. Money ran out, and it was discovered that the land below it was hollow, with a (now flooded) four-level underground passage connecting to the cathedral.

Further north, near the university, is the popular **Bunker Museum** (☎ 536 593; Universitetskaya ul 2; adult/student R40/30; 🕑 10am-6pm), Kaliningrad's German command post in 1945, where the city's last German commander, Otto van Lasch, signed the capitulation to the Soviets.

World Ocean Museum

Another of Kaliningrad's star attractions, this four-section **museum** (☎ 340 244; nab Petra Velikogo 1; each section adult/student R50/25; 🕑 10am-6pm Wed-Sun Apr-Oct, 11am-5pm Wed-Sun Nov-Mar) has some fascinating exhibits hidden among the three ships docked in the river. *Vityaz*, a former expedition vessel, has displays on its past scientific life as well as on other Russian research expeditions. There is also an 'amber cabin', where amber items from around the world are on display. Visits to the *Vityaz* are by guided tour (every 45 minutes or so). There is also a submarine, which you can wander freely through.

Other sights

On the edge of the shimmering Prud Verkny (Upper Pond), the **Amber Museum** (☎ 461 563; pl Vasilevskogo 1; admission R60; 🕑 10am-5pm Tue-Sun) has some 6000 examples of amber artworks, the most impressive being from the Soviet period. In addition to enormous pieces of

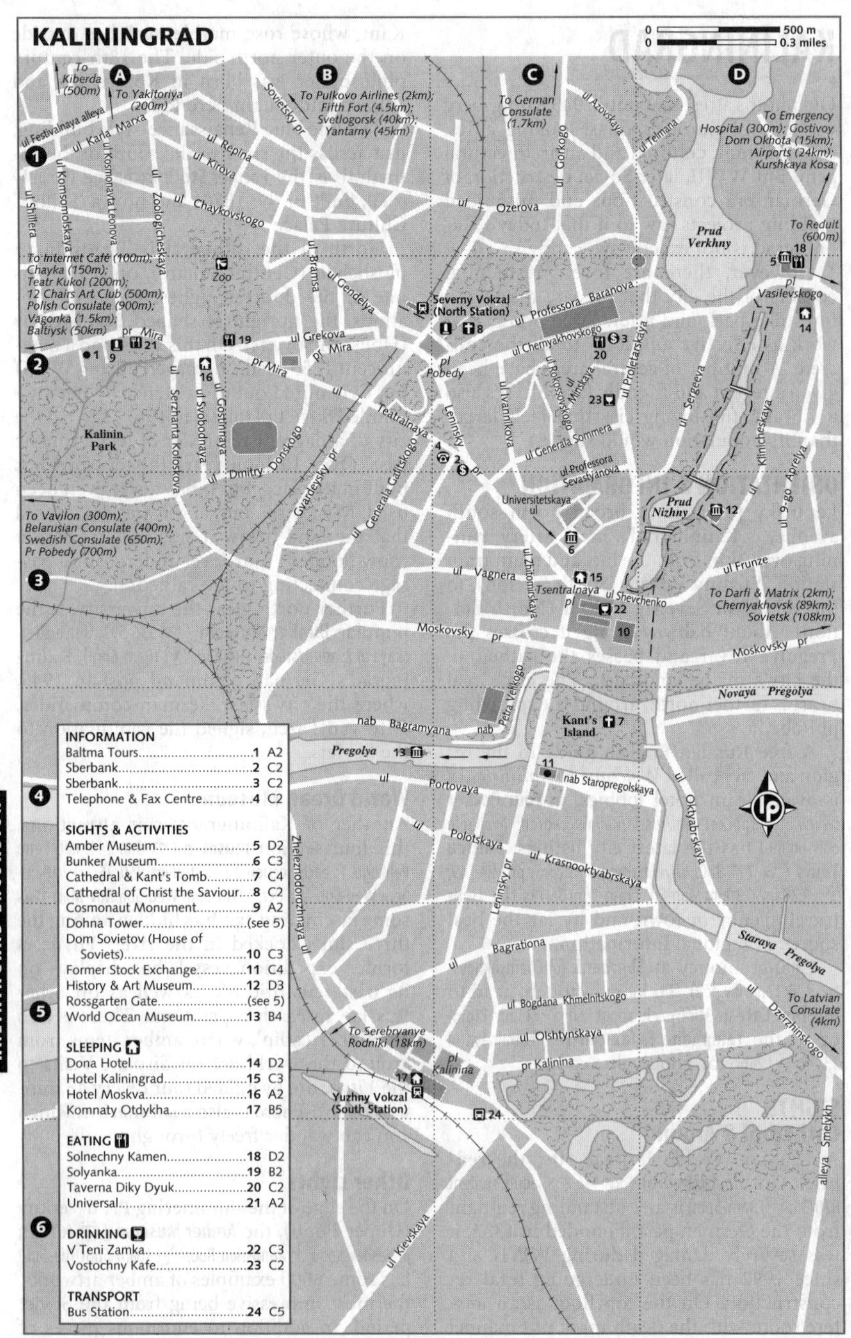
KALININGRAD
0 500 m
0 0.3 miles
A
B
C
D
1
2
3
4
5
6
To Kiberda (500m)
To Yakitoriya (200m)
To Pulkovo Airlines (2km); Fifth Fort (4.5km); Svetlogorsk (40km); Yantarny (45km)
To German Consulate (1.7km)
To Emergency Hospital (300m); Gostivoy Dom Okhota (15km); Airports (24km); Kurshkaya Kosa
To Reduit (600m)
To Internet Café (100m); Chayka (150m); Teatr Kukol (200m); 12 Chairs Art Club (500m); Polish Consulate (900m); Vagonka (1.5km); Baltiysk (50km)
To Vavilon (300m); Belarusian Consulate (400m); Swedish Consulate (650m); Pr Pobedy (700m)
To Darfi & Matrix (2km); Chernyakhovsk (89km); Sovietsk (108km)
To Latvian Consulate (4km)
To Serebryanye Rodniki (18km)
ul Festivalnaya alleya
ul Karla Marxa
ul Kosmonavta Leonova
ul Komsomolskaya
ul Shillera
ul Zoologicheskaya
ul Repina
ul Kirova
ul Chaykovskogo
Sovietsky pr
ul Bramsa
ul Gendelya
ul Ozerova
ul Gorkogo
ul Azovskaya
ul Telmana
Prud Verkhny
pl Vasilevskogo
Zoo
Severny Vokzal (North Station)
ul Professora Baranova
ul Grekova
pr Mira
pl Pobedy
ul Chernyakhovskogo
ul Rokossovskogo
ul Minskaya
ul Proletarskaya
ul Sergeeva
ul Klinicheskaya
ul Serzhanta Koloskova
ul Svobodnaya
ul Gostinnaya
Kalinin Park
ul Teatralnaya
Leninsky pr
ul Ivannikova
ul Generala Sommera
ul Professora Sevastyanova
ul Dmitry Donskogo
Gvardeysky pr
ul Generala Galitskogo
Universitetskaya ul
Prud Nizhny
ul 9-go Aprelya
ul Vagnera
ul Zhitomirskaya
Tsentralnaya pl
ul Shevchenko
ul Frunze
Moskovsky pr
Novaya Pregolya
nab Bagramyana
nab Petra Velikogo
Kant's Island
Pregolya
nab Staropregolskaya
ul Portovaya
ul Oktyabrskaya
ul Polotskaya
ul Krasnooktyabrskaya
Zheleznodorozhnaya ul
Leninsky pr
ul Bagrationa
Staraya Pregolya
ul Dzerzhinskogo
ul Bogdana Khmelnitskogo
ul Olshtynskaya
pl Kalinina
pr Kalinina
Yuzhny Vokzal (South Station)
alleya Smelykh
ul Kievskaya
INFORMATION
Baltma Tours 1 A2
Sberbank 2 C2
Sberbank 3 C2
Telephone & Fax Centre 4 C2
SIGHTS & ACTIVITIES
Amber Museum 5 D2
Bunker Museum 6 C3
Cathedral & Kant's Tomb 7 C4
Cathedral of Christ the Saviour 8 C2
Cosmonaut Monument 9 A2
Dohna Tower (see 5)
Dom Sovietov (House of Soviets) 10 C3
Former Stock Exchange 11 C4
History & Art Museum 12 D3
Rossgarten Gate (see 5)
World Ocean Museum 13 B4
SLEEPING
Dona Hotel 14 D2
Hotel Kaliningrad 15 C3
Hotel Moskva 16 A2
Komnaty Otdykha 17 B5
EATING
Solnechny Kamen 18 D2
Solyanka 19 B2
Taverna Diky Dyuk 20 C2
Universal 21 A2
DRINKING
V Teni Zamka 22 C3
Vostochny Kafe 23 C2
TRANSPORT
Bus Station 24 C5

THE RUSSIAN AMBER ROAD

Amber has been transported along amber roads since before the birth of Christ, and there's nowhere finer to feel its subtle magic than in the Kaliningrad Region – source of almost all Baltic amber. Stunning amber-studded jewellery and the world's second-largest hunk of amber add a sparkle to the Kaliningrad **Amber Museum**, while Kaliningrad's **amber cabin** aboard the *Vitiaz* at the World Ocean Museum is an interesting port of call. A tour of the industrial **Yantarny Amber Mine** (☎ 01153 20392; Gagarin str 11; R70) is a must. Yantarny is about 45km northwest of Kaliningrad, reachable by bus from Kaliningrad.

jewellery containing prehistoric insects suspended within, some of the more fascinating works include an amber flute and a four-panelled amber and ivory chalice depicting Columbus and his ships, *Niña*, *Pinta* and *Santa Maria*. You can buy amber jewellery in the museum or from the vendors outside. The museum is housed in the attractive **Dohna Tower**, a bastion of the city's old defensive ring sitting at the lower end of a small lake surrounded by parkland. The adjacent **Rossgarten Gate**, one of the old German city gates, contains a decent restaurant.

Kaliningrad's outstanding **History & Art Museum** (☎ 453 844; ul Klinicheskaya 21; adult/student R40/30; 🕑 10am-6pm Tue-Sun) is housed in a reconstructed 1912 concert hall by the banks of the pretty Prud Nizhny (Schlossteich, Lower Pond), a favourite recreation spot. The museum displays a fairly open history of the city. Though it mainly focuses on Soviet rule, the German past comes through as the city's spine. There are chilling posters of the castle's destruction.

Prospekt Mira

Ploshchad Pobedy (Pobedy Square) is the current city centre, and is the site of a massive cathedral that should be complete by the time you read this. The gold domes of the **Cathedral of Christ the Saviour** should be visible from many points in the city.

Extending west of the square is pr Mira, a pleasant artery lined with shops and cafés, leading to some of the city's prettiest areas.

Further on is the splendid **Cosmonaut Monument**, a gem of Soviet iconography. This honours the several cosmonauts who hail from the region. Just west, as pl Pobedy branches out from pr Mira, is the entrance to **Kalinin Park**, an amusement centre and a superb, forestlike park on the grounds of an old German cemetery.

SLEEPING

Kaliningrad's hotels are often booked solid by business travellers during the week. To avoid disappointment, call ahead.

Dona Hotel (☎ 351 650; www.dona.kaliningrad.ru; pl Vasilevskogo 2; s/d from R1920/2480) This is Kaliningrad's most stylish hotel, with handsomely furnished rooms and ultramodern design touches worthy of a Philippe Starck protégé. Top-end rooms offer spacious digs, with globe lighting, huge windows and flat-screen TVs. The hallways, with Miro-esque carpeting, are a tribute to sleek modernism. You'll also find a friendly English-speaking staff, pleasant buffet breakfasts and one of the city's best restaurants – Dolce Vita.

Hotel Moskva (☎ 352 300; pr Mira 19; s/d from R1800/2000) This 171-room hotel has been reborn after extensive renovations and boasts bright spacious rooms, friendly atmosphere and a good location.

Hotel Kaliningrad (☎ 350 500; www.hotel.kaliningrad.ru; Leninsky pr 81; s/d from R1000/1200) The town's principal hotel is conveniently placed and offers many services. The renovated rooms are clean and comfortable, but charmless. Try to avoid rooms facing the city centre; these are noisy due to the traffic.

Gostivoy Dom Okhota (☎ 226 994; Petrovo village; s/d R600/800) For those who don't mind staying out of the city, this wooden chalet is a small slice of paradise. Rooms are modern, bright and clean, and the surroundings peaceful. There's horse riding nearby and meals can be ordered. It's on the main road to Zelenogradsk, 15km north along Sovetsky pr.

Komnaty Otdykha (☎ 586 447; pl Kalinina; s/d R280/560) Inside the South Train Station, the rooms here are surprisingly quiet and clean. The shared bathrooms are OK.

EATING & DRINKING

Universal (☎ 216 931; pr Mira 43; meals R100-350; 🕑 10am-3am) This stylish complex comprises a café, restaurant (mains R100 to R150), cinema and nightclub. The restaurant is considered one of the city's top three; if you just want a casual meal, the café, with its various rooms of antique furnishings, makes a fine spot for dishes such as French onion soup, vegetable risotto with mushrooms, and chocolate truffle tart. English menu.

Solyanka (☎ 279 203; pr Mira 24; meals R65-90; 9am-11pm) There may be a doorman here, but this setup is basically caféteria-style (non-Russian speakers can point to what they like), serving tasty dishes at great prices.

Taverna Diky Dyouk (☎ 465 235; ul Chernyakhovskogo 26; meals R190-500) Generous portions of scrumptious Russian, French and Lithuanian dishes are served at this medieval-themed restaurant.

Solnechny Kamen (☎ 539 106; pl Vasilievskogo 3; meals R150-300) In the old Rossgarten Gate, this atmospheric restaurant specialises in seafood, and Russian dishes. As well as the brick walls, stained glass and Teutonic touches in the main dining room, there's a pleasant outdoor terrace at the back.

V Teni Zamka (Tsentralnaya pl, kiosk No 63; cappuccino R40-56) The city's best espresso, coffee cocktails and ice cream are served in this tiny but charming space, seating only 20, inside the aptly named kiosk village.

Vostochniy Kafe (☎ 147 121; ul Proletarskaya 3a; meals R150-300) The sounds of gurgling water-pipes greet visitors upon entering this basement-level tea salon. Gauzy curtains, strings of Christmas lights and New Age music set the scene for lounging over pipefuls of flavoured tobacco and potfuls of green tea. Waiters are summoned via the red button dangling from the paper lanterns.

GETTING THERE & AWAY

Bus

The **bus station** (☎ 443 635; international tickets ☎ 446 261; pl Kalinina) is next to Yuzhny Vokzal. Buses depart from here to every corner of the region. One bus daily goes to Klaipėda (R135) via Sovetsk, and there are two buses daily each to Kaunas (R255) and Vilnius (R360). Daily buses go to Rīga (R360), Tallinn (R670) and Warsaw.

Car & Motorcycle

It is possible to enter Kaliningrad at Kybartai on the Lithuanian border or on the Kurshkaya Kosa at Nida. Petrol is widely available.

Train

There are two stations in the city: **Severny Vokzal** (North Station; ☎ 499 991) and the larger **Yuzhny Vokzal** (South Station; ☎ 492 675). All long-distance and many local trains go from Yuzhny Vokzal, passing through but not always stopping at Severny Vokzal. There are four trains a day to Vilnius (R1000, six hours).

GETTING AROUND

At research time, many of the city's streets were being repaired and transit routes were in flux. By the time you read this, routes should be back in operation. Tickets for trams, trolleybuses, buses and minibuses are sold only on board (R10). To get to the domestic airport, take bus 128 from the bus station (R30). Taxis cost at least R400 from the airport, but less to the airport.

Regional Directory

CONTENTS

Accommodation	381
Activities	383
Business Hours	383
Children	383
Climate Charts	384
Courses	384
Customs	385
Dangers & Annoyances	385
Disabled Travellers	385
Discount Cards	385
Embassies & Consulates	386
Festivals & Events	386
Food	387
Gay & Lesbian Travellers	387
Holidays	387
Insurance	387
Internet Access	387
Legal Matters	388
Maps	388
Money	388
Post	389
Shopping	390
Solo Travellers	390
Telephone	390
Time	390
Toilets	391
Tourist Information	391
Visas	391
Women Travellers	392
Work	392

This chapter contains the nuts and bolts of travelling in the Baltics. Country-specific information can be found in the directories for Estonia (p167), Latvia (p265) and Lithuania (p372).

ACCOMMODATION

Finding a decent place in the Baltics to lay your head is generally not a problem. Tallinn, Rīga and Vilnius all have some stylish choices among the many top-end hotels, with fewer midrange and budget options. Outside the capitals you can find a wide range of guesthouses, B&Bs and hostels. In Estonia and Lithuania old-school sanatoriums have been renovated and reopened as spa resorts. There are a few grey concrete Soviet monsters lurking about (mostly in Latvia), but the Eastern Bloc blues are largely a thing of the past.

In this book, accommodation is ordered under Budget, Midrange and Top End headings. In the Budget category (under €30), you'll find hostels and pretty basic guesthouses with shared bathrooms. Our midrange listings (€30 to €75) run the gamut from family-run guesthouses to large, simply furnished hotel rooms. Most rooms in this category have private bathrooms; some include breakfast in the price. Top-end listings (over €75) comprise historically set hotels, spa resorts and charming places offering something particularly unique (like antique-filled rooms or ocean views). You can expect good service, a prime location and a spacious room in tip-top shape.

The peak tourist season is from June through August. If you come then, you should book well in advance. This is essential in Tallinn, Pänu, Vilnius and Riga – and in other popular summertime destinations.

Rates published in this guide reflect peak prices. From September to May, room prices typically go down by about 30% – sometimes substantially more depending on your powers of persuasion. Also keep in mind that popular seaside spots and other weekend getaway destinations are pricier on weekends than on Monday to Thursday.

B&Bs

Sharing the breakfast table with your host family each morning will give you a keen insight into local life. Sampling traditional cooking is another joy, and one that's hard to find elsewhere.

Several agencies, both within and outside of the Baltics, arrange accommodation in private homes in several cities across Estonia, Latvia and Lithuania. See also agencies listed in Tallinn (Rasastra, p80) and Vilnius (p306).

American-International Homestays (☎ 303-258 3234; www.aihtravel.com/homestays; USA) Homestay accommodation with dinner, transport and an English-speaking guide in any of the Baltic capitals for single/double US$100/175.

Litinterp (☎ 5-212 3850; www.litinterp.com; Bernardinų gatvė, Vilnius, Lithuania) B&B accommodation with local families in Klaipėda, Nida, Palanga and Kaunas; single/double from €23/46.

Rasastra Bed & Breakfast (Map pp70-1; ☎ 661 6291; www.bedbreakfast.ee; Mere puiestee 4, Tallinn, Estonia) Rasastra can set you up in homes in Estonia, Latvia and Lithuania; single/double from €18/32.

Camping

In the Baltics, camp sites are found in some gorgeous natural settings – overlooking a lake or river, or tucked away in the forest – but most are difficult to reach unless you have a private vehicle. Some camp sites have permanent wooden cottages or, occasionally, brick bungalows. Cabins vary in shape and size but are usually small one-room affairs with three or four beds. Showers and toilets are nearly always communal and vary dramatically in cleanliness. Bigger camping grounds have a bar and/or caféteria, and sauna.

Camp sites usually open in mid-May or June and close in mid-September. A night in a wooden cottage typically costs €10 to €20 per person.

Estonia, in particular, has an extremely well-organised outfit overseeing camping. **RMK** (☎ 628 1500; www.rmk.ee; Viljandi maantee 18b, Tallinn) maintains dozens of free camp sites all over the country. You can pick up detailed maps to all of their sites at the head office in Tallinn.

Farmstays

Staying in a private room in a farmhouse, rural manor or cottage is one of the region's most attractive sleeping options. Host families can provide home-cooked meals and arrange fishing, boating, horse riding, mushrooming and berrying, and other activities – for a fee. Each of the Baltic countries has its own rural tourism association through which rural accommodation can be booked.

Baltic Country Holidays (Lauku Ceļotājs; ☎ 761 7600; www.traveller.lv; Kuģu iela 11, LV-1048 Rīga) Arranges B&B accommodation in a variety of rural settings all over Latvia for €12 to €35 per night; it also lets whole farmhouses and cottages, and takes advance bookings for camping grounds, hotels and motels across Latvia.

Countryside Tourism of Lithuania (☎ 37-400 354; www.countryside.lt; Donelaičio gatvė 2-201, Kaunas) Arranges accommodation in farmhouses and rural cottages throughout Lithuania. Most lodgings start at €8 per person. A worthwhile investment is the hefty, illustrated catalogue of the extensive offerings, available in Lithuanian bookshops for 8.75Lt.

Estonian Rural Tourism (☎ 600 9999; www.maaturism.ee; Vilmsi tänav 53b, Tallinn) An umbrella organisation for 220-odd rural tourism organisations in Estonia. The full range of accommodation – from camping and B&B to palaces and castle hotels – can be booked through it. Most B&Bs are on farms and prices start at €15 per person.

> **BOOK ACCOMMODATION ONLINE**
>
> For more accommodation reviews and recommendations by Lonely Planet authors, check out the online booking service at www.lonelyplanet.com. You'll find the true, insider lowdown on the best places to stay. Reviews are thorough and independent. Best of all, you can book online.

Guesthouses

Small private guesthouses are a good bet for affordable travel in the Baltics. Priced somewhere between hostels and standard hotels, guesthouses typically have less than a dozen rooms and usually offer a cosier, less formal setting than other places.

Hostels

There are many hostels scattered across the Baltics, with the largest network in Estonia. Lithuania's hostels have developed in leaps and bounds in the past couple of years, while Latvia has the fewest options. Wherever you decide to stay, book your bed well in advance if you come in the summer. You'll find HI hostels in all of the countries.

For a complete list of hostels in each country visit www.estoniahostels.com, www.hostellinglatvia.com and www.lithuanianhostels.org.

Hotels

There are hotels to suit every price range, although budget hotel accommodation in the increasingly glam capitals has become dishearteningly scarce. As more cheap hotels make the effort to brighten up their image, so nightly rates are being yanked up too.

That's not to say, however, that delightfully horrible relics from the Soviet era – offering cheap accommodation in a glum and shabby setting – don't exist. Head into any town in provincial Latvia, for example, and you'll stumble upon a towering concrete block whose stereotypical customer – once upon a time – was a man in a vest, lying on his bed quaffing vodka, chain-smoking and watching TV. Nowadays, some floors in many of these blocks have been renovated and offer two dramatically different types of accommodation. One flight above a battered hallway crowded with battered rooms, you might stumble across refurbished wood floors which lead into cosy, handsomely lit rooms. The midrange option – both in and outside of the capitals – is marked by a refreshing breed of small, family-run hotels. The only downside of these places is that they get booked up quickly, given the limited number of cosy rooms they offer.

Top hotels are a dime a dozen. Many are under Western management or are part of a recognised international hotel chain, while others – such as Konventa Sēta in Rīga, the Radisson-SAS Astorija in Vilnius and the Three Sisters in Tallinn – are housed in exquisitely renovated, historic buildings dating to the 13th to 19th centuries. Tallinn has plenty of other places to relish the medieval splendour - the Schlössle, the Baltic Hotel Imperial, the Olevi Residents - plus there are other alluring options such as Pärnu's highly polished Tervise Paradiis (p159), whose stylish rooms are just steps from the beach, or the luxurious art-deco masterpiece Ammende Villa (p158), also in Pärnu.

Spa Hotels

One of the newest attractions in the region, spa hotels, are an excellent place to be pampered. Even if you don't stay, you can pop in for treatments – mud baths, massages, herbal baths, and dozens of other options. Estonia has the most selections, and you'll find them in Tallinn (p78-9), Saaremaa (p147), Pärnu (p159), Haapsalu (p132) and other places. Druskininkai (p327) is Lithuania's premier spa connection. Latvia has spas in Jūrmala (p221-3).

ACTIVITIES

You'll never run out of options for outdoor amusement in the Baltics. Cycling across the picturesque countryside, hiking through lush forests, canoeing down meandering rivers, bird-watching, swimming in refreshing lakes, plus cross-country skiing in the winter are some of the region's offerings. For complete details see the Activities chapter.

BUSINESS HOURS

Latvia and Lithuania follow similar hours:

Banks 9am to 5pm Monday to Thursday and 9am-4pm Friday
Bars 11am to midnight from Sunday to Thursday, 11am to 2am Friday and Saturday
Cafés 8am to 11pm
Nightclubs 10pm to 5am Thursday to Saturday
Post offices 8am to 7pm from Monday to Friday, 8am to 3pm Saturday
Restaurants noon to 11pm
Shops 10am to 7pm from Monday to Friday, 10am to 4pm Saturday
Supermarkets 8am to 10pm

Estonia marches to a slightly different beat:

Banks 9am to 4pm Monday to Friday
Bars noon to midnight from Sunday to Thursday, noon to 2am Friday and Saturday
Cafés 9am to 10pm
Nightclubs 10pm to 4am Thursday to Saturday
Post offices 9am to 6pm Monday to Friday, 9am to 3pm Saturday
Restaurants noon to 11pm
Shops 10am to 6pm Monday to Friday, 10am to 3pm Saturday
Supermarkets 9am to 10pm

Listed reviews in this book won't include opening hours unless they deviate from those listed above.

CHILDREN

Travelling through the Baltic region with children in tow isn't as daunting as it used to be. Hotels generally do their best to help make kids feel at home; many have family rooms designed for parents travelling with kids or if not most will gladly place an extra bed in the room. A handful of restaurants have kids' menus though not many. Nappies like Pampers and known-brand baby foods, including some organic ones, are widely available in big supermarkets in the capitals. Unfortunately, you won't find many highchairs, and restaurant changing rooms are yet to be invented here.

Good places to go with kids are the stretches of western coastline found throughout the region. In Estonia, Pärnu boasts a water park, a small amusement park and a lovely sandy beach. In Lithuania the entire coastline is a fabulous playground for kids, be it the merry-go-round of funfair amusements and in-house restaurant entertainers in Palanga and Šventoji or the bikes and boats to rent on the Curonian Spit. See also the sections on kids' activities in Vilnius (p305), Tallinn (p79) and Rīga (p200).

For tips and anecdotes on successful travel with the underage crowd, check out Lonely Planet's *Travel with Children*.

CLIMATE CHARTS

The Baltic climate is temperate but on the cool and damp side. It verges on the continental as you move inland where, in winter, it's up to 4°C colder than on the coasts but in summer may be a degree or two warmer. From May to September, daytime highs are normally between 14°C and 22°C. It's unusually warm if the temperature reaches the high 20s. At these northern latitudes, days are long in summer, with a full 19 hours of daylight around midsummer in Estonia. April and October have cold, sharp, wintry days as well as mild spring or autumn ones.

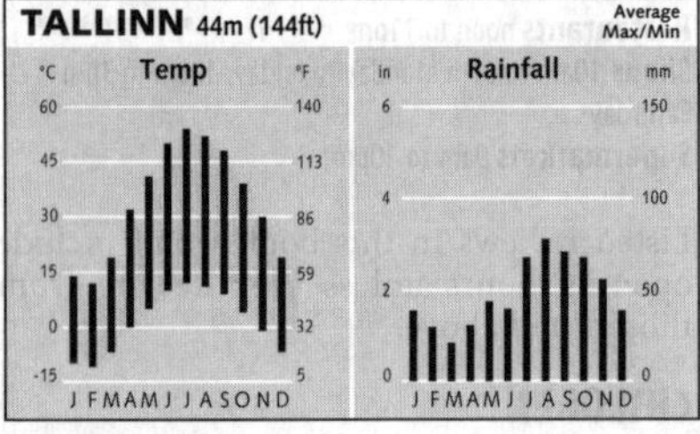

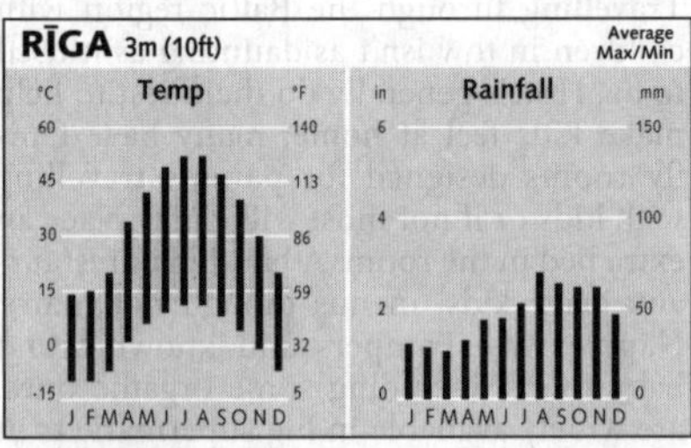

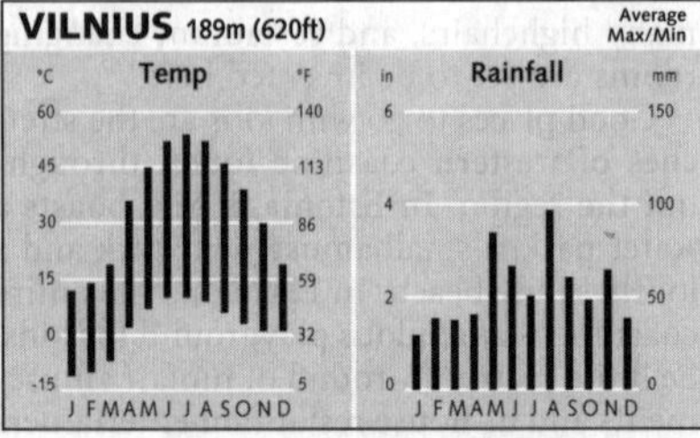

In winter, from November to March, temperatures rarely rise above 4°C and parts of the region may stay below freezing almost permanently from mid-December to late February. Winter hours of daylight are short, and sometimes it never seems to get properly light at all. The first snows usually come in November and there's normally permanent snow cover from January to March in the coastal regions – but up to an extra month either side in the inland east.

Annual precipitation ranges from 500mm to 600mm in the lowland areas to 700mm to 900mm in the uplands. About 75% of it falls as rain, 25% as snow. Winters can be foggy.

Coastal waters average between 16°C and 21°C in summer – July and August are the warmest. The Gulfs of Finland and Rīga freeze occasionally, and the straits between Estonia's islands and the mainland usually freeze for three months from mid-January. The open coast almost never freezes.

See also p14.

COURSES

Crafts

In Lithuania, **Countryside Tourism of Lithuania** (☎ 37-400 354; www.countryside.lt; K Donelaičio 2-201, Kaunas) can organise a variety of classes in rural crafts. Weaving, pottery, carving, knitting and embroidery are some of the things that can be arranged. Various folk-artist workshops in the Lithuanian capital also run courses; see p305 and p313 for details.

Languages

In Lithuania, Vilnius University runs Lithuanian-language courses. An intensive two-/four-week summer course (50/100 hours) costs €377/580, plus €30 registration fee. Accommodation in a student dorm or with a local family can be arranged for a fee. One-year courses are also available. For more details contact the **Department of Lithuanian Studies** (☎ 5-268 7215; www.vu.lt; Universiteto gatvė 5, Vilnius, Lithuania) at Vilnius University.

In Estonia, the **International Language Services** (☎ 627 7170; www.ils.ee; Roosikrantsi 8b, Tallinn) is one of several schools in Tallinn to run Estonian-language courses. A two-week (40-hour) course, costs €256. In the university town of Tartu, intensive two-week courses (54 academic hours) are available for €320 during summer. Contact the **Division of Estonian** (☎ 737 5358; www.ut.ee; room 110, Näitus tänav 2,

Tartu), which also offers one-week classes (20 hours) on Estonian culture for €174.

Those wanting to twist their tongue around Latvian can contact the **Public Service Language Centre** (☎ 721 2251; www.vmc.lv in Latvian; Smilšu iela 1-3, Rīga).

Sculpture

Lithuania has the unique **Centre of Europe Museum** (Europos centro muziejus; ☎ 5-237 7077; www.europosparkas.lt), which runs an artists' residency programme whereby artists from around the world can brainstorm with one another at the open-air sculpture park near Vilnius. Several programmes are held each year and are open to anyone with an interest in applied art or sculpture. Applications must be accompanied by a CV and must be submitted two months before courses start.

CUSTOMS

If you think that a painting or other cultural object you want to buy in one of the Baltic countries may attract customs duty or require special permission to export, check with the seller before purchasing. You may have to get permission from a government office before it can be exported. For country-specific customs information see Estonia (p167), Latvia (p265) and Lithuania (p372).

DANGERS & ANNOYANCES

Theft

Crime is on the rise in the Baltics, though it's rarely of a violent nature. Pickpocketing and petty theft (bag-snatching) is a risk in all of the Baltic capitals, particularly in the busy summer (cash-cow) season. Keep an eye out when you're exploring those enchanting old quarters. Late at night there are occasional muggings on the street. Always be mindful of your surroundings, and be sensible about where you go and who you travel with.

No matter which country you're travelling in, you should always call a taxi rather than hail one on the street. You will definitely save money and worry if you call first. Be especially mindful of taxi drivers at airports and outside the main tourist hotels.

If you're driving, don't leave anything of value in your car. Car theft is less of an issue in Estonia, it's a moderate risk in Lithuania, and it's an integral part of the economy in Latvia: Rīga has one of the highest rates of car theft in the world.

Ethnic Attitudes

Some Estonians, Latvians and Lithuanians have a 'send-'em-home' attitude towards Russians and other ex-Soviet nationalities in their midst. Racist and anti-Semitic statements are likewise not unknown to pass from some Balts' lips.

Mosquitoes

Estonia, Latvia and Lithuania have vast stretches of forest, and yes, swampland, which is home to the mighty Baltic mosquito. Although disease is not a concern here, that may be of little consolation to you as you're being eaten alive on a late summer afternoon. Bring strong repellent (containing at least 20% DEET).

Other Creatures

Ticks are a greater health hazard than mosquitoes, as these can carry lime disease. If you're going hiking in the forest, try to cover up. See p411 for more tips.

DISABLED TRAVELLERS

With its cobbled streets, rickety pavements and old buildings, the Baltic region is not user-friendly for travellers with disabilities. In Estonia the **Social Rehabilitation Centre** (☎ 658 6355; srk@ngonet.ee; Männiku tee 92, Tallinn) gives out advice to travellers with disabilities. In Lithuania, contact the **Disability Information and Consultation Bureau** (☎ 5-261 7277; Teatro gatvė 11/8-13, Vilnius).

Many city hotels have rooms equipped for disabled travellers.

Latvia scores oodles of brownie points from disabled travellers for having the Baltics' most disabled-friendly hotel, adjoining Jūrmala's seaside **Vaivari National Rehabilitation Centre** (☎ 776 6122; nrc3@nrc.lv; Asaru prospketas 61, Jūrmala), which acts as an information centre for travellers with disabilities. Room rates are exceptionally reasonable. Elsewhere it's only really upmarket hotels that have rooms equipped for disabled travellers.

Some beaches on the western Lithuanian coast in Nida and Palanga have ramps to allow wheelchair access to the sand, as does the above-mentioned hotel.

DISCOUNT CARDS

City Discount Cards

Both Tallinn and Rīga offer discount cards to visitors.

TALLINN CARD

The Tallinn Card gives you free or discounted entry to many of the city's sights, discount shopping and free use of all public transport. Prices for one-/two-/three-day cards cost €22.50/26/29 (€11.25/13/14.50 for children) and include a 2½-hour city tour. Cards are sold at tourist information centres, hotels and travel agencies. Further details are available from www.tallinn.ee/tallinncard.

RĪGA CARD

This card offers discounts at restaurants, cafés and theatres. Price includes a walking tour and admission to many museums. Prices for one-/two-/three-day cards are €11.40/17/23 (€6/8.50/11.50 for children). They're sold at tourist offices (www.rigatourism.com), some hostels and travel agencies.

Hostel Cards

A HI card yields discounts of up to 20% at affiliated hostels. You can buy one at some hostels en route; or purchase it before you go, via the national **Youth Hostel Association** (YHA; www.iyhf.org).

Student & Youth Cards

An International Student Identity Card (ISIC) can pay for itself through half-price admissions, discounted air and ferry tickets, and cheap cinema and theatre tickets. Many stockists – generally student-travel agencies – stipulate a maximum age, usually 25. If you're aged under 26 but not a student, you can apply for an International Youth Travel Card (IYTC), which entitles you to much the same discounts as the ISIC. Both cards are administered by the **International Student Travel Confederation** (www.istc.org) and issued by student travel agencies. Within the region, ISIC cards are sold at branches of Student & Youth Travel in Rīga, Tallinn and Vilnius.

Seniors Cards

There are few discounts available to older people – a handful of museums in Tallinn reduce the entrance fee and seniors aged over 70 travel for free on Rīga trolleybuses and trams. But that's about it.

EMBASSIES & CONSULATES

Estonia, Latvia and Lithuania each have numerous diplomatic missions overseas. Likewise, many countries have their own embassies or missions in the Baltic capitals. See Estonia (p167), Latvia (p266) and Lithuania (p372) for details.

It's important to realise what your own embassy can and can't do for you if you get in to trouble. Remember that you are bound by the laws of the country you are in. Your embassy will not be sympathetic if you end up in jail after committing a crime locally, even if such actions are legal in your own country.

FESTIVALS & EVENTS

Estonia, Latvia and Lithuania all enjoy fat festival calendars encompassing everything from religion and music, to song, art, folk culture, handicrafts, film, drama and more. Summer is the busiest time of year, although each of the three Baltic countries celebrates a couple of truly magical festivals at other times of the year, too. The remarkable Day of Setu Lace in the heart of Setumaa in southeastern Estonia on 1 March and the colourful Kaziukas crafts fair in Vilnius to mark St Casimir's Day on 4 March are two worth noting. For a list of the region's top 10, not-to-be-missed festivals see p16.

Most festivals are annual, others are one-off. For a comprehensive list of what's happening in the Baltics see the directories for Estonia (p168), Latvia (p266) and Lithuania (p373). Estonia, Latvia and Lithuania celebrate a number of commemorative days when shops, apartment blocks and offices are obliged by law to fly their national flag.

Above all, however, it is two regular events that are absolutely outstanding: the Baltic song festivals (p33) and the midsummer celebrations (p17).

Folk music and dance performances are also regularly held at Rocca al Mare in Tallinn, the Open-Air Ethnography Museum in Rīga and the Lithuanian Country Life Museum at Rumsiskės near Kaunas.

Baltika Folklore Festival

The Baltic folk festivals, particularly the annual Baltika Folklore Festival, provide a prime opportunity to catch folk songs, music and dance as well as the colourful traditional costumes that are one of the few instantly recognisable trademarks of Estonia, Latvia and Lithuania. The costumes vary, although women generally sport long and colourful skirts, embroidered blouses, jackets or shawls, and an amazing variety of headgear ranging from neat pillboxes to vast, winged, fairy-tale creations. The male equivalent is plainer and more obviously a product of peasant existence. The annual international Baltika Folklore Festival takes place in each Baltic capital in turn (usually in mid-July). The week-long festival is a potent splash of music, dance, exhibitions and parades focusing on Baltic and other folk traditions.

In 2006 the Baltika will be held in Latvia; in 2007 it's due in Estonia; and in 2008 in Lithuania.

FOOD

In this guide, eating entries fall under three price points: budget (less than €10), mid-range (between €10 and €20) and top end (over €20). These are based on the price of two courses and a soft drink. For details on the variety of cuisines on offer, see the Food & Drink sections of Estonia (p62), Latvia (p1640) and Lithuania (p284).

GAY & LESBIAN TRAVELLERS

When it comes to gay rights, the Baltics are still stranded in the shadows of the Dark Ages. While there is a small gay scene in Tallinn, Rīga and Vilnius, there's almost nothing elsewhere. Being 'out' here is largely out of the question, as small displays of public affection can provoke some nasty responses. Tallinn has the most progressive scene (with a single venue openly identifying itself as a gay club). Meanwhile, the Latvian parliament recently took the bold step of adding an amendment to the constitution banning same-sex marriages.

If reading all this has you yearning for a drink, you'll find permanent gay and lesbian bars listed under Entertainment in Tallinn (p87), Rīga (p216) and Vilnius (p306).

Organisations

Estonia's key gay organisation is the **Estonian Gay League** (gayliit@hotmail.com; PO Box 142, EE10502 Tallinn). **Estonian Gay Planet** (www.gay.ee) lists party venues in Estonian only. The **Gay and Lesbian Infocenter** (GLIK; ☎ 645 4545; http://pride.gay.ee; Tartu maantee 29, Tallinn) is also a good source of info.

The Latvian association **Latvian Gay & Lesbian** (☎ 959 2229; www.gay.lv in Latvian; Pastkaste iela 380, Rīga) offers advice on gay issues.

The **Lithuanian Gay League** (LGL; ☎ 5-233 3031; www.gay.lt; PO Box 2862, LT-2000 Vilnius) runs a video library and organises weekend parties, as does the **Lithuanian Lesbian League** (Sappho; www.is.lt/sappho; PO Box 2204, LT-2049 Vilnius).

HOLIDAYS

Public holidays vary between countries; see the holiday information in the directories of Estonia (p169), Latvia (p267) and Lithuania (p374).

INSURANCE

A travel insurance policy to cover theft, loss of property and medical problems is a good idea. The policies written by STA Travel and other travel organisations are usually good value. Some policies offer lower and higher medical expense options. Policies can vary widely, so be sure to check the fine print.

Some insurance policies will specifically exclude 'dangerous activities', which can include hiking.

You may prefer a policy that pays doctors or hospitals rather than you having to pay on the spot and claim later. If you have to claim later make sure you keep all documentation. Some policies ask you to call back (reverse charges) to a centre in your home country where an immediate assessment of your problem is made. Check that the policy covers ambulances and an emergency flight home. For more information on health insurance, see p410.

For further information on car insurance see p416.

Worldwide cover to travellers from over 44 countries is available online at www.lonelyplanet.com/travel_services.

INTERNET ACCESS

The Internet has boomed in Estonia, Latvia and Lithuania in recent years, which, according to reports on the region's so-called 'Tiger Leap', saw enormous advancements as the public quickly adopted the Internet. Estonia leads the way, with 54% of 6 to 74 year olds regularly using the Internet (with a computer in one out of three households). Usage is definitely on the rise in Latvia, where 40% of its citizens are Internet-savvy, along with 30% of Lithuanians.

Today, practically every hotel, restaurant and commercial enterprise is happily hooked up; numerous hotels accept online bookings. Wi-fi is growing in the region with hundreds of sites (some pay per use, some free) scattered across the Baltics. Each of the countries maintains lists of hotspots you can tap into, with the majority of them in Estonia. See Estonia (www.wifi.ee), Lithuania (www.wifi.lt) and Latvia (www.lattelekom.lv) for details.

Public Internet access is available in all three capitals and most provincial towns in the region. Expect to pay around €2 to €3 per hour – or nothing if you visit the public library.

See the country directories of Estonia (p169), Latvia (p267) and Lithuania (p374) for more information.

LEGAL MATTERS

If you are arrested in the Baltics you have the same basic legal rights as anywhere else in Europe. You have the right to be informed of the reason for your arrest (before being carted off to the police station) and you have the right to inform a family member of your misfortune (once you have been carted off). You cannot be detained for more than 72 hours without being charged with an offence, and you have the right to have your lawyer present during questioning.

In Rīga, you can be fined on the spot for straying from public footpaths onto the neatly mowed grass lawns in city parks. In Vilnius, you can sit/lie/sunbathe on the grass in city parks but you can't sleep; police patrol on horseback to check that your eyes aren't shut.

If you're travelling in Latvia, note that it's illegal to buy alcohol anywhere except restaurants, cafés, bars and clubs between 10pm and 8am. In Lithuania and Estonia, public drinking anywhere except licensed premises is illegal.

Tobacco advertising in Lithuania was made illegal only in 2000 (Estonia and Latvia banned it in 1993 and 1998 respectively), while public gambling was only legalised in Lithuania in mid-2001.

LEGAL AGE

	Estonia	Latvia	Lithuania
Drinking	18	18	18
Driving	18	18	18
Sex	14	16	16

MAPS

Decent regional and country maps are widely available outside the region, as are quality city maps in each country. A map covering the region is useful for planning: *Lithuania Estonia Latvia* (Cartographia; www.cartographia.hu), *Estonia, Latvia, Lithuania* (Bartholomew World Map Travel Series; www.bartholomewmaps.com) and *Baltische Staaten* (Ravenstein Verlag, Bad Soden am Taunas; http://reisebuch.de) are very similar 1:850,000-scale maps of the three countries.

Good maps to look for in the region include *Eesti Latvija Lietuva* (1:700,000) published by Vilnius-based Briedis (www.briedis.lt). In Estonia, EO Map (www.eomap) does a pretty mean *Baltimaad* (Baltic States, 1:800,000), which is widely available in Estonian bookshops. In Latvia, map publisher Jāņa sēta (www.kartes.lv) is the market leader, with its pocket-size, spiral-bound, 252-page *Baltic States Road Atlas* (1:500,000), containing 71 city and town maps as well as 24 double-page road maps covering the entire region. Its *Baltic States* (1:700,000) road map is equally indispensable.

On the Internet, www.maps.com is a decent digital map resource. See also p170 for Estonia, p267 for Latvia and p375 for Lithaunia.

MONEY

The local currencies are Estonian krooni (Kr), Latvian lati (Ls) and Lithuanian litų – or litai – (Lt). Since 1992 when the kroon was introduced and 1993 when the lats and litas were introduced (following the dumping of the Soviet rouble), all three have remained completely stable. See the inside front cover for exchange rates.

Lithuania and Estonia pegged the lits and kroon to the euro in 2002 as the first step to joining the euro. Estonia and Latvia are slated to change to the euro on 1 January 2007; Lithuania should follow in 2008.

Regionwide, Western currencies are perfectly acceptable and can be exchanged easily. Exchange rates for Polish złoty, Russian roubles, Ukrainian hrivna and other Eastern European money remain poor. Within the Baltics, it is easy to change one Baltic currency into another, although rates are not always as favourable as those for US dollars.

For information on costs, see the Getting Started chapter. For notes on individual currencies see the country directories, Estonia (p170), Latvia (p268) and Lithaunia (p375.

Although some hotels and tour operators list prices in euros, payment is always in the national currency. In this book, prices are listed in euros where they are advertised as such.

ATMs

ATMs accepting Visa and MasterCard/Eurocard are widespread in cities and larger towns. Some are located inside banks and post offices but the majority are on the streets, outside banks and at bus and train stations, enabling you to get cash 24 hours a day. Most ATMs are multilingual, using the five main European languages.

Credit Cards

Credit cards are widely accepted in hotels, restaurants and shops, especially at the upper end of the market. Visa, MasterCard/Eurocard, Diners Club and Amex all crop up. They are essential for renting a car. With the liberal spread of ATMs, fewer banks are prepared to give cash advances on Visa and MasterCard/Eurocard – those that do, mainly in cities and larger towns, tack a 2% to 5% commission onto the amount of a cash advance. Bring along your passport if you do receive a cash advance.

Moneychangers

Make sure whatever currency you bring is in good condition. Marked, torn or very used notes will be refused. US-dollar notes issued before 1990 are not generally accepted either.

Every town has somewhere you can change cash: usually a bank, exchange office or currency exchange kiosk. The latter crop up in all sorts of places, particularly transport terminals, airports, bus stations and train stations. Rates vary from one outlet to another. Exchange places are generally open during usual business hours.

Tipping & Bargaining

It's fairly common, though not compulsory, to tip waiters 5% to 10% by rounding up the bill. A few waiters may try to tip themselves by 'not having' any change.

Some bargaining (but not a lot) goes on at flea markets. Savings are not likely to be more than 10% to 20% of the initial asking price.

Traveller's Cheques

A limited amount of traveller's cheques are useful because of the protection they offer against theft. It is difficult to find places to exchange them though, once you are out of the cities; most banks charge 4.5% commission. Most banks accept Eurocheques too.

American Express (Amex) has a representative in each capital:

American Express (☎ 212 5809, 24hr service ☎ 8-616 81255; www.amextravel.lt; Vokiec\uių gatvė 13, Vilnius)

Estravel (☎ 626 6266; www.estravel.ee; Suur-Karja tänav 15, EE10140 Tallinn)

Latvia Tours (☎ 708 5001; www.latviatours.lv; Kaļķu iela 8, LV-1050 Rīga)

POST

Letters and postcards from any of the three countries take about two to four days to Western Europe, seven to 10 days to North America and two weeks to Australia, New Zealand and South Africa. Occasionally, as in any other country, a letter or parcel might go astray for a couple of weeks but generally everything arrives.

You can buy your stamps at a post office (Estonian: *postkontor*; Latvian: *pasts*; Lithuanian: *pastas*) and post your mail there. In Estonia, you can bypass the post office, buy stamps in shops and slip the envelope in any post box.

Postal rates for individual countries are listed in the country directories (see p170 for Estonia, p268 for Latvia and p375 for Lithuania). You can also check the websites of the postal companies: **Eesti Post** (www.post.ee) in Estonia, **Latvijas Pasts** (www.riga.post.lv) in Latvia and **Lietuvos Paštas** (www.post.lt) in Lithuania. Expensive international express-mail services are available in the capital cities.

The way addresses are written conform to Western norms, for example:

Kazimiera Jones
Veidenbauma iela 35-17
LV-5432 Ventspils
Latvia

Veidenbauma iela 35-17 means Veidenbaum Street, building No 35, flat No 17. Postcodes in Estonia are the letters EE plus five digits, in Latvia LV- plus four digits, and in

Lithuania LT- plus four digits. For people wanting to receive mail on the move, there are poste-restante mail services in the main post offices in Tallinn and Vilnius, and at the post office next to Rīga train station. All three keep mail for a month. Address letters to Estonia with the full name of the recipient followed by: Poste Restante, Peapostkontor, EE10101 Tallinn, Estonia. Letters to Latvia should be addressed as follows: Poste Restante, Rīga 50, LV-1050, Latvia. Letters to Lithuania: Poste Restante, Centrinis Pastas, Gedimino prospektas 7, LT-2000 Vilnius, Lithuania.

SHOPPING

For traditional handicrafts, Estonia has the best selection. In Tallinn (see p88) and most major centres you'll find traditional items like hand-knitted mittens and socks, lace, leather-bound books, bottles, ceramics, amber, silverware and objects carved from limestone. The syrupy sweet and surprisingly strong liqueur Vana Tallinn also makes a nice gift. *Kaibemaks* is a value-added tax –18% on most items. Medicines and books attract a 5% tax. There is no tax refund for items bought within Estonia although duty-free shops appear at the airport and harbour.

In Vilnius (p312) you'll find an excellent selection of amber jewellery as well as plenty of handicrafts.

Amber, while not as ubiquitous as in Lithuania, is still among one of Latvia's top souvenirs. In fact, the Nordwear shop in Rīga (p217, which sells hand-knitted Nordic sweaters patterned with Latvian national symbols, proudly proclaims itself one of the few amber-free souvenir shops!

SOLO TRAVELLERS

There are enormous advantages to travelling alone: aside from not being yoked to a stick-in-the mud. Solo travellers can see and do whatever they want, wake up in the morning and let the fates decide their next destination. They meet locals and socialise with people they'd probably never have spoken to if they were travelling with others. Estonia, Latvia and Lithuania are no less rewarding for those seeking the freedom of going alone. The only drawbacks are the sometimes lonely and frustrating moments on the road. All of the Baltic countries are fairly safe destinations – Estonia, particularly so – and there's a good network of hostels sprinkled about the region, where you can meet up with other travellers along the way. The lively expat bars in each of the countries are good social places for meeting travellers. You can also check out Thorn Tree postings on Lonely Planet's website (www.lonelyplanet.com), and possibly make a few connections before or even while you're on the road.

Solo women travellers should employ the usual precautions. Though the region has its dark elements, on the whole men aren't terribly aggressive towards foreign women, and travelling in the region is no less safe than travelling through Western Europe.

TELEPHONE

Nowhere is the region's startling transformation from Soviet stagnation to postcommunist capitalism more obvious than in its telephone systems. New exchanges, allowing direct digital connections to the rest of the world, have replaced the slow and decrepit analogue Soviet system that once painfully routed all calls through Moscow.

Calling to/from Estonia, Latvia and Lithuania is like calling to/from anywhere else in the West. International calls can be made from almost every private phone, as well as the public card phones, liberally scattered around the Baltic capitals, cities and towns. Aside from Lithuania, city codes are now a thing of the past in Estonia and Latvia, meaning if you're calling from abroad just dial the country code then the listed number. Precise details on calling as well as the lowdown on the local phone scene (hint: it's mobile-centric in all three countries), can be found in the country directories (see Estonia, p170; Latvia, p268; and Lithuania, p375).

Speaking of mobile phones, Estonia, Latvia and Lithuania all use GSM 900/1800 – compatible with the rest of Europe and Australia, but not with the North American GSM 1900 or the totally different system in Japan. Assuming your phone is GSM 900/1800-compatible, you can buy a SIM-card package from a choice of mobile-phone providers in all three countries. Again, see the country directories for more details.

TIME

Estonia, Latvia and Lithuania are on Eastern European Time (GMT/UTC + 2). All three countries adhere to daylight savings, which runs from the last Sunday in March to the last Sunday in October. At this time it's GMT + 3.

The 24-hour clock is used for train, bus and flight timetables. Dates are generally listed the American way: the month first, followed by the day and the year; ie 01/06/74 refers to 1 June 1974, not 6 January 1974.

Also see the World Time Zones map, p428-9.

TOILETS

Public toilets in the Baltic countries are wondrous things compared to the stinking black holes of the past. Today, you'll find mostly clean, modern systems (no grubby baskets in the corner, just flush the paper). That isn't to say that we recommend spending much time in the public restrooms of train or bus stations; they aren't the most inviting of places – but you should've been here ten years ago! Although there are public toilets in some places, you can also stroll into large hotels in major cities and use the toilets without upsetting the staff too much. Or, do what everyone else does and pop into the nearest McDonald's.

The letter 'M' marks a men's toilet in Estonian, 'V' in Latvian or Lithuanian. 'N' indicates a women's toilet in Estonian, 'S' in Latvian and 'M' in Lithuanian. Some toilets sport the triangle system: a skirt-like triangle for women and a broad-shouldered, upside-down triangle for men.

TOURIST INFORMATION

All three capitals, plus most cities, towns and seaside resorts, sport an efficient tourist office of sorts that doles out accommodation lists and information brochures, many in English and often delivered with a smile. These tourist offices are coordinated by each country's national tourist board, listed under Tourist Offices in the country directories (Estonia, p170; Latvia, p268; and Lithuania, p375).

Overseas, the three tourist boards are represented by the following organisations:

Finland (☎ 0927 84774; latviatravel@kolumbus.fi; Mariankatu 8b, SF-00170 Helsinki) For Latvia only.

Germany (☎ 030 8900 9091; www.baltic-info.de in German; Katharinenstrasse 19-20, 10711 Berlin-Wilmersdorf)

Russia (☎ 095-203 6790; www.litinfo.ru in Russian; Borisoglebskij per 13, Building 2, 121069 Moscow) For Lithuania only.

UK (☎ 207-229 8271; london@latviatourism.lv; 72 Queensborough Terrace, London) For Latvia only.

VISAS

Your number-one document is your passport. Make sure it's valid for at least three months after the end of your Baltic travels. Only some nationalities need visas. Citizens from the European Union (EU), Australia, Canada, Japan, New Zealand and the US do not require visas for entry into Estonia, Latvia or Lithuania.

Other nationalities should check the websites of the **Ministries of Foreign Affairs for Estonia** (www.vm.ee), **Latvia** (www.mfa.gov.lv) and **Lithuania** (www.urm.lt).

Types of Visas

For those who do need a visa, Estonia, Latvia and Lithuania issue transit, single-entry and multiple-entry visas. Fees vary – check the Ministries of Foreign Affairs websites mentioned earlier for updated prices. All visas are best arranged in advance through the respective Baltic consulate or embassy abroad.

At the time of research, sample costs for single-/multi-entry visas were as follows: Estonia €20/35; Latvia €14/24; and Lithuania €35/60.

Applying for Visas

You can get visas in advance at Estonian, Latvian and Lithuanian embassies and consulates in most countries. When applying at an embassy or consulate you need to supply your passport, a completed application form and two photos. Applications often have to be accompanied by an invitation from a registered organisation or proof of hotel/return airfare booking from the tour operator with whom you are travelling; you'll also need to show proof of insurance.

Visa Extensions

Single-entry visas can be extended in the Baltics. In Estonia go to the Tallinn office or a regional branch of the **Migration & Citizenship Board** (☎ 612 6978; www.mig.ee; Endla tänav 13, EE15179 Tallinn). In Latvia there is a visa office inside the **Department of Citizenship & Migration Affairs** (☎ 721 9639; www.pmlp.gov.lv; Raiņa bulvāris 5, LV-1181 Rīga). In Lithuania make your embassy or the immigration department inside the **Ministry of Interior** (☎ 5-271 8695, 271 8785;

www.vrm.lt; Šventaragio gatvė 2, LT-2600 Vilnius) your first port of call.

Russian Visas

Lithuania's neighbour, Kaliningrad Region, is part of Russia; St Petersburg is just a train trip from any of the Baltic capitals. All Western visitors need a visa to enter Russia.

Getting the visa can be time-consuming and is best dealt with before you leave home. A tourist visa requires an invitation, which can be issued from a hotel or some hostels in Russia or from online visa specialists (like www.visatorussia.com). You'll then present your invitation and application to a Russian consulate and receive your visa a few weeks later. It's a lovely bit of leftovers from the glory days of USSR-dom. If you didn't get the urge to enter Russia until arriving in the Baltics, you can obtain a Russian visa from one of the embassies in Tallinn, Rīga or Vilnius. There you'll get a heavy dose of bureaucracy and perhaps a visa, which costs between €40 and €90, depending on your nationality. See Embassies & Consulates in Estonia (p167), Latvia (p266) and Lithuania (p372, or visit the **Ministry of Foreign Affairs of Russia** (www.mid.ru) for more information.

Belarussian Visas

Make sure that before you board a train between Poland and Lithuania that it does not pass through Belarus. If it does, you will need a Belarussian visa, arranged in advance, even to transit the country. Visas are not issued at road borders. Belarussian embassies in all three Baltic capitals issue visas. For more bad news, see the **Ministry of Foreign Affairs for the Republic of Belarus** (www.mfa.gov.by).

WOMEN TRAVELLERS

The Balts have some fairly traditional ideas about gender roles, but on the other hand they're pretty reserved and rarely impose themselves upon other people in an annoying way. Women are not likely to receive aggravation from men in the Baltics, although unaccompanied women may want to avoid a few of the sleazier bars and beer cellars. Many women travel on overnight buses and trains alone but if you're travelling on a train at night, play safe and use the hefty metal lock on the inside of the carriage door.

In larger cities, Latvia particularly, some Russian women walk around with skirts so short you can practically see their bottoms – much to the delight of many male travellers who come to the Baltics mistakenly assuming that *all* young Baltic women are desperate for their attention. Unfortunately, tourists who copy this scanty attire risk being treated as prostitutes. In some tourist hotels prostitution is a fact of life, and a woman sitting alone in a foyer, corridor or café might be propositioned.

Organisations

Lithuania's **Women's Issues Information Centre** (WIIC; ☎ 5-262 8543; wiic@undp.lt; Jakšto gatvė 9, room 303/315, LT-2001 Vilnius) is a fabulous source of information and can put you in touch with other women's organisations in the region. Hot issues of the day for Baltic women are addressed in its quarterly *Women's World* magazine and in other English-language publications.

WORK

The Baltic region has enough difficulty keeping its own people employed, meaning there's little temporary work for visitors. Most Westerners working here have been posted by companies back home. However, these are times of change, and there is some scope for people who want to stay a while and carve themselves a new niche – though, in Western terms, you could not expect to get rich doing so. The English language is certainly in demand, and you might be able to earn your keep (or part of it) teaching it in one of the main cities. On the Internet, there's a wide array of databases where you can search for posts teaching abroad (www.teaching-abroad.co.uk, www.teachabroad.com and www.travelteach.com).

Various volunteer placements – teaching or working in a summer camp, for example – are occasionally advertised on websites such as www.escapeartist.com, an employment overseas index which advertises international jobs and volunteer placements. Very occasionally jobs for English speakers are advertised locally in the **Baltic Times** (www.baltictimes.com).

Transport

CONTENTS

Getting There & Away	**393**
Entering Estonia, Latvia & Lithuania	393
Air	393
Land	396
Sea	400
Getting Around	**403**
Air	403
Bicycle	403
Boat	404
Bus	404
Car & Motorcycle	405
Hitching	407
Local Transport	407
Train	408
Tours	409

THINGS CHANGE...

The information in this chapter is particularly vulnerable to change. Check directly with the airline or a travel agent to make sure you understand how a fare (and ticket you may buy) works and be aware of the security requirements for international travel. Shop carefully. The details given in this chapter should be regarded as pointers and are not a substitute for your own careful, up-to-date research.

GETTING THERE & AWAY

There are numerous ways of travelling into the Baltic countries, and there is certainly no need to stick with the same form of transport. It's perfectly feasible to fly or take a bus to Warsaw and then enter Lithuania by train, or fly to Helsinki and sail from there to Estonia, for example. Within the Baltics, distances are relatively small.

Flights, tours and rail tickets can be booked online at www.lonelyplanet.com /travel_services.

INTERCAPITAL TRAVEL

Buses provide the link between each of the capitals. For details on travel, see Tallinn (p90), Rīga (p218) and Vilnius (p314).

ENTERING ESTONIA, LATVIA & LITHUANIA

Whether you arrive by bus, boat or train, entering procedures are fairly quick and painless when entering any of the Baltic countries.

Passport

All arriving travellers need a passport, valid for three months beyond the planned stay. Very few nationalities need a visa for entering Estonia, Latvia or Lithuania. See p391 for more information.

AIR

Airports & Airlines

The international airports in the region are **Tallinn Airport** (TLL; ☎ 605 8888; www.tallinn-airport .ee), **Rīga Airport** (RIX; ☎ 720 7009; www.riga-airport .com) and, in Lithuania, **Vilnius Airport** (VNO; ☎ 5-720 7009; www.vilnius-airport.lt), **Palanga Airport** (PLQ; ☎ 460-52 020; www.palanga-airport.lt) and **Kaunas International Airport** (KUN; ☎ 46-399 307; www.kaunasair.lt).

The national carriers are **Estonian Air** (code OV; ☎ 640 1101; www.estonian-air.ee), **Air Baltic** (code BT; ☎ 720 7777; www.airbaltic.lv) and **Lithuanian Airlines** (code TE; ☎ 275 2585; www.la.lt).

As well as major carriers, budget airlines like **Ryanair** (code FR; www.ryanair.com) and **easyJet** (code U2; www.easyjet.com) fly into the Baltics.

AIRLINES FLYING TO & FROM ESTONIA, LATVIA & LITHUANIA

Aeroflot (code SU; Lithuania ☎ 232 9300; www.aeroflot .com) Serves Vilnius.

Air Baltic (code BT; Latvia ☎ 720 7777, Lithuania 235 6000; www.airbaltic.lv) Serves Rīga and Vilnius.

Austrian Airlines (code OS; Latvia ☎ 750 7700, Lithuania 231 3137; www.aua.com) Serves Rīga and Vilnius. Hub Vienna.

British Airways (code BA; Latvia ☎ 720 7097, Lithuania 210 6300; www.britishairways.com) Serves Rīga and Vilnius. Hub London, Heathrow.

TRANSPORT

ČSA (Czech Airlines; code OK; Estonia ☎ 630 9397, Latvia 720 7636, Lithuania 215 1503; www.czech-airlines.com) Serves Tallinn, Rīga and Vilnius. Hub Prague.
easyJet (code U2; www.easyjet.com) Serves Tallinn and Rīga. Hub London, Luton.
Estonian Air (code OV; Estonia ☎ 640 1101, Latvia 721 4860, Lithuania 273 9022; www.estonian-air.ee) Serves Tallinn, Rīga and Vilnius. Hub Tallinn.
Finnair (code AY; Estonia ☎ 611 0946, Latvia 720 7010, Lithuania 261 9339; www.finnair.com) Serves Tallinn, Rīga and Vilnius. Hub Helsinki.
KLM (code KL; Estonia ☎ 699 9696, Latvia 766 8600; www.klm.com) Serves Tallinn and Rīga. Hub Amsterdam.
Lithuanian Airlines (LAL; code TE; Lithuania ☎ 252 5555; www.lal.lt) Serves Vilnius.
LOT (code LH; Estonia ☎ 605 8553, Latvia 722 7234, Lithuania 273 9020; www.lot.com) Serves Tallinn, Rīga and Vilnius. Hub Warsaw.
Lufthansa (code LO; Estonia ☎ 681 4630, Latvia 750 7711, Lithuania 230 6300; www.lufthansa.com) Serves Tallinn and Rīga. Hub Frankfurt.
Ryanair (code FR; www.ryanair.com) Serves Rīga and Kaunas. Hub Dublin and London, Stansted.
SAS Scandinavian Airlines (code SK; Estonia ☎ 666 3030, Latvia 720 7777, Lithuania 235 6000; www.scandinavian.net) Serves Tallinn, Rīga and Vilnius. Hub Copenhagen.
Transaero (code UN; Latvia ☎ 720 7738; www.transaero.ru) Serves Rīga. Hub Moscow.

Tickets

Some of the best deals can be found by buying directly from the airlines. This is a departure from the past, where discount agencies often undercut prices. You can buy one-way tickets on no-frills carriers for half the price of a regular ticket, which will give you much more freedom in planning your itinerary.

INTERCONTINENTAL (RTW) TICKETS

Round-the-world tickets are a useful option for long-haul travellers. Tickets are often valid for 90 days to one year. Make sure you understand what restrictions apply: there will be limited stops (or kilometres) allowed, and you won't be able to backtrack.

Australia & New Zealand

There are no direct flights to the Baltic countries from Australia or New Zealand. The best option will nearly always be flying to Western Europe and connecting to your destination from there, although some Asian and Middle Eastern gateways such as Bangkok, Dubai and Hong Kong may also offer good deals. The cheapest fares to Europe are routed through Asia.

Two well-known agents for cheap fares in Australia are **STA Travel** (☎ 1300 733 035; www.statravel.com.au) and **Flight Centre** (☎ 131 133; www.flightcentre.com.au), which have dozens of offices throughout Australia.

Try **Flight Centre** (☎ 0800 243 544; www.flightcentre.co.nz) and **STA Travel** (☎ 0508 782 872; www.statravel.co.nz) in New Zealand also.

Thai Airways International, Malaysia Airlines, Qantas and Singapore Airlines all fly to Europe and have frequent promotional fares. Flights from Perth are usually a couple of hundred dollars cheaper than from east-coast cities.

Continental Europe

Although London is the travel discount capital of Europe, there are several other cities where you'll find a wide range of good deals, namely Amsterdam, Frankfurt, Munich and Paris. Budget airlines have revolutionised European air transport in the past few years. Most budget airlines require you to book online, where you'll get an electronic ticket.

STA Travel (www.statravel.co.uk) has offices throughout Europe where cheap tickets can be purchased and STA-issued tickets can be altered (usually for a small fee); check on the website for contact details. **Nouvelles Frontières** (www.nouvelles-frontieres.fr) also has branches throughout the world.

Russia, Ukraine, Transcaucasia & Central Asia

There are up to four flights daily between Moscow and each of the Baltic capitals including Estonian Air from Tallinn. In Moscow, flights use Sheremetyevo I airport. There are also three to five weekly flights between each of the capitals and Kyiv (Ukraine).

ONLINE TICKETS

Some recommended air-ticket websites include the following:

- www.ebookers.com
- www.flybudget.com
- www.itasoftware.com
- www.opodo.com
- www.statravel.com

IN & OUT OF ESTONIA BY HELICOPTER

One option of arriving in Estonia is by helicopter from Helsinki. **Copterline** (Helsinki ☎ 0200-18181; www.copterline.com; Hernesaari helicopter terminal, Hernematalankatu 2B; Tallinn Map pp66; ☎ 610 1818; www.copterline.ee; Linnahall, Mere puiestee 20) flies between the capitals every hour between 8am and 8pm Monday to Friday, 9am and 5pm on Saturday and 11am and 4pm on Sunday. Flying time is 18 minutes and one-way fares range from €55 to €130. You can book online. Discount tickets are often available at the Copterline desk inside the Sokos Hotel Viru (p82) in Tallinn. Sadly, Copterline had a fatal crash in August 2005.

You can also get to and from dozens of other places in Russia, Transcaucasia and former Soviet Central Asia via a connection at Moscow, which you can book all the way through in one go.

Scandinavia

TO/FROM ESTONIA

Estonian Air and **Finnair** (www.finnair.com) codeshare on five to seven flights daily between Tallinn and Helsinki. Flying time is only 20 minutes but the trip often ends up being no quicker than a hydrofoil (which is substantially cheaper), due to the time spent getting to and through airports.

Estonian Air codeshares with SAS on daily flights to/from the Stockholm. It is cheaper to fly via Helsinki to get to/from Copenhagen.

TO/FROM LATVIA

Air Baltic flies five times a week between Rīga and Helsinki, while Finnair flies the same route once or twice. SAS and Air Baltic codeshare on daily Stockholm–Rīga–Stockholm flights. The two also codeshare on six flights daily to/from Copenhagen.

TO/FROM LITHUANIA

LAL flies once or twice daily between Helsinki and Vilnius; it also services Copenhagen to/from Vilnius (once or twice a day Sunday to Friday) and Stockholm (six a week), while SAS operates twice-daily flights between the Lithuanian and Danish capitals.

Air Lithuania flies from Kaunas, via Palanga, to/from Kristianstad, Sweden (four a week); Oslo, Norway (once a week in summer); and Billund, Denmark (five a week).

UK & Ireland

If you're looking for a cheap flight to or from Eastern Europe, London is Europe's major centre for discounted fares. However, if you are connecting in London, remember that some 'London' airports are a huge distance from the city – you need to check before giving yourself just a few hours in transit. You'll need much more than that to get between Heathrow and Stansted or Gatwick and Luton, for example.

For destinations in the Baltic countries, Ryanair and easyJet offer some of the best deals. Just be mindful of taxes, which can be very high.

Plenty of budget travel agents advertise in the travel sections of weekend newspapers and also in the **TNT Magazine** (www.tntmagazine.com) and the entertainment listings magazine *Time Out*.

STA Travel (☎ 0870 1600 599; www.statravel.co.uk) has 65 branches throughout the UK and sells tickets to all travellers but caters especially to young people and students.

Other recommended travel agents are **Trailfinders** (☎ 020 7937 1234; www.trailfinders.co.uk), which has branches in Manchester, Glasgow and other British cities; **Bridge the World** (☎ 0870 814 4400; www.b-t-w.co.uk); and also **Flightbookers** (☎ 0870 814 0000; www.ebookers.com).

USA & Canada

Any journey to the Baltics entails a flight to Scandinavia or another European transport hub, from where there are ferry or plane connections to the region. In addition to online booking sites like **Orbitz** (www.orbitz.com), **Travelocity** (www.travelocity.com), **Expedia** (www.expedia.com) and the name-your-price service of **Priceline** (www.priceline.com), you can also try the following agents:

Council Travel (☎ 800 226 8624; www.counciltravel.com) America's largest student-travel organisation has some 60 offices in the USA. Call for the office nearest you.

STA Travel (☎ 800 781 4040; www.statravel.com) Has offices in Boston, Chicago, New York, Philadelphia, San Francisco and other major cities.

Travel Cuts (☎ 800 667 2887; www.travelcuts.com) Based in Canada, this outfit has offices in all major Canadian cities.

TRANSPORT

LAND

Bicycle

Bicycles can be carried cheaply (or for free) on the ferries from Scandinavia and Germany to the Baltics; see p400 for more info. Peddlers through Poland face the same choice of routes as drivers; see p397 for more info.

Border Crossings

Now that the Baltic countries are part of the EU, border crossings in the region are simpler. Most visitors don't require a visa to visit the Baltic countries; see p391.

Travelling from north to south, Estonia shares borders with Russia and Latvia; Latvia shares borders with Russia, Belarus, Estonia and Lithuania; while Lithuania borders Belarus, Poland and the Kaliningrad Region (also part of Russia).

Inter-Baltic borders cause little aggravation these days. Public buses get priority over private vehicles and cross immediately, and most trains chug across rail borders without stopping (customs and immigration checks are dealt with on board, while in motion).

If you are travelling by car, don't be alarmed by the kilometres of lorries waiting in line as you approach most crossings. At every border there are separate queues for cars and lorries. The whole procedure should not take more than 30 minutes or so.

Travel to Belarus and Russia is another matter entirely. These borders continue to be rigorously controlled, and you'll need to get a visa in advance. Expect to wait up to an hour regardless of whether you are travelling by bus or car. Entering Russia (including the Kaliningrad Region) or Belarus, you are must fill in a declaration form, specifying how much cash (in any currency) and what valuables you are taking into the country.

At Narva-Ivangorod on the Estonian-Russian border particularly long queues form. The Kaliningrad Region enjoys quieter road borders with Lithuania at Panemunė/Sovietsk, between Kybartai (Lithuania) and Nesterov, and on the Curonian Spit along the Klaipėda–Zelenogradsk road. Queues are known to occur at Lithuania's two border crossings with Poland – between Ogrodniki (Poland) and Lazdijai (Lithuania); and on the road from Suwałki, Szypliszki and Budzisko (Poland) to Kalvarija and Marijampolė (Lithuania). Don't be persuaded to detour through Belarus, however; you'll be delayed at least four to five times as long and have to fork out for a Belarusian visa (not available at any border). Only Belarus' road-borders with Lithuania at Salčininkai, Medininkai and Lavoriskės are open to Westerners.

Bus

With a few exceptions, buses are the cheapest but least comfortable method of reaching the Baltics. There are direct buses to/from Austria, Belgium, Czech Republic, France, Germany, Netherlands, Poland, Russia, Ukraine and Belarus. From much of the rest of Europe you can reach the Baltics with a single change of bus in Warsaw.

International services to/from the Baltics are operated by **Ecolines** (www.ecolines.ee) and **Eurolines** (www.eurolines.ee). See websites for info. Eurolines has more services within the Baltics; Ecolines has more international routes, and you can purchase tickets online. Both companies give 10% discounts for passengers under 26 or over 60. Return tickets cost about 20% less than two one-way tickets.

Eurolines ticketing offices:

Estonia Tallinn Central Bus Station (☎ 680 0909; www.eurolines.ee; Lastekodu 46); Tartu bus station (Map p109; ☎ 734 0075; Turu tänav 2)
Latvia Rīga international bus station (Map pp192-3; ☎ 721 4080; www.eurolines.lv; Prāgas iela 1)
Lithuania Kaunas long-distance bus station (Map p332; ☎ 37-209 836; www.kautra.lt; Vytauto prospektas 24); Panevėžys bus station (☎ 45-582 888; Savanorių aikštė 5); Vilnius bus station (Map pp288-9; ☎ 5-233 6666; www.eurolines.lt; Sodų gatvė 22)

Ecolines ticketing offices:

Estonia Tallinn (Map p70-1; ☎ 610 1570; www.ecolines.ee; Viru Väljak 4/6, Tallinn)
Latvia Rīga international bus station (Map p192-3; ☎ 721 4512; www.ecolines.lv; Prāgas iela 1)
Lithuania Kaunas long-distance bus station (Map p332; ☎ 37-320 2020; Vytauto prospektas 24); Vilnius (☎ 5-262 0020; www.eurolines.lt; Vilniaus gatvė 45, Vilnius)

Other ticketing offices for both companies can be found on their websites.

POLAND & THE CZECH REPUBLIC

Eurolines runs five weekly buses in each direction between Warsaw and Tallinn (around €43, 16 hours), stopping at Rīga (around €32, 11 hours) and Pärnu (€43, 14 hours). Two weekly buses from Tallinn to Krakow, hit the same stops en route. One daily bus connects Warsaw and Vilnius (€27, nine hours). There is also an overnight bus from Vilnius to/from Gdansk (€26, 11 hours).

In Warsaw, buses depart from the **Western Bus Station** (Dworzec Zachodnia; ☎ 822 4811; al Jerozolimskie 144). Tickets are sold at the *miedzynarodowa* (international) ticket window at the bus station.

The Czech Republic has one weekly bus link with Vilnius (€45, 20 hours).

RUSSIA

Estonia, Latvia and Lithuania all have bus links with the Kaliningrad Region (Russia) and the Russian motherland.

From Tallinn, Eurolines runs one bus nightly to Kaliningrad, via Pärnu, Rīga, Šiauliai and Sovietsk (€22, 15 hours). From Rīga, there's one daily bus to Kaliningrad (€14, 10 hours). From Vilnius and Kaunas, there are two buses daily (€8, six to nine hours). Several buses also travel along the Curonian Spit between Klaipėda and Kaliningrad.

Moscow and Rīga are served by two Ecolines buses daily (€25, 15 to 18 hours). Five Eurolines buses connect St Petersburg and Tallinn (€12 to €16, nine hours), passing through Rakvere and Narva en route.

UKRAINE & BELARUS

Vilnius has four daily buses to Minsk (€6, four hours); two daily buses go from Rīga to Minsk (€13, 10 hours). Express buses head from Kaunas, Lithuania, to Hrodna, Belarus (€5, four hours, daily), as well as from Rīga (€10, eight hours, twice weekly) and Vilnius (€4, five hours, daily Friday to Sunday).

Ukraine-bound buses also pass through Belarus. Latvian-based Ecolines runs a four-times-weekly service between Rīga and Kyiv (€44, 17½ hours). Twice a week, the bus continues a further five hours to Odesa (€60).

From Tallinn, three buses go weekly to Kyiv (€40, 25 hours).

All Western travellers need a visa to travel through Belarus. Ukraine has recently eased visa restrictions for some nationalities.

WESTERN EUROPE

There are loads of connections between the Baltic countries and Germany. From Tallinn there is one bus daily to Berlin (€88, 24 hours), five weekly to Aachen (€102, 36 hours), three weekly to Stuttgart (€102, 37 hours) and two weekly to Ulm (€102, 37 hours) and Munster (€102, 34 hours).

There's a daily bus between Rīga and Berlin (€73, 19 hours), Kaunas and Berlin (€63, 17½ hours), and Vilnius and Berlin (€63, 16 hours).

Another handy bus route is the four times weekly link going from Rīga to London (€116, 36 hours), stopping at Vilnius, Kaunas, Amsterdam and Brussels en route.

To Italy, buses from Rīga go twice weekly stopping at Vilnius, Kaunas, Venice, Bologna, Florence and Rome (€117, 44 hours).

Car & Motorcycle

If you do take your own vehicle to the Baltics, get it in good condition before you leave home, and carry a large petrol can and some basic spares. A fire extinguisher, first-aid kit and warning triangle are also advisable. Motoring clubs like the **AAA** (☎ 800 222 4357; www.aaa.com) in the US and **AA** (☎ 0870 600 0371; www.theaa.com) and **RAC** (☎ 0870 572 2722; www.rac.co.uk) in the UK are worth contacting for information on regulations, border crossings, and so on, as are Estonian, Latvian and Lithuanian embassies. For information and tips on driving once you're in the region, see p397.

DOCUMENTS

You need to bring your vehicle's registration document. If you can get it in the form of an international motor vehicle certificate, which is a translation of the basic registration document, so much the better. Motoring associations should be able to provide one. An International Driving Permit (IDP; also obtainable from motoring associations) is recommended, but if you don't have one, your own licence will suffice in most situations. All three Baltic countries demand compulsory accident insurance for drivers.

Insurance policies with limited compensation rates can be bought at the Estonian, Latvian and Lithuanian borders, costing around €25 to €40 for two weeks' insurance. Remember that you'll also need appropriate documentation for all the countries you pass through on the way to or from the Baltics; motoring associations can advise you.

POLAND & GERMANY

Bringing a vehicle into the Baltics from the south entails either a ferry trip from Kiel

TRANSPORT

(Germany) to Klaipėda, Lithuania (ferry details are listed on p400); or a 30-minute to one-hour wait at the Polish-Lithuanian border at Ogrodniki-Lazdijai or the border on the road from Suwałki, Szypliszki and Budzisko (Poland) to Kalvarija and Marijampolė; or a hellish trip through Belarus.

Suckers for punishment opting for the third – and least rosy – motoring option should not attempt to even approach the border or set foot in Lukashenko land without a Belarusian transit visa, only available at Belarusian embassies. No visas are sold at any Belarus border. Those sufficiently privileged to have their visa application accepted can then expect to wait several hours, at least, at the border. A possible route is from Białystok, Poland, to Grodno in northwestern Belarus, then on to Merkinė in Lithuania; other routes include Brest–Lida–Vilnius or Brest–Minsk–Vilnius.

SCANDINAVIA

If travelling from Scandinavia, you can put your vehicle on a ferry (see p400) or drive to the Baltics through Russia.

From the Finnish/Russian border at Vaalimaa/Torfyanovka to St Petersburg is about 220km; from St Petersburg to the Russian/Estonian border at Ivangorod/Narva is 140km. You could do it in a day but there's little point coming this way unless you want to look at St Petersburg on the way through. Don't delay on the Finland–St Petersburg road, as it's said to be plagued by bandits.

Train

Travelling by train can be an interesting way of reaching the region – cheaper than flying and less boring than bussing it. One of the world's most memorable rail journeys figures among the approaches to the Baltics: the Trans-Siberian. Unfortunately, train service both to and within the region have been cut back markedly in recent years.

The *Thomas Cook European Timetable* is the rail-lover's bible, giving a complete listing of train schedules, supplements and reservations information. It is updated monthly and is available from Thomas Cook outlets or from www.thomascook publishing.com. An independent website, with loads of excellent up-to-date tips on rail travel throughout Europe, is the brilliant **Man From Seat Sixty One** (www.seat61.com).

On the Internet, you can also search in English through the timetables of Latvian (www.ldz.lv) and Lithuanian (www.litrail.lt) railways.

POLAND

Surprisingly, the only links between Poland and the Baltic states are the several daily trains running from Warsaw to Vilnius. Travel time is anywhere from 10 to 16 hours (€22). Until recently these trains transited through Belarus, but at research time this was no longer the case. Regardless, you should get the latest on the situation before buying your ticket. If the train does pass through Belarus, you'll have a serious headache if you show up without a visa; see p392 for more info on Belarussian visas.

RUSSIA, UKRAINE & BELARUS

The old Soviet rail network still functions over most of the former USSR. Trains linking Moscow with all the main Baltic cities enable you to combine the Baltics with a Trans-Siberian trip or other Russian or Central Asian travels. For information on types of train, classes of accommodation, how to understand timetables and so on, see p408.

Unfortunately, the Tallinn–St Petersburg service was fazed out in 2004. Estonia's only remaining rail link to Russia is via Moscow. Trains depart Tallinn daily in the late afternoon, arriving the next morning (€33/46 in compartment/first class, 16 hours). From Moscow, you can catch trains to every corner of Mother Russia.

The overnight *Latvijas Ekspresis* (Latvia Express) trundles daily between Rīga train station and Moscow (from €25, 18 hours). A second train, the daily *Jūrmala*, services the same route, while the overnight *Baltija* links the Latvian capital with St Petersburg (from €20, 14 hours, daily). Neither train passes through Belarus.

From Vilnius, there are several daily trains to Moscow's Belarus train station (13 to 17 hours). These pass through Belarus, so you'll need a Belarussian visa (p392). One of the Moscow–Vilnius trains also links to Kaliningrad (Russia). The daily St Petersburg–Kaliningrad train likewise stops in Vilnius, and it does not transit Belarus. There's also a Kaliningrad train that goes to Kharkiv, Ukraine, passing through Vilnius and Belarus along the way.

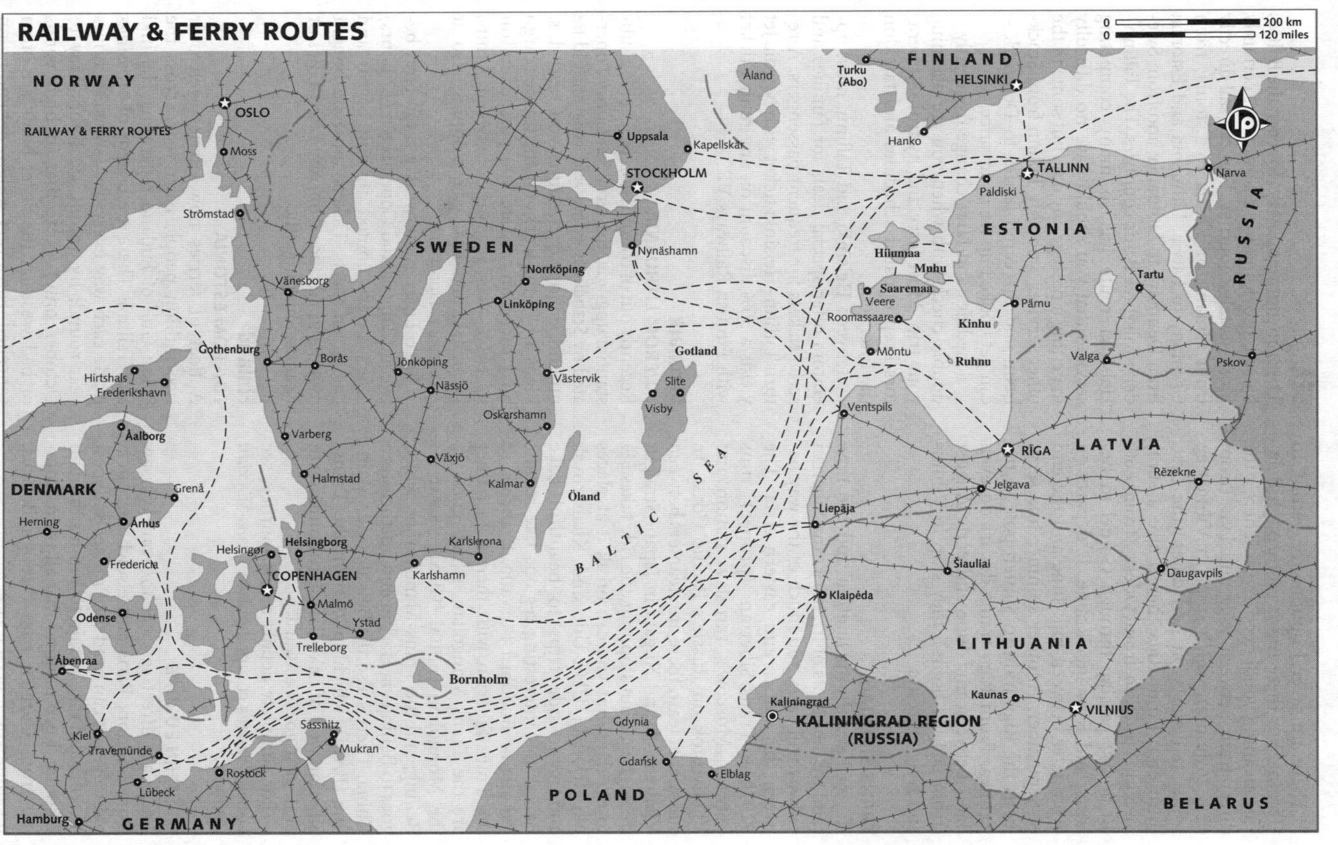
RAILWAY & FERRY ROUTES
0 200 km
0 120 miles
NORWAY
OSLO
RAILWAY & FERRY ROUTES
Moss
Strömstad
Vänesborg
Gothenburg
Borås
Varberg
Halmstad
SWEDEN
Uppsala
Kapellskär
STOCKHOLM
Nynäshamn
Norrköping
Linköping
Jönköping
Nässjö
Västervik
Oskarshamn
Växjö
Kalmar
Karlskrona
Karlshamn
Helsingborg
Helsingør
COPENHAGEN
Malmö
Ystad
Trelleborg
Åland
Gotland
Slite
Visby
Öland
BALTIC SEA
Bornholm
Hirtshals
Frederikshavn
Aalborg
DENMARK
Grenå
Herning
Århus
Fredericia
Odense
Åbenraa
Kiel
Travemünde
Lübeck
Hamburg
Rostock
Sassnitz
Mukran
GERMANY
FINLAND
Turku (Abo)
HELSINKI
Hanko
TALLINN
Paldiski
Narva
ESTONIA
RUSSIA
Hiiumaa
Muhu
Saaremaa
Veere
Roomassaare
Kinhu
Pärnu
Tartu
Mõntu
Ruhnu
Valga
Pskov
Ventspils
RĪGA
LATVIA
Rēzekne
Jelgava
Liepāja
Šiauliai
Daugavpils
Klaipėda
LITHUANIA
Kaunas
VILNIUS
Kaliningrad
KALININGRAD REGION (RUSSIA)
Gdynia
Gdańsk
Elbląg
POLAND
BELARUS

There are several options for getting to Ukraine, but these trains go through Belarus, meaning you'll need a visa. There's the direct train between Rīga and Lviv (from €25, 26 hours), which stops in Vilnius en route. It departs on odd dates (the first, third etc). From Rīga there's also a summertime train to/from Odesa (from €60, 40 hours) passing through Gomel in Belarus, and Kyiv in Ukraine. It departs on even dates between mid-June and the end of September. Another summertime service is the Rīga train to Simferopole in the Crimea. From Rīga trains depart on even dates between mid-June and early August (from €64, 42 hours); they stop in Vilnius and Kyiv en route.

TRANS-SIBERIAN

If you have the inclination and the time (and we mean lots of it), the Trans-Siberian railway will carry you much of the way between the Baltics and eastern Asia. The 9297km Trans-Siberian (proper) runs between Moscow's Yaroslavl station and Vladivostok on Russia's Pacific Coast. In summer at least, there are steamers between Vladivostok and Niigata in Japan. Straight through without stopping, the ride takes 5½ to 6½ days, but you can break it at places like Irkutsk, Ulan-Ude and Khabarovsk and make side trips to beautiful Lake Baikal and interesting regions like remote Yakutia or Buddhist Buryatia. Branches of the Trans-Siberian with their own names are the Trans-Mongolian, which goes via the Mongolian capital, Ulaan Baatar, to Beijing; and the Trans-Manchurian, which goes to Beijing via Harbin and northeastern China. There's also the Baikal Amur Mainline (BAM), which splits from the Trans-Siberian west of Lake Baikal, running north of it, as it goes eastward.

For complete details of the journey, see Lonely Planet's comprehensive *Trans-Siberian Railway*.

WESTERN EUROPE

There are direct services to/from Warsaw from London, Paris and elsewhere. Alternatively, you can head for Prague, Budapest or Sofia and take a train to Vilnius through Ukraine. Keep in mind that all trains coming from Ukraine pass through Belarus, meaning you'll need a visa.

SEA

There are numerous ways to reach the Baltics by sea, providing for a slower but certainly more nostalgic journey. You can sail directly from Finland or Russia to Estonia; from Germany to Latvia, Lithuania and Estonia; from Denmark to Lithuania; and from Sweden to all three Baltic countries. The Tallinn–Helsinki route has so many competing services that you should have no difficulty in getting a passage any day, but some of the other services – notably Tallinn from Stockholm and the cargo ferries to Denmark – can get booked up far in advance.

Schedules and fares change frequently – double-check both when you are planning your trip. Most ferry and hydrofoil operators keep updated schedules and fares on the Internet.

Between Helsinki and Tallinn, most operators offer special deals for families and serial tickets for frequent passengers. A return Tallinn–Helsinki ticket with Nordic Jet yields a 50% discount on any return ticket with Finnish Railways VR.

Denmark

TO/FROM LITHUANIA

Recently out of commission to receive a substantial upgrade, the ferry *Sea Corona* operated by **Scandlines** (www.scandlines.de) should be up and sailing by the time you read this. Plans are in the works for the former cargo boat to accommodate 300 passengers on its twice-weekly voyages between Ârhus, Denmark, and Klaipėda, stopping also at Aabenraa, Denmark.

Lisco Lines' twice-weekly cargo ferry between Klaipėda and Copenhagen (22 hours) offers a very limited amount of car and passenger space. Tickets must be bought months in advance from any Lisco Lines or Krantas Shipping office.

Finland

TO/FROM ESTONIA

A fleet of ferries now carries well over two million people each year across the 80km Gulf of Finland separating Helsinki and Tallinn. There are dozens of crossings made each way every day (ships 3½ hours year-round; hydrofoils 1½ hours May to October only). Note that in high winds or bad weather, the faster boats are often cancelled. Fares vary widely, depending on season, day and time of travel, and other factors – like whether there's a crisis in the world oil market. Fares are generally higher on Friday evening and Saturday.

On most ferry lines, students and seniors can get a 10% discount, children between ages six and 12 pay about half price and those under six ride for free.

Tallink

Year-round, **Tallink** (Map pp70-1; ☎ 640 9808; www.tallink.ee; Laikmaa tänav 5) runs the large passenger and vehicle ferries the M/S *Meloodia* and M/S *Romantika*. Each makes one crossing in each direction daily (3½ hours), using Terminal A in Tallinn and Länsi Terminal in Helsinki. Tickets are cheaper on Monday to Thursday and for departures after 6.30pm from Tallinn or before 1pm from Helsinki. Ballpark high season (July to mid-August) fares for adults start around €18, with a vehicle adding an extra €18. Tickets are available at their office on Laikmaa tänav.

Far more popular than its lumbering old ferries are Tallink's zippy hydrofoils, which transport foot passengers and vehicles. The Autoexpress makes at least 12 departures daily (adult/vehicle from €34/25, 1¾ hours) between 7am or 8am and 10pm (8pm Monday to Wednesday). In Tallinn, these hydrofoils depart from Terminal D.

In Helsinki, Tallink ferries and hydrofoils use Länsi Terminal, where you can buy tickets.

Silja Line

Silja Line's *SuperSeaCatFour* travels five to seven times daily between Tallinn's Terminal D and Helsinki's Olympia Terminal (from €26 to €70, 1¾ hours).

Purchase tickets at the **Silja Line** (☎ 09-180 4685; www.siljaline.se) window at the Makasiini terminal. In Tallinn, the **Silja Line office** (Map pp70-1; ☎ 611 6661; www.silja.ee) is on the 5th floor of the Stockmann Kaubamaja (department store) in Tallinn.

Eckerö Line

Eckerö Line's *Nordlandia* ferry, big enough to hold 2000 passengers and 450 cars, sails once daily back and forth from Tallinn to Helsinki year-round (adult/car from €20/€20, 3½ hours). It uses Terminal B in Tallinn and Länsi terminal in Helsinki.

Tickets are sold in Tallinn at **Eckerö Line** (Map pp70-1; ☎ 631 8606; www.eckeroline.ee) in Terminal B, and in Helsinki at **Eckerö Line** (☎ 09-228 8544; Mannerheimintie 10) at Länsi Terminal.

Nordic Jet Line

Nordic Jet runs two sleek, 450-seat jet catamarans, *Nordic Jet* and *Baltic Jet*, between Tallinn and Helsinki. They sail early May to December (depending on the weather); and there are seven crossings a day (adult/car from €24/€28, 1¾ hours), docking at Terminal C in Tallinn.

In Helsinki, **Nordic Jet** (☎ 09-681 770; www.njl.info) uses the catamaran harbour at Kanava Terminal (Kanavaterminaali). The **Nordic Jet** (Map pp66-7; ☎ 613 7000; www.njl.info) office in Tallinn is in Terminal C.

Linda Line Express

The Linda Line Express is a small, independent hydrofoil company, the vessels of which plough the waters between Tallinn and Helsinki (adult from €22, 1½ hours) seven times daily May to September. All Linda Line vessels stop sailing in October when the waters ice over.

Linda Line Express hydrofoils arrive and depart from the Linnahall Terminal in Tallinn and the South Port (Makasiiniterminaal) in Helsinki. In the Finnish capital, contact **Linda Line** (☎ 09-668 9700; www.lindaline.fi). In Tallinn, purchase tickets from the **Linda Line Express office** (Map pp66-7; ☎ 699 9333; www.lindaliini.ee) in Linnahall Terminal.

Viking Line

Viking Line operates the giant car ferry *Rosella*, which has two departures daily from each port (adult/car from €15/€22, three hours).

The Rosella uses Tallinn Terminal A and Helsinki's Katajanokka terminal. In the Finnish capital, contact the **Viking Line office** (☎ 09-12351; www.vikingline.ee; Mannerheimintie 14). In Tallinn, purchase tickets from the **Viking Line** (Map pp66-7; ☎ 699 9333; www.vikingline.ee) office in Terminal A.

Germany

TO/FROM ESTONIA

Between June and early September Silja Line's passenger ferry, *Finnjet* (one of the world's fastest), sails twice weekly between Tallinn and Rostock (berth from €98, 14 hours). It departs from Terminal D in Tallinn. In Germany, contact **Silja Line** (☎ 0381-350 4350; www.siljaline.de; Am Warnowkai 11, Rostock). In Tallinn, the **Silja Line** (Map pp66-7; ☎ 611 6663; www.silja.com) offices are in Terminal D, and in **Stockmann Kaubamaja** (Map pp70-1; ☎ 611 6661).

TO/FROM LATVIA

A ferry sails twice weekly in each direction between Rīga and Kiel (13 hours). Contact **Hanza Maritime Agency** (Map pp192-3; ☎ 732 3569; www.hanza.lv; Eksporta iela 10, Rīga) for details. In Germany, tickets are sold by **Baltic Seaways** (☎ 0431-239 8511; Ostuferhafen 22, Kiel).

From Lübeck, Germany, **Lisco Lines** (www.lisco.lt) operates a twice-weekly ferry to/from Rīga (car/pullman seat/berth from €80/€60/€91, 34 hours), which also stops at Ventspils. You can buy tickets from **DFDS Tor Line** (www.dfdstorline.lv) at their Latvian offices in **Rīga** (☎ 735 3523; Zivju iela 1, Rīga) and **Ventspils** (☎ 360 7593; Plosta iela 7, Ventspils) and their German office in Lübeck (☎ 451-399 270; Unter der Herrenbrücke 2, Lübeck).

Scandlines (www.scandlines.de) in 2005 rerouted their ferries between Germany and Latvia. Now ferries go between Rostock and Ventspils. Ferries depart from each port four times weekly (car/pullman seat/berth from €110/€90/€145). For tickets, contact the **Rostock Scandlines office** (☎ 381-673 1217; www.scandlines.de; Nam Warnowkai 8, Rostock-Seehafen) or in **Klaipėda** (☎ 46-310 561; N Sodo gatvė 1-111).

TO/FROM LITHUANIA

From Kiel, Scandlines and Lisco Lines run a joint daily service to Klaipėda (car/pullman seat/berth from €110/€70/€110, 21 hours). Each ferry has space for just 40 cars, and tickets should be booked well in advance, particularly if you are taking a vehicle.

In Klaipėda, contact **Lisco Lines** (☎ 46-395 050; www.lisco.lt; Perkelos gatvė 10, Klaipėda) or **Scandlines** (Map p348; ☎ 46-310 561; www.scandlines.de; Naujoji Sodo gatvė 1, Klaipėda).

In Kiel, go to **Lisco Baltic Service** (☎ 0431-2097 6400; www.lisco-baltic-service.de; Ostuferhafen 15, Kiel).

Lisco Lines' *Klaipėda* is a mostly cargo ferry that sails twice weekly between Mukran (Sassnitz) in Germany and Klaipėda (18 hours). When space is available, they can take on 12 passengers, with a berth in a double cabin starting around €120. In Klaipėda, contact Lisco Lines. In Germany, tickets are sold by Lisco Baltic Service.

Poland

TO/FROM LITHUANIA

A weekly ferry operates between Gdansk, Poland and Klaipėda (10 to 14 hours). The ferry is operated by **DFDS Tor Line** (www.dfdstorline.com). In Klaipėda, purchase tickets through **Lisco Lines** (☎ 46-395 050; www.lisco.lt; Perkelos gatvė 10, Klaipėda). In Poland, head to the **DFDS Tor Line office** (☎ 58-340 5019; Gdansk@dfdstorline.com; Majora Henryka Sucharskiego 70, Westerplatte Quay, Gdansk).

Russia

TO/FROM ESTONIA

Silja Line (☎ 611 6663; www.silja.ee) has a passenger ferry that sails twice weekly between Rostock, Germany, and St Petersburg, stopping at Tallinn along the way. The St Petersburg-bound boat departs from Terminal D in Tallinn (from €20, 13 hours). In Russia, contact **Silja Line** (☎ 7-812 331 9826; www.silja.fi; Vasilyevsky ostrov, Ploschad Morskoy Slav 1, St Petersburg).

TO/FROM LITHUANIA

Lisco Lines operates a weekly ferry connecting Baltysk in the Kaliningrad Region with Klaipėda (seven to 11 hours). For ticket info, contact Klaipėda's **Lisco Lines office** (☎ 46-395 050; www.lisco.lt; Perkelos gatvė 10, Klaipėda). In Kaliningrad city, you can book through **BaltFinn** (☎ 0112-728 401; Suvorova 45).

Sweden

TO/FROM ESTONIA

There are direct sailings daily from Stockholm and Västervik to Tallinn, and a cargo ship that accepts passengers between Paldiski and Kapellskär, northeast of Stockholm and linked to the Swedish capital by bus.

Tallink

Tallink's M/S *Regina Baltica* and M/S *Fantaasia* sail every other day (once a day May to September) between Tallinn and Stockholm (adult/car from €32/€53, 17 hours), stopping at the Finnish island of Mariehamn en route. Both ferries make the 17-hour crossing year-round, and leave from Terminal D in Tallinn and the Tallinn terminal at the Free Harbour (Frihamnen) in Stockholm.

Tallink also operates a daily ferry between Paldiski, 52km west of Tallinn, and Kapellskär (adult/car from €20/€53, 11 hours), northeast of Stockholm.

Tallink gets heavily booked, so make your reservation a month or two ahead. Book at Tallinn's **Tallink office** (Map pp70-1; ☎ 640 9808; www.tallink.ee; Laikmaa tänav 5). Alternatively, contact **Tallink's Swedish office** (☎ 08-666 60 01; www.tallink.se; Klaraberdsgatan 31, Sweden).

TO/FROM LATVIA

Between mid-April and mid-September the *Baltic Kristina* ferry sails every second day between Nynäshamn, 60km south of Stockholm, and Rīga (seat/berth from 35Ls/45Ls, 17 hours). The service is operated by **Rīga Sea Line** (RJL; Rīgas Jūras Līnija; Map pp192-3; ☎ 720 5460; www.rigasealine.lv; Eksporta iela 3a). In Sweden, tickets are sold at **Rīga Sea Line** (Rīgas Jūras Līnija; ☎ 08-5100 1500; Magasin 2, Frihamnen).
Scandlines also has a ferry connecting Ventspils and Nynäshamn, in Sweden. Ferries depart five times weekly (adult from €45, nine hours) from both ports. In Nynäshamn, tickets are sold at **Van Ommeren** (☎ 08-5206 0290; Farjeterminalem, Nynäshamn) In Ventspils, you can buy tickets through **Wm H Muller Baltic Ltd** (☎ 360 7358; Plostu iela 7).

Terrabalt (☎ 342 5756; www.terrabalt.lv; Pier 46, Liepāja) runs ferries from Liepāja to Karlshamn three times weekly (pullman seat/berth from €54/€64, 16 hours). In Sweden, contact **Becoship** (☎ 4541 9080; info@becoship.se; Södra Stillerydsvägen 127, Karlshamn).

TO/FROM LITHUANIA

Ferries between Klaipėda and Karlshamn (pullman seat/berth from €70/€95, 15 hours) make the crossing at least five times weekly. In Klaipėda, contact **Lisco Lines** (☎ 46-395 050; www.lisco.lt; Perkelos gatvė 10, Klaipėda). In Sweden, its agent is **DFDS Tor Line AB** (☎ 0454-33680; karlshamn@dfdstorline.com; Sodra Stillerydsvagen 127, Karlshamn).

Yacht

The Baltics – particularly Estonia with its islands and indented coast –attract hundreds of yachts a year, mainly from Finland and Scandinavia. The **Estonian Marine Tourism Association** (EMTA; Map pp66-7; ☎ 639 8933; www.agentuur.ee/sadamad/; Regati 1, Tallinn) has information on sailing to the region, with details on harbour-berth booking and visa services for yachties. Unfortunately, the website isn't kept up to date. In Helsinki, a good contact is the **Estum Sailing Agency** (☎ 09-629 299; fax 09-629 390; Vuorimiehenka 23a, Helsinki).

The harbour at Pärnu was the first in Eastern Europe to get the Blue Flag in 1992. Blue Flag is a green 'eco' label awarded to beaches, harbours and marinas for their cleanliness and amenities. Customs facilities are available at Pirita, Dirhami, Haapsalu, Kuivastu, Kunda, Lehtma, Narva-Jõesuu, Nasva, Paldiski-North, Pärnu, Ruhnu, Roomassaare, Triigi, Vergi and Veere. Approaches to Orjaku, Triigi, Mõntu, Kihnu and Ruhnu should only be made in daylight.

It's also possible to rent yachts throughout the region; see p404 for more info.

GETTING AROUND

AIR

There are plenty of scheduled flights between the three Baltic capitals, listed in the relevant city and town Getting There & Away sections. Flights are reliable but expensive.

Within each country, domestic flights are minimal: Lithuanian Airlines flies between Palanga and Vilnius once weekly mid-May to mid-September. In Estonia, **Avies Air** (☎ 605 8022; www.avies.ee) flies daily to from Tallinn to the islands of Saaremaa and Hiiumaa. Air Livonia operates twice-weekly flights to Ruhnu and flights in summertime to Kihnu from Pärnu. More details are listed in the respective city and town Getting There & Away sections.

BICYCLE

The flatness and small scale of Estonia, Latvia and Lithuania, and the light traffic on most roads make them good cycling territory. On the Estonian islands particularly, you will see cyclists galore in summer. Most bring their own bicycles but there are plenty of places where you can rent a bicycle, including Hiiumaa, Kärdla, Palmse, Pärnu, Sagadi, Tartu and Vormsi in Estonia; Rīga, Jūrmala, Cēsis, Sigulda, Valmiera, Kolka, Kandava and Sabile in Latvia; and in Vilnius, Trakai, Kaunas, Palanga, Nida, Žemaičių Naumiestis (for exploring Nemunas Delta Regional Park), Druskininkai and Palūšė (in Aukštaitija National Park) in Lithuania. For Baltic cycling routes, see p39.

Cyclists should bring waterproof clothing, and perhaps a tent if touring: you may not find accommodation in some out-of-the-way places. Some bike-hire places, such as Valmiera's **Eži** (☎ 420 7263; www.ezi.lv; Valdemāra iela; 9am-7pm Mon-Sat, to 1pm Sun) in Latvia, rent tents, sleeping bags and other gear you might need when out peddling.

Several travel agencies and organisations, both within and outside the region, organise cycling tours (see p409).

TRANSPORT

BOAT

Ferry

The only ferry link between Baltic countries is the new passenger and vehicle line travelling between Ventspils in Latvia and Mõntu on Saaremaa Island, Estonia. **SLK Ferries** (Estonia ☎ 452 4444; www.slkferries.ee) goes four times weekly from May to mid-September (adult/child/car €18/€12/€25, four hours).

Estonia, with its many islands, has plenty of opportunities for sailing. Combined passenger and vehicle ferries sail from the Estonian mainland to the islands of Vormsi, Hiiumaa and Muhu (which is linked by causeway to Estonia's biggest island, Saaremaa). There are also ferry services between Saaremaa and Hiiumaa, and between Saaremaa and Vilsandi Island. You can also take boat trips to the islands of Saarnaki and Hanikatsi, off southeastern Hiiumaa, and to Abruka and Vahase off Saaremaa's southern coast. Full details of all these services are in the Western Estonia & the Islands section.

From Pärnu, you can travel by boat to Kihnu Island; there are also summer ferries between Saaremaa and Ruhnu. Other summer options are sailing from Tallinn to its surrounding islands of Aegna and Naissar.

Boating opportunities within Latvia are few, although you can catch a car ferry (p232) across the Gauja River to/from Līgatne in the Gauja National Park.

Ferries make the short crossing from Klaipėda to Smiltynė in western Lithuania. In southeastern Lithuania, a steamboat ploughs the Nemunas River between Druskininkai and Liškiava. There's also a seasonal hydrofoil daily along the Nemunas River and the Curonian Lagoon between Kaunas, Nida and Rusnė; in summer you can hire a boat along part of the hydrofoil route or from Nida to Klaipėda. You can also explore the Nemunas Delta by boat.

Yacht

Private yachting is a popular way to get around the Baltic Coast, particularly Estonia's coast with its many islands and bays. Yachts can be rented with or without a skipper from the **Tallinn Olympic Yachting Centre** (Map pp66-7; ☎ 639 8981; www.piritatop.ee; Regati puiestee 1, Tallinn). For information and advice on Estonia's dozens of harbours, contact the **Estonian Marine Tourism Association** (EMTA; Map pp66-7; ☎ 639 8933; www.agentuur.ee/sadamad; Regati 1, Tallinn). The EMTA also sells updated navigation charts of the Estonian coast, sold at most Estonian harbours and in Finland at the **Estum Sailing Agency** (☎ 09-629 299; fax 09-629 390; Vuorimiehenka 23a, SF-00140 Helsinki).

In Latvia, Rīga's **Andrejosta Yacht Club** (Map pp192-3; ☎ 732 3221; Eksporta iela 1a, Andrejosta) hires yachts and assists sailors wanting to navigate the country's other nine yacht ports. Detailed information on these can be found on the website of **Latvian Coast** (☎ 348 0808; www.latviancoast.lv) and in the *Yacht Ports of Latvia* guide, sold at the Jāņa sēta bookshop (Map pp192-3; ☎ 709 2277; Elizabetes iela 83-85) in Rīga. Navigation charts for Latvian waters are sold by the hydrographical service of the **Latvian Maritime Administration** (☎ 706 2101; www.maritimeadministration.lv; Trijādības iela 5, Rīga); a full list of charts is posted on its website.

BUS

The region is well served by buses, although services to off-the-beaten track villages are infrequent. Direct bus services link the three capitals – Tallinn, Rīga and Vilnius – and there are plenty of other cross-border services between main towns. To get to Tallinn from Kaunas, you have to change in Panevėžys.

Buses are generally faster than trains and, on the whole, slightly cheaper. Those used for local journeys, up to about two hours long, offer few comforts. Dating from some prehistoric time, many appear to be only fit for the scrap heap. To ensure semisurvival, avoid window seats in rainy, snowy or very cold weather; travel with someone you're prepared to snuggle up to for body warmth; and sit in the seat allocated to you to avoid tangling with a merciless babushka who wants *her* seat that *you're in*. Some shorter routes, however, are serviced by nippier and more modern microbuses, holding about 15 passengers and officially making fewer stops than their big-bus counterparts.

By contrast, buses travelling between the Baltic countries are equal to any long-distance coaches anywhere else in Europe. **Eurolines** (www.eurolines.ee) and **Ecolines** (www.ecolines.ee) have their appointed agents in each Baltic capital. Eurolines buses boast a higher standard than Ecolines, though tickets cost a bit more. Regardless, both are clean and tout a heating system that functions and can be moderated. Most have a toilet, hot drinks dispenser and TV on board. Many scheduled buses to/from Tallinn, Rīga and Vilnius run overnight; a convenient and safe way of travelling, even for solo female travellers.

On buses, carry your luggage on board with you, unless it is too large, in which case you can ask the driver to stash it in the underneath baggage compartment for a small fee.

Tickets & Information

Ticket offices/windows selling national and international tickets are clearly marked in the local language and occasionally in English too. Tickets are always printed in the local language and easy to understand once you know the words for 'seat', 'bus stop' etc.

For long-distance buses originating from where you intend to leave, tickets are sold in advance. For local buses to nearby towns or villages, or for long-distance buses that are in midroute ('in transit'), you normally pay on board. This may mean a bit of a scrum for seats if there are a lot of people waiting.

Most bus and train stations in towns and cities have information windows with staff who generally speak some English.

Timetables & Fares

Timetables can be checked before leaving home on the respective bus company websites or, upon arrival in the region, by checking schedules at the local tourist office. The offices in Tallinn, Rīga and Vilnius in particular mainatin up-to-the-minute transport schedules. The **In Your Pocket** (www.inyourpocket.com) city guides to the capitals include fairly comprehensive domestic and pan-Baltic bus schedules, updated every two months.

Comprehensive timetables are posted in bus stations' main ticket halls. A rare few need careful decoding. Most simply list the departure time and the days (using either Roman or Arabic numerals, the digit one being Monday) on which the service runs.

Fares vary slightly between the three countries. For a 100km domestic trip you pay around 1.70Ls (€2.55) in Latvia, 14Lt (€4.10) in Lithuania and 70Kr (€4.50) in Estonia; fares differ slightly between bus companies, reflecting the speed of the bus and time of day it arrives/departs. Pan-Baltic trips are marginally more expensive, around €5 to €6 per 100km.

CAR & MOTORCYCLE

Driving or riding your own vehicle is an attractive option if you are able to bring or rent a car or motorcycle. It makes some of the region's most beautiful – and remote – places far more accessible, enabling you to discover spots that a 'chug-chug' bus or train would not get you to in a short time – or at all. Indeed, driving in the country is a world apart from the capital cities' manic motorists: zigzag along gravel roads, admire the movie-style dust trail in your mirror and wonder where on earth that solitary passer-by you just passed is walking to.

Main roads linking the cities and towns are generally good, distances are not too great and traffic is far from congested. The number of cars per capita in Latvia is among the lowest in Europe, unlike in Estonia, where car owners toppled the European average (about 300 cars per 1000 inhabitants). In more remote areas there are many gravel roads and dirt tracks, but with a wide range of quality road maps with the different grade roads marked you can easily avoid the rougher roads if you don't feel your suspension is up to it.

Bring Your Own Vehicle

You can take your own vehicle to the Baltics by ferry from Finland, Sweden, Denmark or Germany; or by road from Poland, Belarus or Russia (see p397). Alternatively, you can hire a car once in the region.

Driving Licence & Permits

If you are planning to drive to or in the region, an International Driving Permit (IDP) will be useful, although, if you don't have one, your own national licence (if from a European country) should suffice. Note that licences not bearing a photograph of the holder have been known to upset traffic police, so try to get an IDP before you arrive. You will also need your vehicle's

TRANSPORT

registration document. Accident insurance is compulsory in all three countries.

Fuel & Spare Parts

Petrol stations, run by major oil companies such as Statoil, Shell and Neste, are open 24 hours along all the major roads. Western-grade fuel, including unleaded, is readily available. As elsewhere in the world, the price of petrol has skyrocketed in the Baltics. Count on paying around €0.90 per litre.

Hire

Tallinn, Riga and Vilnius are naturally the easiest places to rent cars, although there are small outlets elsewhere. The major international car-hire companies all have offices in the capitals, often both in town and at the airport, listed in the city and town Getting There & Away sections.

If you are driving across all three Baltic countries, it is cheaper to rent a car in Vilnius. Some companies, such as Avis and Hertz, allow you to pick up a car in one city and drop it off in another.

A variety of different packages and weekend specials is available, so it is worth shopping around. Deals apart, expect to pay around €50 (unlimited mileage) a day in Estonia, and anything from €115 a day (unlimited mileage) with a major rental company to €25 a day with a small private company in the other two capitals.

DOCUMENTS

If you're hiring a car you need a passport and a suitable driving licence, normally an International Driving Permit (IDP), but a national licence from a European country is often acceptable. Some hire companies have minimum ages (usually 19 or 21, but 22 at some places in Estonia) and stipulate that you must have held your licence for at least a year. A major credit card is essential too, as some companies insist on it as the method of payment. Even if they don't, you'll have to leave a very large deposit or make a heavy cash prepayment. See p397 for more on licences and other documents you need if you bring your own vehicle.

Insurance

Third-party motor insurance is compulsory throughout Europe, and the same applies to the now EU Baltic countries. For further advice and more information contact the **Association of British Insurers** (☎ 020-7600 3333; www.abi.org.uk).

You should get your insurer to issue a Green Card (which may cost extra), an internationally recognised proof of insurance, listing all the countries you intend to visit. You'll need this in the event of an accident outside the country where the vehicle is insured. The European Accident Statement (the 'Constat Amiable' in France) is available from your insurance company and is copied so that each party at an accident can record information for insurance purposes. The Association of British Insurers has more details. Never sign accident statements you cannot understand or read; insist on a translation and sign that only if it's acceptable.

Since EU meetings in late 2004, all the Baltic countries should recognise the Green Card; but if the Green Card doesn't list one of the countries you're visiting, you will have to take out separate third-party cover at the border of the country in question.

It's also wise to take out a European breakdown assistance policy, such as the Five Star Service with **AA** (in UK ☎ 0870 550 0600) or the Eurocover Motoring Assistance with **RAC** (in UK ☎ 0800 550 055; www.rac.co.uk). Non-Europeans might find it cheaper to arrange for international coverage with their own national motoring organisation before travelling.

Road Rules

The whole region drives on the right. In Lithuania, driving with any alcohol at all in your blood is illegal – don't do so after even a sip of a drink. In Estonia, a blood-alcohol level of 0.02% (which means you still can't drink) is the legal limit; in Latvia it is marginally higher at 0.05%. Seat belts are compulsory for drivers and for front-seat passengers. Speed limits in built-up areas are 50km/h in Latvia and Estonia, and 60km/h in Lithuania. Limits outside urban areas vary from 90km/h to 110km/h. In Estonia and Latvia, have your headlights switched on when driving on highways, even during the day. In Lithuania, you must have them on during the day – wherever you are driving – for a period of about four weeks starting from 1 September (apparently timed to coincide with the 'going back to school' rush).

Traffic police are fearsome beings who don't need a reason to pull you over. Expect

Road Distances (km)

	Tallinn	Tartu	Pärnu	Narva	Valka/Valga	Rīga	Liepāja	Daugavpils	Ventspils	Vilnius	Kaunas	Klaipėda	Panevėžys
Tartu	190												
Pärnu	130	205											
Narva	210	194	304										
Valka/Valga	276	86	140	268									
Rīga	310	253	180	435	167								
Liepāja	530	473	400	655	387	220							
Daugavpils	540	377	410	559	291	230	450						
Ventspils	510	453	380	635	367	200	119	430					
Vilnius	600	543	470	725	457	290	465	167	584				
Kaunas	575	523	460	715	447	280	230	267	349	100			
Klaipėda	620	538	490	745	477	310	155	477	274	310	210		
Panevėžys	460	403	330	585	317	150	270	168	350	140	110	235	
Šiauliai	465	383	310	565	297	130	192	387	330	220	140	155	80

to be asked to stop at least twice on a trip between Rīga and Vilnius. They are particularly stringent about speeding. Fines are collected on the spot. Fines vary dramatically and the only way you can ensure an officer is not adding a little pocket money for himself onto the official fine is to ask for a receipt. In Latvia, the fine for exceeding the speed limit by up to 20km/h is around 5Ls, up to 40km/h around 10Ls and more than 50km/h anything up to 60Ls. If you don't have enough cash to pay, your passport and car documents can be confiscated until you have paid the fine at the police station stipulated by the penalising officer.

Note that in Latvia and Estonia it is illegal to use a mobile phone while operating a vehicle; chatting to your mates while driving warrants a hefty fine.

Parking meters are still found in some parts of the Baltics, though both Tallinn and Vilnius have moved toward more advanced parking systems. Here drivers pay for parking via SMS, dialling a number and inputting the car's license plate and location number (posted nearby).

There is an hourly fee of 5Ls to drive into the Old Town of Rīga. Driving into the old towns in Tallinn, Vilnius and Kaunas is free, but parking costs 48Kr per hour in Tallinn, 2Lt per hour in Vilnius, and 1Lt per hour in Kaunas. Motorists must also pay a small entrance fee to drive into Latvia's prime seaside resort, Jūrmala (1Ls year-round). The Curonian Spit National Park (p362-70; car, driver and passengers 20Lt, bus passenger or pedestrian 3Lt) in Lithuania also requires an entrance fee from motorists.

Take care driving near trams, trolleybuses and buses in towns. Passengers may run across the road to catch them while they're still in motion. Traffic behind a tram must stop when it opens its doors to let people in and out. Trolleybuses often swing far out into the road when leaving a stop.

HITCHING

Hitching is never entirely safe in any country in the world, and we don't recommend it. Travellers who decide to hitch should understand that they are taking a small but potentially serious risk. People who do choose to hitch will be safer if they travel in pairs and let someone know where they are planning to go.

Locally, hitching is a popular means of getting from A to B. The **Vilnius Hitchhiking Club** (VHHC; ☎ 5-278 3025; www.autostop.lt; Umedzių gatvė 98-19, Vilnius) reckons the Baltic hitcher's average speed to be between 55km/h and 60km/h. It provides practical information and contacts to travellers hoping to hitch a ride in all three Baltic countries.

LOCAL TRANSPORT

Bus, Tram & Trolleybus

A mix of trams, buses and trolleybuses (buses run by electricity from overhead wires) provides thorough public transport around towns and cities in all three countries. All three types of transport get crowded, especially during the early-morning and early-evening rush hours, when so many people cram themselves in that the doors don't shut properly – in Kaunas, some 400 students from the university once squashed into one bus as a publicity stunt to highlight the need for more services!

Trams, trolleybuses and buses all run from about 5.30am to 12.30am, but services get pretty thin in outlying areas after about 7pm. In Estonia, the same ticket is good for all three types of transport; in Lithuania and Latvia, you need different tickets for each type. In all three countries, you validate by punching a flat-fare ticket in one of the ticket punches fixed inside the vehicle. Tickets are sold from news kiosks displaying them in the window and by some drivers (who are easier to find but charge a little more for tickets). Buy five or 10 at once; a single ticket costs 10Kr in Estonia, 0.20Ls in Latvia and 0.90Lt to 1.40Lt in Lithuania. Weekly and monthly travel passes are also available. The system depends on honesty and lends itself to cheating, but there are occasional inspections, with on-the-spot fines if you're caught riding without a punched ticket.

Travelling on all trams, trolleybuses and buses requires a certain etiquette. If you are young, fit and capable of standing on one foot for the duration of your journey, do not sit in the seats at the front – these are only for babushkas and small children. Secondly, plan getting off well ahead of time. The moment the bus/tram rolls away from the stop prior to the one you are getting off at, start making your way to the door. Pushing, shoving, stamping on toes and elbowing are, of course, allowed.

City buses are supplemented by the route-taxi (*liinitakso* or *marsruuttakso* in Estonian, *marsruta taksobuss* or *mikroautobuss* in Latvian, and *masrutinis* in Lithuanian), minibuses that drop you anywhere along a fixed routes for a flat fare: 15Kr in Tallinn, 0.20Ls to 0.30Ls in Rīga and 2Lt in Vilnius.

All airports are served by regular city transport as well as by taxis.

Taxi

Taxis are plentiful and usually cheap: they officially cost 5.50Kr to 7Kr per kilometre in Estonia, 0.30Ls per kilometre in Latvia, and 0.65Lt to 1.30Lt in Lithuania; night-time tariffs, which generally kick in between 10pm and 6am, are higher.

To avoid rip-offs, insist on the meter running. If not, agree on a fixed price before you set off. In any of the cities, it's always cheaper to order a cab by phone.

Train

Suburban trains serve the outskirts of the main cities and some surrounding towns and villages. They're of limited use as city transport for visitors, as they mostly go to residential or industrial areas where there's little to see. But some are useful for day trips to destinations outside the cities.

TRAIN

Estonia, Latvia and Lithuania have railways, although services have been scaled back significantly in recent years.

Trains are slow and cheap, and not terribly comfortable. You can almost never open the windows, which can make things stuffy (and smelly, depending on your travelling companions), while you stand equal chances of freezing or baking, depending on whether the heating is turned on or not. Local trains, known as suburban or electric, are substantially slower and make more frequent stops than long-distance trains.

Routes

The only route between capitals is the three-times weekly train running between Vilnius and Rīga.

Routes within countries include Tallinn–Narva, Tallinn–Pärnu, Tallinn–Tartu, Tallinn–

Viljandi, Rīga–Ventspils, Rīga–Rēzekne, Rīga–Daugavpils, Rīga–Liepāja, Vilnius–Daugavpils–Rēzekne (some terminating at St Petersburg), Vilnius–Druskininkai; Vilnius–Ignalina, Vilnius–Kaunas and Vilnius–Klaipėda. There are other local railways fanning out from the main cities.

Tickets & Information

In Latvia and Lithuania, tickets can be purchased in advance and immediately before departure at train stations. In larger train stations, such as Rīga, you can only buy tickets for certain types of trains or destinations at certain windows. Check under Train in the Getting There & Away section of the city you are visiting for details.

Estonia's train stations are deserted places. There's no ticket agent and no services of any kind. You buy your tickets on the train, and don't head to the train station (which is usually quite far from the city centre) unless you know the exact departure time.

Tickets – upon boarding a long-distance train between the Baltics and elsewhere – must be surrendered to the carriage attendant, who will safeguard it for the journey's duration and return it to you 15 minutes before arrival at your final destination (a handy 'alarm clock' if you're on an overnight train).

Timetables & Fares

The railways of Latvia (www.ldz.lv) and Lithuania (www.litrail.lt) maintain updated train schedules on their websites, as does Estonia (www.edel.ee), though it's only in Estonian. Those displayed at train stations generally list the number of the train, departure and arrival times, and the platform from which it leaves. Some list the return journey schedules, the number of minutes a train waits in your station or the time a train left the place it began its journey. Always study the small print on timetables, too, as many trains only run on certain days or between certain dates. Estonia's train stations aren't really stations, just unstaffed waiting areas with little information for travellers.

Train fares vary. Prices per 100km average 60Kr (€3.83) in Estonia, 1.30Ls (€1.88) in Latvia and 10Lt (€2.90) in Lithuania. Once you get into compartment class, fares start rise from 20% to 50%.

TOURS

Single-city, two- or three-city, country, island and so on, tours and excursions are a dime a dozen in all three countries. Key operators include the following:

Estonia

Estonian Holidays (Map pp70-1; ☎ 627 0500; www.holidays.ee; Rüütli tänav 28/30, Tallinn) Organises thematic group tours, including an Estonian cultural heritage tour, a 'crown tour' featuring the sights depicted on Estonian banknotes, North Estonian manor houses, wildlife and agricultural tours.

Estonian Rural Tourism (Map pp66-7; ☎ 600 9999; www.maatourism.ee; Vilmsi tänav 53B, Tallinn) Organises more alternative four- or five-day tours with farmhouse accommodation, aimed at 'green' travellers into nature and the great outdoors.

Haapsalu Travel Service (Map p131; ☎ 472 4180; www.travel-service.ee; Tallinna maantee 1, Haapsalu) Organises tours of six Estonian cities, western Estonia, Vormsi Island as well as a thematic tour of former Soviet military sites in Estonia, and camping and ecological tours through nature reserves across Estonia.

Kumari (☎ 477 8214; www.kumari.ee) Operating out of Maatsalu Nature Reserve, this is one of the best bird-watching and nature tour outfits in Estonia.

Latvia

Country Holidays (Lauku ceļotājs; ☎ 761 7600; www.celotajs.lv; Kuģu iela 11, Rīga) Organises bird-watching, walking, berry-picking and a host of other nature-loving expeditions around Latvia.

Latvia Tours (Map p197; ☎ 708 5001; www.latviatours.lv; Kaļķu iela 8, Rīga) Runs a bounty of tours, including a classic seven-day coach tour of the three capitals. From May to September it runs daily day trips from Rīga to Sigulda or Rundāle and day trips along the Daugava River to Aglona, Rezēkne and a Latgalian potter's workshop.

Lithuania

Baltic Travel Service (Map p292-3; ☎ 5-212 0220; lcc@bts.lt; Subačiaus gatvė 2, Vilnius) Specialises in countryside tourism, running bird-watching tours, Nemunas Delta trips and the like.

Krantas Travel (☎ 5-231 3314; www.krantas.lt; Pylimo gatvė 4, Vilnius) With branch offices in Kaunas and Klaipėda, Krantas organises cycling, culinary, walking and bird-watching tours in Lithuania's national and regional parks.

Liturimex (☎ 5-279 1416; www.liturimex.lt; Basinavičiaus gatve 11/1, Vilnius) Organises weekend breaks and spa tours to Druskininkai.

Health

CONTENTS

Before You Go	**410**
Insurance	410
Recommended Vaccinations	410
Online Resources	410
In Estonia, Latvia & Lithuania	**411**
Availability & Cost of Health Care	411
Infectious Diseases	411
Traveller's Diarrhoea	411
Environmental Hazards	411
Travelling with Children	411
Women's Health	412
Sexual Health	412

Travel health depends on your predeparture preparations, your daily health care while travelling and how you handle any medical problem that does develop. The Baltic region is, on the whole, a pretty healthy place to travel around, though medical care, particularly outside the capital cities, is not entirely up to Western standards.

BEFORE YOU GO

Illness prevention is the key to staying healthy while abroad. A little planning before departure, particularly for pre-existing illnesses, will save trouble later. See your dentist before a long trip, carry a spare pair of contact lenses and glasses, and take your optical prescription with you: it can be used in the capitals. Bring medications in their original, clearly labelled, containers. A signed and dated letter from your physician describing your medical conditions and medications, including generic names, is also a good idea. If carrying syringes or needles, be sure to have a physician's letter documenting their medical necessity.

INSURANCE

If you're an EU citizen, a European Health Insurance Card (EHIC), available from health centres or, in the UK, post offices, covers you for most medical care. An EHIC will not cover you for nonemergencies or repatriation. Citizens from other countries should find out if there is a reciprocal arrangement for free medical care between their country and the country visited. If you do need health insurance, strongly consider a policy that covers you for the worst possible scenario, such as an accident requiring an emergency flight home. Find out in advance if your insurance plan will make payments directly to providers or reimburse you later for overseas health expenditures. The former option is generally preferable, as it doesn't require you to pay out of your own pocket in a foreign country.

RECOMMENDED VACCINATIONS

The World Health Organization (WHO) recommends that all travellers should be covered for diphtheria, tetanus, measles, mumps, rubella and polio, regardless of their destination. Since most vaccines don't produce immunity until at least two weeks after they're given, visit a physician at least six weeks before departure. If you intend to spend a lot of time in forested areas, including by the coast where pine forest prevails, it is advisable to get a vaccine against tick-borne encephalitis.

ONLINE RESOURCES

The WHO's publication *International Travel and Health* is revised annually and is available online at www.who.int/ith/. Other useful websites include www.mdtravelhealth.com (travel health recommendations for every country; updated daily), www.fitfortravel.scot.nhs.uk (general travel advice for the layperson), www.ageconcern.org.uk (advice on travel for the elderly) and www

TRAVEL HEALTH WEBSITES

It's usually a good idea to consult your government's travel health website before departure, if one is available:

Australia www.smartraveller.gov.au
Canada http://www.hc-sc.gc.ca/english/index.html
United Kingdom www.doh.gov.uk
United States www.cdc.gov/travel

.mariestopes.org.uk (information on women's health and contraception).

IN ESTONIA, LATVIA & LITHUANIA

AVAILABILITY & COST OF HEALTH CARE

Practically all pharmacies in the capitals and larger towns stock imported Western medicines. There are few alternatives to the local medical system, which is short on both facilities and training should you have the misfortune to need serious attention. Private clinics offer Western-standard, English-speaking medical care in the capitals but they are very expensive. In an emergency seek your hotel's help first (if you're in one); the bigger hotels may have doctors on call. Emergency care is free in all three countries.

INFECTIOUS DISEASES

Tick-Borne Encephalitis

Spread by tick bites, tick-borne encephalitis is a serious infection of the brain. Vaccination is advised for those in risk areas who are unable to avoid tick bites (such as campers, forestry workers and walkers). Two doses of vaccine will give a year's protection, three doses up to three years'.

Typhoid & Hepatitis A

These are spread through contaminated food (particularly shellfish) and water. Typhoid can cause septicaemia (blood poisoning); hepatitis A causes liver inflammation and jaundice. Neither is usually fatal but recovery can be prolonged. Typhoid vaccine (Typhim Vi, Typherix) will give protection for three years. In some countries, the oral vaccine Vivotif is also available. Hepatitis A vaccine (Avaxim, VAQTA, Havrix) is given as an injection; a single dose will give protection for up to a year, and a booster after a year gives 10 years' protection. Hepatitis A and typhoid vaccines can also be given as a single dose vaccine (Hepatyrix or Viatim).

TRAVELLER'S DIARRHOEA

To prevent diarrhoea, avoid tap water unless it has been boiled, filtered or chemically disinfected (with iodine tablets) and steer clear of ice. Only eat fresh fruits or vegetables if cooked or peeled; be wary of dairy products that might contain unpasteurised milk. Eat food which is hot through and avoid buffet-style meals. If a restaurant is full of locals the food is probably safe.

If you develop diarrhoea, be sure to drink plenty of fluids, preferably an oral rehydration solution (eg Dioralyte). A few loose stools don't require treatment, but if you start having more than four or five stools a day, you should start taking an antibiotic (usually a quinolone drug) and an anti-diarrhoeal agent (such as Loperamide). If diarrhoea is bloody, persists for more than 72 hours or is accompanied by fever, shaking, chills or severe abdominal pain you should seek medical attention.

ENVIRONMENTAL HAZARDS

Insect Bites & Stings

Bees and wasps cause real problems only to those with a severe allergy (anaphylaxis). If you have a severe allergy to bee or wasp stings carry an 'epipen' or similar adrenaline injection.

Bed bugs lead to very itchy, lumpy bites. Spraying the mattress with crawling-insect killer after changing bedding will get rid of them.

You should always check all over your body if you have been walking through a potentially tick-infested area. Signs along the Lithuanian coast alert walkers and beachgoers to particularly rampant tick areas. If a tick is found attached, press down around the tick's head with tweezers, grab the head and gently pull upwards. Avoid pulling the rear of the body as this may squeeze the tick's gut contents through the attached mouth parts into the skin, increasing the risk of infection and disease.

Water

Tap water may not be safe to drink so it is best to stick to bottled water, or boil water for 10 minutes, use water purification tablets or a filter. Do not drink water from rivers or lakes as it may contain bacteria or viruses that can cause diarrhoea or vomiting.

TRAVELLING WITH CHILDREN

Make sure the children are up to date with routine vaccinations, and discuss possible travel vaccines well before departure as some vaccines are not suitable for children under a year.

In hot moist climates any wound or break in the skin is likely to let in infection. The area should be cleaned and kept dry.

Remember to avoid contaminated food and water. If your child has vomiting or diarrhoea, lost fluid and salts must be replaced. It may be helpful to take rehydration powders for reconstituting with boiled water.

Children should be encouraged to avoid and mistrust any dogs or other mammals because of the risk of rabies and other diseases. Any bite, scratch or lick from a warm-blooded, furry animal should be thoroughly cleaned immediately. If there is any possibility that the animal is infected with rabies, immediate medical assistance should be sought.

WOMEN'S HEALTH

Travelling during pregnancy is usually possible but always consult your doctor before planning your trip. The most risky times for travel are during the first 12 weeks of pregnancy and after 30 weeks.

SEXUAL HEALTH

Emergency contraception is most effective if taken within 24 hours after unprotected sex. The **International Planned Parent Federation** (www.ippf.org) can advise about the availability of contraception in different countries.

When buying condoms, look for a European CE mark, which means they have been rigorously tested, and then keep them in a cool dry place or they may crack and perish.

HEALTH

Language

CONTENTS

Estonian	**413**
Pronunciation	413
Accommodation	414
Conversation & Essentials	414
Shopping & Services	415
Time, Dates & Numbers	415
Transport	416
Latvian	**416**
Pronunciation	416
Accommodation	417
Conversation & Essentials	417
Shopping & Services	418
Time, Dates & Numbers	418
Transport	419
Lithuanian	**420**
Pronunciation	420
Accommodation	420
Conversation & Essentials	421
Shopping & Services	421
Time, Dates & Numbers	422
Transport	422

ESTONIAN

Estonian belongs to the Baltic-Finnic branch of the Finno-Ugric languages. It's closely related to Finnish and distantly related to Hungarian. The complex grammar of Estonian makes it a difficult language to learn – try your luck with 14 cases, declining adjectives and no future tense. Added to this is a vocabulary with no link to any other language outside its own group, save recent borrowings.

A comprehensive and radical reform of the language was undertaken in the early 1900s by Johannes Aavik, somewhat de-Germanising the grammar and adding thousands of new terms. Another language reformer, Johannes Veski, criticised Aavik's liberal borrowing from Finnish, and proceeded to augment the vocabulary by using Estonian roots to create new words. It's a process that is continuing to this day as new Estonian words are invented to suit modern needs. All the same, the last few years have seen an increase in the liberal use of English words in place of their more complicated Estonian translations, or adding Estonian verb endings to English words, eg if you want to *surfima* the Web or *e-mailima* your friends, you'll need to *klikima* the mouse often!

Most Estonians, especially younger people, understand some English and Finnish, but you'll find that Estonians are much more welcoming of visitors who make an effort to speak their language. So don't be shy – there's nothing to lose and much to gain. For trivia buffs, Estonian boasts the word with the most consecutively repeated vowel: *jäääär*, which means 'edge of ice'.

PRONUNCIATION

Vowel & Vowel Combinations

	Pronunciation Guide	
a	ah	as in 'father'
ae	ae	as the 'ie' in 'diet' (two sounds)
ai	ai	as in 'aisle'
e	e	as in 'ten'
ea	ea	as in 'bear'
ee	eh	as the 'e' in 'ten' but longer
ei	ay	as in 'pay'
i	i	as in 'tin'
ii	ee	as the 'ee' in 'see'
o	o	as in British English 'hot'
oi	oy	as in 'ploy'
oo	aw	as in 'dawn'
u	u	as in 'put'
ui	uy	as the 'oui' in 'Louie', but shorter and clipped
uu	oo	as in 'zoo'
õ	y	roughly as the 'i' in 'girl' (without rounding the lips)
õi	yi	roughly as the word 'curly' leaving out the 'c', 'r' and 'l'
ä	a	as in 'act'
äe	aeh	as the 'ae' in 'aesthetic'
ää	aa	as in 'Aaron'
ö	er	as the 'ir' in 'girl' (rounding the lips)
öö	err	as the 'yrr' in 'myrrh' (rounding the lips)
ü	ü	as the 'oo' in 'too' said with a small, round opening of the lips

LANGUAGE

Consonants

Consonants are pronounced as in English, with the exception of the following:

Pronunciation Guide

c	ts	as in 'tsar'
g	g	as in 'good', never as in 'page'
j	y	as in 'yes'
k	k	softer than in English
p	p	between English 'p' and 'b'
r	rr	always trilled, as the Italian 'r'
š	sh	as in 'shampoo'
ž	zh	as the 's' in 'treasure'
t	t	between English 't' and 'd'

Stress

Stress is on the first syllable. There are very few exceptions to this rule, but there's one that's very conspicuous – the word for 'thanks' *aitäh* (ai·*tahh*) stresses the second syllable. Stress is indicated in the pronunciation guides with italics.

ACCOMMODATION

Where can I find a ...?
kus *ah*·sub ... — *Kus asub ...?*

hotel
ho·*tell* — *hotell*

pension
vyy·rrahs·te·mah·yah — *võõrastemaja*

camp site
kam·ping — *kämping*

I'd like a ...
mah *tah*·hak·sin ... *tu*·bah — *Ma tahaksin ... tuba.*

single room
ü·he *vaw*·di·gah — *ühe voodiga*

double room
kah·he *vaw*·di·gah — *kahe voodiga*

room with a bathroom
vahn·ni·toa·gah — *vannitoaga*

How much is it per person?
kui *pahl*·yu *mahk*·sab *vaw*·di·koht
Kui palju maksab voodikoht?

How much is it per night?
kui *pahl*·yu *mahk*·sab *err*·paehv
Kui palju maksab ööpäev?

Does it include breakfast?
kahs *hom*·mi·ku·serrk on *hin*·nah sehs
Kas hommikusöök on hinna sees?

May I see it?
kahs mah vyin *se*·dah *na*·hah
Kas ma võin seda näha?

CONVERSATION & ESSENTIALS

Use the formal 'you', *te* (te) or *teie* (*tay*·e), when addressing strangers or people you've just met. The informal *sa* (sah) or *sina* (*si*·nah) is reserved for children, family and friends. Except with children, don't use it until you are invited to.

Good ...
te·rre ... — *Tere ...*

morning
hom·mi·kust — *hommikust*

afternoon
paeh·vahst — *päevast*

evening
yh·tust — *õhtust*

Hello.
te·rre — *Tere.* (inf & pol)

Welcome.
te·rre *tu*·le·mahst — *Tere tulemast.*

Goodbye.
head *ae*·gah — *Head aega.*

Good night.
head errd — *Head ööd.*

Yes.
yah — *Jah.*

No.
ay — *Ei.*

Thank you.
ta·nahn — *Tänan.*

You're welcome.
pah·lun — *Palun.*

Excuse me/I'm sorry.
vah·bahn·dah·ge — *Vabandage.*

How are you? (How's it going?)
kuy·dahs *la*·heb — *Kuidas läheb?*

Fine.
has·ti — *Hästi.*

What's your name?
mis te *ni*·mi on — *Mis te nimi on?*

My name is ...
mu *ni*·mi on ... — *Minu nimi on ...*

Very nice (to meet you).
va·gah *mehl*·div — *Väga meeldiv.*

Emergencies

Help!
ahp·pi — *Appi!*

Call a doctor!
kut·su·ge ahrrst — *Kutsuge arst!*

I'm ill.
mah *o*·len *hai*·ge — *Ma olen haige.*

I'm lost.
mah *o*·len *ek*·si·nud — *Ma olen eksinud.*

Go away!
min·ge *a*·rrah — *Minge ära!*

Health

Where's the nearest ...?
kus on *la*·him ...
Kus on lähim ...?

chemist	*ap*·tehk	*apteek*
doctor	ahrrst	*arst*
hospital	*haig*·lah	*haigla*

antibiotics
ahn·ti·bi·aw·ti·ku·mid — *antibiootikumid*

condoms
kon·*daw*·mid — *kondoomid*

painkillers
vah·lu·vai·gis·ti — *valuvaigisti*

sanitary napkins
hü·gi·*eh*·ni·si·de·med — *hügieenisidemed*

sunblock cream
paeh·vi·tus·krrehm — *päevituskreem*

tampons
tahm·*paw*·nid — *tampoonid*

Language Difficulties

Do you speak English?
kahs te *rraa*·gi·te *ing*·li·se kehlt
Kas te räägite inglise keelt?

I don't understand.
mah ay saah *ah*·rru
Ma ei saa aru.

Please write it down here.
pah·lun *kirr*·yu·tah·ge seh *see*·ah
Palun kirjutage see siia.

SHOPPING & SERVICES

Where's (a/an/the) ...?
kus on ...
Kus on ...?

bank	pahnk	*pank*
chemist/ pharmacy	*ahp*·tehk	*apteek*
city centre	*kesk*·linn	*kesklinn*
... embassy	... *saaht*·kond	*... saatkond*
market	turrg	*turg*
police	po·lit·*say*	*politsei*
post office	*post*·kon·torr	*postkontor*
toilet	tua·*lett*	*tualett*
tourist office	tu·*rris*·mi·bü·*rroo*	*turismibüroo*

How much does it cost?
kui *pahl*·yu seh *mahk*·sahb
Kui palju see maksab?

Can I pay by credit card?
kahs tayl saahb *mahks*·tah krre·*deet*·*kaahrr*·di·gah
Kas teil saab maksta krediitkaardiga?

Where can I exchange money?
kus mah saahn *vah*·he·tah·dah *rrah*·hah
Kus ma saan vahetada raha?

I need to check my email.
mah pean *vaah*·tah·mah *o*·mah e·*lekt*·rron·pos·ti
Ma pean vaatama oma elektronposti.

What time does it open/close?
mis kell seh *ah*·vah·tahk·se/*su*·le·tahk·se
Mis kell see avatakse/suletakse?

TIME, DATES & NUMBERS

Excuse me, what time is it?
vah·bahn·dah·ge mis kell on
Vabandage, mis kell on?

It's ...	kell on ...	*Kell on ...*
eight o'clock	*kah*·hek·sah	*kaheksa*
one o'clock	üks	*üks*

in the morning	*hom*·mi·kul	*hommikul*
in the evening	*yh*·tul	*õhtul*
today	*ta*·nah	*täna*
tomorrow	*hom*·me	*homme*
yesterday	*ay*·le	*eile*

Monday	*es*·mahs·paehv	*esmaspäev*
Tuesday	*tay*·si·paehv	*teisipäev*
Wednesday	*kol*·mah·paehv	*kolmapäev*
Thursday	*nel*·yah·paehv	*neljapäev*
Friday	*rreh*·de	*reede*
Saturday	*lau*·paehv	*laupäev*
Sunday	*pü*·hah·paehv	*pühapäev*

January	*yaah*·nuahrr	*jaanuar*
February	*vehb*·rruahrr	*veebruar*
March	marrts	*märts*
April	ahp·*rrill*	*aprill*
May	mai	*mai*
June	*joo*·ni	*juuni*
July	*joo*·li	*juuli*
August	*au*·gust	*august*
September	sep·*tem*·berr	*september*
October	ok·*taw*·berr	*oktoober*
November	no·*vem*·berr	*november*
December	det·*sem*·berr	*detsember*

0	null	*null*
1	üks	*üks*
2	kahks	*kaks*
3	kolm	*kolm*
4	*ne*·li	*neli*

5	vees	*viis*
6	koos	*kuus*
7	*sayt*·se	*seitse*
8	*kah*·hek·sah	*kaheksa*
9	*ü*·hek·sah	*üheksa*
10	*küm*·me	*kümme*
11	*üks*·tayst	*üksteist*
12	*kahks*·tayst	*kaksteist*
13	*kolm*·tayst	*kolmteist*
14	*ne*·li·tayst	*neliteist*
15	*vees*·tayst	*viisteist*
16	*koos*·tayst	*kuusteist*
17	*sayt*·se·tayst	*seitseteist*
18	*kah*·hek·sah·tayst	*kaheksateist*
19	*ü*·hek·sah·tayst	*üheksateist*
20	*kahks*·küm·mend	*kakskümmend*
21	*kahks*·küm·mend·üks	*kakskümmend üks*
30	*kolm*·küm·mend	*kolmkümmend*
40	*ne*·li·küm·mend	*nelikümmend*
50	*vees*·küm·mend	*viiskümmend*
60	*koos*·küm·mend	*kuuskümmend*
70	*sayt*·se·küm·mend	*seitsekümmend*
80	*kah*·hek·sah·küm·mend	*kaheksakümmend*
90	*ü*·hek·sah·küm·mend	*üheksakümmend*
100	*sah*·dah	*sada*
1000	*tu*·haht	*tuhat*

TRANSPORT

Where's the ...?
kus on ...
Kus on ...?

airport	*len*·nu·yaahm	*lennujaam*
bus station	*bus*·si·yaahm	*bussijaam*
ferry terminal	*sah*·dahm	*sadam*
train station	*rron*·gi·yaahm	*rongijaam*

Which ... do I take to get there?
mis ... mah *sin*·nah saahn
Mis ... ma sinna saan?

bus	*bus*·si·gah	*bussiga*
tram	*trrahm*·mi·gah	*trammiga*
trolleybus	*trrol*·li·gah	*trolliga*

What time is the next ...?
mis kell on *yarrg*·mi·ne ...
Mis kell on järgmine ...?

bus	buss	*buss*
train	rrong	*rong*

Please give me a ... ticket.
pah·lun ... *pi*·let
Palun ... pilet.

one-way	üks	*üks*
return	e·dah·si·*tah*·gah·si	*edasi-tagasi*

Directions

Excuse me.
vah·bahn·dah·ge — *Vabandage.*

Where is ...?
kus on ... — *Kus on ...?*

How far is it?
kuy *kau*·gel seh on — *Kui kaugel see on?*

Go straight ahead.
ot·se — *Otse.*

Turn left.
vah·sah·ku·le — *Vasakule.*

Turn right.
pah·rre·mah·le — *Paremale.*

Please show me on the map.
pah·lun *nai*·dah·ke *mul*·le *se*·dah *kaahrr*·dil — *Palun näidake mulle seda kaardil.*

LATVIAN

Latvian is one of only two surviving languages of the Baltic branch of the Indo-European language family. Even more than Estonians, the speakers of Latvian regard their language as an endangered species – only about 55% of the people in the country, and just over 45% of the inhabitants of the capital, Rīga, speak it as their first language. Latvian and Lithuanian have a lot of vocabulary in common, but are not quite close enough to be mutually intelligible.

English is a popular foreign language in Latvia so you may find that local people will be more than pleased to practise their language skills with you. If you manage to grasp at least some basic phrases in Latvian you'll be received warmly.

Latvian uses feminine and masculine forms of words. In this language guide the masculine form appears first and is separated from the feminine form by a slash. All phrases are given in the polite form unless otherwise indicated.

PRONUNCIATION

Vowels

A line above a vowel (a macron) indicates that it has a long sound. It's important to make the distinction between short and long sounds as they can change the meaning of a word. For example, *istaba* (a/the room) and *istabā* (in a/the room). Note that there are two different ways of pronouncing the letters **e**, **ē** and **o**, so follow the pronunciation guides carefully.

	Pronunciation Guide	
a	uh	as the 'u' in 'fund'
ā	ah	as in 'father'
e	e	as in 'bet'
	a	as in 'fat'
ē	eh	as the 'ai' in 'fair'
	aa	as the 'a' in 'sad', but longer
i	i	as in 'pin'
ī	ee	as in 'beet'
o	o	as in 'pot'
	aw	as in 'saw'
u	u	as in 'pull'
ū	oo	as in 'pool'

Diphthongs

	Pronunciation Guide	
ai	ai	as the 'i' in 'dive'
au	ow	as the 'ow' in 'now'
ei	ay	as the 'ay' in 'may'
ie	ea	as the 'ea' in 'fear'
oi	oy	as the 'oy' in 'toy'
ui	uy	similar to the 'ui' in 'ruin' (a combination of oo + y, but short)

Consonants

Consonants are pronounced as in English with the following exceptions:

	Pronunciation Guide	
c	ts	as in 'lots'
č	ch	as in 'chew'
dz	dz	as the 'ds' in 'beds'
dž	j	as in 'job'
ģ	jy	a 'dy' sound, similar to the 'dy' sound in British 'duty'
j	y	as in 'yellow'
ķ	ky	as the 'cy' sound in 'cute'
ļ	ly	as the 'll' in 'million'
ņ	ny	as in 'canyon'
r	r	a slightly rolled 'r'
š	sh	as in 'shop'
ž	zh	as the 's' in 'pleasure'

Stress

In Latvian, the stress is almost always on the first syllable. One notable exception is the word for 'thank you' *paldies* (puhl-*deas*). Stress is indicated in the pronunciation guides with italics.

ACCOMMODATION

I'm looking for a ...
es *mek*·leh·yu ... — *Es meklēju ...*

cheap hotel
laa·tu *veas*·neets·u — *lētu viesnīcu*

good hotel
luh·bu *veas*·neets·u — *labu viesnīcu*

youth hostel
yow·nea·shu *meet*·ni — *jauniešu mītni*

Do you have any rooms available?
vai yums ir *bree*·vuhs *is*·tuh·buhs
Vai jums ir brīvas istabas?

How much is it per night?
tsik *muhk*·sah *dean*·nuhk·tee
Cik maksā diennaktī?

I'd like a ...
es *vaa*·laws ...
Es vēlos ...

single room
vean·vea·tee·gu *is*·tuh·bu — *vienvietīgu istabu*

double room
div·vea·tee·gu *is*·tuh·bu — *divvietīgu istabu*

room with a shower/bath
is·tuh·bu uhr *du*·shu/ *vuhn*·nu — *istabu ar dušu/ vannu*

CONVERSATION & ESSENTIALS

Hello. (inf)
svayks/*svay*·kuh — *Sveiks/Sveika.* (m/f)

Good morning.
luhb·*reet* — *Labrīt.*

Good day/afternoon.
luhb·*dean* — *Labdien.* (also a general 'hello')

Good evening.
luhb·*vuh*·kuhr — *Labvakar.*

Goodbye.
uz·*redz*·eh·shuhn·aws — *Uz redzēšanos.*

Good night.
uhr *luh*·bu *nuhkt*·i — *Ar labu nakti.*

How are you?
kah yums *klah*·yuhs — *Kā jums klājas?*

Fine, thank you.
luh·bi puhl·*deas* — *Labi, paldies.*

Yes.
yah — *Jā.*

No.
neh — *Nē.*

Please/You're welcome.
loo·dzu — *Lūdzu.*

Thank you (very much).
(leals) puhl·*deas* — *(Liels) paldies.*

Excuse me.
uht·vai·naw·yeat — *Atvainojiet.*

I'm sorry.
pea·doad·eat — *Piedodiet.*

What's your name?
kah yoos sowts — *Kā jūs sauc?*

LANGUAGE

My name is ...
muhn·i sowts ... *Mani sauc ...*
Where are you from?
naw *kur*·ean·es yoos *as*·uht *No kurienes jūs esat?*
I'm from ...
es *as*·mu naw ... *Es esmu no ...*

Emergencies

Help!
puh·lee·gah *Palīgā!*
Call a doctor!
iz·sowts·eat *ahr*·stu *Izsauciet ārstu!*
I'm ill.
es *as*·mu slims/slim·uh *Es esmu slims/slima.* (m/f)
Go away!
ay·eat *praw*·yam *Ejiet projam!*

I'm lost.
es *as*·mu *uhp*·muhl·dee·yeas
Es esmu apmaldījies. (m)
es *as*·mu *uhp*·muhl·dee·yu·seas
Es esmu apmaldījusies. (f)

Health

Where can I find a/an ...?
kur es *vuh*·ru uht·ruhst ... *Kur es varu atrast ...?*
doctor
ahr·stu *ārstu*
hospital
slim·neets·u *slimnīcu*

I'm allergic to penicillin.
es *as*·mu *uh*·ler·jyisks/*uh*·ler·jyis·kuh pret *pen*·its·i·lee·nu
Es esmu alerģisks/*alerģiska* pret *penicilīnu.* (m/f)

Language Difficulties

Do you speak English?
vai yoos *run*·ah·yuht *uhn*·gli·ski
Vai jūs runājat angliski?
I don't understand.
es *ne*·suh·praw·tu
Es nesaprotu.
Please write that down.
loo·dzu *pea*·ruhk·steat taw
Lūdzu pierakstiet to.

SHOPPING & SERVICES

Where's the ...?
kur *uht*·raw·duhs ... *Kur atrodas ...?*
bank
buhn·kuh *banka*
chemist/pharmacy
uhp·tea·kuh *aptieka*
city/town centre
pil·saa·tuhs *tsent*·rs *pilsētas centrs*
currency exchange booth
vuh·loo·tuhs *mai*·nyuh *valūtas maiņa*
... embassy
... *vehst*·nea·tsee·buh ... *vēstniecība*
market
tir·gus *tirgus*
post office
puhsts *pasts*

How much is it?
tsik tuhs *muhk*·sah
Cik tas maksā?
Can I pay by credit card?
vai es *vuh*·ru *muhk*·saht uhr *kred*·eet·kuhr·ti
Vai es varu maksāt ar kredītkarti?
I'd like to change a travellers cheque.
es *vaa*·laws *iz*·mai·neet *tsely*·aw·yum·uh *che*·ku
Es vēlos izmainīt ceļojuma čeku.
I need to check my email.
es *vaa*·laws *pahr*·bow·deet *suh*·vu *e*·puhst·u
Es vēlos pārbaudīt savu e-pastu.
What time does it open?
naw *tsik*·eam ir *uht*·vaarts
No cikiem ir atvērts?
What time does it close?
tsik·aws slaadz
Cikos slēdz?
Where are the toilets?
kur ir *tu*·uh·le·tes
Kur ir tualetes?

condoms
prez·er·vuh·tee·vi *prezervatīvi*
sanitary napkins
bin·des *bindes*
sunblock cream
sow·les krehms *saules krēms*
tampons
tuhm·po·ni *tamponi*

TIME, DATES & NUMBERS

What time (is it)?
tsik (ir) *pulk*·sten·is *Cik (ir) pulkstenis?*

It's ... ir ... *Ir ...*
two o'clock *di*·vi *divi* (lit: it's two)
five o'clock *peats*·i *pieci*

today *shaw*·dean *šodien*
tomorrow reet *rīt*
morning reets *rīts*
afternoon *pehts*·pus·dea·nuh *pēcpusdiena*
night nuhkts *nakts*

Monday	*pirm*·dea·nuh	*pirmdiena*
Tuesday	*aw*·tr·dea·nuh	*otrdiena*
Wednesday	*tresh*·dea·nuh	*trešdiena*
Thursday	*tsat*·urt·dea·nuh	*ceturtdiena*
Friday	*peakt*·dea·nuh	*piektdiena*
Saturday	*sast*·dea·nuh	*sestdiena*
Sunday	*sveht*·dea·nuh	*svētdiena*

January	*yuhn*·vah·ris	*janvāris*
February	*feb*·ru·ah·ris	*februāris*
March	muhrts	*marts*
April	*uhp*·ree·lis	*aprīlis*
May	maiys	*maijs*
June	*yoo*·niys	*jūnijs*
July	*yoo*·liys	*jūlijs*
August	*ow*·gusts	*augusts*
September	*sep*·tem·bris	*septembris*
October	*ok*·to·bris	*oktobris*
November	*no*·vem·bris	*novembris*
December	*dets*·em·bris	*decembris*

0	*nul*·le	*nulle*
1	veans	*viens*
2	*di*·vi	*divi*
3	trees	*trīs*
4	*chet*·ri	*četri*
5	*peats*·i	*pieci*
6	*sesh*·i	*seši*
7	*sep*·ti·nyi	*septiņi*
8	*uhs*·taw·nyi	*astoņi*
9	*de*·vi·nyi	*deviņi*
10	*des*·mit	*desmit*
11	*vean*·puhds·mit	*vienpadsmit*
12	*div*·puhds·mit	*divpadsmit*
13	*trees*·puhds·mit	*trīspadsmit*
14	*chet*·r·puhds·mit	*četrpadsmit*
15	*peats*·puhds·mit	*piecpadsmit*
16	*sesh*·puhds·mit	*sešpadsmit*
17	*sep*·tiny·puhds·mit	*septiņpadsmit*
18	*uhs*·tawny·puhds·mit	*astoņpadsmit*
19	*de*·viny·puhds·mit	*deviņpadsmit*
20	*div*·des·mit	*divdesmit*
21	*div*·des·mit·veans	*divdesmitviens*
30	*trees*·des·mit	*trīsdesmit*
40	*chet*·r·des·mit	*četrdesmit*
50	*peats*·des·mit	*piecdesmit*
60	*sesh*·des·mit	*sešdesmit*
70	*sep*·tiny·des·mit	*septiņdesmit*
80	*uhs*·tawny·des·mit	*astoņdesmit*
90	*de*·viny·des·mit	*deviņdesmit*
100	simts	*simts*
200	*di*·vi *sim*·ti	*divi simti*
1000	*tooks*·tawts	*tūkstots*

TRANSPORT

Where's the ...?
kur *uht*·raw·duhs ...
Kur atrodas ...?

airport	*lid*·aw·stuh	*lidosta*
bus station	*ow*·to·aws·tuh	*autoosta*
ferry terminal	*puh*·suh·zhea·ru *aw*·stuh	*pasažieru osta*
train station	*dzelz*·ce·lyuh *stuhts*·i·ya	*dzelzceļa stacija*
tram/trolleybus stop	*truhm*·vuh·yuh/ *trol*·ey·bu·suh *pea*·tu·ruh	*tramvaja/ trolejbusa pietura*

I want to buy a ... ticket.
es *vaa*·laws *naw*·pirkt ... *bi*·lyet·i
Es vēlos nopirkt ... biļeti.

one-way	*vean*·virz·ean·uh	*vienvirziena*
return	turp *uht*·puh·kuhly	*turp-atpakaļ*

How much does it cost (to go to ...)?
tsik *muhk*·sah (*aiz*·vest leedz ...)
Cik maksā (aizvest līdz ...)?

boat (ship)	*ku*·gyis	*kuģis*
platform	*pe*·rawns	*perons*
ticket office(s)	*bi*·lye·shu *kuh*·ses	*biļešu kases*
timetable	*vilts*·ea·nu *suh*·ruhksts	*vilcienu saraksts*

Directions

How do I get to ...?
kah es *tea*·ku leedz ...
Kā es tieku līdz ...?

Is it far from here?
vai tuhs *uht*·raw·duhs *tah*·lu
Vai tas atrodas tālu?

Could you show me (on the map) please?
loo·dzu *puhr*·ah·deat muhn (uz *kuhrt*·es)
Lūdzu parādiet man (uz kartes)?

Go straight ahead.
uz *preak*·shu
Uz priekšu.

Turn left/right (at the ...)
puh *kray*·si/luh·bi (pea ...)
Pa kreisi/labi (pie ...)

LANGUAGE

LITHUANIAN

Lithuanian is another surviving language of the Baltic branch of the Indo-European language family. Because many of its forms have remained unchanged longer than those of other Indo-European languages (which cover most of Europe and a fair bit of Asia) Lithuanian is very important to linguistic scholars; it's said to be as archaic as Sanskrit in its grammatical forms. It is also open to free borrowings from other tongues when deemed necessary, as phrases like *ping pong klubas* and *marketingo departamento direktorius* demonstrate.

Low Lithuanian *(Žemaičiai)*, spoken in the west, is a separate dialect from High Lithuanian *(Aukštaičiai)*, spoken in the rest of the country.

Lithuanian has masculine and feminine forms of words, indicated in this language guide by (m) and (f).

PRONUNCIATION

Vowels

	Pronunciation Guide	
a/ą	ah	as the 'u' in 'cut' or longer, as the 'a' in 'arm'
e/ę	a	as the 'a' in 'cat' or longer, as the 'a' in 'amber'
ė	eh	as the 'e' in 'bed' but longer
i	i	as the 'i' in 'it'
y/į	ee	as the 'ee' in 'eel'
o	aw	as the 'aw' in 'law'
	o	as the 'o' in 'hot'
u	u	as the 'u' in 'put'
ū/ų	oo	long, as the 'oo' in 'poor'

Diphthongs

	Pronunciation Guide	
ai	ai	as the 'i' in 'bite' or longer as the 'ai' in 'aisle'
au	ow	as the 'ou' in 'ouch' or longer as the 'ow' in 'owl'
ei	ay	as the 'ay' in 'say'
ie	eah	as the 'ea' in 'ear'
ių	ew	as the 'ew' in 'new'
ui	wi	as the 'oui' in 'Louis'
uo	u·aw	as the 'wa' in 'wander'

Consonants

	Pronunciation Guide	
c	ts	as the 'ts' in 'ants'
č	ch	as the 'ch' in 'chicken'
ch	h	as the 'h' in 'hot'
dz	dz	as the 'ds' in 'roads'
dž	j	as the 'j' in 'jump'
g	g	as the 'g' in 'gas'
j	y	as the 'y' in 'you'
r	r	trilled like the Italian 'r'
s	s	soft, as the 's' in 'kiss'
š	sh	as the 'sh' in 'shop'
ž	zh	as the 's' in 'treasure'

Stress

Stress and tone variations are very subtle and complex in Lithuanian. You'll be understood without having to worry about this too much. The best way to learn is by listening. Stressed syllables are indicated by italics in the pronunciation guides.

ACCOMMODATION

I'm looking for (a) ...
ahsh *yeash*·kow ... *Aš ieškau ...*

hotel
veash·bu·chaw *viešbučio*

somewhere to stay
kur nors ahp·si·*staw*·ti *kur nors apsistoti*

Could you write down the address please?
ahr gah·*leh*·tu·met mahn uzh·rah·*shee*·ti ah·dras·ah
Ar galėtumėt man užrašyti adresą?

Do you have any rooms available?
ahr *tu*·ri·ta lais·*voo kahm*·bahr·yew
Ar turite laisvų kambarių?

How much is it per night, per person?
keahk kai·*nu*·*aw*·yah ahp·si·staw·ti nahk·chay ahs·man·wi
Kiek kainuoja apsistoti nakčiai asmeniui?

Does it include breakfast?
ahr kai·*nah* i·*skai*·taw *pus*·ree·chus
Ar karina įskaito pusryčius?

Can I see the room?
ahr gah·*leh*·chow *kahm*·bah·ri pah·mah·*tee*·ti
Ar galėčiau kambarį pamatyti?

I'd like a ...
ahsh *nawr*·yu ...
Aš noriu ...

single room
veahn·*veah*·chaw *kahm*·bahr·yaw
vienviečio kambario

double room
dvi·*veah*·chaw *kahm*·bahr·yaw
dviviečio kambario

room with a bathroom
kahm·bahr·yaw su prow·*seek*·lah
kambario su prausykla

CONVERSATION & ESSENTIALS

Hello.
svay·ki — *Sveiki.*

Hi.
lah·bahs — *Labas.*

Good morning.
lah·bahs *ree*·tahs — *Labas rytas.*

Good day.
lah·bah *deah*·nah — *Laba diena.*

Good evening.
lah·bahs *vah*·kah·rahs — *Labas vakaras.*

Welcome.
svay·*ki* aht·*vee*·ka — *Sveiki atvykę.*

Goodbye.
su·*deah* — *Sudie.*

Good night.
lah·*baws* nahk·*teahs* — *Labos nakties.* (pol)
lah·*bah*·nahk·tis — *Labanaktis.* (inf)

Yes.
tayp — *Taip.*

No.
na — *Ne.*

Please.
prah·*show* — *Prašau.*

Thank you.
deh·*kaw*·yu/*ah*·choo — *Dėkoju/Ačiū.* (pol/inf)

You're welcome.
prah·*show* — *Prašau.*

Excuse me.
aht·si·prah·*show* — *Atsiprašau.*

Sorry.
aht·*lays*·ki·ta — *Atleiskite.*

How are you?
kaip gee·*vu*·*aw*·yah·ta — *Kaip gyvuojate?* (pol)
kaip gee·*vu*·*aw*·yi? — *Kaip gyvuoji?* (inf)

What's your name?
kaip *yoo*·soo *vahr*·dahs — *Kaip jūsų vardas?*

My name is ...
mah·naw *vahr*·dahs — *Mano vardas*
ee·*rah* ... — *yra ...*

Where are you from?
ish kur yoos *a*·sah·ta — *Iš kur jūs esate?*

I'm from ...
ahsh a·*su* ish ... — *Aš esu iš ...*

Emergencies

Help!
gal·beh·ki·te — *Gelbėkite!*

Call a doctor!
ish·*show*·ki·ta *gee*·dee·taw·yah! — *Iššaukite gydytoją!*

I'm ill.
ahsh sar·*gu* — *Aš sergu.*

I'm lost.
ahsh pah·*klee*·d(usi/as) — *Aš paklyd(usi/ęs).*

Where are the toilets?
kur tu·ah·*lat*·ai — *Kur tualetai?*

Go away!
ayk shah·*lin* — *Eik šalin!*

Health

Where's the ...?
kur ee·*rah* ... — *Kur yra ...?*

doctor
gee·dee·taw·yahs — *gydytojas*

hospital
li·*gaw*·ni·neh — *ligoninė*

I'm allergic to penicillin.
ahsh ah·*lar*·gishk·(ahs/ah) pan·it·si·*lin*·wi
Aš alergišk(as/a) penicilinui. (m/f)

Language Difficulties

Do you speak English?
ahr *kahl*·bah·ta *ahn*·glish·kai
Ar kalbate angliškai?

I don't understand you.
ahsh *yoo*·soo na·su·prahn·*tu*
Aš jūsų nesuprantu.

What's Lithuanian for ...?
kaip leah·*tu*·vish·kai ...
Kaip lietuviškai ...?

SHOPPING & SERVICES

I'm looking for the ...
ahsh *yeahsh*·kow ... — *Aš ieškau ...*

bank
ban·kas — *bankas*

chemist
vais·ti·neh — *vaistinė*

city centre
meahs·taw *tsan*·traw — *miesto centro*

currency exchange
vah·*lyu*·taws — *valiutos*

embassy
ahm·bah·*sah*·daws — *ambasados*

market
tur·gows — *turgaus*

old city
san·*ah*·meahs·chaw — *senamiesčio*

police
paw·*lit*·si·yaws — *policijos*

post office
pahsh·taw — *pašto*

public toilet
tu·ah·*lat*·aw — *tualeto*

How much is it?
keahk kai·*nu*·*aw*·yah
Kiek kainuoja?
What time does it open/close?
kal·*in*·tah *vah*·lahn·dah aht·si·*dah*·raw/uzh·si·*dah*·raw
Kelintą valandą atsidaro/užsidaro?
I need to check my email.
mahn *rayk*·yah pah·si·*tik*·rin·ti al·ak·*tron*·i·ni *pahsh*·tah
Man reikia pasitikrinti elektronini paštą.

condoms
pre·zer·vah·*tee*·vai *prezervatyvai*
credit card
kra·*di*·taw kor·*ta*·leh *kredito kortelė*
sanitary napkins
bin·tai *bintai*
sunblock cream
sow·lehs *kram*·ahs *saulės kremas*
tampons
tahm·*pon*·ai *tamponai*

TIME, DATES & NUMBERS

What time is it?
keahk dah·bahr *lai*·kaw
Kiek dabar laiko?

It's ... (o'clock).
dah·*bahr* ... (vah·lahn·*dah*)
Dabar ... (valanda).

two o'clock	ahn·*trah*	*antra*
5.30	pu·seh shash·*yew*	*pusė šešių*

today	shan·*deahn*	*šiandien*
tomorrow	ree·*toy*	*rytoj*
morning	*ree*·tahs	*rytas*
afternoon	*paw*·peah·teh	*popietė*
night	nahk·*tis*	*naktis*

Monday	pir·*mah*·deah·nis	*pirmadienis*
Tuesday	ahn·*trah*·deah·nis	*antradienis*
Wednesday	trach·*ah*·deah·nis	*trečiadienis*
Thursday	kat·vir·*tah*·deah·nis	*ketvirtadienis*
Friday	pank·*tah*·deah·nis	*penktadienis*
Saturday	shash·*tah*·deah·nis	*šeštadienis*
Sunday	sak·*mah*·deah·nis	*sekmadienis*

January	*sow*·sis	*sausis*
February	vah·*sah*·ris	*vasaris*
March	*kaw*·vahs	*kovas*
April	bah·*lahn*·dis	*balandis*
May	gag·*uzh*·is	*gegužis*
June	bir·*zhal*·is	*birželis*
July	*leah*·pah	*liepa*
August	rug·*pew*·tis	*rugpiūtis*
September	rug·*seh*·yis	*rugsėjis*
October	*spah*·lis	*spalis*
November	*lahp*·krit·is	*lapkritis*
December	*gru*·*aw*·dis	*gruodis*

0	*nul*·is	*nulis*
1	*veah*·nahs	*vienas*
2	du	*du*
3	trees	*trys*
4	kat·u·*ri*	*keturi*
5	pan·*ki*	*penki*
6	shash·*i*	*šeši*
7	sap·tee·*ni*	*septyni*
8	ahsh·tu·aw·*ni*	*aštuoni*
9	dav·ee·*ni*	*devyni*
10	*dash*·imt	*dešimt*
11	veah·*naw*·lik·ah	*vienuolika*
12	*dvee*·lik·ah	*dvylika*
13	*tree*·lik·ah	*trylika*
14	kat·u·*raw*·lik·ah	*keturiolika*
15	pank·*yaw*·lik·ah	*penkiolika*
16	shash·*yaw*·lik·ah	*šešiolika*
17	sap·teen·*yaw*·lik·ah	*septyniolika*
18	ahsh·tawn·*yaw*·lik·ah	*aštuoniolika*
19	dav·een·*yaw*·lik·ah	*devyniolika*
20	*dvi*·dash·imt	*dvidešimt*
21	*dvi*·dash·imt *veah*·nahs	*dvidešimt vienas*
30	*tris*·dash·imt	*trisdešimt*
40	*kat*·ur·as·dash·imt	*keturiasdešimt*
50	*pank*·as·dash·imt	*penkiasdešimt*
60	*shash*·as·dash·imt	*šešiasdešimt*
70	sap·*teen*·as·dash·imt	*septyniasdešimt*
80	ahsh·*tu*·*aw*·nas·dash·imt	*aštuoniasdešimt*
90	dav·*een*·as·dash·imt	*devyniasdešimt*
100	*shim*·tahs	*šimtas*
101	*shim*·tahs *veah*·nahs	*šimtas vienas*
500	pan·*ki* shim·*tai*	*penki šimtai*
1000	*tooks*·tahn·tis	*tūkstantis*

TRANSPORT

Where's the ...?
kur ee·*rah* ... *Kur yra ...?*

airport
aw·raw *u*·*aws*·tahs *oro uostas*
bus stop
ow·*taw*·bu·saw staw·*ta*·leh *autobuso stotelė*
ferry terminal
kal·taw staw·*tis* *kelto stotis*
train station
gal·azh·*in*·kal·yaw staw·*tis* *geležinkelio stotis*

LANGUAGE

When does the ... arrive?
kah·*dah aht*·plowk·yah ... *Kada atplaukia ...?*

boat	*lai*·vahs	*laivas*
ferry	*kal*·tahs	*keltas*
hydrofoil	rah·*kat*·ah	*raketa*

I'd like (a) ...
ahsh naw·*reh*·chow ... *Aš norėčiau ...*

one-way ticket
bil·eah·tah i *veah*·nah *gah*·lah *bilietą į vieną galą*

return ticket
bil·eah·tah i ah·*bu* gah·*lus* *bilietą į abu galus*

I want to travel to ...
ahsh *naw*·ryu nu·vah·*zhu*·*aw*·ti i ...
Aš noriu nuvažiuoti į ...

How much does it cost to go to ...?
keahk kai·*nu*·*aw*·yah nu·vah·*zhu*·*aw*·ti i ...
Kiek kainuoja nuvažiuoti į ...?

Directions

How do I get to the ...?
prah·shom pah·sah·*kee*·ti kaip pah·*tak*·ti i ...
Prašom pasakyti, kaip patekti į ...?

Is it far?
ahr taw·*li*
Ar toli?

Can you show me (on the map)?
gah·leh·tu·met mahn pah·raw·dee·ti (zham·eh·lah·pee·ya)
Galėtumėt man parodyti (žemėlapyje)?

Turn left (at the ...)
su·ki·ta i *kai*·ra (preah ...)
Sukite į kairę (prie ...)

Turn right (at the ...)
su·ki·ta i *dash*·na (preah ...)
Sukite į dešinę (prie ...)

straight ahead
teah·say
tiesiai

Glossary

See the individual destination chapters for some useful words and phrases dealing with food and dining; see the Language chapter for other useful words and phrases. This glossary is a list of Estonian (Est), Finnish (Fin), German (Ger), Latvian (Lat), Lithuanian (Lith), and Russian (Rus) terms you might come across during your time in the Baltics.

aikštė (Lith) – square
aludė (Lith) – beer cellar
alus (Lat, Lith) – beer
apteek (Est) – pharmacy
aptieka (Lat) – pharmacy
Aukštaitija (Lith) – Upper Lithuania
autobusų stotis (Lith) – bus station
autoosta (Lat) – bus staion

baar (Est) – bar
baar (Est) – pub, bar
babushka (Rus) – grandmothers/pensioner ladies in berets
bagāžas glabātava (Lat) – left-luggage room
bagažinė (Lith) – left-luggage room
bāka (Lat) – lighthouse
Baltic glint – raised limestone bank stretching from Sweden across the north of Estonia into Russia
baras (Lith) – pub, bar
baznīca (Lat) – church
bažnyčia (Lith) – church
brokastis (Lat) – breakfast
bulvāris (Lat) – boulevard
bussijaam (Est) – bus station

ceļš (Lat) – railway track, road
centras (Lith) – town centre
centrs (Lat) – town centre
Chudkoye Ozero (Rus) – Lake Peipsi
Courland – Kurzeme

daina (Lat) – short, poetic oral song or verse
datorsalons (Lat) – Internet café
Dievs – sky god
dzintars (Lat) – amber

ebreji (Lat) – Jews
Eesti (Est) – Estonia
ežeras (Lith) – lake
ezerpils (Lat) – lake fortress
ezers (Lat) – lake

gatvė (Lith) – street
geležinkelio stotis (Lith) – train station

hommikusöök (Est) – breakfast

iela (Lat) – street
iezis (Lat) – rock
informacija (Lith) – information centre
internetas kavinė (Lith) – Internet café
interneti kohvik (Est) – Internet café

järv (Est) – lake

kalnas (Lith) – mountain, hill
kalns (Lat) – mountain, hill
kämping (Est) – camp site
katedrāle (Lat) – cathedral
kelias (Lith) – road
kempingas (Lith) – camp site
kempings (Lat) – camp site
kepta duona (Lith) – deep-fried, black-bread garlic sticks
kino (Est, Lat, Lith) – cinema
kirik (Est) – church
krogs (Lat) – pub, bar
Kursių marios (Lith) – Curonian Lagoon

laht (Est) – bay
laipa (Lat) – boardwalk, plank way
LAL – Lithuanian Airlines
Latvija (Lat) – Latvia
Latvijas Ceļš (Lat) – Latvian Way; centre-right political party
laukums (Lat) – square
lidosta (Lat) – airport
Lietuva (Lith) – Lithuania
looduskaitseala (Est) – nature/landscape reserve
loss (Est) – castle, palace

mägi (Est) – mountain, hill
Metsavennad (Est) – Forest Brothers resistance movement
midus (Lith) – mead
muuseum (Est) – museum
muzejs (Lat) – museum
muziejus (Lith) – museum

nacionālais parks (Lat) – national park

parkas (Lith) – park
parks (Lat) – park
pastas (Lith) – post office

pasts (Lat) – post office
Peko (Est) – pagan god of fertility in Setu traditions
perkėla (Lith) – port
Pērkons (Lat) – god of thunder
Perkūnas (Lith) – god of thunder
piletid (Est) – tickets
pilies (Lith) – castle
pils (Lat) – castle, palace
pilsdrupas (Lat) – knights' castle
pilskalns (Lat) – castle mound
plats (Est) – square
plentas (Lith) – highway, motorway
postkontor (Est) – post office
prospektas (Lith) – boulevard
prospekts (Lat) – boulevard
pubi (Est) – pub
puiestee (Est) – boulevard

raekoda (Est) – town/city hall
rahvuspark (Est) – national park
Reval (Ger) – Tallinn
rezervāts (Lat) – reserve
Riigikogu (Est) – Parliament
rotušė (Lith)– town/city hall
rūmai (Lith) – palace

Saeima (Lat) – Parliament
Seimas (Lith) – Parliament
Setu (Est) – ethnic group of mixed Estonian and Orthodox traditions
Setumaa (Est) – territory of the Setu people in southeastern Estonia and Russia
sild (Est) – bridge
smuklė (Lith) – tavern
stacija (Lat) – station

Tallinna (Fin) – Tallinn
tänav (Est) – street
tee (Est) – road
tiltas (Lith) – bridge
tilts (Lat) – bridge
tirgus (Lat) – market
trahter (Est) – tavern
turg (Est) – market
turgus (Lith) – market

vaistinė (Lith) – pharmacy
väljak (Est) – square
vanalinn (Est) – Old Town
Vanemuine (Est) – ancient Estonian song god
Vecrīga (Lat) – Old Rīga
via Baltica – international road (the E67) linking Estonia with Poland

žydų (Lith) – Jews

Behind the Scenes

THIS BOOK

The 1st edition of this guide was written by Nicola Williams and she also coordinated the 2nd edition. In the 3rd edition she was joined by Debra Herrmann and Cathryn Kemp, and for this 4th edition by Becca Blond and Regis St Louis. Dr Caroline Evans wrote the health chapter. This guidebook was commissioned in Lonely Planet's London office and produced by the following:

Commissioning Editor Fiona Buchan
Coordinating Editor Cahal McGroarty
Coordinating Cartographer Valentina Kremenchutskaya
Coordinating Layout Designer Cara Smith
Managing Cartographer Mark Griffiths
Assisting Editors Emma Gilmour, Kim Noble, Charlotte Orr, Laura Stansfeld, Simon Williamson
Assisting Cartographers Clare Capell, Piotr Czajkowski, Julie Dodkins, Emma McNicol
Cover Designer James Hardy
Project Manager Rachel Imeson
Language Content Coordinator Quentin Frayne

Thanks to Imogen Bannister, Helen Christinis, Sally Darmody, Pablo Gastar, Liz Heynes, Jim Hsu, Adriana Mammarella, Kate McDonald, Mik Ruff, Wibowo Rusli, John Shippick, Glenn van der Knijff, Liz White, Gabbi Wilson, Celia Wood

THANKS

NICOLA WILLIAMS

Lithuania was as fantastic as always, thanks in no small part to my dearest friends Nomeda Navaickaitė, Reine Ortiz, Nicolas and Lijana who keep me in the Vilnius loop. Sco, Lina Savranskytė, Bernie ter Braak and Rimas of Rimas Rent a Car were invaluable city sources, as were Neringa Vilutytė and Žygimrontos Vaitkus at the Environmental Projects Management Agency for the Ministry of Environment who unravelled the mysteries of EU funding for me. Elsewhere, thank you to Mindaugas Lapelė of the Dzūkija National Park; Ina Didžiulytė at the Ignalina Nuclear Power Plant; super-efficient Meilutė Požemeckaitė at Šiauliai tourist office; Česlovas Koreiva at Litinterp; Miglė Holliday at Mėja Travel; sweet Lijana in Klaipėda; and Vita Užgalytė. In Nida, Lucia and Igoris Milunai ensured super spit adventures with their bikes and a buggy for the boys; and Jovita at Misko Namas was a wonderful host. At home, big kisses to my parents-in-law who moved mountains to ensure I could finish this book and move house simultaneously, to my sister and parents for superb kid-entertaining skills and to the sweetest of Lüfkens – Matthias, Niko and monkey Mischa – for tolerating the mayhem.

BECCA BLOND

I'd like to dedicate my portion of this book to my great-uncle Bill Lopatin, who passed away recently. He immigrated to the USA as a child from the former USSR and the stories he and my grandmother used to tell instilled in me a desire to explore the region in greater depth. As for thanks, first I've got to thank my boyfriend Aaron, who accompanied me on this trip around Latvia, offered tons of moral support and was always eager to help me brainstorm and research. I'd also like to

THE LONELY PLANET STORY

The story begins with a classic travel adventure: Tony and Maureen Wheeler's 1972 journey across Europe and Asia to Australia. There was no useful information about the overland trail then, so Tony and Maureen published the first Lonely Planet guidebook to meet a growing need.

From a kitchen table, Lonely Planet has grown to become the largest independent travel publisher in the world, with offices in Melbourne (Australia), Oakland (USA) and London (UK). Today Lonely Planet guidebooks cover the globe. There is an ever-growing list of books and information in a variety of media. Some things haven't changed. The main aim is still to make it possible for adventurous travellers to get out there – to explore and better understand the world.

At Lonely Planet we believe travellers can make a positive contribution to the countries they visit – if they respect their host communities and spend their money wisely. Every year 5% of company profit is donated to charities around the world.

thank Richard Baerug, at the Rīga tourism office, for all the info he provided. To all the Latvians and travellers I met on the road, thanks for all the helpful advice. To my co-authors Nicola and Regis, it was fabulous working with you both. To CE Fiona Buchan, big thanks for offering me this wonderful gig! It's been a pleasure working with you. As always, to all the folks behind the scenes at LP – cartos, editors, proofers – lots of appreciation for all the hard work you guys do. To my family, David, Patricia, Jessica, Vera, Jennie and John, thanks for the constant support. To Duke – you and that hedgy have always made me laugh when I'm feeling most stressed out, so thanks buddy, now that this book is done we can go for longer walks.

REGIS ST LOUIS

Many thanks to Steve Kokker for welcoming me to Estonia with open arms (and delicious tea). I'm grateful for his many thoughtful introductions and his friendship along the way. I'd also like to thank Kaarel and Kadri for a lovely Jaanipäev on Hiiumaa; Liisa and family for hospitality (and a memorable horse ride); Piret, Marika, Alar and friends for calisthenics and more celebration; Olev and friends for the unstoppable Audi, a taste of Soomaa and a splendid night in the country. Thanks also to Tõnno and Anton: best wishes on all your endeavors. The many friendly tourist offices (particularly in Põltsamaa) and random acquaintances made my stay in Estonia a real pleasure. Lastly, I'd like to thank Cassandra, my intrepid travelling partner and expert navigator: it was a magical trip, and I hope we can share many more journeys down the road.

OUR READERS

Many thanks to the travellers who used the last edition and wrote to us with helpful hints, useful advice and interesting anecdotes:

B Iris Bezemer, Hilary Bird, Mark Bland, Peter Bolwell, Raymond Boyle, Colin Brown, Attila Bujdoso, John Burke **C** Karen Carlsen, Jemetha Clark, Bjorn Clasen, Robert Cosgrove, Bart Cramer, Philippa Cubison, Bryan Cumner, Drew Cunningham **D** Karsten Dax, Eduardo Delgado, Stephan Dorrenberg **E** Michael Eatroff, Gatis Eglitis **F** Alexandre & Nicole Fauchere, David Fellows, Craig Ford **G** Ansis Gailis, Felix German, Sam Golledge, Ulrike Gorgens, Ignacio Morejon Guerrero **H** Christopher Haslett, Dan Hayon, Frederik Helbo, Lucienne Hellebosch, Lisa & Rune Henriksen, Michael Hensen, Lesley Holmes, Robby Hoskens **J** Loreta Jakonyte, Hango Janika, Jurian Jansen, Joan Joesting-Mahoney, Jakob Jürgensen **K** Paul Keenan, Shum Keith Kai Hay, Ruth Kitching, Helen Kopnina, Hermann Kudrass **L** Ilona Lablaika, Megan Layne, Una Lemeshonok **M** Paul Marcuccitti, Arthur Markham, Francesca Meloni, Edwin Mermans, Dean Meservy, Susanne Michaelsen, Adam Mills, Mike Mimirinis, Jordan Mitchell, Judy Moon **N** Beryl Nicholson, Roger Nierga Frisach **O** Paul Offermanns, Ricardo Olivares, Pal Erik Olsen, Andreas Ort, Bob Otness **P** Rolf Palmberg, Guido Paomees, Erlandas Paplauskis, Jan Pennington, Jakki Postlethwaite, Annika Prangli **R** Kent Raju, Andrew Rejman, Peter Roscoe, Kirstin Rupp **S** Ed Schlenk, Keno Schulte, Anna Sikala, Sidney Sirdiv, Signe Sorensen, Joonia Streng, Donald Sturyl **T** Niels Ten Oever, Lauren Thompson, Alice Tiritas, Rokas Tracevskis **V** Steffan Vaivars, Signild Vallgarda, Monique Van Den Broek, Luk Vanderlinden, Daan Vervoort, Rimas VisGirda **W** Henk Wardenaar, Jonas Wernli, John Wilks, Mark & Ulrike Wilson, Frankas Wurft **Y** Andrew Young, DC Young, Winston Yu

ACKNOWLEDGMENTS

Many thanks to the following for the use of their content:

Globe on back cover ©Mountain High Maps 1993 Digital Wisdom, Inc.

SEND US YOUR FEEDBACK

We love to hear from travellers – your comments keep us on our toes and help make our books better. Our well-travelled team reads every word on what you loved or loathed about this book. Although we cannot reply individually to postal submissions, we always guarantee that your feedback goes straight to the appropriate authors, in time for the next edition. Each person who sends us information is thanked in the next edition – and the most useful submissions are rewarded with a free book.

To send us your updates – and find out about Lonely Planet events, newsletters and travel news – visit our award-winning website: **www.lonelyplanet.com/feedback**.

Note: We may edit, reproduce and incorporate your comments in Lonely Planet products such as guidebooks, websites and digital products, so let us know if you don't want your comments reproduced or your name acknowledged. For a copy of our privacy policy visit www.lonelyplanet.com/privacy.

Index

ABBREVIATIONS

Est	Estonia
Kal	Kaliningrad
Lat	Latvia
Lith	Lithuania

A
A Le Coq Arena (Est) 88
A Le Coq Beer Museum (Est) 111
Abava Valley (Lat) 255-6
Abava Valley Nature Park (Lat) 184
Abruka (Est) 152
accommodation 381-3
activities 38-42, 383, *see also individual activities*
Adamkus, Valdas 271, 276
Aegna (Est) 90
Aglona Basilica (Lat) 241-2
air travel 393-5
  airlines 393-4
  airports 393-4
  to/from the Baltics 393-5
  within the Baltics 403
Alajõe (Est) 105
Alatskivi Castle (Est) 127
Alexander Nevsky Cathedral (Est) 75
Alexandr Nevsky Church (Lat) 199
Alūksne (Lat) 237
Alytus (Lith) 329
amber 35, 175, 282, 379
amber museums
  Kaliningrad 377-9
  Nida (Lith) 367
  Palanga (Lith) 357
  Vilnius (Lith) 297
Amber Road 21, 35
  Kaliningrad 379
  Latvia 175
  Lithuania 282
Ancient Bee-Keeping Museum (Lith) 320
Angla (Est) 145
animals 34
  see also individual animals

000 Map pages
000 Photograph pages

Antanas Mončys House Museum (Lith) 357
Anykščiai (Lith) 345-7
Āraiši (Lat) 234
Arēna New Music Festival (Lat) 267
Arsenāls Museum of Art (Lat) 191
art 32-3
  Estonia 58-9
  Latvia 183
  Lithuania 281
art galleries, *see* museums & galleries
Art Museum of Estonia 76
Art-Nouveau architecture 199, 8
arts 31, *see also individual arts*
ATMs 389
Aukštaitija National Park (Lith) 40, 283, 320-2, **321**

B
B&Bs 381-2
ballet 267
ballooning 230
Baltezers (Lat) 224
Baltic Beach Party (Lat) 16, 263, 267
Baltic culture 29-30, 36
Baltic Glint 59, 95-7, 102
Baltika Folklore Festival 16, 386-7
Balzāms 185
bargaining 389
Baroti Gallery (Lith) 350
basketball
  Estonia 54, 88
  Latvia 180
  Lithuania 278
Bauska (Lat) 244-6, **246**
beaches 34
  Giruliai (Lith) 351
  Järverand (Est) 148
  Jūrmala (Lat) 220
  Karklė (Lith) 351
  Kauksi (Est) 105
  Kloogaranna (Est) 92
  Laulasmaa (Est) 92
  Liepāja (Lat) 263
  Lohusalu (Est) 92
  Melnragė (Lith) 351
  Nida (Lith) 365
  Palanga (Lith) 357
  Pelguranna (Est) 78
  Pirita (Est) 77
  Smiltynė (Lith) 351
  Väna-Jõesuu (Est) 92
Bear Slayer 182
bears 60, 97
beer 36-7
  Estonia 63, 79, 111, 168
  Latvia 185
  Lithuania 285, 323, 345, 353
Beer Summer (Est) 79, 168
berrying 42
  Latvia 238
  Lithuania 285, 319, 320, 328
bicycle travel, *see* cycling
birds 34, *see also individual birds*
  Estonia 59-60, 134, 135, 140, 142, 152, 165
  Latvia 183
  Lithuania 365, 370
bird-watching 41-2
  Estonia 61, 135, 140, 142
  Latvia 41, 253, 254
  Lithuania 329, 365, 370, 371
Birgitta Festival (Est) 79
Bīriņi Castle (Lat) 226
Birštonas (Lith) 339, 373
Biržai Beer Festival (Lith) 345
Bishop's Castle (Est) 130
Black Nights Film Festival (Est) 16, 80, 169
Blues Festival (Est) 169
boat travel
  to/from the Baltics 400-3
  within the Baltics 404
bobsledding 41, 180, 230
books 15, 27, 30, 31, 32, *see also* literature
  Estonia 56
  Latvia 182
  Lithuania 276, 279, 285
border crossings 396
Braki (Lat) 238
Buļļuciems (Lat) 221
bungee jumping
  Latvia 230
  Lithuania 303
Burtnieki (Lat) 236
bus travel
  to/from the Baltics 396-7
  within the Baltics 404-5

bushwalking, *see* hiking
business hours 383

C

camping 382
canoeing 38-40
  Estonia 118-19
  Latvia 230, 235
  Lithuania 40, 320, 323, 324
Cape Kolka (Lat) 7, 253-4
car travel
  driving licence 405
  insurance 406
  permits 405-6
  rental 406
  road distance chart 407
  road rules 406-7
  to/from the Baltics 397-8
  within the Baltics 405-7
Castle Days Festival (Est) 148
castles
  Alatskivi (Est) 127
  Bauska (Lat) 245
  Bīriņi (Lat) 226
  Bishop's (Est) 130
  Cēsis (Lat) 233, **8**
  Dundaga (Lat) 255
  Island (Lith) 316-17, **7**
  Kaunas (Lith) 334
  Kuressaare (Est) 147-8, **6**
  Narva (Est) 104
  Rakvere (Est) 101
  Rīga (Lat) 191
  Toompea (Est) 75
  Turaida (Lat) 228, **202**
  Vastseliina (Est) 124
  Ventspils Livonian Order (Lat) 257
Cathedral of Christ the Saviour (Kal) 379
cathedrals, *see* churches & cathedrals
Centre of Europe Museum (Lith) 385
Čepkeliai Strict Nature Reserve (Lith) 283
Ceraukste (Lat) 246
Cēsis (Lat) 232-4, **233**, **8**
Chapel of the Blessed Mary (Lith) 297-8
children, travel with 383-4
  health 411-12
  Vilnius (Lith) 305
  Nemo Water Park (Lat) 221
  Rīga (Lat) 200-9
  Tallinn (Est) 79
Children's Gallery (Est) 79
Christ's Resurrection Basilica (Lith) 334
churches & cathedrals
  Aglona Basilica (Lat) 241-2
  Alexander Nevsky Cathedral (Est) 75
  Alexandr Nevsky Church (Lat) 199
  Cathedral of Christ the Saviour (Kal) 379
  Chapel of the Blessed Mary (Lith) 297-8
  Christ's Resurrection Basilica (Lith) 334
  Church of the Assumption (Lith) 298
  Dome Cathedral (Lat) 191
  Dome Church (Est) 75
  Evangelical Lutheran Church (Lith) 299
  gothic cathedral (Kal) 377
  Holy Spirit Church (Est) 69-72
  Holy Spirit Church (Lith) 298
  Holy Trinity Church (Lat) 259, 262-3
  Mary Queen of Peace Church (Lith) 351
  Old Gertrude Church (Lat) 199
  Orthodox Church of the Holy Spirit (Lith) 298
  Otepää Church (Est) 117-18
  Romanovs' Church (Lith) 300
  St Anne's Basilica (Lat) 263
  St Anne's Church (Lith) 297
  St Casimir's (Lith) 297
  St Gertrude Church (Lith) 335
  St John's Church (Est) 110
  St John's Church (Lat) 234
  St John's Church (Lith) 296, **207**
  St Joseph's Cathedral (Lat) 263
  St Katrīna's Church (Lat) 259
  St Michael the Archangel Church (Lith) 335, **208**
  St Nicholas' Church (Est) 74
  St Nicholas' Church (Lith) 299
  St Nicholas Russian Orthodox Church (Lat) 257
  St Olaf's Church (Est) 73-4, **202**
  St Peter & Paul's Cathedral (Lith) 339-40
  St Peter & Paul's Church (Lith) 299
  St Peter & St Paul's Cathedral (Lith) 333
  St Peter's Church (Lat) 191, **7**
  St Raphael's Church (Lith) 302
  St Teresa's Church (Lith) 298
  Sts Peter & Paul's Church (Est) 73
  Tartu Cathedral (Est) 111
  Ukrainian-Greek Catholic Church (Est) 74
  Vilnius Cathedral (Lith) 296, **207**
cinema
  Estonia 57-8
  Latvia 181
  Lithuania 280
Citizen's House Museum (Est) 101
City Concert Hall (Est) 88
City Gallery (Est) 77
City Museum (Est) 73
City Theatre (Est) 88
Čiurlionis, Mikalojus Konstantinas 280, 281, 32
classical music 280
climate 14, 384
Clock Museum (Lith) 350
Collishaw, Stephan 32
Communications Development Museum (Lith) 334
consulates, *see* embassies & consulates
cormorants 365
costs 14-15, 37
  discount cards 385-6
  Estonia 45
  food 387
  Internet access 388
  Latvia 173
  Lithuania 271
  tipping 389
courses 384-5
crafts 16, 267, 305, 306
credit cards 389
cross crafting 31, 341
culture
  Estonia 51-3
  Latvia 178-80
  Lithuania 276-8, **206**
Curonian Lagoon (Lith) 42, 362
Curonian Spit (Lith) 8, 16, 39, 347
Curonian Spit National Nature Museum (Lith) 351
Curonian Spit National Park (Lith) 41, 283, 362-70, **363**
customs regulations 385
  Estonia 167
  Latvia 265
  Lithuania 372
cycling 38, 39, 396, 403-4
  Estonia 39, 54, 98, 112, 118
  Latvia 39, 231, 235
  Lithuania 39, 317, 326, 342, 364, 367, 370

D

dance 32
dance festivals 16, 33, 80, 267
Danė River **208**
dangers & annoyances 385
Daugava Valley (Lat) 238-41
Daugavpils (Lat) 242-4, **243**
Days of the White Lady (Est) 16, 132, 169
diarrhoea 411
disabled travellers 385
discount cards 385-6
Dome Cathedral (Lat) 191
Dome Church (Est) 75
Draakoni Gallery (Est) 77
drinks 36-7, *see also* Balzāms, beer
- Estonia 63-4
- Latvia 185-6
- Lithuania 285

driving, *see* car travel
driving licence 405
Druskininkai (Lith) 324-8, **325**
Dundaga (Lat) 255
Dusetos (Lith) 324
Dzūkija National Park (Lith) 283, 328-9

E

economy 22, 23, 45
- Estonia 52
- Latvia 173
- Lithuania 276, 277

electricity
- Estonia 168
- Latvia 266
- Lithuania 373

Elva (Est) 115-16
Elva Vitipalu (Est) 61, 115
embassies & consulates 386
- Estonia 167-8
- Latvia 266
- Lithuania 372-3

emergency services, *see inside front cover*
Endla Nature Reserve (Est) 61, 105
Endla Theatre (Est) 159
environmental issues 16, 32, 34-5
- Estonia 61-2
- Latvia 183-4
- Lithuania 284

Estonia 44-170, **47**
- arts 54-9
- citizenship 53
- costs 45
- culture 51-3
- drinks 63-4
- economy 52
- embassies & consulates 167-8
- environmental issues 61-2
- etiquette 64
- EU 45, 53
- festivals 168-70
- food 62-3, 64
- history 46-51
- Internet access 169
- Internet resources 169
- itineraries 45
- language 63, 413-16
- maps 170
- money 170, *see also inside front cover*
- multiculturalism 52-3
- music 54-5
- national parks & reserves 60-2
- politics 45-6
- population 52
- postal services 170
- public holidays 169
- religion 54
- sport 53-4
- telephone services 170
- tourist information 170
- wildlife 59-60, 97, **201**

Estonia Theatre & Concert Hall 87-8, **204**
Estonian Drama Theatre 88
Estonian Literary Museum 51, 111
Estonian Museum of Architecture 77
Estonian Music Days 168
Estonian National Museum 111
Estonian Puppet Theatre 79, 88
etiquette 16, 30
- Estonia 64
- Latvia 178
- Lithuania 277, 287

EU 22, 29
- Estonia 45, 53
- Latvia 173, 175, 178
- Lithuania 271, 276, 284

Eurovision Song Contest 29, 32, 182
Evangelical Lutheran Church (Lith) 299
exchange rates, *see inside front cover*

F

farmstays 382
ferry travel
- ferry routes 399
- to/from the Baltics 400-3
- within the Baltics 404

festivals 15-16, 33, 386-7
- Arena New Music Festival (Lat) 267
- Baltic Beach Party (Lat) 16, 263, 267
- Baltika Folklore Festival 16, 386-7
- Beer Summer (Est) 79, 168
- Birgitta Festival (Est) 79
- Birštonas Jazz (Lith) 339, 373
- Biržai Beer Festival (Lith) 345
- Black Nights Film Festival (Est) 16, 80, 169
- Blues Festival (Est) 169
- Castle Days Festival (Est) 148
- Dance Festival (Est) 80
- Days of the White Lady (Est) 16, 132, 169
- Estonia 168-70
- Estonian Music Days 168
- Festival of Ancient Music (Lat) 267
- International Baltic Ballet Festival (Lat) 267
- International Jazz Festival (Lith) 336
- International Organ Music Festival (Est) 169
- International Puppet Festival (Est) 168
- Jazzkaar (Est) 16, 79, 168
- Kaziukas Crafts Fair (Lith) 16, 306
- Klaipėda Sea Festival (Lith) 347
- Kuressaare Castle Days (Est) 169
- Lāčplēsis Day (Lat) 267
- Ladies in Jazz Festival (Est) 169
- Latvia 266-7
- Lithuania 373-4
- Matsalu Nature Film Festival (Est) 169
- Midsummer 16, 17, 168, 179
- Muhu Future Music Festival (Est) 169
- Old Town Days (Est) 16, 79
- Opera Music Festival (Lat) 267
- Pärnu International Documentary & Anthropology Film Festival (Est) 158, 169
- Saaremaa Summer Festival (Est) 169
- Student Jazz Festival (Est) 168
- Summer Extravaganza Neringa (Lith) 363
- Tallinn Rock Summer (Est) 169
- Visagino Country (Lith) 16, 322, 374

000 Map pages
000 Photograph pages

film festivals 16, 80, 158, 169
fishing 42, 241, 352, 370
food 35-6, 387
costs 37
Estonia 62-3, 64
Latvia 184-5, 186-7
Lithuania 284-7
football
Estonia 53-4, 88
Latvia 217
Forest Brothers (Est) 50, 166

G
galleries, *see* museums & galleries
Gauja National Park (Lat) 183, 184, 226, 230-1, **227**
gay rights 22-3, 175
gay travellers 387
geography 33-4
Estonia 59
Latvia 183
Lithuania 282
gothic cathedral (Kal) 377
grey herons 365
Grūtas Park (Lith) 326
guesthouses 382
Gulbene (Lat) 237

H
Haanja Nature Park (Est) 122
Haapsalu (Est) 130-3, **131**
Harju (Est) 142
health 385, 410-12
Hiiumaa (Est) 39, 135-42, **136**
Hiiumaa Islets Landscape Reserve (Est) 61, 142
hiking
Estonia 98, 111, 112, 135
Latvia 253
Hill of Crosses (Lith) 5, 341-2
history 23-9
Estonia 46-51
Germanic rule 24-5
Latvia 175-8
Lithuania 273-6
Livonian War 48
Postindependence 28-9
Swedish rule 48
WWI 49
WWII 50
History Museum of Latvia 191
hitching 407-8
holidays 387
Holocaust Museum (Lith) 301
Holy Spirit Church (Est) 69-72
Holy Spirit Church (Lith) 298
Holy Trinity Church (Lat) 259, 262-3
horse racing 373
horse riding
Estonia 99
Latvia 231, 236, 241
hostels 382
hotels 382-3
House of Blackheads (Lat) 194, 7
Hullo (Est) 134

I
ice hockey 180, 217
ice-fishing 352, 370
Ignalina Nuclear Power Plant (Lith) 322
independence
Estonia 49-51
Latvia 176-7
Lithuania 275
insurance
health 410
travel 387
vehicle 406
International Baltic Ballet Festival (Lat) 267
International Jazz Festival (Lith) 336
International Organ Music Festival (Est) 169
International Puppet Festival (Est) 168
Internet access 387-8
Estonia 169
Latvia 267
Lithuania 374
Internet resources 15, 410-11
Estonia 169
Latvia 267
Lithuania 374
Island Castle (Lith) 316-17, 7
itineraries 12-13, 18-21
Estonia 45
Latvia 173
Lithuania 271

J
Jaanipäev, *see* Midsummer
Jägala (Est) 94
Jasmuiža (Lat) 242
jazz 32, 168, 280, 374
Jazzkaar (Est) 16, 79, 168
Jēkabpils (Lat) 240
Jelgava (Lat) 248-50
Jewish history
Latvia 198, 220, 245
Lithuania 274, 275, 296
Jugendstil 199, 8
Juodkrantė (Lith) 364-5
Jūrmala (Lat) 220-4, **222-3**

K
Kaali (Est) 145
Kadriorg Palace (Est) 76
Käina (Est) 140
Käina Bay Bird Reserve (Est) 61, 140
Kalev Stadium (Est) 88
Kalevipoeg 56
Kaliningrad 377-80, **378**
accommodation 379
attractions 377
drinking 379-80
food 379-80
tours 377
travel to/from 380
travel within 380
Kallaste (Est) 127
Kandava (Lat) 255
Kant, Emanuel 377
Kaplinski, Jaan 31
Karaite people 278, 296, 316
Karaites Ethnographic Museum (Lith) 316
Kärdla (Est) 137-8, **138**
Karklė (Lith) 351
Karosta (Lat) 262
Karula National Park (Est) 123
Kassari (Est) 140-2
Kaunas (Lith) 331-9, **332**, **206**, **208**
Kaziukas Crafts Fair (Lith) 16, 306
Ķegums (Lat) 238
Ķemeri (Lat) 253
Ķemeri National Park (Lat) 184, 252-3
Kernavė (Lith) 318
Kihnu (Est) 161-2
kiiking 54
Kiipsaare lighthouse (Est) 151
Klaipėda (Lith) 347-55, **348, 207**
Koguva (Est) 153
Koknese (Lat) 240
Kolka (Lat) 253-4
Kolkja (Est) 127
konick horses 183
Kõpu lighthouse (Est) 139
Košrags (Lat) 254
Kostabi, Mark Kalev 59
Kreutzwald, Friedrich Reinhold 120-1
Kreutzwald Memorial Museum (Est) 121
Kross, Jan 31
Krustkalni Nature Reserve (Lat) 184, 238

INDEX

Krustpils (Lat) 240
Kuldīga (Lat) 259-61, **260**
Kuremäe (Est) 104-5
Kuressaare (Est)146-50, **146**, **6**, **202**
Kuressaare Castle (Est) 147-8, **6**
Kurzeme (Lat) 248-65, **249**

L
Laar, Mart 51
Labanoros Regional Park (Lith) 283, 323
Lāčplēsis Day (Lat) 267
Ladies in Jazz Festival (Est) 169
Lahemaa National Park (Est) 6, 61, 95-101, **96**
Lake Engure (Lat) 41, 253
Lake Peipsi (Est) 59
Lake Peipsi (North; Est) 105
Lake Peipsi (South; Est) 127-8
language
  Estonian 63, 413-16
  Latvian 186, 416-19
  Lithuanian 286, 420-3
  Võro-Seto 108, 124
Latgale (Lat) 238-44, **239**
Latgale Upland (Lat) 241-2
Latvia 172-268, **174**
  arts 181-3
  costs 173
  culture 178-80
  drinks 185-6
  economy 173
  embassies & consulates 266
  environmental issues 184
  etiquette 178
  EU 173, 175, 178
  festivals 266-7
  food 184-5, 186-7
  history 175-8
  independence 176-7
  Internet access 267
  Internet resources 267
  itineraries 173
  language 186, 416-19
  literature 182
  maps 267-8
  money 268, *see also inside front cover*
  multiculturalism 179-80
  music 182-3
  national parks & reserves 183
  NATO 175, 177
  politics 173-5, 177-8
  population 178-9
  postal services 268
  public holidays 267
  religion 180
  sport 180
  telephone services 268
  tourist information 268
  wildlife 183
Latvian Ethnographic Open-Air Museum 199-200
Latvian Photography Museum 195
legal matters 388
lesbian rights 22-3, 175
lesbian travellers 387
Lielvārde (Lat) 240
Liepāja (Lat) 261-5, **262**
Līgatne (Lat) 232
Liiv Museum (Est) 127
Liškiava (Lith) 328
literature 31-2, *see also* books
  Bear Slayer 182
  Estonia 55-6
  Kalevipoeg 56
  Lithuania 279-80
  Latvia 182
Lithuania 270-375, **272**
  arts 279-82, 351
  Centre of Europe 318
  costs 271
  culture 276-8, **206**
  dangers & annoyances 320
  economy 276, 277
  embassies & consulates 372-3
  environmental issues 284
  etiquette 277, 287
  EU 271, 276, 284
  festivals 373-4
  food 284-7
  Hill of Crosses 341-2
  history 273-6
  Internet access 374
  Internet resources 374
  itineraries 271
  language 286, 420-3
  maps 375
  money 375, *see also inside front cover*
  multiculturalism 278
  music 280-1
  national parks & reserves 283-4
  NATO 271-3, 340
  Old Town 296
  politics 271-3, 275-6
  population 277-9
  postal services 375
  public holidays 374
  religion 278-9
  spas 327
  sport 278
  telephone services 375
  tourist information 375
  wildlife 282-3
Lithuanian Energy Museum 302
Lithuanian Ethnocosmology Museum 323
Lithuanian Sea Museum 351
Lithuanian State Jewish Museum of Vilna Gaon 301
local transport 408
Luhasoo Nature Study Trail (Est) 123

M
Maarjamäe Palace (Est) 76
Maironis 279, 333
Maironis Lithuanian Literary Museum (Lith) 333
maps 388
  Estonia 170
  Latvia 267-8
  Lithuania 375
Marijampolė (Lith) 329
Maritime Museum (Est) 74
Mary Queen of Peace Church (Lith) 351
Matsalu Nature Film Festival (Est) 169
Matsalu Nature Reserve (Est) 61, 135
Mazirbe (Lat) 254
Mazsalaca (Lat) 226
Medicine & Pharmaceutical History Museum (Lith) 334
Melnragė (Lith) 351
Merkinė (Lith) 328
metric conversions, *see inside front cover*
Metsavennad, *see* Forest Brothers
Mežotne Palace (Lat) 247-8
Mickiewicz, Adam 274, 279, 297
Mickiewicz Memorial Apartment Museum (Lith) 297
Midsummer 16, 17, 168, 179
Mikkel Museum (Est) 76
Military Museum of Vytautas the Great (Lith) 335
MK Čiurlionis Memorial Museum (Lith) 325
Molėtai (Lith) 323
money 388-9, *see also inside front cover*
  Estonia 170
  Latvia 268
  Lithuania 375

000 Map pages
000 Photograph pages

Moricsala Nature Reserve (Lat) 184, 251
motorcycle travel
insurance 406
driving licence 405
permits 405-6
road rules 406-7
to/from the Baltics 397-8
within the Baltics 405-7
M/S *Estonia* 141
Muhu (Est) 39, 143, 152-3
Muhu Future Music Festival (Est) 169
multiculturalism 30-1
Estonia 52-3
Latvia 179-80
Lithuania 278
museums & galleries
A Le Coq Beer Museum (Est) 111
Amber Gallery Museum (Nida; Lith) 367
Amber Museum (Kal) 377-9
Amber Museum (Palanga; Lith) 357
Amber Museum-Gallery (Vilnius; Lith) 297
Amber Processing Gallery (Palanga; Lith) 357
Ancient Bee-Keeping Museum (Lith) 320
Antanas Mončys House Museum (Lith) 357
Arsenāls Museum of Art 191
Art Museum of Estonia 76
Baroti Gallery (Lith) 350
Centre of Europe Museum (Lith) 385
Children's Gallery (Est) 79
Citizen's House Museum (Est) 101
City Gallery (Est) 77
City Museum (Est) 73
Clock Museum (Lith) 350
Communications Development Museum (Lith) 334
Curonian Spit National Nature Museum (Lith) 351
Draakoni Gallery (Est) 77
Estonian Literary Museum 111
Estonian Museum of Architecture 77
Estonian National Museum 111
History Museum of Latvia 191
Holocaust Museum (Lith) 301
Karaites Ethnographic Museum (Lith) 316
Kaunas Picture Gallery (Lith) 335
Kernavė Archaeological & Historical Museum (Lith) 318
Klaipėda Art Exhibition Palace (Lith) 350
Latvian Ethnographic Open-Air Museum 199-200
Latvian Photography Museum 195
Liepāja History & Art Museum (Lat) 263
Liiv Museum (Est) 127
Lithuanian Energy Museum 302
Lithuanian Ethnocosmology Museum 323
Lithuanian Sea Museum 351
Lithuanian State Jewish Museum of Vilna Gaon 301
Maironis Lithuanian Literary Museum 333
Maritime Museum (Est) 74
Medicine & Pharmaceutical History Museum (Lith) 334
Mickiewicz Memorial Apartment Museum (Lith) 297
Mikkel Museum (Est) 76
Military Museum of Vytautas the Great (Lith) 335
MK Čiurlionis Memorial Museum (Lith) 325
Museum of Applied Arts (Lith) 294
Museum of Decorative & Applied Arts (Lat) 195
Museum of Deportation & Resistance (Lith) 334
Museum of Devils (Lith) 335
Museum of Estonian Photography 69
Museum of Foreign Art (Est) 76
Museum of Foreign Art (Lat) 191
Museum of Genocide Victims (Lith) 302
Museum of Occupation & Fight for Freedom (Est) 75
Museum of Occupation in Latvia 193
Museum of the Estonian Swedes 131
Museum of the History of Rīga & Navigation 191
Museum of Unique Stones (Lith) 360
Museum of War (Lat) 195
Narrow-Gauge Railway Museum (Lith) 345
National Čiurlionis Art Museum (Lith) 335
National Museum of Lithuania 295
Neringa History Museum (Lith) 367
Occupation Museum (Lat) 261-2
Open Air Museum (Est) 78
Open-Air Museum of Lithuania 339
Paneriai Museum (Lith) 315
Pärnu Museum (Est) 157
Pärnu New Art Museum (Est) 157
Pedvāle Open-Air Art Museum (Lat) 255
Peter the Great Home Museum (Est) 76
Railway Museum (Est) 131
Rakvere Museum (Est) 101
Regional Studies & Art Museum (Lat) 243
Rīga Motor Museum (Lat) 199
Russian Old Believers' Museum (Est) 127
Setu Farm Museum (Est) 126
Setu House Museum (Est) 125
Šiauliai Bicycle Museum (Lith) 339
Šiauliai Museum of Cats (Lith) 339
Šiauliai Photography Museum (Lith) 339
Šiauliai Radio & TV Museum (Lith) 339
Sillamäe Museum (Est) 103
State History Museum (Est) 73
State Museum of Art (Lat) 197
Tadas Ivanauskas Zoological Museum (Lith) 335
Tallinn Art Hall (Est) 77
Tammsaare Museum (Est) 76
Tartu Sports Museum (Est) 110
Theatre, Music & Cinema Museum (Lith) 298
Thomas Mann Memorial Museum (Lith) 367
Toy Museum (Est) 111
Turaida Museum Reserve (Lat) 228
Vaal (Est) 77
Viljandi Museum (Est) 164
Vilnius Picture Gallery (Lith) 297
World Ocean Museum (Kal) 377
mushrooming 42
Latvia 238
Lithuania 285, 319, 320, 328, **208**
music 31, 32, 33
classical 280
Estonia 54-5
Eurovision Song Contest 29, 32, 182

INDEX

music *continued*
jazz 32, 280
Latvia 182-3
Lithuania 280-1
pop 32, 280
rock 32
music festivals 33
Estonia 16, 79, 168, 169
Latvia 267
Lithuania 336, 339, 373, 374
Mustvee (Est) 105

N
Naglių Strict Nature Reserve (Lith) 365
Naissaar (Est) 90
Narrow-Gauge Railway Museum (Lith) 345
Narva (Est) 103-4
Narva-Jõesuu (Est) 104
National Čiurlionis Art Museum (Lith) 335
National Ethnic Arts & Crafts Fair (Lat) 267
National Museum of Lithuania 295
national parks & reserves
Aukštaitija National Park (Lith) 40, 283, 320-2, **321**
Čepkeliai Strict Nature Reserve (Lith) 283
Curonian Spit National Park (Lith) 41, 283, 362-70, **363**
Dzūkija National Park (Lith) 283, 328-9
Elva Vitapalu (Est) 61, 105
Endla Nature Reserve (Est) 61, 105
Estonia 60-2
Gauja National Park (Lat) 183, 184, 226, 230-1, **227**
Haanja Nature Park (Est) 122
Hiiumaa Islets Landscape Reserve (Est) 61, 142
Käina Bay Bird Reserve (Est) 61, 140
Karula National Park (Est) 123
Ķemeri National Park (Lat) 184, 252-3
Krustkalni Nature Reserve (Lat) 184, 238
Labanoros Regional Park (Lith) 283, 323
Lahemaa National Park (Est) 61, 95-101, **96**, **6**
Latvia 183
Ligatne Education & Recreation Park (Lat) 232
Lithuania 283-4
Luhasoo Nature Study Trail (Est) 123
Matsalu Nature Reserve (Est) 61, 135
Moricsala Nature Reserve (Lat) 184, 251
Naglių Strict Nature Reserve (Lith) 365
Nemunas Crook Regional Park (Lith) 283, 339
Nemunas Delta Regional Park (Lith) 41, 42, 283, 370-1
Nigula Nature Reserve (Est) 61, 161
Rebala Reserve (Est) 94
Slītere National Park (Lat) 183, 184, 254-5
Soomaa National Park (Est) 40, 61, 165
Teiči Nature Reserve (Lat) 184, 238
Trakai Historical National Park (Lith) 283
Viidumäe Nature Reserve (Est) 61, 150-1
Vilsandi National Park (Est) 61, 152
Žemaitija National Park (Lith) 283, 360-2
Žuvintas Nature Reserve (Lith) 283, 329
NATO 22, 29
Latvia 175, 177
Lithuania 271-3
nature reserves, *see* national parks & reserves
Navitrolla 58-9
Nemirseta (Lith) 355
Nemo Water Park (Lat) 221
Nemunas Crook Regional Park (Lith) 283, 339
Nemunas Delta (Lith) 370-2
Nemunas Delta Regional Park (Lith) 41, 42, 283, 370-1
Neringa History Museum (Lith) 367
newspapers
Estonia 168
Latvia 266
Lithuania 373
Nida (Lith) 365-70, **366**
Nigula Nature Reserve (Est) 61, 161
Noarootsi Peninsula (Est) 134

O
Obinitsa (Est) 125-6
Occupation Museum (Lat) 261-2
Old Believers, *see* Russian Old Believers
Old Gertrude Church (Lat) 199
Old Town Days (Est) 16, 79
Ontika (Est) 102
Open Air Museum (Est) 78
Open-Air Museum of Lithuania 339
Opera Music Festival (Lat) 267
Orissaare (Est) 145
Orthodox Church of the Holy Spirit (Lith) 298
Otepää (Est) 41, 116-19, **117**

P
Padise (Est) 93
Paksas, Rolandas 270, 271, 276
palaces
Jelgava Palace (Lat) 248
Kadriorg Palace (Est) 76
Maarjamäe Palace (Est) 76
Mežotne Palace (Lat) 247-8
Presidential Palace (Lith) 297
Presidential Palace of Lithuania 333
Royal Palace (Lith) 294
Rundāle Palace (Lat) 246-7
Palanga (Lith) 355-60, **356**
Paldiski (Est) 93
Paneriai (Lith) 315
Panevėžys (Lith) 343-5, **344**
Parnidis Dune (Lith) 365, 368
Pärnu (Est) 155-61, **156**, **6**
Pärnu Film Festival (Est) 158
Pärnu International Documentary & Anthropology Film Festival (Est) 169
Pärnu Museum (Est) 157
Pärnu New Art Museum (Est) 157
Pärt, Arvo 32
passports 393
Pedvāle (Lat) 255-6
Pedvāle Open-Air Art Museum (Lat) 255
Peter the Great Home Museum (Est) 76
Piirisaar (Est) 115
Piusa (Est) 125-6
planning 14-17, *see also* itineraries
discount cards 385-6
holidays 387
plants 60, 97, 151
Plateliai (Lith) 361
Plungė (Lith) 361
Podnieks, Juris 181
Pöide (Est) 145

000 Map pages
000 Photograph pages

Põltsamaa (Est) 165-7
Põlva (Est) 119-20
population 29
Estonia 52
Latvia 178
Lithuania 277-9
postal services 389-90
Estonia 170
Latvia 268
Lithuania 375
Presidential Palace (Lith) 297
Presidential Palace of Lithuania 333
public holidays
Estonia 169
Latvia 267
Lithuania 374
Pühajärv 118
Pumpurs, Andrējs 182, 240
Purtse (Est) 102

R

radio
Estonia 168
Latvia 266
Lithuania 373
Radviliškis (Lith) 343
Radvilos' Palace (Lith) 299
rafting 38-40
Railway Museum (Est) 131
railway routes 399
Rainis, Jānis 31, 221, 241, 242
Raja (Est) 105
Rakvere (Est) 101-2
Rastrelli, Bartolomeo 247, 248
Rebala Reserve (Est) 94
Regional Studies & Art Museum (Lat) 243
religion 31
Estonia 54
Latvia 180
Lithuania 278-9
Rēzekne (Lat) 241
Rīga (Lat) 187-224, **188**, **192-3**, **204**, **205**
accommodation 209-11
attractions 189, 190-200
bookshops 190
drinking 214-16
emergency services 190
entertainment 216-17
festivals 209
food 211-14
history 187-9
Internet access 190
shopping 217, 218
tourist information 190
tours 209
travel to/from 217-20
travel within 220
walking tour 200, **200**
Rīga Castle (Lat) 191
Rīga Motor Museum (Lat) 199
Rīga Opera Festival (Lat) 267
Roja (Lat) 253
Roma people 278, 296
Romanovs' Church (Lith) 300
Rõuge (Est) 122-3
Royal Palace (Lith) 294
Ruhnu (Est) 162
Rūjiena (Lat) 226
Rumšiškės (Lith) 339
Rundāle Palace (Lat) 246-7
Rusnė (Lith) 371
Russian Old Believers 54, 115, 127
Russian Old Believers' Museum (Est) 127
Russian rule 26, 274
Rüütel, Arnold 45

S

Saaremaa (Est) 39, 142-52, 169, **143**
Sabile (Lat) 255
St Anne's Basilica (Lat) 263
St Anne's Church (Lith) 297
St Casimir's (Lith) 297
St Casimir's Day (Lith) 373
St Gertrude Church (Lith) 335
St John's Church (Est) 110
St John's Church (Lat) 234
St John's Church (Lith) 296, **207**
St John's Day (Est) 168
St Joseph's Cathedral (Lat) 263
St Katrīna's Church (Lat) 259
St Michael the Archangel Church (Lith) 335, **208**
St Nicholas' Church (Est) 74
St Nicholas' Church (Lith) 299
St Nicholas Russian Orthodox Church (Lat) 257
St Olaf's Church (Est) 73-4, **202**
St Peter & Paul's Cathedral (Lith) 339-40
St Peter & Paul's Church (Lith) 299
St Peter & St Paul's Cathedral (Lith) 333
St Peter's Church (Lat) 191, **7**
St Raphael's Church (Lith) 302
St Teresa's Church (Lith) 298
Sts Peter & Paul's Church (Est) 73
Salacgrīva (Lat) 224
Saulkrasti (Lat) 224
saunas 40, 78
Setu Farm Museum (Est) 126
Setu House Museum (Est) 125
Setu people (Est) 53, 124-5, 126
Setumaa (Est) 124-7
shopping 390
Šiauliai (Lith) 339-43, **340**
Sigulda (Lat) 41, 227-32, **229**
Sillamäe (Est) 103
skiing 40-1
Estonia 118
Latvia 230, 234, 235-6, 256
Slītere National Park (Lat) 183, 184, 254-5
Smiltynė (Lith) 350-1
snowboarding 40-1
soccer, *see* football
song festivals 16, 33
Soomaa National Park (Est) 40, 61, 165
Sõrve Peninsula (Est) 150
Soviet rule 23, 27, 28, 50
spa hotels 383
spas 327
sport, *see also individual sports*
Estonia 53-4
Latvia 180
Lithuania 278
Stalin World (Lith) 326
Stāmeriena (Lat) 237
State History Museum (Est) 73
State Museum of Art (Lat) 197
storks 34, 41, 60, 97, 183, 282, 319
Student Jazz Festival (Est) 168
Summer Extravaganza Neringa (Lith) 363
Suur Munamägi (Est) 137
Suuremõisa (Est) 137
Šventoji (Lith) 355
Swedish Gate (Lat) 195
Swedish rule 25, 48

T

Tadas Ivanauskas Zoological Museum (Lith) 335
Taebla (Est) 133
Taevaskoja (Est) 120
Tahkuna Peninsula (Est) 139
Tallinn (Est) 64-94, **66-7**, **70-1**, **92**
accommodation 80-2
activities 78-9
attractions 69-78
bookshops 67
drinking 86-7
emergency services 68

Tallinn (Est) *continued*
entertainment 87-8
festivals 79-80
food 82-6
history 65
Internet access 67
Old Town 69-75, **201**
shopping 88-9, 201
tourist information 68-9
tours 79
travel to/from 89-91
travel within 91
Tallinn Art Hall (Est) 77
Tallinn Old Town Days (Est) 168
Tallinn Rock Summer (Est) 169
Talsi (Lat) 251-2, **252**
Tammsaare, Anton Hansen 31
Tammsaare Museum (Est) 76
Tartu (Est) 106-15, **109**, 202
Tartu Ski Marathon (Est) 168
Tartu Student Days (Est) 168
taxis 408
Teiči Nature Reserve (Lat) 184, 238
telephone services 390
Estonia 170
Latvia 268
Lithuania 375
theatre
Estonia 56-7
Latvia 217
Lithuania 281-2
Theatre, Music & Cinema Museum (Lith) 298
theatres
City Concert Hall (Est) 88
City Theatre (Est) 88
Daile Theatre (Lat) 217
Endla Theatre (Est) 159
Estonia Theatre & Concert Hall 87-8
Estonian Drama Theatre 88
Estonian Puppet Theatre 79, 88
Lithuanian National Drama Theatre 312
New Rīga Theatre (Lat) 217
Opera & Ballet Theatre (Lith) 312
Oskaras Koršunovas Theatre (Lith) 312
Russian Drama Theatre (Lat) 217
Small Theatre of Vilnius (Lith) 312
Von Krahl Theatre (Est) 88
Youth Theatre (Lith) 312
theft 385
Thomas Mann Memorial Museum (Lith) 367
time 390-1
tipping 389
Toila (Est) 102
toilets 391
Toolse (Est) 102
Toompea Castle (Est) 75
Tori (Est) 160-1
tourist information 391
Estonia 170
Latvia 268
Lithuania 375
tours 409
Toy Museum (Est) 111
train travel
railway routes 399
to/from the Baltics 398-400
within the Baltics 408
Trakai (Lith) 204, 315-18, **316**
Trakai Historical National Park (Lith) 283
traveller's cheques 389
trekking, *see* hiking
Tukums (Lat) 250-1, 267
Turaida Castle (Lat) 228, **202**
Turaida Museum Reserve (Lat) 228
TV
Estonia 168
Latvia 266
Lithuania 373

U

Ukrainian-Greek Catholic Church (Est) 74
Unesco World Heritage Sights 21, 31, 32, 33
Estonia 161
Latvia 178, 187, 199
Lithuania 287, 296, 318, 341
Utena (Lith) 323-4
Užgavėnės (Lith) 373
Užupis Republic (Lith) 298

V

Vaal (Est) 77
vaccinations 410
Vaide (Lat) 254
Vīķe-Freiberga, Vaira 175
Valaste (Est) 102
Valga (Est) 124
Valka (Lat) 236-7
Valmiera (Lat) 234-6, **235**
Varėna (Lith) 328
Värska (Est) 126-7
Vasknarva (Est) 105
Vastseliina Castle (Est) 124
Vėlinės (All Souls' Day) 374
Ventės Ragas (Lith) 371
Ventspils (Lat) 256-9, **257**
video
Estonia 168
Latvia 266
Lithuania 373
Vidzeme (Lat) 224-38, **225**
Vidzeme Upland (Lat) 237-8
Viidumäe Nature Reserve (Est) 61, 150-1
Viljandi (Est) 162-5, 169, **163**
Viljandi Museum (Est) 164
Vilnius (Lith) 287-318, **288-9**, **292-3**
accommodation 306-8
attractions 294-303
bookshops 290
dangers & annoyances 291
drinking 311-12
emergency services 291
entertainment 312
festivals 306
food 308-11
history 287
Internet access 290
Jewish history 296, 300-1
New Town 206
Old Town 296-9
shopping 312-13
tourist information 291
tours 305-6
travel to/from 313-14
travel within 314-15
Užupis Republic 298
walking tour 304-5, **304**
Vilnius Cathedral (Lith) 207, **296**
Vilnius City Days (Lith) 374
Vilnius Jazz Festival (Lith) 374
Vilnius Picture Gallery (Lith) 297
Vilnius Summer Music Festival (Lith) 373
Vilsandi (Est) 152
Vilsandi National Park (Est) 61, 152
Visaginas (Lith) 322
Visagino Country (Lith) 16, 322, 374
visas 391-2, *see also* border crossings
Von Krahl Theatre (Est) 88
Võporzova (Est) 126

000 Map pages
000 Photograph pages

Vormsi (Est) 134-5, 136
Võru (Est) 120-2, **121**

W
water, drinking 411
waterparks 221
weights & measures, *see also inside front cover*
  Estonia 168
  Latvia 266
  Lithuania 373
wildlife 34, *see also individual animals*
  Estonia 59-60, 97, **201**
  Lithuania 282-3
  Latvia 183
women travellers 390, 392, 412
work 392
World Heritage Sights 21, 31, 32, 33
  Estonia 161
  Latvia 178, 187, 199
  Lithuania 287, 296, 318, 341
World Music Days (Est) 168
World Ocean Museum (Kal) 377

Z
Zappa, Frank 287, 299
Žemaičių Kalvarija Church Festival (Lith) 374
Žemaitija National Park (Lith) 283, 360-2
Zemgale (Lat) 244-8, **245**
Zervynos (Lith) 328
Žuvintas Nature Reserve (Lith) 283, 329

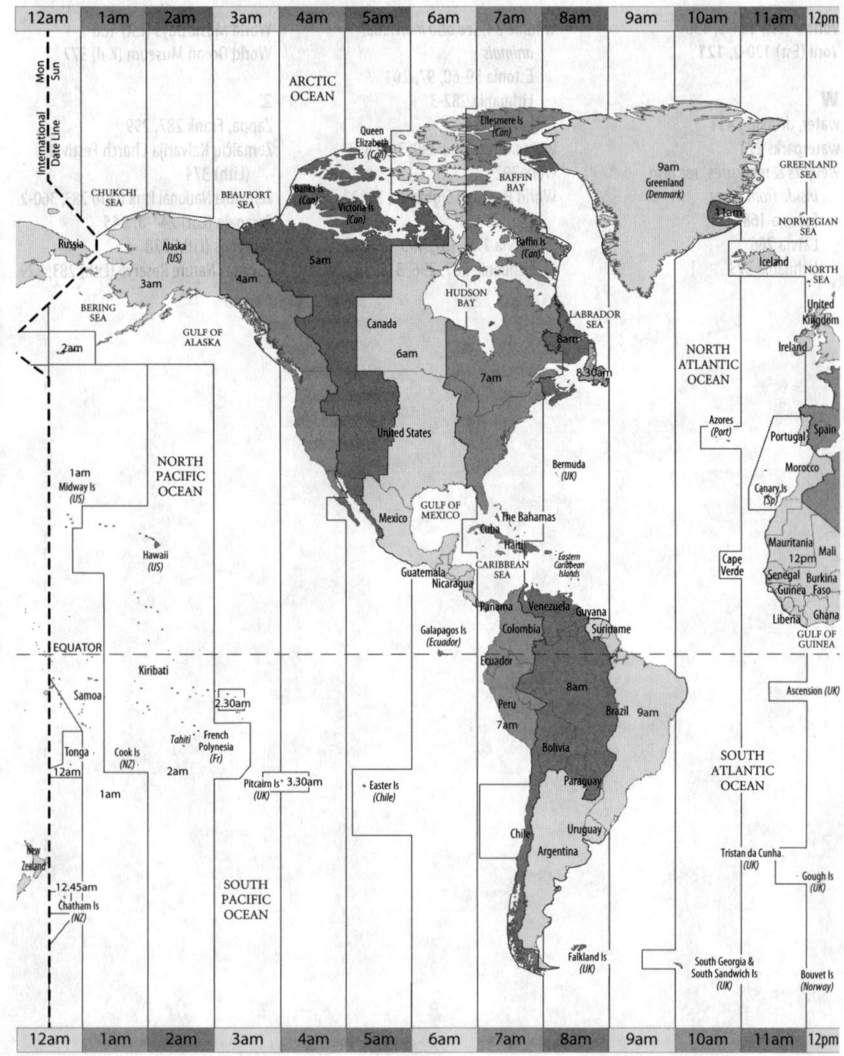
12am
1am
2am
3am
4am
5am
6am
7am
8am
9am
10am
11am
12pm
Mon
Sun
International Date Line
ARCTIC OCEAN
Queen Elizabeth Is (Can)
Ellesmere Is (Can)
BAFFIN BAY
9am
Greenland (Denmark)
GREENLAND SEA
CHUKCHI SEA
BEAUFORT SEA
Banks Is (Can)
Victoria Is (Can)
11am
NORWEGIAN SEA
Russia
Alaska (US)
5am
4am
3am
Baffin Is (Can)
Iceland
NORTH SEA
BERING SEA
HUDSON BAY
United Kingdom
GULF OF ALASKA
Canada
LABRADOR SEA
2am
6am
8am
Ireland
8.30am
7am
NORTH ATLANTIC OCEAN
United States
Azores (Port)
Portugal
Spain
NORTH PACIFIC OCEAN
Bermuda (UK)
Morocco
1am
Midway Is (US)
Canary Is (Sp)
GULF OF MEXICO
Mexico
The Bahamas
Cuba
Haiti
Hawaii (US)
Eastern Caribbean Islands
Mauritania
Mali
12pm
Guatemala
CARIBBEAN SEA
Cape Verde
Nicaragua
Senegal
Burkina Faso
Guinea
Panama
Venezuela
Guyana
Liberia
Ghana
Colombia
Suriname
Galapagos Is (Ecuador)
GULF OF GUINEA
EQUATOR
Ecuador
Kiribati
8am
Samoa
2.30am
Ascension (UK)
Peru
Brazil
9am
7am
French Polynesia (Fr)
Tahiti
Bolivia
SOUTH ATLANTIC OCEAN
Tonga
Cook Is (NZ)
12am
2am
Pitcairn Is (UK)
3.30am
Easter Is (Chile)
Paraguay
1am
Uruguay
Chile
Argentina
Tristan da Cunha (UK)
New Zealand
Gough Is (UK)
12.45am
Chatham Is (NZ)
SOUTH PACIFIC OCEAN
Falkland Is (UK)
South Georgia & South Sandwich Is (UK)
Bouvet Is (Norway)

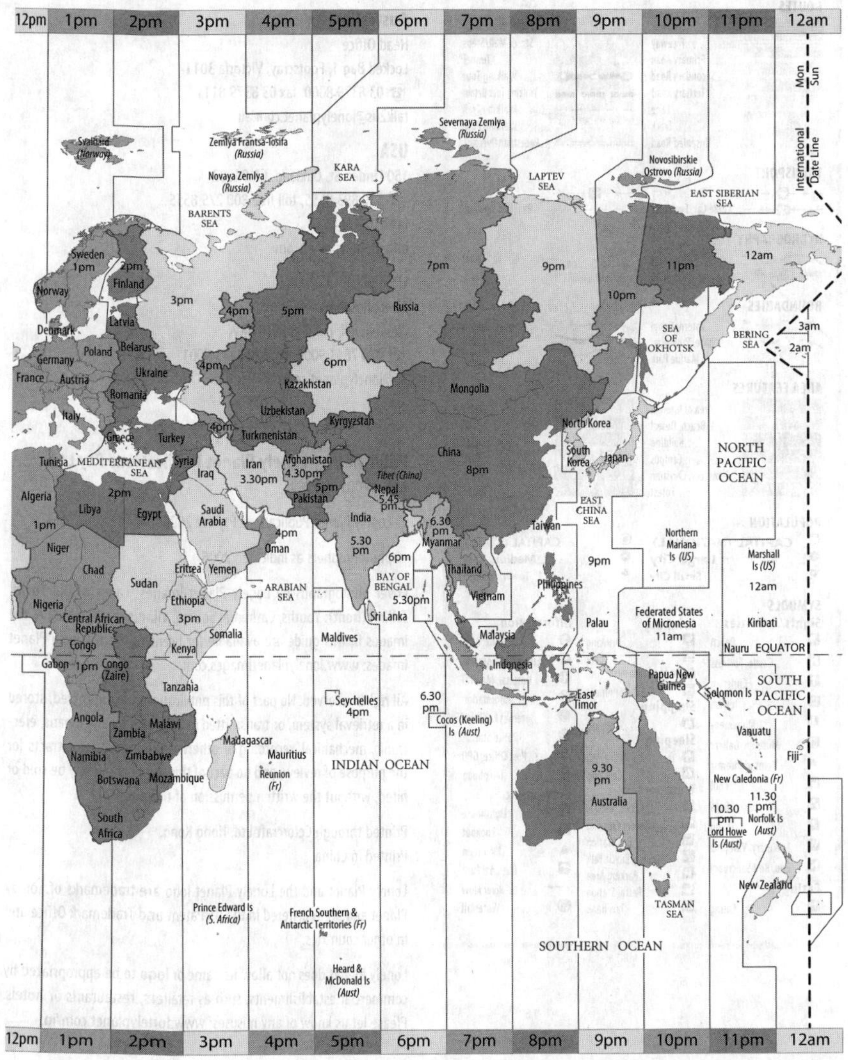
12pm
1pm
2pm
3pm
4pm
5pm
6pm
7pm
8pm
9pm
10pm
11pm
12am
Mon
Sun
International Date Line
Svalbard (Norway)
Zemlya Frantsa-Iosifa (Russia)
Severnaya Zemlya (Russia)
Novaya Zemlya (Russia)
KARA SEA
BARENTS SEA
LAPTEV SEA
Novosibirskie Ostrovo (Russia)
EAST SIBERIAN SEA
Sweden 1pm
2pm
Finland
Norway
3pm
Denmark
Latvia
4pm
5pm
Russia
7pm
9pm
11pm
10pm
12am
Poland
Belarus
Germany
France
Austria
4pm
Ukraine
6pm
Kazakhstan
Mongolia
SEA OF OKHOTSK
BERING SEA
3am
2am
Romania
Italy
Uzbekistan
4pm
Kyrgyzstan
Turkmenistan
Greece
Turkey
North Korea
Tunisia
MEDITERRANEAN SEA
Syria
Iraq
Iran 3.30pm
Afghanistan 4.30pm
China
South Korea
Japan
NORTH PACIFIC OCEAN
Tibet (China)
8pm
Algeria
2pm
5pm
Nepal 5.45 pm
Pakistan
Libya
Egypt
Saudi Arabia
India
EAST CHINA SEA
1pm
4pm
6.30 pm
Taiwan
Niger
Oman
5.30 pm
Myanmar
Northern Mariana Is (US)
Marshall Is (US)
Chad
Eritrea
Yemen
6pm
9pm
Sudan
ARABIAN SEA
BAY OF BENGAL
Thailand
Philippines
12am
Ethiopia
5.30pm
Vietnam
Nigeria
Central African Republic
3pm
Sri Lanka
Palau
Federated States of Micronesia 11am
Kiribati
Congo
Somalia
Maldives
Malaysia
Nauru EQUATOR
Gabon
1pm
Congo (Zaire)
Kenya
Indonesia
Papua New Guinea
SOUTH PACIFIC OCEAN
Tanzania
Solomon Is
Seychelles 4pm
6.30 pm
East Timor
Angola
Malawi
Cocos (Keeling) Is (Aust)
Vanuatu
Zambia
Madagascar
Namibia
Zimbabwe
Mauritius
INDIAN OCEAN
Fiji
Botswana
Mozambique
Reunion (Fr)
9.30 pm
New Caledonia (Fr)
Australia
11.30 pm
10.30 pm
Norfolk Is (Aust)
South Africa
Lord Howe Is (Aust)
New Zealand
Prince Edward Is (S. Africa)
French Southern & Antarctic Territories (Fr)
TASMAN SEA
SOUTHERN OCEAN
Heard & McDonald Is (Aust)

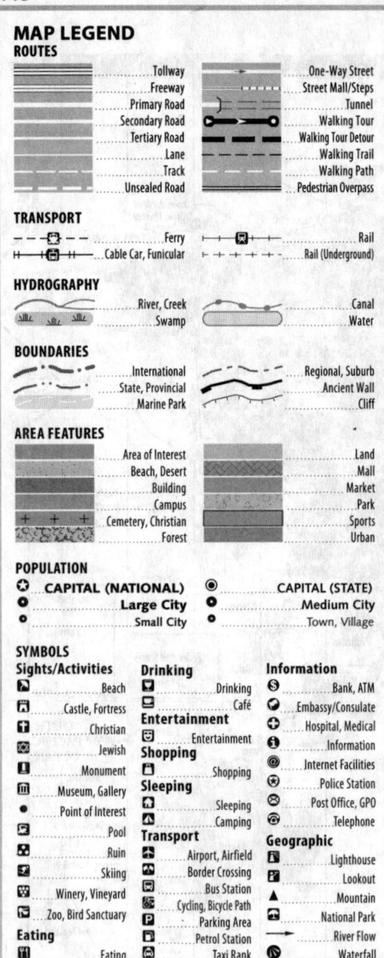

LONELY PLANET OFFICES

Australia
Head Office
Locked Bag 1, Footscray, Victoria 3011
☎ 03 8379 8000, fax 03 8379 8111
talk2us@lonelyplanet.com.au

USA
150 Linden St, Oakland, CA 94607
☎ 510 893 8555, toll free 800 275 8555
fax 510 893 8572
info@lonelyplanet.com

UK
72-82 Rosebery Ave,
Clerkenwell, London EC1R 4RW
☎ 020 7841 9000, fax 020 7841 9001
go@lonelyplanet.co.uk

Published by Lonely Planet Publications Pty Ltd
ABN 36 005 607 983

Cover photographs by Lonely Planet Images: Lanes of Old Town, Tallinn (front); Youths, Cathedral Square, Vilnius (back). Many of the images in this guide are available for licensing from Lonely Planet Images: www.lonelyplanetimages.com.

Printed through Colorcraft Ltd, Hong Kong.
Printed in China